# A SYSTEM

OF

# PENAL LAW,

FOR

## THE STATE OF LOUISIANA:

CONSISTING OF

A CODE OF CRIMES AND PUNISHMENTS,
A CODE OF PROCEDURE,
A CODE OF EVIDENCE,
A CODE OF REFORM AND PRISON DISCIPLINE,
A BOOK OF DEFINITIONS.

PREPARED UNDER THE AUTHORITY OF A LAW OF THE SAID STATE.

## BY EDWARD LIVINGSTON.

TO WHICH ARE PREFIXED

A PRELIMINARY REPORT ON THE PLAN OF A PENAL CODE, AND INTRODUCTORY
REPORTS TO THE SEVERAL CODES EMBRACED IN THE
SYSTEM OF PENAL LAW.

THE LAWBOOK EXCHANGE, LTD.
Clark, New Jersey

ISBN-13: 9781886363830 (hardcover)
ISBN-13: 9781616190736 (paperback)

Lawbook Exchange edition 2010

*The quality of this reprint is equivalent to the quality of the original work.*

## THE LAWBOOK EXCHANGE, LTD.

33 Terminal Avenue
Clark, New Jersey 07066-1321

*Please see our website for a selection of our other publications*
*and fine facsimile reprints of classic works of legal history:*
www.lawbookexchange.com

### Library of Congress Cataloging-in-Publication Data

Livingston, Edward, 1764-1836.
    A system of penal law for the state of Louisiana  :
consisting of a code of crimes and punishments… : prepared
under the authority of a law of the said state  /  by  Edward
Livingston.
        p. cm.
    Originally published:  Philadelphia :  J. Kay, Jun, & Brother ;
    Pittsburgh :  J.I. Kay & Co., 1833.
    ISBN 1-886363-83-8 (cloth : alk. paper)
1. Criminal law—Louisiana.  2. Criminal procedure—Louisiana.
    I.  Title.
    KFL562.L52   1999
    345.763—dc21                                    99-11403
                                                        CIP

*Printed in the United States of America on acid-free paper*

# A SYSTEM

OF

# PENAL LAW,

FOR

## THE STATE OF LOUISIANA:

CONSISTING OF

A CODE OF CRIMES AND PUNISHMENTS,
A CODE OF PROCEDURE,
A CODE OF EVIDENCE,
A CODE OF REFORM AND PRISON DISCIPLINE,
A BOOK OF DEFINITIONS.

PREPARED UNDER THE AUTHORITY OF A LAW OF THE SAID STATE.

## BY EDWARD LIVINGSTON.

TO WHICH ARE PREFIXED

A PRELIMINARY REPORT ON THE PLAN OF A PENAL CODE, AND INTRODUCTORY
REPORTS TO THE SEVERAL CODES EMBRACED IN THE
SYSTEM OF PENAL LAW.

PUBLISHED BY

JAMES KAY, JUN. & BROTHER, 267 MARKET STREET, PHILADELPHIA:

JOHN I. KAY & CO., PITTSBURGH.

Printed by
JAMES KAY, JUN. AND Co.
Printers to the American Philosophical Society,
Race above Fourth Street,
Philadelphia.

# ANALYTICAL TABLE.

## A SYSTEM OF PENAL LAW.

## A CODE OF CRIMES AND PUNISHMENTS.

# AN ACT

OF

# THE GENERAL ASSEMBLY OF LOUISIANA,

RELATIVE TO

## THE CRIMINAL LAWS OF THAT STATE.

APPROVED 10 FEBRUARY 1820.

WHEREAS it is of primary importance, in every well regulated state, that the code of criminal law should be founded on one principle, viz. the prevention of crime; that all offences should be clearly and explicitly defined, in language generally understood; that punishments should be proportioned to offences; that the rules of evidence should be ascertained as applicable to each offence; that the mode of procedure should be simple, and the duty of magistrates, executive officers and individuals assisting them, should be pointed out by law : and whereas the system of criminal law, by which this state is now governed, is defective in many, or all of the points above enumerated, therefore :

Section 1.   Be it enacted by the senate and house of representatives of the state of Louisiana in general assembly convened, that a person learned in the law shall be appointed by the senate and house of representatives at this session, whose duty it shall be to prepare and present to the next general assembly, for its consideration, a code of criminal law in both the French and English languages, designating all criminal offences punishable by law; defining the same in clear and explicit terms; designating the punishment to be inflicted on each; laying down the rules of evidence on trials; directing the whole mode of procedure, and pointing out the duties of the judicial and executive officers in the performance of their functions under it.

Section 2.   And be it further enacted, that the person so to be chosen, shall receive for his services such compensation as shall be determined by the general assembly, at their next session, and that a sum of five hundred dollars shall be paid to him, on a warrant of the governor upon the state treasury, to enable him to procure such in-

A

formation and documents relative to the operation of the improvements in criminal jurisprudence, particularly of the penitentiary system in the different states, as he may deem useful to report to the general assembly in considering the project of a code: he shall account to the general assembly, in what manner the said five hundred dollars has been disposed of.

IN

# THE GENERAL ASSEMBLY OF LOUISIANA.

## 13 FEBRUARY 1821.

WE, the undersigned, secretary of the senate and clerk of the house of representatives of the state of Louisiana, do hereby certify, that on the thirteenth of February in the year of our lord one thousand eight hundred and twenty-one, EDWARD LIVINGSTON, Esq. was elected and appointed by the joint ballot of the general assembly of said state, to draw and prepare a criminal code. In testimony whereof, we have hereunto set our hands.

J. CHABAUD,
Secretary of the Senate.

CANONGE,
Clerk of the House of Representatives.

New-Orleans, March 28, 1822.

# RESOLUTIONS

# THE GENERAL ASSEMBLY OF. LOUISIANA.

## 21 MARCH 1832.

RESOLVED by the senate and house of representatives in general assembly convened, that the general assembly do approve of the plan proposed by Edward Livingston, Esq., in his report, made in pursuance of the act entitled "an act relative to the criminal laws of this state,". and earnestly solicit Mr Livingston to prosecute this work, according to said report; that two thousand copies of the same, together with the part of the projected code thereto annexed, be printed in pamphlet form; one thousand of which shall be printed in French and one thousand in English, under the direction of the said Edward Livingston, Esq., of which five copies be delivered to each member of the present general assembly, fifty copies to the governor, one copy to each of the judges of the supreme court, the district judges, the judge of the criminal court, the attorney-general and district attorneys, the parish judges, two hundred copies to the said Edward Livingston, Esq.; and that the balance shall be for the use of the state, of which one half shall be deposited in the hands of the secretary of the senate and clerk of the house of representatives, and the other half in the office of the secretary of the state.

And be it further resolved, that the governor be requested, and it is hereby made his duty to contract for the printing of said work, and to pay for the same out of the contingent fund.

And be it further resolved, that a sum of one thousand dollars be paid to Edward Livingston, Esq., on his warrant, out of the treasury of the state, to be on account of the compensation to him allowed, when his work shall be completed.

A. BEAUVAIS,
Speaker of the House of Representatives.

J. POYDRAS,
President of the Senate.

Approved, March 21, 1822,

T. B. ROBERTSON,
Governor of the State of Louisiana.

# REPORT

MADE BY

# EDWARD LIVINGSTON

TO

THE HONOURABLE THE SENATE AND HOUSE OF REPRESENTATIVES
OF THE STATE OF LOUISIANA IN GENERAL ASSEMBLY CONVENED.

IN PURSUANCE OF THE ACT ENTITLED "AN ACT RELATIVE TO THE CRIMINAL LAWS
OF THAT STATE."

HAVING been honoured by an appointment at the last session, to perform the duties required by "an act relative to the criminal laws of the state," I have thought it necessary to report to the general assembly, the progress that has been made in the work, and the reasons which have prevented its completion. In undertaking those duties, I relied much on the aid which I expected to derive from the other states; for, although none of them has framed a code on so comprehensive a plan as that contemplated by our law, yet most of them have established the penitentiary system, which is intended to form the basis of our legislation on this subject. Before I could avail myself of the advantage which those experiments afforded, it was necessary to know, with precision, their results. This information could only be obtained by collecting the returns and official reports of the different establishments, and inducing men of eminence and abilities to communicate their observations on the subject. Knowing also the advantage to be derived from a comparison of the opinions of eminent jurists and statesmen on other leading principles, which must be embodied in the system, I addressed several copies of the annexed circular letter to the governors of each state, with the request, that they might be put into the hands of men, from whom the desired information might be expected: these, as well as a number of similar applications, I did hope, would have procured a body of information useful not only to me in framing the work, but to the legislature in judging of it.

This hope has, however, as yet been but partially realized. I have

received returns of the state of the penitentiary only from Massa-
chusets. Governor Wollcott and Judge Swift of Connecticut, Chan-
cellor Kent of New York, Judge Holman of Ohio, Mr Rawle of
Pennsylvania, Mr Bowen of Rhode Island, Mr Brice of Maryland,
and Colonel Johnson of Kentucky, have communicated to me some
useful information; with these exceptions, the gentlemen to whom my
letters were addressed, have been too much occupied in their own
states to attend to the affairs of ours.

Our minister in England has had the goodness to send to me the
reports of the committees of the house of commons, appointed to
inquire into the propriety of a revision of their penal laws ; documents
of great utility, to show the operation of the law we have partially
adopted, in that country from which we have borrowed it.

It appears that these reports are not easily procured, and that Mr
Rush was indebted for them to Mr Jeremy Bentham, whose writings
have thrown so much light on the subject of criminal legislation, and
who, in a note addressed to Mr Rush, on our undertaking, has made
a suggestion which he will find has not been disregarded.

I certainly lost some time in waiting for answers to my letters, but
I cannot, in candour, state this, (even with the necessary attention to
my professional business) to have been the only cause why the task I
have undertaken is not yet fully performed.

I never so far overrated my own powers, as to suppose that the
whole plan would be executed in the short interval between the two
sessions, but I did think, that parts of it might be prepared, and
submitted for the sanction of the present legislature, leaving the others
to be acted upon at a future period. A closer view of the subject,
however, convinced me of my error. In establishing the principles
on which the work was to be framed, and tracing the plan of its different divisions, I found that its parts were so closely connected, and
that continued references from the one to the other were so unavoidable, as to render it difficult fairly to judge of, or decide on any part
without examining the whole. I therefore determined to report to the
general assembly, the progress I had made, to develope the plan on
which I proposed to execute the work, to give them some of the detached parts as specimens of the execution, and then to take their direction whether it should be completed or not.

The introductory notice herewith submitted, gives the different divisions of the code, into books, chapters and sections; the whole is sub-
divided into articles, numbered progressively through each book, so
that citations may be made by referring to the article and book only.
A continued numeration of the articles, through the whole work, has
been found, in other instances, inconvenient, and carrying the numbers
through each chapter or section only, increases the difficulty of reference. In the same notice, will be found some general provisions, made
to obviate the necessity of those repetitions, which increased the bar-
barism of our legal language ; but the omission of which has sometimes
counteracted the intent of the legislature. The instance of two statutes,
which were made in England, to punish, the one the stealing of *horses*,
and the other the stealing of a *horse*, is familiar to lawyers; and indeed
it has been doubted by some, whether a third statute were not necessary, to include the female part of the species.

One other article in this notice points to a method, which will also, it is supposed, tend to render the code both explicit and concise. Technical terms are never used in the work, where common expressions could be found to give the same idea. The employment of them, however, is, in many instances, unavoidable. In all such cases, and whenever a word, or a phrase, is either ambiguous, or employed in any other sense than that which is given to it in common parlance, it becomes necessary to explain the precise meaning which is attached to it in the code. To this end, whenever any such expressions occur in the course of the work, they are to be printed in a particular character, which will serve as a notice, that they are defined and explained. These definitions and explanations form the first book.

This, though necessarily the first in numerical order, it is obvious, must be the last executed. The words requiring explanation are noted, and the definitions written, as the work progresses ; when complete, it will be submitted to men unversed in the language of the law, and every word not fully understood by them, will be marked for explanation. The foregoing parts of the plan are believed to be new, and therefore require the stricter attention to the propriety of their enactment: they suggested themselves to me, as the means of making the work, at once concise, and easily comprehended by those who are most interested in understanding it.

The second book begins with a preamble, which states the reasons that called for the enactment of a criminal code, and which sanctions, by a solemn legislative declaration, the principles on which its several provisions are founded. These principles once studied, and after proper discussion adopted, will serve as a standard to measure the propriety of every other part of the code: with these rules constantly before us, and duly impressed on our minds, we can proceed with confidence and comparative ease, to the task of penal legislation; and we may see at a glance, or determine by a single thought, whether any proposed provision is consonant to those maxims which we have adopted as the dictates of truth. The incongruities which have pervaded our system will disappear; every new enactment will be impressed with the character of the original body of laws; and our penal legislation will no longer be a piece of fretwork exhibiting the passions of its several authors, their fears, their caprices, or the carelessness and inattention with which legislators in all ages and in every country have, at times, endangered the lives, the liberties, and fortunes of the people, by inconsistent provisions, cruel or disproportioned punishments, and a legislation, weak and wavering, because guided by no principle, or by one that was continually changing, and therefore could seldom be right. This division of the code is deemed to be of the highest importance: all the other parts will derive their character from this; it is the foundation of the whole work, and, if well laid, the superstructure raised in conformity to it cannot be essentially faulty. It is the result of much reflection, guided by an anxiety to discover the truth, and to express it with precision.

The remainder of the second book is devoted to the establishment of general dispositions, applicable to the exercise of legislative power in penal jurisprudence; to prosecutions and trials; to a designation of the persons who are amenable to the provisions of this code; to a statement of the circumstances under which acts, that would otherwise be offences, may be justified or excused; to the repetition of offences; to the situation of different persons participating in the same offence, as principals, accomplices or accessaries.

The enunciation of these general provisions, it is supposed, will greatly tend, not only to elucidate, but abridge the work ; by throwing them into a single chapter, memory is assisted, order is better preserved, and repetition very much avoided. Among those which relate to the exercise of legislative power, are some that ought particularly to fix the attention of the general assembly; such is one for the exclusion of that class of offences, which figures in the English, and most other penal codes, under the vague description of offences against the laws of morality, of nature, and of religion. The will of the legislature is established as the only rule ; and the crude and varying opinions of judges, as to the extent of this uncertain code of good morals, are no longer to usurp the authority of law. Connected with this, is the provision which prohibits the punishment of any act not expressly forbidden by the letter of the law, under the pretence that it comes within its spirit.

By the criminal laws which now govern us, most offences are described in the technical words of the English jurisprudence, and we are referred to it for their explanation ; hence our judges have deemed themselves bound to adopt those definitions which have been given by the English courts, and the whole train of constructive offences has been brought into our law. The institution of the trial by jury, the rare infliction of torture ; and in latter times, the law of habeas corpus, gave a decided superiority to the penal law of England over that of its neighbours. The nation, unfortunately, mistook this superiority for perfection ; and while they proudly looked down on the rest of Europe, and reproached them with their tortures, their inquisitions, and secret tribunals, they shut their eyes to the imperfections of their own code. Prisoners were denied the assistance of counsel; men were executed because they could not read ; those who refused to answer, were condemned to die under the most cruel torture. Executions for some crimes were attended with butchery that would disgust a savage. The life and honour of the accused were made to depend on the uncertain issue of a judicial combat. A wretched sophistry introduced the doctrine of corrupted blood. Heretics and witches were committed to the flames. No proportion was preserved between crimes and punishments. The cutting of a twig, and the assassination of a parent ; breaking a fishpond, and poisoning a whole family or murdering them in their sleep, all incurred the same penalties : and two hundred different actions, many not deserving the name of offences, were punishable by death. This dreadful list was increased by the legislation of the judges, who declared acts which were not criminal under the letter of the law, to be punishable by virtue of its spirit. The statute gave the text, and the tribunals wrote the commentary in letters of blood; and extended its penalties by the creation of constructive offences. The vague, and sometimes unintelligible language, employed in the penal statutes ; and the discordant opinions of elementary writers, gave a colour of necessity to this assumption of power ; and the English nation have submitted to the legislation of its courts, and seen their fellow subjects hanged for constructive felonies ; quartered for constructive treasons ; and roasted alive for constructive heresies, with a patience that would be astonishing, even if their written laws had sanctioned the butchery. The first constructive extension of a penal statute beyond its letter, is an ex post facto law, as regards the offence to which it is applied ; and is an illegal assumption of legislative power, so far as it establishes a rule for future decisions. In our republic, where the different departments of government are constitutionally forbidden to interfere with each other's functions, the exercise of this power would be particularly dangerous ; it was therefore thought proper to forbid it by an express prohibition. Some actions, injurious to society, may, by this means, be permitted for a time, but it was deemed infinitely better to submit to this temporary inconvenience, than to allow the exercise of a power so much at war with the principles of our government. It may be proper to observe, that the fear of these consequences is not ideal, and that the decisions of all tribunals, under the common law, justify the belief, that without some legislative restraint, our courts would not be more scrupulous than those of other countries, in sanctioning this dangerous abuse. In another part of the code, it is intended to insert a provision, to bring before the legislature, at stated periods, all those cases in which the operation of the law is supposed to fall short of, or to extend beyond the intention of those who framed it ; the defects, if really such, will then be cured by the power legally authorized to apply the remedy ; the harmony of our constitutional distribution of powers will be undisturbed; and the ends of public justice attained with greater regularity and better effect.

Our constitution, containing a very imperfect declaration of rights, leaves the legislative power entirely uncontrolled in some points, where restraint has, in most free governments, been deemed essential ; a majority may establish their religion as that of the state ; non-conformity may be punished as heresy ; and even the toleration of other creeds may be refused ; without violating any express constitutional law. Corruption of blood may be established, and it is even somewhat doubtful, whether, strictly speaking, it does not, under the general terms in which the rules of the common law are adopted, now exist. No legislative act can apply an effectual remedy to these and other constitutional defects ; but their existence has called for a longer enunciation of general principles in the code, than would otherwise have been necessary. Our successors will not be bound to observe them, but we shall evince our own conviction of their truth ; and by impressing them on the minds of our constituents, render any attempt to undermine or destroy them, more difficult and more odious. Acknowledged truths in politics and jurisprudence, can never be too often repeated. When the true principles of legislation are impressed on the minds of the people ; when they see the reasons of the laws by which they are governed, they will obey them with cheerfulness, if just, and know how to change them, if oppressive. The reporter, therefore, has thought it an essential part of his duty to fortify the precepts of the projected code, by assigning the reasons on which they are founded ; thus to open the arcana of penal legislation, and to show that the mystery in which it has hitherto been involved, was not inherent in the subject, but must disappear, whenever its true principles are developed.

Among the general provisions, is also found one, asserting the right to publish, without restraint, the account of all proceedings in criminal courts, and freely to discuss the conduct of judges, and other officers employed in administering justice. That this may be done more effectually, it is provided that the judge shall, at the request either of the

B

accused or of the prosecutor, state and record his decisions; with the reasons on which they are founded. In a subsequent part of the work, it will be made the duty of a particular officer to publish accurate accounts of all trials, remarkable either for the atrocity of the offence, or the importance of the principles decided in the course of the proceeding. · Publicity is an object of such importance in free governments, that it not only ought to be permitted, but must be secured by a species of compulsion. The people must be forced to know what their servants are doing, or they will, like other masters, submit to imposition, rather than take the trouble of inquiring into the state of their affairs. No nation ever yet found any inconvenience from too close an inspection into the conduct of its officers; but many have been brought to ruin, and reduced to slavery, by suffering gradual imposition and abuses, which were imperceptible, only because the means of publicity had not been secured. In modern times, the press is so powerful an engine to effect this, that the nation which neglects to employ it, in promulgating the operations of every department in government, can neither know nor deserve the blessings of freedom. The important task of spreading this kind of information, ought not, therefore, be left to the chance of private exertion; it must be made a public duty; every one employed in the administration of justice will then act under the conviction, that his official conduct and opinions will be discussed before a tribunal in which he neither presides nor officiates. The effects of such a conviction may be easily imagined, and we may fairly conclude, that in proportion to its strength, will be the fidelity and diligence of those upon whom it operates.

By our constitution the right of a trial by jury is secured to the accused, but it is not exclusively established. This, however, may be done by law, and there are so many strong reasons in its favour, that it has been thought proper to insert in the code, a precise declaration, that in all criminal prosecutions, the trial by jury is a privilege which cannot be renounced. Were it left entirely at the option of the accused, a desire to propitiate the favour of the judge, ignorance of his true interest, or the confusion incident to his situation, might induce him to waive the advantage of a trial by his country, and thus, by degrees, accustom the people to a spectacle they ought never to behold; a single man determining the fact, applying the law, and disposing at his will, of the life, liberty, and reputation of a citizen.

In proposing this change in our law, I may be permitted to make a few reflections, to show its importance. The trial by jury formed no part of the jurisprudence of the different powers which governed Louisiana prior to its last cession. It was first introduced when the province became incorporated with the United States, as one of its territories. By the first act for effecting this union, the trial by jury was established in capital cases; and in all others, both civil and criminal, was left, as in all cases it is now, optional with the parties. In the second grade of government, it was provided, that the people should have the benefit of the trial by jury, but it was not declared the only mode of trial; and our state constitution has adopted it in original cases, nearly in the same words. This indifference in our constitutional compacts, to an institution of such vital importance, has had the most injurious consequences, which have been increased by subsequent provisions. In civil cases it is already banished from our courts, or used only as an engine of delay, or as an awkward and oppressive vehicle for transmitting testimony, to be decided only by the supreme court. This degradation of the functions of jurors, in cases of property, certainly does not tend to render them respectable in cases affecting life and liberty. In criminal cases, the attorney-general, I believe, demands a trial by jury, as he has a right to do, in all serious cases, even where the accused is willing to waive it. But a prosecutor less friendly to the institution, and a judge more desirous to increase his powers than the gentlemen who now fill those stations, could easily find means to make the jury as useless, as rarely employed, and as insignificant in a criminal court, as our laws have already made it in civil jurisdiction.

Those who advocate the present disposition of our law, say—admitting the trial by jury to be an advantage, the law does enough when it gives the accused the option to avail himself of its benefits ; he is the best judge whether it will be useful to him ; and it would be unjust to direct him in so important a choice. This argument is specious, but not solid. There are reasons, and some have already been stated, to show that this option, in many cases, cannot be freely exercised. There is, moreover, another interest, besides that of the culprit, to be considered; if he be guilty, the state has an interest in his conviction ; and whether guilty or innocent, it has a higher interest, that the fact should be fairly canvassed before judges inaccessible to influence, and unbiassed by any false views of official duty. It has an interest in the character of its administration of justice, and a paramount duty to perform, in rendering it free from suspicion. It is not true, therefore, to say, that the laws do enough, when they give the choice (even supposing it could be made with deliberation) between a fair and impartial trial, and one that is liable to the strongest objections. They must do more, they must restrict that choice, so as not to suffer an ill-advised individual to degrade them into instruments of ruin, though it should be voluntarily inflicted ; or of death, though that death should be suicide.

Another advantage of rendering this mode of trial obligatory is, that it diffuses the most valuable information among every rank of citizens; it is a school, of which every jury that is impanelled, is a separate class; where the dictates of the laws, and the consequences of disobedience to them, are practically taught. The frequent exercise of these important functions, moreover, gives a sense of dignity and self-respect, not only becoming the character of a free citizen, but which adds to his private happiness. Neither party spirit, nor intrigue, nor power, can deprive him of this share in the administration of justice, though they can humble the pride of every other office, and vacate every other place. Every time he is called to act in this capacity, he must feel that though perhaps placed in the humblest station, he is yet the guardian of the life, the liberty, and reputation of his fellow-citizens, against injustice and oppression ; and that, while his plain understanding has been found the the best refuge for innocence, his incorruptible integrity is pronounced a sure pledge that guilt will not escape. A state whose most obscure citizens are thus individually elevated to perform those august functions ; who are, alternately, the defenders of the injured, the dread of the guilty, the vigilant guardians of the constitution ; without whose consent no punishment can be inflicted, no disgrace incurred; who can, by their voice, arrest the blow of oppression, and direct the hand of justice where to strike. Such a state can never sink into slavery, or easily submit to oppression : corrupt rulers may pervert the constitution ; ambitious demagogues may violate its precepts ; foreign influence may control its operations ; but while the people enjoy the trial by JURY, taken by lot from among themselves, they cannot cease to be free. The information it spreads ; the sense of dignity and independence it inspires ; the courage it creates, will always give them an energy of resistance, that can grapple with encroachment ; and a renovating spirit that will make arbitrary power despair. The enemies of freedom know this ; they know how admirable a vehicle it is to convey the contagion of those liberal principles, which attack the vitals of their power, and they guard against its introduction with more care than they would take to avoid pestilential disease. In countries where it already exists, they insiduously endeavour to innovate, because they dare not openly destroy; changes inconsistent with the spirit of the institution are introduced, under the plausible pretext of improvement : the common class of citizens are too ill-informed to perform the duties of jurors—a selection is necessary. This choice must be confided to an agent of executive power, and must be made among the most eminent for education, wealth and respectability ; so that, after several successive operations of political chemistry, a shining result may be obtained, freed, indeed, from all republican dross, but without any of the intrinsic value that is found in the rugged, but inflexible integrity and incorruptible worth of the original composition. Men, impanelled by this process, bear no resemblance but in name to the sturdy, honest, unlettered jurors, who derive no dignity but from the performance of their duties ; and the momentary exercise of whose functions gives no time for the work of corruption, or the effect of influence or fear. By innovations such as these, the institution is so changed, as to leave nothing to attach the affections, or awaken the interest of the people, and it is neglected as an useless, or abandoned as a mischievous contrivance.

In England, the panel is made up by an officer of the crown ; but there are many correctives which lessen the effect of this vice. The return, except in very special cases, is made, not with a view to any particular cause, but for the trial of all that are at issue ; and out of a large number returned on the panel, the twelve taken for the trial are designated by lot : in capital cases, also, the extent to which challenges are allowed, is calculated to defeat any improper practices ; and when we add to this the general veneration for this mode of trial, the force of public opinion, guided by a spirit which it has created, and diffused, and perpetuated, we shall see the reason why the trial by jury, though by no means perfectly organized, is, in that country, justly considered as the best security for the liberties of the people ; and why, though they behold with a shameful indifference, a domineering aristocracy, corrupting their legislative, and encroaching on their executive branches of government, they yet boast, with reason, of the independence of their judiciary, ennobled as it is with the trial by jury. We have received this invaluable inheritance from our British ancestors : let us defend, and improve, and perpetuate it ; not only that we may ourselves enjoy its advantages, but, that if this, with the principle of free representation in government, and that admirable contrivance for securing personal liberty, the writ of habeas corpus, should chance to be corrupted or abolished in the country from whence we derived them, we may return the obligation we have received, by offering for adoption, to a regenerated state, those great institutions of freedom established by ancestors common to them and the race of freemen, by whose labours, experience and valour, they will have been perfected and preserved.

In France, this mode of trial was introduced during the revolution, but was afterwards found inconvenient to the exercise of the imperial power. By the code of 1808, it was so modified as to leave scarcely a resemblance of its origin ; it became a select corps of sixty men, chosen by the prefect, who held his office at the will of the crown. It was reduced by successive operations (all by the king's officers) to twenty-one ; out of which the accused had the illusory privilege of excepting to nine ; and the votes of the majority of the remaining twelve, combined, in no very intelligible manner, with the opinions of the bench, decided his fate. Yet even under this vicious constitution, juries have sometimes been found to interpose between executive power and its victims ; and the very name (for it is, in fact, very little more) of the trial by jury, is now, under the monarchy of France, the object of royal jealousy and fear.

With these examples before us, ought we not, in framing a new code, to impress on the minds of our constituents a sacred attachment to this institution ? So venerable for its antiquity ! So wise in theory ! So efficient in practice ! So simple in form ! In substance so well-adapted to its end ! The terror of guilt, the best hope of innocence ! Venerated by the friends of freedom, detested and abhorred by its foes ! Can we too religiously guard this sanctuary into which liberty may retire in times (God long avert them from our country !) when corruption may pervert, and faction overturn, every other institution framed for its protection. Even in such times, the nation need not despair. A regenerating spirit will never be extinct, while this admirable contrivance for its preservation exists ; fostered in this retreat, it will gradually gather strength, and in due time will walk abroad in its majesty over the land, arrest the progress of arbitrary power, strike off the shackles which it has imposed, and restore the blessings of freedom to a people still conscious of their right to enjoy them.

If these reflections should chance to be seen in the other states, they will be considered as a trite repetition of acknowledged truths : here, I have some reason to apprehend they will be thought problematical assertions. But whatever may be their effect, I should, with my ideas of their importance, have been guilty of a dereliction of duty, had I failed to present them. All, however, I think on the subject, more than any language at my command can express, is contained in a single felicitous sentence, written by a man as eminent for learning and genius, as he is admired for the purity of his principles, and his attachment to the institutions of freedom—speaking of jurors, he calls them—

"Twelve invisible judges, whom the eye of the corruptor cannot see, and the influence of the powerful cannot reach, for they are no where to be found, until the moment when the balance of justice being placed in their hands, they hear, weigh, determine, pronounce, and immediately disappear, and are lost in the crowd of their fellow-citizens."*

The other provisions of this book either require no particular elucidation, or will receive it when the work is presented for adoption.

---

*Duponceau's address at the opening of the law academy at Philadelphia.

. It may, however, be proper to notice a change which is proposed in
the law of principals and accessaries. As it now stands, two species
of offenders are designated by this general name; distinguished by an
awkward periphrase, into "accessaries before the fact" and "accessaries
after the fact." As there is scarcely any feature in common between
the offences designated by these two denominations, I have taken away
the general appellation, and called the first an accomplice, leaving the
description of accessary exclusively to the second. In fact, how can
the odious offence of plotting a crime, and instigating another to perform
that which the contriver has not courage himself to execute; how can
this be assimilated to the act of relieving a repentant and supplicant
offender, who invokes our pity, and relies on our generosity? An act,
which, though justice may censure, humanity cannot always condemn.
The first class now includes some acts which are so much identified
with those which constitute the offence, that it was thought more simple, as well more just, to arrange them under the same head, and by
destroying useless distinctions, greatly restrict the number of crimes
of *complicity*.

Under the second head, our law now calls for the punishment of
acts, which, if not strictly virtues, are certainly too nearly allied to
them to be designated as crimes. The ferocious legislation which first
enacted this law, demands (and sometimes under the penalty of the most
cruel death) the sacrifice of all the feelings of nature, of all the sentiments
of humanity; breaks the ties of gratitude and honour; makes obedience to
the law to consist in a dereliction of every principle that gives dignity to
man, and leaves the unfortunate wretch, who has himself been guilty of
no offence, to decide between a life of infamy and self-reproach, or a death
of dishonour. Dreadful as this picture is, the original is found in the law
of accessaries after the fact. If the father commit treason, the son must
abandon, or deliver him up to the executioner. If the son be guilty
of a crime, the stern dictates of our law require, that his parent, that
the very mother who bore him, that his sisters and brothers, the companions of his infancy, should expel nature from their hearts, and humanity from their feelings; that they should barbarously discover his
retreat, or with inhuman apathy, abandon him to his fate. The husband is even required to betray his wife, the mother of his children;
every tie of nature or affection is to be broken, and men are required
to be faithless, treacherous, unnatural and cruel, in order to prove that
they are good citizens, and worthy members of society. This is one
instance, and we shall see others, of the danger of indiscreetly adopting, as a divine precept applicable to all nations, those rules which
were laid down for a particular people, in a remote and barbarous age.
The provisions now under consideration, evidently have their origin
in the Jewish law; that, however, went somewhat further; it required
the person connusant of a crime committed by a relation, not only to
perform the part of informer, but executioner also. "If thy brother,
the son of thy mother; or thy son, or thy daughter, or the wife of thy
bosom, or thy friend, which is as thine own soul, entice thee secretly,
saying, let us go and serve other gods, thou shalt not consent. . . . Neither shall thine eye pity him . . . . neither shalt thou conceal him; . . . .
thou shalt surely kill him; . . . . thou shalt stone him with stones."
Almighty power might counteract, for its own purposes, the feelings

of humanity, but a mortal legislator should not presume to do it; and, in modern times, such laws are too repugnant to our feelings to be frequently executed; but that they may never be enforced, they should be expunged from every code which they disgrace. The project presented to you, does this, with respect to ours. To put an end to that strife, which such provisions create in the minds of jurors, between their best feelings and their duty, their humanity and their oath; no relation to the principal offender, in the ascending or descending line, or in the collateral, as far as the first degree: no person united to him by marriage, or owing obedience to him as a servant, can be punished as an accessary. Cases of other particular ties of gratitude or friendship cannot be distinguished by law: they must be left for the consideration of the pardoning power.

I proceed to the plan of the third book, the most important in the work: it enumerates, classes, and defines all offences.

All contraventions of penal law are denominated by the general term, offences. Some division was necessary to distinguish between those of a greater and others of a less degree of guilt. No scale could be found for this measure, so proper as the injury done to society by any given act ; and as the punishment is intended to be proportioned to the injury, the nature of the punishment was fixed on, as the boundary between smaller offences, which are designated as misdemeanors, and those of a more serious nature which are called crimes. The last being such as are punished by hard labour, seclusion, or privation of civil rights, in addition to imprisonment. All other offences are called misdemeanors. In the progress of the work, I have felt some want of another denomination, to distinguish the lighter offences, which are punishable by pecuniary fines only, from those which are called in the English law by the vague appellation of *high misdemeanors;* and which are punished as well by bodily restraint as by fine. It is possible that in the end, something like the contravention of the French law may be adopted : but I am at present inclined to think, that the single division I have mentioned will be sufficient.

This first division can be of no utility in the definition of offences, and therefore will find no place in that part of the work; it is adopted, principally, from the necessity of such a distinction in the general provisions, and will also be found of use in common parlance, and for the purpose of reference.

Offences, including both crimes and misdemeanors, are next classed, in relation to the object affected by them, into public and private.

Here again the law which divides the two classes must, in some measure, be arbitrary, for scarcely any public offence can be committed that does not injure an individual; and most of the outrages offered to individuals, in some sort, affect the public tranquillity; but the order of the work requires the division, and it is made with as close a view as could be given to the nature of the different offences, as follows:

I. Under the head of public offences are ranked:

Those which affect the sovereignty of the state, in its legislative, executive, or judiciary power.

The public tranquillity ; the revenue of the state ; the right of suffrage ; the public records ; the current coin ; the commerce, manufactures, and trade of the country ; the freedom of the press ; the public health ; the public property ; the public roads, levees, bridges, navigable waters, and other property held by the sovereign power, for the common use of the people ; those which prevent or restrain the free exercise of religion, or which corrupt the morals of the people.

II. Private offences are those which affect individuals and injure them

In their reputation ; their persons ; their political privileges ; their civil rights ; their profession or trade ; their property, or the means of acquiring or preserving it.

Under one or other of these heads, it is believed that all such acts or omissions can be arranged, as it may be proper to constitute offences ; unless, indeed, those which relate to societies or corporate bodies may be found, when they come to be defined, not properly assignable to any one of these divisions ; in which case, a separate class will be created for them and other miscellaneous offences. It is obvious, that the classification cannot be complete until all the offences are enumerated and defined, and, therefore, this sketch is submitted more to give a general idea of the method, than as a complete plan.

Melancholy, misfortune and despair, sometimes urge the unhappy to an act, which, by most criminal codes, is considered as an offence of the deepest die ; and which, being directed principally against the offender himself, would have required a separate division, if it had been admitted in this code. It has not; because its insertion would be contrary to some of the fundamental principles which have been laid down for framing it.

Suicide can never be punished but by making the penalty (whether it be forfeiture or disgrace) fall exclusively upon the innocent. The English mangle the remains of the dead. The inanimate body feels neither the ignominy nor pain. The mind of the innocent survivor alone is lacerated by this useless and savage butchery, and the disgrace of the execution is felt exclusively by him, although it ought to fall on the laws which inflict it. The father, by a rash act of self-destruction, deprives his family of the support he ought to afford them ; and the law completes the work of ruin, by harrowing up their feelings ; covering them with disgrace ; and depriving them by forfeiture of their means of subsistence.

Vengeance, we have said, is unknown to our law ; it cannot, therefore, pursue the living offender, much less, with impotent rage should it pounce, like a vulture, on the body of the dead, to avenge a crime which the offender can never repeat, and which certainly holds out no lure for imitation : the innocent, we have assumed, should never be involved in the punishment inflicted on the guilty. But here, not only the innocent, but those most injured by the crime, are exclusively the sufferers by the punishment. We have established as a maxim, that the sole end of punishment is to prevent the commission of crimes ; the only means of effecting this, in the present case, must be by the force of example ; but what punishment can be devised to deter him, whose very crime consists in the infliction upon himself of the greatest penalty your law can denounce? Unless, therefore, you use the hold which natural affection gives you on his feelings, and restrain him by the fear of the disgrace and ruin with which you threaten his family, your law has no effective sanction ; but humanity forbids this ; the legislator that threatens it, is guilty of the most refined tyranny. If he carries it into execution, he is a savage. It is either a vain threat, and therefore cannot operate, or if executed with an ill-directed rage, strikes the innocent because the guilty is beyond its reach.

Another species of offence is also omitted, though it figures in every code, from the Mosaic downward, to those of our days, and generally with capital punishments denounced against its commission ; yet I have not polluted the pages of the law which I am preparing for you by mentioning it ; for several reasons :

First. Because, although it certainly prevailed among most of the ancient nations, and is said to be frequently committed in some of the modern, yet, I think, in all these cases it may be traced to causes and institutions peculiar to the people where it has been known, but which cannot operate here; and that the repugnance, disgust, and even horror, which the very idea inspires, will be a sufficient security that it can never become a prevalent one in our country.

Secondly. Because, as every crime must be defined, the details of such a definition would inflict a lasting wound on the morals of the people. Your criminal code is no longer to be the study of a select few: it is not the design of the framers that it should be exclusively the study even of our own sex; and it is particularly desirable, that it- should become a branch of early education for our youth. The shock which such a chapter must give to their pudicity, the familiarity their minds must acquire with the most disgusting images, would, it is firmly believed, be most injurious in its effects: and if there was no other objection, ought to make us pause before we submitted such details to public inspection.

Thirdly. It is an offence necessarily difficult of proof, and must generally be established by the evidence of those who are sufficiently base and corrupt to have participated in the offence. Hence, persons shameless and depraved enough to incur this disgrace, have made it the engine of extortion against the innocent, by threatening them with a denunciation for this crime, and they were generally successful: because, against such an accusation, it was known that the infamy of the accuser furnished no sure defence.

My last reason for the omission was, that as all our criminal proceedings must be public, a single trial of this nature would do more injury to the morals of the people than the secret, and therefore always uncertain, commission of the offence. I was not a little influenced, also, by reflecting on the probability, that the innocent might suffer, either by malicious combinations of perjured witnesses, in a case so difficult of defence, or by the ready credit that would be given to circumstantial evidence, where direct proof is not easily procured, and where, from the nature of the crime, a prejudice is created by the very accusation.

In designating the acts which should be declared offences, I could not confine the selection to such as were already prevalent in this country: this would have required, in future, too frequent a recurrence to the work of amendment ; nor could I, with propriety, include all the long list of offences which have been enumerated in the codes of other countries. A middle course has been pursued, embracing such prohibitions only as apply to acts which the present, and probably the future state of society, in our country, may require to be repressed.

The penal laws of most countries have an ample department allotted

C

to offences against religion, because most countries have an established religion'which must be supported in its superiority by the penalties of temporal laws. Here, where no pre-eminence is acknowledged, but such as is acquired by persuasion and conviction of the truth; where all modes of faith, all forms of worship are equal in the eye of the law; and it is left to that of omniscience to discover which is the one most pleasing in its sight; here, the task of legislation, on this head, is simple, and easily performed. It consists in a few provisions for scrupulously preserving this equality, and for punishing every species of disturbance to the exercise of all religious rites, while they do not interfere with public tranquillity: these are accordingly all that will be found in the code.

After thus accounting for the omissions I have remarked, it may be proper to notice a new class, inserted in the enumeration of public offences under the head of offences against the freedom of the press: this is new in the legislation of those governments where the liberty of the press is best established and most prized. It has generally been thought a sufficient protection to declare, that no punishment should be inflicted on those who legally exercise the right of publishing; but hitherto no penalties have been denounced against those who illegally abridge this liberty. Constitutional provisions are, in our republics, universally introduced to assert the right, but no sanction is given to the law. Yet do not the soundest principles require it? If the liberty of publishing be a right, is it sufficient to say that no one shall be punished for exercising it? I have a right to possess my property, yet the law does not confine itself to a declaration that I shall not be punished for using it: something more is done, and it is fenced round with penalties, imposed on those who deprive me of its enjoyment.

Why should there be this difference in the protection which the law affords to those different rights? Not certainly because the one in question is considered as of small moment: every bill of rights since the art of printing has been known, testifies how highly it has been prized. This anomaly may, in states governed by the common law, be accounted for by the reflection, that every breach of a constitutional privilege might there be considered as a misdemeanor, and punished as such, although no penalty were contained in the law. But here, where nothing is an offence but that which is plainly and especially declared to be such by the letter of the law, where we have banished all constructive offences, here our code would be incomplete without the insertion of this class.

All violence or menace of violence, or any other of the means which are enumerated in the code; all exercise of official influence or authority which may abridge this valuable privilege, is declared to be an offence. Nay, the project which will be presented to you goes further. And considering the constitutional provision as paramount to any act of ordinary legislation, and consequently that all laws in derogation of it are void; it declares all those guilty of an offence who shall execute any law abridging or restraining the liberty of the press, contrary to the privilege secured by the constitution. It may be said that this is nugatory, because the same authority which makes the code may repeal it, and that the legislature which could so far forget their duty as to violate the constitution, would certainly abrogate the law by which it was made punishable.   To this I answer, that the consequence does not follow.   Attacks on constitutional rights are seldom openly or directly made; the repeal of this part of the code would be an acknowledgement on the part of those who procured it, that they were hostile to the right secured by the constitution.  This, in a popular government, no representative would dare to avow;  and however desirous a faction might be to get rid of this formidable censor of their principles, operations and plans, they would never dare openly to declare their fears. But by means of these provisions in your code, all those insidious attempts by which valuable privileges are generally destroyed, will be prevented; the people will be put on their guard against them; and the judiciary will be armed with legal authority for their punishment and suppression.

I wish to have it distinctly understood, that the preceding division and classification of offences is introduced to give a method to the work, which will aid the memory; render reference more easy; enable the student to comprehend the whole plan, and future legislators to apply amendments and ameliorations with greater effect.   But that they are not intended, in any manner, to have a constructive operation. Each offence is to be construed by the definition which is given of it, not by the division or class in which it is placed.   The mixed nature of many offences, and the impossibility of making any precise line of demarcation, even between the two great divisions, render this remark necessary.

After the prohibitory and mandatory part of the penal law, we naturally come to consider its sanction or the means of securing obedience to its provisions.

The first of these are the precautionary measures to prevent the commission of apprehended offences, or to arrest the completion of those which are begun.   These are provided for, in the fourth book, and do not, very essentially, differ from those which are known to the English law.

In considering this important branch of the subject, we must refer to the principles established in the preliminary chapter.   If those are right, the law punishes, not to avenge, but to prevent crimes ; it effects this, first, by deterring others by the example of its inflictions on the offender ; secondly, by its effects on the delinquent himself ; taking away, by restraint, his power ; and by reformation, his desire of repeating the offence.   No punishments, greater than are necessary to effect this work of prevention, let us remember, ought to be inflicted ; and that those which produce it, by uniting reformation with example, are the best adapted to the end.   It would be disgusting and unnecessary to pass in review all the modes of punishment which have, even in modern times, been used, rather, it would seem, to gratify vengeance, than to lessen the number of offences. A spirit of enlightened legislation, taught by Montesquieu, Beccaria, Eden, and others; names dear to humanity! has banished some of the most atrocious from the codes of Europe.   But it has happened, in this branch of jurisprudence, as it has in most other departments of science, that long after the great principles are generally acknowledged, a diversity of opinion exists on their application to particular subjects. Thus, although the dislocation of the joints is no longer considered as the best mode of ascertaining innocence or discovering guilt; although offences against the deity are no longer expiated by the burning faggot;

or those against the majesty of kings, avenged by the hot pincers, and the rack, and the wheel; still many other modes of punishment have their advocates, which, if not equally cruel, are quite as inconsistent with the true maxims of penal law; it may, therefore, be proper to pass some of them in review.

They may be reduced to these: banishment; deportation; simple imprisonment; imprisonment in chains; confiscation of property; exposure to public derision ; labour on public works ; mutilation and other indelible marks of disgrace ; stripes, or the infliction of other bodily pain; death.

Banishment, even if it were an efficient remedy, can hardly, I think, be thought consistent with the duties which one nation owes to another. The convict who is forced from one country, must take refuge in another; and wherever he goes, he carries with him his disposition to break the laws and corrupt the morals of the country. The same crimes which make him unfit to reside in his own, render him mischievous to that which he chooses for his retreat. Every nation, then, would have a right to complain of laws that made their territories the retreat of banditti, and other malefactors of their neighbours. Each, at least, would have a right to refuse their entrance. If all do it, then the punishment cannot be inflicted; or must be commuted into that which is denounced against those who return. If no laws are made to expel them, or guard against their entrance, the favour must be reciprocal, and each nation would be bound to receive from its neighbour a number of foreign rogues, equal to that of the domestic villains they send out. The Romans, who commanded the civilized world, might employ this punishment with effect. In modern times, it is only used (and that rarely) for state offences, and then it is generally dangerous; because the man banished for political crimes, has frequently the power of doing more extensive mischief abroad than at home. It is also a very inefficient remedy; to many it would have no terrors, and those upon whose love of country it might operate as a punishment, could find many means of evading it by an undiscovered return.

Deportation, or rather relegation, is more efficient, because return is more difficult than from simple banishment. It also operates favourably sometimes, by producing reformation, and while enforced, effectually prevents a repetition of the offence ; at least on the society where it was first committed. But its effect, as an example, is nearly lost, because the culprit himself scarcely thinks it a punishment ; and because the distance causes both him and his crime to be forgotten as completely as if he was removed by death; and its practical operation in England, where it has been long tried under various forms, does not warrant the conclusion, that it ought to be adopted here.*

The legislature of Pennsylvania have received, very favourably, a plan presented by Dr Mease, recommending this mode of punishment; he has sent me a copy of his papers, which are at the disposal of the

---

* A very respectable witness, examined before the house of commons, says, "as to transportation, I, with deference, think it ought not to be adopted, except for incorrigible offenders, and then it ought to be for life; if it is for seven years, the novelty of the thing, and the prospect of returning to their friends and associates, reconciles offenders to it, so that, in fact, they consider it no punishment, and when this sentence is passed on men, they frequently say, *thank you, my lord.*"

general assembly: they are written with ingenuity, but under the circumstances in which this state is placed, I cannot propose his scheme as either a practicable or an advisable mode of disposing of convicts.

Simple imprisonment has obvious defects; as a corrective, it is nearly the worst that could be applied. If solitary, it is, for most offences, too severe. If it be not solitary, it becomes a school for vice and every kind of corruption. The want of employment, even when men are at liberty, leads them to evil associations, and the proverb does not much exaggerate, which calls it the root of all evil. But when to idleness is joined an association with all that is most profligate and unprincipled, it may be easily imagined how quick must be the progress from innocence to vice, from vice to crime. The band of the guilty thus collected, acquire a knowledge of each other's capacity in the commission of offences; they feel their strength, they recruit their numbers, they organize themselves for their warfare on society, and come out completely disciplined and arrayed against the laws.

Imprisonment in irons has all the evils of simple imprisonment, and adds to them that of inequality, and the danger of arbitrary imposition. The weight of the chains, if regulated by law, must be a torture to the weak, while the robust delinquent will bear them without pain. If they are at the discretion of the jailor, there can be no better engine for petty tyranny and extortion.

Confiscation of property has few advocates, and ought to have none. It has every defect that can attach to a mode of punishment, except that it is in some degree remissible; it is unequal, because it forfeits for the same offence the largest and the smallest fortune. It is cruel, because it deprives numbers of the means of subsistence for the fault of one. It is unjust, for it punishes, without distinction, the innocent as well as the guilty. It is liable to the worst of abuses, because it makes it the interest of the government to multiply convictions. This last characteristic is perhaps the reason why it retains a place in the penal jurisprudence of Europe.

The next four heads may be classed together: the pillory, stocks, and other contrivances for public exposure, labour in chains, and on the public works, indelible marks of disgrace (always attended with bodily pain), and the infliction of stripes, all are liable to the same radical objections; they all discard the idea of reformation; all are unequal, and subject to arbitrary imposition; with the exception of public labour, they are all momentary in their application, and when the operation is over, they impose a necessity on the patient, with the alternative of starving, immediately to repeat his offence; he accordingly, with increased dexterity, commences a new career; forms a corps of similar associates to prey upon society; seduces others by the example of his impunity in the numerous instances in which he escapes detection; swells the list of convictions in those where his vigilance is defeated, and finally becomes a fit subject for the grand remedy—the punishment of death. I approached the inquiry into the nature and effect of this punishment with the awe becoming a man who felt, most deeply, his liability to err, and the necessity of forming a correct opinion on a point so interesting to the justice of the country, the life of its citizens, and the character of its laws. I strove to clear my understanding from all prejudices which education, or early impressions might have created, and to produce a frame of mind fitted for the investigation of truth, and the impartial examination of the arguments on this great question. For this purpose, I not only consulted such writers on the subject as were within my reach, but endeavoured to procure a knowledge of the practical effect of this punishment on different crimes in the several countries where it is inflicted. In my situation, however, I could draw but a very limited advantage from either of these sources: very few books on penal law, even those most commonly referred to, are to be found in the scanty collections of this place, and my failure in procuring information from the other states, is more to be regretted on this than any other topic on which it was requested. With these inadequate means, but after the best use that my faculties would enable me to make of them; after long reflection, and not until I had canvassed every argument that could suggest itself to my mind, I came to the conclusion, that the punishment of death should find no place in the code which you have directed me to present. In offering this result, I feel a diffidence, which arises, not from any doubt of its correctness; I entertain none; but from the fear of being thought presumptuous in going beyond the point of penal reform, at which the wisdom of the other states has hitherto thought proper to stop; and from a reluctance to offer my opinions in opposition to those (certainly more entitled to respect than my own) which still support the propriety of this punishment for certain offences. On a mere speculative question, I should yield to this authority; but here I could not justify the confidence you have reposed in me, were I to give you the opinions of others, no matter how respectable they may be, instead of those which my best judgment assured me were right.

The example of the other states is certainly entitled to great respect; the greater, because all, without exception, still retain this punishment; but this example loses some of its force when we reflect on the slow progress of all improvement, and on the stubborn principles of the common law, which have particularly retarded its advance in jurisprudence.

In England, their parliament had been debating for near a century before they would take off capital punishment from two or three cases, in which every body allowed it was manifestly cruel and absurd: they have retained it in at least an hundred others of the same description; and when we reflect on these facts, and observe the influence which the prevailing opinions of that country have always had on the literature and jurisprudence of ours, we may account for the several states having stopped short in the reform of their penal law, without supposing them to have arrived at the point of perfection, beyond which it would be both unwise and presumptuous to pass. As to the authority of great names, it loses much of its force since the mass of the people have began to think for themselves; and since legislation is no longer considered as a trade, which none can practise with success, but those who have been educated to understand the mystery; the plain matter of fact, practical manner, in which that business is conducted with us, refers more to experience of facts than theory of reasoning: more to ideas of utility drawn from the state of society, than from the opinions of authors on the subject. If the argument were to be carried by the authority of names, that of Beccaria, were there no other, would ensure the victory. But reason alone, not precedent nor authority, must justify me in proposing to the general assembly this important change;

reason alone can persuade them to adopt it. I proceed therefore to develope the considerations which carried conviction to my mind, but which being perhaps now more feebly urged than they were then felt, may fail in producing the same effect upon others. A great part of my task is rendered unnecessary, by the general acknowledgement, universal, I may say, in the United States, that this punishment ought to be abolished in all cases, excepting those of treason, murder and rape. In some states arson is included; and lately, since so large a portion of our influential citizens have become bankers, brokers, and dealers in exchange, a strong inclination has been discovered to extend it to forgery, and uttering false bills of exchange. As it is acknowledged then to be an inadequate remedy for minor offences, the argument will be restricted to an inquiry; whether there is any probability that it will be more efficient in cases of greater importance. Let us have constantly before us, when we reason on this subject, the great principle, that the end of punishment is the prevention of crime. Death, indeed, operates this end most effectually, as respects the delinquent; but the great object of inflicting it is the force of the example on others. If this spectacle of horror is insufficient to deter men from the commission of slight offences, what good reason can be given to persuade us that it will have this operation where the crime is more atrocious? Can we believe that the fear of a remote and uncertain death will stop the traitor in the intoxicating moment of fancied victory over the constitution and liberties of his country? While in the proud confidence of success, he defies heaven and earth, and commits his existence to the chance of arms, that the dread of this punishment will "check his pride;" force him, like some magic spell, to yield obedience to the laws, and abandon a course which, he persuades himself, makes a "virtue" of his "ambition." Will it arrest the hand of the infuriate wretch, who, at a single blow, is about to gratify the strongest passion of his soul in the destruction of his deadly enemy? Will it turn aside the purpose of the secret assassin, who meditates the removal of the only obstacle to his enjoyment of wealth and honours? Will it master the strongest passions and counteract the most powerful motives, while it is too weak to prevent the indulgence of the slightest criminal inclination? If this be true, it must be confessed, that it presents a paradox which will be found more difficult to solve, when we reflect that great crimes are, for the most part, committed by men whose long habits of guilt have familiarized them to the idea of death; or to whom strong passions or natural courage have rendered it, in some measure, indifferent; and that the cowardly poisoner or assassin always thinks that he has taken such precautions as will prevent any risk of discovery. The fear of death, therefore, will rarely deter from the commission of great crimes. It is, on the contrary, a remedy peculiarly inapplicable to those offences. Ambition, which usually inspires the crime of treason, soars above the fear of death; avarice, which whispers the secret murder, creeps below it; and the brutal debasement of the passion that prompts the only other crime, thus punished by our law, is proverbially blind to consequences, and regardless of obstacles that impede its gratification—threats of death will never deter men who are actuated by these passions; many of them affront it in the very commission of the offence, and therefore readily incur the lesser risk of suffering it, in what they think the impossible event of detection. But present other consequences more directly opposed to the enjoyments which were anticipated in the commission of the crime, make those consequences permanent and certain, and then, although milder, they will be less readily risked than the momentary pang attending the loss of life ; study the passions which first suggested the offence, and apply your punishment to mortify and counteract them.  The ambitious man cannot bear the ordinary restraints of government—subject him to those of a prison ; he could not endure the superiority of the most dignified magistrate—force him to submit to the lowest officer of executive justice ; he sought, by his crimes, a superiority above all that was most respectable in society— reduce him in his punishment to a level with the most vile and abject of mankind.  If avarice suggested the murder—separate the wretch for ever from his hoard ; realize the fable of antiquity ; sentence him, from his place of penitence and punishment, to see his heirs rioting on his spoils; and the corroding reflection that others are innocently enjoy- ing the fruits of his crime, will be as appropriate a punishment in prac- tical as it was feigned to be in poetical justice.  The rapacious spend- thrift robs to support his extravagance, and murders to avoid detec- tion; he exposes his life that he may either pass it in idleness, debauche- ry and sensual enjoyment, or lose it by a momentary pang—disappoint his profligate calculation ; force him to live, but to live under those privations which he fears more than death ; let him be reduced to the coarse diet, the hard lodging, and the incessant labour of a penitentiary.

Substitute these privations, which all such offenders fear, which they have all risked their lives to avoid; substitute these, to that death which has little terror for men whose passions or depravity have forced them to plunge in guilt, and you establish a fitness in the punishment to the crime ; instead of a momentary spectacle, you exhibit a lesson, that is every day renewed ; and you make the very passions which caused the offence the engines to punish it, and prevent its repetition.

Reformation is lost sight of in adopting this punishment, but ought it to be totally discarded ?  May not even great crimes be committed by persons whose minds are not so corrupted as to preclude the hope of this effect.  They are, sometimes, produced by a single error.  Of- ten are the consequences of a concatenation of circumstances never likely again to occur, and are very frequently the effect of a momentary hallucination, which, though not sufficient to excuse, ought sometimes to palliate the guilt ; yet the operation of these several causes, the evi- dent gradation in the degrees of guilt which they establish, are levelled before this destructive punishment.  The man who, urged by an irre- sistible impulse of nature, sacrifices the base seducer who has destroyed his domestic happiness ; he who having been calumniated, insulted and dishonoured, at the risk of his own life takes that of the slanderer; are, in the eye of this harsh law, equally deserving of death with the vile assassin who murders for hire, or poisons for revenge ; and the youth, whose weakness in the commission of a first offence has yielded to the artful insinuations or overbearing influence of a veteran in vice, must perish on the same scaffold with the hardened and irreclaimable instigator of his crime.  It may be said, that the pardoning power is the proper remedy for this evil ; but the pardoning power, in capital cases, must be exercised, if at all, without loss of time ; without that insight into character which the penitentiary system affords.  It is therefore, necessarily liable to abuse ; and there is this further objection to its exercise, that it leaves no alternative between death and entire exemption from punishment; but in every degree of crime, some punishment is necessary; the novice, if subject to no reclaiming discipline, will soon become a professor in guilt : but let the corrective be judiciously applied, and its progress will discover whether he may be again trusted in society, or whether his depravity is so rooted as to require continued confinement.

In coming to a resolution on this solemn subject, we must not forget another principle we have established, and I think on the soundest reasons, that other things being equal, that punishment should be preferred, which gives us the means of correcting any false judgment, to which passion, indifference, false testimony, or deceiving appearances, may have given rise. Error from these, or other causes, is sometimes inevitable, its operation is instantaneous, and its fatal effects in the punishment of death, follow without delay : but time is required for its correction ; we retrace our steps with difficulty ; it is mortifying to acknowledge that we have been unjust, and during the time requisite for the discovery of the truth, for its operation on our unwilling minds, for the interposition of that power, which alone can stop the execution of the law, its stroke falls, and the innocent victim dies. What would not then the jurors who convicted ; the judges who condemned ; the mistaken witness who testified to his guilt ; what would not the whole community who saw his dying agonies, who heard, at that solemn moment, his fruitless asseverations of innocence ; what would they not all give to have yet within their reach the means of repairing the wrongs they had witnessed or inflicted ?

Instances of this kind are not unfrequent ; many of them are on record ; several have taken place in our own day, and a very remarkable example which was given but a few years since, in one of the northern states, shows, in a striking manner, the danger of those punishments which cannot be recalled or compensated, even though the innocence of the sufferer is rendered clear to demonstration. A few such instances, even in a century, are sufficient to counteract the best effects that could be derived from example. There is no spectacle that takes such hold on the feelings as that of an innocent man suffering by an unjust sentence ; one such example is remembered, when twenty of merited punishment are forgotten ; the best passions take part against the laws, and arraign their operation as iniquitous and inhuman. This consideration alone, then, if there were no others, would be a most powerful argument for the abolition of capital punishments ; but there are others no less cogent.

To see a human being in the full enjoyment of all the faculties of his mind, and all the energies of his body ; his vital powers attacked by no disease ; injured by no accident ; the pulse beating high with youth and health ; to see him doomed by the cool calculation of his fellow-men to certain destruction, which no courage can repel, no art or persuasion avert ; to see a mortal distribute the most awful dispensations of the Deity, usurp his attributes, and fix, by his own decree, an inevitable limit to that existence which Almighty power alone can give, and which its sentence alone should destroy ; must give rise to solemn reflections, which the imposing spectacle of a human sacrifice naturally produces, until its frequent recurrence renders the mind insensible to the impression. But in a country where the punishment

D

of death is rarely inflicted, this sensation operates in all its force ; the people are always strongly excited by every trial for a capital offence ; they neglect their business, and crowd round the court ; the accused, the witnesses, the counsel, every thing connected with the investigation becomes a matter of interest and curiosity ; when the public mind is screwed up to this pitch, it will take a tone from the circumstances of the case, which will rarely be found to accord with the impartiality acquired by justice.

If the accused excite an interest from his youth, his good character, his connections, or even his countenance and appearance, the dreadful consequences of conviction, and that, too, in the case of great crimes as well as minor offences, lead prosecutors to relax their severity, witnesses to appear with reluctance, jurors to acquit against evidence, and the pardoning power improperly to interpose. If the public excitement take another turn, the consequences are worse ; indignation against the crime is created into a ferocious thirst of vengeance ; and if the real culprit cannot be found, the innocent suffers on the slightest presumption of guilt ; when public zeal requires a victim, the innocent lamb is laid on the altar, while the scape-goat is suffered to fly to the mountain. This savage disposition increases with the severity and the frequency of capital inflictions, so that in atrocious as well as in lighter offences, this species of punishment leads sometimes to the escape of the guilty, often to the conviction of the innocent.

Whoever has at all observed the course of criminal proceedings, must have witnessed what I have just endeavoured to describe ; undeserved indulgence, unjust severity ; opposite effects proceeding from the same cause ; the unnecessary harshness of the punishment.

But when no such fatal consequences are to be the result, the course of justice is rarely influenced by passion or prejudice. The evidence is produced without difficulty, and given without reluctance ; it has its due effect on the minds of jurors, who are under no terrors of pronouncing an irremediable sentence : and pardons need not be granted, unless innocence is ascertained, or reformation becomes unequivocal.

Another consequence of the infliction of death is, that if frequent it loses its effect ; the people become too much familiarized with it to consider it as an example ; it is changed into a spectacle, which must frequently be repeated to satisfy the ferocious taste it has formed. It would be extremely useful in legislation, if the true cause could be discovered of this atrocious passion for witnessing human agonies and beholding the slaughter of human beings. It has disgraced the history of all nations ; in some it gave rise to permanent institutions, like that of the gladiators in Rome ; in others it has shown itself like a moral epidemic, which raged with a violence proportioned to the density of population, for a limited time, and then yielded to the influence of reason and humanity. Every people has given us instances of this delirium ; but the religious massacre of St Bartholomew, and the political slaughters during the reign of terror in France, exemplify, in a striking manner, the idea I mean to convey. The history of our own country, young as it is, is not free from this stain. The judicial murder of the wizards and witches of New England, and of a great number of poor wretches, during what was called the negro-plot at New York, furnish us with domestic lessons on this subject. The human sacrifices which we find in the early history of almost every nation, proceeded from another cause, the idea of vicarious atonement for sins ; but they were attended with the same heart-hardening effect. Human sufferings are never beheld, for the first time, but with aversion, terror and disgust. Nature has strongly implanted this repugnance on our minds, for the wisest purposes : but this once conquered, it happens in the intellectual taste, as it does in that of the senses : in relation to which last, it is observed, that we become most fond of those enjoyments which required, in the beginning, some effort to overcome the disgust produced by their first use ; and that our attachment to them is in proportion to the difficulty which was conquered in becoming familiarized to them. Whatever may be the cause of this striking fact, in the history of the human mind, its effects ought to be studied by the legislator who desires to form a wise and permanent system. If the sight of one capital execution creates an inhuman taste to behold another ; if a curiosity, satisfied at first with terror, increases with its gratification, and becomes a passion by indulgence, we ought to be extremely careful how, by sanctioning the frequency of capital punishments, we lay the foundation for a depravity, the more to be dreaded, because, in our government, popular opinion must have the greatest influence on all its departments, and this vitiated taste would soon be discovered in the decisions of our courts and the verdicts of our juries.

But if this punishment be kept for great occasions, and the people are seldom treated with the gratification of seeing one of their fellow-creatures expire by the sentence of the law ; a most singular effect is produced ; the sufferer, whatever be his crime, becomes a hero or a saint ; he is the object of public attention, curiosity, admiration, and pity. Charity supplies all his wants, and religion proves her power, by exhibiting the outcast and murderer, though unworthy to enjoy existence upon earth, yet purified from the stain of his vices and crimes, converted by her agency into an accepted candidate for the happiness of heaven ; he is lifted above the fear of death by the exhortations and prayers of the pious ; the converted sinner receives the tender attentions of respectability, beauty and worth : his prison becomes a place of pilgrimage, its tenant, a saint awaiting the crown of martyrdom ; his last looks are watched, with affectionate solicitude ; his last words are carefully remembered and recorded ; his last agonies are beheld with affliction and despair ; and after suffering the ignominious sentence of the law, the body of the culprit, whose death was infamy, and whose life was crime, is attended respectfully and mournfully to the grave, by a train that would not have disgraced the obsequies of a patriot or a hero. This sketch, though highly coloured, is drawn from life : the inhabitants of one of the most refined and wealthy of our state capitals, sat for the picture ; and although such exalted feelings are not always excited, or are prudently repressed, yet they are found in nature, and in whatever degree they exist, it cannot be doubted, that in the same proportion, they counteract every good effect that punishment is intended to produce. The hero of such a tragedy can never consider himself as the actor of a mean or ignoble part ; nor can the people view in the object of their admiration or pity, a murderer and a robber, whom they would have regarded with horror, if their feelings had not been injudiciously enlisted in his favour. Thus the end of the law is defeated, the force of example is totally lost, and the place of execution is converted into a scene of triumph for the sufferer, whose crime

is wholly forgotten, while his courage, resignation, or piety, mark him
as the martyr, not the guilty victim, of the laws.

Where laws are so directly at war with the feelings of the people
whom they govern, as this and many other instances prove them to
be, these laws can never be wise or operative, and they ought to be
abolished.

*Quid leges sine moribus, vanæ proficiunt?* But if laws unsupported by the morals of the people are inefficient, how can we reasonably expect that they will have any effect when they are counteracted
by moral feelings as well as by ideas of religion. This is the effect of
capital punishments in a country where they are not commonly inflicted. Let us now see what is their result, where they are unhappily
too frequent.

In England, a great portion of the eloquence and learning, and all
the humanity of the nation are at work, in an endeavour, not to abolish
the punishment of death (that proposition would be too bold in a government where reform, in any department, might lead to revolution
in all), but to restrict it to the more atrocious offences. This has produced a parliamentary inquiry, in the course of which the reports, to
which I have alluded before, were made; one of them contains the examinations of witnesses before a committee of the house of commons.
From one of these, that of a solicitor who had practised for more than
twenty years in the criminal courts, I make the following extracts:

"In the course of my practice, I have found that the punishment of
death has no terror upon a common thief ; indeed, it is much more the
subject of ridicule among them, than of serious deliberation. The
certain approach of an ignominious death does not seem to operate
upon them ; for after the warrant has come down, I have seen them
treat it with levity. I once saw a man, for whom I had been concerned the day before his execution, and on offering him condolence,
and expressing my concern at his situation, he replied with an air of
indifference, 'players at bowls must expect rubbers ;' and this man I
heard say, that it was only a few minutes, a kick and a struggle, and
all was over. The fate of one set of culprits, in some instances, had
no effect, even on those who were next to be reported for execution ;
they play at ball and pass their jokes as if nothing was the matter. I
have seen the last separation of persons about to be executed. There
was nothing of solemnity about it, and it was more like the parting
for a country journey, than taking their last farewell. I mention these
things, to show what little fear common thieves entertain of capital
punishment ; and that so far from being arrested in their wicked courses
by the distant possibility of its infliction, they are not even intimidated by its certainty."

Another of those respectable witnesses (a magistrate of the capital)
being asked, whether he thought that capital punishment had much
tendency to deter criminals from the commission of offences, answered,
"I do not. I believe it is well known to those who are conversant with
criminal associations in this town, that criminals live and act in gangs and
confederacies, and that the execution of one or more of their own body,
seldom has a tendency to dissolve the confederacy, or to deter the remaining associates from the continuance of their former pursuits. Instances have occurred within my own jurisdiction, to confirm me in
this opinion. During one sitting, as a magistrate, three persons were

brought before me for uttering forged notes. During the investigation, I discovered that those notes were obtained from a room in which the body of a person named Wheller (executed on the preceding day, for the same offence) then was laid, and that the notes in question were delivered for circulation by a woman with whom he had been living. This is (he adds) a strong case, but I have no doubt that it is but one of very many others."

The ordinary of Newgate, a witness better qualified than any other to give information on this subject, being asked, "Have you made any observations as to the effect of the sentence of death upon the prisoners?" answers—"It seems scarcely to have any effect upon them; the generality of people under sentence of death are thinking, or doing rather, any thing than preparing for their latter end." Being interrogated as to the effect produced by capital executions on the minds of the people, he answers, "I think, shock and horror at the moment, upon the inexperienced and the young, but immediately after the scene is closed, forgetfulness altogether of it, leaving no impression on the young and inexperienced. The old and experienced thief says, the chances have gone against the man who has suffered ; that it is of no consequence, that it is what was to be expected; making no serious impression on the mind. I have had occasion to go into the press-yard within an hour and a half after an execution, and I have there found them amusing themselves, playing at balls or marbles, and appearing precisely as if nothing had happened."

No colouring is necessary to heighten the effect of these sketches. Nothing, it appears to me, can more fully prove the utter inutility of this waste of human life, its utter inefficiency as a punishment, and its demoralizing operation on the minds of the people.

The want of authentic documents prevents me at present from laying before the general assembly some facts which would elucidate the subject, by examples, from the records of criminal courts in the different states. The prevalence of particular offences, as affected by the changes in their criminal laws ; the number of commitments, compared with that of convictions; and the effect which the punishment of death has on the frequency of the crimes for which it is inflicted; accurate information on these heads would have much facilitated the investigation in which we are engaged. But although from the causes which I have stated, these are not now within our reach; there are yet some facts generally known on the subject, which are not devoid of interest or instruction. Murder, in all the states, is punished with death; in most of them it is, except treason (which never occurred under the state laws), the only crime that is so punished. If this were the most efficacious penalty to prevent crimes, this offence would be the one of which we should see the fewest instances. Is it so ? To answer this question, we must establish a comparison, not between it and other offences,—that would never lead us to a true result; there are some crimes that are so destructive of the very existence of society, create such universal alarm, and suppose so great a depravity, that the perpetrator is always viewed with abhorrence by the whole community, and public execration would inflict a punishment, even if the laws were silent. The number of such crimes, therefore, whatever may be the punishment assigned to them, must necessarily be fewer, in proportion, than those which do not inspire the same horror, or spread the same alarm; of this nature is murder; we must, therefore, look to other countries, to establish our point of comparison.

Unfortunately, the crime is punished in the same manner as it is here, in the only country we have sufficient data to reason upon, and therefore the result of the inquiry cannot be conclusive; but if in that country a number of other offences are punished with death, which do not incur that penalty here, and if those minor offences prevail in a much greater degree there than they do here, where they are not so punished, while murder, and robbery with intent to murder (almost the only crimes punished in that manner here), be more frequently committed in this country than in that which I select for the comparison, then we shall have some reason to doubt the efficacy of this violent remedy.

In London and Middlesex, for sixteen years ending in 1818, thirty-five persons were convicted of murder, and stabbing with intent to murder, which is an average of a fraction more than two in a year. In the city of New Orleans, seven persons suffered for the same crime, in the space of the last four years, which is very little less than the same average; but the population of New-Orleans did not, during the period, amount to more than 35,000, which is to that of Middlesex and London, in round numbers, as one to twenty-seven; therefore, the crime of murder was nearly twenty-seven times as frequent, in proportion to numbers, as in London. Almost the same proportion holds between the whole state and England and Wales, in relation to this crime; nineteen executions having taken place for murder, in the last seven years, in Louisiana, and one hundred and fifty-four during the seven years, ending in 1818, in England and Wales. In London and Middlesex, eight hundred and eighty-five persons were convicted of forgery and counterfeiting in seven years, ending in 1818. During an equal period, seven persons were convicted of the same offence in the whole state, which makes the crime eighteen times more frequent in London, in proportion to number, than it is here. Six thousand nine hundred and seventy-four convictions for larceny took place in the same seven years in London: and for a like period, in the state of Louisiana, one hundred, which is near ten to one more there than here, in proportion to the population. Many capital convictions were had there, for crimes of which none were committed here, and which, if they had been, would have been punished only by imprisonment at hard labour. I well know that the state of society in the two countries, the degree of temptation, the ease or difficulty of obtaining subsistence, and other circumstances, as well as the operation of the laws, may produce the difference I have shown. But does it not raise serious doubts as to the efficacy of the capital punishment, to observe this double effect, that almost the only crime which we punish in that manner, is more frequent in the proportion of twenty-seven to one, while those which are the object of a milder sanction, are almost in the same ratio less than in the country with which we make the comparison?

The laws of none of the states punish highway robbery with death; those of the United States affix this punishment to the robbery of the mail, under circumstances which generally accompany it. Yet it is believed, that this last species of highway robbery is more frequent than the other—another proof that the fear of death is not a more powerful preventative of crime than other punishments.

I do not urge the doubts which many wise and conscientious persons have entertained of the right of inflicting this punishment, because

I am inclined to think that the right can be well established. If this measure be the only one that can prevent the crime, government has a right to adopt it, unless the evil arising from the punishment be greater than that which could be apprehended from the offence. If it were proved, that the fruit in a garden could not be preserved without punishing the boys who stole it with death, the evil to be apprehended from the offence is so much less than that produced by the punishment, that it ought never to be inflicted by the law, much less (as in the case of the English spring-guns) by the party injured; but on the contrary, it is a less evil to destroy the life of an assassin, than to permit him to take that of a man, whose existence is useful to his country, and necessary to his family. Whenever, therefore, in this latter case the alternative is proved to be the only one, I do not think we ought to hesitate from any doubt of the right: but if the necessity of the punishment, as well as the preponderating evil of the crime, cannot be clearly shown, the right cannot exist. The burthen of argument rests here on those who advocate this punishment; they must show that it is the only means of repressing the offence: they must show, that in the cases to which they mean to apply it, the evil of the offence is greater than the punishment. How far they can succeed in the first part of this task, has been already, in part, examined; on the latter branch of the position it may be proper to observe, that in estimating the evil resulting from the impunity of any particular offence, in order to compare it with that of the punishment, we must recollect, that the one is a certain, the other a problematical evil. For instance, a man commits murder; if it were certain, if you did not put him to death, either that he himself would repeat the offence, or that the example of his impunity would induce another to do it, the case both of necessity to prevent crime, and of the preponderating evil of the offence over that of the remedy, would be made out. But it does not follow, because a man has once committed a crime, he will therefore repeat it, nor that another will be seduced by his example to do so; both, I grant, are probable; then we have the probability of two evils to put in competition with the certainty of one; but a strong probability of a great evil ought to countervail the certainty of a smaller one; and if in this instance the probability be great, that society might suffer the loss of its worthiest citizens, this ought not to be placed in competition with the evil of putting an assassin to death. But if by other means, the chance of the uncertain evil can be reduced to a bare possibility, then the certain evil should not be incurred. Admitting, therefore, that the infliction of death is the best means of preventing the repetition of the offence, yet if perpetual imprisonment would as effectually prevent the offender from repeating it, and would also operate as an example, so as to reduce to a possibility the chance of another being induced by the mildness of the punishment to commit the crime, then the certain evil of taking away human life ought not to be incurred, because the remote possibility of even a great evil cannot justify it.

But before we adopt any of these calculations (always liable to the greatest difficulty in practice), we ought to inquire whether the position which alone renders them necessary be true; whether the punishment of death is necessary to prevent offences. In the proper sense of the expression, we know this is not the case; to say that a certain single cause is necessary to produce a given effect, supposes, that if the cause exist, the effect will certainly follow; but it is not pretended that the punishment of death will, in all cases, prevent the crime for which it is inflicted; all that is meant is, that it is better adapted to that end than any other kind of punishment: some reasons have already been given to show that it is not. Let us examine those which are usually given on the affirmative side of this interesting question.

First. There are those who support it by arguments drawn from religion. The divine spirit infused into the great legislator of the Jews, from whose code these arguments are drawn, was never intended to inspire a system of universal jurisprudence. The theocracy given as a form of government to that extraordinary people, was not suited to any other; as little was the system of their penal laws, given on the mysterious mountain, promulgated from the bosom of a dark cloud, amid thunder and lightning; they were intended to strike terror into the minds of a perverse and obdurate people; and as one means of effecting this, the punishment of death is freely denounced for a long list of crimes; but the same authority establishes the *lex talionis*, and other regulations, which those who quote this authority would surely not wish to adopt. They forget that the same Almighty author of that law, at a later period, inspired one of his prophets with a solemn assurance, that might with propriety be placed over the gates of a penitentiary, and confirmed it with an awful asseveration,—" As I LIVE, saith the LORD GOD, I have no pleasure in the DEATH of a sinner, but rather that he should TURN FROM HIS WICKEDNESS AND LIVE." They forget, too, although they are Christians who use this argument, that the divine author of their religion expressly forbids the retaliatory system, on which the punishment of death for murder is founded; they forget the mild benevolence of his precepts, the meekness of his spirit, the philanthropy that breathes in all his words, and directed all his actions; they lose sight of that golden rule which he established : " To do nothing to others that we would not desire them to do unto us ;" and certainly pervert the spirit of his holy and merciful religion, when they give it as the sanction for sanguinary punishments. Indeed, if I were inclined to support my opinion by arguments drawn from religion, the whole New Testament should be my text, and I could easily deduce from it authority for a system of reform as opposed to one of extermination. But although the legislator would be unworthy of the name, who should prescribe any thing contrary to the dictates of religion, and particularly to those of that divine morality on which the Christian system is founded, yet it would be not less dangerous, to make its dogmas the ground-work of his legislation, or to array them in defence of political systems. In a government, where all religions have equal privileges, it would be obviously unjust ; it would lessen the reverence for sacred, by mixing them with political institutions, and perverting to temporal uses those precepts which were given as rules for the attainment of eternal happiness.

Secondly. The practice of all nations, from the remotest antiquity, is urged in favour of this punishment ; the fact, with some exceptions, is undoubtedly true, but is the inference just ? There are general errors, and unfortunately for mankind, but few general truths, established by practice, in government legislation. Make this the criterion, and despotism is, by many thousand degrees on the scale of antiquity, better than a representative government : the laws of Draco were more ancient than those of Solon, and consequently better ; and the practice of torture quite as generally diffused as that of which we are now treating. Idolatry in religion, tyranny in government, capital punishments, and inhuman tortures in jurisprudence, are coeval and coextensive. , Will the advocates of this punishment admit the force of their argument in favour of all these abuses ? If they do not, how will they apply it to the one for which they argue ?

The long and general usage of any institution gives us the means of examining its practical advantages or defects : but it ought to have no authority as a precedent, until it be proved, that the best laws are the most ancient, and that institutions for the happiness of the people are the most permanent and most generally diffused. But this unfortunately cannot be maintained with truth ; the melancholy reverse forces conviction on our minds. Every where, with but few exceptions, the interest of the many has, from the earliest ages, been sacrificed to the power of the few. Every where penal laws have been framed to support this power ; and those institutions, favourable to freedom, which have come down to us from our ancestors, form no part of any original plan, but are isolated privileges which have been wrested from the grasp of tyranny, or which have been suffered, from inattention to their importance, to grow into strength.

Every nation in Europe has, during the last eight or ten centuries, been involved in a continual state of internal discord or foreign war : kings and nobles continually contending for power ; both oppressing the people, and driving them to desperation and revolt. Different pretenders, asserting their claims to the throne of deposed or assassinated kings ; religious wars ; cruel persecutions ; partition of kingdoms ; cessions of provinces ; succeeding each other with a complication and rapidity that defies the skill and diligence of the historian to unravel and record. Add to this, the ignorance in which the human mind was involved, during the early and middle part of this period ; the intolerant bigotry, which from its close connection with government, stifled every improvement in politics as well as every reformation in religion; and we shall see a state of things certainly not favourable for the formation of wise laws on any subject; but particularly ill calculated for the establishment of a just or humane criminal code. From such legislators, acting in such times, what could be expected, but that which we actually find ; a mass of laws unjust, because made solely with a view to support the temporary views of a prevailing party ; unwise, obscure, inhuman, inconsistent, because they were the work of ignorance, dictated by interest, passion and intolerance. But it would scarcely seem prudent to surrender our reason to authorities thus established, and to give the force of precedent to any of the incoherent collections of absurd, cruel, and contradictory provisions which have been dignified with the name of penal codes, in the jurisprudence of any nation in Europe, as their laws stood prior to the last century. No one would surely advise this ; why then select any part of the mass, and recommend it to us, merely because it has been generally practised? If there is any other reason for adopting it, let that be urged, and it ought to have its weight; but my object here is to show, that from the mode in which the penal laws of Europe have, until a very late period, been established, very little respect is due to them merely on account of their antiquity, or of the extent to which they have prevailed. If the criminal jurisprudence

E

of the modern and middle ages affords us little reason to revere either its humanity or justice ; that of the ancient world does not give us more. The despotism of antiquity was like that of modern times, and such as it will always be ; it can have but one character, which the rare occurrence, of a few mild or philosophic monarchs does not change : and in the laws of the republics, there was a mixture of severity and indulgence, that makes them very improper models for imitation.   Yet in Rome, for about two hundred and fifty years, from the date of the valerian law until the institutions of the republic were annihilated by the imperial power, it was not lawful to put a Roman citizen to death for any crime ; and we cannot learn from history that offences were unusually prevalent during that period; but we do know that when executions became frequent, Rome was the receptacle of every crime and every vice. It must, however, be confessed, that we have not sufficient information to determine whether the frequency of capital punishments was the cause or the effect of this depravity.

Modern history affords us two examples which deserve to be attended to in this discussion.   The empress Elizabeth of Russia, soon after she came to the throne, abolished the pain of death in all her extensive dominions ; her reign lasted twenty years, giving ample time to try the effect of the experiment : and Beccaria speaks with enthusiasm of the consequences it had produced. I have not been able to procure the regulations by which this change was effected, but as I believe the *knout* (an infliction more cruel than a speedy death) was preserved, I do not urge this example as having the same weight it would have, if milder punishments had been substituted.   Three years after Elizabeth had ceased to reign in the north of Europe, her great experiment was renewed in the south.   Leopold became grand duke of Tuscany, and one of his first acts was a declaration (rigidly adhered to during his reign) that no offence should be punished with death; he substituted a mild system of graduated punishments, and though I do not think they were very judiciously chosen, yet the consequence was, an immediate decrease in the number of offences.   We are informed, that during a considerable period, the prisons were empty, and no complaints for atrocious offences occurred; and he himself, after an experiment of twenty years, declares, " that the mitigation of punishments, joined to a most scrupulous attention to prevent crimes, and also great despatch in the trial, together with a certainty and suddenness of punishment to real delinquents, had, instead of increasing the number of crimes, considerably diminished that of the smaller ones, and rendered those of an ATROCIOUS NATURE VERY RARE." This passage is extracted from the introduction to a code which he gave to his people in the year 1786 : four years afterwards, he was called to the empire, and the further course of his noble experiment was interrupted.   How far the old system was re-established, I am not accurately informed, but some travellers represent, that the new state of things forms a contrast very much in favour of the Leopold code. These instances, I think, turn the scale of argument as it applies to the authority of example ; if we can rely on that of Tuscany (and it seems perfectly well authenticated), it proves the inefficiency of capital punishments, in great as well as smaller offences, and it is of more weight than the united practice of all the nations of the world where the punishment is retained, but where it has never been found effectual to repress the prevalence of crimes.

The third and last argument I have heard urged, is nearly allied to the second ; it is, the danger to be apprehended from innovation. I confess, I always listen to this objection with some degree of suspicion. That men who owe their rank, their privileges, their emoluments, to abuses and impositions, originating in the darkness of antiquity, and consecrated by time; that such men should preach the danger of innovations, I can well conceive ; the wonder is, that they can find others weak and credulous enough to believe them. But in a country where these abuses do not exist; in a country whose admirable system of government is founded wholly on innovation, where there is no antiquity to create a false veneration for abuses, and no apparent interest to perpetuate them ; in such a country, this argument will have little force against the strong reasons which assail it. Let those, however, who honestly entertain this doubt, reflect that, most fortunately for themselves and for their posterity, they live in an age of advancement: not an art, not a science, that has not in our day made rapid progress towards perfection. The one of which we now speak has received and is daily acquiring improvement ; how long is it since torture was abolished ? Since judges were made independent? Since personal liberty was secured, and religious persecution forbidden ? All these were, in their time, innovations as bold at least as the one now proposed. The true use of this objection, and there I confess it has force, is to prevent any hazardous experiment, or the introduction of any change that is not strongly recommended by reason. I desire no other test for the one that is now under discussion, but I respectfully urge, that it would be unwise to reject it, merely because it is untried, if we are convinced it will be beneficial. Should our expectations be disappointed, no extensive evil can be done ; the remedy is always in our power. Although an experiment, it is not a hazardous one, and the only inquiry seems to be, whether the arguments and facts stated in its favour, are sufficiently strong to justify us in making it. Indeed, it appears to me that the reasoning might, with some propriety, be retorted against those who use it, by saying—" all punishments are but experiments to discover what will best prevent crimes ; your favourite one of death has been fully tried. By your own account, all nations, since the first institution of society, have practised it, but you yourselves must acknowledge, without success. All we ask, then, is that you abandon an experiment which has for five or six thousand years been progressing under all the variety of forms which cruel ingenuity could invent; and which in all ages, under all governments, has been found wanting. You have been obliged reluctantly to confess that it is inefficient, and to abandon it in minor offences ; what charm has it then which makes you cling to it in those of a graver cast ? You have made your experiment ; it was attended in its operation with an incalculable waste of human life ; a deplorable degradation of human intellect ; it was found often fatal to the innocent, and it very frequently permitted the guilty to escape. Nor can you complain of any unseasonable interference with your plan that may account for its failure : during the centuries that your system has been in operation, humanity and justice have never interrupted its course ; you went on in the work of destruction, always seeing an increase of crime, and always supposing that increased severity was the only remedy to suppress it : the mere forfeiture of life was too mild; tortures were superadded, which nothing but the intelligence of a fiend could invent, to prolong its duration and increase its torments; yet there was no diminution of crime; and it never occurred to you, that mildness might accomplish that which could not be effected by severity." This great truth revealed itself to philosophers, who imparted it to the people; the strength of popular opinion at length forced it upon kings, and the work of reformation, in spite of the cry against novelty, began. It has been progressive. Why should it stop, when every argument, every fact, promises its complete success? We could not concur in the early stages of this reformation; perhaps the credit may be reserved to us of completing it; and I therefore make no apology to the general assembly for having so long occupied them with this discussion. In imposing so important a change, it was necessary to state the prominent reasons which induced me to think it necessary; many more have weighed upon my mind, and on reviewing these, I feel with humility and regret how feebly they are urged. The nature of the subject alone will, however, create an interest sufficient to promote inquiry, and humanity will suggest arguments which I have not had sagacity to discover or the talent to enforce.

Having stated the reasons which induced me to discard all the different punishments which have been reviewed, I proceed to a short discussion of those which have been adopted. These are

Pecuniary fines; degradation from office; simple imprisonment; temporary suspension of civil rights; permanent deprivation of civil rights; imprisonment at hard labour; solitary confinement during certain intervals of the time of imprisonment, to be determined in the sentence.

The advantage of this scale of punishment is, that it is divisible almost to infinity; that there is no offence, however slight, for which it does not afford an appropriate corrective; and none, however atrocious, for which, by cumulating its different degrees, an adequate punishment cannot be found.

When to these are added the regulations which are made in certain cases, as to the nature of food and other comforts, during the term of punishment, it has, in an almost perfect degree, the essential quality of being capable of apportionment, not only to any species of offence, but to every offender. Sex, age, habits, constitution, every circumstance which ought to determine the exercise of discretionary power, may have its proper weight.

Reformation of the criminal may reasonably be expected.

He is effectually restrained from a repetition of his crime.

A permanent and striking example is constantly operating to deter others.

The punishment being mild, public feeling will never enlist the passions of the people in opposition to the law.

The same cause will ensure a rigid performance of their duty by public officers.

Jurors, from a false compassion, will seldom acquit the guilty; and if by chance or prejudice they should convict the innocent, their error or fault is not as in the cases of infliction of stripes—permanent stigmas, or death—without the reach of redress.

These are advantages which render the penitentiary system decidedly superior to any other.

To detail the mode in which these different punishments are composed and applied to the different offences, would be to repeat the provisions of the whole book, which cannot be expected from the nature of this report; enough, and I fear more than enough, has been said on this division of the work.

I proceed to the plan of the fourth book, which, as we have seen, is intended to give rules of practice in all criminal proceedings.

It regulates the mode in which complaints and accusations are to be made; designates the proper persons to receive them, and directs their duty in conducting the examination; taking the evidence on the complaint, and ordering the arrest; prescribes the form of warrants; and designates precisely the cases where arrests may be made without them. It prescribes minutely the duties, and defines the authority, as well of officers as of individuals, who assist them in making arrests.

It regulates the mode of conducting the examination, and the manner of making commitments, so as to avoid the frequent escapes of the guilty from the former defective practice on this head.

The manner in which the person is to be treated, during his confinement, is minutely detailed; provisions are introduced to prevent or punish all abuses of authority in those who arrest or have charge of the prisoner.

Rules are laid down for directing the discretion of the magistrate, and ascertaining his duties in admitting to bail.

The manner in which accusations, and the evidence to support them, are to be brought before the proper court, is distinctly described.

Rules are presented for the organization and mode of conducting business before grand juries. Their duties are defined, as are those of the public prosecutor, in presenting indictments before them.

The cases are distinguished which are to be prosecuted by indictment, from those in which information may be filed.

Rules are laid down for drawing acts of accusation, so as to secure a proper degree of certainty in the allegation of the offence, but to prevent the escape of the guilty from formal defects.

The mode of making the arraignment; the manner of pleading; the rules for conducting the trial; the duties of the judge; of the advocate for the accused, and of the public prosecutor, in relation to it, are minutely marked out.

Regulations are made for summoning, swearing, and challenging jurors, and for their government on the trial, and on the delivery of the verdict.

Directions are given for summoning and securing the attendance of witnesses.

The causes are designated for which judgments may be arrested and new trials granted, and all the proceedings subsequent to the verdict are provided for.

A chapter is dedicated to the regulation of the manner in which search-warrants are to be granted and executed, and another to the designation of the cases in which security may be required against the commission of apprehended offences. Contempts are defined, and the mode of trying and punishing them is marked out.

The last chapter of this book contains a system of proceeding on writs of *habeas corpus*.

This chapter will be the first act of legislation in our state on this subject; important enough, it would seem, to have sooner engaged our attention. This writ was known in a remote period of the English

law, but it was a precept without a sanction, and therefore totally inefficient until the statute passed in the 31st year of Charles II. gave it
force and efficacy, and made it a feature in their jurisprudence, of which
any nation might be proud, and which all ought to imitate or adopt.
The mechanism of this admirable contrivance for securing personal
liberty is so simple, its effects are so decisive, that we are led to wonder why it was not sooner put in operation, especially in a nation which
at so early a period made it a stipulation with their king, that "no
freeman should be imprisoned but by the law of the land." Indeed the
writ itself was known in the Roman law by the name of the *interdict
de homine libero exhibendo*; but it was applicable only to the case of
a freeman claimed as a slave; and we do not find that even in that case
there were any provisions to enforce its execution : on the contrary,
there was one which permitted any person to refuse obedience, who
chose rather to pay for the man, estimating his value as if he was a
slave. In no stage of its history, therefore, was this writ of any importance until the spirit of liberty, nearly extinguished under the energetic despotism of the Tudors, rose superior to the weakness of the
Stuarts, and inspired the declaration of those principles of personal
and political rights, on which our republics are chiefly founded. One
of the most important measures which this spirit suggested, was the
habeas corpus act; it directs the manner in which the writ is to issue ;
imposes penalties for disobedience to it, and makes a number of salutary provisions to prevent delays and abuses in criminal proceedings.
In all the Atlantic states, this statute was a part of the law by which
they were governed at the time they became independent ; and it was
either expressly or impliedly adopted with the whole body of their
municipal laws. In those states, therefore, nothing more was necessary than to guard against its suspension by a constitutional clause.
But here the case was different, the common law of England was not
in force here, still less were its statutes. Neither could form part of
our law, unless specially re-enacted. Yet the framers of our constitution, not attending to this difference, contented themselves with tran-
scribing from the constitutions of other states, the provision that "the
privilege of the writ of habeas corpus shall not be suspended, unless
when in cases of rebellion or invasion the public safety may require
it." But no law had before, or has been since passed, defining what
the writ of habeas corpus was, or directing the manner in which it
was to be obtained, how it was to be executed, what was to be its effect, or what the penalty of disobeying it. If the writ alone be introduced without the provisions for enforcing it, it could be of as little use
here as it was in England before the statute of Charles II. ; if the
statute be introduced, do we stop at that of Charles? or are those of
16 George I. and 38 of George III. re-enacted by this laconic legislation ? If either of them are, they involve, as applied to us, great absurdities : for they contain many provisions which are purely local, all of
them referring to courts and to magistrates which do not exist under
our laws; and impose penalties which are not recoverable here;
and yet on which the whole efficacy of the act depends. So that
whatever construction we put on this clause in our constitution, it
must be confessed, that without some statute to define and enforce the
great privilege of which it declares we shall not be deprived, the provision can be of little use. Hitherto the necessity for this remedy has

been so strongly felt, that judges have not scrupulously examined their right to afford it ; and even when improperly granted, so strongly is it supported by public opinion, that parties, though they have sometimes evaded its operation, have never thought proper to question its legality. It has held its authority, therefore, by the moral sense of the people, exerting its influence in support of an institution which they have been taught from their infancy to venerate and admire, rather than by the constraint of law. But times may come ; in the natural progress of human affairs must come ; when public opinion will have less force, and without the aid of law for its support, will prove a feeble barrier against encroachment.

The offences against personal liberty, which are most dangerous, are those that are committed for political purposes, and as the means of silencing opposition to unconstitutional and revolutionary measures. All the energies of the law, armed with its strongest sanctions, and directed by the most efficient measures to secure its execution then become necessary. The magnitude of the evil, therefore, concurring with the probability of its occurrence, calls for the attention of the legislature to this important subject. In examining the different enactments of this justly celebrated statute, every friend of freedom must be grateful to its authors for the extensive, and it is devoutly to be hoped, the lasting benefit they have conferred on mankind. Ten millions of freemen have already consecrated it among their fundamental rights, and the rising republics of the new world will not fail to adopt so precious an institution, when they review and finally establish their constitutional compacts.

This is the greatest glory a wise nation can desire ; to see its principles recognized ; its institutions adopted ; its laws copied, not only by men speaking the same language, and bred in a similarity of manners, but translated into different languages, adapting themselves to different habits ; incorporated in different codes, and in all, acknowledged as the' first of blessings. And the trial of a cause, by an independent jury, on the banks of the La Plata or the Oroonook ; or the writ of habeas corpus adopted by a representative assembly in Mexico and Peru, ought to afford more satisfaction to an Englishman, who loves the honour of his country, than the most splendid triumph of her arms. We must not, however, suffer our admiration of any institution to blind us to its faults or prevent us, when we are about to adopt it, from scrutinizing severely all its provisions, and carefully inquiring whether in its operation, defects have not been discovered, which a prudent attention might amend. In examining the English statute with this view, some important omissions have been observed ; and in the project presented to you, an attempt has been made to remedy them. Some of the most important ought to be enumerated.

1. The great object of this writ ; that, which constitutes its chief excellence, I may say its only use, is the promptitude and efficacy with which it acts. To borrow a phrase from another branch of jurisprudence, it is a writ for " specific performance," or it is nothing. In all civilized countries, there are actions given for injuries to personal liberty : but no nation, until England set the example, provided any means for the immediate cessation of the evil. This law enforces it by attachment, fines and penalties ; in most cases, these are effectual : but there are circumstances in which the party injured would obtain no re-

lief, and the offender would escape punishment, notwithstanding the provisions of the statute. A person may be unlawfully arrested, and forcibly embarked, to be conveyed out of the country ; the writ of habeas corpus may issue ; it may even be served in time, but if the party to whom it is directed choose to make an insufficient return, no other process can issue until that return has been received, debated, and determined to be insufficient ; and then, it is not a compulsory process, but a penal one, which is awarded ; not giving liberty to the prisoner, but punishing the party for his disobedience, who detains him ; in the mean time the sufferer may be conveyed out of the king-dom, or some other irreparable injury may be inflicted on him. This is a case which must probably have often occurred in England, by abuses under their press-warrants ; by military encroachments, and for purposes of private vengeance or public oppression. Recent as has been the establishment of our government, an outrageous and well-known example of this abuse took place here ; an evasive return was made and repeated, and while the court was occupied in determining its validity, a number of citizens were carried out of the state by a military officer, on a groundless charge of political crimes.

To prevent the occurrence of an evil of this kind, an article has been inserted, directing, whenever a case is made out to justify the issuing of this writ, accompanied by proof, that deportation, or any other irremediable injury is apprehended; or whenever the writ is disobeyed, that the magistrate shall, instead of the habeas corpus, issue his warrant to bring the prisoner, and the party in whose custody he is held, be-fore him, that the one may be released and the other committed for trial, in all cases in which those steps may be required by law.

2. Under the English law, the return is taken for true, and the only remedy is an action against the person who makes a false return ; a doctrine utterly subversive of the true intent of the act, and which, in many cases, has rendered it nugatory. This doctrine was established on a reference to the twelve judges, by the house of lords, in 1757, and was enforced in the case of American seaman impressed on board of English vessels ; the captain returned, that they had voluntarily en-listed, and without any other evidence, they were remanded to their slavery, and told, that if they survived the war, and could find any one to bring an action for a false return, on proving it, they might obtain relief. This glaring defect is removed by the law presented to you ; and the mode is prescribed for examining into the truth of a return when it is controverted.

3. The judges in the case alluded to, determined unanimously, that the provisions made for awarding and returning writs of habeas corpus immediately, do not extend to any case but those of a criminal or sup-posed criminal nature. Mr Justice Bathurst, it is true, adds to his opinion, that although the statute did not extend to other cases, yet the justices of the king's bench had, in favour of liberty, extended the same relief to all cases.

To give full effect to this remedy, it is proposed expressly to extend it to every case of illegal imprisonment and restraint.

4. By the English practice, when a prisoner is brought up on habeas corpus, if the commitment be informal, he is discharged, although suf-ficient evidence may exist to justify his detention for trial. The plan proposes a remedy for this evil, by obliging the officer who brings up

the prisoner, to produce the evidence on which he was committed, and directing the judge before whom the writ is returned, to re-commit him if the evidence warrant it.

As the whole of this chapter is submitted, it is not necessary to notice any other of the omissions which have been supplied, or the defects which it has been attempted to remedy. A strong impression of the utility of this great writ, has rendered me particularly desirous to increase the facility of procuring it; to enlarge the sphere of its relief; to give an adequate sanction to each of the provisions that are enacted; to impress upon the people the utility of preserving it and the danger of suffering it to be violated, and to show the value we place on this and other institutions of freedom, not by suffering them to remain imperfect from a blind reverence for their antiquity, but by studying to improve, or, if possible, to perfect them, and by leaving to our children, not only unimpaired, but augmented, those privileges bequeathed to us by the wisdom and patriotism of our fathers.

The great objects in the execution of this division of the work, have been to protect the innocent from ill-founded prosecutions, and even the guilty from vexation, in the manner of conducting those which were necessary to ascertain their guilt. But at the same time, to insure the exact execution of the laws, and as far as possible to destroy the effect of those devices which professional ingenuity has so frequently used to procure the escape of the guilty. Some new provisions have been introduced to effect these objects, but where they could be obtained without innovation, none have been proposed. In those cases my endeavours have been confined to the arrangement of the law applicable to the different divisions, under its proper heads; and to giving precise and intelligible language to the rules of procedure. Even a slight notice of all the points in which changes or modifications of the present law have been suggested, would extend this report, already too long, to an inconvenient size. It may not be amiss, however, to mention a prohibition of those charges, which the judge frequently uses as the means of diffusing his political tenets, displaying his eloquence, and sometimes gratifying his passions; and of those presentments of the same nature, by which the jury recommend candidates to office, denounce public measures, or eulogize the virtues of men in power; such proceedings were thought beneath the dignity of the magistrate, and inconsistent with the sanctity of that body, whose functions of public accusers, and guardians of the liberty and reputation of their fellow-citizens, require calm investigation, undisturbed by intemperate discussions. If an ordinary court of justice be properly called the temple of that high attribute of the deity, we may, without too far extending the metaphor, term the tribunal of criminal jurisdiction, a shrine in that temple; the holy of holies, into which impure or unworthy passion should find no admittance, and where no one ought to officiate until he has put off the habits of ordinary life, and assumed, with the holy robes of his function, that purity of intention, that ardent worship of truth, so inconsistent with the low pursuits of interest, the views of ambition or the vanity of false talent. Party spirit unfortunately will, in some degree, influence every other department; from the nature of our government it must exist, but it will do no material injury, while it is felt in the legislative, or even in the executive branches; but if it once find admittance to the sanctuary of justice, we may be assured, that the vitals of

F

our political constitution are affected, and I can imagine no better means of facilitating this corruption, than permitting your judges to make political harangues to a jury, who reply by a party presentment.

Another article applicable to the trial, restricts the charge of the judge to an opinion of the law, and to the repetition of the evidence, only when required by any one of the jury : the practice of repeating all the testimony from notes, always (from the nature of things) imperfectly, not seldom inaccurately, and sometimes carelessly, taken, has a double disadvantage ; it makes the jurors, who rely more on the judges' notes than their own memory, inattentive to the evidence ; and it gives them an imperfect copy of that, which the nature of the trial by jury requires they should record in their own minds.   Forced to rely upon themselves, the necessity will quicken their attention, and it will be only when they disagree in their recollection, that recourse will be had to the notes of the judge.   There is also another and more cogent reason for the restriction.   Judges are generally men who have grown old in the practice at the bar.   With the knowledge which this experience gives, they also acquire a habit, very difficult to be shaken off, of taking a side in every question that they hear debated, and when the mind is once enlisted, their passions, prejudices, and professional ingenuity are always arrayed on the same side, and furnish arms for the contest.   Neutrality cannot, under these circumstances, be expected; but the law should limit, as much as possible, the evil that this almost inevitable state of things must produce.   In the theory of our law, judges are the counsel for the accused, in practice they are, with a few honourable exceptions, his most virulent prosecutors.   The true principles of criminal jurisprudence require that they should be neither.   Perfect impartiality is incompatible with these duties.   A good judge should have no wish that the guilty should escape, or that the innocent should suffer ; no false pity, no undue severity should bias the unshaken rectitude of his judgment; calm in deliberation, firm in resolve, patient in investigating the truth, tenacious of it when discovered ; he should join urbanity of manners to dignity of demeanour, and an integrity above suspicion, to learning and talent; such a judge is what, according to the true structure of our courts, he ought to be—the protector, not the advocate of the accused ; his judge, not his accuser ; and while executing these functions, he is the organ by which the sacred will of the law is pronounced.   Uttered by such a voice, it will be heard, respected, felt, obeyed ; but impose on him the task of argument, of debate; degrade him from the bench to the bar ; suffer him to overpower the accused with his influence, or to enter the lists with his advocate, to carry on the contest of sophisms, of angry arguments, of tart replies, and all the wordy war of forensic debate ; suffer him to do this, and his dignity is lost ; his decrees are no longer considered as the oracles of the law ; they are submitted to, but not respected ; and even the triumph of his eloquence or ingenuity, in the conviction of the accused, must be lessened by the suspicion, that it has owed its success to official influence, and the privilege of arguing without reply.   For these reasons the judge is forbidden to express any opinion on the facts which are alleged in evidence, much less to address any argument to the jury; but his functions are confined to expounding the law, and stating the points of evidence on which the recollection of the members of the jury may differ.

I pass over other alterations of less importance, and proceed to the consideration of the fifth book.

This, as we have seen in the plan, is devoted to the rules of evidence as applicable to criminal law. In the execution of this part of the work, general principles will be first laid down, applicable to all cases of criminal inquiry, from its incipient to its final stage ; they will be such only as have received the sanction of the learned and the wise, or such as can be supported by the clearest demonstration of their utility and truth. The evidence necessary to justify commitments, indictments, and convictions for each offence specified in the third book, as well as that which may be admitted in the defence, will be detailed under separate heads, and such an arrangement will be studied as to make this part of the work easily comprehended, and remembered without difficulty.

It is obvious, from the nature of this division of the subject, that illustrations of the rules it contains cannot be given without greatly exceeding the limits of an ordinary report. It may be proper, however, under this head, to notice that an attempt is made to enforce the sanction and add to the solemnity of oaths. From the careless and often unintelligible manner in which they are administered, it seems an idle ceremony rather than a sacred promise, accompanied by a renunciation of the blessings of the deity in case it should be broken. Rules are framed on this subject, which it is supposed may, in some measure, correct the evil, and make witnesses more cautious and circumspect in their testimony, by impressing upon the mind a proper sense of the serious consequences of its violation. If this impression should be insufficient to prevent deliberate perjury, it will at least restrain the more prevalent evil of those aberrations from truth which are caused by exaggeration, carelessness or passion.

The sixth and last division of the work, is to contain rules for the establishment and government of the public prisons ; comprehending those intended for detention previous to trial ; for simple confinement, and for correctional imprisonment at hard labour, or in solitude.

Upon these rules, and the proper execution of them, depend the success of the whole system. But it will be useless to make rules, because impossible to execute them, unless the edifice to be prepared for this purpose be on a scale sufficiently extensive to permit the proper classification, the separate employment and proper seclusion of the different offenders. Without these, we can neither produce reformation nor hope for any effect from example. And yet, because it produces neither, we find fault with the system, when we should arraign only our want of attention to its principle. Vice is more infectious than disease ; many maladies of the body are not communicated even by contact, but there is no vice that affects the mind, which is not imparted by constant association ; and it would be more reasonable to put a man in a pest-house, to cure him of a headach, than to confine a young offender in a penitentiary, organized on the ordinary plan, in order to effect his reformation. Considering this interior arrangement as essential to the success of the whole plan, it was deemed improper to leave it to the discretion of the governors or warden ; but by means of precise and somewhat minute regulations, to place the discipline of the prison on a basis that should not vary according to the different theories of those who are to enforce it, taking care, however, to allow a reasonable discretion in cases where considerations of humanity require it.

In order to frame these regulations to advantage, it would be very advisable to obtain more information than we now possess, of the practical operation of those which have been tried in the other states.

For this purpose I intend, if possible, to devote a few months of the summer to a personal examination of the different institutions of the kind in the Atlantic states ; but if my circumstances should not permit me to execute this plan, I shall renew the efforts I have already made to procure the information which the different returns and reports can give.

Every system having reformation for its principal, or even incidental object, is imperfect, if it do not contain a regular and permanent provision for giving education to the young offenders, and moral and religious instruction to all.

Lessons of this nature, inculcated by men of piety and benevolence ; enforced by a life of temperance and labour, and not counteracted by any evil associations, I firmly believe, will make many a discharged convict a more worthy member of society than some who have never committed any offence of sufficient magnitude to incur the same discipline.   But reformation is not enough ; although sincere, it will not be lasting, if the distrust of society shall drive the repentant sinner from its bosom ; deny him the means of subsistence, and force him to seek it in a new association with his former companions in guilt.   To avoid this consequence, means must be found to test by a proper interval of probation, the sincerity of his reformation ; to give him an opportunity of regaining confidence, by acts of gradual intercourse with the public, and after repeated trials, if it be found that he can withstand temptation, to assign him a place in society, which will enable him to subsist without reproach.

This part of the plan will be difficult of execution, but it is not deemed impracticable, and it will be facilitated and enforced by increased severity for a repetition of offences, as well in the duration of punishment as in the increase of privations while it lasts.   Should the regulations which I suggest for this purpose be adopted, and be found efficient, it will complete the system which substitutes amendatory to vindictive punishments.   A reformation in penal jurisprudence which reflects higher honour on modern times, than the greatest discoveries they have produced in arts, literature, or science.

This is the plan of the work, and these are the principles on which it is founded ; if after examining them, it should be perceived that they are inconsistent with the views of the legislature, or that the execution falls short of their expectations, the evil is still within the reach of such remedy as their wisdom may suggest.

From such parts of the code as are in the state of greatest forwardness, I have selected the second book, and the last chapter of the fourth, as specimens of the execution*.   The one being chiefly an enunciation of general principles, and the other necessarily confined to matters of practical detail, the general assembly can the better judge, whether a proper attention to sound theory has been combined with efficient practical details ; and whether the great object I have had in

---

* This report was made before the completion of the " System of Penal Law," the publication of which now renders the insertion of these specimens unnecessary.

view, of rendering every rule intelligible, although concise, has, in a reasonable degree, been attained.

Some parts of the third book are prepared, but the whole of this division is still in an unfinished state.  The fourth is nearly complete. The fifth cannot, without great inconvenience, be put into form until the crimes to which the evidence is to apply are defined and definitively classed ; this book must, therefore, necessarily be unfinished until the completion of the third ; and the want of that information, which I hope to obtain by a personal inspection of the prisons, has unavoidably delayed what I have to add to the sixth and last book.

I have only to add, on this subject, that from the progress already made, I hope that the whole system will be presented at the next session.   And I submit to the legislature, whether it would not be proper to direct, that when finished it shall be printed for the inspection of the members.

This report is intended to apprize the representatives of the people what changes are proposed to be made in their criminal jurisprudence ; to inform them why these changes are deemed necessary ; to lay before them a plan of the whole work ; to announce the principles on which it is established ; and by the exhibition of a part, to show in what manner it may be reasonably expected that the whole will be executed.

In performing this duty, the line traced by the law under which I was appointed, has been scrupulously adhered to.  In its execution, I claim no other merit than that of diligence, and a most conscientious desire to perform it in such a manner as will best reconcile humanity with justice, and the great interests of freedom with both.

The representatives of a free people, although they may do nothing to forfeit the confidence of their constituents, cannot always expect to retain the power of serving them.  A spirit of change is inherent in our government ; it gives it energy, and is even necessary to its existence. We appear in public life ; perform or neglect the duties assigned to us; and then, pushed off the stage by younger, more active, or more popular candidates, we return to the mass of our fellow-citizens ; in common with them, to suffer the evils or enjoy the benefits of the measures we have adopted.  It is not always that, in the brief space allotted to us for the performance of our functions, we have an opportunity of making it an epoch in the annals of our country, by institutions, with which a grateful posterity will identify the names of those by whose patriotic labours they were established.  This rare occasion now presents itself for your acceptance.

If the work which your wisdom has directed, and which your sound judgment, experience and care will modify and correct, should effect the object of giving to your country a penal code, founded on true principles—concise, correct, humane, easily understood, guarding with the same scrupulous care the rights of the poorest citizen and of the most influential member of society ; inforcing firmly, not harshly, a strict obedience to the laws ; repressing with an even hand the abuses of office and the license of insubordination ; protecting the good, restraining, punishing and reforming the wicked ; arraying the best feelings and most powerful passions, as well as the understanding on the side of the law ; making disobedience unwise and inattractive, as well as dangerous ; arming all your institutions with public opinion, and directing its irresistible force against vices and crimes ; rendering your judges venerated as the oracles of justice, and your courts respected as its sanctuary. Should this be the result, few public bodies can boast a fairer claim than you will then have to the approbation of their constituents and the gratitude of posterity. For you will have rendered an essential service, not only to your own country, by securing its internal peace, and establishing its reputation for wisdom and justice, but to the other states, by giving them an useful and honourable example, and to the whole world, by demonstrating the ease and safety with which abuses are corrected, and improvements introduced under a free government, and exemplifying its superiority by this proof of the rapid progress it has enabled you to make in the science of legislation, during the few years you have enjoyed it. And the grateful prayers of the innocent whom you will have saved, of the guilty you will have reformed, and of the whole community whose feelings will no longer be lacerated by public exhibitions of suffering and of death, will combine with your own consciousness of rectitude, in drawing down a blessing on your lives, and diffusing a glow of happiness over that hour, when the remembrance of one measure effected for the interests of humanity or the permanent good of our country, will be of more value than all the fleeting and unsatisfactory recollections of success in the pursuits of fortune or ambition.

All which is respectfully submitted.

EDWARD LIVINGSTON.

# A SYSTEM

OF

# PENAL LAW,

FOR

## THE STATE OF LOUISIANA:

CONSISTING OF

A CODE OF CRIMES AND PUNISHMENTS,
A CODE OF PROCEDURE,
A CODE OF EVIDENCE,
A CODE OF REFORM AND PRISON DISCIPLINE,
A BOOK OF DEFINITIONS.

PREPARED,

UNDER THE AUTHORITY OF A LAW OF THE SAID STATE,

BY

## EDWARD LIVINGSTON.

# INTRODUCTORY REPORT

TO

# THE SYSTEM OF PENAL LAW,

PREPARED FOR

## THE STATE OF LOUISIANA.

I LAY before the general assembly, with unaffected diffidence,. the system which they directed me to prepare. This feeling, however, does not arise from any apprehension that the work has not been framed according to the spirit of the instructions that were given for its execution ; they have been constantly before me. Nor have I entertained any doubt of the correctness of the principles on which those instructions were founded ; on the contrary, every new view that unfolded itself, as I gave them the form of practical precept, convinced me of their wisdom and utility. But in strictly following good rules according to the best of my judgment, that judgment must frequently have erred. To apply general principles to the numerous subdivisions of criminal jurisprudence, so that the same spirit might pervade its different branches of sanction, procedure, evidence, and discipline, presented a task which nothing but the highest presumption could hope to perform without falling into many errors. Of my own fallibility no one can be more sensible than I am, and no one could have taken greater precautions to correct it. Not a provision has been made, without the deepest reflection upon its consequences. Not a line has been written, that was not sent to every quarter of the union in search of amendment. Not a suggestion has been offered, that has not been adopted, without pride of opinion, when it brought conviction to my mind ; and the long list of corrections, at the end of the printed copies, attest how slight my attachment has been to preconceived ideas, or to the language in which they were expressed, when either my own reflection, or the advice of others, convinced me that they might be amended. The codes, as they are now presented, have been produced by the exercise of my best faculties, faithfully and laboriously employed, under the direction of a religious desire to perform the high duty

G

entrusted to me, so as, in some degree, to realize the great views of those by whom I was appointed.

Cheered and encouraged in the very outset of the work by the approbation which the general assembly bestowed on the plan and the specimens which accompanied it, I proceeded with alacrity in the execution of my task ; and in its progress, had the satisfaction to receive testimonials equally calculated to stimulate my exertion. Some of them I have obtained leave to communicate with this report. They all concur in the utility of the projected reform. Some speak in the highest style of encomium on the honour the state has acquired by leading the way in effecting it ; and when the high terms, in which the friendship of some, and the politeness of others, have induced them to speak of the execution of the work, are reduced to their just value, most of them contain reflections that will be found of great use in the discussion of the codes.

Well aware of the difficulties of my task, but feeling a conviction that they were not insurmountable, I undertook it with so much confidence as was necessary to sustain me in its execution ; but with that distrust of my own powers, which made me submit to the test of long reflection and severe scrutiny every principle I laid down and every provision intended to give it effect. I made these my leading rules— to adopt no theory, by whatever specious argument supported, until I should be convinced of its practical utility ; diligently to seek for information, but to admit nothing upon the mere authority of high names ; to make no unnecessary innovation, but boldly to propose every change I should think practicable and useful. This process unavoidably consumed much time ; but, by assiduous labour, in little more than two years after my plan had received the sanction of your predecessors, I had completed the work. Its destruction in the autumn of the year 1824 was communicated to the general assembly, and produced a resolution giving me another year to renew it. This was to be done entirely from recollection, for not a written vestige of my former labour remained ; and the task of recomposition, always irksome, was interrupted and rendered more difficult by the interference of engagements, which, supposing my undertaking finished, I had made for the ensuing year. These circumstances, while they afford a reason, and perhaps an excuse for delay, will render negligent error more unpardonable.

The enunciations of fact as well as of principle, contained in the law under which I have acted, and the resolution approving of the plan which was prepared in conformity with its provisions, might seem to preclude the necessity of saying any thing to show that a reform in our criminal jurisprudence was called for, or that the directions contained in the law were proper in order to effect it. But when it is considered, that the general assembly has been twice changed since those acts were passed, and that all the enemies of reformation have been industriously at work during that period in urging arguments against the contemplated change, it may not be deemed, I hope, improper to attempt, in this report, a refutation of arguments and a disproval of allegations calculated to mislead, and to perpetuate the degrading state of subjection to unwritten, and therefore necessarily unknown laws.

The law of 1820 recites, " that it is of primary importance in every well regulated state, that the code of criminal law should be founded on one principle—the prevention of crime; that all offences should be clearly and explicitly defined in language generally understood; that punishments should be proportioned to offences; that the rules of evidence should be ascertained as applicable to each offence; that the mode of procedure should be simple, and the duty of magistrates, executive officers, and individuals assisting them, should be pointed out by law; AND THAT THE SYSTEM OF CRIMINAL LAW, BY WHICH THIS STATE IS NOW GOVERNED, IS DEFECTIVE IN MANY OR ALL OF THE POINTS ABOVE ENUMERATED." Two years afterwards another general assembly, with the approbation of the governor, resolved, "that they approve of the plan proposed by Edward Livingston, in his report made in pursuance of an act, entitled, an 'act relative to the criminal laws of this state,' and earnestly solicit Mr Livingston to prosecute this work according to the said report;" and thereby added their sanction to a development of the same enunciations contained in the preamble to the code which was submitted for their consideration. This will be frequently referred to, and I therefore quote it at length :

" No act of legislation can be, or ought to be, immutable. Changes are required by the alteration of circumstances; amendments, by the imperfection of all human institutions; but laws ought never to be changed without great deliberation, and a due consideration as well of the reasons on which they were founded, as of the circumstances under which they were enacted. It is therefore proper, in the formation of new laws, to state clearly the motives for making them, and the principles by which the framers were governed in their enactment. Without the knowledge of these, future legislatures cannot perform the task of amendment, and there can be neither consistency in legislation, nor uniformity in the interpretation of laws.

" For these reasons the general assembly of the the state of Louisiana declare, that their objects in establishing the following code are—

" To remove doubts relative to the authority of any parts of the penal law of the different nations by which this state, before its independence, was governed.

" To embody into one law and to arrange into system such of the various prohibitions enacted by different statutes as are proper to be retained in the penal code.

" To include in the class of offences, acts injurious to the state and its inhabitants, which are not forbidden by law.

" To abrogate the reference, which now exists, to a foreign law for the definition of offences and the modes of prosecuting them.

" To organize a connected system for the prevention as well as for the prosecution and punishment of offences.

" To collect into written codes, and to express in plain language, all the rules which it may be necessary to establish, for the protection of the government of the country, and the persons, property, condition, and reputation of individuals; the penalties and punishments attached to a breach of those rules; the legal means of preventing offences, and the forms of prosecuting them when committed; the rules of evidence, by which the truth of accusations are to be tested; and the duties of executive and judicial officers, jurors, and individuals, in preventing, prosecuting, and punishing offences : to the end that no one need be ignorant of any branch of criminal jurisprudence, which it concerns all to know.

" And to change the present penal laws in all those points in which they contravene the following principles ; which the general assembly consider as fundamental truths, and which they have made the basis of their legislation on this subject, to wit :

" Vengeance is unknown to the law.  The only object of punishment is to prevent the commission of offences : it should be calculated to operate—

" First, on the delinquent, so as by seclusion to deprive him of the present means, and by habits of industry and temperance of any future desire, to repeat the offence.

" Secondly, on the rest of the community, so as to deter them, by the example, from a like contravention of the laws.  No punishments greater than are necessary to effect these ends ought to be inflicted.

" No acts or omissions should be declared to be offences, but such as are injurious to the state, to societies permitted by the laws, or to individuals.

" But penal laws should not be multiplied without evident necessity; therefore acts, although injurious to individuals or societies, should not be made liable to public prosecution, when they may be sufficiently repressed by private suit.

" From the imperfection of all human institutions, and the inevitable errors of those who manage them, it sometimes happens that the innocent are condemned to suffer the punishment due to the guilty.  Punishments should, therefore, be of such a nature that they may be remitted, and, as far as possible, compensated, in cases where the injustice of the sentence becomes apparent.

" Where guilt is ascertained, the punishment should be speedily inflicted.

" Penal laws should be written in plain language, clearly and unequivocally expressed, that they may neither be misunderstood nor perverted ; they should be so concise, as to be remembered with ease, and all technical phrases or words they contain, should be clearly defined; they should be promulgated in such a manner as to force a knowledge of their provisions upon the people ; to this end, they should not only be published, but taught in the schools ; and publicly read on stated occasions.

" The law should never command more than it can enforce.  Therefore, whenever from public opinion, or any other cause, a penal law cannot be carried into execution, it should be repealed.

" The accused, in all cases, should be entitled to a public trial, conducted by known rules, before impartial judges, and an unbiassed jury ; to a copy of the act of accusation against him ; to the delay necessary to prepare for his trial ; to process to enforce the attendance of his own witnesses ; and to an opportunity of seeing, hearing, and examining those who are produced against him ; to the assistance of counsel for his defence; to free communication with such counsel, if in confinement, and to be bailed in all cases, except those particularly specified by law. No presumption of guilt, however violent, can justify the infliction of any punishment before conviction, or of any bodily restraint greater than is necessary to prevent escape ; and the nature and extent of this restraint should be determined by law.

"Perfect liberty should be secured of hearing and publishing a true account of the proceedings of criminal courts, limited only by such restrictions as morality and decency require; and no restraint whatsoever should be imposed on the free discussion of the official conduct of the judges, and other ministers of justice, in this branch of government.

"Such a system of procedure, in criminal cases, should be established as to be understood without long study; it should neither suffer the guilty to escape by formal objections, nor involve the innocent in difficulties by errors in pleading.

"For this purpose, amendments should be permitted in all cases, where neither the accused nor the public prosecutor can be surprised.

"Those penal laws counteract their own effect, which, through a mistaken lenity, give greater comforts to a convict than those which he would probably have enjoyed while at liberty.

"The power of pardoning should be only exercised in cases of innocence discovered, or of certain and unequivocal reformation.

"Provision should be made for preventing the execution of intended offences, whenever the design to commit them is sufficiently apparent.

"The remote means of preventing offences do not form the subject of penal laws. The general assembly will provide them in their proper place. They are the diffusion of knowledge, by the means of public education, and the promotion of industry, and consequently of ease and happiness, among the people.

"Religion is a source of happiness here, and the foundation of our hopes of it hereafter; but its observance can never, without the worst of oppression, form the subject of a penal code. All modes of belief, and all forms of worship, are equal in the eye of the law; when they interfere with no private or public rights, all are entitled to equal protection in their exercise.

"Whatever may be the majority of the professors of one religion or sect in the state, it is a persecution to force any one to conform to any ceremonies, or to observe any festival or day, appropriated to worship by the members of a particular religious persuasion: this does not exclude a general law, establishing civil festivals or periodical cessations from labour for civil purposes unconnected with religious worship, or the appointment of particular days on which citizens of all persuasions should join, each according to his own rites, in rendering thanks to God for any signal blessing, or imploring his assistance in any public calamity.

"The innocent should never be made to participate in the punishment inflicted on the guilty; therefore, no such effects should follow conviction, as to prevent the heir from claiming an inheritance through, or from the person convicted. Still less should the feelings of nature be converted into instruments of torture, by denouncing punishment against the children, to secure the good conduct of the parent.

"Laws intended to suppress a temporary evil should be limited to the probable time of its duration, or carefully repealed after the reason for enacting them has ceased."

These different expressions of legislative opinion would seem to preclude the necessity of any argument to show the defects of our present system of penal law, or to establish the truth of the principles upon which the proposed amendments are founded. But as I have taken truth for the foundation of all my statements, utility for the sole object of my provisions, and reason alone as the means of supporting my conclusions, I shall not take shelter behind any authority; but shall endeavour, in this report, to show that the legislative declaration of the defective state of our penal law, is founded in fact, and that the principles they prescribed to remedy the evil were founded in wisdom and practical truth. This will be not only useful but necessary to the proper consideration of the reports, in which the attention of the legislature is called to the principal enactments in the different codes, offered for their consideration. For, without this previous discussion, they cannot determine whether those provisions remedy the existing evils, or whether they are in unison with each other and with the sound doctrines of penal jurisdiction, on which they purport to rest. If the proposed system cannot be supported by reasons showing that it is both practicable and useful, it ought not to be adopted; but let no part of it be rejected on the authority only of influential names; still less by the affected doubts of interested, or the errors of sincere prejudice.

In this report, then, I propose to show THE NECESSITY OF A RE-FORM, FROM A VIEW OF THE ACTUAL STATE OF OUR PENAL LAWS, and to answer the objections that have been made to the establishment of a written system.

The objects of penal law are, to define offences, to prevent their commission, and to designate and direct the mode of inflicting the penalty, when they are committed. To effect these objects, there must be rules established by legislative authority. Those rules must be known; and to be known, they must be promulgated. But the rule can neither be made, nor be known, nor promulgated, unless it be clothed in words. Are those words to be oral or written, is the first question. A strange one, it would seem, in our state of society, yet seriously made; seriously answered in favour of traditional against written law—made and answered by lawyers, by judges, by men whose situation gives influence, and whose opinions have weight. Such are the advocates for retaining the reference to that part of the English common law which forms a part of our criminal jurisprudence. That part is not inconsiderable: it pervades the whole mass of our legislation on this subject: and it is necessary to understand this, that we may know how to value the argument which asserts that our statutes, not the English common law, defines offences and imposes the penalties. This is not the fact. The groundwork of our penal law is the territorial statute of 1805. It enumerates the offences and indicates the penalties; but it does not define. Theft, burglary, murder, and other crimes, are made punishable. But if we want to know what theft, or murder, or any other offence on the list is; if we wish to know what means we may use to prevent either of these crimes; how the offender is to be arrested, how confined, how bailed, how tried, what evidence can be admitted, what is required for conviction; for all these, and an hundred other questions equally important, we are referred to the *common law of England;* that is to say, what one of its greatest panegyrists styles, "the *unwritten* or common law," consisting of "*general customs*"—of *particular customs*—and of "certain particular laws, which *by custom are adopted and used by some particular courts.*" The whole resting, as we see, upon *custom* : and when we come to inquire, how these "customs" are to be known, the same author gives the answer, "by the judges"—who, he says, "are the depositaries of the laws, the living oracles who must decide in all cases of doubt," &c. Here, then, we see what is our law. It is "the unwritten customs of England," which, from the same authority, we are told, it requires twenty years of close study for a judge to understand; and which, without fear of incurring the charge of presumption, I will add, no man ever did or ever can understand—for this plain reason, that, in many instances, it does not exist, until the case arises which calls for its application; then it is pronounced, not by the legislative authority, but by one of these living oracles. It is a maxim with English lawyers, that the common law is the perfection of human reason. No case, therefore, can be supposed to be unprovided for by it, and consequently, whenever any new case occurs, and no preceding response has been given that will fit it, the judge must create one; and although it has never before been spoken, or written, or applied, we must believe it, from time immemorial, to have been a part of the common law; that is to say, as we have just seen, the *custom* of England : which involves the absurdity of supposing that to have been immemorial usage, which we know was never before practised or heard of.

But this is not the only difficulty or absurdity attending a reference to the common law. These oracles, it must be remembered, are not given like those of the sybil, in writing—but like most of those of antiquity, orally. The judge seldom or never writes his decision. The words of inspiration are caught by the reporter, and he publishes them. Here, it would be supposed, an opportunity is afforded of knowing, with some certainty, what the law is. To the people ? No ! The size, the number, the price, and the disgusting verbosity of the volumes, forbid it. To the lawyers, then, at least ? Not even to them ! The same causes operate to prevent many of them from examining more than an index or abridgement; but even the few who are rich enough to buy, and have had leisure to examine, those repositories of the law, with reference to a single point, for a general study of them would consume the longest life, even on that single point will find themselves sadly mistaken if they look for a certainty. Hear what Blackstone—I take my authority only from professed admirers of this system—hear what he says of the credit that is to be given to these reports :—"From the reign of Henry the eighth to the present time, this task (that of reporting) has been executed by many private and contemporary hands; who sometimes through haste and inaccuracy, sometimes through mistake and want of skill, have published very *crude and imperfect*, perhaps *contradictory*, accounts of one and the same determination."

Admit, then, that the judge pronounces the true precept of law, we can have no security that it is truly recorded; and a word omitted or transposed, may alter the whole sense of the rule. But this is not all. Let us suppose the record to be faithfully made, what is to be its effect? Is it binding on future judges, in similar cases ? In other words, is it law ? What say our oracles on this important question ? Blackstone tells us, "it is an established rule to abide by former precedents, but with some exceptions : which are, first, when the precedent is evidently contrary to *reason ;* secondly, when it is clearly contrary to the *divine law ;* thirdly, which seems to be included in the first, when it is *flatly absurd* or *unjust.*" This is the doctrine of the text.

Christian, the able commentator on this justly distinguished book, says, on the contrary, " precedents and rules must be followed even when they are *flatly absurd and unjust*, if they are agreeable to ancient principles :" and he gives an example which places the justice of this admired system in a most striking point of view.   It is a maxim of the common law, that all statutes, whenever passed, refer to, and take effect from, the first day of the session of parliament.   Now, to exemplify his rule, he says, if a statute should have been passed on the last day of the session, making an act a capital offence which before was innocent, any one who had done that act between the first and the last day of the cession, that is to say, perhaps six months before it was made an offence, would have been condemned and executed under the law. " This," he adds, and every body must agree with him, " was flatly absurd and unjust ;" but yet no judge could declare that it was not law; and this absurdity and tyranny, worthy of a Nero or Caligula, continued to form a part of the " perfection of human reason" until the year 1793(a), when one step in the road to common sense was made by enacting that the statute should not be in force before it was made, but gave it effect, when it contained no special provision on the subject, from the day on which it *passed*, without any attention to the time in which it was known by promulgation; so that even at this day, in England, according to the common law, a man at a distance from the seat of government may be punished for doing an act which, in the nature of things, he could not know to be illegal.

Thus the general assembly may form some idea of the nature of that law, to which our present system of criminal proceedings refers us for the definition of certain offences, and for the rules for preventing, trying, and punishing them.   We see that it consists of unwritten rules, promulgated by the judges by precedents often incorrectly reported ; of uncertain authority when known ; to be followed, according to some writers, however unjust or absurd ; and, according to others, to be modified by the principles of *reason* and the *divine law*, that is to say, by the caprice, or the bigotry, or the enthusiasm of the judge.   What more uncertain rules can be referred to than *human reason* and the dogmas of religion ?   What may appear reason to one, is folly to another; and on no one subject does the mind of man take so wide a range as in imagination respecting the divine will. .

But if no other objection existed, that which is contained in its very definition, would, it appears, be sufficient to ask for the substitution of some other ;—it is *unwritten*.   If we like its other provisions (and very many of them are excellent) let us, at least, destroy that characteristic, by reducing them to writing.

Two contradictory objections are commonly raised to this most important operation : the one, that the task is impracticable—that the body of the common law can never be reduced to writing ; the other, that its rules are already written, and that a reference to the reporters and commentators will give a sufficient knowledge of its provisions. Now, of these two opinions, one only can be true ; and if either be true, it presents a state of things that no reasonable being can wish to see continued.   If all the precepts of the common law cannot be reduced to writing, then a part of them are not contained either in the

(a) Statute 33 Geo. III. c. 13.

reporters or other writers, to which we are usually referred. Where are we, then, to find this unrecorded part?—in the unexplored mind of the judge. When is it to be promulgated?—for the first time after the case has occurred to which it is about to be applied. And who is to record or remember it—what is to be its effect and authority—in our state, which of the seven independent judges is to be considered as pronouncing the true oracle when they differ? Can principle be more completely abandoned; can common sense and common justice be more effectually lost sight of; can confusion be worse confounded than by this state of things? Take the other alternative. The precepts and principles of the common law are already reduced to writing. But where are they to be found? In voluminous reports which it requires great diligence to collect, very large sums of money to purchase, a long life to read(a), and a superhuman intellect to understand and reconcile with each other when they are read! They are to be found in commentaries on, and abridgements of, these reports, scarcely less voluminous; in which precedents and arguments may be found for almost every position that may be taken by sophistry, or required for an indiscriminate defence of right and wrong; add to this, that these sources of information are inaccessible to three-fourths of the inhabitants of this state, being written in a language which they cannot understand; and that of the other fourth, a very few only have the time or the means of applying to them; and you have a state approaching to that which has been justly designated as a badge of the most abject slavery, one governed by unknown and uncertain laws.

But even this, bad and absurd and oppressive as it is, this is not the worst. The words of our statute which refer us to this rule, call it the *common law of England*. Now this common law being established in a succession of very remote ages, when manners, religion, society and government were in a totally different state from that in which every succeeding period found them, it necessarily happened that positive laws were made to accommodate it to the change of circumstances. Some of these changes were made at so remote a time, that the most learned antiquary would find it impossible to fix the point in any one given subject where common law first received the aid of positive enactment; in other words, to tell us what is *common*, what is *statute* law. And yet we must at our peril know this; for the first is our rule of action; with the second we have nothing to do. Common sense alone would show the necessity of this research; but being so happy as to find it supported by authority, I gladly avail myself of both. We have reports of cases in penal law for about three years only; and we have them during that period, because the same court, of which the decisions were reported, then had criminal as well as civil jurisdiction. Property, it seems, has not only here, but in most other countries, been considered of so much more consequence than reputation, liberty, or life, that while all decisions that in the slightest

(a) If in the days of Fortescue twenty years of hard study (*viginti annorum lucubrationes*) were required to understand this law, then in its primitive simplicity, it is not unreasonable to calculate that the necessary term must be quadrupled by the reports, commentaries, folio abridgements, books of entries, essays and treatises of practice, which have accumulated in the four centuries that have since elapsed.

H

degree affect the former are collected, those which involve the latter are generally consigned to oblivion ; or, in particular cases, obtain an ephemeral publicity in the gazettes.   The reason of this will be hereafter discussed.   It is here mentioned only to account for the very scanty means we have of collecting authorities on these important points.   But in that short period to which I refer, a decision took place which fully supports my position :—B. was indicted for forging the name of another, as an indorsement, on a promissory note.   The person whose name was supposed to be forged was called as a witness ; he was objected to as being incompetent by the common law ; and many authorities were produced, showing that in England such witnesses had been rejected.   It was answered, that by the common law he was a good witness ; that the decisions relied on as authorities were made since a statute passed in the reign of queen Elizabeth, which had indirectly effected a change in the common law.   Of this opinion was the court, and the witness was sworn(a).   From this it appears that the English authorities were rejected because they were founded on a change made in the common law by a statute ; consequently that the act of 1805 refers to the common law, unamended by statute.   The first evil resulting from this, is that to which I have alluded ; the necessity of drawing, in every contested case, the line between the statute and the common law.   Supposing this difficult task to be accomplished, and that we have reduced the latter to its primitive simplicity by stripping off the statutory shreds and patches by which it was disfigured or adorned, what have we to reward us for our pains ?   First, we have the *benefit of clergy*(b), which assures impunity to every one who can read, for none of our statutes have taken it away.   Next, the right of *appeal* in felony,  and, as a consequence of appeal, the trial by *ordeal and battle ;*  for although you have established the trial by jury, so had the common law, and much in the same manner that you have done, at the option of the party(c).   You have the right of *sanctuary*, by which every offender who can escape to a church or a church-yard, is privileged from arrest, and may *abjure the realm.*  You have the right of *approvement*, by which any criminal who can in a judicial combat knock out the brains of his accomplice, secures his own pardon.   You have the whole doctrine of outlawry, and other incidents to criminal proceedings, which no advocate for the present state of things either understands, or would venture to contend for if he did ; but which they cannot avoid and must learn, and must practise, if the law is to be executed according to its plain letter.   The judges,

(a) 1 Mart. Rep. 214.

(b) Should it be objected that our statute, by directing the punishment of death to be inflicted, abolishes the privilege of clergy ; it is answered, that the same statute introduces the common law which also directed the punishment of death, but admitted the privilege of clergy as an exception.   If, then, the rule and the exception could exist together under the common law, why can they not under our statute ?

(c) The same statute that gives us the trial by jury, at the option of the party, declares that " the method of trial" shall be according to the said " common law ;" but the *said common law* allowed both the trial by battle and the trial by jury—and the former has been demanded in our own day in England, to the great perplexity and astonishment (very probably) of the lawyers, as Spelman says was formerly the case—*non sine magna juris consultorum perturbatione.*  It has within a few years, I believe, been abolished by statute.

THE SYSTEM OF PENAL LAW.

therefore, must dispense with it, and do this to the degree only that they think fit in each case. The court, not the general assembly, must legislate, and they must legislate after the fact(*a*)!

In offering these reflections, it is not intended to excite prejudice against, or pass an indiscriminate censure on the common law of England. On the contrary, it will be seen that many of its provisions are transferred into the system which has been prepared ; and that among them so taken from that law, are those which the most effectually secure liberty, reputation and property. But the subject is discussed to show that your predecessors were well founded in the assertion, that our present laws being neither certain nor accessible, were defective in at least two of the essential requisites to a good system.

The next defect in our present laws was that which the legislature had in view, when they declared that one object of the projected code was, to "remove doubts relative to the authority of any parts of the penal law of the different nations by which this state, before its independence, was governed." Were there any such doubts, and if there were, ought they to be removed ? It is an established rule of national law, that on the transfer, or conquest of a country, the municipal laws remain in force until they are expressly changed by the new government(*b*). When the treaty of 1763, by which Louisiana was ceded by France to Spain, was carried into effect in 1769, the latter power acted on this principle, and solemnly promulgated its own laws(*c*). France, when that power in 1803 received the actual transfer of the country from Spain, in execution of the treaty of St Ildefonso, took only a temporary and provisional possession, in order to deliver it to the United States according to the provisions of the treaty of Paris. No material alteration was made in the laws by this operation.

The first act of sovereignty done by the United States after the cession, was in perfect accordance with the principles laid down. For the law which authorized the president to take possession of the province(*d*), recognizes the force and validity of the existing laws, by vesting in officers to be appointed by the president, *the same* military, civil and judicial powers that were exercised under the Spanish government. The province continued under its old laws, administered by new functionaries, from the time of the transfer in December 1803, until the 1st of October 1804, when the law giving us the first grade of territorial government(*e*) took effect. This act organized the executive, legislative and judiciary branches of a territorial government. It extended to the territory the operation of certain laws of the United States, fixed the qualifications of jurors, and secured the right of trial by jury, and gave the writ of habeas corpus ; but so far from repealing any of the former laws, it contains an express provision that all laws in force in the territory at the passage of the act, and not inconsistent with it, should continue in force until altered, modified, or repealed by the legislature.

(*a*) Our constitution has very wisely guarded against ex post facto legislation by the general assembly. Was it intended that the judiciary should exercise it ?

(*b*) 1 Black. Com. 107; Cowp. Rep. 204.

(*c*) O'Reilly's Pro. 1769.

(*d*) Act of 31st October 1803.

(*e*) Act passed 26th March 1804, to take effect 1st October following.

The next change in the political organization of the territory produced none in our civil or penal laws, the act giving us the second grade of government(a) containing the same clause for continuing them "until altered, modified, or repealed by the legislature." And when the trammels of territorial government were thrown off, our constitution carefully preserved the same provision(b). Thus by uninterrupted succession, the laws by which the Spanish province of Louisiana was governed, with the exception only of such as were inconsistent with the several enumerated acts, were continued through all the different changes of government, and unless since repealed, altered or modified, are the law of the land at this day. That the penal laws formed no exception is evident from the general words which comprehend them, and also from some of the earliest acts of the legislative council, which recognize them in express terms.

One of the first laws passed by the legislative council(c) declares, that "whenever a conviction had taken place or *might take place*, for any crime which by the *existing laws of the territory* would subject the criminal to be sentenced *to the galleys* for life, that such punishment might be *commuted*," &c. Now as no penal law whatever had then passed since the new government was established, and a sentence to the galleys was unknown in our jurisprudence, the "*existing laws*" here mentioned must have meant the Spanish laws—and, of course, the Spanish penal laws.

Another act provides(d), that no suit, either civil or *criminal*, shall be prosecuted against any commandant for any act done subsequent to the 30th September(e) of that year, by virtue of a previous appointment; with proviso, that it shall not protect him from prosecution for *fraud* or *crime* under colour of office. But, at that time, there were no other than the *Spanish laws* for punishing *fraud* or *crime*; therefore, here again the existence of those laws is acknowledged.

Again, on the 4th May 1805, an act was passed for the punishment of crimes and misdemeanors, which, after specifying a number of offences, directs, by the thirty-third section, that all the offences therein named shall be construed and tried according to the common law of England: and by a subsequent statute, passed in the same year, two or three other crimes are added to the list; and it is further enacted, "that all *other crimes, offences and misdemeanors*, committed by free persons, and not provided for by this act or the one to which this is a supplement (act of 4th May 1805), shall be punished, and shall be prosecuted and tried according to the common law of England." There were, then, "*other* crimes, offences and misdemeanors," which were not enumerated in the only two statutes that had then been passed. Against what law were they offences? Clearly against the pre-existent Spanish law. This section was repealed the next year.

(a) Act further providing for the government of the territory of Orleans, 2d March 1805.

(b) 11th section 4th art. Constitution of Louisiana.

(c) Act 2d February 1805, sect. 1.  2 Martin's Dig. 226.

(d) Act 13th December 1804, sect. 1.  2 Martin's Dig. 106.

(e) The reason why the 30th September is the date referred to is, because on the day after, the law organizing the territorial government went into operation; and it was doubted whether the acts done after that time by officers previously appointed, were valid.

The repeal left things in the unsettled state they were in before the section passed, as to the mode of procedure; but it did not change the expression of legislative opinion as to the existence of the ancient laws.

But this is not all. The acts I have quoted were passed under the first grade of government, when the legislative council was appointed by the president. Under the second the elective franchise was extended to the people; and one of the first acts of their representatives was not only to acknowledge the same laws, but to vest in the superior court of the territory the power of punishing crimes that were committed under the Spanish and French governments(a).

Thus, the principles of national law, the acts of congress, the laws of territorial legislatures established by them, and the constitution of the state, all concur in proving that the ancient civil and penal laws of the province continued in force, except in those particulars in which they were modified by our institutions, or repealed by our laws. It becomes, then, highly important to determine what parts of those ancient laws are thus modified; which of them have been repealed; and what are the provisions of those which still exist unaltered. If all those laws have been abrogated, there was no foundation for the apprehensions expressed by your predecessors on that subject. If the abolition is express as to some and presumptive only (and of course doubtful) as to others, their apprehensions were well founded, and the doubts they entertained ought to be removed; and if any parts of that law have neither been expressly or impliedly repealed, all such parts being still virtually in force, ought to be examined; and if good, to be re-enacted in a language that may be understood; or, if bad, to be repealed.

Laws may be repealed either expressly or by implication. But there is nothing that has the appearance of an express repeal in the case before us; unless it be the clauses contained in the several recited acts which continue the existing laws, with the exception of such as are inconsistent with those acts respectively. But this, in truth, is no more than would have been effected without that clause. For a repugnancy between the old and the new law is an implied repeal of the former; and this is the only criterion(b) by which we can judge that there is such repeal; for it has been decided(c) in our courts, in conformity with British decisions, that affirmative statutes, not incompatible in their execution with the old law, and containing no negative or repealing words, do not abrogate the old law.

The Spanish laws, then, have not been expressly repealed. Have they been so by implication? Certainly they have not been so altogether; for there is not the least repugnancy between many of them and our constitution or laws. What classes, then, of them have been repealed?

First, it would seem clear that all those are abrogated by the mere change of government(d), which relate to the prerogative of the crown, and to the mode of making the appointment of officers. As to the du-

---

(a) Laws 1st territorial legislature, 3d June 1806.
(b) 1 Black. Com. 89.
(c) 1 Martin's Rep. (new series) p. 74.
(d) Vattel, lib. 3, c. 13, p. 199.

ties of such officers, in the administration of justice and preservation of peace, they must be performed by those appointed by the new power, having corresponding functions, whether under the old name or with a new designation. Thus, soon after possession was taken by the French in 1803, Mr Laussat, the French prefect, appointed a munici- pality to exercise the powers of the Spanish cabildo within the city, which, on the transfer to the United States, was continued with the same attributes until the town was incorporated by the legislative coun- cil. Thus, too, the governor, immediately after the transfer, appointed an *alguazil mayor* and commandants, who were to exercise as far as was compatible with the new order of things, the same functions with the officers of that name under the Spanish government.

Secondly, all those laws are abrogated which would interfere with any right secured by the constitution or laws of the United States or of the state ; such as the liberty of the press, the right to bear arms, the right of having counsel, of trial by jury, and others of that description.

Thirdly, I am inclined to concede that all those laws are virtually repealed which bear upon the same offences that are prohibited by laws passed since the cession, although there may be nothing absolutely re- pugnant between the two penalties ; there being, in my opinion, a dif- ference between acts passed by the same government on the same subject, (all of which are considered as one act), and the acts of a new power legislating upon an offence which had been defined by the jurisprudence of a former power : in which latter case I am inclined to think, that the new legislation ought to be considered as expressing its whole will, unless there is an express or implied reference to the old law. And finally, the law of evidence, the mode of trial, the rules of procedure, and definition of each of the offences enumerated in the act of 4th May 1805, are changed, *so far as relates to the offences so enu- merated,* because there is a clear repugnancy between the old law and that statute in relation to those particular offences.

The most liberal rules of constructive repeal can go no further ; yet, discarding all that comes within these rules and all that is expressly repealed, when we look into the former law, enough of it will remain to make us reverence the wisdom which directed that all doubts, as to its existence, should be removed. It would be difficult, perhaps im- possible, to give an accurate list of the penal laws of Spain which re- main unrepealed, or to furnish a complete analysis of their provisions. But this very uncertainty is alone a sufficient motive to justify legisla- tive interference. Some cases, however, may be ascertained ; let us examine them. The investigation is both curious and instructive, and it will produce more serious results than at first sight might be sup- posed.

The laws designating offences against sovereignty and the public peace have been generally provided for by our statutes, or by the con- stitution. They, therefore, come within the rules I have laid down, and may be considered as repealed.

But before we enter further into the very cursory examination which it is proposed to make of such offences, affecting reputation, person, property or religion, as by the rules laid down may be supposed yet to be in force, an important title presents itself, which has no corresponding division in our statute law, or that system to which it refers. It operates on the condition or standing in society of those who come within its purview. It is called in the Spanish law, " Enfamamiento;" and, from its definition, is a species of dishonour attached to persons, as well from their birth or course of life, as from having incurred the animadversion of the magistrates, without being convicted or even accused of any offence ; as from the condemnation for an infamous crime. Political disabilities attended this state, which our institutions have, in some instances, virtually repealed ; but the note of ill fame- may still remain, and greatly influence the comfort and respectability of those to whom it is thus attached by law, if those laws are still in force. The subject forms the sixth title of the seventh book of the Partidas. By the second law of this title, the innocent fruit of an illegal marriage, the son whom a father may justly or unjustly have accused in his testament, the suitor to whom the judge may, in court, have addressed an admonition to amend his life, the advocate who may have been warned not to bring a false accusation, the man of good credit who availed himself of his character to ruin that of another by slanders, and the unfaithful depositary, were all declared infamous. By the third law, not only the wife unfaithful to a living husband, but she who forgets a dead one in the arms of a second before her year of mourning is expired, together with her father, if he consent to the marriage, and the too impatient successor of the deceased, come within the penalties of the law. The following law confounds in the same indiscriminate class of infamy, procurers, comedians, mountebanks, usurers, recreant knights, foresworn promise-breakers, gamblers and buffoons. The exclusion from office of all these ill-associated descriptions of persons is, perhaps, remedied by our constitutional laws; but their infamy creates an incapacity to testify, and this again is partially counteracted by the reference to the English rules of evidence in certain enumerated crimes. But in the offences not enumerated in the act of January 1805, beyond which, as I shall show, the reference to the English law does not extend, and in all civil cases, what is to take away the disability to testify? Our civil code(a) renders those incapable *whom the law deems infamous.* What law ? If the answer to this important question .be, as I think it must be, the unrepealed law by which the land was governed; if there should be a doubt on that subject; do those who flatter you with dissertations on the perfection of your present laws, who cry out " peace, peace, when there is no peace," do these blind guides know the depth of the pit to which their counsels are directing you ? Have they calculated, or can they not perceive the evils attendant on this state of things in this one particular? Let it be remembered that these disabilities attach not upon conviction only(b), but from the fact. Let us suppose, then, that a usurer should be appointed to an important office, and it becomes the interest of an individual to make this excep-

(a). Art. 2260. See also the act establishing the superior court, sec. 10.—" No witness, of the age of discretion, shall be disqualified from testifying on the ground of being incompetent, unless such witness be at the time of producing him, interested or infamous."

(b) This law confirms the opinion that a usurer is ipso facto infamous, without any conviction, and as the law does not distinguish whether it speaks of open or secret usury, it must be understood of all." Greg. Lopez, note on the 4th law, and he concludes, *sunt ergo in magno periculo usurarii.*

tion to his official acts, will it be satisfactorily answered by saying that the constitution sets no bounds to the appointing power? But, it may be replied, the same constitution continues all laws which were in force at the time of its adoption until they shall be repealed; but the law declaring infamous persons incapable of exercising office has never been repealed; therefore, if the pre-existing law excluded certain persons as being infamous, there is nothing in the constitution that takes away the disability. With respect to elective offices it is different; where the constitution enumerates certain qualifications, it is reasonable to suppose it expresses all that are required.

Should it be thought, however, that the Spanish law creates no disqualification to office, the more important objection as applied to witnesses remains. In the list of exclusions, how many are enumerated whom it would be in the highest degree unjust and absurd to render incompetent, were a law now to be made on the subject? The accidental circumstance of extra-matrimonial birth—following a profession that has been ennobled by Roscius and Garrick and Talma—or one that, although requiring neither genius nor learning, has yet occasionally had the sanction of great names in ancient($a$) and modern times for its practice—receiving an undeserved reprimand from a choleric judge—solacing the grief of a widow before the time permitted by law for drying up her tears,—are certainly not acts that render one unworthy of belief; not to speak of the numbers who would be excluded under the exception of gambling, or the other incapacities specified in the law. Yet one of these may be the only witness to a transaction on which fortune may depend, or to exculpate from a charge which may effect reputation or life.

I have enlarged more on the consequences of removing doubts as to the existence of this law because of its general operation ; for there is scarcely a litigated question in which it may not be raised, or a person accused, to whose interests it might not prove fatal. Let us now examine whether there are not penal laws, strictly so called, that may not be supposed still in force, according to the principles which have been laid down.

The seventh title of the seventh Partidas treats of the *crimen falsi*, (*falsedades*), and (among many offences which might probably be brought within the purview of our statute against forgery, coining and perjury) forbids, under very heavy penalties, other acts which are not now considered to be indictable, but which may or may not be deemed offences while our laws are suffered to remain in their present uncertain state. Among these are the following: the advocate is guilty of this offence if he betrays the secrets of his client, or if he designedly cite the law falsely($b$). The notary, or other person is

(a) Cato, the censor, would, under this law, have been doubly disqualified as a witness; for, if Plutarch is to be believed, he was not only a usurer but a **** for his own slaves. "Teniendo," (in the expressive language of the Partidas' describing the offence), " sus siervas en su casa faziendolas fazer maldad de sus cuerpos por dineros!" 7 Part. tit. 6, law 4.

The list of exceptions would be greatly swelled, if the commentator's opinion is to be followed, who includes in the class of usurers not only those who, like Shylock, deserve to be "rated about their moneys and their usances"—but even dealers in exchange and bankers, whose counters, he says, " are altars raised to usury and oppression.

(b) 7 Part. tit. 7, l. 1.

guilty, if he deny the deposit of any mystic testament or other writing ; if he hide or deliver it to another ; or if any writing be deposited with him to be kept secret, he read or publish it(*a*). The judge, if he knowingly give a judgment contrary to law ; the person who says mass without being ordained, and he who changes his name to one that is more honourable, are guilty and punishable for falsehood. The next is a falsity of rather difficult execution, and I believe not made punishable by any of our statutes : I must give it in the words of the Spanish lawgiver : " Trabajanse(*b*) a las vegadas algunas mugeres que non pueden aver fijos de sus maridos, de fazer muestra que son prenadas : e quando llegan al tiempo del parto toman enganosamente fijos de otras mugeres e meten los consigo en los lechos, e dizen que nacen dellas, esto dizimos que es gran falsedad ; faziendo e poniendo fijo ageno por heredero en los bienes de su marido bien assi como si fuesse fijo delo."

There are other offences in this class which I do not enumerate, because it may be doubtful whether they do not come within some of our statutes. The punishment is banishment, and confiscation of all the property of the offender to his nearest ascendant or descendant ; if he have no such relation, then to the treasury. A milder punishment is inflicted on the person who(*c*), being appointed to divide lands or apportion other property in dispute, shall make a partial division ; and also on the arbitrator who shall designedly make a false statement of the accounts he is appointed to settle.

Under the next head, of Homicide(*d*), I find the following acts made punishable, which are not so by our statutes.

The first must be a startling one to the faculty of medicine, as one of those I have cited must be to the gentlemen of the bar(*e*). It recites(*f*), that " men give themselves out to be more skilful in physic and surgery than they really are(*g*) ; and that by reason of their being less skilful than they pretend, some of their patients die by their fault." It, therefore, enacts, that if any physician shall give an improper medicine, or too much of a good one, or any surgeon, in dressing a wound, shall break a bone, or divide an artery, and the patient in one or the other case shall die, the offender shall be banished for five years and forbidden to practise. In due order comes the apothecary, after the physician ; without whose orders, if he give a dose to a person who dies in consequence of having taken it, the pharmacopolist is guilty of homicide.

The destruction of our species in the inchoate state of existence is not punishable by any of our statutes. It is so by those of Spain, but

---

(*a*) 7 Part. tit. 7, l. 1.        (*b*) Ib. tit. 7, l. 3.        (*c*) Ib. tit. 7, l. 8.

(*d*) Ib. tit. 8, De los Omezillos.

(*e*) As the presumption is that every man admitted to the bar knows the nature of the law he quotes, it might, perhaps, be argued, that whenever he cited for law that which was not law, he did it designedly, and of course made himself liable to the penalties of the law, " *de las falsedades*," which I have quoted. A law full of peril for the profession.

(*f*) 8 Part. tit. 7, l. 6.

(*g*) This part of the recital would apply to more professions than one. As the law is limited, however, it behoves the advertising part of the faculty particularly to discover whether it be in force.

I

they contain a provision which I have not seen in any other code—that if death is caused by any medicines or herbs, given for the laudable purpose of procuring an heir to the childless, it is a punishable offence.

The title of Defamation (Deshonras)(a) contains some things well worthy of attention in the disquisition we are now making. It divides defamation into two kinds, by word or by deed. Both are made punishable: and the definition includes every thing that is falsely said or done to dishonour another. Defamation by deed includes writing, printing, gestures, and all other acts done with the same intent, including such as would come within the English definition of assault and battery. One of these laws, although perhaps somewhat too strict for the freedom of modern manners, might, in our days, find some careful guardian, jealous husband, or prudent father to put it in force, if it should be deemed one of those that have lost its use, not its authority; and I transcribe it that the gay gallants who are subject to its penalties, may know the peril of their ways:

"Women," says the preamble, "whether widows, wives or maids, who live virtuously in their houses with an honest fame, are frequently injured, grieved and dishonoured by men who take divers means of doing so. Some there are who are continually whispering to them, visiting frequently at their houses, and following them in the streets to the church or other places to which they go; others who dare not pay those public attentions, secretly send jewels to them and to the persons with whom they live, for the purposes of seduction; and others again, strive to corrupt them by the instrumentality of infamous agents, or by other unlawful arts. By these means the weak are led astray, and the virtuous are suspected of evil communication with those who pay them such attentions. Wherefore, we hold that those who conduct themselves in this manner do great wrong and dishonour, not only to the women, but to their parents, their husbands and other relations; and we command that whoever in any such manner offend, shall be fined for the benefit of the woman who is dishonoured: and moreover, the judge shall admonish him who thus follows and dishonours a woman, that he do so no more, and that he desist from such folly, under the penalty of more serious penalty if he do not desist."

Among the other evils which are considered as reflecting dishonour on whom they were practised, are the school-boy tricks of shutting another out of his chamber and sealing the door, smoking out the neighbour in the story above you, or throwing water on him who is below. Contemptuously throwing down a book in the presence of the author, is a dishonour under the law, as well as accusing one of theft ; but from this last the astrologer, who is consulted to find out stolen goods, is exempted, if he be a true astrologer, but not if he is a pretender to that noble art.

It is difficult, in reviewing some of these laws, to preserve the gravity required by the general subject; but it was deemed necessary to show in what manner trivial as well as more serious acts were confounded in the laws, to which we may, by no forced construction, be still liable. Some of those which remain are of a graver nature.

Injuries against the peace are provided for in a separate title (de las

(a) 7 Part. tit. 9.

Fuerças)(a). Most of them are embraced by our statutes. Some, however, are not; and of these last only it is necessary to speak. One of these is the forcible entry into the possession of real or personal property; for which the penalty is the loss of the property, if the party had any in the thing or land forcibly taken, and its value, if he had none. The same law applies to the tenant who holds over by force; and the borrower who, without paying the debt, shall forcibly resume his pledge.

In the title of Theft there is one remarkable provision; by which common gamblers are exempted(b) from punishment for theft, or any other crime, except murder, which they may commit in a house, the master of which receives them, knowing their character. Another makes it a punishable offence to remove a land-mark.

The sixteenth title, of Fraud, specifies a number of acts of this nature, all of which are punishable by our statute; and require no other remark, than that our modern professors cannot claim the merit of originality, several of their most approved stratagems appearing by these laws to have been practised as early at least as the thirteenth century.

Offences against morals have not attracted the attention of our legislature. We have but one statute on the subject. In the Spanish law there are many. Adultery is made a crime. The faithless wife is punished with stripes and confinement(c) for life in a convent. Her seducer with death. The husband may forbid the person he suspects of a design on his domestic peace to visit or speak to his wife; and any interview after this admonition, is conclusive proof of guilt(d). The guardian of a female orphan who marries his ward, or gives her to his son, is guilty of this offence(e).

One of our statutes makes incest a crime, punishable by imprisonment for life; but as it gives no definition of the offence, a reference to the Spanish law may be found necessary. This defines the crime to be an illicit connexion between relatives unto the fourth degree of the canonical law, by consanguinity or affinity, expressly including the sisters-in-law and brothers-in-law; and, by a subsequent disposition(f) a connexion between persons who were sponsors for the same child (compadres y commadres) incurred the same penalty. The punishment was the same as that of adultery, if the offence were committed without marriage; but, if after marriage, banishment for a nobleman, with the addition of stripes for other offenders.

Seduction of a woman(g) of good fame, incurs forfeiture of property and stripes. The husband who sells his own honour and the virtue of his wife, the agent(h) in the seduction of a woman of virtue, and those who educate children for the purpose of public prostitution, are punishable with death.

As the legislation of which I am giving a partial review was made in the thirteenth century, it is not surprising to find that astrology, witchcraft and incantations, love-powders and wax images, make

| | | |
|---|---|---|
| (a) 7 Part. tit. 13. | (b) Ib. tit. 14, lib. 6. | (c) Ib. tit. 17, l. 13. |
| (d) Ib. 1. 12. | (e) Ib. l. 6. | |
| (f) Nueva Recopilacion, lib. 8, tit. 20, l. 7. | | |
| (g) 7 Part. tit. 19. | (h) Ib. tit. 22. | |

a figure in it. Divination is a capital offence, except by astronomy, which is not only permitted, but praised as one of the seven liberal arts, "because the conjectures and presages that are made by this art are drawn from the natural course of the planets and stars, and are taken from the books of Ptolemy and other sages who treat of this science." None, however, but adepts are to meddle with this ; all false pretenders to it, witches, sorcerers, fortune-tellers of every description, enchanters who raise the spirits of the dead, were capitally punished ; but with the proviso, that if the object of the exorcism or of the black art be to cast out a devil, to preserve the crop from hail, or from lightning, or from insects, or for any other good object, the case is altered, and instead of punishment the operator is entitled to reward.

The subject of the few other laws of which I shall speak which were in force here on the change of government, is Religion. There is a general impression, so firmly established as almost to amount to conviction, not only that all former laws on this subject are repealed, but that no law can constitutionally be passed subjecting any one to penalties for his religious belief, or giving any preference to one religion over another. It is to be lamented that this persuasion is unfounded. For however we might rely on the enlightened spirit of the age to prevent the passage of such laws, yet the interest in question is one so essential to the happiness and peace of the people, that it is not only unfortunate but extraordinary, that the liberty of conscience should have been overlooked when the other great interests were secured by the constitutional compact.

This omission is the more surprising, because all the several laws and compacts regulating our political state, prior to our constitution, have contained stipulations on this head. The treaty of Paris declares, that until the inhabitants of the ceded territory shall be admitted into the union, they shall be maintained in the free enjoyment of the religion they profess. The law establishing the first grade of government, and the ordinance which gave the second, both contain restrictions on the legislative power intended to secure religious liberty. But our constitution, careful of every other right, descending to minutiæ which would seem to trench on ordinary legislative power in other cases, is silent in this. That of the United States does not supply the deficit ; it only limits the powers of congress on that subject, but imposes no restraint on those of the states.

In the examination of this subject, which I have made with solicitude, there are two arguments : one that might be used to show that the old laws were repealed ; the other that there exists a restriction on the powers of the legislature. I state them with pleasure, and hope most sincerely that they may always be deemed conclusive with others, although I regret to say they are not so with me.

First, as to the repeal. The act of 1804, giving us the first grade of government, contains the following provision : "The governor and council shall have power to alter, modify or repeal the laws which may be in force at the commencement of this act. Their legislative powers shall also extend to all the rightful subjects of legislation ; but *no law shall be valid* which is inconsistent with the constitution or

(a) Lib. 8, tit. 3, l. 5. Recop. de Castello. 7 Part. tit. 23, l. 1, 2 and 3.

laws of the United States, or which shall lay any person under restraint, burthen, or disability on account of his religious opinions, professions or worship ; in all of which he shall be free to maintain his own, and not burthened for those of another."

I fear that the restriction against laws upon the subject of religion, by the true construction of this clause, operates prospectively only on the laws that might thereafter be passed by the legislative council ; if so, it causes no repeal ; for the eleventh section provides for the continuance of the laws in force in the territory, except those that are inconsistent with it. Now if the restriction is prospective only, the former laws are not inconsistent with it. Should this, however, be a repeal, it is an implied one, and nothing of such importance ought to be left to implication.

The restriction on the powers of the legislature to pass such laws stands on very debateable ground. It is not contained in the construction. But in the ordinance giving us the second grade of government, there are certain articles which are declared to be a compact between the original states and the people and states in the said territory, and which are for ever to remain unalterable, unless by common consent. The first of those provides, that no person, demeaning himself in a peaceable and orderly manner(a), shall be molested on account of his mode of worship or religious sentiments, in the said territory.

By the act authorizing the inhabitants to form a state government, it is provided, among other things, that the constitution to be formed shall contain the fundamental principles of civil and *religious liberty;* and the law admitting the state into the union, contains the proviso, that all the conditions contained in the third section of the last recited act, shall be considered as fundamental conditions and terms, on which the state is admitted into the union. Whether a law passed in contravention of the article of the ordinance or of the proviso in the two laws regulating our admission into the union, would on that account be declared void, when the constitution contains no restriction of power on this subject, is a question requiring an argument that does not come within the scope, and could not be brought within the compass of this report. It is stated to show, that even on this vital subject, the laws respecting religion, there were grounds for the doubts expressed, as one of the motives for directing the work which I have now the honour to present.

The laws on this subject are extremely oppressive and highly penal. Heresy, Judaism and blasphemy, were their principal objects.

The religion of the Jews was tolerated; but an attempt to make proselytes, leaving their houses on holy Friday, buying a Christian slave, and being guilty of the absurd charge of " crucifying young children" at their festivals, were punishable with death; as was the connexion of a Jew with a Christian woman; for, says the lawgiver(b), " if Christians merit death who commit adultery with married women, much more do Jews deserve that punishment for connecting themselves

(a) In bad times this phraseology might give rise to oppression : " he is not to be molested *in his religion,* if he behave in an orderly manner." Do not his religious rights then depend on the order of his behaviour? What would an inquisitor or an inquisitorial judge call *orderly ?*

(b) 7 Part. tit. 24, l. 9. Recop. de Cast. § 2, 3 and 4.

with Christian women, who are all spiritually the wives of our Lord Jesus Christ, on account of the baptism they have received in his name." In one instance the Jews had a protection allowed them which the English laws do not give: they could not be arrested on the day of their Sabbath.

Heresy is defined to be a departure from the Catholic faith as established by the church of Rome, or disbelief in a future state(a). The punishment is death at the stake.

Blasphemy is any thing that is said or done in contempt of God, the Virgin Mary or the saints. The punishment for which, if by words, is forfeiture, according to the rank of the offender and the repetition of the offence; if by deed, with the loss of the hands.

Some of these laws may have been repealed by later Spanish laws; others, doubtless, were added prior to the time that Louisiana was ceded, which have not been brought within our reach. Therefore, the enumeration may not be perfectly correct. This will be of less importance if the object of the detail is kept in view. This was to give a general view of such penal laws only as might not be supposed to be repealed by our constitution or laws; and it must also be remembered that the provisions, exceptions and other details contained in those laws, which would have been indispensable if they had been quoted as rules of action, were not thought so when their existence and general operation only was the subject of inquiry; yet I have been guilty of no voluntary omission, and have followed the text always in preference to the commentary of the law.

Most willingly would I here close this catalogue; but the present state of our jurisprudence renders it a duty with which I reluctantly comply, to add to the list a word at which humanity shudders, and to ask, whether we are as sure as we ought to be that *torture* forms no part of our criminal law? It found, with all its horrors, a prominent place among the laws of Spain; and to determine in what degree they are modified or repealed, the hateful task must be performed of adverting to their provisions.

This diabolical power was vested in the judge, with no other limitation as to the degree in which it was to be inflicted, than that it should not extend to loss of life and limb. Within these limits he was not only empowered but instructed so to direct the operation as to create the most excruciating physical and moral anguish. These monsters studied the human frame, to discover in what part it would feel the acutest pain; they marked the working of the mind, to know where the deepest wounds of the spirit could be inflicted: and they insert the result of their cold-blooded calculation in their laws with minutiæ that sickens the heart. Among several delinquents, the judge is directed to select for this operation of cruelty and horror, the youngest, the most delicately framed(b), the most tenderly educated, and—is this an earthly or a hellish code that I am reviewing?—when there is a father and a son, to rack the limbs of the child in the presence of the parent—" because," says the worthy commentator on this text, " a father(c) can better bear his own torments than those of his child;" and in the same

---

(a) Part. tit. 26, l. 1 and 2. Rec. § 3, 1.     (b) Ib. tit. 30, l. 5. Gom. Var. Res. c. 13.
(c) Greg. Lop. note on l. 5.   7 Part. tit. 30.

spirit, women were made the first victims, until some of these fiends discovered that they bore pain with more fortitude than men. The objects upon whom the application of this engine for beating out the truth, as it is called in their laws (èscodrinar la verdad), was authorized, were, first the accused(a), who was vehemently suspected, or against whom there was no certain proofs, for the purpose of forcing a confession; secondly, a convict to make him discover his accomplice; thirdly, a witness who prevaricates. It would not have been necessary to enter into the details of these laws, if their provisions had been known or attended to by those who framed our constitution. They seem to have entertained the common error that torture was only authorized in order to force a confession from the accused; and they, therefore, thought it would be completely abrogated by the clause which provides, " that the accused shall not be obliged to give evidence against himself," —leaving its application to force testimony against others entirely unaffected by the provision, at least so far as relates to the offences not enumerated in the act of 4th May 1805. I would not be understood as expressing a belief that this mode of obtaining testimony will ever be resorted to. It is too repugnant to our feelings—too inconsistent with our morals and earliest impressions. *Non nostri generis nec sanguinis est.* It is not of our country, and belongs not to our generation or race. It is of foreign growth, and cannot be engrafted on our jurisprudence. Yet the word must not stain its pages. It is yours to purge them of this disgrace; to take away not only the possibility of its being inflicted, but prevent its very sound from offending the ears, or its idea polluting the minds of freemen: or, if it must be remembered, let it be only as one in the list of evils from which our connexion with a confederacy of free states has relieved us. Yes, this task must be performed: for notwithstanding the confidence we all feel that the intelligence and humanity of our fellow citizens would reject these horrors, yet we must not tempt folly or wickedness by placing such weapons within its reach. All the inhuman and ill-assorted and unknown laws must be positively, unequivocally, publicly abrogated. Reason requires it; prudence points out the danger of delay; and experience has added her warning and convincing voice to teach us how little reliance we can place on our fancied security(b). For, in closing this subject, let me answer those who

(a) 7 Part. tit. 30, l. 8. Ant. Gom. ubi supra.

(b) I should have thought the danger almost imaginary on this point, if I had not found the philosopher Voltaire, his disciple Diderot and M. Hautefort, all three commentators on Beccaria, enthusiastic admirers of his humane doctrines, and particularly of his arguments for the abolition of torture against the accused—if I had not found them more or less expressly agreeing, that it ought to be retained as the means of procuring from a convict the disclosure of his accomplices.

" Reserve (says Voltaire) at least this cruelty for acknowledged villains, who have assassinated the head of a family, or the father of his country, to find out their accomplices," &c. —*Comm. Beccaria,* c. 13.

Hautefort says, " It (the torture) can only be employed against a criminal convicted in the most legal manner, in order to discover his accomplices." But he adds, " would it not be essential to examine whether the search after accomplices is not too rigorous."—*Observations sur le Livre des Delites et des Peines.*

Diderot is explicit. He says, " this additional torment is necessary to draw from him

still tell you there is no danger; who can see no mischief until it is felt; who deride as visionaries and false prophets of evil, all those who by a prudent foresight strive to avert them.  Let me tell those incredulous apostles, who will not believe that a stroke has been inflicted until they can lay a finger on the wound, or that what has been dead may be revived, until with their eyes they behold the resurrection—let me tell them, that such revival of dead and obsolete laws requires no miraculous power to effect; that a weak, an ignorant or a conceited magistrate is sufficient for the operation; that it has actually happenèd, and that by such agency one of the worst, the most inhuman and arbitrary of all those ancient laws has been executed under our free and enlightened government.  In a remote parish of the then territory, a human being was, for I know not what crime, by the sentence of a magistrate condemned to be *burned alive;* that the sentence was executed in his presence, and that there was no law passed by the government of the territory authorizing such punishment.  It is true, the victim was a slave.  It is true, that a law of Spain directs that the slave shall be punished with more cruelty(*a*) than the freeman, and the commoner than the nobleman.  But the only law(*b*) I have been able to discover for using this inhuman punishment makes no distinction. It permits the judge in every capital case to designate the punishment.  It may at his discretion, be either " decapitation with the sword (for the statute with great humanity forbids the saw or the reaping hook), or it may be by burning, or hanging, or casting to be devoured by wild beasts." Our judge, in the exercise of the discretion thus humanely given to him, chose the fire and the faggot, and afterwards showed where the writhings of agony had forced the chain of his victim into the bark of the tree that served for a stake.  No name is mentioned, for death has removed the magistrate from the reach of justification or censure; but having strong evidence of the fact, and its bearing being so immediate on the subject of the report, I should have been culpable in suppressing, however reluctant I might be to mention it.

Let me now ask those who have followed me through this rapid detail, whether wisdom, prudence and even necessity did not dictate to the legislature the duty of " removing doubts relative to the authority of any parts of the penal law of the different nations by which this state, before its independence, was governed ;" and of selecting out of them " such statutes as were proper to be retained in the penal code ?"  In the mass to which I have referred, there are some provisions that we should find an advantage in retaining ; but much so inconsistent

(the convict) not only the discovery of his accomplices and the means of arresting them, but an indication of the proofs necessary for their conviction."—*Notes on Beccaria,* c. 12.

When the apostles of reform and preachers of humanity use such language as this in favour of the application of the torture in one of the cases in which, if my argument be correct, it still may be considered as part of our law, is it a very absurd fear which urges its positive abolition ?

(*a*) 7 Part. tit. 31, l. 8.  " Ca mas crumente deven escarmentar al siervo que al libre y al ome vil que al fidalgo."

(*b*) 7 Part. tit. 31, l. 6.  I must in candour state that I am ignorant under pretext of what particular law this execution took place ; but as the one I have cited does authorize it, and there was no territorial statute that could justify it, I thought it fairer to suppose that he acted with than without authority.

with our ideas of justice, so well calculated to become the instruments of oppression, that all doubts of their existence as a part of our law, ought to be put aside. Where there is doubt, there is danger ; and my object in urging that none of the received rules of repeal apply to those laws, has been only to show that doubts may be raised, that in the hands of a more able arguer those doubts may be converted into conviction of their existence, and to the enforcement of such as might suit the party-feeling or other bad passions of the moment. Can the confusion of such a decision be well imagined ? We are now blessed with peace, with exemption from any other party feeling than those neces-' sary for a due vigilance over our servants. We have magistrates incapable of wresting the law to the purposes of interest, ambition or vengeance. Now is the time to act. If those laws are in force, let them be repealed ; if they are not, dissipate all doubts. Do not suffer them, in either case, to remain a snare to the unwary, and instruments in the hands of a corrupt or ignorant judge ; for no oppression is so detestable as that which is exercised under the guise of justice; it is the only tyranny which can be feared under our government. The spirit of the people would soon rise against any open breach of their rights. But their respect for the laws, their reverence for those who administer them, make them slow to perceive the oppression that is clothed in the forms of law; and when it is discovered, it must remain unpunished; for the excuse of error in opinion is always ready to cover every fault in this branch of our government. Place beyond its reach, therefore, all those instruments which would be equally injurious, whether brandished by folly, or directed by malignant design ; leave no doubt as to the existence of those laws which you desire to have enforced ; repeal all those which it is inexpedient, unjust, or impossible to execute. Be assured, legislators, of this truth, that there can be no law of which the existence is a matter of indifference. It must remain in your code for good or for evil : for good, if it be a wise law and carried into effect ; for evil, whether it be good or bad, if it remain unexecuted. In the one case the people are taught the dangerous lesson that the best precepts may be disregarded with impunity ; in the other they are subjected, when the danger is least apprehended, to the unjust operation of a forgotten law.

Indeed, there is scarcely a greater reproach to the jurisprudence of a nation than the existence of obsolete laws(a) ; that is to say, laws that are none—laws that are no rule to guide our actions, because they are unknown to, or forgotten by those upon whom they are to operate ; but which yet may be used to punish them for their contravention, because they are known and remembered by those who are empowered to enforce them, whenever the malice of a prosecutor, or the ignorance, corruption, or party-feeling of a judge may induce him to

---

(a) Hear what the wise Bacon says on this subject: " Dicit propheta *pluet super eos laqueos;* non sunt autem pejores laquei quam laquei legum, præsertim pænalium; si numero immensæ et temporis decursu inutiles non lucernam pedibus præbeant, sed retia potius objiciant." *Aphorismus* 53.—The prophet'saith, *it shall rain snares upon them ;* but of all snares, the snares of the law are the worst, especially of the penal law ; when they have become useless, either by the accumulation of their number or by the lapse of time, they are not a light to guide our steps, but a net to entangle them.

K

draw the rusty sword from its scabbard.   To apply this to our case, as has been seen,

> " We have strict statutes and most biting laws,
> Which(a) for these nineteen years we have let sleep;"

statutes of such number and variety, that there is not a state or condition in life that cannot be affected by them ; not a man in the community that has not made himself obnoxious to the penalties of some of them.   Let the long but imperfect list I have given be perused, and where is he who can say that some of his actions may not be brought within the purview of one or more of the loose and entangling definitions contained in those laws.   But even if they should never be made the instruments of oppression, if they should remain wholly unexecuted, the effect is scarcely less to be deprecated, and is thus well expressed by the high authority whose aphorism I have just referred to in a note : " Here is a further inconvenience of obsolete penal laws ; for this brings on a gangrene, neglect and habit of disobedience upon other wholesome laws, that are fit to be continued in practice and execution, so that our laws endure the torment of Mezentius, the living die in the arms of the dead !"

It is your province, by correcting the evil, to complete what your predecessors began.   This might be effected by a general repeal ; but that would be a small part of the duty which your constituents—which the world requires at your hands.   *Graviora manent.*

The list of defects in our present system is but begun.   They must be faithfully exhibited to your view.   The allegation so frequently repeated, that we want no reform, has, it cannot be concealed, had its effect on the community, on its representatives.   It shall be completely refuted.   I speak with confidence because I know my ground.   The task is not a pleasant one, but it must be performed.   Let us proceed with the detail.

The common law, to which we are referred for definition, procedure, and evidence, has, I may believe, been demonstrated to be rather, to say the least of it, an uncertain guide.   But what shall be said of the legislation that in many cases gives us none(b) ?   Yet such is ours.   This point deserves to be the more seriously considered, because I believe it has not hitherto attracted attention.

---

(a) The slumber in which our Spanish statutes has been plunged, is somewhat longer than Shakspeare has feigned those of Vienna to have been, yet it may happen, that some " precise lord Angelo" may be found,

> " To awaken all the enrolled penalties
> Which have like unscoured armour hung to the wall,
> And none of them been worn ; and for a name
> May put the drowsy and neglected act
> Freshly in execution."

Let our modern Claudios beware, for among the rusty Spanish statutes is one imposing the penalty of death for the very offence which put the gay deceiver of the play in peril of his head.

(b) Bacon, a name which I love to quote, in inquiring into the causes of the law's uncertainty, places this first on the list—" duplex legum incertitudo ; altera ubi lex nulla præscribitur, altera ubi ambigua et obscura."   Unfortunately we have both.

By the 33d section of the act so frequently referred to (4th May(*a*) 1805) it is enacted, " that all the *crimes, offences and misdemeanors herein before named*, shall be taken, intended and construed according to, and in conformity with, the common law of England ; and that the forms of indictment (divested, however, of unnecessary prolixity), the method of trial, the rules of evidence, and all other proceedings whatever in the prosecution *of the said crimes, offences and misdemeanors*, changing what ought to be changed, shall be (except as by this act is otherwise provided for) according to the said common law."

Now although it seems sufficiently plain that the common law is referred to only as relates to the crimes and offences enumerated in that act, the argument is made stronger by the third section of the act of 3d July 1805, being the second law on the subject of offences that was passed by the territorial legislature. It declares, " that all *other* crimes, offences and misdemeanors not provided for by that or the former act, should be punished, prosecuted and tried according to the common law of England." This guarded against the evil ; *but the very next year the legislature* repealed it, thereby adding an express to the former implied declaration of their will, that the common law of England should be applied to those offences only that were enumerated in the act of 1805. Yet that act enumerates only certain offences, and very many more have been created by subsequent statutes, as may be seen by a reference to the schedule annexed to this report. But in no one of these last is there any reference to the common or any other law, for the definition of the crime, the mode of procedure, or the rules of evidence ! What then did the legislature intend should be the rule to govern the courts ? Did they intend the common law ? Certainly, as it is a foreign code, they shall not be presumed to have introduced it without some indication of that intent. The legal conclusion is, that the existing laws were intended to govern in all cases where they are not abrogated or altered. In that case we should have to consult Spanish authorities for the definition of offences and the rules of evidence, and for the mode of proceeding, so far as was compatible with the other provisions of the constitution and statutes of the state. Yet this has great, perhaps insurmountable difficulties. To avoid these difficulties recourse has been had, under the plea of necessity, to the assumption of legislative power by the courts. They have, without scruple and without being questioned, applied the 33d section of the act of 1805 to all the subsequent penal laws; they have restored the third section of this second act which the legislature repealed, and have defined and tried all offences indiscriminately according to the common law. It will not, it is presumed, be denied, that the introduction of this section into the act was the exercise of a legislative power, necessary in order to the application of the common law to the offences enumerated in that statute. If so, it follows that nothing but the exercise of a similar power could legally apply it to offences not enumerated in that act. But it has been so applied to the other offences by the judiciary ; therefore, the judiciary have exercised a legislative power. But the constitution has expressly forbidden, both by affirmative precept and positive prohibi-

(*a*) This act is quoted in Martin's Digest, sometimes under the date of 24th January 1805, sometimes the 4th May 1805. I believe the latter is the true date, but have no means here of ascertaining it correctly.

.tion, in the most precise terms that the language could afford, any such exercise of power.

"The powers of the government of the state of Lousiana shall be divided into three distinct departments, and each of them shall be confided to a separate body of magistracy, viz., those which are legislative to one, those which are executive to another, and those which are judiciary to another. No person being one of these departments shall exercise any power properly belonging to either of the others, except in the instances hereinafter expressly directed or permitted." ·

I do not ascribe this exercise of powers to any improper motive. It may, without any such imputation, be accounted for by the confused state of our criminal laws, which forced the courts either to suffer crimes to go unpunished, or to assume powers not properly belonging to them, but which the proper department would not exercise itself, and took no pains to prevent the exercise by another.

It is thus that the assumption of unconstitutional powers is first exercised, then excused, and in the end insisted on as a right ; and it is as essential to good government that each department should exercise its proper functions as that it should avoid assuming those of another; for power is too precious to be lost. Whatever is abandoned by one is eagerly seized by the other ; and careless legislation will inevitably produce executive and judicial encroachment.

In the case under discussion there is less cause to inculpate the courts of law, because the question has not, it is believed, been hitherto raised for decision ; but whenever it shall be, its importance will be discovered, and the inevitable result be either a solemn decision, which cannot be supposed, that courts have legislative powers, or a confession of that which we are now endeavouring to establish, that a written code is necessary for the execution of the penal·law. To prove this, let us suppose that on the trial of a capital offence created by an act passed since the year 1805, a witness should be offered who is competent according to the common law of England, but inadmissible under the laws which I have rapidly reviewed, either as a usurer, a comedian, a person of illegitimate birth, or as enemy of the accused(a), or a priest(b), a minor(c) under sixteen years of age, a relation in the ascending(d) or descending line, or a collateral within the fourth degree, or for any of the numerous other exceptions that exclude witnesses according to the Spanish law ; by what process of reasoning will any court come to the conclusion that they have the right to adopt the common law as their guide in this question ? What species of testimony is to be admitted ? What makes a competent witness ? are questions which the laws of the country must decide by general rules. Whether any particular testimony offered, any individual witness produced, comes within these rules, are questions for the judge to decide.

On the change of government there were laws which governed the admission of witnesses. The new government changed these laws, as related to certain enumerated crimes. It was silent as to the others. What was the consequence as to those others ? Either, as I believe, that the old law remained in force ; or, if that should not be the case, that they remained without any law to govern them. But in either

(a) Ant. Gom. Var. Res. 3d vol. c. 12, No. 15.      (b) Ib. No. 20.
(c) Ib. No. 14.            (d) Ib. No. 16.

case the common law of England would not be applied to them without a legislative act. The selection of that law for the offences enumerated in the act of 1805 was a legislative act. The application of it to others must be one of the same character; for, as we have seen, it is strictly, emphatically confined by that law to the offences therein enumerated, and for subsequent offences the judiciary have the same right to select the laws of Hindostan as they have to adopt those of England. But if they have not this right, if they cannot exercise it, is there a doubt that the legislature ought and must do it, because there is either no rule, or the one that exists under the laws of Spain is so monstrous, so perfectly inapplicable to our situation that it equally calls for renovation? But 'what remedy can the legislature apply? Is it by the summary process adopted in 1805 of selecting a foreign code? During the territorial government this could have been done; but now the only remedy is a code that shall define the crime, direct the procedure and give the rules of evidence. Attention is particularly necessary to this argument, because, unless the reporter errs, it is conclusive as to the necessity of the work in question.

The framers of our constitution had been witnesses to, and had participated in the anxiety and dismay that pervaded the whole community when an attempt was made, in the earliest stage of our political connexion with the United States, to take advantage of an ambiguous expression in the ordinance given for our government, in order to introduce a new system of jurisprudence(a), totally unknown to, and the knowledge of which was unattainable by the people of the territory. They dreaded the common law of England. They feared another attempt to introduce it. Their escape was too recent not to make them apprehend that in future times the struggle might be renewed. They wisely thought that to be free, a people must know the laws by which they were governed. They were aware of the difficulty, nay, the utter impossibility of this knowledge being acquired when the law was unwritten, or if written, dispersed through hundreds of volumes in a language unknown to three-fourths of their constituents. They saw the danger of permitting a particular class of men to become the sole depositaries of this knowledge and the sole interpreters of the laws; and they did every thing that prudent foresight could do to prevent these evils, by inserting in the constitution the following clause : "The existing laws in this territory, when this constitution goes into effect, shall continue to be in force until altered or abolished by the legislature ; provided, however, that the legislature shall never adopt any system or code of laws by a general reference to the said system or code, but in all cases shall specify the several provisions of the laws it may enact."

By this important amendment, for which the gentleman who introduced it deserves the thanks of his country(b), and by the section which follows it requiring the judges in definitive sentences to refer to the par-

(a) To have had a share in averting this danger gives the reporter a satisfaction that can be equalled only by his being instrumental in the establishment of a system that may promote the honour and happiness of the state that has honoured him with the preparatory duty he is now performing.

(b) Mr Bernard Marigny is the member of the convention to whom the state is indebted for this essential service.

ticular law by which they were governed, an effectual bar was placed to the legislative introduction of unwritten law ; and no act can now constitutionally be passed, extending the 33d section of the act of 1805, which introduces the common law to any offences created by law since that period. If they wish to provide rules on the subjects embraced by that section they must enact them specifically, that is to say, call it by what name it may be convenient to use, they must, in effect, have a code or a law defining crimes, a code of procedure and a code of evidence. This wise provision, while it prevented a repetition of the careless legislation which introduced the common law of England without considering or even knowing its provisions, did not prevent the adoption of all those parts of it which have justly commanded the admiration of the world ; but it imposed the necessity of distinguishing, of selecting, of knowing them and of reducing them to writing ; so that the people might not only be governed by them, but might understand and approve them.

The position, then, with which I set out on this head is fully established: that there is no alternative but this—the legislature must make a code, or they must suffer the courts to legislate on subjects of the most importance to life, reputation, personal liberty and civil and political rights. It will be no escape from this dilemma to say that the legislature, having defined an offence and having designated the punishment, an implied power is given to the court to do all else that is necessary. There are three answers to this argument, all of them conclusive. First, the establishment of rules of evidence is a legislative act; it cannot, therefore, be expressly transferred, much less can it be by implication. Secondly, if a legislative power could be transferred, this power could not, because the power of the general assembly itself is restricted in this particular by the clause I have just quoted. Thirdly, if this power could be transferable from the general assembly, they could not vest it in the judiciary, nor could this latter department execute it, by reason of the express inhibition to which I have referred.

As little will it avail to say that this is not the adoption of a code or system of laws which was forbidden by the constitution, but only the adaptation of a part of such system to a particular part of our law. The evil intended to be guarded against was that of the introduction of laws by a general reference, without seeing and considering their particular import; and most especially (I appeal to all the members of that convention) against the introduction of the common law of England, or *unwritten law*. But of what avail would this provision have been, if, by a general reference to its particular parts the whole might have been introduced ? The argument then would be this:—it is true we cannot introduce the common law by a general reference to the whole; but by taking its parts separately we may effect the same thing, and by the same forbidden means of a general reference to each of them. Thus, without repeating or indeed knowing its details, we will by one act say, the common law rules of evidence shall be introduced; by another, we will adopt its laws of descents; by a third, its whole criminal law; and so of the rest.

Leaving the consideration of these general defects in our criminal law, we must examine its particular provisions; and here, too, we shall find so many omissions to supply, so many faults to correct, as must show the necessity of a thorough reform if we wish to attain a system that will do us honour, or if we aspire only to the humbler merit of avoiding the grossest faults in legislation. A very brief recurrence to our statute-book will show that there is abundant reason to justify the declaration of your predecessors, that our present system " is defective in many or all of the points that are of primary importance in every well regulated state." To begin with one that must strike the most superficial observer. What else could be said of the system which provides no means for inflicting the only punishments its laws denounce against the most numerous and most injurious classes of crimes? Four-fifths of the offences enumerated in the statutes are punishable by im-prisonment at hard labour; yet, for more than twenty years no means have been provided for employing those who may commit such offences. Two evils result from this neglect. The judges are forced to pro-nounce a sentence which they know cannot be carried into effect; and the offender suffers a punishment not denounced by law against his offence; not to speak of another consequence, which will be enlarged upon in the introductory report to the Code of Prison Discipline, the incalculable evil of indiscriminate confinement in idleness.

What shall we say of this system? Shall we say that it is so perfect as to need no amendment—that he was rash and presumptuous who thought he could propose a better—that the legislature which authorized the experiment formed vain theories? Or, shall we deny to the in-congruous mass of written and unwritten law the very name of a sys-tem; and say, that the humblest abilities might, without vanity, aspire to propose something that would replace it to advantage; and that the attempt to amend it did honour to your predecessors? These conclu-sions will appear the more irresistible the further we advance in the examination of our statute law.

From the year 1805 to 1819 we have fourteen statutes, providing for the punishment of more than seventy different acts, or for the same act under different modifications of circumstance and intent; without including the prohibitions of the same act in relation to several objects specified in the statute—as for example, the different instruments, the falsely making of which is declared forgery; besides pecuniary and other forfeitures for infractions of particular regulations interspersed in many other statutes. This period comprises only fourteen years. Yet the want of some fixed principles of legislation, the utter disregard of system and method, and an astonishing inattention to preceding enact-ments, as well as to a due proportion of punishments to crimes, have led us in that short space of time into incongruities, the development of which must excite the wonder of those who have believed the re-peated assertions so confidently made, that our penal laws want no amendment.

When the provisions of the projected codes are compared with the existing laws, their discrepancies will be more particularly pointed out. Here it will be sufficient, generally, to refer to a few instances of this species of legislation.

When we consider the different circumstances attached to the com-mission of homicide, which may characterize it as an innocent or even a meritorious act, when done in defence of ourselves or in the service of our country; as excusable when the effect of accident; slightly pun-ishable when produced by passion arising from adequate cause; or meriting the highest penalty when coming under the denomination of

murder: we must see the necessity of designating with the greatest pre
cision the different circumstances and intentions which give to the same
act the character of a virtue, an excusable fault, a slight offence, or a
crime of the blackest dye; which entitle the accused to reward and esteem, to pity and forgiveness, or consign him to death.  Surely, if there
is any subject on which the law ought to speak in language intelligible
to the meanest capacity, in which it ought to be accessible to all, in
which there should be no doubtful phrase, no contradictory enactments,
it is this.  Let us see how far our boasted legislation complies with
these requisites.

The first act (4th May 1805) declares, that if any person shall commit the crime of *wilful murder* he shall suffer death; and that if he
commit manslaughter, he *shall* be fined, and *may* be imprisoned at
hard labour or otherwise.  The fine may be *one cent* or five hundred
dollars, and the imprisonment one hour or twelve years.  Here are
only two kinds of homicide provided for; and, if it be true that the
Spanish laws cease to operate, this law informs the citizens that every
other killing may be perpetrated without incurring any penalty.  It is
highly important then to know what these terms mean.  At the time
this law passed, four-fifths of the population could understand no English; and a very few only of the other fifth could explain the meaning
of the technical terms *murder* and *manslaughter.*  The only guide,
therefore, for a large majority of the people would be the French version of the law.  There they find that the one is *" homicide premeditée,"* and the other *" homicide non premeditée,"* according to which
the justifiable homicide of a public enemy would be punished with
death, and the accidental shooting of a friend might incur imprisonment
at hard labour for twelve years.  Reason would revolt at this; and it
would be scarcely a sufficient answer for the legislator who might have
been reproached with this slovenly manner of performing his duty to
say, "read on; the 33d section of the statute takes away all cause of
complaint.  You are there referred to a sure guide in all your difficulties.  If you wish to understand these or any other terms in the law,
you have only to consult the *common law of England.*"

" But you have undertaken to give us the explanation.  You have
called murder *premeditated* and *manslaughter unpremeditated* homicide.  Did you intend these as definitions ?  If you did, they lead to
the absurd consequences that have been stated.  If you did not, your
language deceives us; you should have added the other distinctive
characteristics of the several offences.  In either case your legislation
is miserably defective.  Besides, is it not a mockery to refer me to the
common law of England ?  Where am I to find it ?  Who is to interpret it for me ?  If I should apply to a lawyer for the book that contained it he would smile at my ignorance, and pointing to about five
hundred volumes on his shelves, would tell me those contained a small
part of it; that the rest was either unwritten or might be found in books
that were in London or New York, or that it was shut up in the breasts
of the judges at Westminster-hall.  If I should ask him to examine his
books and give me the information which the law itself ought to have
afforded, he would hint that he lived by his profession, and that the
knoweldge he had acquired by hard study for many years could not
be gratuitously imparted. Your law therefore, I repeat, is absurd in its

consequences, if taken literally, and mocks us by a reference to an inaccessible source for an explanation of its obscurities."

What could a candid man say to this reply? Every such man must acknowledge the justice of the reproach, and confess that such laws are a disgrace to the jurisprudence of his country. But this is not all. How shall we characterize the legislation that confounds, under the same denomination of crime(a), intentional and negligent homicide; and permits the judge to punish the same offence by the fine of a cent, or imprisonment at hard labour during a term equivalent to the usual duration of human life; while, for premeditated homicide, under any circumstances, according to the explanation given of it to a majority of the inhabitants, the uniform punishment is death.

A few months after the passage of this law, the same legislature attempted to amend it, by enacting that "'all murder by persons lying in wait, or any other kind of deliberate and premeditated killing,'" or which shall be committed in the perpetration of certain enumerated crimes, "shall be deemed murder in the first degree, and all other kinds of murder shall be deemed murder in the second degree." Here all murder by premeditated killing forms one degree; but premeditation is the only characteristic given by the former statute, and an essential one given by the common law, in the definition of all kinds of murder. What, therefore, is left for murder in the second degree?

The fifth section of this act is a curious specimen of legislative indifference. It provides that a prior offender shall be punished as is directed by this act, or by the act to which it is a supplement, that is, by imprisonment or by death; but whether the alternative is given to the choice of the culprit, to the direction of the court, or to chance, the law mantains a most dignified silence. This statute has been repealed, but it was not until the year 1818 that its absurdity forced itself upon the notice of the legislature. A similar instance may be found in a law passed the 25th March 1813, against carrying concealed weapons. By the second section of which it was enacted, that if any one should "stab or shoot, or in any way disable another by such concealed weapons, or should take the life of any person, he should suffer death, or such other punishment as in the opinion of the jury should be just." I quote the words of this statute as an instance of the style of legislation which put it in the power of the jury to select any species of punishment, from simple fine or reprimand, up to mutilation, torture and death; and that too for giving a slight wound, or in any manner whatever taking the life of a person, even in self defence, for there is no exception in the law. Yet this section was suffered to disgrace our penal law for five years. It was repealed in the year 1818. But the first section is still in force; by which any one who suspects I have a knife in my pocket, may obtain a warrant to take me before a justice, who is authorized to have me searched, and should the *knife* be found, he is *obliged* to make me pay at least ten dollars to the person who gives the important information, and as much to the state; and this sum may at his discretion be more than doubled.

The following provisions, taken without much selection, will suffice to show the want of proportion between punishments and offences that

---

(a) See the different divisions of manslaughter by the English law—into that by sudden provocation, se defendendo, and fortuitously in the performance of an unlawful act.

L

now reigns in our laws.   To break the iron collar(a) of a slave *must* be punished by a fine of at least two hundred dollars and imprisonment for at least six months.   While the court may punish him who kidnaps a free person with a fine of ten cents(b) ; and even for a second conviction for this odious crime there is no maximum, and the imprisonment may be only for a day.

By another statute now in force, "if a woman shall be delivered of *any* issue of her body, and shall endeavour privately, by drowning or secret burying thereof, or in any other way," . . . . "so to conceal the death thereof that it may not come to light whether it be born alive or not," she and those who aid, &c. shall be imprisoned not less than five nor more than fourteen years.   This is a refinement upon the reprobated statute of James 1st, which  is not more objectionable from the severity of its penalty than the want of  principle which made the concealment of the birth  such evidence of the murder as to throw the contrary  proof on the accused.   But even  that statute permitted the unfortunate mother  to exonerate herself by showing that the child was born dead.   Ours, on the contrary, inflicts the penalty for the offence of concealment, or the private burial of a monstrous or abortive birth. That statute confines its provisions to the case of a child which, if born alive, would have been a bastard.   Ours, indiscriminate in its provisions, makes no such distinction ; neither the unfortunate victim of seduction nor her nearest relations are permitted to avail themselves of the accident or the dispensation of providence, which may offer for the concealment of her weakness ; and the modest respectable matron must expose to the world—But  enough, the disgust due to the law would be excited by the work which details its consequences, were the subject to be pursued further.   It cannot escape remark that the same punishment is incurred 'for the crime of *drowning*, which, if I understand  the language, can only be applied to a living  infant, that is denounced for interring a dead one.

A legislation equally vacillating and inconsistent with true principles, is that on the subject of unsuccessful attempts to commit homicide. It began by the law of the 7th June 1806.   By that law, to *administer poison*, to *stab*, or to *shoot*, with intent to *murder*, is punishable, with death.   But by a prior law, to which I have before referred, one species of murder was punishable only by imprisonment.   A strong inducement was here offered the offender if he dreaded death more than labour, to adopt the ferocious motto of the highland chieftain, by making *sure work*.

In 1813, stabbing or shooting with any intent, if done with a concealed weapon, was death.   In 1818 this law was repealed, and the act of 1806 remained unmodified until 6th of March 1819.   It was made punishable with *death*  to *shoot, stab* or *thrust* any one with a *dangerous weapon*, with intent to *murder*, if done by lying in wait or in the attempt to commit any arson, rape, robbery or burglary ; and by the second section, shooting, stabbing, thrusting with a dangerous weapon with intent to  commit murder, under any other circumstances, is punishable by hard labour only from one to twenty-one years, a wide field for the exercise of judicial discretion.

This act creates a serious ambiguity in each of its sections.   What

---

(a) Law 6th March 1819, section 5.          (b) Ib. section 6.

is a dangerous weapon ?   A cambric needle thrust into the spine is as dangerous as a sword.   Yet it can scarcely be called a·weapon.

Again, a thrust with the fist of an athletic man without any weapon at all may be as dangerous as any offensive weapon.   This result then may follow ; if in the perpetration of robbery, the offender attempt to murder a defenceless man or a child by thrusts with his fists, or to commit a rape and murder his victim by endeavouring to smother her with a blanket, although he is prevented from the accomplishment of his crime only by the rescue of the sufferer, he escapes the penalty of the law ; but if in attempting the same crimes he should be attacked and make an effectual thrust with a sword in the heat of a scuffle, with intent to kill (for all killing in the perpetration of the robbery would be murder), he would suffer death, although the attempt should be abandoned as soon as it was made, or although it was only made to defend himself from arrest.

Again, there is no positive repeal of the first section of the law of the 7th June 1806.   But the second section of the one we are considering provides, that to shoot, stab, or thrust with a dangerous weapon, and with intent to murder, shall in all other cases but those provided for by the first section, be punished by hard labour only.   This last enactment, therefore, is not so broad as that of 1806, which does not contain the qualification of a dangerous weapon ; therefore, as the law now stands, a stab with an instrument that·could not come within the description of a weapon, would now under the first act be punished with death, while the more heinous case of a stab with the same intent with a dangerous weapon, might be punished with imprisonment for one year only.

Once more let me respectfully ask whether this part of our jurisprudence does not want revision ?   But this is only one head ; the same or greater defects may be found in all.   The same enacting, explaining, implied repealing and accumulation of provisions on the same subject, until in the short period of twenty years, our legislation has become so confused that the people, and (the truth is so evident that I shall not offend them when I add) their representatives too, are incapable of discovering what the law requires or forbids.   The following instances may justify my assertion.

By the act of 19th March 1818, the punishment of accessaries after the fact(a) to any crime, of course including murder, are to be punished by fine and imprisonment, at the discretion of the court ; and that discretion(b) is limited in all cases to fine of one thousand dollars and imprisonment for two years.   On the very next day a law is passed punishing the accessaries after the fact of burglary(c) by solitary confinement for one year and imprisonment at hard labour for five years. So that you may aid the escape of a murderer, by our laws, at infinitely less risk than you incur by performing the like service to one who has, at night, only lifted the latch of a sugar-house(d) and stolen a pint of molasses.

(a) Act 19th March 1819, section 9.        (b) Ib. section 12.

(c) Act 20th March 1818, section 6.

(d) By the 5th section of the act 20th March 1818, breaking into a sugar-house at night, with intent to steal, is made burglary.

Larceny(*a*) is punished by imprisonment at hard labour for any term not exceeding two years ; while the lesser offence, of obtaining property on false pretences, incurs the corporal punishment of whipping and imprisonment for one year(*b*) ; and by this law, such fraud is somewhat strangely declared to be an offence against the public peace.

By the act of 6th March 1819, the aiding(*c*) a slave to run away is punishable by imprisonment at hard labour, not less than two or more than twenty years ; while kidnapping a freeman(*d*) incurs only fine, not to exceed one thousand dollars, and imprisonment not to exceed fourteen years. The judge must punish the first crime at least by two years imprisonment, but may suffer the greater offender to escape with a nominal punishment.

Not to burthen this report with a longer enumeration of these discrepancies, I have thrown into a tabular form an account of all the statute offences with their present and former punishments. A few other instances of incorrect legislation in our present penal law will enforce the necessity of reform. One embarrassing defect arises from the numerous dissimilar provisions in relation to the same subject in successive statutes which contain no repealing clauses ; leaving it in many instances very difficult to determine whether the penalty was intended to be changed or commuted. Slave stealers, by the act of 1805, are to be publicly whipped and imprisoned at hard labour not less than seven nor more than fourteen years. By the act of 6th March 1819, they are to be imprisoned not less than two nor more than twenty years. Was the intent of the latter statute to take away the whipping, or only to extend the limits of judicial discretion as to the term of imprisonment(*e*) ?

Nearly the same difficulty occurs as to larceny. By the first law, whipping and imprisonment in the alternative of not restoring the goods stolen, is the punishment. The subsequent act only declares that it shall be punished by imprisonment.

Stealing or robbery of bonds, bills or notes, is not larceny at common law. It is made so by statute in England ; and as lacerny was to be defined by the common law, not by statute, they are enumerated in the act of 1805 ; and it is declared that the stealing of them " shall be punished in the same manner, both as to principal and accessary, as robbery or larceny of goods and chattels. Does this relate to the punishment prescribed by that act ? or is it prospective, so as to adapt itself to any other punishment that may afterwards be provided for larceny ? If it is not, stealing of bonds and notes, since the passage of the last statute, is punished differently from other larceny.

In all these instances, and they might be multiplied, there is no express repeal of the prior statutes ; and as there is nothing incompatible between the punishments of whipping and imprisonment, the strongest, perhaps the only good foundation for an implied repeal is taken away. Yet the degrading punishment inflicted by the first law is so repugnant to the feelings of freemen, and I may add, in a country like ours, so

---

(*a*) Act 19th March 1818, section 1.        (*b*) Act 3d July 1805, section 2.

(*c*) Ib. section 3.        (*d*) Ib. section 6.

(*e*) I have an impression that the learned judge of the criminal court of New-Orleans expressed a leaning towards the latter alternative. If I am not mistaken in this, the doubt is supported by very high authority.

dangerous to its peace, that the rules of construction have been disregarded, and a new instance afforded in which the duty of the legislature has been transferred to the judiciary. They have hitherto exercised it with discretion ; but these doubtful laws may hereafter be made engines of oppression as well as of favour.

Another evil in our present legislation is the loose manner in which offences are defined. I will not here repeat the objections arising from the references to the foreign law, although they press upon the mind in every view that is taken of the subject ; but there are cases in which even the obscure light of the common law is denied us. The statute of 22d February 1817 enacts, " that every person who shall commit the abominable crime of incest shall suffer imprisonment at hard labour for life." Here our guide entirely fails us. Incest was a crime unknown to the common law. During the rule of the Puritans in England, that, and every species of incontinence, were made capital crimes. The statute, we are told, was not renewed at the restoration, and I am ignorant what definition it gave to the crime. With us, if the Spanish laws are repealed, the law must be a dead letter, or the judges must make a law explaining the term. If the Spanish laws are not repealed, we *must* look to them for the definition ; and if they are, we *may*. But what will in either case be the serious consequences? In the definition of this crime by that law we have seen that incest means a carnal connexion between parties related, either by affinity or consanguinity, *to* the fourth degree ; and as the degrees are counted by the *canon law*, it would bring within the penalties of this law not only the children but the grandchildren of brothers ; and even if we look to the English law of matrimony, as well as to the Spanish statute, the sister of a wife is included in the prohibition. After the death of the wife it is not uncommon for the husband to marry her sister. Suppose such a connexion to be lawfully made in New York, and the parties remove to New Orleans where they continue to cohabit. By adopting either of these definitions this is the *abominable* crime(*a*) intended by the statute, for which both of them must be consigned to the penitentiary for life. What rule shall we resort to in order to give efficacy to this highly penal statute ? The law gives no guide ; and it would be monstrous to suppose the unconstitutional intent, that it should be framed or adopted by the judges.

By the act of the 7th June 1806, any judge, justice of the peace, sheriff or other civil officer, who shall be guilty of any misdemeanor in the execution of their respective offices, shall suffer fine or imprisonment, or both. Now, without repeating the argument formerly used, that the reference to the law of England does not extend to offences under this law, let us ask what is misdemeanor? Christian, in his notes to Blackstone, says, " in the English law, misdemeanor is generally used in contradistinction to felony ; and misdemeanors comprehend all indictable offences which do not amount to felony." But, by our law, there can be no indictable offence but those created by statute ; but every statute that has created an offence with us has also prescribed the punishment. What therefore has this law to operate upon ? Nothing, if it relate only to offences that were indictable before ; but if it mean something else, and is intended to create a new

(*a*) Vide 7 Part. tit. 18, 1. 1.

offence, that offence ought to have been defined ; or else the court have not only the judicial task of apportioning within the prescribed limits what shall be the punishment, but also the legislative duty of declaring what acts shall be misdemeanors.

Other instances of this defect might be selected, but I hasten to close the catalogue with pointing out another glaring and dangerous fault in our present laws. The almost entire abandonment to the judiciary of that part of the legislative duty, which consists in designating the punishment that shall be inflicted for each species of offence. This is a function perfectly consistent with that which, in all good jurisprudence, is committed to the judge of apportioning within certain limits, the quantity of punishment to the individual case. A wise legislator so arranges and classifies the offences he means to punish, that, as far as may be practicable, a slight variation from the punishment assigned to the designated crime may accommodate it to the least degree of evil that can be attached to its commission ; he gives this discretion in all cases in which different shades of guilt may be supposed to have attended the same act ; he withholds it only in cases where the least degree of depravity deserves the full punishment that is denounced, and it is not convenient to increase the penalty against the more immoral offenders, but he throws all those shades of crime that he can foresee into as many different classes as he can conveniently arrange, and he restricts the discretion he gives to the judge within the narrowest limits in which the distribution of individual justice will permit to be exercised. The reasons for this are evident and conclusive. Every penalty for the infraction of a law ought to be certain. Where the same act may be punished by a slight or a heavy penalty, the offender will always calculate on the slightest punishment ; and the infliction of the heaviest will, for the most part, be considered as an oppression. But there is a more serious objection to giving a wide extent of discretionary power to the judge. To a certain extent his decrees may be considered as having the effect of ex post facto law, for the punishment is not determined until the offence is committed. The prohibition of the law, indeed, existed before, but the sanction is created afterwards. Hatred, envy and the other malignant passions may sometimes influence the mind of the judge ; avarice may corrupt it ; or the more amiable motives of friendship or compassion may give it an unconscious bias in the exercise of his functions ; but the legislator, who cannot know when he frames his law upon whom its penalties may fall, can neither incur nor merit these suspicions. He, therefore, ought to assign the punishment to the offence ; and, in certain cases leave to the discretion of the judge a power of modifying it to the circumstances of the offender. In pecuniary penalties a considerable range must necessarily be given to this power ; for a fine that would be ruin to one, would not be felt as a punishment by another. In a less degree this applies to simple imprisonment, and least of all to penitentiary punishment ; but the difference in their nature between the two first and the last of these punishments is so great, that it very rarely, if ever, ought to be placed in the power of a judge to inflict the one or the other, at his discretion. The circumstances that would render the last proper for offences in which the first would generally be an adequate punishment, ought, if possible, to be detailed and form a different class of crime. The inefficiency of pecuniary fines to punish the rich, without putting them so high as to ruin the poor, renders it indispensable to place the alternative between fine and simple imprisonment in the hands of the judge.

Let us now examine how far our present statutes conform to these principles.

Kidnapping a free person is a crime, which, being destructive of personal liberty, is in the highest degree injurious to society; and moreover supposes a confirmed malignity of heart, and which of all others would seem to admit of no alleviating circumstances; yet the statute permits the court to fine the offender one cent only or to extend it to one thousand dollars, and to add imprisonment at hard labour for fourteen years. Is not this completely giving to the judge the power of legislation after the fact, upon an offence of the deepest die? He may suffer an offender to escape with a nominal fine, or he may imprison him for a term more than commensurate, perhaps, with his chance of life. Let it be remembered, too, that this is a law for the security of personal freedom; and contrast it with the penalty for stealing a slave, which, by a prior section of the same law cannot be less than two years at hard labour. But here again though the criminal cannot escape, as in the other instance, with impunity, his punishment may at the pleasure of the judge be increased tenfold, by a sentence to twenty years imprisonment at hard labour. And it may once more be asked, what circumstance in the crime of stealing a slave can make two years imprisonment a sufficient punishment for one offender, while twenty is not too much for another?.

I can, in this instance, imagine two answers to this question, but each of them disclose a fault in legislation equally grave, at least with the one they might otherwise excuse. The first is that the legislature have not provided as they might have done for the case of a repeated offence, and that the higher grades of punishment are intended to supply this defect. But if such was the intention it ought to have been expressed; the court then would not have had the power which they now have of awarding the same punishment for a first, that was intended for a second or third offence. Secondly, it may be said that the offence described in the statute is not only stealing a slave, but aiding one to escape from his master, which are two very different offences—one deserving the highest, perhaps, and the other the lowest penalty of the law. If this be so, it enhances instead of excusing the incongruity of the act, by confounding two distinct offences in the same clause, and permitting the court to punish one offence by the penalty intended for the other.

Take another instance from the same act. To shoot, stab or thrust by lying in wait, or in the perpetration or attempt to perpetrate arson, rape, robbery or burglary, is death, if done with intent to murder and with a dangerous weapon; but if done with the same intent to murder, but not by lying in wait, or not in the perpetration of either of the crimes above enumerated, it may be punished by simple imprisonment for one year only, or by imprisonment at hard labour for twenty-one years. According to the English definition of terms here can be no gradation of crime. The party, if convicted, must have given the stroke not in the heat of passion only, for then it would be a different offence, but with the deliberate malicious design to murder. The design must have failed, not from any change of purpose in the offender, but contrary to his will. When combined with an intent to commit certain crimes, we see that there is no discretion left to the judge: the punishment is death. Yet, when the same offence is combined with the intention to commit any other crime, perhaps not less atrocious, one year of simple imprisonment may be deemed a sufficient penalty. To exemplify the operation of this law: if, in the attempt to set fire to a building not worth five dollars(*a*), the offender, with intent to murder, should shoot at and wound the person who discovers and prevents him, there is no discretion; the punishment is death. But if he in like manner wound the person who prevents him from assassinating his father, or from poisoning a whole community, it is in the power of the court to let him escape with one year's simple imprisonment.

This example is taken, almost without selection, from a system which is considered by some as too perfect to need any amendment ! We must be at a loss in this species of legislation, however, what most to admire; the severity which punishes the attempt to commit a crime with the same awful penalty that it inflicts on its consummation; the confusion of principle which thus punishes the attempt to commit the highest crime because it is made in the perpetration of an inferior offence; the want of judgment and indifference with which the selection of these lesser offences is made; or the jealous denial of discretionary power to the judge in the one instance, and the prodigality of confidence with which it is lavished on him in the other. The table at the end of this report will give so many examples of this defect in our system, that I need not multiply them here.

It might seem an invidious task to proceed and develope the evils that pervade our penal jurisprudence, from which, however, I should not shrink were it necessary. Enough has been said to show :

That as respects certain crimes, the law to which we are referred for their definition, prosecution and the evidence required on their trial, is not only in itself uncertain, but is placed entirely beyond the reach of the people.

That even that rule, uncertain and difficult of access as it is, has not been provided for offences against any of the statutes passed since that of May 1805.

That if a long list of oppressive and absurd penal laws, forming a part of those by which the country was governed prior to the cession, are not now in force according to the strictest construction of law, at least reasonable doubts may be entertained on that subject, and that in bad times they may be made the instrument of oppression.

That our penal statutes remedy none of these defects :

They repeal none of the ancient laws :

They give new penalties for offences punishable by former statutes, leaving it doubtful whether they are intended as substitutes for the old punishments or as additions to them :

They punish slight offences with undue severity, and impose inconsiderable penalties on more dangerous crimes :

They give in some instances to the judiciary a discretion trenching on legislative power, and wholly deny it in others where justice and humanity requires its exercise :

They leave unpunished many acts and omissions injurious to society,

(*a*) By the act of 22d February 1817, burning any building is made arson.

while some others are made offences which might be repressed by public opinion or private suit.

They are multiplied without necessity on the same, or different modifications of the same offence ; giving occasion frequently to doubts whether the new statute is intended as a substitute for or an addition to the old.

They are deficient in precision of language and in the order required by proper arrangement.

Such laws are unworthy of an enlightened, and dangerous to a free people ; and if you had not given the pledge contained in your law of 1S20; if you had not attracted the attention and excited the hopes of the good, and the wise, and the liberal throughout the civilized world— attention which is still earnestly fixed upon you ! hopes which you cannot without dishonour fail to realize ; if you could be insensible to the noble distinction of emerging from the subordinate rank of the youngest member in the union, taking the lead in a most important reform, making by your example a new era in the history of penal jurisprudence ; if you could consent to renounce the glorious privilege of conducting your country to the best pre-eminence among nations, and associating your own names with those of the benefactors of mankind ; if you could be influenced by the timid fear of innovation or the senseless clamour of prejudice to throw away this rare occasion of founding a glorious reputation for yourselves and for your country, on the solid and permanent basis of public good ; if it were possible for you to be blind to these advantages, deaf to these arguments, yet you could not, without an entire abandonment of official duty, any longer delay to remedy the evils which are thus brought to your view, and others as great which cannot escape your discernment.

Legislative functions are in the most ordinary times attended with high responsibility. Yours, from the duty which your predecessors have imposed upon you, are peculiarly so. From the performance of this duty there is no escape. The defects of your penal laws are arrayed before your eyes. Former legislative acts have declared that they exist, and they have established principles and laid down rules by which laws are to be framed for their removal. Those laws are now submitted for your consideration. You cannot avoid acting. It is impossible to say that the evils are imaginary. You must then either declare that the principles for correcting them, heretofore unanimously established by the representatives of the people, are erroneous, or that the plan prepared is not drawn in conformity with them. In either alternative the duty of correcting the principles or reforming the work is one that must be performed. For, disguise it as we may, it is a truth which must be told'and ought to be felt ; that, circumstanced as you are, should you shrink from the performance of these duties, to you will be attributed the future depredations of every offender who escapes punishment from the ambiguity of your laws ; the vexations of all who suffer by their uncertainty; the general alarm caused by the existence of your unknown and unrepealed statutes; the depravity of those who are corrupted by the associations into which they are forced by your prison discipline; the unnecessary and violent death of the guilty ; and, worse than all this, legislators ! the judicial murder of the innocent who may perish under the operation of your sanguinary laws. All this, and

M

more will be laid to your charge(a), if you do not embrace the opportunity that is afforded to reform them ; for the continuance of every bad law, which we have the power to repeal, is equivalent to its enactment. Whether the mode of reform now offered is the one most proper to be adopted is, with unfeigned diffidence, submitted to the superior wisdom of the general assembly ; but that some change is necessary, is boldly and without fear of contradiction advanced as an irresistible conclusion from the view that has been taken of the state of our penal jurisprudence. Of what nature shall that change be and to what extent shall it be carried, are questions which come now to be considered. A repeal of all the Spanish penal laws, and of such of our own statutes as throw any uncertainty in the construction of those which we choose to retain, would relieve us of part of the difficulty ; but this would be a palliative and give us only a partial relief. Other cases must be provided for by new statutes ; and what security can we have, while this patch-work system continues, that in a few years the same or greater incongruities will not be found in your laws? But supposing this difficulty to be surmounted or not to exist, a greater remains. Where are we to look for our rules and forms of proceeding from the arrest to the execution ? In what statute are contained the rules of evidence, and where shall we find the regulations by which our penitentiaries and other prisons are to be governed ? The Spanish laws of procedure, if they are unrepealed, do not fit our institutions ; their rules of evidence we have seen will exclude nearly all testimony but that forced from the lacerated limbs of a tortured accomplice: and their prison discipline we surely shall not be tempted to establish. We cannot again resort to the concise but comprehensive legislation formerly employed. We cannot refer to and adopt the common or any other law, either *en masse* or generally, on any given branch of jurisprudence. That door is constitutionally closed. No more legislation by reference. This device, excusable from necessity(b) in the infancy of our political existence, is wisely prohibited to our maturer understanding. Representatives can no longer jeopardize the fortunes, reputations and lives of their constituents by the use of an unintelligible phrase ; they must understand and express what they mean ; they must do it clearly and in detail. Foreign laws can no longer be imported by the package, or described in the act of introducing them as goods are in the bill of lading, " *contents unknown*" ; but in the imperative words of the constitution, the general assembly " shall in all cases specify the several provisions of the laws they may enact."

(a) "Lawgivers should reflect that they are immediately, and in effect, the executioners of every fellow-citizen who suffers death in consequence of any penal law."—*Eden. Penal Law.*

(b) The first legislative council—highly respectable men, but not qualified by their education or pursuits to the task of legislation—did all that could be expected from them. They called to their assistance in this branch a gentleman (James Workman, Esq.) whose natural as well as acquired powers eminently fitted him for the task, and whose principles and integrity always direct his exertion in the public service. His high professional as well as private character justified the choice. But they committed the great error of limiting him as to time. What human exertion could do, he performed. He could not, as I know he wished, offer a complete system. All he could give was a general summary, and a reference to other laws for cases unprovided for. It is to be regretted that full scope was not given to the talents of this gentleman ; the humbler exertions of those now employed would have then been rendered unnecessary.

On these parts of the subject then—and they form three-fourths of the system—the question is reduced to one of mere form. We must have detailed laws. Shall they be framed into codes, or dispersed in different independent statutes? By whatever name they may be called, you must enact rules and prescribe forms; you must provide laws to regulate the admission and weight of testimony, and a plan for the government of your prisons.

The advantages of having these reduced to order, under proper heads, and making them component and consistent parts of the same system, are so obvious, the state has already derived so much benefit from a similar improvement in the civil branch of its jurisprudence, that it would scarcely seem necessary to say any thing on this subject; but as this part of the plan has not escaped censure, it may be proper to offer a very few and very brief remarks, to show its utility.

Laws, to be obeyed and administered, must be known; to be known they must be read; to be administered they must be studied and compared. To know them is the right of the people. Their administration is the duty of the magistrate. But that mode which with the least trouble, in the shortest time, and at the least expense, brings the enjoyment of this right and the performance of this duty within the reach of those to whom they are appropriated, that mode is the best; and were two systems submitted to our choice, we should, for the purpose of making a selection, only have to compare them and determine in what degree they severally were calculated to produce these effects. But here the question is not which of two systems is the best; but whether it is better to have a system or none; for there is not, in our present criminal legislation, the least appearance of plan or arrangement. Yet if this character deserves the epithet which is given by the poet, when he calls it emphatically "*lucidus ordo,*" how can we expect that the necessary light will be shed on our laws without it?

A representative is instructed by his constituents, or led by his own observation, to bring in a bill to repress a prevailing vice. A preparatory step is to know whether it has already attracted legislative notice. To discover this he must examine all the acts concerning crimes and punishments, for the titles of none of them designate the particular offence which they forbid. He, perhaps, finds a provision on the subject, crowded into a section(*a*) with others to which it bears not the least relation. But has it not been repealed or modified? Another painful search in which he discovers a second law(*b*). Is it consistent with or repugnant to the first? Another question which he has not the time or skill, or patience to resolve; and he brings in a third bill to increase the doubts and perplexities of his successors.

Is the task easier for the magistrate? Called on, we will suppose, to

(*a*) See the 28th and 31st sections of the act of 4th May 1805. In the first, breach of prison, taking a reward to return stolen goods, compounding felony, and conspiracy to indict an innocent man, are confounded together in a clause not longer than this note, and all these offences are subjected to the same penalty. In the second, rioters, breakers of levees and libellers, are most heterogeneously mixed.

(*b*) See the several acts concerning forgery, larceny, burglary, &c. No reference is made to them here by title or date, that the readers of this report may, in the search for them, and in the task of reconciling them after they are found, have a small specimen of the difficulties mentioned in the text.

perform one of the most ordinary functions of his office, in which he must determine whether the law requires him to deprive a fellow citizen of liberty; whether he has a discretion to discharge him on bail, or whether he is bailable of right. He first consults the digest of our laws up to the year 1816, and in it he searches in vain for such a title as *bail.* Under that of justice he finds something, but it is only the beginning of his labour. He is there told that if the offence be "not punishable by death, or not exclusively cognizable by the superior court," that he must take bail; and afterwards in the same section, that if the offence be punishable by death, that he must commit the accused. But what is to be done with him if the crime be not punishable in that manner, yet is one of those of which the superior court had exclusive cognizance, is not said. He cannot under this law take bail, for it is a case excepted by the first clause. He cannot commit; for the authority is not given by the second, which is confined to the two cases of crimes punishable by death, and a refusal to give security. First difficulty for the magistrate. He happens to look into the constitution, and he finds, "that all prisoners shall be bailable by sufficient securities unless for *capital offences;*" how shall he reconcile this with the law, which excludes other offences, namely, those which are exclusively cognizable by the superior court? Second difficulty for the magistrate. When these are surmounted, he must inquire what is a capital offence, and what offences are exclusively cognizable by the superior court? This leads to an examination of all the penal statutes. As there is no classification, no order, not even a general index, he must examine every law and every section of every law ; for, as we have seen, our statute offences are strangely associated, and there is no knowing where the provision he seeks for may be hid. Third difficulty for the magistrate. But we will suppose him a persevering intelligent man, and that this also is conquered. He has another not less stubborn in his way. If the offence in question is one of those enumerated in the act of 1805, he has to look to the common law of England for its definition, for the rules of evidence which he is to take, and for all those proceedings which are not among those prescribed in the act. If it be an offence against a statute of a subsequent date, he has no rule, and neither Burn, nor Blackstone, nor Coke himself, can tell him how he is to proceed.

As to the citizen who is neither representative nor magistrate, I need not enumerate the difficulties that stand in his way, for he never attempts their encounter; and it is no bold assertion to say, that not one in an hundred, even in the educated part of the community, can, in the nature of things, have even a superficial knowledge of the criminal laws by which he is governed, and which he is expected to obey.

All these and a thousand other evils might be avoided by a simple arrangement of the penal law under its different heads, and in short sentences; where every thing required to be known might be found in its place, and might be understood when it was found; where the eye of the legislator(a) might, at one comprehensive glance, discover, from what was done, what ought to be supplied, corrected or restricted; where magistrates could find simple directions for the performance of their

(a) "The enacting of penalties to which a whole nation shall be subject, ought to be calmly and maturely considered, by persons who know what provisions the laws have already made to remedy the mischief complained of."—*Bl. Com.*

duty; judges, in the precise language of the law, see the limits and extent of their discretionary powers; jurors learn how they are to act, so as neither to abuse nor surrender their important privileges; citizens how to defend their own rights and protect those of others; and the whole community acquire the knowledge of that which all may at some(a) time or other have so high an interest in knowing.

The consideration of expense, too, though of less importance than the others which have been urged, is not without its consequence. Every session of the legislature produces from sixty to an hundred laws; three-fourths of them private acts; and one or two on an average which have some bearing on the penal law. But they are all published in the same volume; so that whoever wishes to possess the statutes on that subject must go to the expense of a whole set of the laws, and think himself fortunate if he can procure them, for the greater part are now out of print; and should duty or inclination induce him to wish for a more perfect and not less necessary knowledge of this branch of our laws, he must procure a common law library at an indefinite expense. All this could be avoided by the adoption of a system in which, without trouble and at a small expense of time or money, the whole penal law would be placed within the reach of all.

No one can be blind to the incalculable advantages our state has derived from its civil code. Yet that code is imperfect and must necessarily be so. The endless variety and ever changing nature of contracts and other civil relations must always make it as difficult to frame, as it must be incomplete, after the utmost care in its construction. But a penal code is susceptible of a nearer approach to perfection. Nothing being an offence but doing that which is forbidden, or omitting to do that which is enjoined by the law. It follows that as the law can only enjoin or forbid by the use of language, there can of necessity be nothing penal, but that which is not only foreseen, but expressed by the legislature; in other words, that which is contrary to written law; and whenever an act is not thus forbidden or enjoined, there can be no punishment for doing or for omitting it. If, therefore, the greater difficulties of framing a civil code have been surmounted so far as to render it an acknowledged blessing to the country, why should objections be raised to the easier operation of making a written system of penal law?

Other general objections, which apply to any written code that could be proposed, have been urged, and must be answered before we consider the particular provisions of the system now offered. They are,

(a) The observations of Blackstone, repeating and enlarging on what was so happily expressed by sir M. Foster, although frequently quoted, cannot be too often repeated for the use of all legislators, who too readily imagining themselves and their connexions beyond the reach of any operation of the criminal laws, pay little attention to the evils which they may produce to the community at large. "The knowledge of this branch of jurisprudence," says this celebrated commentator, "which teaches the nature, extent and degrees of every crime, and adjusts to it its adequate and necessary penalty, is of the utmost importance to every individual in the state; for no rank or elvation in life, no uprightness of heart, no prudence or circumspection of conduct should tempt a man to conclude that he may not at some time or other be deeply interested in these researches. The infirmities of the best among us, the vices and ungovernable passions of others, the instability of all human affairs, and the numberless unforseen events, which the compass of a day may bring forth, will teach us, upon a moment's reflection, that to know with precision what the laws of our country have forbidden, and the deplorable consequences to which a wilful disobedience may expose us, is a matter of universal concern." 4. *Bl. Com.* p. 2.

First, that it is an innovation, and therefore to be avoided.

Second, that we suffer no inconvenience from the present state of our law.

Third, that it will require much time and trouble to become acquainted with a new system.

Fourth, that it may be good in theory but bad in practice.

Fifth, that the terms of the new code will require to be explained by judicial decisions and commentaries, which will produce the same or a greater accumulation of authorities than are now complained of in the common law.

1. The hacknied objection against improvements that they are new, amounts to no more than that they are improvements ; and the fallacy has been so often exposed that the perseverance of those who still use it is truly wonderful, and would deserve our admiration in a better cause.    Their objections hold the very reverse of the wise king of Israel's doctrine, that there is nothing new under the sun.    With them every thing is new, and they use the epithet as synonymous with bad or at least with dangerous.    But the truth is, that with us a body of written, to the exclusion of traditionary laws, is no innovation.    We had them before the cession, and our first care afterwards was to provide them, better suited to our circumstances in civil cases.    An experiment in any of the occult sciences is said to be most successfully made, when the desired effects have been produced, under the most unfavourable circumstances.    It is the same in legislation, and we may consider the favourable result as completely ascertained ; for our experiment has been thus made. It has succeeded in the most difficult branch; succeeded under every disadvantage of imperfect execution, and in opposition to professional and national prejudices; succeeded, too, so completely, as to silence every objection to the measure itself, and leaving none but to some of the details which more mature revision may remove.    This then is no further an innovation, than as it applies the same remedy that has succeeded in the complex case of the civil, to the simpler one of the criminal department.    It is, on the contrary, the removal of one which was formerly made—the mischievous and dangerous reference to a foreign and unwritten code ; and indeed there can be no change which does not destroy something that was itself, when first introduced, an innovation.

The truth is, that by repeating a word or a phrase very frequently, and using it always in a bad sense, an indefinite idea of evil gets attached to it, which makes it a very convenient instrument in the hands of those who are at a loss for more legitimate weapons in argument. This is the case with the word in question ; and many excellent measures have been defeated merely by repeating it, accompanied by some gesture of disapprobation, and reinforced sometimes by the sage observation of " good in theory but bad in practice," a phrase of equal import, which we shall presently analyse.    In the mean time it is put to the recollection of every member of the honourable body to whom this report is addressed, whether these precise words have not frequently been used as objections to the measure now proposed ?

If the objection were, that it is a bad or a dangerous innovation, its merits would immediately come under discussion; and this ought to be the object of every one who proposes a change.    Of this he would have no right to complain, and the question ought to be so stated as to throw upon him the burthen of showing the expediency and practicability of the measure he advocates ; for there is no doubt that every change of laws, or the manner of administering them, must be attended with some inconvenience, and is therefore to be avoided.  And he is justly to be reproached as an idle or mischievous pretender, who proposes any change without being able to show, not only that it would be useful if adopted, but that it is practicable, and that its advantages will more than compensate the evils of the operation.  But he has a right to expect that a good and necessary measure will not be rejected on the vague charge of innovation, which, being strictly true as applied to every change, cannot be denied, and is hurtful only from the improper meaning affixed to the term(a).

2. The next general objection is, that there is no necessity for a change; the peace of the state is as well preserved as that of any other in the union; crimes are not more frequent ; justice is well administered ; and if any evils should result from our present system, it will be time enough to correct them when they arise.  How much of truth there is in the allegations by which this objection is supported, may be determined by referring to a former part of this report, in which the present state of our criminal jurisprudence is detailed.  No comparison can with justice be made, between the situation of other states in this respect and ours. With them the common law is indigenous ; they have grown up under it and modified it to their wants and conveniences.  They have not the embarrassment arising from the laws of foreign countries unrepealed among them.  Their people speak all the same language and are familiar with all the technicalities of the law.  Yet without these pressing inducements, many of them have reduced their criminal code into something like system.  A large majority of them have adopted the penitentiary plan, and have given their laws the shape it requires ; and the legislature of one of the largest and most influential among them is now occupied with the revisal of all their laws, including the criminal code, and throwing them into a methodical form.  But whatever be the comparative situation of ours with other states, as to the condition of their penal laws, we know that ours are extremely defective ; and although the body politic can move on in spite of these defects ; although anarchy does not reign, and the laws, bad as they are, curb offences in some degree, we should scarcely be justified to ourselves, to our country, or to our God, for neglecting the means in our power to remedy the existing and prevent the future mischief of a system, so extremely defective as our own.  The suggestion that all must be right, because we do not see and feel the evil in our own persons, creates a fallacious security, and, it may be, a fatal one.  If it were true that no evil has yet arisen from the effects of a system which we see must eventually produce it, we should

(a) The man who has thrown more light on the science of legislation, than any other in ancient or modern times, speaking of this kind of objection says, " a few words then are necessary to strip the mask from this fallacy : no specific mischief, as likely to result from the specific measure, is alleged; if it were, the argument would not belong to this head. What is alleged is nothing more than that mischief, without regard to the amount, would be among the results of this measure.  But this is no more than can be said of every legislative measure that ever did or ever can pass.  If then it be to be ranked with arguments, it is an argument that involves, in one common condemnation, all political measures whatsoever, past, present and to come; it passes condemnation on whatsoever in this way ever has been or ever can be done, in all places as well as all times."—*Bentham's Book of Fallacies*.

bless God, and hasten, before it is too late, to prevent those ills which we cannot compensate after they have been suffered. To defer it, is as wise as to wait until some traveller has been lost in the torrent that crosses the way, before we build a bridge to pass it.

But is it true that no evil is already felt? Is it only to prevent future, not to remove present mischief that we are called on to legislate? To answer these questions we must look to the general operation of our laws on the character and morals of the whole community as well as to their particular application. Nothing in a free government can be a worse symptom, than an indifference to bad laws, because we do not suffer by their immediate operation. In the people, it evinces a selfish feeling, a carelessness of the welfare of others, and an insensibility to public good, destructive of every patriotic sentiment. This danger-ous apathy is created and fostered by suffering the existence of impoli-tic or oppressive laws, although circumstances may not have called for their application. We become familiar with them and learn to consider as innocent that from which we feel no present inconvenience ; and, presently, as necessary that which has so long continued ; and when in evil times these instruments, ready fashioned for the hand of oppression, are brought into operation, it is illegal to resist, and we know not how to avoid the stroke. But in a community such as ours, there will al-ways be a large proportion who have understanding enough to see and fear the danger. To those this apprehension is a continued evil, at-tended with the humiliating sensation of having life, liberty, reputation, or property at the disposition of another(a), which must always be more or less the case under any but a good system of penal laws. There is, then, evil, positive evil, the evil of political degradation or constant apprehension, even though the laws should never be executed. But that is not the case ; they have a general, active and most pernicious opera-tion; one that never for a moment ceases, and for the continuance of which every legislature that meets incurs a most awful responsibility. The only punishments, with the exception of death(b), now inflicted, are fine and imprisonment. To some crimes the law adds hard labour; but as no means are provided for inflicting this punishment, the only confinement that is suffered is one of idleness, debauchery and vicious association. Of all punishments this is the most unequal and most in-jurious to society and to the individual. As this subject will be fully discussed in the preliminary report on the Code of Prison Discipline,

(a) In some memoir of the reign of Louis XV. we read of a courtier whose duties called him very frequently about the person of the monarch with whom he was a kind of favour-ite ; but far from enjoying this distinction with pleasure, he was observed always to be ex-tremely agitated in the royal presence. On being asked by a friend to account for this feeling, he said, " I have indeed every reason to be satisfied with my treatment ; but whenever I am in company with the king, I cannot avoid saying to myself, there stands a man who whenever he pleases may chop off my head or bury me alive in the Bastile. Judge whether with these reflections I can be happy." The existence of bad laws must have the same effect upon every considerate citizen, that the presence of his master produced on the disturbed faculties of the courtier. The sword, though it never fell, destroyed the festivity of Damocles.

(b) Whipping maintains, as we have seen, an existence of doubtful authority on the stat-ute-book, and the pillory is prescribed as a specific against the disorder of one offence only; neither, however, have, I believe, been administered of late years.

it is not now intended to enter into the reasons which conclusively show, that the laws which permit or direct the indiscriminate association of the innocent with the guilty, before trial, and of those affected with different degrees of guilt, after condemnation, are themselves the great causes of the depravity which they profess to punish. Such laws are ours ; such are and always will be their effects ; and you, legislators ! you have collectively the power to remove this evil, to repeal these laws, to replace them by those which are better—worse, you can scarcely substitute. Each of you, individually, may cast off the responsibility of their continuance, by an earnest, sincere resolve to adopt what is good and amend what is erroneous in the system that is proposed; and by rejecting with disdain the false, and fallacious, and dangerous lullaby that is sung to your consciences, that all is well. All is not well ! The general operation of your laws destroys the morals of the people, saps the foundation of your liberty, and is calculated to spread general alarm. By their particular operation, they endanger the safety of the innocent and favour the escape of the guilty. These last characteristics will be made more apparent in considering the particular provisions of the different codes, more especially that of procedure. Here it will be sufficient to indicate, that the severity of some of your penalties, disproportioned to the offence, and repugnant to the feelings of the people, always have and always will induce witnesses to avoid prosecuting, jurors to acquit against evidence, judges to recommend to undeserved clemency, and the pardoning power to be indiscreetly exercised : that the law which has been prescribed for criminal proceedings, in certain cases, by legislative authority, and adopted without any authority at all, in others, is eminently calculated for the escape of the guilty, by the numerous objections which it admits to the forms of proceedings : that if instances are not produced to you of individuals suffering innocently, you are not, from thence, to conclude that such cases do not exist; for no act being guilt, but one that is intended to be forbidden by the law, whenever that is so ambiguous, or its definition so loose, as to render it doubtful whether one act or another comes within its intent, the chances, —why is it necessary to use this term in speaking of that which ought to exhibit moral certainty ?—the *chances* of a decision in accordance with, or contrary to the meaning of the legislator, are equal, and of course it is as probable that the penalty may fall on the head of the innocent, as of the guilty(*a*): and, finally, that the innocent are made guilty, and the guilty become more depraved, and both suffer incalculable moral and physical evil by their indiscriminate(*b*) confinement.

(*a*) The organization of our criminal courts gives a good reason why instances of erroneous decisions cannot be produced. There is no legal mode of examining them—no review ! —no appeal ! Eight independent judges, each gives his own construction on a mass of laws, the most liable to misconstruction, without any means of comparing or reconciling them. The reporter has not ventured to propose in this system a remedy for this most flagrant evil. He once proposed it, and the bill is on the legislative files. The double influence that defeated it, is still in force. It exists in human nature. Few men like to have their errors exposed, and as few like the trouble of correcting those of others, without additional compensation.

(*b*) This is not a repetition, although the enormity of the evil would excuse its being brought frequently to notice. When formerly mentioned, it was to show its general demoralizing effects on the whole community. Here it is enumerated as one of the causes of individual suffering.

N

3. But we are also told, that the introduction of a new system will be attended with trouble and expense : trouble to learn its provisions ; expense to carry it into effect. Of this there is not the least doubt. All laws that ever were or ever will be made are liable to this objection. But whatever trouble they give in learning them, or whatever sum they cost in making, we must have laws ; and if we are wise, we must have good laws. If those which now govern us are good, he would be mad, or worse, who should propose to change them. The first question, then, is one that has already been discussed, are our present penal laws good or bad ? Their defects have been shown. No man who has considered the subject, can call ours a good system. But as good and bad are relative terms, the present laws not being perfectly bad, nor any that can be offered to replace them perfectly good, our inquiry is reduced to one of expediency. We must compare the present state of things, its advantages and evils, with those of the system that is proposed, and as the scale preponderates decide to remain as we are, or to adopt this or some other code in its stead. The materials for forming the first part of this judgment are already before you. The evils of our present laws have been exhibited ; and if the advantages have not been displayed with equal care, it is because all that has been thought good in the excellent materials which are found in its composition, have been used in the construction of the new system that is offered to replace it. Another part of the operation, the consideration of the advantages and defects of the new system, must necessarily be deferred until we enter on the detail of its provisions.

To dispose of the present objection, we will, first, consider the evils attendant on every change that may be proposed, and compare them with those which we now suffer, or must expect as inevitable, from a continuance in our present state.

First, the prominent objection of the trouble and inconvenience of learning a new system. To give any weight whatever to this reason, we must suppose a state of things which does not exist; we must suppose that the present laws are known—known to those who are to obey, as well as to those who administer them; because, in all evils in government, it is amongst the greatest, that the laws, particularly the penal laws, should be a mystery to the people, and the knowledge of them confined to certain designated classes or descriptions of men. They invariably make a property of them in the strictest sense of the word; a property that must be paid for, whenever it is wanted for use; and, like other articles of commerce, is not always sold in a pure unsophisticated state; and the unfortunate purchaser of the adulterated commodity, has no means of determining whether it be good or bad, until he has incurred some loss, or made himself liable to some penalty by trusting to it. And, to carry on the metaphor, the seller himself may have been equally deceived in them, for a written code is the only public inspection office at which the stamp of authority is given to legal opinions, and by a reference to which, their correctness may be tested. But it has been shown—it is believed to demonstration—that with a very considerable portion of its penal laws, three-fourths of the people of this state cannot, in the nature of things, be acquainted; that the other fourth can know it but partially; and to any one who has attended our courts, it must be evident, from the number of contradictory cases and authorities cited, sometimes on the simplest points(*a*), that even those who have made it the study of their lives to expound these laws, and those whose duty it is to apply them, are not yet masters of their provisions. Each advocate relies on his own authority, and the judge, perhaps, decides according to a third.

The present law, then, is wholly unknown in some of its essential parts to a large majority of the people, because those parts are either not written at all, or written in a language that is not understood; and, to say no more, it is not perfectly known to those who are paid(*b*) to explain and administer it. Here the proposed system has a decided advantage; for it retains almost all that is now known, and renders that accessible which could not be approached before. It can be read in the language of the reader. It can be read in one book, without being obliged to have recourse to a hundred. Its terms are simple and intelligible, or are made so by explanation. It is methodized, and the part that is required, may be found without trouble. If it is adopted, the law no longer is a snare for the

(*a*) For proof of this assertion, if any be wanted, open at random any report of a criminal trial at common law. In the case already referred to, of the Territory *v.* Barran, fourteen cases were arrayed on the one side, and were met by an equal force of fourteen on the other; each of them equally law, because each was pronounced by sir William Blackstone's living oracles; and yet fourteen of them must have been false, if the other fourteen were true.

In another case, the offence was, in the indictment, stated to have been committed "in the city of New Orleans," which we all know to be in the First District; and lest that might be forgotten, the words " *First District*" were put in the margin. A conviction took place on this indictment; but a motion was made to arrest this judgment, because the words " *in the district aforesaid*," were not inserted after the words " New Orleans." Twenty authorities, equally conclusive, were cited on this important question. And it was decided, that the words were necessary; and the defendant, although found guilty, escaped punishment. Will this decision be a rule in future cases? To use a favourite phrase to express judicial legislation, does it *settle* the law? The general assembly may judge from the following statement:

In the case of the Seven Bishops, three judges decided that surety of the peace might be required in a case of a libel. One judge dissented.—In the case of John Wilkes, Lord Camden, in declaring the opinion of the court, according to the report, says, that the dissenting judge (Powell) was the only honest man of the four, and subscribes to his opinion, declaring that " it is absurd to require surety of the peace or bail in the case of a libellous suit."

In the case of Nugent, the superior court of the territory of Orleans, decided contrary to the opinion of the court, as declared by lord Camden, and required the defendant to give security for his good behaviour. What has been decided in the eight several independent courts of criminal jurisdiction, since that time, I cannot say. What sides they have taken between lord Camden and judge Martin, I cannot pretend to know. But I ought to add, that one reason alleged for not subscribing to the opinion of his lordship, was, that it was believed to be inaccurately reported, thereby adding the high authority of our own judiciary, to the support of what I have said, as to this source of uncertainty in the English law—an uncertainty not theoretically feared, but practically felt in forming the decision just quoted.

(*b*) Any reflection derogatory to the learning, ability, or integrity of the respectable judges and other magistrates, who administer our criminal law, would be so unbecoming, not to say unjust and disrespectful, that it is hoped nothing of this kind will be understood by the report, or imputed to its author. What is meant by this, and similar observations in this work, is, that the laws themselves are in such a state, composed of such heterogeneous materials, drawn from such obscure sources, and so confusedly put together, that it is impossible for the most assiduous application and the quickest apprehension to master them.

unwary; all its penalties are exposed; whoever incurs them must do it wilfully; the good citizen clothes himself in their protection, for they teach him all his rights and all his duties; the knave knows and fears them, for he sees that they cannot be evaded nor broken with impunity; the diligent may easily acquire a knowledge of all their contents; the more negligent knows where the provisions that suit his immediate occasions are to be found, when they may be wanted, and no one will have occasion to pay another for expounding laws, which, being intended for general use, are suited to the capacities of all. These will be the effects of a good system. Nearly the reverse is experienced under the present. And I think it may safely be asserted, that less time will be required to obtain a perfect knowledge of any law that is reduced to writing, and framed with a tolerable attention to clearness and method, than would be necessary to learn that part of those which now govern us, which is unknown even to its professors. But should it be conceded that this supposition is unfounded, and that greater trouble would be required than is supposed, to master the differences between the old and the new system, for those who have studied the former, yet this can apply only to ourselves, to those who are now on the stage of public life. But those who are just about to take their places there; the countless succession of legislators, judges, advocates, magistrates and officers, who are to replace them!—the multitude even in the present day, who have not yet studied the present laws, but who are bound to obey them! —the millions who are to follow them in the lapse of those ages which every good citizen must wish his country and its institutions to endure! —is the curse of bad laws, and the odious and painful task of learning them, to be entailed on these for ever, to save ourselves the task of a few days or weeks mental application? But this inconvenience, whatever be its amount, cannot be avoided. The new system must be studied. It cannot be rejected without examining and weighing its provisions; and if in performing this duty, those who study it to find out defects and objections, would give but half the care in amending what is wrong, or pointing out and advocating what is right, we should hear no more of their objections to adopting it. This argument is addressed to enlightened legislators, who know that their labours are not to be confined to the ephemeral operation of the present day. To those upright magistrates who are ever ready to sacrifice their personal convenience to the permanent good of their country; to the high-minded members of an honourable profession, who cannot but see the uncertainties and incongruities of our present laws, and who would scorn to make public evil contribute to their private good : these classes comprise generally all who, having any knowledge of the system now in force, would find some little part of that knowledge useless by the introduction of a new one ; and to either of these it would be insulting to express a doubt of their readiness to devote the time necessary for this new study ; or that they would for a moment put in competition a trifling and temporary personal inconvenience, with a lasting and important benefit to their country. It must be observed, that I am now answering the objection of trouble and inconvenience only, as applicable to any change; and that, therefore, it is permitted to consider the change as an advantageous one; for it will most readily be conceded, that neither trouble nor expense ought to be incurred, for replacing a bad system by one that is not better.

The arguments on this head have hitherto been based on an assumption that we had a choice either to remain as we are, or to change; but if the facts already stated are true, and the deductions from them are correct, there is an absolute necessity for the change. The Spanish laws must be abrogated : the incongruities in your own must be corrected : rules must be provided for defining, prosecuting and trying the offences not enumerated in the act of 1805 : and a penitentiary must be provided and laws must be made for regulating its discipline, or else some other mode of punishment must be substituted for the one to which the criminal is sentenced, but which there are no means to enforce. There is a moral obligation to do this. No part of it can be omitted, consistently with the first duties which representatives owe to their constituents. There is a necessity for all this and more ; unless we choose to abandon the high station on which so lately we were placed by the resolutions of your predecessors ; unless, without motive and contrary to duty, and interest, and reputation, we recede in the path of improvement which we ourselves have traced, while others to whom we led the way advance; unless, after having received by anticipation the prize in the race of reform, we sullenly refuse to proceed and suffer other nations to snatch it from our hands ; unless we cease to be intelligent, great, enlightened and free; cease, in short, to be ourselves, and become, what Louisianians never can be, regardless of national honour, careless of the reputation they have acquired, insensible to their own interest and the happiness of their posterity ; a physical as well as a moral impossibility ! For nature must counteract her own work, must take away the high sentiments of honour and patriotism which she has infused in the minds of my fellow-citizens, before they can submit to any thing that shall derogate from the reputation they have acquired, or be induced to renounce any undertaking that promises future glory and happiness to their country.

Therefore, whatever be the trouble, whatever the expense of the measure, it must be incurred. But the opposers of the system overrate both. The one has already been considered. It has been shown to be converted into facility, as to those who have not yet acquired a knowledge of our laws: and as to those who have, it is believed that little of their former acquirement will prove useless, as the system will be found to contain all those good provisions of the old law, which are familiar to them, with no other alteration than was required for the arrangement of the work ; nothing omitted but what they would not wish to remember ; nothing added but that which was necessary to enforce the great principle on which this branch of jurisprudence ought to rest; and, if the earnest endeavours of the reporter have not failed, they will find at least some order, precision and conciseness introduced, which cannot fail to facilitate study, aid the memory and lessen the difficulty of reference in the same degree that the confusion, ambiguity and prolixity which now characterize our laws render these operations difficult. The expense, as I shall now proceed to show, although nominally of large amount, is yet balanced by so many advantages even in a pecuniary view, as to merit little consideration, and none at all when it is compared with the least of the evils attending our present state, or of those greater evils to which they inevitably lead.

The principal expense attending the reform, will be the establishment of the different prisons, recommended in the fourth code. A schedule to this report, containing the probable cost of erecting those buildings, with the salaries of the officers and attendants ; the expense of food and clothing for the prisoners, and all the other articles of outlay, calculated on the most extensive scale that can be required, will show, when compared with the present expenses, much better than any argument, what additional burthen must be borne by the funds of the state. The moderate amount of which will astonish those who have not calculated the difference between maintaining a prisoner in idleness, or obliging him to labour for his subsistence ; for it will be found that the saving made by the latter mode of treatment, calculated on two hundred prisoners, will very nearly pay the interest of the first expenditure required for all the proposed establishments.

It is true the sum required must be advanced by the state : but if their present funds are relieved to the amount of the interest of that sum, the only present inconvenience is the opening a loan for the principal sum, to be repaid at a future day. Before which time the next and most important pecuniary saving to the state, in the diminution and prevention of crime, will more than enable the next generation to pay it; for it can be shown as nearly to demonstration as the subject is capable of, that every juvenile vagrant or offender that you educate and reform, is on an average a saving to the state treasury of more than two thousand dollars(a), which would be expended under your present system in the expenses of repeated convictions and maintenance during his successive confinements; while there is no calculating the unequal tax that he levies upon particular citizens by his depredations. This subject will be resumed and more fully developed in the introductory report to the Code of Prison Discipline.

4. I now proceed to the objection to a written code—that although good in theory it is bad in practice.

So far as this objection is intended to apply to any part of the system now offered for your consideration, the answer must be deferred until the details of that system come to be examined ; here it must be discussed as an objection to any written code whatever of penal law. This is a common expression, used most frequently without attaching to it any precise meaning. It conveys a vague idea of something wrong, and is employed chiefly to avoid the difficulty of answering cogent reasons that are offered for the adoption of any untried measure. As relates to the present subject, it is a peculiarly unfortunate argument in this state; for, as was formerly observed, it is not untried. It is not theory alone. It is practice in the more difficult branch of civil jurisprudence ; and the facility and success with which that operation was performed, if we may trust to the strongest analogy, must insure the like results to this. Having heard under this head nothing but the naked unsupported assertion, a sufficient answer to it would be, that it carries with it its own refutation; for, if in the terms of the objection, the plan be good in theory, it cannot be bad in practice. A system of laws to be good in theory, must be well adapted to the end proposed(b) ; must be suited to

(a) A committee of the legislature of New-York, state the case of a prisoner in one of the penitentiaries, who was first convicted when he was ten years of age, and had been, for repeated offences, twenty eight years in confinement. This man alone, at the rate we keep our convicts, would have cost the state more than five thousand dollars, besides the expense of removal and conviction.

(b) Lex, bona censeri possit, quæ sit intimatione certa, præcepto justa, executione com

the people they are intended to govern ; must be certain, convenient and constitutional ; in short, must be good when reduced to practice. If the theory fail in any one of those things which are necessary to put it in execution, it must be supported by bad reasoning. There must be some fallacy, which, being exposed, would show it to be bad. Such a theory ought to be assailed, not by asserting it to be good in itself, but incapable of being executed; which is a contradiction in terms; but by showing why it cannot be reduced to practice, that is, by showing it to be a bad theory.

5. The only remaining objection to reducing the laws to writing is this, that every new system necessarily supposes the use of new terms, and those must have their meaning settled by judicial decisions before their import can be understood ; that these will create the very uncertainty which the code is intended to remedy.   And in support of this opinion it is said, that the Code of Justinian, although written, has produced as many contradictory decisions and as voluminous commentaries as the common, which is unwritten law ; and that the Code Napoleon, though but of yesterday, groans under the weight of works intended to eluci- date it.   If the terms of the new law are comprehensive, it is said, they will include more, if precise, less than the legislator intended ; the judge must determine from a wise examinaton of the words, and a prudent attention to the spirit, what was the real intent of the law. This has already been done in the common law.   Its terms are ex- plained.   The cases which come within, and those which are excluded, are known.   To unsettle them would create confusion ; and therefore, we had better suffer the inconveniences we have, than fly to others that we know not of.

There is some truth, but more plausibility, in this argument. It does not, like others, found itself on popular prejudice exclusively, but has weight, great weight, with many prudent men, who do not detect the fallacy of the argument, or perceive how little the facts on which it is founded, apply to our circumstances.   I have some hope of enabling them to do both ; and if the enemies to written law, the partisans of the jurisprudence of decrees, are driven from this position, I shall be justified in believing the field clear for a consideration of the merits of the plan that is now offered.

Before we examine the reasoning we have stated, a preliminary ob- servation or two is necssary, on the difference between the penal and civil law, to which last all their facts and all their reasonings apply. Civil law, from its nature, must govern all cases that may arise in the infinite series of conflicting claims and disputed rights between individ- uals ; claims, which arise from the ambiguity or silence of the laws ; rights, which are created by the continual changes that occur in the state of society, in commerce, in the arts.   Criminal laws, on the contrary, are infinitely more contracted in their operation : emanating from the sovereign will, they admit of no alteration but that which it declares. Neither society, nor commerce, nor the arts, in all their progressive or retrograde movements, be they ever so rapid or important—not even political events, be they ever so destructive of civil associations, can have the slightest effect on the penal law.   They may call for changes,

moda, cum formà politiæ congrua, et generans virtutem subditis.  Bacon was not a vain the- orist.

but can produce none. That law lives in itself, and can neither be changed or modified, so as to be accommodated to any of those circumstances, but by positive legislation. What the law forbids, is an offence ; but the law cannot forbid without being perfectly intelligible, "incertam si vocem det tuba, qui se parabit ad pugnam ?—incertam si vocem det lex, qui se parabit ad parendum ?" The trumpet may sound for ever, but no one prepares for battle unless the appointed signal be given. The laws may speak, but can never be obeyed unless they are understood.

An ambiguous penal law, is no law; and judicial decisions cannot ex-plain it without usurping authority which does not belong to them. To extend the law to a case that does not come within the plain meaning of its words, is to make a new law. Nothing, it appears, can be clearer than the reasoning which shows this. Suppose a law should pass, declaring that if Peter left the state, his property should be forfeited. To declare, by a judicial decision, which of the many men bearing that name was meant, would certainly be a new law ; because the individual really intended could have no notice that the law applied to him ; there was no intelligible prohibition ; the law gave an uncertain sound and he could not prepare himself to obey.

Not quite so in civil law. Its office is to prevent individual rights from being infringed, or to grant compensation for any encroachment upon them ; and in doing this, there is an absolute nesessity of deciding on cases not previously provided for by positive law ; in other words, there must be a power of construction, for this plain reason, that which soever way the judge decides, his sentence affects private right. If it were a right claimed under colour of a positive law, and supposed to be created only by it, and that law were ambiguous, the same reasoning would apply in civil that we have used in criminal cases. The obligation to respect that right, in such case, having no other origin but the positive law, if that were uncertain, the defendant against whom it was claimed, not having any intelligible notice of the duty required of him, could not be constrained either to perform it or to make compensation for omitting it ; and the decree must be against the plaintiff, in the same manner as it would be against the state, on a prosecution under an ambiguous penal statute. But in the decision of ordinary questions this is far from being the case ; there, as has been said, the judge must decide, and his decision must establish a right. Take the common occurrence of a suit on a contract of sale, where the defence is concealment or fraud : here the judge, in deciding for the defendant, takes away the apparent right of the plaintiff to recover on his contract. In giving judgment for the plaintiff he determines, the facts being conceded, that the concealment is not of sufficient importance to vacate the sale. If the case be a new one, he must decide without positive law ; he must frame his judgment by analogical reasoning from the law in similar cases ; and if it be correctly drawn it will be respected for its wisdom, and abridge, by its adoption, the labour of further investigation in subsequent discussions of analogous cases. Thus the jurisprudence of decrees, or the authority of precedent, is by degrees established in civil cases ; first, from the necessity of deciding between conflicting claims, and afterwards from the very great advantage of having settled and fixed principles, *stare decisis* being a maxim that usurps the place of regular legislation ; but its misfortune, like that of all other illegitimate power, is this, that its authority is uncertain and vacillating ; it is law, or not law, according to the discretion or passions of subsequent judges, of which hundreds of examples might be given, more striking than the one hereinbefore referred to.

The effectual and obvious remedy, of a periodical legislative review of these decisions, for the purpose of incorporating any new and convenient principles they may establish, under their proper heads, in the frame of a code previously made, and thus giving them the stamp of legal authority, has not, it seems, ever yet occurred to any legislator; yet it is an effectual mode of clothing judicial wisdom and experience with legislative authority, and making that law, which, under our .constitution, cannot but be considered as an encroachment.   From this glance at the nature, rise, and progress of the law of precedent, and the hint at one of its many evils, with the remedy suggested for it, it will appear, first, that although there is an apparent necessity for giving some authority to decisions in civil cases, there is none in criminal; secondly, that this necessity is only apparent even in civil cases, and arises from the negligence of the legislative branch, to assert its rights and perform its constitutional duties ; thirdly, that any construction which a court can put on the terms of a penal law, must either give them an operation different from that contained in the plain obvious meaning of those terms, or it must be in conformity with such plain meaning, and then it follows conclusively, that, in the first instance, it would be improper to give the authority of law to such construction, and in the last it would be unnecessary ; fourthly, that if a penal law have no such plain obvious meaning in its terms, it is deficient in an essential requisite to its very existence, and can have no sanction.

These deductions all relate to decisions on the text of those laws which impose a penalty for their contravention.   But there are other questions in criminal law, relative to evidence and procedure, in which all the care that may be employed to provide for their solution, will be found insufficient.   To these all that has been said on the subject of precedent in civil cases applies ; and it will be found that means are pointed out to give to every judicial decision, on these points, the force of law, whenever, after a legislative discussion, they shall be found to be correct.   Add to this, that especial care has been taken, in framing the new code, to preserve the terms now in use, where the same sense could, consistently with the order of the work, be applied to them ; and that whenever new terms are found to be necessary, or old ones have a new or more precise signification annexed to them, they are fully explained in the Book of Definitions; and then from a consideration of the whole subject, it will be found, that the objection is more plausible than well founded ; and that if any decisions are necessary to explain the terms of the new system, they will be much less numerous, and will have greater authority, and can be learned at less expense either of time or money, than those which are still necessary to elucidate the dark parts of our present laws.   The argument drawn from the number of commentators and contradictory decisions on the two written codes, those of Justinian and Napoleon, is plausible, and of course very commonly used; but it has little weight even against a civil, much less against a penal code.   And, among many other reasons that might be urged in a dissertation on the subject, for this conclusive one, that both those codes contain the radical fault, of admitting a recourse to an

O

authority beyond that of the codes themselves. The authority of the emperor in the Latin and usage in the French system. The best code that can be provided, is but a frame-work on which a better is to be constructed. It must provide for its own progress towards perfection ; but it provides for its own corruption and final destruction, if it admits judicial decisions, unsanctioned by law, to eke out its deficient parts, to explain what is doubtful, or to retrench what may be thought bad. The remedy is easy, efficacious, if it succeed ; innocent, if, contrary to all reason, it should fail. It will be found at large in the project of a law for adopting these codes ; and it is confidently believed, its operation will show that there is no more force in this last objection than in those which preceded it.

Enough, I hope, has been said to clear the ground of the general and indefinite objections that have been raised to the reformation which was so wisely directed by a former legislature : enough, and more than enough to justify them and their enlightened successors. I have spoken on these subjects with a confidence that might justly be taxed as presumption, if they were my own opinions only that I expressed ; but I am strong in their wisdom, and bold in the assertion of principles which they have sanctioned.

I am now about to approach different ground, and to enter upon the discussion of the different provisions of the system, with very different feelings. So far as concerns the general principles on which they were directed to be formed, I feel the same confidence, for I am supported by the same authority. But in examining how well these principles have been reduced to the form of practical precept, I cannot but feel a diffidence which the uncertainty of receiving the same approbation naturally creates ; though even this is lessened by a consciousness of having exerted every faculty, in the endeavour to make the work worthy of those who directed it, and a blessing to those for whose use it was designed. Before I enter upon this discussion, however, and come to the consideration of the provisions of each particular code, it seems proper that I should conclude these general introductory remarks, with some observations on the characteristics of the whole system, which, although they may have been incidentally adverted to elsewhere, yet merit more particular attention, on account of their novelty, and, as it is also thought, of their importance.

The legislature of Louisiana has given the first example of proclaiming to their constituents and to the world, the principles by which they would be guided in the great work of penal legislation. A very short law contained these principles, concisely, but clearly declared to be the basis of the code which they directed to be prepared. These were developed in a subsequent report ; and both, translated into different languages and published in different countries, have excited an interest abroad which certainly would not have been created by any ordinary change in the jurisprudence of a small and distant state. Nor was there any thing in the report that could account for the attention it has received. The style is not marked by any peculiar excellence, and most of the arguments it contains had been before used and urged with better method and greater force. What then is it that has attracted the attention of the statesmen of Europe to the legislation of one of the least states in our union ; and of its jurists and men of letters to a pamphlet, which has no other merit than that of containing true principles, simply stated, and elucidated without the aid of eloquence? It is the novelty of hearing governors, for the first time, addressing the people in the language of reason, and inviting them to obey the laws, by showing that they are framed on the great principle of utility! It is the imposing spectacle exhibited by a nation, already freed from the shackles of political servitude, bursting those which the prejudice of ages had riveted on the mind! It is the surprise occasioned by the simplicity, and ease, and safety of an operation, which ignorance and interest had represented as perplexed, dangerous, and difficult! Other rulers have sometimes deigned to explain the motive for making a particular law. Ours alone have offered a general system to the consideration of the people; and told them, not only that it was expedient, but explained why they thought it so; invited them to reflect as well as to obey; made their precepts lessons of pure morality as well as of law; and showed that, consistent with the public good, they never can be separated. They say to them, for the first time in the history of jurisprudential legislation—"We are about to frame rules for your government, in your various relations to each other and to your country. Those, by which you and all other nations have hitherto been bound, have hitherto been couched in language only understood by a few, who naturally made a property of their knowledge. All mystery is now at an end. Here are the laws, and here are the principles by which we were guided in framing them! Judge whether the principles are correct! Determine whether we have conformed to them! It has been said by those of old, *sic volo, sic jubeo, stet pro ratione voluntas*—obey the law because it is written; but *we* say unto you, obey the law because it is just, because it is for your benefit, because the principles on which it is founded are wise! The law has its source, not in our will, but in reason, truth, justice and utility: of all which our will is only the organ and the record. When you find that we promulgate precepts not consistent with their dictates, although they must be obeyed while they are in force, yet the evil is remediable, for with the law, we give you the rule in conformity with which it was intended to be made. If, then, the rule be bad, or the law be not conformable to it, the remedy is in your hands: dismiss us and repeal our law." It is the unprecedented nature of this frank, simple language that distinguishes your projected code, and that makes it an object of curiosity and interest; a theme for argument; and possibly, a model for imitation in its leading characteristics.

Another peculiarity in the plan now presented is, that it is a system of which all the parts are connected with, and bear upon, each other. All the written criminal codes hitherto established have been defective in this particular. With those of Draco, Solon and Lycurgus we are not sufficiently acquainted to say more, than that the fragments of them that have descended to us, do not justify a belief that they contained any thing more than a few arbitrary enactments, assigning particular punishments to designated offences, without any provisions for preventing the latter in any other way than by the terror of the former, without any rules of procedure, and mingling together, without order, the civil and criminal branches of jurisprudence. The same characters may be given of the laws of the Twelve Tables; and even that wonderful collection of human wisdom and foresight, to which modern nations still have recourse for the best principles of distributive justice, the body of the Roman Law, was wofully deficient in the arrangement which ought to draw the line between civil and criminal law. The laws of the Partidas in some measure correct this evil; but although the criminal code is there thrown into a separate division, yet penalties are profusely scattered among civil remedies; and these latter are often found usurp- ing the place of punishments.

Of modern codes, the Russian, Prussian, Tuscan and Imperial are more or less liable to the same reproach, but the penal code of Napo- leon in a great degree avoids it. This defines offences, and a code of procedure directs how offenders shall be tried and punished, but here it stops. Yours, on the contrary, in addition to the enunciation of prin- ciples on which I have already remarked, contains the further essentials to a complete plan, a code of evidence and a book of definitions. The book *de verborum significatione* in the code of Justinian, is somewhat analogous to this last feature in yours, but it differs in this, that the whole body of the Roman law being only a digest or compilation of those before in force, the words in which it is expressed were those originally employed, and being the work of different hands, these words were retained, and the book in question was added as a kind of lexicon to explain them. Your code being an original work, the reporter was not restricted in his selection of terms, and when those he used were susceptible of more than one signification, or were in their general use uncertain or ambiguous, he was at liberty to annex to them a precise signification, taking care that, in the course of the work, they should be used in no other. The great utility of this part of the system is obvious, provided it has been executed with the necessary precision. It is that part which has been found the most difficult. The most intense ap- plication was necessary to define terms the most commonly used, but to which many of those who employed them affixed ideas more or less materially different. This difficulty is increased by the nature of the language, which very frequently does not afford terms sufficiently precise to avoid difficulty, even in the periphrase used in the definitions, so that in many instances I have been under the necessity of defining the words employed to explain others. And, in order to approach nearer to that certainty so necessary in all laws, recourse has been had to corollaries, examples, and illustrations, as well in the body of the law, as in the book of definitions. This is also a new feature in legis- lation, and like many others that had not yet received the sanction of experience, it was made the subject of solicitous reflection before it was adopted. An author whose maxims in law and legislation are entitled to the higest respect(*a*), and whose rules I have more than once taken as my guide, has said that the lawgiver ought not to reason, but com- mand : the false construction usually put upon this precept need not now be examined, here it will only be necessary to say that the illus- trations alluded to are not reasonings, and therefore do not contradict the maxim ; they do not purport to give the reason of the rule, but to show clearly what it is. Sometimes this is done by enlarging, some- times by restricting, and sometimes by the elucidation of example, but all are only so many amplifications of the rule in the text ; all are pre-

(*a*) Bacon.

cepts. The lawgiver takes upon himself that part of his duty which has heretofore been improperly devolved upon the judge: the law as it now stands gives the simple precept, the judge makes the deductions ; he declares how far the law is intended to extend, what classes of cases do not come within its purview. If language furnished words sufficiently numerous to express every idea, and sufficiently definite to admit of no other construction than the one intended, the legislative function would end with a simple exposition of its will in the requisite terms ; but unfortunately this is not the case. Languages were formed in the infancy of society, and of course would contain terms commensurate only with the few wants and simple ideas, prevalent in that state of society. As the necessity for other words increased with advancement in civilization, the supply was furnished either by periphrase, by figurative language, by adoption of words or phrases from other tongues, and, in very few instances, by the creation of new terms—all of these, except the last, the fruitful sources of amphibology and doubt. This is not the place to enter into a discussion of the philosophy of language, but it was necessary to advert to the source of this difficulty, in order to show that from this defect in every language, the lawgiver could, in none, find terms sufficiently precise for the expression of his will, in all the cases which might occur. And therefore, although the avowed object of every legislator was certainty, yet in the body of all laws, sometimes from the negligent or unskilful use of the language, sometimes from its internal defects, the legislative intent is so uncertain, that the chief employment of the judiciary power has been, not its proper function of ascertaining facts and then applying to them the provisions of a known law, but in the legislative task of declaring what the law is. Good laws, expressed in precise language, would destroy this confusion of powers. Such laws admit of but one interpretation, or, more correctly speaking, they admit of none. The judiciary power has nothing to do but to ascertain facts, and direct the execution of the law in the particular cases which warrant it. But when the fact is ascertained, and the question is, whether it comes within the purview of a law which does not apply to it in terms, or whether, although it is embraced by the letter of the law, it shall be excluded from its operation—the decision is surely a legislative act, because it must either extend the words so as to embrace the case, or restrict them so as to exclude it. But the extending a statute or restricting it is as clearly a legislative act as the passing of the statute was; a particular legislative act as respects the case under consideration ; a general one, by the doctrine of precedent, as respects all others. Yet this duty has devolved upon the judiciary, even in countries where the division of the several departments is a fundamental principle; so much so, that the abuse has become the rule ; and it is as commonly said that the office of the judge is to interpret the laws, as that it is his duty to apply them.

To avoid misapprehension, let it be clearly understood, that in no part of this system is the judge inhibited from resorting to all the means which grammatical construction, the context of the law, the signification usually given to the words employed, or their technical meaning in reference to the subject matter, will afford for discovering the true sense of the act. This operation must of necessity be performed. It is directed by the text of the code, and indeed is so unconsciously peformed in the common intercourse of life(a) that it cannot be called an interpretation. That which is reasoned against here, and forbidden by the code, is not the application of the rules of grammar and common sense to discover from the language of the law what it intends ; but the encroachment on the legislative functions begins, when judges talk of distinctions between the letter and the spirit of the law, and forget the limits of their authority, so far as to supply omissions and retrench superfluities in statutes. I know that the inaccurate language of many statutes, has, in several cases, reduced the judge to a kind of necessity of exceeding his constitutional powers, because the legislator has neglected his, and thus furnished a plausible excuse for this encroachment, and I acknowledge, that for the most part, it has been beneficially, or at least, not oppressively exercised. But it is not the less an encroachment. In England it is part of the common law that judges should exercise this power. But that part of the common law which regulates the distribution of fundamental powers, is the constitution ; therefore the exercise of this power, is there a constitutional right. In the state of Louisiana on the contrary, it is no part of our constitution—it is expressly forbidden by that instrument. If the act of declaring to be law, and enforcing as such, something which the legislature has not prescribed, or declaring that what they have prescribed shall not have the force of law, under whatever pretexts such acts be done, be the exercise of legislative powers ; then is the act of enlarging or restraining the words of a statute, by a constructive reference to its spirit, expressly forbidden by our constitution, which directs, both in affirmative and negative terms, not only that the three great departments shall be kept separate, but that no person invested with one of these powers shall exercise the functions of either of the others. What, then, is *our* remedy for the evil of ambiguous laws ? The judges cannot, as in England, supply it. The legislature must eradicate the mischief, instead of suffering it to be tampered with by the quackery of judicial legislation. Laws must be brought back to their original simplicity. They must be expressed in purer terms when the language affords them, and when no others can be found but such as admit of a double sense, they must be explained by a periphrasis, elucidated by examples. The exceptions intended must be stated, the true deductions made, and such false conclusions as are apprehended, expressly negatived. This is what has been attempted to be done by the feature in the code now under consideration. If the attempt has been only partially successful, it cannot, it is believed, be doubted that the law will be better understood by this course ; because it is precisely in this way that the advocates for the jurisprudence of decrees contend that the law is better elucidated by the court—every precedent is but an example—every decision it contains is a deduction from the text of the law, declaring affirmatively what is, or negatively what is not, its intent ; and those who say that this task can be well

---

(a) Instances of this are scarcely necessary. " John fell upon Peter and bruised him severely." If the context shows that they were travelling together in a carriage which was overturned, we shall have one sense of this phrase ; if it informs us that they were quarrelling, we shall have another. The instantaneous operation of the mind in connecting the phrase used with the preceding matter can scarcely be called an interpretation, though the words themselves may convey very different ideas.

performed, long after the law has been made, by judges who had no agency in making it, cannot deny that it may be better done at the time of giving the law, by the legislator from whom it emanates, who may reasonably be supposed best to know his own intentions. If after having expressed his will in general terms, he should find, on reflection, that the words he has employed will admit of several constructions, one of which only he intends to enforce ; if he should find that after settling the direct application of the law, deductions may be made from it, which he did not intend to allow ; if, from certain false reasonings which have prevailed, or which circumstances induce him to fear may prevail, he is inclined to apprehend that his law will not be applied to the cases he intended ; or, lastly, although he intends that his law shall apply generally, if he should find there are certain cases which he desires to except from its operation, what, under such circumstances, is it the part of a wise legislator to do ? To devolve upon the judiciary the task of expressing his real intent, of making his deductions, stating his exceptions, and giving to his law all the extension and restriction which it was his object to effect ? Or to perform, as far as may be practicable, his own duty? The only reasonable answer that can be given to this inquiry would justify the course that has been taken. It is scarcely necessary to reply to the objection, that after all the elucidation that can be made, the law may be obscure ; after all the care that can be taken, it may be imperfect ; after all the cases that can be foreseen, others will be found to have been omitted. No duty of society, moral or religious, would be performed, if we were deterred by such arguments. Yet, strange as it may appear, this fallacy has its effect, and we submit, particularly in jurisprudence, to oppressive absurdities, because no remedy can be proposed for removing them, that does not bear the mark of all human institutions, that of having some defect or inconvenience attached to it. But, although new in the simplicity of its form, this feature of the code is not entirely so in substance. It takes the place, advantageously it is hoped, of the loose preambles formerly used, and in some instances retained in our legislation ; of the provisions exempting particular subjects from general enactments ; and in a great measure supersedes the class of statutes whose titles, *an act to explain, an act entitled, an act to amend, an act in addition to, an act to repeal, an act, &c.*, were a puzzle, and the references of which, from one statute to another, were as difficult to trace as the most involved table of descents.

The Introductory Reports to the several Codes of crimes and punishments, of procedure, of evidence, and of reform and prison discipline, which compose this system, will be found to contain a notice of the changes in our present law, on those subjects respectively which are proposed, and the reasons at large for introducing them. They will be longer and more argumentative, as this has been, than would have been necessary, if, still a member of your honourable body, I could meet objections as they are raised, and make the corrections which your superior wisdom would suggest. Having offered nothing without reflection, I have reasons for all I have proposed. Many of them, probably, will be found insufficient to support my conclusions, but those conclusions are honestly if not wisely drawn, and the system which they support is submitted in the full confidence that it will receive a air, a full, and a deliberate consideration. Fair, without prejudice against.the reporter for the opinions he may entertain on other subjects, or against his doctrines for their novelty; full, after a consideration of the whole system and the bearing of its different parts on each other ; deliberate, without rejecting any one provision, until the reasons for proposing it have been maturely weighed and its probable effects calculated. A decision thus made must be wise, and will doubtless prove satisfactory to your constituents, and honourable to your country and yourselves.

# INTRODUCTORY REPORT

TO THE

# CODE OF CRIMES AND PUNISHMENTS.

AFTER noticing and accounting for some variations in the arrangement of the work from the original plan, and giving a slight reference to some of its leading principles, it is proposed in this report to review the CODE OF CRIMES AND PUNISHMENTS, examine the principal changes it purports to make, and offer the reasons on which they are founded.

By the Report on the Plan of a Penal Code(*a*) made in 1822 it was proposed to comprise the whole system of penal law in one code, giving a separate book to each of the four divisions—crimes and punishments, procedure, evidence, and reform and prison discipline, and to appropriate another to the definition of the technical terms used in the body of the work. It was, however, soon discovered, that, by this arrangement, the subdivisions of titles, chapters, sections, and articles, would not be sufficiently numerous for preserving order in the distribution of each of the several great divisions; by throwing them into distinct codes, an additional great division was gained, and an easier mode of reference procured. Each of those great divisions, therefore, in the system now presented forms a separate code, and the book of definitions is a kind of appendix to all, and preserves the form originally given to it.

This is merely a change of form. But there is also a material addition in point of substance : two institutions are provided for in the code of prison discipline, under the titles of the School for Reform and the House of Detention, which were only incidentally referred to in the original report ; the necessity for which is fully explained in the introductory report to that code. With this variation and these additions, the plan contained in the report, which received the sanction of the legislature, has been strictly pursued.

Most of the reflections which would find their place in a general view of the system, have been either anticipated in the report, or will so readily occur to the members of the General Assembly, that it would be abusing their indulgence even to advert to them here. There are some, however, of such importance that they cannot be totally omitted; but in discussing them, all arguments formerly used will either be carefully avoided, or referred to no further than is deemed necessary

(*a*) Report on the Plan of a Penal Code, p. 6.

P

for the understanding of any new course of reasoning, or the application of any new facts, that may be introduced.

At our entrance on the subject we are met by the difficulty of discovering the true theory of penal law. Philosophy must point it out, for it depends on a deep investigation of the faculties of the human mind, and of their usual employment; and wise legislation must adapt it to the use of mankind. At no preceding period has the science of jurisprudence, and more particularly penal jurisprudence, attracted such close attention as at present. At no period has the progression I have referred to, from theoretic truth to practical utility, been more apparent, or promised more important and beneficial results. Learned and good men are directing their time and talents to the subject; and in the intellectual conflict which this interesting discussion has produced, it is highly gratifying to observe, that the principles which you have sanctioned have been confirmed by the best opinions, and supported by the most conclusive arguments. Even those who disagree on other points, unite in approving the general doctrines on which you have directed your code to be prepared; although, as might be expected, they differ in the conclusions that may be drawn from them, and refer their authority to different sources. Thus, while all agree that the true end of penal jurisprudence is to prevent crimes, and that the doctrine of vindictive law is in the highest degree absurd and unjust, some insist that crimes are to be repressed only by the example of punishments; others, that reformation is the only lawful object. Some refer the right to punish to an implied contract between society and its members; others, to the principle of utility alone; and there are those again who admit of no other standard than abstract justice. Each of these has its partisans in the conflict. Without entering into the abstract reasoning to which they lead, we may content ourselves with this important result :—that whether the right to punish be founded on contract, or utility, or justice; whether the object be to punish or reform; whatever be the true doctrine on either of these subjects, we have the satisfaction to know, that by a singular felicity, if either theory be right, the practical results we have drawn from our reasoning cannot be wrong, for all the provisions of our system coincide with abstract justice, with general utility, and with the terms of any supposable original contract; and whether reformation, or punishment, be the true means of preventing crimes, our plan of prison discipline will effect the end, for it embraces both.

If upon a critical examination of the system proposed to you, it should be found to have this extraordinary adaptation to principles that have been considered as discordant, it will certainly go far to prove that the theoretic disputes have turned more upon terms, than on any real difference between them. For instance, if the supposed social contract ever existed, the foundation of it must have been the preservation of the natural rights of its members. And this makes it, in all its effects, the same as the theory which adopts abstract justice as the basis of the right to punish; which, properly defined, is only that which secures to every one his right; and if utility, the remaining source to which this power is referred, be found to be so closely united with justice, as in penal jurisprudence to be inseparable, it will follow that any system founded on one of these principles, must be supported by the other.

In the same manner, as to the means for attaining the object common to all, the prevention of crime, if the most efficacious punishment is that which also best produces reform, then the several theories are reconciled in practice, however they may differ in the arguments they use.

It has therefore been thought more proper to abstain from entering the lists of controversy with either of the disputants, and to adopt, implicitly, the tenets of neither school; but to be content with uniting, if we can, the suffrage of all in the practical results we shall establish. There is, however, one of these results, which, although clearly deducible from the first principles established by all, is not yet generally admitted in practice ; that feature which so honourably distinguishes from the existing laws of any other nation, the plan your predecessors unanimously approved, and which has been one exciting cause of the attention which the European world is now giving to the subject: you may easily imagine that I mean *the abolition of the punishment of death.* Seldom has any doctrine made such rapid strides as this has in public opinion. Although opposed by inveterate prejudices, long habits, mistaken religious opinions, and the general indefinite fear of innovation ; yet its proselytes are becoming every day more numerous; the example of our state is every where quoted ; the future measures of its legislature are expected with the greatest interest; and the final abolition of a punishment, repugnant to our natures, is expected from you with confidence, not unmixed with anxiety, by the whole civilized world. An enlightened citizen of Geneva(a) has published proposals for a prize

(a) Mr Sellon, member of the sovereign representative council of Geneva, as early as 1816, proposed to the Council to abolish the punishment of death ; and in 1826 he offered the prize referred to in the text. In his proposals, after citing the opinions of Beccaria and Bentham, he adds—" I finish these observations by producing a document the most recent and the most conclusive in favour of my proposition. It is the accession of the general assembly of Louisiana to the principles laid down by Mr Livingston in his report. My fellow citizens will there see a republic adopting dispositions, of which the principal one is, *the absolute suppression of the punishment of death.*" He then gives a copy of our law of 1820, the certificate of my appointment, all that part of the report relating to the punishment of death, and the resolution approving of the report. In a note on the law, he says,— " Having no other object in this writing than to convince my fellow citizens that the abolition of the punishment of death would be a measure both useful and honourable for my country, I have thought that this end could not be better attained than by making them acquainted with the report of Mr Livingston, made to the general assembly of Louisiana. Louisiana is a republic. It is a component part of an illustrious union, as we form part of the Swiss confederation ; and the constitution of the United States, as well as our federal act, permits the members to provide for themselves the best laws, even when they differ from those of the other states. We owe to Mr Taillandier the translation of this report," &c. And he concludes his programme by citing the examples of modern nations, in which this abolition has been carried into effect. 1. Russia, under Elizabeth. 2. Tuscany, under Leopold. 3. "*Louisiana*, in America, which, on the report of Mr Livingston, by a solemn resolution of the sovereign assembly, has decreed the absolute suppression of this punishment. This report, in which it will be seen that the author has collected all the experience of the past and present times*, appears to me to be a document of the greatest interest for Geneva, whose position, population, and constitution, have a great resemblance to those of

* He who can accuse me of vanity in making this and similar citations, is incapable of comprehending how utterly this miserable boyish feeling is incompatible with the frame of mind necessary for the consideration of subjects on which the happiness of a nation may depend. Feeling myself superior to such suspicions, I shall not sacrifice any thing that I think may promote the great object, to the fear of incurring them.

Essay on the subject, in which the arguments for the abolition which have been approved by this state, are copied as a text. A society in Paris has followed the example. The several periodical papers of France, England, Germany, and Holland are filled with disquisitions for the most part highly approving of the plan of abolition ; but none, as far as I have perceived, even of those who doubt its success, discouraging the experiment as a dangerous one.

If this principle is retained in our code, it dates back to the vote of approval, and secures to us a name among nations to which our relative population or strength would not, for ages, have entitled us; a distinction more honourable than any that wealth or power or advancement in any other science could give—and I need not observe to the enlightened body I address, how much of that distinction possessed by a country is reflected back upon its citizens ; and in what degree, while they promote the honour of the nation, they augment the happiness of the individuals who compose it. It is the firm persuasion that both will be increased, in an incalculable degree, by the measure in question, that induces me to press it again on the consideration of the legislature, and to add a very few reflections to the arguments which were, on a former occasion, considered as conclusive. I then(a) expressed an opinion that the right to punish by death, might be established in cases where the importance of the object to be obtained, and the necessity of inflicting it in order to attain that object, could both be sufficiently shown; but my argument denied the existence of such necessity. On reviewing that part of the report, I think it requires some elucidation.

Existence was the first gift of Omnipotence to man. Existence, accompanied not only by the instinct necessary to preserve it, and to perpetuate the species, but with a social (not merely a gregarious) disposition, which led so early to the formation of societies, that unless we carry our imagination back to the first created being, it is scarcely possible to imagine, and certainly impossible to trace, any other state than that of the social—it is found wherever men are found, and must have existed as soon as the number of the species were sufficiently multiplied to produce it. Man, then, being created for society, the Creator of man must have intended that it should be preserved; and as he acts by general laws, not by special interference, (except in the cases which religion directs to believe), all primitive society, as well as the individuals of which it is composed, must have been endowed with certain natural rights and correspondent duties, anterior in time, and paramount in authority, to any that may be formed by mutual consent. The first of these rights, perhaps the only one that will not admit of dispute, is as well on the part of the individual as of the society, the right to continue the existence given by God to man, and by the nature of man, to

Louisiana, which member of a federation, as Geneva is, has given to itself good laws without consulting her neighbours on the subject, giving them a noble and wise example to follow, and not fearing that a mild legislation would attract criminals. It is to be hoped, that this example will be followed by us." And he adds,—" It is easy to make this experiment. All the world will approve it. Tho glory will be reflected on the whole nation, and history will certainly make honourable mention of the people which shall first renounce a practice no longer required by necessity, which alone could excuse it."

(a) Report to the Plan of a Penal Code, p. 31.

the social state in which he was formed to live: and the correspondent mutual duty of the individual and of the society is to defend this right; but when the right is given, the means to enforce it must, in natural as well as positive law, be admitted to be also given. If then both individuals and the society have the right to preserve their several existence, and are, moreover, under the reciprocal duty to defend it when attacked, it follows, that if one or the other is threatened with destruction, which cannot be averted but by taking the life of the assailant, the right, nay more, the duty to take it exists: the irresistible impulse of nature indicates the right she has conferred, and her first great law shows that life may be taken in self-defence. It is true the aggressor has the same right to exist; but if this right were sacred while he was attempting to destroy that of another, there would be co-existing, two equal and conflicting rights, which is a contradiction in terms. The right, therefore, I speak of, is proved; but both in the individual and in society it is strictly defensive—it can only be exerted during that period when the danger lasts, by which I mean when the question is, which of the two shall exist, the aggressor or the party attacked, whether this be an individual or the society: before this crisis has arrived, or after it has passed, it is no longer self-defence, and then their rights to enjoy existence would be co-existent and equal, but not conflicting, and for one to deprive the other of it would be of course unjust.

Therefore, the positions with which I set out seem to be proved. That the right to inflict death exists, but that it must be in defence, either of individual or social existence(a); and that it is limited to the case where no other alternative remains to prevent the threatened destruction.

In order to judge whether there is any necessity for calling this abstract right into action, we must recollect the duty imposed upon society of protecting its members, derived, if we have argued correctly, from the social nature of man, independent of any implied contract. While we can imagine society to be in so rude and imperfect a state as to render the performance of this duty impossible without taking the life of the aggressor, we must concede the right. But is there any such state of society? Certainly none in the civilized world, and our laws are made for civilized man. Imprisonment is an obvious and effectual alternative; therefore, in civilized society, in the usual course of events, we can never suppose it necessary, and of course never lawful: and even among the most savage hordes, where the means of detention might be supposed wanting—banishment, for the most part, would take away the necessity of inflicting death. An active imagination, indeed, might create cases and situations in which the necessity might possibly exist—but if there are any such, and they are sufficiently probable to justify an exception in the law, they should be stated as such, and they would then confirm the rule; but by a perversity of reasoning in those who advocate this species of punishment, they put the exception in the place of the rule, and what is worse, an exception of which the possibility is doubtful.

It may be observed, that I have taken the preservation of life as the

---

(a) This explains the part of the report on the Plan of a Penal Code which relates to the comparison between the evil of the offence and the punishment.

only case in which even necessity could give the right to take life, and that for the simple reason, that this is the only case in which the two natural rights of equal importance can be balanced ; and in which the scale must preponderate in favour of him who defends against him who endeavours to destroy. The only true foundation for the right of inflicting death, is the preservation of existence. This gift of our Creator seems, by the universal desire to preserve it which he has infused into every part of his animal creation, to be intended as the only one which he did not intend to place at our disposal. But, it may be said, what becomes of our other rights ? Are personal liberty, personal inviolability and private property to be held at the will of any strong invader ? How are these to be defended, if you restrain the right to take life to the single case of defence against an attack upon existence ? To this it is answered: Society being a natural state, those who compose it have collectively natural rights. The first is that of preserving its existence; but this can only be done by preserving that of the individuals which compose it. It has, then, duties as well as rights; but these are wisely ordered to be inseparable. Society cannot exert its right of self-preservation without, by the same act, performing its duty in the preservation of its members. Whenever any of those things which are the objects of the association, life, liberty or property, are assailed, the force of the whole social body must be exerted for its preservation; and this collective force, in the case of an individual attack, must, in ordinary cases, be sufficient to repel it without the sacrifice of life ; but in extraordinary cases, when the force of the assailants is so great as to induce them to persevere in a manner that reduces the struggle to one for existence, then the law of self-defence applies.

But there may be a period in which individual rights may be injured before the associated power can interfere. In these cases, as the nature of society does not deprive the individual of his rights, but only comes in to aid their preservation, he may defend his person or property against illegal violence by a force sufficient to repel that with which he is assailed. This results clearly from the right to property, to whatever source we may refer it, and from that of personal inviolability, which is (under certain restrictions imposed by nature itself) indubitably a natural right. As the injury threatened may not admit of compensation, the individual may use force to prevent the aggression; and if that used by the assailant endangers his life(a), the question then again becomes one of self-defence, and the same reasoning applies which was used to show the right of taking life in that case. But where the individual attacked can either by his own physical force, or by the aid of the society to which he belongs, defend himself or his property; when the attack is not of such a nature as to jeopardize his own existence in the defence of them ; if he take the life of the aggressor, under these circumstances, he takes it without necessity, and consequently without right. This is the extent to which the natural law of self-defence allows an individual to go in putting another to death. May any association of individuals inflict it for any other cause, and under any other circumstances ? Society has the right only to defend that which the

(a) The existence of danger alone, is not a sufficient justification by the English, nor I believe by other laws for homicide; it must be a danger from which there is no other means of escape.

individuals who compose it have a right to defend, or to defend itself—
that is to say, its own existence, and to destroy any individual, or any
other society which shall attempt its destruction. But this, as in the
case of individuals, must be only while the attempt is making, and
when there is no other means to defeat it. And it is in that sense only
that I understand the word so often used, so often abused, so little
understood, *necessity*. It exists between nations during war ; or a
nation and one of its component parts in a rebellion or insurrection ;
between individuals during the moment of an attempt against life, which
cannot otherwise be repelled ; but between society and individuals,
organized as the former now is, with all the means of repression and
self-defence at its command, never. I come then to the conclusion, in
which I desire, most explicitly, to be understood, that although the
right to punish with death might be abstractedly conceded to exist in
certain societies, and under certain circumstances which might make it
necessary ; yet, composed as society now is, these circumstances cannot
reasonably be even supposed to occur—that therefore no necessity, and
of course, no right to inflict death as a punishment does exist.

There is also great force in the reasonings which have been used to
rebut that, which founds the right to take life for crimes on an original
contract, made by individuals on the first formation of society. First,
that no such contract is proved, or can well be imagined. Secondly,
that if it were, it would be limited to the case of defence. The parties
to such contract could only give to the society those rights which they
individually had ; their only right over the life of another, is to defend
their own ; they can give that to society, and they can give no more.
In this case also, therefore, the right resolves itself into that of doing
what is necessary for preservation. The great inquiry then recurs—
is the punishment of death in any civilized society necessary, for the
preservation either of the lives of its citizens individually, or of their
social collective rights ? If it be not necessary, I hope it has been
proved not to be just ; and if neither just nor necessary, can it be expedient ? To be necessary, it must be shown that the lives of the citizens and the existence of society cannot be preserved without it. But
can this be maintained in the face of so many proofs ? Egypt, for
twenty years, during the reign of Sabaco(*a*)—Rome, for two hundred
and fifty years—Tuscany for more than twenty-five—Russia(*b*), for

(*a*) Diod. Siculus.

(*b*) As I use no historical fact with a desire that it should go for more than it is worth, it
is but proper to say, that I have never relied so much upon the example of Russia as upon
the others to which I refer; because, although I have been able to procure no precise information on the subject, I am yet inclined to believe, that the punishment of the *Knout* was
preserved as an equivalent to that of death in many cases, and to death in its most horrid
form. It is thus described by Howard : "I saw two criminals, a man and a woman, suffer
the punishment of the knout. They were conducted from prison by about fifteen hussars
and ten soldiers. When they arrived at the place of punishment, the hussars formed themselves into a ring round the whipping post. The drum beat a minute or two, and then some
prayers were repeated, the populace taking off their hats. The woman was taken first ; and
after being roughly stripped to the waist, her hands and feet were bound with cords to the
post, a man standing before the post to keep the cords tight. A servant attended the executioners, and both were stout men. The servant first marked his ground and struck the
woman five times on the back. Every stroke seemed to penetrate deep into the flesh. But
his master thinking him too gentle, pushed him aside, took his place, and gave all the re-

twenty-one, during the reign of Elizabeth—are so many proofs to the contrary. Nay, if those are right who tell you that the penal laws of Spain were abrogated by the transfer, this state itself gives an unanswerable proof that no such necessity exists; for if those laws were not in force, it is very clear that there were none imposing the penalty of death, from the time of the transfer in December 1803, to the 5th of May 1805, when our first penal law was passed. Yet during that period, when national prejudices ran high, when one government had abandoned and the other had not yet established its authority, there was not, I believe, a single instance of murder, or of any attempt to destroy the order of society. So that one argument or the other must be given up. Either the Spanish laws existed, or we ourselves furnish a proof that a nation may exist, in peace, without the punishment of death. Societies have then existed without it. In those societies, therefore, it was not necessary. Is there any thing in the state of ours that makes it so? It has not, as far as I have observed, been even suggested. But if not absolutely necessary, have its advocates even the poor pretext that it is convenient; that the crimes for which it is reserved, diminish under its operation in a greater proportion than those which incur a different punishment? The reverse is the melancholy truth. Murder, and those attempts to murder which are capitally punished, have increased in some of the United States to a degree that not only creates general alarm, but by the atrocity with which they are perpetrated, fix a stain on the national character which it will be extremely difficult to efface. I might rely for this fact, on the general impression which every member of the body I address must have on this subject; but as the result is capable of being demonstrated by figures, I pray their attention to the tables annexed to this report, in which, although they are far from being as complete as could be wished, they will see an increase of those crimes that demonstrates, if any thing can do it, the inefficiency of the means adopted and so strangely persisted in, of repressing them. The small number of executions compared with the well authenticated instances of the crime, shows that the severity of the punishment increases the chance of acquittal; and the idle curiosity which draws so many thousands to witness the exhibition of human suffering at the executions; the levity with which the spectacle is beheld, demonstrates its demoralizing and heart-hardening effects; while the crimes committed at the very moment of the example intended to deter from the commission, shows how entirely inefficient it is. One instance of this is so remarkable that I cannot omit its detail. In the year 1822 a person named John Lechler was executed at

maining strokes himself, which were evidently more severe. The woman received twenty-five and the man sixty. I pressed through the hussars, and counted the number as they were chalked on a board. Both seemed but *just alive*, especially the man, who had, however, strength enough to receive a small donation with some signs of gratitude. They were conducted back to prison in a little wagon. I saw the woman in a weak condition some days after, *but could not find the man any more.*" The enlightened successor of Alexander is pursuing, with energy and zeal, a reform in the laws of the empire, which his great predecessor begun. It will, without any doubt, put an end to such scenes as Howard has described; and this code, if completed according to the humane and liberal views of the emperor, will be a monument more glorious than any that was ever erected to a conquering monarch.

Lancaster, in Pennsylvania, for an atrocious murder. The execution was, as usual, witnessed by an immense multitude ; and of the salutary effect it had on their feelings and morals, we may judge from the following extract from a newspaper printed in the neighbourhood(a). The material facts, which are stated in it, having been since confirmed to me by unquestionable authority:

"It has long" says the judicious editor, "been a controverted point, whether public executions, by the parade with which they are conducted, do not operate on the vicious part of the community more as incitements to, than examples deterring from, crime. What has taken place in Lancaster would lead one to believe, that the spectacle of a public execution produces less reformation than criminal propensity. While an old offence was atoned for, more than a dozen new ones were committed, and some of a capital grade. *Twenty-eight persons* were committed to jail on Friday night for divers offences at Lancaster, such as *murder*, larceny, *assault and battery*, &c. besides many gentlemen lost their pocket-books, where the pick-pockets escaped, or the jail would have overflowed.

"In the evening, as one Thomas Burns, who was employed as a weaver in the factory near Lancaster, was going home, he was met by one Wilson, with whom he had some previous misunderstanding, when Wilson drew a knife and gave him divers stabs in sundry places, which are considered mortal. Wilson was apprehended and committed to jail, and had the same irons put on him which had scarcely been laid off long enough by Lechler to get cold."

A letter, in answer to some inquiries I made on the subject, adds to this information, that Wilson was one of the crowd who left his residence expressly to witness the execution : and to take away all doubt that the Gazette account was not exaggerated, that he has since been convicted of the murder.

I pray the advocates for this punishment to reflect on this example, to recollect that, detailed in my former report, of the sale of forged notes in the chamber where lay the corpse(b) of him who was that day executed for a similar offence. I ask them seriously to ponder on them, on the numerous other instances of a like nature that must occur to them, and then to say, whether they can believe the punishment of death an efficient one for murder. The most serious and intense reflection has brought my mind to the conclusion, not only that it fails in any repressive effect, but that it promotes the crime. The cause it is not very easy to discover, and still more difficult to explain ; but I argue from effects—and when I see them general in their occurrence

---

(a) Yorktown Gazette.

(b) The following circumstance, which I find stated by a gentleman at a public meeting in Southampton, in England, as having been detailed by Mr Buxton, is a stronger case :—

"An Irishman, found guilty of issuing forged bank notes, was executed, and his body delivered to his family. While his widow was lamenting over the corpse, a young man came to her to purchase some forged notes. As soon as she knew his business, forgetting at once both her grief and the cause of it, she raised up the dead body of her husband, and pulled from under it a parcel of the very paper for the circulation of which he had forfeited his life. At that moment an alarm was given of the approach of the police; and not knowing where else to conceal the notes, she thrust them into the mouth of the corpse, and there the officers found them."

Q

after the same event, I must believe that event to be the efficient cause which produces them, although I may not be able to trace exactly their connexion.  This difficulty is particularly felt in deducing moral effects from physical causes, or arguing from the operation of moral causes on human actions.  The reciprocal operations of the mind and body must always be a mystery to us, although we are daily witnesses of their effects.  In nothing is this more apparent, or the cause more deeply hidden, than in that propensity which is produced on the mind to imitate that which has been strongly impressed on the senses, and that frequently in cases where the first impression must be that of painful apprehension.  It is one of the earliest developments of the understanding in childhood.  Aided by other impulses, it conquers the sense of pain, and the natural dread of death.  The tortures inflicted on themselves by the fakirs of India ; the privations and strict penance of some monastic orders of Christians ; and the self-immolation of the Hindoo widows, may be attributed, in part to religion, in part to the love of distinction and fear of shame : but no one, nor all of these united, except in the rare cases of a hero or a saint, could produce such extraordinary effects, without that spirit of imitation to which I have alluded. The lawgiver, therefore, should mark this, as well as every other propensity of human nature ; and beware how he repeats in his punishments, the very acts he wishes to repress, and makes them examples to follow rather than to avoid.

Another reason, perhaps not sufficiently enlarged upon in the former report, to show that it cannot be efficient, is drawn from the uncertainty of its infliction—an uncertainty which reduces the chance of the risk to less than that which is, in many instances, voluntarily incurred in many pursuits of life.  Soldiers march gaily to battle with the certainty that many of them must fall—those who commit a crime punishable with death, always proceed with the hope that they will avoid detection. You find men to affront death in all the shapes it can assume(a) ; to pursue the most dangerous trades; to undertake the most desperate enterprises, for the most trifling considerations.  While there is a chance of escape, the happy disposition of our nature makes us always believe it will be favourable to us.  We seize the certain enjoyment that is offered by glory, by profit, or even by convenience, and we trust that we shall escape the uncertain danger.  If this is acknowledged in the common pursuits of life, why should it be denied in the rarer instance

(a) In one of those imaginary characters, drawn by the great modern painter of human passions and pursuits, after his most felicitous manner, we have this reckless contempt of danger admirably personified in the ferocious buccanier :

> " Inured to danger's direst form,
> Tornade and earthquake, flood and storm;
> Death hath he seen by sudden blow,
> By wasting plague, by torture slow,
> By mine, or breach, by steel or ball,
> Knew all his shapes, and scorned them all."

Bertram is the *beau ideal* of a pirate ; but the same contempt of death is found, in a less degree, perhaps, to animate other freebooters—witness the cool reply of one of them to a fellow-sufferer on the wheel:—" Why do you make all this noise; (said he), did you not know that in our profession we were subject to one malady more than the rest of the world ?"

of crime? The great error of our laws is, an obstinate refusal to consider an offender against them as moved by the same impulses, guided by the same motives with the rest of the community; refusing, in short, to consider him as a man. They suppose him a demon or an idiot, and their provisions are, accordingly, for the most part calculated for a being actuated by perversity too incorrigible to be amended, or by folly incapable of pursuing his own happiness when the path is pointed out. If we, on the contrary, were to frame our laws for man as he is, should we consider that the threat of death would be an efficient restraint to him who before he commits the crime, takes every measure that prudence can dictate to avoid discovery ; and who, after that, calculates on the proverbial uncertainty of the law ; while many of us are not deterred by a risk which we cannot flatter ourselves to avoid, for a trifling gain or a momentary gratification. Yet it may be said, the good citizen incurs the risk of death, but not of death in such a form ; he would not for the gratification or reward you speak of, incur the slightest risk of infamy, although the greatest that can be presented of honourable death does not affright him. This is most true, and this is most conclusive in the argument. It is not death, then, that is feared ; it is death with ignominy. But if it be that which makes death dreadful, will it not make life intolerable? If the suffering of shame cannot be endured during the short interval between conviction and execution, how can it be borne spread over a whole life?

But the murderer has no shame !—Then, according to your argument, he has nothing to make him fear death more, in his criminal pursuits, than you do in your honest occupation of inhaling pestilence in an infected hospital, or poison in the manufacture of mercury, or when you are heroically facing it on the ocean or in the field. Why, then, should the lesser risk, against which he thinks he has guarded, deter him, when the greater which you know you must face, has no effect upon you? Let no man whose duty it is to determine on this important measure, evade this question ; if he decide it as I think reason and the slightest knowledge of human nature must direct, the denunciation of death must be acknowledged to be no efficient bar to the commission of the only crime in which you think proper to employ it.

There is no point in the argument on which stronger reasoning and more persuasive authority could be produced than on this, which has more than once been necessarily introduced, for it connects itself with every other. From the operation of the earliest written laws of which history gives us any account, down to the present day, it has been invariably observed by all who would take the trouble to think, that the inexecution of penal laws was in exact proportion to their severity. Those of Draco have become proverbial for this last quality ; and their cruelty has been generally supposed a sufficient reason for their abolition by Solon. But the fact is, that they were abolished, not so much by Solon, as by the impossibility of carrying them into execution. When the stealing an apple incurred the punishment of death, what citizen would accuse—what witness would testify—what assembly of the people would convict—nay, what executioner would be found to present the poisoned cup? We are accordingly told expressly, that these laws were abolished, not by a formal decree, but by the tacit and unrecorded consent of the Athenians(*a*). I make no quotations from modern writers on penal law to this point, for there is not one who has not given his testimony in favour of the position I have taken ; and yet, by a most singular incongruity, each of them has a favourite crime to which he thinks it inapplicable.

This is not an essay to prove the inutility, the danger, and if these are admitted, the *crime* of employing the punishment of death. Such a work would require a methodical arrangement, and a research into the first principles of penal law, which cannot be expected from a mere explanatory report, in which heads of argument are suggested without much order and with little development, leaving to the enlightened minds, to which they are addressed, the task of pursuing to all their consequences, the topics which are raised for consideration. With this understanding, I shall add a few more reflections on this subject, so interesting to our best feelings.

All nations, even those the best organized, are subject to political disorders, during wich the violent passions that are excited avail themselves of every pretext for their indulgence ; and parties, animated with the rage of civil discord, mutually charge each other with the worst intentions, and blackest crimes; but even in the hottest warfare of party rage, the destruction of a rival faction or a dangerous leader, is seldom attempted but by the imputation of some crime ; new laws are not made on such occasions, but the existing laws are perverted and misapplied ; new punishments are not invented, but those already known are rigorously enforced against the innocent. This is the usual state of things in all intestine commotions, and even after they have assumed the shape of civil war, accompanied by all its horrors, those who do not fall in the field are subjected to something like a trial before their lives are sacrificed. Murder, on those occasions, arrays itself in the spotless ermine of justice, covers itself with her robes, mounts her sacred seat, borrows her holy language, adopts her forms, calls its iniquitous sentence the judgment of the law ; and even when it stretches forth its bloody hand for execution, it wields her own weapon, and inflicts on the innocent victim no other punishment than that which previous laws had provided for guilt.

This is necessary, is inevitable in cases of civil discord. Whatever may be the projects of unprincipled leaders, the people who compose their party and their strength, must be made to believe that those to whom they adhere are the friends and supporters of the laws, and therefore no violent open disregard of established forms would be tolerated, even where the essentials of justice are violated ; forms speak to the senses, the substance of justice to the understanding only—this last may be perverted by the passions or imposed on by falsehood in fact, or sophistry in argument ; but the eyes and ears only are necessary to observe a violation of form. In the times I have supposed— and they may afflict our country as they have all others—it is of importance to sanction no penalty that may be used to the destruction of your best citizens ; they are the most obnoxious to all parties ; not partaking the violence of either, they are suspected by both, and become the first victims ; and never has any revolutionary or factious

---

(*a*) " Draconis leges, quoniam videbantur impendio acerbiores, non decreto jussuque, sed tacito illiteratoque Atheniensium consensu, obliteratæ sunt."—*Aulus Gellius*, l. 3, c. 18.

storm desolated any land, without the loss of men lamented even by their mad executioners, after the calm of peace had restored them to their senses.   Beware then, how you sharpen the axe, and prepare the other instruments of .death, for the hand of party violence.   Beware how you so accustom the people to their use, that whenever their judgment may be led astray so as to think the innocent guilty, they may feel no shock in witnessing the last agonies of a man whom they may afterwards deplore as a national loss, and whose death they may feel as a national disgrace.   I dwell upon this, because I deeply feel its force.

History presents to us the magic glass on which, by looking at past, we may discern future events.   It is folly not to read; it is perversity not to follow its lessons.   If the hemlock had not been brewed for felons in Athens, would the fatal cup have been drained by Socrates?   If the people had not been familiarized to scenes of judicial homicide, would France or England have been disgraced by the useless murder of Louis or of Charles?   If the punishment of death had not been sanctioned by the ordinary laws of those kingdoms, would the one have been deluged with the blood of innocence, of worth, of patriotism, and science, in her revolution?   Would the best and noblest lives of the other have been lost on the scaffold, in her civil broils?   Would her lovely and calumniated queen, the virtuous Malsherbes, the learned Condorcet—would religion, personified in the pious ministers of the altar—courage and honour, in the host of high minded nobles—and science, in its worthy representative Lavoisier—would the daily hecatomb of loyalty and worth—would all have been immolated by the stroke of the guillotine; or Russel and Sidney, and the long succession of victims of party and tyranny, by the axe?   The fires of Smithfield would not have blazed; nor, after the lapse of ages, should we yet shudder at the name of St Bartholomew, if the ordinary ecclesiastical law had not usurped the attributes of divine vengeance, and by the sacrilegious and absurd doctrine, that offences against the deity were to be punished with death, given a pretext to these atrocities.   Nor, in the awful and mysterious scene on Mount Calvary, would that agony have been inflicted, if by the daily sight of the cross, as an instrument of justice, the Jews had not been prepared to make it one of their sacrilegious rage.   But there is no end of the examples which crowd upon the memory, to show the length to which the exercise of this power, by the law, has carried the dreadful abuse of it, under the semblance of justice.   Every nation has wept over the graves of patriots, heroes and martyrs, sacrificed by its own fury.   Every age has had its annals of blood.

But not to resort to the danger of the examples in times of trouble and dissension, advert once more to that which was formerly urged, and to which I must again hereafter return—that which attends its regular practice in peace—the irremediable nature of this punishment, when error, popular prejudice, or false or mistaken testimony, has caused its infliction to be ordered upon the innocent; a case by no means of so rare occurrence as may be imagined.   It is not intended to enter into a detail of those which I have myself collected; they are not few, although they must necessarily bear a small proportion to those which were not within my reach.   The author of a book of high(a) authority

(a) Phillips on Evidence, Appendix.

on evidence, has brought together several cases which are well authenticated. In France, in the short space of one year, I have gathered .from the public papers that seven cases occurred, in which persons condemned to death by the primary courts and assizes, have been acquitted by the sentence of a superior tribunal on a reversal of the sentence(*a*). In other states of our union these cases are not uncommon. With us the organization of our courts prevents the correction of any error, either in law, or in fact, by a superior tribunal. But every where it is matter of surprise that any cases should be discovered of these fatal mistakes. The unfortunate subjects of them are, for the most part, friendless ; generally their lives must have been vicious, or suspicion would not have fastened on them ; and men of good character sometimes think it disreputable to show an interest for such men, or to examine critically into the circumstances of their case. They are deserted by their connexions, if they have any; friends they have none. They are condemned—executed—forgotten ; and in a few days, it would seem, that the same earth which covered their bodies has buried all remembrance of them, and all doubts of their innocence or guilt. It is, then, not unreasonable to suppose, that many more such cases have existed than those that have fortuitously been brought to light(*b*).

(*a*) Is not this a striking lesson to teach us the necessity of providing the means of correcting error in criminal as well as in civil cases—of protecting life and liberty as well as property ? The importance of the subject may, perhaps, excuse my referring once more to the bill formerly offered to the general assembly by the reporter.

(*b*) Let me give the substance of this objection to capital punishment in the words of a man to whom the science of legislation owes the great attention that is now paid to its true principles, and to whom statues would be raised if the benefactors of mankind were as much honoured as the oppressors of nations :—" The same objection," he says, " lies against all afflictive penalties, that they cannot be remedied, but they may be compensated. For death alone there is no resource. There is no man, ever so little versed in criminal procedure, who does not feel a kind of terror, when he thinks on how slight a circumstance the life of a man under accusation for a capital crime, depends, and who does not recollect instances in which individuals have owed their lives to some extraordinary circumstance, accidently brought to light at the critical moment of danger. The chances of danger are, without doubt, very different, according to the different systems of procedure . . . but are there any judiciary forms, which can guard, in perfect security, against the snares of falsehood and the illusions of error ? No ! absolute security is a point of perfection which may be approached much nearer than has yet been done without reaching it ; for witnesses may deceive, or be deceived ; the number of those who testify to the same fact is not an infallible safeguard ; and as to proofs which are drawn from circumstantial facts—circumstances the most conclusive, in appearance—those which it would seem impossible to explain, but on the supposition of guilt—even these may be the effect of chance, or of preconcerted circumstances, arranged by interested persons. The only proof which would appear to bring complete conviction, the free confession of the accused, besides its being very rare, does not always give absolute certainty—since men have been found, as in the case of witchcraft, to confess themselves guilty of a crime that it was impossible to commit. Those are not imaginary alarms, drawn from simple possibilities; there are no criminal records that do not present examples of these fatal mistakes—and those which, by a concurrence of singular events, have become known, give us reason to suspect many innocent victims unknown. It may even be observed, that the cases in which the word evidence is most frequently used, are those in which the testimony is most doubtful. When the alleged crime is one of those which excites the most antipathy, or heightens the spirit of party, the witnesses unconsciously become accusers ; they are no more than the echoes of public clamour ; the fer-

Would you retain à punishment that, in the common course of events, must be irremediably inflicted, at times, on the innocent, even if it secured the punishment of the guilty? But that is far from being the effect. While you cannot, in pacticular cases, avoid its falling upon innocence, that very cause, from the imperfection of all testimony, will make it more favourable to the escape of the guilty; and the maxim, so often quoted on this occasion(a), will no longer be perverted in order to effect a compromise between the conscience of the juror and the severity of the law, when your punishments are such only as admit of remission when they have been found to be unjustly imposed.

Other arguments, not less forcible—other authorities, equally respectable, might be adduced to show the ill effects of this species of punishment; but the many topics that are still before me in this report, oblige me to pursue this one no further than to inquire, what good can be expected, or what present advantage is derived from retaining this punishment? Our legislation surrendered it without a struggle, in all cases, at first, but murder, attempt to murder, rape and servile insurrection; and afterwards extended it to a species of aggravated burglary(b). Now as these cases are those only in which it has been deemed expedient to retain this punishment; as it has been abandoned in all others, the serious inquiry presents itself, why it was retained in these, or why abandoned in the others? Its inefficiency, or some of the other objections to it, must have been apparent in all the other numerous offences in which it has been dispensed with, or it would certainly have been retained, or restored. Taking this acknowledged inefficiency, in the numerous cases, for the basis of the argument, let us inquire whether there is any thing which makes it peculiarly adapted to the enumerated crimes, which it is unjust or inexpedient to apply to any of the others? We have three modes of discovering the truth on this subject : by reasoning from the general effects of particular motives on human actions; by analogy, or judging from the effects in one case to the probable effects in another ; or by experience of the effect on the particular case. The general reasoning upon the justice and efficacy of the punishment will not be repeated here, but it is referred to as being conclusive

mentation increases by its own action, and it is no longer permitted to doubt. It was a frenzy of this kind which first seized the people, and was afterwards communicated to the judges in the unfortunate affair of Calas."—*Theory of Rewards and Punishments, Bentham.*

(a) That it is better ten guilty should escape than one innocent suffer, is invariably given to the jury as a maxim in all capital cases, depending on circumstantial evidence ; and where there are no irritating causes, it invariably succeeds.

(b) Act of 20th March 1818, sec. 3. Breaking into a dwelling house in the night time, with intent to steal, &c. so far this crime was already punishable under the act of 1805. The severe punishment of death is added, if any person was lawfully within the house, and if the offender was armed with a dangerous weapon ; or if not so armed, if he armed himself in the house, or made an assault on the person then being in the house ·lawfully. If the occupier of the house was not there *lawfully*, the offender escapes *death!* What a circumstance on which to hang the life of a man. If the tenant has a good lease, the robber is hanged, if he is an intruder, he escapes death. Again, if the robber meets nobody in the house and steals ten thousand dollars, he only suffers imprisonment; but if he sees a servant, and shakes his fist at him, he is hanged, although he should steal nothing. If he breaks in without weapons, and rifles the house of all its contents, he is imprisoned only ; if he finds a fowling-piece, and carries it off in his hand, he is hanged. Another specimen of the laws which nothing but presumption could attempt to amend.

as to all offences, and admitting of no exception that would apply to murder, or either of the three other cases in which our laws inflict it. If we reason from analogy, we should say the only argument ever used in favour of death as a punishment is, that the awful example it presents will deter from the commission of the offence: but by your abandonment of it in all cases but these, you acknowledge it has no efficacy there. Analogy, therefore, would lead us to the conclusion, that if it was useless in the many cases, it would be so in the few. But it is acknowledged, 'that no analogy, or any other mode of reasoning; no theory, however plausible, ought to influence, when contradicted by experience. You have tried this remedy, and found it ineffectual! The crimes to which you have applied it, are decreasing in number and atrocity under its influence! If so, it would be imprudent to make any change, even under the most favourable prospects that the new system would be equally efficient. Let us try it by this test. For the first three years after the transfer of the province, there was not a single execution or conviction for either of these crimes. In the course, however, of the first six years, four Indians, residing within the limits of the state, made an attack on some of the settlers, and were either given up by the tribe, or arrested and condemned, and two were executed as for murder, and one negro was condemned and executed for insurrection. In the next six years there were ten convictions; in the succeeding four, to the month of January 1822, fourteen; so that we find the number of convictions for the enumerated crimes have nearly doubled in every period of six years, in the face of this efficient penalty. But the population of the state doubles only once in twenty years; therefore, the increase of this crime progresses in a ratio of three to one, to that of the population; and we should not forget, in making this calculation, the important and alarming fact, that numerous instances of homicide, and attempts to kill, occur, which are rarely followed by prosecution, and more rarely still by conviction. I mean, all that class that have their origin in a mistaken sense of honour, including not only the lives sacrificed to the tyranny of public opinion in duels, but those less excusable and increasing cases of wounds and death, inflicted in atonement for some injury offered to personal dignity. Under the statute against stabbing, I find but three convictions up to the year 1822; one instance of rape, to the same period; and what is somewhat singular, not a single instance of burglary from 1805 until 1820, in which year, and the succeeding one, there were two cases, just two years after it was made a capital crime. What are we to conclude from this statement? First, I think, that, of burglary, one of the crimes to which capital punishment is annexed, fifteen years' experience, (during which there was not a single conviction, and as far as is known, not a single indictment under the law which denounced imprisonment as the penalty) ought to have convinced us, that the severer punishment was not necessary, while the two convictions which so soon succeeded the promulgation of that law, are strong testimony that the punishment of death is not an effectual remedy for the evil. As to rape, that its rare occurrence is much more properly to be attributed to the manners of the age than to any fear of the punishment annexed; for if that were the efficient cause, we should certainly find it at least as powerful in the case of murder, a crime to which the offender is not stimulated as in the former case, by the strongest sensual appetite.

Besides, this is not the strong hold of those who argue in favour of capital punishment. Driven from every other ground, they defend it as peculiarly applicable to the case of murder. The slow abandonment of it for other offences, is a proof of the gradual advance of true principles, and the pertinacity with which it is adhered to in this, shows the force of early impressions and inveterate prejudice, even in the most enlightened minds : yet that prejudice must in time yield to the evidence which the practical results which have attended this infliction— results which show, almost to demonstration, that the public exhibition of homicide, directed by the sacred voice of the law, so far from repressing, does but encourage it, in private quarrels. · It is commonly advocated on the principle of vindictive justice(a), and can be, with a due regard to facts, on no other. The murderer deserves death ! He that sheds man's blood, by man shall· his blood be shed ! Blood for blood ! These are the exclamations that are used instead of argument. Such sentiments, combined with the spectacle of legal revenge which they dictate, can produce but one effect. Half the odium and horror of taking human life is lost, by the example of seeing it made a public duty, while the motives are sanctified which are but too apt to justify it in the mind of an irritated individual, who magnifies the injury he has received, overlooks the provocation he gave, and thinks himself excusable in doing, to satisfy his passions, that which public justice does from the same motive, revenge. The sensation of horror with which we see a human being suffering a violent death, would certainly be increased, if the hand of justice was never employed in the unholy work; and private vengeance would be checked by the laws, when they no longer encouraged it by their example.

But however this vindictive feeling may betray itself in the warmth of conversation, it is not brought forward in any serious argument; there it is too universally exploded. What then is said ? That it is a punishment proportioned to the crime; that, as murder is the highest of all offences, death, the greatest, of all punishments, ought to be applied to it. But why ought it to be so applied ? To apportion the punishment to the offence, does not mean to make the culprit suffer the same quantity of evil which he inflicted by his crime ; that would be both impossible and unjust. It means, that the punishment should be such as to deter from the commission of the crime, but no greater. If, then, death has not this effect, why ought it to be applied ? But that it has not this effect, is shown by reasoning and by fact. Why then will you continue to apply it ? Pressed by this inquiry, we have the same eternal answer—murder deserves death. Out of this circle no reasoning can drive them. Sometimes, indeed, we are asked, are you sure that if we give up this punishment, your substitute will prove effectual? If

(a) I had once a conversation with an exalted magistrate, a man of high attainments and great liberality, on the abolition of this punishment. He acceded to the propriety of the measure, in all cases but murder ; because of the difficulty of keeping the offender, and the severity of solitary confinement, which was proposed to be substituted. But when these two objections were, as I thought, satisfactorily answered, he replied by one of the exclamations used in the text, and added, very frankly—" I must confess that there is some little feeling of *revenge* at the bottom of my opinion on this subject." If all other reasoners were equally candid, there would be less difficulty in establishing true doctrines.

R

you mean so effectual as to eradicate the crime, I answer, no! But I am as sure as experience and analogy, and reasoning united, can make me, that it will be more effectual. What is it we fear? Why do we hesitate? You know, you cannot deny, that the fear of the gallows does not restrain from murder. We have seen a deliberate murder committed in the very crowd assembled to enjoy the spectacle of a murderer's death; and do we still talk of its force as an example? In defiance of your menaced punishment, homicide stalks abroad and raises its bloody hand at noon-day in your crowded streets; and when arrested in its career, takes shelter under the example of your laws, and is protected by their very severity, from punishment. Try the efficacy of milder punishments; they have succeeded. Your own statutes, all those of every state in the union, prove that they have succeeded, in other offences; try the great experiment on this also. Be consistent; restore capital punishments in other crimes, or abolish it in this. Do not fear that the murderers from all quarters of the earth, seduced by the mildness of your penal code, will choose this as the theatre of their exploits. On this point we have a most persuasive example. In Tuscany, as we have seen, neither murder nor any other crime was punished with death, for more than twenty years, during which time we have not only the official declaration of the sovereign, that "all crimes had diminished, and those of an atrocious nature had become extremely rare ," but the authority of the venerable Franklin, for these conclusive facts ; that in Tuscany where murder was not punished with death, only five had been committed in twenty years ; while in Rome, where that punishment is inflicted with great pomp and parade, *sixty murders* were committed in the short space of three months, in the city and its vicinity(a). "It is remarkable," he adds to this account "that the man-

---

(a) If ever any philosophy deserved the epithets of useful and practical, it was that of Dr Franklin. His opinions must have weight, not only from his character, but from the simple, intelligible reasoning by which they are supported. What says this venerable and irreproachable witness in the cause of humanity, which we are now pleading?—"I suspect the attachment to death, as a punishment for murder, in minds otherwise enlightened upon the subject of capital punishments, arises from a false interpretation of a passage in the old testament, and that is—'He that sheds the blood of man, by man shall his blood be shed.' This has been supposed to imply, that blood could only be expiated by blood. But I am disposed to believe, with a late commentator on this text* of scripture, that it is rather a prediction than a law. The language of it is simply, that such is the folly and depravity of man, that murder, in every age, shall beget murder. Laws, therefore, which inflict death for murder, are, in my opinion, as unchristian as those which justify or tolerate revenge ; for the obligations of Christianity upon individuals, to promote repentance, to forgive injuries, and to discharge the duties of universal benevolence, are equally binding upon states.

"The power over human life is the sole prerogative of him who gave it. Human

---

* "I hope I shall not offend any one by taking the liberty to put my own construction on this celebrated passage, and to inquire, why it should be deemed a precept at all? To me, I must confess, it appears to contain nothing more than a declaration of what will generally happen : and in this view to stand exactly upon the same ground with such passages as the following—'He that leadeth into captivity, shall go into captivity'—'He that taketh up the sword, shall fall by the sword.' The form of expression is precisely the same in both texts. Why then may they not all be interpreted in the same manner, and considered, not as commands, but as denunciations? and if so, the magistrate will no more be bound by the text in Genesis, to punish murder with death, than he will by the text in the Revelations, to sell every Guinea captain to our West India planters."—*Rev. W. Turner.*

ners, principles, and religion of the inhabitants of Tuscany, and of Rome, are exactly the same. The abolition of death alone, as a punishment for murder, produced this difference in the moral character of the two nations." From this it would appear, rather that the murderers of Tuscany were invited, by the severe punishments in the neighbouring territories of Rome, than that those of Rome were attracted into Tuscany by their abolition. We have nothing to apprehend, then, from this measure ; and if any ill effects should follow the experiment, it is but too easy to return to the system of extermination.

One argument, the ferocious character impressed on the people by this punishment, which was insisted on in the first report, has been so strongly illustrated by a subsequent event in Pennsylvania, that I cannot omit stating it. After the execution of Lechler had gratified the people about York and Lancaster with the spectacle of his death, and had produced its proper complement of homicide and other crimes, a poor wretch was condemned to suffer the same fate, for a similar offence, in another part of the state, where the people had not yet been indulged with such a spectacle. They, also, collected by thousands and

laws, therefore, are in rebellion against this prerogative, when they transfer it to human hands.

" If society can be secured from violence by confining the murderer, so as to prevent a repetition of his crime, the end of extirpation will be answered. In confinement he may be reformed; and if this should prove impracticable, he may be restrained for a term of years that will probably be co-eval with his life.

" There was a time when the punishment of captives with death or servitude, and the indiscriminate destruction of peaceable husbandmen, women, and children, were thought to be essential to the success of war, and the safety of states. But experience has taught us that this is not the case; and in proportion as humanity has triumphed over these maxims of false policy, wars have been less frequent and terrible, and nations have enjoyed longer intervals of internal tranquillity. The virtues are all parts of a circle. Whatever is humane, is wise ; whatever is wise, is just; and whatever is wise, just, and humane, will be found to be the true interest of states, whether criminals or foreign enemies are the subject of their legislation.

" For the honour of humanity it can be said, that in every age and country, there have been found persons in whom uncorrupted nature has triumphed over custom and law. Else, why do we hear of houses being abandoned near to places of public execution? Why do we see doors and windows shut the days and hours of criminal executions? Why do we hear of aid being secretly afforded to criminals to mitigate or elude the severity of their punishments? Why is the public executioner of the law a subject of such general detestation? These things are latent struggles of reason, or rather, the secret voice of God himself, speaking in the human heart, against the folly and cruelty of public punishments.

" I shall conclude this inquiry by observing, that the same false religion and philosophy which once kindled the fire on the altar of persecution, now dooms the criminal to public ignominy and death. In proportion as the principles of philosophy and Christianity are understood, they will agree in extinguishing the one and destroying the other. If these principles continue to extend their influence upon government, as they have done for some time past, I cannot help entertaining a hope, that the time is not very distant, when the gallows, the pillory, the stocks, the whipping-post, and the wheel-barrow (the usual engines of public punishment), will be connected with the history of the rack and the stake, as marks of the barbarity of ages and countries, and as melancholy proofs of the feeble operation of reason and religion on the human mind."—*Inquiry upon Public Punishments.*

tens of thousands. The victim was brought out. All the eyes in the living mass that surrounded the gibbet, were fixed on his countenance, and they waited with strong desire, the expected signal for launching him into eternity. There was a delay. They grew impatient; it was prolonged, and they were outrageous; cries like those which precede the tardy rising of the curtain in a theatre were heard. Impatient for the delight they expected in seeing a fellow creature die, they raised a ferocious cry. But when it was at last announced that a reprieve had left them no hope of witnessing his agonies, their fury knew no bounds; and the poor maniac, for it was discovered that he was insane, was with difficulty snatched by the officers of justice from the fate which the most violent among them seemed determined to inflict(a). This is not an overcharged picture; the same savage feeling has been more than once exhibited in different parts of the union, and will always be produced by public executions, unless it is replaced by the equally dangerous feeling of admiration and interest for the sufferer(b). Which of the two is to prevail, depends on circumstances totally out of the power of the lawgiver or the judge to foresee, or control; but by the indulgence of either feeling, every good end of punishment is totally defeated.

I cannot, I ought not, to dismiss this subject without once more pressing on the most serious consideration of the legislature, an argument which every new view of it convinces me is important; and if we listen to the voice of conscience, conclusive: the irremediable nature of this punishment. Until men acquire new faculties, and are enabled to decide upon innocence or guilt without the aid of fallible and corruptible human evidence, so long will the risk be incurred of condemning the innocent. Were the consequence felt as deeply as it ought to be, would there be an advocate for that punishment, which, applied in such case, has all the consequences of the most atrocious murder to the innocent sufferers—worse than the worst murderer! He stabs, or strikes, or poisons, and the victim dies—he dies unconscious of the blow—without being made a spectacle to satisfy ferocious curiosity, and without the torture of leaving his dearest friends doubtful of his innocence, or seeing them abandon him under the conviction of his guilt; he dies, and his death is like one of those inevitable chances to which all mortals are subject; his family are distressed, but not dishonoured; his death is lamented by his friends, and, if his life deserved it, honoured by his country. But the death inflicted by the laws, the

(a) This disgraceful scene took place at Orwigsburgh. The wretched madman who was so near suffering, was named Zimmerman. I have the details from a gentleman of the first respectability in Pennsylvania; my informant adds to his account of this transaction—" Executions in this state are scenes of riot and every species of wickedness; twenty, thirty, and forty thousand persons have been in attendance on such occasions. In country parts, two and even three days are employed in the merry-making, much after the manner of fairs in former times."

(b) The tendency of public executions at times to elevate the sufferer to the honours of saintship, and lose the detestation due to his crime in admiration for the piety of the new convert, is not confined to the United States. The scene described in the first report, of the execution of the mail robbers at Baltimore, has been represented in other countries. A note to that part of the report in a German translation, says—" One would think that the author was an eye-witness to the execution of the murderer Jonas in this place—so exactly is the scene described."

murder of the innocent under its holy forms, has no such mitigating circumstances. Slow in its approach, uncertain in its stroke, its victim feels not only the sickness of the heart that arises from the alternation of hope and fear, until his doom is pronounced, but when that becomes inevitable; alone, the tenant of a dungeon during every moment that the cruel lenity of the law prolongs his life, he is made to feel all those anticipations, worse than a thousand deaths. The consciousness of innocence, that which is our support under other miseries, is here converted into a source of bitter. anguish, when it is found to be no protection from infamy and death ; and when the ties which connected him to his country, his friends, his family, are torn asunder, no consoling reflection mitigates the misery of that moment. He leaves unmerited infamy to his children; a name stamped with dishonour to their surviving parent, and bows down the grey heads of his own with sorrow to the grave. As he walks from his dungeon, he sees the thousands who have come to gaze on his last agony; he mounts the fatal tree, and a life of innocence is closed by a death of dishonour. This is no picture of the imagination. Would to God it were ! Would to God, that if death must be inflicted, some sure means might be discovered of making it fall upon the guilty. These things have happened. These legal murders have been committed ! and who were the primary causes of the crime ? Who authorized a punishment, which once inflicted, could never be remitted to the innocent ? Who tied the cord, or let fall the axe upon the guiltless head ? Not the executioner, the vile instrument who is hired to do the work of death; not the jury who convict, or the judge who condemns; not the law which sanctions these errors, but the legislators who made the law ; those who, having the power, did not repeal it. These are the persons responsible to their country, their consciences, and their God. These horrors not only have happened, but they must be repeated : the same causes will produce the same effects. The innocent have suffered the death of the guilty; the innocent will suffer. We know it. The horrible truth stares us in the face. We dare not deny, and cannot evade it. A word, while it saves the innocent, will secure the punishment of the guilty, and shall we hesitate to pronounce it? Shall we content ourselves with our own imagined exemption from this fate, and shut our ears to the cries of justice and humanity ? Shall " sensibility (as has been finely observed) sleep in the lap of luxury"(a), and not awake at the voice of wretchedness ? I urge this point with more earnestness, because I have witnessed more than one condemnation under false constructions of law, or perjured, or mistaken testimony ; sentences, that would now have been reversed if the unfortunate sufferers were within the reach of mercy. I have seen, in the gloom and silence of the dungeon, the deep concentrated expression of indignation which contended with grief; have heard the earnest asseverations of innocence, made in tones which no art could imitate ; and listened with awe to the dreadful adjuration, poured forth by one of these victims with an energy and solemnity that seemed superhuman, summoning his false accuser and his mistaken judge to meet him before the throne of God. Such an appeal to the high tribunal which never errs, and before which he who made it was in a few hours to appear, was calculated to create a belief of his innocence ; that belief

(a) Eden. Principles of Penal Law.

was changed into certainty ; the perjury of the witness was discovered, and he fled from the infamy that awaited him ; but it was too late for any other effect, than to add one more example to the many that preceded it of the danger, and I may add impiety of using this attribute of the divine power, without the infallibility that can alone properly direct it. And this objection alone, did none of the other cogent reasons against capital punishment exist, this alone would make me hail the decree for its abolition as an event, so honourable to my country and so consoling to humanity, as to be cheaply purchased by the labour of a life.

I cannot quit this part of the subject without submitting to the general assembly the opinion of one whose authority would justify an experiment, even more hazardous than this, but whose arguments are as convincing as his name is respectable. They are not the opinions of one whom the cant, which is used to cover the ignorance of the day, would call a theorist, but of a man whose whole life was spent in the useful and honourable functions of the highest magistracy, whose name is always mentioned with reverence, and whose doctrines are quoted as authority, wherever the true principles of legal knowledge are regarded. Hear the venerable D'Aguesseau :

" Who would believe that a first impression may sometimes decide the question of life and death ? A fatal mass of circumstances, which seem as if fate had collected them together, for the ruin of an unfortunate wretch, a crowd of mute witnesses (and from that character more dangerous) depose against innocence ; they prejudice the judge, his indignation is roused, his zeal contributes to seduce him ; losing the character of the judge in that of the accuser, he looks only to that which is evidence of guilt, and he sacrifices to his own reasonings the man whom he would have saved had he listened only to the proofs of the law. An unforeseen event sometimes shows, that innocence has sunk under the weight of conjectures, and falsifies the conclusions which circumstances had induced the magistrate to draw. Truth lifts up the veil with which probability had enveloped her ; but she appears too late! The blood of the innocent cries aloud for vengeance against the prejudice of his judge ; and the magistrate passes the rest of his life in deploring a misfortune which his REPENTANCE CANNOT REPAIR"(a).

The earnestness for this reform is sometimes reproached to its advocates as proceeding from a childish fear, that magnifies the apprehension of that which we know is appointed to us all. Not so. The value of life is not overrated in the argument. There are occasions in which the risk of its loss must be incurred ; in which the certainty of death must be encountered with firmness and composure. These occasions are presented by patriotism in defence of our country and our country's rights ; by benevolence in the rescue of another from danger ; by religion, whenever persecution offers the martyr's crown to the faithful : and it is not known or believed that those who propose to abolish death as a punishment, either fear it as a natural event or shun its encounter when required by duty, more than those who think it ought to be retained. He who preserved the life of a Roman citizen, was entitled to a more honourable recompense than the daring soldier who ventured his own by first mounting the breach. The civic was preferred to the

(a) D'Auguesseau, 16 Mercuriale.

mural crown.  The Romans, during the best period of their history, reduced this abolition to practice.  "Far," said their great orator, endeavouring in a corrupted age to restore the ancient feeling on the subject, " far(a) from us be the punishment of death—its ministers—its instruments.  Remove them, not only from their actual operation on our bodies, but banish them from our eyes, our ears, our thoughts; for, not only the execution, but the apprehension, the existence, the very mention of these things is disgraceful to a freeman and a Roman citizen."  Yet the Romans were not very remarkable for a pusillanimous fear of death.  In the age of which I speak, they did not want the excitement of capital punishment to induce them to die for their country. On the contrary, it might, perhaps, be plausibly argued, that the servile disposition, which disgraced the latter ages of the republic, was in some measure caused by the change, which made the sacrifice of life the expiation for crime, instead of the consummation and proof of patriotic devotion.

Conscious of having been guilty of much repetition, and certain that I have weakened, by my version of them, arguments much better used by others, I am yet fearful of having omitted many things that might have an effect in convincing any one of those to whom this report is addressed.  The firm religious belief I have of the truth of the doctrine I advance, contrasted with the sense of my incapacity to enforce it upon others, must have produced obscurity where the interests of humanity require there should be light, and confusion where the performance of my great duty demands order.  But the truth will appear in spite of these obstacles.  From the midst of the cloud, with which human imperfection has surrounded her, her voice, like that of the Almighty from the mount, will be heard reiterating to nations as well as to individuals, the great command, " THOU SHALT NOT KILL."

Having more fully than was intended, but much more imperfectly than the subject demands, reviewed the great characteristic that distinguishes the code, the *total abolition of capital punishment*, it will be necessary to advert (which will, hereafter, be very briefly done) to other penalties, which, for reasons nearly as cogent, have been also abrogated.  As to the nature of the punishments, by which these are proposed to be replaced, the principal one, imprisonment in its various grades, is fully discussed in the Code of Prison Discipline.  Fines are retained, but with modifications that lessen the force of the objections usually made to that punishment.  It is certain, that indiscriminately applied to the poor and the rich, this is one of the most unequal punishments that can well be imagined; and that the wide range of discretion which the apportionment of it must necessarily require to be vested in the judge, is another strong objection; but when that discretion is properly exercised, no penalty can be so easily proportioned to the offence and to the circumstances of the offender; it is divisible in the most perfect degree, and admits of complete compensation whenever it has been improperly enforced.  But yet it was foreseen that cases would occur, in which the wealth of the offender might make the highest range of a

---

(*a*) Carnifex et abductio capitis, et nomen ipsum crucis absit, non modo a corpore civium Romanorum sed etiam a cogitatione, oculis, auribus—harum etiam omnium rerum non solum eventus atque perpessio, sed etiam conditio, expectatio, mentio ipsa denique, indigna cive Romano, atque homine libero est.—*Cicero pro Rabirio.*

discretionary fine a penalty too light to be felt; and in which his poverty might change the lowest into utter ruin. To avoid as much as possible these inconveniences, the fine, in most cases, is accompanied by a discretion to commute it into simple imprisonment, which may be inflicted on those whose circumstances would enable them to despise a fine; and on the other hand, to avoid the oppression and ruin of the poor, it is provided that no fine shall ever exceed one-fourth of the clear property of the delinquent; and still further to secure the indigent from ruin, and at the same time to provide for his punishment; where there is no property, the fine is to be commuted into imprisonment, calculating one day for every two dollars($a$) of the fine, limiting it, however, so that whatever may be the amount of the fine, the imprisonment shall not exceed ninety days. Fines are also rendered more equal, when inflicted for a breach of official duty, by apportioning them to the amount of official emolument. There are also general rules, intended to impress on the mind of the judge the principles by which he ought to be guided, in the exercise of the discretion vested in him by the law. These will be found in the Code of Procedure, and the reasons for those directions in the Introductory Report to that Code.

The collection of fines is regulated by the same rules which govern executions in civil cases; giving to the state no preference over other creditors, but from the time of registering the order imposing the fine.

Considering fine as a personal punishment, the death of the offender operates as a discharge at any time before it is paid. Any other arrangement would make it operate as a partial forfeiture upon his heirs.

Forfeiture and suspension of certain civil and political rights are also punishments inflicted by the code. They are applied chiefly to misdemeanours in office, and to such offences as show the want of the proper qualities to perform the duties which are required by them. These are sparingly inflicted, because, if too frequent, it would create a body of men in the community discontented with their situation and ready to promote any violent change.

Among the civil rights, however, which are forfeitable, is not found that of testifying. The reasons of making this change, are set forth at some length in the Introductory Report to the Code of Evidence. Here it will be sufficient to remark, that such a disqualification would be a most serious punishment to persons whose property, reputation, or life, might depend on the testimony of the person disqualified, but could be none to him.

In apportioning punishments to different modifications of the same offence, a mode has been adopted which appeared simple and easily understood. It is that of directing the increase or diminution of the punishment for the simple offence to be made by a fractional proportion; for instance, the punishment for assisting at an unlawful assembly, is fine from fifty to three hundred dollars, and imprisonment from three to twelve months; but as this offence is more reprehensible in a magistrate, or other officer, it is provided, that if any such are guilty of it, the penalty shall be doubled. The same effect might be produced by

($a$) This valuation of a day's imprisonment may seem high, but a just regard for personal liberty induced a belief that double the standard of daily wages would not be deemed excessive.

enacting in the article relating to such modification of the offences, that the punishment should be fine from one hundred to six hundred dollars, and imprisonment not less than six nor more than twelve months. But the contrary course was adopted; because, being equally intelligible, it avoided repetition, which, as all the conciseness consistent with perspicuity was studied in framing the code, made it an object of some importance; and because the precise proportion being enounced in declaring the penalty, the aggravation or diminution of the guilt was more readily impressed on the mind. A reference to the rules for making these apportionments will enable the general assembly to judge of the expediency of the provision. It is one, however, of mere convenience; does not touch any of the essential features in the code, and if disapproved, the same end may be produced by a labour nearly mechanical, of inserting the augmentation and diminution at length in each of the cases where it is directed to be proportionably increased or diminished. The only very material objection to this change would be increasing, without necessity, the bulk of the work, and destroying the association of ideas which it was intended to preserve.

Before entering into the examination which it is proposed to make of the classification and definition of the several offences, one or two of the general and peculiar features of the code must be adverted to. The first is, the enunciation of the general principles on which it is founded. In the first arrangement of the work, this idea occurred as one of the highest utility: and although it was perfectly unprecedented, I was not deterred from the execution by its novelty. The advantages are recited in the chapter itself, and need scarcely any elucidation(a). If it be conceded, that the people ought to know, not only what their agents have done, but their reasons for doing it; that any work, and particularly that of legislation, will be better done when the object is clearly defined, and the means and rules for attaining it have been attentively considered; that uniformity is necessary, and' that it will be better preserved by having a record of the grounds upon which former laws were made;— if any of these things be conceded, then is that part of the code a valuable improvement, provided it contains the true principles of penal legislation—such as cannot change, and which, if good now, will remain so for ever. These, once observed, once acknowledged to be the rule; every future law will be measured by their standard. Then, no more discordant provisions; no more vacillating legislation; no more accumulation of statutes, upon the same matter; none of those evils, in short, which are contrary to these principles. They will perform the office of a constitutional rule, not, indeed, avoiding those laws which are made contrary to it, but preventing their very existence. I rely more on the importance and utility of this part of the work, because it is that which, both in its form and substance, has received the most decided approbation of all those who, both in Europe and America, have made it the subject of examination or criticism.

An introductory notice contains the explanation of certain provisions intended, chiefly, to avoid circumlocution and repetition, in the course of the work. The disgusting tautology of the English statutes, from which our own are not entirely free, is by this means avoided. The strictness with which their judges adhered, at times, to the letter of the

(a) Preamble to the Penal Code.

S

statute, induced the necessity of ringing all the chances which number, gender, and time required, to bring within the words of the statute, every possible case which they could govern, and the inconvenience has been so much felt, that a bill has lately passed, containing in substance(a), the same enactments for avoiding it, that are contained in the third chapter of the code I now present.

One article of this chapter relates to another feature in the system that is entirely new, but it is thought a very important improvement. I mean, the definition of all the technical words or phrases used in the work. The utility of this must be acknowledged by those whose objection to the introduction of the new code is, that it will unsettle the signification that has been affixed, by judicial decisions, to words most commonly used in statutes. Now if this certainty be, as it unquestionably is, an advantage of the first consequence ; then its benefit must be in proportion to the degree of certainty which is given ; but judicial decisions cannot, from their nature, give this certainty in as great a degree as positive law; the book of definitions therefore will be positive law, and in order to know the sense in which any word is used in the code, it will be only necessary to turn to its definition, instead of poring over a countless number of volumes, and endeavouring, from their incomplete or contradictory statements, to find the sense in which it has, at times, been employed in different cases. But it must be observed, that although the endeavour has been to preserve as much as possible

(a) The following extract from Mr Peel's speech, introductory to this bill, will show, that this part of the plan has been deemed worthy of adoption in Great Britain.—" I certainly have set the example to the house of drawing up such bills for the future, in an intelligible manner. Not being myself a lawyer, and possessing, of course no technical knowledge, I do confess, sir, that there is no task which I contemplate with so much distaste; as the reading through an ordinary act of parliament. In the first place, the long recapitulations, the tedious references, the constant repetitions, the providing or designating offences as punishments for the specific case of men, women and children, and for every degree and relation in society, and the necessity of indicating these several personages, and matters by as many appropriate relations and designations—then the confusion resulting from the attempt to describe, and constantly referring to many different descriptions of property. Really, sir, all these various repetitions, recapitulations, and references are so tedious and so perplexing, that I for one, almost invariably find myself completely puzzled before I get to the end of a single clause. The mode I have adopted in this bill to obviate all this confusion and uncertainty, does seem to me, I speak it with submission, much more eligible and precise than the usual phraseology, adopted in these acts, and might, I cannot help thinking, be pursued with advantage in bills which may be brought in hereafter. I will give you an example. It is enacted in my bill, that if any person be convicted of entering into and stealing in any house, room, &c. he shall be liable to a certain penalty; and in the conclusion of the act, that there may be no doubt arising from want of specification of sex or the identity of the offender, there is a clause to this effect: ' And in order to remove all doubt as to the meaning and intention of certain words in this act, be it hereby further enacted, that whenever the words person, party, offender,' and so forth occur, ' they shall each and all of them be deemed to intend and demonstrate any number of persons or parties; and of any sex, being the offender or offenders under this act.' If any person, therefore, commit an offence contemplated by that act, he will, under the general description, be liable to the penalty affixed to such offence. My bill, therefore, will include every person, male, or female, and of every rank or condition of offending under its enactments. Owing to the various lights in which I have considered this provision and the extent which I have thus given to the bill, I am afraid it will be impossible to frame one more comprehensive."

the same words that are used in common parlance, to express the same
ideas, yet, whenever there was any uncertainty, the signification has
been fixed according to the sense in which the expression is used in the
code; and that philological science has always been sacrificed to certainty and precision.   The Book of Definitions, therefore, must not be
consulted as a dictionary of the language of the country, but of that
of the Code, whenever the uncertainty of the former created the necessity of declaring in what sense the term is employed.

I will not attempt to conceal from the general assembly, the extreme
difficulty of this part of my labour; more than any other, it exercised
my closest and intensest attention, and I think it has not been exercised
in vain.   I think so, not only from the satisfaction of my own mind,
but from the approbation of men who have had the kindness to employ
high intellect, enforced by official duty, to the task of close thinking on
legal subjects, in trying to detect the errors of that part of the work:
and who have given me leave to say, that they have found none.   These
venerable names, with the opinions they have given, will be found in
the appendix.   But whatever weight is due to this authority, I disavow
any design of sheltering myself or any thing I have done, behind it.   It
is the duty of the general assembly to judge for themselves, and for the
people to whom they are accountable.   To their judgment I submit.
Another advantage of this feature in the system is this; that however
imperfect it may be at present, the law for giving effect to the code
contains enactments for its amendment and progression towards that
improvement, which all your penal laws, by this arrangement, must
gradually acquire.

The other articles of this chapter need no comment.

We come now to the Code itself.   The first chapter of the first book
contains General Provisions.   Most of them are in exact conformity
with what is generally supposed to be the present laws, but so expressed
as to leave no room for doubt or cavil; some of them, however, deserve
particular notice.   The evil already pointed out, attending the passage
of successive penal laws on the same subject, without repealing the first,
is one so likely to recur, that some general rules were thought necessary
to regulate the effect of such legislation.   Reasoning from what ought
to be, rather than from what is, it might be supposed that when a new
penalty was created without repealing a former law that had, also, imposed one, the legislature intended to preserve both, and such has hitherto been the construction; but, in fact, it is the very reverse; the new
penalty is, nine times in ten, intended as a substitute, and the old law
is suffered to stand merely through haste or negligence.   An article
provides for this, and declares that in such case, unless the contrary is
expressed, the former penalty shall be abrogated.

A more important disposition is that which declares that there shall
be but one mode of construing penal laws, according to the plain import
of the words they employ, and expressly abolishes what are called favourable and strict constructions; in other words, permitting the court
sometimes to say that the law means more, sometimes less, than the
legislature intended.   Common sense acknowledges but the one mode,
when the language is clear and explicit.   When the law is ambiguous,
another article provides the remedy.   Such a law, if it purport to impose a penalty, is void; and he who is accused of contravening it, must
be acquitted.   In the fear, however, that such general terms may some-

times be used as may include an act which the legislature could not have intended to forbid, an article has been added since the code was printed, specially providing, that in such cases, the defendant must be acquitted, and the case reported to the legislature; who may then, more explicitly declare their will to govern future cases.   A perusal of the statute against concealed weapons, will exemplify the necessity of this provision.   There, a *knife* is expressly called a weapon, and the "wearing it in the coat, or any place about the wearer, so that it do not appear in full view," makes him liable to a penalty, and subjects him to search ; wearing a penknife in a man's waistcoat pocket, is an offence within the plain meaning of the words of the statute, employed in their usual sense ; and yet, it evidently could not be the intent of the legislature to make this an offence.   Other cases of the like kind may occur, and the law should provide against inaccuracy, as well as grosser faults.

Another article expressly forbids all convictions for constructive offences ; that is, offences that are created by courts, and not by the legislature.  The latter alone are the proper organ for declaring what acts or omissions shall be punished, and the text forbids the judiciary, for reasons which it assigns, from interfering in their functions.  Whether our courts have extended any offences, by construction, is not known, nor can it be until some means are taken to report and publish their decisions in criminal cases ; but it is certain that they adopt the constructive larcenies and forgeries of the English law(a), and there is every reason to suppose that the same causes will produce the same effects.   Those which we have seen in another country, where the state of society and manners are similar to our own, we may expect here.  It will not be denied, that England has suffered the most cruel evils by this exercise of judicial power.   The restriction, then, in the text was necessary.  We may, hereafter, have a judge who may exercise his constructive ingenuity upon murders or burglary, or other offences, as Jefferies did upon treasons.  Wise laws must look beyond the present day ; and it is their office to foresee and counteract the effects of propensities which tend to disturb or corrupt the order of society.

The second chapter of this book contains provisions which, relating solely to prosecutions and trials, are enlarged on in the text of the code of procedure, and will be elucidated in the introductory report to that code.   One only of these will be mentioned here, that relating to the trial by jury, and this only for the purpose of referring to what has been said on that subject in the first report, to which I need add nothing, and from which all my subsequent reflections have suggested nothing to retrench.

The third chapter contains the general provisions which relate to persons amenable to the penal laws.   Most of them have no novelty to call for any explanation—some, however, do.   Citizens and inhabitants of the state may be punished, as well for acts done out of the state as

---

(a) If one lends a horse to another, who rides away with him, Blackstone declares it is no larceny in 1779 ; and in 1786, by a construction never before heard of, it was declared to be a larceny.  Forgery was originally confined to making the deed of another.  It has been since extended to a very different offence, making a deed in the true name, the offender representing himself to be another person.

for them within ; but in the former case, only when it is so expressly
declared. The state has an undoubted right to forbid and punish any
acts done out of its jurisdiction, which are calculated to produce an injury to its government or the rights of its citizens. On this principle
the government of the United States made it penal(a) for any citizen
of the United States, although residing abroad, to carry on any correspondence with a foreign government, for the purpose of influencing its
measures with respect to the United States; and also under a high penalty, forbids any citizen, without its limits, from fitting out any vessel
to cruise on a power with whom(b) they are at peace. The general
assembly will find this principle acted upon in that part of the code
which relates to fraudulent insurances.

Children below nine years of age, cannot, as formerly, be convicted
of any crime; nor between that and fifteen, unless on proof of sufficient
understanding to know the nature of an offence. The crimes of children
of that age are those of their parents or adult associates ; and whatever
may be the apparent depravity of an infant below that age, the true
correction is education and restraint. These are fully provided for by
the Code of Prison Discipline ; and the subject of juvenile criminality
is so fully discussed in the Introductory Report to that code, that it is
omitted here.

Offences committed by married women, under the influence or by
the command of their husbands, and by minors under the like control
of any one to whom he owes obedience, or by whom he may be supposed to be influenced, present strong cases of extenuation on the one
part, and aggravation on the other, which, in this chapter, are provided
for by a correspondent increase and diminution of punishment : this is
new, but its justice must be so apparent as to need no comment.

There is some analogy between these cases and that of a soldier.
Taught by the severest discipline to obey, without examination, the
commands of superiors, it appeared to me that while such command
ought not to exempt him from punishment for the commission of a
crime, that there would be some cruelty and injustice in making him
liable for acts committed by such command, which are only misdemeanors. In these cases, officers giving or transmitting such illegal
orders, are alone made liable. It is no objection to this, that the officer may escape by leaving the state ; so may the man ; so may any
delinquent.

The circumstances are pointed out in this chapter, and are again enlarged on in another part of the code, which shall be a justification for
executing the order of a magistrate, and for doing unlawful acts under
duress. The want of precise, intelligible and accessible rules on both
these subjects, has led to much litigation and many prosecutions. It
is hoped that those laid down in this chapter, are sufficiently explicit
to avoid many of these evils.

On the propriety of the seventeenth article of this chapter, relative
to acts done by mistake or accident, which would have been offences
had they been intended, there may be some doubts. There is none
that it is in apparent contradiction to the other general provision, that

(a) Act for punishing certain crimes therein specified, 30th January 1799.
(b) Act of 20th April 1818, sect 4.

the will must concur with the act in order to constitute an offence. Here there was both an illegal act and the will to do one, but they did not concur. The will was to do one illegal act; the execution was that of another; therefore, the contradiction still remains. It is supposed, however, to be justified on two grounds; one, that the want of ordinary care and attention supplies the place of malice or design; the other, that there seems to be a propriety in distinguishing between negligent acts, occasioned by a design to do mischief, although not that really done, and the same negligent act done without any intent whatever to injure. It will be observed that article provides, that these provisions do not govern the case of homicide, for which particular rules in this respect are provided under the proper head ; and that there are other limitations reducing the penalty when the intent was to commit a misdemeanor only. Yet, with all this, I am bound to say, that although I think these articles can practically produce no injustice, yet I wish I could have put them in such a shape as to avoid an apparent conflict with principle. They soften, however, the rigour of the present law, which punishes all homicide as murder, although there was no intent to kill or even to injure, if it is done in the attempt to commit a felony.

The attempt to commit an offence, which fails from some circumstance not dependent on the will of the offender, is also made punishable, because every attempt, although it fail of success, must create alarm, which, of itself, is an injury, and the moral guilt of the offender is the same as if he had succeeded. Moral guilt must be united to injury in order to justify punishment ; but as the injury is not, in the case before us, as great as if the act had been consummated, only half the punishment is awarded.

The fith chapter relates to a repetition of offences, and the increased punishment which it directs to be inflicted on those who are not deterred by one punishment from the commission of other crimes, seems so necessary and reasonable, that it may pass without observation.

The sixth requires more consideration. It contains general rules respecting principals, accomplices, and accessaries, making some material changes ; to the introduction of which, however, I have heard of no objection. Its first operation is by defining distinctly who shall be principals and accomplices, to avoid the continual repetition considered to be necessary now in all our penal statues, such as this in the laws against forgery—" Whoever shall forge or counterfeit, *or cause or procure to be forged or counterfeited, or shall willingly aid or assist in the forging or counterfeiting,*" &c. One general provision, applicable to all cases, will render, in future, the use of all these words unnecessary. The persons described by them are principal offenders or accomplices ; they both incur the same punishment, because the guilt is the same, and they cause the same injury ; but the offences are distinguished, and it is thought that the line between them is so accurately marked that no mistake of consequence can occur. They are distinguished, because, although the guilt, the injury and the punishment is the same, yet the act is different, and it is of great consequence, in penal law, not to confound in one denomination acts of a different nature. To counsel the commission of a crime, is certainly a very different act, requiring different evidence from that of actually committing it.

.

The law and the denomination is also somewhat altered, and it seems to me not without necessity. Our law, as it now stands, has two species of accessaries; one "before the fact," the other "after the fact;" but having so-little resemblance either in their definition, in their guilt, or in any other circumstance, that it was deemed expedient to dissolve the connexion, and place accessaries before the fact in the class of accomplices, a denomination which implies closer connexion with the guilt of the principal offender than the accessary, who, as the name implies, can only become criminal *after* the offence has been counselled by the accomplice and executed by the principal. This last offence consists in aiding the offender to escape from justice, a fault that may have many palliating circumstances, originating in the best feelings of our nature. That of the accomplice can have none. Therefore, the punishment is very different; and as those feelings are strongest in certain close connexions, formed as well by society as nature, and which should not be broken without evident necessity by the laws, it is further provided, that certain near connexions, who may follow up this impulse of nature by aiding another in his endeavours to avoid the pain or disgrace of punishment, should not incur this penalty.

In affixing punishments, we should compare the evil of the offence with that necessarily caused by the punishment, and decide as the balance shall incline. In this case the evil of the offence is now and then the escape of an offender; a rare event, and not of much moment, because, by his escape from the punishment ordained by the laws, he inflicts on himself that of banishment, which answers two good ends: it deters almost as effectually as the regular punishment; it rids you of the offender, and prevents a repetition of his offence; and it fails only in the chance of reformation, which a good system might promise; but which, under your present laws, could not be hoped for. If the punishment is incurred, its evil is the conflict between human laws, and in cases of near ties of blood, those which God has implanted in our hearts, in which the former will never prevail, but will be despised for their inefficacy, or abhorred if they are carried into execution. The same observation that was made to show the propriety and convenience of establishing a general rule applying to accomplices in all offences, applies also to accessaries. By the present laws, as has been already observed, accessaries after the fact, in burglary, are subject to a much heavier penalty than those in murder; and owing to the application of the term to two distinct offences, it is doubtful whether a different and greater punishment is not also designated in cases of larceny; for the term used in the law, which directs whipping as the punishment for accessaries in that offence, does not distinguish whether those before, or after the fact are intended.

The whole of this first book, of which I have just finished the very hasty review, is new. In no other code, that I have seen, has the legislator entered into a full and frank explanation with the people; told them what he intended to do, and for what reason; marked out the limits of the right course, and bade them observe whether he exceeded them. In no other has he treated them, in short, like reasonable beings, and told them to reflect as well as obey. The whole of this book was presented with the first report, published by your predecessors, with the stamp of their unanimous approbation, and has been received, both in Europe and the United States, with the most favourable judgment of the profession.

The subject of the second book of this code is offences and punishments, and its first title treats of their general nature and divisions. Its purpose is chiefly that of order and arrangement; an object of more consequence than the confused legislation that has generally prevailed would lead us to suppose. Irregularity is not only an evil in itself, by the loss of time and the errors which it necessarily occasions, but it leads to greater evils; to an ignorance of the laws, because if any difficulty is created in finding them, it is not very frequently overcome. The slightest obstacle is sufficient to make us give up the search for that which does not, and which we flatter ourselves will not, inmmediately concern us; and there is no obstacle more discouraging than the want of arrangement. That which is proposed is simple. The great divisions are few, and their subdivisions grow naturally out of them. An offence is first defined to be an act or omission which is forbidden by a positive law, under the sanction of a penalty. The terms of this definition exclude all offences against unwritten law, all offences growing out of a construction of any law, all contravention of any law which has not provided a penalty for its breach. But it is not enough to know, generally, what are offences. They must, from their nature, be different in degree, and affect different objects. These two considerations call for two general divisions. By the first, which marks the degree of offences, they are divided into CRIMES and MISDEMEANORS; the former designating those which may be punished by imprisonment in the Penitentiary, or by a forfeiture of any civil or political right; the latter, all other offences. These terms have been retained rather than adopted. In the English law they have generally an analogous, although somewhat indefinite, signification. "Crime, properly speaking," according to the language of Blackstone(a), "being used to denote such offences as are of a deeper dye; while smaller faults, and omissions of less consequence, are comprised under the gentler name of misdemeanors." While the terms were retained, it was necessary that a precise idea should be affixed to them. Where is the line to be drawn between offences of a deeper dye and those of less consequence? How deep the dye must be to give to an offence the colour of a crime, or how little the consequence which is to sink its importance into a misdemeanor, the learned commentator does not inform us. Perjury is an offence of deeper dye than an assault; yet, according to Christian(b), they are both misdemeanors. Larceny is an offence of less consequence than murder; yet they are both crimes. The code gives a precise rule, drawn from the nature of the punishment; one that produces no violent change in the usual meaning of the words, but gives them that precision which is necessary in every term employed in a law.

The character drawn from the object against which the offence is directed, gives us the second general division into public and private offences. Here it is impossible that the line of demarcation should be very distinct. Offences which chiefly injure society at large, and come

---

(a) Black. Com. 5.                    (b) Note to Blackstone, p. 5.

under the first denomination, can rarely be committed without also affecting private rights ; nor, in general, can any injury be offered to an individual that does not directly, or in a remote degree, affect the well-being of the community. But it ought to be distinctly understood, that this division is entirely for the sake of order and arrangement in framing the code, and that no mistake in arranging a particular offence, under one or the other of these heads, can be productive of the least injury. No act can be prosecuted as a public or private offence ; the terms are unknown in the procedure, they do not affect the form or the substance, and are merely labels affixed to each offence, that they may be arranged in the proper place, and each offence is defined without any relation to its arrangement under one or the other of these denominations. The same observation applies to the different subdivisions ; they give names to the different titles under which the particular offences are found, but no one can any more be indicted for an offence against the sovereign power of the state, calling it by that name only, than he could for a public offence by that designation ; the particular act forbidden by the law, must be designated, because that alone constitutes the offence. To prevent any error, all this is concisely expressed in the text of the code.

The second chapter of this book has the nature and general divisions of punishments for its object. Much of what may be thought necessary comment on this, has been anticipated in the preceding discussion on the infliction of death, and for a still greater portion, we must refer to the introductory report on the Code of Prison Discipline.

Here, it will be proper to remark on the general features of the scale of punishments that are provided for different offences.

There is an evident distinction in the nature of offences, which demands a correspondent one in punishments. Some show an habitual depravity, which requires long discipline to amend; others are the effect of an occasional disregard of the rights of others, which may be corrected by the privation, pain, or disrepute of the punishment, the remembrance of which may prevent repetition, and the example deter from imitation. On this distinction rests the system of punishments. Penitentiary imprisonment being designated for all offences of the first description, and the other penalties for the others. Of these last, simple imprisonment in close custody is one which is the most frequently employed, because it is applicable to offences which, although they do not evince the degree of depravity which characterises those punishable in the penitentiary, yet require not only correction, but restraint. In these cases solitude is administered long enough to give time for reflection, and to operate as a punishment, but is not prolonged, as in penitentiary confinement, to the period which is there necessary to destroy vicious habits and acquire those of honest industry. It is the connecting link between simple imprisonment, in which nothing but a temporary and slight correction is thought necessary, and the strong remedy of solitude and labour.

Liberty being the best enjoyment of a citizen, its privation, in different degrees, was thought the fittest punishment for faults which disturb social order, by which only it can be preserved ; and the good citizen will value the greatest of all blessings the more, when he sees that its enjoyment is inseparably attached to an observance of the laws, and its loss generally the consequence of their breach.

T

But to some, the privation of personal liberty would be a severer punishment than to others, for the same offence, and for some infractions it would be too great for the offence. Recourse in these cases must, therefore, be had to property, the next great source of human happiness; and its curtailment by fines, forms another grade in the scale of penalties. The principles which have been applied to adapt them to different offences have been already explained. It need only be added here, that in some designated cases the necessary discretion of adopting one or the other, or both, of these punishments, simple imprisonment and fine, is vested in the judge, within certain limits. Because, in all those cases there must be a correction for the offence; and the judge only can determine, from the circumstances of the party, whether the forfeiture of property would operate as such correction, or whether a temporary privation of liberty ought not to be substituted or added.

It has been wisely ordered, that liberty and property, although the principal sources of our enjoyment, should lose the greatest part of their value, if not attended with personal consideration, or the good opinion of those with whom we are associated, and the equal enjoyment of all those rights to which they are entitled. This social feeling gives to the legislator another hold upon the citizen in order to force an observance of the laws, by threatening for their breach a privation of those rights, and of the confidence and consideration by which alone they can be obtained. This forms the third and only remaining class of punishments—privation of office, of civil, of political rights, either for a time or perpetually.

This is all the penal machinery that is employed in the code either for punishment, repression, example, reformation, or prevention. The infliction of bodily pain by mutilation or stripes, indelible stigmas, exposure in the pillory, the stocks, or by public labour, are banished from the code for reasons that are conclusive, and which have once been presented to the legislature and received their approbation. All of them are at war with every principle on which this system is founded; and if either is retained, no good result can be expected from the adoption of it. But there is a reason drawn from our state of society so conclusive against the last, that it cannot be resorted to without danger of the most serious kind. There is a line of demarcation, which it would be rash in the extreme to destroy even in punishments; and the sight of a freeman performing the forced labour, or suffering under the stripes usually inflicted on the slave, must give rise to ideas of the most insubordinate nature. A false economy only could suggest the repetition of an experiment which has every where failed, every where produced increase of misery, degradation and crime; and here might be the cause of evils worse than all these combined.

This part of the plan has, in a very flattering notice taken of it in England, been considered as defective, because it does not combine satisfaction to the party injured by the offence, with the punishment inflicted by public justice.

This idea has been a favourite one with many criminalists. It has been embodied in the French, and some other codes, and once found a place in our laws. But, however plausible the reasons for its adoption may appear, neither the principle on which the system was founded, nor the experience of its effects, would permit me to recommend it.

The distinction between penal and civil laws appears to me to be this, that the first, from their very nature, exclude the idea of private compensation, whereas it is the sole object of the other in all cases of injury; if it were not so, public justice would depend on the vindictive or interested passions for its execution, or might be defeated by the apathy of the individual; and if the old system of pecuniary satisfaction for crimes were not renewed by the laws, it would be by stipulations between the parties. This has been so well acknowledged, that, in most laws, it has been made criminal for the injured party to interfere between the society and the offender against its laws; and after a prosecution has begun, it is only in cases of small importance that the system of compromise is allowed to act.

The foundation of all penal law then is, that the society has received an injury by the breach of its rules. All violations of right are not brought within their purview; those which are not, remain to be compensated by the civil law. Over these it has an exclusive jurisdiction; and although offences for breaches of penal law generally are accompanied by, or consist of, a private injury, yet the rights acquired to the society, and to the individual, by this breach, are totally distinct. The last can only seek for compensation; the first for something else, which may be according to circumstances, either less or more. In case of theft, the owner has a right to ask for restoration or compensation. The society has a right to inflict punishment independent of that restoration. So far has this been carried by the common law, that by one of its extraordinary fictions the private right is *merged*, as they call it, in the felony, and the individual loses the right to his property, as soon as it can be proved that it was stolen from him; that is to say, when that is proven, which shows conclusively that he has a title to it. This distinction existing then in their very nature between civil and penal law, the question is, whether it is better to combine the two operations, so as by the same suit to give satisfaction and inflict punishment? This is a question of mere convenience; and it is to be answered, better perhaps, by experience than by reasoning. If it is to be effected so as to preclude the party from his civil suit, he must be represented in the prosecution. This, in theory, would disturb the order of proceeding, and by confounding the two jurisdictions, cause confusion in our ideas of the nature of public justice, when we saw it so much identified with private interest. It must necessarily produce some irregularity. The wish or the interest of the public prosecutor might be, to bring on the trial when the private party was not ready to show the extent of his loss, and there would be either delay or injustice. It would lessen the dignity of the tribunals of public justice, by making them the arena in which contests were carried on for mere private rights. The attorney for the party in the civil side must necessarily take a part in the conduct of the cause; and the course he thought best, might differ from that preferred by the public prosecutor. This collision must produce disputes, and disputes between those concerned in the administration of justice, ought to be avoided. By not suffering the person injured to be made a party, these inconveniences indeed may be avoided, but then you commit the greater injustice of deciding on his interests without hearing him. These conclusions appear to me to be confirmed by experience on both modes of procedure. In France, the person injured may make himself a party; but as far as a foreigner can judge from the reports of the cases, most of the inconveniences, which might be anticipated, have seemed to follow. And in our state, where the damages were directed to be inquired(a) of by the jury that tried the cause, merely on the prayer of the party, it was found so inconvenient in practice, that the law was soon afterwards repealed.

For these reasons it has been thought most consonant to principle, as well as most convenient in practice, to carry on the prosecution entirely unconnected with the private suit; but, in all cases, to permit the party injured to sue for his damages, and whenever a claim for a fine and those damages come in collision, to give a preference to the private claim.

The discussion of the nature and effects of different punishments has been necessarily irregular. Its anticipation could not be avoided in some degree, when we considered the great characteristic of the code—the abolition of the penalty of death; and a very great part is under an equal necessity postponed, to be treated of in the Introductory Report to the Code of Prison Discipline.

I now proceed to the consideration of the important titles which define the different offences, and assign to each its appropriate punishment.

The first class contains those which affect the sovereign power of the state, and first in that class stands the crime of treason. This is defined by the constitution, and therefore the code could do no more than repeat the definition. But the same offence has the same definition in the constitution of the United States, and in both instruments is described as "levying war" and "adhering to enemies;" but from the nature of the federal union, a levy of war against one member of the union is a levy of war against the whole; therefore it is concluded, that treason against the state, being treason against the United States, it is to be punished under their laws and in their courts.

There are, however, other offences which affect the sovereignty of the state, which do not amount to levying war or adhering to its enemies. The first of these is designated under the name of sedition. It is defined as an attempt by FORCE OF ARMS to dismember the state, or to subvert or change the constitution thereof. This is one of the highest crimes that can be committed; and it must be observed, that here, and elsewhere in this report, the degree of crime is measured by considering as well the moral depravity which it exhibits as the injury it occasions to the community. In this view it stands high in the scale of offences, and the highest punishment (imprisonment for life in the penitentiary) is awarded to it. A milder punishment is designated for him who shall excite others to commit this crime by writing or verbally. The employment of force is a necessary ingredient in the first offence, and expressly exciting others to use force in the second. Neither of these offences are provided for by our present laws.

Next in place, but with scarcely any difference in degree, is the crime of insurrection, which is one of those that have received the attention of our legislature; and, indeed, is one of high consequence in the actual state of our population. It is more precisely defined in the code. It consists, in aiding by a freeman, for this code extends to no others, in any insurrection of slaves against the free inhabitants of the state, or

(a) Act of 1805, section 39.

assisting at an assembly of slaves for the purpose of promoting such insurrection, or exciting them to it. It is punished by the highest penalty of the law—penitentiary imprisonment for life. To prevent any errors, all the material words that admit of different constructions in this, or other descriptions of crimes, are clearly defined. To endeavour to make the slaves discontented with their lot, without actually exciting to insurrection, is also punished by a fine and imprisonment.

Next in order, after offences against the sovereignty of the state, are those which affect its legislative power. The offences arranged under this title are—force directed against either house of the general assembly to dissolve their session, prevent their meeting, or direct their proceeding ; threats of violence to a member to influence his vote, or actual violence in consequence of his official conduct ; bribing or attempting to bribe, any such member, and the receipt of a bribe by him. These are forbidden under appropriate penalties, and with a proper definition of each offence. This class of offences has not yet attracted legislative attention, perhaps, because it was thought that some of them might be sufficiently punished or repressed in the exercise of the authority which is supposed to be inherent in all similar bodies, to punish contempts, without entering into that question which, under our constitution, is not very easily decided ; it may be sufficient to say, that if that power extends beyond the right of removing any immediate obstacle to the proceedings of either house, and of enforcing its constitutional orders, it yet has not the power necessary for the occasion, inasmuch as the warmest partisans for the doctrine of contempts, do not contend, that any punishment the house can inflict, can exceed imprisonment during the session. It seems therefore proper, that an adequate penalty should be provided for the high offences mentioned in this title; and it is moreover consistent with the principles of our government, that every offence should be defined, and that the right of trial by jury, secured by the constitution, should be preserved inviolate. These are effected by the articles of this title, at the same time that whatever privilege is constitutionally vested in either house, remains unimpaired. Giving, offering and accepting a bribe are among the offences enumerated, and the punishment here assigned to it, is a suspension of political rights for five years, or fine equal to four times the amount of the bribe, and penitentiary imprisonment from six to twelve months for the person offering, and forfeiture of political rights, and fine equal to five times the amount of the bribe, for him who accepts it. The difference in the punishment was calculated to suit the probable situation of the several offenders, the tempter being treated more severely by the imprisonment, than him who yields to it ; and the forfeiture of political rights is denounced, in this case, instead of a suspension ; because, he who has once yielded to such a temptation, ought never again to be trusted with political power. Where the value of the bribe offered or accepted cannot be discovered, a standard rule is given in all similar cases for the measure of the fine.

Under the head of offences against the executive power, we have several highly injurious and immoral acts which are not now punishable by any of our statutes. Bribery is confined by the law of 1818, the only act we have on the subject, to bribing or offering to bribe, a " judge or other person concerned in the administration of justice," leaving the accepting a bribe by such judge or person so employed, and the giving, offering, or receiving a bribe by any other totally unprovided for. By this chapter, it is extended to all executive officers, and the following offences, hitherto unnoticed, are added : doing official acts before the oaths and the security required by law are taken and furnished; forcible opposition to official acts; corruptly agreeing to make appointments, or do any other official act in consideration of an *advantage(a)* not allowed by law, and not being an *emolument;* extortion, which is fully defined; receiving an emolument not allowed, or greater than is allowed by law for doing official acts ; committing any act which is an offence under colour of office; negligent performance of official acts, by which injury is received; all these are made offences, and punished by penalties which are supposed to be appropriate and commensurate to them ; and articles are added extending these penalties to deputies, to persons exercising the office, although there may be an informality in their appointments ; and making principals answerable for the acts of the deputy when they are done with his consent. The officers of corporations are also included, as well as those exercising *private offices.* This is an important title, and comprehends several offences, a few only of which will come within the purview of the existing statutes, under the loose description of misdemeanor in office.

First in rank under the head of offences affecting the judiciary power, are those relating to judges and juries, and of them the most important are those which may be committed by these functionaries themselves. The importance of these duties, the dreadful consequences of neglect or corruption in the performance of them, has attached, in all countries, a sanctity to the office of judge, which makes that a crime with him, which would be a venial fault in another. In all ages, therefore, while the public veneration has been readily yielded to the upright magistrate, the unjust judge has been the universal object of detestation and contempt. The highest rewards have not been deemed too great for his merits, nor the most cruel punishments too severe for his faults. Heaven itself must have inspired our British ancestors with the idea of separating the decision of law from that of fact; for nothing could, with so much effect, lessen the danger of corruption. The jury, unapproachable by seduction, because not called into existence in time for it to operate upon them ; the judge, unable for the most part to decide without their intervention. But although this distribution leaves to neither the absolute power over the life or fortune or reputation that is put in the law's jeopardy—yet each of them have sufficient to make it necessary that their integrity should be protected from temptation, and their sense of duty stimulated, by the law. There are some who think, that with respect to the judicial office, it would be degraded by enactments which suppose the possibility of its high functionaries being influenced by such inducements as would bias other men. Confidence, they argue, produces integrity, suspicion provokes to guilt; leave the high characters of your judges to be sustained by their own sense of honour, and do not fetter them by any of the degrading restrictions and penalties, that you devise to bind other officers.

---

(*a*) For the understanding of this article, recourse must be had to the definitions of the words in italics.

These have been the remarks suggested by men whose opinions deserve attention, on the chapter now under consideration ; and they were repeated so earnestly, that I yielded more, I think, to respect than to conviction, and agreed to suppress the third article of this section, which prohibits a judge from receiving gifts of any assignable value, unless by will, or from a near relation. The reasons urged against it have been stated. Those which induced me, at first, to introduce the clause shall be given, that the general assembly may judge of the propriety of reinstating the article which they will find in the first printed copies.

I acknowledge the force of the maxim, that confidence in generous minds begets a disposition to merit it ; but I deny the propriety of its general application. The penalties of law are founded on a supposition, that without them, its precepts would not be fulfilled. Could we count on that generous disposition which the objection supposes, there would be no need of any sanction to our laws. The legislator need only point out his will and express his confidence in the integrity of those to whom it was directed, and the work of legislation would be done. But the argument is not pressed so far ; it is acknowledged that penalties are necessary to insure obedience in ordinary cases ; but it is said, that judges form an honourable exception ; restrain all the rest of the world by the fear of punishment—trust to the integrity of the judge for the performance of his duty. What, will you impose no restraint, no impeachment for corruption, no indictment for bribery ? Yes, these we will allow—but he must not be restrained from accepting presents as the testimonials of friendship, which are no more than common courtesies of life. Now, if you can think it necessary to guard against the gross corruption of direct bribery, why will you permit a practice which is the most common mode of effecting it ? Not to speak of their being made the vehicle for the more glaring crimes, their favourable effect on the mind of man, is evident to any one who has the slightest knowledge of the world. Received as tokens of kindness at first, their slight value excites no suspicion; they are multiplied ; their value is increased, and the obligation goes on augmenting until it can only be discharged by a favourable decree. But the practice ought to be forbidden, if it should have no other effect than that of exciting suspicion. If the judge has been in the habit of receiving presents of game or liquors from a suitor who gains his cause, the loser will not fail to attribute it to the flavour of the venison or the exquisite taste of the wine. Nor is the inhibition either new, or considered as derogatory to officers of the highest trust. It is a constitutional provision that no one, holding an office of trust or profit under the United States, shall accept *any presents* from a foreign power. If this does not degrade the ambassador, why should a similar one degrade the judge ? Besides, be consistent. You have two sets of judges. If those who determine the fact, when they are exhausted with hunger and fatigue, receive the slightest refreshment from one of the parties, you dishonour them by setting aside their verdict, as being corruptly procured, and often punish them for misconduct ; and yet you think it degrading to the other class of judges, to prevent them receiving gifts of much greater value.

The other acts that are made punishable by this section are described with pecision, so as neither to subject the officer to vexatious prosecutions, nor to suffer any judicial oppression or malfeasance to escape the animadversion of the law. This was the more necessary, because, by our statutes, although it is a crime to offer or give a bribe to a judge, there is no penalty denounced against him for accepting it(*a*), unless it be under the vague denomination of misdemeanor(*b*); to understand which, we have not even the resource of a reference to the English law, for the statute which creates the offence was passed since the year 1805, and contains no reference to that law ; and if we had, the matter would not much be mended, as we have seen in former parts of this report(*c*). When a word is used in legislation, that is neither technical nor explained in the law, it must of course be understood according to the signification it has in common parlance ;. but there can be no technical meaning affixed to this word, because there is no body of laws to which we are or can be referred for its explanation. We have no common law, and the statute refers to none, therefore, it must have the same meaning here that it would in common conversation. What is that ? Both etymology and usage give the answer ; any misconduct whatever. A misdemeanor in office, then, is any demeanor that is contrary to official duty. Our present law, therefore, is infinitely more strict than that which is offered as a substitute ; without defining any particular misconduct, by a sweeping clause it makes the minutest inattention punishable by fine, imprisonment, loss of office, and incapacity ever to hold one. A rude or has-. ty word to an advocate, a suitor, or a witness, is misconduct, and so is corruption—both come within the meaning which etymology gives to misdemeanor. Should a judge do that for which he would fine a juror, come too late into court—should he yawn or doze on his bench during the sixth hour of a dull speech, the affronted orator would tax him with misconduct, and he might be vexed, although a jury probably might excuse him for indulging so natural a propensity ; more especially if the speaker were one of those, like Virgil's priest—

" Spargere qui somnos, manu, cantuque, solebat."

Instead, then, of taxing the provisions of this chapter with improper hostility to the judicial character, and with imposing too great restraint upon the exercise of its functions, it ought to be considered, as it truly is, a relief from the danger of an ambiguous law, that creates a penalty which might, without departing from the words of the statute, be made by malice or ignorance to affect the fortune, liberty and reputation of a respectable magistrate, for a trifling misdemeanor. In this section of the code, on the contrary, every thing is defined—nothing made punishable but what is injurious, and the penalties are suited to the offence. In the first copy there was a material omission, by which a judge was inhibited from advising a suit, or giving counsel relative to its management, without making the necessary exception of cases of near relations, or any other in which he could not sit as a judge. This error is corrected.

By this section the necessary penalties are imposed on such misconduct of jurors as by our present law is either not punishable at all, or is

(*a*) Act of 19th March, 1818, sect. 5.          (*b*) Act of 7th June, 1806, sect. 5.
(*c*) Ante, p. 85.

so in a way that precludes the person accused from the benefit of a trial by jury, and the other advantages given by law in other prosecutions.

As, by the section thus reviewed, judges and jurors are restrained by penalties from acts contrary to their duty, so in the next they are protected from all attempts, by bribery, violence or improper persuasion, to seduce or force them from its performance ; and an article gives a precise rule on a subject left very much at discretion by our present practice. I mean the publication of proceedings in court during the pendency of a trial. It is believed, that the provision will secure the dignity of the court, the rights of the parties, and the liberty of the press.

The second chapter of this title is intended to prevent the bribery of ministerial officers of justice, and forcible opposition to them in the execution of their duties. The laws which embrace those offences, did not seem to be sufficiently descriptive of the acts which they forbid, and are totally silent as to a number of circumstances which ought to be explained. What are official acts; what forms the judicial orders must be clothed with to make opposition to them an offence ; in what cases and to what degree opposition is lawful ; what degree of opposition incurs the penalty ; what ought to be the conduct of the officer in the performance of his duty, so as to entitle him to the protection of the law, or to make him forfeit it ; are deficiencies in the present law, which are supplied by that which is offered.

Connected with this is the chapter on Rescue, to which nearly the same observations apply, with this additional reason for the amendment of the present law—that although it punishes the rescue of a person committed for, or convicted·of, any other than a capital offence, yet a rescue for this last offence is only made punishable where the person rescued is indicted or convicted; but leaves the case of his rescue after commitment, but before he is indicted, wholly unprovided for(a). This error is corrected, and other provisions added, to make the law explicit and equal in its operation. In order to effect this latter object, the punishment, with some modifications to adapt it to particular cases, is one-half of that to which the party rescued would have been liable had he been convicted of the offence for which he was in custody, and a certain fine and imprisonment if he were confined on a civil suit.

Escape and breach of prison, are offences analogous to that of rescue. Adopting the principle of the English law, this offence, if committed without violence, is punished by a light fine and imprisonment. By our present law it is not provided against at all. If committed with violence, it incurs the punishment, and comes under the description of a forcible opposition to the officers of justice. If the escape is aided, or voluntarily permitted, by the person having charge of the accused, he incurs one half the punishment which might have been inflicted for the offence with which the accused was charged. The English law makes the punishment of the officer depend, in a great measure, on the conviction of the person escaping; for if such conviction take place, he suffers the same punishment with the delinquent; if he be acquitted or not taken, the keeper only suffers fine and imprisonment as for a misdemeanor. This rule, it was thought, would, in many cases, defeat the ends of justice. The risk of fine and imprisonment was not thought

(a) Act 4th May 1805, section 26, as given in Martin's Digest, 2d vol. 240.

U

sufficient counterpoise to the bribes that might be offered by wealthy delinquents. The punishment assigned to this offence by the code, bears a proportion to the crime for which the person escaping was committed, because the injury to the community is greater in proportion to the magnitude of crime, and the temptation offered always increases in the same proportion, and it is incurred whether the party originally accused be acquitted or be never retaken ; neither of which circumstances can lessen the guilt of the keeper. And allowing either to operate in his favour, would evidently make it his interest that justice should be avoided, either by effectual flight, or by the suppression of testimony necessary for conviction. If the escape be voluntary, the punishment is one half of that incurred by the crime charged on the prisoner; if negligent only, it is one quarter.

It is somewhat singular that an offence of this importance, so deeply affecting the administration of justice, should not be provided against by our laws, otherwise than under the loose head of misdemeanor in office, which can only apply to civil officers ; but if the crime be committed by a sentinel set to guard the prisoner, or by a person having no office at all, it is unprovided against.

To break or attempt to break prison by the prisoner, legally imprisoned, when accompanied by violence, incurs the punishment of from six months in close custody to two years. Breach of prison for the purpose of rescuing another, is punishable by penitentiary imprisonment from two to five years ; and this does not depend on the legality of the imprisonment, as it does in the case of the prisoner himself. A lesser punishment is denounced against furnishing a prisoner with the means of making his escape, whether it be effected or not.

The seventh chapter of this title adapts, to the officers of justice, all offences described in the chapters relating to offences committed by executive officers.

The important duties attached to the profession of the law, have, in all nations where the law was a science, given its members the greatest influence, and sometimes made them obnoxious to the most unworthy suspicions. Deemed worthy to be trusted with the defence of the property, reputation, liberty and life of others; they were yet subjected to have their own reputation blasted, their only means of subsistence forfeited, and, if not their lives, all that makes life desirable taken from them, for offences of all others the worst defined, by a summary process, in which the party injured was the prosecutor and the judge, and his sentence was without appeal. There was, indeed, a corrective in the publicity of judicial proceedings, and the consequent force of public opinion, which prevented any great abuse of this dreadful power ; but this was too uncertain a tenure by which to hold reputation or property. Public opinion, in its sound state, might protect, but when disordered by the madness of party or prejudice, would but stimulate oppression. Such a state of things was so little in unison with the spirit of our institutions, and indeed with the letter of our constitution, that it at length attracted legislative attention ; and the members of an honourable profession were, by a law passed in the year 1823, placed on a footing with other citizens. The benefit of a trial by jury was in all cases, except that of contempts in open court, extended to them; and some definition was given to certain offences which they were supposed to be most liable to commit. This law I have made the basis of the articles of the ninth chapter of the title we have now under review, but the list of offences is extended ; they are more accurately defined ; and while the object has been to protect the honourable members of the profession, a proper increase of punishment has been denounced against those who may disgrace it by their cupidity or chicane.

A short chapter embraces the case of those who may falsely personate an officer of justice, or a suitor, or bail, or any other person. This was provided for by our statute, and also the case of a false personification for putting in bail or confessing a judgment.

Perjury is one of the offences which not only affects the administration of justice, but all the other operations of government in its various departments. By the English law this crime could only be committed by false swearing in some judicial proceeding. Our statute of 1805 wisely extends it to all cases in which depositions or affidavits are taken pursuant to the laws of the territory. Doubts might arise, under this statute, whether affidavits or depositions, taken under laws made subsequent to that statute, were included in it, and also, whether the affidavits and depositions intended were not exclusively such as were taken as evidence in a judicial proceeding. The code, by covering a broader ground, puts an end to those doubts. It defines the crime to be " a falsehood asserted verbally or in writing, deliberately and wilfully, relating to something present or past, under the sanction of an oath, or such other affirmation as is or may be by law made equivalent to an oath, legally administered under circumstances in which an oath or affirmation is required by law, or is necessary for the prosecution or defence of private right, or for the ends of public justice." This definition includes all testimony and judicial oaths whatsoever, whether oral or written ; and it further extends the provisions of our statute so as clearly to embrace all other oaths, which are required by law to attest the truth of any fact, such as declarations under the quarantine laws and the like. In all of which cases the moral evil and the injury to the community may be as great as if the perjury were committed in a court of justice ; yet a deliberate falsehood, asserted under oath, according to our present laws, would not be punishable at all, except it were connected with a judicial proceeding ; unless special provision to that effect should be made in the law requiring the oath, which is frequently neglected where it is necessary, and for want of a general provision, such as the code contains, unnecessarily increases the length of our laws where it is not neglected. The definition excludes the breach of promissory oaths, such as oaths of office, from the guilt of perjury ; because, there the offence is not one that exists in taking the oath, which may be done with the sincerest intentions of keeping it ; but in some act done subsequently, which may be inconsistent with it. If that act be sufficiently injurious to call for the animadversion of the law, it will be found to have been provided against, under its proper head ; if it be not, it is contrary to the principle of this code to punish it, however unconscientious it may be. For we cannot too often repeat, that the endeavour has been to place no acts in the rank of offences, but such as were injurious, and were done either with a design to injure, or with an inattention to the rights of others, that is nearly as reprehensible.

This chapter punishes, under the appellation of false swearing, all deliberate falsehoods, asserted in voluntary affidavits, not taken in the course of judicial proceeding, nor required by law, but yet made the engines of detraction and other mischiefs; for which it is deplored by writers on English law, that it affords no remedy. The punishment of this last offence is, of course, lighter than the former; but the prevalence of the evil seemed to require, that it should be repressed by a penalty, and the nature of the crime suggested the further provision, that a conviction for this offence might be given in evidence against the credit of the party in any case in which he might be sworn as a witness.

On this head of perjury, too close an adherence to the English law led me to insert an article, which further reflection has induced me to wish may be erased. It is the second of the chapter, which provides for a case that will probably never happen, and can cause no injury if it should, the case of a witness swearing to a fact that is true, although at the time he believes it to be false.

The suborner to perjury is made liable to the same punishment with the principal offender. In this the code agrees with the present law; and it adopts the same measure with respect to false swearing. It also adds a lighter penalty on him who makes an ineffectual attempt to procure the commission of either of these offences.

The provisions of the eleventh chapter have excited much attention, and given rise to some severe strictures; on the work, as tending to deprive courts of justice of their only means of self-defence; on the reporter as being actuated by a spirit of hostility to the judiciary. The general assembly, I know, will listen without prejudice to my argument on the first charge, and I hope will excuse me if I add a word or two on the second.

The power of punishing for contempts, in the extent to which it has been carried, it is believed has never been justified by the plea of necessity. Its repugnance to all the fundamental principles which secure private rights in the administration of justice, is so apparent, that no other argument can possibly be used. The offence is the showing a contempt for the court. Of all the words in the language, this is, perhaps, the most indefinite. Every thing that can, by any process of reasoning, be considered as a disrespect to the court, is a contempt. Blackstone enumerates seven different species of consequential, as contradistinguished from direct contempts; each of them comprehending a countless number of different acts as distinct from each other in their nature, as all of them are from contempt, according to its strict definition. For instance, the second division of consequential contempts, comprehends those committed by sheriffs, bailiffs, and other officers of the court, by deceiving the parties—by acts of oppression—by culpable neglect of duty, &c. In short, there is nothing, from an indecorous gesture, or a rude hasty word, up to the most violent opposition to legal authority, that cannot be brought within the purview of the law of contempts. Printing a false account of the proceedings of a court, or a true account while the suit is pending, without permission, as well as speaking or writing contemptuously of the court; treating a piece of paper, under its seal, with disrespect; and, to sum up all in the words of the apologist of the law of England, any thing that shows a gross want of regard and respect.

Now I put it to those who contend that this power ought to be vested in courts, I put it to them to say, what is the conduct that will secure a man against its exercise in the hands of a vain or vindictive judge? "A want of regard and respect!" Regard and respect cannot be commanded but by moral conduct, and not always by that. The most correct conduct will not always secure it; the feeling is involuntary, and cannot be punished. But you must not show that you want it; it is the demonstration that is culpable. But how shall I avoid showing it? When in my own defence, or in the prosecution of my right, I differ from the judge, and show that the opinion he has given is absurd, certainly I treat him with very little regard or respect. I can feel none for a man who, by some miserable sophistry, deprives me of my right; and if I expose it to the world, I show my want of respect; but a want of respect is a contempt: I am, therefore, liable to be punished for defending my right in the only way that justice requires it should be defended. Oh! say the advocates of this tyrannical power, you must distinguish; attack the argument of the judge as much as you please, but say nothing disrespectful of the court. But what jesuit will teach me how I may tell a court, that it has decided against the plainest principles of law, without showing that I think they have been ignorant, careless, prejudiced, or worse? When I know, that by reason of either of these faults they are about to deprive me of my fortune or my life, can I feel regard or respect? When I state the reasons by which I demonstrate it, do I not—clothe it in what language I will—do I not make that want of regard manifest? And is not this, according to the very terms used by the author I have quoted, a contempt? It is amusing to observe the expedients which have been resorted to, to reconcile things that are irreconcilable; great respect for the judge and contempt for his opinion; professions of the highest veneration and regard, coupled with allegations that show the speaker can feel neither; introducing, among other evils, a fawning, hypocritical cant, equally unworthy of the suitors and the judges.

An offence so ill defined, so liable to be imputed, embracing such a variety of dissimilar acts, would be dangerous and oppressive in the extreme, were it to be prosecuted according to the ordinary forms of law; but all these are disregarded; none of them are preserved, and the plainest letter of the constitution is violated in its most sacred provisions. It declares, that "in all criminal prosecutions the accused shall have the right of meeting the witnesses face to face, nor shall he be compelled to give evidence against himself." Yet process of attachment for contempt issues on an affidavit, and when the defendant is brought in, it is not to meet his accuser face to face, but in direct defiance of the constitution to "*give evidence against himself*" if he be guilty, under the penalty of being punished for a "high(a) and repeat-

(a) 4 Bl. 287. The mode of proceeding by attachment and interrogatories is adopted in our courts—1 Martin, Territory v. Thurry—Same v. Nugent. In 10 Mart. 123, De Armas's case, the court punished for an indecorous expression by suspension for a year; and this case expressly supports the argument I have used in the first part of this report, that the Spanish penal laws are unrepealed, unless they are inconsistent with some statute of the state. In this case several points are decided. First, that the law of Spain giving authority to the court, when a lawyer is "*arrogant....*;or is of ill fame, or is *tedious*, contradictory,

ed contempt." The punishment by our statutes is limited to fine of fifty dollars and ten days' imprisonment; but from the case cited in the note, it appears that the Spanish laws are still in force, unless there is an express repeal or incongruity between them and our statutes. With respect to counsellors and attorneys there is such express repeal, but in no other cases(*a*). Now in the variety of offences created by the Spanish statutes, many relate to the courts and judges, and to their officers and process; all these by the sweeping definition of contempts, may be properly considered as such; and as the Spanish law has been decided not to be repealed by our law of contempts, the aggravated punishment may, in those cases, be inflicted as it was in the one referred to in the note. But without this, if the punishment is confined to that directed by our statute—is that nothing? Is it nothing to be deprived of liberty for ten days, without conviction—without jury? Is it nothing to be forced to give evidence against yourself? The magnitude of the punishment is comparatively of little moment. It is the principle that is dangerous. A free citizen ought never to hold his liberty, even for an hour, or the slightest portion of his property, at the will of any magistrate. But those I have noticed are not the worst features of this species of punishment. Vague and uncertain as is the definition of the offence, yet if impartial persons were appointed to decide, whether any given word, look, or gesture, was contemptuous, there would be some security (a slight one I grant) against oppression; but as if it were to make this example one in which every principle of correct procedure was to be violated, the person offended is constituted the only judge—the judge with appeal; and lest his resentment should have time to cool, he is armed with the power of summary process—and if we want evidence, he may force

or *speaks too much*, or any other like crime," is in force, for it is expressly relied* on as justifying the court for suspending the defendant from practice. Secondly, it is decided that this law is a *penal law.* Judge Martin says, "the Spanish law, which thus forbids the judge to suffer any contempt of his authority, is a *penal one*, for it cannot be carried into effect without inflicting some penalty." Thirdly, the full ground I have supposed the doctrine of contempt to occupy, is relied upon as law, for the same judge adds, "and a lawyer guilty towards the court of any contemptuous *action, expression,* or *gesture*," may be instantly punished, by suspension *at least.* Fourthly, the important point I argued for, that the laws of Spain are not repealed, unless there is a perfect incongruity, or an absolute repeal, is declared to be law, supported by at least a dozen authorities. Nay, this case goes further than I thought it necessary to go, and preserves the Spanish law, even where the legislature have made a statute on the same subject; for the defendant was punished for a contempt by suspension for a year, although the legislature had declared that contempts should be punished by fine and imprisonment, because, says the same judge†, "there are no negative words, and the substance of the new act may well stand with that of the Partidas: the two provisions are not contradictory, and may fairly exist together." And he strengthens this reasoning by the authority of the superior court, 1 Mart. 129. Judge Matthew's opinion coincided with that of the other judge‡; and he states the rules of repeal in so clear and methodical a manner, that if the book containing this report had then been within my reach, I should have adopted his reasoning instead of my own when I treated of this part of the subject; but although I recollected the case, I did not choose to quote it from memory.

(*a*) Act 27th March 1823.

* 10 Martin's Rep. 164.          † Ibid. 169.          ‡ Ib. 172.

the defendant to produce it. Let it not be said, as it sometimes is, that this is an advantage; that the defendant may, by his answers to the interrogatories, exonerate himself. Not so. In the case of contemptuous words (and I see no reason why it should not extend to acts also), if he admit the speaking or the writing, the court have the right to judge of the intent as manifested by the words ; and although the party should deny any disrespectful intent in the most unequivocal terms, the court may declare that the answer is false, and proceed to impose the punishment(*a*) ; and this power is given, too, in the very cases where it ought to be withheld. If it were confined to cases of actual injury, not only would the offence be more susceptible of proof— not only would there be a corrective in public opinion, which could be fixed upon the question, whether the injurious act had been committed or not ; but the passions even of the party injured, if he were constituted the judge, would be less liable to be roused. It is a trite, and therefore, probably, a true observation, that men forgive injuries much sooner than insults. Judges (although by vesting them with this power we treat them as angels) are men ; their passions will be more readily roused by real or fancied insults than they would be by injuries, and nothing can be more at war with justice than passion. Another evil—there is no end to them—is, that from the nature of the crime, its existence must depend on the temper of the judge who happens to preside. Words which a man of a cool and considerate disposition would pass over without notice, might trouble the serenity of another more susceptible in his feeling or irritable by his nature. There is no measure for the offence, but the ever variable one of the human mind. The judge carries the standard in his own breast ; and if, by close observation, you have discovered its probable dimensions, your work is but begun, for every succeeding magistrate has his own scale for the weight of an offence, his own measure for the extent of the punishment.

I do but waste the time of the honourable body I address, in showing the dangerous nature of this undefined power ; for its apologists cannot hide its hideous features. Blackstone acknowledges that it " is not agreeable to the genius of the common law in any other instance ;" but he does not attempt to justify it even from necessity, and contents himself with showing that it is of "high antiquity, and by immemorial usage has become the law of the land ;" that is to say, that it is common law, and as that is the perfection of human reason, that it must be good. But here, where we are not satisfied in general with this reasoning, as summary as the process it is used to defend—here, and on this occasion, when we are inquiring, not what is, but what ought to be law—here some other argument must be used to show that we ought to adopt or continue this oppressive absurdity : and that argument is found in a single word—necessity. In the present improved state of human intellect, people do not so readily submit to the force of this word as they formerly did. They inquire—they investigate, and in more instances than one, the result has been, that attributes

(*a*) 1 Mart., Nugent's case. It is true, the words used there, could not be reconciled to the declaration that no disrespect was intended ; but if this case was correctly decided (and there is no reason to doubt it), the court have the right, in all cases, to judge between the answer to the interrogatories and the words used.

before deemed necessary for the exercise of legal power, were found to be only engines for its abuse. Not one of the oppressive prerogatives of which the crown has been successively stripped, in England, but was, in its day, defended on the plea of necessity. Not one of the attempts to destroy them, but was deemed a hazardous innovation. Let us examine whether this power does not partake of the same nature.

A recurrence to the great principle of self-defence, which we have in a former part of this report developed, will serve to show with some certainty, as it is thought, to what extent this power is necessary or proper. Society has, if our reasoning be correct, the right of self-defence. Every department created by that society for its government —every individual composing that society, has the same right, defined to mean the right of defending existence, and the operations necessary to existence. But society, as the superintending power, must have for the purpose of securing these and all other rights belonging to departments and to individuals, the further power to punish. Society alone has this right. Try the law of contempts by this simple rule. Courts of law are the organs of one of the departments of society, and, to avoid confusion, we will select for our example courts of exclusively civil jurisdiction ; such courts have the right to defend their own existence, and to repress every thing that interferes immediately with the exercise of their legal powers. They have this right, as a legitimate part of society, by the principles of natural law ; and if it be curtailed by any constitutional provision, it is a great defect, because self-preservation very frequently requires immediate efforts that would make an application to any other power ineffectual. Every thing, then, that is necessary and proper to defend its existence, and secure the free performance of its functions, can with no greater propriety be denied to a court than there would be in forbidding an individual to defend his life against the attack of an assassin. But neither the court nor the individual have necessarily the right to punish, either after the attempt has been repelled or after it has been carried into execution. That is the duty and the right exclusively vested in the whole society. An individual has the right to defend himself against an attack upon his liberty or life ; but after he has successfully resisted it, he has no right to punish ; yet liberty and life are considered as sufficiently protected by this limited power. Courts of justice have the same right to repel all attempts to interrupt the performance of their functions. They are incorporeal beings, whose existence is only in the performance of their functions—that is their life—that is their liberty. They are, or ought to be, armed with every power necessary to defend them. Noise, interruptions, violence of every kind, must be repressed ; obedience to all lawful orders which are necessary for the performance of their functions, must be enforced. Thus far the law of self-defence goes, but no further. Is the violence over—has the interruption ceased—is the intruder removed—has the order, which was disobeyed, been complied with ?—here the power of the incorporeal being, as well as that of the individual in the analogous case, ceases, and the duty of the sovereign power begins. That alone must punish— that alone can define offences and fix the penalty for committing them. An infringement of the legal rights of a court of justice is an offence, and that government is radically defective which places the power to punish it in the hands of the offended party. Here, then, we find the limit of that necessity, which is so much insisted on, and so little understood. There is a necessity that courts should have the power of removing interruptions to their proceedings, because, unless they can perform their functions, they cannot exist, but there is none that they should have the power to punish those interruptions ; the laws must do that, by the instrumentality of the courts, but in the form prescribed by law.

If the argument has been as clearly expressed as its force is felt, it must be convincing to show—that all those offences, distinguished by the name of contempts, ought to be banished from our penal law, which they disfigure by the grossest departure from principle ; that courts ought to be empowered to remove all obstructions to their proceedings; that all such acts, as well as those tending to interrupt the course of judicial proceeding, to taint its purity, or even to bring it into disrepute, should be punished only by the due course of law ; and that proper punishments, inflicted by the regular operation of law, will deter from these acts much more effectually than the irregular agency of the offended party, who sometimes, from delicacy, will abstain from enforcing the penalty of the law—sometimes, from the indulgence of passion, will exceed it.

It is on these principles that this part of the code has been framed. It vests ample powers of repression in the court. They may remove every interruption to their proceedings ; they may enforce prompt obedience to their orders ; they may, if simple removal is not found sufficient, restrain by imprisonment ; and, after this, a regular trial and punishment follows for the offence. Here is no angry altercation. All is done with the composure necessary to the dignity of justice. The judge is not the accuser ; the accuser is not the judge. All that class of offences, too, which consist in insulting expressions, are provided for. But here again an impartial jury decide, as well on the nature of the words, as on the intent with which they were used. The judge cannot improperly indulge his feelings, or restrain them, to the injury of public justice ; and the offender against laws for preserving the order and dignity of the judiciary, is liable to the same penalties, entitled to the same rights, and judged by the same laws, that apply to other offenders.

This chapter, then, far from derogating from the respect due to the judiciary, is calculated, in all its provisions, to enforce it ; and the insinuation, that its author could be actuated by any hostility to that department, is not only groundless, but absurd. If, indeed, it is hostility to a department of government, to desire that none but its proper powers should be vested in it by law, or still less, should be exercised without law ; if it be hostility to the judiciary to divest them of the odious accumulation of the offices of judge, party, legislator, and accuser, in the same person ; to protect their functions in their exercise, and punish all attempts to interrupt them ; then is this chapter dictated by a spirit of the most determined hostility.

The next class of offences are those which affect the public tranquillity ; and they form the subject of the sixth title. The first chapter comprises two offences of this nature—unlawful assemblies and riots. The first being a preparatory step to the second offence. They are both so clearly defined as not to be easily confounded ; and although both are taken, in their general features, from the English law, there are several modifications introduced, which, it is hoped, will be con-

V

sidered as improvements. If the object of the one or the other offence be in opposition to the collection of taxes, or to a sentence of a court, or for the purpose of effecting a rescue, a definite increase of punishment is ordained, instead of leaving this entirely to the discretion of the court, which would have induced the necessity of an enlargement of that discretion in fixing the original punishment, so as to embrace the two cases. To encourage obedience to the law, it is provided, that if any one, either voluntary or in obedience to the admonition of a magistrate, shall leave an unlawful assembly, without any intent to return, before a riot has been committed, that he shall avoid the punishment due to his assisting in the first offence. An increase of punishment is also directed against those who shall appear *armed* at such unlawful assembly or riot ; and to avoid all equivocation, the term is one of those that are designated as being used in the sense described in the Book of Definitions.

A proceeding, analogous to that of reading the riot act in England, is directed to be had by the magistrate, to disperse an unlawful assembly, or put an end to a riot ; but it is one that, it is thought, is better calculated to strike the attention, while its purport is equally or more intelligible to such an assemblage; and it consists in the display of a flag, accompanied by a short proclamation ; the effect of disobedience to which is pointed out ; and in the correspondent chapter of the Code of Procedure all the forms are given, as well as the mode pointed out for calling out and employing the military, in aid of the civil power, when the first is insufficient to restore order.

An article in this chapter imposes a penalty on those exhibitions of pugilism which disgrace any society in which they are suffered.

Public disturbance is a minor species of this general offence, and it is made punishable by a slighter penalty, and may be repressed by the summary interference of the magistrate.

Articles containing negative provisions prevent any interference with legal meetings.

Offences against the right of suffrage form the important subject of the seventh title. Bribery, violence, undue influence, are endeavoured to be guarded against by enactments, sufficiently explicit to be understood without commentary, and by penalties proportioned and analogous to the several offences.

The eighth title would require much elucidation, if the subject of it had not already been submitted to the legislature, and if its provisions had not received their sanction and produced some strictures ; but being founded in true principles, the more closely it has been examined the more clearly has its utility appeared ; and if a novelty, it is not one of those that can be characterised as dangerous or useless. While we all profess a respect almost amounting to adoration for the liberty of the press, we may be permitted to wonder that it has, as yet, been protected by no penal enactments, while every code abounds with laws to guard against its abuse, and frequently, too, under that pretext, to destroy it. Our state has been more particular than most of the others, in guarding this precious privilege, by its constitution ; but the constitution could, of course, contain no penalty for a breach ; that care was left to the legislature. We cannot too often recur to the very words of our fundamental law on that subject ; full of foresight and wisdom, they are calculated to defeat every attack that might be made by open violence or insidious attempts upon this safeguard of our liberties : "Printing presses shall be free to every person who undertakes to examine the proceedings of the legislature, or any branch of the government, and *no law shall ever be made* to restrain the right thereof"(a). But if such a law should be made ; if a wicked and corrupt legislature should try to repress any discussion of their proceedings by heavy penalties ; and if a subserving judiciary should be found to execute their unconstitutional statutes—where is the remedy ? Should there be none ? Why should disobedience to this constitutional law go unpunished ? Surely the immorality of the act, and most surely its injurious tendency, are sufficiently apparent to call for and to justify repression and punishment. Surely the legislature, which provides a sanction for this wise and highly important law, are performing a sacred duty.

Again—this was a favourite theme with the framers of our constitution. They seem loth to quit it while any thing remains to be said, that could show the high regard they had for this privilege. They add : "The free communication of thoughts and opinions is one of the invaluable rights of man, and every citizen may freely speak, write, and print, on any subject, being responsible for the abuse of that liberty." But if that freedom, thus intended to be secured, is endeavoured to be shackled by threats, by actual violence, by the illegal exercise of judicial power, under pretence of an alleged abuse ? Are not laws, tending to restrain these abuses, worthy of the attention of the legislature when it is forming a system of penal law ? Either the privilege was not worth all the care and attention which has been given to it in the constitution, or it is worth that of the legislature to protect it. Without some law of this kind, the constitutional provision can have no efficient operation. But with the aid of the penal law, it receives the force and effect which its importance merits.

A very superficial attention to one of the articles, has produced an objection that seems to have had some weight, but which is entitled to very little. The article imposes a penalty on any judicial or other officer who, under pretence of any law which contravenes the constitution, in this respect, shall restrain or prevent the exercise of the liberty of discussion secured by the constitution. Now, it is said, if a legislature be found wicked enough to pass such an unconstitutional law, they will also, to secure its execution, repeal that part of your code, and your penalty then goes with it. This objection was anticipated in the first report, and it was answered, that attacks upon the privileges of the people are, for the most part, insidiously made under pretence of public good, and clothed, at least, with a specious regard for constitutional forms ; and that a repeal of this part of the code would take off the mask and put the friends of the people on their guard, and therefore it would not be attempted ; or, if it were, that the repeal of this part of the code, like the attack of an outpost, would put the main body on their guard. Another reason may now be added, that a law infringing that important part of the constitution might be passed, not from any direct hostility to the liberty of the press in general, but for the purpose of some party advantage or other temporary motive, in troublesome times ; and in such case, it would not be

(a) Constitution of Louisiana, art. vi. sect. 21.

accompanied by the repeal of the code. Again—the existence of this article in the code, at least, forms an additional security, for members might be found to concur, from interest or passion, in abridging the liberty of the press, who might not go the length of repealing the article ; and every additional security, which is attended with no inconvenience, and none can be even supposed here, is of the highest importance. And finally, admit that it may be rendered nugatory by a repeal ; yet if it should be of use until that repeal takes place ; if it should defeat one unprincipled attempt to destroy this sacred privilege ; if it should only give time for its friends to rally in its defence—it would be of inestimable value.

As expression, also, of legislative opinion, its importance is not small ; and the vigilance which it testifies in the guarding of constitutional rights, will not only reflect honour on those who pass it, but teach the people how to appreciate those rights which they see thus carefully enclosed with penalties.

One more reflection and I dismiss the subject, with a simple reference to the chapter, which contains nothing that needs an explanation to elucidate any further the several offences and their punishment. That reflection is this, that there is no one possible inconvenience attending the execution of any of the enactments of this chapter. No penalty can fall on any person who does not openly and wilfully violate one of the most important parts of his country's constitution; no ambiguity in the definition of the offences; no undue severity in the punishment. It is new ! This is the "very head and front of its offending ;" but it is not dangerous. It is believed to be necessary and highly useful.

The ninth title relates to offences affecting public records ; on which subject we have now three provisions in the 19th and 20th sections of the act of May 1805, and the 8th section of the act of 19th March 1818. By the first it is forbidden feloniously to steal, take away, alter, falsify, or otherwise avoid any record, writ, process, or any proceeding in any of the courts, under the penalty of fine to three thousand dollars, and imprisonment at hard labour not exceeding two years.

The second provides, that those who shall deface, alter, or embezzle any record, or enrolment, or matter, or instrument recorded, or registry thereof, with intent to defraud, shall pay a fine to one thousand dollars, be imprisoned at hard labour to two years, and be rendered incapable of holding any office.

By the third, if any person shall forge, or counterfeit, any public record or attestation of a public officer, where such attestation is legal proof, he shall be punished by solitary imprisonment to one, and at hard labour not less than two nor more than fourteen years.

Thus, taking these sections together, we find, first, that to steal or alter the record of a court may be punished by a fine of one cent, and imprisonment for one hour, but that the fine cannot exceed three thousand dollars, nor the imprisonment two years ; whereas the minimum punishment, for forging a record of enrolment, is exactly the maximum that is inflicted for stealing or forging the record of a court ; unless the general expression, record, in the third act, should be construed also to include court records ; in which case there would be the difference I have stated, between the punishments for stealing and for forging the same record.

Secondly, that there is a difference in the punishments of the two offences, designated in the first two sections respectively, that does not seem to be warranted by any distinction between them, in moral guilt, or public or private injury.

Thirdly, that in a fair construction of the words employed, all three of the sections include the same offence, to wit, forging the record of a court. The first designates, as one of the acts it forbids, to alter, falsify, or otherwise avoid any record, or other proceeding in any court. The second, to deface, or alter, or embezzle any record, enrolment, or matter of record, &c. The third, to forge, or counterfeit any public record. All of these have different penalties. Are they all to be inflicted? The reasoning of the court(*a*), above quoted, would seem to decide the affirmative of this question, for none of them contain a repealing clause, and two of them are in the same act. Yet, if they are, what confusion must ensue. This evil is remedied by the code; these, and all other offences of the same nature, are clearly described; all the words used in the description are defined; and the distinction, between the guilt and mischief, where an officer, who has the custody of the records, betrays his trust, by falsifying or destroying them; and the same crime committed by any other individual, is marked by an increase of punishment. In this, as well as in a subsequent title, the law is simplified by using a general description of the records intended to be protected against falsification and other injury, rather than by an enumeration, which is generally made imperfect in a few years by other instruments coming in use, which it is also necessary to protect. False certificates of recording officers, personifications to execute, or acknowledge, or prove authentic instruments, are provided against; and a section, describing what shall be deemed a fraudulent use of a forged record, will, it is believed, clear up doubts that have heretofore existed on that subject.

The title of offences against the current coin of the state, is so drawn as to embrace every offence of this nature. There is, among others, a section making it penal to possess counterfeited coin with the intent to pass it as true, either in the state, which is the provision of the present law, or to send it, for that purpose, into any other of the states, or into a foreign country. This is new in penal legislation, but it was thought honourable to the state to prevent its being made a den, in which coiners might carry on their fraudulent manufactory to the injury of other countries, whether enemies or friends; and as one step towards the application of that golden rule, " to do as we would be done by," to nations as well as to individuals. These advances need only be begun; they will be reciprocated; each will promote its interest as well as its honour, by making or meeting these advances, and from the most trifling beginnings, consequences most important to human happiness may result.

The great evil to the revenues of the state, arising from a misapplication of public moneys by those entrusted to receive them, was seriously considered, and a preventive remedy is proposed, which, it is thought, will in a great measure take away the temptation to the offence. A forced deposite of all moneys, by leaving no large sums in the possession of the party, will leave him little inducement to incur the penalty; and the measures described in the code, are such as cannot fail

(*a*) 10 Martin.

to bring on detection in case of disobedience. After the deposite is made, it cannot be withdrawn without a deliberate crime, the commission of which, in the nature of things, cannot remain concealed. In ordinary cases, this breach of trust is made with the design of replacing the money before it can be called for; and this honest intention palliates to the party the irregularity of the conduct. But if this was to be preceded, before any advantage could be made of the money by a false check that must remain on file and insure the conviction of the party, he will, nine times in ten, refrain from the offence, and the revenue will be free from this risk.

Extortion by collectors, or violence against them, are equally provided against.

Under the head of offences which affect commerce and manufactures, we have, first, those which affect foreign commerce.

These are offences against the inspection laws; shipping articles without inspection, when it is required by law; and counterfeiting marks or brands of the proper officers. The frauds which have been but too common in packing articles of little value in boxes or bales, intended for exportation, are punished by an adequate penalty. Destroying a vessel on the high seas, by the master or mariners ; frauds against insurers, either in or out of the state, by shipping articles of inferior value; and any act done in the state, preparatory to a fraud to be completed abroad ; or any such act done out of the state, if the fraud is to be completed within its limits, make the party liable, and this in virtue of a principle that has been before discussed.

A chapter regulates the conduct of tavern-keepers in regard to seamen ; and refers to the existing laws on that subject, it being rather a matter of police than of penal law.

A short chapter contains the usual and simple penalties against using false weights and measures ; and another has some new enactments to punish the fraudulent use of false marks on merchandize, which usually denote the quantity or quality of the article contained in the package.

The next class of offences, which may be distributed under the head of those which injure the commerce, manufactures, or trade of the country, are those affecting the validity of written contracts—a most important title in the criminal law of modern times, although scarcely known in the simple code of our ancestors, in the middle ages. Among the offences of this class, forgery is the most prominent. As was natural, it has closely followed the footsteps of paper credit. It has increased with increasing commerce, and thrives most where the circulation of bank-paper is most widely spread. In England it was an offence at common law ; but it could not be very prevalent at a time when commerce was barter, and when the evidences of public and private credit, being alike unknown, little inducement was offered for the exercise of the ingenuity of the very few who had learning enough to commit the offence ; being then neither felt nor apprehended as a serious evil, it was punished only as a misdemeanor.

By the first statute, (8 Richard II. c. 4.) it would appear, that this crime was only apprehended from judges and clerks, and in the falsification of court records alone. From the provisions of the statute of 8 Henry VI. we may judge that it began to make some progress ; that others, besides judges and clerks, tampered with the records, and that the evil was sufficiently prevalent to require a severe penalty ; for by that statute the offence, by whomsoever committed, is raised in the calendar of crimes to the rank of felony. But by the operation of a clerical privilege, this law had the effect of exempting from punishment the only persons who were enabled to commit the offence ; while its penalties could be enforced against those only who were under a physical incapacity of incurring them : although the crime could be committed by none who could not read, the knowing how to read was the certain means of escaping punishment ; which was only inflicted on those who demonstrated, by their ignorance of that art, that they were not guilty. This absurdity continued until late in the reign of Elizabeth. We then find the government first beginning to pay some attention to the subject. Their statutes, however, protected no species of written contracts, until experience had shown that it became the object of the offence, and its prevalence forced them to legislate ; but even then, they carefully restricted their protection to that species of writing which called for their immediate attention, leaving all others to form the subject of another law, when their introduction into commerce should tempt the hand of the forger to counterfeit them; so that the English statutes might serve as a chronological catalogue of the securities successively in use, from the time of the first statute to the present day.

The first enactments on this subject are, I believe, the statutes of Richard II. and Henry VI., before referred to. Neither of these relates to any other forgery than that of records. From that time no other writing seems to have claimed the attention of the law, until the fifth year of the reign of Elizabeth, when the forgery of deeds, charters, sealed writings, court rolls and wills, by one section ; and by another, that of obligations, acquittances and releases, was punishable by mutilation, imprisonment and forfeiture. During this reign there is but one other law on the subject(a), which relates to soldiers' and mariners' passes, and makes the forgery of them felony, without benefit of clergy. From this time, for more than a century, I find no statute referred to in the treatises on this subject; but they multiply afterwards in an extraordinary ratio. There are two in the reign of William III.—five in that of Anne—eight under the first George—ten in the reign of his immediate successor—and thirty-seven from the 1st to the 45th of George III., since which I have no account, making, in all, more than sixty statutes, bearing on different modifications of the same offence.

This legislation was inevitably confused from its prolixity. It was also, from its nature, in some degree inefficient. By attempting the difficult, perhaps the unattainable, object of protecting every species of writing by name, it constantly left some unprovided for, and, of course, open to the enterprise of offenders ; until the statute, like the ' Pœna pede Claudo' of the poet, came limping behind it with a new penalty. But the application of this penalty was attended with new difficulties from the defects of the system. As each penalty was denounced against those who falsified a particular instrument, it was necessary, in the act of accusation, to charge that the writing in question was one of that particular class. A mistake in this nomenclature has proved fatal to more than one prosecution.

Another source of uncertainty in this system is, that a change of circumstances and habits in the country, may render the law obscure and sometimes unintelligible. The name by which certain writings are

---

(a) Stat. 39 Eliz.

designated in the act, may be well understood at the time of its passage, and afterwards, by disuse, become wholly unknown, at least to
the people ; for instance, in the territorial law of 1805 it is made
forgery to counterfeit a *cotton receipt.* This instrument is understood
in those parts of the state where cotton is the staple commodity, to
mean a kind of negotiable receipt, given by the owners of cotton gins,
to their customers, for cotton brought to be cleaned ; but in the lower
part of the country, I doubt whether it is, even now, generally understood, and certainly it would not be, if either that species of culture
were abandoned, or if, by the invention of some cheap machinery,
every planter should clean his own cotton.   In either of these cases,
the term might be applied  to some instrument for which it was never
intended.

Our legislature might have avoided these inconveniences, but unfortunately they proceeded  on  the same vicious plan, of enumeration,
which had been  adopted in the statute law of England ; and as might
have been expected, with the same effect ; although in framing our law
of 1805 we had the English catalogue  before us, and might cull from
her statutes all the writings which we wish to add to those in use
among ourselves, for the purpose of protecting them against forgery ;
yet since that period, two other statutes(*a*) have been found necesssary
to increase the list ; and in progress of time, our statute book, unless
some other system be resorted to, may on this head, vie in prolixity
with the " statutes at large."

The means of avoiding these inconveniences are so obvious, that I
was, at first, inclined to think that some insurmountable objection,
which I could not discover, must have prevented their adoption.   But
when the most deliberate exercise of my judgment could suggest no
such objection, I ventured upon the description of the offence, not by
enumerating the different writings which should be its object, but by
a definition, intended to embrace all those which it is the policy of the
law to protect by the high penalties attached to the crime of forgery,
and to exclude all those which, from their nature, ought not to be
the subject of that sanction.   This change is offered with some confidence, because the foundation of it is laid in the definition of this
crime by the common law, which, as far as my reading and observation
have gone, has given rise to much less uncertainty of decision, than has
taken place in the practice under the statutes.   By these means all the
uncertainty, arising from an erroneous charge in the indictment, as to
the species of contract, and it is no small item, will be avoided.   It
will be, hereafter, only necessary to describe the effect of the instrument, not to declare to what class of contracts it belongs ; and every
instrument, which the convenience of commerce or the extension of
obligations may introduce, will, at once, be protected by the law,
without a new statute to add its name to the list.   The next change
from the present system, which is proposed, grew naturally out of the
first.   By the thirty-third section of the law of 1805 it is enacted, that
" all the crimes, misdemeanors, and offences, therein enumerated, shall
be taken, intended, and construed according to, and in conformity with,
the common law of England."   This has always been construed into
an adoption of the common law definition, of the several offences which
are made punishable by our statute law, where the statute itself gave

(*a*) Acts of 22d Feb. 1817, and 20th March 1818.

no other definition. But by the common law some acts were considered as forgery, which could not be brought within any reasonable definition of the offence : if a man, who had made a conveyance, should afterwards execute another of a prior date, for the same property, with intent to defraud ; or if he passed a note, signed by himself, pretending that he was another person who bore the same name, but had better credit ; or if he procured the execution of an instrument which had been secretly altered, or substituted one for another before agreed upon ; all of these acts were classed under the head of forgery. They can be placed there, however, only by an arbitrary arrangement, which destroys all systems, and sets definition at defiance. They have this, in common with forgery, that they are all fraudulent acts, and are all committed by means of written instruments; but forging implies falsification of an instrument, and cannot be committed by the fraudulent use of a true one, or by the alteration of a writing before it becomes the act of any one.

I have, therefore, characterized them as offences affecting written contracts, and annexed to them different measures of punishment, proportioned to the offence, but have not considered them as forgeries. In the definition I have offered of forgery, the intent to defraud is equivalent to the actual completion of that part of the offence. In that the new plan coincides with the present system ; but it differs from it in this, that no particular person need to be assigned, as the one on whom the fraud was intended to be practised. The necessity for this designation, and the uncertainty of the proof, leads now to the escape of the guilty. But although the allegations of fraud be general, it can never injure the innocent ; for if it does appear from the instrument, it must always be strictly proved. An inspection of the different articles of this chapter will render any further exposition of them here unnecessary. If its provisions are well drawn, it provides for all those offences affecting the validity of written contracts, which have been deemed worthy of punishment by the English law, or which require it under our state of society. The falsification of other writings not affecting property, such as public records and other official acts, is provided for in other parts of the code.

Although, by the general plan, all the definitions of technical words used in the code are collected in the book designated for that purpose, this order is deviated from, in cases where words or phrases are used exclusively in relation to any particular offence, in which case they are sometimes placed as articles in the section which treats of the offence. This deviation is more perceptible in this chapter than perhaps any other in the code, and it extends in this instance so as to embrace definitions of some words that are not used exclusively in regard to the offences contained in that chapter. It was resorted to in order to bring into one view every thing necessary for the full understanding of an important class of crimes ; but, in all such cases, the same definitions will be found repeated in the Book of Definitions.

In order to give a connected view of all the changes that are proposed, as well in the prosecution as of the definition of this class of offences, I must anticipate here some observations which regularly would find their place in the introductory discourses to the Code of Procedure and the Code of Evidence. As to the first ; that part of the Code of Procedure which relates particularly to prosecutions for

W

offences under this chapter, contains some provisions which require particular notice. . One great inconvenience in the present system, has already been hinted at ; the necessity of giving the false instrument a name in the indictment, in other words, of charging that it purports to be a receipt, a note, or some other of the writings which are specifically enumerated in the various acts. By substituting a definition instead of such a catalogue, this difficulty in the practice is avoided. Another very fruitful source of captious exceptions arose from the necessity of setting forth exact copies of the instrument in the indictment, a mistake in which led always to delay, and sometimes defeated the ends of justice. It is thought that the provisions on this subject will effectually prevent this evil ; while, at the same time, they assure to the accused every degree of certainty in the accusation, necessary to a full understanding of the charge, and every facility which justice and humanity require for making his defence. The hope of escape, by some technical exception, animates every culprit ; he generally overrates his chances of acquittal from this source ; and it is, therefore, a point of the greatest importance to cut off this hope of impunity, to convince the accused that no defect of form can, under any circumstances, procure his escape ; and that the only chance of safety lies in an acquittal on the merits. This conviction, once deeply impressed on the minds of offenders, and counteracted by no examples of impunity from defects of form, will have the happiest consequences, particularly in this description of crime, in which these objects are at present most common, and on which, well or ill-founded, the guilty place the greatest reliance for escape. To effect these important ends, provision is made in the Code of Procedure, that before the defendant can be called to plead, he shall be furnished with a copy of the instrument said to be forged, have an opportunity of comparing it with the original, and at a time assigned be called on to produce his objections, either for any variance, for misnomer, or any other defect of form ; these are to be disposed of in a manner directed by the code, before the plea ; and then the trial takes place, divested of any other inquiry but that on the merits.

This part of the Code of Procedure provides also simple forms of indictment for every offence contained in the corresponding division of the work, and for every modification of these offences ; from which it has been endeavoured to discard all superfluous allegations, but to give to the accused all necessary information of the nature of the charge against him ; but a close adherence, even to these forms, is not rendered essential, and means are taken, and it is hoped effectual means, to remedy every evil arising from exceptions to defects of form. I now pass to the consideration of a few rules of evidence, contained in the Code of Evidence, applicable particularly to trial for offences of this class.

By the English law, the person whose name is forged, was not admitted as a witness to prove the forgery, if any suit could have been supported against him on the instrument, if it were true. This exclusion is, by the English jurists, endeavoured to be reconciled to the general rule, that direct interest alone shall be deemed an objection to the competency.

1st. From the consideration that the forfeiture consequent on conviction, vested all the property of the offender, and, of course, the instrument on which he was convicted, in the crown, who neither could, nor would, enforce the payment of it after conviction ; and that, therefore, there is an evident interest in the witness to procure such conviction.

2d. That it is the practice of the courts to impound the instrument on which a conviction for forgery took place; that is, to keep it in the hands of their officer to prevent a fraudulent circulation, and therefore it would be the interest of the witness to procure a conviction, because, in that case, the difficulty of succeeding in a private suit would be insurmountable.

The first of these reasons cannot apply here, where forfeiture is unknown; and the practice on which the second is founded, is so modified in the new code, as to give facility to the bringing a civil suit, even on an instrument which, in the criminal court, has been declared a forgery. There can, therefore, be no foundation for alleging an interest, that would render the witness incompetent under our law ; and to exclude him for any other of the reasons usually alleged, would be a departure from principle, and destroy the harmony which ought to prevail between the rules of evidence in criminal and civil cases. It is true, that a bias may not unreasonably be suspected in such a case against the prisoner. But it is one that can be appreciated by the jury, and therefore ought to go to credit, rather than competency.

"In adopting this rule you will only sanction what has heretofore been practised in this state, and in several others governed by the principles of common law ; but as there has been a diversity of decision on this point, and as the English rule is at present observed by our courts, it was thought proper, for the reasons alleged, to abrogate it by a legislative provision."

The chapter on fraudulent insolvencies has been framed with a view of making it applicable to the present system of insolvent laws, or to any other that may be substituted for them. The great evils to be apprehended in those cases being; the concealment of property, the fraudulent conveyance of it, and the creation of fictitious debts. All these have been provided against, by penalties applicable as well to the dishonest debtor as to the persons who may colleague with him, to the injury of the creditors. These penalties extend to penitentiary imprisonment for making a false and fraudulent schedule of property or debts, or for wilfully destroying books or papers, with a design to defraud. The other offences being such measures as are, for the most part, resorted to in moments of embarrassment and trouble, not showing such depravity as calls for the discipline of the penitentiary, it was thought would be sufficiently corrected by suspension of certain political and civil rights, and by imprisonment. The circumstances of the insolvent forbade the addition of any fine to his offence; but it forms part of the punishment of those who collude with him, and who may be supposed to have the means of paying one.

By the single article of the thirteenth title, respecting offences affecting public property, it is declared, that all the provisions for the protection of private property, apply also to that of the public. And in the fourteenth title is also comprised one general provision referring to the ordinances of the juries of police, and the public corporations of cities and towns, for the laws respecting the making and enlarging the levees, roads, bridges, streets and public squares, and for the penalties they impose for a disregard of them ; it having been found impossible, in a permanent system, to provide for the varying legislation that the changing nature of the subject would require; or, in a general system, to embrace all the circumstances which the local police might require. But two chapters, under this title, contain the only enactments on this subject, which, from their nature, could be justly made permanent and co-extensive with the state in their local operation. These two chapters are based upon the present law, and, therefore, need no further elucidation.

The fifteenth title relates to offences injurious to public health or safety. At the time it was written the Code of Public Health was in force. As it has since been repealed, it is presumed that the legislature do not consider any provision, against the introduction of infectious and contagious disorders, to be necessary, and the chapter on that subject is suppressed. The first chapter of this title, as it now stands, imposes a penalty on all those who store gunpowder in greater quantity than ten pounds, within one hundred yards of a dwelling-house, or public road, or the land of any person who does not give his consent ; who carry on trades injurious to the health of those who live in the vicinity ; and against those who adulterate provisions, liquor, or drugs, so as to make them injurious to health.

Offences against morals are the subject of a title containing four chapters.

The first relates to disorderly houses, and its provisions coincide substantially with those of our statute, but the offences are more precisely defined.

The second chapter contains prohibitions entirely new in our law, although they form a very comprehensive part of the English common law, under the title of Offences against Decency. This is quite undefined in that law. In the chapter which I present, it is restricted to four cases : indecent exposure of person ; insulting and indecent language to a woman ; deliberate seduction, under promise of marriage ; and the infamous agency of ministering to the vices of others. Seduction is not, I believe, punishable in England, unless preceded by a conspiracy ; nor in any manner whatever by our statutes. Yet, if we consider the base profligacy of the act, by which the most implicit confidence is betrayed, and the most solemn promises are deliberately broken, not only to the utter ruin of the unsuspecting victim, but to the disgrace and misery of her connexions, it is one in which the immorality of the act, and the misery it inflicts, both require exemplary punishment.

Although the private excesses of the passion between the sexes cannot, with propriety, be made the subject of penal law, yet public opinion, in all nations, has marked, by its decided reprobation, him who, without being excited by his own passions, ministers to those of others for gain, and in that vile office frequently seduces innocence, or purchases the influence of infamous or necessitous parents to the dishonour of their child. The indication of public sentiment has, on this occasion, been pursued, and the act has been made penal by the code.

It seems right and proper that the law should lend its aid to punish all acts against individuals that provoke a just resentment, which will naturally vindicate itself, if the law refuses its aid. It is for this reason that the article, imposing a penalty on indecent and insulting expressions to a woman, has been added. It has been considered, by one whose authority and opinions I highly respect, as descending into minutiæ unbefitting a penal code, and as one of those offences to be repressed by public opinion or the fear of private chastisement, rather than by law. If the force of public opinion were a sufficient sanction, I should have proposed no other ; but it is because its insufficiency is acknowledged, and private resentment is proposed to aid its operation, that I propose to substitute the regular action of the law to the uncertain penalty of individual passion.

Whether adultery should be considered as an offence against public morality, or left to the operation of the civil laws, has been the subject of much discussion. As far as I am informed, it figures in the penal law of all nations, except the English; and some of their most celebrated lawyers have considered the omission as a defect.

Neither the immorality of the act, nor its injurious consequences on the happiness of females, and very frequently on the peace of society and the lives of its members, can be denied. The reason, then, why it should go unpunished, does not seem very clear. It is emphatically one of that nature to which I have just referred, in which the resentment of the injured party will prompt him to take vengeance into his own hands, and commit a greater offence, if the laws of his country refuse to punish the lesser. It is the nature of man, and no legislation can alter it, to protect himself where the laws refuse their aid ; very frequently where they do not, but where they will not give protection against injury, it is in vain that they attempt to punish him who supplies, by his own energy, their remissness. Where the law refuses to punish this offence, the injured party will do it for himself ; he will break the public peace, and commit the greatest of all crimes, and he is rarely or never punished. Assaults, duels, assassinations, poisonings, will be the consequence. They cannot be prevented ; but, perhaps, by giving the aid of the law to punish the offence, which they are intended to avenge, they will be less frequent ; and it will, by taking away the pretext for the atrocious acts, in a great measure insure the infliction of the punishment they deserve. It is for these reasons that the offence of adultery forms a chapter of this title.

Different punishments are awarded, to the unfaithful wife—to the inconstant husband, who is so regardless of honour and decency, and public opinion, as to keep a concubine in the house with his wife, or to force her, by ill treatment, to leave it and give place to the usurper of her rights. The reasons for this distinction, between the offence of the husband and the wife, are obvious, and founded in nature. The paramour of the wife is also punished by fine and imprisonment ; and to avoid collusions, no prosecutions against the wife can be carried on unless the partner of her crime is joined in it. This regulation, too, will be some check to the heartless seducer, who might otherwise look with indifference on the penalty suffered by another for the crime of which he was the principal cause.

It is provided, under this head, that no prosecution for this offence shall be commenced but on the complaint of the injured party, and that it shall cease if they become reconciled before sentence.

The respect paid to the bodies of the dead, which from its universality would seem to be a natural sentiment, has suggested, in all countries, laws, or customs having the force of laws, forbidding as a kind of sacrilege the violation of the receptacles for human remains, whether they be embalmed, interred or consumed. The catacomb, the grave, and the urn, were held equally sacred; and any intrusion upon them has always not only been considered as immoral, but punished as a crime. It is in vain that pretended philosophy affects to consider it as prejudice. The feelings of the philosopher belie the language of his wisdom ; and however indifferent he might feel as to his own remains, he would not see, without affliction, the body of a friend or relation torn from the grave, even to promote the progress of science. It is in vain that we are told, and are truly told, that the health and life of the living ought not to be sacrified to a vain respect for the body of the dead, incapable of suffering here, or feeling the ignominy of exposure; the reason may be convinced, but the feeling remains. Science must be content with subjects whose dissection will interest the feelings of none who are alive. The bodies of those few, who, themselves above this prejudice, devote their remains to the cause of science; those of malefactors who die in the imprisonment inflicted by the law, must suffice for the improvement of surgical knowledge. But the laws must protect, in the place of their lasting rest, the remains that are sacred to the memory of surviving relations or friends. This natural feeling has not been neglected in the code which is presented, and a proper punishment is denounced against every violation of the sanctuary of the tomb.

We have now closed the review of those offences which, powerfully affecting the community in general, have been classed as public offences. The seventeenth title commences the other division, distinguished as Private Offences ; and first of these stand such as affect individuals in the exercise of their religion. In most other systems of penal law this title is much more extensive. It there embraces a species of offences carefully excluded from this. In those systems the dominant religion is personified, and rendered by this fiction subject to be injured by investigating its truth, or doubting its divine origin. Nay, the Supreme Being himself is sometimes impiously substituted for the mode of worship or tenets of faith which prevail in the state, and his almighty power is protected by vain laws to punish "offences against God and religion"(a). The code offered to you does not contain this absurdity. The exercise of religion is considered as a right ; an inestimable one. It is restrained only by those limits which must restrict all rights, that they do not encroach on those of another ; or, in other words, do not change into wrongs. All articles of faith, all modes of worship are equal in the eye of the law : all are entitled to equal protection. The fallibility of human laws does not undertake a task to which unerring wisdom alone is competent. The weakness of human laws does not attempt to avenge the cause of infinite power; and injuries and insults to the Deity, are left to the Being who asserts his rights to the exclusive cognizance of such offences : "Vengeance is mine; I will repay, saith the Lord." The code has not ventured to trench on this divine prerogative ; but the provisions of this title will be found to repress or punish any wanton, or intolerant attempt to disturb or persecute; while every necessary authority is secured to religious societies, for the preservation of order among their members. So that the general principles

(a) 4 Bl. 43.

announced in the preliminary chapter to the code, taken in connexion with the provisions of this title, evince that this state will give effect to the noble experiment that has so successfully been tried in these republics—of giving perfect liberty to conscience—perfect protection to all religions, and substituting perfect equality for insulting toleration; an experiment which demonstrates how fallacious is the argument of a necessary connexion between church and state; which shows that true piety may be preserved amid a variety of religious tenets; and proves, that liberty in religion has the same influence on the great virtues, which all sects consider as essential to produce eternal happiness, as liberty, in government, has on those which are the basis of political prosperity.

To repress injuries to reputation, is a duty more incumbent on legislation since the introduction of printing has given so many facilities to assail it; but the task is rendered more difficult, because the same instrument, usually employed in the work of detraction,· is one that is necessary to spread information, promote science, support political and civil liberty, and propagate the truths of religion. To permit its unrestrained employment for these noble ends, and at the same time prevent its being used as a means of destroying reputation, is the task that must be performed, if we wish to preserve consistency in this important division of our Penal Code. This, it was believed, could be done only by defining the offence, and then laying down as deductions from such definition, a set of negative as well as affirmative rules, declaring what species of assertion shall be punishable as illegal attacks upon reputation, and what shall be permitted in order to avoid the greater evil of restraining the proper liberty of speech and of the press. In performing this task, alterations have been made in the present law, which were necessary to adapt it to the letter and spirit of our constitution ; the provisions of which have been adverted to in that part of the report which treats of offences against the liberty of the press. These provisions will be pointed out, although not in the order in which they stand in the chapter.

1. The undefined, and perhaps undefinable, offence of libelling the government, a court, or any other aggregate body, is abolished, as inconsistent with the spirit of the constitution. It gives unqualifiedly the right of using the press for the purpose of "examining the proceedings of the legislature, or any branch of the government," and declares, that no law shall ever be made to restrain this right. But of what avail would this privilege be, if public bodies were guarded by the rules that apply to libels against individuals by the English law? Every thing, according to that law, that tends to bring a person into contempt or disgrace, is a libel ; and although the strictures are true, the guilt is not lessened, but, according to some authorities, enhanced. Therefore, every discussion of a legislative measure, or a judicial decision, which tends to show folly in the one, or injustice in the other, would be punishable as a libel ; and the very end which the constitution had in view would be defeated. The restriction that every one is liable for the abuse of the liberty, clearly does not apply to any latitude of animadversion whatever upon public measures; but to the injury that may be done to private character. As to public measures, there can be no abuse of the right. It must be unrestrained, or it is no right ; for you can rest the right of repression nowhere but in the hands of some pub-

lic functionary ; he must be guided by laws made by the legislative power; and with this power of making the rule and of interpreting the publication that is supposed to be obnoxious to it, the privilege of publishing and discussing would soon be brought within limits too narrow to be of any value, unless it was guarded by the constitutional declaration, and by laws made to give to it its full effect.   Nor can the abuse of this liberty be attended with any great or permanent inconvenience; certainly with none that can be compared with that of the restraint.  A false representation of legislative proceedings can have little or no effect in a country where the press is as free to correct as it is to spread it. In a country where laws are made by a numerous body, whose proceedings are in public, misrepresentation is destroyed the moment it appears, and injures no one but its weak or wicked author.   The terms of a law may be grossly misrepresented.   The next day it is published, and the falsehood is detected.   No injury is suffered by the public; but the penalty falls on. the author, who loses his credit for veracity or discernment.   The reasons which led to the passage of the law, are erroneously and falsely stated ; they are ascribed to ignorance of the true interests of the country—hard at the heels of the calumny comes its refutation in the publication of the debates, and the public sustains no injury from the calumny offered to a public body in its aggregate capacity.   The same reasoning applies to the judiciary, considering courts in their incorporeal capacity.   The publication and the publicity of their proceedings will always correct any false representations that may be made; and the ideal beings which we personify for certain purposes, under the names of legislative and judiciary power, will suffer no more injury, will no more be brought into contempt by false and malicious accounts of their proceedings, than the other power, which we call the executive, and which it has never been thought proper to protect, independent of the persons who exercise it, by any law of libel.   If, then, there be any inconvenience in permitting the widest possible range to the right of verbal or written discussion of public measures, it is one of inconsiderable amount; but the evil of imposing the least restraint is incalculable.   Say that true representations shall be allowed—who will, in order to inform the people, risk any publication of the measures of their rulers ?   If incorrect accounts of judicial proceedings are punishable, who will venture on the task of a reporter ?   Publicity, that great safeguard against corruption, will be destroyed: public opinion, which, even in despotic governments, corrects abuses, will lose its force ; and the law of libel, with this extent, becomes one of the most powerful engines for the overthrow of all free institutions.

But when any of the public functionaries, in either of the great branches of government, are personally attacked—when animadversions on public proceedings are made the vehicle for injury to private character—then the law protects them as it does any other individual ; and, although there can be no libel against the government, or the court, yet the legislator and the judges are not left without the same redress that is given to their fellow-citizens.   The limits of this report will not permit me to offer one-half of the reasons that present themselves to justify the suppression of this species of libel from our codes.   The practical result however from them, observed in the general and state governments, is instructive.   In most, if not in all of the states, libels against the government, and particularly against the judiciary branch of it, are liable to prosecution. Under the general government, since the repeal of the unconstitutional sedition law, they are not. Yet the tribunals of the United States, unprotected by any penalty, are certainly not less respected, and perform their functions with as little interruption, from the licentiousness of the press, as those of the state governments.

In most cases, the connexion between cause and effect exists between the subject of this chapter and that of a subsequent one—Of Duels. Defamation, either real or supposed, is the cause of most of those combats which no laws have yet been able to suppress. If lawgivers had originally condescended to pay some attention to the passions and feelings of those for whom they were to legislate, these appeals to arms would never have usurped a power superior to the laws ; but by affording no satisfaction for the wounded feelings of honour, they drove individuals to avenge all wrongs of that description, denied a place in the code of criminal law. Insults formed a title in that of honour, which claimed exclusive jurisdiction of this offence. It is too late, perhaps, to eradicate; but we may probably, by prudent provisions, lessen the evil. With this view, some have been introduced into this chapter ; all of which are new in our criminal jurisprudence. By one, the court may, if the circumstances of the case render it proper, direct that the whole or any part of the punishment may be remitted, on the defendant's making such apology, or after-amends, as the court shall deem sufficient to the injured party. By another, where the jury find that the accused spoke the words, or made or published the libel, and that the charge is false, they are required specially to state that the charge is false and unfounded, and the court may, on the demand of the prosecutor, cause such declaration to be published at the expense of the defendant. Lastly, if the defendant shall avow himself to have been the speaker of the words, or the author of the libel, and acknowledge that the charge they import is unfounded, or in cases where there is any ambiguity that the charge was not intended to apply to the prosecutor, the punishment shall be confined to the payment of costs and the publication of proceedings. These several provisions, by extending the legal remedy over part of the ground, now exclusively occupied by the principle of honour, it is thought, may, in conjunction with the special enactments in the chapter of duels, have a tendency to check that absurd and fatal practice.

No words should be punishable, unless they are used with intent to injure, or are such as, whatever may be the real intent of the party, naturally have that tendency. But even to this there must be further restrictions, such as charges necessarily made in the prosecution of a public duty, either as a legislator, judge, advocate or witness, and confidentially by way of advice, or called for in self-defence. These and other exceptions are specially declared in the code, and they are generally taken from those English decisions which have been considered as the most consonant to the dictates of reason. A variance, however, from that law will be found in making defamation, by words spoken, as much an offence as if they were written. By the English law, although these give a right of private action, yet be they ever so malicious and injurious, be the charge which they employ ever so atrocious, they cannot be punished as an offence. For this difference it was supposed no substantial reason could be given, and it was believed also that it

X

would lead to other serious inconveniences. The satisfaction by private suit must necessarily be of a pecuniary nature. Men, therefore, who think highly of reputation, are unwilling to have theirs appreciated by that standard. They will, then, either suffer the injury to go unpunished, or they will in this, as in most other cases where no remedy, or an inadequate one is provided, take the law into their own hands ; and it is no improbable conjecture, that a very great proportion of the many breaches of the peace, and deaths by duels, which originate in verbal provocation, might have been avoided, had an adequate satisfaction been provided by law. This distinction, however, is established, that while no action can be sustained for words spoken, unless they are false; yet, when they are deliberately written and published, with a view to injure the character, they are punishable, although they are true, unless they were used from some motive of public good or private duty. This distinction has received the sanction of the highest legal authority, and has been practised under in one or more of the states without any inconvenience. It is a correction of our present law, which forbids the truth to be given in evidence in any case of libel. If the truth were a justification in no case, one half of the utility of the press would be destroyed. The misconduct and incapacity of those already in office, and the want of talent or character of the candidate, would be protected from exposure. If it were a justification in every case, the wanton and malicious exposure of foibles, misfortunes or defects, might, with impunity, make the life of an individual miserable, while the anonymous author remained unknown; and would not, as in the case of the same words spoken, be restrained by the fear of personal vengeance.

The second chapter of this title provides a punishment for an offence, frequent in times of political excitement, the hanging or burning an obnoxious person in effigy, the relique of a barbarous state of society, and the proof of a ferocious disposition, fostered by these riotous proceedings, and which, unless restrained by the laws, would realize the cruel indignities of which they are the symbol. Combinations to destroy reputation by false accusations ; and threats of making them for the purpose of extorting money, are the subject of the third chapter of this title. The fourth, which concludes it, relates to a mode of injuring reputation, not unfrequently resorted to by the ingenuity of malice, by publishing false writings in the name of another, tending to bring him into ridicule or contempt. The happiness of individuals, the quiet of families, and the peace of society, depend so much on the protection given by the laws to reputation, that this title is more minute in its provisions than many of the others. The innovations that have been introduced, it is believed, will be justified by a close examination of their tendency, and that no parts of the present law on the subject have been omitted or changed, but such as can be justified by the most cogent reasons.

We now come to the important title of Offences affecting the Person. And, before we examine the several acts which are made punishable under this head, it may be necessary to remark, that, instead of beginning, as is usually done, with offences of the highest degree in this class and then descending to the lowest, the order in this code is reversed, and the ascending scale has been adopted for reasons which are not those of mere arbitrary arrangement. By beginning with the lowest injury that can be offered to the person, an assault, you lay the foundation for comprehending the definitions and descriptions of all the others which are only aggravations, either in degree or by intent; and having defined all the intermediate degrees between it and murder, you arrive at the simple conclusion that every homicide, which is not included in any of the preceding classes of crimes, is murder. Whereas, by beginning as is usually done at the other end of the scale, you must explain all the lower degrees which are included in that with which. you begin, or your definition will not be understood. For example : if we begin with murder, we can only cause it to be comprehended by saying that it is homicide. We must then anticipate, by defining homicide ; and when we come to the circumstances and intent which distinguish murder from other homicides that are justifiable or excusable or criminal in a less degree, we must travel on untrodden ground, which we must pass over again when we come to speak of these other kinds of homicide. But by advancing regularly, we clear the way as we go ; and by getting a definite idea of the several kinds of homicide, ascending through the different degrees, from the slightest to the highest guilt, our march is uniform ; each definition is the foundation for that which succeeds, until we come to the last ; and we may form a clear conception of the crime of murder, by calling it such homicide as does not fall within any of the preceding classes.

With this notice of the mode of classing the offences against the person, the very few observations that will be made on the details of this title, will be readily understood.

Assault, the lowest injury of this kind, and battery, which usually accompanies it, do not materially vary in their definitions from those contained in the English law ; but the chapter, among other details, contains a minute enumeration of all the circumstances which will justify or excuse violence offered to the person, a matter on which it is of the highest importance that the law should be not only explicit, but well understood by every individual in society. Where the same act may be indifferent, or a duty, or a crime, that legislation is surely imperfect which leaves any thing to conjecture on such important points. Yet however rich our present law may be, in the number of decisions to elucidate this branch of personal duty, it is most wofully deficient in that order, selection and publicity, from which the people can learn its will. The code purports to remedy this evil ; to give to the most prominent and best founded of these decisions the force of positive law ; to give arrangement and order to the principles on which they are founded, and enable the citizen to know what species of violence he may resist, and in what degree ; to what he is bound to submit ; in what cases and in what degree he is, in his turn, justified in exercising it ; and to trace precisely the line which he cannot pass without incurring the penalties of the law. The different sections of this chapter mark, with a precision which it is hoped will prove sufficient, the aggravations of this offence, arising from person, place, intent and degree.

Illegal imprisonment forms the subject of the second chapter. The first section contains the detail of the different modes by which the detention, constituting this offence, may be effected, whether by assault, by actual violence, by threats, or by some natural obstacle opposed to the power of locomotion. Each of these are developed and illustrated;

and the cases in which detention of the person of another may be justified, are set forth in the text. A subsequent section, as in the cases of assault and battery, specifies the aggravation to the offence, caused by the purpose or degree ; and that species of illegal restraint of liberty, applicable only to the female sex, known by the name of abduction, is provided for and defined in the concluding section of this chapter.

The next chapter relates to an offence of the most heinous nature, whether we consider its effects on the sufferer or those with whom she may be connected. Whenever it occurs, the best feelings of our nature are roused against the brutal and ferocious perpetrator, and the detestation in which the ravisher is held, has almost universally induced legislators to increase the severity of the punishment, without considering that his chance of impunity increases in the same ratio. By our present law it is one of the few crimes punished with death. In addition to the general reasons for substituting a milder penalty, which apply to other cases, there is one which makes it peculiarly necessary in this. It is a crime in which conviction, from its nature, must for the most part depend on the testimony of a single witness ; the odium attached to its perpetrator generally supplying the deficiency of other proof. It is of all accusations, therefore, that one in which the innocent have most to fear, and in which an irremediable punishment ought most to be avoided. But though the delinquent ought always to be kept within the reach of the pardoning power, his punishment should not be light : it is imprisonment for life. Some innovation is introduced in the definition of this crime. When the object is attained by fraud, the consent, though apparently given, is as much wanting in reality, as when violence is applied. Two cases, in which such fraud shall be equivalent in guilt to force, are specified : where it is obtained by the administration of soporific or other drugs, and where the perpetrator personates the husband of the sufferer. The other provisions of this chapter are generally accordant with the present law.

The destruction of human life, in its inchoate state, does not come within the definition of homicide. It, therefore, requires a special provision. This is made in the fourth chapter of this title. Whether the object be effected by external violence, or the administration of drugs internally, and whether with or without the consent of the woman, the crime is committed ; the punishment is increased if the delinquent be a physician or surgeon ; and if death is caused by the attempt, it is murder. Exceptions, however, are made of the case where the effect is produced by medical advice, with the intent of saving the life of the mother.

A great personal injury may be sustained by the swallowing or inhaling of deleterious substances. If these are maliciously administered, it constitutes a crime which forms the subject of the fifth chapter of this title, in which the punishment is graduated according to the intent and effect of the offence.

We come now to the consideration of the important title of Homicide. The first section of this chapter lays the foundation for all the others, by the definition of this act, and illustrations and explanations to remove every doubt as to the force of the different words used in such definition. The three great divisions used in our present law are retained, and homicide is considered, in the subsequent sections, as justifiable, excusable or culpable. All of these are defined, explained, and illustrated. The rules by which they are to be distinguished are clearly laid down, and the exceptions specially noted. Homicide is justified, by the requisition of law, in cases where death is legally inflicted as a punishment, or where it occurs in resisting an enemy in the usual mode of warfare, excluding poisoning and assassination, which terms are defined in the text. It is also permitted, and therefore justifiable in the performance of other duties to the state. The first of these is the execution of the lawful orders of magistrates or courts. This general principle is in conformity with our existing law; but there is no part of it in which accessible and clearly intelligible rules are more wanted for the government of the citizens. They are called on by the first duties to the state to obey the orders of the magistrate, if they are legal; if they are illegal, they expose themselves to the highest penalties of the law. One mode of executing the order entitles the citizen, who performs the duty, to the highest praise, and the other subjects him to capital punishment. What in one man, in relation to his condition or offence, is a duty, in another is a crime; and yet the rules by which we are to be guided through these narrow winding paths, bordered by snares and precipices, in which a false step entangles us in ruin or sinks us to destruction; these rules are not to be found in the positive enactment of our law. A few general principles are laid down by elementary writers; numerous and sometimes contradictory practical deductions are made by decisions in particular cases; and the magistrate and the officer, as well as the citizen who is to aid them, are left at their peril to discover the law, in the different volumes in which it is contained, and to reconcile the contradictory opinions and decisions of which it is composed. This defect in legislation is an obvious and fatal one. If the rules cannot be ascertained until the case arises, then no one ought to suffer for contravening them, for they are no rules. It is a solecism to call them such. If they can be established, it is a cruel and a wicked omission to neglect it. It is a tyranny to establish and not promulgate them. But rules laid down in books, which, from their language, their expense, or other circumstances, are not accessible, although they may be printed and published, are not promulgated. The conclusion from these premises is irresistible, easily drawn, and nowise honourable to the state of our criminal jurisprudence.

An attempt is made to remedy this evil in the proposed code. Several subdivisions of this section contain, in order; first, the rules as to the order itself which is to be executed, and the magistrate from whom it emanates; and secondly, those which regard the person executing it, and the manner in which the duty is to be performed. To review these would be to repeat the provisions of the code, which is the less necessary, as most of them are founded on principles established by the best decisions under our present law.

The next duty to the state, in the performance of which homicide may be justified, as analogous to the former, is that which arises from the opposition to rebellion, insurrection and riot. Here again the same importance of regulation is preserved; and is as well in this part of the code, in which the principles are laid down, as in the Code of Procedure, will be found all that is necessary to guide the magistrate in giving; and those whose duty it is in executing his orders on the important subjects of arrests, self-defence, and the suppression of breaches of the peace.

But we have a duty to perform, not only to the state, in obedience to the lawful orders of its magistracy, and in resistance to its foreign and domestic enemies; there is also another which we owe to our families and ourselves, in the necessary defence of person or property. Here again we find the same deficiency in our existing law, that has been pointed out in the beginning of the review of this chapter; and here again that deficiency is attempted to be supplied by the establishment of minute, but intelligible and distinct rules, to designate what resistance may be offered to aggression, and to limit its extent both in nature and degree; and with this ends the division of justifiable homicide.

The designation of that which is excusable, is contained in a single and a short section. The leading distinction between this division and that which preceded it is, that the homicides described in the first were voluntary, but are permitted on some principle of public good or private right; but in this, are involuntary, but unavoidable by common prudence or care. Thus far, from the very definition of an offence, none of the acts coming within the purview of these sections can be denominated such. The next section, however, describes those acts of homicide which assume that character. When we inquire whether any particular act is an offence, this mode of classification gives us, in jurisprudence, the advantage of an operation something like the arithmetical one of proving one rule by another. To show a given act of homicide to be an offence, it must not only be brought within the definition of one of the acts of that nature which are designated as culpable, but it must be excluded from those which it is declared may be justified or excused. The eighth, and last, section of this chapter treats of these culpable homicides, and each of its six subdivisions contains the description of one of these offences, which, beginning with the lowest degree, where no culpable intention can be attributed to the offender, rise to murder in its appalling forms of assassination and parricide.

Those who are satisfied with the provisions of the English law, which knows only two degrees of culpable homicide, must be startled by the number indicated in this chapter. But it is hoped, and believed, that a little attention to the subject will show the necessity of making them. By our present, which is the English law, all culpable homicide is either manslaughter or murder. The first description embraces two kinds of offences that are evidently very different in degree. It confounds voluntary and involuntary homicide in the same name, and applies to both the same punishment. The destruction of human life by want of care, even without any design to do the smallest mischief, is certainly reprehensible; but surely, a wise lawgiver would not say that it was the same offence with that of designedly inflicting death, under the influence of passion, although that passion had adequate cause in a violent provocation; nor would he identify with these, death caused by negligence in the doing of an unlawful act not amounting to a crime. Yet, all this is done by our present jurisprudence; and this, with some other defects, are endeavoured to be remedied by the system which it is proposed to substitute.

The preceding sections having taught us what homicides were justi-

fied, permitted, or excused ; those described in the one we are now reviewing, need no other definition than that they are such as cannot be
brought within any of the preceding classes ; or, in other words, that
those come within the description of culpable homicides which cannot,
according to the preceding provisions, be justified or excused.   Next
comes the designation of the different degrees of culpability.   Here
the first great distinction, between negligence and design, is marked,
and culpable homicides are divided into negligent and voluntary.   But
as different degrees of negligence mark a greater or less attention to
the value of human life, and as extreme provocation, or the want of
any, shows a greater or less degree of malignity in the voluntary infliction of death, so each of these require subdivisions, in order to designate the degree of guilt, and assign its correspondent punishment.
  The first and lowest degree of negligent homicide is one that differs
but little in its circumstances from excusable homicide ; but as it does
differ, it must be an offence.   It is defined as homicide involuntarily
inflicted in the performance of a lawful act, in which there is no apparent risk of life, by ordinary means ; but without that care and precaution which a prudent man would take to avoid the risk of destroying human life.   It will be best understood by a perusal of this division
of the section.   But it may here be generally comprehended by repeating one of the examples by which it is there illustrated.   "When
death is casually inflicted by discharging fire-arms which are believed
not to be loaded, without examining whether they are so or not, it
constitutes this offence.   If the examination be made, and owing to some
unknown cause, although loaded, they appear to be empty ; or, if unknown to the person using them, they have been loaded immediately
after the examination, due caution has been used, and there is no offence."   A very slight punishment is annexed to this offence, and I
doubted long whether, as the definition assumes the absence of any intent
to injure, the horror and grief naturally caused by so fatal a consequence
would not, in itself, be a sufficient punishment for the negligence ; that
these sensations must inflict a suffering much more severe than any the
law could with justice award, cannot be questioned.   But, after much
hesitation, I concluded, that this consideration would not justify me in
omitting to place so fatal an act of negligence in the class of offences.
It would induce us totally to excuse all negligent and even many voluntary homicides.   The depravity that can conquer those feelings of
remorse and mental anguish, with which nature avenges the destruction
of human life, is not suddenly, easily, or frequently attained.   He
who, yielding to sudden passion, takes the life of an adversary who
has provoked him, feels the operation of this internal engine of punishment as keenly as he does who is the negligent or even the casual instrument of a similar event.   Nor is even the deliberate murderer
exempt ; and the poets who have painted the most closely from nature,
have always truly represented the subsequent remorse to augment in
proportion to the previous atrocity of the murder.   Richard is haunted
by the ghosts of his victims.   Macbeth exclaims, " I scarce can think
on what I've done—look on it again, I dare not ;" and the reason of
his tiger-hearted instigator and accomplice reels under the weight of
her remorse.   Indeed, of the two, the homicide from sudden passion
may reasonably be supposed to be endowed with keener sensations, and

therefore more sensibly to feel the pang of remorse, than he does who has shown so much indifference to the life of a human being as not to take the proper precautions for its preservation.

Besides, the frequency of these accidents, as they are incorrectly called, seemed to demand some interposition of the law. At present they are considered and classed as excusable. But when they shall be stigmatized as offences; when the voice of the law shall direct the exercise of that circumspection which prudence now in vain commands, it is believed that greater caution will be the result; and instances are not wanting to show, that a positive inhibition, accompanied by the fear of a comparatively slight punishment, has prevented men from incurring risks and rushing on dangers of the most serious nature(a).

The next offence is negligent homicide in the second degree. It differs from the former only in the greater want of caution. It is defined as that which is involuntarily committed in the performance of a lawful act, but under circumstances, in a manner, or by means, which cause an *apparent danger* of inflicting death, without due precaution to avoid such danger. Every word of this definition that could, by the most forced construction, carry any more than one meaning, is carefully explained in the text; and the whole is illustrated by examples, of the *crime* generally; of the *circumstances;* of the *apparent risk,* as applied to the *manner* of doing the act; and to the *means* used. For all these reference is made to the text. As this is a comprehensive division, much greater latitude of discretion is given to the judge, in the apportionment of the punishment, than is usual in other parts of the code.

The concluding division under this head, of negligent homicides, relates to such offences, of this nature, as are committed in the performance of other unlawful acts. This is only to be remarked inasmuch as it graduates the penalty, according to the nature of the illegal act, in the performance of which the homicide was negligently committed.

We now come to the class of Culpable Homicides that are voluntary.

Still pursuing the same plan, of making the preceding definitions a key to those which follow, voluntary homicide is declared to be a crime in all cases where it cannot be justified or excused by any of the rules before laid down. It comprises two divisions only, manslaughter and murder. These denominations are retained from our present law; but the first, being stripped of the whole class of negligent homicides, nothing remains for it but those acts by which the life of another is taken by one who is under the influence of a sudden passion—a crime so different from that which produces the same fatal effect, after deliberation, as to call for a different name, and to merit a milder punishment. But it is still a crime; one difficult, under certain circumstances, to distinguish from murder; as fatal in its consummation, but drawing the distinction made in its favour by the law from two circumstances: some indulgence to the infirmity of our nature, when passion is excited by

(a) A traveller in Prussia, during the reign of Frederick, has told us, that the cavalry reviews of that great disciplinarian were, at one time, very much embarrassed by the dragoons frequently falling from their horses, whereby many of them had their bones broken or were trampled to death. A general order made a fall punishable with thirty-nine stripes; after which it was found, that their horsemanship was so much improved, that falls became very rare.

an adequate cause, and some reprehension for the injury that provoked the passion. The difficulty of drawing the line that separates this crime from the heinous one of murder ; the high importance that it should be distinctly drawn, were felt in framing the provisions of this séction. The numerous cases in the English law on this subject were studied, and all those principles drawn from them which could give precision to the rules that are laid down. Yet, after all that has or can be done to give precise limits to the definitions of crimes, which depend so much as this does on the ever-varying, and for the most part, the inscrutable workings of the perpetrator's mind, much must be left to the discernment of the judge. But, although we cannot do all, it is our duty to do that which is practicable, and, in cases of this high importance, to leave as little as possible to discretion.

Manslaughter, then, is defined to be homicide committed voluntarily, under the immediate influence of sudden passion, arising from an adequate cause; and it is provided, that all the terms used in the definition are to be strictly construed in applying it to any particular act. Each of these terms is commented upon in the law. General rules are prescribed for deciding what species of injury shall, and what shall not, be deemed an adequate cause for the passion that causes the act; and it is supposed that the intention of the law on this important point, is so clearly expressed, as to leave to the jury only the task of deciding, in each case, whether the acts and intentions of the party bring him within its purview.

Having defined, described, and illustrated by examples, and confined within precise rules, all the other species of homicide, we are now to consider the last and highest description of this crime—murder. The particular attention of the legislature is called to the definition of this crime in the new code, and it is earnestly desired that every word of it may be weighed, and that it may be contrasted with the description of it given by our present law, and that the one may be sanctioned which is the most clear and explicit, and which requires the least reference to other sources for understanding it. By the code it is thus described : "Murder is homicide, inflicted with a premeditated design, unaccompanied by any of the circumstances which, according to the previous provisions of this chapter, do not justify, excuse, or bring it within some one of the descriptions of homicide hereinbefore defined." This description was, as the projected code was first printed, contained in two articles. The sense was precisely the same, but the amendment consolidated and made it more concise, and was therefore preferred. If, then, a clear idea in the preceding parts of this chapter has been given of the other descriptions of homicide, there can be no difficulty in forming one of this, that is not liable to error. An act of homicide occurs. Did the circumstances justify it? Did they excuse it? Does it come within any of the descriptions of negligent homicide? Is it manslaughter? If either of these questions be answered in the affirmative, it cannot be murder. The advantage of this mode of description over that of a simple definition is evident ; for should any words, contained in that definition, be liable to misconstruction, an act, properly coming within the lower degree of that offence, might be brought within the definition of the higher. The act of taking human life is the same in all. The attention should, therefore, if we mean to avoid error, be drawn to all the circumstances that would bring the act into a lower

Y

degree of offence, before we inflict on it the punishment due to the highest; and the law should be so framed as to oblige those who administer it to make this examination. By the new code, no jury can convict—no judge can condemn for murder, until they have carefully examined all the lighter shades of homicide, and are convinced that the circumstances of the case do not bring the accused within any of them. The form of the law imposes this obligation. It cannot be dispensed with; for there is no other description of the crime of murder than that it is homicide that is not one of those before described. Now take the English description of the same crime, and see whether the same result is produced. Coke's description of the crime is the one most generally sanctioned by decisions and commentators. It is this : "when a person of sound memory and discretion unlawfully killeth any reasonable creature, in being, and under the king's peace, with malice aforethought, either express or implied"(a). Now suppose a jury empannelled to try an indictment for murder, and after the circumstances of the case have been detailed by the evidence, this description is read to them, and they are directed by the court, under the sanction of their oaths, to apply it to the case. There is scarcely a word in it that, to a conscientious man, will not afford matter for serious doubt. The perpetrator must have been of *sound memory* and *understanding*. What a scope does this give for equivocation. What a field does it open for inquiry. What has the soundness of memory to do with the act? Be the faculty ever so imperfect, how does it affect the guilt? And as to discretion, if a sound discretion were necessary to constitute guilt, no one could be guilty; for surely he commits the highest indiscretion who takes the life of another, and exposes his own to consequences of detection and punishment. The killing must be also *unlawful*. Here we have one of the features of the description contained in the code, but without the faculty which it affords of determining, by a reference to a few preceding pages, whether the killing be lawful. The person killed, to constitute the crime, must be a *reasonable* creature. Neither a newborn infant, nor an idiot, nor a madman, nor one suffering in the delirium of a fever, or stupified by opium or liquor, comes within this part of this description according to the plain meaning of the words. Again, who is in the *king's peace?* What is *malice aforethought?* Is there any malice that is after thought? What is *express malice?* When shall it be *implied?* Thus we find that there is scarcely a word in the description of a crime so important to be known, that will not raise at least a doubt in the mind of a man of common understanding; and it would be difficult, perhaps, to prove any description of the crime, which would sufficiently give us to understand its precise meaning, without a reference to the definitions of those homicides which were not included in it. I am certainly aware that most of these terms have been expounded by commentators and illustrated by decisions, and that a recourse to these sources of information would teach us what construction the best lawyers and judges have put upon them; but still the evil recurs. There is no source to which we can look for the absolute certainty on which the conscience of a juror ought to rest, who is sworn to decide, and the definition given to him as the text of the law: he has a right to put the construction which his understanding adopts, upon

(a) 3 Inst. 87.

the doubtful words; and there are cases, too, in which the expositors to whom he is directed, are not themselves agreed, more particularly in what respects the construction of malice, express or implied—the great pivot on which this definition turns—and one of which it is so difficult to form a definite idea, that I have purposely excluded it from the description of this offence in the code.

I may be deceived, but if I am not more so on this than on any other provision in the work, the law on the subject of homicides, in their various grades, from innocence up to the deepest guilt, is rendered by the code more clear, more consonant to reason, and more susceptible of easy execution than it is as it now stands.

Our present law knows but one grade of murder. Yet there are evident aggravations which ought to be marked by a discreet legislature. Four have been adopted in the code that is presented to you.

INFANTICIDE, the first grade above that of common murder, is distinguished by its disregard, not only to the feelings of humanity, but of nature; but, on the other hand, its atrocity is so much lessened, by the deep and powerful sense of shame which usually prompts it, that I doubted some time whether it should form a separate class. It, however, after due consideration, seemed properly to occupy a place between that kind of voluntary and culpable homicide, committed under circumstances that would not reduce it strictly to manslaughter, but caused by some provocation, yet distinguishing it from the deeper guilt of ASSASSINATION, which is the next grade.

This characteristic is applied to murderers, from considerations drawn from the purpose of the act, the means by which it was accomplished, or the condition of the person suffering by the crime. The purpose gives it this name when it is committed in order to effect another crime, or to conceal one previously committed, when its object is to obtain an inheritance, or when a reward is given and taken for its commission. The means characterize murder as assassination, when it is perpetrated by lying in wait, by arson, by poison. The condition of the party murdered, and his actual situation, also raise the guilt into that of assassination, under the following circumstances : when the sufferer is a woman; a man above the age of seventy; a minor under the age of sixteen; a person in a dwelling-house at night; asleep any where, or travelling on the high-road. All these situations and conditions imply helplessness and security. They add cowardice and treachery to the guilt which invades them, and therefore rank it in this grade of crime.

But if these cases of implied security and protection demand the severe animadversion of the law, in a much higher degree does that of express trust and confidence, and positive treachery. I have, therefore, incorporated as a third class of aggravated murder, that known to the Scottish law by the express name of MURDER UNDER TRUST, and have described it as " that which is committed by persons standing in the following relation to the party murdered, that is to say: husband, wife, tutor or curator, ward, collateral relations within the second degree inclusive, master, servant, schoolmaster, host, guest, physician or surgeon; and finally, if the murder be committed by one upon another, who has reposed confidence of safety in him, on an express or implied promise of fidelity or protection. Murder committed by a guide or conductor on the land, or by the master of a vessel by water, upon a traveller whom he has undertaken to conduct, are examples of this last description of murder under trust." The code, in this as in other cases, contains articles explanatory of all the words used that might be understood in more than one sense.

PARRICIDE is the last species of murder. The English law, while it punishes the murder of a master by a servant, as a species of treason, expresses by no mark of particular abhorrence that of a father by his son. Solon, it is said, thought it too atrocious to be supposed possible, and therefore omitted the mention of it in his code. Modern times afford too many proofs of its recurrence to justify the same expressive silence with respect to it.

The punishment for murder, unaggravated by any of the circumstances which bring it within either of the denominations above mentioned, is imprisonment for life. The Code of Prison Discipline contains the increased privations, and aggravations of punishment that are applied to higher degrees of this crime.

Suicide does not enter into the catalogue of offences, for the reasons offered in the report on the plan of a penal code(a); but a penalty is provided to operate upon those who aid the unhappy sufferer in committing this act of desperation, or who, having the power, do not prevent its execution.

This title could not conclude without a chapter in relation to duels; that practice which, in modern times, seems to have proved how inefficient are all laws when opposed to public opinion, and to what degree the fear of shame will prevail over that of punishment.

In the whole scope of criminal legislation there is no subject which presents greater difficulties. Severe penalties have been denounced against it in vain; and it is the more difficult to be eradicated, because it prevails most where courage, a fear of disgrace, and a sense of personal dignity, are most perfect.

One cause of this disorder in society has been anticipated in that part of this report which treats of injuries to reputation. Where the law gives no such relief as ought to satisfy those who conceive themselves disgraced by imputations on their honour or integrity, as long as honour and integrity are necessary to happiness in society, human passions will endeavour to supply the deficiencies of the law. But the law, as it now stands, gives a partial remedy in those cases of defamation only, which imply a want of integrity or impute the commission of a gross crime; and we accordingly find that redress is sought by an application to the laws for injuries of that nature more frequently than by appeals to arms; while the charge of mendacity, or of a deficiency in the courtesies of life, are more frequent causes of duels than imputations of serious crimes. Why is this? It is because the law gives some relief in the one case— none in the other. One part of the remedy provided by the code is suggested by this consideration. The other is drawn from the motive that leads to the offence: this is, in most cases, a desire to possess that degree of standing in society which raises the possessor in the esteem of his fellow citizens, and gives him a right to expect those distinctions and offices to which his talents may entitle him.

If then we can procure an adequate remedy by law for injuries to reputation, and make an exclusion from office and civil distinction the consequence of any attempt to usurp the functions of the law: if, by proper penalties, we give to those who reluctantly aid in encounters of

(a) See page 16.

this nature, a good pretext for refusing their co-operation, while we take away that which the law now affords them, for refusing to give evidence against their principals, we shall do much to lessen the frequency of this practice, and by giving a turn to public opinion, in time, to extirpate it.

Beginning at the source of the evil, the first provision of the chapter is to make it punishable to use insulting words, or to make an assault with the intent either of provoking a challenge or disgracing the party if he should not give it ; and in order that a prosecution, for such an offence, may be made the means of producing an honourable satisfaction, the next article provides, that if the defendant shall make any denial, explanation or acknowledgement, which, in the opinion of the court, ought to satisfy the honour of the prosecutor, they shall direct the same to be published, with their opinion, declaring it to be satisfactory, and dismiss the defendant; and where no such acknowledgement is made before judgment, it shall, if given against the defendant, contain a clause that it shall be void as to all but costs, in case the defendant shall make such acknowledgement as shall be satisfactory to the prosecutor; and in any prosecution under this article, if the offence be a charge affecting the honour or reputation of the person making the complaint, and the proof on the trial show such charge to be unfounded, the court shall make that declaration in the sentence, and cause it to be published at the expense of the defendant, and the truth of such charge shall, if the prosecutor desire it, be tried by the jury.

These provisions are entirely new. They give, what the law has hitherto denied, satisfaction for those species of insults which most commonly lead to duels, and satisfaction of a species that the most chivalrous need not blush to seek or to receive ; and insomuch, they are calculated to prevent those fatal encounters which few, if any of those who engage in them, would not avoid, if any other mode were provided by which they could escape disgrace. If, however, the parties refuse this remedy for their wrongs, and give or accept a challenge to fight a duel, although it should not take place, the penalty is imprisonment in close custody from two to six months, and a suspension of political rights for four years; if the duel take place, the penalty is increased by a longer period of imprisonment, and a protracted suspension of rights both civil and political, in proportion to the injury resulting from such conflict ; if it result in death, the imprisonment is extended to four years ; and all political rights, and the civil rights of the first and third class, are forfeited for ever. If the wound which produces death is inflicted by treachery, it is declared to be murder by assassination. The treachery intended by this provision, is defined to be the breach of any rules made for conducting the combat, or by taking any other advantage that could not be supposed to have been intended to be given; and whatever may have been the rules agreed upon, it is declared to be assassination, if the mortal wound be given after the party is disarmed or otherwise incapable of resistance ; or, if the party inflicting the mortal wound have obtained the power of doing it without risk to himself by the effect of a chance previously agreed upon. These two last provisions are intended to put an end to a ferocious practice sometimes resorted to in duels; which it is thought may be done, as much by stigmatizing them by the designation of treachery and assassination, as by the severe punishment assigned to them, which punishment there will, in such cases, be no disposition in the prejudices of jurors to avoid inflicting. However imperative we may make the language of the law, it loses its force when it includes in the same prohibition, by the same name, and under the same penalty, acts different in their motives, circumstances and effects. We may, in our statutes, give the name of murder to death occasioned by a duel; but the world will not adopt the appellation ; and a combat, sanctioned by the irresistible command of public opinion, and marked by no circumstances of peculiar malignity, will never be considered, prosecuted or punished, as an assassination. If you wish to have it punished at all, it must be by its own name, and a proportionate punishment, nor must that be an infamous one. Put what is called a fair duellist on a footing with a thief or a murderer, and you assure his impunity. Consign him to a temporary, close, but not degrading imprisonment; take away from him all hope of political preferment; and seeing that his conviction and its consequences cannot be escaped, he will gladly avail himself of the opportunity offered by the laws, of throwing off, without disgrace, the tyranny of custom ; for there is this peculiarity in the offence of which we now speak, that nine times in ten it is most reluctantly committed by all who are parties to it. Let the severe punishment, then, be reserved for treachery and ferocity; inflict a mild penalty on duels fairly conducted ; punish the insults which lead to them, and you will insure the execution of the law; furnish a fair excuse for even the most high-minded to avoid incurring the disadvantages which it creates, and do more than has been yet done to abolish this barbarous, unequal and unjust mode of settling private quarrels.

If prosecuting officers had always used the same diligence in bringing duellists to justice that they have shown in the case of other offenders against the laws, although the accused might escape the severe penalties of the law from the lenity of jurors, yet the risk, inconvenience, solicitude and expense of the trial, would deter many, particularly those who had aided as witnesses or seconds; but there seems to be a general tacit consent, on the part of the magistrates, attorneys for the state, and grand jurors, that there is something dishonourable in such prosecutions, and that they form an exception to the oath of office, and are not to be prosecuted, unless on the most direct application, and on producing the fullest proof. How else shall we account for the open, notorious, flagrant breaches of the law so frequently taking place almost in the presence of the magistrate, the grand jurors, and the prosecuting officer, without any instance of prosecution. To remedy this evil, the code provides, that the attorney-general and district attorneys shall make a declaration on oath, and also make an honorary declaration, that they consider the execution of laws against duelling as forming no exception to their duty of carrying the laws into effect; and that they will, by all lawful means, prevent any intended duel which comes to their knowledge, and prosecute all offences against that part of the code. Still further to prevent this offence, no person elected or appointed to any office, civil or military, judicial or executive, shall exercise the same, unless he shall declare, on oath, that he has not and will not commit any of the offences described in this chapter. I was not unapprized when these provisions were recommended, that this expedient had been partially resorted to in some of the states, and that it had not been deemed a proper remedy. But I apprehend, that in the cases where it has appeared to fail, it

was not fully or fairly tried ; and I have from the first authority, that
in one state, at least, it had proved so nearly effectual as to render
duels extremely rare where they had formerly prevailed to a most
alarming -degree. ' In a letter, with which I have been favoured by
the chief-justice of the United States, he says : " On the subject of
duelling, some contrariety of opinion prevails.    I am among those
who think that the utmost wisdom is required, and ought to be
exerted, for its.prevention.    Originating in a sense of honour, the passion from which it springs must be consulted, if we hope to suppress it.
We must array ambition against this false honour, as its only equal
competitor in a young and ardent mind.    The privation of political
rights, which you propose,. is, I think, particularly adapted to- this
offence.    The efficacy, as in most other cases, depends on the certainty that the law will be executed.    Were you to rely on public convictions alone, this certainty would not exist.    Even where death
ensues, prosecutions will not always be instituted.    When it does not
ensue, still more where the duel does not take place, the whole affair
will generally be overlooked ; and challenges will not be completely
restrained.    The oath you require from every person appointed or
elected to any office whatever, before he can enter upon its duties, is,
I believe, the best, if not the only measure which human wisdom can
devise.    Its efficacy has been proved in Virginia, where a similar oath
is prescribed and has been rigidly exacted.    The consequence is, that
duelling, formerly so common, is now scarcely known in this state,
and public opinion on the subject, is very much changed."    This
high authority, supported, as it always is, by irrefragable argument for
the doctrines stamped with its approbation, has confirmed me in the
purpose of retaining in the code, which is submitted to you, the provisions I have detailed.    The same false sentiment of honour which
leads to a breach of the laws in committing this offence, renders its punishment more difficult.    Witnesses avail themselves of the principle,
that they cannot be compelled to justify any thing that may inculpate
themselves ; and, therefore, neither seconds, nor surgeons, nor any
others, who were voluntarily present, can be induced to testify ;
so that facts notorious to the world, published in every newspaper,
which must be known and understood in order to exonerate the parties
from the foul crime of assassination, and which, therefore, they cannot
wish to keep secret, can rarely be proved before a court of justice.
In order to obviate this, in another part of the system it is provided,
that those who have served as seconds in a duel, or witnessed one as
surgeons, shall be forced to give testimony against the principals ; and
that no person, so examined, shall be himself punishable for the offence.
This, together with the forfeiture of political and civil rights incurred
by the second, if he be convicted, will make it extremely difficult for
principals to obtain friends to attend them to the field ; and the dishonourable as well as dangerous suspicions that must attach to the survivor,
in a duel without witnesses, will generally prove an insurmountable
obstacle to such encounters.

The frequency of this offence in our state, the many valuable lives
which have been sacrificed ,to this false point of honour, the distress
with which it has overwhelmed whole families, and the particular ferocity which of late years the practice has assumed—all justify the
attention of the legislature, and call for its special interference ; not in

the shape of severe penalties ; not by denouncing punishments which are never inflicted ; but by preventive remedies ; by mild laws, so framed as to secure their execution, and by taking away, in most cases, the pretext for private vengeance which was offered by the deficiencies of public justice.

The twentieth title, " Of offences affecting individuals in their profession or trade," contains only a reference to other parts of the code, in which offences, under that description, were necessarily noticed ; it being found impossible, without repetition, or anticipating on other provisions, to arrange these under a separate head.

The condition of individuals, or that relation in which nature and the institutions of society have placed them with respect to each other, is the source of rights as well as of other enjoyments, which ought to be protected by law.   Our present laws afford this protection but imperfectly in some instances, and totally deny it in others.   The substitution of one infant for another, at such a tender age as renders the exchange and the deceit practicable in the absence of the parent ; the production of a pretended child for the purpose of intercepting an inheritance, are not offences by our present law ; yet the jurisprudence of all nations gives us examples of these deceptions.   The destruction or falsification of registers of births, marriages and deaths, for the purpose of injuring the condition of another, is also made punishable by proper penalties.   The common practice of exposing infants was thought to be not improperly ranged under this head ; for although it is certainly an injury to the person, and as such might have been classed in that division, yet the principal injury is that offered to his condition, by causing him to lose the advantages of the relation in which he would have been placed as the child of his parents.

The conditions arising from the important relation of husband and wife, may be affected in the most cruel and injurious manner, by contracting a second marriage during the existence of a former connexion of the same kind.   While the civil law pronounces the last marriage void, the penal law cannot but add the sanction of a heavy punishment to a fraudulent act, which disappoints the hopes of domestic happiness, deprives the offspring of the first union of a parent's care, and devotes those of the second to unmerited reproach, and all the other evils of illegitimacy.   Our present law is not silent on this last offence; but the statute wants precision, and one of the exceptions would seem by its language to give the means of evading its penalties without much difficulty; for it declares, they shall not attach to any one whose husband or wife shall have absented him or herself from the other for five years, " the one of them (that is the husband or wife) not knowing the other to be living within that time."   So that, if the offending can only keep the injured party in ignorance of his existence for five years, he may contract a second marriage with impunity.   Besides correcting this inaccuracy, by restricting the exception to the innocent party, the nineteenth title contains many other articles to prevent the evasion of the law, and to clear up doubts in a matter so important to the peace of families and the good order of society.

We have now come to the consideration of  a class more numerous and more difficult to repress, than any in the catalogue of offences : those affecting property ; which word is here used precisely in the sense given to it in the Book of Definitions ; that is to say, that it conveys a compound idea, composed of that which is the subject of property and the right to be exercised over it.   In relation to its object, property is either corporeal or incorporeal ; and the right to be exercised over it, is that of possessing and using it with respect to that which is corporeal, and of enforcing and transferring it with respect to that which is incorporeal.   Consequently, the injuries treated of in this title, are acts which interfere with the exercise of the right, which may be done either by destroying or injuring the thing which is the object of property, or by removing it from the possession of the owner, and appropriating it.   On this distinction is founded the division of these offences, into malicious injuries to property, and fraudulent appropriations of it.

1.  In the former, the term malicious is intended to exclude negligent or unintentional injuries, which are left, when the case requires it, to the operation of the civil law.

The most common, as well as the most dangerous offence of this nature, is that called arson by our present law, which imposes the penalty of imprisonment for life on the burning of certain enumerated buildings, and seven years at hard labour for the burning of any other building.   In the new code the severest punishment, for this offence, is fourteen years' penitentiary imprisonment, and this is restricted to the burning of a dwelling-house. A distinction between it, and other buildings not inhabited, being obviously proper.   The destruction of other buildings is made punishable by penalties proportioned to their value; and the chapter contains provisions for the protection of all property real or personal, against every species of malicious mischief.   All the terms used, are defined; the defect in our present law, which punishes no other injury of this kind to property but by burning, is supplied; and two articles are added, which provide for other important omissions; the one, the malicious destruction of title-deeds or evidences of property; the other, the removal or destruction of landmarks.

A second chapter provides for a case analogous to those mentioned in the one that precedes it.   This is the invasion of property by housebreaking; which is defined to be the entry into a house secretly, or by force, or threats, or fraud, during the night, or entry by day and concealment until night, with the intent of committing a crime.   As this is a distinct offence from that of appropriating property after the house has been so entered, and is completed by the entry itself with the intent to commit any species of crime, whether against person or property, it occupies a kind of middle ground between malicious injury to property and the next division, a fraudulent appropriation of it.

2. In this division, it is believed, that several valuable improvements have been introduced, both in the arrangement and the manner.   It is arranged under six heads, and treated of in as many different sections.

The first is the fraudulent appropriation of personal property, which had been delivered to the offender for another purpose.   This section, by several precise articles, is calculated to avoid the uncertainty that has prevailed with respect to constructive thefts, and by providing an adequate punishment, which was totally wanting, for fraudulent breaches of trust, to assign to each of these offences its appropriate penalty and character.

The second section provides for a case that is now either always confounded with theft, or considered as not coming within the scope of

Z

any penal law.    I mean the fraudulent appropriation of property found. Whatever, in strict morality, may be the character of such act, it is clearly less in degree of guilt than theft; while, at the same time, the injury to the owner, and the knowledge which the finder must have that the property is not his, ought to rank it as an offence ; though one deserving a lighter punishment.

A third section relates to the violation of epistolary correspondence; an act not punishable by our present law; but one which, whether we consider the want of principle that must produce it, or the injury it is calculated to do, ought to be repressed by the sanction of the law.    The unauthorized opening and reading of a sealed letter; the publication of such letter so improperly opened; the taking of a letter from another without his consent, whether sealed or not, and the malicious publication thereof, are severally declared to be offences, and are made punishable by fine and imprisonment.    The sanctity of private correspondence, and of the confidential communications of friendship, have been too often violated  by  party spirit or unprincipled treachery, in our day, to require any argument to show why this section has been deemed necessary.

The two next sections are of high importance in this general division of offences; and the attention of the legislature is particularly invited to their provisions.    They relate to two offences that are frequently confounded, but which are here endeavoured to be distinguished by definitions and rules which are minute, and it is hoped, will be found to be intelligible and precise.    These offences are, the obtaining of property by false pretences, and theft, properly so called.    The uncertainty of the English law on this subject was lamented by lord Hale ; and the multiplicity of decisions, since his time, have rather rendered it more obscure.    That great lawyer says : " It is the mind which maketh the taking of another's goods to be felony or a bare trespass only ; but because the variety of circumstances is so great, and the complication thereof so mingled, that it is impossible to prescribe all the circumstances evidencing a felonious intent, or the contrary, the same must be left to the due and attentive consideration of the judges and jury ; whence the best rule is, in doubtful matters, rather to incline to acquittal than to conviction"(a).    These *doubtful matters* alluded to in his lordship's opinion might, it was thought, be much diminished in number, and, of course, the conviction of guilt, and the acquittal of innocence rendered more certain, by adopting precise definitions, drawing practical deductions from them, and elucidating the whole by examples.    It has been my endeavour to do this ; with what success can only be determined, by a close examination of the text.    Simple theft being sufficiently described, and the danger of confounding it with other fraudulent appropriations of property avoided ; the next consideration is the different aggravations of which it is susceptible.    These form the subjects of the three following sections.

The first of these is theft by effraction.    This differs from the crime known  by the name of burglary, by our present  law, in this, that it is committed by breaking into a house by day, or by actually committing the theft therein without breaking ; whereas burglary can only be committed by a nocturnal effraction, and is complete by the intent of en-

(a) Hale's P. C., p. 509.

tering, in which it more resembles the offence which has hereinbefore been described as house-breaking. Stealing by an entry, without effraction, is punished by a mitigated penalty ; but the crime and the punishment are aggravated by the circumstances of actual violence to any person who may resist the offender, or of preventing such resistance by threats. There is an error of the press in placing in this section the two last articles, respecting wrecked property. They properly belong to the section which treats of the fraudulent appropriation of property found.

The next aggravation is that of privately stealing from the person, which I have been induced to place in a separate grade of crime, principally from the consideration that it is one which cannot well be committed, to any extent, without a dexterity acquired only by long practice and instruction ; and also from the difficulty of guarding against the depredations of its exercise.

The last aggravated theft, which it has been deemed proper to notice, is robbery, which is " theft committed by fraudulently taking the property of another from his person, or in his presence, with his knowledge and against his will ; whether it be taken by force, or delivered, or suffered to be taken through fear of some illegal injury to person, property, or reputation, that is threatened by the robber or his accomplice."

The description of these last two offences is so nearly similar to those contained in the English law, as to require no elucidation ; nor does any seem necessary for that treated of in the concluding section, namely, receiving property knowing it to be stolen. But, although the English law has been made the ground-work of these and other provisions, it is not meant to allege that the rules of that jurisprudence have been strictly followed, except where they have been found to coincide, as they for the most part do, with those of justice.

The fourth chapter of this title defines an offence of no unfrequent occurrence in England, and which, it was thought, should be guarded against here ; that of attempting to obtain property or other advantage by such threats, either of injury to person, reputation or property, as do not amount to robbery, according to the definition of that offence contained in this code. The offence chiefly intended to be guarded against by this chapter, is that of sending threatening messages or letters, either to obtain property, to procure service, or merely to alarm.

The last chapter of this book contains a description of offences which it was found impossible to bring within any one division of the code, because it might affect as well the person, the reputation, the property, or the profession or trade of individuals. To have treated conspiracy as a separate offence, under each of these titles, would but have led to a tiresome and useless repetition. It was, therefore, determined to annex it to the whole as a concluding chapter. It is there defined as an agreement, between two or more persons, to do any unlawful act, or any of those acts designated in the law, which become by the combination, injurious to others. Those are further explained to be, agreements to commit offences ; to accuse and prosecute falsely ; to do certain enumerated injuries that are not offences when done by an individual. The object of the first two of these combinations needs no explanation. The offence is the act of combining to do them. If the completion of the design were made necessary to constitute the offence, the evil would, in many cases, be without remedy.  The agreement between two or more persons is an act which shows a settled design ; and is clearly distinguishable from an intent formed in the mind of an individual, not only because of its being more susceptible of proof, but also from the circumstance, that, if the original design of the individual could be made to appear, a change of purpose might have taken place, of which no evidence could be given ; whereas, a combination between two or more must have been communicated by some outward acts, and the renunciation of the project evidenced in the same way ; both being susceptible of proof.  A combination too, although discovered before execution, is injurious, because it excites alarm in the person who was the object of it, and a sense of danger and suspicion in the whole community, which the most determined but secret intention of an individual could never do.  The danger is also increased by the character of the injury to be effected by these combinations ; they being, for the most part, such as individual malignity alone could not accomplish.  For these reasons agreements to do certain acts, although never carried into execution, are, in this and other parts of the code, made punishable as offences.

The third head under which conspiracy is made an offence, although the act agreed to be done would not be an offence, without such previous agreement, requires more elucidation.  Its object is to prevent combinations injurious to trade, by raising or depressing wages.  This subject is one that has engaged some attention lately in England, where the laws, as they now stand, prohibit combinations among workmen for raising their wages, but do not consider, as an offence, a similar agreement among employers to lower them.  To impose as few restraints as possible upon the liberty of action, is undoubtedly a sound rule, in that part of legislation which may operate upon political economy ; and therefore it might, on a superficial view, seem that any regulation, as to the conduct of those concerned in manufactures and trade, in relation to the price they may choose to put on their own labour, or give for that of others, would be contrary to this rule.  But the law interposes here, not to impose a restriction, but to prevent one from being imposed by an incompetent authority.  Every labourer has a right to refuse his services, unless the price which he appreciates them at, be that price ever so extravagant, be paid.  Every employer has the right to refuse the same service, unless the price be reduced to the sum he thinks it worth.  But whenever an agreement takes place among the class of employers or labourers, for regulating these prices, then such an agreement becomes, to the extent to which it can be enforced, a law operating for the reduction or advance of wages, and a law made by parties interested in the imposition of it; and, therefore, necessarily unjust ; and, if permitted, would be, in effect, a usurpation of the powers of legislation, and an unwise and oppressive exercise of them : for, although an agreement be only a law to those who are parties to it, yet, when the object of it is to affect the interest of others in a way in which they would not be effected but for such agreement, it is in its operation, although it may not be in its form, a law operating, though not binding, upon those who are not parties to, but objects of the agreement.  Suppose a law instead of an agreement, and that a statute should render it unlawful in any employer to give more than a certain price to his labourers, the effect upon this last class would be precisely the same; yet such a law would be acknowledged to be one at variance with the principles of free exertion, free use of capital, and free competition. The agreement, therefore, is hostile to these principles, and ought not to be permitted. For these reasons the code, in conformity with the English law, imposes a penalty on any two or more persons conspiring to raise the price of wages; but it adds to that provision, one which is wanting in the English statute, imposing a similar penalty on a combination between employers to reduce the price of labour. Without this, the law would be partial and unjust in its operation. Employers in any one branch of manufacture, being, comparatively to the operators, few in number, an agreement between them is more easily made; more readily enforced among themselves; and, while their wealth enables them to wait the effect of their combination, the poverty of those against whom it is directed, obliges them soon to yield to the dictates of their employers, be they ever so oppressive. This inequality in the effects of this offence, between these two classes of men upon whom it reciprocally operates, requires a correspondent difference in the punishment; and it is, therefore, directed that imprisonment shall always be part of the sentence against employers for a combination to lower the rate of wages, for this cogent reason, that the highest limit which could be given to the fine upon the labourer, would be no punishment to his wealthy employer, who should be guilty of the same offence. It is also provided, that an agreement to require a longer time to labour in the day, or to decrease the number of working hours, without altering the price, shall be considered as a combination to lower or raise the rate of wages; and if the agreement be to inflict any injury on those who will not become parties to it, the punishment is to be doubled. Other articles are contained in the text, calculated to explain, and carry into effect those which have been commented on, and to guard against abuses in enforcing them.

The rapid view I have thought it necessary to take of this important branch of the work committed to me, is now finished. Some comments and arguments that, perhaps, ought to have formed a part of it, have been doubtless omitted. They will readily be supplied by the intelligence of the body to whom it is submitted; but I much fear that the reproach of having unreasonably trespassed on their attention, may have been more justly incurred. Yet nothing has been advanced which was not thought necessary to the elucidation of the great variety of provisions contained in this code, and much was designedly left to be supplied by reflection.

# INTRODUCTORY REPORT

TO

# THE CODE OF PROCEDURE.

I HAVE now the honour to present the second of those codes which your law has directed me to prepare. The legislature, which passed that law, were aware that no system would be complete without a Code of Procedure. Expense, delay or uncertainty, in applying the best laws for the prohibition of offences, would render those laws useless or oppressive. Therefore, this division has been considered of equal importance with any of the others, but more extensive in its operation than either of them. The party committing the offence and the individual injured, rarely the whole community, are the only persons immediately affected by the commission and punishment of a crime. But in the measures prescribed for preventing or prosecuting them, every citizen, however unconnected with the offence, may find himself involved. As a judge, a magistrate, a civil or military officer, or even a private citizen, every one is liable to become an active party in the task of applying the law, after a breach of its provisions has taken place, in preventing the commission of a crime, or in arresting the progress of such as are continuous in their nature. The rules which direct us in what manner, under what circumstances, and to what extent we may use force to protect our own persons and property, or those of another, against unlawful violence, also belong to this division of the law; so that its provisions are more required for daily use than those of any other part of the system; and it may, therefore, without impropriety, be said, that a society, however excellent may be its laws for defining crimes and affixing to them proper punishments, will, if the means of carrying them into effect are expensive, dilatory and uncertain, be worse governed than the community in which the Code of Crimes and Punishments is faulty, but where the rules for executing it, and for preventing and arresting the progress of offences, are easy, cheap, expeditious and just. More attention, therefore, has been paid to this branch of the subject than the little importance, commonly attached to it, would seem to warrant. None of the codes which have come within my knowledge, either ancient or modern, except the French, contain any separate body of laws directing the mode of procedure, either for arrest, trial, punishment or prevention. Our laws, as we have seen, are wofully defective in this particular; giving for acts, which, by some laws, are declared to be offences, no rule whatever; and for the others, referring us to the English common law, unmodified by statute. The necessity, therefore, of a Code of Procedure was much more urgent than that which existed for a Code of Crimes and Punishments. The system adopted in the prosecution of certain offences, by the legislature, and in that of others by the courts, with the modifications introduced by our statutes, is freed from many of the abuses and oppressions to which criminal prosecutions in England are liable : a public officer being appointed to prosecute, the individual who has suffered by the crime, is not, in addition to his loss, put to the expense of bringing the offender to justice : jurors being taken by lot, no improper influence can be exerted in the arrangement of the panel : the assistance of counsel being secured in all cases, the defendant, no matter of what he is accused, is enabled to make his full defence: and the intervention of a grand jury being rendered necessary in every case of a grave accusation, the individual is not exposed to vexatious prosecutions that can materially affect him. Standing mute is considered as a denial, not a confession. Appeals of murder, trials by battle, and many other oppressive and absurd parts of the ancient common law, have never been used in our state. Yet, with all these comparative advantages, our practice requires reform.

First, because the exemption from several of these and other inconveniences is, in many instances, not secured by law ; and, in others, is given to us by the construction of the court, contrary to law. In the Introductory Report to the System of Penal Law, it has been shown, that where the common law of England is prescribed as the law of our procedure, it is spoken of without any of the amendments introduced by the English statutes; and that in all acts, which are created offences since 1805, no mode of procedure whatever has been provided.

Secondly, because, if the present mode of procedure were sanctioned by law, it would require alterations and additions in the several particulars in which they have been introduced in the code, some of which will be hereinafter pointed out, with the reasons for introducing them.

Thirdly, because of the difficulty, expense and inconvenience, before enlarged upon, of referring to foreign laws, written in a language which a majority of our citizens do not understand.

Fourthly, because of the uncertainty inseparable from laws depending for their authority upon judicial decisions.

Fifthly, as incident to the two last, because of the ease, convenience, and indeed necessity, for all those who wish to perform their duty as good citizens, of finding in one book, couched in language easily understood, and arranged in a method making them easily accessible to all ; the rules necessary to direct them in all the cases in which self-defence, the prevention of crime, the arrest of offenders, and their high duties as magistrates or jurors.

The Code of Procedure now offered, sets out, as that of Crimes and Punishments does, with an introductory chapter, containing a brief exposition of the objects which it is intended to effect. To this enunciation I have heard no objection stated, and its utility has been acknowledged by many of those statesmen and jurists to whom the plan has been submitted ; it has, therefore, been retained.

The first of these objects, in order, as well as in importance, is the prevention of intended offences. This may be effected by personal resistance. The cases in which resistance is lawful, the degree to which it may be carried, under what circumstances the interference of private individuals is permitted, when the sanction of a magistrate is required, his right to command the assistance of others, and when he may require the aid of military force, together with the formalities required for effecting these objects, are set forth in the first book.

According to our present jurisprudence, there is either no written law for our direction on these points, which it is so much our interest, as parties, magistrates or citizens, to know, or it is so dispersed in different books, so uncertain when it is found, and of such doubtful authority, as to render it unsafe for any one to trust to his own opinion, or in truth, in many cases, to that of others. Yet the occasions which call for the exercise of these rights and duties, are those of all others in which there is least time to reflect, or opportunity to consult. For this reason, every man ought to be provided with the means of acquiring so much knowledge on these points as is necessary for daily use. Without it, he will neither know how to protect himself, or pay these duties, which he may be urgently called on to perform in the protection of others. He must either act at his peril, submit to injuries which he has a right to repel, or depend on the purchased opinions, and sometimes the 'forked counsel,' of men who disgrace an honourable profession.

The first dictates of common sense inform an individual that he has a right to defend himself. The laws of society impose the obligation upon him of defending others, and of enforcing the execution of the laws. Magistrates and executive officers are required by official duty to prevent or arrest violence and depredation; and the military force is told, that it must assist the civil power when legally called on. All this the general language of the law gives the citizen to understand. But in our state it has never deigned to make such a record of its will as may enable any one, desirous of obeying, to discover boundaries between legal acts and transgression in the performance of this duty. A correct moral sense, a determination to injure no one may, with respect to a man's own actions, render a knowledge of positive law less necessary; but no prudence can foresee or prevent the necessity of self-defence, and every man may be called on in some capacity to protect others or to defend the peace of the state; and yet with every inclination to perform the duties of a good citizen on these occasions, he is continually arrested by the unavoidable doubts which must arise as to the propriety of personal exertion in the particular case, or the extent to which he may carry it. On the vital subject of calling in the military to the aid of the civil powers, there is absolutely no provision; and there is no power liable to a more dangerous abuse. Sometimes necessary for the defence of the constitution and the enforcement of the laws, it is, at the same time, the weapon best adapted for their subversion. The circumstances, therefore, in which its use is permitted, and the mode of its exercise, ought to be impressed on the mind of every citizen to prevent his refusing his aid when it is legally required on the one hand, and of his being made the instrument of his own oppression on the other. It is attempted, in the first book of the code now presented, to provide a remedy for these evils.

The first title treats of the modes of preventing apprehended offences,

2 A

which it is declared may be either by resistance or by the intervention of the officers of justice.

The first chapter, by reference to the corresponding parts of the Penal Code, lays down the rules by which the resistance of the party injured, to offences affecting his person or property, is regulated. The second chapter details the cases in which third persons may interfere, without the sanction of the magistrate, and those in which such interference is not only a right, but a legal as well as a moral duty. In this chapter are contained two provisions which require particular notice. By the first an honorary reward is held out as an inducement for extraordinary exertion in the prevention of crime, or in bringing an offender to justice. This consists in a certificate of the act, recorded on the minutes of the court, and transmitted to the appointing power to serve as a recommendation for any office in which the qualities manifested by it are required; to this, in such cases as the governor and judges think worthy of the distinction, a piece of plate, of limited value, may be added. A very high authority(a) tells us, that recompense, in a despotism, must, to accord with what he terms the principle of the government, be of a pecuniary nature, and honorary in a monarchy; but that in a republic, founded on virtue, and which he seems to think ought to be its own reward, it ought not to be allowed at all. He admits, that in a monarchy the honour is and ought to be accompanied by fortune; but why his doctrine should interdict to republics the agency of both honour and profit, upon the human mind for the public good, it is not easy to imagine. If a republic could be composed of men willing to devote their services to their country from a patriotic desire to see it prosper, without the admixture of any other motive, rewards and distinction would be unnecessary; but such pure attachment to the public good has never been known to pervade any community; and the reward of public esteem, and the distinction to which it leads, must ever be so closely connected in the mind with the most elevated and disinterested patriotism, as to make it extremely difficult to pronounce the latter motive to have been that which predominated in any given exertion for the public service. All that a wise legislator can be expected to do, is to present such motives as will most effectually attain the end, which, in the case under consideration, is extraordinary exertion for the due execution of the laws. But we must take care that these means are not such as will produce a greater evil than the breach of the laws which they are employed to enforce. Such I confess would be a corruption of the morals of the people, or the introduction of any motive that would destroy the fundamental principles of their government.

Let us test the system of rewards for extraordinary services by this rule. There can be no greater incentive to voluntary action than the hope of public applause, and when joined to pecuniary recompense and undiminished by any consciousness of wrong, it comprises all, perhaps, that, independent of religious motives, can most forcibly act on the human mind ; it is, therefore, well calculated to produce the effect. For let it be remarked, that it is proposed solely to operate in cases where the fears of punishment cannot be employed ; no man can justly incur a penalty for not doing more than the law requires ; but the public good may, at times, be essentially promoted by such acts.

<hr/>

(a) Montesquieu, Esprit des Lois, l. 5, c. 18.

Some motive, therefore, should be held out for their performance. Some passion must be enlisted : it cannot, as we have seen, be fear : it must then, as the only alternative, be hope—hope of some enjoyment. Of what nature shall that enjoyment be ? With consciousness of well-doing, pure love of country unconnected with any personal credit or other advantage, and with public esteem without any substantial testimonials of its existence ; legislation can have nothing to do. The first must exist in every uncorrupted mind, whatever may be the operation of the laws ; the second is equally independent of external causes, and the third must in all societies, in a greater or less degree, attend the performance of actions for the public good. But these motives are not sufficiently general or strong to justify us in relying solely on their operation. Laws must be made for men as they are, not such as an exalted theory of imagined perfection suppose them to be ; and although in every community some may be found capable of doing extraordinary acts of public service, without even the hope of reaping the reward of the esteem of those for whose benefit they were performed ; yet the bulk of mankind require something more. The consciousness of a good action, the knowledge of the benefit it has conferred on the country, and even the persuasion that it is known and silently approved, is not sufficient. Good policy, it is thought, as well as justice, requires that this esteem should be expressed by some external mark ; and that pecuniary recompense, the representative of so many other enjoyments, should, in particular cases, be superadded as a testimonial of gratitude. That the hope of these additional rewards would strengthen the motive to action there can be no doubt ; and if they do not counteract the more refined and disinterested impulses, which have the same tendency, they may safely be employed; for although laws cannot direct the operations of the mind, yet those laws may promote or discourage them, by offering other co-operating or counteracting inducements to produce or defeat the end proposed ; and the inquiry is, which of these effects will be produced by the employment of the rewards proposed in this part of the code ? Those held out, for danger incurred, diligence used, or skill displayed in any extraordinary degree, in preventing an offence, or bringing in offenders to justice, are addressed exclusively to love of distinction, and of that distinction only which is founded on public gratitude and esteem. While this passion can be directed to the support of the government, the due execution of the laws and the defence of private right, it supports that which is assumed to be the principle of republican governments : it produces the same effect, excites to the same acts, and cannot be distingushed in its operation from the most exalted public virtue. But the rewards held out by the code, for extraordinary services, are precisely of this nature : a certificate of the fact, recorded, published, and transmitted to the appointing power, to serve as an authentic recommendation for offices requiring the exercise of the qualities displayed. In ordinary cases, this is given by the court ; in those which evince higher merit, the concurrence of the governor, entitles the party to the additional testimonial of a goblet or vase of little pecuniary intrinsic value ; but the inscription, in which the meritorious act is recorded, placed continually before his eyes and those of his family, raises him in his own esteem, increases the reverence of his domestic circle, and gives him a limited local celebrity, which not only adds to his own happiness, but, within a certain sphere, operates as an incentive to promote that of the public.

Honours conferred for brilliant achievements in war, or eminent services in council, may in a republic be said, perhaps with some propriety, to be liable to objection ; not because they are wrong in themselves, but because, by exciting the admiration of the people to a high degree and attaching it to one man, they give him an undue influence that may be sometimes used to the destruction of liberty.   But no such consequence can be apprehended from the unpretending limited popularity and distinction given by the means pointed out by the code.   On the contrary, beneficial political effects may be expected by bringing within the reach of those in the humblest station those testimonials of eminent merit, and by associating public favour in their minds with the execution of the laws.   He who has risked his life in an unequal encounter with ruffians, either to protect another from their violence, or to secure them for the purpose of punishment, every one will allow deserves public esteem ; but it can neither be permanent nor extensive, and, of course, will lose much of its value, if it is confined to the narrow circle of those who happen to have witnessed, or to have been benefited by its exertion.   It is soon forgotten, it loses most of its effect as an example, and it is buried in the same oblivion with the every-day transactions which have nothing to impress them on the memory.

> Paulum sepultæ distat inertiæ
> Celata virtus.

Let the little hero of the hamlet have his celebrity for supporting the laws, and you will have fewer great heroes who seek it by breaking them ; and let it be remembered, that the recorded certificate and the engraved goblet are not given to reward the act, but to keep it in memory.   The only reward is the public consideration, which will not be measured by the worth of these testimonials, but by the merit and utility of the service rendered.

The provisions of the next succeeding articles are founded on other principles, and I confess are liable to stronger objections ; they give a pecuniary reward to him who denounces the commission of certain crimes.

1. In order to bring offenders to justice, two distinct duties are to be performed.   The public officer must prosecute ; but he cannot do this until the private individual, who has suffered by the offence, or knows that it has been committed, shall accuse.   In most cases we may safely rely for the performance of this last mentioned duty upon the feeling of resentment for the injury, or upon a sense of public justice.   There are cases, however, in which neither of these motives exist, or are not sufficiently strong to produce the desired effect, and in which, to secure the execution of the laws, other inducements must be brought to bear. Punishments and rewards are those only, which the legislator has at his disposal.   The first, it was thought, ought not on this occasion to be used, for the general reason, that the denunciation of penalties ought not to be multiplied without evident necessity ; and also, because it was thought proper to make a sensible distinction between the omission to give notice of an intended crime, so as to prevent its commission (which is made punishable by the code) and the failure to denounce a crime already committed.   As the punishment for the first offence was

necessarily placed very low on the scale, the other must either have been rated so low as scarcely to deserve the name of punishment, or else so high as to run the risk of confounding two acts somewhat similar in their nature, but very different in their injurious effects. There was moreover another reason for not employing the sanction of punishment on this occasion. It is a wise maxim in legislation, never to enact laws that the prejudices of the people or other circumstances will not allow you to enforce. Oppressive laws have in most countries, and from the remotest antiquity, caused those by whom they were governed to array themselves against their execution ; and whenever any one of their own number lent his voluntary aid in enforcing them, to consider him as a betrayer of their common interest. For which reason a degree of infamy became attached to the name and office of an informer, which has extended itself in a greater or less degree to those who voluntarily offer evidence of the infraction of the laws, even in countries where they are neither oppressive nor unjust. To impose a penalty, therefore, on those who, guilty of no crime themselves, should shrink from taking upon themselves the task of accusers, would seem unjust even if the penalty be enforced, which, in the common course of things, would rarely happen. First, because it is scarcely ever susceptible of proof. If I have witnessed the commission of the crime and do not inform, who is to accuse me ? Not the offender, surely. Not the injured party : for, if he be alive and desire the prosecution, he is the proper accuser. Not another witness ; for he is in the same predicament with myself if he omit to denounce it, and if he do not, then his information dispenses with the necessity for mine. Besides, while the prejudice against the character of an informer exists, it will attach with tenfold force to him who should assume that office, in order to punish another for refusing to incur the odium that he has voluntarily undertaken.

2. Secondly, if that difficulty be surmounted and a prosecutor be found, jurors will not easily be persuaded to convict ; and when they do, public prejudice will operate upon the pardoning power to interfere. Again—suppose the person to whom I may have confessed that I was the unwilling witness of a crime of which I refused to become the delator, should himself omit to become my accuser, the law will not be executed. Will you enact penalty for him also, and another for the one who omits to accuse him, and so in endless succession? No, you must stop somewhere, and rely on a sense of duty or some other motive to procure the necessary information. This once granted, it is evident that this resting place is at the first link in the chain, and that you will more probably obtain information against the original offender than against those who have not denounced him. The fear of punishment, then, does not seem to be the best means we can employ on this occasion. There remains the hope of reward. We have seen that the prejudice against informers originated in the injustice and oppressive nature of the laws, which forced upon the people the conviction that their interest and that of those by whom they were governed, were totally distinct. But when the laws are evidently made for the benefit of the people, much more when they themselves make the laws, this prejudice ought not to exist ; yet such is the force of habits, of thinking, and the association of ideas to particular terms, that although the reason in a great measure ceases to exist, although the reform of our laws will take it entirely away, yet the effect remains, and we can only hope to

see it entirely destroyed by the operation of time and of wise legislation : it is in vain to attempt to eradicate it by penalties. The first
step is the enactment of good laws, and convincing the people, by
making them intelligible as well as good, that they are so. This will
lead them, by degrees, to the conviction that there can be no dishonour
attached to any legal act by which the public good is promoted. A
worthy citizen will then consider it no more disgrace to inform or
prosecute any infringement of the laws by public offences, than he now
does to complain of injury to his own person or property. No ministry
of the law will then be deemed degrading; and from the bailiff who
arrests, to the judge who sentences the offender, the warden who
superintends his labour, and the divine who conducts him to reformation, all will, in different degrees, be considered as joint labourers in
the same great and honourable work. If your laws for regulating
arrests were just and well understood, the petty oppression of the
constable would cease, and his office would become respectable. Where
the interior of prisons in the United States have been thrown open to
public view, and they have ceased to become the scenes of vice, filth,
and oppression, the keepers have risen to the rank in society to which
their important duties entitle them. Men of respectability and talents
are employed as wardens of your penitentiaries—without repugnance
they become the executioners of the sentence of your courts against
criminals, because the laws which condemn them are just—because the
severity of the punishment does not enlist public feeling against those
who inflict it—and because the good sense of the people has discovered
that the laws are made for their own benefit, and ought to be executed.
He need not be very old to remember the period when the place of
jailor was considered so odious that very rarely would a man esteemed
in society accept it ; yet now the office of keeper of a state prison is
sought for by honourable men as an honourable office. What has
produced this change ? The question is not a difficult one, and the
answer has been anticipated.

We come then to the conclusion, pointed out by reason, and confirmed by experience: that the ministers employed in the execution of
just and mild laws, well understood by an intelligent people, will in no
grade of their rank be considered as dishonourable; and as a just consequence, that the duty of aiding them will not be so considered. The
immediate question then recurs,—will the acceptance of a reward for
such aid attach any odium to the performance of the duty ? The officer receives a salary or fees for the performance of his permanent functions,
why should not the individual receive a compensation for his occasional
service ? In both cases there is a sacrifice of private convenience to
produce a public good : why should it not, in both cases, be compensated ? Public prejudice is against it: this cannot be denied; but the
same prejudice formerly existed against the functions of the regular
officer, yet we have seen this giving way gradually to the force of truth
and the increase of knowledge. Why may not the same effect be expected in this analogous case ? With this hope the text of the law contains the reason for enacting it; it exposes the folly and danger of the
prejudice that would counteract it; and protects those who are independent enough to do the duty and receive the reward, by a penalty against
any defamatory reproaches against them, which the remains of a groundless prejudice might suggest. The reward is pecuniary only; it is mo-

derate, and it is confined to certain offences. To have made it honorary, would have been to destroy the very nature of that recompense, by making it too common. The amount is sufficient in most cases to indemnify for the loss of time and for the trouble attending the service, and not so great as to offer any temptation for false accusations. It is given only for the denunciation of great offences, in the punishment of which the public have a peculiar interest; and it is extended to breaches of the laws against duelling and forgery, because, in the one instance, the prejudices of false honour call for some additional motive to induce persons to give information ; and in the other, an attention to private interest might induce the person who was endeavouring to be defrauded, to make compromises that would defeat the ends of justice, unless it were made the interest of some other person to prosecute. No offence that is only made punishable on the complaint of the party injured, comes within this provision. An accomplice cannot claim the reward, because it would be in vain to offer it to him without adding to it the promise of impunity; nor can the party injured, because, in many cases, his testimony is necessary for conviction, and it was not deemed proper to place him in a situation that must necessarily detract from his credit.

The third and fourth chapters of this title prescribe the manner in which the interference of the magistrate may be required to prevent offences, or to restore to the proprietor articles which may have been illegally and fraudulently taken from his possession. In the first branch (the prosecution of an intended offence by requiring security) the regulations of the English law, as far as they could with certainty be discovered, have been followed; and where its rules were uncertain or defective, provisions have been added in accordance with the spirit of that law, (by which, on this, as on other occasions, I repeat it, I have been guided when I found it to accord with the principles established in the report that has met your approbation). To obtain the required security, the party must declare, upon oath, that he fears some offence will be committed against his person or property by some person whom he must designate ; he must add the reasons which cause his apprehension; and if the cause assigned shall, in the opinion of the magistrate, justify the fear, he shall direct the person complained of to be brought before him. The fear entertained must be that the offence will be committed by violence, because against every other injury to person or property every one is supposed to be able to protect himself by proper care. The duty of the magistrate to hear the party accused, and examine his proof, is pointed out; the security is set forth, and the cases in which courts may exact it on conviction. A provision, entirely new, is introduced, by which the magistrate, before whom complaint is made of an intended offence, when the proof does not show that the complainant had just ground of fear, is directed, before he discharges the accused, to explain to him the nature of the offence which was endeavoured to be guarded against, and the punishment annexed to it by law, and to admonish him that if he should commit the same, he will incur the highest penalty that can be inflicted by law for such offence. Another article directs the like admonition, and prescribes the same consequences in cases of applications setting forth a well founded apprehension of an intended defamation, by speech, by writing, or by printing. The constitution of our state forbids any previous restraint, even when such intent shall be proved ; but as it makes the party liable for the abuse of the liberty it gives, it was thought that the evil might, in some measure, be prevented by the fear of the increased punishment, if the offence should be committed after the admonition.

By the search for property taken by theft or fraud, some of the most important rights of the citizen are at least endangered, if not actually invaded.  Too many precautions, therefore, cannot be taken to prevent the mischiefs that might arise from its abuse ; and if the observance of the forms prescribed should sometimes involve the loss of property, the evil will be less than the vexation which a less restrained power to invade the domicil of the citizen would inevitably occasion.  In framing this chapter the utmost care, therefore, has been taken to guide the judge in the exercise of the discretion which must necessarily direct him in this important function of his office—to point out precisely the cases in which alone he can perform it—to state what evidence he should require in each of those several cases—to direct, with the most minute precision, the material parts of the order he shall issue, and to provide that such order shall confer all the powers necessary for the attainment of the ends proposed, and also every limitation to prevent abuse and secure the innocent from injury, and even those who may afterwards'be found guilty from vexation.  The duties of the magistrate, of the parties, the witnesses, and particularly of the officers who execute the writ, are separately, and it is hoped clearly and accurately detailed; and the penalties for any vexatious complaint, or abuse of authority, or denial of justice, are denounced.

Some of these provisions are new; and those which are not so, appear for the first time in their natural order and connexion with each other; and it is believed, that if they should receive the legislative sanction, much petty oppression, extortion and fraud, will be prevented, of which the ignorant and indigent may otherwise become the victims.  This class, depressed by their circumstances, perhaps by their vices or indolent habits, incapable from their want of instruction, of asserting their rights, are those who most need the protection of the laws, and in most countries they are those who receive the least.

A second title of this book is devoted to the means of putting an end to such offences as are permanent or continuous in their nature.  The first six chapters of which relate to the means of putting a stop to the several offences discussed in the Code of Crimes and Punishments, as those against public tranquillity, public health and safety, the enjoyment of public and common property, morals and decency, and reputation.  These consist chiefly of references to the correspondent parts of that code, which, on these heads, direct the interference of the magistrate, or regulate the exertion of personal defence.  The seventh book is highly important.  Under the title of suppressing offences against personal liberty, it contains the regulations for granting and enforcing the writ of habeas corpus.  No exposition of this chapter is necessary; because it has already received the sanction of your predecessors; and because the subject is fully discussed in the Report on the plan of a Penal Code, which received the approbation of the legislature in 1822.  Detached parts of this book have been enacted into a law, incorporated in the Code of Civil Procedure ; but I submit to the legislature the propriety of repealing so much of that code as relates to this subject, which surely is no part of civil process, and suffering the whole, as now presented and formerly approved, to occupy its place in the present code.  This title closes by a chapter directing the manner in which permanent offences against property are to be suppressed and possession restored to the owners of that which has been seized as stolen or fraudulently obtained.

A short but very important title, consisting of two chapters, contains the regulations for calling out and employing the military, in aid of the civil power. The first chapter designates the cases in which that power may be called for, and the mode of making the application. The second regulates the manner in which the military force may be employed. By military force is intended the militia of the state : and the code provides, that it can only be employed by order of the governor, or, when he is too distant to act, by that of the militia-general commanding the district ; and the order can only be given on the application, in writing, of three magistrates, one of whom must be a judge, supported by an affidavit of two inhabitants stating that a riot or insurrection has taken place in the parish in which they reside, and that it cannot be quelled by the force of the ordinary civil authority. The application must state the circumstances of the case and the number of men that will probably be required to restore order. On this application, the governor or commanding officer is authorized to direct the proper militia force to march to the place indicated, under the command of an officer of requisite rank, and put himself under the direction of the magistrates who made the requisition.

In all riots or insurrections, the immediate, sometimes the ultimate object is violence to some obnoxious person, or the plunder or destruction of property. To protect these, without the useless sacrifice of human life, is the object of the laws on this subject; therefore, all the provisions of this chapter are intended, if possible, to stop the violence by the fear of an armed force, without having recourse to its dreadful execution. The militia are only to be employed where the ordinary civil power has been tried and found insufficient. It is, when practicable, to be stationed between the rioters and the object of their intended violence; to act strictly on the defensive, and under the direction of the magistrate. When the use of weapons becomes necessary, to use only those, such as the bayonet and sword, which may be directed solely against the assailants, without endangering the lives of others; leaving the more dangerous and uncontrollable effect of fire-arms (which may injure the innocent as well as the guilty) for the last resort. In no case can the armed force be brought up, before the magistrate has displayed a white flag, and ordered the rioters to disperse ; and, unless to repel an attack endangering life, no order is to be given for the use of offensive arms, until half an hour has elapsed after the order to disperse, without its being obeyed. The remarks on this chapter cannot be closed without observing the essential difference between the nature of the armed force, the use of which is contemplated by the code, and that employed on similar occasions in England and other countries in Europe. There it is composed of men entirely under the control of the executive branch of the government, upon which they depend entirely for subsistence. Here, except in the circumstances of their being organized and armed, they differ in nothing from the power which is at the daily call of the civil officer. Without arms or military array, they are the common *posse comitatus*, as it is called, or civil power of the country ; the same ties of property, of family, of love of country and of liberty, to make them effective instruments for the suppression of disorder, and the most unfit,

2 B

even when disciplined and armed, that could be chosen to promote any scheme of usurpation. The people can apprehend no danger to their liberties from such a force, even when it is actively employed against themselves—when deceived by the factious, agitated by party, or indignant against real or imagined injury, they are led to oppose the operation of the laws. Yet with all these safeguards, the legislator would be unfaithful to his trust who should neglect other precautions against the necessary evil of employing the weapons of war in the work of peace. According to the erroneous ideas of the ancient jurisprudence, the sword of justice always was unsheathed, always brandished. In our more correct conceptions, it is never placed in her hands, but in the last extreme of necessity.

The review of that part of the code which relates to preventive procedure, is now finished. It is a meagre title in the English, and as sterile in our law, for we have added nothing by statute to that part of the common law which we have adopted ; and in the laws of other nations, with which, however, I am but very imperfectly acquainted, I find little or nothing on this important branch of jurisprudence. Pains and penalties ! Every where penalties ! Every contrivance to punish— scarcely a provision to prevent or repress! If I did not think it, in some measure, disrespectful to the honourable body I address, to express a doubt, that every part of the plan they have directed to be laid before them would receive equal attention, I should venture to request a scrupulous examination of the title we have just reviewed, as one of the most vital importance. I would entreat them to enlarge it by such enactments as their superior wisdom should suggest, for the great, the sacred object of preventing offences, rather than punishing them; and I dare, even at the risk of being thought importunate, and of tiring them by repeating the same argument, earnestly pray them to consider deeply the necessity of early education—general education—religious, moral and literary education, as the great lever for raising the people above the temptation of crime, and the only means by which offences may be prevented by the moral sense, rather than repressed by the operation of law; and in connexion with this important branch of our subject, I refer to the different establishments provided for by the Code of Prison Discipline, under the heads of School for Reform, House of Detention, and House of Refuge ; and to the reasons which will be urged in the Introductory Report to that Code for this establishment.

Having considered the means of preventing inchoate offences, and arresting the course of such as are in operation, we now approach that which may, perhaps, with a stricter propriety, be considered as a Code of Criminal Procedure, that is to say, the mode of conducting prosecutions for offences already consummated. This is the subject of the second book of the Code. The first title of this book contains the law of Arrest and Bail, two very important subjects ; hitherto left, for the most part, without positive legislation to guide the officer, the magistrate and the citizen, in the daily calls upon them to act in the prosecution of alleged offences, or to direct the accused in the assertion of his rights. By this part of the code the omission is endeavoured to be supplied. The first chapter contains definitions and general principles necessary for the full understanding of the provisions which follow, and of the reasons on which they are enacted. The nature of a complaint for an alleged offence, is explained, and its effects pointed out.

What proof of such complaint is necessary to give it the force of a legal accusation, and to justify an order of arrest, is stated. The necessity of such arrest, to ensure the appearance of the witness on the trial, the necessity of the commitment further to secure that end, and the condition of the pledge contained in the contract of bail, is fully explained and elucidated. These follow in regular order and in successive chapters, each one appropriated to a distinct head. The first specifies the mode of making the complaint and accusation, and of granting the order of arrest. This last mentioned subject, the order of arrest, is the subject of a separate section. To deprive a citizen of liberty, before he is convicted of any offence, can only be justified by the necessity of securing his appearance to attend the trial and suffer the penalty, if the charge be well founded. But it cannot be justified at all in the following cases : first, where the punishment annexed to the offence is so light as to destroy the presumption that the accused would avoid it by flight—in other words, where the inconvenience attending flight, would be greater than the evil of the punishment ; secondly, when the evidence is not such as to justify a belief that the accused is guilty ; nor, lastly, where the accused will give such a pledge for his appearance as will render it more probable that he will remain, and either show his innocence or suffer the penalty of his guilt, than that he will forfeit the pledge he has given. The chapter is drawn in accordance with these views of the subject. In case of misdemeanor, where there is no possibility that the party will incur the certain evil of flight, to avoid the comparatively light suffering of the penalty directed by law, there is no arrest, unless it be incurred by wilful disobedience to a citation commanding the party to appear. In accusations of a graver nature, the evidence in support of them must be on oath ; it must be positive that the offence has been committed, and produce belief in the mind of the magistrate that the person designated has committed it, before the order for his arrest can be granted. The complaint, and the evidence in support of it, must be reduced to writing, signed and sworn to by the witnesses. The order must plainly designate the offence charged, that the defendant may be prepared on his appearance before the magistrate with his defence, and it must be delivered to an officer of justice who is to make the arrest. In order, as far as possible, to avoid oppression, to ensure the due execution of the law, to protect the officer against the effects of mistake in the performance of his duty, and to point out to private citizens that which may be required of them when called on to assist him, as well as to designate to the accused the bounds between legal resistance and the submission required by law ; all these points are fully explained under distinct heads in this chapter. Great care has been taken in framing the law on these heads, so as to make it clear to the most common understanding ; because, in the whole course of procedure, there is no circumstance productive of so many vexatious proceedings and serious and frequently fatal effects, as that of arrests. Officers of justice, often uneducated and overbearing men, either do not know, or designedly exceed, the bounds of their authority. The accused sometimes submits to illegal acts, at others, resists those to which he ought to submit. The citizen, when legally called on to enforce the execution of the law, refuses to obey, or makes himself liable to prosecution for aiding in an illegal arrest ; and it is believed, that of all the cases of murder, manslaughter, violent assault and false imprisonment, reported in the books, no inconsiderable proportion will be found to have arisen from ignorance of rights and duties in granting warrants, in making arrests, or resisting them—ignorance inevitable, from the state of our laws ; for where (it is asked on this as it has been on former occasions), where is the necessary information to be obtained ?  The written law is silent ; the oracles who pronounce that which is unwritten, only speak when the case has already happened ; and the unfortunate citizen, called on to act or suffer at a moment's warning, is forced to do it at his own risk ; for those to whom he has confided the care of framing rules for his government, have hitherto obstinately refused, or negligently omitted to dictate them.  It is time that this duty should be done : it is more than time that this reproach should be taken away from our legislation.  You declare, that every man who kills an officer in the legal discharge of his duty, is guilty of murder, and shall suffer death.  You say, that resistance to an unlawful arrest is justifiable ; and you cruelly and wantonly refuse to explain what is a lawful and which an unlawful arrest.  You refer to the contradictory and confused decisions of courts in a foreign country for information on this all-important point.  Do you understand those laws ?  Are they clear ?—deign then to clothe them in the words of legislative authority : publish them to your constituents.  Are the cases contradictory ?—tell us which of them is the law.  Are they confused and uncertain ?—explain them.  Do you not understand them yourselves ?—then how should we your constituents be guided by them, in matters too on which depend life or death ?  If the rules now offered are not approved, frame others.  When obedience is exacted, under such a sanction, the least the people can require is to be clearly and explicitly told what it is they are to obey.  I feel that I am repeating here ideas that have been more than once expressed, and that I am urging former arguments with a zeal that may be deemed indiscreet, and, I hope, is unnecessary ; but I have a great, a holy duty to perform, and I dare not leave any part of it undone, from the fear of giving offence, or the hope of conciliating favour, much less that of gaining applause.  The solemn truth must be told, must be repeated, until it is felt.  "LEGISLATORS ARE IN EFFECT THE MURDERERS OF THOSE WHO PERISH BY THEIR WILFUL NEGLECT TO PROVIDE GOOD, OR TO REPEAL BAD LAWS."  This responsibility cannot be thrown off, or even divided, however numerous the body upon whom it devolves : it attaches to every individual whose vote is counted either against the reform or for postponing it to other matters of minor consideration : and the reflection finds its place very naturally at the close of a review of the chapter relating to arrests, a subject in which so many require the aid of the law to guide them, by clear and precise rules, in order to avoid heavy penalties ; in which so few receive that aid at all, and none in the manner in which it ought to be afforded.

The arrest being made, the next proceeding is to bring the accused before the magistrate, that he may proceed to examine and discharge, commit, remand for further examination, or deliver to bail.  Rules are laid down in the fourth chapter for each of these alternative duties.  The first is the examination.  Our present law prescribes, that the magistrate is to reduce to writing the answers which the accused may voluntarily make to such questions as may be put to him without any threat or promise, and the construction put upon this has, I believe, generally been that no inference against the prisoner is to be made from his refusal to answer such question ; and practice, which with us so frequently usurps the authority of law, has established it as a rule frequently followed, to declare this explicitly to the prisoner, thereby inviting him to silence, and, of course, depriving the prosecution of the advantage to be derived from his communications. The course directed by the code is somewhat different, and requires some discussion.

The great object of all criminal procedure is the conviction of the guilty—but of the guilty only. Every precaution which the wisest legislation can suggest, should be employed to prevent its falling on the innocent. Yet such is the imperfection of all human institutions, that, after these precautions are taken, it must happen that innocence is sometimes mistaken for guilt, and incurs its punishment. To require, therefore, that a code of procedure should be so framed as to prevent the possibility of this error, would be absurd ; and the only mode of affording perfect security from conviction to the innocent, would be to extend impunity to the guilty. All that the best legislation on this subject can do, is to take every precaution consistent with the main object (the conviction of guilt), to secure innocence from being confounded with it before condemnation, and to correct any errors which may afterwards be discovered. Therefore, it is no good objection to any particular part of criminal procedure to say, that it may involve the innocent. That we have seen is, in some cases, inevitable under the best systems. Every question, therefore, of this nature, must be one which presents a choice between two measures, each of which has some portion of evil attached to it, and it must consequently always be one of sound discretion to take that which has the least.

In the examination of the accused, the advantage is, that if guilty, he will frequently betray himself by his own story. The truth would be a confession. He must have recourse, therefore, to falsehood ; but, as error is infinite, he will state some things which can be easily disproved by circumstances or by other witnesses, and the investigation of which would lead to his conviction. Suppose him, on the other hand, to be innocent : his statements will contain the truth, because he has no need of concealment, and the circumstances and witnesses which would detect his falsehood, in the one case, will evince his truth in the other. If the magistrate, who examines, in this preparatory stage, were the tribunal which finally tries, there would be another advantage in permitting the interrogation of the accused, his looks, his manner of answering, his hesitation or promptitude, even his silence, would have their effect in determining on his innocence or guilt. But we are now speaking of the examination before the committing magistrate, who has seldom any agency in the final trial ; and even when the examination is made before the judge who afterwards presides at such trial, the jury, not the judge, are to determine the question of guilt ; therefore, no impression that can be made in favour of the prisoner or against him, from his manner and appearance on his examination, can have any avail on the trial. From this circumstance arises the first item in the detail of disadvantages attending the subjecting the prisoner to examination. That his answers, not being heard by those who are to decide on his innocence or guilt, can only be communicated to them by being reduced to writing. The difficulty of doing this, so as to express precisely the ideas intended to be conveyed, cannot be appreciated but by professional men, who must have witnessed how often inaccuracy of expression in the speaker and carelessness or misapprehension in the scribe, concur in producing the most dangerous errors, even without supposing any intent to mislead or falsify. An unrestrained right of interrogating is also very apt to produce insidious and catching questions. Instead of a cool and impartial attempt to extract the truth, the examination becomes a contest, in which the pride and ingenuity of the magistrate are arrayed against the caution or evasions of the accused, and every construction will be given to his answers that may fix upon him the imputation of guilt. After weighing these and other arguments on both sides of this important question, I came to this conclusion, that it would be unwise to abandon the advantage to be derived from an examination of the accused ; but at the same time, that justice required us to reduce to their lowest term the two inseparable evils attached to this mode of proceeding, and I thought that this might be effected by restricting the magistrate to a prescribed form of interrogatory, so drawn that no innocent person could be entrapped by answering them ; while, at the same time, evasions or untrue answers might frequently lead to the detection of guilt ; and to avoid inaccuracies in recording the answers, the interrogatories are pointed only to such simple circumstances as can be detailed with the greatest simplicity of language, and they are not considered as complete until they have been signed by the party and corrected by him, so as to express exactly the idea he meant to convey ; if we add to this that he has the assistance of counsel, and has heard what the witnesses against him have deposed, it will be found that the accused is in no danger of being circumveuted or intimidated to his prejudice in the preparatory examination. He is first apprized that although he may refuse to answer the interrogatories that are about to be put to him, or answer them in any way he may think fit, yet a false answer, or his refusal to give any, must operate against him on the trial. This consequence is inevitable, and under our present practice, where he is expressly told that he is at perfect liberty to answer or not, as he pleases, which implies that no injury to him can result from his silence, the same result is produced ; and the prisoner is invited to silence by being assured that it will do him no injury, when in the nature of things the jury cannot but infer guilt from false representations, or from silence, without any motive but that of concealing the truth ; either of which circumstances, when they occur, are given in evidence according to our present practice. It was, therefore, thought, that justice to the prisoner as well as to the public, required that full notice should be given of the deductions that would be drawn from his silence or evasions.

It cannot be denied, however, that cases may be supposed in which even the guiltless may be induced, from a strange combination of circumstances, to remain silent, or to give a false colouring to the transaction which has involved them in suspicion. But this reflection did not prevent my adopting the mode of interrogation which I recommend : First ; because the existence of such circumstances must be of very doubtful occurrence ; and if they should happen, the cases in which they occur being, according to other parts of the proposed system, within the reach of remission and compensation, ought not to form an objection to a part of procedure otherwise advantageous. Secondly, because the same objection lies to our present practice, and must attach to any other that may be adopted, there being nothing that can secure the accused, if he is tried at all, from the unfavourable impression that his silence or falsehood may make upon his judges if he is in any way interrogated, or from the effects of circumstances which render guilt probable, if they cannot be explained. With this explanation of the reasons on which it is founded, the attention of the legislature is requested to the fourth chapter, and it is hoped that it will be found to contain every provision necessary to protect the prisoner from any effects injurious to his safety, arising from surprise, intimidation, or false hopes, if he be innocent ; and at the same time secure to the prosecution the advantage of that evidence which a consciousness of guilt will generally furnish in his answers to the interrogatories. A prejudice, but it appears to me a groundless one, and certainly very favourable to the escape of the guilty, exists against procuring testimony from the judicial examination of the party accused before a magistrate ; and yet, without scruple, we admit testimony of his informal and private confessions to individuals, as if he would be more apt to inculpate himself without cause when put on his guard by the admonition of the judge, and a knowledge of the consequences, than he would be in a loose conversation which he must imagine would never be repeated, and as if the record of what he has said, corrected and signed by himself after due deliberation and with the assistance of counsel, were not as high evidence of the fact, as the declaration of a casual witness who may purposely misrepresent the terms of the confession, or unintentionally give it a false colouring. It cannot be denied that an innocent man of very weak nerves may sometimes, in his confusion, give contradictory or false statements that may endanger his safety, or do acts that cannot be accounted for but on a supposition of guilt. So may an innocent man incur the danger of conviction from an untoward combination of circumstances which he cannot explain, or from the misapprehension, or direct perjury of witnesses. Yet the risk must be incurred in both cases, unless we abandon altogether, in the last instance, the prosecution for crimes ; and in the first, all advantage to be drawn, in any shape, from the best source, the acts and confessions of the party accused : and all that can be required in a good system of procedure, is to put these in such a form as will insure authenticity, and guard against error, intimidation, or the effects of false hopes. It is believed this has been done. The prisoner is allowed the assistance of counsel ; he may examine the depositions and question the witnesses against him, before he is called on to answer the interrogatories that are to be propounded to him : the form of these is prescribed by law. He is informed that he cannot be forced to answer them, but he is admonished that silence or falsehood must be a circumstance that will operate against him. His answers, if he give any, are reduced to writing by the magistrate ; they are submitted to his perusal and correction, and he signs them with such additions and alterations as he deems proper ; and if after all any error should have occurred, means are afforded, on the trial, to correct it by explanation, and by the examination of witnesses, before an impartial jury.

The next step, after examination, is to discharge, remand, bail, or commit the prisoner. The first is the duty of the magistrate, when the evidence adduced by the prosecution is not such as leaves on the mind a belief that the crime has been committed, or that the prisoner has been guilty of it. This being only a preparatory proceeding, the magistrate is directed not to require such proof as would justify a conviction : his duty, in this respect, is precisely pointed out.   If there be positive evidence, directly charging the prisoner with the commission of the offence, although he may produce contradictory proof, the magistrate cannot discharge, the task of weighing the exculpatory evidence being reserved for the jury on the trial.   When the evidence is circumstantial only, and does not bring the mind to a belief of guilt, the defendant must be discharged ; but in this case, it is a belief only, not a firm conviction of guilt that is required, by which is meant, that the rule laid down for guiding the conscience of a juror on the trial must be reversed as respects that of the magistrate on the question of discharging him.   In order to convict, the juror must have no doubt of the prisoner's guilt ; to discharge him, the magistrate must have none of his innocence.   The result of an examination may be such as to show that other proof, within the reach of the magistrate, may be required ; in which case the prisoner is remanded, or sent back to the custody of the officer by whom he was arrested, or to the prison in which he was confined ; and at a proper and designated period he is again brought up, and the examination proceeds.   If the magistrate be not convinced of the defendant's innocence, he must either commit him to prison or take bail for his appearance, and the performance of this duty is one in which the highest confidence is necessarily placed in the discretion of the magistrate.   The nature of the contract of bail is too well known to need any explanation.   Its theory was to place the accused in the watchful(a) care of persons who have confidence in him, and who are interested in preventing his escape by the fear of losing the penalty of the bond ; and it was also thought that the confidence reposed in him by his sureties was such proof of good character as formed a presumption that he was not guilty ; but experience, in many cases, shakes the ground-work of this theory.   The bail may always be indemnified when the defendant is wealthy and conscious of guilt ; and the confidence is generally reposed more in his means than his character.   Hence, it is apparent, that where bail is a matter of right, the defendant can always change the penalty of the law into expatriation, and a pecuniary fine to the amount of the bond.   Therefore the law, while it allows bail in cases of doubt or in offences where these consequences would be a sufficient punishment, ought in those of a higher nature, and where the proof is strong, to secure the appearance of the party by other means.   Unfortunately the framers of our constitution have restricted legislation on this subject within very narrow bounds, and on one construction have taken it away altogether, if we should, as I cannot but hope we shall, abolish the punishment of death.   The constitution declares, that " all prisoners shall be bailable by sufficient securities, except for capital offences where the proof is evident or the presumption great."   On the construction I have adopted, the magistrate may refuse bail where the " proof is evident or the presumption strong" in offences which, in the time of making the constitution, were capitally punished : these were murder, rape, exciting insurrection among slaves, and stabbing or shooting with intent to murder. But that in all other cases he is bound to take sufficient bail.   Nor can

(a) The French word *surveillance* expresses the idea I mean to convey, better than even the periphrase I am forced to use, for want of a correspondent word in our language.

any legislative provision, except perhaps that of making the offence capital, enlarge the constitutional restriction. I express myself hesitatingly, because I am not sure what the courts would say on this question; whether the constitution intended such cases as were then capital, or those which the legislature might afterwards declare to be such, or whether when the offence ceases to be punished by death, the constitutional rule with regard to bail remains unchanged. This restriction on the powers of the legislature I consider unfortunate. A highway robber arrested with his pistol at the traveller's breast—a forger taken in the act of passing or making his false bills—every other offender, be his guilt ever so atrocious, or the proof of it ever so apparent, must be let out on bail, and, if he has secured the means of indemnifying his sureties, may change the punishment directed by law, for a fine and expatriation or concealment. Constitutionally, therefore, the magistrate, could be invested by the code with the discretionary power to bail or not to bail in but few cases, and on one construction, as we have seen, (capital punishment being abolished) in none. There, is however, no such restraint upon his discretion as to the amount of the security; and this being the only remedy for the evil, great pains have been taken in the framing of rules for the guidance of the magistrate in the performance of this important duty. If there be any occasion in which it is proper for the legislator to declare what he expects from the judgment, as well as what he commands from the obedience, of a functionary of the law, it is the one now under consideration; because the magistrates, who are to perform the duty, are commonly unused by previous habit or professional education to the consideration of the questions to which it gives rise; and because of the high importance of the due exercise of this discretion, as well to the public as to the individuals more immediately concerned. There are those, however, who consider that the law should do nothing but command, and that its commands should always be sanctioned by some penalty for disobedience. The arguments which enforce this doctrine seem to be founded on the idea that there is some paramount power, even superior to that of a constitutional law, which limits legislative power by certain rules of form as well as of moral duty in the exercise of its functions. Utility prescribes the last, but from what source is the first derived? We feel that there is an obligation not to enjoin the performance of immoral acts, and we are at no loss to discover the source of this duty. But when we are told, you are to prescribe nothing that you cannot or do not enforce by a penalty, we must seek in vain for some good reason for the maxim. The lawgiver cannot foresee the circumstances of every case, and if he could foresee, he could not describe them; he must, therefore, give general rules, and trust, within certain limits, to the discretion of the judge, the power to modify and adapt them to suit particular cases; that is to say, he must delegate that part of his duty which he cannot perform himself; and in making this transfer, it would seem not only right but highly useful to give the rules and lay down the principles according to which he desires it to be exercised. This cannot be done by positive command, because it is to operate on the mind and direct the judgment, not the action; and as this is a delegation of discretionary power, it would be absurd to annex a penalty to an honest, although improper exercise of it, provided the limits of the discretion were not exceeded. To illustrate this reasoning by an example drawn from the

2 C

part of the code which is in question—the magistrate, in admitting to bail, is directed, in general terms, so to apportion the amount as not to suffer the wealthy offender to escape by the payment of a pecuniary penalty, nor to render the privilege useless to the poor; and he is told that this power is, in its exercise, one of the most delicate and important functions of his office, and he is apprized that his sound discretion is to direct it. It is clear that here there can be neither positive command, nor penalty for its breach; if there were, it would no longer be discretion. Yet can it reasonably be said, that legislation derogates from its dignity, or performs a superfluous task when it points out to the magistrate the objects he ought to have in view, and the principles by which he is to be guided, in order to attain it? But the whole duty is not left to the discretion of the magistrate. Whatever could be foreseen, and provided for, by that of the law, is reduced to positive precept, and its breach incurs the penalty attached to disobedience. Thus, where the punishment is fine, the bail must exceed the maximum of the penalty; where it is simple imprisonment, one rule is fixed; where the imprisonment is in the penitentiary, another; other rules are laid down for apportionment in other particular cases; and the discretion of the judge is reduced in this, as it has been the object to do in every part of this code, to the strictest limits, within which it can be exercised consistently with justice. Some of these rules and restrictions are new; others are conformable to present practice; but all are for the first time reduced to the form of statutory legislation.

The bail being completed, the prisoner is suffered to remain at large until the trial; but provision is made, that for the security of the bail, they may, at any time, exonerate themselves by his surrender, and the particular mode of doing this is prescribed.

If sufficient bail be not offered, or if the case be one in which the magistrate rightfully refuses to receive it, the prisoner must be committed to prison, to abide the event of his trial if he be not before that time bailed or discharged by the judge of a superior tribunal, or habeas corpus. The order for commitment is directed to be in writing; its form and essential parts are prescribed, as well as the mode in which it is to be executed; and all the means that experience or reflection could suggest, have been adopted to prevent the discharge of the prisoner, which so frequently happens from formal defects in the warrant, while every requisite security against abuse and oppression have been carefully provided. After commitment, the prisoner may be bailed or discharged, if the nature of his case permit it. But the inferior magistrate has no other agency in this proceeding than to furnish all the evidence of that which was had before him to the judge before whom the prisoner may be brought, on the return of the writ of habeas corpus; to the chapter on which subject the legislature is referred for a minute detail of the duties and rights of all parties and agents, from the judge who decides, to the prisoner whose case is before him; and with this ends the provisions necessary for securing the appearance of the defendant at the trial, by which his guilt or innocence is to be ascertained, and at the judgment, by which it is to be proclaimed. In framing this part of the system, it has never been forgotten, that the guilty were to be brought to punishment with as little inconvenience as possible to the innocent; and that no presumption or other evidence of crime could, before trial and conviction, justify any thing more than necessary restraint. With this view a reverent eye has constantly been kept on those admirable provisions for the security of personal liberty which are to be found in the laws of England, which deserve the gratitude as well as the admiration of the world. Institutions which are every day extending their influence over the happiness of mankind, and which will prove a more lasting and honourable monument of the wisdom, justice and greatness of the nation from whose jurisprudence they are drawn, than any which their splendid victories, their power, their wealth, or even their science, could erect. Of these institutions the writ of habeas corpus is that which applies to this part of our subject. The idea of this remedy is to be found in the Roman law ; but there, as well as in the common law of England, it was ineffectual, until the great statute, of that name, gave it the essential features to which it owes all its utility. These features have been rendered more definite, new provisions and penalties have been added, and, I think, it may now be asserted with truth, that individual liberty can suffer no restraint, which, under this law, will not find an easy, prompt, and unexpensive remedy.

In reviewing the duties of the examining magistrate, among them should have been stated that of taking an obligation from witnesses, under a penalty, to secure their appearance at the trial, and of committing to prison such as refuse to enter into that obligation. Analogous to this is a proceeding which, although an invasion of personal liberty, is practised in most countries, and, I think, justified by the same reasoning which shows the right of taking private property, or coercing personal service, for the public safety. When one who is a necessary witness, in a prosecution for an offence punishable by imprisonment for life, is not a householder, and consequently wants one principal tie to prevent his departure, and has no friends or connexions who will become bound for his appearance, he may be detained in custody until the trial; but in this, and in the Code of Prison Discipline, it is specially provided, that he be properly and comfortably supported at the public expense ; that he suffer no degrading or contaminating associations while detained ; that he be allowed every indulgence, as to occupation, amusement and society, which the good order of the house (for the place of his detention is not characterized as a prison) will allow, and that when discharged, full compensation be made for the loss he has incurred. The duties of the examining magistrate end, with transmitting to the proper officer of the court having cognizance of the case, all the proceedings which have been had before him, including the original examination as well of the party as of the witnesses ; and here opens a new course of proceeding, contained in the second title of this book. It treats of the proceedings subsequent to the commitment or bailing of the-prisoner. The first chapter details the manner in which the appearance, as well of the party as the witnesses, is to be enforced, which, as it differs little, except it is hoped in precision and certainty, from the mode now in use, needs only a reference to the chapter.

The second contains some regulations which it was thought would introduce order in the arrangement of the different cases preparatory to the indictment or information. Among them is one which obliges the prosecuting officer to designate, before the meeting of the grand jury, on a copy of the calendar furnished to him for that purpose, all such cases of misdemeanor as he may choose to prosecute by information ; and the papers, in relation to these cases, are not sent to the grand jury. This is done, as well to avoid any interference between the two accusing powers, as to ensure, on the part of the prosecuting attorney, the performance of his duties. For this officer, after having designated those cases in which he will proceed without the intervention of the grand jury, is bound to file his information before the end of the term ; and the court being made acquainted with them, as the cases which are before him, he cannot, if so inclined, favour any one by delay in the prosecution, or throw off the reproach of neglect upon the grand jury. And that body being obliged, as their exclusive duty, to inquire into all cases of crime, and all those of misdemeanor not selected by the public prosecutor, it follows that every accusation must be disposed of in one or the other mode.

The third chapter is an important one. It relates to the organization and duties of the grand jury. This institution is a favourite one in England and in the United States. But although I consider its advantages outweigh the objections to which it is liable, and have, therefore, preserved for it a place in the system, yet I cannot but suspect that it owes much of its popularity to its name, and to the association which connects it with that invaluable blessing to a free country, the trial by jury. Some part of its utility, too, is traditional only. In the party questions, which at different times have divided the people of England, and which very rarely ended without enlisting the judiciary power on that side which was espoused by the crown, it was sometimes a protection against the combination of royal and judicial oppression, and would have been more frequently so if there had been any means of securing an impartial selection of its members. It is not my intention to present a history of this institution, or a detail of its advantages or inconveniences, in its origin, progress, or present state, in the country from which we have inherited it. It will be sufficient to offer the objections to its establishment here, which have occurred to me, and the reasons in its favour, which I have thought sufficient to countervail them. With such an admirable contrivance for the security of innocence against unjust prosecutions as the trial by jury, where unanimity is required for conviction, any intermediate examination between that made by the committing magistrate and the final trial, would seem an obstruction to the course of justice, of which the necessity, or even the convenience, is not very apparent. The secrecy, too, of that examination and the precautions taken to prevent the slightest responsibility resting on any one of those by whom it is made, it might be argued, give a chance for favouritism, or undue influence, to interpose in favour of those whose guilt would be apparent on a public trial ; while, on the other hand, it might be said that witnesses, according to the usual practice, being heard only to charge the defendant, and heard in secret, he is deprived of the advantage secured to him before the magistrate of showing his innocence by countervailing proof ; and thus, in all cases originating by complaint to the grand jury, he would be subject to commitment and trial, on the evidence of circumstances which he might have fully explained had the examination been publicly had before a magistrate. To this it may be added, that grand juries are very rarely, if ever, composed of men having such a knowledge of the law as will enable them to determine what evidence ought to be admitted, to what credit it is entitled, or whether the facts it discloses amount to an offence ; and that this ignorance of their duties, or an inattention, which

is worse, frequently causes them to mistake or disregard the duties of
their office, and assume the cognizance of matters with which they have
no concern ; sometimes censuring the conduct of political opponents ;
sometimes lending their influence to promote party views.    These
objections are weighty, and some of them not ill-founded.    But after
the fullest consideration, I thought that those to which satisfactory
answers could not be given, might be obviated by alterations, which
would make none in the general outline of the institution ; and,
therefore, for the following reasons I adopted it with the modifications
contained in the code.

1. First, because it participates largely in that prominent characteristic
which distinguishes the trial by jury(a), of spreading general information, and a particular acquaintance with the practical operation of the
constitution and laws; of creating an attachment to the principles on
which they are founded, and, by the periodical performance of an important function, promoting the happiness of the individual by a sense
of self-importance, and that of the public, by a constant vigilance over
its peace.    It might, if necessary, easily be shown that each of these
effects will be produced by the frequent exercise of the duties of a grand
juror; and all of them are objects of the highest consequence in legislation.    For, in a government created for the common good of all its
citizens, that organization of any department is certainly to be preferred, which, while it is equally well calculated with any other, for the
performance of the duties for which it is particularly intended, also
opens new sources for individual happiness, diffuses knowledge, fosters
an attachment to true principles, and adds stability to the government
of which it is a part.    It has appeared to me, that a want of attention to
such considerations is a common fault in the legislation of our country.
We shape our laws to fit the principal end which is proposed, without
sufficiently examining whether the same object could be obtained by
means that produce other collateral effects of equal or perhaps of greater
importance, and avoid dangers which, in our eagerness to attain some
doubtful good by a straight-forward, off-hand legislation, have totally
escaped our attention.    Thus, to raise a revenue for some useful purpose,
we license gambling-houses ; to promote education, and provide for the
building of churches, we establish lotteries ; to avoid the expense of
erecting a penitentiary, we incur that of supporting our convicts in
idleness, and put some of our citizens to death, that we may impress on
the minds of others the great truth that killing is unlawful.    We do this,
without sufficiently inquiring whether the requisite revenue might not
be obtained by some other and better means than giving the sanction of
law to the worst of vices; whether a purer source could not be found,
from which to draw the means of supporting religious and scientific
education, than one that corrupts morals, encourages idleness, and leads
the poorer classes to poverty and vice; whether the crimes which are
fostered in the vicious association of confinement, without labour, are
not infinitely more expensive to the community than the most costly
house of labour ; and whether shedding man's blood is the most effectual
way of showing that it ought not to be shed.

2. Independently of this collateral, but highly important advantage, attached to the institution of grand juries, it was adopted, secondly, because

(a) See Report on the Plan of a Penal Code.

it was already established, and it has been my uniform practice to alter no part of the system but such as could be clearly shown to be defective or inconsistent with other parts of the plan.   Whether the present is of this character must depend upon an examination of the objections which have been stated.   These are in substance, that the intervention of a second accusing power, between the commitment by the magistrate and the trial, is a useless piece of machinery in penal law; that from its particular organization it is cumbrous, and from its secrecy dangerous; that it may, without responsibility, protect guilt and vex innocence; and that the ignorance of its members frequently leads them into erroneous ideas of their power, which creates confusion in the administration of justice.

The error of the first objection lies in supposing that the commitment of the magistrate, in all cases, contains such an exposition of the circumstances and nature of the offence as would enable the party to prepare for his defence, by knowing exactly, not only with what crime he was charged, but also when, where, and in what manner he is accused of having committed it.   But this is far from being the case. If the ministry of the grand jury be dispensed with, that of some other body of men, or of some officer, must be substituted for the performance of this duty.   If it be vested in a known officer, or a permanent body, he or they being previously known, will be subject to the approaches of influence in all its seducing forms, for the purposes of favour or oppression.   Whereas the grand jury, selected by judges totally unconnected in any other manner with the proceeding, cut of a very limited number, taken by lot immediately before the session of the court, are out of the reach of any attempt to seduce or intimidate them.   If, to obviate this, and at the same time the next objection, that the grand jury is inconveniently great, it should be said, draw your accusing judges also by lot, or let them be appointed by the executive immediately before they enter on their duties, but let the number be less: it is answered, this expedient gives us still a grand jury.   If appointed by the executive, you do not take away the danger of an undue influence; you only change the person to whom it may be addressed.   If you take them by lot, in the manner proposed by the code, the only question is, whether the substitution of any smaller number for that now required will be attended with any advantage sufficiently great to justify the change.   It is thought not. If no great reduction be made, the difference will scarcely be perceptible in the mode of proceeding.   If the number be few, some advantage may be gained in celerity; but a greater lost in the want of information, and in the freer scope given to the influence of favour or animosity among a few.   The object of this institution being, not only to make accusations of such infractions of the law as have been prosecuted before the examining magistrate, but the jurors being individually bound to make inquisition into all such as they have reason to think have been committed in the district for which they are assembled, it follows, that a reasonable suspicion, entertained by one of the members and communicated with the circumstances on which it is founded to his fellows, will be sufficient to ground an inquiry; for which purpose they are vested with powers to send for and examine witnesses.   This object will obviously be better attained by a numerous than a small body.

The objection drawn from the secrecy of the proceedings before the grand jury, is one that comes in a more imposing shape than any other, in a country where publicity in every department is justly considered as the greatest security for good conduct in those who direct them. Yet there are reasons why I should hesitate to remove the veil that has been drawn over the proceedings of the grand jury room. To appreciate these reasons, we must consider the constitution of this body and the nature of their duties. The members are not appointed or chosen to perform functions of an office, but designated, as we have seen, by lot to perform a service, an onerous one, which they have not courted, and to which they have not been called by an appointment which they might accept or refuse. It would seem unjust, therefore, to expose an individual, thus performing an involuntary duty, to the odium or suspicion inseparably attached to it, for any erroneous but honest expression of his opinion ; and against the prosecution for corrupt or other illegal conduct, the oath of secrecy taken by his fellows is no protection. It must be remembered, too, that the honest and useful prejudice against secret informers, although it may have contributed to give force to this objection, has in reality no application to the proceedings before a grand jury. When any member of this body prefers an accusation, he becomes a witness, his deposition is taken, and, with that of every other witness, is handed into court. The secrecy is not in the accusation, or in the name of the witness who makes it, but it is confined to the opinion which each juror delivers as to the weight which the evidence ought to have. To make this public, would be to deter the timid from the discharge of an important duty, by exposing him to the animosity of those who might be affected by it, and could be attended with no advantage whatever. If the office were an elective one, it would be important for the people to know how the officer had performed his duties; if it were one held by appointment, the same information would be useful to the executive or appointing power; but in the case before us, responsibility, except for offences, does not and need not exist; and where there is no responsibility, publicity can be of little use.

The want of general knowledge, and especially an ignorance of the law in the greatest number of jurors, is also alleged as a serious objection against their fitness to determine whether a citizen shall be exposed to the risk and vexation of a public trial, or a knave shall be snatched from the conviction that would probably be the consequence of his trial ; and it must be confessed, that if this objection be at all well founded, it is particularly so when applied to a system like the present, in which the jurors are taken by lot. But we must consider that the principal duty of a member of this body is the determination of matters of fact, which requires nothing more than the exercise of a plain sound understanding, a knowledge of the different concerns in common life, an independent spirit, firmness and integrity, acquirements as probably to be met with in any twenty men, who might be selected from three times that number presented by lot, as in any particular class of society. Ignorance of the law must certainly be expected. As our laws now stand, this objection might be made with nearly the same number, chosen with the greatest care from the whole community among those who are liable to this duty. It is obviated, in a great degree, by several provisions : the duties of grand jurors are specially pointed out ; and that part of the code which contains them, is directed to be read to them and a copy sent to their chamber : the written law, upon every one of the offences on which they are to decide, is also laid before them : the public prosecutor is directed to give them his advice on all the cases which he knows from the calendar will claim their attention, and on all other points, whenever it shall be required ; and any further doubts they may entertain, are directed to be cleared up by the court.  With these precautions to avoid error, it seems almost impossible that any of importance should be incurred ; and the necessity of resorting to these sources for information, will every day be diminished by the knowledge of the laws which these measures cannot but diffuse among the people.

One other inconvenience remains to be mentioned.  The abuse encouraged by the courts, and readily fallen into by grand juries,—that of assuming the power of discussing and deciding on extra-judicial and political questions.  This has an unhappy effect, particularly in a popular government, where party spirit is so apt to introduce itself into every assembly, to mix in every deliberation, break the ties of friendship, relax those of kindred, embitter social intercourse, madden public discussion, and unless restrained, impress its character on legislation and pervert the administration of the laws.  The greatest of these evils would be, that it should insinuate itself into the hall of justice ; and, as far as positive interdiction can go, this entrance through the chamber of the grand jury has been closed.  The grand jury, thus organized, is exclusively the accusing power in all cases of crime, and in those of misdemeanor concurrently with the public prosecutor, of whom there is one appointed for each court of criminal jurisdiction, The intervention of this body has been erroneously called a double trial, and it has been stigmatized as an injustice that the accused has not the privilege of being heard before them.  Although the answer to this objection has, in some measure, been anticipated, yet it may be necessary to add, that, until the indictment be found, the accusation is not complete, consequently there is nothing to answer, and nothing to try; and when it is found, there would be an absurdity, as well as glaring injustice, in permitting the truth of the accusation to be tried by the same body that had just preferred it.

It is hoped and believed, that in the chapters describing the mode of proceeding in the grand jury, and enjoining the duties of the court and the several officers of justice in relation to them, many things will be found which may prove useful in establishing and giving certainty to our present practice, together with some innovations that may be deemed improvements on the system, although they are not thought of sufficient importance to be here discussed.  The assent of twelve jurors is made necessary for finding an indictment, but that of a majority of those present is sufficient to decide incidental questions.  The act of accusation being found, must be delivered into the hands of the judge in open court, who, if the defendant be in custody or on bail, shall order it to be filed ; but if he be at large, in order to avoid his receiving notice and escaping, the judge shall issue a warrant for his apprehension, and keep the indictment in his hands until the arrest be made.  Freedom from arrest, during the term of his attendance, and from action or prosecution for any thing said in the performance of his duty, excepting perjury in a deposition made to his fellows, is secured to each grand juror.

A chapter is devoted to the form and substance of indictments and informations—an important division; for, to the want of precision in our law on this subject, may be traced the numerous instances in which men evidently guilty have escaped punishment. In a system which admits the humane maxim, that it is better an hundred guilty should escape than one innocent man be punished, it becomes an imperative duty to avoid all those doubts which make the administration of criminal justice a lottery, with so many chances in favour of guilt. Every man, who has attended our courts, must be convinced of the deleterious effects of this uncertainty, and must have seen the reliance that is placed upon it by culprits on their trials. The first question asked of their counsel, especially by old offenders, is, whether he can find no flaw in the indictment ; and there can be no doubt of its effect in multiplying crimes, by adding one more to the many hopes of impunity. Every endeavour, therefore, has been made for giving to the provisions of this chapter such a character as will make it secure to the accused every information necessary for his defence, but deprive him of all hopes of escaping, in any other manner than by a verdict, which shall declare him innocent: Among the first, is the direction for stating clearly in the act of accusation, whether indictment or information, all the circumstances which enter essentially into the description of the offence charged, the place where it was committed, and, in private offences, the names of those to whose property, person, or reputation, the injury was offered. To render mistakes less frequent, and secure uniformity in this important part of procedure, forms are provided in a subsequent part of the work, applicable to each offence ; but to avoid delay in the few cases in which these forms may have been carelessly departed from, those directions which may be considered as substantial are designated and distinguished from those which are formal only; the latter being amendable of course, and the former, except in a single instance, not operating so as to discharge the accused, if objected to either before or after trial ; that single exception being the one that the indictment charges, a fact which does not amount to an offence. In every other case the indictment is amendable by being referred again to the grand jury, where necessary—and the cases in which it is so, are pointed out—giving the party always time to answer the new allegations. A proper idea of all these provisions can only be formed by a perusal of the chapters which contain them. One alteration, however, demands particular notice. In no cases are exceptions to form more frequent, in none do they more effectually defeat the ends of justice, than in prosecutions for forgery, passing counterfeit bills, and other offences in relation to instruments in writing ; if an erroneous denomination be given to the instrument, by calling it an order when it is really a bill of exchange or a promissory note, or if the tenor of the writing be not exactly set forth in the indictment(a), the proceedings are set aside, and under some circumstance the

(a) To any one who has attended to the proceedings of criminal courts, it would be unnecessary to cite instances of the allegation in the text. One of rather a ludicrous cast lately occurred in England. In an indictment for forgery, a stroke of the pen, which occurred in the instrument, had not been copied in the indictment. The prisoner being convicted, his counsel moved in arrest of judgment, and assigned the omission of this stroke for cause. The paper and the indictment were handed up to the bench, and the judge, not being able with the naked eye to discover any difference, had recourse to a glass, and by the aid of a strong magnifier discovered something which he said was either a *tick* (a word of which I do not profess to know the meaning) or a letter, which he would not or could not determine, but sub-

2 D

defendant, although his guilt has been ascertained by a verdict, is discharged. These consequences are avoided by a simple provision, which has been alluded to in the Introductory Report to the Code of Crimes and Punishments. In all cases, to avoid the delay arising from objections to form, whether made in the shape of motions to quash the indictment, to set aside the proceedings, or to arrest the judgment, a copy of the indictment is directed to be furnished to the defendant, and, at a convenient time before the trial, he is brought into court and informed, that if the indictment contains any defect of form (and what are deemed to be such are explained to him) he must specify them by a day designated; but if he fail to make them then, he will for ever be precluded. In the mean time he has counsel assigned to him, if he have employed none. After the period for deliberation has elapsed, he is again called on for his exceptions; if he make any, and they are such as are designated in the code to be those of form merely, they are amended immediately by the public prosecutor; if of substance, the indictment is sent back to the grand jury. But if no exception be then made, none will afterwards be heard, except the radical defect that the facts charged do not amount to an offence. In prosecutions for offences, founded on writings, the indictment is not required to give any denomination to the instrument; it is not called a note, a bill, or bond, but simply an *"instrument in writing, of which a copy is annexed."* By this means one fruitful source of error, uncertainty and delay is avoided. Another, to which, as has been said, this species of prosecution is particularly liable, is avoided by the proceeding just detailed : the indictment and the copy of the instrument being served on the defendant, when he is brought into court the original is submitted to his inspection and that of his counsel; time is given to compare it with the copy furnished; and, in addition to the notice given in other cases, he is apprised that if he means to make any exception to the correctness of the copy furnished, he must do it in the time limited by the rule before trial. If he make any such exception, and it is found to be well taken, the copy is immediately amended; and it is not until all difficulties of form are thus got rid of, that the defendant is called on to answer to the merits. This is done formally in open court, and the answer can only be a confession or denial of the charge; excepting only, the plea that the defendant has before been acquitted or convicted for the same offence. A refusal to answer, or any indirect or evasive answer, is considered and recorded as a denial of the charge. As but one mode of trial, consistently with this code, will be known to our law, the useless question, which implies an option, is no longer to be put. The trial by jury is established as the only one that can be resorted to. The reasons for this are so obvious and are so fully stated in the Report on the Plan of a Penal Code, made to your predecessors in 1822(a), that nothing need be added to show the importance of this institution, as well in a political as a judicial point of view. A striking exemplification of the views contained in that Report, has lately come to my knowledge, which I think it may be proper to offer in this. The island of Ceylon, inhabited in different

mitted it to the jury, with directions, if they found it to be the one (I forget which) to convict, if the other to acquit; and to aid in the determination of this important question, he handed them his glass—the microscopic powers of which determined them in favour of the acquitting alternative—and the prisoner was discharged : if the judge's glass had not been brought into court, or had been of a lower power, he would have been hanged ! ! !

(a) Report on the Plan of a Penal Code, p. 10.

proportions by Hindoos, Mahometans, and descendants of emigrants from Siam, Ava, and other parts of the eastern continent and its adjacent islands, passed successively under the dominion of the Portuguese, Dutch and English, who have added to the heterogeneous mixture of inhabitants by a number of their descendants, springing from an intercourse with the native women. The English, having conquered this island in 1796, have ever since been in quiet possession of this valuable colony. For the administration of justice, the Dutch had introduced the civil law, by which the country was governed until the year 1811, when sir Alexander Johnston, chief-justice of the island, succeeded in the bold project of introducing the trial by jury into the criminal courts of the colony. Let those who doubt the political utility of this institution—who think it fitted only for the people of highly civilized and well-informed nations— who do not appreciate its power in spreading information and elevating the personal and national character; let those, and they are not few, who have considered the former report on this subject as an effusion of an enthusiastic veneration for a vain theory; let all those peruse the following authentic account, furnished from the highest authority, and confess the almost omnipotent power of this great institution in reforming and elevating the character, overcoming national prejudices, uniting the most discordant materials, diffusing useful knowledge, purifying the sources of justice, and demonstrating, by its effects, that no governments are so strong as those in which the people are suffered to participate. Let the enlightened author of this experiment himself explain its effects. In a letter, written by sir Alexander Johnston to the Board of Control in the year 1815, he says:

" I have the pleasure, at your request, to give you an account of the plan I adopted, while chief-justice and first member of his majesty's council in Ceylon, for introducing the trial by jury into that island, and for extending the right of sitting on juries to every half caste native, as well as to every other native of the country to whatever caste or religious persuasion he might belong. I shall explain to you the reasons which induced me to propose this plan, the mode in which it was carried into effect, and the consequences with which its adoption has been attended. The complaints against the former system for administering justice were, that it was dilatory, expensive and unpopular. The defects of that system arose from *the little value which the natives of the country attached to a character for veracity ; from the total want of interest, which they manifested for a system in the administration of which they had no share ;* from the difficulty which Europeans, who were not only judges of law but also of fact, experienced in ascertaining the degree of credit which they ought to give to native testimony ; and finally, from the delays in the proceedings of the court." The chief-justice then details the remedies he proposed for these evils, which could only be removed, as he thought, by the introduction of the trial by jury. He says, that he then consulted the chief priests of the Budha religion, and the Brahmins, as to the effect it would have on the followers of those religions ; and having submitted his plan to the governor and council, who " thinking the adoption of the plan an object of great importance, and fearing lest objections might be urged against it in England on *account of its novelty*, no such rights as were proposed to grant to the natives of Ceylon ever having been granted to any native of India," sent him to urge its adoption, and he most fortunately succeeded. The chief-justice

then proceeds to explain the qualifications of jurors, the manner of selecting them, and of conducting the trial ; all of which, though highly
interesting, do not so immediately apply to my subject, as the account of the effects, which he thus details : " The native jurymen being
now judges of fact, and the European judges the judges of law, one
European judge only is necessary.  The native jurymen, knowing
the different degrees of weight which may safely be given to their
countrymen, decide upon questions of fact with more promptitude.
*All the natives, who attend the courts as jurymen, obtain so much
information during their attendance, relative to the modes of proceeding and the rules of evidence, that since the establishment of
jury trials, government have been able to find among the half-caste
and native jurymen, some of the most efficient and respectable magistrates in the country.*"  After stating that the saving it produces
to government is at least 10,000*l.* a year, he proceeds :—" No man
whose character for honesty or veracity is impeached, can be enrolled on
the list of jurymen.  The circumstance of a man's name being upon the
jury-roll, is a proof of his being a man of unexceptionable character, and
is that to which he appeals, in case his character be attacked, or in case
he solicits his government for promotion.  As the rolls of jurymen are
revised by the supreme court at every session, *they operate as a most
powerful engine in making the people of the country more attentive
than they used to be in their adherence to truth.*  The right of *sitting upon juries, has given to the natives of Ceylon a value for character which they never felt before, and has raised in a very remarkable manner the standard of their moral feelings.  All the natives
of Ceylon, who are enrolled as jurymen, conceive themselves as much
a part, as the European judges themselves are, of the government of
the country, and therefore feel, since they have possessed the right
of sitting upon juries, an interest which they never felt before in
upholding the British government of Ceylon.*"  He then gives as a
proof of this, their indifference in wars before this privilege, contrasted with their zeal in those after it was conferred.  The writer of this
interesting and highly instructive letter refers, as a proof of his
assertions, to a charge delivered by his successor eight years after the
experiment was tried, in which he ascribes a remarkable decrease of
crimes, " *above all other causes, to the introduction of the trial by
jury.*  To this happy system," he proceeds, " now deeply cherished in
the affections of the people and revered as much as any of their own
oldest and dearest institutions, *I do confidently ascribe this pleasing
alteration ;* and it may be boldly asserted, that while it continues to
be administered with firmness and integrity, the British government
will hold an interest in the hearts of its Singalee subjects, which the
Portuguese and Dutch possessors of this island were never able to
establish."

    The statement of this case, tallying so exactly with the ideas I had
expressed some years before the letter was written, is worth volumes
of arguments, and every reflection I have given to the subject since,
and they have neither been few nor cursory, has convinced me so much
of the danger of tampering with so great a blessing, of injuring in the
attempt to ameliorate what is so positively good, that I could not venture to propose any alterations, although some came recommended by
the most plausible reasons as valuable improvements: among these was
that of substituting for the unanimity now requisite to a decision, a bare

majority of votes, or some other number less than the whole. The absurdity, as well as cruelty, of enforcing that unanimity, under pain of starvation, and the injustice of making the fate of the accused depend on the ability of his judges to resist hunger and thirst, seem so apparent, that, if no other remedy could have been found for the evil, I should, perhaps, have abandoned this characteristic in the trial by jury, and adopted some of the proposed modifications, to avoid the evil. But a practice had been introduced, which, where it prevailed, in a great measure presented the remedy I sought. Courts in the exercise of the legislative power which they held, partly by assumption, partly by the negligent permission of the branch to which it of right belongs, had gradually introduced an important change in this branch of our jurisprudence : when jurors could not agree, instead of being starved, or in some cases carted into unanimity, they were discharged ; and the contest became one of argument and reason, instead of physical force and ability to resist the cravings of nature. The objections to this improvement, for such experience has shown it to be, are, that being entirely without legislative sanction, it depends on the court to determine whether it shall be introduced at all, and when it is, what degree of suffering must be undergone by the jury before they are discharged.

In the code presented to you, rules are prescribed for that purpose. The legislature speaks, and it is no longer imposed upon the court, as some decisions require, to watch, like the medical attendants on a victim of the inquisition, over the struggles between nature and famine, 'and to discharge the juror only when they are convinced that there is immediate danger that death will release him(a). The jurors are no longer to be kept without food ; because it is not considered to be well established, that hunger will bring a man to a correct conclusion, though it may to a speedy one ; and in the system I have adopted, justice is the first, and celerity only a secondary consideration. Jurors are treated like reasonable beings, and with the respect due to a co-ordinate branch with the judges in the administration of justice ; subject, indeed, to their control for the maintenance of order and the advancement of justice but to a legal control, not an arbitary discretion ; their deliberation must be free from the restraint of physical wants—their determination the result of reason and conviction. Perhaps, too, the concurrence of circumstances(b), that probably produced the extraordinary feature in this mode of trial, which requires unanimity for a verdict, has been more fortunate than design would probably have been, in adapting it to the ends of justice in criminal proceedings ; for I am inclined to think, if a bare majority were sufficient to give a verdict, that in a secret consultation, where there is no excitement created by

(a) 7 Johnson's Cases, The People v. Olcot. Chief-justice Kent says, "the power of discharging a jury, in a criminal case, is a highly important and delicate trust, yet it does exist *in cases of extreme and obstinate necessity.*" See the other cases there cited.

(b) It has been conjectured (and I think with reason) that the unanimity afterwards required, formed no part of the primitive institution of juries, which originally, it is argued from the analogy of grand juries, the grand assize, and sheriffs' inquests, must have consisted, like them, of twenty-three, a majority of the whole number (twelve) being necessary for a decision; that afterwards, at some unknown period, probably when suits began to multiply and the attendance of so many jurors was found burthensome, the practice of summoning only twelve was introduced, but that the concurrence of the same majority of twelve continued to-be required.

the presence of auditors or by the prospect of publicity, the decision would, for the most part, be made merely by ascertaining the number of members on each side, without that discussion which is so necessary to elicit truth. Indeed, I have been told by those who have served frequently on juries, and I have made the inquiry in different states, that the first thing generally done, after they retire, is, previous to any debate, to take a vote on the question, and a division of opinion always, under the present system, leads to a revisal of the testimony and a discussion of the arguments that have been offered ; whereas, if a majority were to decide, the vote would have decided the cause.   Another consideration, also, must have some weight in favour of the verdict by unanimity : the evidence that subjects a citizen to the serious consequences of conviction for an offence, ought to be so clear as to convince the understandings of all ; if then it should fail to convince one-fourth, or any other given proportion of the jury, the probability is, that its impression would be the same on the rest of the community ; and the conviction of a man, whom one-fourth or one-tenth of his fellow-citizens believed to be innocent, could not but have effects upon the confidence which ought to be reposed in the administration of justice more injurious than his acquittal could be, if, although really guilty, he should be pronounced innocent by a unanimous verdict.   Reverse the case, and suppose three, or two, or even a single one, of the jury so perfectly convinced, from the evidence, that the defendant has committed the crime, as to be ready to attest his conviction under the sanction of an oath, and consequently refusing to join in the verdict of acquittal, while the rest of the jury doubt his guilt or even believe him to be innocent : to acquit him under such circumstances, would neither restore him to society with the pure reputation that every man, who has been pronounced innocent by his fellow-citizens, ought to enjoy, nor will it remove the alarm which his enlargement will create in a community, a large proportion of which still believed him guilty, and, of course, encouraged by impunity, ready to repeat his former crime.   Thus, whether we consider the effect of an acquittal or conviction by less than the whole number of the jury, upon the community, or the accused, upon the administration of justice, or its reputation, we find nearly the same objections to making any change.   If the defendant is acquitted, he returns with a tarnished reputation, and the community is not relieved from their alarm.   If he is convicted, the chance of his being innocent is increased in proportion to the number of the jury who believed him so ; and the same proportion of his fellow-citizens participating in this belief, will arraign the justice of their country, and consider him upon whom it has been exercised as an innocent victim, not a guilty object of just punishment.   In the actual administration of the laws, we have seen the effect it will produce, of a reliance upon first and cursory impressions, a neglect of due discussion and a careless decision by shifting the responsibility upon a majority, who act in secret, and whose names are not distinguished from those of their fellows.   Where all convict, or all acquit, there is responsibility; upon a secret majority there is none ; and to make them record their names and votes, or to give publicity to all their deliberations, would be attended with inconveniences too obvious to be detailed.   However just in itself, no system of criminal procedure can be good which does not create in the mass of the people a belief that he who is acquitted under it is innocent, and that no punishment can be inflicted but on the guilty. This belief constitutes the reputation of judicial proceeding, and it is as necessary to this branch of government as good character is to individuals ; but we have seen that it will be greatly impaired by any other course than that of requiring unanimity in the jury that decides in criminal cases. It is not my intention to discuss its propriety in those of a civil nature further than to say, that most of the reasons I have urged will not apply to the latter. I have dwelt longer on this subject than I should have done, if I had not found a disposition in the friends of this institution to rest the defence of this particular feature on its antiquity, rather than its wisdom or its use ; and in its enemies, to urge this characteristic as an unanswerable objection to the jury trial in its present form. The legislature will judge whether it has been wisely preserved or not. This discussion has rather anticipated on the regular course of this review, the natural order of which is to follow that of the different chapters of the work ; one, which has before been cursorily mentioned, is connected with the subject we have just left : it regulates the manner in which the grand and petit juries are to be selected—in such a way as to equalize the duty upon all the citizens capable of performing it, and rendering it the means of a gradual diffusion of legal and political information through the whole community. The designation is on the principle, now in such successful operation, of a mixture of chance and selection, which precludes the possibility of any favour in empanelling the jury, and gives little or no opportunity for influence after they are chosen.

The seventh chapter of this title lays down rules for proceedings in court, previous to the trial. The first section gives to the court the discretionary powers of postponing the trial, whenever such circumstances are made to appear, by proper proof, as show that justice requires it, but with the limitation that the defendant, if in custody, must be tried before the end of the second, or, if on bail, before the end of the fourth term, unless the delay has taken place at his instance, or by his fault.

After all the precautions given by the mode of empanelling the jury, it may happen that the forms presented by law, for returning and selecting the jurors, have not been observed ; that one or more of them may not be legally qualified to serve on any jury—or, by reason of interest, partiality, relationship, or some other cause, disqualified to be on the one for which they are drawn. To secure that impartiality which is so essential to justice, the law has provided remedies adapted to each of these cases ; they are taken, with but little alterations, from the English law ; the technical terms are preserved ; but the challenge to the array can, under this system, only be made for a single cause, that the forms of the law for forming the panel have not been followed. Where the names were selected from the community at large, at the discretion of the returning officer, his interests, enmities, and connexions, with the party, formed so many reasons for making this challenge ; all of which are avoided by our mode of making out the panel. Exceptions to particular jurors remain nearly as under the English law. The peremptory challenge, for which the party need assign no reason, is a wise and humane provision, peculiar, it is believed, to the English jurisprudence. There are, in life, so many unfriendly feelings, created by trifles, or for reasons which it would be difficult to assign, but which destroy the perfect impartiality required in a judge, that we cannot too much admire the provision that enables a party to reject him who may be affected by these feelings, without being questioned as to his motive. Considering the little chance there is, under our plan of preparing the panel, that any great number of persons, unfavourably disposed to any individual accused, could be found on it, it was thought that giving the privilege of challenge to nine jurors peremptorily, was a sufficient extension.   The public prosecutor has the same right, but extended only to three jurors ; the reason for this restriction is obvious ; the prejudice against the public can be supposed, and the only undue affection of the mind to be guarded against by the prosecution, is favour to the defendant, which, if made apparent by evidence or by the declaration of the juror, is a disqualification under another head,—the challenge for cause ; this may be made both by the defendant and the prosecutor, and, of course, has no restriction as to number.  The reasons for which it may be made, are set forth at length, and embrace every fact or opinion that can show the slightest bias for or against the prisoner ; and the mode of trying the facts, which evince this bias, or the disqualifying operation they may have on the jurors, is prescribed.

The next chapter, which directs the mode of proceeding on the trial, contains some provisions which call for attention.  The jurors are drawn by lot, not in the order they stand on the panel ; a different practice had obtained in our courts, which it was thought proper to correct, being a deviation from the English law, and liable to obvious abuse.   Any number of jurors, less than twelve, that may be agreed on between the prosecutor and the defendant, may try a misdemeanor, for the purpose of avoiding delay in causes of little importance, wherein a speedy decision may sometimes avoid inconveniences greater than the punishment of the offence, if the party be found guilty ; but it is not allowed in cases of crime, in which the party can neither renounce the trial by jury, nor modify it, for reasons which have been already stated at large.   The order in which the case is opened to the jury, and the proof introduced, is the same as that now in use ; but a material change is made, by giving the closing argument to the defendant.    It was thought that this was proper and just, because it is an *advantage*, that is to say, a benefit to one party, that the other does not and cannot, from the nature of things, enjoy.   To whom shall this be given, to the accuser or the accused, to him who asserts or him who denies ?   Humanity and justice seem to dictate the answer.   Every address to a judge must be supposed to contain a new allegation of fact, a new argument, or a new answer to rebut those which have been offered on the other side ; to close the debate, therefore, without suffering the accused to reply to such allegation or argument, would be in so much as regards it, to decide on his case without hearing him.   The same thing may be said of the prosecution. The remedy would be to suffer the argument to go on until both parties declared they had nothing further to say ; but this would rarely happen, and never until the discussion had been protracted to a length so highly inconvenient as not to be permitted.  It seems, then, as has been said, that the nature of the case imposes the necessity of giving this advantage to the one party or the other.   To give it to the prosecution, sometimes defeats the ends of justice, by enlisting the feelings of humanity on the side of the accused.    There is in human nature, when not perverted, a feeling repugnant to oppression, which generally supposes power to be wrong, and ascribes innocence to weakness, whenever they come in competition with each other ; and few cases give such scope to the imagination to exert itself in this way, as that of a criminal on his trial—squalid in his appearance, his body debilitated by confinement, his mind weakened by misery or conscious guilt, abandoned by all the world, he stands alone, to contend with the fearful odds that are arrayed against him. It is true he has counsel assigned him ; but here again the same feelings operate to lead the judgment astray. This counsel is generally the youngest counsellor at the bar, who is thus made to enter the lists with one of the highest abilities and standing, with a reputation so well established as to have made him the choice of government as the depository of its interests. If you add to all this, the decided advantage of the closing argument, given to a practised advocate, whom long habit has taught to avail himself of every weak argument or suspicious fact, and a zeal in the performance of his duty has taught to believe it proper to do so ;—do this, and of two opposite effects one must be produced, both injurious to the fair administration of justice : either the jury will be swayed by the sentiment I have endeavoured to describe, and feel an undue bias in favour of the prisoner; or if this fails to act, the last impression given with the force of eloquence and professional skill, may, in doubtful cases, have injurious consequences to the innocent. But give the last word to the accused, and you will do little more than counterbalance the disadvantages inseparable from his situation ; while, by this show of humanity and disdain of using the power in your hands, you neutralize the sentiment that would other-wise be felt in his favour. The provision here recommended makes part of the French code of criminal procedure, and it is said to have, in practice, the most beneficial effects.

Another change, of the same character with the one last mentioned, was noticed in the Report on the Plan of a Penal Code made in 1822(a), which received the unanimous approbation of the legislature; yet it has been made the ground-work of an attempt to prejudice the public mind against the work and its author, as if it were a design to lessen the dignity of the judiciary branch of our government, suggested by a spirit of hostility to that department, or of personal enmity to those who fill it. To repel this is necessary, in reference both to the objection itself and the motives that are imputed.

A system of penal law, containing principles or provisions injurious to the power upon which alone it must depend for its execution, would be an absurdity too gross even for imbecility to produce ; and before it is fixed on the code I have now the honour to offer, it ought to be strictly examined. The obnoxious article is in the following words(b): " When the pleadings are finished, the judge shall give his charge to the jury, in which he shall state to them all such matters of law as he shall think necessary for their information in giving their verdict ; but he shall not recapitulate the testimony unless requested so to do by one or more of the jurors, if there should be any difference of opinion between them as to any particular part of the testimony, and then he shall confine his information to the part on which information is required ; being the intent of this article, that the jury shall decide all questions of fact, in which is included the credit due to the witnesses who have been sworn, unbiassed by the opinion of the court." This is the text. I add the reasons as they are given in the first report, that

(a) Page 42.      (b) Code of Procedure, b. ii. c. 8.

2 E

the legislature may see whether the provision was not dictated by the exalted opinion of the judicial character, which, in its purity, it deserves; by a desire to prevent any encroachment by the bench on that feature in our jurisprudence which assigns to the judges the decision of questions of law, to the jury those of fact; and whether in its operation it will not save the judges from degrading altercation, render juries more independent and more attentive to their great duties, and exalt rather than debase the judicial character, and preserve unimpaired the distinctive characters of the jury and the bench.

This is the extract from the Report. "Another article, applicable to the trial, restricts the charge of the judge to an opinion of the law, and allows a repetition of the evidence only when required by the jury, or any one of them. The practice of repeating all the testimony from notes, always, from the nature of things, imperfectly, not seldom inaccurately, and sometimes carelessly taken, has a double disadvantage; it makes the jurors, who depend more on the the judge's notes than on their own memory, inattentive to the evidence, and it gives them an imperfect copy of that which the nature of the trial by jury requires they should record on their own minds. Forced to rely upon themselves, the necessity will quicken their attention, and it will be only when they disagree in their recollection that recourse will be had to the notes of the judge. There is also another and more cogent reason for the restriction. Judges are generally men who have grown old in the practice at the bar. With the knowledge which this experience gives, they also acquire a habit, very difficult to be shaken off, that of taking a side in every question that they hear debated; and when the mind is once enlisted, their passions, prejudices, and their professional ingenuity are always arrayed on the same side, and furnish arms for the contest; neutrality cannot, under these circumstances, be expected; but the law should limit, as much as possible, the evil that this almost inevitable state of things must produce. In the theory of our law, judges are the counsel for the accused; in the practice, they are, with a few honourable exceptions, his most virulent(a) prosecutors. The true principles of criminal jurisprudence require, that he should be neither. Perfect impartiality is inconsistent with these duties. A good judge should have no wish that the guilty should escape, or that the innocent should suffer; no false pity, no undue severity should bias the unshaken rectitude of his judgment; calm in deliberation, firm in resolve, patient in investigating the truth, tenacious of it when discovered; he should join urbanity of manners to dignity of demeanour, and an integrity above suspicion to learning and talent; such a judge is what, according to the structure of our courts, he ought to be—the protector, not the advocate, of the accused—his judge, not his accuser; and while executing these functions, he is the organ by which the sacred will of the law is pronounced. Uttered by such a voice, it will be heard, respected, felt, obeyed. But impose on him the task of argument, of debate; degrade him from the bench to the bar; suffer him to overpower the accused with his influence, or to enter the lists with his advocate, to carry on the conflict of sophisms, of angry argument, of tart replies, and all the wordy war of forensic debate: suffer him to

---

(a) The conduct of some judges would justify this epithet; but, on reflection, I regret that it has been so generally applied as is done in the text; zealous would have better expressed the idea I meant to convey.

do this, and his dignity is lost, his decrees are no longer considered as the oracles of the law ; they are submitted to, but not respected ; and even the triumph of his eloquence or ingenuity, in the conviction of the accused, must be lessened by the suspicion that it has owed its success to official influence and the privilege of arguing without reply. For these reasons the judge is forbidden to express any opinion on the facts which are alleged in evidence, much less to address any argument to the jury ; but his functions are confined to expounding the law, and stating the points of evidence on which the recollection of the members of the jury may differ."

In speaking of the formation and functions of juries, the greater part of that which relates to verdicts, the subject of the next chapter, was anticipated. Some articles deserve consideration. The term, *offences of the same nature*, frequently occurs in this system, and it is important to keep in mind the sense in which it is declared to be used. Offences, we must remember, were arranged in relation to this object under a variety of heads ; as offences against person, property, reputation, and the like. All offences arranged under the same head, are offences of the same nature : of these, some are higher, others lower in degree ; the lowest being the first in numerical order, and ascending on a scale prepared by a view of the injurious effects of each offence combined with the degree of moral depravity evinced in, or usually attendant on, its commission. This explanation is necessary to an understanding of the power, given to the jury, to find the defendant guilty of a lower offence, of the same nature with the one charged in the indictment, provided that the lower offence be produced by the same circumstances ; thus, if one be indicted for murder, the jury may convict of manslaughter or negligent homicide in any of the degrees ; if he be indicted for battery or theft, aggravated by any other circumstances which enhance the guilt of the offender, the jury may convict of any of those offences of the same nature, which are lower in the scale of crime ; but it must be the same homicide, the same battery, the same theft, that is charged in the indictment. On the contrary, on an indictment for negligent homicide in the first degree, the party may not be convicted of manslaughter, murder, or any of the other degrees of homicide ; nor, if indicted for simple theft, can he be found guilty of robbery ; but if on the trial the evidence is found to support a charge of a higher degree than the one set forth in the indictment, the court is directed to discharge the jury and send the witnesses to the grand jury, for the purpose of having an indictment preferred for the higher offence.

In cases of acquittal for insanity, that fact is directed to be certified, and the court is empowered to take proper measures for the confinement of the party or his delivery to his relations.

In the mode in which verdicts are taken, at present, on charges of forgery, a difficulty sometimes arises, where there is an acquittal, to know on what grounds the decision was made ; whether they believe that the instrument was forged, but that the defendant was not the person guilty of the crime ; or that the instrument was made by the person whose act it purported to be, and consequently that no crime had been committed. By the code, whenever the acquittal is made on the last mentioned ground, the jury are directed to declare, and the court to record it ; so that the finding may serve as an authority for the person, whose property the instrument is, to receive it. In the first case, it remains in the hands of the proper officer as the means of prosecuting the offender, whenever he is discovered. But the court is authorized to make such order respecting it, as may be required for the ends of justice, in case any civil suit should be commenced which may make its production necessary.

In cases of conviction, if the court think the jury have mistaken the law, they may order them to reconsider their verdict, after giving them an explanation of the law; but they have not this power given to them where there has been a verdict of acquittal. Directions are given for ascertaining whether the assent of each juror has been given to the verdict declared by the foreman, and for recording it. When the verdict of acquittal is entered and recorded, the defendant is entitled to his immediate discharge, without any detention for fees, costs, for any expenses incurred by his confinement, except only in the following cases: where other charges are legally exhibited against him; where the public prosecutor requires a detention not exceeding twelve hours, to frame such charge on an official allegation to the court, that he has the evidence to justify it; or on the allegation of sufficient causes for a new trial if properly supported by evidence. The causes that are deemed sufficient are precisely enumerated, and all are founded on some malpractice of the defendant, in producing suborned witnesses, or forged papers—in preventing, by fraud or force, the attendance of the witnesses for the prosecution—in giving evidence out of court to the jury—in bribing a juror, or causing an illegal panel to be returned. A much longer list of sufficient reasons is given for setting aside the verdict when it is one of conviction ; and the mode is pointed out by which the facts, in either case, are to be substantiated. The long title of arrest of judgment, under our present system, is abridged to a short chapter ; and all the causes for which the defendant may now hope for impunity, after his guilt has been ascertained, are reduced to a single one—that the act of accusation does not contain the allegation of any fact; or any fact coupled with an intent, that is by law created an offence. But the allowance of the motion in arrest of judgment, only places the party in the situation in which he was before the indictment was found—liable to be again indicted, if the evidence is sufficient for that purpose. If the code has been supposed too favourable to the accused, in some of its features, it has, on the contrary, been considered as too severe in this ; but after the best reflection my mind has been able to give to the subject, it can perceive no injury but to the guilty in thus restraining the effects of allowing a motion in arrest of judgment, nor any unnecessary vexation even to them. Suppose the case of one brought to trial on an indictment which charges facts that do not amount to an offence ; if this defect had been pointed out before the trial, no one supposes that it ought to operate as a discharge from further prosecution. Why should it, after a jury have given their sanction to the truth of the facts, and after the defendant has purposely, perhaps, omitted to avail himself of the exception ? No good reason can be alleged : even the maxim that no one shall twice be put in jeopardy, perverted as it has been, cannot be brought to bear on the question ; for surely no one can be said to be put in jeopardy by a trial for facts not criminal in themselves, and which he might have confessed without incurring any penalty whatever.— Three days, after a verdict of conviction, are allowed for making a motion in arrest of judgment or for a new trial; at the expiration of which time, the prisoner is to be brought into court for sentence : previous to pronouncing it, the prisoner must be interrogated to know whether he can allege any cause why judgment should not be given. The several matters which it will avail him to show, in answer to this interpellation, are only four : a pardon—insanity—inevitable accident, that prevented a motion for a new trial or in arrest of judgment within the three days —or a denial that he is the person convicted. The mode in which these several allegations are to be substantiated and disposed of, is pointed out ; and previous to the sentence it is provided, that such matters in aggravation, as were not necessary to be stated in the indictment, may be shown by the prosecution—and such in extenuation, by the defendant, as would not, on the trial, have proved him to have been entirely innocent.

Before we consider the matters incident to the judgment, it may be proper to review the provisions which characterize the previous proceedings, and which were framed with the view of depriving offenders of every reasonable hope of escaping from defects of form, an inestimable advantage in criminal procedure ; but which would be purchased too dear if attained at the expense of unnecessary risk to the innocent, or any vexation that may be avoided to the party, whether guilty or innocent. As the law is now administered, there is a certain class of defects, not very clearly defined, which are called defects of substance ; for these the defendant may move to have the indictment quashed, that is, declared to be void, before the trial ; or he may take the chance of a verdict in his favour, and if that hope fail, he may move to arrest the judgment after a verdict against him. This latter course he is always advised to pursue, if his advocate thinks the objection a good one, because the effect of quashing the indictment leaves him liable to a renewal of the prosecution ; but when the judgment is arrested, he is for ever discharged, although his guilt be apparent. Now, most of these things called defects of substance, are in reality nothing more than mere defects of form. Sometimes the omission of writing the name of the county in the margin of the indictment, although it be stated in the body of the instrument itself ; sometimes not putting it in the indictment, although it be in the margin, and other omissions of the like nature ; the variance of a letter between the original and the copy of an instrument set forth in the indictment ; sometimes even of a comma, has been held a sufficient cause for setting aside a conviction and discharging the guilty convict without punishment. In England and in this state, which, as we have seen, are governed as to certain crimes by the same law, any defect of form whatever may produce this effect. I say *may* produce it, because this, like other points of practice, depends very much on the will of the judge ; the law having varied in this respect, not by the act of the legislature, but by the changing decisions of the courts ; for Sir M. Hale laments, that " that strictness has *grown* to be a blemish and inconvenience in the law and the administration thereof ; for that more offenders escape, by the over easy ear given to exceptions in indictments, than by their own innocence." Here we have the highest authority, not only for the existence of the evil, but for the fact of its being produced by the decisions of the court, not by any positive law ; and consequently, if one set of judges have altered the law by being over easy in listening to exceptions, other judges may restore it to its original state in which it was before the " strictness grew to be a blemish," or they will have a plausible, if not a legal reason for increasing that strictness, because it is expressly stated to be law(a), that none of the statutes, which allow amendment in civil cases, extend to those of a criminal nature. It is of little consequence, however, to inquire from what cause this strictness, so injurious to the administration of justice, proceeds, provided we guard against its effects in future. This has been attempted not by abolishing the necessity for forms, but by supplying them whenever they have been omitted, and amending them when they are defective. The general enunciation of this feature in the code was so much assailed by the allegation, that allowing the amendments would enable the prosecuting officer to harass by charges that might surprise the defendant to his vexation and injury. An inspection of the provisions by which this characteristic in the plan is to be carried into execution, it is confidently believed, will obviate that objection; no amendment materially altering the charge can be made, but either by the agency of the grand jury, which would never lend itself to vexatious proceeding; or by the act of the defendant himself, when he points out an error arising from misnomer, inaccurate copies, or defects of this nature. Innocence has nothing to fear, nothing to complain of, from this proceeding; guilt, every thing to dread ; public justice, every thing to gain. I consider the adoption of this part of the code so essential to the success of the whole, that I must be excused for pressing the strict examination of it upon the attention of the legislature. Nothing so much fosters the growth of crimes, as the hope in the culprit that some defect of form will enable him to escape ; and nothing encourages that hope so much as the numerous and sometimes frivolous objections that are allowed ; and this is called the tenderness and humanity of the law!—when, in fact, it is, in the words of Sir Matthew Hale, its "greatest blemish and inconvenience." The character of humanity must be acquired, not by facilitating the impunity of offenders, but by the strict infliction of mild punishments, when guilt has been proved ; and it is a strange tenderness to boast of, which suffers a villain to escape his punishment because a clerk has omitted a word, or inserted one too many, in copying an indictment.

We come now to the consummation of the judicial authority in its operation upon offences. The functions of the judge cease when he has pronounced the sentence, unless extraordinary circumstances should require him to communicate with the chief magistrate, in relation to an application for pardon ; but even then, the duty he performs is that of a witness of facts disclosed on the trial, rather than that of a judge. This last office is also the most important. In a system of penal law, which has fine and imprisonment for its chief sanctions, a great scope must be allowed for the discretion of the judge. The circumstances which aggravate or extenuate an offence, which make a punishment ruin to one individual, which would not be felt by another, are too numerous to be detailed, and too much dependent on events to be foreseen. But much may be done, although we confess our inability to do all, and we ought to advance in the path of improvement, although we despair of its leading us to perfection. We have prescribed limits to the discretion of the judge, because we cannot fill up the interval by applying our scale to unknown events. The combination of those events may produce different degrees of depravity for which we cannot anticipate the exact punishment that ought to be applied; but we can foresee and

(a) 4 Black. Com. 875.

can enumerate certain probable circumstances in the commission of every offence, which ought to aggravate or lessen the punishment, although we cannot direct in what precise degree they ought to have that effect. This has been done in the code now offered to you. It contains two opposite details of circumstances, which ought to increase above, and those which ought to diminish below the medium rate of punishment, which is declared to be that which ought to be inflicted where none of these circumstances exist. Thus, if the code direct that the punishment of an offence shall be fine, not less than one hundred nor more than three hundred dollars; the medium is two hundred, which it is the duty of the judge to award, if there be no circumstances of extenuation or aggravation. The nature and extent of the obligation arising from this address to the judgment of the court, is fully explained in the text, and the reason for resorting to it has more than once been adverted to in the report.

The fourteenth chapter is devoted to the forms of conducting .the ordinary business of courts. One of the most important of these, is the oath or affirmation to be administered to jurors and witnesses ; those now in use to officers, are, for reasons that will be given, abolished. These engagements are either promissory or declaratory; the juror's oath being of the first, that of the witnesses of the last description: a breach of the promissory oath not incurring, like that of the other, the punishment of perjury, as we have seen in the penal code. Some changes having been proposed under this head, it will be necessary to make a brief statement of the reasons which have produced them. The necessity of providing some test for the truth of declarations which were to operate as judicial proof, and some bond for the performance of promises, in a very early state of society, suggested, on him who should be guilty of a breach of such engagement, an imprecation of divine displeasure ; which was thought to be inevitable, when the appeal was voluntarily made by the party upon whom the vengeance of heaven was to fall, if his promise was broken, or his declaration false. A belief in a Supreme Being, and in his agency in punishing evil and rewarding virtue, either in this life or another, was essential to this religious sanction of an oath; as it was the first, so it has generally been esteemed the most powerful ; another, however, may be said to be inseparable from the first. The sacrilegious wretch, who had by his broken vows incurred the vengeance of God, could not retain the good opinion of man, and another surety was added in the loss of reputation, which would be incurred by the perjurer. The chastisement which he had invoked upon his head, was observed not always to follow his guilt in this world, and the fear of that which might follow in the world to come, was weakened by doubt, by irreligion, and the prevalence which present advantage generally has over distant and uncertain evil; and it became necessary to add the temporal penalties denounced by human laws against perjury ; thus completing the triple tie of the religious, honorary, and civil sanctions to the obligation of an oath. Some sects from religious principles, and some writers from a specious theory, have rejected the religious sanction : the first, because, according to their tenets, it is contrary to the express precept of the founder of our holy religion ; the second, for reasons which it may be useful to examine. Religious scruples will with difficulty yield to civil laws, and where their indulgence does not operate any great evil to society, a wise legislator will not attempt to overcome them. Throughout the United States, therefore, those Christians who cannot conscientiously take an oath, have the same credit given to their affirmation; which derives its whole force from its civil and honorary obligation. Those who are for abolishing the religious sanction, say, that it is not only useless but injurious, and even profane : useless, because where religious motives produce a determination to tell the truth, they will always operate, whatever be the form of the engagement—and where there is no religion, the form can have no effect.   Injurious, because it creates a false confidence in the declaration of one who has no religious sentiment, and adds nothing to the credit of him who has; because religion cannot be introduced in civil institutions without weakening their effect ; because, with many, religion consists in form, and if that form be varied in the slightest degree, the religious obligation is not incurred, and the other obligations, being considered as inferior, are overlooked : and because, the oath being a religious ceremony, was subject to ecclesiastical control, might be dispensed with, and its breach pardoned or expiated(a).   Profane, not only because it is in opposition to the plain and express command of the Scripture, but because it supposes a power in him who imposes, or him who takes the oath, to direct Almighty vengeance at his pleasure, and often for trifling or even unworthy objects.  When properly developed and coolly considered, these objections have weight; and if I were now, for the first time, devising the formula of a judicial asseveration to declare the truth, I think I should omit the conditional renunciation of God's favour, which it now contains.   The general impression now existing of its necessity, the abandonment of all pretension to right by any ecclesiastical power in our day to dispense with its obligation, and the danger of a sudden change, have combined to induce me to retain this part of the oath in ordinary cases ; but with the proviso of extending the right of dispensing with it in favour of all those who declare they have religious scruples, in the same manner that the same dispensation is now given to Quakers and Memnonists.  But while this part of the form has been retained, it was to be feared, and experience shows that there is some ground for the apprehension, that there are men who do not feel the force of this obligation, and are ready to risk the legal consequences, but who yet might be restrained if an address were expressly made to their honour and integrity.   There are perverse and extraordinary ideas entertained on this subject: one will conceive the oath not binding on his conscience, if administered on any other book than the New Testament; a Jew may think it of no force unless the old be presented to him; this man conceives himself obliged to tell the truth only when he declares that he will do so with uplifted hand; another, who does not mind kissing the book, as he irreverently styles it, will be scrupulously exact in what he declares upon his honour.   These considerations have induced me to incorporate into the form of the oath a clause to bind those of the last description.

As has been observed, all persons belonging to any sect, having religious scruples to take an oath, may substitute an affirmation.   The

(a) Dumont gives an extraordinary instance of this power.  Clement VI., he says, granted to John the III. of France, and Jane his wife, and to all their successors, the right, without incurring any sin, to violate their promises and oaths, as well those they had already made as those they might thereafter make, provided it was not their interest to keep them, and provided also that they commuted the obligation in some work of piety.

declaration of the party that he does belong to such sect is sufficient evidence of the fact; and although that declaration be untrue, the breach of the affirmation carries with it the consequences that the breach of an oath would have done.

A clause is added to the affirmation referring expressly to its legal sanction.

To avoid the frequent repetition of oaths, in judicial proceedings, none are administered to a sworn officer when called on to do a particular duty, such as going out with a juror, or the like.

To give greater solemnity to the obligation, the form is repeated by the person to whom it is administered, during which strict silence is to be observed by all those not concerned in taking or administering it, and no other business is to be transacted in court during the ceremony. The oaths and affirmations of jurors and witnesses are so framed, as to bring their respective duties forcibly before them, as well as the penalties attending a neglect of their performance; and an endeavour is made to enforce the necessity of preserving the requisite solemnity in a ceremonial generally treated with the utmost levity, but which requires every aid that an imposing form can give to enforce the idea of its obligation. One peculiarity in the oath of a witness ought, perhaps, to be pointed out. At present he is sworn to declare the *"whole truth,"* yet when he proceeds to comply with this obligation, he is, perhaps, stopped by the counsel or the court, and told, "what you are now about to say is not legal evidence, and although it is part of the truth, the whole of which you have sworn to tell, yet you are not permitted to tell what we have obliged you to swear that you would tell." This incongruity is remedied by a clause in the proposed form of the oath.

The three remaining sections of this chapter regulate the manner of opening and adjourning the court, keeping the minutes, calling the jurors, witnesses and officers, and imposing fines for their non-attendance; and to supply any omission in this part of the code, authority is given to the courts to make additional rules of practice; but they are to be submitted immediately after to the legislature, to the end that they may prevent any infringement of the law, and preserve a uniformity in the form of proceeding in all the different courts.

The necessary officers of the courts are enumerated in a succeeding chapter, and their several duties specially pointed out. The only addition to those now employed, is the reporter; his duties are, to make reports of all causes that are tried, and all points of law that are determined in the court, and to publish them at stated times, and to make regular returns of all commitments, accusations, indictments, informations and trials, in such form as to give every desirable information of the state of crime and criminal jurisprudence in his district. These returns are to be made to the governor, to be by him laid before the legislature. A mass of information will thus be collected, which will be of the utmost value in future legislation(*a*).

Although publicity is of the highest importance in the administration

(*a*) Both in France and in England these returns are considered as of the highest importance, and the greatest pains are taken to make them as minute as possible. The tables of the state of crime in France, are more perfect in their form than any that have any where been produced.

2 F

of justice, yet public morals require that certain investigations should form exceptions to this rule. A chapter, therefore, provides that, in certain enumerated cases, the details of which would only foster passions injurious to society, or wound the feelings of the innocent connexions of the parties, no persons but the necessary attendants and officers of the court, the witnesses, jurors, and a limited number of persons indicated by the party and the prosecutor, shall be admitted at the trial, and that no report of the details shall be published.

A short chapter directs, that until the system by which magistrates and officers of justice are remunerated for their services, by the payment of fees, be abolished, the state, and not the defendant, shall pay costs in all cases of discharge for want of prosecution, or on acquittal ; and that, in cases of conviction, the court may either exonerate the defendant from the payment of them, or make such an apportionment as may suit the circumstances of the case ; and no person is to be detained for the payment of costs, until after a discussion of his property, and then only for the term limited in the case of fines.

This finishes the review of that part of the code which prescribes the ordinary course of procedure in criminal trials. The concluding chapter of this title relates to a subject which could not be brought properly under any of the preceding heads.

The propriety of allowing any lapse of time to prevent the prosecution of an offence, has frequently been called in question, and for such cogent reasons as have induced the allowance of prescription only in the following cases : misdemeanors for private offences ; crimes which can only be prosecuted on the complaint of designated persons ; attempts to commit crimes when not accompanied by any offence. This plea is allowed in the first case, because the evil of the offence falling chiefly on an individual, it must be presumed to have been too trivial to attract the notice of public justice, if it be not prosecuted within the limited time ; but this presumption is rebutted by showing that the party injured was out of the state, or prevented by force or threats from making the complaint. The same reason partially applies to the second case, Crimes, which can only be prosecuted by designated persons ; as the prosecution could only be made by them, the delay will be presumed to have arisen either from a determination not to accuse, or for the purpose of taking some unfair advantage. The same causes that are enumerated under the third head destroy the prescription ; attempts to commit crimes are prescribed, because they approach so nearly in their nature to private misdemeanors, which enjoy that privilege, that it appeared unjust to make any distinction ; but chiefly because no offence having been actually committed, and the sole question being that of intent, great injustice might ensue from instituting an inquiry of that nature, after a lapse of many years. All other offences may, at any time, be prosecuted, because, allowing them to be barred, would hold out a reward to ingenious villany and address in concealment ; and, as(a) has been very forcibly expressed ; to show the absurdity of suffering any lapse of time to bring impunity, only suppose the law conceived in these terms, " but if the robber, the murderer, the thief, can during twenty years elude the vigilance of justice, their address shall be recompensed, their safety assured, and the proceeds of their crime legalized in their possession."

(a) Traité de Legislation, tom. 1. p. 148

The third and last title of this book contains directions for the mode of procedure in cases not immediately connected with the procedure in courts. The first chapter relates to inquests on dead bodies, found under circumstances that may induce the suspicion of homicide. These do not materially vary from those now in use. The utility of this institution is apparent, and has been tested by experience. The publicity of the proceeding destroys unjust suspicion, which, but for this inquiry, the innocent would have no means of showing to be false ; and it is eminently calculated to bring the guilty to punishment. The inquiry immediately made, before any means can be devised for concealment, the view of the body, the examination of skilful professional men, the power to compel the attendance of witnesses, and the concourse of neighbours and friends bringing with them proof of circumstances that would escape any more tardy or less public inquiry, are most powerful means for bringing to light crimes often committed against human life. The inquest, however, has not, as in England, the effect of an indictment, because the want of time and professional aid frequently render it defective ; but it may be made the foundation for one, and, with all the proceedings, is to be laid before the grand jury, in all cases where death is found to have been occasioned by a crime. The coroner has the same powers conferred, and duties enjoined, as belong to other magistrates, in cases of examination, bail and commitment.

The second chapter regulates the mode in which the examination of a body shall be made in cases of suspected murder. It gives the power to a family meeting, or to a magistrate, and directs the manner of proceeding in the investigation. There are no provisions in our law on this subject, but it was deemed one that required legislative attention.

The fraudulent appropriation of property found, being created an offence, distinguished from theft, with which it is frequently confounded, by extending the doctrine of constructive possession, it was thought just and requisite that the law should direct the honest finder in what manner to proceed, with respect to the property found, so as to avoid unjust suspicion, by observing the rules, and to facilitate the conviction of the dishonest by his breach of them : this forms the subject of the third chapter.

The fourth directs the mode in which vagrancy may he proved, and under what circumstances vagrants may be committed to the House of Industry. This class of men, who hang on to society rather than belong to it, although not absolutely criminals, are yet so near the verge of it, and are so generally the nursery for criminals of every description, that preventive justice is forced, with respect to them, to measures not strictly in unison with its usual course ; but this subject will be so fully discussed in the Introductory Report to the Code of Prison Discipline, to which it properly belongs, that the legislature are respectfully referred to that part of the system, as well for the measures recommended for the employment, restraint and reformation of these people, as for the reasons which suggested these measures.

In criminal proceedings, no question presents itself which is, at times, more difficult of solution, or more important to be accurately answered, than that of alleged insanity. When it occurs as a defence on a trial of the merits, little more need be provided by law, than to direct, that when ascertained to have existed at the time of the act, it takes away an essential quality of guilt. But when the alienation of mind is alleged to have occurred after the act but before the trial,  after the trial but before the judgment, after the judgment but before or during the execution of the sentence, no mode of trial of the fact is provided by law; and yet, at each of these periods, particular provisions are necessary, as well to ascertain the fact, as to direct what is to be the consequence of its being found to exist.   This is done by a chapter in this title, and by it an omission in our law,  important to justice and to humanity, is supplied.

The Code of Crimes and Punishments having directed, in order to avoid collusive prosecutions for adultery, that in all prosecutions for this offence against a supposed adulterer, the offending wife shall be joined, and having referred to this code for the manner of conducting it, it is directed, that where the defendant is so charged, shall have been cited or arrested, but shall not appear, that an attorney shall be named to represent him, and that the trial shall proceed in his absence ; and that if he have left the state, so as not to be served with process, a warrant shall issue and be renewed from time to time until the trial, which, if he do not appear, may proceed against the wife alone.

The collection of small fines, imposed by courts, is not now sufficiently enforced.   The code remedies this defect, requires frequent returns by the collecting officers,  and makes it the duty of the state treasurer to prosecute such of them as are delinquent, and to carry all such sums, as may be collected, to the credit of the "Compensation Fund," which has been referred to in the  beginning of this Report, where it is spoken of as the means of paying the  premiums for extraordinary services and providing the marks of honorary rewards; it is here also burthened with an indemnity directed to be paid to all those who shall receive, on their being discharged  before  trial  of an alleged offence, a certificate from the  judge,  or from the jury who shall acquit them on the trial, that no improper conduct gave reasonable ground for suspicion.   This indemnity is granted on the ground that society is bound to compensate all such  evils as are necessarily incurred for its safety, where they are not the result either of an obligation binding on all the citizens in general, such as assisting  the civil officers in  preserving the peace ;  or of losses so great in amount and general in their nature as  to become too burthensome to the rest of the community, such as granting indemnity for the ravages committed by an invading enemy, or the conflagration of a city to prevent its falling into his hands.   The injury received by a groundless accusation is of another character.   It is  not the result of any duty, and it can be compensated without any great sacrifice. When the prosecution is malicious as well as ill-founded, the state is exonerated from this burthen, for the loss was not incurred for its benefit ; and the indemnity may be recovered against the malicious prosecutor. The state is only bound to pay when there was reasonable ground for suspicion, but which did not arise from any negligence or imprudence of the party accused.   The amount of the compensation is to be fixed by the judge, but under limits which effectually prevent its being made the object of collusive speculation, while it affords  the relief which justice requires to the poor and the oppressed.

Four General Provisions are inserted at the conclusion of this book.  By the first it is declared, that no omission of any matter of form presented in this system, nor any departure from the forms given for proceeding under it, shall render the proceeding void, unless it be so specially provided; or unless the departure from the form has caused some injury to the party complaining of it. The insertion of this article is another attempt, and no good system can contain too many, to counteract the constant and fatal tendency to sacrifice substance to form. The second was, perhaps, superfluous; that when a particular and a general provision conflict, the former must prevail. A rule of true construction would sufficiently enforce it; but true rules of construction are not always those that are adopted. Although a strict adherence to the distribution of the system would have required that all offences whatever, as well as the punishment assigned to them, should have found their place in the Code of Crimes and Punishments, and not elsewhere; yet it was deemed expedient to depart from this rule in many cases, where a penalty is annexed to the non-observance of a rule laid down in any of the other codes. The inconvenience of a constant reference from the one code to the other would have been an inevitable evil, but one of the least attendant on the transfer of the definition of the offence to the former. The two subjects, in their nature distinct, would have been so amalgamated as to create a greater confusion than that which it is the intention of the system to correct. Certain offences, then, being necessarily defined by this code, and the punishment denounced, the third provision of this chapter became necessary, which directs that all offences, created by this code or the Code of Reform and Prison Discipline, shall be prosecuted and tried in the same manner with those which are created by the Code of Crimes and Punishments. The last article gives a rule for calculating the time allowed by the code for certain notices and other proceedings.

The concluding book of this code contains forms for all the proceedings which are directed or authorized by its preceding parts. In framing them, which has been done with much care, the object kept constantly in view, was to unite brevity with so much certainty and precision as would secure the party from any possibility of mistake, as to the precise fact of which he is accused. If the reporter has been successful in this, he has attained a most important object, by closing the door against one of the greatest evils in penal jurisprudence. He offers this branch of the system, with the same diffidence of his own powers that attended the presentation of the first; the same hope, that what is good in it may be preserved, and what is bad corrected; and the same firm reliance on the industry and patient research of the legislature in examining, and on their wisdom in making a decision on its merits.

INTRODUCTORY REPORT

TO

# THE CODE OF EVIDENCE.

No branch of jurisprudence requires greater certainty and more simplicity in its provisions, than that of judicial evidence.  But there is
none in which so little of either is to be found.  The reason is, that,
with fewer exceptions than exist in any other division of the science,
it has been abandoned to the vacillating authority of decisions, for its
creation and amendment, without any superintendence of the legislative power.  This was a natural consequence of the transition from the
semi-barbarism of the middle ages, to the more improved state of the science in modern times.  During the period when the divine power
was invoked, and supposed specially to interpose in litigated questions,
by protecting innocence and making justice prevail in the ordeal and
the battle, human testimony would of course be considered of minor
importance.  In proportion, however, as these miraculous interven-
tions of the Deity ceased to obtain credit, and the agency of human
justice and discretion was called in to supply its place, it became necessary to consider what evidence ought to be received in order to direct them.  But no legislative provision had been made for this change,
which was imperceptibly produced as the mists of ignorance and the
veil of superstition were slowly withdrawn.  In every case in which
the witness was substituted for the champion, and the ordeal of justice for that of the elements, the court was obliged to make some rule
for securing the appearance of the witness; interrogating him to come
at the truth; determining what persons ought to appear in that character, and what degree of credit, under different circumstances, was due
to their testimony.
In the earlier periods of jurisprudential history in Europe, the distinction between oral and written evidence can scarcely be observed.
But when literary education became more common, writing was prescribed by the legislative power, in some cases, as a check upon the inaccuracy of testimonial evidence ; and as the few laws it was found necessary to pass were couched in general terms, and frequently in obscure language, the judges thought themselves authorized to supply deficiencies, and sometimes to restrict what they deemed the too comprehensive words of the text ; and thus the law of written as well as of
testimonial evidence became the creation of judicial decisions, not of
legislative acts.  It is, however, easier to trace its origin with tolerable

certainty than, with any probability, to account for some of the extraordinary features which distinguish it. There is such a moral beauty in truth, it is so necessary to us in all our intercourse with each other, that we have been endowed by our beneficent Creator with a love for it, which, if not innate, is necessarily produced by the circumstances in which he has placed us(a). Man never swerves from truth without some temptation, some real or imaginary good, that he promises himself from the falsehood. Doubt even on matters of little moment, is an uneasy sensation: and there is a corresponding satisfaction in that state of the mind which results from a conviction of truth; so that, as in the ordinary affairs of life, no one makes an assertion of fact, but with the intent of producing belief; so no one hears it without a desire, sometimes imperceptible and involuntary, to be convinced of its truth or falsehood. But this conviction can only be produced by evidence. As long, therefore, as he is deprived of any evidence which is known or suspected to exist, so long will the uneasy state of doubt, in a greater or less degree, continue. If this be true in relation to matters where neither interest nor duty, but a mere love of truth, call upon us to decide; how much more strongly will the desire be felt when life or fortune depends on the correctness of the decision. Yet it is precisely in cases where this longing after truth should be gratified, that is to say, in litigated questions, that the evidence by which it is to be ascertained is most restricted. Every where else, all sources, even the most suspicious, are examined; he who is to judge relying on his own power to discriminate; here alone he is taught to distrust that power, to reject all evidence that may possibly lead him astray, and where he cannot be guided by the full blaze of the noonday sun, to prefer utter darkness to the twilight, in which he might have discovered his path. To trace this leading feature in our law of evidence to its original causes, would be rather a curious disquisition than one leading to important practical results. It most probably is derived to us from the civil and canon law, where this principle is carried to a most extravagant length; and where the secret examination of witnesses by judges unacquainted with the circumstances of the case, made the risk of deception very great; where there was no confrontation, no personal cross-examination, no publicity, and where the parties themselves were not allowed to be present, detection was rendered so difficult, that it afforded a plausible pretext for absolute exclusion in all suspicious cases. The compass of this report will only admit of a reference to such restrictions as now exist, and a notice of those which it has been deemed necessary to retain or to abrogate, with the reasons by which the alterations are supported. These will be developed as we proceed with the details of the system.

This code begins, as those which preceded it have done, by an Introductory Title, laying down rules and making explanations to avoid circumlocution, and to give the perspicuity necessary to a full understanding of the subsequent provisions. Two of the articles are of a different character, and demand particular notice. They are intended to check the legislation of the courts, and to provide for the progressive amelioration of the code by the General Assembly, the only legitimate power for that purpose; while the right of pointing out defects, and suggesting improvements, is conferred on the judges. As the law formerly stood, the whole law of evidence, with very few excep-

(a) In primis, hominis est propria VERI inquisitio atque investigatio.—*Cicero.*

tions, was, as we have seen, the work of the court, over which the legislature very rarely exercised even a corrective power; more frequently the courts corrected the statutory provisions; and by their rules of construction, for enlarging and restricting the operation of the written law, assumed and exercised, by whatever name it may be called, a legislative power. As this is a part, nay the very foundation of the common law, the observation is not intended as a reproach to the judiciary of the country from whence that law is derived. But it cannot be too often repeated, that in our constitution(*a*) it is not only affirmatively declared, that there shall be three separate branches of government—executive, legislative and judiciary; but negatively, that the duties of no two of these branches shall be exercised by the same persons. Every exercise of legislative power by the judiciary is, in this state, unconstitutional, and it is the duty of the legislature to check it. But as all human works are attended with a greater or less degree of imperfection, it must happen that the operation of laws will be found to work injustice; either by embracing, under general expressions, cases not intended to come within them, or, by a too restricted phraseology, not providing for other cases which it was their evident object to include. These defects in laws gave rise to the rules of construction before alluded to, by one of which the court were directed to place themselves in the situation of the legislature(*b*), to inquire whether, if the case before them had presented itself to the mind of the lawgiver, he would have extended or restricted the words of his law so as to provide for it and others of a similar nature. This is called consulting the spirit of the statute ; and the rule, as I have stated it, is every day referred to and received in our courts. While it is evident that this is the exercise of legislative power, inasmuch as it extends or restricts the operation of a statute, it cannot be denied that the defects of all laws are best discovered in their operation, and that, as to all those which relate to jurisprudence, the judges are the persons best qualified to point them out, although, by our institutions, they are not authorized to provide the remedy.

The object of the two articles now under consideration is to secure the advantages to be derived from the experience and wisdom of the judges in the suggestion of defects, while the remedy is reserved to the legislature, the only power to which it can consistently with the constitution be referred. The first of these articles relates to cases in which any positive provision of the code, for the admission or exclusion of evidence, is found to operate improperly, either to the prejudice of the accused, or the ends of public justice in criminal proceedings, or to the injury of any party in a civil suit. In every such case the court is directed to make an accurate report of the same to the legislature, with the reasons for thinking the law imperfect or unjust in its operation. Should the general assembly coincide in opinion with the court, the proper amendment will be made to the code under its appropriate

---

(*a*) Art. 1, § 1. The powers of government of the state of Louisiana shall be divided into three distinct departments, and each of them shall be confided to a separate body of magistracy, to wit—those which are legislative, to one—those which are executive, to another—and those which are judiciary, to another.

§ 2. No person or collection of persons, being one of those departments, shall exercise any power properly belonging to either of the others, except in the instances hereinafter expressly directed or permitted.—*Constitution of the state of Louisiana.*

(*b*) Plowden, 469.

2 G

head; and, instead of a judicial decision of doubtful authority, obligatory or not on their successors, or even on themselves, as they shall think fit, and only to be known through voluminous and costly reports, we shall have positive law, easily understood, to be found in in its proper place, comprised in a few lines, and binding on the courts as well as the community. If, in consequence of such imperfection, the accused shall have been acquitted, judgment in his favour must be entered without waiting for any further legislative proceedings, for it would be unjust to subject an individual to the vexation of a second trial for a defect in the law, even if the amendment required, should be one that could not come within the description of a retro-active law. But if the consequence was an unjust conviction, or verdict in a civil suit, it is directed that no judgment shall be pronounced until the end of the session after the report shall have been made; when, if the provision is altered, new trials shall in both cases be ordered. If no change is made, it is evidence the legislature do not coincide in opinion with the court, and do not think the operation of their law improper or unjust; and as theirs is the supreme will, the courts must carry it into execution.

The first of these two articles having thus provided for the reconsideration and amendment of the code, in such provisions as seem unjust or defective in their operation, the second, in like manner, gives the remedy for omissions. In all cases where legislative enactments, or former decisions, gave no rule on the subject of the admission or exclusion of evidence, the courts necessarily, as has been observed, supplied the omission. They were obliged to admit or reject the evidence offered, and, having no legislation provided, were forced to decide according to their discretion, without one. After the adoption of this article, such an anomaly will no longer exist in our law. The legislator and the judge will each perform his proper duties, and no excuse will exist for the one to usurp, or the other to neglect them; for in every case where evidence is offered, and no rule is provided to direct the judge whether to admit or exclude it, legal authority is given him to do that which is now done without it; and in that case alone the rule, on which some animadversions have been made, is sanctioned, and the judge is directed to suppose himself in the place of the legislator, and to ask what would probably be his opinion if the case had been presented to him, and to decide accordingly; but to make report of the case to the legislature in the manner required by the preceding article, who will in like manner, give or refuse their sanction to the principle adopted by the court, and insert the affirmative or negative provision in the code. Whatever the legislature do in this last case, will not affect the decision if in a civil suit; the ends of justice require that the delay, uncertainty and intrigue, incident to the revision by the legislature of an adjudged case should be avoided. The court decides the case before them, but makes no rule for future cases; that is left to the legislature, whose proper province it is. But if the decision takes place in a criminal cause, and in consequence of the admission or rejection of evidence, not directed by any law, the accused shall be convicted, it is clear that his conviction will have taken place under an ex post facto rule, and is, therefore, illegal. The article consequently provides, that, in such case, judgment shall be arrested and the defendant discharged.

These provisions are deemed to be of the highest importance. They are new, and the attention of the general assembly is respectfully called to a close consideration of them. They offer, it is confidently believed, a complete answer to the objection that has been raised to a written code, from its rigidity, or what has been, by a celebrated jurisconsult, called its want of *malleability*. It cannot, indeed, be worked into any kind of shape that the discretion of a judge, well or ill directed, may deem necessary: but, by this means, it may be accommodated to the changes which take place in society, and adapted to its wants as they arise, and this more effectually, more constitutionally, and equitably, than by the legislation of decrees; more effectually, because the sanction of positive law will not only give it a legitimate, instead of a doubtful authority, but because, being promulgated as a law, it will be universally known; being concise, it will be easily understood, and a knowledge of its provisions may be acquired without expense; more constitutionally, because it will emanate from the proper department of government; and its superior equity must be apparent, when we consider that, in the one case, the rule is made and applied to an existing case, in the other, it has no force until after its enactment and promulgation. This most valuable and simple improvement in legislation was recommended in a former report; and the greatest confidence is felt in its efficiency, because, among the number of lawyers and statesmen to whom it has been proposed, not one was to be found who raised any other objection, than that it was a novelty—a characteristic necessarily attached to every improvement; while, to a very large majority of them, it appeared to promise the most important results.

The profound feeling which the reporter has, that the code he proposes must contain many errors, and that material omissions may be discovered when it goes into operation, induces him to urge the adoption of these two articles with the greater earnestness. The facility they offer of discovering these errors and imperfections and bringing them to the consideration of the legislature, and the ease with which they can be effectually amended, cannot but lessen the reluctance he would have to propose any thing of which the correction would be attended with greater difficulty. He may be allowed, perhaps, to suggest another argument for their adoption, founded on a feeling different from, but not inconsistent with, that which he has just expressed. Conscious that there must be many imperfections in the work, he yet feels a confidence that it is founded on true principles, and that, from the manner in which they are reduced to precept; the general effect cannot but be eminently useful, with the safeguard of these provisions for the gradual perfection of the system. Therefore, the general assembly incur no risk in their adoption. Parts, of which the utility does not seem perfectly apparent, may therefore safely be retained, until their operation is seen: that operation cannot be materially injurious, even if these parts are bad. The evil is instantly perceived, and a check is provided for their operation on the first case in which they are discovered.

After these introductory articles, we come to the body of the work.

Evidence is defined to be that which brings, or contributes to bring, the mind to a just conviction of the truth or falsehood of the fact asserted or denied. Because, in weak minds, conviction may be produced, by that which, addressed to an understanding of common force, would create doubt or conjecture merely; it became necessary to qualify by the epithet *just*, the nature of the conviction to be produced. So far as respects mere speculative opinion, there can be no danger in leaving the determination of what may be termed just to each individual's perception of right and wrong; but as applied to the determination of litigated rights, another qualification was necessarily introduced, and under the denomination LEGAL EVIDENCE, that alone, which is declared by law to be good evidence, forms the subject of the code.

If evidence may, according to the definition, produce, or contribute only to produce, conviction, it must in relation to its effects have different degrees of force. These degrees, producing as many different kinds of evidence, are, under this head, restricted to three, ascending from that created by mere induction, to that which is, by law, directed to have the force of complete proof; PRESUMPTIVE, which, by establishing one fact, renders the existence of another probable, or, in some cases, certain ; DIRECT, which, if true, establishes the fact in question ; and CONCLUSIVE, which, in special cases, is declared to admit of no contradictory evidence.

Considered in relation to the source from whence it is derived, evidence is again of two kinds : first, that which the judge derives from his own knowledge:—secondly, that which is offered to him from other sources, and this last is again composed of TESTIMONIAL, SCRIPTORY, and SUBSTANTIVE evidence.

After these divisions, necessary for the order of the work, it proceeds with a more full explanation of the different kinds into which it is distributed, and an enumeration of the rules applicable to each.

Beginning with the division arising from the source whence the evidence is derived, a short title declares in what cases the judge may act from his own knowledge of the fact on which he is to decide, and in what other cases that knowledge is to be produced as evidence in the cause. In the first case it is provided, that no judge can act merely on his own knowledge of the facts, excepting in those cases in which he is expressly authorized so to do by law. Those cases it is the province of the Civil and Criminal Codes, and their respective systems of procedure, to provide for. Instances, to elucidate the article, are given in the powers vested in the judge to pronounce on the authenticity of a record, in the right given him to commit for an offence, to remove for a disturbance in court, and to employ the military in aid of the civil power. But where the judge has knowledge of a material fact, in any case not so specially provided for, he is to be examined in the same manner as any other witness ; and if he is the sole judge of the court, the judge of the adjoining district is to try the cause, in the manner provided for where the judge is interested. Jurors who are acquainted with any material fact must, in all cases, be examined to give evidence to their fellows. In this title, the law is not materially altered. It is rendered more definite, and the sanction of written law is given to that which is now, in some degree, founded in loose practice.

The next division of evidence, derived from extraneous sources, is in itself more important, and, in this code, is especially so, because of the changes which it proposes in our present system. The first head, that of Testimonial Evidence, is the one in which these changes are of most consequence, and, in the opinion of the reporter, most required. They, however, repose on very simple principles, or, to speak more precisely, on a single principle, and that one drawn from the very definition of evidence.

The organization of courts, the enumeration of rights, the means of asserting, with the denunciation of penalties for infringing them, and the rules of procedure, are only preparatory steps to the trial which, in itself, is but the examination of evidence. Ultimately, then, the whole machinery of jurisprudence, in all its branches, is contrived for the purpose of enabling the judging power to determine on the truth or falsehood of every litigated proposition. This to be done by hearing and examining evidence; that is to say, hearing and examining every thing that will contribute to bring the mind to the determination required. If we refuse to hear what will, in any degree, produce this effect, we must determine on imperfect evidence; and in proportion to the importance of the matter thus refused to be heard, must evidently be the chance of making an incorrect rather than a just determination. But, as in morals, we are forbidden to do evil that good may come of it, so in legislation, we should refrain from doing that kind of good which may produce more than its equivalent in evil. The desirable end to be attained by the admission of every species of evidence, may be more than counterbalanced, in some instances, by the evil attending it; sometimes, in the shape of inconvenience and expense inseparable from its procurement; sometimes, from the danger of error arising from the the deceptive nature of the evidence itself. The great art is to weigh these difficulties, and in those cases where they are most likely to preponderate, but in no others, to exclude the evidence.

Before we enter into an examination of the provisions of the code now presented, it will be necessary to examine those of our present law. On the subject of evidence we have several different bodies of law to consult: one for civil cases, a second for a class of offences created under a particular statute, and a third for all other offences. For the first, we must consult the civil code; for the second, the common law of England; for the third, the laws of Spain(a). On the subject of exclusion, that now under consideration, all these systems materially differ, and all of them are more or less uncertain in their provisions. By the civil code, the exclusions are, interest, relationship in the ascending or descending line, connexion in marriage, and the very vague description of "those whom the law deems infamous." It also forbids the examination of a counsellor or attorney in order to obtain a discovery of what has been confided to him by his client; but somewhat strangely, considering that the Catholic is the prevalent religion in the country, omits to provide for the inviolability of religious confession. These are the only general rules, relating to testimonial evidence in civil cases, that are provided by statute. For the exclusions in those criminal cases which are punishable under the statute of 1805, we must refer to the common law of England. To enumerate them, and note the exceptions with accuracy, would be a difficult, and as far as the ability and research of the reporter is concerned, an impracticable task; and without any endeavour to avoid the reproach of ignorance or want of diligence on the subject, he may venture to assert, that it has never yet been satisfactorily performed, as is manifest from the numerous treatises on the law of evidence which have appeared, become obsolete, and are replaced by others, themselves to become antiquated and laid aside whenever the changing system of decisions

(a) See Introductory Reports, p. 60, et seq. and p. 157, in the note, and De Armas's case, 10 Martin's Reports.

establishes new rules or creates exceptions to those which were in like manner previously established. Fortunately, nothing on this occasion is required more than a general outline, upon which to mark the changes that are recommended by the system now presented.

The circumstances which are generally understood to cause exclusion by the common law of England are, interest, connexion in marriage, infamy, incredulity as to a future state of rewards and punishments, the relation of counsellor or attorney to one of the parties, and conviction for an infamous crime. To the laws of Spain, as has been said, and, as is thought, satisfactorily proved in the Introductory Report to the System of Penal Law(a), we must have recourse, in civil cases, to discover what is meant by the description in the code of "those whom the law deems infamous; and in criminal cases, to direct us in prosecutions for all those acts which may be considered offences under the unrepealed Spanish law, and all those which are created offences by acts subsequent to the year 1805. The list of exclusions under these last mentioned laws, is filled to a most enormous length with every circumstance that can create the slightest suspicion of partiality, prejudice, or a disposition to falsehood. The principle of these laws seems to be, that the weakest inducement to utter falsehood is stronger than the greatest inducement to tell the truth; that all those who are counted infamous ought never to be believed; and that a usurer, a comedian, a slanderer, and all the others, who, by a most extraordinary classification, are involved in the stigma of infamy, as well as those convicted of crimes, ought on no occasion, not even for saving the life of the innocent, or the more favourite object of taking that of the guilty, to be heard. The intimate friend, the frequent guest, the near relation, all of whom were most likely to be acquainted with the circumstances and character of the parties, or accused, as well as the avowed enemy, were, or rather, as this is now our law, are, legally, in the cases above mentioned, excluded.

Without troubling the general assembly with a repetition of the arguments to prove this assertion, I again refer to that Introductory Report, only observing here, that it is no answer to say, that those laws do not exist, because the judges have not yet thought proper to act upon them. The question is not, what has, but what can be done: not what good judges have refrained from doing, from their own sense of right, not from the restriction of law—but what bad men might do in evil times, under the sanction of bad laws; or good men, under the impression that they are bound to execute them.

Omitting the unnecessary task of examining, in detail, the list of exclusions under the Spanish law, and showing their absurdity and injustice, I proceed, at once, to the examination of those which are acknowledged and enforced as part of the law of the state.

The first of these disqualifying circumstances, declared by the code to prevail in civil cases, and making a prominent feature in the common law adopted in criminal cases by our statute, is interest, which is construed to mean an eventual gain or loss that may be estimated in money, by the decision of a cause in which the testimony is produced. By the code now offered, interest shall no longer disqualify, but may be proved in order to lessen, in proportion to its magnitude and to the other circumstances of the case, the credit that may be given to the witness.

(a) Pages 63, 64, et seq., and p. 157, in the note.

This important change demands a full explanation of the reasons for proposing it. For this purpose it will be necessary to revert once more to the nature and effect of all exclusions of testimony. These have been shown to be injurious to the great object of judicial investigation, the discovery of the truth. *Prima facie* then there ought to be no exclusion; but, as has been observed, there may be evils attending the admission of certain evidence, which may be greater than any good such evidence could produce in elucidating the truth. To exclude any species of evidence, therefore, it must be shown that such attendant evil predominates. This evil can only be inconvenience and expense in procuring the testimony greater than the advantage to be derived from its admission; or the probability that, if admitted, it will tend rather to mislead than to enlighten the judge. These probabilities must be weighed whenever we come to consider the propriety or rather the necessity, for that ought to be evident, of creating a rule excluding testimony of any one description.

Now let us apply these rules to that which declares an interested witness inadmissible. This can only be found on the following suppositions: first, that pecuniary interest will be sufficient to induce the witness to incur the inevitable embarrassment and difficulty of sustaining an untruth under the searching trial of a rigorous cross-examination; attended by the liability, too, of being detected, and of the consequent punishment and infamy attending a conviction for perjury, in order to have the chance of the advantage he may promise himself from a judgment to be obtained by his falsehood; for let it be observed, that, if on the one hand, there is no certainty of punishment, conviction or infamy, there is, on the other, no certainty of securing the advantage that prompts him to encounter the risk. Secondly, it must be supposed that the falsehood, thus asserted, will be believed by the judges of the fact. If not believed, the testimony cannot mislead; and we may lay down as a rule which admits of very few exceptions, that with the aids of cross-examination, publicity, and the right of producing counter testimony, the chances are greatly in favour of truth against deception. On this head, too, we must not forget that the judge is on his guard against giving too implicit faith to the witness, because he is aware of the bias which interest would naturally create. The argument supposes the interest to be known, for, if not known, it cannot exclude. Knowing the interest, he will not only be more inclined, but better enabled, to test the truth of the testimony by a rigorous investigation; and what is of more importance, he will be enabled to judge from the nature and amount of the interest, contrasted with the character of the witness, and other circumstances, what effect it will probably have on the testimony. These considerations must, therefore, tend to show, that even in the cases, and it is not denied that they may exist, where interest may induce a departure from the truth, the fear of its misleading the judge is greatly exaggerated by those who make it a ground for utter exclusion. The two assumptions, then, necessary to support the argument, to wit, that interest will always, or even generally, induce the witness to encounter the difficulties and dangers of asserting a falsehood, and that if it should have this operation, the falsehood will most probably be believed, have both been shown to be groundless; and even on this preliminary statement, the disadvantages of shutting out the testimony of an interested witness must be apparent: but many other considerations must be brought into the account before we strike the balance of good or evil attending its admission.   A most profound writer on this subject(a) has argued, and with great force, that so far from leading to deception, the testimony of an interested witness will, in many cases, bring out the truth by the very attempts which he makes to conceal it.   No more falsehood, he contends, will be uttered than the witness thinks necessary to obtain the object he has in view: from these partial disclosures of truth, information of importance may be derived to corroborate or contradict other evidence ; not so much will be uttered as is necessary, if it be highly improbable, or may, from other circumstances, create great risk of detection.   Truth must supply all these intervals, and truth, from the lips of an interested witness, is as valuable as if it were derived from a purer source; but if he dare not tell the falsehood, because it is too dangerous or too easy of detection, and will not tell the truth, because it defeats his interest, he must have recourse to silence or evasion; and either of these expedients are as sure indications of falsehood, in most instances, as a confession of it would be.   Therefore, whether the interested witness declare the truth or utter a falsehood, or recur to evasion or silence, his evidence will more probably lead to a just than an erroneous decision. False testimony is more difficult to frame, and is more easily detected, than those not conversant with judicial proceedings might imagine.   If the witness were at liberty, in secret and at his leisure, to frame his own story, and state only such circumstances as his imagination might supply in a detailed account of all that he thought necessary, without the fear of confrontation, cross-examination, and publicity, he would have nothing but his invention to task, and might, from his own stores, or the suggestion of parties, frame a consistent tale that might impose on the judge.   But, fortunately, this is not the case; he knows, that the strictest scrutiny awaits every allegation that he shall make; that his words, and even his silence, will be the subject of the severest animadversion; that his very looks will not escape the attention of the practised cross-questioner ; and that, during his examination, the gaze of a hundred eyes will be upon him, and he cannot but fear that some one will start forth from the crowd to detect his falsehood.   All this he must anticipate; and under these apprehensions it will require more ready invention, more self-possession, and more courage than falls to the share of ordinary men to persevere in a feigned statement, and render it so consistent as to give it the semblance of truth; so that, if these well-founded fears do not deter him from his purpose, they will at least, for the most part, render him incapable of carrying it successfully into effect.   The part of a false witness is more difficult to act than is generally supposed; and though many rashly and wickedly engage in it from a false confidence in their ability, yet very few can sustain it to the end, and through the great ordeals of cross-examination and publicity.

All this is on the supposition that pecuniary interest will always induce a witness to depart from the truth; but when from the whole number which compose this class, we deduct those to whom the interest is too trifling to be an object compared to their fortune and situation in life—those who, even under the influence of a strong interest, would be restrained by the stronger motives of religion or morality—those who would be deterred by the fear of shame or of punishment—

(a) Bentham, Rationale of Judicial Evidence.

who, without either of these restraints, find their hearts to fail them from the difficulty of performing their tasks: when we deduct all these from the mass of interested witnesses, we shall have very few left willing to sustain the character of perjured ones; and of those few, not many who can do it with any prospect of success. But under the general words of the rule, all these are excluded—all kinds of pecuniary interest disqualifies. He who is worth millions of dollars, cannot be a witness if he is to gain or lose a single dollar of those millions, by the event of the cause: the man of the highest sense of .honour, or the most venerated for his holy life, is equally excluded, if the eventual gain or loss is equivalent only to the hundredth part of those sums which he daily distributes in charity; and even in cases where detection is highly probable, the most timid is, by the rule, supposed ready to encounter the risk of punishment—and the most honourable, to take his chance of infamy, for the uncertain hope of an insignificant gain. Detection is presumed to be impossible, and the credulity of judges and jurors to be so great, that a false tale must, if it be allowed to reach their ears, produce instant conviction that it is true. They forget, who insist on this rule, how difficult it is even for truth to produce its proper effect, although attended with all the advantages it naturally brings with it ; and they argue as if falsehood alone could charm the understanding and lay suspicion asleep.

The question then is this, whether on account of the danger of being deceived by the few who are willing to assume the character of perjured witnesses, a danger diminished by the many powerful means we have of detecting their falsehood, it would be wise to deprive ourselves of the testimony of all those infinitely more numerous classes of interested witnesses, from whom we may expect nothing but truth ? For this is the only alternative. The law can draw no line between interests of different amounts, or between interested witnesses of different characters—it must admit or exclude the whole. Which shall it do ? One consideration, if there were no other, would seem to resolve the question. Exclusion is, in many cases, a certain evil—admission only a problematical one. Where the incompetent witness, whether from interest or any other cause, is the only witness, certain injustice results from a refusal to hear him. Listen to him, and, first, it is not certain that his interest or any other cause will induce him to depart from the truth; and, secondly, if he do, it is not certain that you will believe him. If he is not the only witness, the other testimony will furnish additional means of detecting any false statement that may have been prompted by his interest.

I have said, that the law cannot distinguish particular cases, but must enact a general rule. This is obvious; and it is equally so, that the judges of the fact can. Let them hear the witness. From all the circumstances which they can collect, and which the legislator cannot, they can tell, with tolerable certainty, in which class of interested witnesses he comes—those who may be believed, or those who may not. This they cannot do without hearing him; and when they have done so, and have even assigned him to the latter class, they do more than destroy the ill effect of his testimony, because they draw from it all the information which, as we have seen, may be derived even from false evidence, and run no risk of crediting that which they discover to be inconsistent with truth. They can do, then, effectually, that which the legislative rule does imperfectly—they can let in the interested testimony which

2 H

is worthy of credit, and exclude that which is not. Why does this rule exclude all interested testimony? Because a part only is unworthy of credit. Would wise legislators be guilty of this absurdity, and worse than absurdity, in many cases this injustice and cruelty, if it were possible for them to make the necessary distinction? Certainly they would not. Why not then commit this task to those who can? Why not say to those to whom they delegate the decision of facts, "pecuniary interest has, in some cases, a seductive influence, injurious to the discovery of truth; in many others, it will not be felt. We can draw no line of demarcation between the cases. We cannot make the exclusion depend on the magnitude of the interest, because that is relative. Fix the minimum where we may, there are men on whom the smallest sum would have an improper influence; and others on whom the largest would have none. Wherever we draw the line, we shall admit suspicious evidence and exclude that which is unexceptionable. To be just, a separate rule must be made for every witness, because upon no two will the same amount of interest have the same effect. It is your privilege to determine what degree of credit the witness, under all the circumstances, favourable or unfavourable, in which he is presented to you, is entitled to, because it is your duty to determine according to your conviction of the truth. In prescribing the duty, we will not restrain you from using the means necessary to perform it. You who see the looks and observe the demeanour of the witness, as well as hear what he says; you who can inquire into his circumstances and character; you who can judge how far his testimony is corroborated or contradicted by other evidence; you will be better qualified to determine whether the interest be so great as to render him unworthy of belief, than we are, who have none of these means of forming a correct judgment." This would be the language of reason. Instead of it, what is, in effect, that which is addressed to them? "It is true that you are delegated to decide litigated questions of fact. The greatest confidence must necessarily be reposed as well in your integrity as your judgment, in the general performance of this duty; but there is one point on which we dare not trust your discernment. We will not permit you to hear what an interested witness will say. We are sure, that under all circumstances that may counteract the bias of his interest, and however small that interest may be, we are sure that it will induce him to utter a falsehood; and we are sure that, in spite of all the means we give you to detect it, we are sure, that however improbable it may be, you will believe it. Therefore, whenever a witness is presented to you, ask him first, whether he will gain or lose a cent by the decision of the cause; if he answer truly, that he will—be sure that he will answer falsely on every other point on which you may examine him. It is useless to inquire, what proportion the interest bears to his income; it is useless to ask, what is his character for veracity or religion. The highest standing in society, the best reputation, the largest fortune, are nothing compared to this all-prevailing interest of a dollar, or a cent. Do not give yourselves the trouble to inquire, whether the circumstances do not show a case in which falsehood would meet with certain detection. The fear of punishment—the fear of shame—the restraints of religion—all give way before this irresistible interest of a dollar, or a cent. No matter if the fortune, the reputation, or the life of a citizen depend on the question; it is better they should all be lost, than that you should listen to an interested witness. You may hear the sworn enemy of the party. You may hear his brother, or his most intimate friend. We can trust you with the difficult task of determining what effect all the passions of the mind can have in giving a colour of truth or falsehood to testimony. But interest, all-powerful interest, has no shades of difference—a cent will influence the richest banker in the same degree that a dollar will a beggar. Wherever this appears, you must exclude it—without pity for the ruin it occasions—without remorse for the death it inflicts!" This is the true meaning of the short precept of the English law, and the equivalent provision of our civil code. There is not a word of exaggeration in the comment I have given; and after considering the subject in all its bearings, who can hesitate on the question, whether interest ought not rather to be considered an objection to the credit than to the competency of a witness? In the first case, you can appreciate the bias at nearly its true value, according to the circumstances on which it has to operate; in the last, the strongest and the weakest motives are considered as having equal force.

The truth of this reasoning is evident from the efforts which, of late years, the courts have been making to get rid of the shackles with which they have been bound by their own decisions; unable or unwilling to declare the rule unwise and unjust, they have relaxed it in some cases, but retained it in others, which, for the same reason, ought to have formed an exception, and by hearing interested witnesses in some cases, and rejecting them in others, they have not only abandoned the propriety of the rule, but have established no uniform principle on which another can be founded. Exceptions, the maxim asserts, prove the rule. They may prove the existence of a rule, but never that it is a proper one, unless there is some reason applying to the case excepted, which does not apply to the rule. Where the reason for taking a case out of the operation of a general rule is a good one, and applies with equal force to all that are left within it, there can be no better proof that the rule itself is bad. Let us examine the exceptions in this view; premising, however, that in civil cases there can, in our state, legally be no exception. The legislative will is clearly and imperatively expressed: those who are interested—no matter in what degree, no matter whom the witnesses may be—are all excluded. No enlarging on restrictory construction can here apply. It cannot, under any pretence, be said that the spirit of the law does not apply to any of the cases excepted; while it is acknowledged that they are all embraced by its words: for the spirit of the law, as well as its words, exclude all interests. Yet our courts in civil cases, without any legislative authority, admit all the exceptions contained in the English law. They admit them legally, in all criminal cases, under the act of 1805; and they admit them again, without authority, in the other offences created by legislative statutes. Allowing the exceptions thus generally, with and without express authority, the propriety, or a supposed necessity, must have strongly pressed upon them; and therefore, the opinion of the courts has been clearly expressed against the rule, and in favour of the exception.

The first of those exceptions is the case of a factor in trade, or any other agent, who makes a sale or a contract for another, on the amount of which he is to receive a commission. If the sale itself, or the amount of the sale, be disputed, and a suit be brought to recover the amount, the factor or agent is a good witness. Yet he is evidently and largely interested: if the sale be established, he receives five per cent or one-twentieth part of all that is recovered; if the sale be disaffirmed, he receives nothing. Indeed, the interest in those cases has never been disputed, but he is admitted on the ground of an alleged necessity. It is proper to examine here in what sense this word is used. It is employed by, I believe, all the judges who have sanctioned the doctrine, and can mean nothing more than that if the witness were not heard, there would be a risk that some part of the truth would not appear; for it must be observed, that no inquiry is made previous to the examination of the factor, whether the sale could not be established by other evidence. There may have been twenty witnesses present when it was made, yet the factor is examined : not surely for want of other testimony. Why then ? The only answer that can be given must be, because he is considered as a good witness; because, although largely interested, the probability was in favour of his adherence to the truth; or that, if he swerved from it, his falsehood would be detected. The necessity in this case, then, differs in nothing from that which takes place in every litigated question. The moral necessity of giving to those who are to determine the truth all the means necessary to ascertain it, and if it exist in all others where an interested witness is produced, then the deduction is irresistible, that in all other cases the interested witness ought to be examined, and that the exception should take the place of the rule. That the factor is admitted as a witness, not from the defect of other testimony, is evident from the reason that has been given, that no previous inquiry is ever made on that subject; consequently, he is admitted, not because there is no other proof—but, let us suppose no other evidence to be in existence, he is then, according to the language of the exception, admitted from *necessity* : then it follows, that it is better for the ends of justice to take interested testimony than no testimony. But if it be calculated to mislead, why should it be heard in this case and refused in all others ? But experience has shown, that there is no danger : the evident utility of the exception, which has induced learned and prudent judges to go beyond the bounds prescribed by their constitutional functions in order to establish it, show, that there is no danger—show, that it is useful and necessary in this case; and the reasoning, from the closest analogy, must convince us that it is so in all others.

In every case, either the interested witness is the only one to establish the fact, or he is not. If he be the only witness, then he may be admitted, according to the reason on which the exception is said to be founded, from the necessity in all cases whatever, as well as in that of the agent. If he is not the only witness, then, neither in the case of the rule nor of the exception, will there be any danger in admitting him ; for the other evidence will give the means of detecting his mis-statements ; or the knowledge of its existence, will deter him from making them. Nor will the alleged necessity exist. Thus, every reason that can be advanced in favour of admitting the exception, applies with equal force to the abolition of the rule.

The second exception to the rule, and under the same plea of necessity, is that of a servant, who, in the *way of trade*, is employed to deliver goods to a purchaser ; or a clerk, who is employed to pay money to a creditor. Such servant, in a suit against the purchaser, is a good witness to prove the delivery, and the clerk to prove the receipt of the money ; that is to say, to prove that they did not themselves embezzle the property(a). All the reasoning employed in the preceding case applies with equal, if not greater, force to this ; for here he is prompted to charge the defendant, not only to save himself from loss, but to preserve his reputation. Yet, in other cases in which the necessity would seem equally to exist, the rule is enforced, and the witness is excluded. A master of a vessel is not a competent witness to prove that there was no deviation in an action on a policy(b). The driver of a coach is not a good witness in an action against the owner for injury done by negligently driving. Yet, in these cases, no one so well as the captain or the driver could know whether there was deviation or negligence. It is said, indeed, in defence of this distinction, " that, although the agent is a competent witness to prove that he acted according to the direction of the principal on the ground of necessity, and because the principal can never maintain an action against his agent for acting according to his directions, yet, if the cause depend upon the question whether the agent has been guilty of some tortuous act or negligence in the course of executing the orders of the principal, and in respect of which he would be liable even to the principal if he failed in the action, the agent is not competent without a release." I give the words of the most approved treatise on evidence here to show what stuff the reasons, on which these distinctions are founded, is made of.

The agent is a good witness for the principal to prove the payment of money or the delivery of goods which he himself may have embezzled. Yet he is not a good witness for the owner of the carriage to show there was no negligence. In both cases, by procuring a verdict for the owner, he exonerates himself from any action. In both cases, he is perhaps the only witness of the transaction, and the best witness in the case of the negligence. One, too, who lays a wager on the event of the suit, is a good witness(c). Why ? Because he does not come within the rule ? Surely not. His interest is apparent. Why then ? Another exception is made for his case, and another reason to support it. The party to the suit has a right to the evidence ; and the witness shall not, by his act, deprive him of it. Now what right has the party in this case that every other party has not ? Has not every party to every suit a right to the production of the truth ? But the witness, in this case, produces the interest and apparent disability by his own act ! So much stronger the reason for excluding him. A man must have a strong hostile feeling to a prisoner who lays a wager, not only that he will be convicted, but that he (the witness) will convict him(d). Here are interest, animosity, and perhaps the worst passions, all combined ; yet he is a good witness, because, say other authorities, the interest accrued after the case(e) had arisen in which he is called as a witness. But if bare interest disqualifies, then surely it

(a) 2 Espin. 509.  3 Espin. 48.    (b) Starkie Ev. 1730.
(c) Skinner's Rep. 586.    (d) 1 Strange, 652.
(e) In the strong case of a witness to a will, a good and disinterested witness at the time of making the will, who *becomes interested afterwards,* cannot be a witness to prove the will, and the last intentions of the testator, although accompanied by all the forms of law, become frustrated! 2 Hayward's Rep. 147. It is not, then, the time at which the interest accrues justifies the exception. We have seen that the other circumstance, its being the act of the party, would rather add to, than diminish, the reason for excluding him.

is of no consequence how or when the interest accrued. The argument for the general rule is, that the judge of the fact will be more probably misled than enlightened by hearing an interested witness. If this were true, he ought not to hear any interested witness, still less one who to his interest joins a strong persuasion or prejudice on the side which he is called to support. But it is not true, and this exception proves it ! The truth is, that the disqualification from interest was found to be so inconsistent with principle, that inroads have constantly been making upon it by exceptions, and I refer to the numerous treatises on evidence, for others, none of them supported by reasons that would not justify the total abolition of the rule itself.

Another evil attending it, independent of the injury by the exclusion of evidence, is the uncertainty it has introduced in the law. Cases, either entirely contradictory to each other, or supported by the most flimsy distinctions, give to acute lawyers the means of defeating justice; and to astute judges that of making the balance turn to the one side or the other, as their passions or prejudices may prompt, without, in either case, being liable to the reproach of acting without authority. Abolish the rule in all cases, and no such possibility can exist. The evidence will go to the jury, when they are the judges of the fact; to the court when they are not; in both cases, there will be the check of public opinion, which is either totally lost or greatly weakened when the testimony is suppressed. The reasons for believing or discrediting the witness will have their full weight, because they will be drawn from the circumstances in each case. The advantages will not be lost which arise from the involuntary or necessary admissions of truth, which come from an interested witness, even in the cases in which he is desirous to deceive—from his manner—from his hesitation—even from his silence. The law will be rendered simple on a subject which gives rise now to numerous discussions, and produce great perplexity. The judge will no longer have it in his power to admit or exclude, almost at his discretion, every witness who is at all interested.

This result, so important in itself, so easy of execution, and so general in its operation, is now partially obtained, by a mode which places the interest of the parties frequently in the hands of the witness, by making it optional with him to give up or retain his interest, or with the party to exclude him when he is supposed to be unfavourable by refusing to exonerate him from a liability. This operation for instantaneously transforming a bad into a good witness, for rendering a statement credible, which, if uttered before it was performed, would be unworthy of being even listened to: this operation is called a release; and, according to the circumstances of the case, it must be performed either by the witness or by the party. Where the interest consists in an emolument to be gained by the witness by the event of the cause, it is plain that his own act is required to renounce their advantage. If he has a strong desire that the party should prevail, and his testimony is material, he signs the release, his evidence is taken, and the cause is gained. If his wishes, contrary perhaps to an inconsiderable interest, or a secret interest stronger than the apparent one, should be different, he refuses the release, and the party, whom he might have saved, loses his fortune, his reputation, or his life. The witness, then, is the arbiter of his fate; not by perjury, or other illegal means, but by the exercise of a legal right, for which he can incur neither punishment nor reproach. Again, the interest may arise from a liability to some demand which may be the consequence of a certain decision of the cause. In this case it is evident that the release must come from the party to whom the witness must pay or account. If he give the release, the witness is heard; if he refuse, the testimony is rejected. Here again he becomes the arbiter. But the whole of this is downright mummery, unworthy of a place in the jurisprudence of an intelligent people. So far from adding any thing to the credit of the witness, a release ought nine times in ten to detract from it; because it must always arise from a stipulation expressed or understood, that the witness will state to the jury what he has before stated to the party; and all these contrivances to escape from the operation of the exclusionary rule, must demonstrate that it is unwise and unjust.

Analogous to the extraction of truth from interested witnesses, is that of learning it from the statements of the parties themselves. To a certain extent this is permitted by our present law. In the code now offered it is extended, and alterations are proposed in the manner of obtaining it.

If, on the one hand, the parties are those most strongly tempted to alter or conceal the truth; on the other, they are those whose knowledge of the case best enables them to declare it. These conflicting considerations have, in the jurisprudence of most nations, produced the effects that might have been expected from the same source which excluded the testimony of interested witnesses. A general rule, with exceptions founded on reasons more or less applicable to the rule itself, produced a continual struggle between a conviction that the rule was unjust and the want of courage to avow it, and to break through the trammels it imposed. In England a party may, by an expensive proceeding, in another court, obtain answers, on oath, to such questions as he may propose to the adverse party. In France the same power is given to the party, without the necessity of resorting to another court; and it is there extended to the judge by what is called the decisory oath, when the evidence is, by an artificial scale they have established for graduating it, equally balanced. Here it is given to the party only, but in the same court. In all these cases there are defects, both of form and substance. Of form, in that they all require the questions to be propounded in writing, and answered, with, I believe, the exception of the decisory oath, in the same manner, without cross-examination, and not in the presence of any one but the magistrate who attests the deposition. This is a radical defect. Of substance, in that the right of interrogation is confined to the opposite party, to the total exclusion, in our system and that of England, and the partial exclusion in the French practice, of the judges of the fact. We allow the plaintiff and defendant in civil cases mutually to interrogate each other by the exhibition of written questions; if these are not categorically answered, the facts, it is declared, shall be taken to be confessed. This supposes that a fact must always be stated in the interrogatory, and the affirmance of that fact is to be the consequence of an evasive answer or of silence with respect to it. This is highly inconvenient to both parties(a); but what is more so, is that the answer is final—no explanation

---

(a) Suppose an action on a promise, and the plaintiff, wishing to establish, by the oath of the defendant, that when charged with having made the promise the defendant did not

can be required of what is equivocal—no cross interrogatories to test the truth of what is said, or procure the disclosure of what is omitted: yet the law permits the respondent to go beyond a mere categorical affirmation or negative answer; he may state circumstances closely connected with the subject of the interrogatory; and yet on this matter, be it ever so material or unexpected, the party has no right to question; with the prior interrogatory and the answer to it, the whole process stops.  In considering this head of evidence, it appeared to me, that if it were proper to get that of the party, it should be got effectually, and when we were applying to a source of evidence which is manifestly the most suspicious, that all the means should be applied to render it full, correct, and faithful, which were used in other cases.  I could see no reason why any of the precautions, necessary in cases where the witness is supposed to be impartial, should be omitted.  If we hear the party at all, let us extract from him the whole truth, parts of which his interest may induce him to conceal: let us, by cross-examination, detect all the falsities that same interest may induce him to frame; let us, by the publicity of the examination in the presence of the parties and the judge, and of that faithful guardian of private rights, the keen gaze of the public, deter him from the difficult task of swerving from the truth.

Permit the party to ponder over a written interrogatory, which he is to answer in the same mode; let him call in the assistance of a learned adviser to frame his deposition in such a way as to avoid the danger of perjury on the one hand, or avowals injurious to his interest on the other; let him attest to this in the presence of a magistrate, who is not to judge the suit, who does not read the deposition, and who hurries over the formal words which convert the mere statement into judicial evidence; manage affairs in this manner, and the result will always be that which it is found under our practice, that, in most cases, the one party will not dare to probe the conscience of the other; more especially when, as it were for the express purpose of tempting him to falsehood, he is told whatever you say shall be taken for truth, no matter how improbable it is, if two witnesses cannot be found to contradict, or one witness corroborated by strong circumstantial evidence, or by written proof.  Surely this is a strange inconsistency in our law.  The testimony of a disinterested and impartial witness is left to have what credit the judges of the fact may, from his character or other circumstances, be inclined to give him ; but the oath of the most suspicious witness, the party himself, the one most interested to suppress the truth, is directed by law to be conclusive, unless contradicted by two witnesses, or one witness with strong circumstances, or written proof.  And it seems scarcely a fair answer to say, the party who called for his opponent's oath knew the consequence of his making an unfavourable answer, and was at liberty either to ask for it or not.  The question is not,

---

deny it, put this interrogatory, Did you, on such an occasion, deny that you made the promise ? and the defendant evades the question or refuses to answer it, what is the consequence?  The fact, in the interrogatory is taken to be confessed.  But as far as there is any fact stated, it is that the defendant did deny the debt.  It follows, then, that the refusal to answer, so far from operating as a confession of what the plaintiff wishes to prove, has a directly contrary effect, for it establishes the fact that he did deny the debt, a fact which, perhaps, he would not directly have stated on oath.

whether he knew the consequence or did not know it; but, whether the condition is just, and such as ought to be imposed. The party calling for the answer shows, by that act, his own belief in the fact which he states, and his confidence that the other party will acknowledge it. If disappointed in this, what good reason can be given why he should be precluded from arguing, that other circumstances in the case, that the improbability of the testimony, or its inconsistency, should induce the jury to give it no credit? Why should the jury, who perhaps do not believe a word the party has declared, be forced to consider it as truth? The conviction that no good answer can be given to the queries, has induced the reporter to propose a repeal of the restriction, leaving the judge of the fact free in this, as in other instances, to decide according to his belief of the fact.

The reasoning which has been given for the admission of interested witnesses applies, in a great measure, to that of the parties themselves. But I have stopped short, in the code which is submitted—and perhaps I have done wrong in hesitating—I have stopped short of making the party a witness for himself, except in the case when a piece of scriptory evidence, unsigned by the party, is produced as presumptive evidence against him. In this case, the Code gives him the privilege of stating the circumstance under which it was written, and his intent in writing it. With this exception, he may only be examined by the opposite party, by the judge, or by any one of the jurors; the examination must be under oath, in open court, and subject to cross-examination by the opposite party.

The innovation, made by the code, in extending the right of examining a party to the judges of the fact, as well as to the opposite party, is founded on this reason :—The suitor may decline examining his opposite party from one of two very different motives; because he has no confidence in his integrity ; or because he is conscious of the want of that quality in himself, and fears that the plain tale of his adversary may carry conviction with it. The change proposed puts it in the power of the judge of the fact, to do that which the party fears to do, in the last instance, from a bad motive ; while, in the cases where the reasonable suspicions of the one party prevents his having recourse to the conscience of the other, the extension of the great correctives of oral interrogation, with its concomitants, cross-examination and publicity, lessen, almost to zero, the chance of false statements leaving any impression.

Why the party is not allowed to be examined whenever he himself chooses, is not quite so obviously in conformity with the principles of the code, which, as has been seen, is to allow no exclusion of any thing that is calculated to throw light on the subject; and it has been observed, with much show of reason, the expositions of the parties are what the judge principally requires. It is to this source of evidence that men, in the common affairs of life, most resort when they are called on to decide on any particular fact. They hear the charge, the answer, the reply, the allegations of both parties, with all their circumstances ; then where there is doubt, they look for other proof, compare the whole, and then decide. Why will you deprive the party of the right he ought to have, of being heard, of clearing up doubts, and rectifying errors, which may have been produced by the inattention or design of witnesses, or the ambiguity of other evidence? This objection would have

2 I

great force but for two circumstances, and perhaps has some in despite of them. For the first, we must recur to another provision in the code, which requires that all petitions and answers, in civil cases, must be attested on oath. The second is, that, in most cases, it may be said in all, where the evidence leaves any doubt, the power given to the judge and to the other party, to interrogate, will answer the end proposed.

The article requiring all petitions and answers to be exhibited under oath, was introduced after much reflection, and I ought candidly to state, in opposition to the advice of some professional friends, for whose opinions I have the highest respect. They argued against this, as well as against giving the right of interrogation to the judges of fact, on the ground, that multiplying oaths made them too common, thereby lessening their sanctity and force ; and that an affidavit to the truth of a petition would soon become as proverbially insignificant as a custom-house oath.

1. To this it was answered, that oaths came to be lightly considered, not so much by the frequency of the occasion on which they were exacted, as from other causes; that among these causes was the above, which this very provision was intended to correct; that of allowing any allegation in a judicial proceeding, made by a party, to be considered as a matter of form, which might be false, and yet attach no blame to the person who swore they were true ; that where pleadings were verbose, technical, and founded on fictitious forms, the objection would have great weight, because then the party would generally ill understand the tenor of the instrument to which he attested—the most scrupulous party could find it difficult, in the mass of an English bill in chancery, to distinguish between the material facts and the formal allegations it contains; and the ready excuse, " I was told it was a mere matter of form," is always at hand to satisfy those of an easier conscience. But in a system which discards all fictions, where there is no form inconsistent with truth, which requires facts to be set forth in plain language, as there is no difficulty in distinguishing the truth, neither is there any excuse for falsehood ; and no more evil need be apprehended, because every suitor is obliged to attest to his proceedings, than there is from administering an oath to every witness. Another reason why oaths are treated with inattention, is not their frequency, but the mode of administering them, the essential part of the ceremony being performed by the magistrate or clerk, who in a hurried manner, and often unintelligibly, repeats the words of the attestation, while the deponent is not required to utter even a word of assent to the obligation on his conscience, but signifies it by a gesture, in itself of no meaning. But when, as is provided in the code, solemnity is added to the form of the oath, the words of which the deponent is bound to repeat—when he is reminded that he must submit to cross-examination, and instructed in the consequences of his departing from truth—it may fairly be presumed that the additional number of oaths required by this provision will not lessen their binding force. This last mentioned precaution is quite new, and deserves particular consideration. All the attestations, under oath, to written instruments, as our law now stands, are not only ex parte evidence, but, in most cases, courts will admit of no counter proof, much less counter examination ; and, in many causes, amendments to such affidavits have been refused. The party, or his counsel, prepare the declaration with great care ; so much of the truth, and no more, is set forth as they think necessary to attain the object, and even

if an idea inconsistent with the truth is conveyed, the language in which it may be couched, by its equivocation, secures the party from all fear of prosecution for perjury. Here the whole matter ends. The proof, thus furnished by the party, is presented to the judge, who, on this evidence, grants the order demanded, frequently an order for arrest of the person, for a seizure of goods, or some other proceeding in a cause, equally important. Here is the testimony of the party himself admitted in its worst and most dangerous form. No opportunity for cross-examination; no declaration in full; no appearance of the deponent before the judge; the affidavit most frequently being made before another magistrate. This evil was one of great magnitude, and to correct it as well in cases where affidavits are already admitted as to prevent its recurrence in those now under discussion, the code provides, that whenever an affidavit shall be taken in the course of judicial proceedings, previous notice shall be given, whenever the ends of justice will not be thereby defeated; but when that may be apprehended, the deponent must be informed that, at a convenient designated time, he must attend for cross-examination, and that wilful falsehood will incur the same penalties as if it had been uttered under oath in open court. These precautions, it is thought, will obviate the fear of rendering oaths too common, and making parties regardless of their solemnity. How far it would be proper to abolish the religious sanction given to a judicial declaration, has been matter of some doubt. The regard paid to a simple affirmation by a very numerous part of our comnunity, whose consciences do not permit them to take an oath, would seem to indicate that it might be done with safety. But for the reason stated at large in the introduction to the Code of Procedure, this sanction is preserved in all cases, but those in which the declarent has religious scruples.

2. The other objection urged against requiring the oath of the party to his petition or defence was, that it would be considered as evidence by the judges of the fact, and that an undue influence would thus be given to the powerful, the rich and the influential, over the poor and unknown suitor. I repeat this argument because it was addressed to me from a highly respectable source, and therefore I am inclined to think there must be more force in it than, I confess, I have been able to discover. This is certain, that a declaration under oath of any man, whether witness or party, will derive some credit from his character and the absence of motives to falsehood, which his situation in life suppose; but so will his word when not under oath. If the plaintiff, who is rich and esteemed, presents his petition, under oath, in like manner does the poor and unknown defendant attest his answer. The relative credit of the parties is preserved. Indeed, of the two modes, the present affords the greatest advantage to the man of credit; his simple assertion will, sometimes, have more weight than the oath of one of bad or unknown character, but would, certainly, other things being equal, be more readily believed than the simple declaration of the latter. Requiring the oath of both parties restores, in a great measure, the equality. But if the objection be good for any thing, why not apply it to witnesses as well as parties? And for fear that the oath of the influential man should preponderate over that of the poor and humble, why not banish the oath in this case also? As the law now

stands,. there is. nothing, it is believed, to forbid any individual from swearing to his pleadings; and thus it is optional with any, who thinks he can derive an advantage from it, to throw his oath into the scale.

.Having disposed—how satisfactorily the general assembly will determine—of the only two objections made to the change, let us inquire what are the advantages proposed by its adoption. . In order fully to appreciate these advantages, we must consider the objects which a wise legislator ought to aim at in providing a mode for the decision of contested rights. These are, that no one should be vexed by the commencement of unjust suits; or delayed or defeated by a false defence in the prosecution of those which are well founded. The means to attain these important ends are, first, that the language of all law proceedings should be simple and certain, neither involved in the mystery of technical language, nor disfigured by ridiculous fictions ; that there should be as much celerity as is consistent with proper deliberation ; no more than inevitable expense; and that every suitor should be responsible for every injurious act wilfully committed. To effect which last and important purpose, it is essential that, as far as possible, there should be no intervening party between him and the judge. Without this responsibility how can any of the great objects of practical jurisprudence be obtained ? A frivolous suit is commenced, to the great injury of the defendant. The plaintiff says truly, " I never saw the declaration that has been put in." Or, he may say, " I did see it, but I did not understand a word it contained. My lawyer signed it, and told me it was in the necessary and usual form. If it contains falsehoods, I am not answerable for them." This would be a good excuse for the client, and the advocate might avoid all responsibility by alleging, that he had only put in technical form the instructions of his client. The proposed change avoids this difficulty. It secures responsibility; when the client is obliged to attest what he alleges on oath ; when he is told by the magistrate, who administers it, "'Take care that you tell nothing but the truth, for your falsehood will incur the punishment of perjury. Take care you tell all the truth, for what you may endeavour to conceal will be brought out on a cross-examination before the judge who is to try the cause, and the public who will form their opinion of you from the correctness of your assertions." In the face of these cautions, falsehoods and vexatious suits will be extremely rare. Responsibility, under this arrangement, can no longer be shifted off; and the certainty and simplicity so desirable in legal language, will be inevitably attained. We have the honour of being the first in the union, and that in the incipient state of our freedom, while we were yet a territory, to reduce legal procedure to a degree of simplicity unknown, perhaps, in any other country(a) : and if the plain intent of the laws for

(a) While the practice under the territorial law, which the reporter prepared at the request of the legislative council, was uncorrupted by the introduction of the common law counts, a young gentleman, from one of the Atlantic states, applied to him to be admitted into his office for the purpose of becoming acquainted with the routine of practice, previous to his examination ; and inquired, with much apparent solicitude, in how long a time, with great assiduity, he might hope to make himself master of its intricacies? The answer was, " It is not easy to calculate to a minute, but if you call on me to-morrow at two, as I do not dine until four, I believe the task may be accomplished before we sit down." The surprise

that purpose had been adhered to, in practice, this strong reason for the proposed change would not exist. But, although those laws directed the parties to state the facts on which they relied, according to the truth of the case, with the necessary circumstances of time and place, yet imperceptibly all the common law counts came to be introduced ; and instead of a plain statement, which every body can understand, of the manner in which, and the time when, and the place where, a sum of money became due from the defendant to the plaintiff, we have a number of *counts*, as they are called, contradictory to each other, but all relating to the same transaction, and unintelligible except to the initiated. Counts for money had and received, for money lent, money laid out and expended, as a ground-work, on which is raised the superstructure of an alleged promise to pay, never necessary to be proved. The necessity of swearing to the truth of the demand will, as a first advantage, bring back the practice to its original purity, and banish the fictions which the common law education of most of our lawyers has introduced. The suitor is required to swear, not merely that the material facts in his pleadings are true, which he frequently does on the statement of his advocate, that the parts which he does not and cannot understand, are matters of form only, but he must swear to the truth of the whole allegation ; and, in order to do this, he must understand what is alleged ; but, to understand it, it must be written in plain and simple language, according to the fact. Thus several important points are gained—clearness, simplicity and the absence of all technical jargon in your proceedings. But this is not all. To diminish the number of suits has always been, professedly at least, a great object with lawgivers; but unfortunately they have imagined only one mode of effecting this ; increasing the expenses, vexations and delays of applications for justice. Suits will certainly be diminished in number, if, to recover ten pounds, as in England, a disbursement of that or a greater sum is required. But it is not the interest of any state that suits should be diminished in that manner. Its true interest is, that every man should be deterred from asking what he has no right to receive ; but should recover what is due at the smallest possible expense, and with the least degree of vexation and inconvenience ; and that no man should be encouraged by the uncertainty of the law, or the hope of gaining an unfair advantage from any defect of form or want of evidence in the prosecution to withhold a just debt, or compensation for a wrong. The proposed alteration, it is thought, will most materially lessen the number of suits; not by a denial of justice, but by its certain, easy and cheap administration. This will be effected in the following manner.

First, all those suits will, it is supposed, be completely prevented, or so nearly prevented as to be reduced to a most inconsiderable number, which are brought without any other hope of success than that which arises from the defendant's supposed want of the necessary proof to discharge himself from an apparently just demand; for instance, the plaintiff having the evidence that a sum of money was once due to him, but having reason to believe that the defendant has lost the evidence which had been given of its discharge, brings his experimental suit, which he gains if his conjecture of the loss of evidence was well founded ; and if

of one, who had just passed some laborious years in learning the fictions of the common law, may easily be conceived at this reply, in which there was little or no exaggeration.

he finds himself mistaken, he loses nothing but the costs. Now, suppose this plaintiff obliged, before he can commence his suit, to make oath to the truth of the charge, will he risk the searching interrogatories of his adversary, the danger of the evidence of the discharge being produced, the punishment, the infamy, that will await his detection? Certainly not. This whole class of cases, then, may be considered as struck off from the docket.

Next to those are the less numerous cases in which suits are brought merely for purposes of vexation. As greater risk, nay a certainty of failure, must attend these; and the same consequences follow the support of them by a false oath, we may as reasonably suppose that these also will be swept away.

In the cases considered, the party is supposed to be conscious of his want of merits. A more numerous class is composed of those in which, from irritated feelings or false information, he really believes himself injured and entitled to relief. Under these impressions he has nothing to do but to direct the suit. The man who stands between him and the judge, for the most part, does not examine very closely into the proof by which the suit is to be supported: it is not his interest to do so. He commences the suit; and to commence it he has no need in other states, in any case, and since the introduction of the common law counts, he has no need in many cases here, of any precise information as to the cause of action. He files his petition, stuffed with a variety of counts or statements, some one of which he hopes the evidence will fit; and when, in due time, the cause is ready for trial, he begins to call for the testimony, and finding that it will not support the cause, it is either dismissed, continued with the vague hope that some evidence may in time be discovered, or it is brought on with no prospect of success but that which the uncertainty of the law will afford. Instead of this careless, precipitate mode of proceeding, impose the necessity of such a precise statement as must be attested on oath and supported by the examination of the party making it under the interrogatory of his adversary, and the causes of this description also will be greatly diminished in number.

There are other causes which may be readily supposed will, under the proposed regulation, restrain plaintiffs from bringing experimental, vexatious and hasty suits. The same causes will operate on defendants to make compromises and settlements before suit brought, or prevent a frivolous or vexatious defence afterwards. It will no longer be sufficient for an attorney to say for a party, that he owes nothing, or to put in any other plea or allegation that he knows to be false, in order to retard or avoid the payment of a just debt; or the performance of any other legal obligation. The previous oath, the all-searching subsequent interrogation under the inspection and in the hearing of the public, will effectually prevent any false pretence being made. The creditor, not being irritated by the delay, the vexation, and the expense of a groundless defence, will be more lenient; and the debtor, knowing that he cannot rely on these shifts, will be more punctual; and thus the same measures which facilitate the recovery of a legal demand, will prevent those from being made which are unfounded or vexatious.

Having demonstrated, as it is hoped, the utility of requiring that all the judicial allegations of the parties should be substantiated by their oaths, under the correctives of publicity, cross-examination, and the right of interrogation given to the judge and the jury; and having pointed out the analogous reasoning which would require the admission of the testimony of the parties in the cases in which that of interested witnesses is permitted ; it remains only, under this head, to give the reasons why the code has not permitted the parties to offer themselves as witnesses in all cases without restriction. It has been a principle, in preparing this plan, not to be deterred from proposing any useful change by the mere consideration that it was new ; but, at the same time, to respect existing institutions, so much as to innovate no further than was necessary ; and never where the useful end proposed could be obtained without shocking established opinions or prejudices in favour of known forms, although they might be, in some degree, inconvenient.

In the present instance, the maxim, that no one should be a witness in his own cause, had been so long established, as a self-evident proposition, that it was supposed much more feasible to add to the exceptions, which, as we have seen, were admitted in practice, than to deny its truth ; while, at the same time, nearly all the advantages that could be expected from abolishing it entirely, were secured by the extensions which have been enumerated ; to which may be added, that although the party cannot, except in the cases and in the manner specially provided for, support his case by his own testimony, yet the faculty given to the judge and jury to examine him, will in very nearly all cases supply the deficiency ; because, having his oath in support of his own statement, as set forth in the pleadings, if that statement should be denied or explained away by other testimony, the judge or jury will naturally apply to the party to know how he accounts for the difference, and thus he will have the same advantage which a right to offer his own testimony would give.

The exclusion of interested testimony having been examined, and found to be injurious to the investigation of truth, and its admission to be attended with no inconvenience which may not be reduced to one of a quantity that has no assignable value ; it, of course, finds no place in the proposed code ; and with it disappears one of the most fruitful sources of uncertainty, expense, delay and inconvenience, in the law.

If the search after truth requires that interested witnesses, and even the parties themselves, should be interrogated to discover it, are there any relations, in which the offered witness may stand to the parties, that ought to exclude his testimony ? By the English law, and of course, in the several cases which have been noticed, by ours, there are several : husband and wife—attorney and client—parties in the same cause.

1. The code now offered does not contain the exclusion of husband or wife, as witnesses, for or against each other; because the reporter does not find any one sufficient among the reasons by which it is supported in the English decisions or commentaries. The first of these alleged reasons is, that their " interests are identical"(a). But in a system which discards interest as an objection to competency, this reason falls of course. The second is said, by the same authority, to be " on grounds of public policy" to prevent distrust and dissension between them, and to guard against perjury. It is said, that individual interest and individual rights

(a) 2 Starkie, 706. 1 Bl. 443.

may sometimes, by a wise legislation, be made to yield to the good of the whole community, which is understood to be meant by the expression *"public policy ;"* but those cases are not numerous, and generally admit of compensation, and ought only to be allowed when the public advantage is evident and so important as greatly to overbalance the individual inconvenience which is incurred to promote it. In the case before us, the public evils are designated : first, the danger of domestic dissension; secondly, the danger of perjury. The first, if the evidence should be against the party connected with the witness ; the second, if it should go to exonerate him. The argument supposes, that if the husband or wife be called as a witness in a suit to which the other is a party, one of two things must happen ; either unfavourable truths will be told, which it is said will disturb the family peace ; or perjury will be committed, to preserve it. Now these are two opposite and contradictory reasons. If the danger be, that family dissensions will grow out of the testimony, then that of perjury is avoided; if the danger be perjury, then that of family discord need not be apprehended. But legislation must be founded on the general application of its reasons ; not on the tendency of its measures to good or evil in particular instances. If the connexion by marriage be so close as to make the parties incur the danger and disgrace of giving false testimony for the other, then let the case be examined solely with a view to the evil of placing the witness in a situation where strong motives are offered to him to commit a crime. If the predominant risk be that of destroying domestic harmony, let that be assigned as the reason. But to allege both, when they are contradictory, is a strong presumption that neither can safely be relied upon. Both, however, will be examined, and both contrasted with the evils which attended the exclusion.

First, let us suppose that domestic dissension is the danger ; that is to say, that one spouse will quarrel with the other for telling the truth, in a court of justice, when it makes against the interest of the other. But in most cases the interest is common between them ; therefore, there is little probability that any ill will can be created in the mind of the one against the other for not committing perjury, in order to protect a common interest. The supposition that a domestic broil may ensue from a cause like this, is to suppose the party raising it corrupt, in expecting falsehood from his or her spouse, and malevolent in resenting his disappointment; and the law cannot reasonably be required to make any great sacrifice for preserving the harmony of so ill-assorted an union as that which such a case supposes. The dissension arises from the performance of a duty—bearing open testimony of the truth ; and avoiding a crime—the commission of perjury: and, because a brutal, corrupt, or passionate husband, may quarrel with his wife for avoiding the crime, shall the law declare, that the wife shall not perform the duty ? It will watch over domestic peace by punishing those who disturb it, and for proper causes, by dissolving the bond of an ill-assorted connexion : but it ought never to say, the one party shall be exempted from the performance of an important public duty, because the other is tyrannical and unjust. The argument supposes, too, that there is greater danger to domestic happiness from this than from any other source ; but is there any foundation for the belief ? Not one case in a thousand, it is believed, will occur in practice where any improper excitement will be created by an adherence to the truth, although it should militate against the wife or the husband of the party who states it. Why should it more in this case, than in that of any other witness? Mutual affection, the knowledge that it was the performance of a duty required by law, and that it could only be avoided by a crime, are so many and such cogent reasons to prevent ill-will on the occasion, that it is astonishing how this reason could find favour with the great lawyers who have assigned it as an argument in favour of their rule; more especially when they themselves most explicitly discard this reason by declaring, that the wife shall not be allowed to appear as a witness against the husband, even if he consents, or after a divorce; nor against the interest of his heirs after his death(a). How connubial happiness can be disturbed by a compliance on the part of the wife with her husband's request while united, or by any act after the connexion has been dissolved by death or divorce, these learned doctors of the law alone can explain.

Examine the opposite reason—the danger of perjury; that is to say, the matrimonial union is so strict, that the one party to it will incur all the dangers of punishment and infamy rather than tell the truth when it is injurious to the other; and the law, it is said, holds out this irresistible temptation to the witness when it permits him to be examined. Yet, by the preceding argument, the temptation is easily resisted, the truth will be told, and this strong connexion is so weak, that it is broken merely on that account.

But the arguments must be destroyed, not by opposing the one to the other, but both of them to the truth. There is no doubt that in this, as in many other cases, minds may be found that will waver between the declaration of a truth that may hurt their interests or their feelings, and the assertion of a falsehood that, in their opinion, may secure both from injury; but can the law be said to hold out a temptation to perjury when it orders a party, under those circumstances, to tell the truth? If there were no temptations to conceal the truth, or assert a falsehood, there would be no need of oaths. Oaths, and the penalties for breaking them, were made for the purpose of counteracting that disposition. If they were to be dispensed with in cases where that disposition exists, there would be no need for them in any others. In every such case, then, it may with equal reason be said, that the law holds out a temptation to perjury, because it exacts the oath to tell the truth, when there is an inclination to conceal it; and the argument would extend with equal reason to the abolition of oaths, and the penalties for the breach of them. This exclusion is at variance, too, with other provisions of the law as they already exist. The party himself may be interrogated in chancery in England, and in all cases at law here. The wife may be interrogated to support an accusation made by herself against her husband for a personal injury, in some cases affecting his life; yet she is not permitted to prove a fact that would save him from an ignominious death, on a charge brought against him by another. Now in all these cases the danger of perjury is equally great, or greater, unless we suppose the attachment of a wife to her husband's interest superior to his own; or her desire to make good her own charge less intense than that she would feel to support the accusation brought by another. The danger of perjury is no greater in this than

(a) 2 Stark. 706.  6 East, 192.

2 K

in othér cases in which it is incurred, without scruple, in the dearest connexions of nature ; father and son, mother and child, brother and sister, friendships of the most intimate kind, habits of intimacy during a long life—the parties to all these are every day arrayed for and against each other as witnesses, and the law interposes no other safeguard to their consciences, than its penalties, and the danger of infamy by detection.    No rule of exclusion protects the witness against the influence of his affections or his interest.    He is heard, and the degree of connexion is weighed against his character and the probability of his story; the counsel cross-examine; the public inspect; the jury interrogate, and calculate, and determine ; and no inconvenience is felt in those cases. Why should there be in this ?

Having stated the general principle, that every party to a suit has a right to all the information in relation to his cause, of which he ought not to be deprived but for reasons of great public or private inconvenience; and examined by discussing the reasons for exclusion in this case, whether it offers any such inconvenience; let us now examine the particular evils attached to the rule as it now stands.

In criminal cases the evil is most apparent.    Suppose the husband, accused by positive, but perjured testimony, of a crime affecting his life, and the wife, the only witness of a fact that would prove his innocence; no matter what circumstances she could adduce to corroborate her testimony, no matter what intrinsic evidence it contained, no matter what perfect conviction it would produce of its truth, it is sternly excluded ; and the innocent husband is executed because " *public policy requires that the peace of families should not be disturbed, and that no temptations should be held out to perjury.*"    In this case, by no means an improbable one, there is positive evil, cruel injustice, heart-rending distress.    In the case which the law attempts to guard against, inconvenience only, if it occurs, but an inconvenience highly improbable to happen, inasmuch as it is supposed to affect domestic union; and as it is believed to be a temptation to perjury, not one strong enough to produce the effect, or should it be yielded to, would be capable of detection by the usual means.    But even without supposing the extreme case of life or death, the suppression of testimony is, in all cases, an evil ; and the law deprives the party of a certain right, to avoid a problematical inconvenience.

On the other hand, suppose the testimony of the wife necessary to procure the conviction of the husband : she is the only witness to a murder which he has committed.    This I consider the strongest ground for the exclusion; it enlists the feelings, and they are most frequently found on the right side.    Shall a wife be forced to give testimony that will condemn her husband, the father of her children, to infamy and death, or take refuge in the crime of perjury to avoid it ?    I confess that if the alternative could be avoided, a humane lawgiver would not enjoin it; but if sympathy for individual distress should not be entirely rejected, it ought never to be entertained when its indulgence would lead to more extensive injuries to the community.    A wise and provident legislator must have the consequences of every legal provision as present to his mind, as its immediate operation is to his senses ; and in applying this rule to the subject under consideration, he should not, in tenderness to the feelings of conjugal affection, permit the husband or wife to escape punishment for a crime, or defraud another of his right, by declaring that the only witness of the offence, or the wrong, shall not be heard. Some crimes cannot be perpetrated without the aid of an accomplice. The accomplice may betray the principal. The fear of this treachery, in many instances, may prevent the crime ; or a person may not be found willing to engage in the enterprise. But, by the rule of exclusion, the law furnishes an assistant, who can never betray, and one who is always at hand; and thus gives a facility to the commission of offences which no other circumstance could possibly offer. Besides, public justice requires, and common sense would seem to point out, that those persons who are the most likely to be acquainted with the fact should be first called on to prove it; but who so probable to know the guilt or innocence of the party accused as the companion of all his hours, the depository of his most secret thoughts ; and what better calculated to prevent an intended crime, than the knowledge that those from whom it is so difficult to conceal it, may be made the unwilling witness of its disclosure ? Precisely in the proportion that a man would be encouraged to commit a crime by the knowledge that the person to whom he finds it necessary to confide it, cannot become a witness against him, will be his fear of committing it, when he knows that there is no person in whom he may confide, that may not be forced or be willing to betray him.

So sensible of this have been the judicial lawgivers of England, that they have imposed no bar to the receiving the testimony of father and son, mother and daughter, brother and sister, and all the other relations of consanguinity or affinity. They have had no regard to the confidences of friendship, and have thought that the affections of nature, as well as those of habit and sympathetic feeling, should afford no obstacle to the attainment of the ends of public justice. They have gone farther, and made an exception to the rule which they laid down, as one inviolable, even by consent(a), in the case of husband and wife ; and as we have seen, have allowed the wife to be produced as a witness against the husband on a prosecution for an injury done to herself. Now mark the reason! It is a convenient and a ready one: from the "*necessity of the case;*" which must mean, if it mean any thing, that there is a necessity that crimes should be punished, and that unless the testimony of the wife were admitted, they would, in those instances, be unpunished. Now, admit this reasoning, and see whether it does not go to the utter destruction of the rule to which it is offered as an exception. There is no greater necessity for punishing a crime committed by the husband against his wife than there is for punishing the same crime committed by him against another ; and if the wife is the only witness that can convict in the last case, her testimony is as necessary as it is in the first; and being necessary in both, it should not be admitted in one and excluded in the other. But, in truth, the inquiry is never made ; and in this, as in all the other cases founded on the convenient argument of necessity, although there may have been twenty other witnesses present, the pretended necessary witness is admitted ; and, although there may be none but him conversant of the fact, he is rejected where it has not yet been deemed convenient to admit the argument of necessity.

2. The advantages of receiving testimony from this source so greatly overbalance its evils and the inconveniences, and the injustice of re-

(a) 2 Starkie, 706. Rep. Temp. Hardw. 264.

jecting it are so manifest, that I have not hesitated to give this exclusion no place in the code. Not so with that arising from the next relation —that of counsel or attorney and client. In this I have offered little or no alteration to the existing law, as laid down by the latest decisions ; and this course has been the result of much reflection, and has been preceded by more doubts of its correctness, than I have found on any other provision of the work. Although I have earnestly endeavoured to discard all unfounded prejudices in favour of established and injurious errors, merely because they were established, it is yet possible that I may not, in this instance, have succeeded, and that ideas entertained during a professional course of more than forty years may have so fastened themselves upon the mind, as to give them a force they are not entitled to, and induced me to retain a provision which ought to be abolished. The legislature must judge of this ; and that they may do so, the arguments, which besides are not devoid of interest, for abolishing and retaining the provision must be stated.

The foundation for the reasoning against the exclusion is the acknowledged principle, that in judicial proceedings every thing calculated to bring the mind of the judge to a just conviction of the truth ought to be produced, unless the evil of its production should be greater than the good to be expected from it. In this case, say the arguers on this side of the question, the evil is all on the side of the exclusion. The object is truth ; who so like to know it as the confidential adviser of the party ? If the client have a just cause, the advocate can disclose nothing to his prejudice. If he is in the wrong, there is no reason why it should not be disclosed. This is the great object of the law ; nor will it be attended with that which the advocates for exclusion consider as the great evil, the violation of confidence ; for all the communications between client and counsel will be made with the knowledge that, if called on, the latter must declare them. The exclusionists, say their opponents, seem to consider that the great object of the law, in criminal cases, is the escape of the guilty ; for their objection is founded on the supposition that the client has confessed his guilt to his legal adviser ; and their rule is framed in order to conceal that confession, and thus to favour his escape. Whereas, its sole aim is the punishment of guilt ; and the confession of the party being the strongest evidence, ought not to be suppressed. So far, they add, from the declarations being dangerous to innocence, it is one of its strongest safeguards. If the client be really innocent, he will make no confessions ; and the declaration of his counsel that he has made none to his professional friend, cannot but be a presumption in his favour. Nor is there any thing derogatory to the dignity of counsel, or that ought to affect the delicacy of his feelings, to be called on for the confessions of his client. As a minister of the law, his desire must be that they should be faithfully executed ; and whether conviction takes place on his declaration of a fact communicated by his client, or known from any other source, is perfectly immaterial in both cases. He does his duty in declaring the truth, and he ought to feel equally free from self-reproach in both. On the contrary, the profession is degraded by making the advocate, in effect, the accessary after the fact, to a criminal, by aiding him to escape the penalty of the law, with a knowledge that he has incurred it. Why, too, it is asked, will you extend this privilege to attorneys and counsellors, when you deny it in the case of physicians, friends, or the nearest relations ? In these cases there is equal confidence reposed, and, in many instances, necessarily reposed ; yet there is no exclusion. Besides, the contract between counsellor and client ought to be governed by the same rules that are applied to other contracts in relation to the legality of their object. A contract to enable one to defeat the known operation of law, would be reprobated by the courts. But the object of this contract, where the party is guilty, is precisely one of that description, and ought not to have any binding force.

These are the main arguments, greatly abridged and undoubtedly weakened in the operation, by which it is contended, that in all cases the counsellor and attorney ought to be admitted as witnesses against their client. These reasons are forcible, and some of the arguments, at first view, unanswerable ; but when maturely considered, they seem to me to rest, for the most part, on the untenable ground that, if the client be innocent, he has nothing to fear from the disclosures of his counsel ; and that if he be guilty, he ought not to be protected against them. I have applied the term untenable to this basis of the argument from a belief that, in many supposable cases, the most perfect innocence may suffer from the disclosure of circumstances necessary to be communicated to a professional adviser. In a civil case, concerning the title to land of which the client is in possession, and which he holds under an ancestor, whose title, though acquired in good faith and for a valuable consideration, is defective in form, the client, ignorant of the forms required by law, thinks the title is good, but having occasion to make some family settlement, shows it to his counsel, who immediately perceives the defect. What is the consequence ? Is the professional man bound to secrecy or not ? Whatever be the answer to this question, it seems to be decisive, at least in such a case, of the propriety of the exclusion. If he be not bound to secrecy, he may, without blame, immediately communicate his discovery to the party interested, and his innocent and confiding client is ruined. Every feeling of justice, honour and humanity, would be shocked at this ; and one of the most ingenious opponents of the exclusion seems to admit, that the uncalled for communication of a fact of this nature would be improper, for he excludes it expressly from his argument, which he confines to the propriety of obliging the counsel to answer when interrogated in court(a). But if the counsel be bound to secrecy before the trial, why should he be absolved from the obligation on the trial? To admit the obligation out of court, is to acknowledge that it arises from some professional duty ; and if it be a duty, it ought to be enforced at all times and in all places, for it would be a strange provision which imposed secrecy under pain of disgrace, and perhaps the censure of the court, for communicating that at one moment which the next it directed to be proclaimed to the world. For if it be a duty to keep the secrets of a client, it must be a professional duty, and can only be founded on the injury that would arise to him from the breach of his confidence. But the greatest of all injuries would be caused by bearing testimony to the fact he wished to conceal. Therefore, to admit that there exists a professional duty to keep the communications of a client secret before trial, is a fortiori admitting that the same duty requires them to be kept secret at all times when the communication of them would injure

(a) Editor of Bentham's Rationale of Jud. Evid., 5th vol. page 315.

the client. It does not appear to be a fair answer to say, that the client himself might be forced to declare the fact upon oath, and that, therefore, there can be no impropriety in drawing the same declaration from the counsel : for, by the case supposed, and others which might be put, the adverse party had no notice of the defect, and therefore could not have made it the foundation of his suit ; and the client himself being ignorant of the want of form in his title, could not disclose it.

Again, take a criminal case. Money has been stolen, consisting of coins not very common in the place where the fact occurred. The accused has been seen to pass some pieces of the same description; other circumstances cause him to be suspected. He has no proof of the manner in which he acquired the pieces in question. He is innocent ; but he confesses to his counsel, that about the time of the loss he was in the chamber where the theft was committed. The other circumstances would not be sufficient for his conviction ; but this, added to them, would have that effect ; and there is no other proof but his confession to his counsel. Shall he be forced to cause the conviction of the innocent man whom it is his duty to defend? That the testimony of any other, to whom the prisoner may have made the same confession, would have the same effect will scarcely be deemed a good answer, because the case supposes that he has made no such communication ; and because it was necessary to state his whole case to his professional adviser ; but no such necessity existing as to any other, it would have been an act of imprudence to do so, for the consequences of which he could not blame the law. We must suppose, say those who argue against the exclusion, that all laws are good, and, of consequence, that they ought to be executed ; and the truth, by whatever means brought to light, can never injure the innocent , because no good law can ever direct a punishment to be inflicted on any but those who are convicted on true testimony. The disclosure of the truth, therefore, can only injure the guilty, whom it is the object of the law to punish, but the innocent have nothing to fear. But the question does not turn on the justice or injustice of the law, but on the sufficiency of the evidence to show a breach of it. The law, in the criminal case supposed, that forbids theft, is a good law and ought to be executed ; but the effect, upon the minds of a jury, of the circumstantial evidence, adduced to show the guilt of the accused, cannot be regulated by law ; and the true circumstance of the presence of the party at the place where the fact was committed, might lead to a false conclusion that he was the offender, and therefore might, with great propriety, be convicted. So in civil cases, circumstances of common occurrence may be supposed, which, though true in themselves, might probably lead to a false conclusion ; and which therefore could not, without injustice to the client, be disclosed by his advocate. An estate depends upon the question of the sanity of mind of a testator. The law annulling testaments made by persons labouring under insanity is a good law, and ought to be executed ; yet a defendant, holding lands under a testament made by a person of sound mind, may communicate circumstances, such as acts or speeches of the testator, out of the common course, which to a jury, ignorant of his habits, might seem indicative of derangement ; and thus endanger the client's good title. If it be said that in all these and other cases that might be imagined, the reaction of the circumstances would be accompanied by a denial of the main fact which they might render probable, and that as it is a rule that the whole confession must be taken together, the danger would be obviated ; it is answered, that the rule cited is a good one, but that there is a general disposition to believe so much of a confession as make against the party, and to disbelieve the rest ; and that moreover the client in a confidential conversation with his counsel, might not always so connect the parts of his communication which were injurious to his interests with those which supported them, as to render them inseparable, and that if they are not so connected, the rule will not apply.

All the reasoning hitherto has been under the improbable supposition that, if the law were changed, the client would go on to make, and the advocate to receive, the confidential communications in question. But take away the rule of exclusion and what happens ? The client does know, or does not know, that his counsel is obliged to discover all he may communicate to him. If he do not know it, but proceeds to state circumstances that show his guilt, what is the counsellor to do—stop him short by a refusal to hear the story ? But why should he do this ? If the duty of carrying the law into effect obliges him to disclose what he hears, the same duty should induce him to listen to the communication. Remember also the principle is, that no dishonour should be attached to any thing that enforces the execution of the laws, that this is the first duty of a good citizen, and that it must follow, as I have said, that the counsellor is as much bound to listen to the communication as he is to disclose it afterwards. For, I think, it has been sufficiently shown, that, if it be a legal obligation to state the confession when interrogated, there is a moral obligation to discover it before the interrogation; because they both stand on the same foundation—the duty of causing the laws to be executed ; and, indeed, the voluntary revelation, if it be a good act, would be more meritorious than the forced discovery under interrogatories : and the consequence is, that the professional man of high honour, selected by the accused to defend him, or assigned by the court to that honourable office, must listen to the story of his confiding client, must treasure up the circumstances which tend to inculpate him, and then hasten to the public prosecutor with the information he has thus obtained. What man of humanity or honour would accept of such an office ? The laws must be executed—yes! but by such means as are not repugnant to those sentiments of self-respect which every good citizen ought to entertain. To creep into the confidence of even a guilty man, under pretence of being his defender, for the purpose of bringing him to justice, is an act that never can be viewed in a moral or respectable light. A public enemy must be destroyed, but not by poisoned weapons. The means, in both cases, are more injurious than the end is useful.

Take the other, and the more probable, alternative. The law is known to both client and lawyer, and what happens ? There will be nothing communicated, and the advocate will have nothing to declare. Public justice, then, acquires nothing by removing the rule of exclusion. But is there nothing lost on the score of humanity ? Are no advantages taken from the innocent by this fruitless attempt to gain one over the guilty ? The advocate warns the client not to utter any thing that may injure him on the trial. The client replies : " In order to enable you to make my defence, I wish to lay before you the whole transaction in which this suit, or this accusation is founded ; but I am an ignorant man. I do not know whether some of the circumstances I may relate cannot, by the ingenuity of my adversary, be made to bear against me. It will be best, therefore, for me to keep them to myself. I must forego the benefit of your advice, because I cannot, without fear of being entrapped, tell you all you ought to know." Thus the great benefit which is the boast of modern criminal law, allowing counsel to the accused, is in most cases impaired, in many rendered of no avail. In the work to which I have before referred(a) it is acknowledged, that, if the exclusive rule were abrogated, no confessions would be made, and, of course, little or no information would be obtained. But it is further contended, that the exclusion creates a combination between client and lawyer, to protect the former, although guilty, from the penalty of the law ; that the advocate becomes, in effect, the accessary after the fact, by concealing the guilt which had become known to him, and by aiding the culprit to escape ; and thus an act which would be culpable in one, is made the subject of boast in another. There is some force in these observations, so far as they apply to the devices by which solicitors degrade themselves and their honourable profession for the purpose of suppressing or perverting testimony, in order to procure the acquittal of their client, whom they know to be guilty. Whether any remedy can be found for this inconvenience, consistently with the preservation of the rule of exclusion, may, perhaps, be doubtful ; but although the secrecy it requires may sometimes be abused in this manner, yet it is not the necessary consequence of it. An honourable and conscientious advocate may contend for the acquittal of a client whom he may yet,from circumstances disclosed to him in his instructions, believe to be guilty. He may, under the operation of the present rules of evidence, do this from two considerations : first, because he cannot properly make himself the judge of the man whose case he has undertaken to defend, not to decide upon. Secondly, because, while the rule of exclusion lasts, the confession of the accused to his counsel is no evidence, and it is the professional duty of the advocate to see that the accused is condemned by legal evidence only. This supposes no other combination between client and counsel than one which goes to support, not to defeat the law. If the evidence, independent of the confession to counsel, be defective, and the confession be no evidence, surely there is no immorality in urging an acquittal. On the contrary, the immorality and illegality would be in procuring a conviction which was not justified by legal evidence. The repeal of the rule of exclusion, then, is not required from this consideration; and not believing that any positive good would result from its abrogation, it has been retained in the code—but confined strictly to cases of communication for professional aid, either in the conduct of, or preparation for, a suit or defence, or for advice in some *lawful* occasion.

3. The next exclusion of testimony applies to religious confessions, made to a priest of the catholic religion. The reasons for this are obvious. To force the disclosure, if it could be done, would be a tyrannical invasion of the rights of conscience; and the law would be useless if it could be executed; because, in that case, as in the case of counsel and client which has just been examined, no confessions would be made, and there would be nothing to disclose. But, independent of the protection of the religious duties and opinions of a numerous class of our fellow citizens,

(a) Editor of Bentham's Rat. Jud. Proof.

much positive good has resulted from the institution of this religious rite: confession is calculated to produce repentance and reformation; crimes have been prevented, restitutions made, and unjust litigation averted, by its means; and moreover,+the penance imposed by the priest, furnishes the means of inflicting some penalty for offences that, being unknown, would otherwise be unpunished. This rule of exclusion is not acknowledged by the English law(*a*), although it has been enforced by a decision in the state of New York(*b*). In confining this protection to the priests and penitents of a particular sect, I was guided by the belief that, in no other sect was auricular confession made obligatory as a religious duty, and consecrated as one of the solemn rites called sacraments, as it is by that description of Christians. Professors of other religions, and of other sects of the same religion, may seek to disburthen their consciences by confession to a minister or priest, but as secrecy in those cases is not a religious duty in the clergyman, his conscience would not be violated by exacting a disclosure ; and as the confession is not obligatory on the penitent, it must be considered as a voluntary communication; and it would be difficult to draw a distinction between this and any confidential confession to another individual. Whenever a religious sect shall arise, among whose tenets confession is held to be a religious duty, and concealment of the matter in confession an obligation of the most sacred kind, then the same protection ought to be extended to the professors and priests of such sect.

4. Other descriptions of persons, excluded from testifying by the English law, and of course by ours, are those who are deemed infamous. We have seen the numerous classes which this vague description embraces in the Spanish law, which, it is necessary to repeat, is also ours in civil cases, and in those of other criminal causes than those designated in the law of 1805. Nor is the legal import of the term well defined by the English decisions(*c*); so that, if it were proper to exclude the testimony of the infamous, a law would be necessary to designate what persons ought to come under that description. But it is thought that this will be rendered unnecessary, when the propriety of continuing the exclusion comes to be considered.

Let us recur to the position made in the argument against one of the former rules of exclusion, that no man will, without some motive, make a false statement in preference to one that is true; and having seen that, even when that motive exists in the shape of interest, there were so many antagonist motives always at work as to render it more probable that truth would be extracted from an interested witness, than that he should either endeavour to deceive or succeed if he did attempt it. Having come to this conclusion in cases when the motive for falsity exists, why should we hesitate in a case when no such motive appears? One who has been guilty of falsehood, perjury if you will, ninety-nine

(*a*) 2 Starkie, 396. M'Nally, 258. Peake, 77. 2 Atkins, 524.

(*b*) Smith's case. Philip's case.

(*c*) Where a man is convicted of an offence, which is inconsistent with the principles of honesty and humanity, the law considers his oath to be of no weight, and excludes his testimony, &c. 2 Starkie, 713. This is the text on which commentaries have been made by numerous decisions, none of them denying any future judge the right of declaring any other offence to be contrary to the principles of honesty and humanity, and of course, rendering those guilty of it, incompetent witnesses.

2 L

times, will tell truth the hundredth, if he expects no advantage from concealing it or telling a falsehood.   Remember that we are now speaking of infamy alone as a ground of exclusion, not infamy coupled with interest in the shape of a bribe, or any other motive directly operating on the witness.   To justify the exclusion in such a case, we must suppose that because a witness has, for some advantage received or expected, told a falsehood once, he, without any advantage to himself, without any motive, for ever after will persevere in telling falsehoods rather than truths.   Nay, more, we must suppose that after having been detected and punished for the falsehoods which he was induced by the hope of gain to utter, for it is the conviction only which creates the incompetency, he will, without the hope of gain, incur the same risk merely for the love of falsehood.   This is so improbable, that some inducement must be added, to render the perjury probable, and justify, on that ground, the exclusion.   What shall that be ?   An interest in the event ?   But we have seen that this alone is not sufficient cause; nor is the conviction for an infamous crime alone a sufficient cause. If the union of the two produces that effect, then the rule should be, not that an infamous, but that an infamous and interested witness ought not to be heard.   But the rule, even thus modified and restricted, would be a bad one, on account of the effect it would have on the right of third persons, and on the security of the person and property of the party who had been convicted.   The most approved authorities, from which the rule is derived, add, as the reason on which it is founded, "that the law considers the testimony of one so convicted as of too doubtful and suspicious a nature to be admitted in a court of justice *to affect the property or liberty of others*"(a).   This supposes the testimony of the witness always to be intended to take away the property or liberty of another.  But how if its being heard be the only means of preserving property, or liberty, or life itself?   How then ?   Is it of too suspicious a nature to effect these good ends ?   It would rather seem that the reason may, in many cases, be traced to the inconsiderate legislation of early ages, which made the disability to testify a part of the penalty for the offence, intended to affect the offender alone, without considering the extensive operation it might have on the interests of others; for we find the same clause introduced into modern statutes, adding, after other penalties,   "and shall be incapable of testifying in any court of justice." But whatever be its origin, there is no good argument for its continuance.   If there are some occasions on which we may choose our own witnesses, there are many others, and quite as important, on which this is regulated by chance.   If the only and casual witness of a transaction, on which fortune may depend, happens to have been convicted in this, or even in a foreign(b), country of an infamous crime—no matter what time has elapsed, or what the character of the witness may be—he is

---

(a) Starkie, 714, cites Gilb. L. E. 256.   2 Bulst. 154, Br. b. 4, c. 19.  Ib. b. 4, c. 8. Blackstone gives one of those fanciful reasons, too frequently found in his excellent work, in support of the common law rules, that " because the person convicted of an infamous crime could not have served as a juror, he should not be permitted to give evidence to a jury, with 'whom he was too scandalous to associate."

(b) This point has been differently decided in Massachusetts and in Maryland.  In the state first named, the foreign conviction did not disqualify ; in the last, it operates as an exclusion.  17 Mass. 515.  2 Har. & M'H. 120.  Ib. 373.  1 Har. & J. 572.

incompetent. No matter whether his testimony is corroborated by circumstances so as to render it evidently true, or whether it is enforced by being clearly contrary to his interest, nothing can render it fit to be heard; truth itself—evident, uncontradicted, and incontrovertible truth—must not be received from lips that have once been polluted by falsehood, if that falsehood have received the condemnation of law; for, unless sentence have been passed, an hundred falsehoods, proclaimed in the market-place every day of the witness's life, will not disqualify him. But, even in the cases where the witness is selected, there is no security; his previous conviction may be unknown, or a subsequent judgment may incapacitate: and cases are not wanting where testaments, regularly executed in the presence of the requisite number of witnesses, have been set aside(a), and the will of the testator disregarded, because one of those witnesses had, either previously or subsequently, been convicted of a crime, the chief punishment for which has thus fallen on the innocent. Even life itself may fall a sacrifice, the life of the innocent by an ignominious death, to an adherence to this rule, and that by no violent supposition of circumstances. A homicide has been committed which, according to appearances, would be murder, but which facts, known only to the convicted witness, prove to have been a justifiable act; but that witness cannot be heard. Thus fortune, liberty, life itself, are sacrificed to the maintenance of a rule which is absurdly invoked as their support.

5. Thus far the exclusion of the witness has been considered only as it may affect others. But consider the more probable operation it may have on the witness, and through him on the public peace. In the long list of offences against person or property, how many are there to the conviction for which the testimony of the party injured is indispensable? All these may be committed with impunity against a person disqualified by this rule from giving testimony, and thus a short imprisonment, which the law may have affixed as a sufficient punishment for the crime, is changed into an outlawry of the most rigorous kind, by which the party is put completely out of the protection of the law, and subjected to depredation on property, to insults, to personal injury, and, if a female, to the most brutal violence, without the hope of redress.

Here again, as in the case of interest, we find by our present law, exceptions introduced, founded on reasons which apply with equal force to the rule. By statute, in England, a conviction for petit larceny shall not disable the witness ; by the court it has been decided, that the affidavit of a person incapacitated as a witness by conviction for perjury shall be received as evidence, in defence of a charge brought against him ; the judge, Holt, making this natural reflection—" because he has been convicted of perjury, must he, therefore, suffer all injuries and have no way to help himself ?" Yet it never occurred to the learned judge, that this effect which he agreed to give to the convicted defendant's affidavit, for a purpose which concerned himself, and where, of course, the two objections of interest and infamy were combined, ought to be extended to the case where the interest or the life of a third person were in jeopardy, and where the convicted witness had no interest to disguise the truth. Still less did it occur to him that the very words of his decision would permit the convicted person

(a) Mackender v. Mackender, Hill. 23. Geo. II. M'Nally, Ev. 208.

to make a complaint for an injury done to himself, or to support the prosecution by his oath, the only testimony, perhaps, in existence ; for it is only in the case of an affidavit to be used on an incidental question, that the exception is made : a case which, of all others, ought not to have been made an exception ; that of affidavit, made with deliberation, in secret, and attended by no opportunity for cross-examination. Therefore, we have the strongest case in favour of the rule made an exception to it ; and the rule itself applied to those only where there is the least danger from the admission of the testimony.

Another, and no less incongruous, exception is, that made in favour of the accomplice, who is every day admitted to testify against the principal. Here we have interest of the highest kind—the hope, often the assurance, of pardon—joined to the acknowledged infamy of a participation in the crime ; and yet the witness is heard. For what reason, if the generale rule of exclusion be a good one, should the exception be made ? Necessity ? What necessity ? The necessity of convicting the accused by false testimony ; for it is on the supposition that it will be false that you exclude it in other cases. If the evidence be too suspicious to be heard to preserve fortune, liberty, or life, can it be pretended that there is a necessity for using it for depriving one of these blessings ?

. The uncertainty of the rule has been hinted at, as one of the reasons for abolishing it. To what offences shall it apply ? Particular circumstances, enumerated in different books, all agree that felony is one of them. This comprehensive and ill-defined term embraces so many acts, each employing a different degree of depravity, from treason down to. petit larceny, that it cannot well be conceived that all suppose the want of veracity in those who are guilty of them, more especially of a general disposition to utter falsehood or conceal the truth, without any special motive. To preserve the rule, therefore, with any appearance of consistency, it must be modified : a line must be drawn between such offences as suppose a particular proneness to falsehood, and those which evince only other species of depravity. To have taken the losing side in a political struggle and have incurred the crime of treason, certainly does not create a presumption of the disposition to perjury; and perjury without motive, for the purpose of depriving an innocent stranger of his fortune or his life, or for the destruction of his reputation. We must distinguish : and when we come to analyse the different offences, in order to discover in which of them lies this latent disposition to mendacity, we shall find it in none, and we shall come to the conclusion at which I have arrived—that the exclusion, in this case also, ought to be abolished.

6. One more ground of exclusion remains to be discussed: that arising from religious opinion. The doctrine on this subject, after having gone through several changes, is settled as far as any thing depending on judicial decisions can be settled into this rule, that a disbelief in a future state of rewards and punishments is the only cause of religious exclusion. It is certain that this state of the mind destroys one of the sanctions for the efficacy of the oath ; but that it is compensated by the additional weight which may reasonably be supposed to be given to one of the others, the moral, honorary, or penal sanction just as the privation of one sense adds accuracy and sensibility to the others. The man who is so unfortunate as not to believe in a future state, will be con-

THE CODE OF EVIDENCE.

scious of the disadvantage attending this disbelief upon his reputation, and will endeavour, by a more scrupulous attention to his conduct and conversation, to show that his want of faith does not derogate from his respectability. But, without having recourse to this supposition, of an increased force in the other sanctions from the suppression of one, ought we to believe that the man who doubts whether he will be punished in a future state for false testimony given in this, will, therefore, feel himself bound by no obligation to tell the truth ; or, to state the position more truly, will, on that account, be more inclined to falsehood than to truth ? May he not dread the reproaches of his conscience in this life ? May not a moral sense show him the utility and beauty of truth ? May not a sense of honour make him disdain the idea of falsehood ? May not the fear of infamy or of punishment deter him ? No, say the inexorable exclusionists; we must have every security for the truth of the testimony, or we dare not trust ourselves with hearing it ; or rather, we must have this and we will dispense with all the other. A man of profligate character, who laughs at all moral duties ; a dishonoured and notorious liar, who has no regard for reputation ; a witness who resides out of the reach of the tribunals which might bring him to punishment for his perjury, and therefore has no fears for the consequences; all these may be heard ; but the man of honour, of integrity, and the most fearful of the temporal consequences of an aberration from truth, cannot be heard if he cannot believe in the immortality of the soul—a most unfortunate state of mind, but certainly not one that supposes a want of veracity. Belief in a future state must arise either from reasoning on probabilities, or from a conviction of the truth of revealed religion. Some minds may be so framed as not to yield to the evidence which most of us think sufficient on these points ; but surely an inability to draw a just conclusion from abstract propositions, does not imply such a degradation of moral principle as would render it more probable that, without motive, he would prefer falsehood to truth. The religious sanction is the only one which, by this reasoning, will secure the truth. But yet, you will believe a quaker, who rejects even the form of the oath ; yet you will in a thousand instances, as in customhouse declarations, put no faith in the oath, which is unaccompanied by the other sanctions, and because little dishonour is attached to their breach, and punishment rarely follows their violation. If the truth could be demonstrated, it would appear that the fear of the consequences in a future state is not half so operative, taken by itself, as the fear of dishonour and punishment here. Therefore, in itself, this disbelief does not destroy the credibility of the witness. On the contrary, from the mode in which alone it can be proved, it must add to his credit. To avow this disbelief requires some courage. The atheist is a character not favoured in society. A repugnance to utter a falsehood, for the most part, would be the motive for making the avowal ; yet, the moment he has given this evidence of his regard to truth, he is declared unworthy of belief. If, being an unbeliever, he answers falsely that he believes, he is a good witness. If he answers truly on this point, the presumption is, that he will answer untruly to every other question that may be put to him ; for, remember, that whatever proof you may have to convict him of disbelief, it must all end in that to be derived from his own examination. What he may have said or written yesterday is no proof of his belief to-day. It is the actual state of

mind at the time of examination that must be inquired into, and if
be believes then, he is a good witness ; and this state of mind can only
be known from himself.

In itself, then, the exclusion is absurd.   In its consequences it is
more dangerous than any we have reviewed.   Not only is the unbeliever, in common with the witness convicted of crime, put out of the
protection of the law, as to all injuries to his person or property that
require his own evidence to punish or repress ; not only in this case,.
as in that, is the party entitled to his evidence deprived of it, when it
may be necessary for the protection of his property or his life ; but in
this case every kind of outrage may be committed, not only upon the
person who wants the necessary faith, but in the presence of others of
the same description.   There is no more risk than if it were committed before so many statues.   All those who, knowing the offender's
guilt, might wish to avoid giving testimony against him, but are unwilling to expose themselves to the punishment of perjurers by false testimony, have the ready means of avoiding the examination—an avowal
of unbelief is all that is necessary.   If it be false, there can be no
detection or punishment, for as it is a matter of belief only, no one can
contradict this assertion.

There is another view in which the inquiry into religious belief,
which must precede the exclusion, appears highly reprehensible.   All
kinds of religion are by our laws and constitution put on a perfect
equality.   He who believes, he who doubts, and he who disbelieves,
have the same civil rights.   Every speculation, as to the existence or
non-existence of a future state, of the probability or duration of rewards
or punishments we may expect there, all the infinite modifications from
mere conjecture to perfect faith, are all so many species of religious
tenets.   No one sect has a right to say to another, mine is the true doctrine, and therefore I am entitled to temporal advantages of which you
ought to be deprived.   But the right of appearing as a witness against
one who has committed a crime affecting the party, is a civil and temporal right ; to deprive him of it, for a want of uniformity of faith in
any one point with the rest of the community, is to deprive him of it
for a difference in religious belief, which is contrary to the constitution
and laws.

For these reasons, all exclusions of particular persons, as witnesses,
are abolished by the code, except in the instance of persons insane, and
the analogous one of infants whose minds are not sufficiently developed
to give information on the subject inquired of.   But in these cases
modifications of the present law are introduced, which require the
attention of the general assembly.

As the law now stands, the court decides on the fact which is to
cause the exclusion of the witness ; and, although the jury may be quite
convinced of the sanity, or maturity of judgment of the witness, he
cannot be heard, if the court believes him either to have lost, or not
yet to have acquired, the intellectual powers necessary to distinguish
and relate the truth.   By this code the determination of these questions
is vested in those who are to determine the principal question ; they
are to examine the persons said to be insane, and, if they think it necessary, other witnesses.   They are also to examine the infant, and to
determine, not by the usual inquiry, whether he understands the nature

of an oath, but, by questions which may satisfy them "whether his faculties are sufficiently developed to receive correct impressions *of the fact relative to which he is interrogated*, to relate those impressions *correctly*, and to feel the obligation of doing it *truly.*" These are the only cases of total exclusion. Those who, under certain circumstances, cannot testify, are slaves, in cases affecting free persons; counsellors and attorneys, in the cases before mentioned; priests of the Catholic religion, in cases of religious confession; and parties to the suit, under the modifications contained in the code, and hereinbefore fully explained.

The constitution also creates another partial exclusion, or rather privilege, which a witness has of refusing to give his testimony, whenever the answer to a question put to him will make him liable to prosecution for a crime. It is true, that the words of the constitution only extend this privilege to *criminal prosecutions* and to the *accused;* but the incongruity of forcing a witness to do that which the accused was protected against, seemed to call for the provision contained in the code, which, however, modifies the rule, as now understood, so as to restrict the objection to such answers only as would furnish evidence against the witness on a prosecution for a CRIME.

To appreciate properly the reduction of the exclusionary rules to this narrow compass, we must not only consider the advantages it will have in the investigation of truth on the trial, which, it is hoped, have been sufficiently demonstrated; but we must also consider the effect it will have in simplifying the law, rendering a recourse to it less expensive, giving it certainty and stability, and diminishing the number of suits. That these consequences must necessarily follow, will be apparent to the most hasty observer. Whoever has opened one of the English treatises on evidence; whoever has looked over the index to a volume of reports, or into any of the abridgements, and examined its contents on that subject, will have seen how large a proportion is occupied with cases in which the competency of witnesses is discussed; not only for causes which would disqualify generally, but for those which make them incompetent to particular points, or in particular suits. Most of the arguments depending on nice, and often fanciful, distinctions, and the decisions doubted, or confirmed, or overruled, according to the judgment or caprices of a succeeding judge; and sometimes, we may venture to say, according to his respect for, or jealousy of, his predecessor(a). But when the rule is abolished, all the exceptions go with it, and the simplicity, which we have claimed for the new system, is apparent. Its certainty and stability are derived from the same source. When the law is simple and precise, the courts can make no exceptions, as they did when they themselves legislated on the subject; and from those exceptions arose all the uncertainty and instability of the law of evidence. I need scarcely add a word to prove another of the characteristics I have ascribed to this change in the law; that a recourse to it would be had with less expense; for a few short articles, and a single page, contain all that must now be sought (and frequently without any certainty of success) in many volumes, and numerous decisions: its probable effect, in diminishing the number of suits, has been already, and it is hoped successfuly, discussed.

(a) See, in the English Reports, the numerous cases before lords Kenyon and Mansfield.

Having determined the few cases in which persons are actually or partially excluded from appearing as witnesses, the code next regulates the manner in which they are to be examined; and here the entrance into a boundless field of debateable ground is prevented by a provision, that, with the exceptions contained in the articles that have already been examined, and the single additional one in relation to leading questions, every interrogatory, pertinent to the issue, may be put, and must be answered. No more debates as to what is proper evidence in one cause and what in another. The simple inquiry is, will the answer to the question elucidate the fact in dispute ? No rules are given on this point, because none can be framed that would direct the judge through the infinite variety of circumstances in which they must be applied. Whether the question proposed, therefore, is pertinent to the issue or not, is of necessity left in every case to the discretion of the judge.

Leading questions, or those which suggest facts to the witness, are forbidden; but what shall be deemed such is again, of necessity, left to the decision of the court, but with a general direction not to prevent suggestions necessary to recall facts to the memory of the witness when the transaction is remote—when from its nature, it was not likely to have made a strong impression on the mind of the witness ; or when, from age, indisposition, timidity, or other cause, his mind is weakened or disturbed.

The witness is also permitted to refresh his memory by written notes made by himself, or another by his direction; and in all cases, when his testimony relates to accounts or calculations, he is permitted to refer to the papers or books containing them.

He is put under the protection of the court, to guard against harsh language, or what is called browbeating; and provision is made for giving him time for reflection when necessary, and for rectifying errors in his testimony.

He who alledges a fact judicially, must, if it be litigated, prove it ; but if, in the same manner confessed, no proof need be adduced. If neither confessed nor denied judicially, it must be proved ; the oath of the party alleging, in this case, forming presumptive proof.

The rule requiring that the best evidence of the fact alleged shall, in all cases, be produced, is modified and restricted to the following cases :

1. When a positive law has declared, that to give validity to any species of contract, it shall be made in writing, then no other proof shall be admitted; unless it be proved, that the writing was made, but has been casually lost or destroyed, or, without the fault of the party, placed without his reach.

2. When scriptory evidence of the fact has been made, and was in the possession of the party; unless it has been lost or placed out of his reach, in the manner above stated.

3. When positive law has declared certain evidence necessary for the proof of the facts designated in the law.

4. When the fact which is alleged, if true, must have appeared by an authentic act.

In all other cases where evidence shall be produced, which the judge or jury shall deem inferior to other evidence which is not produced, it shall, if legal evidence be heard, and the nonproduction of the other shall operate as presumptive evidence, to have the weight it may deserve according to the circumstances of the case, against the party failing to produce it.

These provisions were deemed necessary to avoid much useless and perplexed investigation, as to the relative authority of evidence, which frequently causes great injustice in the exclusion of testimony, and always much perplexity in the argument. The first of them was drawn with the view to prevent the liberties that are taken by courts with the legislative will, as expressed in such laws as are known by the name of the Statute of Frauds in England, and the analogous provisions in the civil and other codes of law : sometimes enforcing the written law according to its terms; at others, creating exceptions, which weaken, if they do not destroy, its efficacy. Whether the Civil Code itself ought not to contain some exceptions to the strictness of this rule ; and whether, while it declares, in general terms, that the omission of formalities shall vacate the act, it should not still provide for the cases where it was not in the power of the party to comply with them—are questions worth considering when the revision of that code shall again come before the legislature. In the mean time, its will, clearly expressed, must be obeyed. It is better that individuals should suffer from the operation of a law, acknowledged to be bad, than that the remedy should be applied by unconstitutional means. The one is a partial, the other a general and fundamental evil.

The second modification of the rule provides for cases in which the parties have made evidence of their intentions, and reduced the same to writing; in which case testimonial evidence cannot be produced, without proving the loss of the writing. In this the present law is not changed.

The two other cases need no explanation.

Another rule of evidence productive of much uncertainty of decision, is that which declares, " that parol evidence shall not be admitted against or beyond what is contained in a written act, nor of what may have been said before or at the time of making it." To this, important qualifications are added by the system now proposed. It is confined in its operation exclusively to writings containing obligations or donations, and to testamentary dispositions. These, it is supposed, will comprehend all the cases in which the parties may be supposed to have expressed all they intended on the subject matter on which they wrote. Error, fraud, violence, threats, or any other circumstance that, by the provisions of the Civil Code, would avoid or modify a written contract, evidently ought to be proved by extraneous evidence. Although no party, except in the designated cases, shall be permitted to qualify by testimonial evidence that which he has deliberately committed to writing, yet, as his will constituted the obligation of which the writing is only the evidence, the opposite party may resort to that higher evidence of will, which resides in the mind of the other, by calling on him to declare, on oath, what was his true meaning. Circumstances are pointed out which are necessary to be considered, whenever for the purpose of defeating a contract, an allegation is made of error, fraud, violence, or threats ; but the effect they are to have is left to the discretion of the judges of the fact.

The sanction of an oath, or an equivalent affirmation, is required for

2 M

the reception of testimonial evidence, from which it follows, that one witness, who is himself under that sanction, ought not to state what another had said who was under no such obligation to tell the truth, and whose veracity cannot be tested by cross-examination, or the other means of discovering it.   But there are necessary exceptions to this rule, and the code has not left them to be ascertained by judicial legislation.   They are the following.

A witness may declare what the party to the suit, his agents, or other persons, who could have bound him by their contracts, or those, under whom such party claims, have said, when such proof is required by the opposite party.   What has been said relative to the matter in dispute in the presence and hearing of one party to the suit, may be given in evidence by the other, as a foundation for a presumption to be drawn from what he said, or did, or from his silence.   What a witness has said when he was not under oath may be proved, to show that it was consistent or inconsistent with his testimony.   If a witness has been examined on a former trial between the same parties, for the same cause, what he has said may be related by another, if such witness be dead, or his testimony cannot be procured.   In cases of homicide, what the deceased has said, after receiving the wound, in relation thereto, may be given in evidence, if his deposition could not, from circumstances, have been taken. When the declarations of a party, or a witness, under the first or second of the exceptions before mentioned, are given in .evidence, any thing said by another person, which is necessary to contradict or explain what was said by such party or witness, may be given in evidence.   As proof of the hand-writing of a witness, who is dead or absent, may, in certain cases, be admitted as a presumption that he would not have signed if he could not prove the execution ; so. any material declaration of such witness, to rebut this presumption, may be related. In cases not depending on scriptory evidence, a party is permitted by the code to give evidence of what he himself said or did at the time of the transaction, in relation to the matter in litigation, in order to explain his intentions; but in this, as in other cases, he may be examined on the trial by the adverse party.   There is a species of evidence that is only acquired by information from others ; it is that usually called a fact of public notoriety—such as pedigree, and other facts of the same nature. These are enumerated in the code, and the proof of them allowed.

A short section declares, that the rules for receiving the oral declarations of a witness, apply to their examination on interrogatories ; and direct, that, whenever the deposition of a witness is taken in writing, the question as well as the answer shall be written, and the answer recorded as given.

This finishes all the provisions of the code in relation to testimonial evidence.

The next head is that of scriptory evidence, which includes all kinds of written proof, except the examination of witnesses when their evidence is reduced to writing ; the term SCRIPTORY having been used to designate this division, because that of *written evidence* would have comprehended testimonial evidence, when reduced to writing, as under our code of practice it always may be.

To argue the advantages of this species of evidence, to speak of its certainty and durability, would be a useless task, when addressing the legislature of a state in which those advantages have been so wisely secured by laws directing its employment in so many instances, and under such a variety of sanctions as in this. Of writings, which may become matter of evidence, some purport to express the will of those by whom they are made ; others are only declarations of facts. Of the first kind are those which are called the *acts* of the parties whose will they purport to declare. Of the second, are the attestations of public officers, declaratory that certain of the acts were really made by those parties ; and also, the written depositions of witnesses. With the last, the depositions, we have nothing, as has been said, to do in this division. The mode of taking them, and their effect, and the persons by whom they may be made, are pointed out in the Code of Procedure, and in the former part of this report. The other kinds of scriptory evidence, properly so called, are divided by the code into two kinds, authenticated and unauthenticated.

I. Authenticated acts are defined to be "such instruments in writing as are attested by a public officer, legally authorized for that purpose in the form prescribed by law." It will readily be seen that the evidence here is of two kinds. The expression of the will of the party, as contained in the act, and the declaration of the attesting officer, that such writing does contain the will of the party, and to avoid any misunderstanding of the effect of such evidence, the code provides, that it shall be proof only of that which is specially attested by the officer to have been done in his presence, and nothing more, and exemplifies its intent by some of the most common cases in which this species of evidence is produced. A bill attested by the signatures of the president of the senate, of the speaker of the house of representatives, and of the governor, is an authentic act; but the signatures prove only that the bill, to which they are affixed, has been passed by the two houses respectively, and has been approved by the governor. The signature of the governor to a proclamation, under his seal of office, offering a reward for apprehending a person accused of murder, is authentic evidence that such proclamation was issued on the day it bears date, that complaints were made to him of the commission of the offence, the flight of the defendant, or any other fact which he certifies to have been done in his presence; but it is not evidence that the crime was actually committed, or that the party fled.

The code divides authentic acts into four kinds : legislative acts ; records of courts ; records of the different executive governments, made in the legal administration of its different departments, which are declared to be authentic acts ; and written instruments, made in the presence of, and attested by, such public officer as is for that purpose commissioned according to law, and purporting to testify what is said, done, or contracted by those whose acts they are.

1. A section directs the manner in which legislative acts are to be proved. In this the present law is not changed, as now the production of the original of an attested copy, or of the statutes printed by the state printer, are considered good evidence. The provision that an error in either of the kinds of copy may be alleged and proved by collating them with the original, is also, I apprehend, the law at this time ; but it was thought advisable to insert it in terms. The mode of proof of public and of private acts, is declared to be the same. The court is

directed, ex officio, to take notice of public acts, and to carry them into effect, whether pleaded or not; but the party relying on a private act for the support of a right, or the privilege of an exemption, must allege and prove it.

Private legislative acts are those which concern designated individuals only. All others are public acts. All acts of incorporation, made for regulating the police or local government of any part of the state; for the establishment of the banks; for authorizing the imposition of a toll, of tonnage, wharfage, or other duty; for the establishment of hospitals, or other purposes of charity, or the promotion of religion, education, or science, are specially declared to be public, and all other incorporations to be private acts. But it is provided, that this enumeration is intended solely for the purposes of this title in the code, and does not affect the nature or definition of corporations established by law.

2. Judicial records are, in a section under that title, defined, and the mode of authenticating them in the several cases of their being those of a court in this state, in another state, or in a foreign country. A new provision is introduced to guard against surprise and fraud. It directs that whenever the certified copy of a foreign judgment is intended to be produced as evidence, it must be filed a specified time before the trial, and notice given to the opposite party; and if he shall object to the introduction of such copy, the party introducing it must have it collated with the original and proved, either by a witness or on commission; and that if the copy filed shall be thus proved to have been a true one, the additional expense shall be borne by the objecting party. The effect of judgments, in other states of the union, or in foreign countries, as evidence, is declared to be the same as is directed in the code, in the chapter on Resjudicata, in relation to judgments in this state. But it is specially provided, that no judgment rendered in a suit, commenced by a proceeding in rem, whether by attachment or otherwise, shall have any effect of the resjudicata, except so far as respects the thing seized, unless the party have appeared either in person or by attorney and defended the suit.

To avoid the enormous expenses attending the introduction of proceedings in admiralty, when necessary as evidence, it is provided, that whenever the object is to prove a condemnation in a foreign court of admiralty, no other part of the record but the libel and condemnation need be produced for that purpose; and that no evidence taken in such cause shall be evidence between the same parties of any other fact than that in contestation in such cause.

3. The next section provides for what is thought to be a desideratum in our present law. It gives an enumeration of the acts of the executive government which are to have the force of authentic evidence, and the mode of their authentication. This needs no elucidation. A reference to the section itself is all that is necessary, both for its purport and for the reasons of the different provisions it contains. It may be proper, however, to remark, that while special laws provided for giving the force of authentic acts to the records of courts and notarial proceedings, the equally important documents of an executive nature were left for their authenticity to the discretion of the courts; which admitted or rejected them, and gave what degree of force to them that their judgment directed,

without any fixed rules, which, for the first time, are established by the proposed code.

4. Notarial acts, and the various provisions necessary to establish their validity, provide against their abuse, designate their effects, and point out the cases in which they may be declared void, are necessarily a most important subject in the Code of Evidence. Forming, as they do by our law, the principal means by which sales, contracts, donations, testaments and declaratory dispositions, in all their various forms, are to be witnessed; every provision in relation to them ought to be generally and minutely known; and for that purpose should be clearly and particularly expressed. This it has been the endeavour of the reporter to do in the three subsequent sections of this chapter.

The first of them describes the nature and prescribes the requisites of a notarial act, in which there is little to claim particular attention, as the provisions are chiefly those contained in different laws and decisions on the same subject, collected in one view, and enforced by precise enactment, which a reference to the section will fully explain without comment.

The same observation, in substance, may be made on the subject of the next section, which treats of the effect of notarial acts, in relation to those who are parties to them; and in the few cases in which they may bear upon the rights of others, the laws and decisions on the subject are embodied and reduced to short, and, it is hoped, clear precepts, which are illustrated by examples, and some new provisions are introduced which require no explanation.

" For what causes and in what manner notarial acts may be declared not authentic," is the title of the last section relating to this matter. The silence of our present law on this important topic, required the greatest care in the reduction(a) of this part of the code, and imposes the necessity of some elucidations.

The distinguishing characteristic of a notarial act, that it is authentic evidence, in other words, that it is conclusive evidence, against those who are parties to it, rendered it necessary that many formalities should be required in passing it to secure the parties, as well as the public, from imposition. These are minutely directed in a section which has already been referred to. No officer at all attentive to his duty, no party not entirely negligent of his interest, can mistake them. When they are not attended to, a presumption will naturally arise that they have been omitted for some sinister end, and the natural corrective would be punishment. This, as regards the officer, has been provided for by the Code of Crimes and Punishments, in the shape of a personal penalty. As respects the parties, the remedy is not so clear. To inflict a punishment on both would be clearly unjust, for one must be the party injured. To inflict it on either would, in many cases, have the same character. The party really consenting to the omission, may be the one injured by the neglect; while the other, naturally careless of what it was the peculiar interest of the one with whom he contracted to observe, would overlook the

(a) This word is not English, but I have ventured to employ it, from the absolute want of one to express the act of preparing for publication a work, neither entirely compiled from pre-existing materials, nor entirely of original composition, but like the code I now present. If there be an equivalent term in the English language, it does not occur to me.

omission of formalities, by the neglect of which he could only gain. To illustrate my meaning by an example. A sale is made before a notary, who does not call on the witnesses required by law to sign the act. The notary is justly punishable for a neglect of official duty; but a personal penalty on either the purchaser or seller, would be unjust: on the purchaser, because he is the loser by his defect of title; on the seller, because, having received his consideration, he would leave the examination of the conveyance to the purchaser, contenting himself with the perusal of the act, to see that he conveyed what he had a right to convey. As to the parties themselves, some other provision was necessary to excite their attention to the observance of forms, rendered necessary by the general policy of the law. The means for enforcing the provisions of the law, which first present themselves, are those which operate on the act itself. The contract depends on the consent alone of the parties; the means of enforcing it on the legislative will. To this there is no injustice in annexing conditions. "I will provide," says the lawgiver, " an officer who shall draw your contracts, who shall give them legal forms and put you on your guard against imposition, who shall record and preserve them, who shall furnish you with copies when you want them, which copies shall have all the force of originals; but it is on condition that the plain rules which I prescribe, to guard against fraud, error and confusion, shall be strictly observed. It is your interest as well as your duty, if your intentions are correct, to observe these rules on your parts, and to see that they are observed by those with whom you deal. If you do not, the condition is broken, and you lose the advantages you would have had by observing them. I will punish my officer when he wilfully or negligently omits to perform his duty ; but unless there is evidence of fraud against you, the only penalty you incur is the loss of that character to your contract which the observance of the rules would have attached to it. Prove your contract in any other way, if it be a legal one, my laws do not affect them. I will even allow you to consider the assent given to it by your signatures as binding ; but it cannot be enforced as an authentic act." Such language seems to be appropriate to the occasion in the mouth of a just legislator, and its substance is contained in this part of the code. A notarial act, wanting any of the enumerated formalities, may be used as an instrument under private signature, if it have those of the parties; but it is not authentic.

The omission of a necessary formality, which ought to appear on the face of the instrument, is one of those facts which the judge is empowered to ascertain by his own inspection, without other evidence. Other omissions, or defects, which would destroy the authenticity of the instrument, may be proved by other evidence, the nature of which is designated in the code.

The cases in which notarial acts may be declared not authentic, for causes not apparent on the face of the instrument, are specially enumerated. For any of which, or for any such defect appearing on the face of the instrument, as is by this section declared to destroy its force as an authentic act, it is provided, that a suit may be brought by any one interested, in which suit the objection to the act must be particularly set forth, or the party may rely on such objection as a bar to any suit commenced upon it ; but in every such case, as well as where the suit is brought to have the act destroyed, the petition or answer, and the causes for considering it defective, specially stated. Provision is also made for the production of the instrument and giving notice of the objections to it, when it is used for some collateral point in a cause, and is not the foundation either of the suit or of the defence.

Another article specifies the cases in which authentic acts, not notarial, may be declared invalid. This, with the provision that the sentence of a court, declaring any act to be invalid shall be noted in the margin, both of the copy produced and of the original, concludes what is contained in the proposed code on this subject; but I cannot dismiss the notice of it, in this report, without felicitating the legislature on our finding already established, a system so admirably adapted to its purpose as that of transfers by notarial acts. With the firmest conviction of its advantages over every other intended for the same ends, it would have been difficult, if not impossible, without the experience we have had, to have forced the same conviction on the people : and the maintenance of the defective system of registration, which prevails in all the other states with more or less of inconvenience attached to each, is a convincing proof of the difficulties we should have had to encounter if we had been under the necessity of removing the one of these plans to make way for the other.

II. We come now to consider scriptory evidence, of less authority than that which is declared to be authentic. This inferior evidence is of two kinds; that which is attested by the signature of the party whose act it purports to be, and is called an act under private signature; and all other written evidence not so attested.

1. The difference between authentic acts and those now under consideration, with the reason for their different weight in the scale of evidence, is explained in the code. No writing, it is said, is in itself evidence of the truth of that which it contains : it shows that certain covenants are written, and that certain names have been subscribed to them; but it contains no proof that those names were subscribed, or that those covenants were agreed to, by the parties. To give them any validity, there must be some extrinsic evidence. This evidence, in authentic acts, is supplied by the credit which the law attaches to the certificate of the public officer, and to the seal of his office, which the courts are bound, ex-officio, to be acquainted with. But to acts under private signature no such credit is given. The production of them does not even raise a simple presumption of their validity. Proof of their execution is required. This proof, in ordinary cases, is either the testimony of a subscribing witness, or of one who knows the handwriting of the party. The code has introduced another and more simple mode of proof, to be used at the discretion of the party. It directs that whenever a suit is brought on an instrument made under private signature, the original shall be annexed to the petition for the inspection of the party who shall be summoned to acknowledge or deny the signature. If it purport to be his own, he must answer directly to the question, under the penalty of having an evasive answer construed as a confession. If the signature do not purport to be his own, but that of some one whose engagement would bind him, and he is acquainted with the handwriting, he must answer whether he knows or believes the signature to be genuine. If he is not acquainted with the handwriting,

he must say so.   If acknowledged, the instrument then becomes an authentic act.   But evidence may be received of any fact which would show that, from any cause, it ought not to be enforced.   If not acknowledged, proof must be made as in ordinary cases.   These different effects are particularly set forth in the code, as well as the circumstances under which recourse may be had to proof by comparison of hands, and the mode in which such evidence is to be received.

The perfection with which the handwriting may be imitated has led to a provision that a comparison of hands alone, unsupported by other circumstances, shall not of itself be sufficient evidence, where the handwriting is denied.   The provisions of this chapter are but a development of the one which has been already sufficiently commented upon, that which requires the oath of the party in support of his defence. Few men would have the hardihood to deny their own signatures, even without oath, if it were not for the pernicious practice of throwing the defence of a suit upon the attorney, who, in the name of his client, every day, without any blame attaching either to his client or himself, asserts what they both know to be false, by denying a signature which, in a few weeks, is proved or confessed to be true.   According to the plan proposed, the party must speak for himself; the instrument is offered for his inspection, and he must, first by his answer, and afterwards, if required, openly, in the presence of his fellow-citizens and the magistracy of his country, on his own responsibility, make his declaration of the truth.   Thus, independently of the gain, on the score of public justice, the members of an honourable profession are no longer made the instruments of falsehood ; and, if any is asserted, the risk, the shame and the odium, is incurred and borne by those to whom it properly belongs.

Another and a very full chapter relates to copies of written instruments as evidence.

It is enacted that attested copies of authentic acts are exceptions to the rule, that transcripts are not to be received when the original can be procured.   In favour of copies of other acts no such exception exists.   The different kinds of copies invested with different degrees of authenticity, are pointed out, and a mode is provided for giving a certain degree of authenticity to acts under private signature, which is new and requires particular attention.

Whenever the holder of an act, under private signature, fears the loss of the instrument, or of the evidence by which he expects to substantiate it, he may, at his own expense, present a petition to a court of competent jurisdiction, praying that the party who has signed the instrument may be summoned to appear at the office of some designated notary, to witness the registry of the act.

If the party summoned answer that he denies the signature, its authenticity is tried as in common cases, and if found for the plaintiff, the registry of the act shall be decreed with costs.   If he confesses the signature, or do not answer, the notary, on seeing a certified copy of the record, shall proceed to register the act by making a full copy on his records.   Copies, thus authenticated, are full proof of the signature, but do not entitle the party to prompt execution, as is the case with authentic acts.   They are called *copies in form*, but cannot be produced without proof that the original is lost or destroyed.   On proof of loss only, security is required against the appearance of the instrument in the hands of a bona fide holder, after public notice. When destruction is proved, no such security is required.

Acts under private signature may also be authenticated and registered by the consent of the parties, testified by their signatures in the presence of the notary, so as to produce the effect of copies in form.

Even without any judicial order, and without the consent of the party signing an act under private signature, it may be transcribed in his register by the notary at the request of the holder. This is called an informal copy, and can serve only the following purposes: to become the foundation for a prescriptive right from the time of the registry; when the original is produced, but the time of its execution is in dispute, to verify that execution up to the time of its registry; after ten years' uninterrupted enjoyment under it, it has the force of an authentic act; and, connected with other circumstances, it forms presumptive proof of the execution of the original and of its contents.

The originals of acts under private signature may also be placed in deposit on the records of the notary, preceded by the declaration of the depositor, signed by the parties making the same, and attested by the notary. Attested copies of such act are authentic evidence against all who have signed the same.

A concluding section of this chapter directs the mode in which acts under private signature should be signed and attested; declares that they may be made the evidence of all kinds of obligations or declarations, except those that are specially by law declared to be made by authentic acts; and contains provisions to guard against fraud and imposition upon the illiterate.

2. Writings, even not signed by the parties, may furnish evidence of the presumptive kind. This species of evidence is of two descriptions. Those which appear to have been prepared for signature, but, not having received it, are imperfect; such as wills, contracts, declarations of trust, &c., and to those which from their nature were not intended to be signed; of this kind are entries in books, family records of births, &c.

Writings of the first kind are never admitted as direct proof of the disposition of which they would have been the evidence, had they been perfected. They may be presumptive evidence—first, of the intent to make the contract or disposition, when such intent is material to the issue; and secondly, of the truth of any enunciation in the writing, or of the knowledge which the party had of such fact. But in no case can such writing be admitted at all, unless it be in the hand-writing of the party against whom it is offered, or proved to have been made by his direction, or approved by him after it was made.

Writings of the second kind, when made by the party, by his direction, or approved by him, may also be admitted as presumptive proof of that which they enounce. But in both cases, the party may be admitted to state, on oath, the circumstances under which such writings were made, and to explain their intent.

All the kinds of scriptory evidence we have been considering, are such as were made by the parties against whom they are offered, or by their direction. Of another description are those writings, including printed papers and engravings, which are made by others. These are:

2 N

Historical works to elucidate any public fact that may become material in a litigated case.

Books of art or science—when any thing appertaining to the branch of learning of which they treat is in dispute.

Maps or plans, to elucidate questions of locality; but these are subject to restrictions contained in the code.

Accounts stated, or calculations made by persons who prove them to be correct.

Nautical or other almanacs, whenever material to the issue.

This finishes a review of the important title of Scriptory Evidence: a source from which the most contradictory effects have flowed. If on the one hand it gives the means of precision and permanence to engagements, those very qualities make it, in many instances, the instrument of fraud and imposition upon ignorance. Its quality of precision makes verbal explanation in most cases dangerous, and the rectification of error inconsistent with rules which it would be improper, in general, to violate; and its permanence makes it outlast the evidence, which might serve to show the causes why it ought to be declared invalid even in the few cases where such evidence would have been permitted. Its superior rank in the scale of evidence, too, makes it a stronger temptation to fraud, in the shape of forgery. These and other disadvantages should be considered, and, as far as possible, counteracted by legislation. No means of effecting this desirable end appear to promise such good results as a wise system of registration; and of all those systems, none appear equal to that which is in force in this state. The provisions contained in the proposed code have been framed for the purpose of bringing it nearer to that perfection to which, by adopting the plan for gradual improvement pointed out in the beginning of this report, it is devoutly hoped it may answer.

In no other state is any provision made to counteract a fraud, which has been practised, and will be practised, in spite of all general laws against that offence. This is the process: a deed is forged, or fraudulently altered; it is proved by a perjured, mistaken, or ignorant witness, before a magistrate—in some states, even before a magistrate residing under another jurisdiction, and therefore not amenable to its laws; this magistrate allows it to be recorded; it is transcribed on the record, and returned to the party, and by him destroyed. The copy from the record is then evidence; and the means of detection, by showing the signatures to be forged from a comparison of hands and other circumstances, is lost. In our system, which ought to be examined, and deserves to be imitated by the other states, no such frauds can be committed. Publicity is secured in all cases in which the general welfare requires it; secrecy provided for, when the public interest will not suffer; permanence and security given to the originals of all important papers; and imposition upon the ignorant and illiterate prevented by the scrutinizing supervision of a public and responsible officer.

A short title of one chapter contains all that seemed necessary relating to substantive evidence.

When we reflect that from the very definition of this kind of evidence it must always be supported by testimony, to show the connexion of the object produced with the circumstances of the case; it will be evident, that it must be governed by the rules laid down in relation to that kind of evidence which serves to introduce it. A few illustrations and examples are given in the code to give a full understanding of the nature of this evidence. The mark on a tree coinciding with that stated by scriptory or testimonial evidence, in cases of disputed boundary, is substantive evidence of a land-mark. The number of concentric circles in the wood that has grown over the mark, is substantive evidence of the number of years that have elapsed since it was made. Yet the mark itself is no evidence, unless supported by proof of the circumstances under which it was made.

Having considered all the divisions of evidence in relation to the source from which it proceeds, we come now to consider it in relation to the degree of weight it is calculated to have in producing that conviction in the mind, which is the object of all judicial evidence. The divisions in this view, and in the ascending scale, are, as we have seen, presumptive, direct and conclusive. But for one consideration this division would not be necessary, except for developing the nature of evidence, not for directing the mode of its admission; because, conviction of the truth, being the result of an intellectual operation, the degree in which evidence of any kind is to operate can never be prescribed; and it would, therefore, have been proper only in a theoretic view to have indicated these divisions, but for certain positive enactments which, forming part of our civil code, it does not come within the intent of the legislature to alter or repeal by this code. These enactments declare what evidence, in particular cases, shall be considered as presumptive, and what others conclusive testimony. This can, in effect, be no more than directing what judgment shall be given when particular testimony is adduced; because, as has been said, no law can control the operations of the mind. Yet as the effect of the different descriptions of evidence is directed, it became necessary, in a code on that subject, to give these divisions a place. In another point of view, also, it would seem to be proper. The authority of nature, as well as that of positive law, has decreed that on a well organized mind, all events happening according to her invariable course, should be considered as true; and allegations of fact, contrary to such course, as false; hence a second source to which we can refer conclusive, and in some instances presumptive, evidence. These considerations have induced the insertion of chapters corresponding to the three degrees of evidence which have been enumerated.

1. The first of these, presumptive evidence, is of two kinds, which cannot be brought under the same general definition : the one, simple presumptions, arising from the operation of the mind of the judge drawing from the existence of one fact, which has been proved, the inference that another, which has not been proved, exists also ; the other, legal presumptions, are those which are made by the law itself, and which the judge is forced to adopt, whatever may be his own conclusions from the facts. Illustrations of the former are given in presumption, drawn from the structure of the human mind ; such as that a man of good character will not do an unworthy act—that a mother will not abandon her child—and, from the common course of business, that if the obligation be delivered to the debtor, the debt has been paid. As examples of legal presumptions, are given the following, which are directed by law : that he who has possessed real estate for a year, is the owner ; and that when no time is expressed for the continuance

of a predial estate, it shall be deemed to have been intended for a year-
The effect of these presumptions is directed to be, that the fact pre.
sumed shall be considered as proved, unless the contrary be shown by
other evidence.

Presumptions can only be raised by legal evidence ; therefore, nothing can be the legal foundation for a presumption but that which can be
legally given in evidence ; and it is further provided, that simple
presumptions must be founded, first, on the establishment of some fact
by legal testimony ; secondly, by such deduction from that fact as is
warranted by the usual propensities or passions of men—by the particular habits or passions of the individual whose act is in question—by
the usual course of business, or by the ordinary operations of nature.

2. Of direct evidence, little more need be said than to give its definition, which is, that which, if true, conclusively establishes the fact in
question.  It, therefore, can give rise to one inquiry only—whether
the fact stated be true ; and as this inquiry must be pursued in the ordinary form, the rules for conducting it must be sought under other
heads.

3. Conclusive evidence forms a more comprehensive title.  Every
species of proof may produce conviction in the mind of the judge, and
any evidence producing that conviction would, in one sense of the
word, be deemed conclusive.  But in this code, that term is applied
exclusively to that which is declared to be such by it, or by other provisions of law which it does not alter or repeal.

It may, perhaps, seem inconsistent with the principles on which this
code· is founded, for the legislature so far to interfere with judicial
discretion in judging of the force of evidence as to declare, that any
proof shall be considered as conclusive of any litigated fact.  In many
cases, as has been observed, the interference is but nominal ; and the
legislative phraseology would be more correct, if, instead of declaring
that such a fact, or such evidence, shall be presumptive proof of such
another designated fact, it were to direct, in cases of legal presumptions,
that when such a fact should appear in evidence to the judge, then he
should give judgment in the manner directed by the law, unless counter evidence were produced by the opposite party ; and in case of
conclusive evidence, that whenever the designated fact should be proved,
he should give judgment in the manner designated, without hearing
other evidence.  But in whatever manner the legislative will is expressed—whether in the incorrect mode of directing the judge what
to believe, or in the more proper manner of directing him what to decide—is not so material as to inquire for the reasons why any such
directions should be given in any form.  Uniformity in judicial decisions, it will be allowed, is a very desirable object in the exercise of
jurisprudence.  By this is meant, the same deductions from the same
facts, applied to similar circumstances.  The cases in which this can be
procured by legislative interference, without injustice, are few; and the
probability of the reverse—that is, of different decisions, although the
proof and the circumstances may be the same—is very great ; because,
the minds of men being differently organized, there are not many
things in which all would agree.  If this be the case, when not only the
evidence but the circumstances of the case on which it is to operate are
the same, how much more is it to be expected where these circum-

stances exhibit shades of difference? Yet there are cases in which, at
the risk of producing particular inconvenience, the general welfare
requires that this uniformity should be preserved ; which can only be
done by directing that, whatever may be the opinion of the judge, his
decree shall be rendered in conformity with the directions of the statute,
whenever the evidence it, for public purposes, considers as conclusive,
shall be produced. Without multiplying examples, that of the
authentic act may sufficiently illustrate what has been said on this subject. The authentic act, as we have seen, is conclusive evidence of
the truth of all that is certified by it to have been done in the presence
of the public officer, before whom it has been passed. Different judges,
from different views of the subject, might not receive an equal conviction of the truth of what is declared by it. To such it would not be
conclusive evidence. There would, then, be no uniformity of decision on the validity of such instruments; but public convenience and
utility require, that the holder of such an act should rely upon the
faith of the officer's certificate ; therefore, the law wisely declares, that
it shall be conclusive testimony, although, in some instances, carelessness or ignorance may have consented to its execution, when it did not
contain the stipulations that were intended. In this, however, as in all
other cases where evidence is declared to be conclusive, provision is
made for annulling the act whenever fraud, error or force has intervened. So the record of a judgment is conclusive evidence that the
party in whose favour it was rendered, was entitled to the relief which
it purports to give. Yet the judgment, in some particular case, may
have been unjust, and the judge, before whom it is produced as evidence, may be convinced that it was so. But the individual interest,
in this case, must be sacrificed to the stability of the general rule, it
being more expedient that one unjust judgment should be carried into
execution, than that all judgments should be open to contestation,
whenever they were produced as evidence of the claims which they
have sanctioned.

This code only refers for illustration to some enactments belonging
to the Civil Code and other general laws, by which certain evidence is
declared conclusive. It does not detail them, but it enforces their provisions ; shows that the objects they are intended to attain are to
diminish litigation and lessen the temptations to perjury ; and divides
them into positive enactments for the purposes just mentioned, and those
which are declaratory of the usual course of nature. Examples of the
first are offered in the authority given to judgments, to authentic acts,
and to judicial confessions ; and of the last, in the provision of our
existing law, that the birth of a child, more than three hundred days
after the death of the husband, is conclusive proof that the child is not his.

In the enumeration of evidence, declared to be conclusive, the item
of judicial decrees is the most important, both for the frequency of its
occurrence, and the difficult questions to which it gives rise. A whole
chapter is devoted to this subject. It contains few provisions entirely
new; but, it is believed, that the several sections, directing what judgments are valid as res judicatæ—which cannot have that effect, and
against whom they may be given in evidence, will obviate many of the
difficulties that have hitherto attended this subject; and that, if adopted,
a ready solution will be found to most of the questions to which it has
given rise.

Another species of evidence which, under certain circumstances, is conclusive, arises from the confession of the party. Confession, in relation to the manner in which it is made, is either judicial or extra-judicial. The former, being that which is made in some writing forming a part of the judicial proceedings in a cause; or when it is made before a person authorized by law to receive the same, and reduced to writing in the manner prescribed by law. The latter, are confessions made in any other manner.

In relation to the matter, confessions are either full, or partial only. Full confession, is that which acknowledges the fact alleged with all its material circumstances, so as to leave nothing to be supplied by other evidence. Partial confession, is that which acknowledges some circumstance from which an inference may be drawn, so as to make it presumptive evidence.

In civil cases, where every proceeding made by the parties is in writing, and after full deliberation, a judicial confession is declared to be conclusive evidence, if not recalled, and after a reasonable term for deliberation shown to the satisfaction of the judge to be erroneous; but restrictions are added, to prevent vexation by making and capriciously retracting confessions.

In criminal cases, however, no confession, whether judicial or extra-judicial, is conclusive testimony of guilt. The reason of this difference is evident. Insanity, promises, fear, hope of liberty or pardon, may produce a confession contrary to the fact; and therefore, although the confession is strong evidence, it is always open to be rebutted by any other that would lessen its force.

Even the answer of *"guilty"* to the arraignment is not a sufficient ground for passing sentence, until the necessary inquiries as to the sanity of mind in the prisoner and the existence of the other causes, have been made. When we reflect on the numerous instances in which men have confessed themselves guilty, not only of crimes which they had not committed, but which were impossible to be committed by any one, the necessity of these precautions will be admitted. The inexplicable state of mind which produced, in so many instances, confessions of sorcery and witchcraft, may take place in other cases, although those delusions are over.

By the declaration, that no evidence should be deemed conclusive but that which is declared to be such by law, that which operates as such by our present law under the title of estoppel, is of course abolished; but for greater certainty, that effect is declared by a special provision.

A concluding article contains the necessary notice, that nothing in the code shall be construed so as to dispense with the proof required by the Civil Code or other statutes, to give effect to certain contracts or testamentary dispositions, or to enforce the registry or recording of acts, or prove legitimacy, filiation or civil condition. A detail of the evidence, required in these and similar cases, did not form a part of this code, because they could not have been inserted without repeating the provisions of the laws of which they form a part, which would have intermixed two distinct branches of legislation, required by the policy of our law to be kept separate.

Before I close the report, it may be necessary to account for an omission in the work—that of not designating the evidence required or permitted in each separate species of civil action and criminal procedure.

It is easy, however, to show that this would have been unnecessary and injurious to the simplicity of the plan that has been adopted.

By our excellent system of civil law, a plaintiff can succeed only by stating such facts as entitle him to relief according to law; and by proving those facts. In these two operations he must be directed by two different codes. The Civil Code informs him what circumstances give him the right to recover; and it is the province of the Code of Evidence to direct in what manner the proof shall be made; not of the facts in that suit only, but of all facts in any action. To direct what facts are necessary to be proved, in order to be restored to a possession which is wrongfully withheld, to enforce the payment of a debt, or obtain damages for a wrong—could only be done by repeating the substance of the Civil Code, and would, therefore, be misplaced in the law of evidence, which ought to contain only general rules, applicable to the different species of evidence, not to particular actions in which that evidence may become proper or necessary. It is the same as regards the defence: the Civil Code directs what circumstances will justify an act that would otherwise be wrongful: and the Code of Evidence tells us, by the application of its general rules, how those circumstances are to be proved. So in criminal prosecutions ; the acts or omissions which constitute an offence, are designated in the Code of Crimes and Punishment, and consequently we need no other guide to discover what is necessary to be proved in any particular prosecution. Why, then, should it be repeated in the Code of Evidence ?

A contradictory practice on this point, together with the necessity of arranging and weighing the authority of the contradictory or explanatory decisions, in every controverted case, has rendered the English law of evidence so extremely voluminous and contributed to increase its uncertainty.

# INTRODUCTORY REPORT

TO

# THE CODE OF REFORM AND PRISON DISCIPLINE.

In offering to the legislature a system of penal law, the principal sanction of which is imprisonment, it is scarcely necessary to remark, that its whole efficacy must depend on the manner in which confinement is to be inflicted as a punishment, or used as a means of detention; in other words, on the wisdom of the Code of Prison Discipline.   In preparing the plan now submitted, I kept in view, as the great objects to be attained—restraint, example and reformation.   To discover what species of seclusion would best produce these ends, rigidly to direct every privation necessary to attain them, but to inflict no evil greater than was required to produce these consequences, would seem at first view a comparatively easy task; but the selection of proper means, and the details required for their application, presented difficulties in the execution only to be overcome by the closest attention to facts, and the most cautious calculation of consequences.   A statement of these facts, and an exposition of the consequences drawn from them, will enable the House better to understand and decide on the plan which I have the honour to propose.

At a time when the penal law of Great Britain, still liable to the reproach of unnecessary severity in its enactments, and barbarity in its executions, had received none of those improvements which the true principles of jurisprudence have since produced, the benevolent heart and enlightened mind of the legislator of Pennsylvania, suggested the substitution of solitary imprisonment and labour for the punishment of death.   The beneficial effects of this change were felt until they were counteracted by the intolerant and sanguinary system of the common law of England, enforced by the paramount authority of the mother country.   But no sooner did independence confer the power of consulting the public good, than the people of Pennsylvania made the reformation of the penal code a constitutional obligation on their representatives; and, amidst the confusion produced by foreign invasion and civil discord in the Revolutionary war, a society worthy of the city of "brotherly love" was formed for the relief of distressed prisoners. With persevering benevolence, they not only relieved the victims of the inhuman system that then prevailed, but, by unceasing appeals to true principles, induced the legislature of that state to begin the great reform.   In all but two or three cases, the punishment of death was

2 O

abolished : labour was substituted for loss of life and stripes; but, contrary to the opinion early expressed by the society in favour of solitary labour, that on the public works was adopted.  The error was a radical one: debasement, corruption, and an immediate repetition of crime, were the consequences; and the failure of this experiment with any but a wise and reflecting people, might have been fatal to the system.  But, happily for Pennsylvania, and perhaps for the world, she had enlightened men to frame her penal laws; and happier still, she had a class of citizens admirably calculated to execute them with the zeal of enthusiasm.  The founder of that state, and his first associates, belonged to a sect which fitted them, by its principles, and by the habits and pursuits which it created and prescribed, to be the agents of a reform in jurisprudence similar to that which they adopted, and perhaps, carried to excess, in religion.  Their descendants, with less of that enthusiasm which, in their ancestors, was exalted by persecution, had all the active benevolence and Christian charity necessary to prompt, and the perseverance and unwearied industry to support their exertions.  Abstracted by their tenets from the pleasures which occupy so large a portion of life among other sects ; equally excluded from other pursuits in which so many find occupation ; freed from the vexations of mutual litigation, by submitting every difference to the umpirage of the elders, and from the tyranny of fashion by an independent contempt for its rules; the modern quakers devote all that time which others waste in dissipation, or employ in intriguing for public employment, to the direction of charitable institutions, and that surplus wealth which others dissipate in frivolous pursuits, to the cause of humanity.  In every society for promoting education, for instructing or supporting the poor, for relieving the distresses of prisoners, for suppressing vice and immorality, they are active and zealous members; and they indemnify themselves for the loss of the honours and pleasures of the world by the highest of all honours, the purest of all pleasures—that of doing good.

To these men, and others who participated in their principles, was committed the task of uniting reformation and punishment, when secluded was substituted for the public labour to which the convicts had before been exposed.  The most encouraging results justified the change in the law, and the selection of persons to whom its execution was committed; and from the year 1790, when it took place, until 1793, we have the official attestation of one of the inspectors(a), that, out of two hundred convicts who had been pardoned, only four were returned on a second conviction; that only two cases of burglary, and not one of privately stealing from the person, had occurred; that the streets and roads were freed from robbers, and that in all the prisons for the populous city and county of Philadelphia, immediately before the sitting of the court, only four persons were in custody for trial.  This last is a striking fact.  The city and county of Philadelphia, at that time, contained upwards of sixty thousand inhabitants, and, prior to that time, more than thirty had been condemned at a session, a number which supposes at least fifty commitments ; so that, in the short space of two years, the effect of the system was the entire suppression of some

(a) A member of the Society of Friends, who has rendered the name of *Lowndes* as celebrated for active, enlightened benevolence, as a late lamented statesman has since done for eloquence, patriotism and integrity.

crimes, and the reduction of others in the proportion of ten to one, in the place where the example might be supposed to have had the greatest effect. The operation of the system in the whole of the state, was nearly as encouraging. Although its population was increasing in a very rapid ratio, yet conviction decreased from one hundred and twenty-five, in the year 1789, to the respective numbers of one hundred and nine, seventy, sixty-three, forty-five(a), in the four succeeding years. Thus we find that, although the population of the state was increasing in a ratio of four and a half per cent a year, offences(b) had decreased in the proportion of forty-five to one hundred and twenty-five, or nearly two-thirds less; and in the last year I have mentioned, there were no convictions for one half of the crimes that had figured on the preceding calendars. So remarkable a diminution of crime in a regular decreasing series, is a fact worthy our most profound attention, when we are considering the effects of this species of punishment. Nothing can develop the true principles of legislation on this subject more clearly than the history of the reform in Pennsylvania in all its stages. In 1786, we find that the various system of labour in the public works was established. Under it, in the three years of its operation, and the first year after its repeal, but before the effects of the system could cease, the average number of convictions in each year was one hundred and nine; in 1791 it decreased under the new system to seventy-six; in 1792 to sixty-three; and in 1793 to forty-five: all this while the population of the state and, what is more worthy to be noted, of the city, was rapidly increasing. This was the lowest point of depression: from that time the increase has been in a more rapid ratio than the diminution: for the first four years afterwards, the average was one hundred and nineteen, and it has gradually progressed until the average of the last twelve years is three hundred and eleven; that is, within a fraction of eight times as many as it was in 1793; but the population of the state in that time had very little more than doubled(c), so that crime has increased in proportion to the population nearly as eight is to two. Most fortunately for the cause of truth, humanity and wise legislation, the cause of this ebb and flow of crime is not difficult to discover ; and when pointed out, it will be more persuasive to show that there is a check that may be effectually applied to the increase of offences than the most ingenious argument that could be suggested.

In the three years previous to the year 1790, when Philadelphia prison was first used for the purpose of inflicting punishment by solitary confinement, three hundred and twenty-eight convicts had been confined. Of these, about two-thirds were committed for short terms, and others were discharged by pardon; so that at the commencement of the year 1790, not more than about two hundred remained. The accommodations of the prison afforded the means of separation for this small number, and the humane zeal of the inspectors, quickened by the natural desire to give efficacy to the plan which they had themselves formed, urged on the labour and superintended the instruction of the convicts. In that year, the first of the experiment, but before its result could be known, one hundred and nine convictions took place. In the next, its

---

(a) Vaux's Notices.                    (b) Seybert's Statistics.
(c) Four hundred and ninety-five thousand one hundred and eighty-five, in 1793. One million forty-nine thousand four hundred and fifty-eight, in 1820.

beneficent effects began to be felt; the convictions were reduced to seventy-eight, and in the two successive years to sixty-three and forty-five. But in the mean time(a) the prison began to be crowded, solitary labour was necessarily abandoned, even classification became impossible ; the same prison serving for vagrants, fugitive apprentices(b), and those committed for trial; a relaxation of discipline was the natural consequence of the indiscriminate association, and the increase of convictions, in every succeeding term of four years, bears an exact proportion to the increased numbers in the prison. This double result of a rapid and before unheard of decrease while the convicts were separated and employed, and an increase almost in the same ratio when they were suffered to associate, seems to solve the great problem of penal jurisprudence, and points to seclusion and labour as an effectual remedy for the prevention of crime : for these effects were produced without any change in the state of society at the two periods, that could be favourable to such results; on the contrary, an increase of population while crimes were decreasing, and the same increase, but only of one half, in the numbers of the people during the other period, when crimes increased fourfold. This practical result, so decisive of the truth of the theory, founded on a consideration of human nature, with other corroborating facts, has confirmed me in the design, not only of persevering in my first recommendation of imprisonment, solitude and labour, in different degrees, and under different modifications, as the principal sanctions of the code, but it has become the basis of my whole system of prison discipline; and from the well attested fact that a plan, by no means perfect, persevered in for only four years, banished some crimes, and rapidly reduced the number of others nearly two-thirds, I draw the cheering conclusion that, by giving to the system the improvements of which it is susceptible, the sum of human happiness may be increased by the repression of crimes and of the evils which result both from their commission and punishment.

My position is, that imprisonment, with seclusion and labour, as a punishment, will diminish the offences for which it is inflicted; but that imprisonment without seclusion will increase them. What will be the effect of solitary confinement without labour, remains to be tried. The Pennsylvania experiment proves conclusively, that while the numbers were not too great to admit of seclusion, offences diminished; and when it was no longer practicable, they increased. In all the other states a similar result has been observed, during the first years. When there was room for classification, the most sanguine hopes of humanity were surpassed by the effect(c). But with the promiscuous intercourse of the convicts, offences increased both in number and atrocity. This great truth, then, is supported in both its parts by experiment, the most conclusive of all proof, when it has been so oftened repeated, under different circumstances, as to show the uniform result is produced by the same cause, and when it confirms a theory to which no abstract objection can be conclusively urged. But here the theory is emphatically one of

(a) No provision had been made for the increased number of prisoners, which, of all descriptions, amounted, in 1793, to the average number of 450.

(b) Petition of the Society for Public Prisons, 1801—1803.

(c) See reports to the Senate of New-York, and the reports of all the state prisons in the different states.

that kind.   Of all the crimes in the catalogue of human depravity, four-fifths are, in different forms, invasions of private property: and the motive for committing them is the desire of obtaining, without labour, the enjoyments which property brings.   The natural corrective is to deprive the offender of the gratifications he expects, and to convince him that they can be acquired by the exertions of industry.   The remaining proportion of offences are such as arise from the indulgence of the bad passions, and for those also solitude and employment are the best correctives.   But whatever corrects the desire or the passion that prompts the offence, acts in the double capacity, first of punishment, until the desire is repressed, and, afterwards, when it is effected, of reformation.   As an example, too, it is infinitely more efficacious than any other penalty.   When it is seen that offences which were committed to avoid labour and to increase the enjoyments of society, lead only to solitude and labour, and that the passions which caused the more serious crimes, are to be kept under the rigid restraint of abstinence and reflection, in. the fearful loneliness of a cell; when these examples are permanent, and by a rigid administration of justice believed to be inevitable, who that studies human nature can doubt the effect ?  Therefore, the experiments of Pennsylvania and of the other states, in the first years of their operation, as well as their subsequent failure, have but confirmed a theory true, because it was drawn from the workings of the human mind.   They succeeded at first exactly in the proportion to the strictness of the seclusion; they failed precisely in the ratio of its relaxation.

Solitude and labour, then, are the two great remedies.   How are they to be employed ?   Is the confinement to be a rigid, unbroken solitude, or only a seclusion from the corruption of evil counsel and example ?  Is it to be permanent for the whole term of the sentence, or to be mitigated by proofs of industry and amendment ?   Is the labour to be forced or voluntary, and is its principal object pecuniary profit to the state, or the means of honest support to the convict?   These are the great questions to be decided before we enter on the consideration of a multitude of subordinate details.

When imprisonment and labour were substituted for corporal punishment, the evils of promiscuous association became apparent.   The separation most obviously required was that of the sexes, and this seems to have been universally introduced.   But it required little observation or knowledge of human nature to discover that something more was necessary ; that, as a place of punishment, a penitentiary would soon lose its terrors, if the depraved inhabitants were suffered to enjoy the society within, which they had always preferred when at large ; and that, instead of a place of reformation, it must become the best institution that could be devised for instruction in all the mysteries of vice and crime, if the professors of guilt are suffered to make disciples of those who may be comparatively ignorant.   To remedy this evil, what is called classification was resorted to ; first, the young were separated from the old, then the analogous division was made between the novice and the practised offender ; further subdivisions. were found indispensable, in proportion as it was discovered that in each of these classes would be found individuals of different degrees of depravity, and, of course, corrupters, and those ready to receive their lessons.   Accordingly, classes were multiplied, until, in some prisons in England we find them amounting to fifteen or more. But, all this while, the evident truths seemed not to have had proper force : first, that moral guilt cannot always be discovered, and if discovered, so nicely appreciated as to assign to each one infected with it, his comparative place in the scale ; and that if it could be so discovered it would be found that no two would be found contaminated in the same degree. Secondly, that if these difficulties could be surmounted, and a class could be formed of individuals who had advanced exactly to the same point, not only of offence, but of moral depravity, still their association would produce a further progress in both, just as sparks produce a flame when brought together, which separated, would be extinguished and die. It is not in human nature for the mind to be stationary ; it must progress in virtue or in vice : nothing promotes this progress so much as the emulation created by society; and from the nature of the society will it receive its direction. Every association of convicts, then, that can be formed, will in a greater or less degree pervert, but will never reform, those of which it is composed : and we are brought to the irresistible conclusion that classification once admitted to be useful, it is so in an inverse proportion to the numbers of which each class is composed ; and is not perfect until we come to the point at which it loses its name and nature, in the complete separation of individuals. We come, then, to the conclusion that each convict is to be separated from his fellows. But is he to be debarred from all other society ? In discussing this question we must always have before our eyes the ends we propose to attain by the discipline we inflict—punishment and reformation. So much punishment as is necessary to deter others from committing the crime, and the offender from repeating it ; every alleviation not inconsistent with those objects, that will cause the culprit gradually to prefer a life of honest industry, not from the fear of punishment, but from a conviction of its utility. That system of prison discipline will make the nearest approach to perfection that shall best attain these objects. In order to judge in what degree the plan I propose is entitled to this distinction, it will be necessary to examine other systems, and a discussion of their defects will enable us to discover how far that which is proposed as a substitute avoids them.

Imprisonment and labour have been adopted, as a punishment, in fourteen out of twenty-four states. In none of these has there been, until very lately, any individual seclusion, except for breaches of prison discipline, and, during different periods, for the more atrocious offences : the consequences of this radical fault were such as might have been expected—an increase rather than a diminution of crime ; and the prodigal, indiscreet and ruinous exercise of the pardoning power, combined to render abortive the best experiment ever made for the suppression of vice. The people who were taxed for the support of these institutions, saw in them only the nurseries of crime, and were naturally desirous of throwing off the burthen ; and it was made, in one important state, a serious question whether they should not resort to sanguinary and infamous punishments. The calm reasoning and spirit of investigation, which sooner or later resume their place in the councils of our republics, soon discovered that the experiment had not been fairly tried ; the cause of its failure became apparent ; and all agreed that imprisonment without separation would never serve either for punishment or reform. Two different systems were proposed to remedy the evil; one is in the course of experiment; the other has not yet been examined, but preparations are nearly completed for carrying it into effect on a most extensive scale, and in a degree that must completely test its utility.   In New-York there are two penitentiaries, and a third is now constructing: one of them, in the city, is, from its construction, and the numbers confined in it, necessarily conducted on the old vicious plan, which is to be abandoned as soon as the third prison is finished; the other, at Auburn, a village in the interior of the state, is the model for the new penitentiary, and by the partisans of the system on which it is managed, is declared to be one that ought to serve as a pattern for all others.   That system is briefly this: absolute solitude during the night ; joint labor during the day, but without any communication with each other by word or sign ; meals taken at the same table, but so disposed as not to see the faces of those opposite to them ; religious instruction on Sundays, received in a body ; and a Sunday school in the same manner, twice a day ; both in church and school the same prohibition of intercourse ; a full diet of meat, bread and vegetables ; comfortable bedding, in very narrow but well-aired, well warmed cells, and the utmost attention to cleanliness in every department of the prison ; visiters are admitted, but without permission to speak to the convicts—who on their discharge receive a sum not exceeding three dollars, without any relation to their earnings ; their work is uninterrupted during the day, except by their meals, and is generally contracted for by mechanics, who find the materials.   This enumeration is not one of what is required but what is actually done. And the strictness with which these rules have been enforced is such, that it is asserted that, among thirty or forty, working together for years in the same shop, no two of them know each others names. Mr Elam Lynds, a gentleman who formerly served in the army, has the credit of introducing this order—it was begun with his appointment as keeper of the Auburn prison, and he has executed it with most astonishing success in superintending the building of the new prison at Sing Sing, where he has had two hundred convicts employed, with no other place of confinement than a wooden shed, in which they slept, and with only eight or ten under keepers and guards, and yet the same industry, order and obedience, was preserved as there was within the walls of the prison.   Nothing can be more imposing than the view of a prison conducted on these principles.   Order, obedience, sobriety, industry, religious and literary instruction, and solitary reflection, all seem to promise beneficial effects on the convict, while important points of secure detention and economy are attained for the state.   Yet with all these advantages I cannot offer this system for adoption ; and my chief objection arises from the means employed to procure them.   It is by the lash(a), put into the hands of the keeper, to be used at dis-

(a) " It has already appeared that, as a mode of punishment, and as the means of enforcing prison discipline, in this prison, STRIPES are generally resorted to as a punishment, in the presence of the inspectors ; and to enforce obedience, *by the keepers, at all times when necessary.*   These stripes are required by the present agent to be inflicted by the keeper with a raw hide whip, and applied to the back, &c."—*Power's Account of the State Prison at Auburn*, p. 60.

" At Auburn stripes are almost the only mode of punishment."—*Report of Massachusetts Society.*

cretion, and by a power strangely I think declared to be legally vested in the turnkey(a). The objections to this system are obvious. And first, the anomaly presents itself, not to call it by a harsher name, of permitting a punishment to be inflicted at the discretion not only of a man at the head of the institution, but by his under officers, at their discretion, and that too for disrespect, or the vague charge of disobedience, which punishment the law has abolished as too ignominious, unequal and cruel, to be inflicted by the court for dangerous crimes. The discretion is limited, say the court in their opinon, under which it is to be considered to be legal, to the enforcement of obedience for its object, and in degree to the punishment necessary to secure it. Can any thing be more vague? Obedience to what? Lawful commands is the answer; but it is unlawful to break any, the minutest regulation of the prison; it is unlawful to deny any breach of them when the convict is accused by the turnkey; therefore, if a convict speak to his neighbour he is whipped, and if he should deny having done so he is whipped. The very case in which the stripes were declared lawful, was one in which they were severely inflicted to make the convict confess, and when he had confessed, they ceased.—Here is every character of the torture, applied by the lowest officer in the prison—and this by the court of the state of New-York was declared to be lawful, if the jury should think that the chastisement was not greater in degree than was necessary to enforce obedience. Now the obedience required in this case was the confession; and it follows according to the decision of the court, that such force as was necessary to this end was justifiable; in other words, that torture by infliction of stripes might legally be used in the state of New-York, by a turnkey against a convict, according to the *common law*, although the legislature has enacted, "That if any prisoner in either of the state's prisons shall refuse to comply with the rules, it shall be lawful, and is declared to be the duty of the keepers, under the direction of the inspectors, to inflict corporal punishment by whipping, not to exceed thirty-nine lashes, or to confine them. Provided, that, when corporal punishment is inflicted on any person by whipping, it shall be the duty of at least two of the inspectors to be present." Then according to the discipline of the prison, as declared by the court to be lawful, only thirty-nine stripes can be inflicted at a time for any offence, and that by order of the inspectors, and in the presence of two of them; but a turnkey, whenever it is necessary to enforce obedience, or a confession, may inflict as many as he pleases, without any witness of his proceedings. I have enlarged upon this head, more, perhaps, than was necessary, to enforce the position that the punishment by stripes was an anomaly even as it is permitted by law; and I have detailed the practice independent of the statute, for the direct purpose of showing the principle on which the discipline of this prison rests; and for the incidental one of illustrating, by a striking example, the difficulty of enforcing a statute in countries governed by unwritten law. Here, because the common law permits a school-master moderately to correct his pupil, and an officer his soldiers, the learned judge declares it to be law, that the turnkey of a penitentiary, an institution utterly

(a) Decision of the court in the case of The People *v.* An Under Keeper at Auburn.—*Power's Account*, p. 62.

unknown to the common law, has a right to chastise a convict, nay, more, whip him until he confess himself guilty of an offence ; and this, too, although the legislature has expressly directed that when he is whipped it shall be by the direction of other officers, and in their presence. Yet this decision is law in the state of New York, and is published as the authority by which the discipline of this prison is maintained.

The next objection to this system is its evident liability to abuse. The talent and firmness, tempered by moderation, the knowledge of human nature, and personal courage of captain Lynds, who introduced it, and who began by procuring a waiver of all interference with his plans by the inspectors, have done much present good; he has introduced order, economy, industry and cleanliness ; he has banished many abuses ; and his system, under his own direction, although liable to strong objections, is yet so much superior in effect to any hitherto practised, that it has been considered as a model(a) for the imitation of the world ; and in his hands, I have no doubt, that many beneficial effects will result from it.    But what security have we that the same rare qualities will be found united in another ?    In the communications I have had with him, he says, that his method may be easily taught. This may be true, but unless he can impart his integrity and moderation(b) as well as a knowledge of his discipline, it will be unsafe to adopt a system, that must depend entirely for its success on the personal qualities of the man who is to carry it into effect.

But, even if we were sure of commanding all the requisite qualities and talents united in the same person, still there are faults, inherent in the plan, which no administration can cure.    Fear is the great principle of this institution, and chastisement of the most degrading kind is the instrument to excite it.    If the sole objects were to preserve order in the prison, it is perhaps as effectual, but certainly not as proper a mode as can be devised.    But, as a punishment, it fails in two essential points; in most cases it will not deter the party from a repetition of his crimes, and very rarely will it take away by reformation his inclination to relapse.    A superficial view of this subject has led to the belief, that the great secret of penal legislation is, to annex a penalty of sufficient severity to every offence ; and, accordingly, all the variety of pains that the body of man could suffer, infamy and death, have figured as sanctions in the codes of all nations; but although these have been in a train of experiment for thousands of years, under every variety that government, manners and religion could give, they have never produced the expected effect.    The reason is to be found in that insurgent spirit with which man was endowed by his beneficent Creator, to answer the best ends of his nature.    The same feeling that elevated, refined, and applied to the noblest purpose, animates the patriot to resist civil tyranny, and the martyr to defy the flames, when it is perverted, and made the incentive to vice and crime, goads on the convict to arraign the justice of his sentence, to rebel against those who execute it, and to counteract its effects with an obstinacy in exact proportion to the severity of the punishment.    If the grossest

(a) Report of the Massachusetts Society.
(b) The case of the keeper, above alluded to, took place, I believe, after Mr Lynds had left the Auburn prison, and is itself a strong illustration of the danger of unlimited delegation of power.

2 P

follies and absurdest fancies of enthusiasm, as well as the clear truths and pure principles of religion, are extended and confirmed by severe punishments and persecution, what more evident proof can we require, that this character of the human mind braces itself with an equal energy against bodily suffering, whether inflicted for the correction of error or the suppression of truth? The convict, therefore, who has performed his daily labour, even for years, under the pang or the dread of the lash, will be rather less deterred from the repetition of his crimes, whenever he thinks himself secure from detection, than he would have been by a milder discipline, because the spirit of hatred, revenge, and a desire to retaliate on society, are stimulated and strengthened by the principles which I have supposed to be inherent in our nature. But, as the object of punishment is not only to prevent the repetition, but also the commission of offences, we must inquire whether this discipline is calculated, in any degree, to have this effect? Its peculiar characteristic is severity. We are told, indeed, that its actual application to individuals is not frequently required, because of the certainty with which punishment follows the offence ; but the dread of it is always there, and the uplifted lash, although its stroke is avoided by submission, is, perhaps, as great a punishment as the actual pain, because it is attended with the moral suffering of degradation. We must repeat then that the nature of this discipline does no more than add severity to the punishment ; and he must be blind to the uniform history of penal jurisprudence, who can believe that increased severity diminishes the recurrence of crimes. The same operation of the mind, to which I have alluded, that gives the energy of mental resistance to the sufferer, operates by a sympathy invariably called into action, on all who, by their state in society, their education or manners, have any feelings in common with him ; and by the same system of severity converts are made to religion, proselytes to impostures, and accessaries to offences. The system, therefore, to judge from analogy, will not deter. Will it reform? Judging by the same rule, for, as yet, we cannot have, in any conclusive degree, the light of experience, I think it cannot: The force of habits on the mind is proverbial ; but those which have this power, are such as were either formed in early life, or were produced by repeated voluntary acts ; few instances, it is thought, can be found in which any series of constrained acts, have produced the habit of continuing them after the force was removed ; but this part of the subject will be more fully discussed, when I shall explain the reformatory system contained in the code which I submit for consideration. I will only now remark that, so far as the force is applied to coerce the convict into a knowledge of some trade, by which he may earn a subsistence, so far it may produce amendment ; but then if the same labour can be made a voluntary act, the skill attained in it will probably be more perfect, and undoubtedly there is a greater chance of its being persevered in.

I conclude then that this system, although it avoids the obvious defect of promiscuous confinement at night, and by the strictness of its discipline, prevents many of the evils attending associated labours by day, still has defects, that will not permit me to agree with the committee of the Massachusetts Society, in considering it as a model for imitation. Before I develope the features of one, in which I think these defects are remedied, while all its advantages are retained, it will be necessary to examine the rival plan proposed in Pennsylvania. This consists in solitary confinement, strictly so called, by which, say the committee who proposed it, we mean "such an entire seclusion of convicts from society, and from one another, as that during the period of their confinement, no one shall see or hear, or be seen or heard, by any human being, except the jailor, the inspectors, or such other persons as, for highly urgent reasons, may be permitted to enter the walls of the prison"(a). To carry this plan into execution a prison has been erected at Pittsburgh, and another is nearly completed, on a most extensive scale, at Philadelphia. This last is most admirably contrived for perfect seclusion : the purposes of cleanliness do not demand the entrance of an attendant, or the egress of the prisoner. His food is furnished without his seeing the hand that brings it ; and a complete inspection of every part of the cell is had, while the prisoner can neither see nor hear the approach of his keeper ; all is silence and solitude, and, if these alone can work reformation, there was never a building better calculated to produce the effect. Whether labour is to be permitted or enjoined does not seem to be determined. There is a court, however, annexed to each cell, in which solitary labour may be performed, without much danger of communication between the prisoners. This system is simple, and has few details beyond those I have mentioned in describing it. The advantages expected from it are described in the report to which I have referred. Reformation it is hoped will be produced by the reflections inseparable from solitude, and the severity of the punishment is well described in the report, as one that will almost make the patient " *the victim of despair,*" while he is " shut up in a cell for weeks and months and years alone, to be deprived of all converse—while he counts the tedious hours as they pass, a prey to the corrodings of conscience and the pangs of guilt :" and this, it is supposed, will effectually deter the convict from repeating his crime, and make the vicious fly from a region " *where conviction produces so much misery.*" As the severity of the punishment is increased, its duration is proposed to be diminished ; which will produce a saving that the committee believe will compensate for the loss incurred by the difference between solitary and social labour, if the former should be allowed. It is evident that here the contagion of evil associations is effectually prevented without the degrading discipline of the New York plan ; that the security is more perfect, and at less expense ; and, if they should make such relaxation from the strictness of solitude as to permit instruction and labour, that it is liable to much fewer objections than the other. If, on the contrary, the plan of the committee, in their understanding of what is meant by solitude, be carried strictly into execution, without instruction, without labour, those objections would be of the most serious nature. Their force will be better understood when I show in what points the plan I propose differs from those I have thus reviewed.

I premise that no plan of jurisprudence, combining the prevention of crime with the reformation of the criminal, has ever yet been attempted on such a scale as would embrace all the different stages and departments of criminal procedure. The only experiment that has been made, that which is called the penitentiary system, has been ap-

(a) Report, 1821.

plied solely to the substitution of imprisonment for other more acute bodily suffering as a punishment after conviction, in the expectation that it would not only deter but reform ; and the results, during the first years of the trial, gave encouraging proof that, if conducted on proper principles, it must have the most beneficial effect. But the wretched economy that refused the accommodations for separate confinement ; the exercise of the pardoning power, ill-advised in many instances, in others resulting from a necessity created by that economy ; and the neglect of moral instruction, co-operated to arrest the course of this first great improvement ; and all the different state committees unite with that of Pennsylvania, in the declaration, that the great penitentiary system is no longer in operation. But this, even if it had been fully tried, is but one part, though an important one, of a reformatory code that deserves the name. To be perfect in its object, such a system should begin by prescribing a plan of public education, not confined to the elements of literature, but extended particularly to the duties of a citizen towards the state, and of men towards each other in every relation in life, and to those principles of religion which are equally acknowledged by all sects. It would only be repeating trite maxims and acknowledged truths, were the necessity of an early education to be enlarged upon ; but it is its operation, when extended to all classes of society, in preventing offences, that is here considered ; early youth is the season in which the germs of cupidity are to be eradicated :

> Eradenda cupidinis
> Pravi sunt elementa : et teneræ nimis
> Mentes superioribus
> Formandæ studiis————

It is there our legislation on this subject must begin, if we wish that its foundation should be stable. A prejudice has been entertained against religious instruction in public institutions, from a fear of their being made the engines of proselytism to sectarian doctrines—a fear well founded in countries where there is a dominant sect, but utterly groundless here, where the only establishment is that of perfect equality, and where there would be no practical difficulty in leaving to the parents and pastors of every pupil, the care of instructing him in the particular dogmas of his church, at the same time that the principles in which all concurred might be inculcated in the public school not only as duties of morality but of religion. It is astonishing how little use has been made of this powerful, I might say, when properly used, this omnipotent engine, in promoting the temporal concerns of society, as well as the most important welfare of the individuals who compose it. When it has been called into action, it has been either in aid of temporal, often absolute power, or for the aggrandizement of a particular church. In our happy country no such result need be feared ; and if this important part of a system for diminishing offence was within the compass of my undertaking, I should offer the project of a statute on this subject, that I think would secure the most perfect equality of religious rights, while it added the inestimable advantages of religious sanction in the prevention of crime. These advantages cannot be placed in a stronger point of light than is done by a gentleman to whose publications on this subject I have been indebted for much information

In fact, as well as instruction in argument. "If" he says " the inflic-tion of human punishment were as certain as their promulgation, crimes would be prevented altogether. But as it is impossible for any government to institute such a system of laws as can detect and punish all offences, the daring criminal perceives the imperfection ; and, trust-ing to his own precautions, and availing himself of time and circum-stances, flatters himself with the prospect of impunity. Not so with the denunciations of divine punishment ; which, when daily impressed on the mind, possess a sanction at which mere human authority can never arrive, and bring with them the *certainty of detection* and certainty of punishment, which alone can, in *all cases* and under *all circumstances,* prevent the perpetration of crime. If, then, we are once able to produce upon the mind a thorough conviction of the ex-istence of one supreme, intelligent, superintending being, the creator of all things, who sees through all his works, and perceives the deepest recesses of the human heart, and who *will reward or punish every one according to his deeds,* this will not only remedy the defects in mere human institutions by providing that continual inspection, discovery, and punishment, which such institutions endeavour in vain to supply ; but will correct innumerable offences of every kind which they do not pretend to punish, and which are wholly beyond their reach(*a*)." Such a plan of general religious instruction, embracing the doctrines common to all the Christain sects, and excluding all sectarian doctrine, is not mere theory. It has been for years practised in the city of Bos-ton, where nearly 100,000 dollars are appropriated to the public instruc-tion of children of every denomination, and where the forms of reli-gious instruction have been settled by the pastors of the several sects on the principles I have laid down ; and such success has attended this honourable and liberal experiment, that, although the schools have been in operation for more than ten years, and on an average more than three thousand have been educated in them annually, not one of those educated there have been even *committed* for a crime(*b*). And in New York a similar effect has been observed. Of the thou-sands educated in the public schools of that city, taken generally from the poorest classes of society, but one, it is asserted, has ever been con-victed, and that for a trifling offence(*c*).

I should apologize for drawing the attention of the legislature to a subject that might seem foreign to the plan which this report is intend-ed to elucidate, if public education were not found to be one of the best means of preventing crimes, and if the reflections here made did not apply to the instruction which forms so large a part of the prison discipline

(*a*) Roscoe. Additional Observations on Penal Jurisprudence.

(*b*) As far as the reporter is informed, the United States have given the first example, in modern times, of provision for education, furnished at the public expense to all the commu-nity. The early colonists of New-England set the example; the system is coeval with the first settlement of Massachusetts, and has with the most enlightened spirit of legis-lation been adopted by other states. The liberal arrangement with respect to religious in-struction is not confined to the period of ten years mentioned in the text—it was made much earlier; but the fact of its operation in preventing crime was derived from a gentleman, (S. L. Knapp, Esq.) who spoke from knowledge, acquired during that period, by a personal attention to the schools, and a close professional attendance in the courts.

(*c*) Letter from Thomas Eddy to the commissioners, 1825, containing very judicious re-flections on this subject.

which I propose. Adverting, then, only to this as to a subject connected with, but not embraced by, the matter of this report, I proceed to develop the system which, after the maturest reflection, I have submitted for consideration. Its objects are extensive and many, but are so closely connected, that to strike out any one would destroy the unity that must give it effect. Instead of confining it, as has been hitherto done, to considering imprisonment and labour as the means of punishing crimes already committed, I draw the attention of the legislature to the means of preventing them, by provisions bearing upon pauperism, mendicity, idleness and vagrancy, the great sources of those offences which send the greatest numbers to our prisons.

Political society owes perfect protection to all its members in their persons, reputations and property ; and it also owes necessary subsistence to those who cannot procure it for themselves, penal laws to suppress offences are the consequences of the first obligation, those for the relief of pauperism of the second; these two are closely connected, and when poverty is relieved, and idleness punished whenever it assumes the garb of necessity, and presses on the fund that is destined for its relief, the property and persons of the more fortunate classes will be found to have acquired a security, that, in the present state of things, cannot exist.

This truth has attracted the attention of most civilized nations, but by always making the laws of pauperism a distinct branch of legislation, never connecting it with their penal jurisprudence, with which it has so intimate a relation, it has been a source of more perplexity and confusion, has given birth to more bad theory and ruinous practice than any other question in government. Many of these difficulties, it is supposed, will be obviated by the application of sound principles, before the evil has become so incorporated in the system as to make it difficult to be eradicated.

In relation to this subject, society is formed of two divisions ; those who by their industry or property, provide subsistence for themselves and their families, and those who do not. The latter must of necessity draw their support from the former, either by depredations on property which brings them within the purview of the laws for punishing crimes ; or under the reality or pretence of pauperism by levying a tax on public or individual charity. It is to this last description that I now draw the attention of the legislature. They may be divided into three classes.

Those who can labour and are willing to labour, but who cannot find employment.

Those who can labour, but are idle from inclination, not for want of employment.

Those who are unable to support themselves by their labour, from infancy, old age, or infirmity of body or mind.

The first and last of these classes are to be relieved, not only by force of the obligation before referred to, but from a social duty not less imperative, because it is founded on humane feelings, and is enforced by perhaps the best precept of that religion which places charity in the highest rank of the virtues it inculcates. This relief must be given by providing means of employment for the industrious, and gratuitous support for the helpless. The middle class includes those who, under the name of vagrants and able bodied beggars, are placed in society on the verge between vice and crime, vicious enough to require inspection and restraint, not so palpably guilty as to justify severer punishment : abounding in large cities, they are the hot-beds, in which idleness and profligacy are forced into crime, and are properly the object of coercive justice, but they cannot become so without adopting the means necessary to distinguish and separate them from the innocently poor, and it is this necessity which brings that class also within the scope of the measures for preventing crimes.   It was thought that a good system should not only restrain the vicious, and punish and reform the guilty, but, by relieving and employing the poor, put an end to one of the strongest inducements to commit offences.   For these reasons the Code of Reform and Prison Discipline provides, that a building shall be erected to be called the House of Industry, with two distinct departments, one for voluntary the other for coerced labour ; the first department is intended as a place of employment for all those who are capable of gaining, by their bodily exertions, a complete or partial support ; and for the few who are totally helpless.   Its character, as a HOUSE OF REFUGE, will be hereafter explained ; the second department is designated as a place in which vagrants and the able bodied mendicants shall be forced to labour for their support.

This establishment enters most essentially into the plan I propose. Its different departments, under the name of poorhouses, workhouses, and bridewells, are known not only in England and the states which derive their jurisprudence from that country, but in different parts of Europe, but they are there distinct institutions, and want that unity of plan from which it is thought their principal utility will arise.   This requires elucidation.   If the duty of supporting its members be once acknowledged to be one incumbent on society to the extent that has been assumed, and if the classification I have made is correct, the necessity becomes apparent of distinguishing in what degree the different applicants are entitled to relief ; but that system would be obviously imperfect that was confined to making this distinction, and granting relief only to the one class without making any disposition of the others. Every applicant, if my premises be true, must belong to one or the other of those classes; and the same magistrate who hears his demand of support, or before whom he is brought, on an accusation of illegally obtaining it, is enabled at once to assign him his place.   Is he able and willing to work, but cannot obtain it ?   Here is employment suited to his strength, to his age, his capacity.   Is he able to work, but idle, intemperate, or vicious ?   His habits must be corrected by seclusion, sobriety, instruction and labour.   Is he utterly unable to provide for his support ? The great social duty of religion and humanity must be performed. One investigation on this plan puts an end to the inquiry.   Every one applying for alms, or convicted of illegal idleness and vice, necessarily belongs to one or the other class, and immediately finds his place ; he no longer remains a burthen on individuals, and society is at once relieved from vagrancy and pauperism.   Instead of this simple process, the poor laws are generally administered by agents whose duty is confined to a selection of proper objects of charity, without power to punish the impostor who preys on the fund provided for the poor and the helpless; and without any means to enable the honest labourer or artisan to earn his subsistence.   This establishment once made, on a proper scale, the plan for supporting it faithfully executed, the second degree in this scale of preventive justice will be obtained. By the first, your rising generation will be taught habits of industrious obedience to the law, a respect for religion, and a love of justice and moral duties. By this, which is the second, those who have grown up without these advantages, those who have not profited by them, and the numerous class of adventurers from other countries, will be arrested in the earliest stages of their profligacy, and taught to be industrious before they become criminal.

I am not unaware that this plan is, in some points, founded on principles that are much questioned by many who have written on this part of social economy. Without making this report a vehicle for the full discussion of those principles, it will be necessary briefly to state the objections that have been made, with my reasons for not yielding to their force.

The policy, and sometimes the obligation, of a public provision for the poor, has been forcibly assailed in England, and by men of high reputation here. The argument is shortly this. The duty to provide for the poor is rather a moral than a civil obligation: it binds, successively, relations, friends, wealthy individuals, and, last of all, society, which can be called on to support those only who are not provided for by individuals. But if this obligation upon society be once acknowledged and acted on, the individuals who stand in a nearer relation to the pauper will at once disregard a duty which has only a moral sanction, and the government will have the exclusive charge of the burthen. And this, according to the argument, is not all: the certainty of an ultimate support will lead to idleness, extravagant speculations, imprudent marriages, and all the improvident acts that naturally produce poverty; and, in time, the number of paupers will be so great as to consume the resources of the state, or, if quartered on smaller divisions of the country, to reduce the individuals composing it nearly to the state of those whom they are forced to relieve. And the theory is supported by reference to England, where, at times, every fifth man is a pauper, and the poor-rates equal one-tenth($a$) of the whole revenue of the kingdom.

In a country with a population so great as to reduce the full price of labour to a bare subsistence, and at the same time employing that labour in the production of articles for which the demand is uncertain, there is no doubt, that, at times, a permanent provision for the poor must be extremely burthensome on the community; and in such a country, an establishment to provide labour for all those whom the vicissitudes of trade should throw out of employment, would be, perhaps, impracticable, and certainly very difficult of execution. But besides its inapplicability to a different state of society, the argument is founded on the false principle, that the moral obligation of charity in individuals, whether related to the pauper or not, is superior in degree, as well as prior in the time of its exercise, to that social duty which every nation owes to the individuals which compose it; which duty is not only protection, but mutual support. That society owes protection to all its members, is not denied. But what is that protection? Certainly its

(*a*) In the year 1821, the poor-rates were 7,325,611*l*; the income 72,811,862*l*; the number of paupers 2,493,423; and the whole population 12,218,500.

chief object is life; but whether life be assailed by the sword or by famine, it is equally important for the individual, and for the community too, that it should be preserved.   There are mutual obligations between society and the members who compose it, which are not written covenants; they result from the nature of the connexion, from the object to be attained by the association, which is the protection of life and property.   But the preservation of life is the first object, property is only a secondary one; and if a contract is to be supposed, can it be imagined to be of a nature that would impose on any one of the contracting parties the loss of that which it was the chief end of the contract to preserve ; and that too for the preservation to the others of a portion of that which was only the secondary object ?   In other words, can it be supposed that any just contract could stipulate that one of the contracting parties should die of hunger, in order that the others might enjoy, without deduction, the whole of their property ?   The obligation, then, if derived from the only source to which we can look for its conditions, includes support as well as protection; and although this obligation may, by the operation of positive law, be justly modified by imposing the burthen of support on relations capable by their fortune of supporting it, yet, whenever these means are either deficient, or have not been provided, the duty returns in its full force upon the community.

That this duty is sometimes very onerous, cannot be denied.   A redundant population, by which I mean more people than can be so employed as to earn their subsistence, is a cause of this evil, that can only be avoided by emigration, when it is the result of a natural increase ; but generally it is the effect of false principles in political economy ; of that system which, by premiums and duties, pampers one branch of industry into an unnatural growth, and seduces so many to pursue it, that the market is soon overstocked with the proceeds of their labour, and they are then left to starve, or become the objects of public charity. A temporary foreign demand may also have the same effect ; but, in that case, the community, which must have been enriched by the effects of that demand, will be better able to bear the burthen, and ought not to complain that it is forced to give occasional support to the unfortunate instruments of its prosperity.   But, in a country where the ordinary price of labour is more than sufficient for maintenance of the poor, they can only be a serious burthen in consequence of the want of true principles, or a good system of enforcing them, and the whole secret lies in the finding employment adapted to every applicant for relief. The number of those who are incapable in any degree of contributing by labour to their own support, is very small ; and it is evident that, when none are idle, the cost to the state will be only equal to the difference between the proceeds of such labour and the expense of support; but the proceeds of ordinary labour are supposed, by the state of society, to be more than sufficient for maintenance ; therefore, making all proper deductions for forced labour, and the other disadvantages of public institutions, the proceeds of labour, then, if they are properly conducted, will not fall so far short of the expense as to create any fear of the ruinous consequences which attend the increase of the poor-rates in England.

At present, the duty of supporting needy relations is, by the law as well of England as of the different united states, confined to ascendants and descendants only.   To extend this obligation, so as to oblig

2 Q

collaterals within the second, or perhaps the third degree, to contribute to their support, would, it is thought, not only lessen the burthen on the public, but prevent, by the advice and interference of friends, those imprudent engagements which are the principal causes of poverty. Should it have this effect, it will lessen the weight of the objection that a public provision for the poor will increase the numbers, by rendering men adventurous in speculation, improvident in marriage, and careless in the conduct of their affairs. Most of the writers on this subject, state that this effect is produced by the poor laws of England ; but it would seem that the natural love of independence, and the sense of degradation inseparable from a reliance on public charity, would always prevent this provision being calculated on as a desirable resource ; and we might rather conclude that the numbers who are reduced to this extremity by extravagance, would have been equally prodigal if no such provision had existed. However this may be, in a country where the sense of shame is deadened by misery and extensive companionship in its degrading effects, and where support is afforded without exacting its equivalent in labour, it is believed that nothing of this nature need to be apprehended, in one where the natural repugnance to live on charity is strengthened by the ease with which labour can procure not only support, but competence and ease ; and where the relief that it is proposed to afford, can only be procured by bodily exertions proportioned to the ability of the party. Such are the reasonings and facts on which I have ventured to propose, as part of my plan, the house of refuge and of industry. I deem it a most essential part of the system. As prevention, in the diseases of the body, is less painful, less expensive, and more efficacious than the most skilful cure ; so, in the moral maladies of society, to arrest the vicious before the profligacy assumes the shape of crime ; to take away from the poor the cause or pretence of relieving themselves by fraud or by theft ; to reform them by education, and make their own industry contribute to their support, although difficult and expensive ; will be found more effectual in the suppression of offences, and more economical, than the best organized system of punishment. An offence perpetrated, incurs the loss sustained by its commission, and frequently that of its repetion added to the expense of its punishment. To prevent an offence requires only the previous expense of education and confinement. These reasons have induced me to suggest the plan of general education, and to combine with the system I offer, establishments for the relief of paupers, and the seclusion and instruction of the vicious and idle. These institutions, although they may conveniently be placed under the immediate direction of the same superintendent, are essentially different in their character : the one is a prison, the other a place of refuge. The object of one is instruction, of the other relief : education and industry are ends common to both. Therefore, the regulations for the one prescribe strict seclusion and coerced labour, while the confinement and classification of the other is merely such as is necessary for the maintenance of order ; and the only penalty for idleness is discharge, with the certainty of being classed in the next application for relief with those who are wilfully idle. The great objection usually made to establishments of this kind, is the expense. This, in a great measure, will be obviated by a wise and prudent administration, by which labour, suited to every degree of strength and skill may be provided.   In our country there are great facilities for this : gardening, poultry yards, and the different occupations of agriculture necessary for the supply of a large city, offer employments of the most healthful kind, and in which some occupation suited to every individual may be found.   Add to these, a brick or tile yard, a rope walk, chair making, all the manufactures of straw, cotton spinning, weaving, and other manufactures, of which more particular mention will be made when we speak of the penitentiary ; and it will be seen that, by proper management, means will be found to employ all the tenants of this establishment, whether in the seclusion of the house of industry, or the more relaxed discipline of the house of refuge : few are so weak and infirm as to contribute nothing towards their support ; and the great object will be that there shall be no idleness that is not the effect of infirmity.   By these means, the actual expense will be much lessened, and the comparative account truly stated, between the cost of suffering them to live in idleness by contributions levied upon private or public charity, or depredations upon property, and the expense of this establishment will show a balance greatly in its favour.

We are come to that part of the system of prison discipline applicable to penal law, in that restricted sense which confines it to the prosecution and punishment of offences.   In the project which I submit to the legislature, I begin with a part of the subject that has generally been most unaccountably, most injuriously neglected.   The danger of vicious association is universally acknowledged ; its corrupting influence has been pourtrayed by every figure that rhetoric could supply, and enforced by the most energetic language of eloquence ; but its deleterious effects seem to be feared only after condemnation, and no efficient plan has hitherto been adopted, or, as far as I am informed, proposed to any legislature, to apply a corrective to it in the incipient stages of criminal procedure.   Yet here, emphatically, it is calculated more widely to spread its infection.   After condemnation there can be no association but of the guilty with the guilty ; but in the preliminary imprisonment, guilt is associated with innocence.   The youth who is confined on suspicion only, whose innocence at the time of his arrest is attested by his subsequent acquittal, leaves the den where he was imprisoned, with tainted morals, depraved habits, passions excited to vengeance, and fit associates to aid him in pursuits that makes his second entrance to the house of detention only a passage to the penitentiary, or, in our present system, to the gallows.   In our great cities, where this reform is most necessary, it seems least attended to.   Vices the most disgusting, brutal intemperance, crime in its most hideous and appalling forms, are there congregated, and form a mass of corruption, rendered more deleterious from the mixture of imported depravity and native profligacy of which it is composed.   The bridewell of a large city is the place in which those representatives of human nature, in its most degraded shape, are assembled ; brought into close contact, so that no art of fraud, no means of depredation, no shift to avoid detection, known to one, may be hid from the other; where those who have escaped receive the applause due to their dexterity, and he who has suffered, glories in the constancy with which he has endured his punishment, and resisted the attempts to reform him. Here, he who can " commit the oldest crime the newest sort of way,''

is hailed as a genius of superior order, and having no interest to secure
the exclusive use of the discovery, he freely imparts it to his less instructed companions. Thieves, and all the other offenders whose crimes
are committed upon property, here receive the most useful instructions,
not only for perfecting themselves in their vocation, but of the proper
objects on which it may be exercised; and the comparatively short detention of a large majority, gives them the means of immediately practising the lessons they have received: for it may be fairly calculated
that, of those committed for trial, three-fourths(a) escape conviction
after being detained just long enough to receive instruction in all the
mysteries of crime. This view of the danger of increasing guilt, by
communication between the guilty in different degrees, has been often
considered, and is in a great degree applicable to the association of convicts in a penitentiary as well as in those prisons we are now considering. But, when we add to it the serious consideration that innocence
and youth are at all times exposed to this contaminating influence; that
laws which profess to preserve the morals and purity of the citizen, are

(a) In New York, in the year 1822, there were committed to the bridewell prison, on accusations for crimes and misdemeanors, 2361 persons. Of these, fewer than 541 were
brought to trial, for that is the whole number of persons tried, including those who were not
committed but bailed ; of these 541, 180 were acquitted ; which produces this result.

| | |
|---|---:|
| Committed for trial, | 2361 |
| Convicted, | 361 |
| Discharged or acquitted, | 2000 |
| In 1823, were committed, | 1928 |
| The whole number tried that year was 599, of whom 177 were acquitted, so that the number of those convicted was | 422 |
| Total discharged or acquitted, | 1506 |
| In 1824, committed, | 1961 |
| Tried 586, acquitted 169, convicted, | 417 |
| Total discharged or acquitted, | 1544 |
| In 1825, committed, | 2168 |
| Tried 547, acquitted 161, convicted, | 386 |
| Total discharged or acquitted, | 1782 |
| In 1826, there were committed, to the 20th November, | 2046 |
| Add in the same proportion for the rest of the year, | 227 |
| | 2273 |
| Tried 662, acquitted 200, convicted, | 462 |
| Total discharged or acquitted, | 1811 |

This is sufficient to show that, in every year in one of our cities, from 1500 to 2000 persons of both sexes, all of whom are legally presumed to be innocent, and a large proportion
must be really so, are annually forced, by the operation of the laws, into the closest association with the most abandoned of their species; they must eat, drink and sleep with them.
They have no retreat from the infectious atmosphere of their society; and, after having been
thus forced to enter the school of vice and criminality, the 2000 disciples are turned out to
practise the lessons they have learned! And this is the wise system of laws that needs no
amendment! This is the humane administration of them in a rich and enlightened city!

made the instruments of their destruction ; what expression can be too strong to mark our astonishment at the apathy or indolence of legislators, who, knowing the evils of the system, can suffer it to continue, or who will not take the trouble to inform themselves on the subject ?   Indiscriminate confinement, preparatory to the trial, has, in this report, hitherto been considered only in its contaminating effects ; and those effects are sufficiently dreadful.   But there is another view of its consequences, its inevitable consequences, which not only shocks the understanding, but lacerates the best feelings of the heart.   The only discrimination made between the white tenants of these places of confinement is that of the sexes.   The women are kept in a separate apartment, the men in as many others as the prison can afford, but without any distinction between them.   The innocent stranger, unable to find security, is joint tenant of the same chambers with three times convicted convicts ; vagrants sunk in vice, and brutified by intoxication; perpetrators of every infamous crime, and even with murderers taken in the fact.   Women of innocence and virtue are sometimes forced, by this unhallowed administration of justice, into an association with all that is disgusting in female vice ; with vulgarity in its most offensive form ; with intemperance sunk to the lowest depth of degradation ; with every thing that can be conceived most abhorrent to female delicacy and refinement. This is no picture of the imagination : the reporter has seen it.   It is realized in a greater or less degree in all the cities of the Atlantic states: and even legislators, patriotic statesmen, and benevolent philanthropists, who have for years been legislating, and reasoning, and devoting their time and talents to the application of solitary imprisonment to the purposes of punishment after conviction, have never yet taken one efficient step to prevent the demoralizing effects attending indiscriminate association before trial, or to rescue the innocent not only from the infection of such society, but from the punishment it inflicts.   For what greater punishment could be devised for a man of education and morals, used to the refinements of good society, than to shut him up night and day, for weeks and months, in a room crowded with the vilest of the vile, with men stained with every crime ? or to a woman, not sunk herself in vice, to be associated with the most abandoned of her sex ?   Yet such is the humanity, the justice of our boasted jurisprudence.   We begin by inflicting this moral punishment on one presumed, by the first principle of our law, to be innocent : we add to it the physical evil of close confinement, without any of the conveniences of life, for an unlimited period ; and when perhaps his morals are corrupted by the society which the justice of his country has forced him to keep, and his health is destroyed by the rigour of imprisonment, his innocence is declared, and he is restored to society either to prey upon it by his crimes, or burthen it by his poverty.   What greater moral or physical evil, it may be asked, would have been inflicted on the guilty, than this which the innocent is made to suffer ?   An eye witness to more than one of the scenes he has described, and which, he repeats, are not exaggerated in the description, the reporter was deeply impressed with the necessity of a radical reform in the system of detention before trial, and has embodied it in the code which he presents.   Persons whose liberty, for the good of society, must be restrained, are either those upon whom imprisonment is imposed merely for the purpose of securing their appearance when the purposes of justice require it, or those upon whom it is inflicted as a punishment.

The detention of those of the first description, to be just, must not only be necessary, but must be attended with no privation that is not absolutely required for the end proposed, and for the preservation of order.

Each of these two divisions is composed of several subordinate classes, for the government of which different rules are necessary. None are comprehended in the first, who are able to find a sufficient pledge that their personal attendance will be given when it is called for. The purposes of the projected code require, that those comprising this division should form three classes.

1. Persons whose testimony is necessary for the investigation of some important charge.

2. Those accused of misdemeanor.

3. Those charged with crime.

The first of these classes is separated from the two others by an evidently marked distinction. Those who compose it are not presumed to be guilty of any offence; the temporary privation of their liberty is a necessary sacrifice for the safety of society; it is taken on the same principle that justifies the appropriation of private property for public purposes, and it carries with it the same right of indemnity; which indemnity the code does not fail to provide.

With respect to the two other classes, there is this difference, that, in these, there is a presumption of guilt, arising from an accusation on oath. The maxim, that every man is presumed innocent before conviction, is, like many other legal maxims, true only to a certain extent. In its application, it can mean only that proof must precede conviction, and that accusation alone is not one of those presumptions which throws the burthen of proof on the accused, and cause him to be believed guilty, unless he shows himself innocent. But it is not true as respects persons accused on oath in a legal form. This is sufficient to justify every measure for securing the person, because it creates such a presumption of guilt as raises a probability of an attempt to escape punishment, and on the degree of this probability is founded the distinction between the second and third classes: the motive to attempt an escape being greater, in proportion to the magnitude of the punishment. For these reasons, the code directs that prisoners of the first class, to whom no offence is imputed, shall enjoy every alleviation of their misfortune, not incompatible with the maintenance of order, that their own means can procure. The second class being accused of an offence, punishable when proved, by a comparatively light penalty, neither the temptation to escape, nor the evil consequences to society, should it be effected, are so great as to justify a rigour of confinement equal to that which is necessary to secure the third class, accused of crime. These degrees are distinctly marked in the code, but it carefully provides that none of those comprehended in this division, shall suffer any other inconveniences from their detention, than those necessary to secure their personal appearance, and to prevent the evil association, no less requisite to protect their own morals against the contagion of vice, for this classification is essential to the other and no less important design, which has been before stated in this report, that of separating the persons composing the two first classes from any communication with those of the third, and the individuals of this last from any intercourse with each other. The presumption, before alluded to, also justifies this measure. It is one of protection, from which the innocent have every thing to gain, and of which the guilty cannot complain: for it imposes no unnecessary restraint, and takes from them only the power of corrupting and being further corrupted. The danger of guilty associations; the duty of avoiding them by a careful separation of the innocent from those who labour under a presumption of guilt; of those accused or convicted of offences, implying no great degree of moral turpitude, from those who are presumed or known to be guilty of crimes which evince depravity of mind and manners; of the young from the old offender; are considerations on which the Code of Prison Discipline rests ; and on the Code of Prison Discipline depends the whole system of penal law. It is for this reason that classification before trial has been provided for with the same care that is required after conviction; and it has been particularly urged in the report, from a conviction that its importance in penal jurisprudence has not hitherto been properly appreciated. It is proposed, not only that the place for this confinement shall be separate from that in which it is inflicted as a punishment, but it is called, not a prison, but a HOUSE OF DETENTION merely, that the name may not carry with it any idea of infamous punishment. The marked distinction in the penal code, between crimes and misdemeanors; the degree of moral guilt in the former, with which the latter is, for the most part, not infected ; renders a correspondent difference necessary in the plan and nature of the punishment inflicted on them respectively.

After considering imprisonment as a necessary restraint merely, the only just character which, before trial, it can have, and showing the provisions in the Code of Prison Discipline adapted to this end, it remains to be considered in its double capacity, as a punishment and the means of reform.

The nature, properties and efficacy, of imprisonment, as a means of punishment, have been so fully discussed in the Introductory Report to the Code of Crimes and Punishments, that no more will be said here than is necessary to elucidate its modifications and combinations with the reformatory part of the plan.

Of imprisonment, the Code of Crimes and Punishments directs four grades : simple imprisonment, simple imprisonment in close custody, imprisonment with labour, and imprisonment in solitude.

The two first are applied to offences involving no great degree of moral wrong, and therefore ought not to be confounded with others in which depravity is apparent. Some loss of reputation, when the laws are just and impartially administered, necessarily is incurred by the infliction of every punishment. But disgrace ought to be attached to those only which are inflicted for crimes implying moral depravity. Hence the distinction which the law has drawn, and which the Code of Prison Discipline must execute, between misdemeanors and crimes. To mark this distinction, different places, as well as a difference of treatment, are necessary.

It would be approximating these degrees of offence too closely, to commit to the same prison the criminal and the misdemeanant. A man of worth and integrity may be guilty of breaking the provisions of mere positive law; but it would be confounding all ideas of proportion in punishment to conduct him to the same prison with the thief or assassin. A department, therefore, in the house of detention is designated for offenders of this description, whether the sentence be simple confinement or imprisonment in close custody. The discipline applicable to them is also necessarily different from that required in the penitentiary : as no great moral guilt is implied in the offences of which they have been guilty, and the detention is limited to short periods, so the imprisonment is intended more for punishment than reformation. In this, as in all other places of confinement, under this system, complete separation at night is strictly enforced ; the means of education and religious instruction are provided; seclusion is graduated according to the sentence; good wholesome food and comfortable lodging are provided at the public expense ; labour is permitted but never enforced ; vicious associations precluded, but close confinement never resorted to but when directed by the judgment, or rendered necessary to preserve the order of the prison. The distinction between simple imprisonment and confinement in close custody, is sufficiently explained in the Code of Crimes and Punishments; and the precise rules laid down in the Code of Prison Discipline for the treatment of prisoners under these punishments is calculated to prevent oppression, on the one hand, and on the other, strictly to enforce the execution of the sentence. How different in its very nature! How infinitely so in its effects, is imprisonment, under these regulations, from the same punishment as usually inflicted for slight offences! The horrors of a bridewell have been faintly described, yet it is such that the misdemeanor under the present system, in most of the states, is committed, to pass the period of his confinement without labour or instruction; and either in the congenial association with vulgarity and vice to forget that he is in a place of punishment, or, shrinking from their abhorred contact, to find the physical evil of imprisonment increased beyond calculation by a moral evil which is inflicted without being ordained by the law: whereas, on the plan I propose, no greater evil being suffered than precisely that directed by the sentence, and nothing left to the discretion of turnkeys or keepers, the judge is enabled, with a precision before impossible, to apportion the punishment to the offence. Heretofore, however slight the infraction of law that involved the penalty of confinement, an indefinite evil of bad association was necessarily annexed to it: and if a respectable man, for an imprudent breach of the peace, or for intemperate expression in court, should be committed to prison for a few days, it depended on the accidental circumstance of the numbers in the bridewell, and sometimes on the disposition of the keeper, or, what is worse, on the wealth of the party, to determine whether he should pass those days in a comfortable apartment, making merry with his friends, or should drag them on in the society of felons. Now, the magistrate will know the extent of the punishment he awards. Simple imprisonment is defined, its privations, its indulgences, the penalties attending the abuse of them ; every thing is accurately marked. Within certain limits traced by the law, these indulgences may be restricted or enlarged by the judge, not by the jailer; according to the circumstances of the offence, not according to the caprice of a turnkey, or the capacity of the prisoner to purchase his favour. And simple imprisonment, the lowest grade of corporal punishment, formerly an engine of torture to some, to others a mockery of justice, to all the means of depraved and depraving associations, becomes, in the hands of a discreet judge, an elastic instrument of coercion that may be made to press on the smallest transgressions, or expand to fit the highest misdemeanor to which it is applied.

Imprisonment in close custody is the next grade; and here the same strict rules to limit the discretion of the keeper, are applied.   In all the provisions of this code the great truth is never lost sight of, that every evil inflicted, beyond that which is necessarily included in the sentence, is illegal, is cruel, is tyrannical.   Hence the care in the codes that are submitted, first, to make the judge confine himself in his sentence strictly within the limits of the discretion that is given him, and to exercise that discretion as much as possible by the application of the general rules that are prescribed to guide his judgment ; and afterwards, when he has pronounced, to take away all other discretion that might alleviate, increase, or in any manner alter the punishment, except in the cases specially provided for.   In the case of simple imprisonment in close custody, these rules and exceptions, it is thought, will be found to answer these ends.   This grade of punishment is the last and highest of those inflicted for misdemeanors ; as it is intended by the Code of Crimes and Punishments to approach the severity, but not to be attended with the degradation of penitentiary confinement in solitude, so the Code of Prison Discipline, to give effect to this distinction, has prescribed a treatment that should mark, both to the sufferer and to others, that although the law punished his act as an offence, and doomed him to a prison for punishment, and to solitude and reflection for repentance, yet it does not confound his offence with those which, by the general consent of the civilized world, has been characterized as infamous.   This important distinction, fully discussed in the preliminary report to the former Code, is referred to here, only to mark the reason of the different places assigned to these two species of close custody, and to account for the different discipline by which they are respectively regulated.

We come now to the beaten ground of penitentiary discipline.   The first remark necessary to explain the nature of that system I have ventured to recommend is this: that the penal code assigns this punishment to no offences but such as suppose in the offender a depravity and corruption of mind which requires the application of reformatory discipline as well as punishment—they must not be separated.   And with the respect due to the great writers who have devoted their talents to this interesting subject, it may be permitted perhaps to suggest, that most of them err in considering the true end of penal laws to be either punishment alone, or reformation alone.   A good system must combine them: and the great excellence of the penitentiary plan is, that the process of reformation cannot be carried on but by privations and sufferings which, if they do not succeed so as to reform, must necessarily deter from a repetition of crime in as great a degree as any other bodily infliction could.   If the reformation is complete, we have the double assurance arising from the moral restraint and the remembrance of the physical as well as mental suffering.   As an example to deter others, penitentiary imprisonment has been considered to be defective in this, that here the real is greater than the apparent suffering ; whereas, it ought to be directly the reverse ; the apparent should exceed the real pain ; because the object of deterring others would be attained with as little injury as possible to the sufferers—it being a principle that no more evil than is necessary to produce that effect ought to be inflicted.

2 R

The principle is true when modified so as to require the real suffering to be sufficient for deterring the criminal himself, and the apparent not to be so great as to shock by a belief that it is cruel or disproportioned to the offence: but is the application of it to penitentiary imprisonment well made? The prisoner is not, say those who use this argument, always exposed to view, and, when he is seen, his appearance may not indicate the suffering which he undergoes. The misery of a restraint for years, perhaps for life, cannot show itself in the few moments of a casual visit; he appears well fed, well clothed, and the labour which he is seen to perform is moderate; there is nothing therefore in the aspect of the man to show the wretchedness that must be created by a whole life doomed to forced labour and degrading subjection. In this reasoning, however, we lose sight of two operations; the one going on in the mind of the convict, the other in that of the man upon whom his punishment is intended to be as an example; both of which essentially lessen the force of this objection. By the first, the sufferer becomes by habit, if not reconciled to his punishment, at least much better able to bear it. Some "strange comfort" finds its way into his cell, and illuminates it with a hope which, though long deferred, does not always sadden the heart: employment interrupts uneasy thoughts during the day, and produces the total oblivion of them by sound sleep at night ; and the misery of confinement for life, spread in equal proportions over each day, is so much less in any particular time, that, in many cases, the apparent is greater than the real suffering of the convict. On the other hand, he who is tempted to offend, and may be restrained by the fear of punishment, will add to that which he knows to exist, but which he does not see, all those horrors by which mystery always aggravates apprehended evils. Circumstances, too, may be superadded, to strike the imagination and increase this effect, without increasing the real suffering of the prisoner, while they augment its apparent intensity. Thus imprisonment even tested by this rule, is far from being so inefficient an engine of punishment, whether considered as the means of deterring the offender himself or others, as the objection supposes. And, even if we should discard the idea of reformation, penitentiary imprisonment has advantages which few other modes of punishment possess. It is permanent ; the prison is always seen ; and even if we do not visit its gloomy cells, the imagination will people them with tenants of its own creation, more squalid in appearance and hopeless and dejected in mind, than the real culprits who inhabit them; these too will have enough of suffering (discarding any but that authorized by law), to leave a lasting impression, and to prevent, if any thing short of reformation can prevent, a repetition of guilt. Whatever advantages penitentiary imprisonment, however, may possess as a punishment, it is certain that all punishments, considered merely as such, have failed in preventing offences; and the severest have always, without exception, been found the least efficacious. But, if punishment alone is inefficient, the reformation of the offender, if it were possible to effect it without punishment, would be so in the same or a greater degree ; the reformation of one offender would have little effect on his fellows, unless indeed as an additional inducement to proceed : but to refute this argument is nugatory, because no means of reformation have been proposed, or can well be imagined, that can be applied without imprisonment or other restraint ; but imprisonment or restraint is an evil to the sufferer, and all evil imposed in consequence of crime is punishment: all reformatory discipline therefore is necessarily connected with punishment; and it would, but for one consideration, be investigating the truth of a theory inapplicable to the subject if found to be true, were we to inquire whether reformation ought to be the sole object of penitentiary discipline. The consideration which alone renders the inquiry proper, and at the same time highly important, is this: that if reformation of the offender be the only object, and the example of the punishment is not to be considered, then the endeavour in establishing a mode of discipline should be to render it as light as possible, consistent with the end to be attained, which, by the argument, is reformation alone; because it is a true principle, that no greater evil ought ever to be inflicted than is necessary to the end; and therefore, if some legislator, a proselyte to this doctrine, should believe that mild persuasion and indulgence were better instruments of reformation than coerced labour and restraint, and should act on this belief, the example of the punishment to deter would be lost; and though one convict might go out a real or pretended saint, seven sinners would pursue his track of profligacy, secure that, even if detected, instead of punishment they would receive only advice and indulgence. The doctrine, therefore, that reformation is the sole end of penitentiary punishment, deserves to be examined. If it mean the reformation of the culprit, and of all who might follow his example, as the language used by one of its advocates(a) would perhaps justify us in believing, the dispute is one only of words; for if the punishment of one, or the reformation of one, prevents the other from committing the crime, it must be because he fears the evil of the reformatory discipline; he is then deterred by the example; and we arrive by different roads to the same point. But, more fairly considered, the argument is this: crime is an evil, punishment is an evil; to punish, therefore, is to multiply instead of diminishing it, unless it will deter the offender as well as others: but it is proved, by long experiment, that punishment has failed in this effect: therefore it is useless. Again, experience has proved that severe are much less efficacious than milder punishments; it is fair, then, to believe that the more you diminish the severity of your laws, the more efficacious will be their operation: and by one consequence further, if crimes decrease in the same ratio with the severity of penalties, that it is not the penalty that deters; and if it does not deter, it is not only useless but wrong, because we set out with the incontrovertible position that this is the only legitimate object of punishment: if crimes have been diminished by penitentiary imprisonment, then it could not have been the punishment that operated, it must have been something else, and that something should be the great object to keep in view—it is reformation.

A great error at the bottom of all this reasoning is one already referred to, that reformation is considered abstractedly, without any consideration of the means by which it is to be brought about, which is the evil or the punishment of seclusion, and which is inseparable from it: another not less striking is, that, supposing reformation effectually to prevent a repetition of the crime by the offender, the reasoning gives us no means of discovering how this will operate to deter others, except through the fear of the reformatory discipline, which, being from its nature a punishment, is discarded by the argument from hav-

(a) Roscoe.

ing effect. The other fallacies are, first, in placing crime and punishment as evils of the same nature. Crime is an evil operating on society; punishment, in the just degree that will prevent or lessen crime, so far from being an evil, is a good ; its pain is only felt by the delinquent : the immediate pain of the crime may perhaps only affect the individual sufferer by it, but the alarm it creates, the certainty that, unless repressed, it will be repeated, spreads through the whole community, and the uncertainty who will be its next victim, makes it an evil to all. The error lies in taking that for granted which is in dispute, that the dread of punishment does not deter from offences. And when that comes to be proved, it is done by another fallacy ; there have always been punishments and there have always been and still are offences ; if punishment would prevent them, there would be none. But my argument is, not that punishment will totally prevent, but that it will diminish crimes ; and in order to prove that it has not this effect, it would be necessary to show a state of society in which there was neither punishment nor crime. Besides, to convince us that punishment in its nature can have no effect, it must be shown to have failed when applied in its most perfect form. But no one pretends that this experiment has been ever tried: on the contrary, those who contend for its efficacy, when properly applied, have demonstrated that, throughout the world it has, in all ages, been wofully deficient. No one has yet gone so far as to draw the conclusion that, because mild have generally been found more efficacious than severe punishments, therefore no penalty ought to be annexed to offences ; and yet, if we assert that reformation is the only object, this is the plain and inevitable result : for then every pain, however small, inflicted as a punishment, would be a useless, and therefore an improper evil.

Imprisonment, therefore, is to be used, in the plan I propose, to punish as well as to reform. But to make imprisonment, especially if coupled with labour, a proper sanction, its details must be strictly defined by the law. Any discretion left to the jailer as to the mode of inflicting it, makes him, and not the judge, the arbiter of the culprit's fate. He may, without proper limits to his authority, change the sentence of a few years confinement into the same period of exquisite misery, followed by loss of health or of life ; and he may do this without incurring any penalty : for where a full discretion is given, there can be no penalty except in extreme cases for its abuse. If he may, at his discretion, inflict stripes for disobedience or want of respect ; if, in the language held from the bench in New York, it is his duty, "by all the means in his power, to make the convicts feel the awful degradation and misery to which their vicious courses had reduced them," and "that the ordinary sympathies of our nature could not be extended to them ;" if this be permitted, or especially if inculcated as the duty of the keeper, imprisonment is the worst of all punishments, because the most unequal. It is, then, no more the wisdom of the law applied to the case by the discretion of the judge that apportions the punishment, but the caprice or passion of an individual in the exercise of the fearful duty of forcing a convict to feel the *awful misery and degradation* of his situation. If labour be superadded as a punishment, the danger of this discretion is greatly increased. The same labour may be misery and death to one, and no more than wholesome exercise to another ; and the greatest abuse and oppression may be justified by enforcing a literal execution of the sentence. The law, then, must, in every particular that can be foreseen, regulate the conduct of those to whose keeping the prisoner is to be committed ; and after every precaution that human prudence can take, the carelessness, or passion, or pride of opinion in the keeper, may greatly counteract the operation of a good system, and his intelligence, firmness, humanity and strict attention, may correct some of the evils, and supply some of the omissions, which even the best cannot escape.  For this reason the importance of this office is inculcated in the text of the code ; and the qualities required for its exercise are pointed out as a guide to the selecting power, and a lesson to him who is chosen, that the one may not commit the fatal error of underrating the talents necessary for the employment, and that the other may feel the dignity with which he is invested, as well as the responsibility imposed on him by the law.  This was the more necessary in order to counteract a prejudice against the employment of those to whom the custody of prisons has been for many ages confided.  A well-founded prejudice, while the jailer was only appointed to prevent the escape of the promiscuous assemblage of vagrants of both sexes, consisting of unfortunate debtors, of innocent or guilty prisoners committed for trial, and of convicted felons awaiting an ignominous death, who were placed in his custody ; while he had no moral duty to perform, and was the mere Cerberus to guard the doors of a terrestrial Tartarus, such a prejudice was just and unavoidable ; and as one part of the duty of a jailer to prevent escapes, necessarily continues to be vested in the warden, the enunciation in the code becomes proper, in order to break the chain of ideas which might otherwise, from that circumstance, assimilate the character of an office calling for high talents, and honour and integrity, with that of an employment the natural tendency of which was to make him who exercised it an extortioner and a petty tyrant.

I return to the position, from which I may seem perhaps to have digressed, that the law should be so framed as to restrict as much as possible the discretionary power of the keeper ; it must designate the punishment due to the offence, either by an invariable rule, or by a discretion left to the judge to make one within certain limits.  The judge must apply this rule, by declaring the punishment, if it be fixed; by apportioning it to the degree of the offence, if he have a discretion. The punishment once ordered, that system is strangely defective which unnecessarily permits it to be aggravated or alleviated by an inferior officer, at his will.  It deserves a worse epithet if it hold out temptations for him to do it ; and the strongest that could be used to express disapprobation, would be merited if it is inculcated as a duty.  But the system of social forced labour makes this discretionary power unavoidable ; for nothing, we are told, (and I believe told truly), nothing but the lash can preserve the proper discipline in such an association.  The punishment, then, necessary to execute the sentence of the law is on this plan, so far from being directed by the sentence, is one expressly prohibited by the law under which that sentence is pronounced, and therefore ought never to enter into any subordinate part of the system. What could be more incongruous than to snatch the scourge from the hands of justice to place it in those of caprice ; to declare it too severe, and degrading, and demoralizing, and unequal, to be applied as a punishment for CRIME, at the sound discretion of the judge, and, at the same time, direct that it shall be inflicted for disobedience to a subaltern officer of a prison at his pleasure ?  I could not, therefore, offer any plan of imprisonment that would make this absurdity necessary. Other disadvantages which are inseparable from this discipline, have been detailed when I described that of the New York prisons, of which it forms so prominent a feature. I discard it, therefore, being firmly convinced that, as an instrument of punishment, it is not only defective and dangerous, but that it cannot be brought to produce that reformation which is one of the essential parts of my plan. But social labour, whether general or in classes (if those classes are at all numerous), cannot be carried on without it, unless the security and order of the prison be put at hazard. Social labour, therefore, must be abandoned, or so modified, and admitted with such precautions, as to render this anomaly unnecessary. The manner in which this has been attempted, requires some previous examination of the principles on which it is founded.

We have, in former parts of this report, considered the question whether punishment, as an object distinct from reformation, should not enter into the sanction of penal laws; and were brought to the double conclusion, that it was necessary, and that no reformation could be produced without it. Imprisonment has been examined as a means of inflicting punishment, and in this and in the introductory report to the Code of Crimes and Punishments, has been compared with other corporal punishments, and been found to possess, in a greater degree than any other, the essential properties to render it effectual. Here we need only add, that there is no other means by which a reformatory process (necessarily requiring time and a succession of operations) can be carried on; no labour, no instruction, without detention, no reformation without employment, without instruction, religious, moral and literary. It must be remembered that we are now speaking of the prison discipline proper for convicts, for men already corrupted; to whom, for the most part, labour was necessary for support, and who resorted to crime in order to avoid it. Labour consists of a number, of a succession of bodily exertions, always painful when first endured, becoming tolerable only by the habit of making them, and never voluntarily resorted to but from the hope of some enjoyment they are to produce; these two causes combined give to an occupation painful in itself, all the characteristics of a pleasurable pursuit; habit destroys the sense of bodily pain; hope anticipates the reward it is to bring, identifies the enjoyment with the means of procuring it, and, by a wise use of the faculties bestowed by our beneficient Creator, labour becomes cheerful, and its pain a pleasure. This might be further illustrated by investigating the cause of pleasure resulting from the chase, and other laborious recreations, which are often voluntarily pursued so far as to become toilsome and fatiguing in a degree not frequently suffered by the severest labour. In these pursuits, indeed, the exhilarating effects of fresh air, of society, and a view of the beauties of nature, give a present enjoyment that is not found in daily employment; but these would never induce us to go beyond the point of agreeable exercise: they are pushed into fatigue by the causes that have been stated, and by the self-satisfaction arising from a consciousness of dexterity and skill. The anticipation of the applause he will receive, of the festivity, or the domestic comfort, that awaits his return, is identified in the mind of the sportsman with the fatigue he undergoes, the pain of which habit has already alleviated; so that the toils and the pleasures of the chase have become terms that are nearly synonymous.

The great painter of human passions has beautifully delineated this association, in the picture of a young lover toiling through a servile employment, with the hope of being rewarded by the presence of his mistress, and referring the patience and even the pleasure with which his toil was endured to this very illustration :

> There be some sports are painful; but their labour,
> Delight in them sets off.

Whenever this association of ideas is broken, labour is regarded as an evil unmitigated by any alleviating circumstance ; no habit will induce a continuance of it, and it will never be resorted to but in moments of pressing distress, the idea of which then becomes incorporated with it and embitters its pains.    Labour forced by stripes must always produce this dreadful concatenation of ideas ; and whenever the coercion ceases, the natural aversion to fatigue will combine with the remembrance of the evils with which it was embittered, and make the culprit fly to vice to forget, or to crime to avoid it.

If these reflections be well founded, employment should be offered as an alleviation of punishment, not superadded to aggravate it. Although labour is painful, yet the separate exertions, of a succession of which it is composed, are not so in themselves ; it is their repetition only which makes them irksome: there is an innate love of action in human nature, which renders its restraint the principal evil attending imprisonment : and involuntary idleness, unbroken by any mental or bodily occupation, creates a degree of suffering which, setting aside acute physical pain, can only be aggravated by uninterrupted solitude.    Solitude without physical employment may be rendered tolerable, if the mind can be diverted from its own reflections by receiving intellectual instruction from others, or amusement from books: these, also, except so far as concerns a future life, are indulgences withheld from the convict by the tenor of his sentence.

Next to the privations of liberty and employment, and perhaps superior in intensity to the last, is that of the usual indulgence of the appetite for food and drink : to inflict this, so far as to make the patient suffer by hunger or thirst, would be at war with the first principles of this system; it would be causing an evil, the degree of which could never be measured so as to be directed by the sentence ; and if left to the discretion of an executive officer, would cause a suffering not directed by the law or the judge ; and in most cases would change a sentence of confinement into one carrying with it loss of health or life: food, therefore, wholesome in quality, and in abundance sufficient to satisfy the appetite and support life, but of the plainest kind, without any variety to stimulate, or delicacy to gratify the appetite, is allowed to the convict, but it is all he is entitled to; and thus another privation is added to those already enumerated, as concomitants of the punishment directed by law. But this is not all : men desire not only liberty, recreation, and the indulgence of the appetite; but also a shelter and clothing, fitted to the variations of the season : and in civilized life there are certain refinements of indulgence in these articles, the privation of which becomes a severe punishment, when we are reduced to what is strictly necessary. The action of these natural inclinations, their restriction, and partial indulgence, constitute the moving power of my system of punishment and reformation.

Imprisonment, solitude, want of occupation, either for the mind or body, coarse aliments, hard lodging, clothing of the roughest kind, are the evils of which punishments are composed ; their duration, their intensity, their cumulation, are the means provided·by the Code of Crimes and Punishments, for adapting them to the different offences ; their alleviation in different degrees are those designated in the Code of Reform and Prison Discipline, for producing reform.

If the reasoning already employed be correct, no succession of involuntary acts to which adults may be coerced is likely to produce permanent habits of reformation : they must be the effect of the will, operated upon by the judgment, producing a conviction that such acts are beneficial; and experience must enforce this conviction, by giving the actual enjoyment of some, and the certain hope of other benefits, that are the result of these acts.  With evil habits it is different : for the most part they are acquired by a repetition of acts procuring sensual enjoyment; and the judgment has so little agency in producing them, that it must be silenced or perverted before the acts of indulgence are done or repeated.  It is for this reason that the work of reformation is more difficult than that of perversion : the one requires intellectual power sufficient to prefer a distant and moral good, to a present and physical enjoyment: the other coincides with the natural propensity for present enjoyment, reckless of what an uncertain futurity may produce.  And for this reason also it is that the work of reformation is slower in its operation than that of corruption.  A single instance in which distress has been alleviated, or expected good has been realized by labour or exertion, would have but a temporary effect; the operation must be repeated, and be made always to produce the same result, and the judgment must be thoroughly convinced that this result is invariable, before it can counteract in the will the natural preference of present enjoyment to future good.  But to produce this effect, the mind must be improved by intellectual instruction; it must be taught that there are other pleasures besides those of sense ; and religion must be brought to bear its part in the work of amelioration.  The deep solitude of the prisoner's cell, the awful impression which must be made on his mind, by contrasting the fleeting enjoyment produced by his crime with the lasting evil in which he is plunged by its consequences; the privation of factitious excitements; with no companions to applaud his perseverance in wrong; no means of drowning reflection by intemperance ; no acute or disproportioned pain to brace him up against real or fancied oppression; the heart must necessarily be softened, and the spirit subdued, and the mind prepared to receive those great truths, which, under such circumstances, may be inculcated to the highest advantage, more especially when this, combined with literary instruction, is offered, not as a part of the sentence, but as an alleviation of its rigour.

This spring, then, which sets in motion my whole machinery for producing reform, is this: that all the acts which, by their succession, are to produce habits of good, are to be performed voluntarily, and are offered as alleviations of the severity of the sentence: the will must act, or the repetition will produce no effect.  But, to operate on the inclination, sufficient inducements must be held out to overcome the natural repugnance to labour: and this brings me back to the detail of those modifications of imprisonment, and its concomitant labour, which I offer instead of the strict seclusion of the Pennsylvania(a), or the severe discipline of the New York system.

To understand them, a clear idea must first be given of the place of confinement.   It consists of an arched cell for each prisoner, of small dimensions, but well ventilated, and comfortably warmed, communicating with a small court, surrounded with a high wall.   The sentence of the law is confinement to the cell, supported by wholesome but coarse food, in sufficient quantity to satisfy hunger, but without occupation, and with no other society than the attendance of those officers who minister to the physical wants of the prisoner, and to his religious instruction.   Privation of employment is denounced as a part of the punishment; and this circumstance alone would, with most men, cause it to be considered as an evil, and the experience of its effects will soon cause it to be felt as such; of course it will be connected with the idea of suffering; and occupation being denied, will, from the propensity to wish for that from which we are expressly debarred, be estimated as a good, and desired with an intensity proportioned to the strictness and length of the privation.   To strengthen this natural desire, other inducements are offered.   He who labours lessens the expense of his support, he who works skilfully and diligently may more than repay it.   The advantage of this beneficial result must be felt by the prisoner as well as the state: if the proceeds of his work should not be sufficient to cover his expenses, it yet produces for him a better diet; and if persevered in, and accompanied with good conduct, for certain probationary periods of six and twelve months, during which he is permitted in the day to leave his cell and pursue his solitary employment in the court, he is indulged with the privilege of working, and receiving instruction in a small class, not exceeding ten: but, if he acquires such proficiency in his business as to make the proceeds of his industry exceed the expense of his support, he is allowed the immediate enjoyment of a part, to be laid out in books, or such other articles as he may desire.   Those of food or drink are excepted, in order to avoid irregularities that would otherwise be unavoidable; and the residue of the surplus is an accumulating fund to be paid to him on his discharge.   To give the greater effect to these inducements, they are not offered to the convict on his commitment to the prison: first he must know and feel the unmitigated punishment; his own reflections must be his only companions for a preliminary period, during which he is closely confined to his cell ; he must live on the coarse diet allowed to the unemployed prisoner ; he must suffer the tedium arising from want of society and of occupation, and when he begins to feel that labour would be an indulgence, it is offered to him as such; it is not threatened as an evil, nor urged upon his acceptance as an advantage to any but to himself; and when he is employed, no stripes, no punishments whatever, are inflicted, for want of diligence; if not properly used, the indulgence is withdrawn, and he returns to his solitude and other privations, not to punish him for not labouring, but merely because his conduct shows that he prefers that state to the enjoyment

(a) Mr Roberts Vaux, one of the commissioners for building the new prison, a gentleman to whose instructive publications and conversation 1 am indebted for much useful information, has informed me that the plan of strict seclusion which I have quoted has never received the sanction of the legislature, and that there is a probability it will be so modified as to admit labour and instruction.

2 S

with which employment must always be associated in his mind, in order to produce reformation. If it has been shown that involuntary acts of employment will not produce a lasting habit, then, if there be any such as will not accept these alleviations of their imprisonment, upon them the imprisonment must operate solely as a punishment But experience shows that these exceptions will, if any, be very few: for employment, even under the lash, is in most cases preferred to solitude.

It is no unimportant-part of this plan, that education and intellectual improvement, as well as mere physical enjoyments, are held out as inducements for the exercise of industry, skill, and good conduct. These are to be rewarded by the use of books combining entertainment with instruction; the instruments, and other means, of exercising the mind in science, or the hand in the delicate operations of the fine arts, of developing talent or improving skill. Such pursuits offer, perhaps, the most efficient means of reformation ; they operate by reconciling the convict to himself, which is the first and most difficult point to be gained. The daily exercise of mental powers, the consciousness of progress in useful knowledge, must raise him in his own estimation ; and this honest pride, once set at work, will do more to change the conduct and purify the heart, than any external agency, however constantly or skilfully applied.

Let it not be said that this is a theory too refined to be adapted to depraved and degraded convicts. Convicts are men. The most depraved and degraded are men : their minds are moved by the same springs that give activity to those of others ; they avoid pain with the same care, and pursue pleasure with the same avidity, that actuate their fellow mortals. It is the false direction only of these great motives that produces the criminal actions which they prompt. To turn them into a course that produces the criminal actions which they prompt. To turn them into a course that will promote the true happiness of the individual, by making him cease to injure that of society, should be the great object of penal jurisprudence. The error, it appears to me, lies in considering them as beings of a nature so inferior as to be incapable of elevation, and so bad as to make any amelioration impossible ; but crime is the effect principally of intemperance, idleness, ignorance, vicious associations, irreligion and poverty—not of any defective natural organization ; and the laws which permit the unrestrained and continual exercise of these causes, are themselves the sources of those excesses which legislators, to cover their own inattention, or indolence, or ignorance, impiously and falsely ascribe to the Supreme Being, as if he had created man incapable of receiving the impressions of good. Let us try the experiment, before we pronounce that even the degraded convict cannot be reclaimed. It has never yet been tried. Every plan hitherto offered, is manifestly defective, because none has contemplated a complete system, and partial remedies never can succeed. It would be a presumption, of which the reporter's deep sense of his own incapacity renders him incapable, were he to say, that what he offers is a perfect system, or to think that it will produce all the effects which might be expected from a good one ; but he may be permitted, perhaps, to believe, that the principles on which it is founded are not discordant ; that it has a unity of design, and embraces a greater combination of provisions, all tending to produce the same result, than any that has yet been practised.   Whether those principles are correct, or the details proper to enforce them, the superior wisdom of the legislature must determine.   But, to think that the best plan which human sagacity could devise will produce reformation in every case; that there will not be numerous exceptions to its general effect, would be to indulge the visionary belief of a moral panacea, applicable to all vices and all crimes; and although this would be quackery in legislation, as absurd as any that has appeared in medicine, yet, to say that there are no general rules by which reformation of the mind may be produced, is as great and fatal an error as to assert that there are in the healing art no useful rules for preserving the general health and bodily vigour of the patient.

A reference to the text of the code is all that is necessary for the details by which it has been endeavoured to temper the rigour of solitary confinement, by useful employment and instruction, as a favour, to be withdrawn when neglected or abused; by the hope of enjoying society after a probationary period ; and by the immediate rewards of labour and skill, in procuring social comforts and other conveniences.   The indulgence of society in labour and instruction, which is offered as the greatest inducement to good conduct, has its value enhanced by the delay and perseverance in industry, which are prescribed as necessary to its attainment ; and, when granted, the number in each class is so small as to preclude the necessity of any severe discipline to maintain order, which, it is supposed, may be preserved by the precautions that are prescribed, by the fear of forfeiting the privilege, and by the advance towards reformation, which must be made before the indulgence is granted.

The average term of confinement may be assumed to be from four to six years, for such crimes, affecting property, as are attended with no circumstances in their commission to show greater depravity than the crime itself supposes; of this time, six months must necessarily be spent in solitude, with no alleviation but labour ; twelve more in the same confinement, unless a desire for intellectual improvement (the evidence of the first step towards reform), should have diversified it by intervals of social instruction ; and the remainder of the term, in continuing those lessons, and in perfecting that dexterity in mechanical employment which is best acquired in society.   A period thus passed, without any possibility of corrupting associations, with the daily experience of the actual enjoyments gained by diligence, hearing no precepts but those of religion, morality and science, and those inculcated not in the harsh language of reproach, but in the mild yet firm accents of advice, pronounced by men who take an interest in the welfare of the convict; and with the cheering prospect of regaining, by honest industry, that good opinion of society, which no one ever lost without regret: a period thus passed, it is confidently believed, must efface bad impressions, must create lasting habits of industry and virtuous pursuit, must discharge the subject of this discipline from the prison a better, a wiser and a happier man than he entered.   But these happy effects will be counteracted; the care, labour and expense, of your reformatory discipline, will have been uselessly incurred; if your proselyte to virtue and industry is to have the one exposed to the seduction of his former associates, and the other rendered useless by the want of means to exert it.   It will be in vain that you have given him the skill necessary for his support, if no one will afford him an opportunity of using it; or that you have made him an honest man, if all the world avoids him as a villain; his relapse is certain, unavoidable, and his depravity will be the greater, from the experience that reformation has been productive only of distrust, want and misery. "Seven evil spirits" will take possession of the mind that has been "swept and garnished" by your discipline, and "the last state of that man shall be worse than the first." To avoid this result, so destructive of the whole system, an asylum is provided in the House of Refuge and Industry, (the other departments of which have been already described). Here the discharged convict may find employment and subsistence, and receive such wages as will enable him to remove from the scenes of his past crimes, place him above temptation, confirm him in his newly acquired habits of industry, and cause him safely to pass the dangerous and trying period between the acquisition of his liberty and restoration to the confidence of society. Independently of this resource, the industrious convict receives, at his discharge, a proper proportion of his surplus earnings; he receives friendly advice as to his future pursuits, and a certificate (if he has merited it) of such conduct as will entitle him to confidence; the consequences of reconviction are solemnly represented to him, and his conduct, if he remain in the neighbourhood of the prison, is carefully watched, so that if he return to habits of idleness and intemperance, his career to crime may be stopped by a commitment to the House of Industry as a vagrant. The cause, the temptation, or the excuse for relapse, being thus removed, it is hoped that instances of return to vicious pursuits will become more rare, and that many will become useful members of society, who, under the present system, either burthen it by their poverty, or prey upon it by their crimes. The House of Refuge is rendered the more necessary, because a man of prudence will no more receive or employ a convict discharged from one of our present penitentiaries, than he would shut up with his flock a wild beast escaped from its keepers: but the reformatory plan, once fairly in operation, its principles studied, developed, steadily adhered to, improved by the light of experience, and its beneficial effects upon morals perceived, the man who has undergone its purifying operation will, in time, be no longer regarded with fear or contempt, and society, by confiding in his reformation, will permit him to be honest; the House of Refuge will then become less necessary, and its expense, of course, diminished(a).

Before I quit the consideration of this establishment, it may be necessary to dispose of an objection sometimes raised to it, as well as to the penitentiary : that the products of mechanical operations, which may be carried on there, will be sold cheaper than they can be afforded by the regular mechanic, who is burthened with the support of a family, with rent, taxes and other charges, and thus injure the innocent, in

(a) This theory is confirmed by experience in the House of Refuge at New York. Although admission into that school is obtained only by vagrancy on conviction; yet, such reliance is placed upon the reformatory effect of the discipline, that the applications for apprentices of both sexes are so numerous that they cannot be complied with. Nor is the confidence misplaced. A single instance only having been known in which the employer was dissatisfied with the conduct of his apprentice. After making all due allowance for the docility of children, the same effects may reasonably be expected, in a great degree, upon adults, by a longer and severer course of discipline.

order to find employment for the guilty. This objection could only have weight if all the convicts were employed in one business, and that in a country where there is a greater supply of labour than there is a demand for it; but here the very reverse of this is the fact. Again, if all the convicts should be employed in a single occupation, it must be because there is an excess of demand for that species of labour over the supply ; and while that continues, there can be no injury : when that demand is reduced, the business will be abandoned both within and without the prison. As respects the public interest, there can be no doubt, for the question reduces itself to this—whether the convicts are to be maintained in idleness, or suffered to contribute by labour to their own support? And even as regards particular classes of mechanics, the same reasoning which would prevent their trade being carried on in prison, would go to show that it ought to be limited without. But the best answer to the objection is, that experience has never realized any of the evils that have been apprehended.

Having passed through the different stages of confinement with the prisoner committed for a term; having shown the hopes and fears, the occupation, instruction and discipline, by which he is to be punished and reformed; and, having unlocked the door of his cell, and restored him to the world a renovated man; we must return once more to the interior of the prison, to visit those who have by their atrocity rendered it unsafe to trust them in that society, the very existence of which their crimes have put to hazard. They are those whose offences are now punished with death. Reformation enters no farther into their treatment than as it concerns them individually. Shut out for ever from civil society, its laws provide no means for their future employment ; it is indifferent as to their habits, and solicitous only that, for their own sake, they should make their peace with Heaven : for, in avoiding to punish with death, it would not " kill the soul."

The confinement of this class is intended for two purposes only : first, by actual restraint, to secure society against a repetition of the crime. Next, to deter others from committing a similar one, by the severity of the punishment. These two purposes are attained by absolute seclusion, under circumstances varied according to the enormity of the offence. These circumstances are calculated to strike the imagination with horror for the crime, without awaking any dangerous sympathy for the sufferer.` A gloomy cell; inscriptions recording the nature of the crime and the intensity of the punishment; so much of mystery as excites the imagination; real suffering enough to deter when the veil is withdrawn, not so much as to enlist the feelings of the community and make them arraign the cruelty of the law ; perfect security from escape ; a gradation in the discipline to show, by strong features, the different degrees of atrocity of the crime ; such are the characteristics. of the punishments substituted for that of death, now inflicted for the different species of capital homicide. These convicts are considered, for many purposes, to be as much dead to the world as if no commutation of their former punishment had been made ; their property is divided among their heirs ; they are buried in their solitary cells, and their epitaph is contained in the inscription that records their crime, and the daily renewal of its punishment. Their existence is preserved by the policy of the law, for reasons which it has proclaimed ; and, although they are kept within the reach of the pardoning power, yet.

that policy will be counteracted by any remission of the sentence, the case of acknowledged innocence alone excepted.

Those who are confined for life, for a repetition of minor offences, are considered more in the light of incurables, than atrocious offenders whose ferocious disposition makes perpetual restraint necessary for the peace of society. Yet a very long and uninterrupted curative process may sometimes succeed in cases that were deemed desperate, and the subjects of this observation have, therefore, the same advantages of instruction and employment offered to them, that are given to the other convicts, in the hope that, by unequivocal evidence of reformation, after a very long probatory period without relapse, they may be discharged by the pardoning power. It is highly important, however, that this should not be lightly or frequently exercised. Few circumstances have tended more directly to disappoint the friends of the penitentiary system, than the counteractive operation of this prerogative : parsimonious legislative provisions have furnished an excuse for its exercise, to a degree that renders every attempt to punish or reform by imprisonment, equally abortive; and, if the unhappy facility of granting pardons be not checked, it is in vain to hope that the best organized plan will produce any good effect. Restraint will be suffered with impatience, instruction will be unheeded, labour neglected, and counsel derided, while the mind is kept in the feverish state of expectation, which the daily release of fellow convicts, more guilty, perhaps, but better befriended, must produce on those who remain. In some states this abuse has become so prevalent, that the culprit has not only in his favour the chance of escaping detection, or, if detected, the chance of acquittal, but, after conviction, it has become more probable that he will be discharged by pardon(a), than that his sentence will be executed. With so many chances in his favour, the felon continues his game without fear or scruple. The prison loses its terrors as a place of punishment, and its discipline becomes a mockery to those who remain, cursing their ill fortune, and hoping that, in the next lottery of pardons, they may gain the prize of discharge. Before I passed from the penitentiary discipline to another branch of my subject, it was necessary to advert to this radical, and, unfortunately, in most of the states, this constitutional evil, to which, of course, no other remedy can be applied by the legislative, than the voice of expostulation with the executive power. A very able report on this subject, made by the direction of a society for the prevention of pauperism in the city of New York, in the year 1822, contains the opinions of the most celebrated jurists and magistrates in every state in the union, all of whom concur in stating frequent pardons to be the greatest obstacle that the penitentiary system has to encounter. Out of it has arisen another evil ; soliciting pardons, has, in some places, become a business; men who disgrace an honourable profession, hang about the doors of the prison, bargain with the convict, to be paid, perhaps, out of the proceeds of his crime; by importunity or false statements, procure the signatures of respectable men to petitions, deceive the executive power by false allegations of reformation, and procure the pardon of the most hardened offenders ;

(a) In five years, *seven hundred and forty convicts* were discharged by pardon from the New York prison, and only *seventy-three* by the expiration of their sentence, making the chance of impunity after conviction, more than ten to one in favour of the convict.

who use their liberty only to commit new depredations, in the hope of again being released ; and, strange to tell, this hope has been realized after a second and even a third sentence.   Out of sixteen committed for a second offence to the New York penitentiary, in 1825, eleven had been discharged by pardon, and of those committed in the same year, for a third offence, every one had been previously twice pardoned.   To arrest, if possible, the progress of this abuse, which totally counteracts every attempt to punish or reform, the text of the code is made to express the wishes of the legislature, and a provision is introduced, making the soliciting of pardons, for reward, a punishable offence.

One other institution remains to be described; one of perhaps quite as much importance as any other in the system.   It is the School of Reform ; designed for the confinement, and discipline, and instruction of juvenile offenders and young vagrants.   Of all the establishments suggested by the charity, and executed by the active and enlightened benevolence of modern times, none interests more deeply the best feelings of the heart.   Whether we consider the evil avoided, or the positive good bestowed, it is equally worthy of our admiration.

The provisions of law have heretofore denounced the same punishment against the first offence of a child, that they awarded to the veteran in guilt; the seducer to crime, and the artless victim of his corruption, were confounded in the same penalty, and that penalty, until lately, was here, and in the land from whence we derive our jurisprudence still is—death.   We have substituted imprisonment; but our laws make no other distinction between adults and children, than that contained in the common law, by which all above a certain age, and that a very tender one, are supposed to have sufficient discretion to know both the law and its penalty; and as to those who have not attained that age, it is a matter of inquiry to be determined by evidence, and an instance is recorded, in which an infant of nine years was convicted and executed for murder.   For the minor offences, affecting property, indictments against children are frequent; and humanity is equally shocked, whether they are convicted, or, by the lenity of the jury, discharged, to complete their education of infamy.   In the penal code which you have under consideration, some material changes are introduced on this subject; an age is fixed, below which guilt cannot be supposed, and the inquiry as to discretion can only take place when the accused is above that age, but below another, at which sufficient capacity may always be presumed.   It also contains other provisions, which govern the case in which a child does the prohibited act, in the presence, or under the influence of a parent or superior.   But, with all these modifications, nothing materially good, under this head would be effected, if, after conviction, the same discipline were indiscriminately applied to children and adults.   The necessity of a different course, whether for punishment, or education or reform, is so clearly pointed out by nature, that he must be an inattentive observer of her laws, who does not perceive it; and it should be considered, that, when a child of tender age commits an offence against the law of society, he acts, for the most part, in obedience to one which with him has a paramount force—that of nature—who has given him strong desires to possess an ardent passion for novelty, and a free spirit, that with difficulty submits to restraint; while she has withheld that discretion which alone can give a voluntary control over those passions. For acts committed before this discretion is acquired, or when, by the visitation of Providence, it is taken away, it is unjust to punish, although the good of society requires that we should restrain. Paternal, or any other authority that represents it, stands in the place of this discretion, until it is conferred by instruction, experience, and the natural expansion of the faculties. To this domestic lawgiver and judge, is confided, during this interval, the task of repressing all the faults of infancy; and when they become hurtful to others, he, not the child whom he ought to have restrained, is answerable; civilly, if the injury were done without his connivance or permission; criminally if it were. These are the dictates of most laws, applicable to a period of infancy more or less indefinite, according to different systems ; but, after that period, they all abandon these sound principles, and hold the child personally accountable to the penal law; and if he has shown dexterity in committing the crime, or used shifts to avoid detection, it is, by the common law, counted sufficient evidence of a consciousness of moral guilt, and of a discretion that ought to have prevented the offence. But they do not consider that the moral sense is, in childhood, produced by instruction only, and the force of example, and that, with the children who are generally the objects of criminal procedure, instruction has either been totally wanting, or both that and example have been of a nature to pervert, not form, a sense of right ; so that, if the want of discretion entitles to the protective power of the law, it is due to the adolescence of children quite as much as it is to their infancy. Either they have parents who entirely neglect the task, or abuse the power given to them by nature, and confirmed by the laws of society; without relations, they are thrown friendless and unprotected into the most contaminating associations, where morality, religion and temperance, are spoken of only to be derided, and the restraints of law are studied only to be evaded. In either of these cases, these unfortunate victims to the vices of others, have a right to demand that the community shall supply the place of their natural protectors, and teach them the sanction of the law before they are punished for its breach. In a country governed by wise laws, faithfully executed, this class of children would be very small ; moral, religious and literary education would be brought, in such a country, within the reach of every individual, and he would be forced to avail himself of these advantages; ours, in this respect, is not yet such a country. We are rapidly advancing towards this degree of perfection; but, until we attain it, the defect in this part of our system increases the obligation on the community to be a father to the fatherless ; to snatch the innocent child from the hands of depraved parents, and the orphan from the contamination of vice and infamy; and, instead of harsh punishments, inflicted for offences which its own neglect of duty has occasioned, to remove their cause by the milder methods of instruction and useful employment.

The place for the confinement of juvenile offenders, for these reasons, is to be considered more as a school of instruction than a prison for degrading punishment; a school in which the vicious habits of the pupil require a strict discipline, but still a school; into which he enters a vicious boy, and from which he is to depart a virtuous and industrious youth; where the involuntary vices and crimes with which his early childhood was stained, are to be eradicated, their very remembrance lost; and, in their place, the lessons inculcated, and the examples given, which would have guided him, had the duties of nature and society been performed. From hence he begins his career of life; and as it would be unjust to load him, on his outset, with the opprobrium which would be inseparable from an association, in the same place of punishment, with hardened offenders, it became necessary, as well from this circumstance as from the different nature of the discipline, to separate this entirely, both by locality and name, from the other prisons.

To argue the utility, or to descant on the humanity, of this establishment, after demonstrating its justice, would be a useless task. Every mind that has investigated the causes and progress of crime, must acknowledge the one ; every benevolent heart must feel the other.   And even economy, cold, calculating economy, after stating the account in dollars and cents, must confess that this is a money-saving institution. If it is wise to prevent an hundred atrocious crimes by removing the opprobrium of a venial fault, and substituting instruction for punishment; if it is the highest species of humanity to relieve from the misery of vice and the degradation of crime, to extend the operation of charity to the mind, and to snatch with its angel arm innocence from seduction ; if it be a saving to society to support an infant for a few years at school, and thereby avoid the charge of the depredations of a felon for the rest of his life(a), and the expense of his future convictions and confinements ; then is the School of Reform—a wise, a humane, and an economical institution.

I need not enlarge this report by the details for the government of this school ; they are minutely contained in the code.   One principle pervades the whole, which has been sufficiently enlarged upon : that the offences of children may be sufficiently corrected, both for the

(a) There is hardly a child who will be condemned to it (the New York House of Refuge), who, if left to the course which would bring him to it, would not finally be supported by the state as a convict.   The evidence of this is, that a very large proportion who are now confined in our state prisons, commenced their career in crimes when they were children, in some of our large cities.   One person in particular, who is now confined in the prison at Auburn, was first convicted when he was only ten years old, and has since been, at different times, twenty-eight years a convict, supported by the state, at an expense of not less than two thousand dollars.—*Report of the New York Committee.*

In the Arch street prison at Philadelphia there is now awaiting his trial, for felony, a boy of eleven years of age, who already passed a year in the penitentiary of New Jersey for horse stealing: during this period the only lessons he received, were the details given by his fellow convicts of their exploits ; some of which he repeated to us, with a satisfaction but ill repressed.   I cannot avoid adding to this note an extract from a report on the state of the French prisons made by Mr Deappert, which strongly exemplifies the necessity of a complete separation of juvenile from other offenders.   " There were in the same room, at Douay, several youths, who had been sentenced to imprisonment by the correctional tribunal, together with men of different ages, and also a man condemned to death for murder: he requested to speak to me in private ; " I wait," said he, " the moment of execution ; and since you are the first person who has visited us, I wish to address you with confidence, and to conceal nothing from you.   I am guilty of the crime for which I have been condemned; I have committed robbery and murder.   From my infancy my parents neglected me.   I fell into bad company ; my undoing was completed in a prison; and I am now about to expiate all my faults.   Among the persons whom you see in this room there are some youths, who, with pain I observe, are preparing themselves for the commission of new crimes, as soon as their term of confinement expires.   If you could get them removed into a separate room, this, sir, would be the greatest benefit that you could confer upon them."

2 T

ends of punishment and example, by education and employment. If this be wrong, the whole plan must be remodelled ; but in establishing it, I have been guided by something better than the best reasoning. In the city of New York there is an establishment of this kind, which can never be visited but with unmixed emotions of the highest intellectual pleasure. It now contains one hundred and twenty-five boys and twenty-nine girls, for the most part healthy, cheerful, intelligent, industrious, orderly, and obedient; animated with the certain prospect of becoming useful members of society, who, but for this establishment, would still have been suffering under the accumulated evils attendant on poverty, ignorance, and the lowest depravity, with no other futurity before them than the penitentiary or the gallows. I ought not to omit mentioning here, that the female department is superintended by a visiting committee of ladies, who, at regular and frequent periods, examine the school, converse with the scholars, encourage the diffident, reprove the disorderly, reward the industrious, and inspire all with their own virtues. The code I submit, invites a similar superintendence, from which the highest advantages, such as nothing but the benign influence of female character can give, are expected.

The plan of indenting the scholars to useful trades has been recommended, from the practical effect that has been observed at New-York. It might at first be supposed, that an aversion would be found to taking apprentices from such a place ; but experience has proved that the confidence inspired by the mode of education pursued, is so great, that applications are more numerous, for children of both sexes, than the rules of the institution will permit them to supply. And, although twenty-eight boys and fifteen girls have been indented, the most favourable accounts have been received of their behaviour ; two having received what they thought ill usage from their masters, left them, but returned to the school, and only one has resumed his former bad habits. What renders the reformation of these children the more extraordinary, is, that thirty of them had before been sentenced to the penitentiary, from one to five different times. A register is kept of the behaviour of the different boys, and of as much of their previous history as can be discovered. Extracts from this are annually published, and they contain a number of facts of the most interesting kind ; all proving the practical utility of the plan. Some of these are selected from the last report of the managers(a).

(a) W. H. O.—This boy's history exhibits one of the most striking instances of juvenile depravity that we have on the records of this institution. He, at the early age of nine years, commenced his career of stealing, and with the assistance of some, more hardened and older in crime than himself, he continued it for three years, with the most undeviating success. Of his short life, two and a half years in three separate terms, have been served in the penitentiary, besides having been several times in bridewell. The associations he formed in those schools of vice, instead of reclaiming him, served only to strengthen his vicious propensities, and, at his discharge from them, he recommenced his depredatory acts with renewed skill; in short, with him stealing seemed to be an instinctive principle. Thus he continued until the establishment of this institution. He fortunately became one of its first inmates. Upon his introduction he evinced a settled determination to escape (in which he succeeded three several times). The most rigid treatment was for a long time successfully applied. At length he began gradually to yield to the restraints, and submit to the regulations required of him ; from January to December 1826, he so far improved that we considered him one of the most amiable boys in the house : the person who contracted for

It will be observed, that, contrary to the rules laid down for the penitentiary, personal castigation is permitted in the school. This exception was introduced because the infliction of that punishment in childhood, is not attended with the degradation which characterises it when applied to adults ; because it is permitted to teachers, with respect to their scholars ; to masters, as respects apprentices ; and because the rules laid down for regulating the punishment are such as will effectually prevent its abuse. Yet, if experience should prove, as I think it will, that, even in these cases, it may be dispensed with, it

his services, said, that his attention to his work was such as to afford him much pleasure ; that he was entirely obedient, agreeable, and active in the discharge of his duties. Conceiving that the object of the institution, in the effect of his reformation, was completed, and that a better state of mind could not be effected in William, he was indentured to a highly respectable mechanic, living in Connecticut. Some time previous to his indenture, he was asked whether he would ever redarken his character by the commission of crime, if selected to be bound out ; his reply was, that he was then influenced by the *wicked one*, but that he now felt his mind to be in a different channel ; and if a modest and humble deportment for several months, together with a knowledge of his frequently practising devotional exercise, are proper criterions by which to judge, we feel perfectly safe in saying that William was truly an altered boy. Since his indenture, a very favourable report has been received from him.

S. T.—Aged sixteen years, born in Patterson, N. J.; he lost his father and mother when quite young, after which he was left to the care of guardians, who neglected him. He in a short time acquired a degree of celebrity among his companions, by his skill in stealing old rope, iron, copper, &c. from around the docks. His career, however, was made short by the superintending care of the city authority, by whom he was committed to the alms-house, as a vagrant. He twice escaped from that institution, and when retaken the second time, he was sent here. Soon after his commitment it became evident that the discipline of the house was all that was requisite to make him obedient. After conducting himself to the entire satisfaction of the superintendent, he was indented to a farmer in the country. Since his indenture, we have been informed by the gentleman with whom he lives, that "he is industrious, attentive and kind ; and such is the state of his mind, as relates to religion and morality, that he will reprove his men for using profane language, in a prompt, though modest and becoming manner, often referring to the precepts he received from his recent friends."

D. B. L.—Aged fifteen years, born in New York, committed from the police, on suspicion of having stolen a shawl. He was brought up in the vicinity of Baucker street, and for some months played the tambourine in those receptacles of vice and misery, the dancing-houses of Corlears Hook. He acknowledges having stolen some few articles, but denies stealing the article for which he was sent here. From the time he was committed until his discharge he conducted in an entirely satisfactory manner. In October he was indentured to a respectable gentleman residing about sixty miles north of this city.

L. S.—Aged about sixteen years, born in Ireland ; his parents emigrated to this country about eight years ago. His father has since died. His education was entirely neglected by his parents, and the choice of his companions left exclusively to himself. He has worked at several mechanical branches of business, to none of which his restless disposition could attach itself. He was committed to the Refuge in March, 1825, from the police office, for stealing a copper kettle, for which he had been confined in Bridewell eight days, where he had been four times before. The character of a notorious thief cannot with justice be attached to this boy, though he had been a habitual pilferer for several years. Upon his entry into the house, he gave no evidence of a disposition palpably wicked, yet he was a source of much trouble to the superintendent ; in mischief he was almost invariably first ; to the rules and regulations of the house he was perfectly indifferent, and in one instance he absconded. After a few days he was returned, severely punished, and put in irons for forty-three days, when his irons were taken off. In December his improvement was so

ought to be abolished.   But, while this power is granted by law to the master over the scholar or apprentice, it would not be prudent to deny it to the warden, who acts in this capacity towards the children under his care.

There is also another difference that will be remarked, in comparing this institution with the penitentiary : here public worship is directed, while, in the penitentiary, no provision is made for its performance. The advantage to be derived from an habitual attendance on this duty is so great, that it ought not lightly to be given up ; but, after the best reflection I could give to the subject, I determined that it might safely be allowed in the school, but could not, without danger, be permitted in the penitentiary.   The discipline necessary to preserve order in the work-shops, and during the hours of instruction, will be sufficient for the same purpose, in the chapel, during divine service.   In the habit of seeing and conversing with each other during the week, the association in the church, on Sunday, will not be made, by the children, the means of communicating plans for escape, or other unlawful combination.   But, in a penitentiary, instituted for solitary confinement,

great that he was promoted to the situation of night watch, and day guard, the duties of which he faithfully performed until July 1826, when he requested to be sent to sea; his request was complied with, and he was indentured to a highly respectable ship owner of this city. After an absence of three months, he returned to the Refuge on a visit, stated that he was perfectly contented with his situation, and that he had often reflected while at sea, that, instead of enjoying the blessings of liberty, he might have now been in the state prison, had it not been for the establishment of a House of Refuge.

D. S.—Aged fifteen years, born in New York ; his father died while he was yet an infant ; his mother since married an oysterman, now living in the vicinity of Bancker street.   David has lived with three different persons, who kept oyster-cellars ; after leaving them, he returned to his mother.   He commenced his thefts by stealing wood from about the docks ; has also been in the habit of stealing old junk, copper, &c.   He has been three several times committed to bridewell, the last time for stealing a copper kettle, in company with the foregoing boy ; it was for this offence that he was committed to the Refuge.   He was at first very refractory, constantly plotting how to escape, and endeavouring to persuade others to accompany him.   He was for some months treated with much strictness ; from June 1825 to February 1826, his conduct was entirely satisfactory ; at this time an opportunity offering to give him an advantageous situation, it was deemed incompatible with the object of the institution to detain him longer.   He was consequently indented to a gentleman residing in the western part of this state, who, in a letter directed to his mother, two months after the date of his indenture, says he has much reason to be pleased with David's conduct.

J. D. S.—Aged eleven and a half years, born in New York.   This child, notwithstanding his extreme youth, has committed many errors.   He was first led to the perpetration of crime by the persuasion of one older than himself, in whose company he stole many articles ; he was once in bridewell for stealing, and was frequently punished by his parents, but to no effect.   He was committed here, at the solicitation of his father, in April 1825.   He conducted himself with uniform propriety until October 1826, when he was returned to his parents for the purpose of indenturing to a gentleman who was instrumental in his reformation, and who was well acquainted with his disposition.   Here is another instance in which the preservation of a child from ruin may be attributed to the establishment of a House of Refuge. Had this boy's thieving practices been permitted to degenerate into a habit, they doubtless would have procured for him a residence in our state prison or penitentiary, where the object is punishment, and not reformation ; he must have been thrown in the company of old and hardened offenders, the contaminating influence of whose conversation would eventually have banished every virtuous and generous sentiment from his tender bosom.   What reflecting mind but must admit the utility of such an institution, and what generous soul but would contribute to its support ?

the meeting of all the convicts on Sunday would be entirely inconsistent with the first principles of the plan ; order could not be preserved without recourse being had to corporal chastisement ; the convicts would anticipate the return of their periodical re-union, not to listen to the truths of religion, but to enjoy the society of which they had been deprived ; the utmost vigilance could not prevent communication by whispers or signs; they would become acquainted with each other's faces, and be ready to renew, after discharge, those associations, which it is one object of the plan to prevent ; and it has been asserted, and I believe with truth, that most of the combinations for insurrection and escape have been formed in the chapel.

In all these institutions, whether for restraint, punishment or education, so much must depend on the integrity, attention and ability, of the warden, that not only are the greatest care and judgment necessary in selecting him, but the most watchful superintendence after he is chosen. It may be stated as a general rule, to which, unhappily, there are few exceptions, that, if neglect in the performance of official duties incurs no loss of emolument, they will be neglected, unless the state of public opinion is such as to make it an equivalent sanction; this last is a powerful agent ; but it cannot always be depended upon ; and it operates least upon those that are most in want of a supervising power. A sensibility to public opinion is connected, for the most part, with a moral sense that would, of itself, enforce a performance of the duty ; and a lax morality is seldom attended with any great reverence for the opinions of others. But, in framing laws, we cannot count on the constant operation of this high sense of duty or regard to public approbation. They must be made for men as they are ; and unfortunately the disposition to gain as much as possible, with as little trouble as possible, is that which we shall find most general, and which, therefore, we must counteract, or direct to our purpose, if we expect our institutions to be useful and permanent. A superintending power, therefore, has, in most systems of law, been provided to secure the execution of official duty; this is easily done, and were the remedy an effectual one, nothing could be more simple than this branch of legislation ; but what can assure us that the supervisors will do their duty ?

Custodes ipsos, quis custodiet?

In our legislation, we way create a system of successive responsibilities and inspections; but a foundation must be laid for the last. We may place the weight on the elephant, and support him by the tortoise, but here our theory, with that of the Indian cosmogonist, ends. Sound philosophy alone can, in both cases, direct us to the great principles, which effect the different ends, without this cumbrous and useless machinery. Individual interest draws all to a central point ; a desire to promote the public good, enforced by the fear of censure and the hope of applause, gives an impetus in a different direction ; and these powers combined, will restrain aberrations from the circle of official duty just as the order of the heavenly bodies is preserved by the divergent operation of mutual attraction and the projectile force.

Self-interest, then, must be so combined with the public good, as to make them inseparable; and public inspection must be secured, to keep this great spring of human action in its proper direction. This has been endeavoured in the plan of administration for the several houses of confinement provided for by this system.

The whole are placed under the superintending care of the same board, because, being parts of the same system, its general principles could only be enforced by a common head. The number of the institutions required an attention that a single person could not well perform ; a board of inspection, therefore, was created, and, considering the nature of the duties, the number of five was fixed on as that which would best unite the advantages of deliberation with the requisite despatch of business ; and a distribution of the duties into classes, that some might be performed by one member, making two necessary for others, and a majority for those which were most important, was considered as a convenient and safe arrangement. This board, in addition to its general superintending power, has the direct management of all the pecuniary concerns of the several prisons, but under regulations, which, it is thought, must prevent the possibility of any corrupt appropriation or negligent dilapidation of the funds. Among other precautions, is one that ought, I think, to be adopted in all cases of trust, whether arising from office, or contract, or testamentary disposition; the deposite of all moneys held for another, or for the public or any institution, in a safe public bank, in the name of the trust, or of the person in his quality as officer or agent, to be drawn out only by checks, expressing the purpose to which the money is to be applied, and making it a criminal breach of trust if the deposite is not made, or if the funds are drawn for any other purpose than that of the person or institution for whose use it was received. The advantages of such an arrangement in commercial agencies, and private and public trusts, need not be descanted on here : it is intended, in connexion with other provisions, prohibiting any kind of concern in purchases or sales made for the prisons, any profit or convenience from the employment of the prisoners, to take away all temptation of making the office a pecuniary speculation, and what is of as much consequence, perhaps, to prevent its being thought one.

The board of inspection must be permanent ; its duties are arduous ; they require experience as well as diligence ; the undivided attention of the members must be given to the subject; the close and unremitted labours required by the important business entrusted to them, cannot be expected to be gratuitously given. Few men, in our state of society, can afford to divert the time required for this purpose from their private affairs ; and those who can afford it, are not always the best fitted for the task. They must, therefore, be paid, and so liberally paid, as to command the talent and integrity required. Philanthropy, public spirit, humanity or religion, may inspire individuals to volunteer services ; but it is a natural tendency of zeal gradually to cool, when the service which excited it is one requiring patient attention, a daily intercourse with the most degraded of our species, and a close attention to dull detail, more especially when it requires no exertion of those talents that command public applause: besides this, if the service is unpaid, its negligent performance rarely incurs the penalty of public censure, which never falls very heavy on those who have gratuitously given any part of their time or attention to the business; whereas, the salary being an equivalent for the service, legal punishment, as well as loss of reputation, will generally attend neglect. The particular powers given to the board of inspectors, need not be here detailed ; they are, it is thought, clearly designated in the text. As theirs is chiefly a su-

pervising power, and not so direct an agency upon the prisoners as that
of the other officers, it was not deemed necessary to give them any
interest in the labour of the convicts; the number, too, of their members would have rendered this extremely onerous to the institution.
But with the warden it was different; to him it was deemed necessary
to apply those principles I have endeavoured to establish, which make
the interest of the officer and of the public to coincide. The interest of
the public is, first, that all the regulations in the code, for punishment
and reformation, should be strictly observed ; secondly, that as much
as possible of the expense of the institution should be paid by the labour
of the convicts. To give the warden an interest in the first branch,
he has a premium on the decrease of reconvictions, the best mode of
testing the efficiency of the system. To stimulate him in promoting
the industry and skill of the convicts, he has a per centage on the gross
amount of their labour ; while the superintendence of the inspectors,
their periodical examination of the prisoners, and of the other officers,
the observation of the chaplain and physician, and of the official visiters,
will effectually prevent his urging that labour by any other means, or
in any greater degree, than is prescribed by the code. It is also a great
object, that by preserving the health of the prisoners, the punishment
should not be carried further than is directed by the sentence ; for this
purpose, cleanliness, wholesome food, exercise and proper relaxation
from labour, are prescribed. To enforce their execution, the proper
system of inspection is provided ; and to combine private interest and
the love of distinction in the performance of this duty, honorary and
useful premiums are given for different grades of decrease in the usual
mortality of the prisons. These rewards are extended to all the officers
whose agency can at all contribute to the end.

It may be necessary, before the conclusion of this report, to give
some idea of the number of officers, and the duties of those which have
not yet been mentioned.

The plan, as has been seen, comprehends,

A House of Detention, with two departments ;

A Penitentiary ;

A School of Reform ;

A House of Refuge and Industry, with two departments.

All of these are under the general superintendence of five inspectors;
one warden and one matron will be required for each institution. One
chaplain and one physician will be sufficient for the four ; a clerk for
the Penitentiary; one teacher for the School for Reform and another for
the Penitentiary. In the other institutions, the detention is not long
enough to require a regular establishment for education, and one of the
inmates will always be found competent for this purpose ; so that, independent of the underkeepers, the number of which will depend, in
some measure, on that of the prisoners, the four institutions will require
thirteen officers. The manner in which the prisoners are proposed to
be confined, will preclude the necessity of a military guard; and unless
the number shall multiply much beyond our hopes and reasonable expectations, one underkeeper for the House of Detention, one for the
School of Reform, two for the House of Industry, and six for the Penitentiary, ten only in all, will be required. In this calculation, neither
the inspectors nor their agent are included.

A regulation of much importance in the code may need some explanation, which has not been given in its place. Solitary confinement, although accompanied by the permission to labour in an uncovered court, may, if the labour be sedentary, be injurious to the health. To counteract this effect, a machine is directed to be made that will require strong muscular power to put in motion ; and at this, each of the male prisoners is directed to work, but only for one hour in each day. This is made compulsory; but as the only penalty is solitary confinement to the cell, and as it is considered and intended only as a preservation to the health, this compulsion is not at war with the principles before laid down on 'that subject. The prisoners are to be brought to the machine separately, and it must be so contrived as not to permit them to see or hear each other while at work. Its effects will be not only to preserve general health, but to fortify the muscular powers, and fit the convict on his discharge for any species of laborious employment.

The tread-mill, although a favourite engine of punishment in many institutions, finds no place in this, for the following reasons : it cannot be employed without breaking in upon the system of solitary confinement, which is the basis of the system ; its injurious effects upon the health are supported by strong testimony(a), and although there is, a contrariety of evidence on the subject(b), yet it may be fairly inferred from the whole, that it does not fortify the constitution and prepare the convict for any of the ordinary pursuits of laborious life, the principal muscular action being in the legs only. It teaches the convict nothing that can be useful to him on his discharge. It is not a profitable employment of human power. If it have any effect on the morals, it must be a bad one, from the associations inseparable from it, and from the degradation which is considered to be attached to it. As a punishment it must be unequal ; to give it the velocity necessary to punish one of a robust constitution, would make it a torture to a weaker convict.

The Code of Reform and Prison Discipline, and the reasoning in support of its provisions, are now before the legislature; their wisdom will determine on the propriety of its adoption. Many parts of the plan have at different times been proposed, and some of them have been partially executed, but they have never before been consolidated and presented as component parts of a whole system; a characteristic which it is thought constitutes its chief value : for it must be apparent, from the nature of the subject, that, without a continuity of operation, as well as uniformity of principle in the plan, no infliction of punishment or discipline for reformation can have any great effect. In all legislation we must first form a clear idea of that which we wish to accomplish, and then determine on the best means of effecting it. These being well understood, they must be explicitly enounced, not only for our own guidance in forming the plan, but for that of our successors in correcting, of the judges in expounding, and of our constituents in obeying it. In that which I offer, its great object has been constantly kept in view, and has been repeated perhaps oftener than was necessary; and the means proposed to effect it are such only as have been recommended either by experience or the maturest reflection. But, as this

(a) Sir John Cox Hippeslie on the tread-mill.
(b) Sixth Report of the Society for the Improvement of Prison Discipline, appendix.

object is the prevention of crime, it is clear that this would be but imperfectly effected by any discipline applied after conviction only. Conviction supposes the prior existence of crime, and the discipline that corrects it is punishment; but punishment is only one of the means of attaining the end of preventing crimes: to avoid their commission, therefore, we must go one step further back; we must prevent contaminating association before trial, more carefully than we would after it; we must never confound innocence with unconvicted guilt, by imposing any unnecessary restraint upon either. But even accusation is most commonly founded on the evident commission of an offence, although trial is necessary to designate the offenders. We must begin, then, at an earlier stage in our efforts to prevent it; we must relieve that extreme want which is sometimes the cause, and oftener the pretence for crime; and we must find employment for the idleness which generally produces it. And when this is done, our work is not yet complete; religious, moral and scientific instruction must be not only provided but enforced, in order to stamp on the minds of the people that character, that public feeling, and those manners, without which laws are but vain restraints.

The recapitulation of the several institutions embraced by the Code of Reform and Prison Discipline, has been made to show their close connexion, and that each part is so necessary to carry into effect the great objects of the system, that an omission of any one would, in a great measure, defeat the good effect that might be expected from the others. If we mean to guard the community from the inroads of crime, every avenue must be defended. A besieged city, fortified on one side, leaving the others open to hostile attacks, would be a just image of a country in which laws are made to eradicate offences by punishments only, while they invite them by neglect of education, by the toleration of mendicity, idleness, vagrancy, and the corrupting associations of the accused before trial, as well as after conviction. Yet such is the lamentable state of criminal jurisprudence, that all nations are more or less in this state. Here great severity is used to punish offences, but no means are provided to prevent them: there mild punishments and a reformatory discipline are applied after judgment; but severe imprisonment and contaminating associations are indiscriminately inflicted on the innocent and on the guilty before trial. Between some states the contest seems which shall raise the greatest revenue from the labour of the convicts: in others the object is to degrade and make them feel their misery. No where has a system been established consisting of a connected series of institutions founded on the same principle of uniformity, directed to the same end; no where is criminal jurisprudence treated as a science; what goes by that name, consists of a collection of dissimilar, unconnected, sometimes conflicting expedients to punish different offences as they happen to prevail; of experiments directed by no principle to try the effect of different penalties; of permanent laws to repress temporary evils; of discretionary power, sometimes with the blindest confidence vested in the judge, and at others with the most criminal negligence given to an officer of executive justice. All these and other incongruities would cease, were the lawgiver to form correct principles; enounce them for his own guidance and that of his successors; and, with them constantly before his eyes, arrange his system of criminal jurisprudence into its natural divisions, by providing for the poor, employing the idle, educating the ignorant, defining of-

2 U

fences and designating their correspondent punishment, regulating the mode of procedure for preventing crimes and prosecuting offenders, and giving precise rules for the government and discipline of prisons.

With such a system it may reasonably be expected, not that offences will be eradicated, but that their recurrence will be much less frequent, and that the rare spectacle will be witnessed of a retrograde movement in vice and crime. But the desultory attempts which have been made, and are daily making, to carry some of its detached parts into execution, do but retard the progress and endanger the success of reform ; they are troublesome, they are expensive; the false reliance that is placed upon them by their advocates, excites high expectations, which must be disappointed, because a disease pervading the system cannot.be cured by topical remedies; and the disappointment produces despair of final success, an abandonment of the plan of reformation, and an inclination to return to the old sanguinary system.

The code now submitted completes the System of Penal Law, which is respectfully offered for consideration.

The task was undertaken with an unfeigned distrust of my own powers, which nothing could have conquered but the conviction that a simple enumeration and development of the principles on which the system is founded, would force a conviction of their truth.

It has been prosecuted with laborious and unremitted application for several years, with a respectful attention to the opinions of others, and a close observation of practical results.

Its conclusion was attended with the gratifying consciousness of having taken every precaution to guard against the pride of opinion, and neglected no means that could be suggested by the deepest sense of its importance, and a religious desire that it might advance private happiness, by establishing the true principles of public justice.

It is now respectfully offered for consideration, in the hope that after legislative wisdom shall have supplied the omissions, and corrected the errors of the work, it may be made the basis of a system, by which instruction may be promoted, idleness and vice repressed, crimes diminished, and the sum of human happiness increased.

EDWARD LIVINGSTON.

# A SYSTEM OF PENAL LAW.

# INTRODUCTORY TITLE.

## CHAPTER I.

### *Preamble.*

No act of legislation can be, or ought to be immutable. Changes are required by the alteration of circumstances ; amendments, by the imperfection of all human institutions; but laws ought never to be changed without great deliberation, and a due consideration as well of the reasons on which they were founded, as of the circumstances under which they were enacted. It is therefore proper, in the formation of new laws, to state clearly the motives for making them, and the principles by which the framers were governed in their enactment. Without a knowledge of these, future legislatures cannot perform the task of amendment, and there can be neither consistency in legislation, nor uniformity in the interpretation of laws.

For these reasons the general assembly of the state of Louisiana declare, that their objects in establishing the following code, are—

To remove doubts relative to the authority of any parts of the penal law of the different nations by which this state, before its independence, was governed.

To embody into one law and to arrange into system such of the various prohibitions enacted by different statutes as are proper to be retained in the penal code.

To include in the class of offences, acts injurious to the state and its inhabitants, which are not now forbidden by law.

To abrogate the reference, which now exits, to a foreign law for the definition of offences and the mode of prosecuting them.

To organize a connected system for the prevention as well as for the prosecution and punishment of offences.

To collect into written codes, and to express in plain language, all the rules which it may be necessary to establish, for the protection of the government of the country, and the person, property, condition, and reputation of individuals ; the penalties and punishments attached to a breach of those rules; the legal means of preventing offences, and the forms of prosecuting them when committed; the rules of evidence, by which the truth of accusations are to be tested; and the duties of executive and judicial officers, jurors and individuals, in preventing, prosecuting, and punishing offences: to the end that no one need be ignorant of any branch of criminal jurisprudence, which it concerns all to know.

And to change the present penal laws, in all those points in which they contravene the following principles, which the general assembly consider as fundamental truths, and which they have made the basis of their legislation on this subject, to wit :

Vengeance is unknown to the law. The only object of punishment is to prevent the commission of offences : it should be calculated to operate.

First, on the delinquent, so as by seclusion to deprive him of the present means, and by habits of industry and temperance, of any future desire, to repeat the offence.

Secondly, on the rest of the community, so as to deter them by the example, from a like contravention of the laws. No punishments, greater than are necessary to effect these ends, ought to be inflicted.

No acts or omissions should be declared to be offences, but such as are injurious to the state, to societies permitted by the laws, or to individuals.

But penal laws should not be multiplied without evident necessity ; therefore acts, although injurious to individuals or societies, should not be made liable to public prosecution, when they may be sufficiently repressed by private suit.

From the imperfection of all human institutions, and the inevitable errors of those who manage them, it sometimes happens, that the innocent are condemned to suffer the punishment due to the guilty. Punishments should, therefore, be of such a nature that they may be remitted, and as far as possible compensated, in cases where the injustice of the sentence becomes apparent.

Where guilt is ascertained, the punishment should be speedily inflicted.

Penal laws should be written in plain language, clearly and unequivocally expressed, that they may neither be misunderstood nor perverted ; they should be so concise, as to be remembered with ease; and all technical phrases, or words they contain, should be clearly defined. They should be promulgated in such a manner as to force a knowledge of their provisions upon the people; to this end, they should not only be published, but taught in the schools; and publicly read on stated occasions.

The law should never command more than it can enforce. Therefore, whenever, from public opinion, or any other cause, a penal law cannot be carried into execution, it should be repealed.

The accused, in all cases, should be entitled to a public trial, conducted by known rules, before impartial judges and an unbiassed jury; to a copy of the act of accusation against him ; to the delay necessary to prepare for his trial ; to process to enforce the attendance of his own witnesses; and to an opportunity of seeing, hearing, and examining those who are produced against him; to the assistance of counsel for his defence; to free communication with such counsel, if in confinement, and to be bailed in all cases, except those particularly specified by law. No presumption of guilt, however violent, can justify the infliction of any punishment before conviction, or of any bodily restraint greater than is necessary to prevent escape ; and the nature and extent of this restraint should be determined by law.

Perfect liberty should be secured of hearing and publishing a true account of the proceedings of criminal courts, limited only by such restrictions as morality and decency require ; and no restraint whatsoever should be imposed on the free discussion of the official conduct of the judges and other ministers of justice, in this branch of government.

Such a system of procedure, in criminal cases, should be established as to be understood without long study; it should neither suffer the guilty to escape by formal objections, nor involve the innocent in difficulties, by errors in pleading.

For this purpose, amendments should be permitted in all cases, where neither the accused nor the public prosecutor can be surprised.

Those penal laws counteract their own effect, which, through a mistaken lenity, give greater comforts to a convict than those which he would probably have enjoyed, while at liberty.

The power of pardoning should be only exercised in cases of innocence discovered, or of certain and unequivocal reformation.

Provision should be made for preventing the execution of intended offences, whenever the design to commit them is sufficiently apparent.

The remote means of preventing offences, do not form the subject of penal laws. The general assembly will provide them in their proper place. They are the diffusion of knowledge, by the means of public education, and the promotion of industry, and consequently of ease and happiness among the people.

Religion is a source of happiness here, and the foundation of our hopes of it hereafter ; but its observance can never, without the worst of oppression, form the subject of a penal code. All modes of belief, and all forms of worship, are equal in the eye of the law ; when they interfere with no private or public rights, all are entitled to equal protection in their exercise.

Whatever may be the majority of the professors of one religion or sect in the state, it is a persecution to force any one to conform to any ceremonies, or to observe any festival or day, appropriated to worship by the members of a particular religious persuasion : this does not exclude a general law, establishing civil festivals or periodical cessations from labour for civil purposes unconnected with religious worship, or the appointment of particular days on which citizens of all persuasions should join, each according to the rites of his own religion, in rendering thanks to God for any signal blessing, or imploring his assistance in any public calamity.

The innocent should never be made to participate in the punishment inflicted on the guilty; therefore, no such effects should follow conviction as to prevent the heir from claiming an inheritance through or from the person convicted. Still less should the feelings of nature be converted into instruments of torture, by denouncing punishment against the children, to secure the good conduct of the parent.

Laws intended to suppress a temporary evil should be limited to the probable time of its duration, or carefully repealed after the reason for enacting them has ceased.

## CHAPTER II.

*Plan and division of the system of penal law.*

Art. 1. This system comprises four distinct codes, and a Book of Definitions. The first, called the CODE OF CRIMES AND PUNISHMENTS, is divided into two books, containing :—General Principles ; and the description of all acts or omissions that are declared to be offences ; with the punishment assigned to each.

Art. 2. The second is called the CODE OF CRIMINAL PROCEDURE. It is divided into two books. It contains the means provided for preventing offences that are apprehended, and for repressing those that exist ; and it directs the mode of proceeding for bringing offenders to justice.

Art. 3. The third is the whole law of evidence, applicable as well to civil as to penal cases, and is called the CODE OF EVIDENCE.

Art. 4. The fourth contains a system of prison discipline, in all the stages in which imprisonment is used, either as the means of detention or punishment. It is designated as the CODE OF REFORM AND PRISON DISCIPLINE.

Art. 5. The concluding division of the system is a BOOK OF DEFINITIONS, which defines all the technical words or phrases that are used in the several codes.

## CHAPTER III.

*Introductory notice.*

Art. 6. Whenever the office, trust, state, or relation, of tutor, ward, administrator, executor, ancestor, heir, parent, child, ascendant, descendant, minor, infant, master, or servant, and the relative pronouns, he or they, as referring to them, are used, they are intended to mean as well females as males, standing in those relations, or exercising the same offices, trusts, or duties, unless the contrary be expressed.

Art. 7. The general terms—whoever ; any person ; any one ; and the relative pronouns—he or they, when they refer to them, are intended to include females as well as males, unless there is some expression to the contrary. The word *man* is used in this system, not as a generical term, but to express a person of the male sex, of whatever age. The term woman includes females of every age.

Art. 8. Whenever any thing is forbidden or directed, by using the general terms—any one ; one ; any person ; whoever ; or the relative pronoun—he ; referring to any such general term, the same prohibition or direction (if the contrary be not expressed) is extended to more persons than one, doing or omitting the same act.

Art. 9. Whenever any thing is directed or forbidden with respect to one object or thing, the same direction or prohibition extends to

more than one of the same objects or things, and a direction or prohibition as to more objects than one, includes the same prohibition as to
a single one of the same objects.

Art. 10. All words printed in small capitals, are defined and explained in the Book of Definitions; and in all other parts of the system
are used in no other sense than that given to them by such definition
or explanation.

Art. 11. Every word or phrase, other than those so printed, is to be
taken and construed in the sense in which it is used in common parlance, taken in connexion with the context, and the subject relative to
which it is employed.

Art. 12. It is not intended that each article should contain in itself
a complete expression of legislative will, on the subject of which it
treats, independent of the other articles of the same section; the whole
are to be considered together; to avoid repetition, a provision in one
article sometimes relates to something expressed in another; an example of which is found in the article immediately preceding this, where
the words "so printed" relate to printing in "small capitals," provided
for in the section preceding it.

Art. 13. Whenever the degrees of relationship between persons are
referred to, the degrees by AFFINITY, as well as CONSANGUINITY, are
intended, unless the contrary be expressed.

Art. 14. Whenever any thing is forbidden or commanded for the
protection of property or interest, and the general term "person" or
any other general term, is used, to designate the party whose property
or interest it is intended to protect by such prohibition or command;
in all such cases, the state, and all public and private bodies corporate
are included.

2 V

# A CODE OF CRIMES AND PUNISHMENTS.

# INTRODUCTORY TITLE.

THIS code is divided into two books, and each book into titles, chapters, sections and articles, numbered throughout the whole code.

The first book contains general provisions, applicable to prosecutions and trials ; to the persons who are amenable to the penal laws of the state; to the circumstances under which all acts that would otherwise be offences may be justified or excused; to the repetition of offences; and to the case of different persons participating in the same offence, as principals, accomplices and accessaries.

The second book defines offences, and designates their punishments.

# BOOK I.

CONTAINING GENERAL PROVISIONS.

## CHAPTER I.

*Containing general provisions relative to the operation of the penal laws of this state.*

Art. 1. No act or omission done or made before the promulgation of the law which forbids it, can be punished as an OFFENCE.

Art. 2. If an act or omission be created an offence by one law, and the penalty be altered by another, no breach of the first law, committed before the promulgation of the second, can be punished by inflicting the penalty of the latter.

Art. 3. After a PENAL LAW is repealed, no person can be arrested, imprisoned, tried or condemned, for a breach of it while it was in force, unless the repealing law has an express provision to that effect.

Art. 4. The distinction between a favourable and unfavourable construction of laws is abolished. All penal laws whatever are to be construed according to the plain import of their words, taken in their usual sense, in connexion with the context, and with reference to the matter of which they treat.

Art. 5. When a second penal law shall direct a NEW PENALTY, the penalty of the first law shall be deemed to be abolished, unless the contrary be expressed.

Art. 6. A law which simply commands or forbids an act to be done, but which contains no denunciation of a penalty, can have none but civil effects; the act or omission which is forbidden cannot be punished as an offence.

Art. 7. The legislature alone has the right to declare what shall constitute an offence; therefore it is forbidden to punish any acts or omissions, not expressly prohibited, under pretence that they offend against the laws of nature, of religion, morality or any other rule, except written law.

Art. 8. Courts are expressly prohibited from punishing any acts or omissions which are not forbidden by the plain import of the words of the law, under the pretence that they are within its spirit. It is better that acts of an evil tendency should for a time be done with impunity, than that courts should assume legislative powers; which assumption is itself an act more injurious than any it may purport to repress. There are, therefore, no constructive offences. The legislature, when the necessity appears, will bring such acts as ought to be punished within the letter of the law.

Art. 9. If, however, any penal law shall be so inaccurately drawn, as to bring within its penalty an act that it could not, in the opinion of the court, have been the intention of the legislature so to punish ; the accused must be acquitted, but the court shall report such case to the legislature at their next session, or within eight days if they be in session.

Art. 10. When a competent tribunal, judging in the last resort, hath rendered a final judgment, acquitting or condemning the accused, on the merits of the charge against them, he can never be again prosecuted for the same offence.

Art. 11. An accusation being an affirmation of guilt, it must be proved to the satisfaction of those whose province it is to decide.

## CHAPTER II.

### General provisions relative to prosecutions and trials.

Art. 12. No person accused of any offence shall be compelled by violence or menace, to answer any interrogations relative to his innocence or guilt; nor shall his confession, unless it be given freely, without violence, menace, or promise of indemnity or favour, be produced in evidence against him.

Art. 13. No person shall be arrested to answer for any offence, but in the manner and on the evidence specially set forth in the Codes of Procedure and Evidence.

Art. 14. No SEARCH WARRANT shall issue in any case but in those provided for, and in the manner directed, in the Code of Procedure.

Art. 15. The accused, in every stage of the prosecution, is entitled to have advice of such counsellor at law, or other person, as may be employed by him for his defence. If he declare himself unable to procure counsel, the court shall assign him an advocate in the manner directed by the said code.

Art. 16. No trial for any CRIME shall be had, but in the presence of the accused. No examination of witnesses shall be used on such trial, but such as is taken in the joint presence of the court, the jury, the public prosecutor and the accused ; all of whom shall have leave to question the witness. Those cases in which testimony is allowed to be taken by commission, and those which are specially provided for in the Code of Procedure, are excepted from the provisions of this article.

Art. 17. All trials for offences shall be held in public. All persons under no legal disability or restraint, have a right to be present at such trials ; provided, however, that the court may, on the prayer of the prosecutor or the accused, direct witnesses to withdraw until they are called for examination ; and may also, in the manner directed by the provisions of the Code of Procedure, remove such persons as shall obstruct the administration of justice.

Art. 18. The preceding article is subject to the restriction required by decency and morals, which are particularly provided for in the Code of Procedure.

Art. 19. All final judgments in trials for offences, with the reasons on which they are founded, shall be distinctly pronounced in open court, in the presence of the accused (if he be in custody), and they shall be entered at large on the minutes of the court. And in like manner all other judgments, orders or decisions, shall be pronounced and entered on the minutes, whenever either the public prosecutor or the accused shall require the same.

Art. 20. After a cause, whether civil or criminal, is decided, it shall be lawful for any one, by printing and in writing, as well as by speech, to discuss the reasons of any judgment, order or decree, given in the course of any such suit or prosecution, and to call in question the legality or propriety of the same.

Art. 21. The process to which the accused is entitled by the constitution, to compel the attendance of his witnesses, shall be granted for witnesses who may be in any part of the state, and the sheriff of any parish to whom the same may be directed, shall serve and return such process, and such witnesses shall be paid by the state, whenever the accused shall be acquitted, and whenever it shall appear to the court that the accused, if convicted, is unable to pay them.

Art. 22. All witnesses summoned to attend the trial of any offence, shall be protected from arrest in any civil suit, and in any penal suit for a misdemeanor, other than a breach of the peace, while attending on the court, and for a reasonable time, while going to or returning therefrom ; unless it shall appear that the witness was summoned by collusion merely to protect him from arrest. And in case of any arrest, contrary to this article, any judge of any court of this state, either of criminal or civil jurisdiction, except justices of the peace, may grant relief by discharging the person arrested, first giving notice to the person causing the arrest, or to his agent.

Art. 23. No person after being acquitted or ordered to be discharged, shall be detained for the payment of any fees or costs attending the prosecution for which he has been discharged, or for the reimbursement of the sum allowed by the law for his support, or for any sums whatever due for his maintenance, or for services or supplies while he was in prison. Nor shall any court or magistrate give judgment in any suit against a person who has been acquitted or discharged for want of prosecution, if he shall be sued for any such fees, or for any such sum as is allowed by law for the maintenance of prisoners.

Art. 24. The trial by jury, as regulated in the Code of Procedure, is declared to be the mode of trial for all offences, and it cannot be renounced.

Art. 25. There shall be no trial for any CRIME but on indictment, nor for any MISDEMEANOR but on indictment or information, in the manner directed by the Code of Procedure.

## CHAPTER III.

*Of persons amenable to the provisions of this code, and of the circumstances under which all acts that would otherwise be offences, may be justified or excused.*

Art. 26. All persons, whether they be inhabitants of this state, or of any other of the United States of America, or aliens, are liable to be punished for any offence committed in this state against the laws thereof. Citizens or inhabitants of the state may be punished for acts committed out of the limits thereof, in those cases in which there is a special provision of law, declaring that the act forbidden shall be an offence, although done out of the state.

Art. 27. An offence is a voluntary act or omission, done or made contrary to the directions of a penal law. There can, therefore, generally be no offence, if the will do not concur with the act ; but the law has established exceptions to, and modifications of, this rule : but no modifications or exceptions, other than those expressly provided, are to be allowed.

Art. 28. After the promulgation of a law, no one shall be excused for a breach of it on an alleged ignorance of its provisions.

Art. 29. No person shall be convicted of any offence committed when under nine years of age ; nor of any offence when between nine and fifteen years of age, unless it shall appear by proof to the jury, that he had sufficient understanding to know the nature and illegality of the act which constituted the offence.

Art. 30. If a minor shall commit an offence by command or persuasion of any relation in the ascending line ; of his tutor or curator, or any person acting as such ; or of his master, if he be an apprentice or servant, then the minor shall be punished for such offence by simple imprisonment, during one half of the time to which he would have been sentenced had he been of full age. Provided such minor have attained the age of fifteen years at the time of the commission of the offence ; if under that age, the command or persuasion of either of the persons, standing in either of the relations to him which are above enumerated, shall excuse him from punishment, if the offence committed be a misdemeanor only ; but if the offence be a crime, such minor, under fifteen years of age, shall be committed to the school of reform, for the purpose of being instructed in some trade, in the manner particularly provided for in the Code of Reform and Prison Discipline. And in all cases of crimes committed by minors, under the age of eighteen years, except those punishable by imprisonment for life, the court may direct that the offender be, either in lieu of, or in addition to, the punishment generally provided for the offence, be so committed to the school of reform.

Art. 31. In like manner, a married woman committing an offence by the command or persuasion of her husband, shall suffer no greater punishment than simple imprisonment, for one half of the time to which she would have been sentenced, if she had committed the offence

2 W

without such command or persuasion. The relation of husband and wife, for the purposes of this article, need not be proved by testimony of the celebration of the marriage contract. Living together at the time, and general reputation of marriage, shall be sufficient to reduce the punishment of the reputed wife, and to increase that of the reputed husband, in the manner hereafter directed.

Art. 32. Offences punishable by imprisonment for life, are excepted from the operation of the two last preceding articles.

Art. 33. In all cases where a minor shall be AIDED in the commission of an offence, by either of the persons standing in the relation to him hereinbefore enumerated ; or if the husband or the reputed husband, shall aid the wife in the commission of the offence, or shall be PRESENT during the time of its commission, without endeavouring to prevent it, either of these circumstances shall be proof that the offence was committed by their command or persuasion.

Art. 34. If any minor or married woman shall have committed any offence, and the persons standing in the relations to such minor, which are above enumerated, or the husband of the wife, shall be convicted of having persuaded, commanded, or aided in the said offence, then said persons so convicted shall be punished as follows, that is to say:—

If the minor be under fifteen years of age at the time of committing the offence, then the duration of the punishment, if the same shall consist of imprisonment, and the amount of the fine, if any, which would otherwise have been inflicted on such persons, shall be increased one half. And if the minor shall be above fifteen years, then one-fourth ; and in either case, if the punishment for such offence be imprisonment for life, then one month of such imprisonment, in every year, shall be in solitude.

Art. 35. No act done by a person in a state of INSANITY, can be punished as an offence. No person becoming INSANE after he has committed an offence, can be tried for the same. No person becoming insane after he has been found guilty, shall be sentenced while in that state. No person sentenced shall be punished, if he afterwards become and continue insane.

And during the continuance of the punishment, if the convict is deprived of his reason, so much of the punishment as may consist of hard labour, shall, during such insanity, cease; and the court shall make such order with respect to the convict, as is provided in the Code of Reform and Prison Discipline.

In all the cases mentioned in this article, the court having cognizance of the offence, shall make order for securing the person of the accused. The manner of ascertaining whether insanity is feigned or real, is provided for in the Code of Procedure.

Art. 36. Private soldiers and non-commissioned officers in the army, or in the militia when in actual service, are not liable to punishment for misdemeanors committed by the order of any officer, whose legal military order they were bound to obey; but all officers giving or transmitting the command, are liable to the penalties of the law.

Art. 37. The order of a military superior is no justification or excuse for the commission of a crime.

Art. 38. The order, warrant or writ issued by a magistrate or court, shall justify the person executing it for any act done in obedience thereto, only in cases wherein the following circumstances concur:

1. The court or magistrate must have JURISDICTION of the cause or COGNIZANCE of the matter, in which the order, warrant or writ was issued.

2. The writ, warrant or order, if written, must have all the substantial requisites prescribed by law for such writs as it purports to be.

3. The person executing it must be an officer bound to execute, by virtue of his office, such writs as it purports to be ; or he must be a person to whom such writ is legally directed; or he must be one legally called upon by such officer, to aid in the execution of the order, warrant or writ.

4. He must have no knowledge of any illegality in obtaining or executing the order, warrant or writ.

Art. 39. The legal order of a COMPETENT magistrate or court, if executed by a person DULY AUTHORIZED, will justify those acts which are expressly commanded by such order, and also all those acts which are the necessary means of carrying the order into execution, but it will justify no other acts ; the means allowed as necessary by law, are detailed in the Code of Procedure.

Art. 40. If one be forced by threats or actual violence to do any act, which, if voluntarily done, would be an offence, he shall be exempted from punishment, by proving the following circumstances:

1. That he was threatened with the loss of life or limb, if he did not perform the act ; and that he had good reason to believe that such threat would be executed.

2. That he made every endeavour which could be made by any man of common courage, to resist or escape from the power of the person using the threats.

3. That the act of which he is accused, was done while he was in the presence of the person using the threats or violence, and during the continuance of the same.

Art. 41. If one intending to commit an offence, and in the act of preparing for, or executing the same, shall, through MISTAKE or ACCIDENT, do another act, which, if voluntarily done, would be an offence, he shall incur the penalty for the act really done. Provided, that if the act intended to be done, be a misdemeanor, he shall only incur the highest penalty provided by law for the offence he intended to commit, although the act done would, if he had intended it, have been a crime.

But if the intent was to commit a crime, although INFERIOR IN DEGREE, he shall incur the penalty provided by law for the act really done.

Art. 42. No event happening through MISTAKE or ACCIDENT in the performance of a lawful act, done with ORDINARY ATTENTION, is an offence.

Art. 43. An act forbidden by law, though done through MISTAKE or ACCIDENT, from the want of ORDINARY CARE AND ATTENTION, is punishable.

Art. 44. The provisions of the last preceding article are subject to modifications in the case of homicide, which are expressed in the part of the code which treats of homicide.

Art. 45. The intention to commit an offence shall be presumed whenever the means used are such as, in the common course of events, must produce the event which is forbidden.

Art. 46. The fact which constitutes an offence being proved, all facts or circumstances on which the accused relies to justify or excuse the prohibited act or omission, must be proved by him.

Art. 47. If any person who shall ATTEMPT TO COMMIT an offence, fail in completing the same, or is interrupted from any cause, not depending on his own will, he shall suffer ONE HALF OF THE PUNISHMENT to which he would have been sentenced if he had completed the whole.

Art. 48. Military offences are not comprehended in this code.

Art. 49. The Indian tribes residing within the boundaries of this state, being governed by their own usages, no act done within their boundaries by individuals belonging to such tribes, in their intercourse with each other, or with other tribes, and not affecting any other person, is considered as an offence against this code: in other respects they are considered in the same light with other persons in the state, both as to protection and liability to punishment.

Art. 50. Offences committed by slaves, form the subject of a separate code : such offences are not included in any of the provisions of this system.

Art. 51. The Second Book of this code contains modifications of the general provisions contained in this chapter, which control them.


## CHAPTER IV.


### *Of a repetition of offences.*

Art. 52. Any person, who having been convicted of a misdemeanor, shall afterwards repeat the same offence, or commit any other misdemeanor of the same nature, shall suffer ADDITION OF ONE HALF to the punishment he would otherwise have suffered. If the first conviction was for a crime, the punishment for the second offence of the same nature, shall also be INCREASED ONE HALF.

Art. 53. And if any person, having been twice previously convicted of crimes, no matter of what nature, shall a third time be convicted of any crime afterwards committed, he shall be considered as unfit for society, and be imprisoned at hard labour for life.

Art. 54. A previous conviction in any of the United States of America, operates the same effect as to the increase of punishment for subsequent offences, as if the same conviction had taken place in this state.

Art. 55. By offences of the SAME NATURE, in this section, are intended all such as are comprised within the same title in the Second Book of this code.

Art. 56. Where the punishment of the crime of which the offender is a second or a third time convicted, is imprisonment for life, the increased punishment must consist in seclusion, or such other privations as the judges are empowered in the Second Book to direct, with respect to offenders in general.

# CHAPTER V.

*Of principals, accomplices and accessaries.*

Art. 57. An offence being the doing of an act which is forbidden under a penalty imposed by law, or omitting to do some act, which under like penalty is directed by law to be done ; those are principal offenders who do the forbidden act, or who being bound to do the act enjoined, are guilty of the omission.

Art. 58. If the forbidden act be done by several, all are principal offenders. If several are bound to perform the act which is enjoined, all who omit it are principal offenders.

Art. 59. When the act constituting the offence is actually done by only one or more persons, but others are present, and knowing the unlawful intent, aid them by acts, or encourage them by words or gestures; or if not being actually present, others shall keep watch to give notice of the approach of any one who might interrupt the commission of the offence; or shall be employed in procuring aid, or arms, or instruments for the performance of the act, while it is executing ; or shall do any other act at the time of executing the offence, to secure the safety or concealment of those who perform the offence, or to aid them in its execution : all such persons are also principal offenders, and may be prosecuted and convicted as such.

Art. 60. When the offence is committed by SECONDARY MEANS, without employing the agency of a person who may be convicted as a principal offender, the person employing and preparing those secondary means is a principal offender, although he may not be present when the means he had prepared took their effect.

Art. 61. Laying poison where the person whom it is intended to murder may take it himself; employing a child, or other innocent person, to give it ; setting a spring-gun, so that the party may fire it himself; are examples of the secondary means intended by the last preceding article.

Art. 62. Those persons are also principals, who, having counselled or agreed to the performance of the act, shall be present when it is done, whether they aid in the execution or not.

Art. 63. There may be accessaries to all offences committed with premeditation, and accomplices to all except manslaughter, and offences occasioned by neglect.

Art. 64. There can be neither accomplice nor accessary, except in cases where an offence has been committed.

Art. 65. All those are accomplices who are not present at the commission of an offence, but who, before the act is done, verbally or in writing, shall advise or command, or encourage another to commit it:

Those who agree with the principal offender to aid him in committing the offence, although such aid may not have been given :

Those who shall promise money, or other reward, who shall offer any place or particular favour, or any other inducement; or shall menace any injury or loss of favour, in order to procure the commission of an offence :

Those who shall prepare arms or instruments, men, money or aid of any kind, or do any other act prior to the commission of the offence, to facilitate its execution, and knowing that it is intended : all these persons are accomplices.

Art. 66. No person can be found guilty as an accomplice to any offence, other than such as have aided, promoted, advised or encouraged it by some of the means set forth in the last preceding article; but it is not necessary that the advice should be strictly pursued : it is sufficient if the offence be of the SAME NATURE and for the same object, as the offence advised or encouraged.

Art. 67. If in the attempt to commit an offence, the principal offender shall make himself liable to punishment for any other act committed by mistake or accident, according to the provisions for that purpose hereinbefore contained, his accomplices shall be punished only as they would have been had the offence been committed which he intended to commit.

Art. 68. The punishment of an accomplice is the same as that designated for the principal offender, excepting the increase of such punishment provided for in the next article.

Art. 69. If the principal offender be under fifteen years of age, whether he be found of sufficient intelligence to understand the nature and illegality of the act or not, and there be an accomplice of full age, the punishment of such accomplice shall be INCREASED ONE HALF and if the principal offender be a minor, above fifteen, then the punishment of the accomplice shall be INCREASED ONE QUARTER.

Art. 70. Accessaries are those who, knowing that an offence has been committed, conceal the offender, or give him any other aid, in order that he may effect his escape from arrest or trial, or the execution of his sentence; he who aids the offender in preparing and making his defence at law; or who procures him to be bailed, although he may afterwards abscond, shall not be considered as an accessary.

Art. 71. The following persons cannot be punished as accessaries.

1. The husband or wife of the offender.

2. His relations in the ascending or descending line, either by affinity or consanguinity.

3. His brothers or sisters.

4. His domestic servants.

Art. 72. The accessary shall be punished by fine and simple imprisonment in the manner directed by the Second Book.

Art. 73. The accomplice may be arrested, tried and punished before the conviction of the principal offender, and the acquittal of the principal shall .be no bar to the prosecution of the accomplice, but on the trial of such accomplice, the commission of the offence must be clearly proved, or the accomplice cannot be convicted.

Art. 74. The accessary may be arrested, but not tried without his consent before the conviction of the principal, and the acquittal of the principal shall discharge the person named as accessary.

# BOOK II.

## TITLE I.

OF THE GENERAL DIVISIONS AND DESCRIPTIONS OF OFFENCES AND PUNISHMENTS.

### CHAPTER I.

*Definition and divisions of offences.*

Art. 75. Offences are those acts and omissions which are forbidden by positive law, under the sanction of a penalty.

Art. 76. There are two divisions of offences; establishing distinctions drawn, the one from the degree of the offence, the other from its object.

By the first division, all offences are either CRIMES OR MISDEMEANORS.

By the second, they are PUBLIC OR PRIVATE OFFENCES.

Art. 77. All offences punishable by confinement at hard labour, or by a forfeiture of any civil or political right, are crimes ; all other offences are misdemeanors.

All offences to which either of the punishments enumerated in the last preceding article are expressly assigned, or to which the court have a discretionary power to apply them, are punishable in that manner within the meaning of that article.

Art. 78. Offences, in relation to their object, are public or private offences.

Art. 79. Those are public offences which principally affect the state or its government in any of its branches, or any of its institutions, or operations for the benefit of the citizens. Those are public offences which affect,

1. The sovereign power of the state.
2. The legislative power.
3. The executive power.
4. The judiciary power.
5. The public tranquillity.
6. The right of suffrage.
7. The freedom of the press.

8. The public records.
9. The current coin and public securities.
10. The public revenue.
11. The commerce and manufactures.
12. The public property.
13. The public roads, embankments, navigable waters, and other property held by the sovereign power for the common use of the people.
14. The public health.
15. The morals of the people.

Art. 80. Those are private offences which principally affect individuals, or such societies as are either established or permitted by law; they are such as affect them,

1. In the exercise of their religion.
2. In their honour and reputation.
3. In their persons.
4. In their profession and trade.
5. In their civil and political rights and conditions.
6. In their property.

Art. 81. The division of offences marked out by this chapter, is intended only for the establishment of order in the arrangement of the code; each offence will be hereinafter particularly defined and illustrated; and no act or omission is an offence, which does not come within some one of those definitions as they are explained and illustrated.


# CHAPTER II.


## *Of punishments.*

Art. 82. To enforce the performance of a duty, or to give compensation for or prevent the infraction of a right, is the province of civil law. Penal law designates such infractions as require coercion or punishment to prevent or repress them; and it provides for each wrong thus designated, the requisite remedy of prevention, removal of the evil, or penalty for its commission. This code is strictly penal: compensation forms no part of its sanction. But no punishment deprives the party who is injured by an offence, of his civil remedy; the reservation of such right to civil redress, is no where expressly made, but is in all cases understood.

Art. 83. The claim of the party injured by an offence, when it becomes liquidated by a judgment, is preferred in cases of insolvency, to the claim of the state for a fine imposed for the same offence. And if the fine be levied, and there is no property sufficient to satisfy the execution on the private suit, the amount of the fine, or as much of it as may be necessary, shall, on petition against the officer of government in whose hands it may be, be paid over to satisfy the judgment obtained by the party injured.

Art. 84. The civil remedy for the wrong occasioned by an offence may be pursued, either against the offender (when he is not confined at hard labour), or against the curators of his estate, when they are appointed according to the directions hereinafter contained.

Art. 85. The punishments and penalties to be incurred for offences under this code are,

1. Pecuniary fines.
2. Simple imprisonment.
3. Imprisonment in close custody.
4. Deprivation of office.
5. The suspension of some one or more political or civil rights for a limited period.
6. The forfeiture of some one or more political or civil rights.
7. Imprisonment and hard labour for a limited time.
8. Imprisonment at hard labour for life. Both these last punishments, with or without the addition of solitary confinement and other privations, as are directed in different parts of this code.

Art. 86. In addition to these punishments, where the offence is of a continuous nature, there must be judgment for its discontinuance.

Art. 87. In conviction for offences that affect honour or reputation, the judgment may, in addition to, or as an alternative for the punishment assigned, grant an honorary reparation, in the manner designated in that class of offences.

Art. 88. Pecuniary fines imposed for offences shall be levied by execution in the name of the state ; in the same manner as is directed by the practice in civil cases, for enforcing the execution of a judgment for debt, in the highest court of original jurisdiction in the state ; and the fine shall be a lien upon real property, from the time it is registered in the office of the register of mortgages, in the manner directed by law for the registry of judicial mortgages.

Art. 89. The death of the offender operates as a discharge of all pecuniary fines imposed upon him : even if execution be issued, the officer shall proceed no further therein. If the offender die before a sale on such execution, the lien created by the registry of such fine shall, by order of the court, be taken off, on proving the death of the offender ; unless real property shall have been sold, subject to such lien, and the amount thereof shall have formed part of the price ; in which case, the amount of such fine shall be levied by sale of the said real property, notwithstanding the death of the person on whom the fine was imposed.

Art. 90. A pecuniary fine shall in no case exceed one fourth part of the value of the property, real and personal, of the person on whom it is imposed ; and such person may, in all cases, have any pecuniary fine reduced to that amount, on showing the true value of his property, to the satisfaction of the court ; in which case the court must commute the part of the fine that is deducted into imprisonment ; calculating one day's imprisonment for every two dollars deducted from the fine, and the imprisonment, or any part of it, may be in close custody with the limitation contained in the next article.

Art 91. The wearing apparel, implements of trade, and household furniture of the delinquent, shall not be seized on an execution to satisfy a pecuniary fine, nor shall his arms or accoutrements as an officer or private in the militia. If no other property be found, the court imposing the fine may, on such return being made on the execution, direct that the offender be imprisoned (either in close custody or in simple imprisonment, for the whole or a part of the time, at their discretion) one day for every two dollars contained in the amount

2 X

of the fine imposed ; provided, that such imprisonment do not exceed the term of ninety days, whatever be the amount of such fine ; and such imprisonment shall operate as full satisfaction of such fine.

Art. 92. Simple imprisonment is inflicted by the mere confinement of the offender in the common prison, appointed for that purpose by law, which shall be in a building or apartment distinct from the penitentiary. This punishment consists simply in the confinement of the person within the walls of such prison, the prisoner being debarred neither the use of books, nor the means of writing, nor the society of such persons as may desire to see him during the hours established by the general regulations for the prison.

Imprisonment in close custody is an imprisonment within a single chamber of the common prison, during which the prisoner is to be allowed no other sustenance than the common prison allowance, and is debarred all visits, except such as may be specially allowed by the judge in particular cases of business or sickness.

Art. 93. The civil rights, which may be forfeited or suspended by virtue of any sentence importing such forfeiture or suspension, are divided into three classes :

1. The right of exercising the duties of executor, administrator, tutor, curator, attorney at law, attorney in fact, or being appointed to any PRIVATE OFFICE, which is now, or may hereafter, be established by law.

2. The right of appearing in person, or by attorney, in any court, as party to a suit, either as plaintiff or defendant.

3. The right of bearing arms in defence of the country, and of serving on juries.

Art. 94. All political rights are suspended by a sentence of imprisonment at hard labour, during the period for which such imprisonment is directed; if such sentence be for life, all those rights are forfeited.

Art. 95. A sentence of imprisonment at hard labour suspends, during the term of such imprisonment, all civil rights. If such sentence be for life, all civil rights are forfeited. Forfeiture or suspension of civil rights is directed in certain cases, which are specially provided for.

Art. 96. A suspension or forfeiture of political rights, whether expressly pronounced or implied, by the operation of the two last preceding articles, deprives the offender of any PUBLIC OFFICE he may hold at the time.

Art. 97. When sentence of forfeiture or suspension of civil rights, or of those of the first-class only, has been expressly pronounced or implied by a sentence of imprisonment at hard labour, all the duties, trusts, or PRIVATE OFFICES, coming within the first class of civil rights, are vacated by the sentence; and some other person shall be appointed to fulfil the same, in the same manner as if the vacancy had been occasioned by death.

Art. 98. During the term of imprisonment at hard labour, the administration of the affairs of the convict is committed to a curator, named in the manner directed by the Code of Procedure.

Art. 99. Imprisonment at hard labour is inflicted in the following degrees :

1. At labour in classes of convicts, in the manner directed by the Code of Reform and Prison Discipline.

2. At labour in solitude.

3. In solitude, with occasional labour.

Art. 100. When any one convicted of murder under trust, assassination, or parricide, shall die in prison, his body shall be delivered for dissection; and the court may, at their discretion, add the same provision to their judgment in the case of simple murder or rape.

Art. 101. The punishment of imprisonment at hard labour admits of aggravation and alleviation, in different offences, as to food, dress, hours of labour, solitude and other particulars which are described in this code, and in the Code of Reform and Prison Discipline.

Art. 102. For different modifications of the same offence, aggravations and alleviations of punishment are directed in this code, by a reference to the punishment assigned to the principal offence; which it orders to be increased or diminished in a certain proportion. To apply this proportion, the following rules are to be observed :

1. If the direction be to diminish the punishment of imprisonment for life, the proportion shall be taken on a period of twenty-four years.

2. If the punishment directed to be increased or diminished leave a discretion to the court between a longer and a shorter term of time, or a greater or a smaller fine, the highest and the lowest terms or sums shall be diminished or increased in the proportion directed.

3. When no lower term or sum is fixed, the highest term or sum must be increased or diminished in the proportion directed, as the highest limit. The court must determine what judgment they would have probably rendered for the simple offence, and take that as the sum or term on which to calculate the proportion of punishment for the modified offence.

4. In all cases where a discretion is given to the court, they must observe the last preceding rule; and within the increased or diminished limits, calculate the increase or diminution of punishment for the modified offence, upon the term or sum they would have assigned to the simple offence.

5. Where the punishment is a forfeiture of civil or political rights, and a diminution is directed, the proportion shall be determined by a suspension of those rights, calculated on a number of twenty-four years as the whole.

6. When the judgment is a suspension of such rights for a definite time, the proportion shall be calculated on that time.

All the other incidents of the whole punishment are annexed to the proportion during the period it lasts.

Art. 103. Fines for certain offences are directed to bear a certain proportion to the income or emoluments of the office held by the offender. To determine the amount of these fines, the court may examine witnesses as to the reputed emoluments, which may be reduced, if higher than the truth, by the oath of the defendant, which it is optional with him to give.

Art. 104. Where for the offence of bribery a fine is directed to be imposed, bearing a certain proportion to the value of the bribe offered or received, and such value cannot be ascertained, or if the bribe is something which cannot be appreciated in money, the fine imposed shall not be less than five hundred dollars, nor more than three thousand dollars, unless there be a special provision to the contrary.

Art. 105. No other punishments can be inflicted for any offence than those enumerated in this chapter, and only in the cases provided for by this code.

Art. 106. Where one person shall be guilty of several offences before he has been convicted of any, the punishment for each successive offence is cumulative; but the augmented punishment prescribed for the repetition of offences is not thereby incurred ; and where the punishment for a former offence is less than imprisonment for life, the imprisonment incurred for the second conviction shall commence at the expiration of the first imprisonment.

Art. 107. The person of a convict who is condemned to imprisonment, which brings with it a forfeiture of his civil rights, is under the protection of the law, as well as in its custody. Any restraint or violence to his person, beyond that necessary to the execution of the sentence of the law, is punishable in the same manner as it would be if he were not convicted.

Art. 108. The privation of the right to bear arms in defence of the country, does not give an exemption from military duty. Persons under this disability are forced to serve, but without arms, on working parties, and in the drudgery of the service.

# TITLE II.

OF OFFENCES AGAINST THE SOVEREIGN POWER OF THE STATE.

## CHAPTER I.

### *Of treason.*

Art. 109. Treason is defined by the constitution of the state. It consists in levying war against the state, or in adhering to its enemies, giving them aid and comfort; but as by the nature of the union between the different states, the levying war against one state is a levy of war against the whole, and the constitution of the United States having made that act treason, and vested the cognizance of the crime in the courts of the United States, no provisions are deemed proper to be made respecting that offence.

## CHAPTER II.

### *Of sedition.*

Art. 110. Whoever shall, by FORCE OF ARMS, attempt to DISMEMBER the state, or to SUBVERT OR CHANGE the constitution thereof, shall be imprisoned at hard labour in solitude for life, and after death his body shall be delivered for dissection.

Art. 111. To constitute this offence, there must be not only a design to dismember the state, or to subvert or change its constitution, but an attempt must be made to do it by FORCE.

Art. 112. The attempt consists in enlisting men, preparing arms, or making an assemblage of men, armed or otherwise arrayed, in such a manner as to show the design to effect their object by force. This is sufficient evidence of the attempt, whether any actual violence be committed or not.

Art. 113. If any one shall, by writing, printing, or verbally, counsel or EXCITE the people of this state, or of any part thereof, to commit either of the offences described in the preceding part of this chapter, or to resist by force the legal execution of any constitutional law of the state, he shall be fined not less than five hundred dollars, nor more than two thousand dollars; shall be imprisoned in close custody not less than three nor more than twelve months, and be suspended from his political rights for four years.

Art. 114. It is not necessary, to constitute this offence, that the crime advised should be committed.

## CHAPTER III.

### Of exciting insurrection.

Art. 115. Any free person who shall aid in any insurrection of slaves against the free inhabitants of this state, who shall join in any secret assembly of slaves, in which such insurrection shall be planned, with design to promote it, or shall excite or persuade any slaves to attempt such insurrection, shall be imprisoned at hard labour for life.

Art. 116. By "insurrection," is meant an assembling with ARMS, with intent to regain their liberty by force.

Art. 117. The term "excite" in the description of this offence, means to offer any persuasion or inducement, which has insurrection for its immediate object. It excludes the construction that would make those guilty who only use language calculated to render the slaves discontented with their state. This, if done with design to promote such discontent, is an offence punishable by fine, not less than fifty, nor more than two hundred dollars; or imprisonment, not less than thirty days, nor more than six months, in close custody.

## TITLE III.

### OF OFFENCES AGAINST THE LEGISLATIVE POWER.

Art. 118. If any one shall designedly, and by FORCE, prevent the general assembly of this state, or either of the houses composing it, from meeting, or shall, with intent to prevent such meeting, by the use of personal violence or threats thereof, prevent any of the members of the general assembly from attending the house to which they may belong, or shall by force or threats thereof force either of the said branches of the general assembly to adjourn or disperse, or to pass any resolution or law, or do any other act; or to reject any resolution or law which they constitutionally might pass; he shall be fined not less than five hundred dollars, nor more than two thousand dollars; be confined not less than five, nor more than ten years at hard labour, and shall forfeit his political rights.

Art. 119. Whoever shall use any threats of violence to any member of the general assembly, with intent to influence his official conduct, or shall make any assault on him in consequence of any thing he may have said or done, as a member of the assembly, or of his conduct as a member thereof, shall be fined not less than one hundred dollars, nor more than five hundred dollars; and be imprisoned in close custody, not less than one, nor more than six months.

Art. 120. Whoever shall BRIBE or offer to BRIBE any member of the general assembly, shall be fined in a sum equal to four times the value of the bribe, and if the amount thereof cannot be ascertained, or cannot be appreciated in money, then in a sum not less than one thousand, nor more than two thousand dollars; shall suffer imprisonment at hard labour, not less than six months, nor more than one year, and be suspended from all political rights for five years.

Art. 121. If any member of the general assembly shall receive or agree to receive a BRIBE, he shall be fined in a sum equal to five times the value of the bribe, and if the value thereof cannot be ascertained, or cannot be appreciated in money, then in a sum not less than two thousand, nor more than five thousand dollars; shall forfeit his political rights, and be imprisoned in solitude and at hard labour, not less than one, nor more than two years.

# TITLE IV.

## OF OFFENCES AGAINST THE EXECUTIVE POWER.

## CHAPTER I.

Art. 122. If any person elected or appointed to any EXECUTIVE OFFICE, shall do any official act, before he shall have given security, if any is required by law, or before he shall have taken the oaths of the office, when they are required by law, he shall pay a fine equal to one half year's emolument of his office.

Art. 123. Any person who shall BRIBE, or offer to BRIBE AN EXECUTIVE OFFICER, shall be suspended from the enjoyment of his political rights, for not less than four, nor more than six years, be fined not less than three times the value of the bribe offered, and be imprisoned in close custody, not less than two, nor more than six months.

Art. 124. If any one by VIOLENCE OFFERED TO THE PERSON of any executive officer, or by threats of violence, shall induce, or force him to do any official act, in an illegal manner, or to do under colour of his office any other act, which he is not authorized to do, or to omit the performance of any official act, which he is bound to perform, the offender shall be imprisoned in close custody, not less than three, nor more than twelve months, and shall be fined in a sum not less than fifty, nor more than two hundred dollars : in addition to the punishment provided by law for the act or omission, to which he compelled the officer, if it be an offence, and in addition also to the punishment directed by law for the violence itself, considered as unconnected with the motive for offering it.

Art. 125. If any one shall by force resist any executive officer in the performance of his office, or attempt by force to commit either of· the acts made punishable by the last preceding article, without succeeding in such resistance or attempt, he shall suffer one half the punishment directed by the said article.

## CHAPTER II.

### *Of offences committed by executive officers.*

Art. 126. Any EXECUTIVE OFFICER who shall receive a BRIBE, shall forfeit his political rights, and be imprisoned, not less than one, nor more than two years ; one-fourth of the time in close custody ; and shall be fined not less than four times the value of the bribe received.

Art. 127. If any executive officer shall corruptly agree to make any appointment, or do any other official act in consideration of some AD-VANTAGE (which is not incident to the act) given or promised to him for such act, but which ADVANTAGE does not come within the definition of an EMOLUMENT, he shall forfeit the amount of the emoluments of his office for not less than six months, nor more than two years.

Art. 128. If any executive officer shall EXTORT money, or OTHER REWARD, for the performance of acts he was obliged by law to perform, and for which no remuneration is given by law, or shall extort more than is allowed by law for the performance of any service, or shall EXTORT money or other REWARD from any one, under the pretence that he has performed services for which a remuneration is given by law, when in fact no such services have been rendered, he shall be imprisoned in close confinement, not less than two months, nor more than one year, and shall moreover forfeit the office he holds, and be fined in a sum equal to one year's salary or emoluments of the said office.

Art. 129. If any executive officer shall RECEIVE, or agree to RECEIVE, any EMOLUMENT whatever, though voluntarily given, for doing any act required to be done by virtue of his office, or for refraining from doing any thing, which he is not authorized to do, if the law does not expressly authorize the receipt of such emolument ; or shall receive any emolument greater in value than the sum determined by law for any services rendered by virtue of his office, although such emolument be voluntarily given, he shall forfeit the amount of one half year's salary or emoluments of his office.

Art. 130. If any executive officer shall, under pretence of performing the duties of his office, do any act which amounts to an offence, he shall suffer an additional punishment of one half, to that which is by law provided for the offence when committed by another.

Art. 131. If any executive officer shall undesignedly do any act, under colour of his office, which he is not authorized by his office to perform, or shall negligently omit to do any act which he ought by virtue of his office to perform, by which act or omission any individual or society receives such injury as would entitle them to a civil action, such officer shall be fined, in a sum not less than two months, and not more than six months, of the emoluments of his office. This article does not extend to any other such act or omission, as by any other part of this code is created an offence.

Art. 132. If any of the acts or omissions described in the last preceding section shall be intentionally done, or made the party guilty thereof, shall, in addition to the fine, be suspended from his political rights, for not less than two, nor more than four years.

Art. 133. All the articles of this title, which impose penalties upon executive officers for offences, extend to the deputies and clerks of such officers who shall commit the same offences.

Art. 134. Every person entrusted by the officer with the performance of his official duties, is considered as a deputy for the purpose of this section, whether the officer had a right to appoint a deputy or not.

Art. 135. Every person who publicly exercises the duties of any office, is subject to the penalties imposed by this section; although there be such defect or informality on his appointment or election, or any such omission to comply with the formalities required by law, as would render his official acts invalid.

Art. 136. The principal officer is considered as himself guilty of all such offences committed by his deputy, in relation to his office, as are committed with his knowledge or consent; and he shall be presumed to have known and consented to such offence, if it can be shown that the deputy had, before the act complained of, committed a similar official offence, while in his service, to the knowledge of the officer; and that after such knowledge, he continued to employ him in the performance of his official duties.

Art. 137. The provisions of this and of the last preceding chapter, relating to bribery; extend to those who exercise any CORPORATE or PRIVATE office, and to those who may bribe or attempt to bribe them.

# TITLE V.

OF OFFENCES AFFECTING THE JUDICIARY POWER.

## CHAPTER I.

*Of offences committed by and against judges or jurors in their official capacity.*

### SECTION I.

Of offences committed by judges or jurors.

Art. 138. If any judge or juror shall take a bribe, he shall be fined five times the value of the bribe received, shall suffer imprisonment, in close confinement, not less than six, nor more than twelve months ; and shall forfeit his political rights.

Art. 139. If any judge shall maliciously, but without being bribed, do any official act, or render any judgment, which he is not by law authorized to do or render, or shall maliciously omit to do any act which he ought, by virtue of his office, to perform, he shall forfeit his political rights, and be fined to the amount of his income of office for one year.

Art. 140. If any judge shall corruptly agree to give any judgment, or to do any other official act, in consideration of some advantage (which is not incident to the official act) given or promised to him for rendering such judgment or doing such act, which advantage shall not come within the definition of an emolument, he shall forfeit his office and be fined in the amount of the income thereof for one year.

Art. 141. If any judge shall receive from any person whatever, unless he be a relation in the ascending or descending line, or a collateral relation within the second degree, any gift or donation whatever, of any assignable value, unless it be made by last will and testament or codicil, he shall be fined in a sum equal to six months' income of his office.

Art. 142. If any judge, whose duty it shall or may be to assist at the drawing of jurors to form the panel for the grand jury, or the petit jury in any court in this state, shall designedly put, or consent to the putting of any name on the said panel not drawn according to law, or shall omit to put on such panel any name which shall be legally drawn, or shall sign or certify any panel of names not drawn according to law, such judge, or any other person who shall designedly aid therein, shall be fined not less than two hundred dollars, nor more than one thousand dollars, and shall be imprisoned not less than one, nor more than six months ; and if the offence shall be committed at the solicitation of any person accused of an offence, or of the prosecutor, or any

2 Y

party in a civil suit; the offender shall also be suspended from the exercise of his political rights for five years.

Art. 143. If any juror shall (except in the deliberation with his fellow jurors) make any promise or agreement to give a verdict for or against any one accused of any offence, or for or against any party to a civil suit; or shall receive any papers or evidence from the prosecutor or the accused in any criminal suit, or either of the parties in any civil suit, other than such as shall be delivered in open court, he shall be fined not less than fifty, nor more than four hundred dollars, or may be imprisoned not exceeding thirty days, or both.

Art. 144. If any judge, who is allowed to take fees or compensation for any official act that he is authorized to do, whether of a judicial or executive nature, shall exact and receive more for such service than by law he is authorized to receive, he shall pay a fine equal to one year's income of his office, and shall forfeit his political rights.

Art. 145. If any judge, even with the consent of the party paying the same for any official act, whether of a judicial nature or executive nature, for which he is authorized to take any fees or compensation, shall receive any greater sum than that allowed by law for such service, he shall be fined in a sum equal to six months' income of his office.

Art. 146. No judge shall take any part, either by sitting as judge, or deciding any point, or advising with the other judges, either in or out of court, in the trial or hearing of any cause in which or in the controversy out of which it has arisen he shall have been employed either as counsellor or attorney, or which or in the controversy of which it shall have arisen he shall have acted as ARBITRATOR, or on any former trial of which he shall have been sworn as a juror, or in which he has any interest, or to which any of his ascendants or decendants, or any collateral relation, either by consanguinity or affinity, within the third degree, are parties, or are anywise interested; nor shall any of the other judges of the same court consult with, or take the opinion of such other, in or out of court, in any such cause as is above described. And any judge who shall designedly offend against any provision of this article, shall be fined in a sum equal to his salary and emoluments for six months.

Art. 147. The first article of this chapter relates to ARBITRATORS as well as judges; and all the preceding articles of this chapter, except the fourth, relate to justices of the peace as well as judges.

SECTION II.

Of offences against judges or jurors in their official capacity.

Art. 148. If any one shall bribe or offer to bribe any judge, justice of the peace or arbitrator or juror, either of the grand jury or trial jury, he shall be confined in close custody, not less than two, nor more than six months, and shall be fined in a sum equal to four times the value of the bribe offered or given.

Art. 149. If any one by violence or threats of bodily harm, or illegal injury to property or reputation, shall attempt to oppose or influence any judge or justice of the peace in the execution of any official act, or shall in like manner attempt to force or influence any judge, justice of the peace or ARBITRATOR or juror to render or find any judgment, order, verdict, or indictment, or to do any other official act, he shall be fined not less than fifty, nor more than four hundred dollars ; or be imprisoned, not less than twenty days, nor more than six months, or both ; and the imprisonment, or any part of it, may be in close custody, in addition to any punishment that may be incurred by the violence used.

Art. 150. If any one, with intent to influence the verdict of a jury in a criminal or civil suit, shall any where but in open court, or by leave of the court, exhibit to any person drawn or summoned to serve as a grand juror or petit juror during the term at which such suit is to be tried, knowing or believing him to be so summoned or drawn, any evidence in such suit, or use any arguments in favour of, or against either of the parties in such suit, he shall be fined not less than twenty, nor more than one hundred dollars, and shall be imprisoned not less than five, nor more than thirty days ; and if the offender be an officer of justice, or an attorney or counsellor, or an officer of the court, the punishment shall be double.

Art. 151. If any one shall, during the pendency of any civil suit, or criminal prosecution, publish or print any argument, statement or observations relating to such cause, of such a nature as to influence the verdict of a jury, or to excite any public prejudice for or against either of the parties in such cause, he shall be imprisoned, not exceeding thirty days, or fined not exceeding two hundred dollars.

Art. 152. But nothing in the preceding article contained, shall prohibit in any stage of a criminal prosecution, the publication of a true statement of any judicial proceeding, or the examination of witnesses judicially taken, with the exceptions contained in the Code of Procedure, in cases affecting decency and morals.

## CHAPTER II.

### *Of offences against officers of justice and officers of courts.*

Art. 153. Whoever shall BRIBE or offer to BRIBE any officer of justice, or any clerk, translator, or other officer of a court of justice, he shall be imprisoned not less than one, nor more than six months, shall be fined not less than one hundred, nor more than five hundred dollars, and be suspended from his political rights for five years.

Art. 154. Whoever shall forcibly oppose any officer of justice, knowing him to be such, in the lawful execution of an official act, he shall be imprisoned not less than ten days, nor more than six months ; and shall be fined not less than fifty, nor more than five hundred dollars ; and the whole or any part of the imprisonment may be close custody.

Art. 155. Persons to whom a special warrant is directed in the manner prescribed in the Code of Procedure, and those who are by the provisions of the same code, authorized to make arrests, without warrant in the cases allowed by law, are officers of justice within the purview of this title, while actually employed in executing such warrant or making such arrest.

Art. 156. To constitute this offence, it must be known not only that the person opposed is an officer of justice, but that the act he is doing is an official one ; this knowledge may be proved by other circumstances, but no other proof is necessary than that the officer (if he were one) at the time gave notice of his official character, and of the purpose of his act.

Art. 157. The offence is not committed by an opposition to any others than official acts, therefore the penalty is not incurred by opposing an officer of justice, when he attempts to do any act that is not authorized by his legal powers, or to do an authorized act by illegal means, the opposition, if confined in purpose to that part of the act which is illegal, and in degree to the force necessary to prevent its execution, does not amount to this offence.

Art. 158. No other error in a warrant, or order, will justify an opposition to it than the following :

1. That it was not issued by either a court or magistrate.

2. That the person named or described in the warrant is not the person against whom the warrant or order is attempted to be executed.

3. That the person executing it is neither the one to whom it is directed, nor an officer of justice ; if he be an officer of justice, he may execute the warrant to whomsoever it may be directed.

4. That the warrant or order is issued or allowed by a magistrate, whose authority does not extend to the place in which it is attempted to be executed.

Art. 159. Force used against an officer of justice while in the legal execution of his duty, does not amount to this offence, unless the intent be to prevent the execution of his duty, although the force should have that effect.

Art. 160. In making an arrest under a warrant, a forcible opposition to it is not justified by a refusal to deliver the warrant out of the officer's hands, provided he show it when required.

Art. 161. If by reason of the opposition the officer of justice is prevented from executing his duty, the punishment shall be increased one half.

Art. 162. This offence may be committed as well by a person not concerned in the official act which is opposed, as by the party against whom it is directed.

Art. 163. All official acts that can be lawfully done by an officer of justice, either in obedience to the lawful order of a court or magistrate, whether of a civil or criminal jurisdiction ; or such as he is required to do as conservator of the peace, or for the prevention of offences, or securing the persons of offenders, come within the purview of this chapter.

Art. 164. Threats of such violence as the party has it in his power to execute, and as would be sufficient to intimidate a man of common firmness, amount to a forcible opposition within the meaning of this and the next chapter, as to rescue.

# CHAPTER IV.

## *Of rescue.*

Art. 165. Whoever shall by force set any one at liberty, who is in custody on a lawful arrest for any offence, shall suffer one half of the punishment assigned by law to the offence for which the person rescued was charged. If the arrest was on a civil suit, the punishment shall be fine, not less than fifty nor more than five hundred dollars, or imprisonment in close custody not less that thirty days, nor more than six months, or both; provided, that whatever may be the punishment assigned to any offence for which the person rescued shall have been arrested, no judgment, on a conviction for rescuing one who was arrested for an offence, shall be less than that assigned for the rescue of one arrested in a civil suit.

Art. 166. If the warrant, under which the arrest was made, be so defective as to justify the party arrested in resisting it, according to the previous disposition of this code, and he does so resist; those who aid him in a legal manner are not guilty of a rescue.

Art. 167. In like manner, those who aid a person in resisting an arrest made without warrant, under circumstances which do not legally justify such arrest, are not guilty of a rescue.

Art. 168. There can be no rescue, unless there has been an arrest; any forcible opposition to making a lawful arrest is another offence already provided for.

Art. 169. If the party arrested make no opposition, and the officer or other person making the arrest is proceeding with the prisoner to a magistrate for examination, when he is forcibly set at liberty, it is a rescue, although the original arrest were unlawful.

Art. 170. If the rescue be after a commitment is made out, and before the prisoner is actually received in prison, no defect whatever in the commitment can justify the rescue.

# CHAPTER V.

## *Of escape.*

Art. 171. If any one lawfully arrested for whatever cause, shall escape from custody, without being legally discharged, he shall be fined not exceeding one hundred dollars, or imprisoned not exceeding sixty days; provided such escape be not effected by breach of prison or by violence.

If the escape be effected by violence, it shall be punished in the manner hereinbefore directed with respect to those who oppose executive officers of justice in the performance of their duty.

Art. 172. Any executive officer of justice, or other person having the legal custody of any one who has been lawfully arrested for any offence, who shall voluntarily suffer such person to escape or to be rescued, shall suffer one half of the punishment of the offence with which the person escaping was charged ; and if an officer, he shall be suspended from his political rights for four years.

Art. 173. If the escape or rescue be owing to negligence, the punishment shall be one-fourth of that which would have been incurred by the person escaping, had he been found guilty.

Art. 174. Offenders against the provisions of either of the two last preceding articles may be convicted, although the person escaping should not be retaken or should be acquitted on trial.

## CHAPTER VI.

### *Of breach of prison.*

Art. 175. If any one legally committed to any PUBLIC PRISON, either before or after conviction, for any offence or in any civil suit, shall, by breaking the prison or by violence offered to any person employed to keep or guard such prison, escape or attempt to escape from such prison, he shall be imprisoned in close custody, not less than six months, nor more than two years, to commence after the expiration of his original imprisonment.

Art. 176. If any one shall rescue or attempt to rescue any other person who is confined in any public prison, by breaking such prison, he shall be imprisoned at hard labour, not less than two nor more than five years, in addition to the punishment assigned for the offence of rescuing such prisoners, should the rescue be effected.

Art. 177. The penalty of the last preceding article is incurred whether the prisoner be legally or illegally committed.

Art. 178. If any one shall, by any means not amounting to breach of prison, aid any prisoner legally confined in a public prison to escape, or shall supply instruments for breaking the prison, or other means of escape, for the purpose of attempting it, whether the escape be effected or not, he shall be fined not less than one hundred nor more than five hundred dollars, and be imprisoned not less than one nor more than six months in close custody, or by simple imprisonment for the whole or part of the time.

Art. 179. If the breach of prison be effected by the means set forth in the last preceding article, the person aiding or providing the means may also be punished as an accomplice in that offence.

## CHAPTER VII.

*Of offences committed by officers of justice and officers of courts in their official capacity.*

Art. 180. All the articles of the first and second chapters of the fourth title of this book, entitled, " of offences committed by executive officers," apply to officers of justice and officers of courts, they being comprehended in the definition of executive officers.

## CHAPTER VIII.

*Of counsellors and attorneys at law.*

Art. 181. If any of the offences enumerated in the other chapters of this title, and not provided for in this chapter, shall be committed by an attorney at law or a counsellor at law, the punishment assigned to such offence shall be increased one half.

Art. 182. Any counsellor at law, or attorney at law, or any attorney in fact, charged with the prosecution or defence of a civil suit, who shall receive a bribe, shall be fined a sum equal to five times the value of the bribe received, shall be imprisoned not less than six nor more than twelve months, and shall forfeit his political rights, and his civil rights of the first class.

Art. 183. If any attorney at law, or counsellor at law, or any attorney in fact, who is charged in any prosecution or defence of a civil suit, or the defence of any one accused of an offence, shall designedly divulge any circumstance which came to his knowledge in virtue of his trust, to the injury of his client ; or shall give counsel to the opposite party, to the injury of his client ; or after having engaged to prosecute or defend any civil suit, and been consulted on the merits of the case, for any one, shall, on account of the non-payment of fees, or for any other cause or pretext, appear for the opposite party, either as his attorney or counsellor in court, or secretly as his adviser ; or shall, with intent to injure the party for whom he is employed, do any other act which he is not legally required to do, that is injurious to the interest of such party, or omit to do any other lawful official act, whereby his client shall suffer in his interest or reputation ; he shall, for either of these offences, be imprisoned not less than twenty days, nor more than six months ; and if an attorney or counsellor at law, be suspended from the exercise of his profession not less than three nor more than twelve months ; and if an attorney in fact, in addition to the imprisonment, be fined not less than one hundred nor more than five hundred dollars.

Art. 184. If any attorney at law, or counsellor at law, or any attorney in fact, employed to conduct a suit or defence in court, shall, within five days after demand in writing, by a person legally authorized to make such demand, refuse or neglect to pay the balance due on any sum of money, or deliver any notes or other securities he may have received for the person by whom he was employed, on any suit in court, or on any demand he was professionally employed to make, or any papers with which he was intrusted in his official capacity, he shall, if an attorney in fact, be fined not less than one hundred, nor more than three hundred dollars; and if a counsellor at law, or attorney at law, shall be suspended from the exercise of his profession, not less than six, nor more than twelve months, and until he shall have paid the sum due, with interest.

Art. 185. No attorney or counsellor at law, or attorney in fact, shall be liable, under the preceding article, for retaining out of the moneys by him received, any sum due to him by his employer, for any liquidated debt due to him, or for legal or customary and reasonable fees and costs or commissions; nor shall he be guilty of any offence in retaining any papers or securities he may have received until such sums be paid, as may be due for costs or fees in any suit or controversy, for the defence or prosecution of which the papers were delivered to him; nor for not delivering papers that have been casually lost or destroyed.

Art. 186. If any attorney or counsellor at law shall fraudulently commence, prosecute or defend any suit in any court in this state, in the name of any person by whom he has not been authorized to prosecute or defend such suit, he shall be suspended from the exercise of his profession, not less than six months, nor more than two years.

Art. 187. Whoever shall bribe or offer to bribe any attorney or counsellor at law, or any attorney in fact, who is charged with the conducting a suit in court, shall be imprisoned in close custody, not less than one nor more than six months, and shall pay a fine equal to four times the amount of the bribe given or offered.

Art. 188. All offences committed by counsellors or attorneys at law, shall be tried in the same manner as other offences, except as is hereinafter provided, in the case of offences committed in the courts of justice.


# CHAPTER IX.


*Of offences by falsely personating another in judiciary proceedings.*

Art. 189. If any one, not being an officer of justice, shall fraudulently pretend to be such, and in such assumed character shall commit any assault, or false imprisonment, or receive or attempt to receive property, he shall be imprisoned at hard labour not less than three, nor more than six years, in addition to the punishment incurred by the other offence he may commit.

Art. 190. If any one shall falsely PERSONATE ANOTHER, and in such assumed character shall become bail, confess judgment, or do any other act in the course of any proceeding in any suit or prosecution, he shall be imprisoned at hard labour not less than two nor more than five years, in addition to the punishment he may incur by any other offence he may commit in such assumed character.

# CHAPTER X.

## *Of perjury and false swearing.*

Art. 191. Perjury is a falsehood, asserted verbally or in writing, deliberately and wilfully, relating to something present or past, under the sanction of an oath, or such other affirmation as is or may be by law made equivalent to an oath, legally administered, under circumstances in which an oath or affirmation is required by law, or is necessary for the prosecution or defence of private right, or for the ends of public justice. Perjury is punished by penitentiary imprisonment, not less than three, nor more than seven years; by a forfeiture of all political rights, and of civil rights of the first and third class. But if any one by means of perjury shall cause another to be convicted of a crime, he shall suffer the same punishment that is incurred by the commission of the crime of which such person has been convicted by means of the perjury.

Art. 192. Falsehood in this definition refers to the belief of the party attesting; therefore if he believes what he swears to be false, and it should happen to be true, he is as guilty of the offence as if he had sworn that to be true which he knew to be false.

Art. 193. The declaration must be deliberate; a false statement made inadvertently, or under agitation, or by mistake, is not perjury.

Art. 194. It must be with design to make the falsehood believed by another, the party taking the oath knowing or believing it to be false; and this design is presumed whenever the falsehood of the declaration is proved.

Art. 195. The oath or affirmation must be administered in the manner required by law, and by a magistrate, or other person duly authorized to administer oaths in the matter or cause in which the oath was taken.

Art. 196. The declaration, to constitute perjury, must be of something present or past; a promissory oath, although broken, is not perjury. An oath of office is one of this last description.

Art. 197. The occasion of taking the oath, in the description of the offence, includes those taken in every stage of a judicial proceeding, either civil or criminal, either in or out of court; and all declaratory oaths required by special laws, whether they impose the penalty of perjury or not.

Art. 198. As the falsehood must be wilful and deliberate to constitute the crime; the assertion of any circumstance, so immaterial to the matter in relation to which the declaration is made, as reasonably to induce a belief that it was not intended to conceal the truth or assert a false hood, is not perjury; although the circumstance be not true.

Art. 199. It is not necessary to complete this offence, that any credit should be given to the false declaration.

Art. 200. Whoever shall deliberately and wilfully, under oath, or affirmation, (in cases where it is by law equivalent to an oath), legally administered, declare a falsehood, by a voluntary declaration or affidavit, which is neither required by law nor made in the course of any judicial

2 Z

proceeding, is guilty of false swearing, and shall be confined in close custody not less than one nor more than six months; and the conviction of such an offence may be produced as evidence against his CREDIT in any court where he may be offered as a witness.

Art. 201. The punishment for the offence mentioned in the last preceding article is independent of any that may be inflicted for the publication of the affidavit, should it be a libel.

Art. 202. The term declaratory oath, or declaratory affidavit, in this section, means an oath made to the truth of something present or past, and is used in contradistinction to promissory oath, which is a stipulation confirmed by oath, that some act shall be done or omitted, or some event take place in future. The breach of this last description of oaths, does not amount either to perjury or to false swearing, except as will be hereafter provided in the case of officers of justice for duties done in court.

Art. 203. Whoever shall designedly, by any MEANS whatever, induce another to commit perjury, or to. be guilty of false swearing, shall undergo the same punishment as if he had committed the crime himself.

Art. 204. Whoever shall endeavour, by offering any INDUCEMENT or persuasion whatever, to procure another to commit perjury, or to be guilty of false swearing, shall be fined not less than fifty nor more than three hundred dollars, and imprisoned in close custody not less than thirty days, nor more than six months.

## CHAPTER XI.

### Offences against the judiciary power committed in a court of justice.

Art. 205. If any one shall, during the session of any COURT OF JUSTICE, in the presence of the court, by words or by making a clamour or noise, wilfully obstruct the proceedings of such court, or shall refuse to obey any legal order of such court made for the maintenance of order or to preserve regularity of proceedings in court, it shall be lawful for the said court to cause the offender to be removed by the proper officer of justice from the building in which the sessions of such court are held ; and if such offender shall persevere in returning to and disturbing said court, it shall also be lawful for them to cause him to be imprisoned during the time the court shall be in session during the same day; and the party offending against this article, is guilty of a misdemeanor, and shall be punished by fine not exceeding twenty dollars, and by imprisonment not exceeding three days.

Art. 206. If any person shall, either verbally in court, or in any pleading or other writing addressed to the judges in any cause pending in any court of justice, use any indecorous, contemptuous or insulting expressions, to or of the court or the judges thereof, with intent to insult the said court or any of the said judges, he shall be punished by simple imprisonment not more than fifteen days, and by fine not exceeding fifty dollars; and the fact of the intent, with which the words were used, and also whether they were indecorous, contemptuous and insulting, shall be decided by the jury, who shall try the cause. The said punishment shall be doubled on a second conviction for an offence under this article; and for a third, the party shall, in addition to the said punishment, if an attorney or counsellor, be suspended for not less than one nor more than four years from practising in the said court as attorney or counsellor at law, or as attorney in fact.

Art. 207. If any one shall obstruct the proceedings of a court of justice by violence, or threats of violence, offered either to the judges, jurors, witnesses, parties, or attorneys or counsellors, he shall be fined in a sum not less than one hundred and not exceeding five hundred dollars, and by imprisonment, in close custody, not less than ten days nor more than six months ; and if the offender be an attorney or counsellor at law, he shall be suspended from practising in such court for not less than one nor more than three years, either as attorney or counsellor at law, or as attorney in fact.

Art. 208. Courts of justice have no power to inflict any punishment for offences committed against their authority, other than those specially provided for by this Code and the Code of Procedure. All proceedings for offences, heretofore denominated contempts, are abolished. All offences created by this chapter, shall be tried on indictment, or information, in the usual form.

# TITLE VI.

OF OFFENCES AGAINST PUBLIC TRANQUILLITY.

## CHAPTER I.

*Of unlawful assemblies and riots.*

Art. 209. If any three or more persons shall ASSEMBLE with intent to aid each other by violence, either to commit an offence, or illegally to deprive any person of the enjoyment of a right, such assembly shall be called an unlawful assembly, and those guilty thereof shall be fined not less than fifty nor more than three hundred dollars, and shall be imprisoned not less than three nor more than twelve months, in close custody.

Art. 210. If persons, assembled for either of the purposes mentioned in the last preceding article, shall, by VIOLENCE, commit any illegal act, they are guilty of a riot, and in addition to the punishment to which they may be liable by reason of the illegal act they may commit, if it be an offence, they may be suspended from their political rights for three years, shall be fined not less than fifty nor more than five hundred dollars, and imprisoned not less than three nor more than eighteen months in close custody, for at least one half the time, or more, at the discretion of the court.

Art. 211. If the purpose of the unlawful assembly be illegally to oppose the collection of any taxes, tolls, imposts, or excises legally imposed, or the execution of any law of the state, or any lawful sentence of a court, or to effect the rescue of a prisoner legally arrested for any crime, the punishment for that offence shall be increased one half.

Art. 212. If a riot be committed for either of the purposes set forth in the last preceding article, the punishment hereinbefore imposed for that offence shall be doubled.

Art. 213. If any person engaged in an unlawful assembly, before the unlawful object of such meeting, or any other offence except such unlawful meeting, has been committed by them, or those with whom they are combined, shall either voluntarily, or on being warned by a magistrate, retire therefrom, without the intent to return, he shall not be prosecuted for being concerned in the unlawful assembly, or for any riot or other offence of which any persons concerned in it may afterwards be guilty, provided he do not return to the said assembly.

Art. 214. Any one person concerned in an unlawful assembly, may be indicted and convicted before the others are arrested ; but it is necessary to state in the indictment, and prove on the trial, that three or more persons were assembled ; if known, they must be described or named ; if unknown, it must be so alleged.

It is necessary to state, in an indictment for either of those offences, the illegal act which was the object of the meeting, or which they proceeded to do if the assembly was originally for a lawful purpose.

Art. 215. If three or more persons assemble for a lawful purpose, and they afterwards proceed to commit any act that would amount to a riot, if it had been the original purpose of the meeting, all those who do not retire when the change of purpose is known, are guilty of a riot.

Art. 216. If two or more persons engaged in an unlawful assembly or riot are ARMED, the punishment of the person so armed shall be doubled ; and of those who assisted in such assembly, when part were armed, although they themselves were unarmed, shall be increased one half.

Art. 217. If any judge, military officer or executive officer, or officer of justice, shall be engaged in an unlawful assembly or riot, his punishment shall be doubled.

Art. 218. When proof shall be made to any magistrate, by the oath of two or more credible witnesses, of the existence of any unlawful assembly or riot, consisting of more than twenty persons, it shall be the duty of such magistrate to go to the place where the unlawful assembly is, and he shall there proclaim the office which he holds, and order such unlawful assembly to disperse ; and that he may be the better known and distinguished, he shall display a white flag ; and if the offenders shall, after being so warned, proceed to commit a riot, they shall be imprisoned at hard labour, not less than one, nor more than three years, in addition to the other punishment for any other offence of which they may be guilty by such riot or illegal assembly.

Art. 219. Any one being in the said assembly at the time such order was given, or having joined it afterwards, (provided this last have notice of such order), who shall be found therein after the expiration of half an hour, shall, if no other offence be committed, be imprisoned, in close custody, not less than one nor more than six months, or fined not less than fifty, nor more than three hundred dollars.    And immediately after the expiration of the said half hour, or before, if any other illegal act be committed, it shall be lawful for any magistrate, or minister of justice, to arrest any of those composing the said assembly who shall disobey such order, or to cause them to be arrested with or without warrant; and for that purpose, any magistrate may call for the assistance of any person who may be within three miles of the place where the said unlawful assembly shall be, to aid him in the arrest of the said offenders; and such arrest shall be made in the manner directed by the Code of Procedure, in the chapter relative to Arrests.

Art. 220. If any free, able-bodied male person, above eighteen years of age and under fifty, shall be called on to aid in arresting the offenders in the manner directed by the last preceding article, and shall refuse or neglect so to do, such person shall be fined fifty dollars.

Art. 221. Any assembly, for the purpose of witnessing a boxing match, is an unlawful assembly.

If any boxing match takes place at such assembly, it is a riot, for which the combatants, and each of those who lay a wager on the event of such combat, shall be fined not less than ten, nor more than one hundred dollars, or may be imprisoned not less than ten, nor more than twenty days, in close custody, or both; and those who are guilty of the riot, without laying a wager on the combat, shall be fined not less than five, nor more than fifty dollars; or may be imprisoned ten days in close custody.

## CHAPTER II.

### Of public disturbance.

Art. 222. Those are guilty of making a public disturbance, who, without any such intent as would give to a meeting the character of an unlawful assembly, shall, to the number of two or more, meet or assemble in a tumultuous manner, in a public place, and by vociferation, quarrelling, or fighting, disturb the inhabitants of the place in the prosecution of their lawful business, or in their necessary repose. Public disturbers shall be fined not exceeding twenty dollars, or imprisoned not exceeding ten days, or both.

Art. 223. All magistrates and officers of justice are required to arrest, or cause to be arrested, persons guilty of this offence, on their own view, or on complaint, with or without warrant.

Art. 224. No public meeting, for the purpose of exercising any political or private right; no assembly for the purpose of legal recreation, or the expression of dissatisfaction or approbation made in such assembly in the usual manner, although it may disturb those in the vicinity, is an offence under this chapter.

Art. 225. The police of places of public amusement continues under the superintendence of the mayors, or other first magistrates of cities and towns.

# TITLE VII.

OF OFFENCES AGAINST THE RIGHT OF SUFFRAGE.

## CHAPTER 1.

*Of bribery and undue influence.*

Art. 226. Whoever shall offer or give a BRIBE to any elector, for the purpose of influencing his vote at any PUBLIC ELECTION, and any elector entitled to vote at such election who shall receive such bribe, shall be fined not less than one hundred, nor more than five hundred dollars, shall forfeit all his political rights, and be confined in close custody not less than six months, nor more than one year.

Art. 227. Whoever shall give or offer a bribe to any JUDGE or clerk of any public election, or any executive officer attending the same, as a consideration for some act done, or omitted to be done, or to be done or omitted contrary to his official duty in relation to such election, shall pay a fine not less than one hundred, nor more than five hundred dollars, shall forfeit all political rights, and shall be confined in close custody not less than one, nor more than two years.

Art. 228. If any one shall offer or give a reward to any person whatever, for the purpose of inducing him to persuade, or by any other means not amounting to bribery, to procure persons to vote at any PUBLIC ELECTION, for or against any person, the person so giving or offering, and he who shall receive such reward, shall forfeit not less than fifty, nor more than one hundred dollars.

Art. 229. Whoever shall procure or endeavour to procure the vote of any elector, or the influence of any person over other electors at any public election, for himself or any candidate; by means of VIOLENCE, threats of violence, or threats of withdrawing custom or dealing in business or trade, or of enforcing the payment of a debt, or bringing a suit or criminal prosecution, or any other threat of injury to be inflicted by him or by his means, the person so offending, shall forfeit not less than fifty, nor more than three hundred dollars, and be confined in close custody, not less than one, nor more than six months, and shall be suspended from the exercise of his political rights for four years.

## CHAPTER II.

*Of offences committed by the judges or other officers of elections.*

Art. 230. If any judge or clerk of any public election, or executive officer attending the same, shall knowingly make or consent to any false entry on the list of voters; put into the ballot box, or permit to be so put in, any ballot not given by a voter; or take out of such box, or permit to be so taken out, any ballot deposited therein, except in the manner prescribed by law; or by any other act or omission, designedly destroy, or change the ballots given by the electors; the offender shall pay a fine of not less than five hundred, nor more than one thousand dollars, forfeit his political rights, and be imprisoned in close confinement, not less than six months, nor more than one year.

Art. 231. Any such judge who shall proceed to any such election, without having the ballot box locked and secured in the manner directed by law; or who shall open and read, or consent to any other person opening and reading any ballot given to him to deposit in the box at such election, before it is put into the box, without the consent of the voter giving the same, shall be fined one hundred dollars.

Art. 232. Any judge of a public election, who before the votes are counted, shall dispose of, or deposit the ballot box, in a manner not authorized by law; or shall at any time after the election has begun, and before the ballots are counted, give the key of the ballot box with which he is intrusted to any other, the person so offending shall pay a fine of five hundred dollars.

Art. 233. When any one who offers to vote at any such election, shall be objected to by an elector, as a person unqualified to vote, if any judge of such election shall permit him to vote without producing proof of such qualification, in the manner directed by law; or if any such judge shall refuse the vote of any person, who shall comply with the requisites prescribed by law to prove his qualifications, knowing him to be entitled to vote, he shall forfeit for such offence, one hundred dollars, and if the offence be committed for the purpose of favouring or injuring the election of any candidate, shall moreover be suspended from the exercise of his political rights, for five years.

Art. 234. If any judge, or clerk, or executive officer, shall designedly omit to do any official act required by the law, or designedly do any illegal act, in relation to any public election, by which act or omission the votes taken at any such election in any city, parish or district, shall be lóst, or the electors thereof shall be deprived of their suffrages at such election, or shall designedly do any act which shall render such election void, he shall be fined not less than one hundred nor more than five hundred dollars, shall forfeit his political rights, and shall be confined in close custody not less than six months nor more than one year.


# CHAPTER III.


*Of violence and riots at elections, and of the protection of electors from arrest.*

Art. 235. It shall not be lawful for any military officer, or other person, to order or bring, or keep any troops or armed men, at any place within a mile of the place where any public election is held, on any day during which the same shall be held, under the penalty of five hundred dollars; unless it be for the purpose of quelling a riot or insurrection, in the manner provided by law, or for the purpose of defence in time of war, and if the offence shall be committed with intent to influence such election, he shall moreover be imprisoned not less than thirty nor more than sixty days in close custody, and shall forfeit his political rights. This article does not apply to troops of the United States, usually stationed within a mile of the place of election, and kept there during the same.

Art. 236. If any one shall, by illegal force, or threats of such force, prevent or endeavour to prevent any elector from giving his vote ; or shall, at the place of election, commit any assault or battery on any elector, he shall be fined not less than fifty nor more than two hundred dollars, shall be imprisoned in close custody not less than thirty days nor more than six months, and shall be suspended from his right of suffrage for two years.

Art. 237. If any riot be committed at any place of any public election or within half a mile of such place, during the time that the polls are open, the offender shall, in addition to the punishment imposed by law for a riot, also suffer imprisonment, in close custody, for not less than thirty nor more than sixty days ; and if the riot shall have been made for the purpose of influencing the election, shall be suspended from the right of suffrage for two years.

Art. 238. No elector shall be arrested at any civil suit, or on any warrant, except for a crime or a breach of the peace, or in order to obtain surety of the peace, during any day on which a public election is held, or while going to or returning from such election ; and any executive officer of justice, or other person, making or causing such arrest, contrary to this article, knowing the person arrested to be an elector, shall be fined not less than fifty nor more than two hundred dollars.

# TITLE VIII.

### OF OFFENCES AGAINST THE LIBERTY OF THE PRESS.

Art. 239. The constitution of this state having declared, that "printing presses shall be free to every person who undertakes to examine the proceedings of the legislature or any branch of the government," and that "the free communication of thoughts and opinions is one of the invaluable rights of man," and that "every citizen may freely speak, write, and print, on any subject, being responsible for the abuse of that liberty," it is declared to be a misdemeanor for any one by violence, or threats of violence, or threats of any injury to person, property or credit, to prevent, or endeavour to prevent any person from exercising any of the rights asserted in the parts of the constitution above recited, and the offender shall pay a fine of not less than fifty nor more than five hundred dollars.

Art. 240. If any member of the general assembly, or any judge or judicial or executive officer, shall be guilty of the offences created by the last preceding article, in order to prevent an investigation of his official conduct, or that of the branch of the government to which he belongs :

Or, if any judge or judicial or executive officer shall, by the exercise of any act of his office or the threat thereof, prevent, or endeavour to prevent any person from exercising any of the rights declared in the parts of the constitution above recited, he shall be fined not less than three hundred nor more than one thousand dollars, shall suffer imprisonment not less than sixty days nor more than six months, in simple imprisonment or close custody, at the discretion of the court, and be suspended for four years from the exercise of his political rights.

Art. 241. Nothing in this chapter contained shall render it unlawful for any person, who is apprehensive that a libel is about to be published, or that any literary property is about to be invaded by any publication, from endeavouring to prevent it by threats of a suit or prosecution, or from commencing such suit or prosecution for any such libel, should it be published, or for such invasion of literary property, should it be made.

Art. 242. The constitution having declared, that no law shall ever be made to restrain the right to examine the proceedings of the legislature, or any branch of the government, any judicial or executive officer or other person, who, under pretence or colour of any existing law, or laws that may hereafter be passed, shall prevent, restrain, or attempt to restrain or prevent the exercise of the right asserted in that part of the constitution above recited in this article, shall be fined not less than three hundred nor more than one thousand dollars.

Art. 243. If any court, judge or other officer, shall enjoin, restrain or prevent the printing and publishing of any WRITING whatever, under the allegation, whether true or false, that such writing contains a libel or seditious words, or under any other pretext, or for any other reason than is contained in the next article, the judges of such court assenting to such order, and the judge (if done out of court) or other officer, offending against this article, shall severally be fined not less than five hundred nor more than one thousand dollars, and shall be suspended from their political rights for two years.

Art. 244. It is no infringement of the last article to grant an injunction against the publication of any literary work, on the application of a person who shall satisfy the court or judge granting the injunction, that he is the author or proprietor of the work intended to be published, and that the publication will be injurious to his rights; nor shall it be considered as a breach of the said article for a court of justice, in which any one shall be convicted of publishing a libel, to require security in the manner directed by the chapter of this code concerning libels, nor for a magistrate to make an admonition in the manner provided by the Code of Procedure against the publication of a libel or publication against decency.

3 A

# TITLE IX.

Art. 245. If any one shall FORGE, or FRAUDULENTLY carry away, deface or destroy any PUBLIC RECORD, or shall FORGE any official CERTIFICATE of any OFFICER having the custody of any public records of registry, he shall be imprisoned at hard labour not less than seven nor more than fifteen years, and shall forfeit his political rights.

Art. 246. To FORGE, in the sense in which that word is employed in this chapter, is to make a false record or official certificate, or without authority to alter a true one in such a manner as that, if such false record were true or such alteration were legally made, some public or private right, or the condition of some individual, or the rights or immunities of some society, corporation, or general description of individuals, or some purpose of public utility, would be injured, altered or destroyed, or some right, immunity, privilege, condition or property would be vested, by such false or altered record.

Art. 247. The public and private rights mentioned in the last preceding article, are all those that are protected by the penal code, or for an injury to which a private suit is given by the civil code.

Art. 248. If any officer intrusted with the custody of PUBLIC RECORDS, shall commit any FORGERY of or upon such records, shall intentionally destroy or deface them, or conceal or carry them away, so that persons interested therein cannot have access to them, or shall advise or consent to such forgery, destruction, concealment or carrying away : or,

Shall fraudulently make and certify any entry or other act on such records in the name of one who was not present, or did not consent to such act : or,

Shall place any ACT, either AUTHENTIC or under PRIVATE SIGNATURE, on such register or record, under a date at which it was not registered or recorded, with intent to take away a right, give an illegal advantage to any one : or,

Shall knowingly permit any one falsely to PERSONATE another in the execution of any act entered or to be entered on any such register or record ; he shall be imprisoned at hard labour not less than seven nor more than fifteen years.

Art. 249. If any such officer as is described in the last preceding article shall, undesignedly, but through want of proper care, suffer the records intrusted to him, or any part of them, to be altered, defaced, taken away or lost; or shall negligently do any act, by virtue or under colour of his office, which he is not authorized to do, or omit to do some official act which he ought to do, by either of which acts or omissions any one is INJURED in his property, condition or reputation, he shall be fined not less than one hundred nor more than four hundred dollars.

Art. 250. If any notary or other officer, authorized by law to reduce to writing any authentic acts, or receive and record any acts under private signature, shall falsely, in his official capacity, certify any thing to be true which is false, whereby any one is injured in his property, condition or reputation, he shall be fined not less than one hundred nor more than four hundred dollars, shall be imprisoned in close custody not less than sixty days nor more than one year.

Art. 251. If the offence described in the last preceding article be FRAUDULENTLY committed, the punishment, in addition to the fine, shall be imprisonment at hard labour not less than seven nor more than fifteen years.

Art. 252. If any one shall use any record of any act, so forged, or fraudulently entered, made, registered or recorded, or any such false declaration, as is described in this chapter, either by offering the same in a court of justice, or endeavouring by any other means to procure any advantage therefrom, knowing such act to be forged, or fraudulently entered or recorded, or such certificate to be false ; he shall be fined not less than six hundred nor more than two thousand dollars, and imprisoned at hard labour not less than seven nor more than fifteen years.

# TITLE X.

OF OFFENCES AGAINST THE CURRENT COIN AND PUBLIC SECURITIES.

## CHAPTER I.

*Of offences against the current coin of the state.*

Art. 253. Whoever shall counterfeit any GOLD OR SILVER COIN, whether such coin be of the United States, or of any other government; or,

Whoever shall PASS, or offer to pass any such counterfeit coin, knowing it to be counterfeit ;

Shall be imprisoned at hard labour not less than seven nor more than fifteen years.

Art. 254. Whoever, with the intention of committing the crime of counterfeiting, or of aiding therein, shall have in his possession any die, or other instrument, such as is usually employed solely for the coinage of money, or shall make or repair any such die or other instrument, or shall prepare, or have in his possession and conceal any base metal prepared for coinage, shall be imprisoned at hard labour not less than two nor more than four years ; provided, that if any of the acts specified in this article shall be accompanied by circumstances which would render the accused liable, as an accomplice, for either of the crimes designated in the first article of this chapter, he may be prosecuted for such offence.

Art. 255. To counterfeit, under the provisions of this section, means, to make in the semblance of a true gold or silver coin, one having in its composition a less proportion of the precious metal, of which the true coin intended to be imitated is composed, than is contained in such true coin, with intent that the same should be passed as true, either in the United States or elsewhere. To alter any coin of a lower value, with the like intent, so as to make it resemble one of a higher value, is also a counterfeit. It is not necessary, to constitute the offence, that the resemblance should be perfect.

Art. 256. The gold or silver coins mentioned in this chapter mean any pieces of gold or silver, or of which gold or silver is the principal component part, and which pass as money in the United States, or in any foreign nation, although such pieces may not be made current by any law of the United States.

Art. 257. Whoever shall have in his possession any counterfeited gold or silver coins, with intent to pass them as true, or to cause them to be passed either in the United States or any other nation, he shall be imprisoned at hard labour not less than two nor more than four years.

Art. 258. If any one shall, with intent to profit, diminish the weight of any gold or silver coin, and shall afterwards pass it for the same value it had before it was so diminished, or shall send or carry it to be so passed to any other place, whether in the United States or elsewhere, he shall be fined not less than two hundred, nor more than five hundred dollars, and be imprisoned not less than one nor more than three years.

Art. 259. To constitute the crime of PASSING, under the provisions of this section, it is not necessary that the counterfeit coin should have been given at the full value of the true coin of the same denomination; the crime is complete by delivering the counterfeit coin, knowing it to be counterfeit, to another, if such delivery is made either for the purpose of defrauding the person to whom it is delivered, or for the purpose of enabling him to deceive others.

Art. 260. The general provisions in this code, relative to attempts to commit offences, and to accomplices and accessaries, apply to the offences mentioned in this chapter.

# CHAPTER II.

### Of offences against the public securities.

Art. 261. All offences coming under this head are provided for in the chapter concerning offences against the public revenue, or in that concerning offences affecting written contracts.

# TITLE XI.

### OF OFFENCES AFFECTING THE PUBLIC REVENUE.

Art. 262. If any OFFICER, or other person legally empowered to receive any money, or SECURITY FOR MONEY, for the state, or for any public corporation, shall illegally appropriate any such moneys or securities for money to his own use, or to the use of any other person, and shall, by rendering false accounts, or producing false vouchers, or in any other manner endeavour to conceal such illegal appropriation, with intent to defraud the state or the public corporation, to whom the said moneys belonged, of the same, or any part thereof, he shall pay a fine equal to double the yearly emolument of his office, shall be imprisoned not less than two nor more than six months, and shall forfeit his political rights.

Art. 263. No public officer or other person who is or shall be authorized to collect or receive moneys, or securities for the payment of money for the state or any public corporation, shall appropriate the same, or any part thereof, to his own use, or to the use of any other person, even although he may intend to restore the same; and whoever shall offend against this article, if he do not pay the sum so illegally appropriated within three days after demand made by a person legally authorized for that purpose, shall pay a fine equal to double the amount which he shall neglect to pay, and be suspended from his political rights for not less than two nor more than four years.

Art. 264. Although any person who may offend against the provisions of the last preceding article, shall, before the expiration of the three days after demand, or even before any demand, replace or repay the money or security so illegally appropriated, he shall pay a fine equal to the amount of the said money, or the value of the said security.

Art. 265. In order to render offences against the preceding articles more difficult, and to detect them when they occur, every such receiver of moneys or public securities, who shall receive any sum or sums of money, or any such security, whenever and as often as they in the whole shall amount to the value of three hundred dollars, shall, within three days after such receipt, either pay or deliver the same to the officer appointed by law to receive the same, or deposite the same in some incorporated bank, if any be within three leagues of the place of such receiver's abode, to his credit, in the capacity or office in which he shall receive the same: and such money or security shall not be drawn out but by a draft or order specifying to whom and for what purpose it is to be paid. And any such officer or other person shall, for any offence against this article, pay a fine not less than two hundred nor more than six hundred dollars.

Art. 266. If the receiver of any such moneys or securities reside more than three leagues from the place where such bank is kept, he shall have fifteen days to make the deposite, payment or delivery, mentioned in the last preceding article ; and in cases where greater distance than twenty leagues, or difficulty of travelling may render it necessary, in the opinion of the treasurer of the state, to enlarge such time in any particular case, he may at his discretion extend it so as not to exceed thirty days.

Art. 267. If any person, employed to receive taxes or other moneys due to the state or any public corporation, shall EXTORT or attempt to extort, from any one a larger sum than is due; or shall demand or receive any sum of money, emolument, service or favour, as a consideration for granting any delay in the collection of such dues, or for doing or omitting to do any act whatever in relation to the collection of such money, other than such emolument as may be allowed by law, he shall pay a fine not less than one-half nor more than the whole of the amount of his yearly emoluments, be dismissed from his office, and rendered incapable of being re-appointed or re-elected to any public office for not less than one nor more than two years.

Art. 268. If any one shall by force attempt to prevent any officer or other person, authorized to enforce the payment of any tax or other debt due to the state, or to any public corporation, from performing the duties required of him by law, relative to the collection of such tax or debt; or shall by force, or threats of force, actually prevent any such officer or person above described from performing such duties—he shall be fined in a sum double to that of which he prevented or attempted to prevent the collection, and shall be imprisoned not less than ten nor more than sixty days, in addition to the other penalties which may be incurred for any act of violence committed in the course of the opposition forbidden by this article.

# TITLE XII.

## OF OFFENCES WHICH AFFECT COMMERCE AND MANUFACTURES.

## CHAPTER I.

### *Of offences which affect foreign commerce.*

Art. 269. If any one shall export from this state, or ship for the purpose of exportation, any article of commerce which, by the laws now in force are, or by any laws hereafter to be passed may be, required to be inspected by a public inspector, without having caused such article to be inspected, according to the direction of such laws, he shall be fined one hundred dollars.

Art. 270. If any one shall counterfeit the mark, or brand or stamp, directed by any such law to be put on any article of commerce, or on the cask or package containing the same, he shall be fined not less than one hundred nor more than three hundred dollars, and be imprisoned at hard labour not less than one nor more than three years.

Art. 271. If any one shall, with intent to defraud, put into any hogshead, barrel, or other cask, or in any bale, box or package, containing merchandise usually sold by weight, any article whatever of less value than the merchandise with which such cask, bale, box or package is apparently filled; or shall sell or barter, or give in payment, or expose for sale, or ship for exportation, such cask or bale, or package of merchandise, with any such article of inferior value concealed therein, with intent to DEFRAUD ; he shall pay a fine not less than five hundred nor more than one thousand dollars, and be imprisoned at hard labour not less than one nor more than three years.

Art. 272. If any one, being a citizen of or a person DOMESTICATED in this state, shall, on the high seas; or if any person whatever shall, within the limits of this state, injure or DESTROY any VESSEL of which such person is the owner, part owner, or freighter, or on board of which he shall be employed as master, supercargo, under officer, seaman, or in any other capacity whatsoever, with intent to defraud or injure the owner of such vessel, or of the cargo on board, or the underwriters on such vessel or cargo, or any part thereof, or any other person interested in such vessel or cargo, or in the voyage, or the freight or other profits of such ship or vessel ; he shall be imprisoned at hard labour not less than six nor more than fourteen years.

Nothing in this article applies to any act that would be piracy by the laws of the United States.

Art. 273. If any one shall cause insurance to be made in this state on any merchandise, represented as shipped, or about to be shipped, at any place, whether within this state or elsewhere ; or shall cause such insurance to be made at some place not within this state, on goods said to be shipped or about to be shipped within this state, and shall, with intent to defraud the insurer, ship articles of less value and different from those insured, or, if of the same kind, being less than one-half of the value of the articles insured, pretending that the articles so shipped are of the kind or of the quality with those insured ; he shall be fined not less than one hundred nor more than five hundred dollars, and shall be imprisoned not less than sixty days nor more than six months in close custody.

Art. 274. Any person, not a citizen of or resident in this state, is guilty of an attempt to commit either of the offences described in the preceding articles, who shall make any agreement for the commission thereof within this state, and shall DO any ACT PREPARATORY thereto, whether the act be done in this state or elsewhere ; or who shall make such agreement out of the state, and do the preparatory act within this state. A citizen of or a resident in this state is guilty of such attempt, if he make the agreement or does the preparatory act, above described, any where.

Art. 275. No person shall be punished under either of the two last preceding articles who shall have been tried and acquitted, or punished, on an accusation for the same offence either in any court of the United States, of either of the United States, or of any foreign country having cognizance of the offence.

# CHAPTER II.

*Of offences against the laws regulating seamen in the merchant service, and the police of the port.*

Art. 276. If any keeper of a tavern, or lodging or boarding-house, shall lodge, entertain or conceal any seaman who has deserted from any merchant vessel, in any port of this state, within one month after such desertion, and knowing that he had so deserted, he shall forfeit one hundred dollars; and for a second offence, in addition to such fine, be imprisoned for thirty days.

Art. 277. Any master of any ship or vessel who shall in or at any port of this state, ship any seaman, who has not produced a discharge in the form required by law from the master of the vessel with whom he last sailed, in the cases in which such discharge is by law required, shall pay a fine of fifty dollars.

Art. 278. The police of the ports of this state is regulated by ordinances, passed by the corporations of the cities and places where such ports are situated.

# CHAPTER III

### Of false weights and measures.

Art. 279. Whoever shall use a false balance, weight or measure, in the weighing or measuring of any thing whatever that shall be purchased, sold, bartered, or shipped or delivered for sale or barter, or that shall be pledged or given in payment, knowing such balance, weight or measure to be false, and with intent to defraud, shall be fined not less than twenty nor more than two hundred dollars, and shall be imprisoned in close custody not less than ten nor more than ninety days.

Art. 280. The false weights and measures intended by the last preceding article, are such as shall not be conformable to the standard of weights and measures of length or capacity which are or may be established by law; the false balance thereby intended is any machine whatever used for ascertaining the weight of any personal property, which is so constructed as to make the article weighed appear to have more or less than the real weight.

Art. 281. Any person who shall sell bread or meat by a false weight or balance, shall incur double the punishment directed by the first article of this chapter.

Art. 282. The magistrate, granting the warrant or arrest for this offence, shall also direct the seizure of the false weights, balances or measures ; and if the party be convicted, or they be found to be false, they shall be broken, or otherwise destroyed.

# CHAPTER IV.

### Of false marks.

Art. 283. If any one shall falsely alter any stamp, brand or mark, on any cask, package, box or bale, containing merchandise or produce, made by a public officer appointed for that purpose, in order to denote the quality, weight or quantity of the contents thereof, with intent to DEFRAUD, he shall be fined not less than two hundred nor more than five hundred dollars, and shall be imprisoned at hard labour not less than one nor more than three years.

Art. 284. Any one who shall counterfeit any mark, stamp or brand, intended to imitate one, such as is described in the last preceding article, with intent to defraud, shall incur the same punishment as is directed by the said article.

Art. 285. Any one who, with a fraudulent intent, shall use any cask, package, box or bale, so marked, stamped or branded, for the sale of merchandise, of inferior quality, or less in quantity or weight, than is denoted by such mark, stamp or brand, shall incur one-half the punishment designated by the last preceding article.


# CHAPTER V.


*Of offences affecting the credit of written instruments.*

Art. 286. Whoever shall be guilty of the crime of forgery, shall be imprisoned at hard labour not less than seven nor more than fifteen years, and shall forfeit his political and civil rights.

Art. 287. He is guilty of forgery, who, without lawful authority, and with intent to injure or defraud, shall either make a false INSTRUMENT in writing, purporting to be the ACT of another, or alter an instrument in writing then already in existence, by whomsoever made, in such a manner that the false instrument so made (if the same were true), or the alteration in the true instrument (if such alteration had been legally made), would have created, increased, defeated, discharged, or diminished, any PECUNIARY OBLIGATION, or would have transferred or in any manner have affected any PROPERTY whatever.

Art. 288. He is guilty of making, under the last preceding article, who, knowing the illegal purpose for which it is intended, shall write, or cause to be written, the SIGNATURE, or the whole or any part of the forged instrument. Therefore several persons may be each guilty of making the same forged instrument.

Art. 289. He who, under a void authority, but which he shall suppose good, shall make an instrument in writing in the name of another, is not guilty of making a false instrument, although it may be made without lawful authority. But if any one, without a legal authority, or without an authority which he shall have good reason to believe to be a legal one, shall make any writing over a blank signature, or on the back of a paper containing a blank signature of another person, such writing is a false instrument in writing, and if the other parts of the definition concur, is forgery.

Art. 290. The words, "instrument in writing," comprehend every writing purporting to testify the will or intent of the party whose act it purports to be, whether of RECORD by AUTHENTIC ACT, under seal, or PRIVATE SIGNATURE, or in whatever form it may be couched. It must be on paper, vellum, or parchment, or on some substance made to resemble one of them, and it comes within the definition, whether the words be traced with a pen, or stamped, or made by any other device to resemble a manuscript. An instrument, partly printed and partly written, is a written instrument. But if the whole, including the signature, be printed with types or plates, not made to resemble manuscript, it is not a written instrument, as that term is used in this chapter.

3 B

Art. 291. A name, or commercial firm, or the style of a corporation, without any other writing, is an instrument, when made for the purpose of conveying, creating, or destroying an interest.

Art. 292. In order to constitute the making a false instrument, it must purport to be the act of another. Therefore no one can be found guilty of forgery for making an instrument signed by himself, or by his authority, in his true name. Such act, when done with a fraudulent intent, is a different offence, hereinafter provided for.

Art. 293. The word "another," in the definition of the crime of forgery, includes the United States, each of the states and territories of the union, and all the several branches of the governments of either of them, including this state; all public or private bodies, politic and corporate; all partnerships in trade; all courts; all officers, public or private, in their official capacities; and all persons whatever, whether real or fictitious, except the person making the forgery, as is provided in the last preceding article.

Art. 294. The word "whomsoever," in the said definition, as applied to the person by whom the altered instrument was originally made, is used in its most extensive sense, and includes not only all those mentioned in the last preceding article, but (in cases where the instrument at the time of making the alteration was the property of another) it includes also the person whose act it purports to be.

Art. 295. The word "alter," in the said definition, signifies not only erasing or obliterating some words, letters, or figures, or extracting the writing altogether, but the substituting other words, letters, or figures, for those erased, obliterated, or extracted, and also the adding any other words, letters, or figures, to the original instrument, or making any change therein that shall have any of the effects pointed out in the said definition.

Art. 296. The words, "if the same were true," in the said definition, in describing the effect of an instrument falsely made, apply as well to the person whose act the instrument purports to be, as to the instrument itself; therefore, although the writing be made in a fictitious name, it is forgery, if the instrument would have had any of the effects detailed in the said definition, in case it had been made by a real person of the same name, or description, and if the act be done with a fraudulent intent.

Art. 297. The words, "PECUNIARY OBLIGATION," used in the said definition there, and throughout this system, mean not only such as have money for their object, but every obligation for the breach of which damages might be legally, equitably, or justly demanded.

Art. 298. The words, "which would have transferred, or in any manner have affected any property whatever," are used in the most extensive sense. All property, REAL or PERSONAL is included, as those terms are defined in this system; and the transfer or affecting such property, includes every species of disposition, whether to take effect immediately, or in future, on condition, or absolutely, by sale, delivery, will, donation, exchange, pledge, mortgage, release, discharge, or any other act that supposes a right to dispose of, or change the condition of said property.

Art. 299. The limitation, at the beginning of the said definition, is strictly to be adhered to: no act is a forgery, unless done with an intent either to injure or defraud.

Art. 300. The injury mentioned in the last preceding article, means injury affecting one in his PROPERTY, REAL, PERSONAL or mixed, corporeal or incorporeal, not an injury to person or reputation ; false writings, having the latter tendency, are provided for in another part of this code.

Art. 301. No design of refunding the money, or restoring the property received, or of preventing or compensating any damage or loss that might be occasioned by any of the offences described in this chapter, shall avoid the presumption of fraud created by the acts constituting those offences : but such design, if actually executed before any discovery of the crime, shall diminish its punishment one-half.

Art. 302. If any one shall make any written instrument in his own name, intended to create, increase, discharge, defeat or diminish any pecuniary obligation or transfer, or affect any property whatever, and shall put a false date to the same with intent to injure or defraud—he shall be fined not less than two hundred nor more than five hundred dollars, and shall suffer imprisonment at hard labour not less than two nor more than six years.

Art. 303. If any one shall, with intent to injure or DEFRAUD, make any instrument in his own name, intended to create, increase, discharge or diminish any pecuniary obligation, or to transfer or affect any property whatsoever, and shall UTTER or PASS it, under the pretence that it is the act of another who bears the same name—he shall be fined not less than two hundred nor more than five hundred dollars, and confined at hard labour not less than three nor more than six years.

Art. 304. All the terms of the two last preceding articles, which are contained in the definition of forgery in the second article of this chapter, are to be understood in the same sense in which they are used in the said definition.

Art. 305. If any one, having in his power a paper containing the true signature of another, shall, on the other side of the same, make a promissory note or bill of exchange in his own name, so as to make the said signature appear as an indorsement on such bill or note, with intent to defraud—he shall suffer the punishment assigned to such as are guilty of forgery.

Art. 306. Any one who shall, with intent to DEFRAUD, UTTER as TRUE, or PASS, any forged instrument in writing, or any other instrument in writing, the making of which is by this section made an offence, knowing such instrument to be forged, or made contrary to the provisions of this section, shall suffer the same punishment that is assigned to the offence of forging or making the same.

Art. 307. Whoever shall, in this state, engrave any plate, or prepare any implements, or materials, for the purpose of their being employed in the forging any notes of any bank, whether this bank be in or out of this state, or whether such bank be incorporated or not, and knowing such purpose, and with intent to defraud ; or shall have in his possession any such plate, implements or materials made or prepared for such purpose, knowing the same, and with intent that they shall be used in the forging of any such notes—he shall be imprisoned at hard labour not less than one nor more than three years.

Art. 308. Whoever shall have in his possession any forged instrument in writing, or any instrument, the making of which is created an offence by this code, knowing the same to be forged, or made contrary to the provisions of this code, with intent fraudulently to utter or to pass the same—shall be imprisoned at hard labour not less than one nor more than three years.

Art. 309. If any one shall, with intent to defraud, either by falsely reading, or falsely interpreting any instrument in writing ; or by misrepresenting its contents, induce any one, who, either from ignorance or infirmity, is incapable of reading an instrument in writing, or who, if he can read, does not understand the language in which it is written, to sign such instrument as his act, or give such assent to it as would, if there had been no error, make it his act ; by the means of which false reading, false interpretation or misrepresenting, any PECUNIARY OBLIGATION purports to be created, increased, discharged or diminished, on the part of the person signing the same, or any of his property whatever, purports to be transferred or in any manner affected—the person so offending shall be imprisoned at hard labour not less than one nor more than three years.

Art. 310. If any one, with intent to defraud, shall induce another to sign any such instrument as is described in the last preceding article, by falsely and without the knowledge of such other, substituting it for another instrument, materially different therefrom, which the said person intended to sign—the person so offending shall be imprisoned at hard labour not less than one nor more than three years.

Art. 311. If either of the offences described in the two last preceding articles shall be committed by a public officer, whose duty it is to take or to record public acts, or by any counsellor or attorney at law, the term of imprisonment shall be doubled, and he shall forfeit his political rights.

Art. 312. If any one shall falsely personate another, whether bearing the same name or not, and in such assumed character or name shall give authority to a notary or any other person to sign such assumed name to any act, or to insert it therein, or to do any other thing implying a legal assent to any act, which, if it were the act of the party so personated, would have created, or increased, diminished or discharged, any pecuniary obligation, or transferred, or in any wise affected any property—he shall be imprisoned at hard labour not less than seven nor more than fifteen years.


## CHAPTER VI.

### Of fraudulent insolvencies.

Art. 313. Whoever shall institute any proceedings in any court of justice for the purpose of obtaining relief, under the laws now in force for giving relief in case of insolvency, for granting a respite, for making a cession of goods, or for giving relief from imprisonment for debt : or under any other laws that may be passed for any of the purposes above mentioned, and shall in the course of such proceeding, with intent to defraud, make a false schedule or account of his credits, property or debts, and exhibit the same in such court as true, or shall fraudulently conceal or destroy his books of accounts, or papers relative to his estate, in cases where by law he is bound to produce the same for the use or inspection of his creditors, he shall suffer imprisonment for not less than two nor more than four years at hard labour.

Art. 314. The filing of the said schedule or account with the clerk of a court of justice, is exhibiting the same, under the above article.

Art. 315. It is a false schedule or account under the said article,

1. If the party making the same shall fraudulently omit to insert on the said schedule any property, REAL or PERSONAL, to which he is entitled, and which by law ought to be placed on the said schedule or account, of the value of ten dollars or upwards.

2. If he shall place on the account of his debts any sum as due from him which he does not owe, for the purpose of defrauding his true creditors.

But the mere omission of any property on the schedule, shall not make the party liable, unless, from the circumstances of the case, it appear that it was done with design, and in order to defraud.

Art. 316. Any one who, not having property of sufficient value to pay his debts, shall make any simulated conveyance, mortgage or other disposition of any part of his property for his own use or the use of his family, and in order to prevent the same from becoming liable to the payment of his debts, shall be imprisoned for not less than sixty days nor more than six months, and shall be suspended from the exercise of his civil rights of the first class, and of his political rights for four years ; and the imprisonment, or any part of it, may be in close custody.

Art. 317. A simulated conveyance, mortgage or disposition, is one sufficient in form for the alienation or affecting of the property, but made without consideration, or for an inadequate consideration, and under a secret understanding between the parties that it shall operate for the benefit of the person making the same, either by a reconveyance afterwards to be made, or by a destruction or redelivery of the instrument by which it was conveyed or affected, if it be property requiring a written conveyance, or of the property itself, or by holding or conveying the same to his use, or that of his wife or any relation in the ascending or descending line.

Art. 318. Any person who shall receive any such simulated conveyance, mortgage or disposition for the purposes aforesaid, knowing the said purpose, shall pay a fine equal to the full value of the property so intended to be conveyed, or the amount for which it was intended to be affected, to be ascertained by three appraisers appointed by the court, and sworn to make a true appraisement.

Art. 319. The word " disposition," in the three last articles, means every species of contract by which property may be subjected to any alien or onerous condition, whether by mortgage, pledge or otherwise.

Art. 320. Any one who, not having sufficient property to pay his just debts, shall voluntarily suffer a judgment to be entered in favour of any one, that shall bind or encumber any real property, or on which any personal property shall be seized, for a sum not due, or without consideration, or for an inadequate consideration, shall convey, or mortgage or affect by any onerous condition any of his property, or for a larger sum than is really due, with intent to defraud his creditors, or some one or more of them, shall be imprisoned not less than sixty days nor more than six months, shall be suspended from the exercise of his political and of his civil rights of the first class for four years, and the imprisonment may in the whole or in part be in close custody.

Art. 321. The person who shall, collusively with such debtor, recover such judgment, shall be fined in a sum equal to the amount of such judgment, and he who knowing the intent of such conveyance, mortgage or onerous disposition, shall receive the same, shall be fined in a sum equal to the value of the property if conveyed, or the amount of the incumbrance if only mortgaged or burthened.

Art. 322. All the dispositions of the six last preceding articles take effect only in cases where the inability to pay debts appears by a forced or voluntary cession of property, or petition for a respite, or a discussion of all the property of the debtor.

# TITLE XIII.

### OF OFFENCES AFFECTING PUBLIC PROPERTY.

Art. 323. All the provisions for the protection of the property of individuals against fraudulent or malicious injury, apply to the property of the state, and of public and private corporations.

# TITLE XIV.

### OF OFFENCES AFFECTING THE PUBLIC ROADS, EMBANKMENTS, BRIDGES, NAVIGABLE WATERS, AND OTHER PROPERTY HELD BY THE SOVEREIGN POWER FOR THE COMMON USE.

## GENERAL PROVISION.

Art. 324. The ordinances which the juries of police in the different parishes and the public corporations in the cities and towns are authorized to make, contain the regulations of police for the making and enlarging the embankments or levees, roads, bridges, streets, and public squares, and the penalties which are incurred by disobeying them.

## CHAPTER I.

*Of the levees and embankments of rivers.*

Art. 325. If any one shall maliciously break down any levee or embankment made to confine the waters of any river or bayou, he shall be fined not less than fifty, nor more than five hundred dollars, or imprisoned not less than one month nor more than one year, or both.

Art. 326. Every breach in such levee or embankment shall be deemed to be maliciously made, if it shall be attended with any injury to the property of another, and if it be done in a manner or for a purpose forbidden by the ordinances of police.

## CHAPTER II.

### *Of the roads, bridges, and navigable waters.*

Art. 327. Whoever shall make any embankment, wharf, or other construction in the bed of any navigable river, bayou, or lake, that shall impede the navigation thereof, or that shall not be allowed by the legal ordinances of police, of the police juries in the parish in which it is made, shall be fined not less than fifty nor more than five hundred dollars.

Art. 328. Whoever shall erect any fence or building, or dig any ditch, or throw up any mound of earth in any street or public road or square, or do any other act that shall obstruct the public use thereof, or shall unlawfully destroy any bridge erected thereon, shall be fined not less than five, nor more than one hundred dollars.

Art. 329. Whoever shall erect on the space set apart by the police regulations for a tow path, along any navigable waters, or on the levee or embankment of the same, or on its banks, any building, enclosure, or other construction, or any other works whatever, that shall prevent the public use thereof, or render it less convenient, unless thereunto authorized in the manner directed by law, or by the ordinances of police, shall be fined not less than fifty nor more than five hundred dollars.

Art. 330. All persons guilty of any of the offences designated in this chapter shall also be subject to such regulations as are or shall be lawfully made by the police ordinances, for the repair of any damages that may be occasioned by such offences, and the removal of the works that are forbidden by this chapter.

# TITLE XV.

## CHAPTER I.

*Of acts injurious to public health or safety.*

Art. 331. No one shall carry on a manufactory of gunpowder, or shall keep more than ten pounds of gunpowder at one time, in any building within three hundred yards of any dwelling-house, or of any public road, or of any land belonging to any other person than the proprietor of the land on which such manufactory or building is erected, unless the owner of such adjacent land shall permit such manufactory to be carried on, and will agree not to build any dwelling-house within three hundred yards of such manufactory or building in which such gunpowder is stored. Any one offending against the provisions of this article, shall be fined five hundred dollars ; and on conviction, may be enjoined by the court from carrying on such business.

Art. 332. Whoever shall carry on any trade, or business, or do any act that is injurious to the health of those who reside in the vicinity, or shall suffer any substance which shall have that effect, to remain on any real property possessed by him, shall be fined not exceeding three hundred dollars, and the party may be enjoined proceeding in the operations that are offensive to health, and ordered to remove such substances.

Art. 333. Whoever shall wilfully ADULTERATE for the purpose of sale, or shall sell, knowing it to be adulterated, any wine, beer, spirits of any kind, or other liquor intended for drinking, with any substance that renders them injurious to the health of those who drink them, shall be fined not exceeding three hundred dollars, and the liquor so adulterated shall be forfeited and destroyed.

Art. 334. If any person shall fraudulently adulterate for sale, or shall sell, knowing them to be so adulterated, any drugs or medicines in such a manner as to lessen the efficacy or change the operation of such drugs or medicines, or to make them injurious to health, he shall be fined not less than one hundred nor more than five hundred dollars, and imprisoned not less than ten days nor more than six months, and the imprisonment may be in close custody.

# TITLE XVI.

OF OFFENCES AGAINST MORALS.

## CHAPTER I.

*Of disorderly houses.*

Art. 335. If any one shall keep a disorderly house, he shall be punished by fine not exceeding two hundred dollars, or by imprisonment in close custody not more than sixty days.

Art. 336. The houses that are punishable as disorderly, are:

1. Houses kept for the purpose of public prostitution, and DISTURB-ANCE.

2. Houses kept as taverns, or for the sale of spirituous liquors by retail, without license.

3. Licensed houses of the description last above mentioned, in which any act forbidden by the license, is permitted to be done.

4. Houses in which gambling is permitted in a manner contrary to some express law.

Art. 337. Any part of a building, appropriated to either of the purposes above enumerated, is a house within the meaning of this chapter.

Art. 338. There must be more than one act of the kinds that are above forbidden, done in a house, to constitute it a disorderly house.

Art. 339. The wife may be punished with the husband, for keeping a disorderly house of the first description; but no house shall be comprehended in that term unless such acts are habitually permitted therein, as come within the description of those public exhibitions of person, which are made punishable by the next chapter, or unless acts are habitually done therein, which, if done in a public place, would amount to the offence of PUBLIC DISTURBANCE.

## CHAPTER II.

*Of offences against decency.*

Art. 340. If any one shall make, publish or print any obscene print, picture or written or printed composition, manifestly designed to corrupt the morals of youth, or shall designedly make any indecent or obscene exhibitions of their persons or of those of another, in public,

3 C

by which pudicity is offended ; he shall be imprisoned not more than six months, or fined not more than one thousand dollars, or both ; and the imprisonment, or part of it, shall be in close custody.

Art. 341. If any one shall, with design to insult, in the hearing of any person of the female sex, utter any obscene or lascivious expressions, such as must shock the natural pudicity of that sex; he shall be imprisoned in close custody not less than five nor more than thirty days, or fined not exceeding fifty dollars, or both.

Art. 342. Whoever shall be guilty of SEDUCING a woman of good reputation under a promise of marriage, and shall violate his promise, shall be fined not less than one hundred nor more than one thousand dollars, or shall be imprisoned in close custody not less than one nor more than six months.

Art. 343. Whoever shall, for hire, procure the means of illicit connexion between persons of different sexes, or shall solicit or procure a woman to prostitute her person to another, shall be imprisoned not exceeding three months in close custody.


## CHAPTER III.

### *Of adultery.*

Art. 344. Adultery is a term of which the meaning, as affixed by this code, is precisely that which it bears in common parlance; it therefore needs no other description. When committed by the wife, it is an offence for which she forfeits all the matrimonial gains, to which she would otherwise be entitled: which immediately, on the conviction, are vested in those who would have been her legal heirs had she died on the day of conviction ; she also forfeits her civil rights of the first class.

Art. 345. The person with whom a woman commits adultery shall suffer fine not less than one hundred and not exceeding two thousand dollars, or imprisonment not more than six months, or both.

Art. 346. The husband who commits adultery, by keeping a concubine in the house with his wife, or by forcing her by ill-treatment to abandon his house, and keeping his concubine in it, shall be fined not less than one hundred nor more than two thousand dollars ; and his civil right of being tutor or curator to any minor, including his own children, is suspended from the time of conviction, for one year, and as much longer as he shall live with his concubine in the same house.

Art. 347. No prosecution for adultery shall be commenced, but on the complaint of the husband or wife; and the prosecution shall cease if the parties are reconciled before judgment.

Art. 348. A sentence of separation, in person and estate, for cause of adultery, must always be preceded by a conviction for that offence.

Art. 349. The indictment or information for adultery against the wife must be a joint one, against the woman and the man with whom the adultery is said to have been committed, if he be alive, and the one cannot be found guilty without the other—subject to the modifications, contained in the Code of Procedure.

# CHAPTER IV.

## *Of the violation of places of interment.*

Art. 350. Whoever shall open a grave, or other place of interment, for the purpose of stealing the coffin, or any part thereof, or the vestments, or other articles, interred with any dead body which is deposited in such place of interment; shall be imprisoned at hard labour not less than one nor more than three years.

Art. 351. Whoever, for the purpose of sale, exposure or dissection, shall remove any dead body from the grave, or other place of interment—shall be fined not less than fifty nor more than three hundred dollars, or imprisoned not less than thirty nor more than ninety days.

Art. 352. The last preceding article does not extend to cases where a dead body shall be disinterred in the manner directed by the Code of Procedure, for the purpose of examination into the means by which the deceased lost his life.

Art. 353. Whoever shall purchase, or sell, or otherwise than is hereinafter provided, shall dissect any dead body before its interment—shall be fined not less than fifty nor more than two hundred dollars, or shall be imprisoned not more than ninety days.

Art. 354. The last preceding article does not extend to cases where a dissection is ordered in case of suspicion of murder, according to the provisions of the Code of Procedure:

To cases where the deceased has himself directed it.

To cases where it is performed by the permission of the next of kin to the deceased.

Or, to cases where dissection is ordered by law to be perfomed upon the bodies of those who die in prison, under conviction of certain offences.

Art. 355. The dead body, intended by this chapter, is that of a human being.

# TITLE XVII.

OF OFFENCES WHICH AFFECT PERSONS IN THE EXERCISE OF THEIR RELIGION.

Art. 356. If any one shall MALICIOUSLY prevent any person from doing any lawful act that is required by the religion he professes ; or shall, by force or threats of force, or of injury to person or property, oblige, or endeavour to oblige, any one to follow any forms of worship, or to profess any mode of religious belief, or to perform any religious rites or ceremonies ; he shall be fined not less than twenty nor more than two hundred dollars, or imprisoned in close custody not exceeding forty days, or both.

Art. 357. If the offence, described in the last preceding article, shall be committed by a judicial or executive officer, under COLOUR of authority derived from his office, or by any priest or minister, or preacher of any religious congregation or sect, the punishment shall be doubled.

Art. 358. Nothing in this chapter contained shall prevent a parent or tutor, or curator, or master, from obliging his child, or ward, or apprentice, being a minor, by all such means as are permitted by law for the enforcement of his other legal commands, to conform to the forms of worship in which such minor was educated.

Art. 359. Nor do the provisions of this chapter prevent the enforcement of the rules, canons, or ordinances, made by different churches, or religious congregations or societies, for the preservation of discipline or order among their members : provided, that such enforcement shall not be made by the infringement of any civil or political right, or by any act declared by this code to be an offence.

Art. 360. If any act which by this code is made an offence, shall be committed in a place of public worship during the celebration thereof, so as to disturb any religious society in the legal performance of their worship, or their religious rites and ceremonies. The punishment for such offence shall be doubled and shall not in any case be less than a fine of fifty dollars or imprisonment in close custody for fifteen days.

Art. 361. If such disturbance be intentionally made by any act which is not otherwise created an offence, the punishment shall be fine not exceeding fifty dollars, or imprisonment not exceeding thirty days.

# TITLE XVIII.

OF OFFENCES AFFECTING REPUTATION.

## CHAPTER I.

### *Of defamation.*

Art. 362. Whoever shall defame another, shall be punished by fine and imprisonment, or both.

If the defamation impute a CRIME, it shall be punished by fine not exceeding three thousand dollars, or by imprisonment not more than twelve months, or by both ; and the imprisonment may, for the whole or a part of the time, be in close custody.

If the defamation do not impute a CRIME, the punishment shall be lessened one-fourth.

If the defamation be by libel, imprisonment in close custody shall always form a part of the punishment.

Art. 363. Defamation is an injury offered to the reputation of another, by an allegation which is either untrue, or, if true, is not made with a justifiable intent.

Art. 364. Defamation may be made verbally or by signs, which is called slander ; or by writing or painting, which is called libel.

Art. 365. This offence consists in the injury offered to reputation, not in any probable breach of the peace or other consequence that may result from it.

Art. 366. There must be some injury offered in order to constitute the offence ; therefore, the words used, or the figures represented, must convey the idea, either—

1. That the person, to whom they refer, has been guilty of some crime.

2. That he has done some act, or been guilty of some omission, which, although not a crime, is of a nature to make people in general avoid social intercourse with him, or lessen their confidence in his integrity.

3. That he has some moral vice, or physical or mental defect or disease, that would cause his society to be generally avoided : or

4. That his general character is such as to produce either of the effects mentioned in this article.

Art. 367. It is also an injury, coming within the definition, if the natural tendency of the words or representations used is to bring upon the person, to whom they refer, the hatred, ridicule, or contempt of the public ; or to deprive him of the benefits of social intercourse.

Art. 368. To make false representations, importing that the party referred to wants the necessary talents, or is otherwise incompetent to perform or conduct the office, business, profession, or trade, in which he is engaged ; or is dishonest in his conduct therein ; is also an injury within this part of the definition.

Art. 369. But it is not an offence to make true statements of fact, or express any opinion, whether such opinion be correctly formed or not, as to the qualifications of any person for any public office, with a bona fide intent to give information to those who have the power of making the appointment or election to such office.

Art. 370. Nor is it an offence to make true statements of fact, or express the opinion which he who gives it entertains relative to the integrity or other qualifications to perform the duties of any station, profession, or trade, when it is done by way of advice to those who have asked it, or to those whom it was a duty, arising either from legal or social connexion, or from motives of humanity, to give such advice.

Art. 371. Nor shall it be deemed an offence, to make or publish any criticism or examination of any work of literature, science, or art ; or to express any opinion on the qualifications, merits, or competency of the author of such work, in relation thereto ; although such criticism, examination, or opinion, shall be ill-founded and prove injurious to the party to whom it refers : provided, such criticism or expression of opinion be not intended to cover a malicious design to injure the party to whom it refers.

Art. 372. If the injury spoken of in the definition be OFFERED, it is sufficient to constitute the offence ; by which is not meant, that the injury must be actually suffered ; but that the words or representations are such as, in the ordinary course of affairs, tend to cause such injury, according to the definition and explanation of that word in this chapter.

Art. 373. All those who make, publish, or circulate a libel, are severally guilty of the offence of defamation.

Art. 374. He is the maker of a libel, who originally contrived, and either gave it form himself, by writing, printing, engraving, painting, or any other of the modes which may constitute a libel, or caused it to be so done by others.

Art. 375. He is the PUBLISHER, who executes the mechanical labour of writing it when dictated by the maker, or who paints or engraves, or in any other manner gives it form under his direction, who copies, or prints it.

Art. 376. He circulates who sells a libel, or who, knowing the contents, gives or distributes, or reads, or exhibits it to others.

Art. 377. If the libel be in a printed form, and is printed or sold in an office, or shop, where books, or other printed works are usually printed or sold, the person on whose account the business of such office or shop is carried on, is presumed to be the person who published or circulated it, until he remove that presumption by contrary proof.

Art. 378. In like manner, if the libel be an engraving, or painting, and is made and sold in an office or shop, in which paintings or engravings are usually made or sold, the person on whose account the business of such office or shop is carried on, is presumed to be the person who published or circulated it.

Art. 379. No one shall be convicted merely on evidence of his having made a manuscript copy of a libel, or of having performed the mechanical labour of printing it, who can prove that he made such printed or written copy without any intent to injure the person to whom it refers ; but he, for whose account, or by whose order it is printed, shall be presumed to have known the intent of publication, and shall be liable for the offence.

Art. 380. He is not guilty of the offence, who only lends or gives a book or paper containing a libel, or reads it to another after it is already in general circulation, unless some circumstances are proved to show that it was done with design to injure.

Art. 381. The injury to constitute the offence, must be offered to the REPUTATION. Words, or representations which injure the party in his title to property only, form a different offence, provided for under its proper head.

Art. 382. The words " of another," in the definition of this offence, comprehends every person in possession of his CIVIL RIGHTS, as also aliens, whether resident within the state or not.

Art. 383. The dead are also included in this term, but subject to the following formality and proviso :

1. No prosecution shall be commenced, but on the complaint of a family meeting, called at the request of a descendant, collateral relation, or friend of the deceased, in the manner directed by the Code of Civil Procedure.

2. No prosecution can be supported, for the statement of any historical facts, or delineations of character in any literary work, whether the party to whom they refer be dead or alive, provided such statements be made in the fair prosecution of historical or other literary disquisition, and not for the purpose of defamation.

Art. 384. The word "allegation," as used in the definition, comprehends not only the direct assertion of a fact, but every mode of speech or device, by which the hearers or spectators may understand what is intended.

Art. 385. The words or representations by which the allegation is expressed, are to be understood in the sense in which they were intended by the person using them : intent and signification are matters of fact to be determined from a consideration of all the evidence in the case.

Art. 386. An important part of the definition is that which determines that the uttering of truth may sometimes constitute defamation. The truth may be expressed in all cases in which it is not forbidden by law, but the allegation of falsehood is not always an OFFENCE ; it is sometimes made the cause of private suit, sometimes left to the sanction of the moral sense, or of public opinion. For the development of this branch of the definition, the following rules are established :

1. True statements of the OFFICIAL conduct of members of the general assembly, or of public officers, and of the proceedings of all legislative bodies, PUBLIC CORPORATIONS, and courts of justice, may be legally made.

2. Observations on the tendency of the official acts of members of the legislature, and of public officers, and on their motives in performing them, are permitted, even if the author should mistake such tendency or motives ; but a false allegation or suggestion of such motives, as would, connected with the act, constitute a crime, is defamation.

3. Allegations, having no natural connexion with the case, provided for by the two last preceding articles, which would amount to defamation, if made or exhibited alone, are offences, although they may be

contained in publications which treat or propose to treat of the conduct of public measures and public officers.

Art. 387. Allegations, in writing, made with respect to all other than the official acts above provided for, which would, if they were false, be defamation, shall, although true, constitute that offence, if they are made from motives of revenge, hatred, envy, or ill-will of any other kind, entertained by the party making them, or to gratify either of those passions in any other ; and they shall be deemed to have been made from such motive in all cases in which the defendant cannot show that he was actuated by some motive of public good, or private duty, in making the allegation.

5. No true allegations but such as are described in the last preceding rule, and no false allegations but such as are declared to be offences by this code, are declared punishable by law.

6. No prosecution can be maintained for defamation, on account of any thing said or written, either as judge, attorney, counsel, party or witness, in a court of justice in the course of a legal proceeding, provided that what is said or written be relevant to the matter before such court, and is not introduced for the sole purpose of injuring the party to whom it refers.

7. Inquiries and suggestions, made even out of court, if done with a bona fide view of investigating a fact, necessary for the party's interest in a civil, or defence in a criminal prosecution, and not from malice towards the party to whom they refer, are not an offence, although they may injure such party.

8. Nothing said by a party to a civil suit or criminal prosecution, in confidence to his attorney, solicitor or counsel, relative to such suit or prosecution, while it is pending, or with a view to its commencement or defence, is an offence under this chapter.

9. The constitutions of the United States and of this state severally, protect members of congress and of the general assembly from prosecutions for any thing said in either of those bodies. The same rule is to be observed with respect to members of the legislatures of the different states, and those who may publish their proceedings.

Art. 388. The word "verbally," used in the definition of slander, means the utterance of words by the voice ; and the words "by signs," comprehend every motion of the fingers or other gesture, that is understood by the party using it, and by them to whom it is addressed, to signify words, or otherwise to communicate ideas.

Art. 389. It is slander to repeat the contents of any libel, or the words of any slander, unless the defendant show that he was not actuated in doing so by any desire to injure the person defamed.

Art. 390. The word "writing," in the definition of libel, comprehends not only manuscript, but printing, engraving, etching or any other means now known, or which may hereafter be discovered or invented, to make words visible. The word "painting," in the same definition, includes not only the art usually so called, but drawing, engraving or representing figures in any other way. It also comprehends hieroglyphics, or the representation of words by objects which they signify.

Art. 391. Offences enumerated in this chapter can only be punished by indictment, and never but on complaint of the party injured, or his legal representative, if he be alive ; or if the defamation be against the reputation of the person deceased, then in the manner hereinbefore provided.

Art. 392. In all the offences created by this chapter, the jury decide not only all the facts that are in question, but the intent when it is material, subject to the general powers given to the court in the Code of Procedure.

Art. 393. Nothing in this chapter contained shall be so construed as to prevent or punish the free discussion of the proceedings of the legislature, or any other branch of the government, which is secured by the constitution ; and nothing shall be considered as an abuse of the liberty, to speak, write and print on any subject which is referred to in the constitution, but such acts of that nature as are specially constituted offences by this code.

Art. 394. There is no such offence known to our law as defamation of the government, or either of its branches, either under the name of libel, slander, seditious writing or other appellation. When such allegations amount to defamation of the representatives of the people, or public officers, they are provided for by the preceding articles. When they amount to the crime of complicity in sedition, or in opposition to law, they are made punishable by the general provisions respecting accomplices.

Art. 395. There is no such offence as defamation of a body corporate or politic, or of public justice, or religion, or good morals, either by libel or otherwise.

Art. 396. In all cases of prosecution under this chapter, the court may, at its discretion, make it a condition that the whole or any part of the punishment which is awarded, may be remitted on the offender's making apology and amends to the person injured in such form and manner as the court shall by its sentence declare ; and if the person injured shall accept of any pecuniary amends, it shall be a bar to any private suit for defamation, founded on the same offence.

Art. 397. On the trial of any prosecution for a defamation, if the jury find that the defendant is the author of the libel, or the speaker of the defamatory words, and that the matter which constitutes the libel is false in the whole or in part, they shall specially so declare it in their verdict; declaring the allegations of the defendant to have been unfounded, and, where the case requires it, malicious ; and the charge made by the defendant, the verdict and the judgment of the court, shall, when required by the prosecutor, be published at the expense of the defendant.

Art. 398. Whenever the defendant, in any prosecution for defamation, shall avow himself the author or speaker of the words alleged, and shall acknowledge that the charge they import is unfounded ; or that they were not intended to apply to the prosecutor ; or in cases where there is either ambiguity in the expression, or uncertainty as to their application that they were not used in the sense in which they were understood by him, but in another sense, stating it. In either of these cases, the punishment shall be confined to the payment of costs, and of the publication of the proceedings ; unless the defendant shall make it appear that the words, according to their true import, did not imply any defamation, or did not apply to the prosecutor ; in which case he shall be exempt from any costs ; but the proceedings may, in like manner, be published.

3 D

## CHAPTER II.

### *Of other injuries to reputation by effigies or dramatic representations.*

Art. 399. Whoever, with intent to bring another into contempt, or to excite ridicule or indignation against him, shall exhibit, or shall make, with intent that it shall be exhibited, any effigy or figure, intended to represent such other person, shall be fined not exceeding one thousand dollars, or imprisoned not exceeding ninety days, or both; and part or the whole of the imprisonment may be in close custody. And if more than twelve persons are collected to witness such exhibition, it shall be deemed an unlawful assembly, and a riot, if they refuse to disperse when thereto legally required.

Art. 400. If any one, with intent to bring another into contempt, or to excite ridicule or indignation against him, shall perform, or cause any dramatic work to be performed, in which such person is represented and personated, either by an imitation of his person, or of any peculiarity in his manner, gesture, language, or otherwise, so as to make it apparent to those who know him that he is the person intended by such personification, the offender shall be fined not exceeding one thousand dollars, or imprisoned not exceeding ninety days, or both; and part or the whole of the imprisonment may be in close custody.

## CHAPTER III.

### *Of false accusation, and threats of prosecution.*

Art. 401. If any two or more persons shall combine falsely to accuse another of a crime, and in consequence of such combination shall either verbally or in writing make such accusation, whether judicially or not, they shall be fined not less than one hundred nor more than three thousand dollars, and imprisoned at hard labour not less than one nor more than four years, besides incurring the penalty of perjury, if that crime should be committed in the prosecution of their design.

Art. 402. If the intent of such combination be to extort any pecuniary advantage by such false accusation, or the threat thereof, the punishment shall be doubled.

Art. 403. If any one, with intent to extort money or procure other profit, shall falsely accuse, or threaten to accuse another of any crime, or of the doing of any act which, if the accusation were true, would bring him into contempt, or excite public indignation against him, the person making such threat or accusation, knowing the same to be false, shall suffer the same punishment as is set forth in the last preceding article.

## CHAPTER IV.

### *Of fabricating defamatory papers.*

Art. 404. Whoever, with intent to injure the reputation of another, shall, without any lawful authority, publish or circulate, or make, with the intent to publish or circulate, any false writing, purporting to be the act or work of such other person, which does not constitute the crime of forgery, but which would, if the same were true, bring the person, whose act or work it purports to be, into contempt, cause his society to be generally avoided, excite public ridicule or indignation against him, or injure him in his office, profession, or trade, the offender shall be fined not exceeding four thousand dollars, and shall be imprisoned not exceeding one year in close confinement.

Art. 405. The words used in the last preceding article, which occur in the first of this title, are used in the same sense in which they were explained in that, and are subject to the same limitation.

## TITLE XIX.

### OF OFFENCES AFFECTING THE PERSONS OF INDIVIDUALS.

## CHAPTER I.

### *Of assault and of battery.*

#### SECTION I.

##### Of simple assault, or simple assault and battery.

Art. 406. No one has a right to use any VIOLENCE on the person of another, except in the cases and to the degree allowed by law ; such violence used in any other case or to a greater degree, with intent to inflict an injury, is an offence called a battery ; it may be a misdemeanor, or a crime, according to the measure of violence or the intent with which it is offered.

Art. 407. By the term " violence," in the above definition, is meant any physical force applied either immediately, by any part of the body of the person using it, or by the instrumentality or intervention of any other matter, whether animate or inanimate, and it comes within the definition whether the violence be produced by SECONDARY MEANS, intentionally prepared by the offender, or be caused by his immediate act.

Art. 408. The explanation in the last article may be illustrated thus: a blow with the hand is an example of physical force applied immediately by the body of the person using it; a bullet shot from a gun, a stroke given with a cudgel, water thrown from a bowl, are examples of the employment of inanimate matter; and one man injured by pushing another against him, or by beating or assaulting the horse which draws or carries him, are instances of battery committed by the entervention of animated matter, and a wound given by a spring-gun or trap purposely set, or an injury caused by falling into a pit or over an obstruction intentionally dug or placed in a highway, are illustrations of what is meant by the words of SECONDARY MEANS.

Art. 409. A menacing gesture, showing either in itself or by words which accompany it, an immediate design coupled with the ability to commit a battery, is an assault; which is a misdemeanor, whether followed by a battery or not.

Art: 410. The person of every free person being entitled to perfect protection from the exercise of illegal force, the degree of such force applied to it does not enter into the definition; it is a battery, however slight, if done with intent to injure.

Art. 411. The injury meant by the definition is not only bodily pain, constraint, or inconvenience, but alarm, a sense of degradation, or other disagreeable emotion of the mind.

Art. 412. Whenever injury is caused by violence to the person, the intent to injure is presumed, and the burthen of proving accident, or another intent, is thrown on him who alleges it.

Art. 413. It is sufficient to constitute the offence if the intent be to injure any one, although not the person to whom the violence was actually offered.

Art. 414. When an injury has been done to the person, by an act, which, although not intended to injure, was such as, in the usual course of things, might be expected to produce such injury to some one, it is an offence which shall be punished by fine, not exceeding two hundred dollars, or imprisonment not exceeding sixty days, or both.

Art. 415. Violence offered to the person does not amount to the offence of battery, where it is done in either of the cases, or for either of the purposes hereafter enumerated in this article; that is to say,

1. In the execution of that right of moderate restraint or correction which is given by law to the parent over the child: the tutor or curator over his minor ward: the master over the apprentice or servant: the schoolmaster over the scholar: or by persons duly authorized to use such restraint or correction towards minors, by persons standing in either of the above relations to them;

2. By the curator of a person insane, for the necessary restraint of the ward, although such ward be of full age;

3. For the preservation of order in any meeting either for religious, political, literary, social or any other lawful purposes;

4. For the necessary preservation of the peace, or to prevent the commission of any crime;

5. To prevent or put an end to an intrusion on a legal possession;

6. To make a lawful arrest, and to detain the party arrested in lawful

custody, in cases where, by the Code of Procedure, arrests are permitted without warrant;

7. In obedience to the lawful order of a magistrate, or court of competent authority;

8. To overcome resistance to the execution of any such lawful order.

9. In self defence, or the defence of another, against unlawful violence, offered to his person or property.

In each of the preceding cases, the force used, to effect either of the purposes thereby declared to be lawful, must be such as does not exceed what is necessary for the purpose, otherwise it will amount to the offence of battery. That degree of force shall be esteemed to have been necessary, which would have appeared so to one of ordinary prudence and firmness, placed in the situation in which the accused was.

Art. 416. An assault or battery cannot be justified by any verbal provocation; but under certain circumstances, such provocation may be submitted to the court in the manner directed in the Code of Procedure, in mitigation of the punishment.

Art. 417. No prosecution shall be commenced for simple assault or battery, but on the complaint of the party injured, or some one representing, or duly authorized by him: when attended with any other circumstance or intent which aggravates the offence, it may, with the exceptions hereinafter contained, be prosecuted on the complaint of any person whatever.

Art. 418. The punishment for simple assault or battery is fine, not exceeding one thousand dollars, or imprisonment not exceeding six months, or both, and the imprisonment may be in the whole, or in part, in close custody.

Art. 419. The terms, "degree of force," mean as well the instrument, or other secondary means employed, as physical or bodily power.

## SECTION II.

Of assault and battery in relation to the person on whom, or by whom it is committed.

Art. 420. The law gives protection to all persons against illegal violence, but different remedies are applied according to the effect of the offence upon society, when committed by, or upon particular persons who are either appointed to preserve order, or on those who are particularly exposed to violence.

Art. 421. If assault or battery be committed on any public officer while in the legal execution of his office, the punishment assigned to the species of assault or battery that is committed, shall be doubled.

Art. 422. No act is an offence under this section, unless it was known to the party accused, that the person assaulted was a public officer, and was in the execution of his office; and he shall be deemed to have known it when it was so openly declared in his presence, or when, from the circumstances of the case, he could not have been ignorant both of the character of the officer, and of the nature of the duty he was performing.

Art. 423. If any public officer shall, under pretence of executing his office, exercise any violence against any other person, in cases where no force is permitted to be used, or shall exceed, in cases where force is permitted, that degree thereof which is allowed by law, the punishment assigned to the species of assault and battery that is committed, shall be doubled.

Art. 424. If assault or battery be committed by a relation in the descending line against his ascendant; or by a man against a woman; or by a ward against his tutor, the punishment assigned to the species of assault or battery that is committed, shall be doubled.


## SECTION III.

### Of assault and battery, aggravated by its commission in a particular place.

Art. 425. If an assault or battery be committed in a court of justice, the punishment assigned to the species of assault and battery that is committed shall be doubled; but the fine shall not be less than one hundred dollars, nor the imprisonment less than sixty days, in close custody.

Art. 426. If any one shall go into a house occupied by another, with the intent of committing an assault or battery on him, or on any one of his family, or any sojourner in such house, and shall there commit such assault, or assault and battery, the punishment assigned to the species of assault and battery that is committed shall be doubled; but the fine shall not be less than one hundred dollars, nor the imprisonment less than sixty days, in close custody.

Art. 427. The word, " family," in the last article, comprehends all persons who habitually reside, or are guests in such house. By the term, "house," is intended, not only the dwelling-house, but shops, stores, and other buildings, which are used for carrying on business, or for domestic purposes. By "sojourners," is meant any person who lodges in, boards in, or occupies any part of such house.

Art. 428. In all cases of offences, under this and the last preceding section, imprisonment in close custody shall form a part of the punishment.


## SECTION IV.

### Of assault and battery aggravated by the intent.

Art. 429. If an asault or battery be made with an intent to commit murder or rape, the offender shall be imprisoned at hard labour not less than six nor more than ten years.

Art. 430. If the assault or battery be made with design to DISMEMBER, DISFIGURE or inflict a PERMANENT INJURY, the offender shall be fined not less than two hundred nor more than two thousand dollars, and imprisoned in close custody not less than sixty days nor more than one year.

Art. 431. If any one shall commit an assault or battery, with intent to commit any other crime than murder and rape, he shall be imprisoned at hard labour not less than two nor more than six years.

Art. 432. An assault or battery, with intent to force the party injured to commit an offence, shall be punished by one-half of the punishment assigned to the offence intended to be committed.

Art. 433. If the assault or battery be committed against a woman, attended with any circumstances, either of words or action, that are calculated to wound the modesty of her sex, not amounting to an attempt to ravish ; the offender shall be fined not less than two hundred nor more than two thousand dollars, and imprisoned in close custody not less than one month nor more than one year. If the offence, designated by this article, be committed by a tutor or curator against his ward, or a SCHOOLMASTER against his scholar, the imprisonment shall be at hard labour, and for a term not less than one nor more than two years.

Art. 434. If an assault or battery be committed, with intent to DISHONOUR ; or in consequence of a refusal to fight a duel, or to provoke another to fight a duel, or to give a challenge ; the punishment, assigned to the species of assault or assault and battery that is committed, shall be doubled; but the fine shall not be less than two hundred dollars, nor the imprisonment less than sixty days, in close custody.

## SECTION V.

Of assault and battery, aggravated by the manner and degree in which it is inflicted.

Art. 435. If assault and battery be committed with a DEADLY WEAPON, and in consequence of a premeditated design, although there be no design to kill actually proved ; the punishment shall be fine, not less than two hundred nor exceeding two thousand dollars, and imprisonment, in close custody, not less than sixty days nor more than one year, in addition to the punishment assigned to the species of assault or assault and battery that is committed.

Art. 436. If the offence be committed in the execution of a premeditated design, but not with a deadly weapon ; the punishment shall be fine, not less than fifty dollars, and imprisonment not less than twenty days, in addition to the punishment assigned to the species of assault and battery which is committed.

Art. 437. If the premeditated design be shown by LYING IN WAIT ; the punishment, assigned to the species of assault or assault and battery which is committed, shall be doubled; but shall not be less than a fine of one hundred dollars, and imprisonment in close custody, for thirty days.

Art. 438. If, in consequence of any assault or battery, the person against whom it is committed shall be DISFIGURED, or shall be deprived of or lose the use of any MEMBER OF HIS BODY, or receive such other injury as shall render it certain or probable that he will for the rest of his life labour under some bodily infirmity, although there be no design proved of doing such particular injury—the punishment shall be fine, not less than one hundred nor more than two thousand dollars, and imprisonment in close custody, or at hard labour, not less than three months nor more than two years.

Art. 439. If either of the injuries, mentioned in the last preceding article, shall be committed by premeditated design to do that particular injury, or by LYING IN WAIT, although no design to do that particular injury shall be proved—the punishment shall be fine, not less than five hundred nor more than three thousand dollars, and imprisonment, in close custody, not less than three months nor more than two years.

## SECTION VI.

### General provisions.

Art. 440. All the punishments assigned for the offences described in the second, third, fourth and fifth sections of this chapter, are CUMULA- TIVE in cases where the different circumstances, constituting such of- fences, concur in the same offence, and the lighter species of imprison- ment shall be made to commence after the expiration of the heavier.

Art. 441. No prosecution for simple assault and battery, as described in the first section; or for assault, with intent to ravish ; or for the of- fence described in the two last articles of the fourth section—shall be commenced but on the complaint of the party injured, or his legal re- presentative, or some one duly authorized by him ; unless such offence was committed in public, that is to say, in the presence of six or more persons, or in any dwelling-house, shop or store—in the first of which cases, any person—in the latter, the occupant of the house, shop or store, may make the complaint.

Art. 442. Where two persons agree to fight, unless it be with deadly weapons, no prosecution shall be commenced for assault and battery committed in consequence of such agreement, on the complaint of either of the parties, or any other person, unless the assault and battery took place in public, or in a dwelling-house, shop or store ; in which cases the prosecution may be commenced as is directed in the last preceding article.

## CHAPTER II.

### Of false imprisonment.

#### SECTION I.

##### Of simple false imprisonment.

Art. 443. Any intentional detention of the person of another, not ex- pressly authorized by law, is false imprisonment.

Art. 444. The detention to constitute this offence, may be either—
By assault.
By actual violence to the person.
By some impediment opposed to the power of locomotion.
By threats.

Art. 445. The assault and violence mentioned in the preceding article, are such as are defined in the last chapter ; but to constitute this offence, they must be such as to show the intent, and to have the effect of detaining the party against his will.

Art. 446. The material impediment must be such as is not applied immediately to the person ; in which case it would be actual violence, but it must be of such a nature as to prevent the free exercise of the right of locomotion, without having recourse to extraordinary means. A door merely closed with a latch, or in any other usual mode, so that the party complaining might, without any unusual effort, open it, would not be such an impediment ; but if bolted or locked on the outside, it would come within the definition, although the party imprisoned might escape by the window, or was strong enough to break the door.

Art. 447. Threats, to constitute the means of false imprisonment, must be such as would materially operate on a person of ordinary firmness, and inspire a just fear of great injury to person, reputation or fortune. The age, sex, state of health, temper and disposition of the party complaining, and all other circumstances that may be calculated to give greater or less effect to the violence or threats, must be taken into consideration ; and the threat must be to inflict the injury if the person departs from the bounds prescribed.

Art. 448. A detention of the person shall not be deemed illegal, if made in any of the nine cases set forth in the first section of the first chapter, and nineteenth title of this book; provided, under the circumstances of such case, a detention of the person was necessary to effect the object relied on as a justification, and was not continued longer than was so necessary. The rule for determining the necessity established by the said section, also applies to this.

Art. 449. The punishment for this offence is fine not exceeding five thousand dollars, or imprisonment not exceeding two years, or both, and the whole or part of the imprisonment may be in close custody.

SECTION II.

Of false imprisonment aggravated by the purpose or the degree.

Art. 450. If the party falsely imprisoned be conveyed, while so imprisoned, out of the state, the punishment shall be doubled, but shall not be less than five hundred dollars fine, and six months imprisonment, one-half in close custody.

Art. 451. If the offence be committed with intent to convey the person imprisoned out of the state, although the purpose be not actually effected, the punishment shall not be less than three hundred dollars fine, and three months imprisonment in close custody.

Art. 452. If the offence be committed against a free person for the purpose of detaining or disposing of him as a slave, knowing such person to be free, the punishment shall be fine, not less than five hundred dollars nor more than five thousand dollars, and imprisonment at hard labour, not less than two nor more than four years.

Art. 453. If false imprisonment be used as the means of forcing one to do an act which, if voluntarily done, would be an offence, the punish-

3 E

ment shall be the one-half of that designated in this code for the offence which it was intended to force the party to commit.

Art. 454. If this offence be committed with intent to commit a crime or misdemeanor, the punishment shall be one half of that designated by this code for the offence intended to be committed.

Art. 455. If false imprisonment be used as the means of forcing a woman to do an act or submit to treatment injurious to the modesty of her sex, the punishment, besides the fine, shall be confinement at hard labour not less than one and not exceeding three years; and if the offence described in this article be committed by the tutor or curator against his ward, or a schoolmaster against his scholar, the confinement at hard labour shall not be less than three nor more than six years.

Art. 456. If an imprisonment, otherwise legal, shall be used for the purpose expressed in the preceding article, it shall be deemed a false imprisonment.


## SECTION III.

### Of abduction.

Art. 457. Abduction is false imprisonment of a woman with the intent to force her into a marriage, either with the offender or some other, and that whether the marriage takes place or not.

Art. 458. If any female, under the age of fourteen years, be taken away from her father, mother, tutor, or other person having legal charge of her person, without their consent, either for the purpose of marriage, concubinage or prostitution, it is an abduction, although the female should consent, and although a marriage should afterwards take place between the parties.

Art. 459. The punishment for this offence is a fine not less than one hundred nor more than two thousand dollars, or imprisonment not less than sixty days nor more than two years, or both; and the imprisonment may be, in the whole or in part, in close custody, and in case the abduction be for the purpose of prostitution, the imprisonment may be at hard labour.


# CHAPTER III.

## Of rape.

Art. 460. Rape is the carnal knowledge of a woman, obtained against her consent, by force, menace or fraud.

Art. 461. The force used to constitute this crime must be such in kind as would constitute a battery, and in degree such as may reasonably be supposed sufficient to overcome resistance, taking into consideration the relative strength of the parties, and other circumstances of the case.

Art. 462. The menace must be such as may reasonably be supposed to inspire a just fear of death, or great bodily harm, taking into consideration the age and strength of the parties ; the state of health, temper and disposition of the party injured, and all other circumstances that may have increased or diminished her fears, into consideration.

Art. 463. A carnal knowledge obtained by fraud, does not amount to the crime of rape, unless the fraud consist,

1. In causing the woman, against whom the offence is committed, to believe during its commission, that the offender is her husband.

2. In forcibly, or without her knowledge, administering to the woman who is injured, any substance that produces an unnatural sexual desire, or such stupor as to prevent or weaken resistance, and committing the crime while she is under the operation of that which is so administered.

Art. 464. Consent cannot be presumed to have been given, from an acquiescence in the sexual connexion, when produced by either of the means mentioned in the definition.

Art. 465. Carnal knowledge is accomplished by the commencement of a sexual connexion ; proof of the circumstance that usually terminates it is not required.

Art. 466. No person can be convicted of this offence, or of an assault with intent to commit it, who had not, at the time the offence is said to have been committed, attained the age of fourteen years.

Art. 467. Carnal knowledge of a female under the age of eleven years, is in itself a rape, without any evidence of force, menace, imprisonment or frand.

Art. 468. The punishment of rape is imprisonment in the penitentiary for life.


# CHAPTER IV.


## *Of abortion.*

Art. 469. Whoever, by violence, or by any means, externally or internally applied to any pregnant woman, with her consent, shall designedly procure an abortion, shall be imprisoned in the penitentiary not less than three nor more than six years. If it be done without her consent, the punishment shall be doubled.

Art. 470. He who furnishes such means, knowing the purpose to which they are intended to be applied, is guilty of this offence.

Art. 471. He who designedly furnishes or administers the means intended to produce abortion, when they are administered, but fail in their effect, shall suffer one half the punishment that the crime would have incurred, had it been completed.

Art. 472. If the offender be a physician or surgeon, or practising as such, he shall suffer the highest punishment that can be inflicted for the offence.

Art. 473. Nothing herein contained shall extend to the case of an abortion procured by medical advice, for the purpose of saving the life of the mother.

Art. 474. If death ensues, by reason of the attempt to procure abortion, it is murder, except in the case provided for in the last article.

# CHAPTER V.

## *Of injury to the person by malicious potions.*

Art. 475. If any one shall maliciously cause another, without his knowledge, or against his will, to swallow or inhale any substance which causes any interruption or violent change in the usual functions of his body, or injures his health, he shall be fined not less than one hundred dollars nor more than one thousand dollars, and imprisoned in close custody not less than ten days nor more than three months ; and if such substance was given with intent to murder, he shall be punished in the manner hereinafter directed in the chapter concerning murder.

Art. 476. If such substance so maliciously adminstered, causes any malady of which the party to whom it is administered shall die within one year, although there was no intent to kill, the offender shall be punished by imprisonment at hard labour not less than four nor more than ten years.

Art. 477. If the malicious intent was not to kill, and the substance so administered shall be the immediate cause of the death of the person to whom it was given, the offender shall be punished by imprisonment at hard labour not less than seven nor more than fifteen years.

Art. 478. If such substance, although not coming within the definition of POISON, be given with intent to kill, and it shall have that effect, it is murder.

# CHAPTER VI.

## *Of homicide.*

### SECTION I.

#### Of homicide in general, and of its different divisions.

Art. 479. Homicide is the destruction of the life of one human being, by the act, procurement or culpable omission of another.

Art. 480. The life which is destroyed must have been complete by the birth of the being who is deprived of it. The destruction of a child before its birth is an offence specially defined.

Art. 481. The destruction of human life at any period of its existence after birth, is homicide, however near it may be extinction from any other cause.

Art. 482. The destruction must be by the act of ANOTHER ; therefore self-destruction is excluded from this definition.

Art. 483. It must be operated by some act; therefore death, although produced by the operation of words on the imagination, or the passions, is not homicide. But if words are used, which are calculated to produce and do produce, some act which is the immediate cause of death, it is homicide. A blind man, or a stranger in the dark, directed by words only to a precipice, where he falls and is killed ; a direction verbally given to take a drug that it is known will prove fatal, and which has that effect; are instances of this modification of the rule.

Art. 484. Homicide by omisssion only, is committed by voluntarily permitting another to do an act, that must, in the natural course of things, cause his death, without apprising him of his danger, if the act be involuntary, or endeavouring to prevent it if it be voluntary. He shall be presumed to have permitted it voluntarily, who omits the necessary means of preventing the death, when he knows the danger, and can cause it to be avoided, without danger of personal injury or pecuniary loss. This rule may be illustrated by the examples put in the last preceding article : if the blind man is seen walking to the precipice by one who knows the danger, can easily apprize him of it, but does not ; or if one who knows that a glass contains poison, sees him about to drink it, either by mistake or with intent to destroy himself, and makes no attempt to prevent him ; in these cases the omission amounts to homicide.

Art. 485. The exposing another to causes either natural or adventitious, which in the natural course of things must probably produce and do actually produce death, is homicide ; and this may be either by act, or by omission ; the placing an infant or other helpless person, in the open air during a winter's night by which he is frozen to death, or in the midst of a frequented high way where he is killed by the wheel of a carriage, is an illustration of this species of homicide by act.

He who shall with the knowledge of the danger leave a person of such description to perish in either of those situations when he could have been removed without personal danger or pecuniary loss commits this kind of homicide by omission.

Art. 486. Every being of the human species, of whatever age or condition, is included in the relative terms, "one human being," and "another," in the definition of this article. Therefore no death is homicide that is not caused by human agency. If the agent or sufferer have never attained, or have been deprived of reason, it is still homicide.

Art. 487. Human agency must be the cause of the death; therefore, he who gives a slight wound, which from neglect becomes a mortification, and proves fatal, is not guilty of homicide. If the same kind of injury proves fatal by the administration of improper remedies, the homicide is not the act of him who inflicted the wound, but of the one who applied the remedy, and may be criminal or not, according to the intent and other circumstances.

Art. 488. Although the injury that caused the death might not, under other circumstances, have proved fatal, yet if without any evident neglect, or treatment manifestly improper, it causes death, it is homicide. Thus, if an artery be cut, and the party bleed to death for want of aid, it is homicide, although, if proper assistance had been obtained, the artery might have been secured. What shall be proper or conclusive evidence of the cause of death in questions of homicide, is found in the Code of Evidence.

Art. 489. Death, or the total extinction of life, is a necessary part of the definition. If the act produce disability of any kind, or even the extinction of any or all of the senses, it is not homicide, while life remains.

Art. 490. The nature of the means or instrument by which death is caused or inflicted, is not essential to constitute homicide. All means by which life is destroyed, are within the definition.

Art. 491. Homicide is justifiable, excusable, or culpable.

## SECTION II.

#### Of justifiable homicide.

Art. 492. That is justifiable homicide, which, although committed voluntarily, is inflicted in cases where it is required or permitted by law. These cases are enumerated in the following section.

## SECTION III.

#### Of homicide justified by the requisition of law.

Art. 493. Homicide of a public enemy in the prosecution of war, is justified by the laws of nations. An enemy in the act of hostile invasion or occupation of any part of this state, is not within the protection of its laws ; but an enemy, although one of an invading force, who is within the state as a prisoner of war, as a deserter, as the bearer of a flag of truce, or in any other character which does not show a design to commit hostilities, and all enemies' subjects, brought within the state by force, coming there without any hostile intent, or found there at the commencement of the war, are entitled to the same personal protection of the laws as citizens are, excepting only the degree of personal restraint that may be imposed by the laws of the United States, or the rules and usages of war.

Art. 494. Neither the laws of the United States, nor the laws of nations, justify the homicide even of an invading enemy, by poison, by assassination, or by the use of poisoned weapons.

Art. 495. By assassination, in the preceding article, is meant homicide, committed on a public enemy by one who has come under an express or implicit obligation to refrain from any hostile act ; if one who should be received as a deserter in the enemy's camp, or should go there in the disguise of a person bringing provisions, or who being a prisoner should be suffered to go at large on his parole, and should, under such circumstances, put an enemy to death, afford an example of what is meant by the term as here employed.

Art. 496. Those are PUBLIC ENEMIES, who are declared such by the constitutional authority, and those who have declared themselves such, either in the manner usual among nations, or by a hostile invasion of the territory of the nation.

Art. 497. It may also be required by law, that persons convicted of certain offences, be punished by death. Whenever such laws, either of the United States or of this state, exist, the execution of a criminal, in pursuance of the unreversed sentence passed by a competent court, in the manner, at the time, and by the officer, prescribed by the law and the sentence, is justifiable homicide.

Art. 498. The preceding articles of this section describe the only cases in which homicide can be justified, as being required by law. It is permitted, as a necessary alternative, to avoid a greater evil in the following cases, that is to say, in the execution of certain public duties, specially designated : to prevent the commission of certain enumerated crimes, and in defence of person or property, against the injuries, and in the manner designated by law. The circumstances under which homicide will be justified in each of the above cases, is more fully developed in the following sections.

SECTION IV.

Of homicide, permitted in the performance of a duty to the state.

Art. 499. There are certain public duties of such importance to society, that those upon whom the obligation to perform them devolves, are bound to it at the risk of their lives. Justice, therefore, requires, that the law should permit all proper means of defence against the dangers to which they are exposed. On this principle is founded the impunity allowed by law to the class of homicides, treated of in this section, which designates what public duties come within its purview, and under what circumstances homicide, done in the performance of them, shall be justified.

Art. 500. The first of these duties is the execution of the lawful orders of MAGISTRATES and courts ; and in such cases, homicide, by the person legally charged with that duty, is justifiable where it is violently resisted, and he has a JUST REASON to fear, that his own life will be in danger if he persevere in executing the order ; subject, however, to the modifications and restrictions contained in the following rule :

§ 1.

*As to the order itself.*

1. The order must be that of a MAGISTRATE or court, having legal power to issue it.

2. It must have so much of the form prescribed by law as is declared necessary to give it validity.

3. Whether the court or magistrate have judged erroneously or not in making the order : it is a justification to the person executing it, if it emanate from a proper authority, and is made in legal form, or with all essential requisites.

§ 2.

*As to the person executing the order, and his conduct in performing that duty.*

4. The person must be an OFFICER OF JUSTICE, or some other legally

authorized to perform the duty in question, according to the provisions contained in the Code of Procedure.

5. If an officer of justice, and performing an act which none but an
officer could do, he must have taken the oath of office, and given security
when they are required by law.

6. He must execute the order in the manner prescribed by law, and
must in all cases, whether it be elsewhere prescribed or not, at the time
of performing the duty, and before doing the act which caused the
homicide, have declared to the person making opposition, that he was
an executive officer of justice, or had other authority (designating it) to
perform the duty.

7. If the order be by written warrant, and the party against whom it
is issued, submits, but desires to see it, or hear it read, the person charged
with its execution, is bound to produce, and show, or read it, according to the request ; and if he refuse such request, and persevere in
executing the order, it shall be no justification to him for any homicide
committed after such refusal.

8. If the order be to make an arrest, the person executing it is bound
not only to show the order where it is in writing, and is required, in
the manner prescribed in the last preceding rule, but to declare in all
cases, at least to the person he is about to arrest, for what offence, or
whose suit, (if in a civil suit) the arrest is made.

9. At or after the arrest, if any resistance be made by force, the
officer, or other person making the warrant, is bound to oppose to such
resistance, a force sufficient so to overcome it, as to be enabled to perform the duty required of him by the writ, and no greater force ; but if
the resistance be of such a nature as to give him JUST REASON TO FEAR
THE LOSS OF LIFE if he persevere, he may then use such force as is
necessary for his own defence, and if homicide ensues, he is justified.

10. An endeavour to escape before or after an arrest, by flight only,
will not justify the infliction of death, or the use of DEADLY WEAPONS
to prevent it ; but if the fugitive be armed with a deadly weapon, and
the pursuer has JUST REASON TO FEAR, from the threats or gestures of
the person pursued, that his own life will be endangered by continuing
the pursuit, he may then use deadly weapons to stop the flight ; and
if they produce death, he is justifiable.

11. The case of prisoners attempting to escape from a public prison,
is an exception to the last preceding rule. Deadly weapons may be
used, and death inflicted on any prisoners legally committed, who shall
endeavour, BY BREACH OF PRISON, to escape, but not until previous
warning has been given, and the prisoners persevere in their attempt.

12. These rules apply as well to the justification of those who are
legally aiding an executive officer of justice in the execution of a legal
order, as to that of the officer, or other person, specially charged with
the duty. They also apply to the homicide of any other person opposing the execution of the order, as well as to him against whom the
order is directed.

13. They apply also to orders in civil suits, as well as in criminal
prosecutions, and to courts and magistrates of the United States, lawfully acting in this state, as well as to the state magistrates and courts.

14. The words "just reason," as used in this section, mean such
reasons as would impress a man of ordinary understanding and firm-

ness, if placed in the same circumstances, with a belief that he, was in great hazard of losing his life.

Art. 501. Another duty to the state, which justifies homicide when necessary to its performance, is the opposition to rebellions, insurrections and riots. Death inflicted by any one acting in pursuance to the provisions of this code, or to those of any other law of the state that may be made for the suppression of riots, is justifiable homicide..

Art. 502. Whenever any law of this state, or of the United States, shall require an officer or any other person to perform a public duty, and, from the law, or the nature of the duty, the legislative will plainly appears to be that the duty should be performed, notwithstanding any forcible opposition, then homicide in the performance of the duty is justifiable, provided the directions of such law be strictly pursued, and subject to such of the rules laid down in this section for the execution of judicial orders as can be applied to the case, although it may not be a judicial order ; but if it be a case of judicial order, then subject to all those rules; and all those which designate the nature of the opposition, and to limit the lawful resistance that may be applied to overcome it, are hereby declared to apply to all cases provided for by this article.

Art. 503. Whenever any law of the state, or of the United States, shall give authority to any officer or other person to call for the aid of the country or the military power, to enforce its execution, it shall be deemed, without any other indication, such a case as is contemplated by the last preceding article.

Art. 504. Homicide by a military or a naval officer, or by any one under the command of either of them, or by an officer or soldier of the militia on actual service, is justifiable if it happen in the lawful arrest of a deserter or other person amenable to the military laws to answer for a military offence ; but in such case the rules laid down in this section with respect to judicial arrest must be observed.

## SECTION V.

### Of homicide permitted in defence of person or property.

Art. 505. Homicide is permitted in the necessary defence of person or property under the circumstances and restrictions set forth in the following articles.

Art. 506. For the prevention of the crimes of murder by violence, rape, robbery, arson, burglary and nocturnal theft ; the necessity of the case permits the infliction of death on those who have begun to commit either of them, subject to the following rules, that is to say,

1. The intent to commit the crime must be unequivocal, and apparent by acts, or by acts coupled with words.

2. The homicide for this cause cannot be justified, unless it be done before the crime is completed, and after it is begun to be executed, that is to say, after some act is done showing unequivocally either by itself, or by words coupled with it, an intent immediately to commit the crime.

3. The crime is not completed in the sense of the last preceding article, while the offender, in the case of murder, is still committing violence, although the mortal stroke may have been given ; in the case of rape, while the ravisher is continuing his violence, although he may

3 F

have done enough to make himself guilty of the crime; in the case of robbery, while the robber is still in the presence of the party robbed, or is flying with his booty; and in the cases of arson, burglary, and nocturnal theft, while the offender is still in the building where the crime has been committed.

4. The beginning to commit either of the crimes above mentioned, is prima facie evidence of the necessity of inflicting death, to prevent the completion of it; but if the crime would have been prevented, or the persons of the offenders secured by means within the knowledge and power of the person doing the homicide, without resorting to that act, and without danger of life, it is not justifiable homicide; but receives its designation from the circumstances of extenuation or criminality attending it, according to the rules hereafter established in this code.

5. The rules contained in this article relate to death inflicted by design; the use of weapons or other means calculated to produce death, is presumptive evidence of the design to inflict it.

Art. 507. When any other crime, but one of those enumerated in the last preceding article, is attempted, it is not lawful to inflict death for its prevention, until all reasonable endeavours have been made to avoid the danger, if the crime be one of those which endanger the person, or to prevent it by other means, if it affect property.

Art. 508. The endeavour to avoid the danger, in the case of a crime attempted against the person, which are mentioned in the preceding article, are,

1. The use of such means as are in the party's power to repel the assault, short of such as are of a nature to produce death, if the nature of the attack, the weapons with which it is made, the relative weakness of the assailant, or other circumstances, enable the person assailed to secure himself without resorting to the infliction of death, or the use of such means as will probably produce it.

2. If he have not the means to repel the attack without endangering the life of the assailant, or do not think proper to use those means, if he have them, he must retire from the assailant; the idea of dishonour being attached to such means of avoidance will not excuse the neglect of it; the laws can acknowledge no dishonour in obedience to what they command. This retiring must be with a bona fide intent to avoid the danger: it must be continued until it is stopped by some material obstacle, or the want of physical power to continue it. But in cases where retreat would expose to greater danger than facing the attack, it is not required.

Art. 509. Even after using the endeavours above mentioned to avoid personal dangers without effect, it is not lawful to inflict death in order to repel every attack, or avoid every species of personal danger: it must be such an attack as gives a JUST FEAR of death, or of permanent bodily injury.

Art. 510. Whatever circumstances are by this section declared to be a justification for homicide, in the party against whom the crime is committed or intended, will be a justification for others interfering with a bona fide intention to prevent the commission of a crime.

Art. 511. Homicide is also justifiable in the necessary defence of property, although the attempt to take it do not amount to the crimes above provided for, of murder by violence, robbery, rape, burglary, and nocturnal theft. Every man has a right to his legal possession of property ; he is not bound to yield it to the force of any invaders. If, therefore, any one attempt by illegal force to deprive another of property, either real or personal, in his actual, corporal and legal possession : the legal and actual possessor may defend his possession by a force proportioned to that with which it is attacked, and if the aggressor persist in his unlawful attempt in a manner that gives the party attacked a JUST FEAR of death, he is justified in defending himself and his possession by killing the invader.

This article is to be construed by the following rules, and modified as follows, that is to say,

1. The possession must be of a corporal property, not a mere right ; and must be an ACTUAL not a mere CONSTRUCTIVE possession.

2. The possession must be a legal one ; but it is not necessary that the actual property be vested in the possessor, but he must have acquired the right of possession.

3. The resistance must be made to the illegal force during its exercise ; if the actual possession be once lost, it will be no justification of a homicide that it was inflicted in an attempt to regain it.

4. No resistance that would probably produce death, can be justified in this case, unless the attack is made in such a manner as to create in the possessor a JUST FEAR of death, in case he should persevere in the defence of his possession.

5. Every endeavour in the power of the possessor must have been used to induce the aggressor to desist, both by words and such physical means as were in his power, before resorting to the means that produced death.

6. Every thing in this article which relates to the nature of the possession, or the degree of force that may be justifiably used, applies to any person aiding the possessor to maintain his possession.

7. Nothing in this article contained, relates to the defence of property against an attempt to rob, which is heretofore provided for.

Art. 512. Except in the instance provided for, by the last preceding article, homicide is not permitted by law for the prevention of any offence that is not a crime ; thus, neither simple assault and battery, nor trespass, will justify homicide, nor will any crime not accompanied by force ; thus, neither private stealing, nor even poisoning, can be lawfully prevented by homicide.

SECTION VI.

Of excusable homicide.

Art. 513. Homicide is excusable, and consequently not criminal, whenever the death of one human being, though caused by the act of another, can be attributed neither to negligence nor design, but happens in the prosecution of a lawful act by lawful means ; and is caused by some accident which ordinary human prudence could not foresee nor avoid. If in shooting at game on his own grounds, a man kill another who is hid unknown to him in the wood, he commits homicide, for it comes within the definition of that act; but it is excusable, for it was involuntary, and was not caused by negligence; but if the shot is fired across a highway, and one travelling thereon is killed, there is negligence, and the homicide is not excusable.

Art. 514. The lawful act which causes the death must be done by lawful means, used in a lawful degree. It is lawful to correct a scholar, or an apprentice; but if this be done with an instrument likely to produce death, or if with a proper instrument the chastisement be cruelly inflicted, and death ensue, it is not excusable homicide.

## SECTION VII.

### Of culpable homicide.

Art. 515. Every homicide that is neither justifiable nor excusable, according to the foregoing definitions and illustrations, is a culpable homicide.

They are negligent or voluntary.

## § 1.

### Of negligent homicide.

Art. 516. The species of homicide thus called, is that which is inflicted without design to kill either the person actually killed or any other.

Art. 517. This is an offence, of which the several grades are distinguished by the degree of negligence and the nature of the act, in the performance of which the homicide happens; each degree forming a separate class of offences.

## § 2.

### Of negligent homicide in the first degree.

Art. 518. The first degree of this offence, is homicide involuntarily inflicted in the performance of a LAWFUL ACT, in which there is no apparent risk of life, by ordinary means, but without that care and precaution which a prudent man would take to avoid the risk of destroying human life.

Whoever is guilty of this offence, in this degree, shall suffer imprisonment, not less than two months nor more than one year, of which such party may be in close custody as the court may direct.

Art. 519. The following rules, derived from the foregoing definition, are to be observed:

1. The act, in the performance of which the homicide happens, must be lawful; by which is meant, any thing that is not forbidden by the penal law, or which would not give just cause for a civil suit.

2. It is an essential part of this definition, that the danger of causing death, in doing the act, should not be apparent. Where there is such apparent danger, the offence becomes a crime.

3. The terms, "ordinary means," in the definition, are not confined strictly to such as are usually employed ; they are intended to admit the employment of means different from those ordinarily used, provided they are not more dangerous.

4. The want of care and precaution distinguishes this from excusable homicide, and places it in the first or incipient degree of culpability. In all that regards the preservation of human life, a greater degree of caution is required, by law, than it demands in other cases. By "caution," is meant a consideration of probable consequences, and the use of means to avoid them, if they appear injurious. Therefore, in order to avoid the guilt of this offence, it is not enough to abstain from acts, or from the use of such means, in performing them, in which a risk of homicide is known or apparent ; but where, from the nature of the case, it is as reasonable to believe, that danger of destroying life may exist, as that it may not exist, the law requires a previous examination.

5. The degree of caution described, as that which a prudent man would use, must be determined by a consideration of the circumstances as they appeared before the event ; if the event alone were sufficient to prove want of caution, all casual homicide would be culpable.

1st Example. When death is casually inflicted, by the discharge of fire arms which are believed not to be loaded, without examining whether they are so or not, it constitutes this offence. If the examination be made, and owing to some unknown cause, although loaded, they appear to be empty ; or, if unknown to the person using them, they have been loaded immediately after the examination, due caution has been used, and there is no offence.

2d Example. If one, in blasting a quarry, although at a distance from a public way, makes the explosion without examining whether any persons are so near as to be injured by it, the offence is incurred. If he make the examination and discover no one, he is innocent, although a person concealed from his view, or one who came suddenly on the spot, should be killed. If the quarry be in a frequented place, or he knew there were bystanders, another offence would be incurred.

Art. 520. Death caused by any kind of fire-arms, purposely directed against any one, without intention to kill or injure, but merely in sport, is negligent homicide of the first grade, whether any examination of the arms have been previously made or not.

## § 3.

### Of negligent homicide in the second grade.

Art. 521. Homicide of the second grade, is that which is involuntarily committed in the performance of a lawful act, but under circumstances, in a manner, or by means, which cause an apparent danger of inflicting death, without due precaution to avoid such danger. It is punishable by imprisonment, not less than two nor more than four years, in the penitentiary, or in close custody, at the discretion of the court.

Art. 522. An important distinction between this and the first grade of negligent homicide is, that in this the risk of causing death, or other great bodily harm, must be apparent; by which is meant, that it must necessarily be perceived by a common observer, without inquiry or examination, merely by witnessing the act, and reflecting on its consequences.

Art. 523. The words, "lawful act," used in the definition, have the same meaning as is explained in that of the first grade of this offence.

Art. 524. The word, " circumstances," used in the description of this offence, relates to the time, place, and such other concomitants of the act as make it dangerous, although it would not be so at other times, in other places, or attended by other accompaniments.

Art. 525. The word " manner," relates to the mode in which the act is done, or in which the instruments, or means that produce it, are used or employed.

Art. 526. The term, " mean" is intended to include the instruments with which the act is performed, or the other modes employed to effect it.

Art. 527. The " act," intended by that term, in the last four preceding articles, means the act in the performance of which the homicide takes place.

Art. 528. The " due precaution," mentioned in the description of this offence, is such as a prudent man would deem effectual to prevent the danger.

Art. 529. It is no justification for omitting such necessary precaution as is above described, that time or other circumstances did not permit them to be taken, but that the party did every thing else in his power to avoid the homicide. In such case the act itself, in the doing of which the death happened, ought to be omitted, unless it be one of those acts which are necessary for such defence of person or property as renders homicide justifiable : in which case, the best precaution that circumstances permitted, is sufficient.

1st Example. Of the crime generally. If one prove a cannon in a public road, and it burst and kill a passenger, it amounts to this offence, whether the passenger had notice of the intended explosion or not; for no one has a right to stop the passage of a highway, for the purpose of doing an act that ought to be done elsewhere.

But if the operation were performing in a proper place, and one who had notice chose to remain, and is killed, it is no offence, for due caution has been used.

If an act that cannot be done but in a public place, such as pulling down a house, cause the death of a passenger, who perseveres in passing after due notice, it is no offence. If no notice be given, the killing in this case is negligent homicide in the second grade.

2d Example. Of the " circumstances" which give the character of apparent risk.

The common case of a workman throwing materials from the roof of a house exemplifies this part of the definition. The criminality of the homicide there depends on the circumstance of the PLACE in which the act is done; if in the country, or other unfrequented place, without previous inquiry and examination whether any one be in the way, it is ranked in the first grade of this offence ; if in the streets of a populous city, without the precautions required by this code, or by the police of the city, it is a negligent homicide in the second grade; if in either place, with the caution required under the circumstances of the respective cases, it is no offence.

3d Example. Of the apparent risk, as applied to the MANNER.

It is lawful for a master to correct his apprentice by ordinary means; yet if such correction be repeated or continued in a manner apparently cruel or dangerous, and it causes death, although no improper instrument be used, it comes within the definition of this offence.

4th Example. Of risk apparent from the MEANS used.

If death is caused by the employment of deadly weapons, or using greater force than is necessary to repel the attack of an unarmed man upon person or property, the risk of death is apparent, and the party inflicting it is guilty of this offence.

Art. 530. In all the examples of the different kinds of offences designated as negligent homicide, it is understood, as an essential part of such case, that there is no intent to kill, and in all (except the example taken from the law of self defence) that there was no design to do a bodily harm.

## § 4.

### Of negligent homicide in the performance of unlawful acts.

Art. 531. All the definitions, rules, and provisions, with respect to negligent homicide in the first and second grades, except those which regard the legality of the act, in the doing or attempt to do which the homicide is committed, apply to the homicides described in this division of the offence, in all things in which they are not contrary to the following provisions.

Art. 532. Where negligent homicide in the second grade has been committed, in the doing or the attempt to do an act which is an injury, but not an offence, one-fifth shall be added to the punishment. If the act done or attempted, be a misdemeanor, but not an offence against the person, one-fourth shall be added. If it be one of those designated as an offence against the person, but not one of those offences designated as murder, one-half shall be added. If it be a crime punishable with imprisonment at hard labour for any term less than life, the punishment shall be doubled, and the imprisonment shall be at hard labour. And if the act done or attempted to be done, be a crime punishable with imprisonment for life, the homicide shall be punished by imprisonment at hard labour for life.

Art. 533. It is intended, by the preceding article, that the homicide must have been done in the attempt to offer the injury or commit the offences therein specified, that is to say, must have been the consequence of some act done for the purpose of offering or committing such other injury or offence. If the act which caused the death had no connexion with the injury intended to be offered or committed, it does not come within the definition. The same rule of construction applies to the words, "in the doing or in the attempt to do," whenever they are used as giving a character to any act actually done.

## § 5.

### *Of criminal voluntary homicide.*

Art. 534. Voluntary homicide is a CRIME in all cases, where it is neither justifiable nor excusable, according to the rules heretofore laid down. There are two degrees of this species of homicide, each degree forming a distinct class of crime. They are,

1. Manslaughter.
2. Murder.

Art. 535. Manslaughter is voluntary homicide, committed under the immediate influence of sudden passion, arising from an adequate cause.

In considering and applying this definition, the following rules are to be observed.

1. To constitute manslaughter, the homicide must be intentional. Those involuntary homicides, occasioned by want of due care, or occurring in the prosecution of some unlawful act, which were heretofore distinguished by this name, are in this code distinct offences.

2. Manslaughter is homicide committed under the immediate influence of sudden passion; all the terms of this part of the definition are to be strictly observed in its application to any particular act. If the passion be not sudden, that is to say, arising in the same interview in which the act was committed, but entertained before that time ; or if thus arising, and the act be not done under the immediate influence of that passion, but after such an interval of time as in the common course of human feelings would give time for reflection, or with the intervention of such circumstances as must naturally produce it : in either of these cases the crime is not manslaughter. That the act be done "under the influence" of such passion, is also a necessary part of the definition. This means, that the passion is the cause of the act ; not merely that it is done during the time that the mind is agitated by passion; from which it follows, that passion against one will not qualify the homicide of another with the appellation of manslaughter.

3. The passion intended by the above definition, includes all those called choler, rage, anger, sudden resentment, terror or fear; their great characteristic being a sudden and temporary agitation of the mind, that renders it incapable of cool reflection during the prevalence of this passion.

4. It is not sufficient that the act be committed under the influence of passion, to give to homicide the character of manslaughter : the passion must have an adequate cause. The law admits only such as adequate causes, which it defines as such.

The cause, to be adequate, must be one that in men of ordinary tempers, commonly produces an irritation of mind which renders them incapable of calculating the consequences of their acts. No words whatever are an adequate cause; no gestures, merely showing derision or contempt.

No assault and battery, so slight as to show that the intent was not to inflict great bodily pain.

An assault and battery made by the deceased, causing great pain or bloodshed, is an adequate cause.

A serious personal conflict, in which great bodily pain was inflicted by means of a weapon or other instrument, used by the person killed, or by means of a great superiority of personal strength or skill, is an adequate cause, even if the person guilty of the homicide were the aggressor in such conflict, or in any manner provoked the contest, provided such aggression or provocation was not made with the intent to bring on a conflict for the purpose of killing.

A discovery of the wife of the accused, in the act of adultery with the person killed, is an adequate cause.

Passion, occasioned by lawful correction of the person accused, is not an adequate cause.

Provocation given by a relation in the ascending line to his descendant, is not an adequate cause; although it would have been such, if given by a person not standing in the same relation. This does not extend to relations by affinity only.

Injury to property, unaccompanied by violence, is not an adequate cause.

Passion occasioned by the legal performance of duty by an officer of justice, or other person legally authorized to perform any executive duty of justice, is not an adequate cause.

Art. 536. Manslaughter is punished by imprisonment not less than one nor more than five years, at hard labour or in close confinement.

## § 6.

### Of murder.

Art. 537. Murder is homicide, inflicted with a premeditated design, unaccompanied by any of the circumstances, which, according to the previous provision of this chapter, do not justify, excuse or bring it within some one of the descriptions of homicide hereinbefore defined.

Art. 538. There are different grades of guilt in the commission of this crime, which are called,

Infanticide,
Assassination,
Murder under trust,
Parricide.

Art. 539. Infanticide is the murder of an infant for the purpose of concealing its birth.

Art. 540. Murder is characterized as assassination, either by the purpose intended to be obtained, by the means used to effect it, or by the condition of the person murdered.

### 1. By the purpose.

When the murder is committed for the purpose of effecting another crime.

When it is committed for the purpose of concealing another crime previously committed.

When it is committed for the purpose of obtaining an inheritance.

When it is committed for HIRE ; and in this case, he who gives and he who receives the reward is guilty of assassination.

### 2. By the means used.

When the murder is done by LYING IN WAIT; by burning the house in which the person murdered is; by POISON.

3 G

### 3. By the condition of the person murdered.

When the crime is committed on a woman, a man above the age of seventy, a minor under the age of sixteen, a person asleep, or in a dwelling-house by night, or travelling on the high road.

Art. 541. Murder, under trust, is that which is committed by persons under the following relations to the person murdered, that is to say: husband, wife, tutor or curator, ward, collateral relation within the second degree inclusive, master, servant, schoolmaster, host, guest, physician, or surgeon; and finally, if the murder be committed by one upon another, who has reposed confidence of safety in him, on an express or implied promise of fidelity or protection. Murder, committed by a guide or conductor on the land, or by the master of a vessel by water, upon a traveller, whom he has undertaken to conduct, are examples of this last description of murder under trust.

Art. 542. Illegitimate children of the same mother, and of the same father by another mother, if acknowledged by the father, are comprehended in the above description of collateral relations.

Art. 543. The word "host," includes as well the gratuitous receiver of the guest, as the one who receives him for hire.

Art. 544. Parricide is murder committed by a relation by consanguinity, in the ascending line upon his descendant, or by a descendant upon his relation by consanguinity, in the ascending line.

Art. 545. Illegitimate children, and such of their parents as have acknowledged them, are included in the above definition.

Art. 546. Punishment for murder is imprisonment for life.

Each of the aggravated species of murder described in this section, has appropriate privations and aggravations of discipline allotted to it in the Code of Reform and Prison Discipline.

Art. 547. An attempt to murder, by administering poison, although it fail in its effects, shall be punished by imprisonment at hard labour, for fifteen years.


### SECTION VIII.

#### Of suicide.

Art. 548. No punishment can be inflicted on him who commits this act; and by the principles on which this system is founded, the law cannot make an innocent survivor suffer for the rashness of another. But any one who shall aid in the act of suicide, or who shall provide the means of executing it, knowing the purpose for which they were intended, or be guilty of any omission with respect to the act or means of suicide, that constitutes homicide by omission, according to any of the preceding provisions of this chapter, shall be imprisoned, at hard labour, not less than three nor more than six years.

# CHAPTER VI.

## *Of duels.*

Art. 549. If any person shall use any insulting words or gestures of or to, or make an assault upon another with intent, either to provoke any one to give a challenge to FIGHT A DUEL, or as an alternative, to dishonour him, he shall be fined not less than fifty, nor more than three hundred dollars, or imprisoned not less than five, nor more than thirty days, in close custody.

Art. 550. If the defendant, in any prosecution under the last preceding article, shall make any denial, explanation, or acknowledgment, that the court shall think ought to satisfy the honour of the prosecutor, they shall direct the same to be recorded and published, with their judgment declaring the same to be satisfactory ; and may, at their discretion, direct the defendant to be dismissed, on the payment of costs.

Art. 551. Whenever judgment shall be pronounced on, for any offence under the said article, it shall contain a clause that it shall be void as to every thing but costs, in case the defendant shall make such acknowledgment as shall be satisfactory to the prosecutor.

Art. 552. No conviction on judgment for any offence under the said article, shall be a bar to any prosecution or suit for defamation or assault for the same cause, unless the satisfaction made by the defendant shall be accepted, as is provided in the last preceding article.

Art. 553. In case any offence under the said article should imply a charge affecting the honour or reputation of the person making the complaint, and the investigation on the trial show such charge to be unfounded, the court shall make that declaration in the sentence, and cause the same to be published at the expense of the defendant ; and if the party complaining request it, the question, whether the charge be true or false, shall be decided by the jury.

Art. 554. Whoever shall give a challenge to fight a duel, or shall, on receiving such challenge, ACCEPT the same, shall be imprisoned, in close custody, not less than two, nor more than six months, and be suspended from his political rights for four years.

Art. 555. Whoever shall fight a duel, if he in such fight inflicts no wound, shall be imprisoned, in close custody, not less than six, nor more than twelve months, and shall be suspended from his political rights for six years. If he wound his adversary, and such wound do not occasion death, or any permanent bodily disability, the imprisonment shall not be less than twelve, nor more than eighteen months, and the suspension for eight years. If he fight a duel, and shall inflict a wound on his adversary that causes a permanent disability, he shall be imprisoned not less than twelve months, and be suspended from the exercise of his political rights, and his civil rights of the first and third class, for seven years. If in such fight he kill, or inflict a mortal wound on his adversary, he shall be imprisoned not less than two, nor more than four years, and forfeit for ever his political rights, and his civil rights of the first and third class. And if such death or mortal wound be inflicted by treachery, he shall be deemed guilty of murder by assassination, and suffer the punishment in this code directed to be inflicted on those convicted of that crime.

Art. 556. If any one shall advise another to fight a duel, or shall use any reproachful or contemptuous language to or concerning any one for not sending or accepting a challenge, or for not fighting a duel, he shall be fined not less than fifty, nor more than five hundred dollars, or be imprisoned not less than thirty days, nor more than six months.

Art. 557. If any one shall bear a challenge, either written or verbal to another, knowing the intent with which it was sent, he shall be fined not less than one hundred, nor more than one thousand dollars, be imprisoned, in close custody, not less than two, nor more than six months, and suspended from his political rights for three years.

Art. 558. If a challenge shall be given and accepted in this state, and the parties go out of the state and fight a duel, the punishment for giving or accepting such challenge, shall be the same as if the whole offence were committed within the state.

Art. 559. It is an offence within the meaning of the first article of this chapter, if the insulting words or gestures be used relative to, or the assault be committed upon, either the person whom it is intended to provoke, or any other so nearly connected with or related to him as to show the intent in the said article expressed.

The dishonour, in the same article, means a loss of the esteem of those who think that offences of that nature ought to be avenged by a challenge to fight a duel.

Art. 560. The words " to fight a duel," in this chapter, are used in their common and general acceptation : they mean, to enter into a voluntary combat, one man against another, with deadly weapons.

Art. 561. A challenge is any proposal, either 'verbal or written, or by message, in whatever language it may be couched, to fight a duel, provided that, from the circumstances attending the proposition, it appeared to be so understood by the party accused whether he be the party giving or the party accepting it.

Art. 562. The acceptance of a challenge, is an agreement to the proposition to fight a duel, either given by express words or by other terms, either written or oral, from which such agreement may clearly be inferred on by circumstances which show such agreement.

Art. 563. It is treachery, if the death be occasioned by the breach of any rules made for conducting the combat, or by any other advantage, which, although not expressly provided against in those rules, was yet one that could not be supposed to have been intended to be given.

Art. 564. It is assassination, if the mortal wound be intentionally inflicted on a party, after he is incapable of further resistance, either from being disarmed, or any other circumstance, with a knowledge of such incapacity by the party inflicting it, whether it be done in pursuance of any previous rule for the combat or not.

Art. 565. It is assassination, and not a duel, if the death or mortal wound be inflicted by a party who has obtained the power of inflicting it without risk to himself, by the effect of a chance previously agreed on. Death inflicted by a party who has obtained a loaded pistol by a chance agreed on, while the one used by his adversary is not loaded, is an example of what is intended by this rule.

Art. 566. In order more effectually to secure the execution of the provisions of this chapter, the attorney general and district attorneys of this state, and all officers of justice when they are sworn into office, and such of them as are in office at the time of the promulgation of this code, or within fifteen days afterwards, and all grand jurors when they are sworn, shall sign a declaration in the following form :—"I declare, that I consider the obligation, which my duty requires, of bringing to justice all offenders against the laws, as containing no reservation with respect to duels. And I promise on my honour that I will, within the local bounds to which my official functions extend, by all lawful means prevent so far as shall be in my power, any duel which I may have reason to suppose is intended, and prosecute all offences which come to my knowledge, against the sixth chapter of the nineteenth title of the second book of the Code of Crimes and Punishments of this state, entitled, ' Of Duels.' "

The word "prosecute," in the said declaration, shall, in the case of grand jurors, be changed for "indict;" and in the case of officers of justice, it shall be changed for the words " enter complaint against."

Art. 567. And all officers, civil or military, judicial or executive, now in office, shall, within thirty days after the promulgation of this code, if in office at that time, and those appointed or elected afterwards, shall, at the time they take their oath of office, and before they enter on the duties of their office, take before a magistrate, and subscribe a declaration, under oath, in the following form :—"I do solemnly swear, that I have not fought a duel, or given or accepted a challenge to fight a duel, since the promulgation of the Code of Crimes and Punishments of the state of Louisiana ; and that I shall hereafter consider myself as bound by the ties of honour, as well as the sanction of this oath and of the laws, not to commit any offence against the provisions of the sixth chapter of the nineteenth title of the second book of the said code, entitled, ' Of Duels.' " And every person elected or chosen to any office, who shall refuse or neglect to take such oath and subscribe such declaration, within the period and at the time above directed, and to send the same to the office of the secretary of state, as is directed in the next article, shall be considered as having resigned or refused to except the office to which he is elected.

Art. 568. As to all officers appointed or elected, the oath and declaration aforesaid shall be taken and subscribed before the magistrate who administers the oath of office, and shall be deposited, recorded and transmitted, as is by law directed concerning oaths of office. And as to all officers in office at the time of the promulgation of this code, the oath shall be taken before any magistrate, and deposited, recorded and transmitted, as is now by law directed with respect to oaths of office.

# TITLE XX.

OF OFFENCES AFFECTING INDIVIDUALS IN THEIR PROFESSION OR TRADE.

Art. 569. All direct offences of this nature are comprehended in the twelfth and eighteenth titles, and the chapter "Of Conspiracies," and those having the same effect indirectly, in other titles of this book.

# TITLE XXI.

## CHAPTER I.

*Of the substitution, exposure of infants, and of falsifying registers.*

Art. 570. If any person to whom an infant, under the age of six years, shall be confided for nursing, education, or other purpose, shall, with intent to deceive the parents, tutors, or curators of such infant, substitute, or attempt to substitute another child in the place of the one so confided, he shall be imprisoned at hard labour not less than three nor more than seven years.

Art. 571. The word substitute in this chapter means, to deliver to the person confiding the child, another instead of the one so confided, under the pretence that it is the same.

Art. 572. If any one, to whom such a child shall be so confided, or its father or mother, shall expose or desert such child, with intent wholly to abandon it, in a place where its life will be endangered, the punishment shall be imprisonment at hard labour not less than five nor more than ten years.

Art. 573. But if such abandonment be made without the knowledge of the father, mother, tutor or curator of the child, by the person to whom it shall have been confided, by fraudulently depositing it in an inhabited house, one half of the punishment, mentioned in the last article, shall be inflicted.

Art. 574. If such child shall die in consequence of such exposure, it is infanticide, murder, or murder under trust, depending on the person who commits the crime. If it receive any other bodily injury, the offence shall be punished in the same manner as the same injury would be, had it been done with intent to kill.

Art. 575. If any one shall, for the purpose of intercepting an inheritance in the whole or in part, fraudulently produce an infant, falsely pretending it to be born of parents, whose child would stand in the order of successsion to such inheritance before or equally with another person, whose condition and civil rights it was intended to intercept, the persons so offending, and those who shall aid and assist in the deception, shall be imprisoned in close custody not less than six nor more than twelve months, and shall be suspended from the exercise of their civil rights of the first and third class for five years.

If any one shall, for the purpose of injuring another in his civil or political rights, or in his right to property, destroy, or alter any certificate of birth, or marriage, or burial, he shall be imprisoned not less than seven nor more than fifteen years at hard labour, and shall forfeit his political rights.

If any person, whose duty it is, by law, to make, a record of births, marriages, or deaths ; or any curate, priest, minister, or parson, who in any church or religious congregation, is charged with keeping a register of births, marriages, or funerals, celebrated for the members of such church or religious congregation, shall fraudulently make a false entry in such record or register of any such birth, marriage, death, or funeral, with intent to injure any one in his condition, civil or political rights, or his right to property, he shall be imprisoned at hard labour not less than seven nor more than fifteen years.

Art. 576. Other offences affecting political rights will be found in the title of offences against the right of suffrage.

# CHAPTER II.

## *Of bigamy.*

Art. 577. A person having a wife or husband living, who shall, without having a reasonable cause to believe such wife or husband to be dead, contract a second marriage, is guilty of bigamy, and shall be imprisoned at hard labour not less than one, nor more than five years.

Art. 578. If the first wife or husband had, at the time of the subsequent marriage, been absent for five years, and during that time the accused had not received any intelligence of his or her being alive, this shall, for the purposes of this chapter, be considered such a reasonable belief of death, as to take away all criminality from the act.

Art. 579. What other cause to believe the death of the former husband or wife shall be deemed a reasonable cause, is matter of fact, to be decided according to the circumstances of the case.

Art. 580. It is not necessary, to constitute this offence, that the first marriage should have been contracted within this state ; but it must, wherever celebrated, have been a valid marriage, according to the laws of the country in which it was contracted.

Art. 581. The subsequent marriage must also be made according to the forms prescribed by law to give validity to marriages in this state.

Art. 582. If a citizen of this state, residing therein, having a husband or wife living, either here or elsewhere, shall go out of this state, and contract a second marriage, with the intent of returning to reside within this state, and shall so return—he or she shall be deemed guilty of the crime of bigamy.

Art. 583. If the first marriage be not null in itself, but only voidable, a second marriage, during the lives of the parties to the first, is bigamy ; unless such first marriage had been declared void by a competent authority, or had become so by the operation of law or the act of the party, before the time of contracting the second marriage.

Art. 584. No other divorce but one, from the bonds of matrimony, is such a dissolution of the first marriage as will exempt the party from the guilt of bigamy or a second marriage, while both parties to the first are living.

Art. 585. A third marriage, during the lifetime of the parties to the second, is bigamy, although the second marriage was contracted during

the lifetime of the parties to the first, and in a manner to make it bigamy ; and in case of three or more successive marriages, any of the
persons, with whom the party accused, contracted either of the former
marriages, being alive, at the time of celebrating a subsequent one, he
or she may be convicted of bigamy.

# TITLE XXII.

### OF OFFENCES AFFECTING PERSONS IN THEIR PROFESSION OR TRADE.

THE offences coming under the purview of this title, will be found
in the titles, " Of offences affecting commerce and manufactures," and
in the chapter of " Conspiracies."

# TITLE XXIII.

### OF OFFENCES AFFECTING PRIVATE PROPERTY.

## CHAPTER I.

### *Jf burning and other malicious injury to property.*

Art. 586. If any one shall MALICIOUSLY SET FIRE to any DWELLING-
HOUSE, with intent to destroy the same; or shall destroy such house by
an explosion of gunpowder or any other explosive matter, he shall be
imprisoned, at hard labour, during life. If the house be not a dwelling house, but contain personal property of the value of one hundred
dollars, he shall be imprisoned, in like manner, not less than seven
nor more than fourteen years : and if it be empty, or contain personal
property of less value than one hundred dollars, the punishment shall
be a like imprisonment, not less than five nor more than ten years.

Art. 587. A house, within the meaning of this chapter, is any edifice
so built as to come within the denomination of real estate, according
to the definition of that term in this code, being closed in on all sides,
and having the area, which is enclosed by its sides, covered with a roof.
This definition excludes a tent, a booth or an open shed.

Art. 588. A dwelling-house is one in which some person habitually
sleeps or eats his meals, or one that is built and intended for that purpose, although not actually inhabited.

Art. 589. This offence of setting fire to a dwelling-house, is also
committed by setting fire to any building that communicates, by any
combustible matter with the inhabited building, or that is so near to
it as, if the one burns, to cause the other to take fire.

Art. 590. If any one shall, in like manner and with like intent as is above expressed, set fire to any building, not coming within the description of a house, or to any stack of grain or hay, any heap of firewood, or timber, or other collection of combustible produce of the earth, standing or being on the land of another, and of the value of ten dollars or upwards—he shall be imprisoned not less than six nor more than twelve months, or fined not more than five hundred dollars, or both, at the discretion of the court.

Art. 591. The intent must be malicious; therefore, if the house be the property of the person who does the act, and no other person has any interest therein, he is guilty of no offence. But if there be any other person interested as joint owner, usufructuary, lessee, or in any other manner whatever; or if another have an incumbrance on the house, or have made insurance thereon—the offence is incurred, although the person committing the act may have some estate in the house. This article applies to all the offences described in this chapter.

Art. 592. If one set fire to his own house, with the intent that the fire shall communicate to that of another, and it does so communicate—he is guilty of this offence.

Art. 593. The offence is not complete merely by the burning of the combustible matter placed for communicating the fire. It must actually have communicated to the house; but it is not necessary for this purpose, that it should be completely destroyed.

Art. 594. If any building destroyed by fire, contrary to the provisions of this section, contain any DOMESTIC ANIMALS, which are destroyed with the building—the punishment shall be increased one-half.

Art. 595. If any one shall, designedly, and with intent to injure, illegally set fire to, or destroy or injure by explosion, any ship or other vessel, boat, flat-boat or raft, which with the cargo, if any there be, is of the value of one hundred dollars or upwards—he shall be imprisoned, at hard labour, not less than three nor more than seven years.

Art. 596. The "intent to injure," mentioned in the articles of this section, means an intent to cause a PECUNIARY loss to some person (other than the offender) having an interest in or upon the property when the act is designedly done. The circumstance that another has an interest in or upon it, is conclusive proof of the intent to injure.

Art. 597. Where death is occasioned by any of the offences described in this section, the offender is guilty of murder; and of assassination, if he intended the death of the party.

Art. 598. If any bodily injury, less than death, is suffered by the fire or explosion, in the execution of the offence—the punishment shall be doubled in all cases where the punishment is less than imprisonment for life.

Art. 599. If any of the offences described in this section be committed during the NIGHT, the punishment shall be increased one-half.

Art. 600. Whoever shall MALICIOUSLY destroy any personal property exclusively belonging to, and in the possession of another, if of any of the kinds hereinbefore described, by any other means than by fire, or if of any other kind, by any means whatever, being of the value of ten dollars or more; or in like manner injure it to that amount, he shall be imprisoned not less than one month, nor more than one year, or shall be fined not exceeding five hundred dollars, or both, and the im-

3 H

prisonment or part of it may be in close custody. If the offence described in this article be committed by poisoning, killing or disabling any animal of any kind usually employed in husbandry, or raised for sale, the punishment shall be doubled, but shall not be less than imprisonment for thirty days in close custody, or a fine of two hundred and fifty dollars.

Art. 601. If any one shall MALICIOUSLY destroy the fences or enclosures of any real property belonging exclusively to another, and in his separate possession, or shall destroy any trees, shrubs or any CROP of any kind growing thereon, if the fences or other things so destroyed are of the value of ten dollars or upwards, he shall be imprisoned not more than one year, or fined not exceeding five hundred dollars, or both; and the imprisonment, or any part thereof, may be in close custody.

Art. 602. If any one shall MALICIOUSLY destroy any original written obligations or original acts, giving an interest in, or a right to any real or personal property, of the value of one hundred dollars, belonging to another, or shall in like manner destroy the copy of any such obligation or act, when by reason of the destruction of the original or other legal cause, such copy is the only proof of the obligation or act, he shall be imprisoned not less than one month, nor more than one year, or be fined not less than fifty, nor more than one thousand dollars, or both, and the imprisonment or any part of it may be in close custody.

Art. 603. If any one shall maliciously or fraudulently remove or destroy any post, stone, tree, or other thing serving as a land-mark to designate a boundary between two different tracts of land, he shall be imprisoned at hard labour not less than one nor more than three years, and shall forfeit his political rights.

Art. 604. Injuries to property by negligence are not the object of penal law.

## CHAPTER II.

### *Of house-breaking.*

Art. 605. Whoever enters a HOUSE secretly, or by force, or threats, or fraud, during the NIGHT, or in like manner enters a HOUSE by day, and conceals himself therein until the NIGHT, with the INTENT in either case of committing a crime, is guilty of the crime of house-breaking, and shall be imprisoned at hard labour not less than ten nor more than fifteen years.

Art. 606. The qualifications of secrecy, force, or fraud, as applied to the entry, in the description of this offence, are intended to exclude every kind of entry but one made by the free consent of the occupant, or of one authorized to give such consent for him, fairly obtained and expressly or impliedly given.

Art. 607. Although a consent be given to an entrance into one part of a house, yet an entrance into any other part, by any of the means and with the intent described in the first article of this section, constitutes the crime of house-breaking.

Art. 608. The term "house," as used in this chapter, comprehends all such as are built for public as well as private use, whether the property of the state, the United States, or any public or private corporation or society.

Art. 609. The entry, in the description of this offence, is not confined to the entrance of the whole body ; the introduction of any part, for the purpose of committing a crime, is sufficient.

Art. 610. If any one shall discharge any fire-arms, or any missile weapon, into a house, with the intent of doing bodily injury to any one in such house, or introduce any instrument for the purpose of drawing out any personal property, it is an entry intended by the description of this offence, although no part of the body of the offender should come within the house.

# CHAPTER III.

*Of the acquisition or appropriation of property by fraud or force.*

Art. 611. Offences of this nature may be committed in the following manner.

1. By the fraudulent appropriation of personal property, which had been delivered to the offender for another purpose.

2. By the like appropriation of property which came to the possession of the offender by finding.

3. By the violation of epistolary correspondence.

4. By obtaining personal property under false pretences.

5. By theft or robbery.

6. By receiving property knowing it to be fraudulently obtained.

## SECTION I.

### Of fraudulent breach of trust.

Art. 612. The following are the acts which may severally constitute this offence:

1st. The fraudulent appropriation of personal property by any one, to whom it shall have been delivered on deposite, sequestration, pledge, or to be carried or repaired, or on any other contract or trust, by which he was bound to deliver or return the thing received.

2d. The fraudulent appropriation of certain specific personal property by any one, to whom it shall have been delivered on a contract of loan for use, or of letting and hiring, after the time at which, according to the contract, the right of use acquired thereby has ceased, or before that time, by a disposition not authorized by such contract.

Art. 613. These two cases refer to a receiving, with an intent to comply with the contract under which the delivery is made, and a subsequent determination of fraud ; if the contract be intended merely as the means of procuring possession, with the intent of making a fraudulent appropriation, it is theft.

Art. 614. The punishment for the offences described in the first article of this section, is imprisonment in close custody, not exceeding six months, if the property be of the value of thirty dollars or under ; and if above that value, the like imprisonment, not exceeding one year.

Art. 615. The giving to another the charge or care of property, subject to the immediate orders of the owner, or the use of it in his presence, or for the purposes of his trade, is not a delivery within the meaning of any articles describing this offence. A fraudulent appropriation of property so placed is theft.

## SECTION II.

### Of fraudulent appropriation of property found.

Art. 616. If any one shall come, by finding, to the possession of any personal property, of which he shall know, or have reason to believe any DESIGNATED person to be the owner, and shall fraudulently appropriate the same, or any part thereof, he shall be imprisoned in close custody, not less than sixty days nor more than six months, and shall be fined in a sum equal to double the amount of the property so appropriated.

Art. 617. Where property has been casually lost, and the finder has no reason to believe any designated person to be the owner of the property found, if it is of the value of more than twenty dollars, and the finder shall conceal the same, and appropriate it to his own use, he shall be fined in a sum equal to double the amount of the property appropriated.

Art. 618. If the property be found in a place where property of the same description is usually placed, or suffered to be ; or if in an unusual place, in one where the finder knows it to have been designedly put by the owner ; or if the property be domestic animals, and they are found in a place in which they are usually kept, or to which they are suffered to go, or may reasonably be supposed to have strayed, this is not finding within the meaning of the preceding articles ; and if the person taking the property fraudulently appropriate it, he is guilty of theft.

Art. 619. If any one shall fraudulently appropriate property, taken or driven on shore from any vessel, wrecked, stranded or burned, on the sea-coast, or on any of the rivers, lakes or harbours of this state, he shall be imprisoned, at hard labour, not less than one nor more than three years.

Art. 620. The property, described in the last preceding article, shall be presumed to be fraudulently appropriated, within the meaning of that article, in all cases where the property is concealed and the directions contained in the Code of Procedure, on the subject of wrecked property, are not pursued.

## SECTION III.

### Of the violation of epistolary correspondence.

Art. 621. If any one shall open and read, or cause to be read, any sealed letter, without being authorized so to do either by the writer of such letter or the person to whom it is addressed, or by law—he shall be fined not more than fifty dollars, or imprisoned not less than ten nor more than thirty days.

Art. 622. Whoever shall MALICIOUSLY PUBLISH OR CIRCULATE the whole or any part of a letter so opened, knowing the manner in which it was obtained, and without legal authority—shall be fined not less than fifty nor more than two hundred dollars, or imprisoned not less than one nor more than three months.

Art. 623. If property of any assignable value be taken from such letter, it is theft.

Art. 624. If any one shall TAKE any letter, whether sealed or not, or any writing whatever, from the legal possession of another, without his consent, and shall maliciously publish the same—he shall be fined not less than one hundred nor more than five hundred dollars, or imprisoned not less than one nor more than six months.

## SECTION IV.

### Of obtaining property by false pretences.

Art. 625. If any one, with a fraudulent intent, shall obtain any personal property, or the release of any right, of any ASSIGNABLE value, with the consent of the owner or possessor thereof, by means of any false pretences, without the use of which such consent would not have been given—he is guilty of this offence.

Art. 626. No mere declaration of the value, or cost, or quality, or quantity of the property sold, although such declaration should be false: no promise of a consideration for the delivery of personal property, although such promise be not performed: no mere declaration that the party is able to pay, or perform or deliver the consideration : is a false pretence under the above definition.

Art. 627. The owner's consent to the delivery of the property is an essential part of the definition of this offence, and a characteristic that distinguishes it from theft. A temporary possession for examination, or any other purpose, while the contract for the transfer is pending, is not such a delivery, by consent, as is required by the description of the offence. And if the fraudulent appropriation be made before such final consent be given, it is theft.

Art. 628. This consent is presumed to have been given, whenever the consideration is received, and the property is left, or put in the power of the person to whom by the purport of the contract it appears to be transferred, although such consideration should prove worthless or fraudulent. It is also presumed to have been given whenever credit has been given for the price, however short the time.

Art. 629. Credit is presumed to have been given when, although the sale or other transfer was made on a stipulation of paying cash, the seller shall have taken a draft or order, or other security for the amount, and voluntarily left the property in the hands of the vendor.

Art. 630. It is a false pretence for any one to assign or deliver any written contract as his own property, when, to his knowledge, it belongs to another bearing the same name.

Art. 631. It is a false pretence to assume any false description, which would, if true, give greater credit to the party assuming it. By "description," is meant profession, trade, office or employment.

Art. 632. If any one shall commit this offence by falsely personating another, he shall incur the highest punishment designated for the same.

This modification of the offence is committed,

1. By assuming to be another, whose name or credit shall induce the owner to deliver the property.

2. By assuming to be another person bearing the same name as the person who commits the offence.

Art. 633. The assumption need not be by positive words; it is sufficient if, by any device whatever, the person delivering the property, or releasing the right, is designedly made to believe that he who receives such property, or release, is the person whose name or character he assumes.

Art. 634. It is an offence, under the first article of this section, after a sale of personal property and before delivery, to substitute other property of less value than that sold, with intent to defraud the purchaser of the price paid, or to be received.

Art. 635. It is a false pretence to promise immediate payment for personal property, and, after obtaining possession thereof, to refuse either to restore the property or to pay the price. The offence, described in this article, is committed by a refusal to pay or to deliver the property, on demand, at any time within three days after the purchase, if the property be then in the possession of the purchaser, or within one hour if demand be then made, whether the property be in his possession or not.

Art. 636. It is sufficient to make the party liable under the preceding article, if the demand be made at the place where payment was promised to be made, and the not making the payment there is a sufficient refusal within the meaning of the said article.          -

Art. 637. It is a false pretence to give in payment, for any personal property sold and delivered as for cash, any check, bill or order, which the person, giving the same, affirms will be paid at sight, but which he shall, at the time, know to be of no value ; unless such check, bill or order, be taken on the credit of the parties thereto, or some of them, and it shall be presumed to have been so taken whenever it is made payable otherwise than at sight or on demand.

Art. 638. It is a false pretence to sell any merchandize by a sample, taken not from that actually sold, but from other merchandize of a greater value, with intent to defraud.

Art. 639. It is a false pretence to produce a false invoice of merchandize sold, or to produce an invoice of other goods of the same description, affirming it to be the true invoice of the goods sold, for the purpose of deceiving the purchaser as to the cost and value of the property purchased.

Art. 640. It is a false pretence to make, or knowingly to produce, any false letter or other paper, not amounting to forgery, in order to influence another in the purchase or sale, or other disposition of property.

Art. 641. It is obtaining property under a false pretence to procure it by any game, either of skill or chance, or of both, by any other means than those which are given by the regular chances of the game, if it be one of chance ; or by the fair exercise of skill and knowledge of the game, if it be not a game of hazard.

Art. 642. It is a false pretence fraudulently to make any false reports, for the purpose of raising or depressing the price of the public funds, or the stock of any incorporated company ; or to circulate them, knowing them to be false.

Art. 643. The enumeration, contained in this chapter, and in other parts of the code, of certain acts which shall constitute the offence described, does not exclude other acts coming within the definition. Nor does the declaration, that certain other acts are not considered as offences, restrict the exception to those particular acts.

Art. 644. If the value of the property, obtained by an offence under this section, shall not amount to more than thirty dollars, the punishment shall be imprisonment, at hard labour, not exceeding three years; and if the value exceed that sum, the imprisonment shall not be less than one nor more than four years.

SECTION V.

Of theft.

Art. 645. Theft is the FRAUDULENTLY TAKING OF CORPORAL PERSONAL PROPERTY, having some ASSIGNABLE value, and belonging to another, from his possession and without his assent.

Art. 646. The subject on which this offence can operate, is exclusively PERSONAL PROPERTY ; but it embraces every species of that property that can be taken, and excludes only incorporeal rights.

Art. 647. The "TAKING," mentioned in the description of this offence, is that which designates it from the other fraudulent appropriations of property heretofore described. The following rules and illustrations show the nature of the taking intended, and the circumstances under which it constitutes the offence:

1. There must be to constitute this offence a taking, and that taking must be from the possession of the owner; therefore, although there has been a fraudulent appropriation, yet, if the possession was acquired by the accused in such a way as to bring the case within the description of either of the offences made punishable by the preceding part of this chapter, it is not theft.

2. But every fraudulent taking from the possession of the owner, and subsequent appropriation of personal property, which does not come within the description of some one of the offences described in the former sections of this chapter, is either theft or robbery.

3. If any servant or clerk, or person employed as such by any person, receive on account of his employers, from any other person, or from the employer himself, in trust or charge, to be kept or disposed of under the direction of the employer, any such property as is described in the definition of this offence, the possession of such clerk or servant is, as relates to this offence, the possession of his employer; and if the servant or clerk fraudulently appropriate it, it is theft.

4. Whenever the delivery is extorted by fear, it is a taking, within the definition of this offence, and one of those circumstances which constitutes the offence of robbery.

5. The possession of a factor or agent, entrusted with the sale or other alienation of property, is not such a possession of the owner as will make the factor or agent guilty of this offence, if he appropriate the proceeds.

6. Taking alone, without carrying away, is sufficient within the definition.

7. Taking may be either by a removal, or simply by laying hold upon the article, either directly with the hand or by means of any instrument, in such a way as to evince a design to remove it.

8. The offence is complete by the taking; therefore, a voluntary return of the property will not prevent conviction; but it shall lessen the punishment one half.

9. No one can be convicted of theft or robbery for any taking of property, in which he has a joint interest with the person from whose possession it was taken.

10. He who has the general property, of personal property, may commit this offence, by taking the same fraudulently, from one who has a special property in it, with intent to make him answerable for the value.

11. If one of several persons, having a joint interest in personal property, either as partners, husband and wife, or otherwise, deliver it voluntarily to another, who takes it with a fraudulent intent against the other persons interested, it is not theft.

12. Where husband and wife are separated in person and estate, the delivery by the husband of the wife's property, over which she has given him no control, without her assent, to a person who is connusant of the facts, and who takes it with a fraudulent intent, it is theft in both.

13. But where the separation is of property only, no one can be convicted of theft of the wife's property, who shows a voluntary delivery by the husband.

14. The last two preceding rules apply equally to property of the husband, delivered under similar circumstances by the wife.

15. The dispositions of law, in the case of thefts or other offences committed by the wife in company with the husband, are found in the third chapter of the First Book.

16. Neither the ownership nor the legal possession of property is changed by theft alone, without the circumstances required in such case by the Civil Code, in order to produce a change of property; therefore, stolen goods, if fraudulently taken from the thief, are stolen from the original proprietor.

17. The possession of articles of dress or ornament, which are personally used by minor children, who are not of sufficient discretion

to know the value of property, is the possession of the parent or guardian; therefore, such property fraudulently taken, although with the consent of the child, is theft.

Art. 648. Although nothing but corporal personal property, as the same is defined in this code, is the subject of this offence, yet if any one shall sever from any BUILDING, fixed on the land of another, any of the materials of which it is formed, or shall take any produce of the soil, growing on such soil, of the value of five dollars or more, for the purpose of fraudulently appropriating the same ; and in pursuance of such intent, shall remove them from the said land, such severance is sufficient to bring the materials, or other produce taken, within the description of personal property, and make the person taking the same, guilty of theft.

Art. 649. Simple theft, if of property not exceeding in value thirty dollars, is punishable by imprisonment, at hard labour, not exceeding three years. If the property be above the value of thirty dollars, the punishment shall not be less than two nor more than four years.

## SECTION VI.

### Of aggravated theft.

Art. 650. The crime of theft may be aggravated by several circumstances, which are described in the following sections. If theft be not accompanied by any of them, it is simple theft.

## SECTION VII.

### Of theft by effraction.

Art. 651. If any one shall, in the DAY-TIME, with a fraudulent design, enter a house, or a SHIP or other VESSEL, without breaking or other violence, and shall then and there commit a theft, he shall be imprisoned not less than three nor more than six years, at hard labour.

This article does not relate to domestic servants, or other inhabitants of the house in which the theft is committed.

Art. 652. The last article only relates to property being in the house or ship, not in the personal possession of any one in it. Taking property of this last description may be either simple theft, private stealing from the person, or robbery.

Art. 653. If any one break into a house, or into any ship or other vessel, in the day-time, with intent to commit a theft, whether the theft be committed or not, he shall be imprisoned, at hard labour, not less than four nor more than seven years.

Art. 654. If any one be in the house, or in the ship or other vessel, either at the time the offence mentioned in the last two preceding articles is committed, and resist the offender, or be restrained from resisting by fear, the punishment shall be increased one-fourth.

Art. 655. The breaking intended by the last three preceding articles, means—first, that the entry must be made with actual force—the slight-

3 I

est force brings the offender within their purview—the lifting of a latch of a door that is shut—the raising a window—the entry at a window, chimney, or other unusual place—the introduction of the hand or any instrument to draw out the property, through any aperture made for the purpose, although the whole body does not enter, is a breaking.

Art. 656. If any theft shall be committed by breaking any closet, box, or other place of the like nature, in which the property stolen was contained, the punishment shall be not less than four nor more than seven years, at hard labour.

The breaking meant by this article must be by actual force. Not merely lifting the lid of a box, or opening a door, when either are unfastened, the use of false keys, or of the true one fraudulently obtained, is a breaking.

## SECTION VIII.

### Of stealing from the person.

Art. 657. If the theft be committed by privately stealing property from the person of another, the offender shall be imprisoned, at hard labour, not less than two nor more than six years.

Art. 658. By "privately," is meant either without the knowledge of the party whose property is taken, or so suddenly that he has no time to make resistance before the property is carried away.

Art. 659. If the party perceive the theft, and attempt to resist it, and the theft is completed by violence, it is robbery; if not completed, after violence or threats, it is an attempt to rob.

Art. 660. If the article be TAKEN, under the definition heretofore given of that word, the crime of private stealing is complete, although, owing to the difficulty of extricating it from the person of the possessor or from his detection of the attempt, it be not actually carried away.

Art. 661. The theft must be from the person; if the property stolen be in his presence only, it does not amount to this offence.

## SECTION IX.

### Of robbery.

Art. 662. Robbery is theft, committed by fraudulently taking the property of another from his person or in his presence, with his knowledge and against his will; whether it be taken by force, or delivered or suffered to be taken through fear of some illegal injury to person, property or reputation, that is threatened by the robber or his accomplice.

Art. 663. The audacity of an open infringement of the laws, and the alarm and danger it creates, are the characteristics of this species of theft. Wherever either of these occurs, in any degree in the commission of theft, the additional guilt is incurred; therefore, the law gives no measure for the degree of violence necessary to constitute this crime. Any force that accomplishes the object, is sufficient.

Art. 664. No device will be sufficient to give another character to this crime. If the property be fraudulently taken by violence, or thus received when it is surrendered through fear, it is immaterial whether it be done by a direct command, or by a request to give as alms, or under any other pretence.

Art. 665. If, by any of the means which constitute robbery, one is forced to give property for an inadequate price, it is robbery.

Art. 666. If property be stolen by simple theft, and before it is carried away, the owner is forced, by any of the means which constitute robbery, to give up his attempts to recover possession of the property, it is robbery.

Art. 667. Any threat, in order to be an effectual cause for the fear mentioned in the definition of this offence, must be to do some illegal act, productive of injury, either to person, property or character. A threat of withdrawing favour, or doing any other lawful act, is not sufficient.

Art. 668. The threat need not be direct; it is sufficient, if it be expressed indirectly, or by gestures only, so as to produce the effect.

Art. 669. The punishment for this offence is imprisonment, at hard labour, not less than seven nor more than fifteen years.

## SECTION X.

### Of receiving property, knowing it to be fraudulently obtained.

Art .670. Whoever shall receive, either by way of purchase or on any other contract, or for safe keeping or concealment; or shall conceal, or endeavour to conceal any property, knowing it to be fraudulently obtained by any of the acts which, by this chapter, are created offences—shall be punished in the same manner with the principal offender.

Art. 671. It is no objection to the conviction of a receiver, under this section, that the principal offender has not been convicted; but if any one be indicted, and in custody or on bail, for stealing, or otherwise fraudulently obtaining the same property, the person accused as receiver shall not be tried, without his consent, until the prosecution against the principal offender is disposed of.

Art. 672. The offence, described in this section, is a distinct and substantive offence, not governed by the rules which apply to accessaries.

Art. 673. If any one, knowing that property has been taken by theft, aid the thief in removing it to its final destination or place of concealment—such person is an accomplice in the theft, and not a receiver.

Art. 674. An accomplice in a theft, who is not present at the act, and afterwards receives the property, is punishable as an accomplice.

Art. 675. Nothing in this chapter contained, applies to the taking of property, which the person taking believes to be his own, or that of another who has authorized him to take it.

# CHAPTER IV.

### *Of attempts to defraud by threats.*

Art. 676. Whoever, with a FRAUDULENT intent, shall threaten another with any injury to his person, reputation or property, accompanied by a demand of property, or of service, as the means of avoiding the execution of such threat, shall be imprisoned at hard labour, not less than one nor more than five years, provided such offence do not amount to robbery.

Art. 677. The injury intended by the last preceding article, means not only a direct injury, by means of actual violence, but also that which is indirect, such as a threat of bringing an accusation for some offence, either juridically, or by public defamation.

Art. 678. The injury need not be threatened directly against the property, person, or reputation of the person to whom the threat is addressed, if it be against the reputation or person of the wife or husband, ascendant or descendant, of the person whom it is intended to defraud, it is sufficient to constitute the offence.

Art. 679. A threat to vilify the memory of a deceased ancestor, is a sufficient threat to constitute this crime.

Art. 680. This offence is committed, whether the threat be verbal or written ; and if written, whether with or without a signature.

Art. 681. It is not necessary that the demand of property, or the threat, should be in direct terms, if such be the plain meaning, it is sufficient.

Art. 682. If any one shall make any such threats by writing, printing, sending or delivering a letter or writing, whether in his own name, in a fictitious name, or anonymously, or shall procure such letter to be written, printed, sent or delivered, without any intent to DEFRAUD, and without any demand of property, as the means of avoiding the execution of the threat, but merely from MALICE, he shall be imprisoned not less than one nor more than six months, and fined not less than fifty nor more than three hundred dollars, and the whole or part of the imprisonment shall be in close custody.

# CHAPTER V.

### *Of conspiracy.*

Art. 683. Conspiracy is an agreement between two or more persons to do any unlawful act, or any of those designated acts which become, by the combination, injurious to others.

The several conspiracies that are punishable by law, are :

1. A conspiracy to commit an offence.
2. Falsely to accuse and prosecute another of committing an offence.

3. To do certain injuries that are neither crimes nor offences if done by an individual.

Art. 684. The agreement constitutes the offence, and it is a distinct offence from any other that may be committed in carrying it into effect; and to complete the offence, it is not necessary that any act should be proved to have been done in furtherance of the agreement.

Art. 685. But if the accused show that the design was abandoned, before any act was done towards its execution, voluntarily, and not from any obstacle, the punishment shall be lessened one-half.

Art. 686. Where the conspiracy is to commit an offence, the punishment shall be one-half of that denounced by law against the offence which it was the object of the agreement to commit, if it be not carried into effect, and in addition to such punishment, if it is committed.

Art. 687. Where the conspiracy is falsely to accuse and prosecute another of an offence, the punishment shall be one-half of that which would have been inflicted if the offence had been proved.

Art. 688. It is not necessary, for supporting an indictment for a conspiracy, to accuse and prosecute; to show that the party has been acquitted on such prosecution; but if the prosecution, which is alleged to be false, be pending, the defendants in the indictment for conspiracy are entitled to have it tried before they are themselves put upon trial.

Art. 689. The cases not comprehended in the foregoing articles of this chapter, and in which conspiracies become unlawful, are as follows, to wit:

1. Every one has a right, individually, to determine what he will give as a consideration for services or property to be furnished to him: he has the same right to withhold his own service or property, unless the value he shall place upon them be paid. But an agreement, stipulating that the parties to it will not give more than a certain price for any particular species of service or property, or that they will not furnish or render any such property or service for less than a stipulated price, is injurious to that free competition necessary to commerce. And if such agreement be made between two or more persons not being partners, it is a conspiracy, and shall be punished by simple imprisonment, for not more than three months, or by fine not exceeding three hundred dollars, or both.

2. If the agreement be made between employers, not to give above certain wages to workmen, imprisonment shall always form part of the sentence, and the imprisonment cannot be for less than ten days.

3. If the agreement constituting the conspiracy, in any case whatever, purport to inflict any injury on the person, property or reputation, of those who will not enter into such agreement, the punishment shall be doubled.

4. Any malicious combination or agreement to injure any individual, or description of persons, in their reputation, or profession, or trade, or property, by agreeing not to employ them, or by other means that would not otherwise amount to an offence, is a conspiracy, and shall be punished by fine, not exceeding two hundred dollars, or imprisonment, not exceeding sixty days, or both.

5. Any combination or agreement to raise the price of any articles of food, fuel or drink, is a conspiracy, and is punishable by fine, not

exceeding five hundred dollars, and imprisonment, not exceeding three months.

6. An agreement of partners, solely between themselves, is not such an agreement as can constitute this offence, unless the partnership be specially entered into for the purpose of making such conspiracy ; in which case, or whenever the benefit (if any) to be derived from the conspiracy is agreed to be participated, the punishment shall be doubled.

7. An agreement to abridge or increase the quantity or time of labour, comes within the description of limiting the price to be given, or determining that which must be received.

## GENERAL PROVISION.

### *Of accessaries.*

Art. 690. All accessaries shall be punished by one-fourth of the punishment that would have been suffered by the principal offender ; provided, that it shall, in no case, exceed a fine of three hundred dollars, and imprisonment, in close custody, for one year

# A CODE OF PROCEDURE.

# INTRODUCTORY TITLE.

## CHAPTER I.

### *Preamble.*

Art. 1. It is not enough-to have defined offences and designated the punishments adapted to them : every citizen must not only be taught what actions he is to avoid as offences, but must also be informed by what means he may prevent an injury he apprehends, or bring the offender to justice if the wrong be already suffered.

Judges, other magistrates, and ministers of justice, must have their duties defined not only for their own guidance, but that, being generally understood, they may receive the high reward of public approbation, or suffer disgrace or punishment ; as those duties are performed, neglected, or wilfully abandoned.

These considerations have induced the general assembly of Louisiana to enact this Code of Procedure, forming a part of their System of Penal Law. It is divided into three books :

The first contains the means of preventing offences, and of putting an end to such as continue ; it designates the cases in which the military force may be employed in aid of the civil power, and prescribes the rules by which it shall be governed in that service.

The second directs the mode of proceeding for bringing an offender to punishment, from the complaint to the final judgment.

The third gives the forms to be used in all the judicial proceedings prescribed or authorized by this code.

## CHAPTER II.

### *General provisions.*

Art. 2. This code being a part of the general system of Penal Law, all the words used herein, are employed in the same sense that is given to them when they are used in any other part of the system.

Art. 3. All the general provisions in the second chapter of the first book of the Code of Crimes and Punishments, and all such general provisions in other parts thereof as apply to the subject of this code,

3 K

have the same force in this that they have in the Code of Crimes and Punishments.

Art. 4. The objects which the general assembly has endeavoured to effect by this code, are:

1. *The prevention of intended offences.*—This is attained by pointing out on what occasions, and by what means an individual may call for the interference of the magistrate, or of his fellow citizens, or may use his own physical powers to resist any attempted invasion of his rights or those of others.

2. *The protection of innocence against unjust accusations.*—No laws can in all cases protect against perjury, error, or the combination of circumstances which sometimes gives to innocence the appearance of guilt; but they can, and ought to provide every facility that human prudence can suggest, and human power can effect, for making truth evident, and detecting error; they should also, by avoiding all entangling forms, insure an acquittal to every one who is accused unless his guilt be made apparent.

3. *To take away from the guilty all hope of escape by a resort to formal or technical objections.*—The great object of penal law is the prevention of offences by the example of punishment, the intent of all codes of procedure is to insure this end; therefore, every system must be imperfect which permits the form to defeat the substance of the law, and suffers a criminal ever to escape punishment, from any defect of form in his prosecution.

4. *To give to criminal proceedings the greatest degree of despatch that is consistent with the prosecution of public justice on the one side, and the defence of private rights on the other.*—Delay inflicts punishment on the innocent, or lessens the force of example, by punishing the guilty after the crime he has committed is forgotten.

5. *To subject the innocent to no expense, and to impose none on the guilty but such as may be measured and apportioned to the offence.*—To add to the evil of an unjust accusation the obligation of paying for it, would be an absurdity and an injustice that no law should sanction; and the indiscriminate infliction of costs on every conviction without regard to the circumstances of the offender or the nature of his offence, is scarcely less unjust.

6. *To abolish all forms, that produce vexation to the prosecutor, to the accused or to the witnesses; and to subject no one who is concerned in a criminal proceeding to any inconvenience, but such as are absolutely necessary for the execution of the law.*—The obligations and restraints imposed by the most perfect laws, are necessarily attended with inconvenience to those who are called on to execute them, or have become subject to their animadversion; to reduce them to the lowest degree consistent with public safety, is one object of the present code.

7. *To render the whole form of proceeding simple and perfectly intelligible to all.*—The utility of this object is so apparent as to render no illustration necessary.

Art. 5. These objects: security to the innocent, not only from the danger of an unjust conviction, but the apprehension of it; the prevention of intended offences; the destruction of all hope of escape from merited punishment by a resort to formal objections; despatch; economy; the abolition of all vexatious proceedings, and the establishment of simplicity in forms, have been the principal objects in the formation of this code, and they are conspicuously placed here that future legislatures may weigh their importance, examine how far the different provisions of this code are in conformity with them, and in what points they are not adhered to, in order that the proper amendments may be made to give them effect.

# BOOK I.

OF THE MEANS OF PREVENTING OFFENCES; OF SUPPRESSING THOSE WHICH ARE CONTINUOUS, AND OF EMPLOYING THE MILITARY IN AID OF THE CIVIL POWER.

## TITLE I.

### OF PREVENTING OFFENCES.

Art. 6. Offences may be prevented,
1. By lawful resistance.
2. By the intervention of the officers of justice.
Art. 7. Resistance to the offender in the commission of the offence may be made in the cases and in the manner prescribed by law, either by the person about to be injured or by others, without the intervention of the officers of justice.

## CHAPTER I.

### Of resistance by the party offended.

Art. 8. Resistance, proportioned to the degree of aggression, may be used to prevent any of those acts described in the Code of Crimes and Punishments, as "Offences against the person."
Art. 9. The same degree of resistance may be opposed to prevent any illegal attempt by force to take or injure property in the lawful possession of the person holding it.
Art. 10. By the resistance proportioned to the aggression in the above articles is meant, such as is sufficient for the purpose of preventing the offence, and no more.
Art. 11. The Code of Crimes and Punishments in the titles relative to offences affecting person and property, contains rules by which the exercise of this right is elucidated and modified.

## CHAPTER II.

*Of the rights and duties of third persons in preventing the commission or continuance of offences.*

Art. 12. It is the duty of every citizen not only to abstain from offences himself, but to prevent their being committed by another, if he can do so without injury to himself: if he voluntarily incur the risk of such injury it is a merit which entitles him to public esteem and in certain cases provided by law, to an honorary reward. The cases in which this duty of interfering to prevent offences is permitted, and those in which it is enforced under a penal sanction, are detailed in the following articles of this chapter.

Art. 13. In all cases where an offence is seriously threatened or intended, it is a moral duty in him to whose knowledge such intent may come, to prevent its execution by notice given either to the party who may be affected, or to a magistrate. It is an offence to have omitted such notice, in all cases where the crime is subsequently committed, and is one of those punishable by imprisonment for life, provided, the intention has been made manifest by express words, or by doing some act preparatory to the commission of the crime : whoever shall be guilty of this offence shall be fined not exceeding one hundred dollars or imprisoned not exceeding sixty days.

Art. 14. In cases in which the intention has been shown by an act which itself is an offence, (such as a conspiracy) and the intent is to commit a crime punishable by imprisonment for life : the person having a knowledge of such conspiracy or other preparatory act, who shall not give notice of it to a magistrate or to the party about to be injured, shall incur the punishment denounced by the last preceding article, whether the intended crime be committed or not.

Art. 15. After an offence has been committed, the mere omission to denounce it is not punishable, if not accompanied by such an act as renders the person an accessary.

Art. 16. Every species of such illegal violence to the person or property as is by the Code of Crimes and Punishments constituted an offence, may be suppressed after it has begun to be exercised, by the resistance not only of the party injured, but by that of others who may come to his aid, but they are bound in exercising this right to proportion the means and degree of resistance to the violence offered, according to the rules that are prescribed to the party injured in the last preceding chapter, and the parts of the code to which it refers.

Art. 17. All those who are legally called on by any magistrate or officer of justice in the execution of his duties, are not only justified in giving their aid in suppressing acts of illegal violence, and arresting offenders, but are bound to do so, under the penalty of a fine not exceeding fifty dollars.

Art. 18. If any one shall voluntarily incur any great danger, or use extraordinary diligence, or show unusual skill in preventing or suppressing an offence, or in arresting an offender, he shall be entitled to

an honorary certificate made by the court, having the highest penal jurisdiction in the district of his residence, which certificate shall be entered on the minutes of the court, and published three times in three
successive years, and authenticated copies shall be sent to the governor
of the state, and to the president of the senate, to serve as recommen-
dations for an appointment to any office in which the qualities he has
shown may be useful.

Art. 19. In cases of extraordinary exertion, coming within the intent
of the last preceding article, which in the opinion of the judge, and of
the governor of the state, shall merit such distinction, a piece of plate
of the value of one hundred dollars, with a suitable inscription, to be
executed under the direction of the governor, shall be added to the
honorary certificate.

Art. 20. Whoever shall give such information to a magistrate as
shall lead to the conviction of any one guilty of fighting a duel, or giving or accepting a challenge, or forgery, or any crime punishable by
imprisonment for life, shall be entitled to receive, on the certificate of
the judge and public prosecutor in the court where the conviction was
had, the sum of fifty dollars, from the treasurer of the state, out of the
moneys received for fines.

Art. 21. Neither the party immediately injured by any of the crimes
referred to in the last article, nor an accomplice in the crime, are entitled to the recompense therein mentioned.

Art. 22. The crime of rape being one of those that can only be prosecuted on the complaint of the party injured, is not included in those
for the discovery of which the recompense is offered.

Art. 23. When laws are just, whoever contributes to their execution,
renders an acceptable and an honourable service to his country, and he
ought no more to be reproached for receiving a recompense for the
trouble of denouncing an offender, than for taking a salary for any other
public service ; therefore, to repress the effects of a vulgar and injurious
prejudice, it is declared to be an offence for any one in writing or in
any other way by which defamation may be committed, to use reproachful or insulting words against any person, or endeavour to bring him
into contempt, or excite the public indignation against him for having
given information against any offender, or for having received the recompense granted by law ; and the offender shall be punished by fine
not less than twenty nor more than one hundred dollars.


CHAPTER III.


*Of the prevention of offences by the intervention of officers of justice.*

Art. 24. When any one fears, with JUST REASON, that another intends
to commit an offence against his person or property, with violence, he
may apply to a magistrate, who shall without delay take the declaration
of the applicant, under oath, reduced to writing ; and if it appears that
he has any reason to fear the commission of such an offence as is above
described from any DESIGNATED PERSON, he may cause such person to

be arrested and brought before him by warrant, which must substantially state the application.

Art. 25. When any one so arrested is brought before the magistrate, he shall hear any statement or proof the accused has to offer, and if from such statement and evidence it appear that the complainant has mistaken the intention of the accused, and has no cause of fear, the prisoner shall be discharged ; if he fail in showing that the application is groundless, the magistrate shall direct him to give bond with sufficient security that he will commit no offence against the person or property of the complainant.

Art. 26. The penalty of such bond shall be determined by the rules laid down in this code, for the government of magistrates in taking bail.

Art. 27. If the bond be not executed according to the order of the magistrate, the prisoner shall be committed to prison, and shall remain in custody until the bond shall be executed according to the order.

Art. 28. If from the nature of the evidence offered, or from the demeanour of the prisoner, the magistrate has just reason to believe that the prisoner intends an offence against the person or property of any persons who cannot be particularly designated, he may order the bond to be conditioned that he will commit no offence against the person or property of any one.

Art. 29. The bond shall be limited in its operation to the term of twelve months ; but it may be for a shorter time ; and at any time within the last month, the complainant may renew his application, and the order for security may be renewed on the oath of the party, declaring that he still fears the execution of the prisoner's former designs, provided the magistrate, after hearing the circumstances of the case, shall deem such fear well founded.

Art. 30. Any magistrate who is present when any offence, accompanied with violence, is committed, may, without any other proof, order the offender to be arrested, and compel him to give security in the manner above directed, to refrain from the exercise of any illegal force.

Art. 31. Any person who knows or has reason to suspect that an offence, such as is distinguished in this code as one of those against person or property is intended to be committed, may apply to a magistrate, who shall hear the proof, and if he be convinced of the existence of such intention, shall cause the person accused to be arrested, and compelled to give security in the manner before directed.

Art. 32. Courts may on any conviction add to their sentence that after the execution of the punishment is complete, and before the defendant, if in custody, be discharged, he shall give security in the form and for the time above directed, either that he will not commit any particular offence or any designated species of offences, or generally, that he will commit no offence for the time limited. But this power is only to be exercised where, from the character of the party or his conduct in committing the offence, there is good reason to apprehend a repetition of that offence, or the commission of some other.

Art. 33. If the condition of the bond be forfeited, it shall be put in suit by the public prosecutor, who must specify in his petition in such suit the offence which caused the breach of the condition of the bond, with the same certainty that is required in an indictment, and must prove the same by the same evidence that would be required on a trial for the same offence.

Art. 34. At any time before the breach of the condition of such bond, the surety may discharge himself by surrendering the principal, in the manner herein directed in the case of bail for appearance.

Art. 35. Individuals have also a right to prevent the consequences of a theft by seizing any personal property which has been stolen, or which there is good reason to believe has been stolen, and bringing it with the supposed offender, if he can be taken, before a magistrate for examination, or delivering it to an officer of justice for that purpose ; but this must be done openly, and the whole without delay.

Art. 36. When the nature of the case and the proof offered to the magistrate, of any intended injury to person or property, justifies and requires it in his opinion, he may order a sufficient number of officers of justice to guard the person or property threatened, or may, according to the directions hereinafter contained, require military aid for that purpose.

Art. 37. If any one be brought before a magistrate by virtue of an application under the first article of this chapter, where the complainant has made oath that he fears violence, but it does not appear to the magistrate that from the circumstances such fears are well grounded, he shall, nevertheless, before discharging the prisoner, admonish him of the nature and consequences of the offence which the applicant fears he will commit, and if after such admonition the prisoner shall commit such offence, he shall suffer the maximum of the punishment assigned to the same.

Art. 38. The constitution of the state gives to every citizen the right "freely to speak, write and print on any subject, being responsible for the abuse of that liberty ;" therefore, no law can be made to prevent any intended defamation in either of those modes ; but if any one shall make oath that he is informed and believes, and shall convince the magistrate that he has good reason to believe that another is about to PUBLISH, SELL or CIRCULATE, or is continuing to sell, publish or circulate any libel against him, or any such publication as is forbidden by the Code of Crimes and Punishments, in the chapter of offences against morals and decency, the magistrate shall cause the person accused to be summoned to appear before him, and shall admonish him of the nature and consequences of the offence which the applicant fears he will commit ; and if after such admonition the accused shall commit such offence, he shall suffer the maximum of the punishment assigned to the same.

Art. 39. On a conviction for a libel, or for any publication forbidden by the chapter of the Code of Crimes and Punishments concerning offences against morals and decency, the court shall order all the copies of the publication on which the conviction was had ; and which remain in the hands of the defendant, to be seized and destroyed ; and if it shall appear that after the commencement of the prosecution was notified to the defendant, he shall have sold or circulated any copies of such publication, he shall suffer the maximum of the punishment assigned to the offence.

Art. 40. The court shall, in like manner, on a prosecution for selling unwholesome provisions or liquors, or adulterated medicines, order them to be seized, and after conviction they shall be destroyed ; and any sale made by the accused during the pendency of the prosecution, shall produce the same effects as to the punishment that is directed in the last preceding article with respect to libels.

Art. 41. Another case in which the court must interfere to prevent offences is, by ordering the removal of all such obstructions in public and common property, and all such establishments injurious to public health, as shall be found by a conviction of the offender to have been made.

## CHAPTER IV.

*Of search warrants, as the means of preventing the commission of crimes and the loss of property by theft.*

Art. 42. A search warrant is an order in writing made by a magistrate, directed to an officer of justice, commanding him to search for certain specified articles, supposed to be in the possession of one who is charged with having obtained them illegally, or who keeps them with the intent of using them as the means of committing a certain designated crime.

Art. 43. The power of granting this writ is one in the exercise of which much is necessarily left to the discretion of the magistrate ; he is, however, bound by the following rules in granting the warrant, and the ministerial officer by those which are afterwards laid down for his conduct in executing it.

*Rules for the magistrate in granting a search warrant.*

1. Search warrants can only be granted for the following purposes, that is to say :

To discover property taken by theft or under false pretences, or found and fraudulently appropriated.

To seize forged instruments in writing or counterfeited coin intended to be passed, or the instruments or materials prepared for making them.

To seize arms or munitions prepared for the purpose of insurrection or riot.

To discover articles necessary to be produced on the trial of one accused of a crime under the circumstances hereinafter stated.

2. A search warrant can be granted in no case but on an AFFIDAVIT, made by a credible person.

3. If the application be to search for property taken by theft or under false pretences, the affidavit must state that the property has been lost by one of these offences ; it must describe the property, and state a belief and the reason of such belief, that the property is concealed in a certain place, describing it.

4. If forged papers, false coin, or the instruments or materials for making them, form the object of the application, the affidavit must state a belief and the reason on which it is founded, that those articles or some of them are concealed in a certain place, describing it, with intent to commit a crime.

5. If the application be to search for arms or munitions prepared for insurrection or riot, the affidavit must state a belief and reasonable

3 L

grounds for such belief, that a conspiracy has been formed, or an unlawful assembly held, for the purpose of preparing the means for executing those offences, and that the arms or munitions were part of such preparation ; and must also describe the place in which it is suspected they are deposited.

6. When any one accused of a crime before a magistrate, to whom it shall appear from the circumstances in evidence before him, that the production of some weapon, implement or other article, will be necessary on the trial of the accusation, if it shall appear by the oath of at least one witness, that there is good reason to believe that such article is concealed in a certain place, this warrant may also issue.

7. The designation of a house by the name of the owner or the occupant, or by the number or situation, is a sufficient description of place under the preceding articles.

8. If the magistrate be satisfied of the truth of the allegations in the affidavit, he shall make his warrant in the form prescribed for that purpose in this code, but no variation from that form shall affect the validity of the warrant, provided it be not deficient in one of the following requisites :

*First.* It must be in WRITING, and signed by the magistrate with his name ; and the designation of the office he holds, must appear either by the signature or in the form of the warrant.

*Second.* It must be directed to the sheriff or to some other officer of justice : if to the sheriff, it may be by the designation of his office ; if to any other officer of justice, his name as well as his office must be put in the direction.

*Third.* It must direct him to search for and bring before the magistrate to be disposed of according to law, the property or articles specified in the affidavit, describing it as set forth in the affidavit.

*Fourth.* The place to be searched must be specified with reasonable certainty.

*Fifth.* The officer must be directed to execute the warrant in the day time.

*Sixth.* The officer must be directed to bring the property described, and the person in whose possession it may be found, before the magistrate for examination, without delay.

9. When the property is brought before the magistrate, if upon the examination and evidence offered him it shall be identified to be the same with that described in the affidavit, and that it was taken or held for the purpose mentioned therein, he shall cause an inventory to be publicly taken thereof, in the presence of the party in whose possession it was found and of the applicant for the warrant, if they choose to attend ; one copy of which shall be given to each of them, one kept by the sheriff, and another filed by the magistrate, with his proceedings, for the purpose of being sent with the articles seized to the court that shall try the offence.

10. If the magistrate discovers either that the property seized is not the same with that described in the affidavit and warrant, or that there is no good reason for the suspicions set forth in the affidavit, he shall direct the property to be restored, and the possessor, if brought before him, discharged.

11. If the person in whose possession the property was found, shall be brought before the magistrate in obedience to the writ, he shall pro-

ceed to his examination in the manner directed for examinations on arrests, and shall either discharge, commit or let him to bail, as is directed in that part of this code.

*Rules for the government of officers of justice in the execution of search warrants.*

1. If the warrant be directed to a sheriff, it may be executed by him or any of his known deputies previously appointed, but if he make a special deputy for the purpose of the deputation, the name of the person shall be written on the warrant.

2. If the warrant be directed by the magistrate to any other officer of justice, he must see that his name as well as his office is written in the warrant, and in all cases the officer must see that the warrant contain all the requisites above stated, to give it validity ; if it do not, he is not bound to execute it.

3. Before executing the warrant, the officer must give notice of its execution to the person who applied for it, that he may be present and identify the property if it be found.

4. The warrant must be executed in the presence of two inhabitants of the parish, who shall sign the return as witnesses.

5. It can only be executed in the DAY TIME.

6. No other place than that designated in the warrant can be searched, but the whole of that may be examined.

7. The officer charged with the warrant, if a HOUSE is designated as the place to be searched, may enter it without demanding permission if he find it open ; if the doors be shut, he must declare his office and his business, and demand entrance ; if the doors be not opened, he may break them. When entered, he may demand that any other part of the house, or any closet, or other closed place in which he has reason to believe the property is concealed, may be opened for his inspection, and he may break them if it is refused.

8. If required, the officer must show his warrant.

9. He makes himself liable to damages and to the penalties prescribed by the Code of Crimes and Punishments in cases of misbehaviour in office, by any unnecessary force, harshness or ill usage in the discharge of this duty.

10. An inventory of the property seized must be made before it is removed, and signed by the officer and the two witnesses.

11. No other property but that specified in the warrant must be seized.

12. If the property specified in the warrant be seized, the person in whose possession it was found must be arrested, according to the forms in this code for making arrests, and with the property brought for examination before the magistrate who issued the warrant.

13. A return shall be indorsed or annexed to the warrant, stating what was done in obedience to it, and signed by the officer and the two witnesses.

Art. 44. Whoever shall maliciously and without reasonable cause, procure any search warrant to be issued and executed, shall be fined not less than fifty nor more than three hundred dollars, or imprisoned not less than thirty days nor more than six months, and the imprisonment, or any part of it, may be in close custody.

Art. 45. If any magistrate shall issue a search warrant without a previous affidavit, as required by this chapter, he shall suffer the punishment mentioned in the last preceding article, and be deprived of his office.

Art. 46. Any officer of justice, who in executing a search warrant, shall exceed his authority to the injury of any one, shall be imprisoned not exceeding sixty days, besides suffering the punishment assigned to any other offence he may have committed by such illegal conduct.

# TITLE II.

## OF SUPPRESSING PERMANENT OFFENCES.

Art. 47. Permanent offences are such as are renewed by a continued succession of the same acts which first created them. They may affect the public tranquillity, the public health, the public property, or the person, the reputation, or the property of individuals.

# CHAPTER I.

*Of suppressing permanent offences against the public tranquillity.*

Art. 48. The mode in which magistrates and officers of justice are to proceed in the suppression of offences of this nature, is declared in the title that treats of those offences in the Code of Crimes and Punishments, and will be further provided for in the next title of this book.

# CHAPTER II.

*Of suppressing permanent offences against public health and safety.*

Art. 49. Whenever an indictment shall be found against any one for carrying on a business injurious to the health of those in the vicinity, if the indictment shall charge that any persons have actually suffered in their health from the exercise of such business, the court on the application of those interested and after hearing the person accused and receiving statements on oath on both sides, may in their discretion enjoin the person accused, in such penalty as they may deem reasonable, not to carry on the said business, or to carry it on in a place or in a manner that will not prove injurious to the health of others until the trial; and if a conviction shall be had on such indictment, the injunction shall be perpetual in conformity with the provisions of the third chapter of the first title of this book.

Art. 50. In like manner if an indictment be found against any one for carrying on a manufacture of powder or other dangerous operation, contrary to the provisions of the Code of Crimes and Punishments, a like injunction, and an order for the removal of the dangerous substance to a safe distance may be made by the court in which the indictment is found.

## CHAPTER III.

*Of suppressing permanent offences against the public enjoyment of property held for common use of all the citizens.*

Art. 51. If any one shall erect any building or make any other permanent obstruction which shall prevent the free use of any public property held for the common use of all the citizens, and which shall have been in such common use for twelve months next preceding the time of erecting such obstruction, the judge of the court of the highest criminal jurisdiction in the district may on complaint and proof of the facts above stated, cite the party accused of making such obstruction, to appear before him, and in a summary way shall take evidence of the facts, and if the inconvenience to the public from the obstruction be so great, as in his opinion to render it improper to wait the event of a trial for the offence, and the fact of one year's previous possession and use in the public is clearly proved, he may order such obstruction to be removed by the sheriff.

Art. 52. No further penalty can be imposed until a conviction take place, on an indictment or information for the offence.

Art. 53. If no indictment or information be filed against the party whose building has been removed, or if on the trial he shall be acquitted by showing title to the property on which it was erected, he is entitled to an indemnity from the person making the complaint, for any damage he may have suffered by the removal.

## CHAPTER IV.

*Of the suppression of permanent offences against morals and decency.*

Art. 54. In cases of publications which come within this description of offences, the suppressive remedy is set forth in the      article of the third chapter and first title of this book ; if the offence be committed by indecent exposure, it is suppressed on complaint and arrest, in the manner directed for other offences, and by taking security for good behaviour.

# CHAPTER V.

## *Of suppressing permanent offences to reputation.*

Art. 55. The only cases and the only manner in which the suppression of the offences mentioned in the title of this chapter can be made, are those detailed in the        articles of the third chapter and first title of this book.

# CHAPTER VI.

## *Of the suppression of permanent offences affecting the person by assault and battery.*

Art. 56. The continuance of assault and battery may be suppressed in the manner heretofore indicated in this and in the Code of Crimes and Punishments, by resistance of the party aggrieved, or of those who come to his aid, and by the arrest of the offender, and forcing him to give security to keep the peace.

# CHAPTER VII.

## *Of suppressing offences against personal liberty.*

Art. 57. The suppressive remedy for offences of the nature indicated in the title of this chapter, is by writ of *habeas corpus;* the nature of which remedy, and the mode of applying it, are detailed in the following sections of this chapter.

### SECTION I.

#### Definition and form of this writ.

Art. 58. A writ of *habeas corpus* is an order in writing, issued in the name of the state, by a judge or court of competent jurisdiction, directed to any one having a person in his custody, or under his restraint, commanding him to produce such a person at a certain time and place, and to state the reason why he is held in custody, or under restraint.

Art. 59. The writ of *habeas corpus* is to be, as nearly as circumstances will permit, in the following form, *to wit :—*

The state of Louisiana to A. B. You are commanded to have C. D. in your custody, as is said, detained, or under your restraint, kept, before E. F. judge of, (describing the office of the magistrate issuing the writ, or if issued by a court, inserting the style of such court) on the day of        at        o'clock, in the forenoon or afternoon (as the case may be) of the same day, at (naming the place) or forthwith (as the case may be), and that you then and there state in writing, the cause of detaining the said person, and produce your authority for so doing, and hereof you are not to fail under the heavy penalties denounced by law against those who disobey this writ. E. F. judge, &c. or G. H. clerk of the court of, &c.

Art. 60. The writ of *habeas corpus* (if issued by a judge) must be signed by him, or (if issued by a court) must be signed by the clerk, and sealed with the seal of such court.

Art. 61. The proceedings under this writ are considered as the most effectual safeguard of personal liberty against public or private attempts to invade it. It is therefore declared, that in all cases where there may be any doubt on the construction of any provision in this chapter, that construction must be given which is most favourable to the person applying for relief under it, and which will give the most extensive operation in all cases, to the remedies hereby provided against illegal restraint.

Art. 62. The writ of *habeas corpus* is not to be disobeyed for any defect of form. It is sufficient ; 1st, If the person to whom it is directed, be designated, either by the style of his office (if he have any), or by such other appellation or description as may make it understood by one of common understanding, that he is the person intended, and any one who may be served with this writ, who has, in fact, the custody of the person directed to be produced, or who exercises a restraint over him, cannot avoid obedience thereto, although the writ may be directed to him by a wrong name, a false description, or even although it be directed to another. 2d, It is sufficient if the person who is directed to be produced, be designated by name, or if the name be unknown or uncertain, if he be described in any other way so as to make it be understood by one of common understanding, who is the person intended. 3d, The name and office of the judge, or the STYLE of the court issuing the writ, must be either stated in the body of the writ, or by the signature thereof, so as to show sufficiently the authority for issuing the same. If the time of making the return should be omitted, the writ is to be obeyed without delay ; if no place be inserted, it must be obeyed, by making the return at the dwelling of the judge or the usual place of holding the sessions of the court, whichever issued the same.

Art. 63. The insertion of words in the writ, other than those contained in the above given form, or the omission of any which are inserted in such form, shall not vitiate the writ, provided the substantial parts enumerated in the preceding article are preserved.

Who has authority to issue writs of *habeas corpus*, and in what case and how they are to be applied for.

Art. 64. The district courts and the criminal court, as now established, and all other courts which may hereafter be established, having jurisdiction in civil causes, to the amount of more than three hundred dollars, or of criminal cases where the punishment is more than one year's imprisonment at hard labour ; and the judges of such courts have power to issue writs of *habeas corpus*, directed to any person within their respective districts.

Art. 65. When the judge of any district is absent, interested or incapable, from whatever cause, of acting, and there is no judge of a criminal court in such district, a writ of *habeas corpus* may be issued by a judge of competent authority, in any of the adjoining districts ; provided, the absence, interest or inability of the judge of the district, where the illegal imprisonment is said to exist, be made to appear by the oath of the party applying, or other sufficient evidence.

Art. 66. The writ of *habeas corpus* may be obtained by petition addressed to any court or judge, having authority to grant the same, signed either by the party, for whose relief it is intended, or any other person on his behalf. ˙The petition must state in substance :

1. That the party is illegally imprisoned or restrained in his liberty, and by whom, naming both parties, if their names are known, or designating or describing them, if they are not.

2. If the confinement or restraint is by virtue, or under colour of any judicial writ, order or process, a copy thereof must be annexed, or it must be averred that such copy has been demanded and refused.

3. If the confinement or restraint be by virtue of judicial process, regular in form, but illegally obtained or executed, it must be set forth in what the illegality consists.

4. If the confinement or restraint is not by virtue of any judicial process, then the petitioner need only state that the party is illegally confined or restrained.

5. The petition must contain a prayer for the writ of *habeas corpus*.

6. It must be sworn to be true, at least according to the belief of the person making the application.

Art. 67. Any court or judge empowered to grant writs of *habeas corpus* on receiving such petition, shall, without delay, grant the same ; unless it appear from the petition itself, or from documents annexed, that the party can neither be discharged, nor admitted to bail, nor in any other manner relieved.

Art. 68. A writ of *habeas corpus* is granted in court by the signature of the clerk, and affixing the seal of the court to the writ. It is granted by the judge, by his signature only.

Art. 69. Whenever the court or judge, duly authorized, shall know, or have reason to believe, that any one, in the district of such judge or court, is illegally confined or restrained in his liberty, they shall issue a writ of *habeas corpus* for his relief, although no petition be presented, or application made for such writ.

Art. 70. Whenever it shall appear by the oath of a credible witness, or other satisfactory evidence, that any one is held in illegal confinement or custody, and there is good reason to believe that he will be carried out of the state, or suffer some irreparable injury, before he can be relieved in the usual course of law ; or whenever a writ of *habeas corpus* has been issued and disobeyed, any court or judge, empowered to issue writs of habeas corpus, shall make a warrant, directed to any sheriff or other executive officer of justice, or any other person who may agree to execute the same, commanding him to take and bring the prisoner, so illegally confined, before such judge, to be dealt with according to law.

Art. 71. Where the proof mentioned in the preceding article, is sufficient to justify an arrest of the person, having the prisoner in custody for any offence against the provisions of the Code of Crimes and Punishments, in favour of personal liberty, the judge may add to the warrant an order of arrest of such person for such offence, who shall be brought before the judge, and shall be examined and committed, bailed or discharged, according to the directions contained in the first title of the second book of this code.

Art. 72. Any officer, or other person to whom the warrant mentioned in the two last preceding articles shall be delivered; shall execute the same by bringing the person held in custody (and the person who detains him, if so commanded by the warrant), before the judge or court, issuing the same, who shall inquire into the cause of his imprisonment or restraint, and either discharge, bail, or remand the party into custody, as directed in this chapter in cases of returns of writs of *habeas corpus.*

Art. 73. The person, to whom the warrant mentioned in the three last preceding articles may be directed, shall, for the execution thereof, have the same powers, and be bound by the same rules as are designated in the chapter of this code which relates to the execution of warrants of arrest ; but the said warrant may be executed in any parish of the state, into which the party for whose relief it issued, may have been carried, without any indorsement of such writ, as is required in cases of arrest.

Art. 74. No fees or emolument whatever shall be received by any judge, clerk or other officer, for granting a writ of *habeas corpus,* but the expences of conducting the prisoner before the court or judge, must be tendered to the person having charge of him, at the rate of twenty-five cents for each mile, unless the judge granting the writ, be satisfied that the applicant is unable to pay such expences, and shall by writing on the back of said writ, direct that they be advanced by the person having the custody of the prisoner, and the judge may on the return, either direct that such expenses be paid by either party, or by the state, or the parish, as circumstances may render proper.

Art. 75. In all cases where the law does not otherwise specially provide, every one has a right to dispose of his own person UNCONTROLLED by any other individual. When the right is interfered with by detaining the person against his will, within certain limits, either by threats, by the fear of injury, or by bonds, or other physical and material obstacles, the party is said to be CONFINED or IMPRISONED and to be in CUSTODY of the person who continues such detention. A person also has the CUSTODY of another, who does not confine him within

3 M

certain limits, but by menace or force, directs his movements, and obliges him-against his will, to go or remain where he directs.

When no such detention within certain limits exist, but an authority is claimed and exercised of general control over the actions of the party against his consent, he is said to be under the RESTRAINT of the person exercising such control.

In all cases whatever, where such imprisonment, confinement, custody or restraint exists, which is not authorised by positive law, or is exercised in a mode or degree not authorised by law, the party aggrieved may have relief by writ of *habeas corpus*.

Art. 76. When a person claiming to be free, shall be held as a slave, relief may be granted by *habeas corpus*, and his discharge shall be full evidence of his liberty against the person claiming him as a slave, unless he shall within ten days after such discharge, institute a civil suit, in which he may obtain a sequestration of the body of the party so discharged, provided he give the security required by law in case of SEQUESTRATION, and produce such evidence of his property, as will satisfy the judge of any court having cognizance of the cause, that the party is a slave, and that the plaintiff is entitled to his services.

But unless such suit be instituted, within the time aforesaid, the party who held him as a slave, shall be forever barred from making any claim to the services of the person so discharged ; and on the trial of such suit, the discharge shall be presumptive evidence of the liberty of the party discharged, and throw the burthen of proof on the person claiming him as a slave.


SECTION III.

How the writ of *habeas corpus* is served and returned.

Art. 77. This writ is served by delivering the original to the person to whom it is directed, or to him in whose custody, or under whose restraint the party for whose relief it is intended, is detained. If he refuse to receive it, he must be informed verbally of the purport of the writ. If he conceal himself, or refuse admittance to the person charged with the service, the writ must be fixed in some conspicuous place on the outside, either of his dwelling-house, or of the place where the party is confined.

Art. 78. Any free white male person, capable of giving testimony, may serve the writ.

Art. 79. Its service is proved by the declaration on oath, and in writing of the person making the service.

Art. 80. It is the duty of the person upon whom a writ of *habeas corpus* is served, whether such writ be directed to him or not, to obey and return the same without delay.

Art. 81. This is done by producing, as directed, the person intended to be released, if in his custody, or under his power or control, and by making a return in writing on the back of the writ, or annexed to it, which must state plainly and unequivocally:

1. Whether he have or have not the party in his power or custody, or under his restraint.

2. By virtue of what authority, or for what cause he took or detains him.

3. If he had the party in his power or custody, or under his restraint at any time within three days prior to the date of the writ, but has transferred such custody or restraint to another ; then stating particularly, to whom, at what time, for what cause, and by what authority such transfer took place.

4. If he have the party in his custody, or under his restraint, by virtue of any writ or warrant, or other written authority, the same must be annexed to the return.

Art. 82. The return must be signed by the persons making the same, and attested on oath.

Art. 83. Whenever a writ of *habeas corpus* shall be taken out for any one in custody, by virtue of an order or execution issued for carrying into effect the final judgment, sentence or decree of any COMPETENT tribunal, either of civil or criminal jurisdiction, the officer having legal custody of such person, need not produce him, unless specially directed to do so, notwithstanding such execution or order, in the cases hereafter provided for ; but it shall be sufficient to make a return in writing, annexing the order or execution, by virtue of which the party is detained. Provided always: that for any special cause for which relief may legally be granted, either set forth in the affidavit, on which the writ of *habeas corpus* is issued, or appearing on the return, the judge may order the prisoner to be brought up, notwithstanding such final judgment, sentence or decree, and may proceed to give the relief to which the party is entitled.

Art. 84. The return to a writ of *habeas corpus* must be made within twelve hours after the service, or sooner, if required by the writ, if the party to be relieved by it is within twelve miles of the place of return. If he be at a greater distance, then he must make the return, allowing one day for every twenty miles distance, which the party must travel, in order to make the return, and in proportion for a greater or less distance.

## SECTION IV.

### The mode of enforcing a return.

Art. 85. When it appears to the court or judge, issuing the writ, that it has been duly served, if the person intended to be relieved, is not produced at the time, which is required by the provisions of this chapter, the judge, who issued the writ, or if issued by a court, the said court, or any judge thereof, shall make a warrant, directed to any executive officer of justice, or other person willing to execute the same, commanding him to take the person, who has disobeyed the writ, into custody, and to bring him before the judge or court, which issued the warrant, to be dealt with according to law ; and if, on being brought before the court or judge, he shall refuse to return the writ, or does not produce the person he was ordered to bring up, in the cases wherein he is by the provisions of this chapter obliged to produce him, he shall be committed to prison, and remain there until the effect of the writ shall be produced, and until he shall pay all the costs of the procedure, and shall moreover be liable to the penalties imposed by law, for disobedience to the said writ, and for any other offence against personal liberty, of which he may have been guilty, in the imprisonment or detention complained of.

Art. 86. In the case provided for by the last preceding article, the person intended to be relieved by the writ of *habeas corpus*, must be brought up in the manner directed by the second section of this chapter.

Art. 87. Whenever, from sickness or infirmity of the person directed to be produced, he cannot, without danger of his life, be brought before the judge, the party in whose custody he is, may state that fact in the return of the writ; and if it be made to appear, by the certificate of a physician regularly admitted to practice, and the testimony of two other witnesses, and the signature of the party intended to be relieved, if he can write; then, if the judge be satisfied of the truth of the allegation, and if the return be otherwise sufficient, it shall be good without the production of the person, and the judge may either go to the place where the prisoner is confined, if he think justice requires it, or he may proceed, when he is satisfied with the truth of the allegation, as in other cases, to decide on the return.

Art. 88. The death of the prisoner, or any other INEVITABLE ACCIDENT, or SUPERIOR FORCE, will be a good return to excuse the production of the prisoner ; provided proof of such fact be given to the perfect satisfaction of the court or judge, issuing the writ ; but this as well as any other matter alleged in any return, may be contested in the manner hereinafter mentioned.

Art. 89. When any one shall die, while under imprisonment, it shall be the duty of the person in whose custody he was at the time of his death, without any delay, to give notice thereof to the coroner of the parish, or in case of his absence or inability to attend, to a justice of the peace, who shall summon a jury of householders in the said parish, to consist of not less than nine, nor more than eighteen, who shall view the body, and being first duly sworn, shall inquire into the manner in which the person came by his death ; and the said jury shall, in all cases, cause the body to be inspected by a surgeon or a physician duly admitted, and examine him as well as all other persons they may call as witnesses, and if they do not appear, compel their attendance by warrant. And the said jury, or a majority of them, shall make and sign an inquest or certificate, stating that they have examined witnesses, and are satisfied that the body produced to them, is that of such a person (naming him) and setting forth the manner in which he came by his death, unless it shall appear to the said inquest, that the death of such prisoner was caused by a crime ; in which case the coroner or justice shall send the inquest to the court having cognizance of the crime, and shall immediately issue a warrant for the arrest and commitment of the party, who shall appear by such inquest to be guilty. And wherever the death of a prisoner is returned as a reason for not producing him in the return of a *habeas corpus*, the inquest proving such death must be annexed to the return.

## SECTION V.

### Of the proceedings on the return.

Art. 90. The judge or court before whom a person is brought on a *habeas corpus*, shall examine the return and the papers, if any, referred to in it, and if no legal cause be shown for the imprisonment or restraint ; or if it appear, although legally committed, he has not been prosecuted, tried or sentenced, within the periods for those purposes respectively limited by law, or that for any other cause the imprisonment or restraint cannot legally be continued, he shall discharge him from the custody or restraint under which he is held.

Art. 91. If it appear that the party has been legally committed for an offence, BAILABLE OF RIGHT, or if he appear by the testimony offered with the return, to be guilty of such on offence, although the commitment be irregular, or there be no commitment, he shall bail the prisoner, if good bail be offered.

Art. 92. In cases which are not BAILABLE OF RIGHT, the judge has a discretion, the exercise of which involves a high responsibility. It must of necessity be left to his sagacity and prudence to distinguish between those presumptions, which leave a strong probability of guilt and those which are too slight to justify imprisonment, previous to the trial. In the latter case only of presumptions, which are not strong, he may admit to bail. This discretion, however, cannot be exercised at all. 1st, Where the crime has been freely confessed before a magistrate. 2d, Where it is positively and directly charged by the oath of a credible witness present at the act. 3d, Where an indictment has been found, charging the prisoner with an offence not BAILABLE OF RIGHT.

Art. 93. If the party be not entitled to his discharge, and cannot be bailed, the judge must remand him to the custody, or place him under the restraint from which he was taken, if such custody or restraint be legal, or otherwise place him in the custody or power of such person, as by·the law of the state, he is entitled thereto.

Art. 94. If the judge cannot immediately determine the case, he may until judgment be given on the return, either place him in the custody of the sheriff of the parish where the return is made, or place him under such care, and in such custody, as his age or other circumstances may require.

Art. 95. If it be shown by the return that the person is detained by virtue of an informal or void commitment, yet if from the documents on which it was made, or from other proof, it appear that there is good cause for commitment, the prisoner shall not be discharged— but the judge or court before whom he is brought, shall either commit him for trial, or admit him to bail, in cases where, by law, he may be bailed.

Art. 96. In order to enable the judge, before whom a return to a writ of *habeas corpus* is made, to perform the duty required by the last preceding section, the officer having the custody of any person committed for any offence, for whose relief such writ is granted, must show the same to the magistrate who made the commitment, or to the clerk of the court, (if the papers relative to the commitment have been delivered to him,) and it shall thereupon be the duty of such magistrate or clerk, to attend at the hour and place of the return, and exhibit to the judge or court, to which the same is made, all the proofs and documents relative to the said commitment; and if such magistrate or clerk neglect to attend, the judge or court is authorized, on proof of his having had the notice required by this article, to enforce his attendance by warrant of arrest, and the party when arrested, shall be kept in custody until he perform the duty required by this article.

Art. 97. When it appears by the return that the person soliciting his discharge, is in custody, on any civil process, or that any other person has an interest in continuing his imprisonment or restraint, no order shall be given for his discharge, until it appear that the plaintiff, in such civil suit, or the person so interested, or their attorneys or agents, if either are within twenty miles, have had reasonable notice of the issuing of such writ of *habeas corpus.*

Art. 98. The party brought before the judge on the return of the *habeas corpus*, may deny any of the material facts set forth in the return, or allege any fact, to show either that the imprisonment or detention is unlawful, or that he is entitled to his discharge, which allegations or denials must be on oath; and thereupon the judge shall proceed in a summary way, to hear testimony, and the arguments, as well of the party interested, civilly, if any there be, as of the prisoner, and the person who holds him in custody, and shall dispose of the prisoner as the case may require.

Art. 99. If it appear on the return, that the prisoner is in custody by virtue of process from any court legally constituted, he can be discharged only in one of the following cases:

1. Where the court has exceeded the limits of its jurisdiction, either as to matter, place, sum or person.

2. Where, though the original imprisonment was lawful, yet by some act, omission or event, which has taken place afterwards, the party has become entitled to his liberty.

3. Where the process is defective in some substantial form required by law.

4. Where the process, though in proper form, has been issued in a case, or under circumstances where the law does not allow process or orders for imprisonment, or arrest to issue.

5. Where, although in proper form, the process has been issued or executed by a person either unauthorised, or improperly authorised to issue or execute the same, or where the person having the custody of the prisoner under such process, is not the person empowered by law to detain him.

6. Where the process appears to have been obtained by false pretences or bribery.

7. Where there is no general law, nor any judgment, order or decree of a court, to authorise the process, if in a civil suit, nor any conviction, if in a criminal proceeding.

But no judge or court, on the return of a *habeas corpus*, shall in any matter inquire into the legality or justice of a judgment or decree of a court legally constituted, and in all cases where it appears that there is a sufficient legal cause for the commitment of the prisoner for an offence, although it may have been informally made, or without due authority, or the process may have been executed by a person not duly authorised, the judge shall make a new commitment, in proper form, and directed to the proper officer, or admit the party to bail if the case be bailable.

Art. 100. The order of discharge made by a court or judge, on the return of a *habeas corpus*, has no other effect than that of restoring the party to liberty, and securing him from any future imprisonment or restraint for the same; it is not conclusive, as to any other civil right, except with respect to persons claimed as slaves, which is herein specially provided for.

Art. 101. No person who has been discharged by order of a court or judge, on a *habeas corpus*, shall be again imprisoned, restrained or kept in custody for the same cause, unless he be afterwards indicted for the same offence. But it shall not be deemed to be the same cause.

1. If after a discharge for defect of proof, or for any material defect in the commitment, in a criminal case, the prisoner should be again arrested on sufficient proof, and committed by legal process for the same offence.

2. If in a civil suit, the party has been discharged for any illegality in the judgment or process, and is afterwards imprisoned by legal process, for the same cause of action.

3. Generally, whenever the discharge has been ordered on account of the non-observance of any of the forms required by law, the party may be a second time imprisoned, if the cause be legal, and the forms required by law observed.

Art. 102. When a judge, authorized to grant writs of *habeas corpus*, shall be satisfied that any person in legal custody, on a charge for any offence, is afflicted with a disease, which will render a removal necessary for the preservation of his life, such judge may order his removal, on his giving bail with two securities, in such sum as shall be ordered by the judge, that he will surrender himself to the same custody, whenever he shall be thereunto required, or the judge may in such case, where the prisoner is manifestly unable to procure bail, put him in the custody of an executive officer of justice, whose duty it shall be to watch over the said prisoner in the place to which he may be removed, to prevent his escape. Provided, that the fact of such disease, and the necessity of removal, shall appear by the oaths of two physicians or surgeons duly admitted to practice, and that the physican who shall attend on such prisoner after his removal, shall also take an oath that he will give notice to a magistrate as soon as in his opinion the said prisoner may safely be returned to his imprisonment, which magistrate shall, on receiving such notice, issue a warrant for his removal to the place in which he was formerly confined.

## SECTION VI.

### General provisions.

Art. 103. No person shall be discharged under the provisions of this chapter, who is in custody on a commitment for any offence exclusively cognizable by the courts of the United States, or by order, execution or process, issuing out of such courts, in cases where they have jurisdiction, or who is held by virtue of any legal engagement, or enlistment in the army, or who, being subject to the rules and articles of war, is confined by any one legally acting under the authority thereof, or who is held as prisoner of war, under the authority of the United States.

⊕Art. 104. There is no other writ of *habeas corpus* known in the law of this state, but that described and provided for in this chapter. Courts having occasion to direct the production of prisoners before them, either to prosecute, to give testimony, or for any other purpose than that of examining into the cause of their imprisonment, may command the production of such prisoners by an order of court, entered on their minutes, and certified to the officer having charge of such prisoner.

### SECTION VII.

#### Penalties for the breaches of the duties enjoined by this chapter.

Art. 105. Any judge empowered by this chapter, to issue writs of *habeas corpus*, who shall refuse to issue such writ, when legally applied to, in a case where such writ may lawfully issue, or who shall unreasonably delay the issuing of such writ, or who, in cases where such writ is allowed to issue without any proof, shall WILFULLY omit to issue, or wilfully and unreasonably delay the issuing such writ, shall for every offence be fined in the sum of two thousand dollars.

Art. 106. Any judge so authorized, who shall refuse, or wilfully omit to perform, any other of the duties imposed on him by this chapter, or shall unreasonably delay the performance thereof, by which refusal, omission or negligence, any illegal imprisonment is caused or prolonged, shall be fined in the sum of one thousand dollars.

Art. 107. Any executive officer of justice to whom a writ of *habeas corpus*, or any other warrant, writ or order, authorized by this chapter, shall be directed, delivered or tendered, who shall refuse, or neglect to serve or execute the same, as by this chapter is directed, or who shall unreasonably delay the service or execution thereof, shall be fined in the sum of one thousand dollars.

Art. 108. Any one having the person in his custody, or under his restraint, power or control, for whose relief a writ of *habeas corpus* is issued, who, with the intent to avoid the effect of such writ, shall transfer such person to the custody, or place him under the power or control of another, or shall conceal him, or change the place of his confinement, with intent to avoid the operation of such writ, or with intent to remove him out of the state, shall be fined in the sum of two thousand dollars, and may be imprisoned at hard labour, not less than one nor more than five years.

Art. 109. In a prosecution for any penalty incurred, under the last preceding article, it shall not be necessary to show that the writ of *habeas corpus* had issued at the time of the removal, transfer or concealment therein mentioned, if it be proved that the acts therein forbidden, were done with the intent to avoid the operation of such writ.

Art. 110. Any one having the person for whose relief a writ of *habeas corpus* is issued, in his custody, or under his power or control, who, (without being guilty of any of the acts made punishable by the last preceding article) shall, after being legally served with such writ, neglect or refuse to produce such person, in cases where, by the provisions of this chapter, he is bound to produce him, shall be fined in the sum of one thousand dollars.

Art. 111. Any person to whom a writ of *habeas corpus* is directed, and on whom it is duly served, who shall neglect or refuse to make a return thereto, in the manner directed by the third section of this chapter, shall be fined in the sum of five hundred dollars, even if he have not the party whom it is intended to relieve in his custody, or under his power or control.

Art. 112. Any sheriff or his deputy, any jailor or coroner, having custody of any prisoner, committed on any civil or criminal process of any court or magistrate, who shall neglect to give such prisoner a copy of the process, order or commitment, by virtue of which he is imprisoned, within three hours after demand, shall be fined in the sum of five hundred dollars.

Art. 113. Any magistrate who, on receiving notice of the issuing of a *habeas corpus* for any person committed by him for any offence, shall neglect to attend at the return of the *habeas corpus*, in the manner directed in this chapter, shall be fined in the sum of three hundred dollars ; unless, before receiving such notice, he shall have returned the papers relative to such commitment, to the clerk of the court having cognizance of the cause.

Art. 114. Any person who, knowing that another has been discharged by order of a competent judge, on a *habeas corpus*, shall, contrary to the provisions of this chapter, arrest or detain him again for the same cause, which was shown on the return of such writ, shall be fined in the sum of five hundred dollars for the first, and one thousand five hundred dollars for a second offence.

Art. 115. Any able bodied male inhabitant of this state, above the age of eighteen and under fifty years of age, who shall, when legally called on for that purpose, refuse to aid a magistrate, executive officer of justice, or other person, legally authorized to serve or execute any writ, commitment or order, issued by virtue of this chapter, in the service or execution of such writ, warrant or order, shall be fined in the sum of fifty dollars.

Art. 116. The recovery of the said fines shall be no bar to a civil suit for damages, or to a criminal prosecution, for such of the said acts or omissions as may, in the third book of this code, be declared to be an offence.

# CHAPTER VIII.

*Of suppressing permanent offences against property, and of the disposition of personal property, seized and supposed to be stolen.*

Art. 117. Permanent offences against personal property, by a criminal taking, may be suppressed either by civil suit for its restoration, or by the means hereinbefore directed of a search warrant, or by resistance to the unlawful taking.

3 N

Art. 118. In all cases of a conviction for a criminal taking or detention of personal property, which is taken with the offender or in his possession, or where without such conviction the property is found on a search warrant, or is detained in the hands of an officer of justice on suspicion of being stolen; on satisfactory proof of ownership, it shall be restored to the owner.

Art. 119. No property coming to the possession of a magistrate, court or officer of justice, by any of the means described in the last preceding article, shall be restored to any one claiming as owner until after notice published for fifteen days, describing the property and designating the person from whom it was taken, or the place where it was found, and requiring all persons having any claims, to make them known.

Art. 120. If no more than one claimant appear, the property shall, without prejudice to any other civil claim, be delivered to him on his making oath to the ownership. If more than one claimant appear, the property shall remain sequestered in the hands of the sheriff, until by a civil suit the rights of the parties be determined.

Art. 121. If no claimant appear, the property shall be sold at auction, and the proceeds paid to the treasurer of the state, and if no claim be made on him by any person claiming as owner within one year, it shall be carried to account of the Recompense Fund, hereinafter designated.

Art. 122. If an indictment or information be presented against any one for a violent dispossession of real property, contrary to the provisions of the Code of Crimes and Punishments, it shall be tried in preference to any other, except those for offences punishable with imprisonment for life; and an information may be filed when the court is not in session by permission of the judge, who shall thereupon hold a special court for the trial of such offence.

Art. 123. If the defendant be convicted, the person aggrieved shall be restored to, and maintained by the court in, possession of the property against the person convicted, until the right shall be determined by a civil suit, if any be brought.


# TITLE III.


## OF THE MANNER OF CALLING FOR AND EMPLOYING THE MILITARY FORCE OF THE STATE IN AID OF THE CIVIL POWER.


Art. 124. Neither the militia nor any other military force shall be employed in the aid of the civil power, or brought to act in a military capacity against any persons in the state, unless it be called for in the manner directed by this title; and when so called for shall be subject to the regulations hereinafter prescribed.

# CHAPTER I.

*Of the manner and cases in which the military force may be required.*

Art. 125. When any three magistrates, of whom a judge must always be one, shall be convinced by the affidavits of two inhabitants of the state, that a RIOT or INSURRECTION has taken place in the parish in which the persons making the affidavit reside, and that the persons engaged therein cannot be arrested or dispersed by the ordinary force of civil authority, they shall make a written application to the governor, requesting military aid.

Art. 126. If the governor be at such a distance from the place at which the riot or insurrection exists, as is two great to enable him to give the necessary orders in time for its suppression, a copy of the application shall be also sent to the nearest field officer of ordinary militia or of any independent corps, containing the same request.

Art. 127. The application must be signed by the magistrates, must state the substance of the testimony offered to them, and the place and probable object of the riot or insurrection, and it must designate the number of men required for the purpose of suppressing it.

Art. 128. Immediately after receiving such application, the governor or officer to whom it is directed, shall order the number of men specified therein, to march with arms and ammunition under the command of the requisite officer, and place themselves under the direction of the magistrates signing the application.

Art. 129. The governor or the officer to whom the application is made, may, notwithstanding the designation of the number of men in the application, order as many more as he may deem necessary, to be embodied and hold themselves in readiness, if those sent for the purpose should prove insufficient to overcome the resistance that may be offered; and if the resistance should be continued, the men so kept in readiness may be employed without further requisition from the magistrate.

# CHAPTER II.

*Of the manner in which the military force is to be employed.*

Art. 130. The officer commanding the troops detailed in compliance with the application of the magistrates, shall immediately repair to the place designated, and post the troops in such a manner as to intervene between the persons or the property that it may be the intention of the rioters or insurgents to attack. He shall then act entirely on the defensive, not suffering the men to fire, and permitting them to use their edged or pointed weapons only to repel actual violence, except in one of the following cases.

1. If an attack be made on any one of the militia by which his life is in danger, or if an attempt be made to disarm him, which he cannot otherwise avoid, he may defend himself by discharging his fire-arms.

2. If a general attack be made by the insurgents or rioters upon the militia with fire-arms, or by missile or other weapons, by which the lives of the men are indiscriminately put in danger, the officer may order the men to fire, but not until an endeavour has been made to disperse the rioters by means less dangerous to persons who may not be engaged in the offence.

3. If the troops cannot be so placed as to intervene between the rioters and the persons or property which they apparently intend to attack, and the illegal purpose of the riot is persevered in, by means evidently dangerous to the lives of others, although no attack be made on the troops themselves, the magistrates, or any two of them, may direct the officer to disperse the rioters, which he is authorised to do, by ordering the men first to use the bayonet or sword, and if they prove ineffectual to disperse the assembly, but not otherwise, then to discharge their fire-arms against them.

4. The troops shall not be brought up to the place until the white flag has been displayed by a magistrate, and warning given to disperse, in the manner directed by the            article of the Code of Crimes and Punishments, and unless in defence against an attack dangerous to life, no order shall be given or obeyed to make any discharge of fire-arms, or other use of any other arms than for defence, until half an hour shall have elapsed after the displaying of the white flag and the giving the warning to disperse.

5. Every endeavour must be used both by the magistrates and officer commanding the troops that can be made consistently with the preservation of life, to induce or force the rioters or insurgents to disperse before any attack is made upon them by which their lives may be endangered.

# BOOK II.

## TITLE I.

OF ARREST AND BAIL.

## CHAPTER I.

*Definitions and general principles, relative to the subject of this title.*

Art. 131. A complaint is the allegation made to a proper officer, that some person, whether known or unknown, has been guilty of a designated offence.

Art. 132. No complaint can have a legal effect, unless it be supported by such evidence as shall show that an act which constitutes an offence has been committed, and renders it certain or probable, that it was committed by some person named or described in the complaint. It is then called an ACCUSATION.

Art. 133. The evidence mentioned in the last preceding article may be taken without the knowledge of the party accused, or the effect of the law might be evaded by his escape. But he cannot be condemned on such evidence; he must have an opportunity of explaining or contradicting it before the judges who are finally to decide on his innocence or guilt. This investigation is called the TRIAL. It necessarily requires some delay, but public justice requires that during this interval, the person of the accused should be secured, in order that he may undergo the penalty of the law, if he be found guilty. This is affected by an ARREST.

Art. 134. As it would be oppressive in most cases to deprive the accused of his liberty before trial and conviction, if he can give a sufficient pledge for his appearance at the trial, the law restores him to his liberty on his giving such pledge. This pledge is called BAIL.

Art. 135. There are cases in which the accused is bailable of right, others in which it is discretionary with the judge to admit to bail, and some in which no bail can be taken. The rules relative to these several distinctions are laid down in a subsequent chapter of this title, and in the chapter of the preceding book relative to writs of *habeas corpus*.

# CHAPTER II.

*Of the mode of making a complaint and accusation, and of ordering an arrest.*

## SECTION I.

### Of complaints and accusations, and who may receive them.

Art. 136. Any judge of any court, any mayor or justice of the peace, of the state, is authorized to receive complaints and accusations for offences; to issue warrants, order arrests, make commitments, and take bail in the manner directed by this code. They are designated under the general term, MAGISTRATE.

Art. 137. Any person, even those incapable of giving testimony, may make complaint to a magistrate.

Art. 138. When a complaint shall be made to a magistrate, he shall reduce the declaration of the complainant to writing, and if he be a person capable of giving testimony, shall administer an oath, that the said declaration contains the truth, and shall cause it to be signed in his presence, and shall then proceed to take such other testimony as shall be offered him to prove the offence, or designate the offender, causing each declaration to be SIGNED by the declarant, and attested on oath.

Art. 139. If it appear probable to the magistrate than any other persons have knowledge of any material fact or circumstance relative to the complaint, it is his duty to summon and examine them on oath, touching the matter of the complaint.

## SECTION II.

### Of warrants of arrest, and citation.

Art. 140. When a magistrate from the complaint or accuation, or other evidence taken before him, is convinced that an offence has been committed, and has reason to believe, that any person who can be sufficiently designated by name or description, has committed such offence, it shall be his duty to issue a WARRANT OF ARREST, or CITATION, according to the discretion hereinafter vested in him.

Art. 141. When an offence is committed in the presence of a magistrate, he may issue a warrant of arrest, although no complaint or accusation be brought before him; but in such case the warrant must be *returnable* before some other magistrate, and the magistrate signing the same, must reduce his own testimony to writing, and prior to any commitment or holding to bail, attest the same before such other magistrate on oath.

Art. 142. A warrant of arrest is an order in writing, directing a person, accused or suspected of having committed an offence, to be brought before a magistrate or court of examination.

Art. 143. This warrant may be issued by the governor of the state, by any court having any criminal jurisdiction, or any magistrate.

Art. 144. It must be directed to the person who is to execute it, either by name, or by his official designation. In the latter case it may be directed specially to a particular officer, or generally to all officers of the same description : when so generally directed, any officer of that description, to whom it is delivered, must execute it.

It must describe the party suspected or accused, by name, or by such other designation, as may sufficiently distinguish him, and it must contain an order to arrest and bring him before some court or magistrate for examination. The offence of which the person to be arrested is accused or suspected, must be set forth, either by its legal appellation, or it must be substantially described.

It must be signed by the magistrate, or by the clerk of the court which issues it.

Art. 145. Warrants of arrest may be directed to a sheriff or his deputy, or to a constable. These are called officers of justice, and they are bound to execute any legal warrant directed to them. Warrants may also be directed to individuals, who are not such officers, but they are under no obligation to execute such warrant unless they have undertaken so to do ; in which case they are bound by the same rules, and are subject to the same penalties for neglect or misconduct, as officers are.

## SECTION III.

### In what cases an arrest may be made without warrant.

Art. 146. Where a CRIME, or a BREACH OF THE PEACE has been committed, and the offender shall endeavour to make his escape, if there is a good reason to believe that he will effect it, before a warrant can be obtained, he may be arrested by virtue of a verbal order of any magistrate, or without such order, if no magistrate be present.

Art. 147. Any one in the act of committing a crime, may be arrested by any person present, without a warrant.

Art. 148. Whenever a CRIME is committed, and the offenders are unknown, and any person shall be found near the place where the crime was committed, either endeavouring to conceal himself, or endeavouring to escape, or under such other circumstances as justify a REASONABLE SUSPICION of his being the offender, such person may be arrested without warrant.

Art. 149. In cities and towns, even in cases where it is not certain that an offence has been committed, it is the duty of officers of justice and persons employed in such cities and towns as watchmen, without warrant to arrest and detain for examination, such persons as may be found at night, under such circumstances as justify a reasonable suspicion that they have committed or intended to commit an offence.

*Of citations.*

Art. 150. In cases of misdemeanour, when no danger appears of the defendant's absconding, the magistrate, instead of a warrant of arrest, may issue a citation in the form provided for by this code.

Art. 151. The citation may be served, either by leaving a copy with some person above the age of puberty who shall be found at the dwelling house of the defendant, or by delivering such copy personally to him.

Art. 152. If the defendant do not appear at the time and place of the return of the citation, when it has been duly served, the magistrate shall issue a warrant of arrest.

# CHAPTER III.

*Of the duty and powers of officers of justice and others in making arrests.*

Art. 153. At or before the time of making an arrest, the person who makes it must declare that he is an officer of justice, if such be the case. If he have a warrant, he must show it if required ; or if he make the arrest without warrant in any of the cases in which it is authorized by law, he must give the party arrested clearly to understand, for what cause he undertakes to make the arrest, and must require him to submit and accompany him to the magistrate.

Art. 154. The arrest is complete as soon as such notice is given as is required by the last preceding article ; provided, the party intended to be arrested, from his situation and other circumstances, may reasonably be supposed to have heard the said notice, and to have known that it was addressed to him.

Art. 155. In all cases where the person arrested refuses to submit to the arrest, or to proceed to the magistrate for examination, or attempts to escape, such degree of force may be used as is necessary to compel his appearance. But when he submits to the arrest, and neither attempts to escape nor make resistance, PERSONAL VIOLENCE shall not be used, nor shall BLOWS, STRIPES or WOUNDS be inflicted in any case, as a means of enforcing submission to the arrest, except so far as is hereinafter specially provided.

Art. 156. He who makes an arrest, may take from the party arrested all OFFENSIVE WEAPONS which he may have about his person, and must deliver them to the magistrate who takes the examination, to be disposed of according to law.

Art. 157. No person who shall kill or wound another, intentionally

or unintentionally, by the use of such means as would probably produce death, shall be justified or excused for such killing or wounding,
although he prove that the party killed or wounded endeavoured to
escape from an arrest ; but if the party arrested or attempted to be
arrested, shall, after receiving the notice provided for in the first article
of this chapter, make resistance with DEADLY WEAPONS, the person
making the arrest may also use such weapons, where they are necessary for his defence and to repel any forcible opposition to the execution of the arrest; and in such case, if wounds or death ensue, the
party making the arrest shall be justified. This article does not
extend to prisoners breaking out, or endeavouring to break out of
prison when lawfully arrested ; in such case, the person having custody
of the prisoner, and others employed by him, may lawfully use offensive weapons to prevent the breach of the prison.

Art. 158. If, after a lawful arrest has been made, any one shall, by
force, rescue or attempt the rescue of the prisoner, or before the arrest
has been made, shall by force attempt to prevent it from being made,
the person having the prisoner in custody, or authorized to make the
arrest, and others who may be lawfully aiding him, may resist such
force, and in doing so may use deadly weapons, whenever it may be
necessary to prevent this rescue, or overcome resistance to the arrest.

The provisions of this article extend to all cases where a person is
in lawful custody.

Art. 159. In all cases of arrest for examination, the person making
the same must, without unnecessary delay, conduct the party arrested
before the court or magistrate by whom the warrant was issued, or, if
the arrest was made without warrant, before the nearest magistrate
in the parish.

Art. 160. Until the person arrested can be brought before the
court or magistrate, and during the examination he remains in the
custody of the person making the arrest, or of some officer of justice
appointed by the magistrate or court.

Art 161. Watchmen in cities or towns, and officers of justice having
charge of prisoners any where, are authorized to receive persons
arrested for examination, when necessary, for their safe custody during the night or at other times when they cannot be brought before
the court or magistrate for examination, and to deliver them again to
the party who made the arrest ; but in all such cases, the person having charge of the prison, shall take a copy of the warrant if the arrest
is made by warrant, or of a declaration of the cause of the arrest in writing, signed by the party making the arrest, if it be one made without
warrant.

Art. 162. If the magistrate who shall issue any warrant of arrest,
shall be absent at the time when it is returned, or unable from whatever cause, to examine the prisoner, the person, in whose custody he
is, must conduct him before some other magistrate in the same parish,
and in such case the complaint and affidavit on which the warrant was
granted must be sent to the magistrate before whom the prisoner was
taken, or if they cannot be procured, the complainant and witnesses
must be summoned to give their testimony anew.

Art. 163. Warrants of arrest may be executed in any parish of the
state, provided the person authorized to execute such warrant shall procure the allowance of some magistrate in such parish, which he is re-

3 O

quired to give on being satisfied that the warrant is not forged, and that the person presenting it, is the person to whom it is directed.

This allowance shall be made by writing on the warrant the word "allowed," with the name of the parish and the date of the allowance signed with the name of the magistrate who makes it. In whatever parish the arrest be made, the prisoner shall be brought to the parish in which the warrant for his examination was issued.

Art. 164. Arrests may be made on any day and at any hour of the day or night, and at any place within the state, under the several modifications provided in this section.

Art. 165. If the person accused shall fly into any HOUSE, or other BUILDING, in order to avoid arrest, any one having authority in the manner directed in this chapter to arrest him, may follow him into the said house, and when entered, he may, for the purpose of making the arrest, break any inner door of any apartment, in such house where the accused may be, if entrance be refused.

Art. 166. If the door be not opened when required, it is a refusal of entrance.

Art. 167. No one is authorized to break the outer door of a house in order to make an arrest, but an officer or other person having a warrant of arrest, and those who are lawfully assisting him, except as is provided in the next article.

Art. 168. In cases where, by any of the preceding articles, arrests are authorized to be made without warrant, the person so authorized, may justify breaking the outer door of any house, or in any other manner forcing an entrance therein, without warrant, in cases of such crimes only as are punishable by an imprisonment for life.

Art. 169. No outer door of any house can in any case be broken, or an entrance forced therein, in order to make an arrest, without the following formalities :

Entrance must be demanded in a loud voice.

Notice must be given in the same manner that the party is the bearer of a warrant of arrest.

Or if it is a case in which the arrest is lawful without warrant, that information must be substantially given in an audible voice.

If the arrest is attempted to be made *at night*, two householders of the parish, required for the purpose, must be present, who must announce their names to those within.

Art. 170. All inhabitants of the state when called on by a magistrate or officer of justice, are bound to assist in making arrests and securing the persons arrested, and are justified in doing all acts in rendering such aid, which the officer himself might do.

Art. 171. If any person who has been lawfully arrested shall escape or be rescued from custody, either before or after commitment, the person from whose custody he escaped may lawfully pursue and arrest him by virtue of the original warrant or commitment in any part of the state, and convey him back to his former custody.

## CHAPTER IV.

*Of the duty of magistrates in taking examinations and making commitments.*

Art. 172. When the person accused is brought before a magistrate for examination, he shall be informed of the accusation against him ; the examinations of the witnesses, which have been taken, shall be read to him ; and, if he request it, the witnesses (if they are yet alive and within the state) shall be summoned to attend, and they, as well as any additional witnesses who are produced, may be cross examined by the acccused or his counsel.

Art. 173. The magistrate shall then proceed to the examination of the person accused in the following manner :

1st. · He must be informed that, although he is at liberty to answer in what manner he may think proper to the questions that shall be put to him, or not to answer them at all, yet a departure from the truth, or a refusal to answer without assigning a sufficient reason, must operate as a circumstance against him, as well on the question of commitment as of his guilt or innocence on the trial.

2d. The magistrate shall next put the following interrogatories to the person accused :

What is your name and age ?

Where were you born ?

Where do you reside, and how long have you resided there ?

What is your business or profession ?

Where were you at the time the act (or omission) of which you are accused is stated by the witnesses to have taken place ?

ιDo you know the persons who have been sworn as witnesses on the part of the accusation, or any, and which of them, and how long have you known them ?

Give any explanation you may think proper of the circumstances appearing in the testimony against you, and state any facts that you think will tend to your exculpation.

3d. If any writing, or any article of property, be produced in evidence, it must be shown to him, and he must be asked whether he recognises it.

4th. The answers of the accused to the several interrogatories shall be reduced to writing by the magistrate, or some one by his order. They shall be shown or read to the accused, who may correct and add to them; and when made conformable to what he declares is the truth, may be SIGNED by him'; but if he refuses to SIGN, his reason shall be stated in writing, as he gives it, by the magistrate himself ; and the examination shall be signed and certified by the magistrate, whether the accused sign it or not. This examination is not to be on oath.

Art. 174. After the examination of the accused is finished, his witnesses, if he have any, shall be sworn and examined, and their examinations reduced to writing and signed by them respectively, after they have been read, corrected (if necessary by them), and approved.

Art. 175. The witnesses shall not be present at the examination of the person accused ; and while one of them is examined, the others shall be kept apart.

Art. 176. All the examinations, depositions, and other proof, shall be kept by the magistrate, to be disposed of as is hereinafter directed.

Art. 177. If the accused or the public prosecutor request that a further examination take place, the magistrate may, at his discretion, postpone the examination to a future day ; and either continue the prisoner verbally in the custody of the officer by whom he was brought before him, or give a written commitment to the keeper of the prison of the parish ; in which commitment it will be necessary only to state, that the party is committed for further examination on a complaint of (stating the offence).

Art. 178. After being once committed for further examination, the prisoner may be verbally ordered to be brought up and REMANDED from time to time, as long as the examination continues.

Art. 179. The effect which the examinations and depositions, taken before the magistrate, is to have on the trial, is set forth in the Code of Evidence.

Art. 180. It is the duty of the magistrate, before whom a prisoner is brought for examination, to address him without passion. He must neither use menace, nor hold out hopes of impunity or reward, in order to influence him.

Art. 181. In cases of difficulty, other magistrates of the same parish may assist at the examination and offer the sitting magistrate their advice, but he must decide, except on questions of bail, as is herein after provided.

Art. 182. The prisoner may have the assistance of such counsel as he may employ, but the magistrate has no authority to assign counsel.

Art. 183. Whenever the accusation is for a crime, the magistrate shall, and on all other occasions may, give notice to the public prosecutor to attend the examination; and it shall be his duty, on such occasions, to attend and examine the witnesses, and argue all questions of law and fact that may arise in the course of the investigation.

Art. 184. The magistrate has the same powers for preserving order, during the examinations, that are vested in courts by the chapter of the Code of Crimes and Punishments relative to offences against the judiciary power committed in a court of justice ; and the magistrate may, on his own view, immediately make a commitment for trial for any of the said offences.

Art. 185. The magistrate shall, on the application of the accused or the public prosecutor, issue summonses to the witnesses that may be required by either, which shall be served by any officer of justice ; and if they refuse to attend, they may be brought up by warrant ; and any witness refusing to answer a legal question, may be committed to prison until he shall agree to answer.

Art. 186. After hearing the proof, and considering the allegation, if any be made by the accused, the magistrate must determine, whether he be legally charged with the offence of which he is accused, or any other offence, or there be sufficient reason to believe him guilty thereof. In either case, that is to say, if the charge be positively proved by a credible witness, although there be exculpatory proof, or although there be no such direct proof, but the circumstances detailed induce a belief that he is guilty, he must be bailed or committed.

Art. 187. A commitment is an order directed to the sheriff of the parish, commanding him to keep the prisoner in safe custody, to answer a charge for the offence of which he is accused (specifying the same particularly), until he shall be released by law. This commitment must, in substance, contain a direction to the sheriff or his deputy, or the keeper of the jail, either by the style of his office, or by name, or both.

An allegation that the person (naming or describing him), is charged on oath with an offence, (specifying it either by the legal appellation of the offence, or substantially stating the act which has been charged.)

An order to receive the prisoner and detain him until he shall be discharged by law.

It must be signed by the magistrate issuing it, or if issued by a court, the commitment must be under its seal and signed by the clerk.

Art. 188. No person shall be discharged for any defect of form in the commitment, if it can be sufficiently understood from the language thereof, in its usual signification, that the officer detaining him is the person to whose custody persons accused of offences may be legally committed; that the prisoner is legally charged with some offence; and that the commitment be signed by a magistrate authorized to make commitments.

Art. 189. The commitment shall be delivered to an officer of justice, whose duty it shall be to take charge of the prisoner, without other warrant, and convey him without delay to the officer who is directed to receive him.

Art. 190. But if the offence be BAILABLE OF RIGHT, or if not bailable of right, and the proof is not evident nor the presumption great, the magistrate cannot commit the prisoner, if he offers good bail. His duty, in taking bail, is set forth in the next chapter.

Art. 191. If it appear from the testimony, that the prisoner is guilty of any other offence than the one of which he was originally accused, he shall be committed or bailed for such offence.


# CHAPTER V.


## *Of the duty of the magistrate in taking bail.*

Art. 192. The constitution declares, that "all persons shall be bailable, except for capital offences, whenever the proof is evident or presumption great." At the time of adopting the constitution the capital offences were murder, rape, exciting insurrection among slaves, and stabbing or shooting or poisoning with intent to murder; therefore, all other offences are and must be bailable. Persons accused of the offences above enumerated, are also to be bailed when the proof is not evident nor the presumption strong.

Art. 193. A single justice of the peace may admit to bail in all cases of misdemeanor, and in cases of crime where the punishment is imprisonment at hard labour for a term not exceeding six years. In cases where the punishment exceeds that term, but is less than fifteen years, the assent of two justices is necessary for determining the amount of bail and approving the security. In all other cases the bail must be taken before a judge.

When homicide is directly proven or admitted on an examination before a justice, the prisoner cannot be admitted to bail by the justice alone without the assent of a judge, notwithstanding any allegation or proof of justification, excuse or alleviation. He must, in such case, be committed; and, if the circumstances require it, afterwards bailed, or relieved on *habeas corpus.*

Art. 194. Bail is given by the prisoner and his surety signing a RECOGNIZANCE, conditioned for the appearance of the prisoner at the next session of a court of competent jurisdiction, to be named in the condition, and to abide the judgment of such court.

Art. 195. When bail is given, the prisoner must be discharged without exacting from him the payment of any fees.

Art. 196. In all cases where a crime is charged, and from the nature of the offence any proof or presumption of guilt may reasonably be supposed to be drawn from any article in the possession of the prisoner, the magistrate may direct him to be searched in his presence, and shall preserve all things found on him which may be useful to be produced on the trial, and afterwards disposed of according to law.

Art. 197. Where the offence charged is the illegal infliction of a wound, or any other injury, which may terminate in the death of the person injured, and the offence be proved or confessed, the magistrate cannot discharge, if it appear from the examination of surgeons that there is a probability that death will ensue in consequence of such injury. In this case the party must be committed for further examination, until the consequences of the injury can be ascertained.

Art. 198. No justice of the peace can let any prisoner to bail after he has been committed for trial; the power of these magistrates, on this subject, is confined to cases where persons are brought before them for examination.

Art. 199. The amount of bail cannot be apportioned by law to the circumstances of every case. It forms one of the most important and delicate exercises of judicial duty. It should be so performed as neither to suffer the wealthy offenders to escape by the payment of a pecuniary penalty, nor to render the privilege useless to the poor. In order to make it a sure pledge for the appearance of the party, it must be determined by considering:

1. The nature of the punishment to be inflicted on conviction.

2. The pecuniary circumstances of the party accused.

If the offence be punishable by hard labour, imprisonment or privation of civil rights, the desire to avoid punishment being greater, it should be counteracted by an increase of penalty.

The wealth of the party must also be considered. The poor might be oppressed by requiring an amount of security which would be no pledge whatever for the appearance of the rich. For these reasons, the law leaves to the discretion of the judge to determine the amount of bail, guided by the above principles, and within the limits contained in the following articles.

Art. 200. Where the punishment of the offence is a pecuniary penalty only, the bail must be greater than the highest fine that can be imposed.

Art. 201. When simple imprisonment forms a part of the punishment, one dollar at least must be added to the amount of bail for every day that the party may be sentenced, if not exceeding one year; if the imprisonment may exceed one year, then any further addition must be left to the discretion of the magistrate.

Art. 202. If hard labour form part of the punishment on conviction, then two dollars at least is to be added to the amount of bail for every day to which the party may be sentenced, not exceeding one year ; if the punishment may exceed one year, then any further increase must be left to the discretion of the magistrate.

Art. 203. If a suspension or forfeiture of political or civil rights, without imprisonment at hard labour, form a part of the punishment, then the sum of five hundred dollars at least must be. added to the amount of the bail.

Art. 204. The five last preceding articles shall also govern the judges who may bail prisoners on writs of *habeas corpus*.

Art. 205. No person shall be received as surety for the appearance of the party accused, who is not a HOUSEHOLDER who has resided at least one year in the state, and who does not own or possess property either real or personal to double the amount of the sum for which he is bound to prove by his oath, in all cases where the magistrate has any doubt of his sufficiency.

Art. 206. A woman cannot be received at bail.

Art. 207. In all cases of crime, two sureties are required.

Art. 208. A single surety will be sufficient, if he possess and own unincumbered real property to double the amount of the sum for which he is bound.

Art. 209. When the person admitted to bail is a minor or a married woman, the engagement shall, notwithstanding, be valid.

Art. 210. If, owing to mistake or misrepresentation, insufficient bail has been taken, or if the sureties become afterwards insufficient, the accused may be ordered to find sufficient sureties by any magistrate, and on his refusal, may commit him for trial.

Art. 211. In all cases where a magistrate shall either commit for trial or bail the accused, he must cause each of the witnesses who has been examined, and has testified to any material fact or circumstance in the case, to enter into a recognizance, without surety, in a sum fixed by the magistrate, conditioned for his appearance at the next sitting of the court, at which the accused is bound or committed to appear ; and if a witness shall refuse to sign such recognizance when required, he may be committed to prison by the order of the magistrate, and shall be confined until he shall be brought before the court to testify, or until he shall sign the recognizance.

Art. 212. Those who may have become bail for any one, may at any time discharge themselves by surrendering him to the custody of the sheriff of the parish in which the court at which he was bound to appear, shall sit.

Art. 213. The magistrate who took the recognizance of bail, is bound, on request, to deliver a copy thereof to the bail, if he have not yet transmitted the same in the manner hereinafter directed, or if he have so transmitted it, then the clerk of the court having custody thereof, must, on like request, deliver such copy, which shall be a sufficient warrant for the bail to arrest the person for whom they have become bound. In making which arrest the bail are authorized to do the same acts and are bound by the same rules as are hereinbefore prescribed to persons having warrants of arrest for examination on accusations for the same offences.

Art. 214. The sheriff to whom a surrender is legally made, as authorized by the preceding articles, is bound to receive the person so surrendered, and the bail must deliver to him with the prisoner the certified copy of the recognizance of the bail, as his authority for detaining such prisoner, and he shall on the request of such bail, give them a transcript of the recognizance with an acknowledgement that he has received the person mentioned therein, in discharge of his bail. Which transcript and acknowledgement being proved by the oath of two witnesses to have been executed by such sheriff, shall be a sufficient warrant for the officer or magistrate having custody of the recognizance to cancel the same.

Art. 215. The magistrate who shall make any commitment or let any person to bail, shall without any unnecessary delay, at the furthest within three days, transmit to the clerk of the court, which has legal cognizance of the offence charged, all the complaints, accusations, depositions, recognizances of bail, bonds for the appearance of witnesses, and all other documents in his possession relative to the accusation.

Art. 216. If there be proof made before a magistrate of the commission of any offence, and the party accused shall not be found on the warrant of arrest for examination, it shall notwithstanding be the duty of the magistrate to transmit to the court having cognizance of the offence, all the depositions and other documents he has taken in the manner directed by the last section, in order that the same may be laid before the grand jury in the manner hereinafter directed. But the said depositions and other documents need not in this case be transmitted to the court until the first day on which it shall sit, after the said depositions shall have been taken.

Art. 217. Further rules respecting bail are given in the chapter regulating the practice on writs of *habeas corpus*.

# TITLE II.

## OF THE PROCEEDINGS SUBSEQUENT TO T E COMMITMENT OR BAIL.

# CHAPTER I.

*Of appearance and the manner of enforcing it against parties and witnesses.*

Art. 218. The names of all persons who have given bail or have become bound by recognizance to appear in any court of criminal jurisdiction, shall be called in open court on the day they are respectively bound to appear, and if they fail to appear before the adjournment of the court, and no sufficient cause is shown according to the provisions of the next article, their defaults shall be entered, and such entry shall be evidence of the breach of their appearance, bonds or recognizances.

Art. 219. If it be satisfactorily shown on the part of the sureties or of the accused, that he is prevented from appearing by inevitable necessity, the court must direct an entry to be made on the back of the appearance bond, that time is given for the accused to appear until such day as the court, under a consideration of the circumstances of the case, shall appoint.

Art. 220. Courts may also, on the motion of the public prosecutor, order the sheriff to arrest and bring before them any person who has been bound by recognizance or summoned to appear and give testimony, and who has not attended at the time appointed; and when so arrested the said witnesses may be also fined in any sum not exceeding fifty dollars for their neglect, and must remain in custody until they give their testimony and are discharged from further attendance, or until they give such security as shall satisfy the court (either by their own recognizance or with sureties) for their appearance to testify. Provided, that if a witness shall show that he was prevented from appearing by inevitable necessity, the court must remit the fine, and take the witness's own recognizance for his appearance.

Art. 221. Witnesses bound to appear, and persons let out on bail, must not only attend on the day appointed in their respective obligations, but at such other times as the court shall direct, and the obligation continues, until they are discharged by the court.

Art. 222. If the public prosecutor discover that it will be necessary to have any person examined before the grand jury, who has not been bound by recognizance to appear, he may apply to a magistrate, who shall summon such witness and cause him to enter into recognizance for his appearance, to testify in the manner prescribed in the first chapter of this book, or he may obtain a summons from the clerk of the court under his signature and the seal of the court, commanding such witness to appear at a day therein to be appointed, to give testimony in such cases as shall be required of him, and courts and magistrates may, whenever they think proper, cause witnesses to enter into recognizance for their appearance to testify.

## CHAPTER II.

*Of the duty of public prosecutors, sheriffs and clerks, preparatory to the meeting of the grand jury.*

Art. 223. On the first day of each term of any court, at which a grand jury is summoned, the sheriff of the parish in which the court shall sit, shall make out and deliver to the judge of such court, two copies of a calendar, on which shall be entered the names of all the persons in his custody committed for trial for any offence, stating when they were committed, by whom, and for what offence, and entering on the said calendar the names of all such persons as having been committed for any offence were bailed, since the last term of the court, and by what judge. And the clerk of the said court shall also make out (and deliver to the judge) two copies of a calendar, on which he shall enter the names of all the persons who appear by the returns of the magis-

3 P

trates to have been either committed, or bailed, or who have been accused without having been arrested, for any offence, together with the dates of the accusation, the name of the magistrate who committed or bailed, and distinguishing whether each person was committed or bailed, or could not be found; and the judge shall deliver to the grand jury, as soon as they are sworn, one copy of each of the said calendars, together with all the examinations, depositions and other documents returned by the magistrate, and shall also send to them all such other returns as shall be afterwards made by any magistrate during the session of the grand jury.   Provided that the said calendar before it is sent to the grand jury, shall be submitted to the public prosecutor, who shall mark thereon such cases of misdemeanor as he shall choose to prosecute by information, and the papers and documents relative to such cases shall not be sent to the grand jury, and it shall be the duty of the public prosecutor to file informations in all such cases before the end of the term.

## CHAPTER III.

### Of the grand jury, its organization and its duties.

Art. 224.  The grand jury is a body of men, taken at stated periods, from the mass of citizens, to perform a most important function in the administration of justice.   It is their duty to protect the innocent from accusation, but to discover and bring the guilty to trial.   They have no political nor any other civil powers, and must confine their deliberations to inquiries whether there have been infractions of the penal laws of the state, and who have been the offenders : no other presentments or expressions of their opinions can be received in a court of justice, except in cases where special duties may be imposed upon them by law.

Art. 225.  The grand jury consists of twenty-three members, who are selected in the manner prescribed by special laws for that purpose: the consent of a majority of the whole number is necessary to make an indictment ; but a majority of those present may decide on any other question arising in the course of their deliberations.   No grand jury can proceed to any business, unless thirteen members at least are present.

Art. 226.  The grand jurors, before they enter on the exercise of their duties, shall each take the oath prescribed for that purpose by this Code.

Art. 227.  A judge of the court in which the grand jury shall be convened, shall immediately after they are sworn, give them such information as he may deem proper as to the nature of their duties, and draw their attention to such offences as are on the calendar, or as he has reason to believe will be brought before them ; confining his observations to the subjects connected with their duties as jurors, and carefully avoiding all topics of political or party nature : he shall read to them such parts of the Penal Code as relate to the several offences on their calendar, together, with the whole of this chapter.

Art. 228.  When the grand jury has received the address of the court, they shall retire to the chamber appointed for their deliberations.  Two constables or deputies of the sheriff shall be appointed to be constantly in attendance on them, the one as door-keeper, the other as messenger to carry the orders and citations which they may issue.

Art. 229. The first act of the jury, after having retired, shall be to organize themselves, by electing two of their members, the one to preside at their sittings, to be called the foreman of the grand jury, the other to be their clerk : this choice shall be made by ballot, and the members having the greatest number of votes for these places, shall respectively be elected. If two persons shall have an equal number of votes for the same place, this fact shall be reported to the court, and the judge shall determine which shall be elected. As soon as an election shall be made, a message shall be sent by one of the members of the grand jury to the court, stating which members have been respectively chosen.

Art. 230. The deliberations of the grand jury shall be secret: no one shall be admitted while they are sitting but the public prosecutor, and such persons as may be sent for or appear as witnesses, or may come to make complaint or give information relative to the infraction of any penal law. Every one announcing himself as complainant or informant against such infraction, must be admitted and heard at such time as the grand jury will permit.

Art. 231. The public prosecutor shall have access to the grand jury whenever he may have any information or advice on any point of law to give, or any complaint or evidence to lay before them, or whenever his attendance is required by the grand jury or any member thereof who may desire his advice ; but he must not be present at their deliberations or decisions.

Art. 232. The grand jury are to decide on all the cases on the two calendars whether there is matter for accusation ; this is not left to the discretion of the public prosecutor: therefore, it shall be the duty of the public prosecutor to prepare bills of indictment in all cases of crimes appearing on the calendars, and in all such cases of misdemeanor as he shall not choose to prosecute by information, and to send them to the grand jury, beginning with the cases of those who are in actual custody, and among those, sending in first the cases of crimes highest in degree. He can only depart from this order when material witnesses summoned or under recognizance to appear, have not appeared, and he has reason to expect their attendance. For the purpose of preparing these indictments, copies of the examinations, depositions and other papers returned by the magistrates, shall be sent to him by the clerk within three days after they are filed, and except in cases in which the returns are made within three days of the meeting of the grand jury, it is the duty of the public prosecutor to prepare all such bills of indictment by the first day of the term.

Art. 233. If any of the grand jury know or have reason to believe that an offence has been committed, within the jurisdiction of the court in which they are sworn, he is bound by his oath to declare the same to his fellow jurors, excepting such offences as can be presented on the complaint of the party injured only, and the jury shall thereupon take up the consideration thereof in their order.

Art. 234. Any individual having a knowledge of the commission of any offence, may apply to the grand jury, who are bound to hear his complaint and take his own declaration or oath, and that of such other witnesses as he may point out to them.

Art. 235. The grand jury may issue a summons ordering the attendance of any witness, and if he fail to attend, may issue an order directing the sheriff to arrest and bring him before them, and if he shall refuse to be sworn or to testify, they may by a like order commit him to prison, and he shall not be released until the grand jury are finally discharged, unless he consent to be sworn and give testimony as ordered, and he shall moreover be liable to such punishment as in such case is provided by the Code of Crimes and Punishments.

Art. 236. Every summons, order of arrest or other order of the grand jury, shall issue in the name of the grand jury, (specifying the parish or district for which they are sworn) and shall be signed by the foreman and attested by the clerk.

Art. 237. When the foreman or clerk are disabled from sickness, or for other cause have been discharged or excused from attendance by the court, other members of the jury may be chosen in their places during such disability.

Art. 238. When an indictment is found or the jury decide in the manner hereinafter provided, that there is matter of accusation for any offence against a person who is neither in custody nor on bail, or if on bail, is bailed for an offence less in degree than that found, it shall be the duty of the public prosecutor to apply for, and of the judge to grant a warrant of arrest for the offence stated in the indictment or presentment, commanding the sheriff to arrest and keep in safe custody the person therein named, who is charged with the commission of an offence (naming it) by the grand jury.

Art. 239. The warrant shall be in the form hereinafter prescribed, and shall be executed in the manner directed with respect to ordinary warrants for arrest, except that no examination can take place before the magistrate on any other point than that of the identity of the person; if no objection of this nature be made, or if made, be not supported by proof, the magistrate must either commit or bail the prisoner, according to the rules established for that purpose on ordinary arrests.

Art. 240. In their deliberations, the grand jury are to proceed in the following order: the calendars are to be read and they shall take up for consideration, first: the causes of those who are in custody, beginning with the greatest in degree. The indictment sent in by the public prosecutor shall be then read, together with the examinations and other documents returned by the magistrates. The witnesses shall then be examined, and if any member requires the advice of the public prosecutor, he may be called, heard, and after he has retired, the foreman shall again read the indictment and put the following questions to the jury:

1. Whether they find that the offence stated in the indictment has been committed.

2. Whether it was committed by the person accused in the indictment.

Each of these questions shall be debated and decided separately, and on each the jury may, with the assent of twelve members, make any amendments or alterations in the indictment, either in the description and circumstances of the offence, according to their view of the testimony and law, or in the name or description of the offender, if another person than the accused in the indictment appears to have committed the offence.

If both the questions above stated are decided in the affirmative by twelve jurors, the indictment shall then be signed by the foreman and clerk, respectively by each, adding to his name the quality in which he signs. When thus signed, the indictment is said to be found.

Art. 241. In cases where the public prosecutor has not sent an indictment, the grand jury, after hearing the testimony, shall in like manner decide, 1. Whether an offence has been committed, and what that offence is; and, 2. Who is the offender. And if it result from the decision of these questions, that twelve jurors are of opinion, that any designated person has been guilty of an offence, the clerk shall certify that there is matter for accusation against the person (naming him) for such an offence (designating it), and shall deliver such certificate with a minute of the evidence to the public prosecutor; who shall immediately send an indictment to the grand jury, conformable to the fact and law, which indictment, before it can have any force, must be found in the manner above directed.

Art. 242. If the grand jury decide that they have not sufficient evidence, either that the offence was committed, or that it was committed by the person accused (whether this decision be made on an indictment or under the last preceding clause, where no indictment has been presented), a certificate shall be sent to the court, stating that the grand jury find no cause of accusation against such person (naming him) for the offence of which he is charged (specifying it), which certificate shall be signed by the foreman and attested by the clerk. Whereupon such person, if in custody, shall be discharged, or if bailed, the bail bond shall be cancelled ; but such finding and discharge shall not prevent another accusation for the same cause, if other testimony be produced ; nor shall the party be discharged either from custody or from his bail, if he be detained or bailed for any other cause than that which has been examined by the grand jury: Provided also, that no discharge shall be ordered on any such certificate until the public prosecutor have had notice thereof, and if he shall declare to the court that he has other evidence against the accused, which in his opinion will justify a commitment, the discharge shall be delayed twelve hours to enable him to produce such testimony.

Art. 243. No record shall be kept of the manner in which any member of the grand jury has voted on any question before them ; nor can any member be obliged or allowed to declare, even in a court of justice, in what manner he or any other member of the grand jury voted on any such question, or what opinions they expressed. But they may be called on in any court of justice (in cases where evidence of that nature is otherwise legal) to show that the testimony of a witness examined before the grand jury was different from or consistent with that given before such court.

Art. 244. Every indictment found by the grand jury shall be delivered by the clerk into the hands of the presiding judge in open court, and if the person indicted be in custody or bailed for the offence of which he is indicted, the judge shall deliver the indictment to the clerk to be filed. But if the person indicted, be not in custody or not bailed for the offence of which he was indicted, then the judge shall retain such indictment until the party be arrested, or until the last day of the term, if he be not arrested before, and shall then deliver it to the clerk to be filed.

Art. 245. The grand jury cannot be discharged during the term, until they have decided on all the causes on the calendar, and on all complaints before them, nor then without the order of the court; until discharged, they must meet every day while they have any business before them; but they may determine their own hours of meeting and adjournment. When they have no business immediately before them, but are waiting for witnesses, or on any other account, they may adjourn with leave of the court, for any term not exceeding three days.

When the term of the court to which the grand jury is summoned, expires, eithier by its limitation or the adjournment of the court, the functions of the grand jury cease.

Art. 246. The grand jury has a right to ask the instruction and opinion of the court on any point of law on which one-third of the grand jurors present may be dissatisfied with the opinion of the public prosecutor. In order to obtain such instruction the grand jury shall come into court, and if the matter on which they desire to consult the court, requires secrecy, the foreman shall so state to the judge, and thereupon the judge shall cause all persons to leave the court until he shall have heard the questions of the grand jury and given his opinion and instruction thereon. After hearing which, the said jury shall retire to thir own chamber to deliberate, but are not bound to decide in conformity with such opinion or instruction.

Art. 247. Fines not exceeding for any one infraction thirty dollars, may be imposed by the court on such grand jurors as fail in their attendance at any time during the term. The grand jury may themselves, in addition thereto, impose fines not exceeding ten dollars, to insure punctuality in attending at the hour to which they may have adjourned. Such fines to be collected in the same manner with other fines by the sheriff, on the warrant of the foreman, and appropriated to such charitable institution, as the grand jury shall direct.

Art. 248. Grand jurors cannot, during the time of their attendance as such, be arrested for any misdemeanor, nor on any civil suit, except for a breach of the peace committed during the time they are thus privileged; nor for five days previous to the day for which they are summoned, nor two days after their discharge: and any one who shall arrest or cause to be arrested, any person summoned as grand juror, knowing him to be such, contrary to the provisions of this act, shall be fined not less than thirty nor more than one hundred dollars; and the grand juror so arrested shall be discharged from such arrest, and may recover such damages as he may be entitled to by a civil suit.

Art. 249. The functions of a grand juror require to be exercised with the most perfect freedom of opinion, of debate and action; therefore it is his duty to keep secret whatever he himself or any other juror may have said, or in what manner he or they may have voted, on any particular question or matter legally before them; and any person offending against the provisions of this article is guilty of a misdemeanor, and shall be fined not less than thirty dollars nor more than one hundred dollars.

Art. 250. No grand juror shall, directly, or indirectly, give information to any one that an accusation or complaint is pending before the grand jury, if the person accused has not been arrested on such accusation or complaint; and any one offending against this provision, is guilty of a misdemeanor, and shall be fined not less than fifty nor more than two hundred dollars, unless such information was given with intent that the person accused should escape or avoid an arrest, in which case, the juror giving such information shall also be deemed to be an accessary to the offender, whose escape he intended to promote.

Art. 251. No grand juror shall be prosecuted or sued for any thing he may say or any vote he may give, in the grand jury, relative to any matter legally pending before the jury ; provided, that nothing herein contained shall prevent the prosecution and punishment of any grand juror who shall be guilty of perjury in making any accusation or giving any evidence to his fellow jurors ; and in the case contemplated by this proviso, the jurors are not bound by their oath nor by any of the preceding articles, to keep such perjury secret.


# CHAPTER IV.

## *Of indictments and informations.*

Art. 252. No OFFENCE can be prosecuted except by indictment or information. This rule is modified in cases of certain fines and of contempt, in the manner specially provided for.

Art. 253. An indictment is an act in writing made by a grand jury legally convoked and sworn, declaring that a person therein named or described, has done some act or has been guilty of some omission which is by law declared to be an offence.

The indictment shall be in the following form :

" To the district court of the district (or the criminal court, giving the style of the court as the case may be).

" The grand jurors for the (name the parish and district) on their oath present, that A. B. on the        day of        in the year
in the parish of        did (here insert the act constituting the offence) contrary to the laws of this state and the peace and dignity of the same.

C. D. Foreman.

E. F. Clerk."

Art. 254. No indictment shall be deemed deficient in form for any variance from that contained in the preceding article, provided it can be understood :

1. That the same was presented to some court having jurisdiction of the offence stated in the indictment, although the title of the said court may not be accurately set forth.

2. That it may be also understood from the said indictment that it was found by a grand jury, convened for the parish or district in which such court sat.

3. That the person accused is named, or if his name cannot be discovered, that he be described as "a person refusing to discover his name," which shall be sufficient description ; but if on his arraignment the accused, so described, shall assume some name, the name so assumed shall be inserted in the indictment and taken as the true name. No addition is necessary to the name, but if a false one be given,

it can only be corrected in the manner stated under the head of arraignment.

4. That the offence is alleged to have been committed at some place which is within the jurisdiction of the court, except in cases where the act, though done without the local jurisdiction of the court, is made cognizable therein by law.

5. That the offence is alleged to have been committed at some time which is prior to the time of finding the indictment, and where there is a limitation of time for commencing the prosecution, within such limitation.

6. That the act or omission charged, be so clearly and distinctly set forth, as to enable a man of common understanding to know what is intended.

7. That the indictment be signed by the foreman and the clerk of the grand jury, and that the day on which it was presented to the court be noted thereon.

8. That the name be set forth of the party injured, if a private offence, but if the names are unknown to the grand jury, it may be so stated.

9. That it concludes with the words " contrary to the laws of this state, and the peace and dignity of the same," which are required by the constitution.

Art. 255. The words used in an indictment, shall be taken and construed in their usual acceptation in common language, except such words and phrases as are particularly defined, which are to be taken in the sense herein given to them.

Art. 256. It is not necessary to state in the indictment any particular place in the parish for the commission of the offence, or to aver that it was done within the jurisdiction of the court, but it will be sufficient to state that it was done within the parish, naming it, if such parish be actually within the jurisdiction of the court.

Art. 257. Where the offence shall have been begun in one parish or district, and become complete in another parish or district, the offender may be tried in either of the districts or parishes, and the offence may be stated to have been done in either of the said parishes or districts, and proof that the offence was either begun or completed in the parish or district where it is charged to have been done, shall be sufficient to support the indictment.

Art. 258. Accomplices and accessaries to offences begun in one parish or district, and which become complete in another, may in like manner be prosecuted in either of the said parishes or districts, and the offender may also, as in case of principals, be stated in the indictment to have been done in either, and proof thereof shall in like manner support the indictment.

Art. 259. Where any act done out of the state is made an offence by the Penal Code, the offender may be tried in the parish or district in which he is apprehended.

Art. 260. If any one out of the state or in one parish or district of the state, shall procure another person to commit an offence within another parish of the state, he may be indicted and tried in the place where the offence was committed, and that whether the person doing the act, were an innocent or guilty agent.

Art. 261. It is not necessary to state the place in which an indictment is found in the margin of the indictment.

Art. 262. Every thing necessary to be stated must be truly stated in the indictment : there are no legal fictions.

Art. 263. Every indictment must describe the offence with such certainty, as to enable the accused to plead the judgment that may be given on it, in bar of any prosecution for the same offence.

Art. 264. The precise time at which the offence was committed need not be stated in the indictment, provided it be laid to have been done before the time of presenting the indictment ; but where the time is material to the description of the offence, it must be alleged with the same certainty that is described in the definition of the offence.

Art. 265. Rules and forms are given in a subsequent chapter for drawing indictments and informations, in each particular offence ; where those forms or rules vary from those contained in this chapter, the particular rules or forms are to prevail in that offence for which they are intended.

Art. 266. When any circumstance is expressly made an aggravation of the offence, such circumstance must be set forth in the indictment.

Art. 267. Where a repetition of the offence is intended to be relied on as an aggravation of the punishment, the indictment must set forth the preceding conviction, with the exceptions hereinafter mentioned.

Art. 268. Where the intent is a material part in the description of the offence, it must be stated in the indictment.

Art. 269. Every indictment for forgery, or for making, altering, passing, or having in possession any instrument in writing, contrary to any of the provisions of the chapter of the Code of Crimes and Punishments relative to "Offences affecting the credit of written instruments," or for any other offences founded on written instruments, shall, with the exception contained in the next article, contain an exact copy of such instrument, expressing in words whatever is so expressed in the instrument, and in figures, what in the instrument is expressed in figures, but no ornamental engraving or writing contained in the instrument, need be imitated in the copy.

Art. 270. The only case in which an indictment for either of the offences mentioned in the last article, shall be good without containing a copy of the instrument, is, where the instrument has been destroyed by the act or procurement of the accused, in which case that fact may be charged in the indictment, and must on the trial be proved ; and instead of the copy, the instrument must be described in the indictment with so much certainty as to make it appear that it was one of those which are made punishable by the system of Penal Law.

Art. 271. To every indictment for any of the offences above enumerated, except in the case mentioned in the last article, and in the case of forgery or other offence relating to a public record, the foreman of the grand jury shall annex the instrument on which the indictment is found, and shall mark the same, by writing on some part thereof, the initials of his name, and the said instrument shall remain annexed to the said indictment, unless it shall be withdrawn by leave of the court.

Art. 272. In the case above of an offence relating to a public record,

3 Q

the book in which it is kept shall be produced and marked by the foreman of the grand jury ; and shall again be brought into court, and verified to be the same, without alteration, as it was produced to the grand jury ; and shall be exhibited to the defendant, previous to his arraignment, when he is called on for his exceptions to the indictment, in the manner prescribed in the next chapter.

Art. 273. In case of any defamation by writing or printing, painted or inscribed on a building, or on an article, too bulky to be produced in court, a copy or description may be inserted in the ACT OF ACCUSATION, and proof of the fact be given on the trial, without producing the painting or writing, or showing it to the accused.

Art. 274. In cases of libel, the indictment or information need not contain the whole of the work, but only so much as is charged to be libellous, but the whole must be annexed to the act of accusation.

Art. 275. In an indictment for any of the offences created by the said chapter of offences affecting the credit of written instruments, it shall not be necessary to charge that the instrument on which the indictment is brought, would, if true, have had any of the effects enumerated in the article containing the definition of the offence, or specifying what the effect would be, or to name any particular person, whom it was the intent of the accused to defraud ; or to state otherwise than by the copy thereof, what the said instrument purported to be, or in any act of accusation whatever, to charge that the offence was committed against the form of any particular statute.

## CHAPTER V.

### Of the proceedings between the indictment and the trial.

Art. 276. It shall be the duty of the clerk of the court, in which any indictment or information for any offence is filed, within three days after the same shall have been filed, to make a copy thereof, and to deliver the same to the sheriff, to be served on the accused, or on his bail ; and no one shall be, without his assent, arraigned or called on to answer any indictment or information, until three whole days have elapsed after the copy shall have been served as aforesaid exclusive of the days of service and arraignments.

Art. 277. Two days, at the least, after having received the copy of the indictment, and one day at the least before his arraignment, the accused shall be brought into court, and the instrument (if there be any) annexed to the indictment shall be exhibited to him ; and he and his counsel shall, in the presence of an officer of the court, have reasonable time allowed them to compare the said instrument with the copy set forth in the indictment, and to consider of any exception they may think proper to make to the indictment.

Art. 278. After the exhibition of the instrument, as is above provided for, and after the expiration of the time allowed for the examination thereof, in cases where there is any instrument annexed, and in cases where there is no instrument annexed, then at such time as the court shall direct, at least two days after the service of the indictment, and at least one day before the arraignment, the accused shall be brought into court, and he must be told by the clerk that if he has any exception to make to the indictment, for any want of substance or form, or for any variance between the said indictment and the instrument thereunto annexed, or for that he, the accused, is not indicted by his true name, that he must then make such exception, or that no such exception will hereafter be heard.

Art. 279. If the accused shall make no such exception, an entry shall be made on the back of the indictment to that effect, and the accused shall be remanded to prison if in custody, or to his bail, if he be out on bail, until the time of his arraignment; and no motion for quashing the indictment, or for an arrest of the judgment, shall be made on account of any of the exceptions mentioned in the last article, except as is hereafter provided in this chapter.

Art. 280. If the accused shall allege for exception, that he is not indicted by his true name, he must state what such true name is; and the prosecuting officer may then immediately amend the indictment by inserting such name, which the accused shall not be permitted at any time afterwards to disavow.

Art. 281. If the accused shall make any exception to any want of form in the indictment, or to any variance between the instrument of writing and the copy in the indictment, the public prosecutor may, if he think the said exceptions well taken, immediately amend such defect of form or variance.

It shall be optional with the accused to make the exceptions mentioned in the preceding articles, verbally or in writing; if verbally made, the judge shall take a note of them in writing, which shall be read to the accused.

Art. 282. In case any amendments shall be made, either in virtue of the two preceding sections, or by permission of the court, as is hereinafterwards provided for, the court may allow such further time for the arraignment and trial, as they may deem necessary to enable the accused to prepare for his defence.

Art. 283. Whether the accused except to any irregularity in the form of the indictment, or to any variance between the indictment and the copy of the instrument annexed to it, or not, the public prosecutor shall be permitted to amend the same, at any time before the arraignment. If the public prosecutor shall not choose to amend the indictment according to any exception made by the accused, or if the court shall be of opinion that such exception relates to matter of substance, and is not amendable under the provisions of this chapter, a day shall be assigned for the argument of such exceptions, previous to the arraignment; and if the court shall allow such exception, and consider them as matter of substance, the accused may be again indicted for the same offence, and shall not be, on that account, discharged; but if the court shall allow the exceptions, after argument, but consider them as matter of form only, the public prosecutor may immediately amend them.

Art. 284. If the grand jury which found the indictment was illegally constituted, or not drawn or selected in the manner directed by law, or not sworn; the accused may except thereto, in the manner directed by the        article; but if such exception be allowed, it shall be considered as a matter of substance, and no amendment shall be allowed.

Art. 285. If the exception be that it does not appear by the indictment, for what district the grand jurors were summoned, or in what court, or whether they were sworn or not, or whether they were drawn and impanelled in the manner directed by law ; it shall be considered as matter of form and amendable, unless the exception state, that in point of fact the grand jury were not summoned from the proper district, or were not sworn, or that they were impanelled in another court, or that the forms prescribed by law were not pursued in the drawing or impanelling their names, in which case, if either of the said last mentioned exceptions of fact are allowed, it shall be considered matter of substance, and shall not be amendable.

Art. 286. If the exception be that the copy of the instrument in writing on which the prosecution is founded, is not contained in the indictment, or that the original is not annexed in cases where, by law, such copy ought to have been inserted, and such original annexed ; or that the time and place is not set forth at which the offence is said to have been committed; or that the action or omission alleged, is not one that is by law created an offence : or that where the intent is made a material part of the offence, such intent is not charged; either of these exceptions shall be considered as matter of substance, and shall not be amendable.

Art. 287. All exceptions, other than those enumerated in the three last preceding articles, and therein designated as exceptions to matter of substance, shall be considered as exceptions to matter of form ; and shall be amendable in the manner hereinbefore provided for.

Art. 288. After a conviction, no judgment shall be arrested for any allegation of a defect, either in substance or form, other than this; that the act of accusation contains no charge of any thing amounting to an offence, and if such objection be allowed, another indictment or information may immediately be filed, and the defendant shall not be discharged, if the proof adduced on the trial be sufficient to have warranted his arrest.

Art. 289. At the time when the accused is called to make his exception to the indictment, he shall be asked by the court whether he has counsel; and if he shall allege that he is unable to procure counsel, the court shall assign some licensed attorney to conduct his defence under his direction. But the accused may in all cases have the advice and assistance of any one whom he may have engaged, whether licensed or not, to aid him in his defence. But such employment shall not deprive the prosecutor of the right of examining such person as a witness, to state any facts which came to his knowledge, either prior to the prosecution, or which were not confided to him by the accused, after such prosecution was commenced.

Art. 290. If the defendant make no exceptions to the act of accusation, or if, having made any, they are overruled, he must next be arraigned: this is done by the clerk, who must read to him the act of accusation in an audible voice, and the judge must interrogate him by asking, "Are you guilty of the charge you have just heard read, or not guilty?"

Art. 291. This form must not be dispensed with, either on a suggestion that the defendant knows the contents of the act of accusation, or out of delicacy to any defendant.

Art. 292. To this interrogatory of the arraignment, unless he plead the special plea mentioned in the next article, the defendant can only answer in the negative or the affirmative: a refusal to answer, or an evasive or explanatory answer, shall be taken and recorded as an answer of not guilty.

Art. 293. If the defendant have before had judgment of acquittal, or been convicted of the same offence, he must state that matter specially in writing, and to this plea the public prosecutor may either demur if it be deficient in substance, or reply either that there is no record of any such conviction or acquittal as is pleaded, and on the trial the defendant must produce the record and prove that he is the same person mentioned therein.

Art. 294. If the defendant answer in the affirmative, it shall not be recorded until the court shall have explained its consequence, and desired him to reflect, and if he wishes it, to consult with his counsel : if after this he persevere, the confession shall be recorded; provided there is no reason to suppose the confession proceeds from insanity, for which purpose, in all cases of CRIME when the party making the confession is in custody, the officer in whose charge he was, shall be interrogated.

Art. 295. When the plea of not guilty is recorded, the public prosecutor shall, under the direction of the court, designate to the defendant a day for the trial, which shall not, without the consent of the defendant, be less than the third day after that on which the notice is given, and this time may be prolonged at the instance of the defendant or of the public prosecutor, under the limitations hereinafter contained.

Art. 296. On application to the clerk, process for summoning the witnesses, as well on the part of the defendant as the public prosecutor, shall be made out directed to the sheriff of any parish where the witness may be found, who shall be bound to execute the same.

## CHAPTER VI.

*Of the mode of drawing and summoning the jury.*

Art. 297. All offences whatever must be tried by jury.

Art. 298. All free white persons of full age and not exceeding sixty years of age, who have resided one year in the parish in which they are called to serve, and have paid taxes or been rated on the tax list either for parish, city or state tax, or who have resided six months in the parish and own real property therein, whether they have paid taxes or not, are qualified jurors.

Art. 299. The names of all grand jurors and petit jurors, must be drawn by lot before they are put on the panel.

Art. 300. For this purpose, in each of the parishes of this state in which a court, having criminal jurisdiction, shall sit, the parish judge, the sheriff, and two justices of the peace to be designated by the judge, or a majority of them, shall within thirty days after the promulgation of this code, form and sign a list containing the names of the persons having the qualifications above enumerated, who are in their opinion the best qualified, from their education and character, to serve on juries. Such list shall contain a number of names equal at least to two thirds of the number of voters at the last general election in such parish.

Art. 301. In forming such list, the persons aforesaid shall consult the assessment roll of taxes, and the list of votes taken at the general election next preceding the time of making the list.

Art. 302. No name on the tax list or list of voters, shall be excluded from the list so to be formed but by the unanimous consent of all the persons hereby appointed to form it.

Art. 303. Any inhabitant of the parish, having the qualifications required, whose name has been omitted on such list for one year, may, if he desire it, have it inserted in the next year's list, by applying either to the sheriff or the parish judge.

Art. 304. When the list is so signed, the same shall be delivered to the parish judge to be filed, and the sheriff shall immediately, in the presence of the judge, of at least one justice and of as many other citizens as choose to attend, proceed to write each name contained on such list on a separate ballot, all as nearly as may be of the same size and appearance.

Art. 305. The sheriff shall also provide two boxes, each having an opening in the top that may be closed and locked with two different locks, and shall deposit the said ballots in one of the boxes and lock the openings of both, delivering one of the keys of each to the judge, and keeping the other himself, and shall keep both boxes in his own custody.

Art. 306. At some day, to be designated by the parish judge, between thirty and fifteen days before every session of any court of criminal jurisdiction in the parish, the said judge shall cause notice to be given to the sheriff and to two justices of the peace, to meet at such place as he shall direct ; and the judge shall, in their presence or that of a majority of them, as often as a grand jury shall be required for such court, draw at hazard from the box containing the ballots the names of fifty persons, out of which the sheriff shall select ten and the judge seven, and the justices of the peace each three names, which shall be inserted on a list to form the panel for the grand jury, but if only one justice attend, he shall select six names, and the ballots containing the names so selected shall be put in the second box, and the residue of the ballots returned to that from which they were taken.

Art. 307. Forty ballots shall in like manner be taken from the first box, and the names contained on them shall be written on a list to form the panel of petit jurors, for the trial of causes in such court at its next session ; and the ballots shall be put in the second box and both boxes shall then be locked, the keys delivered as before, and the boxes kept in the custody of the sheriff.

Art. 308. The two lists, or the one (in case no grand jury is drawn), shall then be certified by the judge, the sheriff and at least one justice, to contain the names of those who were drawn and selected to serve as grand jurors or drawn to serve as petit jurors, and shall be delivered by the sheriff to the clerk of the court, who shall file and record the same.

Art. 309. Any court may by rule direct grand or petit jurors to be summoned at other periods, where the business of the court renders the attendance of one set for a whole session too oppressive.

Art. 310. Every year, within thirty days of the time the first list was made out, a new list shall be in like manner made, and the ballots containing the names shall be put into the box after destroying those of the first year.

Art. 311. So many of the names contained on the list of one year, may be put on that of the succeeding year, as the persons intrusted with the duty may deem proper.

Art. 312. As often as the first box shall be exhausted, the ballots contained in the second shall be transferred to the first.

Art. 313. On receiving such lists, it shall be the duty of the clerk to make out a writ in the form hereinafter in this code contained, with a schedule annexed containing a true copy of the list of grand jurors, commanding the sheriff to summon the persons named in such list to attend as grand jurors at the next session of the court.

Art. 314. The clerk shall in like manner make out a writ for summoning the petit jury.

Art. 315. The sheriff shall execute such writs in the manner they command, by leaving a printed notice, containing the day and place of attendance, with each juror, or at his place of abode, at least six days before the return of the writ.

Art. 316. Jurors who do not appear when regularly summoned, or who depart without leave of the court, or who violate any legal rule for preserving order in the course of judicial proceedings, may be fined, for each offence, not exceeding ten dollars, and the court may command process to issue immediately for collecting it.

## CHAPTER VII.

*Of proceedings in court previous to the trial.*

### SECTION I.

#### Of postponing a trial.

Art. 317. At any time before the trial, the public prosecutor or the defendant may apply to put it off to a future day, which shall be granted whenever such circumstances shall appear to the court by affidavit, as show justice requires it. But the defendant, if in custody, may be discharged, if he is not brought to trial in the second term after his arrest; and if on bail, during the fourth term after such arrest : provided the delay have not taken place on his application, and that he have been guilty of no contrivance to deprive the prosecutor of his testimony.

Art. 318. The trial must also be postponed if it appear that a copy of the panel of jurors has not been delivered according to the provisions hereinafter contained.

Art. 319. On the day of the trial, the defendant shall be called, if he be on bail, or brought into court, if in custody: the names of the jurors shall then be called, and if not challenged, or if the challenge be overruled, shall be sworn.

Art. 320. If the trial be for a misdemeanor, it may proceed if the defendant appear by his counsel ; if it be for a crime, the defendant must be personally present ; and if on bail, must then be surrendered into the custody of the sheriff, and remain in custody until discharged by due course of law. But the court may at their discretion, when sex, age, or state of health require it, permit the defendant to remain in the custody of his bail during the recess of the court, if the cause cannot be finished in one sitting, or while the jury are out, if any great delay should take place in rendering the verdict.

SECTION II.

Of challenge.

Art. 321. A challenge is an objection made to the jurors who are returned to try the cause, and is of two kinds.

1. To the panel.

2. To any individual juror.

Art. 322. The panel is the list of jurors, either for the grand or trial jury, made by the officers authorized for that purpose, when the names are drawn according to law.

Art. 323. A copy of the panel of the trial jury must be delivered by the sheriff to every defendant, if in custody, or to his bail, if he be delivered to bail, at least three whole days before the day of trial, for the purpose of enabling him to make his challenge.

Art. 324. A challenge to the panel is an objection made to all trial jurors who are summoned; it can only be grounded on some material departure from the forms prescribed by law for drawing and empanelling juries. But it is not a good cause of challenge to the panel, that one or more persons not having the legal qualifications, have been put on the jury list.

Art. 325. A challenge to the panel must be made in writing, stating the cause of challenge, before any juror is sworn, and the officers, whether judicial or ministerial, as well as any other persons, may be examined to prove or disprove the irregularity alleged, if the public prosecutor deny the fact. If he admit the fact, but deny the irregularity complained of is material, he may demur to the challenge.

Art. 326. Challenges to individual jurors are of two kinds; peremptory and for cause.

Art. 327. A peremptory challenge is an objection made to a juror for which no reason need be given; it is enough for the defendant to signify his desire that any particular juror who is about to be sworn, shall not serve on the jury, and he shall be set aside; but this right can be exercised only with respect to nine jurors.

Art. 328. Where there are several defendants, each one is entitled to his challenge, both peremptory and for cause; but if they do not agree to let one challenge for the whole, they must be separately tried.

Art. 329. A challenge for cause is an objection made to a particular juror on the allegation of some circumstance that renders him either incapable to serve as a juror in any case, or unfit to serve as such in the one about to be tried. Of the first kind are:

1. Conviction of any offence which by the Code of Crimes and Punishments incurs a forfeiture of the right of serving as a juror.

2. A want of qualifications designated by law as necessary for a juryman.

3. Insanity, or such defect in the organs of hearing, seeing or speaking, or other bodily or mental defect or disease as renders him incapable of performing the duties of a juror.

All these are called principal causes of challenge. When a particular exemption from service on juries is granted by law, it is not a cause of challenge to such person, but a right of which he may avail himself or not.

Art. 330. The causes of challenge of the second kind are either in chief, by the allegation of a fact, which if proved is a disqualification by law, or to the favour, by the allegation of some circumstance which is supposed to evince the want of that perfect impartiality necessary in a juror. The causes of challenge in chief are:

1. Relationship within the ninth degree to the person alleged to be injured or attempted to be injured by the offence charged, or to the person on whose complaint the prosecution was instituted, or to the defendant.

2. Standing in the relation of husband, master or servant, landlord or tenant, tutor or curator, sponsor for the child of one of the said parties, in his employment on wages, or plaintiff or defendant against him in any civil suit, or having complained against him, or being accused by him in any criminal prosecution.

3. Having served on the grand jury which found the indictment against the defendant on which he is about to be tried.

4. Having served on a petit jury which has convicted or acquitted another person charged with having committed the same offence now about to be tried.

5. Having been one of a jury which was sworn in the same cause against the same defendant, and which jury either gave a verdict which was set aside, or was discharged after hearing evidence for any other cause, except in the case hereinafter provided.

6. Having served as a juror in a civil suit brought against the defendant for the same act.

7. Having formed such an opinion of the guilt or innocence of the defendant, as in the opinion of the juror himself, renders him not an impartial judge.

Art. 331. If either of the facts stated as causes of challenge in the two last preceding articles, be alleged and proved to the satisfaction of the court, the juror challenged for such cause shall not be sworn.

Art. 332. The juror challenged may be sworn, and other evidence may be produced, to show the truth of the cause of challenge, and in the case of the seventh cause above enumerated for challenges in chief, if the juror have formed an opinion but does not think it disqualifies him, this may be made a case of challenge to the juror in the manner provided by the next article. But no juror shall be obliged to answer, whether he has been convicted or not of a certain crime that would disqualify him.

Art. 333. A juror must come to the performance of his high duty with a mind perfectly unbiassed; therefore, if no challenge in chief be made, or being made, is not proved, the defendant, if he can prove any other circumstance that shows either prejudice against him, or favour to his accuser, may make it a cause of challenge to the favour.

Art. 334. This challenge, like those in chief, is made verbally, and if it be to the first juror who appears, it must be tried by three

3 R

persons called triers, to be named by the court : if one juror has been sworn, he, together with two persons named, are the triers ; if two are sworn, the court must name another trier, and when three jurors are sworn, they are the triers of all subsequent challenges to the jurors.

Art. 335. The triers shall be sworn to decide whether the juror challenged is perfectly unbiassed, and free from all prejudice against the defendant, and as a majority of the said triers decide, the juror shall be sworn or the challenge allowed.

Art. 336. A juror against whom a challenge in chief or the favour has been overruled, may be challenged peremptorily.

Art. 337. The public prosecutor may make challenges to the panel or for cause to individual jurors, for the same causes, in which they are allowed to the defendant. He has also a right of peremptory challenge to three jurors.

Art. 338. All challenges to individual jurors must be made when they are called to be sworn, but before they are sworn.

## CHAPTER VIII.

### Of the trial.

Art. 339. The names of all the jurors on the petit jury panel, shall be called, and those who do not appear shall be fined not exceeding ten dollars, which fine on the subsequent appearance of the juror and on his offering a sufficient excuse, to be approved at the discretion of the court, may be remitted.

Art. 340. Either the public prosecutor or the defendant may require, before proceeding to trial, that an attachment issue against the jurors who have made default, on which they shall be arrested and brought forthwith into court.

Art. 341. After waiting such time as the court shall deem reasonable for the return of the attachment, the clerk shall in open court put the names of all the jurors on the panel, each written on a separate ballot, folded as near as may be of the same size and shape, into a ballot box, from which they shall be drawn successively, and, if not challenged, sworn in the order in which they are drawn, until the number of twelve shall be complete.

Art. 342. The court has power to excuse any juror from attendance, for reasonable cause, and whenever any number exceeding five have been so excused, or when a sufficient number cannot be brought up on attachment for the trial of a cause, the court may direct the names of a sufficient number of other jurors to be drawn from the box, and order them to be summoned to attend immediately, and their names shall be put into the court box and drawn for the trials as is before directed.

Art. 343. Any less number than twelve that may be agreed on between the public prosecutor and the defendant, may try a misdemeanor, but a crime shall not be tried by less than a full jury, drawn by lot in the manner above directed.

Art. 344. The trial shall proceed in the following order :

1. The clerk shall read the indictment or information to the jury, and inform them what answer has been recorded.

2. The public prosecutor shall open the case by reading from the code the description of the offence, and stating summarily, by what evidence he expects to prove the guilt of the defendant.

3. The public prosecutor shall offer the evidence in support of the prosecution.

4. The defendant, or his counsel, shall open his defence, state in what facts or law he intends to rely, and whether he thinks the evidence for the prosecution insufficient or inapplicable.

5. The defendant shall produce his testimony.

6. The public prosecutor may then introduce testimony to rebut any that has been introduced by the defendant, or if he do not, he may offer his concluding argument.

7. The defendant closes the argument; previous to which he may introduce testimony to repel that last offered by the prosecutor.

Art. 346. The public prosecutor may at any time during the term request the court to give a direction to find a verdict for the defendant, if he finds that the prosecution cannot be supported, and if the court give such direction, the jury are bound to acquit the defendant, and if they refuse, a new trial shall be immediately granted, or, at the option of the defendant, entry made that the public prosecutor will no longer prosecute for the offence.

Art. 347. The court cannot, for any defect or supposed deficiency of testimony, prevent the jury from giving a verdict.

Art. 348. If a juror on any trial for a crime should be taken with some malady, that prevents his performing his duty, the court may order him to be discharged; and in that case a new jury must be sworn, and the trial must begin again : the same jurors may, if drawn, serve on the new jury, but may be challenged although they were not before.

Art. 349. In misdemeanor, a new juror may be added, or the trial may proceed with those who remain by the consent of the prosecutor and the defendant.

Art. 350. The court has a discretionary power of adjourning the trial from day to day, if from the length of the proceedings it cannot be conveniently finished in one or more sittings, or if any unforeseen circumstance should make it necessary for the attainment of justice to do so.

Art. 351. In the case provided for by the last preceding article, the jury must, unless by consent, be kept together during the recess of the court, at the public expense, under the charge of an officer, who shall be sworn not to permit any one to speak with them touching any matter relative to that trial. This consent cannot be given in cases of crimes punishable with imprisonment for life.

Art. 352. The court may also discharge the jury : 1st. Whenever it appears to them by the examination of a physician that a witness on either side, who has not been examined or discharged, and who is proved to be a material one, has been taken sick since the commencement of the trial, and cannot be examined in court without danger to his life, and there is no probability of his speedy recovery. 2d. Where the defendant himself is so taken sick. 3d. Where a material witness on the part of the prosecution has been concealed, or induced to abscond or conceal himself by the defendant, or any one employed by him ; or where such witness for the defendant is concealed, or has been induced to conceal himself, or abscond, by the public prosecutor, the complainant, or the person supposed to be injured by the offence, or by any one employed by either of them.

Art. 353. The judge shall decide all questions of law arising in the course of the trial, and shall keep notes of all the testimony offered on either side.

Art. 354. When the pleadings are finished, the judge shall give his charge to the jury, in which he shall state to them all such matters of law as he shall think necessary for their information in giving their verdict. But he shall not recapitulate the testimony unless requested so to do by one or more of the jurors, if there should be any difference of opinion between them as to any particular part of the testimony, and then he shall confine his information to the part on which information is required, it being the intent of this article that the jury shall decide all questions of fact, in which is included the credit due to the witnesses who have been sworn, unbiassed by the opinion of the court.

Art. 355. After hearing the charge, the jury may either decide in court or retire for consultation. If they cannot immediately agree, an officer must be sworn in the manner set forth in the subsequent chapter, to take charge of them ; and they must then retire to a chamber prepared for them.

Art. 356. Before leaving the court, the jury must appoint one of their number to be foreman ; whose duty it is to preside in their debates, to deliver the verdict, or ask any information from the court that may be required by the jury. If a majority do not agree in the appointment of a foreman, he shall be named by the court.

Art. 357. Whenever in the opinion of the court it may be deemed proper and convenient that the jury should have a view of the place in which the offence is said to have been committed or of any other place in which any other transaction material to the inquiry on the trial took place, an order shall be made to that effect, and the jury shall be conducted in a body under the care of the sheriff, to the place, which shall be shown to them by a person appointed by the court, and it shall be the duty of the sheriff to suffer no other person to speak to the jury, and they shall when the view is finished, be immediately conducted into court.

## CHAPTER IX.

### *Of the conduct of the jury after receiving the charge.*

Art. 358. When the jury have retired, they must proceed to deliberate of their verdict. If there be any disagreement between them as to any part of the testimony, or if any juror wish to be informed of any point of law arising in the cause, the officer having charge of them shall bring them into court ; where the information asked shall be given in the presence of, or after notice to, the defendant or his counsel, and to the public prosecutor.

Art. 359. After having received the information required, the jury may again return, and shall not be discharged until they are all agreed on their verdict, unless it shall appear to the court that there is no probability that they will agree, and that the health of one or more of the jurors will be endangered by the confinement.

Art. 360. The jury to be kept during the time of their retirement without any other sustenance than bread and water, except during the adjournments from day to day, mentioned in the last chapter ; and they are to speak to no one, except in case of such adjournment, but the officer who attends them, and with him they are to have no other communication than necessity requires.

Art. 361. If one of the jurors, after they have retired, should be taken so sick as to prevent the continuance of his duty, the jury must be discharged, unless in cases of misdemeanor it is agreed between the public prosecutor and the defendant, that the remaining jurors shall decide the cause. This agreement cannot be made in case of crime.

Art. 362. In all cases where power is given to the court to discharge a jury, it operates no discharge of the defendant, but a new jury must be sworn to try the cause.

Art. 363. The court may adjourn while the jury are deliberating on their verdict, and if the jury should agree before the next meeting of the court, if the cause in which they are empanelled be a misdemeanor, they may write and sign their verdict, which must be left with the foreman, sealed, and the jurors are then at liberty to disperse, but must be all present in court at its opening ; when the foreman must deliver it to the court, which shall be openly read, and if agreed to by all the jurors, shall be recorded.

Art. 364. A sealed verdict cannot be given in cases of crime even by consent.

Art. 365. The jury shall take with them all papers that have been received as evidence in the cause, or copies of such parts of public records, books or other documents as cannot without inconvenience be taken from the persons having charge of them. They may also take with them notes of the testimony which one or more of them have taken, but none made by any other person.

Art. 366. If a juror have any personal knowledge respecting any fact in controversy in the cause, it is his duty to make the declaration in open court during the trial. If during the retirement any juror declare any fact that could be evidence in the cause, to his fellows, as of his own knowledge, it is the duty of the other members to return with him into court ; and in both cases, the juror making the statement must be sworn as a witness, and examined in the presence of the parties.

Art. 367. A mere declaration of the credit or want of credit any juror gives to a witness, does not come within the last preceding article.

Art. 368. The court may punish by fine not exceeding twenty dollars, any such breach of the duties prescribed to grand or petit jurors as are imposed upon them by law, other than such as are specially created offences, which must be prosecuted by information.

Art. 369. No juror shall be punished for any opinion or vote he may have given in deliberating on or in giving his verdict.

## CHAPTER X.

### *Of the verdict.*

Art. 370. When the jury have agreed in their verdict, they shall be conducted by the officer having charge of them into court ; when their names shall be called, and if all do not appear, the rest shall be discharged without giving a verdict.

Art. 371. If the whole jury appear, the defendant shall be called if he be out on bail, or brought into court if he be in custody.

Art. 372. In case of misdemeanor, the defendant may answer when called by his attorney or counsel, both at the trial and when the verdict is brought in, and the bail is answerable in the amount of the recognizance if the defendant do not surrender himself to receive judgment. When imprisonment forms a part of the judgment, it may at any time afterwards be inflicted if the defendant be found, notwithstanding the payment of the penalty of the recognizance.

Art. 373. When the jury have returned into court, they shall be asked whether they have agreed on their verdict, and if the foreman answer in the affirmative, they shall, on being required, give the same verbally, or if it be written, the foreman shall read the same.

Art. 374. The form must be either "guilty" or "not guilty," which is a general verdict and imports an acquittal or conviction on all the facts charged ; or in cases where the jurors are in doubt whether the facts that have been proved, amount to any offence on which they can decide under the charge in the act of accusation, they may find a special verdict.

Art. 375. A special verdict is a statement of the facts which have been proved to the satisfaction of the jury, with a conclusion that, being uncertain whether such facts are sufficient to establish in law the guilt of the defendant, they submit that point to the decision of the court.

Art. 376. A special verdict shall be argued at such time and in such manner as shall be directed by the rules of court, but the counsel for the defendant shall conclude the argument.

Art. 377. If, after argument, the court shall be of opinion that the facts found prove the defendant is guilty of the offence charged in the act of accusation, or of any other of which he could be convicted under that act of accusation, according to the rules hereinafter established, they shall proceed to pronounce judgment accordingly.

Art. 378. If the facts found show, that the act does not amount to any such offence as the defendant could have been convicted on, under that act of accusation, they shall pronounce a judgment of acquittal.

Art. 379. In either of the cases mentioned in the two last preceding articles, the judgment shall be a bar to any future prosecution for the same offence.

Art. 380. If the jury do not pronounce affirmatively or negatively on facts necessary to establish the guilt or the innocence of the defendant, the court shall direct a new trial.

Art. 381. On an act of accusation for any offence coming within the general description of homicide, the jury may find the defendant guilty of homicide in any degree lower than that charged in the indictment ; the degrees are measured by the order in which the offences are described in the code, those first described being lowest in degree.

Art. 382. On acts of accusation for battery, aggravated by any of the circumstances which enhance the guilt of the offender, the jury may find him guilty only of simple assault and battery ; if several circumstances of aggravation are charged in the act of accusation, they may find him guilty of one or more ; but no one can be found guilty of an act of aggravation not charged.

Art. 383. If the charge made by the act of accusation be of theft, aggravated by any of the circumstances which would enhance the guilt of the offence, whether such circumstances as give it another denomination (such as robbery or stealing from the person) or not, the defendant may be found guilty of simple theft, or of theft aggravated by any one or more of the circumstances charged.

Art. 384. If the charge be simple theft, a verdict may be given for any fraudulent appropriation of property that by law is created an offence.

Art. 385. In the cases coming within the purview of the three last preceding articles, the acquittal or conviction is a bar to any other prosecution for the same act, although the subsequent accusation should add a charge of other intent or circumstance.

Art. 386. If a former conviction be changed either in the act of accusation or by notice, it may negative that fact, or affirm it specially, or by a general verdict.

Art. 387. In every other case not herein specially provided for, the defendant may be found guilty of any offence the commission of which is necessarily included in that of which he is accused, in the act of accusation.

Art. 388. If the defence in any accusation of crime be insanity in the defendant, and the jury acquit him on that ground, they must add that finding to their verdict, and thereupon the court is authorized to make such order for the confinement of the defendant in a hospital or otherwise, or for the delivery of him to his relations, as humanity and public safety may require.

Art. 389. If on the trial for any offence it should appear by the testimony that an offence of a higher nature has been committed than the one charged as arising from the same circumstances, the court must direct the jury to be discharged, and a new indictment sent to the grand jury for the higher offence.

Art. 390. They may also direct the jury to be discharged where there is any such defect in the indictment or other proceedings, as will prevent a trial on the merits, and may, in such case, order the defendant to be committed for any offence that the testimony may have shown he had committed.

Art. 391. If a verdict of acquittal shall be given on any act of accusation, so defective that no judgment could have been given against the defendant if he had been convicted, he shall not be discharged, but may again be indicted and brought to trial for the same offence.

Art. 392. When the jury shall find the defendant not guilty on an accusation, for any offence founded on a written instrument, under the chapter of the Penal Code entitled "Of offences affecting the credit of written contracts," the court shall inquire, and the jury must declare whether they find such instrument to be false or forged, or made contrary to any of the provisions of that chapter ; and if they find that the instrument is not false nor forged, nor made contrary to any of those provisions, the instrument shall be delivered to the person from whose possession it was taken.

Art. 393. If on such accusation the defendant is convicted, or if the jury, under the direction of the last preceding article, have found that the instrument was false, forged, or made in contravention of any provision in the chapter above referred to, the instrument shall remain attached to the indictment, until the court shall make other order, which they may do in case any civil suit be commenced which may render the production thereof necessary to any party in such suit ; but on such terms and on such security, as the court may deem proper to prevent fraud.

Art. 394. When there is a verdict of acquittal, the court cannot require the jury to reconsider it ; but when there is a verdict of conviction, in which it appears to the court that the jury have mistaken the law, they may explain the reason why they think so, and direct the jury to go out and reconsider the verdict ; but if after such reconsideration they return with the same verdict, it must be entered.

Art. 395. In like manner, if the jury bring in a verdict that is neither an acquittal nor a conviction, nor a special verdict, the court may direct the jury to reconsider the verdict, and it shall not be recorded until it is brought in in some form from which it can be clearly understood what is the intent of the jury, whether to acquit, to convict, or to state facts and leave the judgment to the court.

Art. 396. If the jury persevere in finding an informal verdict, from which, however, it can be clearly understood that their intent is to acquit, it shall be entered in the terms in which they found it, and the court shall give judgment of acquittal ; but no judgment shall be given against a defendant unless the jury expressly find him guilty, or judgment be given against him on a special verdict.

Art. 397. If the court or either of the parties think that all the jurors have not agreed to the verdict that may have been given by the foreman, they shall severally be asked whether they agree, and if any one answers in the negative, the whole jury shall be sent out for further deliberation.

Art. 398. When the verdict is given, and is such as the court must receive, the clerk records it on the minutes of the court, which he must do immediately, without attending to any other business ; and when it is recorded in full, he must read it to the jury, and demand whether they all agree : if any juror disagree, the record must be cancelled, and the jury again sent out ; if no objection be made, the jury must be discharged.

# CHAPTER XI.

*Of the proceedings after verdict to judgment.*

Art. 399. If the defendant be acquitted, and is not detained for any other legal cause, he is entitled to his discharge as soon as the verdict is recorded, except in the cases hereinbefore provided, where the court may order a detention and a new act of accusation ; unless the public prosecutor shall declare that he intends to move for a new trial for some of the legal causes hereinafter set forth, or shall request that he may be detained on an allegation that he has other charges to exhibit against him : but such motion must be made, or such charges must be exhibited in a legal form, within twelve hours after the acquittal, or the defendant must be discharged, if in custody, and his bail is exonerated if he be delivered to bail.

Art. 400. No prisoner acquitted by a verdict or discharged for want of prosecution, shall be detained for any costs or fees of office, or any debts incurred for his subsistence while in custody.

Art. 401. If the defendant be convicted, he must be remanded, if in custody, to the prison, until judgment shall be pronounced.

# CHAPTER XII.

*Of new trials and motions in arrest of judgment.*

### SECTION I.

#### Of new trials.

Art. 402. A new trial is a rehearing of the cause before another jury, after a verdict has been given on the same act of accusation.

Art. 403. The allowance of a motion for a new trial places the parties precisely in the state in which they were immediately before the first trial. All the testimony must be heard again ; and the first verdict cannot be made use of either as evidence or in argument.

Art. 404. Courts have power to grant new trials in the cases enumerated in this section.

Art. 405. After acquittal, either by general verdict or when a special verdict is found, new trials may be granted on the motion of the public prosecutor in the following cases, and no other :

1. When the defendant, or any one for his benefit, has bribed a juror, or suborned or bribed a witness, or has given any forged paper in evidence, on the first trial, which might, in the opinion of the court, have changed the verdict.

3 S

2. When the defendant, or any one for his benefit, has either by force, threats or persuasion, prevented any material witness from appearing against him on the first trial ; or has destroyed or secreted any written document, material to the prosecution, and which might otherwise have been produced.

3. When evidence in favour of the accused shall have been given to the jury out of court, without the order of the court and the consent of the public prosecutor.

4. When by the procurement of the defendant, or of any one for his benefit, the jury which tried the cause was illegally impannelled, but no illegality in the panel unless caused by such procurement, shall be a good cause for a new trial after an acquittal.

Art. 406. No irregularity committed by the jury shall be a good cause for setting aside a verdict of acquittal.

Art. 407. New trials, after a verdict of conviction, may be granted on the application of the defendant, in the following cases and no other :

1. When the defendant, being in custody, was not brought into court at the trial or at the time the verdict was delivered.

2. When he has been tried without being called on to make his exceptions to the act of accusation and other proceedings in the manner directed in the fifth chapter of this title.

3. When any one has bribed a juror to give a verdict against the defendant ; or has forged an instrument in writing which has been produced in evidence against him ; or when any of his material witnesses have by force, threats or persuasion, been prevented from attending on the trial ; or when a written instrument, material to his defence, has been intentionally destroyed or secreted for the purpose of procuring his conviction—provided in this last case, that the instrument was legal testimony, and that the defendant had reason to expect its production on the trial.

4. When material evidence has been discovered since the trial which may be procured on a new trial, which could not by due diligence have been discovered before ; and which, in the opinion of the court, might have changed the verdict had it been produced.

5. When the jury has received any other evidence, out of court, than that resulting from a view as hereinbefore directed, without leave of the court and the consent of the defendant ; when they have decided their verdict by chance ; or have separated after they had retired to consult of their verdict, and before they have given it in, except in cases of sealed verdicts, as is hereinbefore provided.

6. When the verdict is, in the opinion of the court, contrary to law or evidence : but no more than two new trials shall be given for this cause alone.

7. When the defendant has been tried without the assistance of counsel, when he has prayed that counsel should be assigned him.

8. When the court has misdirected the jury on any point of law, or given them any direction how to find any point of fact, to the prejudice of the defendant.

Art. 408. No new trial shall be granted on the allegation of the perjury of a witness, or the production of forged papers, unless the fact of perjury or forgery appear by the oath of two credible witnesses, or of one witness and strong circumstantial proof ; and unless it shall appear, that the party making the application was surprized by the production of such false evidence, and could not, by reasonable diligence, have been apprized of the intention to produce it ; or that the evidence to prove the forgery or perjury came to his knowledge after the trial, and could not, by reasonable diligence, have been discovered before.

Art. 409. In all cases of applications for a new trial, such of the facts on which it is founded, as may reasonably be supposed to be within the knowledge of the party making it, must be declared by his affidavit, supported by such other testimony, where the case admits of it, as may be satisfactory to the court.

Art. 410. Applications for a new trial, on the part of the defendant, must be made within three days after the entry of the verdict on the part of the prosecution ; it must be made in the manner and within the time specified by the first article of the eleventh chapter of this title. All applications for new trials must be in writing.

## SECTION II.

### Of motions in arrest of judgment.

Art. 411. A motion in arrest of judgment is a request made to the court, after conviction, praying that no judgment be rendered on the verdict. It must be founded on a defect apparent on the act of accusation.

Art. 412. No judgment can be arrested for a defect of form.

Art. 413. The only matter of substance for which a judgment can be arrested is this, that the act of accusation contains no charge of any fact, or of any fact coupled with an intent, that is by law declared to be an offence. The court may, on its own view of this defect, arrest the judgment without motion.

Art. 414. The effect of allowing a motion in arrest of judgment is to place the defendant in the same state, with respect to the prosecution, in which he was before the indictment was found, or the information was filed. If from the testimony, on the trial, there is sufficient reason to believe him guilty of the offence for which he was first arrested, a new indictment shall be sent to the grand jury ; or a new information shall be filed, as the case may require ; and the defendant shall remain in custody, or be delivered to bail. If the evidence show him guilty of another offence, he shall be committed or bailed on such charge : and in neither case shall the verdict bar a new prosecution. If no evidence appear sufficient to charge him with any offence, he shall be discharged, and the arrest of judgment shall operate as an acquittal of the charge on which he was arrested.

Art. 415. Motions in arrest of judgment must be made within three days after the entry of the verdict.

# CHAPTER XIII.

*Of the judgment and its incidents.*

## SECTION I.

### Of the judgment.

Art. 416. If within three days after a verdict has been entered no motion in arrest of judgment, or for a new trial, has been made, or having been made has been over-ruled, the court shall proceed to render judgment.

Art. 417. For this purpose the defendant shall be brought into court, if in custody ; or surrendered, if delivered on bail.

Art. 418. In cases of misdemeanor where the defendant has been bailed, and has appeared by attorney or in person at the trial, and when the verdict was delivered ; but does not appear to receive judgment, sentence may be pronounced in his absence. If the sentence be fine only, it shall be recovered from the bail, but only to the amount of the recognizance and after DISCUSSION of the property of the defendant.

Art. 419. If under the circumstances set forth in the last preceding article, the judgment be fine and imprisonment, or imprisonment alone, and the defendant does not surrender himself before the return of the process of execution, the bail is liable to the amount of the recognizance, and the sentence of imprisonment may afterwards be executed whenever the defendant is found.

Art. 420. The defendant being at the bar, the verdict shall be read to him, and he shall be asked whether he have any legal cause to show why judgment should not be pronounced against him.

Art. 421. It will be good cause to show, in answer to this address :

1. That the defendant has received a pardon from the constitutional authority. On the production of which, legally authenticated, the defendant shall be discharged, if the pardon be unconditional, and if there be no other legal cause for his detention but that on which the pardon operates ; but if the pardon be conditional, and the fulfilment of any of its conditions requires his further detention, he shall be recommitted.

2. It may be alleged in behalf of the defendant, that he is INSANE ; and, if the application be supported by such proofs as satisfies the court of the fact, judgment shall not be pronounced, unless a jury, to be impannelled for that purpose in the manner herein after directed, shall decide that he is not insane.

3. The defendant may state, that he has good cause to offer either in arrest of judgment or for a new trial, and that by some unavoidable accident, or cause, over which he had no control, he was prevented from submitting the motion in the time prescribed ; and if such accident, or cause, be shown to the satisfaction of the court, the

judgment shall be deferred ; and they shall proceed, as in other cases, to decide on the motion in arrest of judgment, or for a new trial.

4. He may allege, that he is not the person against whom the verdict was pronounced, and pray that his identity may be inquired of by a jury ; and if he shall make affidavit of the truth of such allegation, a jury shall be impannelled to try and determine on the identity of the person, at such time as the court shall direct.

Art. 422. If a defendant, sentenced to imprisonment, shall escape before he has been committed, the sentence cannot be executed on any person who shall be apprehended under an allegation, or suspicion of his being the delinquent, until he has been brought before the court and asked if he have any cause to show why the sentence should not be executed. When, if an allegation of non-identity be made, and supported by affidavit, the same proceedings shall take place as are provided for by the last article ; and until such decision he shall be kept in custody.

Art. 423. In cases where the court has a discretionary power as to the measure or selection of the punishment, if either the public prosecutor or the defendant shall allege that he has matter to offer which ought to produce an increase or diminution of the punishment, which did not appear on the trial ; the court may hear the same, or in their discretion give time to produce it ; provided it apply to some one of the points set forth in the next following section. But no evidence shall be taken of any circumstance in aggravation which was, or ought to have been alleged, in the act of accusation ; or in alleviation, which might have been produced on the trial to show the defendant not to be guilty.

Art. 424. If no application, in either of the modes above provided for, shall be made for arresting or suspending the judgment, or if being made they should be overruled, the court shall proceed to enter their judgment on the minutes of the court, and to declare it to the defendant, which is called passing the sentence.

Art. 425. In all cases of crime, and of misdemeanor prosecuted separately, the sentence of each prisoner shall be pronounced severally, but in the presence and hearing of all who may have been convicted during the same term of the court.

Art. 426. The judge who pronounces sentence must perform this duty in a manner that he may deem the best calculated to give effect to the example upon the hearers ; the strictest silence must be observed by those who are present ; and it should be accompanied with such reflections as may impress on the mind the importance of obedience to the laws, and the dangers and infamy of infringing them.

Art. 427. When sentence is pronounced for murder, the seat and table of the court shall be hung in black, and the prisoner shall, immediately after the sentence is pronounced, be enveloped in a black mantle that shall cover his whole body, with a cowl or veil drawn over his head ; and shall be thus conveyed in a cart, hung with black, to the place of his confinement.

Art. 428. If the judgment be the imposition of a fine, the clerk, shall, without delay, issue execution for its recovery in the manner directed by law.

Art. 429. If the sentence direct the forfeiture of, or suspension from, the exercise of any office, or of any political or civil right, one copy of the judgment shall be sent to the governor, who shall cause it to be filed and recorded in the office of the secretary of state, and published for one week in the gazette printed by the state printer.

Art. 430. If the sentence be for imprisonment, the sheriff shall deliver a copy of the judgment, together with the body of the defendant, to the keeper of the prison in which the sentence is to be executed.

## SECTION II.

*Of the exercise of the discretionary power given to the court in the selection and apportionment of punishments.*

Art. 431. Laws apparently equal in their provisions become unequal and unjust if indiscriminately applied, without modification, to all who become subject to their operation. A difference of physical force or moral feelings, in several culprits, may render the same punishment light to one which would be intolerable to another. Certain circumstances, moreover, attending the commission of the same kind of offence, may render it more or less immoral, injurious or difficult to be repressed. No legislation can be sufficiently minute to provide for all these gradations. The deficiency can only be supplied by vesting in the judge, who applies the law, a discretionary power, within certain limits, to select the kind of punishment adapted to the case, and to increase or diminish its degree. The exercise of this discretion forms one of the most important and difficult functions of the judiciary power : in practice, it must of necessity be irregular ; but, in order to render it as uniform as the nature of the case will admit, the following rules are established, and these principles are enounced in order more effectually to impress on the mind of the judge that the discretion, vested in him by law, is not an arbitrary power, to be exercised according to his caprice, or his feelings, or to gratify his passions ; but that it is required to be an act of sound judgment, guided by views of utility, justice, and good morals ;—and that in using the power vested in him, of selecting, of increasing, and of diminishing the punishment, he must act as he supposes the legislature would have done had it been possible for them to provide for the particular case under his consideration.

Art. 432. The scale of punishment, in this system of penal law, is so graduated, that the medium between the highest and lowest punishments, where a discretion is given, is intended to be applied to offences marked by no circumstances of extenuation or aggravation.

Art. 433. The following are to be considered as circumstances of aggravation. The effect they are to have in the increase of punishment cannot be prescribed, but is left to the discretion of the judge, within the limits given by law, in each case.

1. If the person committing the offence was, by the duties of his office, or by his CONDITION, obliged to prevent the particular offence committed, or to bring offenders committing it to justice.

2. If he held any other public office, although not one requiring the suppression of the particular offence.

3. Although holding no office, if his education, fortune, profession, or reputation, placed him in a situation in which his example would probably influence the conduct of others.

4. When the offence was committed with premeditation.

5. Or in consequence of.a plan formed with others.

6. When the defendant endeavoured to induce others to join in committing the offence.

7. When the CONDITION of the offender created a trust which was broken by the offence, or when it afforded him easier means of committing the offence.

8. When, in the commission of the offence, any other injury was offered than that necessarily suffered by the offence itself; such as wanton cruelty, or humiliating language, in cases of personal injury.

9. When it was attended with the breach of any other moral duty than that necessarily broken in committing the offence ; such as personal injury accompanied by ingratitude.

10. When the injury was offered to one whom age, sex, office, conduct, or CONDITION, entitled him to respect from the offender.

11. When the injury was offered to one whose age, sex, or infirmity rendered incapable of resistance.

12. · When the general character of the defendant is marked by those passions or vices, which generally lead to the commission of the offence of which he has been convicted.

13. Whenever the injury has been offered without any provocation on the part of the person suffering by it, and no other circumstances of aggravation or extenuation appear, the medium punishment is that which ought to be inflicted. The existence of such provocation is hereinafter made a motive of extenuation ; but when the act was done from mere malignity of disposition, and not under the influence of any of those passions which generally actuate mankind, it is an aggravation of the offence.

Art. 434. There are also circumstances which ought to enhance the punishment, although they form no aggravation of the offence ; these are:

1. The frequency of the offence. In most cases where the law is well administered, this can only take place when the gratification derived from the offence is more than equivalent to the evil produced by the punishment. When the observation of the magistrate induces him to believe that this is the cause of the increase of the crime, it should be a motive with him to exercise the discretion given him to augment the punishment.

2. The wealth of the offender. Where this is great, in all cases of fine, the penalty must be increased in proportion. In all cases where the punishment is an alternative of fine or imprisonment, or cumulation of both, and the wealth of the offender is so great as to render the payment of the highest fine that can be imposed a matter of little importance to him, imprisonment ought to be inflicted, unless some of the other circumstances, which are herein directed to be considered, should render it improper.

Art. 435. The following circumstances are to be considered in alleviation of the punishment:

1. The minority of the offender: if so young as to justify a supposition that he was ignorant of the law, or that he acted under the influence of another, although he may have attained the age fixed by law for rendering him responsible, and although he have not committed the offence by such command, persuasion, or aid, as by the "Penal Code" entitle him to a certain diminution of punishment.

2. If the offender was so old as to render it probable that the faculties of his mind were weakened.

3. The CONDITION of the offender. This in the several relations of wife, child, apprentice, and ward, is specifically provided for under certain circumstances, in the Penal Code. Those CONDITIONS under other circumstances than those there detailed; and all other CONDITIONS, which suppose the party to have been influenced in committing the offence by another, standing in a correlative superior situation to him, afford inducements for diminishing the degree of punishment.

4. The order of a superior military officer, is no justification for committing a crime, but under circumstances of misapprehension of the duty of obedience, may be shown in extenuation of the offence.

5. When the offence was committed under a combination of circumstances, and under the influence of motives which may not probably recur either with respect to the offender or to any other.

6. The measure of increased punishment for a repetition of offences of the SAME NATURE, is prescribed by the Penal Code; therefore, the medium punishment is that which is intended for the first offence when it is not attended by any circumstance of aggravation or extenuation: but if the party, convicted for the first offence, have previously sustained a good character, and that offence be the only one of ANY NATURE that he has committed, such good character and exemption from other offences, is a motive for lessening the punishment.

7. When the offence has been caused by great provocation, or other cause sufficient to excite in men of ordinary tempers such passions as require unusual strength of mind to restrain.

8. The state of health of the delinquent and the sex (if a female) must be considered in the nature and duration of imprisonment, where that is a part of the sentence.

Art. 436. In selecting the particular kind of punishment, where there is a discretion, attention should be paid to the sex, the constitution, the fortune, the education, and habits of life of the offender. It is apparent that hard labour is not the same punishment, when applied in the same degree, to one used all his life to bodily exertion and to another bred up to literary pursuits; to a robust man and to a delicate woman. That incapacity to be elected to public office will be a greater penalty to one used to public life, than to him whose pursuits and education have fitted only for attention to his own affairs; and that the possessor of a large fortune will consider a moderate fine as no punishment.

Art. 437. This section is from its nature recommendatory; and obligatory only on the conscience of the judge; it is intended to direct, not to confine, the exercise of his discretion. The only obligation it creates is the moral one of exercising his power on this subject so as to apportion the punishment, not only to the offence, but to the motives and other circumstances of the offender; so as to equalize, as far as possible, the effects of the punishment, and cause it, by a proper selection, to counteract the passions which produced it.

Art. 438. All matters in aggravation, which form no part of the charge in the act of accusation, and matters of extenuation which do not amount to a legal defence, and which have not necessarily or incidentally appeared to the court on the trial, may be produced, either by the examination of witnesses in open court, or by their affidavits, as the court may deem most conducive to justice in each particular case; but the opposite party must, in all cases, have an opportunity of cross-examining the witnesses, if he require it, and of producing counter-proof.

## CHAPTER XIV.

*Of forms to be used in judicial proceedings in court.*

### SECTION I.

#### Of oaths and affirmations.

Art. 439. An affirmation is a solemn declaration made before a person or court authorized to receive it, attesting the truth of a statement already made, or about to be made, by the affirmant, or the truth or sincerity of a promise made by him.

Art. 440. An oath is a similar declaration, accompanied by a religious invocation of the Supreme Being to bear witness to the truth of the declaration or the sincerity of the promise, and agreeing to renounce the blessing of God and the respect of man if the engagement should be broken.

Art. 441. In order the better to enforce the obligation of an oath upon those who might disregard its religious penal sanctions, an honorary engagement is expressly added in the form established by this Code.

Art. 442. An oath or affirmation can be legally administered, only by a court, a magistrate, or some one specially commissioned to perform that function.

Art. 443. If the person to whom the oath is to be administered profess the Christian religion, the oath shall be taken in the following form. The deponent shall lay his hand on the scripture of the New Testament, and shall, with an audible voice, repeat the following formule : "I swear, in the presence of Almighty God, and by His holy word ; and on the faith of a person of probity and honour declare that [here he shall repeat the purport of the oath]—and may God so bless and man so honour me as this oath is truly and sincerely made."

Art. 444. If the person to whom the oath is to be administered be one of the Jewish religion, he shall take it with his head covered, with one hand on the gospels of the Old Testament, and shall repeat the formule denoted by the last preceding article.

Art. 445. If the deponent profess any religion, according to the tenets of which, any other ceremony is necessary to give the sanction of religion to the oath, such ceremony shall be observed.

Art. 446. The sanction of religion is added only to strengthen the legal force of the engagement; any error, therefore, in that part of the form, either as respects the Christian or any other religion, will not affect the civil obligation or the penal consequences of its breach, nor can any ecclesiastical power dissolve or lessen its force.

3 T

Art. 447. If the person professing the Christian religion, to whom an oath is tendered, shall declare that he has religious scruples against swearing with his hand on the scriptures, that part of the ceremony shall be omitted ; but he shall raise his right hand, repeat the same formule that is above directed for those professing that religion, omitting only the words "and by his holy word."

Art. 448. Instead of an oath, in all cases where it is required or permitted by law, an affirmation shall be made by those who are members of any religious sect, according to the tenets of which it is considered irreligious to take an oath, and such affirmation is declared, in all respects, to be equivalent to an oath; and its breach, or falsity, incurs the same penalties with the breach, or falsity, of an oath.

Art. 449. The declaration of the affirmant that he belongs to such sect as is mentioned in the last preceding article, shall be sufficient proof of the fact; but, although it should be false, the affirmation shall be as valid, and its breach or falsity shall produce the same consequences as if his declaration had been true.

Art. 450. The affirmant shall pronounce, in an audible voice, the following formule : "I do solemnly, sincerely, and truly, declare and affirm, that [the purport of the affirmation must be here enounced.]"

Art. 451. No oath need be administered to an executive officer of justice (after he has taken his oath of office), that he has done or will do any act that is required of him by the duties of his office; a declaration to that effect, signed by the officer in cases where his signature is required, is sufficient; and the breach, or falsity, of such declaration incurs all the penalties that would have ensued on the breach or falsity of an oath.

Art. 452. Nothing in the last article contained shall prevent the swearing and examination of an officer of justice as to the manner in which an official act was performed, when those circumstances become a matter of controversy ; the intent of the said article being to avoid the multiplicity of oaths which occurs by the swearing of executive officers, to the truth of their returns, in order to fine witnesses or jurors for non-attendance, making affidavits to the service of notices, swearing them to go out with a juror, or with the jury when they retire to deliberate, and other official acts of the like nature ordered by the court.

Art. 453. All returns of the manner in which any written order has been executed, or any written notice has been delivered, must be in writing, endorsed on or annexed to the order or notice, or on copies thereof, and signed by the officer who has executed it.

Art. 454. When the duty which has been performed, is not the service of any written order or notice, it shall be proved by verbal declaration of the officer, in open court, and noted on the minutes.

Art. 455. The formule of the verbal declaration of any official act that has been performed, and referred to in the preceding article, is as follows : "I do declare, under the sanction of my oath of office, that I did, &c. [enounce the particulars of the service performed.]"

Art. 456. When the duty is an official one, but to be performed by an officer especially designated by the court for the purpose, the obligation to perform it is incurred by the clerk stating, in the form prescribed, the duty that is to be performed, and the assent of the officer verbally given to perform it.

Art. 547. The formule for the statement to be made by the clerk, under the last preceding article, is as follows, addressing himself to the officer he shall say : "You are required, under the sanction of your oath of office, to [keep this jury, &c. or any other official act]. Will you perform this duty?" To which the officer shall answer, "I will."

Art. 458. The oaths, affirmations, and declarations, to be administered in the course of judicial proceeding, in a court of criminal jurisdiction, are the following, each of them to be begun and concluded by the formule hereinbefore prescribed for each of these engagements:

1. That of a grand juror. "I swear, &c., as one of the grand jurors for this district, I will diligently inquire, and true presentment make, of all such offences as this court has cognizance of: that I will present no one from hatred or malice, nor leave any one unpresented from favour, affection, reward, or the hope of reward. But that I will, to the best of my ability, perform all the duties enjoined upon me as a grand juror, and may God so bless, &c."

2. The oath of a petit juror. "I will, without passion, prejudice, or favour, hear the proofs and arguments offered in this cause, and determine on the truth of the accusation submitted to my decision ; and give a true verdict according to law and the evidence, and, &c."

3. The oath of a witness. "The evidence I am about to give, shall be the truth, the whole truth, and nothing but the truth, under the direction of the court as to the legality of the testimony."

4. The oath of a deponent to an affidavit. "What is stated in this affidavit, as of my own knowledge, is true [if any other matter be stated, add] and all the other matters stated as true, I believe to be true."

5. Declaration of an officer of the service of a verbal order or notice. "That I did, on the          day of          now last past, give notice to A. B. that his attendance was immediately required in this court as a juror or witness."

6. Statement and direction to an executive officer to perform the duty of going out with a juror or jurors during a trial. "You are required, &c. to go out with such of the jurors as have leave of the court. You shall not suffer any one to speak to them, nor shall you yourself speak to them, unless it be to require their return to the court, and you shall return with them without any unnecessary delay."

7. The like direction to keep the jury during their retirement. "You are required, &c. to keep this jury in some convenient place, without food and drink, save bread and water, unless with leave of the court. You shall suffer no one to speak to any of them, neither shall you speak to them yourself, without such leave ; unless it be to ask them whether they be agreed on their verdict ; and you shall return with them into court when they are so agreed ; [in cases where a secret verdict is permitted, the following clause shall be added,] or you shall suffer them to disperse after having made a secret verdict, if they shall obtain leave of the court for that purpose."

Art. 459. All affidavits must be certified to have been sworn or affirmed by the clerk of the court, if taken in court, with the style of the court ; or by the magistrate or commissioner, with the addition of their offices ; and must be signed by the deponent in his hand-writing if he can write, or with his mark if he cannot.

Art. 460. An oath, taken in court, shall be administered by the judge or the clerk, by either enouncing the formule of the oath to the person who takes it, and causing him to repeat it after him, or giving it to him in writing that he may read it aloud.

Art. 461.  Strict silence shall be observed by all but those occupied in administering and repeating the oath ; and the court shall, during that time, transact no other business.

Art. 462.  If any one who is legally called on to take an oath, or affirmation, or to be examined as a witness in any court of civil or criminal jurisdiction, shall refuse so to do, he may be committed to prison, in close custody, until he shall consent, besides incurring such other penalties as are provided by law ; provided, that such imprisonment shall not continue longer than the end of the term in which he was committed, unless the commitment be within three days of the end of the term ; in which case, the imprisonment may continue for three days after.

SECTION II.

Of the opening and adjournment of courts, and of the form in which the minutes are to be kept.

Art. 463.  No court, according to the definition of the term, can do any legal act before it is opened by a public proclamation, which may give notice that the persons authorized to constitute the court have met, under the circumstances necessary to give existence to that body; which opening must be entered on the minutes, stating the day, hour, and place, at which it took place.

Art. 464.  Adjournments must, in like manner, be made by proclamation, entered on the minutes ; and if, from the continuance of a trial or other cause, the court shall continue its sessions until after twelve at night, the entry shall be made in this, as in all other cases, according to the truth.

Art. 465.  The minutes of a court are a record of all the proceedings of such court ; and, in order to secure their correctness, a book shall be kept by the clerk, in which he shall enter a note of each proceeding at the time it takes place.  This book shall be open for the inspection of all persons interested, until the opening of the court on the next day ; and immediately after the opening, the minutes of the preceding session shall be openly read by the clerk, and all errors therein shall be corrected by order of the court, and the minutes shall then be fairly copied into the record-book of minutes.

Art. 466.  The names of the defendants in each trial, of the witnesses, and of the jurors who are sworn, and of the counsel who appear, shall be entered on the minutes, distinguishing the witnesses called for the prosecution from those called by the defendant.

Art. 467.  When any instrument in writing is produced in evidence, a short note or description of it, containing the general tenor, the parties, and the date, shall be entered on the minutes, and some mark made on it by the clerk to identify it.

Art. 468.  All the orders, and judgments, and every other act of the court whatever, shall be recorded on the minutes.

Art. 469.  A note of every application made to the court during its session, and by whom made, and for whom, must be entered on the minutes, together with the decision of the court thereon, whether granting or refusing the application.

## SECTION III.

### Of the order of proceeding on the first day of the term.

Art. 470. The judge having taken his seat, shall order the court to be opened. The clerk shall then say, "Crier, make proclamation." The crier then, with a loud voice, proclaims, "Silence! while I proclaim the orders of the court. This court [repeating the STYLE of the court] is now open : of this all persons are required to take notice, and to demean themselves with the reverence due to the laws and the respect they require to be paid to the important functions of those who administer them."

Art. 471. The clerk shall then, after entering the opening of the court on the minutes, order the crier to call the officers of justice, whose duty it shall be, according to law, to attend ; which he shall do by repeating the formule, "Silence! while I proclaim the orders of the court"—which formule shall introduce all proclamations hereby directed to be made. He shall then say, "All officers of justice, whose duty it is to attend this court, answer to your names, or you will incur the penalties of law." He shall then call each name three times, and the clerk shall enter on the minutes the appearance or default of each.

Art. 472. On the appearance of the officers the sheriff shall assign to each his separate duty.

Art. 473. The clerk shall then order proclamation to be made for calling the grand jury, which shall be done in the following form: "You good men, who have been selected to perform the important duties of grand jurors, answer to your names, and take your seats as you are called." If a sufficient number of the jury appear, they shall be sworn.

Art. 474. When the grand jury are sworn, the court shall proceed to give them their charge, and to have that part of this code read to them which concerns their duties, and to deliver them the copy of the calendar as is herein before directed. Previous to which the clerk shall direct proclamation of silence to be made when the charge is giving to the grand jury.

Art. 475. When the grand jury has retired, the clerk shall order proclamation to be made for the calling of the petit jury, in the following form: "You good men, whose duty it is to decide, as jurors, between the state of Louisiana and those who are accused of offences against the laws, answer to your names as they are called." The names on the panel shall then be called, and the clerk shall take note of the defaulters.

Art. 476. When any grand juror shall appear, after the others are sworn, the oath shall be administered to him, and he shall, with a certificate of its being taken, be sent to the grand jury.

Art. 477. Proclamation shall then be made, requiring all magistrates who have taken any recognizances or examinations, which have not been delivered to the clerk, forthwith to bring them into court.

Art. 478. Persons bound by recognizance shall then, by proclamation, be called as follows : "All you who are bound by recognizance to appear at this court to answer complaints against you, come forth when your names are called, or your recognizance will be forfeited." The defaulters shall then be noted, and proclamation shall be made, with respect to such defaulters, in the following form: A. B. and C. D. [repeating the names of the bail] produce E. F. [the person delivered to bail] for whose appearance you are answerable, or you will forfeit your recognizance."

SECTION IV.

Of the forms to be used after an indictment or information has been filed.

Art. 479. When an act of accusation has been filed, founded on any written instrument, the original of which is annexed according to the former provisions of this code, the defendant, at the time for that purpose prescribed, shall be brought into court, and the court shall inquire whether he has employed counsel for his defence ; if he has not, counsel shall be assigned him. The clerk shall then address him to this effect : "A. B. an indictment [or information] has been filed against you, of which you have been served with a copy ; here is the original of the instrument annexed to that act. You are at liberty, under the. inspection of an officer of the court, to examine the said instrument, and to compare it with the original, to see that the copy is correct."

Art. 480. After the defendant shall have had an opportunity of examining the instrument when one is annexed, and in all cases when no instrument is annexed, the clerk shall, at the time for that purpose herein before prescribed, address the defendant to this effect : "A. B. if you have any exception to make to the indictment [or information] of which you have received a copy, either for any defect of substance or form [or "because there is a variance between the copy of the instrument in the indictment and the original which you have seen," in cases where there is an instrument,] or because the name by which you are called in the act of accusation is not your true name, this is the time to make such exception ; hereafter it will be too late."

Art. 481. If no exception be made, the clerk shall write on the back of the indictment : "This          day of          the defendant in this indictment was personally called on to make exceptions, if any he had thereto, and warned that they would not hereafter be received, but made none."

Art. 482. The arraignment shall be made in the form before prescribed.

Art. 483. On the day appointed for the trial, the witnesses, as well on the part of the prosecution as of the defendant, shall be called ; and if any do not attend, process may be applied for, to compel their attendance ; or if an application to postpone the trial be intended, it must be made before a juror is sworn.

Art. 484. If the trial is ordered on, the clerk shall address the defendant to this effect : "A. B. the jurors who are now to be called are those who are to decide on your innocence or guilt. If you do not desire to be tried by any particular jurors, you may set aside nine of them, without assigning any cause ; and if you have good cause to set aside any others, you may do so by declaring it : what is good cause, your counsel will explain to you. If you have any objection to make to the manner in which the jury has been drawn, you must now do so, or you will hereafter be precluded. Your objections to individual jurors must be made when they come to be sworn, but before they are sworn."

Art. 485. The clerk shall then proceed to draw the names of the jurors, and as each shall come to be sworn, the clerk shall, in cases of CRIME, say, " Defendant, look on the jury ! Juror, look on the defendant !"—And if no challenge is made, shall proceed to administer the oath.

Art. 486. When a full jury shall be sworn, the clerk shall address them thus : " Gentlemen of this jury, an indictment [or information, as the case may be,] has been filed against A. B. [the defendant] ·in the following words. To this accusation he has pleaded not guilty. You are the persons upon whom the task is imposed of deciding whether he be guilty or not guilty. This you are to determine according to the evidence which will be offered to you."

Art. 487. Courts of criminal jurisdiction may make such rules for the order of proceeding therein ; but copies of all such rules must be sent to the governor, the senate, and the house of assembly, on the first day of the session after they shall have been made, or if the legislature be in session when such rules are entered, within five days afterwards ; provided, that no such rule shall be contrary to any provision in this system of penal law.

## CHAPTER XV.

### *Of the officers of courts of criminal jurisdiction.*

Art. 488. There shall be in every court of criminal jurisdiction the following officers : a clerk, an interpreter, a reporter, a crier, and a sheriff with his deputies.

### SECTION I.

#### Of the clerk.

Art. 489. The duties of the clerk are, to keep correct minutes under the direction of the judge ; to preserve all the papers and records of the court ; to administer oaths in court ; to direct the crier to call the persons whose attendance may be required ; to file all papers directed to be filed, by endorsing on them some description by which they may be known, together with the date of their being filed ; to receive and record all indictments and informations, and to arraign the defendants ; to demand, receive, record their answers ; to give authenticated copies of the minutes and records ; and to do all other things as he may be required by law to perform.

Art. 490. The clerk may appoint a deputy, whose official acts shall be valid ; provided the deputation be in writing and recorded on the minutes of the court. When neither the clerk nor his deputy appears, the judge may appoint some person to officiate, whose appointment shall be entered on the minutes of the court, and whose official acts shall be valid.

Art. 491. The clerk is civilly liable for all the acts of his deputy, and criminally for all such as he shall have authorized, or knowingly permitted, in the manner described in the criminal code.

Art. 492. The clerk shall keep an office, in which all the records and papers of the court shall be kept, and methodically arranged in such manner as the judge shall order ; and the court shall, by rule, direct at what hours such office shall be kept open ; and during such hours the clerk is bound to show any paper filed in such office, to any person who may require to see the same ; but no acts of accusation, or evidence in support of the same shall be shown, or copies thereof given, to any but the court, the party accused, the grand jury, or the public prosecutor, before the trial of the cause.

## SECTION II.

### Of the interpreter.

Art. 493. An interpreter shall be appointed for each court of criminal jurisdiction, who shall be well acquainted with the English, French, and Spanish languages, and who shall be sworn faithfully to perform the duties of his office.

Art. 494. It shall be the duty of the interpreter to translate such papers as are produced, and to interpret such declarations and proceedings as are made in court, so that they may be understood by the court, the jury, the parties, and others present who ought to know the contents ; if any of them are ignorant of the language in which such papers are written, such declarations given, or such proceedings had.

Art. 495. Whenever the defendant cannot understand English, a translation, of the act of accusation and of all papers annexed to the same, into some language which he understands, shall be given to him, with the copy herein before directed to be served on him ; and if he require it, his arraignment shall be postponed until such copy be given.

Art. 496. Whenever any translation or interpretation is required into, or from, a language with which the interpreter is unacquainted, or in the absence or sickness of that officer, or of a vacancy in the office, the court may appoint a proper person to do the particular service required, first administering an oath for the faithful performance of the duty.

## SECTION III.

### Of the reporter.

Art. 497. A reporter shall be appointed by the governor for each court having criminal jurisdiction, who shall receive such emolument as the legislature shall, by special law, direct : he shall be sworn faithfully to perform the duties of his office. The reporter shall not practise as counsellor or attorney in any criminal cause in that or any other court.

Art. 498. The duty of the reporter shall be to attend at all the sittings of the court ; to take notes of all the acts of accusation, testimony, arguments, verdicts, judgments, and other proceedings, in each criminal cause that shall be brought before such court ; to perform which duty a convenient seat shall be assigned to him ; and from these notes he shall make a faithful report.

Art. 499. Within one month after every term of such court, or oftener at his discretion, he shall publish such reports in some gazette printed in the city of New Orleans.

Art. 500. The governor is authorized to contract with the proprietors of a gazette for the publication of such reports ; and as an equivalent for the expense—all judicial orders, directed to be published by any court—all advertisements for sheriff's sales, either on execution or for taxes—all advertisements directed to be made by syndics—shall be published in such gazette, at the usual rates now allowed by the court.

Art. 501. The proceeding in the causes designated or presented in the chapter next following, are excepted from the operation of the three last preceding articles, and from any other provision in the system of penal law, contrary to the directions of the said chapter.

Art. 502. It shall also be the duty of the reporter to make and deliver to the governor, and the attorney general, once in every three months, a return of names of all the persons bailed or committed to prison by any court or magistrate in the district, designating, in separate columns, the offence charged ; whether bailed or committed, and whether the accusation has been followed up by an indictment or information, and whether the indictment or information be for the same offence as originally charged by the commitment ; whether the party has been discharged, and by what authority, and for what cause ; and whether tried and acquitted, or convicted, and if convicted, of what offence ; and how sentenced, and whether sentence has been executed, and how : designating also, the sex, age, place of nativity, and profession or trade, of the defendant ; whether he could write or read, together with the dates of the commitment and other proceedings, according to forms to be furnished by the governor, who may require by them such additional information as may show the prevalence or suppression of different offences, and the general operation of the penal laws.

Art. 503. Once in every year the governor shall cause an abstract to be made of all the returns, omitting the names in cases of misdemeanor, and cause the same to be published ; to which abstract shall be added (from the return directed by the Code of Reform and Prison Discipline to be made by the keeper) opposite to the name of each convict, who

3 U

has been committed to the state prison, whether he-is still in custody, or discharged, and how ; and if in custody, whether at labour, or in solitude ; and if at labour, how employed.

## SECTION IV.

### Of the sheriff and other officers of justice.

Art. 504. It is the duty of the sheriff of the district in which any court of criminal jurisdiction shall sit, to attend its sessions by himself or his deputy ; and he, or such deputy who acts for him, shall have at least two other deputies constantly in attendance, to execute the orders of the court.

Art. 505. The sheriff shall also present to the court, at the opening of its session, a list containing the names of all the constables ; and the court shall also designate the number of them required for daily attendance, who shall serve in rotation.

Art. 506. The constables, during the session of the court, shall be under the direction of the sheriff.

Art. 507. The judge may, in or out of court, whenever he shall deem it expedient for the preservation of the peace or the execution of the orders of the court, appoint any number of special constables he may think proper, who shall continue in office during the time, or for the occasion, for which they are named.

Art. 508. The sheriff's officers and constables may, when the sheriff or the court deem it necessary, be armed with staves ; but no man, armed in any other manner, shall be allowed to enter the hall in which the court is sitting. An armed guard may, with the approbation of the judge, be employed by the sheriff, to guard a prisoner to and from the court whenever there is danger of a rescue, but they cannot enter with their arms. Nothing in this article shall prevent officers in the army or navy from entering the court with their usual side-arms.

Art. 509. The crier is an officer of justice appointed by the court ; his duty is to make proclamations for opening and adjourning the court ; to call and swear the jurors and witnesses ; to preserve silence and order in court, and to remove those who disturb its proceedings : the whole under the orders of the court.

## CHAPTER XV.

*Of cases in which the publicity of legal proceedings may be limited.*

Art. 510. In all prosecutions for the following offences, that is to say: for assault, accompanied by any of the circumstances set forth in the fourth article of the fourth section of the first chapter nineteenth title and second book of the Code of Crimes and Punishments ; for assault with intent to ravish ; for rape, adultery, offences against decency, and defamation implying a charge of either of the offences. During the examination of witnesses, previous to the commitment for those offences, no person shall be present but the magistrate before whom the complaint shall be made, and such other magistrates as he may request to aid him in the examination, the public prosecutor, the accused and his counsel, the person complaining, the sheriff, and other officers of justice attending on the magistrate, the witnesses, and such persons, not exceeding ten for each party, as the complainant and the accused may desire to have admitted.

Art. 511. On the trial, the persons admitted into court shall be restricted to those mentioned in the preceding article, with the officers of court, and the jurors sworn to try the cause.

Art. 512. In making the report of any such trial, the reporter shall not give the details of the evidence, or publish the names of the witnesses.

Art. 513. Any person who shall publish any account of such trial, containing any indecent or wanton details, shall be fined not exceeding two hundred dollars, and imprisoned not exceeding sixty days, if the account be substantially true ; but if it be false, the punishment shall be doubled, and the prosecution and trial for such offence shall be conducted according to the rules laid down in this chapter.


# CHAPTER XVI.

## Of costs.

Art. 514. Until the system by which magistrates and officers of courts and of justice are remunerated for their services by fees, shall be abolished, the state shall pay costs in all cases where the accused is discharged on an acquittal or for want of prosecution.

Art. 515. The payment of costs is not to be awarded in all cases on conviction. The defendant may, in some cases, be exonerated from them altogether, or he may be directed to pay a certain sum towards the payment of costs. This is at the discretion of the court, and must be exercised so as to proportion the amount of costs to the punishment inflicted.

Art. 516. Costs can only be recovered by execution, in the manner directed for the recovery of a fine ; and no one shall be detained in prison to enforce the payment of costs, until after the DISCUSSION of his property, and then only in the manner directed in cases of fines.


# CHAPTER XVII.

## Of prescription as applied to offences.

Art. 517. There is no prescription against prosecutions for any offences other than those especially provided for in this chapter.

Art. 518. Prosecutions for all misdemeanors, except public offences, are prescribed by the lapse of three years after the commission of the offence.

Art. 519. Whenever the indictment is for a crime, and the party is found guilty of a misdemeanor, according to the rules hereinbefore established in the chapter of Verdicts, the prescription does not apply.

Art. 520. Prosecutions for injuries to reputation, for rape, assault with intent to ravish, assault aggravated by injury to pudicity, are prescribed by one year.

Art. 521. Prosecutions for an attempt to commit a crime, if no other offence is committed by the attempt, are barred by one year.

Art. 522. The prescription is barred in two cases :

1. If complaint was made of the offence within the time prescribed, although it was not followed by further prosecution, if the offender was either unknown or could not be found, or was rescued, or escaped.

2. Where the party injured, or the person whose duty it was to prosecute, was absent from the state, or was prevented by force or imprisonment, or debarred by threats, from prosecuting ; in either of which cases the prescription begins from the time the party shall return, or the disability shall cease.

Art. 523. When the defendant shall, according to the rules hereinbefore prescribed, except to the form of any act of accusation, that the time at which the offence is alleged to have been committed is beyond the time limited by the prescription. Such exception shall not be allowed if the public prosecutor shall undertake to show, on the trial, either of the circumstances (designating which) that are in the last preceding article declared sufficient to rebut the prescription ; and if he shall fail so to do on the trial, or to show that the offence was committed within the time limited, the defendant must be acquitted.

Art. 524. Although there is no prescription for prosecutions for offences not enumerated in this chapter, yet provision will be found in the Code of Evidence to check any attempts to oppress, by delaying the accusation.

# TITLE III.

### OF THE MODE OF PROCEDURE IN CERTAIN CASES NOT IMMEDIATELY CONNECTED WITH PROSECUTIONS.

## CHAPTER I.

### *Of inquests on dead bodies.*

Art. 525. Whenever death shall be caused by violence, or a dead body of any person shall be found, and it is not known in what manner he came by his death, notice shall be given to the coroner of the parish, or, in his absence or inability to serve, to a magistrate.

Art. 526. Immediately after receiving such notice, it shall be the duty of the coroner, or magistrate, to summon a jury of inquest, consisting of eighteen persons qualified to serve as petit jurors, to meet at the place where the dead body is.

Art. 527. Officers of justice, and deputies whom the coroner may appoint, are bound to execute all his legal warrants for summoning the jury of inquest, and for making such arrest and serving such orders as he is authorized to make.

Art. 528. When twelve or more of the jury are assembled, they shall be sworn, in the form hereinbefore prescribed, diligently to inquire into the cause and manner of the death of the person whose body is before them, and to make a true inquisition according to the evidence offered to them, or arising from the inspection of the body.

Art. 529. A surgeon or physician shall also be summoned and sworn, if any can be found within ten miles, as a witness, who shall, in the presence of the jury, inspect the body and give a professional opinion as to the cause of the death.

Art. 530. The coroner shall also summon and examine as witnesses, on oath, all such persons as he or any of the jury shall reasonably suppose to have any knowledge of facts to be ascertained by the inquest.

Art. 531. After hearing the testimony, the jury shall determine when and in what manner, and by the act of whom it shall appear to them that the deceased came to his death; and when a majority of such jury shall agree in making any such statement, the same shall be reduced to writing by the coroner and signed by the jurors agreeing to the same. This statement is called the coroner's inquest.

Art. 532. If by the inquest it shall appear that any DESIGNATED person has been guilty of an offence in producing the death of the deceased, either as principal or accomplice, the coroner shall immediately issue his warrant for the arrest of such person, which shall be in the form of warrants of the like nature issued by magistrates, and shall be executed and proceeded on in the same manner.

Art. 533. The coroner has power to summon witnesses, and issue all such process to enforce their attendance and that of the jury, and to punish a refusal to attend, or to testify, in the same manner as a magistrate may in cases submitted to his jurisdiction. He has also the same power to issue a search warrant for any article necessary to the investigation before him, that is by this Code given to magistrates.

Art. 534. The inquest, together with any evidence that may have been taken by the coroner, the return of the warrant, shall be transmitted to the clerk of the court having cognizance of the offence; and all material witnesses shall be bound over by the coroner to appear at such court; and in relation to the arrest, examination, and other proceedings, after an inquisition, the duties of the coroner and the officers of justice shall be the same as those prescribed generally by this Code in cases of warrants of arrest issued by magistrates.

## CHAPTER II.

*Of the disinterment and dissection of dead bodies in cases of suspected murders.*

Art. 535. Whenever a FAMILY-MEETING of the relations or friends of the deceased, convened according to law, shall determine that it is expedient to make an examination of the dead body of any person who has been already interred, in order to discover the cause of his death, and shall make application to a judge for that effect ; or whenever the judge shall himself deem it necessary, in consequence of evidence presented to him, he shall appoint two surgeons to perform any chirurgical operation that may be necessary, and shall issue his order to the sheriff to have the body disinterred and examined.

Art. 536. The surgeons shall make a VERBAL PROCESS of the whole professional proceeding, which they shall sign, and the sheriff shall also make minutes of the whole of his proceeding, which shall be signed by him, and at least three persons who were present at the operation.

Art. 537. The VERBAL PROCESS of the surgeons and the minutes of the sheriff shall be returned to the judge who issued the order, and may serve as corroborating testimony to found a warrant of arrest, but shall not be evidence on the trial.

Art. 538. The family-meeting may, in like manner, apply for the examination of the dead body before interment, and when the order is granted, the same proceedings as are before directed shall take place.

## CHAPTER III.

### Of the proceedings in case of property found, where the owner is unknown.

Art. 539. When any one shall come by finding to the possession of any personal property, greater in value than twenty dollars, of which he has no reason to believe any designated person to be the owner, he shall be deemed to have concealed the same, and to have appropriated it to his own use, so as to incur the penalties directed by the        article of the Code of Crimes and Punishments, unless he shall pursue the directions of this chapter.

Art. 540. He must within three days give to the parish judge a written notice, containing a description of the property found, with its marks (if any), and the time and place of finding the same.

Art. 541. If the property be above the value of one hundred dollars, he must either deliver it to the sheriff of the parish, or give such security as the judge shall approve, to restore the same if legally claimed within six months.

Art. 542. If it be of greater value than three hundred dollars, consisting of money, jewels, gold or silver bullion, notes or other instruments in writing, or any article of small bulk, he shall deposit the same in some bank, if there be one within five miles, which will take charge of the same as a deposit for safe keeping—if there be no such bank within that distance, it shall be deposited with the parish judge, unless the finder give the security mentioned in the last preceding article.

Art. 543. A particular inventory of the property must be made by the parish judge and recorded in his office.

Art. 544. Within eight days after the report made to the parish judge, he shall cause an advertisement of the finding, describing the property particularly, to be published, with a notice to the owner to claim the same within six months from the time of finding; which advertisement shall be continued once every month during the six months.

Art. 545. If the owner appear within the six months, and prove his property to the satisfaction of the judge, it shall be restored to him on his paying all the costs of preserving the same, all the expenses attending the procedure decreed by this chapter, and ten per cent on the value of the property to the finder.

Art. 546. This chapter applies to property found stranded or drifting in any lake or stream of water within the state, except only that, in this last case, the owner shall be bound to pay a reasonable salvage, proportioned to the trouble and risk of saving and securing the property, over and above the ten per cent on the value; which salvage shall be determined by the parish judge.

Art. 547. If no owner appear to claim the property within six -months, it shall be delivered to the finder, if not in his possession, and if it be, his bonds shall be cancelled, and he shall not be criminally liable for any use he may make of the same.

# CHAPTER IV.

*Of the mode of proceeding in cases of vagrancy.*

Art. 548. A vagrant is one who, having no visible means of subsistence, lives in idleness, or in the practice of drinking, or gaming, and who, by the whole of his conduct and character, gives just reason to believe that he gains his subsistence by illegal means.

Art. 549. On the complaint of three householders to a magistrate, stating, that they have reason to believe, and detailing those reasons, and that they do believe that any designated individual comes within the description abovementioned, the magistrate shall issue his warrant to bring the person before him, and shall require him to give an account of the means by which he gains his living.

Art. 550. The account required by the last article may, if the party implicated desire it, be given to the magistrate in private, but it must be on oath, and supported by at least one credible witness; and if such account show legal means of subsistence, to the satisfaction of the magistrate, the party shall be dismissed. But if the party refuse to render any account, or render one not satisfactory to the magistrate, he shall be required to report himself to the magistrate, and to show, within three days, that he has adopted some regular means of livelihood, or to leave the district, or to give security for his good behaviour.

Art. 551. If the party fail in performing one of the conditions prescribed by the last section, the magistrate shall issue his warrant to send him to the HOUSE OF INDUSTRY, there to be employed for sixty days, or until he shall find security for his good behaviour, or that he will leave the state and not return within two years.

Art. 552. If after his discharge the party shall again be found in a state of vagrancy, either in the same or in any other district in the state, he shall, after the like inquiry, be sent to the house of industry for six months ; and the same process shall be repeated as often as the same kind of life shall be resumed.

Art. 553. No person shall be deemed a vagrant, under the provisions of this chapter, who, from bodily infirmity, or infancy, or old age, is unable to gain a livelihood by labour. Persons of this description, if without the means of subsistence, are under the care of the police of the parish to which they belong.

## CHAPTER V.

### *Of the mode of proceeding in cases of alleged insanity.*

Art. 554. Insanity alleged on the trial to have existed at the time of committing the offence, must be determined like any other ground of defence by the jury impannelled for the trial of the cause ; but if the defendant be acquitted on that ground, it should be specially so found, that the court may make order for his safe custody, according to the provisions of the Code of Crimes and Punishments.

Art. 555. If insanity be alleged, or observed by the court, to exist at any other stage of the proceeding, it must be inquired of by a jury specially sworn for that purpose, who shall be drawn from the panel of petit jurors in the same manner as they are drawn for the trial of causes.

Art. 556. If the insanity be alleged or discovered before the trial, or after conviction and before judgment, the question to be submitted to the jury shall, in the first case, be, whether the defendant is of a sufficiently sane mind to make his defence, or give instructions for it ; in the second case it shall be, whether he have sufficient sanity of mind to show cause against the judgment, and take those other measures he is allowed to take for the diminution of the punishment.

Art. 557. If the insanity be alleged after judgment, the inquiry shall be, if it exist in such a degree as to make him dangerous to others or unconscious of the nature and consequences of his offence.

Art. 558. Whenever, in any of the cases mentioned in the three last preceding articles, the insanity of the defendant shall be alleged, or shall be observed by the court, they shall name a physician to attend him, in order that he may be examined as a witness before the jury.

Art. 559. Counsel shall be assigned to the defendant on such inquiry if none have before been employed or assigned.

Art. 560. The jury may interrogate the defendant on such inquiry.

## CHAPTER VI.

### *Of the mode of proceeding in trials for adultery.*

Art. 561. In order to avoid collusive attempts between the husband and a pretended adulterer to obtain a divorce, to the injury of the wife ;

or between the husband and wife, to injure an innocent person, charged as the adulterer; the Code of Crimes and Punishments has provided, that prosecutions for adultery shall be joint against the wife and the supposed adulterer (if he be alive); and that there can be no conviction of the one without the other, under the modifications to be contained in this code : these are the following :

1. If the defendant, who is charged with being the adulterer, shall have been either summoned or arrested, but he should not appear, an attorney shall be named for his defence, who shall enter a plea of " not guilty" for him, and the trial shall proceed in his absence.

2. If he be alive, but shall have left the state before the prosecution is commenced, a warant or citation shall issue against him, and be renewed, from time to time, for six months, until it shall be served, and until the trial shall actually take place.  If he be not found, the trial may proceed, after the expiration of the six months, against the wife alone.


# CHAPTER VII.


*Of the application of moneys collected for fines, and of compensations for services to prosecutor, and for losses incurred by innocent defendants.*

Art. 562.  The mode in which fines are to be collected, is prescribed in the chapter of punishments in the Code of Crimes and Punishments.

Art. 563.  Sheriffs, coroners, and the marshal of the city court of the city of New Orleans, must, once in every three months, render to the treasurer of the state, an account of all fines either of them may have received prior to that time ; or if they have received none, make a return to that effect, in writing, signed by them respectively.

Art. 564.  At the time of rendering such account, the balance in the hands of the officer rendering it shall be paid to the treasurer of the state, who shall carry the same to account of a fund, called the " compensation fund"—which shall be applied, first, to the payment of warrants for recompense drawn by the governor, or by the judge, and public prosecutor, in cases authorized by the second chapter, first title, first book of this Code ; secondly, to such other uses as the legislature may direct.

Art. 565.  If any sheriff, coroner or marshal shall neglect or refuse to render such account, and to pay the balance that may be due thereon, or to make such return, he shall forfeit a sum of fifty dollars.

Art. 566.  It is hereby made the duty of the treasurer to cause prosecutions to be commenced for the offences against this chapter ; and also, to file petitions in a court of competent jurisdiction for an account of fines that may have been received ; and in such suits the defendants shall pay costs, although it may appear that no money was due to the state ; unless the defendant can show, that he had made the returns, required by this chapter, before the commencement of the suit.

Art. 567.  Suspicion of guilt sometimes subjects the innocent to the vexatious expense and privation of liberty incident to the measures

3 V

preparatory to the trial, by which their innocence is ascertained. Justice requires that such persons should be compensated by the public, because the loss and inconvenience was caused by its officers, and in attempting to secure its peace and safety. To do full justice in the few cases where it will be found due, would expose the treasury to petitious demand in so many others, that the law can only give relief in such a manner as to aid the more needy class of sufferers, while it offers no temptation to fraudulent combinations :

Art. 568. Therefore, whenever the judge who, before trial, shall discharge a person who has been committed, or bailed, for any offence—or whenever the jury, who shall acquit any defendant—shall certify, that he did not, by any improper conduct, give reasonable ground for suspicion that he had committed the offence, he shall be entitled to such compensation for the losses he has sustained by reason of the prosecution, as the judge shall think reasonable ; but such compensation shall in no case exceed an amount of emoluments which he might have made during the time that he was confined, or necessarily employed in his defence, to be ascertained according to the following circumstances :

1. If the defendant have no trade or profession, the compensation shall be calculated according to the wages of day-labourers.

2. If he be a mechanic, the average rate of wages for hired workmen of his trade shall be the measure, without any regard to the particular skill of the defendant.

3. If the defendant pursue any other calling or profession, the compensation shall not exceed twice the amount which could be allowed to a mechanic.

Art. 569. The sum allowed shall be paid by the treasurer out of the compensation fund, on the judge's warrant, countersigned by the clerk of the court, to the person in whose favour the allowance is made.

Art. 570. In such cases the acquittal shall always be published, and the expenses paid by a similar draft on the same fund.

## GENERAL PROVISIONS.

Art. 571. No omission of any matter of form, prescribed by this system, nor any departure from the forms given for proceeding under it, shall render the proceeding void, unless it be so specially provided ; or, unless the departure from the form has caused some injury to the party complaining of it.

Art. 572. Where a particular provision is made in any part of this system, contrary to a general provision, the particular provision must be observed.

Art. 573. All offences which are created by the Code of Procedure, or the Code of Reform and Prison Discipline, shall be tried in the same manner with those which are created by the Code of Crimes and Punishments.

Art. 574. Whenever a notice or interval of a certain number of days is directed to be given or to elapse, three whole days, exclusive of the two terms referred to, must intervene, unless the contrary be expressed.

# BOOK III.

CONTAINING THE FORMS TO BE USED IN ALL THE JUDICIAL PRO-
CEEDINGS PRESCRIBED OR AUTHORIZED BY THIS CODE.

## TITLE I.

OF THE FORMS TO BE USED IN THE PROCEEDINGS AUTHORIZED BY THE FIRST
BOOK, TITLE FIRST, FOR THE PREVENTION OF OFFENCES.

### CHAPTER I.

*General provisions.*

Art. 575. Where the forms given in this book are filled up, the
parts within brackets are to be changed according to the circumstances; the real names are to be substituted for the letters used to
represent them in the forms, and the real dates for the blanks or the
fictitious dates used in the forms.

Art. 576. The certificate of the attestation of the magistrate to affidavits, the seals to writs, and the signatures of parties, clerks and magistrates, are omitted in most of these forms. The cases in which
they are necessary, in practice, are either declared by the law on the
subject, or result from the nature of the instrument.

Art. 577. Where the beginning or conclusion of any form has been
given before, it is omitted in the subsequent forms of the same nature.
The part of the form omitted in the beginning of any precedent, is to
be supplied by copying the formal part that had before been given,
down to the recurrence of the word with which the new form begins.
Thus, in the precedents of an indictment, the formal part must be
copied in each case down to the word "did," with which word some
of the forms, given for the different officers, begin in the subsequent
precedents; or to the word "that," with which others begin. The
formal conclusion is supplied by "&c."

## CHAPTER II.

*Of the forms to be used in the proceedings under the third chapter of the title and book aforesaid.*

Art. 578. The honorary certificate, directed to be granted by the article, shall be in the following form :

"*State of Louisiana—certificate of merit.*

"A. B. having [here insert the act with such circumstances as in the opinion of the court rendered it worthy of recompense], the criminal court of said state [reciting the style of the court] have, according to the laws of the said state, caused this certificate to be made out, under their seal, to record the merit of his conduct, and to have the other effects provided for by law. Witness, J. T. judge of the said court, this          day of          in the year          ."

Art. 579. The certificate directed by the          article, to entitle the person giving information of an offence to the reward thereby directed, shall be as follows :

"We certify, that A. B. gave the first information which led to the conviction of C. D. of the offence of [here insert the description of offence] ; and that, pursuant to the directions of the Code of Criminal Procedure, he is entitled to receive from the treasurer of the state, out of the compensation fund, the sum of fifty dollars. Dated the          day of          in the year          ."

Art. 580. The several proceedings for the prevention of offences by the intervention of officers of justice, which are authorized by the third chapter of the title and book mentioned in the title of this chapter, shall be according to the following forms :

1. The form of an affidavit required by the first article of that chapter :

"I, A. B., do hereby declare, that I do fear that C. D. intends to commit an offence against my person [or property, designating which] by [designating the act which is apprehended] ; and that I have just reason for this fear, because [here insert the circumstances which cause the apprehension.]"

2. Form of the warrant :

"To H. H. one of the constables," &c.

"Whereas, A. B. hath made oath before me, C. D. [designating the office of the magistrate], that he has just reason to fear and does fear, that E. F. intends to [here insert the nature of the offence] : You are, therefore, ordered to arrest the said E. F., and bring him before me to answer the said allegation, and to be dealt with according to law. Given under my hand, this          day of          in the year          ."

3. The form of the bond :

"We, E. F. and G. H., acknowledge ourselves bound in solido to the state of Louisiana in the sum of          to be paid by us, or our heirs, if the said C. D. shall commit any offence against [the person] of A. B. within the term of one year."

4. The form of commitment, if the accused do not find security.

"To the sheriff of the parish, &c. By C. D. [one of the justices, &c.]

"Keep in safe custody, until he shall be discharged by law, E. F. herewith delivered to you, charged, on the oath of A. B., with an intent to [here insert the charge]. Witness my hand, this day of        in the year        ."

Art. 581. Any one committed by virtue of such commitment, may be brought up by order of the magistrate who committed him whenever he finds security, and on executing the bond aforesaid shall be discharged.

5. Warrant for arrest, on the view of the magistrate, under the article.

"To H. H. one of the constables," &c.

"Whereas, E. F. in the presence and view of me, C. D., one of the justices [insert his style of office], did commit illegal violence on the person of A. B.: You are, therefore, commanded to arrest the said E. F., and bring him before me to answer for the said offence, and to be dealt with according to law. Given under my hand this        day of        in the year        ."

6. Application for a summons, in case of an intended libel.

"To C. D. one of the justices," &c.

"A. B. complains that E. F. as he is informed and believes, is now printing a libel against him, which he intends to publish [or that he has written and intends to print, or continues to sell and circulate, some such libel, or some such publication as is forbidden by the Penal Code, as the case may be]; he therefore prays, that the said E. F. may be summoned, for admonition, according to law."

7. Summons on the above complaint.

"To I. K. one of the constables," &c.

"Summon E. F. to appear before me, [one of the justices, &c.] on the        day of        next, at        o'clock in the morning, at my office, to hear the complaint of A. B. against him, for intending to publish [or for continuing to circulate, &c., as the case may be] a libel against him [or other publication forbidden by the Code of Crimes and Punishments, as the case may be]. Witness my hand, this day of        C. D."

Art. 582. If the person summoned do not appear, and the officer to whom it was directed shall return, that it was duly served, such summons and return shall have the same effect as to the punishment, in case of conviction, that the admonition would have had.


# CHAPTER III.


*Form of the proceeding authorized by the fourth chapter respecting search warrants.*


Art. 583. The forms to be used for proceedings authorized by this chapter are as follows :

1. Affidavit for procuring a search warrant for stolen goods, or goods taken on false pretences or fraud :

"A. B. being duly sworn before me, C. D. one of the justices, &c. [insert the office of the magistrate], doth depose, that the following property, viz. [describing it], the property of [insert the name of the owner], has been stolen, [or has been taken by false pretences, or has been forced and fraudulently appropriated, as the case may be], in the parish of        ; and that the deponent believes, that the said property is concealed in the house of I. K., [or, as the case may be, in a particular chamber, or in a barn, or other place, describing it], in the said parish; and he so believes because [here state the circumstances on which the belief is founded.]

2. Affidavit for procuring a search warrant for seizing forged instruments in writing, or counterfeit coin, or the instruments and materials for making them.

"A. B. being duly sworn before me, C. D. [insert the magistrate's office], doth depose, that he believes that certain forged bank notes [or counterfeit coin, or instruments, or materials for making them, as the case may be] are concealed in the house of [describing the place] with the fraudulent intent of passing the same [if it be bank notes or coin] or of [employing the said instruments or materials in committing the crime of forgery or counterfeiting, as the case may be]; and he also believes [state the circumstances on which he founds his belief.]

3. Affidavit for procuring a search warrant for arms and munitions prepared for insurrection or riot.

"A. B. being duly sworn before me, C. D. [insert the magistrate's office] doth depose, that he believes that certain arms [or munitions, as the case may be] consisting of [describe of what kind the arms or munitions are], are concealed in [describe the place]; and that they are intended to be used for the purposes of a riot [or insurrection, as the case may be], which he also believes certain persons have conspired to make [or have actually made, if such be the case]; and that his reasons for believing as aforesaid are [insert the reasons for believing in the insurrection, or riot, or the conspiracy, to effect them, as well as the concealment of the arms for that purpose.]

4. Affidavit for a search warrant for some article, the production of which may be necessary on a trial :

"A. B. being duly sworn, &c. [as before] doth depose, that on the trial of E. F. now under examination, [or lately committed or bailed, as the case may be], on an accusation of [state the offence] a certain silver-mounted pistol [or any other article, describing it], will, as he believes, be necessary to be produced, and that the same, as he believes, is now in the house occupied by G. H. situate in [describing the place]; and that his reasons for believing that the production of the said article will be necessary are [here state the circumstances.]

5. Warrant to search for goods stolen, taken under false pretences, or forced :

"To the sheriff of the parish        [or to A. B. one of the constables
          of the parish of                .]

"Whereas, affidavit hath this day been made before me, C. D. one of the justices, &c. [insert the office of the magistrate] by A. B. that certain property belonging to        was stolen [or obtained by false pretences from him, or had been fraudulently appropriated, as the case may be,] and that he had good reason to believe and did believe, that the said property was concealed in the house of        situate in [or other place, describing it]: You are therefore required, without delay, to make search in the said house [or other place] in the day-time for the said property; and if you find the same, or any part thereof, that you bring the same, with the person in whose custody the same was found, before me without delay, to be examined and dealt with according to law. Given under my hand and seal, this        day of in the year

6. Search warrant for seizing forged instruments in writing, or counterfeit coin, or the instruments and materials for making them.

" To the Sheriff, &c.

" Whereas, an affidavit has been made, &c. [as in the preceding form] that certain forged bank bills [or counterfeit coin, or instruments or materials for making forged bills or counterfeit coin, as the case may be, reciting the affidavit], are concealed, &c. [as in the affidavit, de-scribing the place particularly], with the fraudulent intent of passing the said bills or coin [or employing the said materials or instruments in committing the crime of forgery or counterfeiting, as the same may be stated in the affidavit]: You are therefore required," &c. as in the last form.

7. Search warrant for seizing arms and munitions prepared for in-surrection or riot.

" To the Sheriff, &c.

" Whereas, &c. [the direction and recital as in the preceding forms] affidavit has been made before me, &c. by A. B. stating that he believes, and has good reason to believe, there are certain arms [or munitions, describing them as in the affidavit] are concealed in [describing the place as in the affidavit], and that they are intended to be used for the purposes of an insurrection, [or riot, as the case may be] which certain persons have conspired to make [or have made] as he also believes, and has good reason to believe : You are therefore required," &c. as in the preceding forms.

# TITLE II.

OF THE FORMS TO BE USED IN THE PROCEEDINGS AUTHORIZED BY THE FIRST BOOK, TITLE SECOND, FOR SUPPRESSING PERMANENT OFFENCES.

## CHAPTER I.

*Forms of proceeding to be used for giving effect to the directions for suppressing permanent offences against public tranquillity, public safety, public health, public property, morals, and de-cency, and reputation.*

Art. 584. Affidavit of the existence of an unlawful assembly or riot :
"A. B. and C. D. of the parish of [New Orleans], being sworn say,

that E. F., G. H. and I. K. and others to the deponent unknown, to the number of more than twenty, are now assembled in [the public square of the city of New Orleans] with the intent to aid each other in violently and illegally [rescuing from the sheriff one J. S. who has been legally committed on an accusation of murder, which intent was openly expressed by numbers of the said assembly in the presence of these deponents."]

Art. 585. In case of a riot this clause is to be added, "and that the said persons have begun to execute their purpose [by assaulting and beating the officers of justice who have the custody of the said J. S."]

Art. 586. Proclamation and order of a magistrate for the dispersion of an unlawful assembly or a riot.

The magistrate shall, according to the directions of the Penal Code, display a white flag, which shall be carried either by him or by an officer of justice, or other person appointed by him. The flag bearer shall then proclaim "Silence! while [F. T. judge of the criminal court] speaks in the name of the law!" The magistrate shall then make his order in the following form: "In the name of the state of Louisiana, and by virtue of the powers vested in me by law as [the judge of the criminal court,] I order this assembly to disperse; and I warn each of you, that by remaining he makes himself liable to imprisonment at hard labour for any riot that may be committed by himself or his associates, and to fine and imprisonment for not retiring in half an hour after this warning, even if no other offence be committed; and if any or other crime should be committed in the prosecution of the illegal purpose for which you are assembled, all of you will incur the guilt and the punishment. Again I command you, in the name of the law and the state, to disperse."

Art. 587. All the consequences of not dispersing are incurred if the magistrate is by violence prevented from making the proclamation, or displaying his flag; or if he should not make the proclamation in the form prescribed, provided (if not prevented by violence) he shall display the flag, cause his office to be known, and give the order to disperse. But the magistrate is guilty of a neglect of duty who does not pursue the forms above directed.

Art. 588. After making the proclamation and order, the magistrate shall take notice of the precise time at which such order was given, and as soon as possible shall make a minute thereof in writing, signed by himself and other witnesses.

Art. 589. If the proclamation be made to those actually engaged in a riot, the magistrate shall cause those to be arrested who shall persevere in the unlawful act after the proclamation has been made.

Art. 590. If the proclamation be made to an unlawful assembly, but before any riot has been committed, he shall arrest those who remain in the said assembly after the expiration of the half-hour from the time of the order to disperse, as well as those who before the expiration of that time shall commit any act that amounts to a riot.

Art. 591. Application to procure an injunction against any trade, or continuing any act or cause injurious to public health.

Such application must be made in the following form:

" To the [judge of the criminal court]:

" The petition of A. B., C. D. and E. F. inhabitants of [the Bayou

St John in the city of New Orleans], showeth, that G. H. of the same place, hath lately been indicted in this court for [suffering the blood which he uses in refining sugar to putrefy] in a manner injurious to the health of the inhabitants in the vicinity ; that notwithstanding such indictment, the said G. H. continues the said practice to the great danger of your petitioners and others in the vicinity : they therefore pray, that the said G. H. may be enjoined from continuing the said unhealthy process."

Art. 592. Citation on the above petition to be served on the defendant :

" G. H. you are cited to appear before [the criminal court of the state of Louisiana] on the          day of          next, at ten o'clock in the morning, to show cause, if any you have, why the prayer of the petition, a copy whereof is annexed, should not be granted.   Dated the          day of          in the year eighteen hundred and          ."

Art. 593. Injunction on the above petition :
" The state of Louisiana to G. H.

" Whereas, an indictment hath been presented against you in the criminal court, charging [that in carrying on the business of refining sugar you suffer the blood used in that process, to putrefy] so as to injure the health of persons residing in the vicinity ; and whereas it hath been represented to our said court, that notwithstanding such indictment, you still continue the said [process] to the great injury of the persons in the neighbourhood of your works : you are, therefore, commanded to desist from continuing such [mode of carrying on the said business] as is complained of under the penalty of fine, imprisonment, and sequestration of your [works].   Witness, F. T. judge of the said court, the          day of          in the year          ."

Art. 594. If it shall appear to the court that this injunction is wilfully disobeyed, they may order the works, or other cause of injury to public health, to be sequestered until the trial of the indictment, or until the defendant shall give security to obey the order of the court.

Art. 595. In all cases where any one shall wilfully disobey any lawful writ of injunction, issued by a competent court in a criminal cause, he may be fined not exceeding fifty dollars, and imprisoned not exceeding ten days, by the court, on hearing, in a summary manner, without the intervention of a jury.

Art. 596. Writ of sequestration for disobedience to the injunction.
" The state of Louisiana to the sheriff of [the parish of the city of New Orleans :]

" You are commanded to take into your possession [the buildings situate at the Bayou St Johns, in which G. H. now carries on the business of refining sugar, and that after causing the putrid blood to be removed therefrom], you safely keep the said [building] until the further order of this court.   Witness," &c.

Art. 597. The form hereinbefore prescribed shall be used in cases of manufacturing or storing articles, dangerous from their explosive nature to human life, except that in the petition the injunction and the sequestration, the charge shall be according to fact of the manufacture carried on, or the article stored, and that it endangers the lives

3 W

of the inhabitants in the vicinity, instead of their health, as is stated in the forms above prescribed.

Art. 598. Petition for the removal of a building or obstruction of public property, held for the common use of all the inhabitants :

"To F. T. [judge of the criminal court.]

" A. B. complains that C. D. has lately erected a [house] which permanently obstructs the free use of [a street called Lafayette-street, in the city of New Orleans]; that the said [street] is public property, held for the common use of all the citizens, and that the part thereof on which the said [house] is erected has been in such common use for twelve months next preceding the time of erecting the said [house], of all which the said A. B. is ready to make proof, and he prays that the said C. D. may be cited, and that the said obstruction may be removed."

Art. 599. The citation shall be in the following form :

" C. D. you are cited to appear before me, at [my dwelling-house in the suburb St Mary,] on the          day of          at ten o'clock in the morning, to show cause, if any you have, why the prayer of the petition, a copy whereof is annexed, should not be granted.   Dated the          day of   .  in the year          ."

Art. 600. The order for removal shall be in the following form :

"By [F. T. judge of the criminal court.]    To the sheriff of the parish [of the city of New Orleans.]

" Whereas, complaint has been made to me that C. D. has lately erected a [house] which permanently obstructs the free use of a [street called Lafayette-street, in the city of New Orleans] ; that the said street is public property, held for the common use of all the citizens ; and that the part thereof on which the said [house] is erected has been in such common use for twelve months next preceding the time of erecting such [house] ; all which allegations have been clearly proved, and the inconvenience to the public being, in my opinion, so great from the obstruction aforesaid as to render it improper to wait the event of a trial for the offence, I do therefore, by virtue of the powers vested in me as judge of the court of the highest criminal jurisdiction in this district, command you, that you cause the said [house] to be removed, so that it may no longer obstruct the said street."

Art. 601. Complaint of an intended libel, or of publication injurious to morals and decency :

"To A. B. one of the justices of the peace for the parish of Plaquemine :

" C. D. of the said parish, complains that E. F. of the said parish, hath written or printed a false and malicious libel concerning the deponent, which he is continuing to sell or publish, [or has written a false and malicious libel against the deponent, which he intends to publish, as the case may be] [or that the said E. F. has prepared and intends to publish an obscene print (or picture) or a written composition called, as the case may be] which manifestly tends to corrupt the morals of youth; all which the complainant has good reason to believe and does believe ; wherefore he prays, that the said E. F. may be cited before you, and that he may receive the admonition in such case directed by law."

Art. 602. Citation in the above complaint ;

" [E. F. of the parish of Plaquemine,] you are hereby cited to appear before me [A. B. one of the justices of the peace for the said parish,] on the        day of        at ten o'clock in the forenoon, to hear such things as may be addressed to you in relation to a libel against C. D. [or a publication contrary to morals and decency, as the case may be]. Dated the        day of        in the year        ."

Art. 603. Admonition on the above citation :

" E. F. affidavit having been made before me, that there is good reason to believe that you intend to publish or sell a libel against C. D. of this parish, [or as the case may be, a publication against decency, manifestly tending to corrupt the morals of youth] or [that you have prepared and intend to publish some work of that description,] it is made my duty to admonish you, which I hereby do, that although no restraint can be laid on the liberty secured to every one by the constitution, "freely to speak, write, and print on any subject," yet the same constitution makes you liable for the abuse of that liberty, and the laws have empowered and directed me to warn you that if, after this admonition, you should commit the offence that is apprehended, you will suffer the highest punishment that can be inflicted, that is to say [if the apprehended offence be a libel purporting the accusation of a crime] imprisonment for twelve months and a fine of three thousand dollars ; [if the apprehended libel does not import the accusation of a crime, then say, imprisonment for nine months and a fine of two hundred and fifty dollars,] [and if the apprehended offence be one against decency, then say, imprisonment for six months and a fine of one thousand dollars.]"

## CHAPTER II.

*Of the forms to be used in the suppression of permanent offences against personal liberty.*

Art. 604. The suppressive remedy for offences against personal liberty is the writ of *habeas corpus*. The directions for obtaining and proceeding under that writ are minutely detailed in the first book of this Code, title second, chapter seventh. The forms are herein given to preserve uniformity in practice ; but no part of such forms are essential but such as are declared to be so in the chapter above referred to.

Art. 605. Petition for a writ of *habeas corpus* by the party imprisoned, where the imprisonment is under colour of judicial process, but irregular in form :

" To J. L. [district judge of the state of Louisiana for the first district.]

" The petition of A. B. of the city of New Orleans, showeth, that he is imprisoned in the prison of the city of New Orleans, in the custody of the sheriff of the said city, by virtue of [an order purporting to be a commitment made by C. D. one of the justices of the peace for said city,] a copy of which [order] is hereunto annexed, [or if the copy has been refused to be given, say, a copy of which commitment is not hereunto annexed, because on application to the keeper of the prison the same was refused to be given]; and your petitioner is advised and believes, that his imprisonment, or under colour of the said [order], is illegal. Your petitioner, therefore, prays, that a writ of *habeas corpus*, directed to said sheriff or the keeper of the said prison, may be granted, ordering him forthwith to bring your petitioner before you, that he may be discharged according to law."

Art. 606. When the petition is made by any other than the person imprisoned, it may state the fact of imprisonment and illegality, according to the best of his information and belief.

Art. 607. Petition when the imprisonment is by virtue of judicial process, regular in form but illegally obtained, and where a third party is interested in the discharge.

As in the last form to "in the custody of the sheriff of the said city, by virtue of a writ purporting to be a writ [of capias ad satisfaciendum, issuing out of the parish court for the parish of the city of New Orleans, at the suit of C. D. to satisfy a judgment pretended to have been obtained in the said court, for the sum of one thousand dollars ; but in truth no such judgment was ever entered, nor is there any judgment, order, or decree, to authorize the said process.] Wherefore he prays, that the said C. D. may be cited according to law, and that a writ of *habeas corpus* be granted," &c.

Art. 608. On the above petition the judge issuing the *habeas corpus* shall indorse these words, "the within named A. B. must be brought up, notwithstanding the [execution] within mentioned," otherwise the sheriff need only send up the [execution], as is provided by the third section of the seventh chapter of this Code, above referred to.

Art. 609. Citation to the plaintiff at whose suit the execution mentioned in the preceding petition was taken out, conformably to the directions in the said chapter, regulating proceedings on *habeas corpus*.

"By J. L. district judge of the state of Louisiana for the first district.
        To C. D. of the city of New Orleans.

"You are hereby cited to appear before me, at the court house of the district court, at nine o'clock to-morrow morning, to show cause, if any you have, why A. B. confined, illegally as is said, at your suit in the prison of this city, should not be discharged on a writ of *habeas corpus*. Dated," &c.

Art. 610. Petition where the imprisonment is not under colour of any judicial process.

"That he is illegally confined by J. W. [in the fort of Plaquemine, in this district] ; he therefore prays," &c.

Art. 611. Petition where the party is claimed to be held as a slave.

"That he is a free person, but is illegally held to service as a slave by C. D. Therefore he prays, that a writ of *habeas corpus*, directed to the said C. D., may issue, commanding him," &c. as in the preceding form.

Art. 612. The form of the writ of *habeas corpus* is set forth in the     article of this code in the chapter relating to "the suppression of offences against personal liberty."

Art. 613. Proof of the service of a writ of *habeas corpus* when a copy has been kept.

"A. B. being duly sworn, doth dispose, that on the                day of             , about the hour of ten before noon, he delivered to C. D. the original writ of *habeas corpus*, of which a true copy is hereunto annexed."

Art. 614. Proof service where no copy has been kept.

As above. "That on the         day of         , at about the hour of ten in the forenoon, he did serve on C. D. a writ of *habeas corpus,* allowed by J. L. district judge, directed to the said C. D. by which he was ordered [forthwith] to produce A. B., said to be in his custody, before the said judge, at the court room of the first district court, in this city ; that the said service was made by delivering the said writ to the said C. D."

Art. 615. Affidavit in cases where the person to whom the writ is directed refuses to receive it.

As above. " That he offered the writ which is hereunto annexed, on the         day of         at about the hour of ten before noon, to C. D. to whom the same is directed, but that he refused to receive the same, whereupon the deponent verbally informed the said C. D. of the contents of the said writ."

Art. 616. Proof in cases where the person to whom the writ is directed conceals himself, or refuses admittance to the person charged with the service.

As above. " That he went to the dwelling house of C. D. to whom the writ of *habeas corpus,* of which a copy is hereunto annexed, was directed, with the said writ in his possession, but that he was refused admittance into the said house, [or that having entered the said house he sought for the said C. D. in order to serve the said writ, but that the said C. D. was not there to be found, and the deponent believes that he conceals himself to avoid the service thereof ; whereupon the deponent proclaimed aloud his business, and fixed up the said writ on the outside of the said house, on the outer door thereof, where he left the same]."

Art. 617. In this last case, if the deponent have kept no copy, he must, instead of saying "a writ of *habeas corpus* of which a copy is annexed," describe the same as in the form above prescribed for proof of service when no copy was kept.

Art. 618. Form of a return when he to whom the writ is directed, has not the person he is directed to produce in his custody, or under his control.

" I, C. D., to whom the within writ is directed, do return, that I have not now, nor within three days before the date of the said writ, have not had the within named A. B. within my power, restraint, or control.          (Signed)          " A. B.

" Sworn before,

" E. F. justice of the peace," &c.

Art. 619. Form when he had the custody or control of the party within three days, but has transferred him to another.

" I, C. D., to whom the within writ is directed, do return, that I have not the within named A. B. now in my custody, or under my restraint or control ; but that on the         day of
[the said C. D. was delivered to me as a deserter from the first regiment of United States infantry, by J. S. a sergeant in the first company of said regiment, I being at that time commander of the fort of St Phillips in this state, and that I afterwards, to wit, on the
day of         transferred the custody of the said A. B. to L. M. a captain in the said regiment, before the issuing of the said writ, and before I had any notice of an intent to apply for the same]."

Art. 620. Form when the party is in custody on judicial process.

"I, C. D., to whom the within writ is directed, do return, that in obedience thereto I have the within named A. B. at the time and place within mentioned in my custody, and that the cause of his detention is a certain [order or commitment] which is annexed to this writ, to me directed as [keeper of the prison of the city of New Orleans."]

Art. 621. Form of return when the applicant is held as a slave.

"I, C. D., [as above] and that the cause of his detention is this, that he is a slave, legally acquired as my property, and I pray that his claim to freedom may be inquired of and determined according to law."

Art. 622. Form of return when the party is too sick to be produced.

"I, C. D., to whom the within writ is directed, do in obedience thereto return, that the said A. B. is detained in my custody by virtue of [an order of commitment to me directed as keeper of the prison of the city of New Orleans, which is hereunto annexed], and that I have not produced the said A. B. because it could not be done without danger to his life from the sickness which he now suffers, as appears by the testimony of the physician and witnesses hereunto annexed."

Art. 623. Certificate of physician.

"I. D. H., a physician regularly admitted to practice, certify, that I have visited A. B. now in the custody of [the keeper of the prison at New Orleans,] and found him suffering with a [bilious fever], and that, in my opinion, he cannot be brought before the judge on the annexed writ without danger of his life."

"We, I. K. and L. F. being duly sworn, do depose, that we have seen the within named A. B. and believe, from the state of his health, that he cannot be produced in obedience to this writ, without danger to his life. In witness whereof, as well we the said witnesses as the said A. B. have signed this deposition."

Art. 624. Form of a warrant to bring up the prisoner when the writ of *habeas corpus* has not been obeyed.

"By J. L. [district judge of the first district court.]	To A. B.
[one of the constables of the city of New Orleans.]

"Whereas, a writ of *habeas corpus* was lately allowed by me, directed to C. D. of the city of New Orleans, directing him to bring before me A. B. in his custody, as was said illegally detained, and the said C. D. having disobeyed the said writ,—These are to command you, to take the said A. B. out of the custody, or from under the restraint or control of the said C. D. or of any person to whose custody he may have transferred him, and to bring him before me without delay, to abide such order as I may make in the case. Witness my hand, this	day of	in the year	."

Art. 625. Warrant to arrest the person to whom the *habeas corpus* was directed, for not bringing up the prisoner.

Direction and recital as in the preceding form. "These are to command you, that you arrest the said C. D. and bring him in safe custody before me without delay, to be dealt with for his said default according to law. Witness," &c.

Art. 626. Commitment, where the party on being brought before the judge, on the preceding warrant, refuses to return the writ or to produce the prisoner.

"By J. L. district judge, &c.	To [ the keeper of the prison of the city of New Orleans.]

"Receive in your custody C. D. herewith sent to you for refusing obedience to a writ of *habeas corpus*, by me issued, directing him to produce A. B. in his custody as was alleged, and him the said C. D. safely keep until discharged by due course of law. Witness," &c.

Art. 627. Petition for a warrant to bring up the prisoner when there is danger of his being carried out of the state, or of irreparable injury, and to arrest the person in whose custody he is.

" To J. L. district judge, &c.

" The petition of A. B. showeth, that C. D. is now in the custody or power of one J. S. [who has put him on board of a vessel called the Tartar, lying at the levee of this city, now ready to sail ; and that the said J. S. intends, as the deponent is informed and verily believes, forcibly to convey the said C. D. against his will and without any legal authority, out of this state ;] and the deponent verily believes, that if a writ of *habeas corpus* issue it will be disobeyed, and the said C. D. will, notwithstanding such writ, be conveyed out of the state, [or suffer irreparable injury, as the case may be ;] and the petitioner shows, that the said J. S. hath knowingly and illegally deprived the said C. D. of his liberty, with intent to [convey him out of the state :] wherefore he prays, that a warrant may issue to bring before you the said C. D. to be discharged according to law, and to arrest the said J. S. to answer for the said offence.

" Sworn," &c.

Art. 628. Warrant on the above petition.

"By J. L. &c. To the sheriff, &c.

" Whereas proof has been made before me, that [one C. D. is illegally confined on board a vessel called the Tartar, lying at the levee of this city, and by one J. S. who intends illegally and forcibly to convey the said C. D. against his will out of this state, before he can be relieved by the due course of law :] these are, therefore, to command you to take the said C. D. out of the custody of the said J. S., or of any other person to whose custody he may have transferred him, and to bring him before me, [at the court-room of the first district court,] without delay, to abide such order as I may make in the case : and you are also commanded to arrest the said J. S. and bring him before me, without delay, [at the said court-room,] to answer for the said offence. Witness," &c.

Art. 629. When the petition does not expressly charge, that the person in whose custody the prisoner is has committed an offence, in the arrest and detention of the person detained, then the part of the warrant ordering his arrest is to be omitted.

Art. 630. Return when the party ordered to be produced has died in imprisonment, with record of the inquest.

"I, C. D., to whom the within writ is directed, do in obedience thereto return, that the within named A. B. was committed to my custody [as keeper of the prison of the city of New Orleans] on the     day of     last, by virtue of [a warrant of commitment] which is hereunto annexed, but that I cannot produce him, as I am directed, because on the     day of     last he departed this life [by the visitation of God,] as appears by the proceedings herewith returned."

Annex the inquest.

Art. 631. Notice to the coroner of the death of the prisoner.

" To the coroner of the parish of New Orleans.

" Please to take notice, that last night, about the hour of twelve, C. D.

a prisoner, confined in the prison under my charge, departed this life, that his body now remains in the said prison in the situation in which he died, and that I request you will summon a jury of inquest to perform the duties in such case required by law."

Art. 632. The summons for the jury and the inquest shall be in the form herein before prescribed for inquests on dead bodies.

Art. 633. Discharge when no sufficient cause of detention is shown by the return.

"By J. L. judge of the district court, &c.    To the keeper of the prison of the parish of New-Orleans.

"Discharge out of your custody C. D. of the said city, if detained for no other cause than that shown by your return to the writ of *habeas corpus*, allowed by me on the           day of           last, and for your so doing this shall be your sufficient warrant. Dated the           day of           in the year           ."

Art. 634. Order to remand when sufficient cause of detention is shown.

"To the keeper of the prison, &c.

"C. D. brought before me on a writ of *habeas corpus*, dated the           day of           instant, is remanded to your custody, the cause shown by you, in your return to the said writ, being sufficient in law for his detention."

# TITLE III.

OF THE FORM TO BE USED IN THE PROCEEDING AUTHORISED BY THE FIRST BOOK,. TITLE THIRD, FOR CALLING FOR AND EMPLOYING MILITARY FORCE.

## ONLY CHAPTER.

### *Forms of information and requisition.*

Art. 635. Information of the existence of a riot or insurrection.

"To J. L. district judge, and I. K. and L. M. justices of the peace.

"A. B. and C. D. inhabitants of the city of New Orleans, being duly sworn, say, that a number of men, consisting of more than twenty, [that is to say, one hundred and more,] according to the best estimate the deponent can make of their numbers, are now assembled [in Chartres-street in this city, many of them armed with swords and pistols, and others with clubs, and bricks, and other missiles, with the intent, as avowed by many of them, to break into the prison of the said city in order to liberate the persons legally confined therein ; that they have already begun to execute their threats by breaking the outer door of the said prison,] and that they have refused to disperse, although they were ordered so to do by proclamation, solemnly made in the manner directed by law by a magistrate ; and the deponent further says, that the said rioters cannot be arrested or dispersed by the ordinary form of civil authority, such arrest having been attempted by the officers of justice, who were always resisted by force and with deadly weapons, [and some of them wounded and others killed in the attempt."]

Art. 636. Application of the judge and other magistrates to the governor for the employment of a military force.

"To his excellency H. J. governor of the state of Louisiana.

"We, J. L., judge of the district court, and I. K. and L. M., justices of the peace for the city of New Orleans, being convinced by the affidavits of two inhabitants of this state, that a riot has taken place in the parish [of the city of New Orleans,] where they reside, and that the persons engaged therein cannot be arrested or dispersed by the ordinary force of civil authority ; all which, as well as the object of the said riot, appears by the affidavit aforesaid, which is hereunto annexed and to which we refer : we therefore request, that you will be pleased to order a military force of at least two hundred men, to repair to the place where the said rioters are assembled, and to act under our direction, according to law."

# TITLE IV.

### OF THE FORMS USED IN THE PROCEEDINGS AUTHORIZED IN THE SECOND BOOK, FOR PROSECUTING OFFENCES.

## CHAPTER I.

*Special forms of complaints, accusations, citations, and warrants of arrest.*

Art. 637. Form of a complaint where the complainant is not sufficiently acquainted with the circumstances to make oath of the fact.

"Be it remembered, that on this            day of before me, P. B., associate judge of the city court of the city of New Orleans, personally appeared A. B. of the said city, who made complaint, that [his store, situate in Royal-street, was broken open last night between the hours of ten and twelve, and that ten pieces of Irish linen were stolen and carried away] by some person or persons to him unknown, but that he believes [his opposite neighbour C. D.] can give testimony that may designate the offenders.

(Signed)                    "A. B.

"Sworn this day before me."

Art. 638. Citation for witnesses to appear before the magistrate.

"Mr C. D., you are commanded to appear forthwith before me, [G. P., one of the associate judges of the city court of the city of New

3 X

Orleans, at my office in the city-hall,] to testify what you know relative to a complaint made by A. B., of [house-breaking]; and hereof fail not under the penalties imposed by law of fine, imprisonment, and constraint. Given under my hands, this                day of          in the year          „

Art. 639. Return of the service.

"I, H. R., one of the constables of the city of New Orleans, certify, on my oath of office, that I did on this day deliver a copy of the within citation to C. D. therein named, about the hour of ten in the morning."

Art. 640. If the witness does not appear according to the citation, the magistrate is authorized to impose a fine not exceeding five dollars, and to issue a warrant of attachment to constrain his appearance ; and if he appear and refuse to give testimony, he may commit him to prison until he shall submit to be examined.

Art. 641. Warrant of attachment to compel the appearance of a witness before the magistrate.

"By G. P., associate judge of the city court of New Orleans. To          any officer of justice of the said city :

"You are commanded to take into your custody C. D., and bring him forthwith before me, that he may be examined as a witness in the complaint of A. B. entered before me of the [crime of house-breaking]; and for so doing this shall be your warrant. Witness my hand, this          day of          in the year          „

Art. 642. Complaint by a person incapable of giving testimony.

"Be it remembered, that on this          day of          before me, G. P., one of the associate judges of the city of New Orleans, appeared [Robert, a mulatto slave, late belonging to J. S. deceased], who declared, that last night, at about eleven o'clock, two white men, who were at work on the plantation of the said J. S., entered his chamber, when he was in bed, and with an axe gave him several mortal wounds, of which he soon after died ; that he, the appearer, came into the chamber and saw the last blow given, immediately after which the said persons fled ; that their names were G. H. and I. K.—the first a very tall spare man, about thirty years of age—and the other short, and about the age of sixty ; that a free mulatto man, named John Clark, also saw the stroke given, and endeavoured, with the deponent, to arrest the murderers, but that they could not effect it ; and that the said John Clark refused to accompany this appearer to make complaint."

Art. 643. Ex officio complaint by the public prosecutor.

"Be it remembered, that on the          day of          in the year          , before me, J. P. &c. came J. P., attorney-general of the state, who gave me to understand, that he had reason to believe that [A. B. and C. D. would, if examined, prove that the offence of giving and receiving a challenge to fight a duel had been lately committed by E. F. and G. H. of the city of New Orleans, respectively]; he therefore required, that a citation should be issued to the said A. B. and C. D. to appear and testify what they know in the premises."

Art. 644. Form of an accusation where the defendant's name is not known.

"Be it remembered, that on the          day of          in the year   , before me, G. P., one of the justices of the peace, &c. personally appeared A. B. of the said city, who on his oath declared, that on [this day, at nine o'clock in the morning, he was attacked in the high road in this parish, and by violence was robbed of ten dollars in silver and a gold watch, which were taken from his person by a man unknown to the deponent, with red hair, and a large scar over his left eye, marked with the small pox, and appearing to be about six feet high, and dressed in a sailor's jacket and trousers."]

## CHAPTER II.

*Forms of proceeding in offences against the sovereign power of the state, from the complaint to the indictment ; but applicable in the formal parts to the other offences mentioned in this title.*

Art. 645. Form of an accusation of sedition.

"Be it remembered, [as in the above form], who on his oath declared, that J. S. [of the parish of St Mary's, now in this city, hath enlisted in this city more than one hundred men, and arrayed and furnished them with arms], for the purpose of subverting and changing the constitution of the state by force of arms, [so as to abolish the senate and make other changes in the said constitution ; that the deponent was applied to by the said J. S. to enlist for the purpose aforesaid, and saw him enlist ten other persons, to whom he gave arms in the presence of the deponent."]

Art. 646. Form of complaint for exciting sedition by a writing.

——"That J. S. of this city has confessed himself as the author and publisher of a writing, published in handbills in this city on or about the  day of  last, a copy of which is hereunto annexed, by which he excites the people of this city to resist, by *force*, the execution of a constitutional law of the state, that is to say, [to resist the execution of an act imposing a tax on the real estate in this city, passed the  day of  .]"

Art. 647. Complaint for exciting insurrection, by joining a meeting of slaves with design to promote.

——"That J. S. on the  day of  was present at a meeting of slaves held in this city, at which meeting an insurrection of the slaves against the free inhabitants of this state was planned, with design to promote such insurrection ; that the deponent was concealed and heard the said J. S. persuade the said slaves then present to attempt such insurrection by [seizing the arms in the city and the powder-magazine on the other side of the river."]

Art. 648. Complaint for designedly using language calculated to make the slaves discontented with their state.

——" That J. S. in a discourse addressed himself to a number of slaves assembled in the street of the Esplanade, on Sunday, the  day of  last, in the hearing of the deponent, and used the following words, or words to the same effect—'Poor fellows ! you serve hard masters in this country—you can never know the blessings of liberty—your life is a life of misery'—with intent to render the said slaves discontented with their state of slavery."

Art. 649. Warrant of arrest in sedition, on the above accusation.

"By G. P. one of the associate judges of the city court of New Orleans. To the sheriff of the said city.

"You are commanded forthwith to arrest, and bring before me, J. S., of the parish of St. Marys, charged on oath with sedition in enlisting men and furnishing arms, for the purpose of subverting the constitution of the state by force—that he may be examined and dealt with according to law. Given under my hand, the day of                    in the year           ."

Art. 650. Examination of the prisoner.

"Be it remembered, that on the                day of                in the year           J. S. being brought before me, on my warrant, issued on the complaint of A. B. on a charge of [sedition in attempting to subvert the constitution of the state by force of arms,] I did, according to law, inform him of the nature of the accusation against him, and read to him the examinations of the witnesses which had then been taken ; who, that is to say, I. K. and H. H., were at his request summoned and were cross examined by him, as appears by the said examinations hereunto annexed ; and I did then inform him, that although he was at liberty to answer the questions I was about to put to him in what manner he thought proper, or not answer them at all, yet a departure from the truth, or a refusal to answer without assigning a sufficient reason, must operate as a circumstance against him as well on the question of commitment as of his guilt or innocence on the trial. I then put to him the following interrogatories :

1. What is your name and age ?

To which he answered, ['My name is J. S. and I am twenty-five years of age.]'

2. Where were you born ?

To which he answered, [' in the city of New Orleans.]'

3. Where do you reside, and how long have you resided there ?

[Insert answer.]

4. What is your business or profession ?

[Insert answer.]

5. Do you know the  persons who have  been sworn as witnesses on the part of the accusation, or any, and which of them, and how long have you known them ?

To which he answered, &c.

6. Where were you at the time the act of which you are accused is stated by the witnesses to have taken place ?

To which he answered, [' I was at the town of Natchez.]'

7. Give any explanation you may think proper of the circumstances appearing on the testimony against you, and state any facts that you think will tend to your exculpation.

To which he said, [state the answers of the defendant.]

G. P. Judge," &c.

Art. 651. If, after examination and hearing evidence, the magistrate shall think there is not reasonable ground for committing the defendant, he shall write on the warrant, immediately after the return, " Let the within named J. S. be discharged, the evidence, on examination, not being sufficient for commitment," and shall then sign the same.

Art. 652. Commitment when the evidence warrants it.

"By G. P., one of the associate judges of the city of New Orleans. To the keeper of the prison of the city of New Orleans.

"Receive into your custody, J. S. herewith delivered to you, charged, on oath before me, [with the crime of sedition, by enlisting men and furnishing them with arms for the purpose of subverting the constitution of this state by force of arms ;] and him safely keep until he shall be legally discharged. Witness my hand, this day of        in the year        ."

Art. 653. When the offence is bailable of right, or the proof in a case not bailable of right is not evident, nor the presumption strong, the defendant must be bailed, if he offer good security ; which is done in the following form :

"We, J. S. as principal, and G. P. and I. D. as securities, do acknowledge that we are indebted, in solido, to the state of Louisiana in the sum of        to be paid if the said J. S. should not appear at the next [criminal court,] to be held at [the city of New Orleans,] on the        day of        next, to answer those things that shall be objected to him, and particularly to a charge of [sedition] whereof he is accused, and to abide the orders of such court ; but if he should so appear and abide, then this recognizance to be void. Witness our hands, this        day of        in the year        ."

Art. 654. The witnesses are also to enter into recognizance in the following form :

"I, A. B., acknowledge that I am indebted to the state of Louisiana in the sum of        to be paid if I should not appear at the next [criminal court,] to be held in the city of New Orleans, on the        day of        next, to give testimony in an accusation against J. S. for sedition, and to abide the order of the court ; but if I so appear and abide, this recognizance to be void. Witness my hand, this        day of        in the year        ."

Art. 655. If any witness should refuse to sign such recognizance, he may be committed by the magistrate in the following form :

"By G. P. &c. [as above.] To the keeper, &c. [as above.]

"Receive in your custody, A. B. herewith delivered to you, he having refused to enter into recognizance to appear and give testimony [against J. S. on a charge of sedition] ; and him safely keep until he shall enter into such recognizance before me, or some other magistrate, or shall be otherwise released by law. Witness," &c.

Art. 656. If any one shall make oath, that another is a material witness on behalf of the prosecution in a case of CRIME, and that there is good reason to believe that he intends to depart the state, or otherwise to avoid attendance on the trial, the magistrate may direct him to find security to be recognized with him for his appearance to testify ; and on his refusal, or inability to do so, may commit him by an order in the form of that prescribed by the last article, altering only the cause of commitment according to the circumstances of the case.

Art. 657. Any one committed under the last article, for inability to find security, shall receive out of the recompense fund, on the warrant of the judge, a compensation for the time he is imprisoned, to be calculated according to the rules established for compensation to persons acquitted.

Art. 658. The forms and the provisions of the ten last preceding articles apply to all prosecutions, (changing the description of the offence where it occurs in any of the said forms).

Art. 659. Form of indictment for sedition.

The beginning and conclusion shall be according to the form prescribed in the chapter of this code, entitled *"Of indictments and informations."*

The charge in this offence shall be "did [design and attempt to subvert the constitution of this state by force of arms ; and did, on the day and year and at the place aforesaid, enlist one hundred men, to the jurors unknown, and furnish them with arms, for the purpose of changing and subverting the constitution by force of arms," &c.]

Art. 660. Another charge for the same.

——" Did design and attempt, by force of arms, to dismember the state by [forming a government, in defiance of the authority of the state, in that part of the same lying west of the Mississippi river, and for that purpose, on the day and year and at the place aforesaid, collected an assemblage of men armed and arrayed,] with the intent of carrying such design into effect by force of arms, and so the jurors say," &c.

Art. 661. The form of commitment on the accusation for exciting the people to resist the execution of the laws or commit sedition, is the same as that given above for sedition, except the charge, which is " charged on oath, before me, of having published a writing exciting the people of the city of New Orleans to [resist the legal execution of a constitutional law of this state for the levying a tax in the said city] ; or, [to dismember the state by force of arms]; or, [to subvert the constitution of the state by force of arms."]

Art. 662. The form of examination, summons, and proceedings against witnesses, and recognizance, are the same, for this offence, and for the offences hereafter mentioned in this chapter, as those before contained in this chapter, changing only the names and description of the offences where they occur.

Art. 663. Form of the charge in the indictment for exciting the people to commit sedition.

The formal parts are the same in all cases.——"That J. S. on the day of in the year , at the parish of New Orleans, did excite the people of the city of New Orleans to resist, by force, the legal execution of a constitutional law of this state, entitled, 'an act for levying a tax on the real property in the city of New Orleans,' by a certain writing printed and published by him, of which the following is a copy,[insert the particulars]; contrary," &c.

Art. 664. When the charge is of a verbal excitement, instead of " by a certain writing," in the indictment insert [" by using these expressions, addressed to a number of inhabitants of the said city assembled to prepare a petition against the said tax, 'We are fools to think of petitioning. Let us do ourselves justice. Take arms and put any officer to death who will attempt to levy the tax. I will be the first to set the example.' Thereby verbally counselling and exciting the people of the city of New Orleans, a part of the people of the state, to resist the legal execution of the said constitutional law] ; contrary," &c. And in the commitment, instead of the words "having published a writing," &c. insert " having used a verbal discourse," &c.

Art. 665. Commitments for offences under the chapter in the Code of Crimes and Punishments, relating to " Exciting Insurrection."

———" Charged on oath, before me, with having [aided in an insurrection of the slaves against the free inhabitants of this state], or [having joined a secret assembly of slaves, in which an insurrection of the slaves against the free inhabitants of this state was planned; with design to promote such insurrection]; or, [having persuaded and excited the slaves to attempt an insurrection against the free inhabitants of this state]; or, [having used language calculated to make the slaves discontented with their state, with design to promote such discontent]; contrary," &c.

Art. 666. Charge in the indictment for offences mentioned in the last article.

———" Did [aid in an insurrection of slaves against the free inhabitants of this state, by providing the said slaves with arms and ammunition to forward the purposes of the said insurrection]; or, [did join a secret assembly of slaves, held in the parish aforesaid, in which assembly an insurrection of slaves against the free inhabitants of this state was planned, with design to promote the same] ; or, [did excite and persuade certain slaves in the said parish, to the jurors unknown, to attempt an insurrection against the free inhabitants of this state]; or, [did use language to certain slaves, to the jurors unknown, calculated to make them discontented with their state, by saying to them, ' Poor. fellows,' &c. or words to that effect, [as in the affidavit], with design to promote such discontent."]

## CHAPTER III.

*Of the forms of complaint, warrant of arrest, commitment, and indictment, on prosecution for offences against the legislative power.*

Art. 667. Complaint for preventing the house of assembly from meeting, &c.

" Be it remembered, &c. [as in the preceding forms of complaint] that A. B. [on the first day of February now last past, at nine o'clock in the morning, came to the government-house of the state, situate in the city of New Orleans, followed by a guard of soldiers, and placed a soldier at each door of the chambers usually occupied by the house of representatives of the said state, and gave orders to such soldier not to permit any one to pass into the said chamber ; and this deponent further saith, that the house of representatives had adjourned on the twenty-ninth day of January last to meet on the said first day of February, at ten o'clock in the morning ; and that this deponent being a member of the said house, as well as a majority of the members thereof, presented themselves about the said hour to enter into the said chamber, but that they were by force of arms prevented by the said soldiers under the command of the said J. S., and that the said house of representatives did not and could not meet that day."

Art. 668. In like manner when the complaint is of any of the offences created by the third title of the second book of the Code of Crimes and Punishments, relating to " Offences against the legislative powers," state the circumstances thereof in the complaint particularly.

Art. 669. Form of charge in the warrant of arrest on the above complaint.

——" Charged on oath, before me, with [having designedly and by force prevented the house of representatives of this state from meeting."]

Art. 670. The charge in the commitment for this offence, is the same as that directed for the warrant of arrest.

Art. 671. Charge in the indictment.

——"[Did designedly and by force prevent the house of representatives, being one of the houses composing the general assembly of this state, from meeting] ; or according to the fact stated in the complaint, [did with intent to prevent the meeting of the house of representatives of this state, being one of the houses composing the general assembly of this state, by the use of personal violence offered to A. B., C. D. and E. F., members of the said house of representatives, prevent them from attending the said house] ; or, [did by force and the threats thereof force the senate] [or the house of representatives], being one of the branches of the general assembly of the state of Louisiana, then and there in session, to adjourn [or disperse], or [to pass a law, entitled an act, &c.] giving the title ; or [to reject an act, entitled an act, &c. which they constitutionally might have passed] ; or, [did threaten A. B. then a member of the house of representatives, that he, the said J. S., would beat and otherwise ill treat him, unless he voted for the passage of a bill then before the said house, entitled an act, &c. with intent to influence his official conduct as a member of the said house of representatives] ; or, [did make an assault upon A. B. late a member of the house of representatives, and did beat and ill treat him in consequence of the conduct of the said A. B. while he was a member of the said house]; or [did offer to bribe A. B. then a member of the house of representatives of this state, by promising that if the said A. B. would vote for the passage of a certain law then under consideration in the said house, entitled " an act for incorporating an insurance company called the Safety Company," he the said A. B. should have ten shares in the stock of the said company]; or, [did bribe A. B. a member of the house of representatives of this state, by transferring to him ten shares in the stock of an insurance company called the Safety Company, as an inducement to the said A. B. to vote for an act then before the said house for continuing the charter of the said company]; or, [did offer to one C. D. the sum of one thousand dollars, (or the right to subscribe ten shares in a certain bank, called the Fog Bank, when the said bank should be incorporated), for the purpose of securing his, the said C. D.'s interest with the general assembly, or with some members thereof, in order to procure an act incorporating the said bank]; or, [that the said J. S. on the     day of     in the year     at the parish of New Orleans, did receive from A. B. the sum of     or the promise of ten shares in the Fog Bank, as a compensation for exerting his influence with the general assembly to pass an act incorporating the said bank]; or, [that A. B. being a member of the house of representatives of the state of Louisiana, did on the     day of     in the year     at the city of New Orleans, receive from J. S. a transfer of ten shares in a certain bank called the Specie Bank, as the consideration for a promise then and there made by him the said A. B. to vote for the passage of a law then pending before the said house, entitled an act, &c.] contrary to the laws," &c.

## CHAPTER IV.

*Forms for prosecution of offences against the executive power.*

Art. 672. Complaint against officers.

" To A. B. justice of the peace, &c.

" C. D. being duly sworn says, [that E. F. lately appointed to the executive office of inspector of flour in the city of New Orleans, on the    day of    in the year    , at the city of New Orleans, performed an official act by inspecting and marking one hundred barrels of flour for G. H. of the said city, merchant, he the said E. F. not having then taken the oath of office required by law."]

"Sworn," &c.

Art. 673. Citation to E. F.

" You are cited to appear before me A. B. justice of the peace, &c. on the    day of    next, at ten o'clock in the morning, to answer to a complaint entered against you for having, as inspector of flour for the city of New Orleans, inspected and marked one hundred barrels of flour, before you had taken the oath of office required by law."

Art. 674. Charges in indictments for offences under this title.

——" Did offer the sum of one hundred dollars to A. B. register of mortgages, to induce him to give a certificate that a certain parcel of land, belonging to him the said    , was free from incumbrance, when, in fact, the same was incumbered to a large amount."

——" Did by threats of violence to the person of A. B. [one of the constables of the city of New Orleans,] force him [to make an arrest of one A. B. without any warrant or other legal authority," &c.]

——" Did attempt to force," [as in the preceding form.]

——" Did by force resist and attempt to prevent A. B. [a notary public, from entering on his minutes an act of sale legally made by I. K. to L. M." describing it.]

——" Did, he being then a [notary public], receive the sum of [one hundred dollars] from A. B. as a bribe for [making an entry in the register of his office of a sale made to him the said A. B. by C. D. as of a date prior to the true time of recording the same."

——" Did, he being then legally appointed and exercising the office [of inspector of tobacco], extort and receive from one A. B. the sum of [ten dollars for inspecting five hogsheads of tobacco], being more than is allowed by law for performing such service]; or [for doing any act (describing it) which he was by law obliged to perform, and for which no remuneration is given by law]—that he did extort and receive ten dollars when, in fact, he had not made such inspection; or [did receive the sum of ten dollars for inspecting five hogsheads of tobacco], being more than the sum allowed by law for that service, which were voluntarily given to him by one A. B. for [making such inspection."]

——" Did receive [the sum of ten dollars] from one A. B. for refraining from [condemning ten hogsheads of tobacco], which he was not authorized by law to [condemn], and which sum the law did not authorize him to receive."

3 Y

———"Being an executive officer, to wit, a notary for the city of New Orleans, he negligently [or intentionally, as the case may be] omitted [to enter on his register a certain act of sale, under private signature made, &c. (describing it) which was acknowledged and left with him for that purpose], by which omission such an injury accrued to the said                         as would entitle him to a civil action against the said E. F."

———"Being [sheriff of the city and parish of              ] did, under pretence of performing the duties of his office, [arrest one A. B. and keep him in prison from the said        day until the        day of the same month], he the said E. F. falsely pretending that he had a [writ or other process for arresting and detaining the said A. B."]


## CHAPTER V.

*Forms relating to offences against the judiciary power.*

Art. 675. Form of information against a judge or juror for receiving a bribe.

"That J. S. had a cause pending in the                court of this parish, against the deponent, which was tried by [the court or a jury, as the case may be], and that the said J. S. on the        day of        , during the pendency of the said suit, gave to A. B. [the judge of the said court, or a juror summoned to try the said cause] a promise in writing to pay to the said A. B. the sum of one thousand dollars when he the said J. S. should obtain judgment (or a verdict) in the said cause]; which written promise the said A. B. then and there received, and did promise to give a judgment (or verdict) for the said J. S. against the deponent."

Art. 676. Commitment thereon.

———"Charged on oath with having, as judge of        or as juror, received a bribe from one J. S. in a suit between him and one C. D."

Art. 677. Indictment.

———"That A. B. being appointed to the office of [parish judge of the parish of L.] and exercising the duties of that office, did on the        day of        in the year        , at the parish aforesaid, [receive from one J. S., who then had a suit pending undetermined in the said court, a written promise to pay to him the said judge the sum of        dollars in case the said suit should be determined in favour of the said J. S.] as a bribe to influence the official conduct of him the said A. B."

Art. 678. Complaint for corrupt or malicious conduct, not amounting to bribery.

———"That A. B. being appointed [parish judge of the parish of L.] and exercising the duties of that office, on the        day of        in the year        , at the said parish of L. with design to injure this deponent, and maliciously to have him declared an insolvent debtor, and by a forced surrender to deprive him of the possession of his property, did persuade one C. D. of the said parish, a creditor of the deponent, to present a petition for a forced surrender against the deponent, to him the said C. D., alleging in such petition that the deponent had suffered his notes to be protested, and had committed other acts of bankruptcy, which petition the said C. D. did present, but, although he did not make oath to the truth of such petition, or give any other proof thereon, the said A. B., under colour of his office, ordered a provisional seizure to be made of the deponent's property, and other proceedings to be had as in case of a forced surrender against him."

Art. 679. The same transaction may be stated to be corruptly done, alleging the motive instead of a desire to injure, to be that of securing some emolument or advantage to himself, [describing it], or to another, (by giving him the management of the estate at Syndic, or some other means.)

Art. 680. Warrant and commitment.

——"Charged on oath, with having officially as parish judge [or maliciously] granted an order of seizure, as in case of a forced surrender, against C. D."

Art. 681. Indictment.

——"That A. B. being appointed to the office of [parish judge of the parish of L.] and exercising the duties of that office, on the day of       in the year       , at the said parish of L, did [corruptly, for the purpose of securing emolument to himself, or to another, stating what emolument, as the case may be], or [maliciously, for the purpose of injuring one C. D., grant under colour of his office, but in a manner unauthorized by law, an order of seizure, as in a forced surrender, against one C. D."

Art. 682. Complaint of an offer to bribe.

——"That the deponent is, and since the       day of       last, has been clerk of the parish court of the parish of L., and that C. D. of the said parish, on the       day of       in the year       , in the parish aforesaid, offered to the deponent that if the deponent would permit him the said C. D. to alter a certain record of a judgment obtained in the said court, and then in the official custody of the deponent, [describing it,] by erasing the word "hundred," and inserting the word "thousand" instead thereof, he would give to the deponent the sum of three hundred dollars, which the deponent refused to do."

Art. 683. Warrant of arrest and commitment.

——"Charged on oath, with having offered to bribe A. B. clerk of the parish court of the parish of L."

Art. 684. Indictment.

——"That one A. B. having been before the       day of       in the year       , legally appointed clerk of the parish court of the parish of L., and being on that day in the legal exercise of the duties of the said office, one C. D. of the said parish, on the day and year and in the parish aforesaid, did offer to give to the said A. B. three hundred dollars as a bribe, if he would permit him the said C. D. to alter the record of a judgment entered in the said court in favour of the said C. D. against one E. F., for five hundred dollars, by erasing in the said record the word "hundred" and inserting in the place thereof the word "thousand," so as to falsify and forge the said record, and make it appear to be a judgment for five thousand dollars."]

Art. 685. Complaint of forcible opposition to an officer of justice.

——"That the deponent is [sheriff of the parish of L. and was so on the       day of       last, that having in his hands a warrant in due form of law, issued by G. P. one of the justices of the peace for the said parish, to arrest one E. F. charged with the crime of forgery, and being about to execute the said warrant on the said E. F., who was then in the house of G. H. in the said parish, he was by force of arms opposed by I. K. and L. M. in the lawful execution of the said official act, and prevented by force from entering the said house to search for and arrest the said E. F. they the said I. K. and L. M. knowing, at the same time, the office of the deponent and his authority to make the said arrest."]

Art. 686. Warrant for arrest and commitment.

——" Charged with having forcibly opposed A. B. sheriff of the parish of L. in the lawful execution of an official duty."

Art. 687. Indictment.

——" Did by force oppose A. B. then being sheriff of the said parish of L. in the lawful execution of an official act, that is to say, by forcibly preventing him from making the arrest of one E. F. by virtue of a warrant in due form of law, issued by G. P. one of the justices, &c. commanding the said sheriff to arrest the said E. F. and bring him for examination on a charge of forgery, they the said I. K. and L. M. well knowing that the said A. B. was sheriff of the said parish, and had legal authority to make the said arrest."

Art. 688. Complaint where the opposition was made in a case when the arrest was authorized to be made without warrant.

——" That on the     day of     last, A. B. was murdered in the said parish, by a blow with an axe on the head of the said A. B., of which he instantly died, given by C. D. of the said parish ; that the said C. D. immediately fled, and that the deponent having good reason to believe that he would effect his escape before a warrant could be obtained, and there being no magistrate present, the deponent pursued the said C. D. with the intent to arrest and bring him before a magistrate for examination and commitment, but that I. K. and L. M. well knowing all that is above stated, forcibly opposed the deponent in the lawful execution of the said duty."

Art. 689. Warrant for arrest and commitment.

——" Charged on oath with having forcibly opposed E. F. legally acting as an officer of justice, in the lawful execution of the official act of arresting C. D. who fled after having committed murder, the circumstances under which the said E. F. acted being then known to the said I. K. and L. M."

Art. 690. Indictment.

——" That on the     day of     in the year    , in the parish of L. the crime of murder was committed on one A. B. by a certain C. D. who instantly endeavoured to make his escape, and there being good reason to believe that he would effect it before a warrant could be obtained, and there being no magistrate present, E. F. pursued the said C. D. with the intent to arrest him ; but that I. K. and L. M. well knowing the premises, on the day and year and at the place aforesaid, forcibly opposed the said E. F. in making the said arrest," &c.

Art. 691. Complaint of rescue.

——" [That the deponent being sheriff of the parish of L. had on the     day of     last a warrant in due form of law, issued by G. P. one of the justices, commanding the deponent to arrest A. B. charged on oath with the crime of forgery ; on which warrant the said A. B. was lawfully arrested and in the custody of the deponent, who was proceeding with him to the said justice as by the said warrant he was commanded, and that] I. K. and L. M. did on the day and year and the place last aforesaid, by force of arms, rescue the said C. D. from the deponent's custody and set him at liberty."

Art. 692. Warrant and commitment.

——" Charged with having rescued from the custody of the sheriff of the parish of L. one C. D. lawfully arrested by the said sheriff on a [warrant for forgery," &c.]

Art. 693. Indictment.

The same as the complaint, substituting the name of the sheriff for the words " the deponent," whenever they occur.

Art. 694. Complaint of escape.

——"That A. B. being lawfully arrested and in the custody of the deponent, [by virtue of a warrant to him directed and delivered, issued in due form of law by G. P. one of the justices, &c. commanding the deponent to arrest the said A. B. charged on oath with the assault and battery upon G. H.] and being so in custody the said A. B. privately escaped therefrom without being legally discharged," &c.

Art. 695. Warrant and commitment.

——" Charged on oath with having escaped from a lawful arrest," &c.

Art. 696. Indictment.

——" Did, after being lawfully arrested, on a charge of [assault and battery committed upon one G. H.] escape from the custody of the sheriff of the parish of L. without being legally discharged."

Art. 697. Complaint for breach of prison.

——" That he is the keeper of the public prison of the parish of L., and that A. B. was legally committed to his custody in the said prison on the          day of          last, by a commitment in due form of law, issued by G. P. one of the justices, &c. charging the said A. B. [with the crime of house-breaking ; and that in the night of the          day of          last, broke the said prison by taking out two of the iron bars which formed the window-grates of the said prison], and escaped [or attempted to escape] out of the said prison by the breach he had so made."

Art. 698. Warrant and commitment.

——" Charged with breach of prison and attempt to escape [or with having escaped."]

Art. 699. Indictment.

——" That on the          day of          in the year          , being [legally] confined in the public prison of the parish of L. in the said parish, and in the custody of the keeper thereof, on a charge of [house-breaking], he did then and there forcibly break [the bars which formed the window grates thereof], and escape through the breach he had thus made."

Art. 700. Indictment for aiding the prisoner to attempt an escape.

——"That one A. B. was on the          day of          in the year          , lawfully confined in the public prison of the parish of L. by virtue of a commitment made by a magistrate, for the [crime of theft], and that I. K. and L. M. did, on the day and year and in the parish aforesaid, furnish the said A. B. with [a hammer and saw] for the purpose of attempting his escape, by breaking the said prison with the instruments aforesaid."

Art. 701. Warrant and commitment for the above offence.

——" Charged with having furnished to A. B. a prisoner legally confined in the public prison of the parish of L. instruments for attempting his escape by breaking the prison."

Art. 702. In all the proceedings under this chapter, if the defendant be an attorney at law or a counsellor at law, these words must be inserted after his name in the charge of the offence, " he being at that time an attorney at law," or " counsellor at law," or both, as the case may be.

Art. 703. Complaint against an attorney, for malpractice.

——"That A. B. being on the        day of        last, an attorney and counsellor at law, duly admitted to practise in the parish court of the parish of L., and having been charged with the prosecution of a suit brought by the deponent in that court against one C. D. for the recovery of a tract of land ; on the day and year and in the parish aforesaid, during the pendency of the said suit, did designedly divulge to the said C. D., to the injury of the deponent, a circumstance that came to his knowledge by virtue of this trust, to wit, [that I. K. under whom the defendant claimed the land in question, had resided for two years in this state, the knowledge of which fact enabled the said C. D. to avail himself of a plea of prescription against the deponent's] title ; or, [did give counsel to the said C. D. to plead prescription against the deponent's title] ; or, [did, after having been consulted on the merits of. the case for the deponent, under pretext that the deponent had not paid his fees, (or under some other pretext, stating it,) appear for the said C. D. as his counsellor in court in the said cause]—[or secretly as his adviser, as the case may be] ; or, [did in the prosecution of the said cause, with intent to injure the deponent, (agree to put off the trial of the said cause) when he was not obliged by law so to do, by which the deponent suffered great injury] ; or, [did with intent to injure the deponent, omit to bring on the trial of the said cause, which he lawfully might have done, by which the deponent suffered great injury] ; or, [did receive from the said C. D. the sum of one thousand dollars, under colour of a fee for advice to be given for services to be rendered by the said A. B., but in reality as a bribe for betraying the trust reposed in him as attorney and counsellor to the deponent."]

Art. 704. In the warrant and commitment, it will be sufficient to say, in either of these complaints—

——" Charged with malpractice as an attorney at law, or a counsellor at law, or both, [or charged with receiving a bribe], as the case may be.

Art. 705. Indictment.

The same charge as in the complaint, substituting the name of the complainant for the words " the deponent," whenever they occur.

Art. 706. The above forms will serve for all prosecutions against attornies or counsellors, changing only the charge according to circumstances, retaining in all cases the words of the article, under which the prosecution is made, where the sense will admit.

Art. 707. Complaint for personating an officer of justice.

——" That one A. B. not being an officer of justice, but fraudulently pretending to be [one of the deputies of the sheriff of the parish of L., in such assumed character on the        day of        in the year        , in the parish of L., made an assault on the deponent, and kept him in custody and imprisonment for the space of two hours] ; or, in such assumed character, exacted and received, [or attempted to receive, as the case may be], the sum of five dollars from the deponent, for fees due to the said sheriff."

Art. 708. Warrant and commitment.

——"Charged on oath with falsely and fraudulently personating an officer of justice."

Art. 709. Indictment.

The same charge as in the complaint, substituting the name of the complainant for the words "the deponent," whenever they occur.

Art. 710. Complaint for falsely personating another in a judicial proceeding.

——"That A. B. without having received any authority from the deponent, falsely personated him, and in such assumed character, [on the          day of          in the year          , in the parish of L., put in a plea of confession of judgment in a suit brought by one J. S. against the deponent, in the parish court of the parish of L.;] or [put in bail for one C. D. in a suit brought against him by one J. S. in the parish court of the parish of L."]

Art. 711. Complaint for perjury in a court of justice.

"Be it remembered, that on          this          day of          in the year of our Lord          , before me, ·G. P. judge of the city court of the city of New Orleans, came I. K. and L. L. who being sworn, do say, that [on the          day of          last, they were present in the district court of the first district of this state then sitting in this city, and that they saw and heard J. S. sworn as a witness in the said court in a cause then there pending, between A. B. plaintiff, and C. D. defendant, and that the said J. S. did then and there, under the sanction of the oath so administered, falsely, deliberately, and wilfully assert and give in evidence in the said cause, that he heard the defendant acknowledge on the first day of January last, in the city of New Orleans, that he owed the sum of one hundred dollars to the plaintiff in the said suit, which assertion the deponents declare to be a falsehood, because they say that on the said first day of January the said J. S. was not in the city of New Orleans, but was seen by both the deponents on that day in the city of New York."]

Art. 712. Warrant and commitment.

——"Charged on oath with the crime of perjury."

Art. 713. Indictment.

——"That J. S. being, on the          day of          in the year          , at the parish of New Orleans, sworn as a witness, on oath legally administered to him [in the district court of the state of Louisiana for the first district], in a suit pending in the said court between A. B. plaintiff and C. D. defendant, did under sanction of the said oath declare and assert as evidence in the said cause, that [here insert the particular part of the evidence which is found to be false] ; which evidence and assertion so given and made the jurors present, was a deliberate and wilful falsehood, inasmuch as [the said J. S. was not at New Orleans at the time asserted in his said evidence, but at the city of New York, and did hear the defendant acknowledge that he owed the said sum to the plaintiff."]

Art. 714. In proceedings for perjury on a written instrument, such as an accusation before a magistrate, an examination before commissioners, or answers to interrogatories, the whole instrument need not be copied in the complaint or the indictment, but only that assertion which is alleged to be false ; the whole instrument must, however, be produced and shown to the defendant previous to the arraignment in the manner herein before directed with respect to forged instruments, with the modifications contained in a subsequent chapter prescribing the forms of proceeding on prosecutions for forgery.

Art. 715. Complaint for perjury, in answer to interrogatories put by a plaintiff.

———"That the deponent on the            day of            in the year            , presented a petition to the parish court of the parish of L. against J. S, for the recovery of a sum of money due to him, by promise, for goods sold ; that, according to the forms prescribed by law, he annexed to his said petition certain interrogations to be answered by the said J. S. on oath ; among which interrogations was the following: ' First interrogatory—did you not on the            day of            , or at any other time, acknowledge that you had purchased the goods mentioned in the petition and promise to pay the amount to the ‑ plaintiff ?'—which interrogatories were allowed, and ordered by the judge of the said court to be answered, and that the said J. S. made answers thereto in writing ; and in answer to the interrogatory herein before set forth, on the            day of            last, in the parish of New Orleans, under the sanction of an oath legally administered, that is to say, by G. P. one of the judges of the city court of the city of New Orleans, did deliberately, and wilfully, and falsely allege and declare, in writing, as follows : ' In answer to the first interrogatory the respondent [meaning the said J. S.] answers—that he never made such acknowledgement as set forth in the said first interrogatory'—which allegation *the deponent declares* is a falsehood, inasmuch as the said J. S. did make such acknowledgement as is stated or inquired of by the interrogatory above recited."

Art. 716. The charge in the indictment is the same as the complaint, inserting the name of the complainant instead of the words " the deponent," and the words " the grand jury present," instead of the words " the deponent declares," in the conclusion of the statement.

Art. 717. Complaint for false-swearing.

———"That J. S. on the            day of            in the year            , in the parish of New-Orleans, made a voluntary affidavit under the sanction of an oath, administered by H. P. one of the justices, to the following effect, [recite the part of the affidavit alleged to be false] ; and the *deponent declares*, that the allegation aforesaid, contained in the said affidavit, is a falsehood, deliberately and wilfully made, inasmuch as in truth [insert the true statement as above."]

Art. 718. The indictment pursues the complaint, changing as is above directed in the last precedent.

Art. 719. Complaint for subornation or perjury.

———" That [as in the case of perjury by a witness in court] ; and that W. S. of the said parish, did, by means unknown to the deponent, procure the said J. S. to make the false declaration and commit the perjury aforesaid."

Art. 720. Indictment.

———" That [the same as the indictment for perjury by a witness in court ; and add,] and the jurors aforesaid do further present, that W. S.

of the said city, did, on the said          day of          in the year          ,
at the parish of New-Orleans, by means to the said jurors unknown, induce the said J. S. to make the false declaration and commit the perjury aforesaid."

Art. 721. Complaint for endeavouring to suborn.

——"That J. S. on the          day of          in the year          , in the parish of L., by offering a reward of one hundred dollars to him, endeavoured to persuade one W. S. to commit perjury by declaring, under the sanction of an oath as a witness in a certain cause then pending and to be tried before the parish court of the parish of L., brought by this deponent against A. B., that he the said W. S. had [insert the fact endeavoured to be proved,] he the said J. S. well knowing that [if the said W. S. had wilfully and deliberately made the said declaration, under the sanction of an oath lawfully administered in the said court,] he would have been guilty of perjury."

Art. 722. Indictment.

——"That J. S. on the ·          day of          in the year          , at the parish of L., by offering a reward of one hundred dollars to one W. S., did endeavour to persuade him the said W. S. to commit perjury by declaring, under the sanction of an oath to be legally administered to him the said W. S. as a witness in a certain cause then pending and to be tried in the parish court of the parish of L. between one I. K. plaintiff and A. B. defendant," &c. as in the complaint.

Art. 723. Complaint and indictment for obstructing the proceedings of a court of justice.

——"That J. S. during the session of the parish court of the parish of L. on the          day of          in the year          - , in the parish of L. did [by loud speaking or making a clamour and noise] wilfully obstruct the proceedings of the said court ; or [that the parish court of the parish of L. on the          day of          in the year          , made a legal order for the maintenance of order (or to preserve regularity of proceedings therein), which order directed [insert the purport of the order] ; and that the said order was signified to one J. S. for his government, but that he the said J. S. did refuse to obey the same, and did," [insert the act of disobedience.]

Art. 724. Indictment for using indecorous expressions, &c.

——"That J. S. on the          day of          in the year          , in the parish of          in the [parish court of the said parish] then open and in session, did verbally use the following [indecorous,] [contemptuous,] or [insulting] expressions, addressed to the judge of the said court, [of,] or [to,] the [judge of the said court,] or said [court,] that is to say, [recite the expressions complained of."]

Art. 725. Indictment for indecorous expressions in writing.

——"That J. S. on the          day of          in the year          , in the parish of New-Orleans, in a written argument or pleading, addressed to the [judges of the supreme court of the state of Louisiana,] in a suit then pending in the said court between A. B. plaintiff and C. D. defendant, did use the following [indecorous,] [contemptuous,] or [insulting] expressions of or [to] the said court, or [the judges thereof,] that is to say," [insert the language complained of.]

Art. 726. If the party complained of be an attorney or counsellor, and the indictment be on a third offence, the circumstances of his being an attorney or counsellor must be set forth in the indictment.

·3 Z

Art. 727. Indictment for obstructing the proceedings of courts.

——"That on the        day of        in the year        , at the parish of L. the parish court of the said parish being then open, J. S. [by threats of violence] or [by violence] offered to A. B. the [judge of the said court,] or [summoned to attend the said court as a juror,] or [as a witness,] or attending the said court to [prosecute] or defend a suit as a party or [as an attorney or counsellor,] obstructed the proceedings of the said court."

Art. 728. If the person accused in the above indictment be an attorney or counsellor, that fact must be stated.

## CHAPTER VI.

*Forms of proceeding on prosecutions for offences against public tranquillity.*

Art. 729. Indictment for an unlawful assembly.

——"That A. B., [together with C. D., E. F., &c.] or together with three or more persons, to the jurors unknown, did, on the        day of        in the year        , in the parish of L. assemble with intent to aid each other by violence illegally to [pull down a house erected by A. B. in the said parish,] or [to do any other illegal act, reciting it."]

Art. 730. For a riot.

——"That A. B. [as in the preceding form to the end]; and that being so assembled, the said A. B. and the others of the said assembly, did actually, by violence and illegally, [pull down the said house, or do any other illegal act, reciting it."]

Art. 731. When the original assembly was not unlawful.

——"That A. B. together with three or more persons, to the jurors unknown, having assembled on the        day of        in the year        , in the parish of L. for a lawful purpose, did, afterwards and before the said assembly was dispersed, on the same day and year and at the place aforesaid, proceed to aid each other in committing, and did commit the unlawful and violent act of [recite the unlawful act."]

Art. 732. An unlawful assembly for the purpose of witnessing a boxing match.

——"That A. B. with three or more others, to the jurors unknown, on the        day of        in the year        , at the parish of L., assembled together for the purpose of being present at and witnessing a boxing match, made up and agreed to be fought between [C. and D.], or [between two persons to the jurors unknown."]

[If the fight actually takes place, add,] " and the jurors further present, that a single combat with fists, or a boxing match, was then and there fought in the presence of the said assembly, whereof the said A. B. was one, and that he and the other persons composing the said assembly witnessed the boxing match ; and [if wagers were laid, add,] that the said A. B. then and there laid a wager on the event of such combat or boxing match."

Art. 733. Indictment for public disturbance.

——"That A. B. and C. D. on the        day of        in the year

, in the parish of L., did meet in the public highway, near to the houses of I. K., and J. S., and G. H, and other inhabitants of the said parish, and being so met [by vociferation, quarrelling,] or fighting with each other, greatly disturbed the said inhabitants of the said place in the prosecution of their business ; [or if at night, say,] in their necessary repose."

Art. 734. The enumeration of the names of the inhabitants in the above, is made only to designate the place, but is not necessary if the neighbourhood be otherwise designated, as a square or street in a city.


## CHAPTER VII.


*Forms used in prosecutions for offences against the right of suffrage.*

Art. 735. Indictment for bribing at an election.

——"That A. B. on the          day of          · in the year          , at the parish of L., was an inhabitant of the said parish entitled by law to vote at public elections for members of the          and for governor of this state, and that J. S. on the day and year and at the place aforesaid, for the purpose of influencing the vote of the said A. B. at the public election then about to be held on the          day of          then next thereafter for the election of [a governor of the state of Louisiana], did offer to the said A. B. [the sum of ten dollars, or any other advantage or emolument which would constitute bribery, according to the definition of that term in the book of Definitions, describing what such advantage or emolument is], as a BRIBE, if he would consent to vote at such election for C. D. as governor."

If the charge be given for a BRIBE, insert " did give" instead of " did offer;" and instead of the words, " if he would consent to vote," insert " for consenting to vote."

If the charge be for receiving a BRIBE, add at the end of the last form, " which the said A. B. received, and promised, in consideration of such bribe, to vote for the said C. D."

Art. 736. Indictment for offering or giving a bribe to a judge or clerk of the election, or the officers attending it.

——"That A. B. being [parish judge of the parish of L., is by virtue of his office constituted by law one of the judges of the public elections for members of the general assembly and governor of the state, in the said parish of L.]; and that J. S. desiring to influence the said A. B. to betray the said trust reposed in him by law, on the day of          in the year          , at the parish aforesaid, proposed and offered to the said A. B. [to procure for him by the influence of him the said J. S. the place as cashier of the bank of          in the city of New Orleans, as a bribe, if he the said A. B. would, at a public election for governor of the state then about to be held in the said parish, on the          day of          then next, put into the ballot-box one hundred ballots with the name of X. Y. written thereon, and take out an equal number that had been legally deposited therein, containing the name of some other person."

If the charge be bribery against the judge, clerk, or other officer, add, "which proposal the said A. B. did then and there accept, and promised to perform the illegal act so requested to be done as a consideration for the said bribe."

Art. 737. The above form will serve for indictments against clerks and other officers of elections, changing only the allegation of the office.

Art. 738. Indictment for hiring persons to procure votes.

——"That J. S. on the  day of  in the year  , in the parish of  did offer or [give, as the case is], to one A. B. [the sum of fifty dollars] as a reward for his services in persuading or procuring persons qualified to vote as electors for [governor] to vote at an election then about to take place for X. Y. as [governor], or, as the case may be, [to vote against A. Z."]

Art. 739. Indictment for endeavouring to procure votes by threats.

——"That A. B. of the parish of L. on the  day of followed the business of a grocer, and in the way of his business, then and for a long time before, had the custom of one J. S. and made lawful gains by supplying him with groceries for his family, and that the said A. B. on the  day of  last aforesaid, was entitled to vote at a public election for members of the general assembly of this state then about to be held on the  day of  then next in the said parish; and the jurors further present, that J. S. of the said parish, being desirous of procuring the vote and influence of the said A. B. at the said election in favour of C. D., E. F., &c. as members of the house of representatives, on the day and year and at the parish first aforesaid, threatened the said A. B. to withdraw his custom or dealing from him in his said trade of grocer, if he the said A. B. did not, at the said election, vote for the said C. D. and E. F. as members of the house of representatives."

Art. 740. Indictment against a clerk of election for making a false entry.

——"That J. S. being appointed clerk of the public election began to be held on the  day of  in the year  , at the parish of L. for members of the house of representatives of the state of Louisiana, and being in the exercise of the duties of the said office on the   day of  in the year aforesaid, did knowingly make a false entry on the list of voters at the said election, by inserting thereon [insert the false entry."]

Art. 741. If against a judge.

——"That J. S. being a judge of the public election, began to be held, &c. [as in the above form] did knowingly put into the ballot-box a ballot not given by an elector, or [did permit a ballot, not given by an elector, to be put into the ballot-box;] or [did take, or permit to be taken, out of the ballot-box, in a manner not prescribed by law, a ballot deposited therein]; or [did designedly change the ballots given by the electors]; or [did designedly destroy the ballots given by the electors at such election by burning the same]; or [did designedly, by omitting to seal the box, or any other omission or act, describing it], destroy or change the ballots given at the said election."]

Art. 742. The other offences under the second chapter of the seventh title of the Penal Code, may be indicted according to the above form, stating in the same manner the office of the defendant, and the act or omission as nearly as possible in the words of the article creating the offence.

Art. 743. Indictment for bringing armed men within a mile of the place of election.

———"That A. B. having under his orders [as colonel of the militia of the state, or other military office, if he hold one, stating it], a body of troops or armed men, did on the          day of          in the year          , at the parish of L. order and bring, [or did keep, according to the fact], the said troops within one mile of the [courthouse] of the said parish, where a public election for [members of the general assembly] of the state of Louisiana was on that day held, and [if such be the charge, add] with intent to influence the said election."

Art. 744. Indictments for riots at elections, must be in the form of indictments for riots on other occasions, only adding to the charge that such riot was within half a mile of the place at which a public election was then held.

Art. 745. Indictments for other offences committed at elections, must state the holding of the election in the form above given, and the offence as nearly as possible in the words of the article which forbids the offence.


CHAPTER VIII.


*Of forms used in prosecutions for offences against the liberty of the press.*

Art. 746. Indictment for preventing any one from publishing by threats, &c.

———" That A. B. having the intention, according to the right secured to him by the constitution, of freely speaking, writing, and printing on any subject, to write, or to publish, or verbally to make [an investigation into the public character and conduct of J. S. as governor of the state of Louisiana, (or as judge or member of the general assembly, or as any other officer, stating the office), or any other speech, or publication, or writing, describing its nature], J. S. of the parish of L. on the          day of          in the year          , in the parish aforesaid, in order to prevent, or endeavour to prevent the said A. B. from exercising the right secured to him as aforesaid, did threaten him, that if he printed, [wrote, or spoke, as the case may be], the said investigation, [or other matter, according to the fact], he the said J. S. would beat him the said A. B. [or do some other injury to his person, property, or credit, describing the nature of the injury,"] &c.

If the offender be a member of the general assembly, or a judge, or judicial or executive officer, then add, if his intent will warrant the charge, "he the said J. S. being [state the place or office], and having made the said threats, in order to prevent an investigation of his official conduct, [or if he be a member of the general assembly, the investigation of the branch to which he belongs, stating it,"] &c.

If the offence be committed by a judge, and the publication be prevented by an official act or the threat of one, follow the above form down to and including the words, "that he the said J. S. would," after which insert " he being then [state his office] by virtue of his office, arrest, [or state any other official act that was threatened."]

If the publication was prevented, or attempted to be prevented, by the actual exercise of the official act, state,——" did by virtue of his office, he being then [state the office], arrest or [state the official act] the said A. B., and did thereby prevent, or attempt to prevent, the said A. B. from speaking, [printing, or writing, as the case may be], what he so intended."

Art. 747. Indictment against a judge for granting an injunction against a publication, under an allegation that it was a libel.

——" That J. S. being judge and [state the office] did [insert the date and place] issue an injunction commanding A. B. to desist from publishing a writing which he intended to publish, entitled or purporting to be [describing the writing] under pretext [that the same was a libel or a seditious writing on,"] [stating the cause for granting the injunction.]

Art. 748. Indictment for preventing the investigation of legislative, judicial, or executive proceedings.

——" That J. S. [being a judge, and state his office if he have any], intending to restrain the right, given by the constitution, to examine the proceedings of the legislature, or of any branch of the government, and intending also to give effect to an act of the general assembly, entitled ' an act,' [insert the title], passed in contravention of that clause in the constitution which declares, that no law shall be made to restrain the right aforesaid, did," [here insert the act done in obedience to the unconstitutional law.]

## CHAPTER IX.

*Of the forms to be used in prosecutions for offences against public records.*

Art. 749. Indictment for forging a public record.

——" That A. B. on the             day of             in the year
            , at the parish of L. forged a public record, purporting to be the record of an act of the general assembly of Louisiana, of which forgery the following is a copy [insert an exact copy of the forged record], with intent to injure or defraud, and so the said jurors say, that the said A. B. hath committed the crime of forgery, contrary," &c.

Art. 750. When the forgery consists in altering a record, the indictment shall be :

——" That among the records of conveyances and other authentic acts, kept in the notary's office now under the care of A. B. notary public, in [state the place] there was prior to the             day of
            in the year             , a certain [act of sales], made by I. K. to L. M. of which the following is a copy [insert a copy of the record as it was before the alteration], and that J. S. on the
day of             in the year             , at the parish of L. made, without any legal authority, and with intent to injure or defraud, made such alterations in the said record as to make it appear to be of

the following tenor [insert a copy of the record as altered], and so the said jurors say, that the said J. S. hath committed the crime of forgery."

Art. 751. When, from obliterations made in the original record it is difficult to prove what its exact tenor was before the alterations, the form shall be :

——" That among the records [designating them as above] there was one purporting to be [describe the nature of the altered record as it was before the alteration], and that J. S. on the day [state the date] at the parish of L., without lawful authority, and with design to injure or defraud, made such alterations in the said record as to make it appear to be of the following tenor," [insert a copy of the record as altered.]

Art. 752. Indictment for forging an official certificate of an officer having the custody of public records.

——"Did make and forge a false certificate, of which the following is a copy, [insert an exact copy of the forged certificate], with the design to injure or defraud, and so the said jurors say, that the said J. S. hath committed forgery, contrary," &c.

Art. 753. Indictment for carrying away, defacing, or destroying a public record.

——" That A. B. on the      day of      in the year , in the parish of      did fraudulently [carry away], [deface], or [as the case may be, destroy], a public record, that is to say, the record of [the death of A. B. kept by the recorder of births and deaths in the city of New Orleans], [or any other public record," describing it.]

Art. 754. If either of the above offences be committed by the officer having the custody of the record, in relation to which the crime was committed, it must be thus stated, after describing the offence: "with design to injure or defraud : he the said J. S. being at that time the officer entrusted with the custody of the said public record."

Art. 755. If the offence be concealing or carrying away the record by an officer, the description of the offence must be, "did [conceal] or carry away a public record, [describing it], so that persons interested therein could not have access to it;" or, as the case may be, "did advise or counsel to such [forgery], [destruction], or [carrying away]," according to the case.

Art. 756. Other forms against officers for offences affecting public records.

——" That J. S. being an officer entrusted with the custody of public records, that is to say, [describe the office], did, knowingly and fraudulently, certify the entry of an act on the said records, in the name of one A. B. who was not present at the time such act purports to have been passed ; or [who did not consent to such act], which act is in the words following, [insert copy of the act."]

Or, ——" did intentionally and fraudulently place on the said register or records, an act in words following, [copy the act], under the date of the      day of      in the year      , which was not the date at which the said act was, in truth, registered or recorded, with intent to give an illegal advantage to [naming the person favoured by the fraud ; or say, to some one to the jurors unknown."]

Or, ——"did fraudulently permit A. B. or [some person, to the jurors unknown,] to personate one I. K., and in his name and without his authority, in the execution of an act, entered or intended to be entered on such record or registry."

Or, —— " did undesignedly, and for want of proper care, suffer the said records, so entrusted to his care, [or some part of the records, describing it,] to be [defaced,] or [taken away,] [or lost,] or to be altered, so that a certain [act] which was truly entered on the said record or registry, in the following words, [insert a copy of the original (act)], appeared, after such alterations, to be an [act] in the words following, [insert the (act) as altered]; by reason of which [alterations,] [defacement,] [obliterations,] or [loss,] one A. B. was injured in his [property,] [condition,] or [reputation,"] according to the case.

Or, ——did, in his official capacity, certify as true that [insert the act falsely certified] when, in fact and truth, the part so certified was false ; by reason of which false certificate one A. B. was injured," &c. [as in the last charge].

If in the last case the accusation be, that the falsehood was fraudulently certified, it must be so stated ; but need not, unless specially intended inasmuch as the mere falsehood is a misdemeanor, and the doing it fraudulently is a crime.

Art. 757. Indictment for using a record so forged, or fraudulently made, or entered.

——[Charge the offence according to to the circumstances, as set forth in one of the preceding forms of this chapter, and then add,] "and the jurors aforesaid do further present, that Y. Z. well-knowing the premises, afterwards, on the          day of          in the parish of L. [used the said record or act, so (forged,) or fraudulently entered,] or [made,] or registered, or [recorded] on the said [false declaration,] [as the case may be,] producing the same in a court of the parish of L. [stating the court] as testimony, or by [state the means by which advantage was endeavoured to be derived from the fraudulent act."]

# CHAPTER X.

*Of the forms used in prosecutions for offences against the current coin and public securities.*

Art. 758. Indictment for counterfeiting.

——" Did counterfeit [two gold coins of the United States, called eagles ; or one silver coin of the Kingdom of Spain or of the Republic of Mexico, called a dollar ; or one gold coin of Portugal, called a half-johannes ; or any other gold or silver coin, according to the case, describing them only by their popular names, without adding their value or any other description."]

Art. 759. Indictment for passing or offering to pass.

——That J. S. one, &c. [as in the form] having in his possession one counterfeited gold coin of the United States, called an eagle, or one [describing the counterfeited coin as above], and knowing the same to be counterfeited, did, on the day and year last aforesaid, at the parish of L., pass or offer to pass the same [as the case may be] to one I. K. or to some person to the said jurors unknown," &c.

Art. 760. Indictment for having in possession dies or other instruments.

——" That J. S. on the          day of          in the year         , at the parish of L., had in his possession a die [or some other instrument, describing it as a punch, screw, or other implement, by name,] such as is usually employed solely for the coinage of money, with the intent of committing the crime of counterfeiting, or of aiding therein."

Or, ——" did, on the          day of          in the year         , at the parish of L., repair a die [or other instrument, describing it, as a *punch, screw*, or other implement, by name,] such as is usually employed solely in the coinage of money, with the intention of committing the crime of counterfeiting, or of aiding therein."

Or, ——" had in his possession and did conceal certain base metal prepared for coinage, with the intention," &c. [as above.]

Art. 761. Indictment for having counterfeit coins in possession with intent to pass them.

——" That J. S. on the          day of          in the year         , at the parish of L., had in his possession [three counterfeited gold coins of the United States, called half eagles, and ten counterfeited silver coins of the Republic of Mexico, called dollars], with intent to pass them as true, or cause them to be passed as true, contrary to the laws," &c.

Art. 762. For diminishing the weight of coins.

——" That J. S. having in his possession [ten gold coins of the United States, called eagles,] with intent to profit, did, on the day of          in the year         , in the parish of L., diminish the weight of the said coins, and did afterwards, on the same day and year, at the place aforesaid, pass [or attempt to pass, according to the case], the same for the value the said coins had before the weight was so diminished." [Or, after the charge of diminishing the weight, as above stated, insert,] " did send or carry the same to [stating the place] to be passed for the value the said coins had before they were so diminished in value," &c.


## CHAPTER XI.


*Forms used in prosecutions for offences against the public receivers.*


Art. 763. Indictment against receivers of public money for the fraudulent appropriation thereof.

——" That J. S. being a person legally empowered to receive money or [security for money] for the state, or for the corporation of [giving the title of the corporation], by virtue of his office [state the description or name of the office] did, on the          day of          in the year         , and on sundry other days between that time and the day of commencing the prosecution for this offence, ille-

4 A

gally appropriate certain large sums of money [or certain securities for money, describe them], amounting in all to one thousand dollars, which he had before that time received for the state of Louisiana, [or for the public corporation, naming it] ; and did, on the          day of in the year          , last aforesaid, at the said parish, by rendering a false account, or [as the case may be] by producing false vouchers [describing them,] or by other means [describing those means,] did endeavour to conceal such illegal appropriation, with intent to defraud the state of Louisiana, [or the corporation of (naming it)], of the said moneys [or securities, as the case may be."]

Art. 764. Indictment for illegal appropriation with intent to restore the same.

As in the preceding form, omitting the charge of rendering a false account and all the subsequent part of the charge, and instead thereof state, " and the jurors further present that on the          day of in the year          , at the parish of L., demand was made by A. B. a person legally authorized for that purpose by the state [or the corporation] from the said J. S. of the sum [or of the securities] so illegally appropriated by him ; but that he did not, within three days after such demand, pay the same."

Art. 765. Indictment for not depositing public money.

——" That J. S. being a person legally empowered to receive money or securities for money for the state, [or for the corporation of (naming it)] by virtue of his office [state what it was], did, on the          day of in the year          , at the parish of          receive a sum [or sums, as the case may be], of money [or securities] to the amount of three hundred dollars and upwards, and did not, within three days after having so received the said sum of money or securities, deposit the same in an incorporated bank, according to the directions given by law, although a bank of that description, to wit, the bank of L. was within three leagues of the place of abode of the said J. S."

If the bank was more than three leagues and not more than twenty from the receiver's abode, then the charge must be, " that he did not make the deposit within fifteen days after receiving the same, and that the treasurer of the state did not enlarge the time allowed for making the said deposit."

Art. 766. Indictment for extortion by a receiver.

——" That J. S. being a person legally appointed, by virtue of his office [state the office] to receive taxes for the state [or for the corporation of L.] on the [state the date and place], did, under pretence of collecting the said tax, extort from one A. B. the sum of          , which was not due for such tax; or [did attempt to extort from A. B. a sum of more than was really due for such taxes]; or did demand a sum of          or an emolument of [describing the nature of the emolument,] or [a service or a favour, describing the nature thereof particularly,] from A. B. as a consideration for granting a delay in the collection of a sum of          then due from the said A. B. for taxes to the said state [or corporation]; or as a consideration [stating any other consideration in relation to the collection of such money, for which the said sum was paid, or such emolument, service, or favour was granted, unless it were paid or given for the emolument allowed by law for such collection,"] &c.

Art. 767. Indictment for preventing the collection of public moneys by force.

——"That on the          day of          in the year          , at the parish of          one A. B. was duly authorized as [sheriff of the said parish, or other office, designating it], to enforce the payment of taxes [or other debt, stating of what kind], due to the state [or to a public corporation, naming it], and J. S. on the day and year and at the place aforesaid, did, by force, attempt to prevent, or [did, by force or threats of force, prevent] the said A. B. from seizing the goods of one C. D., [or state any other act which he was prevented from doing], with intent to enforce the payment of a sum of          due from him to the said C. D. to the state, [or to the corporation, naming it], for taxes, [or for any other debt, stating it], which seizure [or other act in which he was obstructed, stating it,] was a duty required of the said A. B. by law relative to the collection of taxes [or debt."]

## CHAPTER XII.

*Forms of indictment for offences which affect foreign commerce.*

Art. 768. Charge for exporting flour without inspection.

——"Did export from this state [or ship for the purpose of exportation] on board the ship called the [Andrew Jackson] [one hundred barrels of flour] without having caused the same to be inspected, according to the directions of the laws of the state in such case provided."

Art. 769. For counterfeiting the mark of an inspector.

——"Did COUNTERFEIT the [mark], or [brand], or [stamp], directed by the laws of this state to be made or placed on all flour exported from the port of New Orleans, and made or placed such counterfeit [mark, or brand,' or stamp,] on [one hundred barrels of flour,"] &c.

Art. 770. For placing articles of inferior value in a package, with intent to defraud.

——"Did, with intent to defraud, put into a [hogshead] apparently filled with [tobacco], or [a bale apparently filled with cotton], or [a box apparently filled with spermaceti candles], or [a package apparently filled with cochineal], or [any other cask, bale, box, or package, describing it, with apparent articles], being merchandize usually sold by weight, a quantity of [rubbish], [or any other article, describing it], being of less value than the said tobacco, [or other article], with which the said hogshead, or [bale], or [package], or [box], was apparently filled," &c.

Art. 771. For selling merchandize with articles of inferior value concealed therein.

——"Did [sell], or [barter], or [give in payment], to A. B., or [expose for sale], or [ship for exportation in a certain ship called A. J.] a [bale apparently filled with cotton, or other articles as above], being merchandize usually sold by weight, with a quantity of [rubbish] concealed therein, with intent to defraud, contrary," &c.

Art. 772. For destroying or injuring a vessel, with intent to defraud.

——"That J. S. within the limits of this state, that is to say, in the river Mississippi, below the Balize, in the parish of Plaquemines, he being then and there the owner, [part owner], [freighter], of a certain [schooner] called the [Bee], or being then and there employed as [master], [supercargo], [seaman], or as [state any other capacity], on board a certain schooner called the [Bee], with intent to defraud or injure A. B. who was [or some person or persons, to the jurors unknown, who was or were] the [owner or owners of the said vessel] or [of the cargo on board, or of any part thereof], or [the underwriters on the said vessel, or the cargo on board, or some part thereof,] or those interested in the said schooner, or the said cargo, [or in the [voyage], [freight], or [profits] of the said [schooner]] ; did [destroy the said schooner], or did injure the said [schooner,] by [running her on shore], or [cutting away the masts], or [doing other injury, describing it."]

If the offence be committed on the high seas, it must be so stated, and it must be averred that the offender, at the time, was a citizen of this state, or domiciliated within it.

Art. 773. For fraudulent insurance.

——"That J. S. on the      day of      in the year      , at the parish of New Orleans, caused insurance to be made for one thousand dollars, by the insurance company called the New Orleans Insurance Company, on one hundred hogsheads of rum, which he represented to the said insurance company as shipped [or about to be shipped] at Jamaica in the West Indies, for New York, and pretended that the said hogsheads contained Jamaica rum of the first proof, with intent to defraud the said New Orleans Insurance Company, had actually shipped one hundred hogsheads containing water, [or rum of less than one half the value of Jamaica rum of the first proof], instead of one hundred hogsheads of Jamaica rum of the first proof, contrary," &c.

If the insurance were made at some place not within this state, the goods must be stated as having been represented as shipped, or about to be shipped, within the state of Louisiana, and goods of inferior value to have been actually shipped there.

Art. 774. Against an inn-keeper for concealing a seaman.

——"That J. S. being the keeper of a tavern, or [lodging-house, or boarding-house], did, on the      day of      in the year      , at the city of New Orleans, entertain, [lodge], or [conceal], A. B. a seaman who had, within one month previous to the day last aforesaid, DESERTED from a merchant vessel called the .D. in the port of New Orleans, he the said J. S. knowing that the said A. B. had so deserted."

Art. 775. Against a master of a vessel shipping a seaman who has deserted.

——"That J. S. being the master of a ship called the D., lying in the port of New Orleans, on the [insert the date and parish], did SHIP as a mariner on board the said ship, one C. D. who did not produce his discharge from the master of the vessel in which he last sailed, he the said C. D. having deserted from a ship called the Bee, in the said port of New Orleans, within one month before he was so shipped by the said J. S."

Art. 776. For using false weights and measures.

——"That A. B. in the weighing of a quantity of sugar sold to C. D. on the      day of      in the year      , in the parish of L., did use a false weight, knowing the said weight to be false, with a design to defraud."

The same form as to a false balance.

Art. 777. For a false measure.

——"That J. S. on the      day of      in the year      , at the parish of      in the measuring a quantity [of whiskey], or [of cloth], sold on that day to C. D., did use a false measure, knowing the same to be false, with intent to defraud."

Art. 778. Warrant of arrest and for the seizure of false weights, or measures.

"By A. B. [one of the judges, &c.] To the [sheriff of the city and parish of New Orleans.]

"You are commanded to arrest J. S. charged on oath before me, with having fraudulently used a false weight in the weighing of a certain quantity [of sugar] sold to C. D., knowing such weight to be false ; and you are also commanded to seize the weights used by the said J. S. in weighing the articles sold by him in his trade of [a grocer, or other trade, as the case may be] ; and to bring as well the said weights as the said J. S. before me, on [insert the return of the warrant], to be dealt with according to law."

Art. 779. When the weights, or balances, or measures, are brought before the magistrate, in pursuance of the above warrant, he shall cause the measures and weights to be compared and tested in his presence, by the officer appointed to keep the standard of weights and measures ; and if it be a balance that is the subject of prosecution, he shall examine it, and shall retain all those that appear to be false, to be used on the trial, and afterward destroyed according to law.

Art. 780. The above forms are to serve for purchases by false weights, measures, or balances, changing the words "*sold to*" for the words "*purchased from.*"

Art. 781. For altering marks.

——"That J. S. having [one hundred barrels of flour, which had been inspected by the officer appointed for that purpose by virtue of the laws of this state, and which barrels had been marked by the said officer with a mark, denoting that the flour contained in the said barrels was of inferior quality, did, on the                    day of in the year          , at the parish of New Orleans, falsely alter the said marks, so as to make it appear that the said officer had put on the said barrels a mark denoting that the flour contained in the said barrels was of the best quality,"] &c.

Art. 782. Form of indictment for counterfeiting a mark or brand.

——"Did, with intent to defraud, counterfeit the brand or mark used by the public officer appointed to inspect tobacco, [and by him to denote that tobacco was of a good quality] by marking the said counterfeit brand or mark on one hundred hogsheads of tobacco."

Art. 783. Fraudulently using a marked cask, or box, &c.

——"That J. S. having in his possession [ten pipes marked, by one of the officers of the customs of the United States in the port of New Orleans, as containing French brandy], did, on the                    day of             in the year          , at the parish of L. fraudulently use the same for the sale of liquor of an inferior quality than that denoted by the said mark,"] &c.

Art. 784. Forging a written instrument.

——"Did make a false instrument in writing, of which the following is a copy, [insert copy of the instrument], with intent to injure or defraud," &c.

Art. 785. For forging by altering.

——"That A. B. on [insert the date and place] having in his power a certain instrument in writing in the following words and [figures], to wit, [insert copy of the instrument as it was before it was altered], made such alterations in the said instrument as to make it appear to be of the following tenor [insert copy of the instrument as altered] with intent to [injure] or [defraud,"] &c.

Art. 786. When from obliteration in the original instrument it may be difficult to prove its exact tenor, it will be sufficient, instead of inserting the copy of the original instrument, to state, "that having in his possession a certain instrument in writing, by which, among other things, [he promised to pay to the said J. S. at the time mentioned in the said instrument the sum of one thousand dollars], [or insert any other part of the instrument that was altered], but of which the other contents are not sufficiently known to the jurors to enable them to set the same literally forth, the said J. S. on the             day of             in the year          , in the parish of L., altered the said instrument so as to change the same into an instrument of which the following is a copy, [insert the copy of the instrument altered], with intent to · [injure] or [defraud,"] &c.

Art. 787. For forgery by writing over or on the back of a true signature.

——" That J. S. having in his possession a paper on which was written a true signature of A. B., without any legal authority and with intent to defraud, wrote over the said signature, [or on the other side of the paper that contained such signature], the words following, to wit, [insert the instrument], with intent to injure or defraud."

Art. 788. For forgery by adding a signature.

——" That J. S. on the             day of             in the year    , at the parish of L., having in his power an instrument in the following words, [insert the copy of the instrument], written by A. B. [or by some person to the jurors unknown, as the case may be], altered the same by adding thereto the false signature of the name of A. B. with intent to injure or defraud."

Art. 789. For forgery by altering an instrument made by the offender himself.

——" That J. S. having before that time made a certain instrument in writing, of which the following is a copy, [insert the copy], delivered the same to A. B., and that on the             day of   in the year          , at the parish of L., the said instrument then being the property of [insert the name of the holder] he the said J. S. with intent to defraud [or injure], altered the said instrument so as to make it appear to be one of the tenor following, [insert copy of the instrument as altered,"] &c.

Art. 790. When the forgery consists in making an instrument in the name of a fictitious person, the indictment must be in the form above prescribed, for "forging a written instrument" without any special avowal that the name of the person was fictitious, and it may be proved on the trial without such special averment.

Art. 791. Form of the charge for making an instrument with a false date.

——" That J. S. on [insert the date and place] made a certain instrument in writing, of which the following is a copy, [insert it], which instrument was falsely dated, with intent to [injure] or [defraud] a certain A. B. [insert the name of the person whose interest would have been affected by the false dating of the instrument if the same had been true,"] &c.

Art. 792. Form of charge for uttering an instrument under pretence that it was the act of another.

——" That J. S. on the          day of          in the year
, at the parish of L., made a certain instrument in writing, of which the following is a copy, [insert it], and with intent to defraud [uttered or passed it, as the case may be], to A. B. as the act of another person bearing the name of J. S."

Art. 793. Form of a charge for making a note in the offender's name on the other side of a paper containing a blank signature.

——"That J. S. having in his power a paper containing the true signature of one A. B. on the          day of          in the year          , at the parish of L., wrote on the other side of the paper, containing such signature, a [promissory note or bill of exchange, as the case may be], purporting to be the bill [or note] of him the said J. S. and signed with his name [or firm, as the case may be], so as to make the said signature appear as the indorsement of the said [bill or note], without any lawful authority and with intent to defraud [or injure."]

Art. 794. Form of charge for uttering or passing illegal instruments in writing.

——"That J. S. on the [insert date and place] having in his possession, or under his control, an instrument in writing, of which the following is a copy, [insert it], and knowing the same to be [forged] [or to have been *fraudulently made*, if it be not a forgery, but is one of those instruments the making or uttering of which, by any disposition of the Penal Code, are declared to be an offence], [uttered] or [passed] the said instrument to one C. D. with intent to defraud."

Art. 795. For engraving a plate, or preparing implements or materials for the purpose of forging bank notes.

——" That J. S. on [state the date of time and place], did engrave [or as the case may be, had in his possession] a plate, or [did prepare paper], [a rolling press], or other implements or materials, [declaring what they were], for the purpose of [their or its] being employed in forging the notes of a bank [called the Bank of New York, doing business in the city of New York], or [called the Bank of Canada, doing business at Montreal], or [any other bank wherever situated], knowing such purpose, and with intent to defraud."

Art. 796. For having a forged or fraudulent instrument in possession, with intent to utter.

——"That J. S. on the          day of          in the year          , at the parish of L., had in his possession a certain instrument in writing, of which the following is a copy [insert it], and knowing the same to have been forged, [or to have been *fraudulently made*, if it be not a forgery, but is one of those instruments the making or uttering of which, by the Code of Crimes and Punishments, is declared to be an offence], with intent to utter or pass the same, and to defraud or injure."

Art. 797. For procuring a signature by a false reading or false interpretation of the instrument.

——"That one A. B. being a person who from infirmity or ignorance [as the case may be] could not read, [or who was ignorant of the language, naming that in which the instrument was written], J. S. on the          day of          in the year          , at the parish of L., with intent to defraud, induced the said A. B. to sign as his act a certain instrument in writing, of which the following is a copy [insert it], by falsely pretending to [read, or to interpret the said instrument, or by misrepresenting its contents, as the case may be], so as to cause the said A. B. to believe that the said instrument purported to be materially different in this, to wit, [state the misrepresentation, or the false reading, or the false interpretation], contrary," &c.

Art. 798. If in the case provided for by the last preceding form, the act was not signed but assented to in a manner that would, if there had been no error, have made the instrument the act of the party, it must be so stated, instead of charging that it was signed.

Art. 799. Charge for falsely substituting an instrument instead of the one intended to be signed.

——"That A. B. having the intention of signing or giving his legal assent to a certain instrument in writing, so as to make it his act, which was prepared by him or by his direction, and purported to be [insert copy of it if it can be procured, if not, state the general purport thereof, and particularly the parts in which it differed from the substituted instrument], one J. S. falsely and without the knowledge of the said A. B. substituted for the instrument so intended to be signed, or legally assented to, another instrument in the following words [insert copy,] and by means of such false substitution induced the said A. B. to sign [or assent to, as the case may be], the said last mentioned instrument, with intent to defraud," &c.

Art. 800. If either of the offences, charged by the two last forms, shall be committed by a public officer whose duty it is to record public acts, or by a counsellor or attorney-at-law, that circumstance must be charged.

Art. 801. Charge in an indictment for falsely personating another.

——"That J. S. of the city of New Orleans, broker, pretending to be [J. S. of the parish of St Francisville, planter], or [pretending to be A. B.] on the        day of        in the year        , at the parish of L. before [I. K. being parish judge of the said parish, acting as notary public], in the name of the said [J. S. of St Francisville, or of the said A. B.] gave his assent to an act of which the following is a copy [insert it], and declaring that he could not write, authorized the said notary to record his assent, he personating the said [J. S. of St Francisville, or the said A. B.] to the said act, with intent to defraud."

Art. 802. Indictment for making a false schedule in case of insolvency.

——"That J. S. having presented to the [district court of the first district] a petition praying for a meeting of his creditors, in order [that they might receive a cession of his effects], or [grant him a respite] made a false account of his [credits], [property] or [debts] in the schedule annexed to his petition, in this, that the said J. S. omitted to place on the said schedule [a tract of land or other property, describing it], or [a credit of a debt due to him from A. B. of one hundred dollars], or [a debt due from him to C. D. for one hundred dollars], or [did place on his said schedule a sum of one hundred dollars as due by him to I. K. when in fact no such sum was due], and did exhibit the said false account, in such court, as true, with intent to defraud," &c.

Art. 803. For fraudulently destroying or concealing books of account in cases of insolvency.

——"That J. S. having presented his petition to [state what court], in order to procure a meeting of his creditors, for the purpose of making to them a cession of his property, [or obtaining a respite], and obtaining the relief in such cases granted by law, did fraudulently destroy [or conceal] a certain book of accounts [or papers] relative to his estate, which, by law, he was bound to produce for the use and inspection of his said creditors, that is to say, one book of account called a ledger, containing accounts from the to [or otherwise, describing the book or papers destroyed or concealed."]

Art. 804. Making simulated conveyances.

——"That J. S. not having property of sufficient value to pay his debts, did on the day of in the year , in the parish of L., in order to prevent the property hereinafter mentioned from becoming liable to the payment of his debts, make an act of which the following is a copy [inserting it], which act the jurors present was simulated, and intended for his own use, or for that of his family."

Art. 805. If the property was personal property, and no written conveyance was made, say, "made a verbal sale and delivery of [describing the property], which sale the jurors present was simulated," &c.

Art. 806. Form of indictment for receiving a simulated conveyance.

Follow the preceding form, and at the end add, "and the jurors further present, that I. K. knowing the purposes for which the said [conveyance,] [mortgage,] or [disposition,] was made, and that it was simulated, received the same for the purposes aforesaid, contrary," &c.

Art. 807. For suffering fraudulent judgments.

——"That J. S. not having sufficient property to pay his just debts, on the day of in the year , with intent to defraud his creditors, or some one or more of them, did voluntarily suffer a judgment to be entered in the [parish court of the parish of L.] in favour of one I. K. the sum of by which the [real property of the said J. S. in the said parish was bound] and [personal property belonging to him was seized], which judgment the jurors present was for a sum not due, or for a larger sum than was really due, contrary," &c.

Art. 808. For recovering such judgment.

——"That one J. S. being on the day of , in the year , at the parish of L., not having sufficient property to pay his debts, I. K. in collusion with the said J. S. and with intent to defraud the creditors of him the said J. S. or some one or more of them, did recover a judgment in the parish of L. for the sum of which was voluntarily suffered to be entered by the said J. S. with intent to defraud his creditors, or some one or more of them; and the jurors further present, that the said I. K. recovered the said judgment for a sum not due, or for a sum larger than was due from the said J. S., and that [real property of the said J. S. has been incumbered], and [personal property belonging to him has been seized], under the said judgment."

Art. 809. For conveying without consideration to defraud creditors.

[Beginning as in the last form.] "Did without any consideration [or for an inadequate consideration,] [convey,] [mortgage,] or [affect by an onerous condition, stating it,] all that [describe the property sold, mortgaged, or affected,] to one I. K."

Art. 810. For receiving such conveyance.

[Add to the last preceding form, "which [conveyance,] [mortgage,]
4 B

or [onerous condition,] the said I. K. did on the day and year last aforesaid, at the place aforesaid, receive, he then well knowing the said fradulent intent."

# CHAPTER XIII.

*Forms of indictments for offences affecting public property held for common use.*

Art. 811. Form of indictment for maliciously breaking levees.
———" Did maliciously break down the levee, or embankment of the river Mississippi, opposite to the plantation of A. B. in the said parish."
Art. 812. For impeding navigation by embankments, &c.
———" Did make a certain wharf [or other construction, describing it, in the bed of the river Mississippi, opposite to the lands of A. B. in the said parish, by which the navigation of the said river was impeded, [or which was made contrary to an ordinance of the police, being legally made on the          day of          in the year          ,] contrary to the laws," &c.
Art. 813. For erecting obstructions in a street or public road.
———" Did erect a [fence,] [or dig a ditch,] [or make any other obstruction, describing it,] in the public road, [or street] [or square] in the said parish, [near to or opposite the house or land of A. B., or otherwise describing the place,] by which the public use of the said [street,] [or road,] [or square,] was obstructed ; [or did unlawfully destroy a bridge erected on the street or public road, at (describing the place,)] in the said parish."
Art. 814. For obstructing the banks of navigable rivers.
———" Did on the [bank,] [or on the embankment,] [or the space set apart by the police regulation on the banks of the river Mississippi for a tow path,] erect a house, [or any other obstruction, describing it,] by which the public use of the said [bank, embankment, or tow path, as the case may be,] was prevented [or rendered less convenient."]

# CHAPTER XIV.

*Forms of indictments for offences against public health and safety.*

Art. 815. Indictment for illegally carrying on a manufactory of gunpowder.
———" Did carry on a manufactory of gunpowder, [or did keep more than ten pounds of gunpowder at one time] within three hundred yards of a public road, [or of a dwelling house, to wit, the dwelling house of A. B. in the said parish,] [or of land of A. B. he the said A. B. not having permitted the said manufactory to be carried on,] contrary to the laws," &c.
Art. 816. For carrying on trade in a manner dangerous to health.

——"That J. S. [being a manufacturer of parchment in the parish of L., did on the          day of          in the year          , in the parish aforesaid, suffer the water, in which the skins used in the said manufactory are soaked, to remain and putrefy,] in a manner injurious to the health of those who reside in the vicinity of the said manufactory, contrary," &c.

Art. 817. For adulterating liquors in a manner injurious to health.

——"Did adulterate, for the purpose of selling the same, [one pipe of wine intended for drinking,] by mixing therewith a substance called [sugar of lead] which rendered the said wine injurious to the health of those who should drink thereof."

Or ——"Did sell to one A. B. [one pipe of wine which had been adulterated with (as in the foregoing form)] knowing the same to be adulterated."

Art. 818. For adulterating drugs.

——"Did fraudulently adulterate, for the purpose of selling the same, a certain quantity, to the jurors unknown, of a drug [called quinquina or Peruvian bark, or jesuit's bark,] by mixing therewith a quantity of bark of the oak tree in the said drug, [or to make the same injurious to health."]

Art. 819. For selling adulterated drugs.

——"Did sell to one A. B. one ounce of a drug or medicine called quinquina or jesuit's bark, or Peruvian bark, which had been fraudulently adulterated by mixing therewith a quantity of bark of the oak tree, in such manner as to lessen the efficacy [or change the operation] of the said drug, [or to make the same injurious to health."]

## CHAPTER XV.

*Charges in indictments for offences against morals and decency.*

Art. 820. Keeping a disorderly house.

——"That J. S. on several days between the          day of          and the          day of          in the parish of L., did keep a disorderly house for the purpose of public prostitution."

Or ——"Did [keep a public tavern, or a house for the sale of spirituous liquors, without having the license required by law."]

Or ——"That J. S. having a license for keeping a tavern in the parish of L., [or for the sale of spirituous liquors by retail,] did on the          day of          in the year          , and at divers other times afterwards, in the parish of          permit [here insert the act forbidden by the license or by law to be done in the town,] in the said tavern."

Or ——"That J. S. having a license to keep a gambling house in the parish of L., did on the          day of          in the year          , and at divers other times afterwards, permit [insert the act forbidden by the license or the law to be done in the gambling house."]

Art. 821. For publishing obscene prints or pictures.

——"Did [make, publish, or print, as the case may be,] a certain obscene [print] [or picture] which [was shown to the said J. S. on his examination, if the defendant was arrested or summoned previous to the finding of the indictment,] is now exhibited to the said jurors and will be produced on the trial of this indictment, but which cannot be decently described in words, and which was manifestly designed to corrupt the morals of youth."

Art. 822. On the examination of any one accused of this offence, the print or picture must be exhibited to the defendant on his examination, and marked by the magistrate and others, so as to be identified, and shall also be exhibited to him in court previous to his arraignment.

Art. 823. Form of charge on an indictment for an obscene written or printed composition.

——" Did [make,] or [publish,] or [print] an obscene composition [of which the following is a copy,] which composition the jurors present was manifestly designed to corrupt the morals of youth."

Art. 824. For making an obscene exhibition of the person in public.

——" Did in the public-highway to a number of persons then present designedly make an indecent exhibition of his person, or [of the person of A. B.] whereby the modesty of those present was offended, contrary," &c.

Art. 825. For uttering obscene expressions with intent to insult one of the female sex.

——" Did in the presence and hearing of one or more persons of the female sex, with design to insult them, utter divers obscene expressions as follows, [repeating them,] contrary," &c.

Art. 826. For seducing a woman under promise of marriage.

——" That A. B. being a woman of good chaste reputation, at the parish of L. one J. S. addressed her with proposals of marriage, which the said A. B. received favourably, and the said J. S. thereupon made a promise that he would marry the said A. B. ; and under the faith of that promise, on the        day of        in the year        , at the parish of L., seduced her, and afterwards failed to comply with his said promise."

Art. 827. For soliciting prostitution.

——" Did for hire received from one A. B. procure the means of illicit connexion between him and a certain woman named C. D. [or a certain woman to the jurors unknown."]

Or, when all the parties are unknown, state, " did for hire procure the means of illicit connexion between two persons of different sexes, to the jurors unknown."

Or, " did for hire [solicit] [or procure] a woman [named A. B.] or [a woman to the jurors unknown,] to prostitute her person to a man named C. D. [or to a man to the jurors unknown."]

Art. 828. For adultery against the wife and the person with whom the crime is committed.

——" That Anne B. being the lawful wife of C. D. on the        day of        in the year        , at the parish of        committed adultery with J. S., and so the jurors present the said Anne B. and C. D. did together commit the offence of adultery."

Art. 829. For adultery by the husband.

——" That A. B. being the lawful husband of C. D. did on the        day of        in the year        , at the parish of L. commit adultery with one E. F. and did during the time he so committed the said offence, keep the said E. F. as his concubine in the house with his said wife ; [or did, by ill-treating his said wife, force her to leave the house in which he resided, and did, after her departure, keep the said E. F. as his concubine in it."]

Art. 830. For violating a place of interment for the purpose of stealing.

——"Did open the [grave,] or [vault,] or [tomb,] in which the dead body of one A. B. had been interred, with the intent of stealing the coffin or vestments with which the said A. B. had been interred, [or some article, describing it, which was interred with the said body."]

Art. 831. For removing a dead body for the purpose of exposure or dissection.

——"Did, without legal authority, remove from the [grave,] or [vault,] or [tomb,] in which it had been interred, the dead body of one A. B. for the purpose of selling, or exposing, or dissecting the same."

Art. 832. For purchasing, selling, or dissecting a dead body before interment.

——"Did purchase the dead body of one A. B. from C. D., or from certain persons to the jurors unknown ; [or did sell the dead body of one A. B. to C. D. or to a certain person to the jurors unknown,] before the said body was interred."

Att. 833. For dissecting a dead body before interment.

——"Did, without being authorized in any manner provided by law, dissect the dead body of one C. D. which had not been interred."

## CHAPTER XVI.

*Of the forms of indictments for offences which affect persons in the exercise of their religion.*

Art. 834. For restraining the free exercise of religion by force or threats.

——"Did by FORCE [or THREATS, stating of which kind,] prevent A. B. from attending divine service in the Protestant Episcopal Church, which attendance was a lawful act required by the Protestant Episcopal religion, which the said A. B. professed."

Art. 835. For maliciously preventing the free exercise of religion. · .

——" That A. B. being a person professing the [Roman Catholic religion, and being confined by sickness to his bed, was desirous of having the sacraments of that religion administered to him by C. D. a priest of that church, and had a note written to him requesting his attendance for that purpose, but that one J. S. maliciously destroyed the said note before it was delivered to the said C. D. with intent to prevent the said A. B. from doing the lawful act of receiving the said sacraments, which was required by the religion professed by the said A. B."]

Art. 836. For forcibly obliging another to perform religious rites.

——"Did by force [or threats of injury to person or property, stating what the threats were,] oblige or endeavour to oblige one A. B. [to receive the communion according to the rites and ceremonies of the church."]

Art. 837. If the offender be a judicial or executive officer, and the act be done under colour of his office ; or if he be a priest, or minister, or preacher of any religious sect or congregation, the fact must be stated in either of the preceding forms in this chapter.

# CHAPTER XVII.

*Of the forms of indictments for offences affecting reputation.*

Art. 838. Charge for slander, charging a crime.

———" Did in the presence of sundry persons make the following false and defamatory allegation of one A. B.—' he is the man who murdered C. D.'—intending thereby to convey the idea that the said A. B. had committed the crime of murder."

Art. 839. For slander, by signs, imputing the vice of habitual drunkenness.

———"That J. S. being in company with A. B., I. K., and others, on the          day of          in the year          , at the parish of L., [a discourse arose of and concerning persons addicted to the vice of habitual drunkenness, whereupon the said J. S. in order to make it falsely be believed that the said I. K. was guilty of the said vice, raised his right hand to his mouth as if in the act of bringing a glass to his lips, and at the same time, unperceived by the said I. K., with the other hand pointed him out to the observation of the persons there present ; and the jurors further present, that the said A. B., one of the said company, asked the said J. S. whether the said I. K. was a drunkard, to which question the said J. S. nodded his head in the manner usually done to give an assent,] and that by the said signs the said J. S. did falsely impute to the said I. K. the vice of [habitual drunkenness] in order to cause his society to be avoided by people in general."

Art. 840. For a libel, by painting, imputing a crime.

———" Did make and publish a certain engraved and printed picture, by and in which a figure, intended to represent one I. K., was represented as [picking the pocket of another of a purse, thereby intending to convey the idea and make it be believed that the said I. K. had committed the crime of stealing from the person], which picture or engraving is annexed to this indictment."

Art. 841. To every indictment for libel by a PICTURE, the same shall be annexed to the indictment, and shown to the party accused before his arraignment, in the manner and for the purpose set forth in the chapter of this Code respecting indictments, unless such picture was painted on a building, or on some article too bulky to be brought into court, or has been destroyed by some other means than the act of the prosecutor, or by his procurement.

Art. 842. For a libel charging moral guilt.

———" Did make and publish [or circulate, as the case may be], a certain writing of and concerning one I. K. in the words following, [' of the character of this Mr K. you may judge from this circumstance, that he was treasurer of a charitable society in New Orleans last year, and that a Flemish account was given of the funds ;' meaning thereby that the said I. K. had appropriated to his own use the funds of some charitable society that were entrusted to him as treasurer thereof."]

Art. 843. For a libel imputing a mental defect that would cause the society of the party to be avoided.

———" Did make, publish, and circulate a certain writing concerning one I. K., printed in the public paper [called the Daily Gazette,] in the words following, to wit : [' To Mr I. K.—I should be surprised at your conduct if I did not know the unhappy state of your mind ; that no intimacy can render any man safe in your society ; that you abuse and defame, according to your caprice, every man who has the misfortune to associate with you, without provocation and without mercy.' "]

Art. 844. Where the charge is direct, as in the last form, there is no need of any explanatory allegation ; where the words, importing the charge, are not perfectly clear, or their application is not apparent, the meaning must be alleged. The Code of Evidence gives rules as to the cases and manner in which those allegations are to be proved.

Art. 845. Injury to reputation by exhibiting an effigy.

———" Did, with the intent to bring I. K. into contempt, and to excite ridicule and indignation against him, exhibit [or make with intent that it should be exhibited] an effigy or figure intended to represent the said I. K."

Art. 846. If more than twelve persons are collected to witness the exhibition and refuse to disperse, they may be indicted as an unlawful assembly, by adding to the above form, "And that the said J. S. [the person above indicted] and A. B., C. D., and others to the jurors unknown, were unlawfully assembled to aid each other in making the said unlawful exhibition. And in case they refuse to disperse, the indictment may be for a riot, by adding to the charge of an unlawful assembly the following : " And the jurors further present, that the persons so unlawfully assembled, then and there committed a riot, by remaining together for the purposes aforesaid half an hour and more after they had been warned by a magistrate to disperse in the form required by law."

Art. 847. For injury to reputation by dramatic performances.

———" Did, with intent to bring one I. K. into contempt, and to excite ridicule and indignation against him, perform [or cause to be performed] a certain dramatic work, called ' the Tartuffe,' in which the said I. K. was represented or personated by an imitation of his person, dress, manners and gestures, in such a manner as made it apparent to those who were present, and who knew the said I. K., that he was the person intended by such personification."

Art. 848. For combining to make a false accusation of a crime.

———" That J. S. and C. D. on the          day of          in the year          , at the parish of L., did combine falsely to accuse one I. K. of the crime of stealing ; and in pursuance of such combination, they the said J. S. and C. D. [or one of them, stating which,] did declare [state whether verbally or in writing] that [the said I. K. had stolen ten sheep from him the said J. S."]

If the combination should be to extort any pecuniary advantage, then insert, " Did, for the purpose of extorting some pecuniary advantage from one I. K., combine falsely to accuse [or to threaten to accuse] the said I. K. of the crime of stealing, and in pursuance of such combination, did, for the purpose aforesaid," &c. as above.

Art. 849. For false accusation with intent to extort.

———" Did, with intent to extort money or procure some other profit, [threaten one A. B. that he the said J. S. would accuse him the said A. B. of the crime of rape ;] or [did falsely accuse one A. B. of having committed the crime of rape ;] or [did falsely accuse or threaten to accuse, as charged in the preceding form,] one A. B. of [having sold the favours of his wife, or other act that would bring him into contempt."]

Art. 850. For fabricating defamatory papers.

——"Did, without any lawful authority and with intent to injure the reputation of one I. K., publish or circulate, or make with intent that it should be circulated, a false writing, purporting to be a letter written by the said J. S. in the words following, to wit, [insert copy."]

## CHAPTER XVIII.

*Of the forms of indictments for offences affecting the person of individuals.*

### SECTION I.

#### Simple assaults and batteries.

Art 851. Form of indictment for a simple assault.

——"That J. S. on the        day of        in the year        , at the parish of L., upon one A. B. did make an assault by striking at the said A. B. with a cane, [or in any other manner that by law will constitute an assault, describing it."]

Art. 852. For a simple assault and battery.

——"Did, with intent to injure, make an illegal assault on one A. B. and struck him with his fist in the face, [or with a cane on the head,] [or by throwing water in his face,] [or by pushing another person against him,] [or by firing a pistol and wounding him with the ball, or in any of the various ways in which this offence may be committed, describing the act without fiction or exaggeration."]

### SECTION II.

#### Assault and battery in relation to the person.

Art. 853. For an assault and battery against a public officer in the execution of his office.

——"Did, with intent to injure, make an illegal assault on one A. B. [one of the constables of the city of New Orleans, at the time of the said assault being in the legal execution of his office, to wit, destraining certain goods of the said J. S. by virtue of a warrant legally issued by G. P. one of the judges of the city court,] he the said J. S. well knowing the office of the said A. B. and that he was in the legal exercise of them."

Art. 854. For assault and battery committed by an officer under pretence of executing his office.

——" That J. S. on the          day of          in the year          , in the parish of L., he being then and there [sheriff of the said parish,] under pretence of executing his office by [serving a summons on one A. B. to appear as a witness in the parish court of the parish, did make an illegal assault on the said A. B., and with intent to injure, did seize him by the collar and drag him in the street towards the said court."]

If, in a case where the officer had authority to use force but exceeded the necessary degree, say, "then being sheriff of the said parish, by virtue of his office arrested one A. B. on a warrant, [describing it,] and although no resistance was offered to the said arrest, yet the said J. S., under pretence of executing the said warrant, illegally assaulted and beat the said A. B. by," [describing the assault.]

Art. 855. For assault against an ascendant—against a woman—a tutor.

——" Did, with intent to injure, make an illegal assault on A. B. the [father,] [mother,] [grandfather,] [grandmother,] [tutor,] of him the said J. S." &c.

In the indictment for assault and battery by a man against a woman, no particular averment is necessary, the names, and the relative personal pronouns used in the indictment are a sufficient indication of the sex.

## SECTION III.

### Assault and battery in relation to the place.

Art. 856. Assault and battery in a court of justice.

——" Did in the parish court of the parish of L. make an assault."

Art. 857. Assault and battery committed in the house of another.

——" Did go to the house of one I. K. with the intent of committing an assault and battery on one A. B. then residing in the said house as [a guest,] and did then and there, in pursuance of such intent, illegally and with design to injure, make an assault on the said A. B." &c.

Art. 858. Assault and battery in a church during the celebration of public worship.

——" Did, during the celebration of public worship in the [Catholic church,] with intent to injure, make an illegal assault in the said church upon one A. B. &c. whereby the congregation of [Catholics] was disturbed in the performance of their worship, or religious rites and ceremonies."

## SECTION IV.

### Assault and battery in relation to the intent.

Art. 859. Assault and battery with intent to murder or ravish.

——" Did, with intent to commit the crime of [murder] or [of rape,] make an assault," &c.

4 C

Art. 860. With intent to dismember or inflict a permanent injury.

——"Did, with intent to dismember one I. K. by cutting off his ears, make an assault on him the said I. K., and with a penknife made several cuts in his head and cheeks."

Art. 861. If the intent be to disfigure, say :

——"Did make an illegal assault upon one A. B. with intent to disfigure him by slitting open his nostrils, and in attempting the said injury did wound the said A. B. in several parts of his face."

Art. 862. If the intent be to do a permanent injury, not amounting to dismembering or disfiguration, say:

——"Did make an illegal assault upon one A. B. and with design to inflict a permanent injury by [laming the said A. B. in the right leg, did attempt to cut the tendons of the said leg with a knife."]

Art. 863. If the design of the assault and battery, or the assault alone, be to commit any other crime than murder or rape, such intent must be specified in the same form as is given above for an assault with intent to commit those crimes.

Art. 864. For assault and battery with intent to force another to commit an offence.

——"Did make an illegal assault on one A. B. with intent to force him to commit the crime of theft by stealing the horses of a certain C. D., and did beat and wound the said A. B. and threaten to kill him unless he would consent to commit the said crime."

Art. 865. For an assault and battery on a woman, attended with immodest words or actions.

——"Did make an illegal assault upon one Anne B., and did accompany the said assault by words and gestures calculated to wound the modesty of the female sex, and by violently laying his hands on the said Anne."

Art. 866. If, in the case stated in the last form, the offender was tutor or curator and the person injured was his ward, or if the offender was schoolmaster and the person injured was his scholar, those circumstances must be stated, thus :

——"That J. S. on the          day of          in the year          , at the parish of L., was the tutor [or curator] of Anne B., a minor ; [or was the schoolmaster of Anne B., employed to teach her reading and writing,] [or music,] [or any other art or any science,] and that on the day and year and at the place aforesaid, the said J. S. made an assault upon the said Anne," &c. as in the last form.

Art. 867. For an assault or battery with intent to dishonour or provoke a duel.

——"Did make an illegal assault and battery upon one A. B. by pulling his nose with intent to dishonour the said A. B. [or to force the said A. B. to accept or to give a challenge to fight a duel."]

SECTION V.

Forms in assaults aggravated by the degree or the manner.

Art. 868. For assault by design and with a deadly weapon.

——" Did, in consequence of a premeditated design to [wound and otherwise ill-treat one A. B.] [or to disfigure, or to dismember, or to inflict a permanent injury, stating particularly the design,] make an assault upon him the said A. B. with a deadly weapon, to wit, [with a sword,] and did wound the said A. B. in the arm."

Art. 869. For assault and battery by premeditated design, but not with a deadly weapon.

——"Did, in consequence of premeditated design to beat and ill-treat one A. B. [or to disfigure, or dishonour, stating the intent particularly,] make an illegal assault upon the said A. B. [and with a cane struck and bruised him in his face and head."]

Art. 870. If the offences, described in the preceding forms of this section, be committed by lying-in-wait, that circumstance must be charged, thus :

——"Did, in consequence of a premeditated design [to beat and ill-treat, or to disfigure or dismember, or to dishonour, &c.] lie-in-wait for the said A. B. and make an illegal assault," &c.

Art. 871. Assault and battery, attended by disfiguration, dismembering, or other permanent injury, when no design to inflict that degree of injury is proved.

——"Did make an illegal assault upon one A. B. and with design to injure him did [strike,] or [thrust,] or [cut the said A. B. with a sword, state the nature of the injury and the weapon,] so that the said A. B. in consequence of such battery was dismembered by the loss of [or losing the use of] an [eye, a leg, or other members, stating which;] or was [disfigured by a large wound, leaving a scar under the right eye, which drew it from its natural position, or otherwise, stating how ;] or [did receive such injury in his right leg as makes it certain that he will, for the rest of his life, be lame,] or such bruises in his chest as renders it probable that he will labour for the rest of his life under the infirmity of weakness in the lungs, or other permanent bodily hurt, describing it."]

SECTION VI.

Forms of indictment for false imprisonment.

Art. 872. Form of indictment for false imprisonment by assault.

——" Did illegally and intentionally detain one A. B. in [the high-way, or other place, describing it], by making an assault on him with a drawn sword opposed to his breast, by which the said A. B. was illegally prevented from moving from the place where he then was, by the just fear of death or great bodily injury, for the space of one hour."

Art. 873. By actual violence.

——" Did illegally and intentionally detain one A. B. in [describe the place] by [violently seizing him by the collar with his hands, or by binding him with a rope,] [describing the manner of the detention], and kept the said A. B., so detained as aforesaid, for the space of [two hours."]

Art. 874. By some material impediment to the power of locomotion.

——" Did illegally and intentionally detain and imprison one A. B. in [a [chamber] or cellar, or other place in the said parish], by locking or barring the doors and windows of the said [chamber] when he the said A. B. was therein, in such a manner as to prevent him from leaving the said place, and kept him so imprisoned for the space of [ten days."]

Art. 875. By threats.

———"Did illegally and intentionally detain one A. B. in [describe the place] by threatening, that if he should leave the said place [naming it] he would [describe the threat], and by means of such threats did detain the said A. B. in the said　　　　　for the space of [six hours,"] &c.

Art. 876. False imprisonment may be charged to have been inflicted when such is the case, by a combination of all the means stated in the preceding forms ; and may also be joined in the indictment with all the different kinds and degrees of assault and battery, stating therein the forms above given.

SECTION VII.

False imprisonment aggravated by the purpose or the degree.

Art. 877. Indictment for false imprisonment and conveyance out of the state.

———"Did illegally and intentionally detain one A. B. [by making an assault on him with a drawn sword, or other weapon, or by seizing him with his hands, or any of the other modes above described] and did forcibly convey the said A. B., so imprisoned, out of this state to [the city of Natchez], or [to some place to the jurors unknown."]

Art. 878. If the charge be an intent to convey out of the state, after stating the imprisonments as above, add :

———" Did keep the said A. B. in form aforesaid during the space of [two days] with intent to convey him by force out of this state, [to the Havanna], or to some place without this state to the jurors unknown."

Art. 879. Form of charge in an indictment for detaining a free person as a slave.

———" Did, &c. [charge the imprisonment according to the fact in either of the above forms, and add], and did detain the said A. B. in form aforesaid during the space of [two days] for the purpose of keeping or disposing of him as a slave, he the said J. S. knowing the said A. B. to be free."

Art. 880. For false imprisonment used as the means of forcing another to commit an offence.

———" Did illegally and intentionally detain one A. B. [for the space of　　　　] by [insert the means] with the intent to force the said A. B. to [aid the said J. S. in forging bills of the bank of B. or any other offence, describing it."]

Art. 881. For false imprisonment with intent to commit an offence. —[After the charge of the false imprisonment, as in the above form, say, " with the intent to [rob the said A . B., or to murder, or any other crime describing it."]

Art. 882. If the intent of the imprisonment is to force a woman to do an immodest act, after the charge of the imprisonment, as above, add, " with intent to force the said A. B. to do some act, or submit to some treatment, injurious to the modesty of her sex."

Art. 883. In the case provided for by the last form, if the person accused be the tutor, .curator, or schoolmaster of the party offended, it must be specially so stated in the form, prescribed in the fourth section of this chapter.

Art. 884. Form of indictment when the imprisonment was legal, but used with the intent set forth in the two last forms.

———" That Anne B. on the       day of       in the year      , in the parish of      having been guilty of a [misdemeanor, or crime, stating it], or [having threatened injury to any one, or done any other act (stating it) which would justify a complaint and accusation,] one J. S. procured a warrant to be issued against the said Anne B. by G. P. one of the justices, &c. for the said offence, and caused her to be arrested and imprisoned thereon, with intent and for the purpose of," &c. as in the last form.

## SECTION VIII.

### Forms of indictment in cases of abduction.

Art. 885. Indictment for false imprisonment and abduction.

———" Did, [state the false imprisonment according to the forms in the preceding section, and add,] with the intent to force the said A. B., by means of such detention, to consent to a marriage with the said J. S. or with a certain 1. K."]

Art. 886. Abduction of a female under fourteen years.

——— " Did take and carry away from the care, superintendence, and custody of her [father,] [mother,] [tutor,] [or other person having legal charge of the minor, stating his quality with respect to her,] one Anne B. a female minor, under the age of fourteen years, without the consent of the said [father, &c. or other person having legal charge of the said minor], and [without the consent of the said Anne B., if such be the case], with the intent of marrying the said Anne B., [or keeping her as a concubine], [or inducing her to prostitute her person to others."]

## SECTION IX.

### Forms of indictment in cases of rape.

Art. 887. Rape by force.

———" Did make an assault upon one Anne B., and her, against her consent, did by force and violence carnally know."

Art. 888. Rape by menace.

———" Did ravish one Anne B., and against her will did carnally know her by threatening her with instant death, [or with putting out her eyes, or other great bodily harm, stating it."]

Art. 889. Rape by fraud.

———" Did approach one Anne B. she then being asleep, [or the room in which she lay, she being in bed, being dark, or state such other circumstances as favoured the fraud,] and causing the said Anne B. to believe that he the said J. S. was her husband, the said Anne B. thus fraudulently did ravish and carnally know."

Or, ——"Did designedly administer to one Anne B. a certain drug or substance, to the jurors unknown, [or called        ], by which an unnatural sexual desire was produced in the said Anne B. [or by which she was thrown into such stupor or weakness as weakened or prevented resistance], and while she was under the influence of the said drug or substance, her the said Anne did ravish and carnally know."

SECTION X.

Forms of indictment for procuring a miscarriage or abortion.

Art. 890. For procuring without the consent of the woman, by violence.

 ——"That on the         day of         in the year        , at the parish of        , one Anne B. being pregnant, J. S. of the same place, with intent to procure the said Anne to miscarry of the child with which she was then pregnant, without her consent or knowledge, did cause her to swallow a certain drug or substance called         , or [did apply to her body a certain substance called         ,] or [did by violence and against her consent forcibly compress the body of the said Anne], and by those means caused the said Anne to miscarry of the child of which she was then pregnant."

Art. 891. If done with the consent of the woman, the above form may be used, substituting only the words " with her consent," for the words " without her consent or knowledge."

Art. 892. For furnishing the means, knowing the purpose.

The same form as above. Instead of charging that he "did cause her to swallow," &c. say, "did furnish to her [to be taken with her consent], [or to J. S. to be administered to the said Anne B. without her consent or knowledge,] a certain drug or substance called which was taken [or applied] by [or to] the said Anne B., and caused her to miscarry of the child of which she was then pregnant, he the said J. S. knowing the purpose to which the said drug or substance was intended to be applied."

Art. 893. For furnishing the means when they fail in their effect.

As in the last preceding form to the words "which was taken [or applied] by [or to] the said Anne B.," after which add, "for the purpose of causing her to miscarry of the child with which she was then pregnant, but which failed in producing such miscarriage, he the said J. S. well knowing, at the time of furnishing the said drug or substance, the purpose to which it was intended to be applied."

Art. 894. If the offender be a physician or surgeon, or midwife, or practise as such, that fact must be charged.

## SECTION XI.

Form of indictment for maliciously giving a potion injurious to health.

Art. 895. ——"Did maliciously cause one I. K. to swallow, or inhale, without his knowledge, a drug called      , or some drug or substance to the jurors unknown, which caused a violent change in the usual functions of his body, [or injured his health."]

## SECTION XII.

Forms of charges in indictments for homicide.

Art. 896. Indictment for negligent homicide in the first grade.

——"That J. S. on the      day of      in the year      , in the parish of L., being about to repair the barrel of a musket, believing the same not to be loaded, but without examining whether it was loaded or not, negligently put the breach of the said musket-barrel into a heated furnace; and the jurors present, that the said musket-barrel was, unknown to the said J. S., loaded with powder and ball, and that owing to the heat of the furnace the powder exploded and drove the ball through the heart of one I. K. who was accidentally passing, and inflicted a mortal wound, of which wound, made by the said ball, the said I. K. instantly died: therefore the said jurors present, that the said J. S. is guilty of negligent homicide in the first grade."

Art. 897. Negligent homicide in the second grade.

——"That J. S. on the      day of      in the year      , at the parish of L., [caused one of his slaves to mount on the back of an unbroke colt, for the purpose of breaking him, in the public street or high-way, where, at the time, a number of persons were passing on their lawful business, to the evident danger of the lives of such persons, without taking any precaution to avoid the danger to which the said persons were exposed; and the jurors present, that the rider of the said colt being unable to govern it, the said colt ran violently against one I. K. then passing in the said [high-way] or [street], and inflicted on him the said I. K. a mortal bruise on the breast, of which the said I. K. afterwards, that is to say, on the      day of      in the same year, in the parish aforesaid, died: therefore the said jurors present, that the said J. S. is guilty of negligent homicide in the second grade.

Art. 898. For negligent homicide, in the first grade, in the attempt to do an unlawful act.

——"That J. S. on the [insert date and place], intending unlawfully [and maliciously to kill an ox belonging to one I. K. in an unfrequented field, fired with a rifle loaded with ball at the said ox, without having previously examined whether any person was concealed by a bush which grew in the said field; and the jurors present, that the said I. K. was concealed from the view of the said J. S. by the said bush, and that the ball discharged from the said rifle, as aforesaid, after killing the said ox, entered the right side of the said I. K. and inflicted a mortal wound] of which the said I. K. afterwards, on the same day and year, at the place aforesaid, died : wherefore the said jurors present, that the said I. K. has committed the first grade of negligent homicide in the commission of an unlawful act."

Art. 899. Negligent homicide, in the second grade, in the commission of an unlawful act.

――"That J. S. on the [insert date and place] [intending and attempting to kill and steal a turkey belonging to I. K. then feeding near the door of the dwelling-house of the said I. K. negligently fired a fowling-piece, loaded with powder and small shot, at the said turkey, but in the direction of the window of the said house, and that some of the shot, so fired from the said fowling-piece, passed through the window and inflicted a mortal wound on the right temple of A. K. a female child of the said I. K., aged five years or thereabouts, of which wound the said A. K. afterwards, on the same day and year and at the place aforesaid, died] : therefore the jurors present, that the said J. S. hath committed the second grade of negligent homicide, in the [attempt] to do an unlawful act."

Art. 900. In all indictments for homicide, in doing or attempting to do an unlawful act, the circumstances of such unlawful act must be detailed with as much precision as if the indictment were for doing such act; and also, it must be stated whether the unlawful act were accomplished, or only attempted, because it is from a knowledge of these circumstances only that the court can determine the degree of the offence and the manner of punishment."

Art. 901. Indictment for manslaughter.

――"That J. S. on the      day of      in the year      , at the parish of L. under the immediate influence of sudden passion, arising from an adequate cause, did [strike one I. K. on the head with a bar of iron, and did thereby inflict a mortal wound, of which the said I. K. afterwards, on the same day and year, and at the parish aforesaid, died] : wherefore the said jurors present, that the said J. S. the said I. K. then and there unlawfully did kill and slay."

Art. 902. Charge in an indictment for murder.

――"That J. S. on the      day of      in the year      , in the parish of L. with a premeditated design to kill one I. K. made an assault upon the said I. K. and with a dirk inflicted a mortal wound on the left breast of him the said I. K., of which wound he the said I. K. afterwards, on the      day of      in the year aforesaid, at the place last aforesaid, died : wherefore the said jurors present, that the said J. S. the said I. K., in manner aforesaid, with a premeditated design, did kill and murder."

Art. 903. Indictment for infanticide.

――"That J. S. on the [insert date and place], in order to conceal the birth of a male child, born on the      day of      in the year of [insert the name of the mother], or [if the person accused is the mother, say, of the said J. S.] did, with a premeditated design to kill, expose the said child to the inclemency of the weather in an unfrequented field in the said parish, on the night of the said      day of      and left the said child so exposed during the whole of the said night, of which exposure the said child, on the same night, died : wherefore the said jurors present, that the said J. S. the said male child did, in manner aforesaid, with premeditated design, kill and murder."

Art. 904. For assassination to conceal a crime.

——" That J. S. [insert date and place] having committed the crime of robbery by violently and fraudulently taking from the person of A. B. against his will, one gold watch and fifty Mexican dollars, in order to conceal the said crime, with premeditated design to kill, did make an assault on the said A. B. and by discharging a pistol, loaded with powder and ball and buckshot, against the head of him the said A. B., with the said ball and buckshot, inflicted a mortal wound under the right eye of the said A. B., of which wound the said A. B. afterwards, on the          day of          died : therefore the jurors say, that the said J. S. the said A. B. did, in manner aforesaid, with a premeditated design, kill, murder, and assassinate."

Art. 905. Assassination in the commission of a crime.

——" That J. S. on the          day of          in the year          , at the parish of L., for the purpose of committing the crime of robbery of one I. K. by violently and fraudulently taking from the person of the said I. K., against his will, one gold watch, did, with premeditated design to kill, make an assault upon one A. B. who then and there endeavoured to prevent the said robbery, and with a sword inflicted a mortal wound on the right side of the said A. B." &c. [as in the preceding form.]

Art. 906. Assassination for the purpose of obtaining an inheritance, and by hiring to murder.

——" That J. S. being the next of kin to one I. K. for the purpose of obtaining the inheritance of the said I. K. on the          day of          in the year          , did hire P. L. and N. O. for a reward promised to them by the said J. S. to kill the said I. K. and that the said P. L. and N. O. agreed to murder and assassinate the said I. K. for the said hire, and in pursuance of such agreement on the night of the day last aforesaid, entered the bed-room of the said I. K. and did make an assault upon him the said I. K. there lying in his bed, and the said I. K. with a pillow pressed by them on his face did suffocate, of which suffocation the said I. K. then and there died : wherefore the said jurors present, that the said J. S. and the said P. L. and the said N. O. the said I. K. with a premeditated design then and there, in manner aforesaid, did kill, murder, and assassinate."

Art. 907. Assassination by the means used to murder; lying-in-wait, arson, poison.

——" That J. S. on [set forth the date and place] with a premeditated design to kill one I. K. did lie in wait for him in a wood through which the J. S. expected that the said I. K. would pass, and did then and there make and assault on the said," &c. [as in the preceding form.]

Art. 908. By arson.

——" With a premeditated design to kill one I. K., did set fire to the dwelling-house of the said I. K. in which he the said I. K. then was, and by means of such fire did burn and consume the said dwelling-house, and by the fire and smoke caused by the burning of the said house the said I. K. was suffocated and burned, and of which burning and suffocation the said I. K. then and there died : wherefore the said jurors present, that the said J. S. the said I. K. with a premeditated design then and there did kill, murder, and assassinate."

4 D

Art. 909. By poison.

——"That J. S. having the premeditated design to kill one I. K. on the        day of        in the year        , did, in order to effect such design, mix a certain poison, called opium, in the soup prepared for the dinner of the said I. K., and the said I. K. having, on the same day and year, at        without any knowledge of such mixture, swallowed a portion of the said soup with the said poison mixed therein, by the effect of the said poison became disordered in his body, and afterwards of such disorder, caused by the said poison, to wit, from the day last aforesaid until the        day of        now last past, languished, and then of the said disorder, so caused as aforesaid, in the parish aforesaid, died: wherefore the jury present," &c. [as in the last.]

Art. 910. In charging murder and assassination by poison, it is necessary to state that the poison was taken by the deceased without knowing that it was poison, otherwise it might amount only to a charge of aiding in suicide, which is another offence. It is also necessary to state the time of giving the poison and the time of death.

Art. 911. If the indictment state one kind of poison, and the proof is death by another, it will support the indictment.

Art. 912. When any circumstance in the situation or the condition of the person killed gives to murder the character of assassination, it is sufficient to state that circumstance in the indictment, after the name of the person killed. The same rule applies as to murder under trust, where the trust arises from the relative conditions or relationships of the murderer with the person murdered; such condition or relationship being stated after the name of the person accused. When the trust arises under a special or implied promise, it must be stated thus:

——"That J. S. on [inserting the date and place], being [the master of a vessel called the Fly, then bound on a voyage from New Orleans to Havanna, took on board the said vessel, as a passenger, one I. K. and promised to convey him (the danger of the seas excepted) from the said port of New Orleans to the Havanna ; but the jurors present, that the said J. S. violating the trust so reposed in him, and with premeditated design to kill, did, on the        day of        last, on board the said vessel called the Fly, then lying in the river Mississippi, within the parish of Plaquemines, make an assault upon him the said I. K. and by force threw the said I. K. from the deck of the said vessel into the water in the said river, where the said I. K. sunk and was suffocated by the said water, and then and there, in consequence of such suffocation, instantly died and was drowned:] wherefore," &c.

Art. 913. Attempt to kill by poison.

The charge is the same as that of assassination by poison, omitting only the latter part which charges the death.

Art. 914. Charge for aiding in suicide.

——"That A. B. on the        day of        in the year        , at the parish of L., committed suicide by [swallowing a quantity of poison, which then and there killed him]; and that J. S. before that time, that is to say, on the        day of        in the parish aforesaid, [procured the said poison and gave it to the said A. B. for the purpose of enabling him to commit the said suicide, he the said J. S. well knowing that it was the intention of the said A. B. to destroy his own life [by swallowing the said poison.]

## SECTION XIII.

*Forms of indictments and other proceedings against the provisions of the Penal Code respecting duels.*

Art. 915. Using insulting -words or gestures, or making an assault to provoke a duel.

——" That J. S. on [insert date and place], intending to provoke one I. K. to fight a duel, or if the said I. K. should not fight a duel in consequence of such provocation, that the said I. K. should be dishonoured, did use the following words, speaking to the said I. K., ['you are a coward']; or did use an insulting gesture, by [snapping his fingers in the face of the said I. K.]; or did make an assault upon the said I. K., by striking him in the face with the palm of his hand, or other insult, assault, or insulting gesture," [describing it,] &c.

Art. 916. Answers and explanations of the defendant.

" To the district court of the second district of the state of Louisiana.

"The answer and explanation of J. S. to the indictment [or information] filed against him for using insulting words [or gestures] to [or of] I. K., [or assaulting him, as the case may be,] with intent to provoke the said I. K. to fight a duel, or as an alternative to dishonour him—this defendant saith, that the [words or gestures, as the case may be,] charged in the said indictment were used [in the heat of passion, that he is truly concerned for having used them, and that he has the highest respect for the said I. K., and never seriously intended to impeach his courage"]—[or any other denial or explanation that he may deem satisfactory.]

Art. 917. Certificate when the court is satisfied with the explanation.

" By the district court of the second district, &c.

" Whereas an indictment was filed in this court, on [insert date,] charging [insert the charge] ; and whereas the said J. S. afterwards presented to this court an answer and explanation [or acknowledgment] [or denial] hereunto annexed, which answer and explanation, in the opinion of this court, ought to satisfy the honour of the said I. K. It is therefore ordered, that the said answer be recorded and published, together with this judgment."

## CHAPTER XIX.

*Forms of indictments in offences against civil and political rights and conditions.*

Art. 918. Against a nurse for substituting a child.

——" That A. B. on the  day of  in the year  , at the parish of L., confided an infant male child of him the said A. B., aged one month or thereabouts, to J. S. of said parish, for the purpose of suckling and nursing the said child ; and that the said A. B. having been absent from the state for a long time, to wit, for five years and upwards, the said J. S. afterwards, on the day of          in the year          , and at the parish aforesaid, with intent to deceive the said A. B. the [father, or mother, or tutor, or curator], of the said child, substituted [or attempted to substitute] another child for the one confided to her."

Art. 919. For exposing an infant, under the age of six years, with intent to abandon it.

———" That A. B. having on the          day of          in the year          , at the parish of L., confided a [female child, named C. B., aged two years or thereabouts, the daughter of the said A. B.,] for the purpose of having the said child nursed and educated ; [and that the said J. S. afterwards to wit, on the day of     ,     in the year          , in the parish aforesaid, exposed and deserted the said child in a wood in the said parish], where the life of the said child was greatly endangered, with the intent the said child then and there wholly to abandon," &c.

Art. 920. Against the father or mother for exposing an infant, with intent to abandon it.

———" That J. S. being the [father] [or mother] of an illegitimate male child, born of the said J. S. [or, if the indictment be against the father, born of one J. S.] on the          day of          in the year          , at the said parish, did, on the day and year and at the place aforesaid, expose and desert the said child in a certain highway where the life of the said child was endangered, with intent wholly to abandon the said child."

Art. 921. For fraudulently producing a child with intent to intercept an inheritance.

———" That A. B. of the parish of L., long before and on the day of          in the year          , was the owner and possessor of a large real and personal estate in this state, and that the said A. B. on the day aforesaid, had only two descendants, to wit, C. and D. his sons ; and that the said C. on the day last aforesaid died without leaving any legitimate descendants, whereby the said D. became the presumptive heir to the said A. B. ; and the jurors present, that one J. S. afterwards, to wit, on the          day of          in the year          , at the parish aforesaid, with design to intercept half of the inheritance of the said A. B. from the said D. fraudulently produced an infant male child, falsely pretending that the said infant was the legitimate child of the said C. deceased, and which child would, if he had really been the legitimate child of the said C., have stood in the order of succession to the inheritance of the said A. B. equally with the said D."

Art. 922. If the offence be committed against a collateral presumptive heir, and the child produced be alleged to be a descendant, the charge must be "of a design to intercept the whole inheritance."

Art. 923. For making a false entry on register of births.

———" That J. S. on [insert date and place] being then minister of the Protestant Episcopal Church in the parish of L. and charged with keeping the register of marriages for the members of the said church, did fraudulently make a false entry on such register, falsely registering therein that on the          day of          in the year          , A. B. was married to C. D. by him the said minister, [or by I. K. formerly minister of the church], with intent to injure one E. F. in her condition and civil rights [as legitimate wife of the said A. B."]

Art. 924. For bigamy.

——" That J. S. on the            day of            in the year      , at the parish of            being then married to Anne, the daughter of J. B., and the said Anne being then living, contracted another marriage with C. D. of the said parish, according to the form required to give validity to marriages in this state, he the said J. S. having, at the time of his contracting the said second marriage, no reasonable cause to believe that the said Anne, his wife, to be dead."

## CHAPTER XX.

*Forms of indictments for offences affecting private property.*

### SECTION I.

Forms of indictments for burning and other malicious injuries to property.

Art. 925. For maliciously setting fire to a dwelling-house or other property.

——" That J. S. on the            day of            in the year      , at the parish of L., did maliciously set fire to a dwelling-house belonging to [or inhabited by] one I. K. with intent to destroy the same," &c.

Art. 926. If the house be not a dwelling-house, but contains property of the value of one hundred dollars, it must be thus described : " a certain house belonging to [or occupied by] I. K., situated in the same parish, containing personal property of the value of one hundred dollars."

If the house be empty, and be not a dwelling-house, it must be described as a " house."

Art. 927. For destroying a house with gunpowder or other explosive matter.

——" Did maliciously place gunpowder [or other explosive matter, designating it,] under [or in] a certain house, [or a house containing personal property of the value of one hundred dollars,] [or a dwelling-house] belonging to [or occupied by] I. K. situated in the said parish, and put fire to the said gunpowder [or other explosive matter] thereby causing the same to explode, with intent to destroy the said house," &c.

Art. 928. The above forms answer for the offence of setting fire to the other objects which the Code of Crimes and Punishments makes it an offence to set fire to, adding a charge of the value.

Art. 929. When bodily injury is suffered by any one, by the commission of the offence of malicious burning of a house or other property, or the offence be committed in the night, or if the buildings contain any domestic animals, those circumstances must be added to the charge.

Art. 930. For the destruction of a ship or other vessel, or raft, by fire.

———"Did, designedly and with intent to injure, illegally set fire to [or destroy by explosion of gunpowder, stating the manner,] a certain boat, [raft, schooner, or other vessel, describing it,] with the cargo on board, [if any, describing it,] being, together with such cargo, of the value of one hundred dollars."

Art. 931. For the malicious destruction of property by other means than by fire.

———"Did maliciously destroy a certain boat, commonly called a pirogue, with the cargo, consisting of fifty hogsheads of sugar, being then and there in the exclusive possession of one I. K., and being, together with such cargo, of greater value than ten dollars, by boring a hole in the bottom of the said pirogue and sinking it in the river Mississippi."

Art. 932. For fraudulently removing a land-mark.

———"That J. S. on the       day of       in the year       , at the parish of       did fraudulently [or maliciously, as the case may be,] remove a [cypress post] which had been placed to serve and did then serve as a land-mark to designate the boundary between two parcels of land in the said parish, the one in the possession of [the said J. S.] and the other of the said tracts in the possession of one A. B."


SECTION II.

Forms of indictments for house-breaking.

Art. 933. House-breaking by force, in the night.

———"That J. S. on the night of the       day of       , in the year       , in the parish of L. about the hours of eleven, by force, entered into a house occupied by I. K. in the said parish, with intent to steal, [or burn the said house, or to commit murder, or any other crime, naming it."]

Art. 934. For entering in the day and concealment until night.

———"That J. S. on the       day of       in the year       , at the parish of L., entered, in the day-time, secretly and fraudulently into the house of one I. K. situated in the said parish, and concealed himself in the said house until the night of the same day, with the intent to steal," &c.

Art. 935. For entering by discharging fire-arms or throwing a stone.

———"Did, with intent to do a bodily injury to one I. K. then being in a certain house [occupied by him the said I. K.] in the parish aforesaid, discharge a pistol, loaded with gunpowder and a ball, into the said house, through the door thereof; [or throw a stone through the window of the said house, or other missile, as the case may be."]


SECTION III.

Forms of indictments for the forcible or fraudulent acquisition of property.

Art. 936. For a fraudulent breach of trust.

———"That J. S. on [insert date and place] having before that time, at the parish of Point Coupee, received [ten bales of cotton, belonging to one I. K.] of the value of fifty dollars each, [to be carried by him the said J. S. from the said parish of Point Coupee to the said parish of L. to be there delivered to one A. B.] did, on the day and year and at the place first above mentioned, fraudulently appropriate the said [ten bales of cotton] to his own use."

Art. 937. When the property was received on a contract of loan, or letting or hiring.

——"That J. S. on [state the date and place] received from one I. K. on a contract of letting and hiring a certain [bay horse with a gig, of the value of          ] to be used by him the said J. S. for the purpose of conveying him to the Bayou St Johns in the said parish, and to be returned to the said I. K. on the same day ; and the jurors further present, that the said J. S. did not on the said day return the said [horse and gig] to the said I. K., but did, on the day and year and at the parish aforesaid, fraudulently appropriate the said [horse and gig] to his own use"

Art. 938. For the fraudulent appropriation of property found.

——"That J. S. [insert date of time and place] found a certain [red morocco pocket-book, containing bank-notes to the value of          ,] which had before that time been casually lost by one I. K., and that the said J. S. then and there knowing, or having good reason to believe, that the said I. K. was the owner of the said [pocket-book and its contents,] fraudulently did then and there appropriate the same," &c.

Art. 939. Where the finder has no reason to believe any designated person to be the owner.

[As before to the words "lost by one I. K."] "and that the said J. S. did then and there conceal and appropriate the same to his own use."

Art. 940. For opening and reading a sealed letter.

——"That J. S. [insert date of time and place] did open and read [or cause to be read] a sealed letter, written by I. K. to A. B., he the said J. S. not being authorized so to do by the said I. K., or the said A. B., or by law."

Art. 941. For malicious publication—add,

——"And that the said J. S. [or one C. D.] did maliciously and without authority publish the said letter [or a part of such letter] by printing the same in the words following, [insert the printed letter,] which publication is hereunto annexed, he the said J. S. [or C. D.] knowing the manner in which the said letter was obtained."

Art. 942. If, in the preceding form and that immediately following, the publication was in any other mode than by printing, there is no necessity of inserting a copy of the published letter in the indictment, or giving any other declaration of the letter than the names of the writer and of the person to whom it was addressed.

Art. 943. For taking and publishing a letter.

——"Did take from the legal possession of I. K. without his consent, a certain letter written by one A. B. to him the said I. K., and did maliciously publish the same by printing it in the following words, [insert copy of the published letter,] which printed letter is hereunto annexed."

Art. 944. For obtaining property by false pretences.

——"That J. S. [insert date of time and place,] did, with a fraudulent intent, and by the consent of one I. K., obtain from him one pair of silver candlesticks, belonging to him the said I. K., by falsely pretending that he the said J. S. was the servant of one A. B. a person well known to the said I. K., and that the said A. B. had sent him the said J. S. to borrow the said candlesticks for him the said A. B.; and the jurors further present, that the said I. K. would not have consented to deliver the said candlesticks to the said J. S. if he had not made use of the said false pretence.

Art. 945. For false pretences by personification.

——"That one J. S. with a fraudulent intent, and under the false pretence that he was G. H. of the parish of Point Coupee, planter, a man of great wealth and credit, on the                 day of
in the parish of L., induced one I. K. to deliver to him the said J. S. thus personating the said G. H., five hundred yards of raven's duck and ten pieces of Scotch plains, which he falsely asserted were wanted as supplies for the plantation of the said G. H. whom he falsely personated, and the jurors present," [as in the last form.]

Art. 946. If the false pretence be that he is another person of the same name, instead of charging the false pretence as above, say, "falsely pretending that he the said J. S. was another person, also named J. S. of," &c. [as in the last form.]

Art. 947. Charge for obtaining goods on the false pretence of immediate payment.

——"That J. S. on [insert date of time and place] with a fraudulent intent, induced one I. K. to deliver to him [describe the goods] under the false pretence that he would immediately pay the sum of
dollars for them in cash ; and the jurors further present, that the said J. S. refused to return the said goods or to pay the said sum, although he was afterwards, on the same day and year, at the parish aforesaid, within one hour after the delivery of the said goods, required so to do." [If the demand was made after one hour, state, "although he was afterwards, to wit, on          the          day of          in the same year,] [stating some time within three days of the delivery] required so to do, the said goods then being in the possession of the said J. S. ; and the jurors further present, that the said I. K. would not have consented to deliver the said goods if the said J. S. had not made the said false pretence of immediate payment in cash, &c.

Art. 948. For giving a check of no value in payment.

——"That J. S. on [insert date of time and place] purchased from one I. K. [insert description of property] and with intent to defraud, did give to the said I. K. in payment for the said property a check or draft, drawn by him the said J. S. [or by A. B.] on the bank of
payable on demand for the sum of          which he the said J. S. falsely pretended and affirmed would be paid at sight, he the said J. S. then and there well knowing that the said check or draft then was of no value ; and the jurors further present, that the said check was of no value, and that the said I. K. would not have delivered the said property if the said J. S. had not made the said false and fraudulent pretences, contrary," &c.

Art. 949. For false pretences by producing false papers.

——"That J. S. being desirous of purchasing one hundred bales of fair Louisiana cotton from one I. K., with a fraudulent design to induce him to sell the said cotton at a low price, produced a writing which he

falsely pretended was a Liverpool price current [or letter from C. &
Co. of Liverpool] dated the     day of     last, in which
false paper [or writing] it was stated that the price of fair Louisiana
cotton, on the day of the date thereof, was seven pence sterling per
pound ; and the jurors present, that the said paper [or writing] was
false and fraudulent, and that giving credit to the false pretence of the
said J. S. he the said I. K. sold and delivered to him one hundred bales
of cotton at the price of fourteen cents a pound, which he would not
have done if the said J. S. had not made the false pretences, and by
which the said I. K. was defrauded of the sum of     dollars."

Art. 950. False pretences by cheating at cards.

——" That J. S. on [insert date of time and place] fraudulently obtained from one A. B. the sum of     dollars at a game of [skill
and chance called whist] by means of packing the cards in such a manner [as to keep in his own hand all the court cards, or other means,
describing them,] which means the jurors present were other than those
which would have been given to the said J. S. by the regular chances
of the said game, or by the fair exercise of his skill therein, he the
said J. S. falsely pretending that the said sum of money was won by
the regular chances of the said game, and the fair exercise of his skill
therein ; and the jurors further present, that the said A. B. would not
have delivered and paid the said sum of     dollars if the said
J. S. had not made the said false and fraudulent pretences."

Art. 951. Charge in indictment for theft.

——" That J. S. or [insert date of time and place] one piece of lace,
of the value of     dollars, the property of A. B., from his possession fraudulently did take without his assent."

Art. 952. Theft by effraction.

——" That J. S. [insert date of time and place] in the day time,
with a fraudulent design, did enter into a certain house occupied by A.
B. [or ship called the Bee] and one piece of lace of the value of
dollars the property of A. B. and in his possession, then and there being, fradulently did take without the assent of the said A. B."

Art. 953. Breaking into a ship or house with intent to steal.

——" That J. S. on [insert date of time and place] with intent to
commit a theft, a certain house belonging to [or occupied by] one A.
B. did break and enter," &c.

If theft be committed, add, " and one piece of linen of the value
of     belonging to the said A. B. from his possession fraudulently did then and there take, without the assent of the said A. B."

If any one were in the house or ship, then add, " and the jurors
further present, that C. D. was at the time of the said entry in the
said house [or ship,] and did resist the said J. S. [or was prevented by
fear from resisting him, as the case may be."]

Art. 954. For entering a house and stealing by breaking a chest or
box, &c.

——" That J. S. on, &c. in the day time, with a fraudulent intent,
into a certain house belonging to [or in the occupation of] one A. B.
did enter, and a certain box [or chest, or other enclosed place] did forcibly break, and a piece of gold coin, then in the said box, belonging to
A. B., being found, did fraudulently take, without the assent of the
said A. B."

4 E

Art. 955. For fraudulently appropriating property taken from a wrecked vessel.

——"That a certain ship or vessel, of which the name and the owners are to the jurors unknown, was wrecked [or stranded] [or burned] on the west shore of the Lake Pontchartrain, in this state, on the day of          in the year          in the parish of New Orleans ; and that J. S. on the day and year and at the place last aforesaid, ten bales of cotton, driven on shore from the said wreck, did fraudulently appropriate, knowing it to have proceeded from the said wreck."

Art. 956. For privately stealing from the person.

——" That J. S. on [insert date of time and place] one [gold watch of the value of fifty dollars, belonging to and in the possession of I. K.,] privately from the said I. K. did fraudulently take, without his assent."

Art. 957. For robbery.

——" That J. S. [date, &c.] from the person of one I. K. by force and against his will, one gold watch of the value of fifty dollars, belonging to him, did fraudulently take."

Art. 958. For robbery by threats of violence.

——" That J. S. [date, &c.] from the person of one I. K. one hundred gold coins of the United States, called eagles, belonging to him the said I. K. did fraudulently take, and did force the said I. K. to deliver by threatening the said I. K. [to accuse him of the crime of rape]; or [to burn the house of the said I. K.] ; or [to assassinate him] or [to do any other injury to his person, property, or character, describing it."]

Art. 959. For receiving property, knowing it to be fraudulently obtained.

——" That J. S. on [date &c.] did fraudulently receive [or did fraudulently conceal or endeavour to conceal] one gold watch, belonging to one I. K. of the value of fifty dollars, which had been fraudulently taken [or obtained] from him by [theft,] or [fraudulent breach of trust,] or [by the fraudulent appropriation of property found,] or [by false pretences,] he the said J. S. well knowing that the said property had been so fraudulently taken [or obtained."]

Art. 960. For attempts to defraud by threats.

——" That J. S. with a fraudulent intent did, on [insert date, &c.] threaten one I. K. that he would [set fire to the dwelling-house of] him the said I. K. if he the said I. K. did not [give him a sum of one hundred dollars,] or [did not procure for him the place of under-sheriff of the parish], as the means of avoiding the execution of the said threat."

Art. 961. If the threat be of injury to person or reputation, or any other injury to property than the one above specified, it must be particularly set forth.

Art. 962. If the threat be in writing, it must be in the following form :

——" That J. S. on [insert date, &c.] did, with a fraudulent intent, make an instrument in writing, and send the same to one I. K., which instrument is in the words following, to wit : ['Mr. I. K., if you wish to avoid the burning of your house, or the infamy of having made an attempt to suborn a witness, you will do well to enclose a bank-note for one hundred dollars, by post, directed to A. B. at L.']—meaning thereby to demand of the said I. K. the sum of one hundred dollars as the means to avoid the destruction of the house of the said I. K. and an accusation of having attempted to suborn a witness to commit perjury, contrary," &c.

Art. 963. For writing a malicious threatening letter, without any design to defraud.

———"That J. S. [insert date] maliciously intending to vex and disquiet one I. K. wrote [or caused to be written and sent or delivered, as the case may be,] to the said I. K. a certain writing, in the words following, to wit, [insert the letter."]


# CHAPTER XXI.

*Forms of indictments for conspiracy.*

Art. 964. Conspiracy to rob and murder.

———"That J. S. and N. O. on [insert date] fraudulently intending to rob and murder one A. B. agreed together, or with other persons to the jurors unknown, [according to the fact] [that the said N. O. he being then and there a domestic servant of the said A. B. should admit the said J. S. at midnight, on some subsequent day into the house of the said A. B., and that they should then and there strangle and kill the said A. B. in his bed, and should carry off and steal all the money and other valuable property found in the said house."]

Art. 965. Conspiracy to make a false accusation.

———"That J. S. and N. O. on [insert date] intending maliciously to injure one A. B. agreed together, or [with others, as above,] that they the said J. S. and N. O. would accuse the said A. B. of having committed the crime of rape upon one C. D., they the said J. S. well knowing that the said A. B. was innocent of any such crime."

Art. 966. Conspiracy to lower wages.

"That J. S., N. O. and L. M. on [insert date] being master-shoemakers in the said city of New Orleans, entered into an agreement and combination with each other, and with other master-shoemakers in the said city to the jurors unknown, that they would give to the journeymen shoemakers, whom they should severally employ, no more than [the sum of          for each day's work, or for each pair of shoes, &c. stating the substance of the agreement; and if any penalty be imposed by the agreement for a breach of it, state the same particularly."]

Art. 967. Conspiracy to raise wages and abridge the time of labour.

"That J. S., N. O. and R. P. being persons usually working as journeymen in the trade of shoemaking, did, on [insert date] enter into an agreement and conspiracy to and with each other, and to and with divers other persons to the jurors unknown, that they would not work at their said trade unless they were paid at the rate of          for each pair of shoes, and          for each pair of boots, or          for each day they should work at their said trade ; [or that they would work only ten hours for a day's work;] [state, as above, the substance of the agreement, and if it contained any penalty for a breach of it, or any proceeding to oblige others to enter into the conspiracy, state the same."]

Art. 968. The agreement is the offence, but if any thing be done in consequence of it to carry it into execution (as if the penalty imposed by the agreement be enforced, or any injury be offered to others to force them to join in the conspiracy,) it should be stated, that the court may apportion the punishment.

Art. 969. Conspiracy to raise the price of flour.

" That J. S. and I. K. being merchants dealing in the purchase and sale of flour, on [insert date] did enter into a conspiracy and agreement to and with each other, and to and with other persons to the jurors unknown, that they would purchase each of them one thousand barrels of flour, and would not sell the same for less than twelve dollars for each barrel, [insert the conditions of the agreement and the penalty, if any, for its breach."]

## CHAPTER XXII.

*Forms of indictments against principals who become such by aiding or encouraging the act, against accomplices and accessaries.*

Art. 970. Whenever any one, who hath not himself committed the offence, hath made himself a principal by any of the acts enumerated in the third article of the fifth chapter of the first book of the Code of Crimes and Punishments, he is a principal in the second degree, and he may be indicted jointly with the one who personally committed the offence, or separately; but, in either case, the commission of the offence and the act which made the abettor liable, must be stated according to the truth; but if he be present at the act, it will be sufficient to state, that he was so, and that he aided or encouraged the others, without stating in what manner particularly.

Art. 971. The person becoming liable, as a principal, under the provisions of the above recited article, may be indicted, tried, and punished, although the one who personally committed the offence should have escaped, or be acquitted, or pardoned, but the commission of the offence must be proved.

Art. 972. Indictment against principals in the first and second degree, jointly, for murder.

———" That J. S. on the     day of     in the year     at the parish of L., with a premeditated design to kill one I. K., made an assault upon the said I. K., and with a dirk inflicted a mortal wound on the left breast of him the said I. K., of which wound he the said I. K. afterwards, on the same day and year, at the place aforesaid, died: and that L. M. during the time that the said J. S. was committing the said offence stood at a short distance from the place where the said murder was committed, knowing that the said J. S. was engaged in the perpetration thereof, and with the intent to keep watch and give notice to the said J. S. of the approach of any one who might interrupt the commission of the said offence; whereupon the jurors aforesaid present, that the said J. S. and L. M. the said I. K. in manner aforesaid did kill and murder, contrary," &c.

Art. 973. Indictment against the principal in the second degree alone.

" That, &c. [insert the charge against the person who actually committed the offence, according to the forms prescribed for such offence, then add,] and the jurors aforesaid do further present, that L. M. at the time the said offence was committed was present [and by words and gestures did encourage the said J. S. to commit the said offence, he the said L. M. well knowing the unlawful intent of the said J. S. in committing the said offence."]

Art. 974. Indictment against an accomplice for having committed the offence, &c.

" That, &c. [state the offence, according to the proper form, and then add,] and the jurors further present, that L. M. before the said offence was committed, to wit, on the          day of
in the year aforesaid, at the parish aforesaid, did unlawfully advise, command, and encourage, [or did agree to aid,] or [did promise the sum of          dollars to,] or [offer his interest in procuring the office of sheriff of the county of L. for,] or [did prepare and furnish the pistol to, &c. as the case may be,] the said J. S. in order to induce him to commit the said offence."

Art. 975. Indictment against an accessary.

" That, &c. [state the offence, according to the proper form, after which add,] and the jurors aforesaid do further present, that L. M. well knowing the said J. S. to have committed the said offence as aforesaid, afterwards, to wit, on the          day of
in the year aforesaid, at the parish of L. did conceal the said J. S. or aid him, in order that he might effect his escape [from arrest, or trial, or the execution of his sentence, as the case may be."]


CHAPTER XXIII.


*Of informations.*


Art. 976. Form of an information by the attorney-general, or district attorney.

" Be it remembered, that on the          day of          in the year          , in the criminal court of the state of Louisiana, came J. P, attorney-general of the state of Louisiana, and gives the said court to be informed, that," &c. [as in an indictment.]

Art. 977. After an information has been filed, the prosecution cannot be dismissed but by leave of the court, on motion of the public prosecutor, who must state his reasons for such motion, which motion with the reasons must be entered on the minutes of the court, together with the decision of the court on such motion whether it be allowed or rejected.

Art. 978. All the provisions respecting indictments in this Code apply to informations in cases where by law they may be filed, unless the contrary is expressed or results from the nature of the two modes of proceeding.

## CHAPTER XXIV.

*Of joining different offences and persons in the same indictment,*
*and of different courts, for the same offence.*

Art. 979. No indictment can contain a charge for more offences than one, under the modification hereinafter in this chapter contained.

Art. 980. The practice of inserting different charges or counts in an indictment for the same offence, is abolished ; but where there is evidence before a grand jury sufficient to prove a fact which is an offence, and the evidence renders it doubtful whether it was done with one or the other of several intents, either of which would aggravate the offence, the jury may charge the intent in the alternative, and the accused may be convicted on the proof of either on the trial.

Art. 981. Form of indictment charging the intent in the alternative.

" That J. S. on &c. [insert date] at the parish of L., upon one A. B. did make an assault by seizing the said A. B. by the throat with his hands and striking him, &c. with the intent either to murder the said A. B. or to disfigure him, or to do a permanent injury by laming him," &c.

Art. 982. In cases of libel it will be sufficient to charge in the indictment that the defendant "*made*," "*published*," or "*circulated*," the libel ; and proof of either, according to the definition of those terms in the Penal Code of Crimes and Punishments, will be sufficient. In like manner, an indictment will be good which charges that the defendant either made the counterfeit coin, or a forged instrument, or had the same in possession, with intent to pass, (in cases where such possession is made an offence); or that he knowingly uttered or passed the same, naming the person to whom.

Art. 983. In indictments for all offences against private property in which, according to the forms herein before prescribed, it is necessary to aver the name of the owner or possessor of the property, it will be sufficient to state in the alternative that either A. B. or C. D. was such possessor or owner ; and in like manner, proof of either will be sufficient.

Art. 984. The several persons may be joined in the same indictment in the following cases :

The person who gives and he who receives a bribe.

·The principal, the accomplice, and accessary.

The suborner and the perjurer.

The employer and the actual assassin, (in cases of assassination for hire.)

The adulteress and her paramour.

Joint rioters, conspirators, and all others who jointly commit an offence.

Art. 985. Although several be joined, yet each defendant may demand and have a separate trial, except in case of adultery, as is before provided for.

## CHAPTER XXV.

*Of the mode of making the charge in cases of repetition of the offence.*

Art. 986. That the party accused has been before convicted of an offence of the same nature may be stated in the indictment according to the following form : after the charge of the offence add, "and the jurors do further present, that the said J. S. was heretofore in the court of [state the court] in or about the year        convicted of [state the offence, and if he was more than once convicted, state the same in like manner, and conclude,] wherefore the said jurors present, that the said J. S. hath [a second or third time] committed an offence affecting [private property, according to the nature of the offence."]

Art. 987. If the prior convictions are discovered after the time of finding the indictment, but before the trial, the public prosecutor may give notice to the defendant, at any time before the trial, that he will give evidence of such conviction, specifying the offence and the time as is above set forth, and shall then be allowed to give such evidence.

Art. 988. If the prior conviction be discovered after conviction, whether sentence be passed or not, the record of the conviction shall be received by the court, and the defendant shall be brought up and required to show cause why the additional punishment should not be inflicted, which he may do by denying that he is the person formerly convicted. If the identity is denied, it shall be tried by a jury, and the burthen of proof shall be on the public prosecutor.

·

# A CODE OF EVIDENCE.

# INTRODUCTORY TITLE.

Art. 1. The Code of Evidence, which is applicable as well to civil as to criminal cases, will direct judges, other magistrates, ministers of justice and jurors, what proof is sufficient to commit, to indict, and to convict an offender, against the Code of Crimes and Punishments.

Art. 2. Where, in this Code, examples are given to illustrate certain rules of evidence, they are never intended as an enumeration of all the cases coming within such rules. When a limitation to certain enumerated cases is intended, it is unequivocally so expressed.

Art. 3. The substantive word *judge* in this Code means the power which has the right of deciding on the subject matter to which the article in which it is used applies; it may, according to the subject, mean either the magistrate, the jury, or the arbitrator or referee.

Art. 4. All the rules of evidence which are laid down to regulate the introduction and declare the effect of proof adduced on the principal matter in dispute in judicial investigation, apply also to the introduction and effect of the same kind of proof on any incidental question, except when it is otherwise expressly provided.

Art. 5. Particular provisions in this Code control general rules, but in the particular case only in which they are introduced.

Art. 6. By the expression "immoveable estate," or "immoveables," is meant all that is made such by destination or provision of law, as well as by nature.

Art. 7. When the word "*evidence*" is used in this Code, it always means "*legal evidence*," as herein defined.

Art. 8. In all cases whatever where any thing is declared to be legal evidence, it must be understood to be with the proviso that it is applicable to the issue or fact in litigation. Whether so applicable or not (when there is no express provision) it is left to the discretion of the court to determine. But in the exercise of this discretion great liberality must be used, and no legal evidence excluded that has even a remote application to the question.

Art. 9. If in any criminal case the provisions of this Code, for the admission or exclusion of evidence, shall in the opinion of the court be found to have operated unjustly ; and in consequence thereof any one is convicted, judgment shall not be pronounced until after the report has been made to the legislature, in the manner hereinafter provided. But if such provision shall operate, in the opinion of the court, in favour of the accused, who shall, in consequence of evidence admitted or excluded conformably to such provision, be acquitted, judgment of acquittal shall be rendered: and in either of these cases (as well as in civil cases, where a verdict has, in the opinion of the court, been unjustly given in consequence of evidence admitted or excluded conformably to such provision) a full report shall be made to the legislature of the case, together with the reasons of the court for thinking the particular provision unjust or inexpedient; and if the legislature shall, at the first session after the report, make the alterations, in substance, as suggested by the court, a new trial shall be given in the civil suit, and to the party convicted in a criminal cause; otherwise judgment shall be given on the verdict.

Art. 10. If in the trial of any cause a question shall arise, relative to the admission of evidence for the decision of which no provision is made in this Code, the court shall decide according to such principles as they believe the legislature would have been guided by had the case been foreseen; and shall, in like manner, report the case and their decision, with the reason thereof, to the legislature. And although the legislature should amend this Code in consequence of such representation, or should omit so to do, it shall not affect the decision if it be made in a civil cause.

Art. 11. But if the case provided for by the last preceding article be a criminal one, and the principle adopted by the court shall have admitted or excluded evidence, to the prejudice of the accused, which evidence would not have been so excluded or admitted as the Code now stands, and the accused shall, in consequence thereof, be convicted, no judgment shall be had on such conviction, but the defendant shall be discharged.

Art. 12. The last three preceding articles relate only to questions on the admissibility of evidence; all questions, as to its credit and weight, when admitted, must be decided by the judge or the jury, to whichever the fact is submitted, except in cases of evidence declared by law to be conclusive.

# BOOK I.

OF THE NATURE OF EVIDENCE, AND OF ITS SEVERAL KINDS.

## TITLE I.

### GENERAL PRINCIPLES AND DEFINITIONS.

Art. 13. Evidence is that which brings or contributes to bring the mind to a just conviction of the truth or falsehood of any fact asserted or denied.

Art. 14. From the above definition it results that judges of fact, except in cases of proof declared to be conclusive, are not bound to decide in conformity with the declarations of any number of witnesses, which do not produce conviction to the mind, against a less number, or against presumptions which do satisfy the mind.

Art. 15. A conviction produced by evidence, which ought not, according to the rules of true reason, to have that effect, is not a just conviction. But different minds may have different conceptions of what is true reason; the law, in order to secure uniformity of decision on this point, declares what evidence ought, in given cases, to produce, or contribute to produce such conviction, and that evidence is called legal evidence.

## TITLE II.

### DISTRIBUTION OF THE SUBJECT.

Art. 16. LEGAL EVIDENCE, in relation to its nature, is of two kinds: that which the judge receives from his own knowledge, and that which he derives from other sources; the latter is either testimonial, scriptory, or substantive.

TESTIMONIAL EVIDENCE is that which is offered by the relation of any other person, whether communicated to the judge orally or in writing.

SCRIPTORY EVIDENCE comprehends all written evidence other than the declarations of witnesses reduced to writing.

SUBSTANTIVE EVIDENCE is that which is produced by the exhibition of any object which from its nature, situation, or appearance, creates a belief of the truth or falsehood of the allegation in dispute.

Art. 17. Evidence being different in the degree of effect which it ought to produce, is therefore divided into three kinds : presumptive evidence, direct evidence, and conclusive evidence.

Art. 18. Presumptive evidence is that, which by directly proving one fact, renders the existence of another fact probable.

Art. 19. Direct evidence is that, which if true, conclusively establishes or destroys the proposition in question.

Art. 20. Conclusive evidence is that, which by law is declared to be such proof of that which it asserts, as cannot, while it exists, be contradicted by other testimony. The law does not and cannot in this case command belief ; but on the exhibition of certain evidence it does command such decision, as would be the result of a belief in the existence of the fact which such evidence purports to prove.

Art. 21. These degrees may be produced by either of the kinds of evidence above enumerated ; the actual inspection or perception of the judge, the declaration of witnesses, the exhibition of written proof, or of substantive evidence. The law under each of these divisions is declared in the subsequent titles.

Art. 22. Every offence being in this system clearly defined and directed to be distinctly charged in the act of accusation, all rules of evidence applicable to one, are applicable to all ; therefore, in criminal cases, whatever constitutes the offence, whether act, omission, or intent, must be supported by such LEGAL EVIDENCE as proves the allegation.

Art. 23. So in civil cases, all fictions being in like manner discarded, and the demand and defence being required to be set forth according to the truth, the same rules of evidence are applicable to all actions.

Art. 24. It results from the two preceding articles, that no provisions are necessary in this Code to designate what evidence is required or permitted in each kind of action or division of offence.

# BOOK II.

## OF THE RULES APPLICABLE TO THE SEVERAL KINDS OF EVIDENCE.

## TITLE I.

### OF THE EVIDENCE OFFERED TO A JUDGE FROM HIS OWN KNOWLEDGE.

Art. 25. Under some circumstances the judge is allowed to frame his decision upon the conviction brought to his mind by means of his own senses without the intervention of any other proof. But he can do this only in cases particularly provided by law; these are éspecially designated in the different codes of this system.

Art. 26. In all other cases than those so specially provided for, the judge hears the testimonial, sees the scriptory, or the substantive, evi-. dence, and must decide (not from his knowledge, but) from the conviction produced on his mind by this evidence.

Art. 27. The power given to a magistrate to arrest when an offence is committed in his presence; to a judge, to determine on the authenticity of a record, to order the removal of a person who interrupts the proceedings of a court, and the authority given to the magistrates to determine when the military may be directed to act in support of the civil power, are examples of cases in which the judge is empowered to act on evidence derived from his own knowledge.

Art. 28. In all other cases where facts material to the decision of the cause have come to the knowledge of the judge, and he is not specially authorized to act on such knowledge, he must state the facts in open court under oath, and is liable to cross-examination like any other witness. When there is but one judge, and the fact is to be tried by the court, if the testimony of the judge is necessary, the cause shall be tried by the judge of an adjoining district in the manner provided for in cases where the judge is interested.

Art. 29. Jurors are not permitted to act on the evidence of their own knowledge. Whatever has come to the knowledge of either of them, must be stated under oath in open court.

# TITLE II.

Art. 30. Rules for procuring the personal attendance or the written testimony of witnesses, are contained in the Codes of Civil and of Criminal Procedure. This chapter directs what persons may be produced as witnesses : to what points they may be examined, and the mode of conducting the examination.

## CHAPTER I.

### *What persons may be examined as witnesses.*

Art. 31. The only persons who, under all circumstances, are excluded from giving testimony are:

1. Those who are of INSANE MIND at the time of examination.

2. Children under fourteen years of age, whose faculties do not appear to be sufficiently developed, to receive correct impressions of the fact relative to which they are interrogated, to relate those impressions correctly, and to feel the obligation of doing it truly.

Art. 32. Whether a child under the age of fourteen has attained the intellectual powers required by the preceding article, or whether the person offered as a witness be of sane mind or not; must be determined by those who are to decide on the principal fact in question between the parties, and to come to such determination, they must examine the person who is offered as a witness, and other witnesses if it be deemed necessary. If the trial is by a jury, a majority shall determine whether a witness objected to for either of these causes shall be examined.

Art. 33. The circumstances and cases in which certain persons otherwise permitted to testify, are excluded from giving testimony, are the following :

1. A slave is not admitted to testify in any case but one in which another slave is prosecuted for some offence ; but the declaration of a slave is received as a complaint in the manner directed by the Code of Criminal Procedure.

2. A counsellor or attorney at law shall not be interrogated to disclose any fact that has come to his knowledge by communication from his client. But this rule is subject to the following limitations and explanations : viz.—It shall apply only to facts which were communicated to the counsellor or attorney for the purpose of conducting or defending some judicial proceeding pending, or apprehended. It shall not apply to any other person than a licensed counsellor or attorney, although the purpose of the communication may be the defence or prosecution of a suit.

3. A priest of the Catholic religion shall not be forced to reveal any thing which he knows only by its being confided to him in religious confession by his penitent.

# CHAPTER II.

*Of the different modes of taking testimonial evidence.*

Art. 34. Testimonial evidence may be exhibited in three different forms :

By affidavit.

By oral examination.

By written deposition or interrogation.

## SECTION I.

### Of testimony by affidavit.

Art. 35. In all cases in which the affidavit of the party or a witness is by the Code of Civil or Criminal Procedure, allowed as a sufficient ground for the issuing of any process order, or other judicial proceeding, the party making such affidavit may be cross-examined by the party opposed in interest before the judge of the court from which such order or process issues, and evidence may be produced to disprove the facts stated in such affidavit.

Art. 36. In order to carry the preceding article into effect, if no injustice will in that particular case be suffered by the delay, the judge shall require reasonable notice to be given to the opposite party of the time and place of examination, together with a copy of the affidavit before the order or process shall issue.

Art. 37. If the judge shall be of opinion that the ends of justice will be defeated by delay or by giving the notice required, he may, if the proof warrants it, give the order required; but shall, at a proper time, cause the notice required by the last article to be given, and if by the cross-examination of the deponent or the production of opposite proof, the alleged facts shall be disproved, the order shall be rescinded, and the party who has obtained it shall pay the costs and damages sustained by the other party in consequence thereof, to be awarded by the court, or by a jury if either party require it.

Art. 38. Notice shall be given to every person making an affidavit, or swearing to the truth of any pleading or paper whatever to be used in any judicial proceeding, before the oath is administered, that he will be liable to cross examination, and that he subjects himself to the penalty of perjury if the statement be designedly false ; and the magistrate who administers the oath shall give such notice and insert in the certificate of attestation the words "after the notice required by law," or words to that effect, under the penalties prescribed by law for a neglect of duty.

Art. 39. It is the duty of every magistrate who shall administer the oath of attestation to any affidavit, to inquire of the deponent whether he has read the same ; and if the answer be that he has not, or cannot read, then to cause him to read, or to have it read to him distinctly, and after giving the notice required by the last article, to cause him to sign his name, if he can write, and if he cannot, then to make a mark

4 G

at the foot of the said affidavit, opposite to which the magistrate shall write the name of the deponent.

Art. 40. The oath or affirmation to all affidavits shall be according to the form prescribed by the Code of Procedure, with additions required by this section.

SECTION II.

Of the examination and attestation of those who are parties to judicial proceedings in civil causes.

Art. 41. All fictions being expressly discarded from the judicial proceedings of this state, no party to a suit shall be permitted to make any allegation of fact in a court of justice of which he is not willing to declare his knowledge or belief under oath. Therefore, all petitions, or answers intended to be used in any suit, and containing any allegation of fact, or the belief of any fact by the party in the suit on whose behalf such petition or answer shall be exhibited, shall be sworn to in the form prescribed for affidavits by the preceding section, and the same notice shall be given that the party is liable to cross examination and the penalties of perjury in case of wilful falsehood.

Art. 42. In addition to the discovery directed to be mutually furnished by the parties in answer to interrogatories, as provided by the laws regulating the practice of the courts in civil cases, (or in lieu thereof) any party to a suit may summon another party or any one having an adverse interest and being within the state, to attend the trial in order to be examined touching the matters in controversy; and if such party be not within the state, or do not attend, the same proceedings shall be had either to procure the deposition of the said party, or to put off the trial, as are directed with respect to witnesses who are absent or refuse to attend.

Art. 43. The deposition of any party to the pleadings, or his answers to interrogations or on oral examination in court, shall have no other force than the judge or jury who try the fact shall deem it entitled to ; therefore, that part of the present law which directs that to countervail such testimony drawn from the party, the oath of two witnesses, or of one witness with circumstantial evidence shall be necessary, is repealed.

Art. 44. In every trial where the parties, or either of them, have appeared, whether in pursuance of such provisions or not, he or they, at the request of the opposite party, or of any juror, or by direction of the judge for his own satisfaction, may be sworn to answer such proper questions as shall be put to him or them relative to the matter in dispute.

Art. 45. On the trial of any cause, if the judge or a majority of the jury shall deem it necessary to form a true decision after hearing the testimony, that any party not present shall be examined, the trial shall, at the discretion of the court, be postponed, and the usual measures taken for obtaining the attendance or the deposition of the party upon interrogatories, to the point deemed to be important by the judge or the jury as aforesaid. All questions pertinent to the matter in dispute may be put to a party examined in the manner aforesaid, which might be put to a witness.

Art. 46. When any party to a suit shall be examined in pursuance of the provisions of this section, the same rules shall be observed for conducting the examination as are laid down for the examination of witnesses by the third section of this chapter.

Art. 47. This section relates exclusively to civil causes.

## SECTION III.

### To what points and in what manner witnesses may be examined.

Art. 48. If the witness be a Catholic priest, he shall not be interrogated for the purposes of revealing any thing that has been confided to him by confession ; but he may be examined as to knowledge obtained from any other source.

Art. 49. The counsellor or attorney employed by the defendant or assigned to him by the court, shall not be interrogated for the purpose of revealing any thing that he knows only by its being communicated to him by his client in relation to the cause in which he is employed, and for the purpose of conducting or defending the same, or for the purpose of procuring professional advice on some lawful occasion. What he knows in any other manner, although it may also have been communicated by his client, or what he knows by communication from his client, before he became his counsellor or attorney, or at any time, if the fact so communicated have no relation to the cause or matter in which it was communicated to him, he shall be obliged to declare whenever the question is otherwise pertinent.

Art. 50. If it should become material in any suit to require information of a fact which it would be dangerous to the public safety to disclose at the time of trial, this is a good cause for postponing the trial until such danger shall cease.

Art. 51. No witness shall be obliged to answer any questions but such as are immediately pertinent to the issue between the parties, or which may elucidate or establish some incidental fact necessary to be inquired into in the cause. Questions as to the character of a witness, and questions which, though unconnected with the merits of the case, may be put to test the veracity of a witness, are examples of such incidental inquiry. But of the pertinency of any question, the court, in its discretion, must judge according to the circumstances of the case.

Art. 52. The constitution having provided, " that in criminal prosecutions the accused shall not be compelled to give evidence against himself," the legislature feel themselves bound to extend the same protection to witnesses in all cases, and to declare, that no witness shall be compelled to answer any interrogatory, if the answer he would give, would furnish evidence to justify a prosecution against him for a CRIME.

Art. 53. With the exceptions contained in the five last preceding articles, and the restrictions hereafter put upon leading questions, all other interrogatories may be put to any witness.

Art. 54. The rule that no one shall discredit his own witness, is abolished. The party calling a witness may cross-examine him to test his veracity, and call witnesses to his character in the same manner as if he had not been called at his instance.

Art. 55. Leading questions are not permitted to be put. Such only shall be deemed leading questions as suggest to the witness some statement (inconsistent with the truth,) which the party proposing the question wishes to prove. This is a matter left to the sound discretion of the court. But it must be so exercised as not to present suggestions necessary to recall the facts in question to the memory of the witness, when the transaction is remote, when from its nature it was not likely to have made a strong impression on the mind of the witness, or when from age or indisposition, timidity, or other cause, the mind of the witness is weakened or disturbed.

Art. 56. The witness may, on his examination, refer to written notes made by himself or by his direction, for the purpose of refreshing his memory as to events mentioned in them; he may refer to writings made by others for the same purpose; but in that case he must speak from his own recollection of the fact, thus revived by the writing; not from the evidence of the writing itself; and he must in all cases declare when, and by whom, and for what purpose, the writing to which he refers, was made; and he shall not be permitted to refer to them if they appear to have been made by either of the parties in the suit, or by their direction, for the purpose of suggesting to the witness what he ought to say.

Art. 57. In all cases where a witness is examined to prove or disprove any matter of account or calculation, he must be permitted to refer to the papers or books containing such account or calculation.

Art. 58. It is the duty of the judge to prevent any harsh or threatening language to be used towards a witness for the purpose of confusing or intimidating him. Reasonable time shall be given to the witness to recollect himself before he is urged to answer. After his testimony has been given, he may rectify any mistake in his answers, within a like reasonable time, to be judged of by the court.

Art. 59. Whenever the testimony of a witness is reduced to writing, he may, before signing it, correct any inaccuracies which may have been made in reducing it to writing, or any error which he may himself have made; and such correction may be made even after signing the deposition, within a reasonable time, to be judged of according to circumstances by the court.

Art. 60. He who judicially alleges a litigated fact, must produce evidence to support it, whether it be a fact in charge or discharge.

Art. 61. No fact judicially alleged by one party and in the same manner confessed by the other, need be proved by other evidence.

Art. 62. A fact judicially alleged by one party and neither confessed nor denied by the other, must be proved by the alleging party; but the oath of the party alleging, shall be presumptive evidence, to have such weight as the judge or jury, to whichever the fact is submitted, may think it deserves.

Art. 63. The evidence required by the preceding articles, is any of the several kinds specified in the Code as legal evidence.

Art. 64. The judicial allegation above mentioned means the affirmative declaration made in the course of written judicial proceeding, that a fact or state of things exists or has happened, on which the one party relies to support his charge, or the other to exonerate himself from it. An affirmative assertion of innocence amounts only to a negation of a charge made, and is not, therefore, such an affirmative declaration as the party making it is bound to support by proof.

Art. 65. The rule of evidence which required that the best evidence, or as it is sometimes stated, the best attainable evidence, shall be produced, shall hereafter operate to the exclusion of other evidence only in the following cases :

1. When the law shall have declared that to give validity to a contract, it shall be made in writing, no other proof shall be admitted of such contract, unless it be proved that the writing required by law was made, and that it has been casually lost or destroyed, or has been placed, without the default of the party offering the inferior evidence, out of his reach.

2. When it is proved that SCRIPTORY EVIDENCE of the matter in question has been made, and was in possession of the party offering the inferior proof, unless he show that it has been casually lost or destroyed, or without his default has been placed out of his reach.

3. When the legislature shall have declared certain evidence necessary for the proof of designated facts.

4. When the fact alleged is one which, if true, must have appeared by AUTHENTIC ACT.

Art. 66. In all other cases where evidence is offered, which the judge or jury shall deem of an inferior nature to other evidence which is not produced, such inferior evidence, if legal, shall be admitted, and the non-production of the other shall operate only as presumptive proof against the party failing to produce it, to have such effect as such judge of the fact shall, according to circumstances, give to it.

Art. 67. In all cases where a writing is proved to be in the possession of the opposite party, who, on proper notice being given, does not produce it, evidence may be given of its contents.

Art. 68. The rule established by the Civil Code, that parol evidence shall not be admitted against or beyond what is contained in the acts, nor what may have been said before or at the time of making them, is to be taken with the following modifications :

1. It applies exclusively to writings, containing obligations or donations, and to testamentary dispositions.

2. Parol evidence, in all cases of written instruments, shall be admitted to prove error, fraud, violence, threats, or any other circumstance which, by the Civil Code, would avoid or modify a contract.

3. It may be admitted to remove any ambiguity, whether apparent on the face of the instrument, or arising out of the application of its terms.

4. Any one of the parties to a written instrument may be called on by another to explain, on oath, either by parol evidence on the trial, or by answer to interrogatories, at the option of the party making the inquiry, any point in litigation between them, arising out of such instrument, and that, whether the interrogation goes to contradict, explain, or add to, or diminish the obligation specified in the writing.

Art. 69. Whenever error, fraud, violence, or threats are alleged as reasons for setting aside a contract, the following points must be inquired into by the judge, and considered, if he is to decide or give in charge to the jury, in addition to the evidence of the direct fact alleged.

1. If error is the reason alleged, the character as to caution and prudence in conducting his affairs, of the party alleging that he was deceived ; his knowledge of the particular business which formed the subject of the contract ; the deliberation or haste with which it was effected.

2. If the objection be fraud, violence, or threats, the character of

both parties must be the subject of inquiry, as presumptive evidence of the fraudulent or violent practices on the one side, or of a submission to them on the other.

3. In all cases of this kind, the time that has elapsed after the error or fraud was discovered, or the violence or threats had ceased, before the proceedings were had, or complaint made for redress, and the reason for the delay, if any.

Art. 70. Parol evidence is not admitted unless the witness be under the sanction of an oath. Therefore the witness is only to be interrogated as to his own knowledge or belief, and not as to what he has heard from others, upon whom none of the sanctions to secure veracity could operate. This is a general rule, to which there are the following exceptions :

1. A witness may declare what a party has said, if the testimony be called for by the opposite party ; and this extends not only to the declarations of the actual parties to the suit, but those of the persons under whom they claim ;· and also to the declarations of such agents or other persons as could have bound them by their contracts in the matters in contest ; but no declaration of one under whom the party claims shall be given in evidence unless it was made while such person was interested, or of the agent except while he was in the employ of the party.

2. What has been said relative to the matter in dispute by others, in the presence and hearing of one party to the suit, may be given in evidence by the other as a foundation for presumption to be drawn from what was said or done by the party, or from his silence ; but in all such cases the party implicated may require that he be allowed to explain upon oath.

3. What a witness has said before he was sworn, may be shown to prove that it was consistent, or inconsistent, with his declaration on oath.

4. What a witness has declared on a former trial between the same parties for the same cause, if the witness be dead, or his testimony cannot be procured.

5. When the declarations of a party, or a witness, are admitted under the first or second exceptions above mentioned, any thing said by another person in the same conversation, which is necessary to counteract or explain what was said by such party or witness may be given in evidence.

6. Proof of the hand-writing of a subscribing witness to an instrument who is absent or dead, may, in certain cases, be admitted on the presumption that he would not have signed if he could not prove the execution. To rebut this presumption, any material declaration of such witness may be given in evidence.

7. In cases not depending on scriptory evidence, a party may give as evidence what he himself said or did in relation to the matter in litigation at the time of the transaction on which it is founded, in order to explain the intention with which any thing was said or done, that he is charged with in the proceedings or by the evidence ; but in this case he may himself be examined under oath by the adverse party.

Art. 71. When the fact inquired of is one of which the knowledge is generally acquired by information of others, or by information joined to personal observation, forming what is usually called facts of public notoriety, they may be stated on such information by parol evidence :

of this nature are—pedigree, boundary, births and deaths, cohabitation, residence, profession or trade, possession with reputation of ownership, general reputation, custom, course of trade, prescription, public historical events. In all these cases, and others of the same description, the witness may testify, not only as to the public notoriety of the fact, but may specify the persons from whom he has derived his information.

Art. 72. What a person, who is dead at the time of trial, has said or done in relation to the subject in controversy, may be given in evidence, if such act or declaration was, at the time of making it, contrary to his pecuniary interest.

Art. 73. In prosecutions for homicide, the deposition of the deceased may be given in evidence, or what he was heard to say after receiving the wound, if he do not live long enough to have his deposition taken, or if circumstances prevent its being taken.

## SECTION IV.

#### Of evidence to the character of parties and witnesses.

Art. 74. In all criminal prosecutions the general character of the party accused may be shown by evidence, but to such points only as would evince a disposition or indisposition to commit the offence with which he is charged. Thus, if the prosecution be for a battery, the defendant may show that his general reputation is that of mildness and forbearance; and on the part of the prosecution, the reverse may be proved.

Art. 75. The general character of witnesses for veracity, or the contrary, may be also shown, both on the part of those who introduce them and on the opposite part.

Art. 76. Evidence of general character may be introduced to discredit a witness, by showing that he is habitually addicted to any vice that evinces a disregard to moral character ; such as intoxication, or that he is a common vagrant ; or if the witness be a woman, that she is a common prostitute.

Art. 77. Particular facts may also be given in evidence ; but they must be of a public and notorious nature, such as conviction for a CRIME ; but this must be proved, either by the production of the records or the oath of the witness himself ; or if the conviction took place out of the state, by testimonial proof.

Art. 78. All facts which would show the incapacity of the witness, either to perceive accurately, or correctly to relate, what he states, may also be shown ; such as a natural imperfection in any of the senses, want of memory or of skill, usual inattention to subjects of the nature of that in question, or general ignorance of them, or a temporary disability arising from disease or intemperance.

Art. 79. Any particular bias, arising from interest, affection, relationship, from fear, enmity, favour, or affection, or intimate friendship to or with either of the parties, or having had disputes with them, or being under their control or influence in the relation of ward, servant, tenant, debtor, or obligated by past favours.

Art. 80. The examinations of the witnesses, taken before the examining magistrate, may be produced to contradict what they may say on the trial, or to show that they have been consistent.

Art. 81. The depositions of such witnesses, taken in the presence of the defendant, pursuant to the directions of the Code of Criminal Procedure, may be read as evidence, if the witness is since dead or cannot be found in the state.

Art. 82. The examination of the defendant, taken before the examining magistrate, if made according to the directions of the Code of Criminal Procedure, may also be produced.

## SECTION V.

### Of written depositions on interrogatories.

Art. 83. All the rules for receiving the oral declarations of witnesses, apply to their examination taken in writing on interrogatories.

Art. 84. When the oral testimony of witnesses is taken down in writing, in the cases provided by law for regulating the practice of the courts, the question shall be taken down as well as the answer, and the answer recorded as it is given.

# TITLE III.

## OF SCRIPTORY EVIDENCE.

Art. 85. Scriptory evidence is of two kinds—AUTHENTICATED and UNAUTHENTICATED.

# CHAPTER I.

## *Of authenticated acts.*

### SECTION I.

### Of the different kinds of authenticated acts.

Art. 86. Authenticated acts are such instruments in writing as are attested by a public officer, legally authorized for that purpose, in the form prescribed by law. They are evidence of that which is attested to have been done in his presence by the officer whose attestation gave them validity; but of nothing more.—Thus, the joint attestation of the speaker of the house of representatives, of the president of the senate, and of the governor, is authentic evidence that a bill has become a law of the state. The attestation of the governor and secretary of state, under the seal of the state, is authentic evidence that the copy to which it is affixed is a true copy of the statute. The signature of the governor to a proclamation issued by him, under the seal of office, to apprehend a person accused of murder, is authentic evidence that such proclamation was issued on the day it bears date, that complaints were made to him of the commission of the crime and of the flight of the defendant, or of any other fact which he certifies to have been done in his presence ; but it is not evidence that the crime was committed or that the party fled.

Art. 87. They are of several kinds :

1st. Legislative acts, passed by the constitutional authority, and attested in the manner prescribed by law.

2d. Records of courts.

3d. Such records of the different branches of the executive government as are made in the legal administration of their different departments, and as are declared to be authentic acts.

4th. Written instruments, made in the presence of and attested by such public officer, as is for that purpose commissioned according to law, and purporting to testify what is said, done, or contracted, by those whose act it is.

## SECTION II.

### Of legislative acts.

Art. 88. Legislative acts are proved, either by a production of the original act deposited in the archives of the state ; by a copy attested by the signature of the person exercising the executive authority of the state, and by the secretary of state, or other proper officer having the custody of the said archives, under the seal of the state ; or, by the printed copy contained in the statute book, or the gazette printed by the printer of the state. Provided, that on the production of either of the said copies of a legislative act, it shall be lawful for any party, alleging a mistake in the printed or other copy, to prove it by producing the copy under the seal of the state, or in such attested copy, by collating it with the original archives, and procuring, in this last case, a correction of the attested copy; but the party alleging such mistake must prove it ; and, until the error be shown, such copy shall be deemed a true one, and shall have its full and entire effect.

Art. 89. There is no distinction in the mode of proof between public and private legislative acts. The court, however, is bound to take notice of and carry into effect all public acts which apply to the facts before them, whether they are pleaded or offered in evidence or not ; but a party claiming a right or exemption, under a private act, must produce it.

Art. 90. A private legislative act is one that concerns certain designated individuals only. All other legislative acts are public.

Art. 91. All acts of incorporation made for regulating the police or local government of any particular part of the state, for the establishment of banks, for authorizing the imposition of a toll, tonnage, wharfage, or other duty, for the establishment of hospitals, or other purposes of charity, or for the promotion of education, religion, or science, are public acts. All other acts of incorporation are private acts.

Art. 92. The enumeration contained in the last article relates solely to the purpose of this title: it does not affect the nature or definition of corporations established by law.

4 H

Art. 93. Judicial records arc all the written proceedings in a court legally constituted and directed to record its decrees. They comprehend, not only the orders and judgments of such courts, but the written pleadings and allegations of parties; the proofs and documents they have produced, when the same are made part of the written proceedings; and the certificates and returns of the officers of such courts ; the verdict of jurors, and all other proceedings, which are entered on the minutes or preserved among the records of such court.

Art. 94. Judicial records of courts, within this state, are proved by a production of the original record, or by a copy attested to be a true copy by the clerk of such court, under the seal of the same, to which must be annexed a certificate signed by the presiding judge of such court, declaring that the person who has attested the same is clerk of such court; but any error or omission in such copy may be rectified by a collation with the original record ; but, unless such error be shown, the copy is a conclusive evidence. All records from other states, must be authenticated in the manner directed by the laws of the United States, in order to be received as proof in this state. Legislative acts from other states, may be proved by the production of such printed statute books as are proved to be received in the courts of such state.

Art. 95. Records of judgments on proceedings in foreign countries, other than the states of the Union, are proved by the certificate of officers, whose duty it is, by the laws of the country in which such court is situated, to give such certificates, together with such other attestation as is required by the laws of such country, to make such copy evidence in other courts of the same country; which fact, to wit, that the attestation is in such form, must be certified by the minister for the proper department of such government, and his signature and office must be certified by the minister of the United States, if there be one in such country; or, if there be none, by some consul of the United States for that district of such country in which the decree was given, under his hand and consular seal; and in countries where there is neither American minister nor consul, the substance of such certificate must be proved by two witnesses, examined on commission or in open court.

Art. 96. Whenever a foreign judgment is made the foundation of a suit or of a defence, and the party wishes to produce the copy, whether authenticated in the manner set forth in the last preceding article or only by the certificate of the clerk or judge, he must, at the time he files his petition or answer, deposit in the court the said copy, and give notice to the opposite party that he intends to produce such copy in evidence ; and if the opposite party shall, within ten days, give notice, in writing, that he will oppose the introduction of such copy, then the party offering the same must prove such record by an examination of the proper officer on a commission ; but, in such case, all reasonable expenditures, made in the execution of such commission, whatever may be the event of the suit, shall be borne by the party opposing the introduction of the copy; provided such copy should, by the return to the commissioner, be proved to have been complete and correct. But if no such notice of opposition be given, the copy certified as aforesaid shall be evidence of such judgment.

Art. 97. If such foreign judgment be not the foundation of the suit, or of the defence, but may be necessary to be produced on some collateral point arising in the cause, then the copy, authenticated as is beforementioned, must be deposited at least fifteen days before the day appointed for the trial of the cause ; and notice must be given as is set forth in the last preceding article, and the same proceedings must be had by the parties as is provided for in the said article.

Art. 98. Nothing in the preceding articles shall prevent the admission of the copy of any foreign record, certified by the recording officer of the court in which it was given and by the judge, as itself good evidence when proved to be a true copy by the oath of a competent witness, taken according to law, who has collated it with the original.

Art. 99. As evidence, a judgment rendered in either of the United States, or in a foreign country, has the same effect, and is subject to the same rules, as are established in the section on resjudicata for judgments rendered in this state ; but no judgment rendered in any court whatever, in a suit in rem, whether by attachment or otherwise, shall have any other of the effects of the resjudicata, except so far as respects the thing, the seizure whereof was the first process in the cause; unless the party appeared and defended such suit, either in person or by attorney.

Art. 100. If the only object be to prove a condemnation in a foreign court of admiralty, it is not necessary to produce copies of any other part of the proceedings than the libel and the final decree of condemnation; and none of the evidence, taken in such court, shall be evidence even between the same parties to prove any other point than the one in contestation in the original cause.

## SECTION IV.

### Of records of the executive branches of government.

Art. 101. The following are the acts of the different departments of executive government, which have the force of authentic acts.

1st. Commissions, or special authority to perform any civil duty, given by the governor, pursuant to law, or any proclamation issued by him. They must be under the seal of the state, and must be signed by the governor, and attested by the secretary of state.

2d. Certificates of election directed by law to be given to persons chosen to fill any place in office, signed by the persons who are authorized to determine the result of such election.

3d. Certificates of the administration of oaths of office, and other oaths necessary to be taken previous to the performance of the duties of any place or office, signed by the persons authorized to administer such oaths.

4th. Entries in the proper books of the registry and cancelling of mortgages. Donations and other acts directed by law to be registered, and such certificate as by law the officer appointed to make such registry, is entitled to give.

5th. Entries in the proper book of the registries which may be

made of births, baptisms, marriages, and deaths, by any officer who is
or may be appointed by law to enregister the same.

The commissions, proclamations, special delegations of authority,
certificates of election, and certificates of administration of oaths, are
themselves the original authentic acts; and those given by the proper
officers in this state, and in the form prescribed by law, need no additional proof, it being the duty of all judges in this state, ex officio,
to know the seals and signatures of the officers whose acts they purport to be. Where the original of these acts cannot be produced, a
copy of the record of the commission or certificate of election, under
the seal of the state, certified by the secretary of state, is authentic
evidence. With respect to the certificate of the administration of
oaths of office, if the original cannot be produced, the fact may be
proved by other testimony, which may be or may not be authentic
according to its nature.

Art. 102. Entries in the proper books of the register of mortgages,
or other officers appointed to enregister any description of acts of baptisms, marriages, births, or deaths, are proved by the official certificates
of such officer, with the addition of his seal of office where he is authorized to keep such seal ; and such copy is an authentic act, as are
also all such official certificates as he is by law authorized to give.

Art. 103. The registry of a mortgage, or of any other act which is
directed to be registered for the purpose of giving notice to those who
may be interested, or the authenticated copy of such registry, is not
evidence of the act itself: it is evidence only, that the law which
directs the registry has been complied with. Therefore, the registry,
or an authenticated copy of it, does not dispense with the introduction
of the act itself, or other legal evidence of its having been made.

SECTION V.

Of notarial acts.

Art. 104. Written instruments, made in the presence and attested
by a public officer duly appointed and commissioned for that purpose,
purporting to testify what is said, done, or contracted by the parties
to such act, are authentic acts, as are the copies of such acts attested by
such officer in the form prescribed by law. These acts are called
"notarial acts ;" but they have the same effect when passed before
any other officer authorized by law, although not a notary ; and
whenever the term notary is used in this chapter, it includes all such
officers as are empowered by law to authenticate private contracts.

Art. 105. All acts passed before a notary shall be written in his
registry, and signed by the contracting party, by the notary, and two
witnesses at least. This written instrument is called the original
notarial act ; it remains as a record in the hands and on the books of
record of the notary. A copy of this notarial act, certified to be a
true copy by the notary or his successor in office, and under his official seal, is full proof of such act in any court within the jurisdiction
of which such officer exercises his functions ; but in any other court
the signature of the notary must be certified to be true, either by the
judge of the court of highest original civil jurisdiction within which
the notary resides, or by the governor under the seal of the state.

Art. 106. In order to give to any notarial instrument the form of an authentic act, it must have the following requisites, the want of either of which destroys its authenticity :

1st. It must contain in the body of the act the name and office of the notary, or other officer, before whom it is passed, and the place for which he is appointed.

2d. The place at which, and the day, month, and year when it was made.

3d. The names and places of abode of the parties ; or, if they have no fixed residence, the last place of their permanent abode.

4th. It must appear that the act was passed within the district of country for which the notary was appointed.

5th. It must be stated to be passed in the presence of at least two witnesses, citizens of this state and inhabitants of the place for which he is appointed.

6th. It must be signed by the party obligated if it be an UNILATERAL contract, or by the declarant if it be a protest or declaration, and by all the parties if it be a SYNALLAGMATIC contract ; and if either of the said parties cannot sign his name, either from want of knowledge, accident, weakness, or disease, he must declare his incapacity and from which of the said causes it proceeds, and such declaration must be inserted in the act. It will not be sufficient for the notary to certify such incapacity, he must certify the declaration of the party.

7th. It must be signed by the notary, and by the witnesses who are named as such in the act. No person is a competent witness for this purpose who cannot write.

8th. Where either of the parties to an act cannot read, the notary must certify that he has read the act to such party in the presence of the witnesses, and that he consented thereto ; and when the party incapable of writing can make a mark, he shall do so, and the notary, or one of the witnesses, shall write opposite thereto the name of such party, stating that it is his mark. When, from whatever cause, the party cannot make the mark, it must be stated in the instrument.

9th. All signatures, as well of parties as of witnesses and of the notary, must be at the end of the instrument ; but for the approval of any correction in the instrument, the signature may either be put in the margin or at the end of the instrument, and a signature by initials will be a sufficient approval of a correction which creates no material change in the instrument ; but every material correction must be approved by a full signature.

10th. All interlineations, erasures, obliterations, or apparent changes, in any part of the act which is necessary to give it validity, in the names of the parties or witnesses, in the expression of any sums, or the description of the thing which is the object of the act, in the date, in the time of any payment, or in any other part of the act, which alters the obligation, or increases or lessens the responsibility of either party, must be enumerated and approved by the signatures of all the parties.

11th. The act must appear to have been passed before one duly authorized by law to give authority to such acts.

Art. 107. All the matters and forms set forth in the last preceding article, are necessary to give to any act, passed before a notary, the force of an authentic act ; but there are some notarial acts, such as testaments, to the validity of which other formalities are specially required, in addition to those above enumerated.

Art. 108. A notarial act is also invalid, as an authentic act, if, on its face, it appears to have been executed by a married woman, without the assent of her husband, or of the judge in cases where such assent is required ; or by a minor, or other person incapable of contracting, without the assistance of a tutor or curator, if such curator or tutor be no party to the act.

Art. 109. Signature, in this title, means the name of the party, written by himself; as evidence of his assent to an instrument as a party, or to attest it as a witness : the family name must be written at length —the baptismal or prenominal name may be abbreviated, or indicated only by the initial letter, or altogether omitted, if such has been the usual mode in which the signer has subscribed his name.

Art. 110. No party to an instrument shall avoid any obligation created thereby, by showing that he has not signed it in his true name, or in the manner in which he usually signed the same, provided the signature be made by him.

## SECTION VI.

### Of the effect of notarial acts.

Art. 111. Notarial acts, passed in the form required by law before an officer duly authorized, are authentic acts, and have the following effects :

1st. As to all persons, even those not parties to the act, it is conclusive evidence that every thing which the notary certifies to have been declared, acknowledged, or done in his presence, and in that of the witnesses, was so declared, acknowledged, and done by the parties ; but against any but the parties and those who succeed to them or to their rights, it has no other effect.   Thus, a bona fide purchase made by an authentic act from a person in possession, who has no title, although it can give no right against the true owner, who was no party to the sale, is yet conclusive evidence against him, for the purpose of establishing a prescription and giving a title to the fruits during the time that the purchaser possessed in good faith.

2d. As to all who were parties to such act, and those who succeeded to them, or to their rights, it is conclusive proof of that, which is the object of such act ; and also of every thing relating immediately to the object of the act—which is therein acknowledged by both parties—or which is recited or enounced by one party and acknowledged by the other, either expressly or by necessary implication.   That recital or enunciation by one party shall be said to be acknowledged by necessary implication, which the other must, from the nature of the transaction, have known, and which it would be his interest to deny if untrue, which is suffered to remain uncontradicted by the act.

That recital or enunciation relates immediately to the object of the act, which, if omitted, would make a material change in the obligations incurred, or rights acquired by either of the parties.

Thus, for the illustration of the different parts of the last rule :—If a sale is made by a notarial act for a certain price, which is promised to be paid in a given time, (this purchase and sale being the object of the act,) it is conclusive proof of that transaction between the parties, so that the purchaser needs no other proof of the sale, nor the seller of the promise to pay the price, than the production of the act itself.

If the thing sold was subject to a yearly rent or charge, and the seller declare that he has deposited the money in the hands of a third person for the payment of the arrears up to the day of sale, this enunciation is not the immediate object of the act; yet it relates immediately to it, because the omission of it would have made a change in the rights and obligations of the parties; but it is not conclusive against the purchaser, unless he expressly acknowledge that it is true, because it is not a fact, which he is supposed to know. If he expressly acknowledge it, it is conclusive, and he can never afterwards call in question the truth of such deposit. But if, in the last example, the rent-charge had, before the sale, been due to the purchaser himself, and the seller had, in the act, declared that all the arrears were paid; this declaration, if uncontradicted by the buyer, would of itself, without any express acknowledgment, by necessary implication, be conclusive evidence that the declaration was true; because the fact, from the nature of the case, was within the knowledge of the purchaser, and it was an enunciation which, if not true, it was his interest to contradict.

If in the sale the vendor declare that he had acquired the property as instituted heir of A. B., and the legal heir of A. B. should bring a suit for the property against the purchaser, alleging that the will, under which the vendor claimed, was void—this enunciation in the act would not be conclusive evidence that it belonged to the estate of A. B., for this enunciation did not immediately relate to the object of the act, which was the sale; nor was it a matter, either within the knowledge of the purchaser, or which he was interested in denying if it was untrue.

3d. Any enunciation made in a notarial act, is evidence against the party making the enunciation in favour of the person who is no party to the act, whether it relate to the object of the suit or not; but it is not conclusive evidence; it amounts to an extrajudicial confession only, and, as such, is ranked in the class of presumptions, which have more or less weight, according to the circumstances under which the declaration was made.

4th. A declaration or enunciation made by one party to an act, and either expressly or by necessary implication acknowledged by another, forms the same kind of proof against both, as set forth in the last preceding article.

5th. An act signed by the parties, intended for a notarial act, but not valid as such for want of some formality required by law, is still good as an act under private signature, if it have the requisites to give it force as a private act; nor can the defect of its not being signed in as many copies as there are parties in interest, be opposed to its validity as a private act.

6th. The mention in an inventory, made by notarial act of any obligation or other paper, forms no such proof against one not a party to the inventory, as to dispense with the production of the original. The entry in the inventory proves that a paper purporting to be such an obligation was produced, but it is not conclusive evidence that it was the act of the party. Where the original has, by other proof, been shown to have existed, and has since been destroyed, and there are circumstances to prove its identity with the paper mentioned in the inventory, it may be admitted as presumptive proof of the contents of such obligation.

7th. Although the enunciations made by the parties are, in the cases above stated, sometimes conclusive and sometimes presumptive proof between the parties, and are sometimes presumptive proof in favour of third persons; they form no species of proof whatever against third persons, and cannot injure their rights or obligate them.

To this rule there is one exception: an enunciation in an act, made many years before it is offered, may at the discretion of the judge, under the limitation hereafter expressed, be admitted as presumptive evidence between those who are not parties to it in questions of age, relationship, descent, affinity, filiation, absence, or death; but in no other questions.

Thus, an ancient notarial act of a family assembly may be admitted as presumptive proof between third persons, that the parties who composed it stood in the various degrees of relationship which they severally enounced. So, too, the enunciation of the deceased, in an authentic and ancient certificate of burial, of the age of the child; in the like certificate of baptism, the time of the death of a person in the act of partition between his heirs, may be permitted as presumptive proof of the enunciations therein contained.

But the discretion of the judge, to admit the testimony mentioned in the exception to the rule, is limited to cases in which, from the date of the act and from other circumstances, he is convinced that the parties making the enunciation had no motive to declare a falsehood.

8th. Notarial acts take effect immediately after their signature. Therefore, no alteration of an act, once perfected, is lawful even if done with the consent of the parties; any modification they desire must be made by a separate act; but such an act cannot affect any rights acquired by third persons by the act itself, or derived from one of the parties after such act.

## SECTION VII.

For what causes and in what manner a notarial act may be declared not authentic.

Art. 112. No notarial act, which contains on the face of it any omission of any of these things which have been herein before enumerated as necessary to give it validity, shall be considered as an authentic act; and the evidence of this shall be the inspection of the authenticated copy, or of the original in cases where it is required to be produced, or of other evidences taken according to the directions of the following article.

Art. 113. When, on the presentation of the copy of a notarial act duly certified, if the party against whom it is produced will declare, on oath, or otherwise make appear to the court that there are defects in the original of the said act, which do not appear on the copy, it shall be the duty of the judge, if the facts are material, and also in all cases where the hand-writing of the parties, witness, or notary, may be legally brought in question, to cause the original to be brought into court, if the same be within the jurisdiction of the court, but if otherwise, then to appoint three proper persons to make a collated copy of such original, and to report specially whether there are any, and if any, what variation between the original and the copy which had been produced, and also between the handwriting of the notary, parties, or witnesses, in question—to compare the acknowledged handwriting of the party whose hand is disputed with that which is in dispute, and to report thereon ; which persons shall be sworn before some magistrate to perform the duty faithfully ; and their report, or that of a majority of them, shall be a legal presumption of the truth of what it contains. After hearing the report of the persons commissioned as aforesaid, and such other legal proofs as may be adduced by the parties, the judge shall determine on the validity of the original act, in cases where it is not within the jurisdiction of the court, in the same manner as he would by inspection if the original had been produced.

Art. 114. There are cases in which a notarial act, although it may contain apparently all the requisites to make it an authentic act, ought not be admitted as such. These are :

1st. Where the signature of the notary, parties, or witnesses, or either of them, are forged.

2d. Where the act has been altered, or a material part, since the execution.

3d. Where either the notary, or either of the witnesses, were not present when the act was signed by the parties or by either of them.

4th. Where the act was falsely read in a material part to a party, who could not read ; or falsely translated in a material part to a party who could not understand the language in which it was written.

5th. Where it was executed out of the limits for which the notary was appointed.

6th. Where the act is signed by one personating the party whom it purports to bind, whether the one so personating him bears the same name or not.

7th. Where the act purports to create any obligation upon, or to dispose of, or affect the property of any person incapable by law of contracting without the aid of a curator or tutor, and no such tutor or curator was party to the act.

8th. Where the act was made in fraud of creditors.

9th. Where it was made without consideration, or for an inadequate consideration, in order to avoid any law regulating successions.

10th. Where it is made under any other circumstances, which, by the laws in force at the time of making the act, shall be declared to render it void.

11th. Where any of the requisites necessary to give validity to the act, have been falsely certified by the notary.

12th. Where the act wants any of the parts or clauses which are necessary by law to give effect to such contract as it purports to be. But this shall not prevent an act, invalid as to one intent, from being operative in another, in cases where it is otherwise allowed by law.

13th. Where either of the parties were in a state of mind, either from bodily weakness, derangement of intellect by intoxication, or other cause, which rendered him incapable of understanding the nature and consequence of the act, and such incapacity must have been apparent to the notary and witnesses.

14th. Where the witnesses have not the qualifications required by law.

15th. Where the consideration, declared to have been paid by the act,

4 I

has not been paid ; and this whether there is a renunciation of the exception of non numerata pecunia, or not.

16th. Where the act contains any disposition of property, or any pecuniary obligation in favour of the notary, or any of his relations, by affinity or consanguinity in the ascending or descending line, or collaterally to the relationship by consanguinity or affinity, of uncle or nephew, inclusively ; and this extends to the case where the disposition is made in the name of a person interposed for the benefit of the notary or any such relation.

17th. Where the act purports to dispose of property which cannot, by law, be conveyed—such as the dotal property of a married woman.

Art. 115. For any one of the causes mentioned in the last preceding article, or for any of the defects apparent on the face of the act, which are in this title declared to destroy its authenticity, a suit may be brought by any one interested in having the said act declared invalid. In which suit the objections made to the same shall be particularly set forth ; and all persons, interested in supporting the validity of the act, must be made parties.

Art. 116. Whenever a notarial or other authentic act is the foundation of any suit, or of the defence to any suit—that is to say, whenever, to support the claim for which the suit is brought, or the defence which is made to the suit, it is necessary to produce such authentic act. In all such cases, a copy of the act, intended to be relied on, shall be filed with the petition, answers, or other pleading in which a reference is made in the same ; and if the party against whom it is produced, intends to object to the same, he must do so specially and in writing, specifying the particular cause of nullity on which he intends to rely ; otherwise no such objection, other than those apparent on the face of the act, can be heard on the trial.

Art. 117. Wherever it may be necessary to introduce an authentic act in evidence, on some collateral matter, not being the foundation of the suit ; or, if introduced by the defendant, of the defence, the party, if he can reasonably be supposed according to the circumstances of the case to have foreseen the necessity of producing such act, shall file a copy thereof ten days at least before the trial, and shall give notice to the opposite party, who may then make his objections in the manner directed by the last article.

Art. 118. If the party who ought, according to the preceding articles, to file the copy of a notarial act on which they mean to rely, do not file it, the court may force its production, on the application of the opposite party ; or, at his option, he may make his objections verbally at the trial ; and if they are supported either by inspection or evidence, the act must be rejected as evidence, and the party whose duty it was to have filed the act, cannot in such case object to the want of notice of the objections.

Art. 119. If it appears that the party could not reasonably have foreseen the necessity of producing such authentic act, and an objection be taken to its authenticity for any cause not apparent on the face of the act, the court, if they think the act material evidence, and if the objection be supported by affidavit either of the party or other person, may, according to circumstances, give the necessary time to make and answer the objections.

Art. 120. In all cases of objections to the validity of any act, which appears on the face of it to have all the formalities required by law to give it authenticity, the burthen of proving the defects lies on the party objecting to the validity of the act.

Art. 121. On the question of the validity of an authentic act, the persons whose names are subscribed as witnesses, when not otherwise incompetent, are competent witnesses.

The notary is also a good witness in all cases where no objection has been made to the act in any point that implies a want of integrity, misconduct, or inattention on his part; or where, if made, they are entirely unsupported.

Art. 122. Authentic acts, not notarial, may be declared invalid for either of the following causes:

1st. Forgery of the signatures, or either of them, or of the body of the act.

2d. Want of legal authority in the party making such act.

3d. Making the act out of the limits for which the officer was appointed.

4th. If the authentic act be a commission, or other authority given under a law, the want of the qualifications required by law in the person commissioned or designated to perform the duty, including the objection to the want of security, and the taking of the oaths of office where they are required.

5th. Fraud in obtaining the act by a false personification, or such other false pretence as would make the party practising it liable to punishment if they had been used to procure the delivery of goods or money, under such penal laws as may be in force at the time of using such false pretences.

6th. Bribery, either to the officer making the act, or any other person, to do any thing necessary to procure the act to be made.

Art. 123. Suits for invalidating all authentic acts (not notarial) and oppositions to their introduction in evidence, shall be governed by the same rules as are laid down respecting notarial acts.

Art. 124. Forgery and bribery, mentioned as causes for invalidating a notarial or other authentic act, shall be construed according to the definitions of those offences given in such penal law as shall be in force at the time such acts were made.

Art. 125. When a notarial act, or other authentic act, shall, by final sentence of a court, be declared void for any cause, the court pronouncing such sentence shall direct that it shall be noted in the margin of the original of such notarial act, and of the record of such other authentic act, if any such record shall have been kept, and on the certified copy which was produced in court.

## CHAPTER II.

*Of unauthenticated scriptory evidence.*

### SECTION I.

#### Of the different kinds of unauthenticated scriptory evidence.

Art. 126. Unauthenticated scriptory evidence is of two kinds:

1. That which is attested by the signature of the party whose act it purports to be, called an act under private signature.

2. All other written evidence not so attested.

## SECTION II.

### Of evidence under private signature.

Art. 127. All written instruments, signed by the party whose act they purport to be, which are not authentic acts, are called acts under private signature.

Art. 128. Independent of positive law, no written instrument is, in its nature, evidence of the truth which it contains. It shows that certain covenants are written, and that certain names are subscribed to them ; but in itself it contains no proof, not even of the presumptive kind, that those names were subscribed by the parties, or that the covenants were made by them. In authentic acts this proof is supplied by the credit which the law declares shall be given to the attestation of a sworn officer. To acts under private signature, no such credit is given ; the production of them does not raise even simple presumptions of their validity.

Art. 129. But although the law creates no presumption from the production of such an act, yet to avoid unnecessary delays and expenses, it permits the party against whom it is produced to be interrogated whether the signatures are true. From this permission result the different effects produced by the confession, the denial, or the ignorance of the fact, stated in the answer of the defendant, or of his refusal to acknowledge or deny the writing.

Art. 130. In every case where any party to a suit finds it necessary to produce a writing under private signature, either to support his action or maintain his defence, and wishes to have the answer of the opposite party, as to the truth of the signature, he must annex the original instrument to his petition or answer, and must pray that the opposite party may declare whether the signature be true or false.

Art. 131. If the signature which a party is thus called on to confess or deny, purports to be his own, the answer must be explicit, either that he confesses it to be his, or that it is forged. An answer which does not directly deny the signature, shall be deemed to be a confession.

Art. 132. If the signature purports to be, not that of the party himself, but of some other person, for whose obligation the opposite party endeavours to make him liable, either personally or by virtue of some office, duty, or trust, then the party interrogated is not obliged to answer explicitly, as in the former case. If he have seen the party write whose signature is in question, or is, from other circumstances, acquainted with his handwriting, he must say so, and declare whether he believes the signature to be true or false. It is only when he declares himself utterly ignorant of the handwriting that he is dispensed with declaring his belief.

Art. 133. The answers to these interrogatories need not to be on oath, unless it is required by the opposite party ; and when it is, the effect is regulated by special provisions for that purpose.

Art. 134. The recognition or denial of a signature must be made by the party himself, who is interrogated. A wilfully false answer, not only incurs the civil effects herein provided, but is considered as an offence, and is punishable by the Penal Code.

Art. 135. The following are the effects produced by the answers, or by the refusal to answer, to the interrogatory demanding the recognition of a signature.

1st. If the party avow the signature, whether it be his own or that of another for whose obligation he is responsible, it makes the act, as to him and his representatives, an authentic act, and judgment may be immediately rendered thereon, without any other proof or trial—if such avowal be not accompanied by some legal defence, in the manner hereinafter provided; and it has, with respect to third persons, the same effect that an authentic act in any other form has by law.

2d. If it purport to be the act of one for whose obligation the respondent is liable, and he say that he is acquainted with the signature and believes it to be true, it creates a legal presumption in favour of the act.

3d. If the signature be denied, or if in cases where he is permitted to say so, the respondent answers, that he is ignorant whether the signature be true or false ; then no presumption is to be raised on either side. But the burthen of proving the signature true lies on him who asserts it.

4th. If the party interrogated do not answer in the time prescribed by the rules of court, the default is equivalent to a confession, and gives authenticity to the act.

5th. If the party avowing the signature have a legal defence to make against the operation of the instrument, supposing the signature to be true, he may set forth the same in his answer, and then the obligation of the act shall not be carried into effect until such obligations be decided on. A legal defence, in the meaning of this article, is any such as might be made on an ordinary trial, after the signature to the instrument has been proved.

Art. 136. In all cases, whether under this section or not, when it becomes necessary to prove handwriting, it shall be done in the manner following :

§ 1st. If there be one or more subscribing witnesses, one of them at least must be examined, if he be within the state, and his testimony that he saw the party sign, is direct evidence, as is also the testimony of a witness to the same fact, although he was not a subscribing witness.

§ 2d. If the names of subscribing witnesses appear to the act, and they are dead or not within the state, the handwriting of one at least of the said witnesses, and of the party to the act, must be proved in one or all of the modes following, that is to say—by a witness who has seen the party write, or who has acquired a knowledge of his handwriting by correspondence, (by which is meant, writing letters and receiving answers, under such circumstances as give no suspicions of deception.)

Handwriting may also be proved by a comparison with some authentic act, or other instrument acknowledged by the party, or positively proved by witnesses in the same cause to be his. This mode of proof may be resorted to at the request of either party, and the comparison is made by the judge on his own inspection ; but he may, at the like request, be assisted by persons, skilled in the knowledge of handwritings, named by the court, and sworn to compare the papers and truly to give their opinion to the judge. But no writing can serve as an instrument of comparison which has been judicially denied by the party, although it may have been proved to be his.

§ 3d. If there are no subscribing witnesses to the act, and none who can give direct evidence of the signature, then the handwriting may be proved in either or all of the modes set forth in the last preceding paragraph.

§ 4th. An act, under private signature, may also be proved by an authentic act, if it be therein either recited or referred to in such a manner as that its identity is clearly established. Thus, if in a notarial act of inventory, a promissory note, given to the deceased, by a person who signed the inventory, as executor or tutor, is particularly set forth, and the note itself is referred to by a mark at the time of making the notarial act; this sufficiently identifies the note, and renders no other proof necessary. But if the act, under private signature, be merely recited in an authentic act to which the maker of the note is party, but the note be not produced and marked at the time of making the authentic act, then other proof must be resorted to, to identify the act under private signature which is in dispute, with the one recited in the authentic act.

§ 5th. None of the above modes of proving an act under private signature exclude the admission of the testimony of witnesses, who, although they were neither present at the making of the act, nor are acquainted with the handwriting, yet testify to facts to prove or disprove the act, which could not reasonably be supposed to have happened if the signature were in the one case, and in the other were not that of the party.

§ 6th. The proof by comparison of hands alone, unsupported by other circumstances, is not a sufficient evidence of the validity of an act under private signature, where the signature has been denied.

Art. 137. No suit can be brought for the purpose of making the party to an act, under private signature, acknowledge or deny it, so as to give it the effect of an authentic act, before the time limited in the obligation for it to become due has elapsed, unless in cases where by law it is made exigible before, except as is provided in the following section.

SECTION III.

Of copies.

Art. 138. It is a general rule of evidence, that copies are not evidence when the original can be resorted to. Copies of certain authentic acts are modified exceptions to this rule. There is no exception as to acts under private signature. There are, however, different kinds of copies of such acts entitled to different degrees of credit, in cases where the original cannot be produced. There are formal and informal notarial copies, and unattested copies.

Art. 139. If the holder of an act, under private signature, thinks the original is exposed to risk of loss, or fears that the evidence may not be procured when wanted, he may, at any time at his own expense, present a petition to any court of competent jurisdiction, and pray that the party who has signed the act may be summoned to attend at the office of some notary, at a given time, in order to witness the registry of such act, a copy whereof must be annexed ; and the party shall be summoned to attend accordingly.

Art. 140. If the party summoned shall file his answer to such petition, and deny the signature to the act, then that fact shall be tried as in ordinary cases, and if found in favour of the petitioner, judgment shall be rendered for him with costs, directing that the instrument shall be registered.

Art. 141. If the party summoned does not deny the signature, but (in cases where such answer is permitted) shall say, that he is ignorant whether it be true or false, then evidence must be produced as in common cases ; and if it be found that the act is valid, it shall be ordered to be registered.

Art. 142. If the party make no answer, and shall attend at the time and place directed for the registry, whether he then acknowledge the act or not, the notary, on production of a certified copy of the petition and the judge's order, of the return of the proper officer certifying that the party was duly summoned, or in cases where after proof of the act in court, it shall be ordered to be registered, on production of that judgment, shall register the act in his ordinary register, and shall annex thereto the certified copies of the previous judicial proceedings.

Art. 143. If the party, after being summoned, do neither answer nor attend, the notary shall, in like manner, proceed to copy the act and annex the proceedings. Authenticated copies of records, thus made, are called copies in form, and they have the same force and effect as the originals, if the said originals should be lost or destroyed ; but, if not proved to be so lost or destroyed, they must be produced in any suit brought thereon. The said copy and proceedings shall be authentic evidence of the signature ; but this shall not entitle the plaintiff to prompt execution thereon ; it only dispenses him with the proof of the signature and with the production of the original, in case it be lost or destroyed.

Art. 144. Proof of the destruction of an original act has a different effect from that which is produced by showing that it is lost. In the first case, the court may, on production of the formal copy or other legal proof, give immediate effect to the obligation of the act. In the last, they must direct that security shall be given to repay the money, if the original should be produced in the hands of a bona fide holder, within such time as the court, in their discretion, shall direct, or order that the judgment shall not be executed until public notice shall have been given for such a time and at such places as the court shall direct, describing the instrument, setting forth the judgment and calling on all persons to allege any reasons why it should not be carried into effect. The provisions of this article apply to all cases where judgment is given, or evidence of the contents of an instrument lost or destroyed, as well as in cases coming under this section.

Art. 145. Acts may also be recorded without any judicial proceeding, if done in the presence of the party obligated, testified by their signature, and attested in the common form by the notary. Authenticated copies of such records are also copies in form, and have the force and effect with the copies mentioned in the preceding article.

Art. 146. Acts under private signature may also be transcribed on the registry of a notary, without any judicial order, and out of the presence of the parties. This registry, and notarial copies thereof, are called informal copies. They do not fully replace the original, in case of its loss, as the formal copies do. They have, however, the following effects :

1. They serve, as the foundation of a prescriptive right, from the time of the registry only.

2. They verify the existence of the act, back at least to the period of its registry, where the time of the execution is in question.

3. Where the party has enjoyed or exercised the right given, or possessed the property purported to be conveyed, by such act, for ten years from the time of registry, without interruption, it has the force of an authentic act.

4. Connected with other proof of the execution of the original act and its loss, and of the identity of the paper which was registered with such original, they may form, according to circumstances, presumptive evidence of the contents of such original.

Art. 147. An informal copy, without the intervention of a justice or of a public officer, is called an unattested copy, and it may, when the loss of the original is proved, be admitted as presumptive evidence, to show what were its contents, in cases where it can be established, by legal proof, that the copy is correct, and that the original, from which it was taken, was executed by the party against whom it is produced.

Art. 148. In case it is proved that the original was purposely destroyed by the party offering the copy, or by him under whom he claims ; no copy, not even a formal one, shall be admitted in evidence.

Art. 149. When the original is proved to be in the possession of the opposite party, an informal copy is presumptive evidence of the contents, if the original is not produced after due notice. In such case, even parol proof may be resorted to for that purpose in the manner hereinafter provided.

Art. 150. Original acts, under private signature, may also be deposited in the office of a notary, who must enter in his register an act of deposit.

Art. 151. The act of deposit must declare at whose request it is made, and designate the parties to the act who were present at such deposit ; it must be signed by those parties, by the notary, and two witnesses, in the form of other notarial acts. The notary must annex thereto the act deposited, having first made his paraph at the foot of every page of writing contained in such act, and carefully noted all interlineations, erasures, or obliterations, appearing thereon.

Art. 152. Acts thus deposited, and copies thereof duly attested, have the force of authentic acts against the parties who have signed such act of deposit, from the date of the act deposited. Against third persons they have the same effect which authentic acts are declared to have, only from the date of the deposit.

Art. 153. Acts deposited by one party alone have no effect as authentic acts, except against him ; but they have all the other effects which, in a preceding article, are ascribed to informal copies.

Art. 154. The ex parte depositions of witnesses to the execution of an act, under private signature, give it no additional validity, nor are they a sufficient warrant for a notary to make a copy in form.

## SECTION IV.

### Of the form and effect of acts under private signature.

Art. 155. GENERAL PROVISION.—All the rules contained in the succeeding section apply exclusively to acts under private signature, unless the contrary be expressed.

## SECTION V.

### Of the requisites to an act under private signature.

Art. 156. An act under private signature may be made the evidence of all kinds of obligations or declarations, excepting those which by law are directed to be made by authentic act only ; it must be signed with the names of those whom it purports to obligate, or by the declarant if it be a mere declaratory act.

Art. 157. The signature must be made at the end of the act, in the proper handwriting of the party, if he can write; it must consist of the name commonly subscribed by such party to his other writings; but no act shall be invalidated because the party has falsely pretended that he could not write, or has made his signature differently from his usual manner.

Art. 158. If the party cannot write, his signature shall consist of a mark made by him at the end of the act, in the presence of two witnesses, and of his name written by one of them, with a declaration that it is the mark of the party. This signature must be attested by that of the two witnesses.

Art. 159. If the party can read, but from whatever cause, is unable to write, he must, before affixing his mark, declare in the presence of the witnesses that he has read the instrument, or that it has been read to him. If he cannot read, the instrument must be read to him intelligibly by one of the witnesses in the presence of the other.

Art. 160. No instrument, purporting to be the act of a person who has not himself signed the same with his name, shall have any validity against such person, unless the requisites prescribed by the last two preceding articles have been complied with, or the party shall judicially avow the validity of the act, after having the same read to him by an officer of the court.

Art. 161. If an act be defective, for the want of any of the formalities above described, its execution is no bar to a suit founded on the obligation of which it was intended as the evidence, if such obligation can be sustained by other proof.

Art. 162. It is not necessary to the validity of such an act, that any part but the signature should be in the handwriting of the party obligated.

Art. 163. In an instrument containing an obligation respecting money, or any other article of which the sum, quantity, or number, is expressed in words in the body of the instrument, and repeated elsewhere on the paper in figures, if there be any difference between such a repetition and the body of the instrument, the latter shall be esteemed the

4 K

true numeration, unless an error of calculation appears on the face of the act. If the numeration, both in the body of the instrument and out of it, be in figures, other evidence may be admitted to prove the intent of the parties.

Art. 164. Acts containing no other than communicative, or other synallagmatic contracts, must have the legal signatures of all the parties who, by the terms of the act, are obligated to each other thereby; if any of the signatures of such parties are wanting, the act is invalid as to the others.

Art. 165. If the act purports to contain communicative, or other synallagmatic contracts, between certain parties, and also a unilateral contract, relative to the same thing, by which they are jointly bound to another, it need not be signed by the party to whom the obligation is made by the unilateral contract.

# CHAPTER III.

*Of scriptory evidence not attested by the signature of party.*

## SECTION I.

### Of the different kinds of unattested scriptory evidence.

Art. 166. Evidence, coming under this division, is of two kinds:

1. Writings which, from their form and nature, show that they were intended to receive the signature of a party, and are therefore imperfect without it. Of this kind are unsigned contracts of any kind, declarations of trust, testaments, and codicils.

2. Writings which, from their nature, do not appear to have been intended to be attested by any signature. Such are entries in account books, family records of births and deaths, and memoranda of other events.

## SECTION II.

### Of writings intended to be signed by the parties.

Art. 167. Writings of the first kind are never to be admitted as direct proof of the contract, or disposition of which they would have been the evidence, if they had been perfected. They may be admitted as presumptive evidence—

1st. Of the intent to make the contract, or disposition in case where such intent is material to the issue.

2d. Of the truth of any other enunciation contained in the writings.

3d. Of the knowledge which the party making such writing had of any fact therein stated.

But such writing cannot be admitted at all, unless it is in the handwriting of the party whose act it purports to be, or is proved to have been made by his direction, or to have been approved by him after it was made.

## SECTION III.

### Of writings not intended to have been signed by the parties.

Art. 168. Writings of the second kind may be admitted (against the party making them) as presumptions of the fact they purport to state, when they are proved to be in his handwriting, or to have been made by his direction, or to have been read and approved by him.

Art. 169. The party against whom either of the two kinds of unattested writings is produced, may be admitted to give an explanation, on oath, of the circumstances under which the same were made, and the intent of making them—subject to cross-examination.

Art. 170. These kinds of written evidence can be admitted for the party who made them, only when it appears that they were made at a time and under circumstances which show that they were not intended to create legal evidence for the party making them.

Art. 171. When any written evidence is produced, under the preceding article, the opposite party may demand that the other be examined on oath.

## SECTION IV.

### Of writings not made by the parties to the suit.

Art. 172. All the previous provisions of this chapter relate to writings made by one of the parties to the suit, or by some one under whom he claims, or by the direction of one of them. Writings made by others, in which are included those which are printed, and maps and plans, can be introduced in the following cases:

1st. Historical works—to elucidate any historical fact that may become material in a litigated cause.

2d. Books of art or science—when any thing, appertaining to the branch of learning of which they treat, is in dispute.

3d. Maps or plans—to elucidate questions of locality.

When made by persons who had no interest in making erroneous representations to the prejudice or advantage of either of the parties, and who are either dead or so situated that their testimony cannot be procured. Or,

When legally attested to be accurate by the persons who made them, or by others who have verified the delineations they contain.

4th. Accounts stated or calculations made by persons who prove them to be accurate.

5th. Nautical and other almanacs—whenever the calculations they contain are material to the issue.

# TITLE IV.

## OF SUBSTANTIVE EVIDENCE.

Art. 173. Substantive evidence being that which arises from the existence or position of an object in relation to the fact in dispute, it follows, that unless it comes within the scope of that evidence which is offered to the senses of the judge in the situation and under the circumstances which make it material to the cause, it requires other evidence for its introduction. A bloody dagger is substantive evidence: if the judge saw it in the hand of the assassin immediately after the blow was struck, it would be the foundation of evidence coming within his own knowledge; otherwise, it must be supported by testimony to show when and where it was found, and the instrument itself forms the substantive evidence.

Art. 174. The following are examples of substantive evidence : the mark on a tree, coinciding with that stated by testimonial or scriptory evidence in cases of disputed boundary, is substantive evidence of a land-mark. The number of concentric circles in the wood, that has grown over the mark, is substantive evidence of the number of years that have elapsed since it was made.

The inscription on a monument or tombstone, is presumptive evidence of the time of birth or death, and the other material facts it commemorates.

# TITLE V.

## OF PRESUMPTIVE EVIDENCE.

Art. 175. Presumptions are of two kinds : such as are the result of the reason only of the judge, exercised on the circumstances which are proved, without any express direction of law to guide him in his conclusions, which are called simple presumptions ; and legal presumptions, which are such as the law expressly directs to be drawn from certain circumstances.

Art. 176. The difference between a simple and a legal presumption is this, that the first is an inference drawn by the judge, from the circumstances by the unrestrained exercise of his reason ; the last is a deduction made by the law itself, which the judge is forced to adopt, whatever may be his own conclusions from the facts :

That a man of good character will not tell a falsehood ;

That other things being equal, a man will do that which is most conducive to his interest and happiness ;

That a mother will not abandon her infant ;

Are examples of simple presumptions, drawn from the structure of the human mind.

That, if the obligation is delivered to the debtor, the debt has been paid ;

That the rent due from former years has been paid, when a receipt is produced for the last year ;

Are other instances of simple presumptions, drawn, not like the former from nature, but from the common course of business and affairs. All these, although natural conclusions, are simple presumptions, because there is no positive law directing them to be drawn.

That the person who has been in the peaceable possession of real property for more than a year, is the owner ;

That, when no time is expressed for the duration of a lease of a predial estate, it shall be for a year ;

Are examples of legal presumptions, which the law expressly orders to be drawn.

Art. 177. The effect of a presumption, whether simple or legal, in favour of any affirmative or negative proposition, is, that the proof of such proposition is considered as established, until the contrary is shown by direct proof, or rendered doubtful by other presumptions.

Art. 178. When the party, who alleges a fact, brings no evidence of any kind to support it, the want of such evidence creates a presumption in favour of the party who denies.

Art. 179. When the existence of one fact necessarily supposes the existence of another, so that, if one be true the other cannot, in the nature of things, be false, the induction drawn from the establishment of the first fact is not a presumption, but conclusive evidence.

Art. 180. The division of presumptions heretofore known in our law, under the name of *presumptiones juris et de jure*, is abolished. Evidence, heretofore arranged under that head, will be found in its proper division in this title.

Art. 181. A legal presumption (unless declared by law to be conclusive) has no greater force of itself than a simple presumption, and may be counteracted by one if sufficiently strong.

Thus, the lease of a predial estate, when no time is expressed, creates a legal presumption that it is to continue for a year ; but if the lessor, at the time of making the lease, with the knowledge and assent of the lessee, makes another to a third person, to commence at the end of three months from the time of making the first, the first presumption is counteracted by the second.

Art. 182. Presumptions can only be raised from facts, which appear by legal testimony ; therefore, a matter that cannot be given in evidence, cannot be a legal foundation for any presumption.

Art. 183. Simple presumptions must be founded :

First, on the establishment of some fact by legal testimony.

Secondly, by such deduction from that fact as is warranted by a consideration of the usual propensities or passions of human nature ; by the usual course of business ; by the particular habits or passions of the individual, whose act is in question ; or by the course of nature.

# TITLE VI.

## OF DIRECT EVIDENCE.

Art. 184. Direct evidence being that which, if true, conclusively establishes the proposition in question, it follows that this kind of evidence gives rise to one inquiry only, to wit—Whether the fact be true? The mind once convinced of this, has no other operation to perform, in order to arrive at the truth of the proposition asserted, which must be true, if the evidence be true. In all cases, therefore, where any doubt remains of the fact in question, after the mind of the judge is fully satisfied that the evidence, offered in support of it, is true; such evidence is not direct, but presumptive only.

Art. 185. Although the effect of direct evidence, when established to be true, is conclusive of the fact in question; yet the truth of such evidence (in cases where it is not declared by law to be conclusive) depends on presumptions more or less strong. The declaration of a witness, that he saw the act in controversy done, is direct evidence, and (if the judge have no doubt that the witness tells the truth) is conclusive. But whether the judge will give credit to the witness, must depend on the presumptions in favour of, or against his veracity, arising from character and other circumstances. Thus, too, the authority of written testimony, even of records, (independent of positive law,) depends on the presumption, that the witnesses who prove, or the public officer who recorded them, would not attest a falsehood.

Art. 186. It results, from the preceding articles, that direct testimony (when not declared by law to be conclusive) may be counteracted, not only by other direct contrary evidence, but by presumptions.

# TITLE VII.

OF CONCLUSIVE EVIDENCE.

## CHAPTER I.

*Definition and division of the different kinds of conclusive evidence.*

Art. 187. Proof of any kind may produce conviction in the mind of the judge of the truth or falsity of any proposition; but no evidence is called conclusive in this code, but that which is declared to be such by it or by anterior law.

Art. 188. When the law has declared that certain proof forms conclusive evidence of any fact, the judge, whatever may be his own conclusion, can make no other than such as has been drawn by the law. He can admit no presumptions or direct proof to weaken the effect of evidence, so declared to be conclusive;· but in the manner prescribed by law, in particular specified cases, he may admit evidence to disprove its existence.

Art. 189. Conclusive evidence is classed under several heads :

First—Such as arises from the uniform course of nature.

Second—That which is expressly declared to be such by law.

Third—That which is produced in the mind of the judge by the clear and unequivocal exercise of his senses.

That, where maternity is proved, there must have been cohabitation, is an example of the first class.

Where there is no personal incapacity, cohabitation is conclusive proof of the second class, that the issue of the wife is the issue of the husband.

And an example of the third class may be given in the case where the issue is, record or no record, and the judge decides it by inspection.

Art. 190. In order that the course of nature should be the foundation of conclusive proof, it must be the invariable course of nature; its general course only gives rise to presumptions. Proof that an absentee was born two hundred years ago, is conclusive proof that he is dead, because no instance has been known of human life extended to that period. If it be shown that he was born one hundred years before, the law creates a presumption of his death, which may, however, be counteracted by proof, because, though it be the general course of nature for men to die before that age, it is not invariable.

Art. 191. When the law, by the enactment of positive rules, declares certain evidence to be conclusive, it is done to avoid litigation or fraud, and prevent the temptation to perjury.

Some of these rules are declaratory of the conclusions drawn from the invariable course of nature, mentioned in the preceding articles; others are positive provisions, established by legislative wisdom, for the object above stated in this article.

The birth of a child more than three hundred days after the death of the husband, is conclusive proof that such child is not his, and is an example of the declaratory rule above mentioned, as the same is contained in o﹒ law as it now stands.

The authority given to a judgment between the parties, to an authentic act, and to a judicial confession, are examples of the positive rule.

## CHAPTER II.

### Of resjudicata.

#### SECTION I.

##### What judgments are valid as resjudicata.

Art. 192. Resjudicata is whatever has been finally decided by a court of competent jurisdiction—proceeding according to the forms of law—by a valid sentence—on a matter alleged and either denied or expressly or impliedly confessed by the other; and it is conclusive evidence of that which it decides, between the same parties or those that represent them, litigating for the same thing, under the same title, and in the same quality.

Art. 193. Such judgment may be used, either as a plea (in which case it bars any other suit brought for the same cause) or as evidence, and is then conclusive of that which it decides, under the modifications contained in the following articles.

Art. 194. The decision must be final, that is to say, it must be such as the court, rendering it, could not alter, on the application of either party, or reconsider it of its own accord; therefore, an interlocutory order that a party account ; a judgment that needs confirmation; the verdict of a jury, or even a final judgment, before it is signed, and before the time has elapsed within which it may be set aside on a motion for a new trial or rehearing, has not the force of resjudicata. A judgment appealed from has not the force of resjudicata, and is not even presumptive proof ; but a final judgment, although the time for appealing may not have elapsed, is conclusive proof until the appeal be made.

Art. 195. By appeal, in this title, is meant any legal process whatever, by which the judgment of an inferior court may be reconsidered and modified or annulled.

Art. 196. The judgment, to form conclusive proof, must have been rendered by a competent tribunal. A sentence, having all the other requisites, is no proof, if the person who rendered it had no power to decide on the subject matter in dispute between the parties ; but this want of jurisdiction must appear by an examination of the proceedings in the court in which the judgment was rendered, and of the law by which the court rendering it was empowered to act : and no allegation of any matter not appearing from the said laws and proceedings, shall be admitted to show a want of jurisdiction, although such allegation would have deprived the court of its jurisdiction, had it been pleaded and proved in the original cause.

Thus, a judgment given for more than one hundred dollars by a justice of the peace, under our present laws, is no evidence that the defendant owes that sum, because the court has no jurisdiction ; or that he owes any smaller sum, because the whole judgment is void.

But a judgment rendered in a court of the United States, in a suit brought by a person styling himself an alien against a citizen of the state, would be conclusive evidence, although in fact he was not an alien ; nor can any evidence of that fact be admitted in opposition to the judgment.

Art. 197. Where the court, in which the judgment relied on as evidence has been given, is one of limited jurisdiction, either as to sum, person, place, or the nature of the suits of which it can take cognizance, its decisions are no proof, unless the circumstances necessary to confer jurisdiction appear on the record of the suit.

Art. 198. The courts of this state will ex officio take notice of the jurisdiction given to the different tribunals within the same ; but where a judgment given in another state, or in a foreign country, is relied on, the production of the judgment, duly authenticated, is presumptive evidence that the court had a competent jurisdiction, unless the contrary appear on the record ; bnt such presumption may be removed by showing the want of jurisdiction by such evidence as is allowed by law.

Art. 199. Whenever a judgment is offered, either as presumptive or conclusive evidence, all the proceedings in the suit, in which such judgment was rendered, must be produced.

Art. 200. Every judgment to operate as evidence of the thing judged, must have been rendered in the forms which are prescribed by law, in order to give validity to the judgment, unless the matter which is alleged as want of form has been either impliedly or expressly assented to by the party who alleged it.

Thus, the want of a citation is a defect that would render the judgment void ; but if the party has expressly acknowledged service of the petition, or impliedly waived the necessity of a citation, by putting in an answer, this shall not be made an objection.

Art. 201. The want of form, prescribed by law for the validity of a judgment, must (in order to bar its operation as resjudicata) be such as is apparent on the face of the record. No other evidence can be resorted to, in order to prove any such defect.

Art. 202. A sentence to produce the effect of resjudicata, must not only have been rendered, but must be in itself valid, according to the forms of law.

Art. 203. Judgments may be erroneous and unjust without being invalid, within the purview of the last article. Whether the error be in the construction of law, or the deduction from fact, the judgment is valid, unless appealed from ; but an invalid judgment is one that appears on the face of it to be void.

## SECTION II.

### What judgments are invalid to produce the effect of resjudicata.

Art. 204. Judgments, under the following circumstances, are not valid under the preceding articles :

1st. When the judgment is uncertain, and is not rendered certain by some part of the record. Thus, a judgment that the defendant pay the damages which the plaintiff sustained, is uncertain; but if the judgment had been to recover what the plaintiff demanded, it would be rendered certain, by referring to the plaintiff's demand. If it were to recover damages as A. should determine, it would not be ·void, but could not operate as resjudicata for another reason, because such judgment would not be final.

2d. When the judgment pronounces something expressly contrary to the law ; by which is meant, when it declares that what is acknowledged by all to be law, shall not be observed : as if on a plea of infancy, to avoid a contract, it should declare, that because the defendant was twenty years of age, he should be bound. But a decision on the construction of law is still binding, although the judge may have been wrong in his construction. Nor is the force of a judgment lessened, although the evidence should not warrant the conclusion drawn by the judge.

3d. When there is an evident error of calculation appearing in the judgment itself : as if in a suit for the value of three hogsheads of sugar, the sentence should be, that the defendant pay, at the rate of $70 per hogshead, the sum of 250 dollars.

4th. Where the judgment is contrary to the judicial confession of the party in the same suit : as if the decree should declare, that a defendant should go quit of a debt demanded by the plaintiff, and which the defendant had confessed in his answer to be due.

5th. Where the decree is given against one not a party to the suit.

6th. Where the judgment has been rendered against one who appears in the suit to be a minor, or other person who is not, by law, competent to defend his own interests without the intervention of his curator or tutor, or other person designated by law to watch over his interest. This rule includes married women, who appear without being author-

4 L

ized by their husbands, or by the court, in cases in which authorization is required.

7th. Where the party can show, in the manner hereinafter prescribed, that the judgment has been obtained by forgery or fraud, and the party had no notice in time to avail himself of the objection in the court where the judgment was rendered.

Art. 205. The judgment must also be in a matter alleged by the parties in the suit in which it is given. Thus, if the demand be for one acre of land, and the judgment is that the plaintiff recover three acres, this judgment would be neither conclusive evidence of his title to the two additional acres, nor a bar to the defendant if he should sue to recover them.

Art. 206. It is not sufficient that the matter on which the judgment is given be alleged by one party; it must also be denied or admitted by the other party: but a general denial of all facts alleged, is sufficient for this purpose, without specially negativing the several facts alleged.

Art. 207. The denial or admission, referred to in the last two preceding articles, may be either express or implied. A denial of the fact in question is implied when it is a necessary consequence from the denial of another fact. Thus, a denial that the party was ever indebted, is an implied denial of the charge of a sum alleged to be due for interest; but an allegation that the principal sum has been paid, is no negative of the interest being due.

Art. 208. A refusal or neglect to answer in the time prescribed by the rules of procedure, creates an implied admission of the allegations to which the answer is required. Therefore, a judgment by default, rendered definitively, is resjudicata, although the fact, on which it is pronounced, was neither expressly denied or admitted.

Art. 209. A judgment absolving a party from that which he has judicially confessed to be due in the same suit (provided such confession has not been set aside) is not resjudicata in favour of the person making the confession.

Art. 210. Such judgment as is described in the foregoing articles is conclusive; that is, it is a bar when pleaded, and conclusive proof when offered in evidence, of that which it decides ; but of nothing else contained in such judgment : therefore, nothing alleged by way of inducement, illustration, argument, or example, in giving the judgment, has the force of a judgment.

Art. 211. The pleadings in each cause are the only evidence of what was alleged, and denied, or confessed, and the decisory part of the judgment of that which was decided.

SECTION III.

Against whom the resjudicata may be given in evidence.

Art. 212. The effect of resjudicata is confined to the parties in the suit, or to those who succeed to their interest. There are, however, exceptions to this rule, which will be particularly noticed.

Art. 213. Parties are those only who appear in the suit and allege or answer ; who have been cited in the manner prescribed by law, although they do not appear or answer, or who have intervened in the suit to contest or prosecute the same.

Art. 214. No person can be concluded by a judgment, although a party to it, unless for the amount of the interest, which, at the time of rendering such judgment, he had or claimed in the matter in controversy. No interest accruing after such judgment, by any party, is affected by it. Thus, if the heir or executor sue one for effects belonging to the succession, and it should appear that the defendant had no property belonging to the estate, and judgment be thereupon rendered in his favour, this judgment shall be no bar to a subsequent suit, against the same defendant, who may afterwards have got possession of part of the estate.

Art. 215. But every person cited to show what right he has in any matter in controversy, is, as to the other parties in such suit, and as to any claims he may then have, bound by the judgment rendered therein, although he do not set forth his right.

Art. 216. Not only the parties, but those who succeed to the interests in the subject in controversy, are bound by the judgment; but they must succeed to them—that is, they must hold or claim under them. Thus, the sentence against the ancestor, binds the heir—against the seller, binds the purchaser; but a sentence against or in favour of the possessor, does not bind him who recovers the property from such possessor, or acquire it in any other manner, which does not suppose the property to have been in him at the time of such judgment.

Art. 217. Every one is a party to a suit who appears as such, either in person, by a mandatory duly constituted, or by an attorney at law duly licensed to practice in the court in which the suit is pending and employed by him ; and it shall be presumptive evidence that such attorney at law was employed by the party, if he had in his hands the papers necessary for the prosecution or defence of the cause, or if the party knew that such suit was prosecuted or defended in his name, and did not disavow the attorney in such court.

Art. 218. To be bound by a judgment, it is not sufficient to have been a party to the suit only, but to the judgment ; therefore, a party who, before the judgment, is allowed to discontinue—whose name is struck out of the proceedings—who is otherwise dismissed before a hearing on the merits—or who, on the hearing, is dismissed as having improperly been made a party—is not bound by a judgment afterwards rendered ; but if the order of dismissal be appealed from and reversed, and such party's name is afterwards reinstated in the pleadings, he shall be bound by the judgment.

Art. 219. A judgment on an appeal against the party in the original suit, who has neither cited, nor appeared, nor in any manner waived a citation in such court of appeals, is not resjudicata against such party.

Art. 220. The exceptions to the rule, that none but parties to a judgment are bound by it, are the following :

1st. Where a suit has been brought for the purpose of determining a right of common or servitude claimed by several persons, either by one or against one or more of the persons claiming such right, the judgment shall be conclusive for or against all the other commoners or persons claiming the same servitude or right of common, under the same title ; but not, if they claim under a different title.

2d. When a public or private corporation, or body politic, shall claim a right of laying or receiving any toll, tax, duty, wharfage, tonnage, or any other contribution or imposition whatever, a judgment rendered in a suit to try the legality of such claim, between the said corporation or body politic and any individual interested therein, shall be conclusive as to the right of such public or private corporation or body politic.

Provided, that in the two cases, above mentioned in this article, the decision shall not be conclusive, except against those who are individually made parties, unless two concurring judgments have been pronounced on the same right; in which case the judgment shall be resjudicata as to all; but if the servitude claimed be indivisible, a single judgment is conclusive.

3d. A judgment against a principal debtor shall bind his surety, although he be no party to it; and, in like manner, a judgment in favour of the principal shall be conclusive evidence for the security.

4th. If one who has acquired by purchase, donation, exchange, or any other contract, suffers the former proprietor to prosecute or defend a suit affecting such property, the person so acquiring such property, having notice of such suit, he shall be bound by the judgment, if it be given against the former proprietor, although he, the purchaser, be no party; but a judgment given in favour of the former owner, in such suit, shall not prejudice the title of the true owner. The same rule applies to the creditor, who suffers the owner of property, who has pledged or mortgaged it to him, to litigate respecting it with his knowledge. In this case, the creditor shall be bound to the amount of his interest by the judgment given against the owner; and, in like manner, if the owner of the property pledged or mortgaged suffers the creditor to litigate respecting it, he shall be bound by the sentence.

Provided, that the said judgments, mentioned in this article, be rendered on a fair contestation of the right, and not collusively, or by default or confession; and therefore, in any such case, the party against whom any such judgment is opposed, either as an exception or evidence, may show that it was entered by collusion, and defeat its effect.

Art. 221. There are no other causes than those expressed in the last preceding article, in which one who is not a party to a judgment, or who does not succeed to the rights of those who were parties to it, is bound thereby.

Art. 222. Where, in a suit brought by one plaintiff, judgment has been given against him, and he afterwards brings another suit for the same cause of action jointly with another, the former judgment shall be conclusive against the former plaintiff, if his interest be a divisible one, and under the same title with that brought in question in the former suit. If his interest be indivisible, or if the last claim is under a different title, the former judgment is not conclusive.

Art. 223. To give a judgment the force of resjudicata, when pleaded or offered in evidence in another cause, it must appear that the subject matter in controversy, in both causes, is the same. If it be essentially the same, although demanded in a different form, the judgment is conclusive. Thus, if a personal action is brought on a debt due by mortgage, and it be decided that nothing is due, this judgment is a bar to a subsequent hypothecary suit for the same debt. In like manner, if the first suit be a hypothecary action, and the decision is that nothing is due to the plaintiff, such judgment shall bar a personal suit for the same thing.

Art. 224. There are, however, exceptions to, and modifications of, the rule contained in the last article, as follows:

1st. Where the matter in dispute is an aggregate body, of which the parts are changeable by nature, without changing the character of the whole. Thus, a judgment relative to a flock, is conclusive between the parties, although the individual animals composing the flock may not be the same at the time of both suits.

2d. Where the party, who has failed in a demand for the whole, shall afterwards bring a suit for a part, the first judgment is a bar ; and this, whether the controversy be for a certain price of property, a sum of money, or an incorporeal right. Thus, if a suit be brought for a tract of land, and judgment be rendered for the defendant, the judgment will be a bar to an action brought under the same title for any part of the same land, either for an undivided part, or for a certain designated portion. The same rule applies where a suit is brought for two separate pieces of property and judgment be rendered for the defendant, the plaintiff cannot afterwards sustain a suit for either of them separately. The rules laid down under this second head also apply to the defendant ; if the judgment be rendered against him for the whole, he can never sustain an action for any of the parts separately.

3d. Where a suit has been brought for a distinct part and under a PARTICULAR TITLE, and a demand is afterwards made for the whole, the judgment, in the first suit, is resjudicata only for that part which was in controversy in the first suit. But if the first judgment were for a demand for a part, under a UNIVERSAL TITLE, such judgment, if against the plaintiff, is no bar to the suit for the whole.

4th. There is an exception to the second rule of this article, in the case of a suit brought in the cases allowed by law for the materials which have been employed in the construction of a house. This demand is not barred by a judgment given against the plaintiff in a suit brought by him for the house.

Where what is demanded by the second suit, although not the same with that which was the subject of litigation in the first, yet is incident to, or grows out of it, or by law belongs to him, who is the owner of that which was the object of the first suit. There the first judgment is a bar to the second suit. For example :

It having failed in a demand of a female slave, the plaintiff should, under the same title and by virtue of the law which gives the issue of a female slave to the owner of the mother, claim a child born of such slave.

Or, if in a demand for a principal sum it has been adjudged that it was never due, the same plaintiff should sue for the interest of such sum. In both these cases the first judgment would bar the second suit, although the demand was not for the same thing. But if in the first example, the child was claimed, not by virtue of the principle of law which gives the issue of a slave to the owner of the mother, but by some other title, even by virtue of a sale by which both the mother and child were conveyed, the judgment in the first suit, by which the mother was demanded, is no bar to the second. And in the second example, if the judgment in the first suit had been, not that the capital had never been due, but only that it had been paid, then the first judgment is no bar to the second suit, under the law relative to resjudicata ; but it is a bar under another principle, that to avoid circuity of actions the right to interest shall always be determined in the same suit by which the principal is demanded. Thus, too, a judgment settling the title to land, is a bar to a subsequent suit for alluvial soil added to it since, or to a claim for trees which have been cut, demanding them as the growth of the land, by virtue of the same title under which the land was claimed.

5th. Whenever the thing demanded by a second suit is so included in that which was decided 'by a former judgment, that the decree rendered must confirm or annul that which was given in the first, then, although the same thing be not nominally demanded, yet the first judgment shall be considered as resjudicata between the parties.

For example—If, in one suit respecting a servitude of view, it has been determined that the party has no right to raise his wall ten feet, this judgment will bar a claim to raise his wall twenty feet; for, if the second judgment should be against the right claimed in the second suit, it affirms the judgment given in the first; if it allows the right, it annuls the first decision.

6th. In determining whether the same thing be demanded by a second action, courts must determine by the substance, not the form of the demand. Thus, if judgment be rendered on a written obligation for the payment of money, this judgment shall be a bar to a subsequent suit for money lent, founded on the same transaction, unless, in this case, the obligation be declared void for some reason not affecting the original cause of action.

7th. But if a plaintiff fails in a suit, because he has mistaken the manner in which it ought to have been brought, such judgment is no bar to a suit brought in the proper form for the same thing.

Art. 225. A judgment on a claim of ownership, or for possession of property, is no bar to a suit for a usufruct or servitude, or use on the same land. Nor is a judgment on a claim for such usufruct, servitude, or use, any bar to a suit for the property or possession.

Art. 226. A judgment in a suit for possession is no bar to a suit for the property; but a recovery in a suit, where both property and possession are claimed, is a bar to a subsequent suit for possession.

Art. 227. A judgment in a suit for one species of servitude is not a bar to a suit for different servitude, although that which was first demanded, may include the last. Thus, a suit for a right of footway is not barred by a judgment that the party claiming it had no right to a servitude for the passage of cattle.

Art. 228. Another requisite to the conclusiveness of a judgment is, that the thing demanded must, in both suits, be not only the same, but demanded under the same title.

Art. 229. The last requisite to give effect to a decision as resjudicata is, that the parties should, in both suits, prosecute or defend in the same quality; if in the first suit, the party, against whom the judgment is opposed or defended, sued as executor, curator, tutor, attorney in fact, or garnishee, and in the second appeared in his own name, the judgment can neither be a bar, nor evidence for or against him, although the same thing be the object of the suit, and it be against the same party.

Art. 230. Yet, if a quality be assumed or given in either suit which would make no alteration in the party's right, the judgment shall have its effect as a bar or as evidence. As if a man bring a suit, on a promise made to him personally by another, or for personal injury done to him, and in such suit call himself heir or executor of another, or give other of those qualities to the defendant, judgment in such suit would be conclusive in another, which might be brought for the same cause, unless the first judgment were given as an exception taken to the quality assumed, and not on the merits.

## CHAPTER III.

### *Of confession.*

Art. 231. Confession in relation to the manner in which it is made is, either judicial or extra judicial. In relation to its nature, it is either full or partial only.

Art. 232. A judicial confession is that which is made by a party in some writing forming part of the proceedings in a cause, or which is made before a person authorized by law to receive the same, and reduced to writing by him, or under his authority, in the manner prescribed by law. Extra judicial confessions are those which are made in any other manner.

Art. 233. Full confession is that which acknowledges the fact alleged, with all its material circumstances, so as to leave nothing to be supplied by other evidence. Partial confession is that which acknowledges some circumstance from which an inference may be drawn to operate as presumptive evidence.

Art. 234. In civil cases, every proceeding being usually made with due deliberation and a knowledge of facts, a judicial confession, whether full or partial, is conclusive evidence of what is so confessed, but with the following provisions to guard against error.

1. Whenever a judicial confession has been made by the party himself, which on reflection he deems to be erroneous, he may on application within a time which the judge shall deem reasonable, and on showing cause to his satisfaction, obtain leave to amend such confessory proceeding.

2. When the confession has been made by an attorney or agent, such amendment shall be of course, if the party shall without unnecessary delay, after the proceeding comes to his knowledge, state the error on oath, and apply to have the same amended.

3. The condition of such amendments shall always be, that the adverse party shall be paid all costs and expenses he may have incurred in consequence of the error, and have time allowed him, if he require it, to supply other evidence of the facts at first confessed.

Art. 235. In criminal cases, no confession, whether full or partial, is conclusive evidence to the jury on a trial. The answer of "guilty" to the charge, if persevered in after the admonition and inquiry hereinafter directed, is such evidence as justifies the court in pronouncing sentence, without the intervention of a jury.

Art. 236. When the accused, on his arraignment, shall plead "guilty," it shall be the duty of the court to admonish him of the consequences of such answer, and to inquire, as well from him as from others, and particularly if he be in custody from the officer having charge of him, whether his acknowledgment has been produced by any threat or promise; and also when there is any reason to suppose insanity or imbecility of mind, to inquire into that fact.

Art. 237. In all other cases of a full or partial confession, whether judicial or extra judical, the accused may show, to avoid the effect of such confession, not only by other evidence that it was not true, but that it was produced by error, by threats, promises, false hopes, confusion of mind, or any other efficient cause. And in every such case, the confession is to have such weight as the judges of the fact shall, in their discretion, give to it, under a consideration of all the circumstances of the case.

Art. 238. In all cases the whole confession must be taken together; that is to say, every thing said, done, or written, at the time of the confession, tending to enlarge, restrict, or modify it, must be received as part of the evidence.

## CHAPTER IV.

### *Of estoppels.*

Art. 239. There being no other conclusive evidence than in the cases especially provided for by the legislative authority of this state, that species of conclusive evidence known in the English law of evidence by the name of "Estoppel," is abolished, and can operate as direct, or, according to its nature, presumptive, evidence only.

## GENERAL PROVISION.

Art. 240. Nothing in this Code contained shall be so construed as to dispense with the proof required by the Civil Code, or other statutes, to give effect to certain contracts, or testamentary or other dispositions, or to enforce the registry or recording of certain acts, or to prove legitimacy or filiation, legitimation or civil condition.

# A CODE OF REFORM AND PRISON
# DISCIPLINE.

.

.

# INTRODUCTORY TITLE.

## CHAPTER I.

*Design of the code of reform and prison discipline.*

Art. 1. The Code of Reform and Prison Discipline will regulate the manner in which prisoners of different descriptions are to be confined and treated, as well before as after judgment.

Art. 2. This Code is intended not only to direct the structure and police, of the prison for the confinement of convicts, but also of those which are rendered necessary for the detention of the accused before trial, for the education of juvenile offenders, and of a House of Refuge and employment for those who have undergone the sentence of the law. All these objects are necessarily connected : no one part can be abstracted without materially injuring the effect of the others.

Art. 3. Safe custody is an object common to the prisons; but reform is the intent of all the institutions. Punishment also enters into the design of the Penitentiary, the School of Reform, and that department of the House of Detention destined to receive those convicted of misdemeanors; but forms no part of the system, so far as it applies to the custody of the accused before trial, and to their relief and employment after having suffered the sentence of the law.

Art. 4. In all these establishments the means by which reformation is expected, are, reflection, instruction, habits of industry, and religion. To promote these is one of the first duties of the men who are charged with the important and honourable task of superintending the different departments of these institutions.

Art. 5. Reformation cannot be expected while the vicious are permitted to associate with each other or with the innocent. This kind of seclusion, therefore, is a protection not a punishment; and is consequently necessary in the House of Detention and Refuge, as well as in the Penitentiary and School of Reform.

Art. 6. All the officers appointed under this Code, from the inspector to the under-keeper, have a moral as well as a legal duty to perform. In no department of the government is there a greater call for the best qualities of the mind—a strong moral sense and unfeigned belief in religion (for they must be teachers of both,) firmness in preserving order, moderation and temper in enforcing it, close attention to discover the evil propensities that have led to the crimes of the convicts, and a knowledge of human nature to apply the proper correctives. The officers of a prison are no longer jailors and turnkeys charged with the custody of the body only ; they must minister to the diseased minds and correct the depraved habits of their patients. The law raises them to their true station. They have higher functions, and on the manner in which they shall perform them depends the success of the whole system to which this Code is intended to give vigour and effect.

Art. 7. This view of the intent of the law and of what it expects from the ministers who are to execute it, are placed at the introduction of the Code to impress them with a true view of the spirit which dictated it, and direct them, in those points in which the law may be made more efficacious, by a zealous and enlightened performance of their several duties.

Art. 8. From the magistrates and others, who are constituted visiters, much also is expected; the right given by this Code is not intended as a complimentary privilege, conferred only to satisfy curiosity. Publicity and the superintending care of upright magistrates and intelligent men, is the best incentive to a zealous performance of duty. Faithful and active officers will court their investigation; those who are negligent or corrupt, will fear it.

Art. 9. The progress of reform in the female department will depend chiefly on those of their own sex, who may accept the invitation given by the law, to carry their example and precept, and persuasive exhortation to the place of punishment, and convert it into a school for religion, industry, and virtue.


## CHAPTER II.

### *Division of the work.*

Art. 10. This Code is divided into three books. The first treats of the different places of confinement, their construction, and officers; the second directs the treatment of the persons confined; and the third contains the regulations for the House of Refuge.

# BOOK I.

PLACES OF CONFINEMENT—OF THEIR CONSTRUCTION AND OFFICERS.

## TITLE I.

OF PLACES OF CONFINEMENT.

### CHAPTER I.

*Of the different denominations of places of confinement.*

Art. 11. There shall be provided at the expense of the state, in such place in the first judicial district as the general assembly shall direct, three separate and distinct places of confinement.

Art. 12. One of them shall be called the House of Detention. In this shall be confined:

1. Persons who, in the cases allowed by law, are detained in order to secure their attendance as witnesses on criminal trials in the first district.

2. Those who are committed for trial on an accusation of MISDEMEA-NOR in the first district.

3. Persons sentenced to simple imprisonment (whether in close custody or not) for any period, whether in the first district, or in any other district, for more than sixty days.

4. Those who may be committed for a disturbance in court, for any such disobedience to the orders of a court or a magistrate as may be punished by imprisonment, for the non-payment of a fine, or for the breach of a recognizance, or any other engagement entered into in the course of a prosecution for an offence, in the first district, in the cases where such confinement is authorized.

5. All those who may, in the first district, be committed for trial on an accusation of CRIME.

Art. 13. Another of the said places of confinement shall be called the Penitentiary. In which shall be confined all those convicted of crime in any part of the state, who, at the time of conviction, had attained the age of eighteen years.

Art. 14. The third shall be called the School of Reform. In it shall be placed:

1. All those convicted of crime (not punishable by imprisonment for

life) who have not attained the age of eighteen years, in whatever part of the state the conviction may have been had.

2. All persons under the age of eighteen years who shall be sentenced to be placed in the said prison, on conviction, for misdemeanor, in cases where power for that purpose is specially given by law.

3. All young vagrants whose commitment shall, under that denomination, be permitted by law.

Art. 15. Prisoners committed before trial, and offenders sentenced to simple imprisonment for a term less than sixty days, in any of the other judicial districts, except the first, shall be confined in the jail of the parish in which they shall be committed, or in which they shall be sentenced.

Art. 16. Offenders sentenced to simple imprisonment in any part of the state, for any term exceeding sixty days, shall be confined in the House of Detention.

Art. 17. While imprisonment for debt continues to be authorized by the laws of the state, it must be regulated by the CIVIL LAW, and this Code contains no other provision in relation to it than that contained in the following article.

Art. 18. No person shall be imprisoned in any of the three places of confinement directed to be provided by this chapter, in pursuance of a final judgment, or for want of bail, in a civil suit.


CHAPTER II.

*Of the construction of the different places of confinement.*

Art. 19. The House of Detention shall be so constructed as to keep in four divisions, entirely separate the one division from the other, the prisoners comprehended in the following classes :

1. The first class shall consist of the male persons described in the first, second, third, and fourth numbers of the enumeration contained in the second article of the preceding section.

2. The second class shall consist of female prisoners of the above description.

3. The third class shall consist of male persons committed for trial on an accusation of CRIME.

4. And the fourth class shall consist of female prisoners confined for trial on an accusation of CRIME.

Art. 20. This building must also contain separate accommodations for each individual of the third and fourth classes, and for each of the persons who shall be sentenced to simple imprisonment in close custody ; and two enclosed yards—the one for the male and the other for the female prisoners of the other classes, in which they may take exercise and pursue such employment as is hereby permitted.

Art. 21. The Penitentiary shall be so constructed as to contain :

1. Cells for those sentenced to solitary confinement for murder.

2. Ranges of separate cells, one for each convict, with an enclosed court for each cell.

3. A hydraulic or other machine to be put in operation by manual labour, so disposed that a convenient number of prisoners may work at it, separated from each other by a wall.

4. School-rooms sufficient for the instruction of a class of persons.

5. An infirmary.

6. All other necessary buildings for the safe-keeping and support of the prisoners, and for the preservation of their health.

Art. 22. The Penitentiary shall also have a separate enclosure, containing similar cells for female convicts, so disposed as to prevent all means of communication with the male convicts.

Art. 23. The School of Reform shall contain :

1. Separate divisions for the sexes.

2. A separate dormitory for each prisoner.

3. Proper courts or shops for the employment of the prisoners.

4. A school-room for each division.

5. An infirmary.

Art. 24. Each of the three places of confinement described in this section shall be so constructed as to be separate from the others ; and if for the convenience of building they should be contained in the same outer wall or enclosure, they must be so arranged as to give the prisoners in the one no means of communication with those in any other.

Art. 25. All the prisons must be so constructed as to be at all times completely ventilated, and in winter warmed by flues communicating with the different cells.


# TITLE II.


OF THE OFFICERS AND ATTENDANTS OF THE SEVERAL PLACES OF CONFINEMENT
AND THEIR SEVERAL DUTIES.


## CHAPTER I.


### *Of the appointment of the officers.*

Art. 26. There shall be appointed by the governor, for the several places of confinement above mentioned, the following officers and attendants :

Art. 27. For the House of Detention, a warden and a matron. The warden, with the approbation of the inspectors hereinafter mentioned, shall name so many under-keepers, and the matron, with the like approbation, so many assistants as by the inspectors shall be deemed necessary for the safe-keeping of the persons committed to their charge, and for the necessary attendance on them.

Art. 28. For the Penitentiary, a warden, a matron, a teacher, a physician, two chaplains, and a clerk.

Art. 29. The warden and matron shall respectively appoint so many assistants as the inspectors shall deem necessary.

Art. 30. For the School of Reform, a warden, a matron, and a female teacher ; and the keeper and matron shall respectively appoint so many assistants as the inspectors shall deem necessary.

Art. 31. The physician and the chaplains appointed for the Penitentiary shall also attend the two other places of confinement; and the teacher of the Penitentiary shall instruct such of the persons confined in the House of Detention as choose to receive lessons, at such times as shall be directed by the inspectors.

## CHAPTER II.

### Of the board of inspectors and their duties.

Art. 32. The governor shall appoint five persons to form a board of inspectors.

Art. 33. The duties of the inspectors shall be to visit the House of Detention, the Penitentiary, and the School of Reform, at least once in every week, to see that the duties of the several officers and attendants are performed—to prevent all oppression, peculation, or other abuse, in the management of the several institutions; and to report to the legislature such means as may suggest themselves for their improvement.

Art. 34. They shall also, with the approbation of the governor, form rules for the government of the several places of confinement and the employment of the persons confined therein, not inconsistent with this Code. They shall direct the purchase of all implements and materials for the manufactures carried on therein, and the sale of the articles manufactured which are not wanted for the use of the prisoners, and they shall direct the manner in which all purchases of provisions and other supplies for the prisoners shall be made.

Art. 35. The inspectors shall cause accurate accounts to be kept in separate sets of books of all expenditures and receipts in each of the places of confinemeut.

Art. 36. They shall on or before the first day of December, in every year, make a report in writing to the legislature, of the state of the said places of confinement and of the House of Refuge. The report shall contain the name, age, sex, place of residence and nativity, time of commitment, term of imprisonment, profession or trade prior to commitment, and employment in prison, of each person who has been committed during the preceding year to either of said places of confinement: noticing also those who may have escaped, or died, or who were pardoned, or discharged, designating the offence for which the commitment was made, and whether for a first or repeated offence, and when and in what court, or by whose order: and in such return the inspectors shall make such observations and give such information as they may deem expedient for making the said institutions effectual in the punishment and reformation of offenders.

Art. 37. The inspectors have power to examine any person on oath, relative to any abuse in the said places of confinement, or other matter within the purview of their duties.

Art. 38. They have power to make rules for the preservation of prison discipline and for promoting industry, morals, and education, in the said several institutions, which shall not be contrary to any provisions of this Code or of other law, and to impose and cause to be inflicted the punishments they shall have ordained for the breach of such rules, and for all such infractions of prison discipline, as are made punishable by this Code.

Art. 39. They shall direct in what manner the rations for the subsistence of the prisoners shall be composed, in conformity with the general directions on that subject hereinafter contained.

Art. 40. They shall also perform such duties as are required of them in the subsequent parts of this Code.

Art. 41. Each inspector shall have the right to visit and inspect the said places of confinement and the House of Refuge whenever he shall deem it expedient ; and the keepers, wardens, clerks, and other officers of the several prisons are bound to submit to them, or either of them, whenever called on, the books, papers, and accounts, belonging to the prisons, to which such officers belong, and to admit them to the prisoners therein confined.

Art. 42. It is the duty of the inspectors to call at least once in every three months upon the proper officers of each place of confinement for an exhibition of the accounts, to examine the same, and compare the entries with the vouchers ; to examine the persons employed in the said places of confinement on oath, whenever it shall be deemed necessary, and to report any abuses or oppressions that may come to their knowledge, to the governor, if any of the officers appointed by him are implicated therein, or themselves to reprimand or dismiss any other person employed when it is found necessary.

Art. 43. The inspectors in their weekly visits to the several places of confinement shall speak to each person confined therein, out of the presence of any of the persons employed therein ; shall listen to any complaints that may be made of oppression or ill conduct of the persons so employed ; examine into the truth thereof, and proceed therein according to the directions of the last preceding article when the complaint is well founded ; and on such visits they shall. have the calendar of the prisoners furnished to them by the warden, and see by actual inspection whether all the prisoners named in the said calendar are found in the said prison in the situation in which by the said calendar they are declared to be.

Art. 44. They shall also hear and determine all charges of breach of prison discipline that shall be reported against any prisoner, when the punishment to be inflicted is close confinement for more than twenty-four hours.

Art. 45. A majority of the said inspectors shall constitute a board, and may do any of the acts required of the said inspectors by this Code. Two of the inspectors shall be a quorum for the weekly visitations hereby directed to be made.

Art. 46. The governor, the president of the senate, the speaker of the house of representatives, the mayor of the city of New Orleans, the judges of the supreme court, of the criminal court, and of the first district, the attorney-general, and the directors of the Asylum for Orphan Boys, are authorized to attend the meetings of the inspectors, to take part in their deliberations, but not to vote, to attend their weekly inspections ; and each of the persons abovementioned may do any act which the said inspectors individually are authorized to perform.

Art. 47. Each of the directresses of the Poydrass Asylum, and the members of any female society that shall be formed for that purpose, are permitted and requested to exercise all the powers and perform all the duties with respect to the female prisoners in either of the establishments, that any individual inspector is hereby authorized to perform.

4 N

Art. 48. Each inspector shall receive for every day's attendance in the performance of the duties required by this act the sum of ................ dollars, provided the same shall not amount, in any one year, to more than ............... dollars.

Art. 49. It is made the important and special duty of the inspectors, in their individual or joint visits to the convicts, to enter into friendly conversation with them, to impress on their minds the importance of moral and religious instruction, of industry, and orderly conduct, and to encourage them to a perseverance in this course by a promise of aid and patronage, in the manner hereinafter directed on their discharge.

Art. 50. The inspectors shall have power to make contracts for the labour of the convicts in the Penitentiary and School of Reform with such mechanics as will learn them a useful trade, under the restrictions prescribed in the title concerning the treatment of the convicts.

Art. 51. No inspector, nor any officer or other person employed in any of the said places of confinement, shall sell any article for the use of either of them, or of the persons confined therein during their confinement, or shall purchase any of the manufactures made therein, or derive any emolument from such purchase or sale either to himself or to any relation in the ascending or descending line, or any collateral within the third degree, other than such emolument as is hereinafter expressly allowed ; and any offender against this provision shall be fined five hundred dollars and imprisoned in close custody thirty days.

Art. 52. No work shall be performed nor any article manufactured by any of the prisoners for the use of any of the inspectors or officers of either of the prisons, or of any of the attendants employed therein, or for the use of the families of either of them ; nor shall they or either of them receive under any pretence whatever from either of the said prisoners, or any one on his behalf, any sum of money or gift of any assignable value, under the penalty of five hundred dollars fine, and six months' imprisonment in close custody.

Art. 53. The inspectors have power, in case of the necessary and temporary absence or disability of either of the wardens, or of any of the officers employed in either of the prisons, to employ a substitute during such absence or disability ; which substitute shall, for the time being, perform all the duties, have all the authority, and be liable to all the penalties as the officer himself.

CHAPTER III.

*Of the duties common to the wardens of the penitentiary, house of detention, and of the school of reform.*

Art. 54. Each of the said wardens shall reside in the prison over which he presides.

Art. 55. Each of them shall visit every cell and apartment, and see every prisoner under his care, at least once in every day, and when he visits the female prisoners, he shall be accompanied by the matron.

Art. 56. They shall each keep a journal, in which shall be regularly entered the reception, discharge, death, pardon, or escape, of any prisoner; and also, the complaints that are made and the punishments that are inflicted for the breach of prison discipline, as they occur, the visits of the inspectors, the chaplain and the physician, and all other occurrences of note that concern the state of the prison, except the receipts and expenditures, the account of which are to be kept in the manner hereinafter directed.

Art. 57. On the commitment of a prisoner accused of CRIME in the House of Detention, and when convicted of a crime on his entrance in the Penitentiary or School of Reform, there shall be entered on the journal the sex, age, apparent height, and accurate description of the person, last place of abode, and nativity of the prisoner.

Art. 58. On the death of any prisoners, the warden shall immediately give notice to the board of inspectors, and shall take the measures directed by the Code of Procedure for summoning a jury of inquest.

Art. 59. The wardens shall severally make a report in writing to the governor every six months of all the persons in custody, specifying the times of commitment and discharge, by pardon or expiration of sentence, or acquittal, and the escape or death and removal from the one prison to another of each person who has been in their custody, severally, during the preceding six months, together with the general state of the prison, and such observations and information as the warden may think necessary, or as the governor or inspectors shall direct.

Art. 60. The wardens shall appoint the under-keepers, and dismiss them at their pleasure.

Art. 61. They shall see that the duties required by this Code in their respective prisons are performed by the several officers thereof, and shall report any default both to the governor and to the board of inspectors.

Art. 62. The wardens severally have power to arrest and conduct before a magistrate for commitment any person who shall make himself liable to any penalty under this Code.

Art. 63. Each warden shall put up in every apartment and cell of the prison under his care a printed copy of the rules for the government thereof, and shall cause them to be explained to those who cannot read or are unable to understand them.

Art. 64. He shall report all infractions of the rules to the inspectors, and with the approbation of one of them, may punish the offender in the manner directed in the chapter concerning the treatment of prisoners.

Art. 65. No warden shall absent himself from the prison under his care for a night, without permission, in writing, from one of the inspectors, or in the execution of some duty that requires such absence, or by reason of some unforeseen accident which renders it necessary; and whenever such accident occurs, it is to be noted on the journal.

Art. 66. The warden shall not be present when the inspectors make their stated visits to the prisoners under his care.

Art. 67. The further duties and powers of the wardens in their respective prisons, are detailed in the chapter relative to the reception and treatment of prisoners, and in other parts of this Code.

## CHAPTER IV:

*Of the duty of the under-keepers in the penitentiary and house of detention.*

Art. 68. The under-keepers must be men of sobriety, honesty, and industry. They must understand reading, writing, the first rules of arithmetic, and must speak, for the common purposes of life, the French and English languages.

Art 69. It is the duty of the under-keepers to visit each prisoner three times in every day, to see that his meals are regularly delivered according to the prison allowance; to set those to work who are permitted or condemned to labour; and to see that they are instructed therein, according to the rules established by this Code, and to the further directions of the warden.

Art. 70. Whenever any convict shall complain of such illness as to require medical aid, the under-keeper shall immediately give notice to the physician.

Art. 71. Each under-keeper shall have a certain number of prisoners assigned to his care.

Art. 72. He shall make a daily report to the warden, of the health, conduct, and industry of the prisoners, and a like report to the inspectors when required.

Art. 73. No under-keeper shall be present when the warden or the inspector visit the prisoners under his particular care.

Art. 74. The under-keepers shall obey all legal orders given by the warden for the government of the prison. They shall be removeable by him at pleasure; and by the inspectors on proof of ill conduct in their offices. All orders to the under-keepers must be given through or by the warden.

Art. 75. They must remain in the prison night and day, and shall not be employed either by the warden or the inspectors in any other place. They shall not absent themselves without permission from the warden.

Art. 76. The under-keepers shall act also as guards; for which purpose arms and munitions shall be provided by the state, to be put into their hands by the warden when they are on guard, and at other times when circumstances require it; but in their daily occupations they are not to be armed.

Art. 77. No under-keeper shall receive from any one confined in either of the said prisons, or from any one in behalf of such prisoner, any emolument or reward whatever, or the promise of any, either for services or supplies, or as a gratuity; under the penalty of fine of one hundred dollars and imprisonment for thirty days; and when any breach of this article shall come to the knowledge of the warden or inspectors, the under-keepers offending shall be immediately discharged.

Art. 78. The compensation of the under-keepers shall be

## CHAPTER V.

### *Of the duties of the chaplains.*

Art. 79. The chaplains shall be, the one a clergyman of the Catholic church, the other of some one of the Protestant persuasions; each shall receive a salary of

Art. 80. The Catholic chaplain shall, at least twice in every week, visit every person of his own persuasion in the Penitentiary and School of Reform, and such persons as are confined in the House of Detention in close custody.

Art. 81. The Protestant chaplain shall, in like manner, perform the same duty to all the prisoners who are of any Protestant persuasion.

Art. 82. It is the duty of both to instruct the prisoners under their care in the duties of religion and morality ; to exhort them to repentance and amendment ; to show the folly and danger of vice ; and to encourage those who are confined for a term of years with the hope of being reinstated in the good opinion of the world by a perseverance in the principles of honesty and the practice of industry ; to impress on their minds that it is not their punishment but their crime that has degraded them, and that sincere repentance and amendment may cause both to be forgotten by man, as the sin will surely be forgiven by God. To those sentenced to confinement for life, they must hold out no fallacious hope of pardon, but teach them to fix their hopes on another world, and prepare for it by contrition and repentance.

Art. 83. The Catholic chaplain shall have free access to the cells of all the Catholic convicts ; and the Protestant chaplain to those of the Protestant convicts ; and either of them to the cell of any convict of any religion who requests it.

Art. 84. Any clergyman of any religion or religious sect may be admitted to see any convict who may require his attendance, or at his own request, at proper and reasonable hours, under the direction of the warden or inspectors.

Art. 85. The chaplains shall be furnished with forms of returns which shall contain the names of the prisoners, with blank columns, in which shall be entered, by the chaplain, the date of each visit he shall pay, and opposite to each name the observations he may make on the character and demeanor of the convict with respect to his moral and religious improvement.

Art. 86. Each of the said chaplains shall perform divine service at least once on every Sunday in the School of Reform.

Art. 87. Selections from Scriptures, and such other books of religious and moral instruction as shall be recommended by the chaplains and approved by the inspectors, shall be distributed among the convicts.

## CHAPTER VI.

*Of the qualifications of the teachers, and the duties of the teacher of the penitentiary.*

Art. 88. The teachers must be men of good moral characters ; they must understand the French and English languages, and be capable of teaching reading, writing, arithmetic, book-keeping, navigation, and land-surveying. They need not reside in the prison.

Art. 89. The teacher of the Penitentiary, for the first six months after the convict shall be confined therein, must attend at the cells and working courts of all the male convicts who cannot read and write, and give separate lessons, in turn, to as many of them as his time will permit, calculating seven hours in each day, in every day, Sundays included.

Art. 90. At the end of the said six months he may form classes, not exceeding eight in each class, of such of the convicts as shall have obtained favourable certificates of conduct during that period, as to industry, morality and order, from the warden and chaplain, which class he shall assemble, at least once in every two days, in the school-room for instruction, for the space of one hour.

Art. 91. No convict shall be admitted into a class until after he has obtained such certificate, and shall be degraded therefrom for misconduct for a greater or less interval, according to the nature of the offence and the sentence of the inspectors.

Art. 92. Those convicts who can write and read, but who are desirous of instruction in any of the other branches taught by the teacher, may also be instructed in their cells after three months' good behaviour, certified as aforesaid, and may be admitted into a class on a like certificate of six months.

Art. 93. Convicts condemned to imprisonment for life cannot be admitted into a class. They may receive such instruction, if they need and deserve it, as will enable them to read, but it must be given in their cells or courts.

Art. 94. The teacher shall make rules for the preservation of discipline and order in the several classes, which he shall submit to the inspectors and the warden, and, if approved by them, shall be in force; but no punishment shall be inflicted greater than those directed by the rules established in this Code.

Art. 95. The individuals who are to compose the different classes shall be designated by the teacher with the approbation of the inspectors, after they shall have consulted the warden.

Art. 96. One rule of the instruction by classes shall be, that no conversation shall be permitted between the individuals composing it on any other subject than that relating to the art or science in which they are instructed; and to enforce this rule, it is made the duty of the teacher never to leave the class while they, or any two of the individuals composing it, are assembled.

Art. 97. The individuals composing the class shall be conducted by an under-keeper separately to and from the place of instruction, and shall not, on any pretence whatever, be suffered to speak to any one by the way.

Art. 98. The teacher may, with the approbation of the inspectors, select one or more of the convicts of sufficient instruction and ability, who has been committed for a term of years, to assist in the duties of his office, provided no person shall be selected who has not a certificate of good behaviour for at least two years, both from the chaplain and warden; and until the expiration of the said two years, and until such selection shall be made, the inspectors are authorized, if they deem it necessary, to employ such assistant, at a salary not exceeding two-thirds of that given to the principal teacher.

Art. 99. If any convict shall have, prior to his commitment, cultivated any of the arts, of painting, sculpture, or architecture, as a profession, or, in the opinion of the inspectors, shall have a decided genius for either of them, he shall, after obtaining a certificate of six months' good behaviour, be permitted to employ a portion of the time allotted for labour, not exceeding one hour in each day, to his improvement therein; and      per cent. of his earnings, after paying for his support, shall, if he request it, be appropriated to the purchase of implements and materials for the business; provided, that this indulgence shall be suspended or forfeited, at the direction of the inspectors, by any breach of the rules of the prison.

Art. 100. Convicts committed for a term of years, who cannot read, write, and cipher, may be punished, by order of the inspectors or the warden, for refusing to receive instruction therein. All other scientific instruction is an indulgence to be obtained only by a perseverance in good behaviour.

Art. 101. The female convicts who are uninstructed in reading and writing and the first rules of arithmetic, shall be taught by the matron, or such assistant as the inspectors may direct, and at such hours as they shall appoint.

## CHAPTER VII.

*Of the duties of the teacher of the school of reform.*

Art. 102. The teacher of the School of Reform must possess the same qualifications that are required in the teacher in the Penitentiary. He need not reside in the establishment.

Art. 103. He shall instruct the male and female departments of the School of Reform in the several branches of learning, at the times and in the manner prescribed for that purpose in the chapter of this Code relative to instruction in the School of Reform.

Art. 104. He shall receive a yearly salary of          dollars.

## CHAPTER VIII.

*Of the duties of the physician.*

Art. 105. The physician shall visit every prisoner in the prisons twice in every week, and oftener if the state of their health requires it, and shall report once in every month to the inspectors.

Art. 106. He shall attend immediately on notice from the warden or keeper that any person is sick.

Art. 107. He shall examine every prisoner that shall be brought into the Penitentiary and School of Reform before he shall be confined in his cell.

Art. 108. Whenever, in the opinion of the physician, any convict in the Penitentiary or School of Reform, is so ill as to require removal, the warden shall direct such removal to the infirmary of the institution in which he is confined; and the prisoner shall be kept in the infirmary until the physician shall certify that he may be removed without injury to his health, and he shall then be removed to his cell.

Art. 109. He shall visit the patients in the infirmary at least once in every day, and he shall give such directions for the health and cleanliness of the prisoners as he may deem expedient, which the warden shall have executed, provided they shall not be contrary to the provisions of this Code, or inconsistent with the safe custody of the said prisoners ; and the directions he may give, whether complied with or not, shall be entered on the journal of the warden and on his own.

Art. 110. The physician shall inquire into the mental as well as the bodily state of every prisoner; and when he shall have reason to believe that the mind or body is materially affected by the discipline, treatment, or diet, he shall inform the warden thereof, and shall enter his observations on the journal, herein after directed to be kept, which shall be an authority for the warden for altering the discipline, treatment, or diet, of any prisoner until the next meeting of the inspectors, who shall inquire into the case, and make orders accordingly.

Art. 111. He shall have power to cause any one infected by a contagious or infectious disorder to be separated from the other prisoners; and if three other licensed practitioners of physic shall certify, that the disease is infectious, and that the prisoner cannot, without danger to the others, be kept within the walls of the prison, the inspectors shall make an order for his removal and confinement elsewhere, until he shall die or recover.

Art. 112. The physician shall keep a journal, in which, opposite to the name of each prisoner, shall be entered the state of his health; and if sick, whether in the infirmary or not, together with such remarks as he may deem important; which journal shall be open to the inspection of the warden and the inspectors; and the same, together with the return provided for in the first article of this section, shall be laid before the inspectors once in every month, or oftener if called for.

Art. 113. The prisoners, under the care of the physician, shall be allowed such diet as he shall direct.

Art. 114. No prisoner shall be discharged while labouring under a dangerous disease, although entitled to his discharge, unless by his own desire.

Art. 115. The infirmary shall have a partition between every two beds, and no two patients shall occupy the same bed; and the physician and his attendants shall take every precaution in their power to prevent all intercourse between the convicts while in the infirmary.

Art. 116. The physician shall select from among the young delinquents in the School of Reform two or more who have given evidence to the satisfaction of the warden, the teacher, and the chaplain, of determination to reform, and who shall have made sufficient progress in their education, as his assistants in the two infirmaries, to whom he shall teach the art of compounding and administering remedies, and such other branches of medical knowledge as they may be capable of acquiring; which assistants shall be employed in the care and attendance on the sick, and shall be exempt from all other labour while they preserve the confidence of the physician, and are guilty of no breach of the rules of prison discipline.


CHAPTER IX.

*Of the duties of the clerk of the penitentiary.*

Art. 117. The clerk shall, under the direction of the inspectors, keep regular accounts of all the expenses of the Penitentiary, of the proceeds of the articles manufactured therein, and of the purchase of materials to keep the convicts employed, when they do not work by contract, as is hereinafter provided. He shall also open an account with each convict, in which such convict shall be charged with the cost of his prosecution and conviction, and with his maintenance in prison, including only his food and clothing and such drugs and medicines as he may be supplied with ; and shall be credited with his labour at such estimation of its value as shall be equitable, according to its quantity and quality, agreeable to the rates paid for like labour in the city of New Orleans ; or (when he works by contract) according to the contract price of such labour.

Art. 118. The inspectors shall direct the mode in which the accounts shall be kept, and shall direct the agent they shall employ for making purchases and for selling the articles.manufactured in the Penitentiary, (which agent shall in no case be the clerk); to furnish the clerk with accounts and bills of all such purchases and sales.

Art. 119. The clerk shall deliver to the agent all such articles manufactured in the prison as are not done for manufacturers by contract, and which are not wanted for the use of the same, keeping an account as well of what is so wanted and retained, as of what is delivered.

Art. 120. The books of accounts shall be kept in the prison, and shall be open to the inspection of the warden and the inspectors.

Art. 121. The clerk shall keep a regular account of all the furniture, tools, and implements of trade provided for the prison, and shall submit the same to the inspectors.

Art. 122. He shall receive such remuneration for his services as shall be determined by the inspectors, not exceeding       dollars per annum.

## CHAPTER X.

### *Of the duties of the matrons.*

Art. 123. The matrons shall reside in their respective prisons. They and their female assistants shall, under the direction of the inspectors, have the exclusive care and superintendence of the female convicts. No male person, except the chaplain, shall be permitted to visit them, but in the presence of the matron.

Art. 124. She shall employ them in making,· mending, and washing the clothing for the prisoners. She shall cause them to be taught needle-work and other employments of housewifery, keeping them all apart at night, and as much as the nature of their employment will allow during the day. She shall report daily to the warden all infractions of order, or other material occurrence ; and shall inflict such punishment, consistent with this Code, as the inspectors and teacher shall direct.

4 0

# BOOK II.

OF THE TREATMENT OF THE PRISONERS IN THE SEVERAL PLACES OF
CONFINEMENT.

## TITLE I.

OF THE PRISONERS CONFINED IN THE HOUSE OF DETENTION.

Art. 125. The prisoners of the first class, that is to say, those confined in order to secure their attendance as witnesses, shall be under no other restriction than that which is absolutely necessary to prevent their escape from the prison.   Good and wholesome food, comfortable bedding, and other necessaries, shall be provided for them at the public expense ; or they may be allowed to provide it for themselves ; and every such prisoner shall be immediately liberated on his giving the security for his appearance to testify, that is required by law.

Art. 126.  Those who are committed for want of bail, in the first district, on an accusation of misdemeanor :

Those who are condemned to simple imprisonment (not in close custody), in the first district, or who are removed on a like sentence from any other district :

Those who may be committed for the non-payment of a fine, or for the breach of a recognizance, or other engagement, entered into in the course of a prosecution for an offence :

Form a second class of prisoners.   They need not be separated from each other during the day, but each shall be lodged at night in separate dormitories, unless the numbers in the prison shall render it impossible.

Art. 127.  Those who are committed for want of bail on accusations of crime, form a third class.   These shall be kept in separate cells or apartments both night and day, and shall have no communication whatever with each other.

Art. 128.  All the above classes of prisoners shall be entitled to good wholesome food and drink, according to the prison regulations hereinafter provided for, and to beds and bedding, at the public expense ; or they shall be permitted to purchase or receive such food and beds, of a better quality, at their own expense, also under the restrictions contained under the prison regulations.

They may receive the visits of their families and friends, and their counsel, at all reasonable hours.

They shall be allowed the free use of books, of pen, ink, and paper, at their own expense.

Art. 129.  The prisoners sentenced to close confinement, shall each be confined in a separate apartment or cell, furnished with the prison allowance of bedding, and a chair, and a table ; but may provide their own bedding if they think fit. They shall be restricted to the prison allowance of drink and food, unless the court shall order differently in the sentence, or the physician shall officially certify that their health will be impaired by confining them to it.

They shall not be permitted to receive any society in their places of confinement, without permission of two of the inspectors in writing, and the time of such visit shall be prescribed and limited in the permission, and shall in no case exceed one hour at a time.

They shall not be debarred the privilege of consulting with their counsel, or receiving the visits of their physician and chaplains, at all reasonable times.

Art. 130. No prisoner in this house shall be forced to perform any labour. No prisoner shall be confined in irons ; but if he shall have made an attempt to break the prison, or have assaulted the keeper or other person employed in the house, he may be confined in a straight-jacket or arm straps.

Art. 131. All the prisoners in this house may be permitted to work at such trades and manufactures as they may desire and may be deemed by the inspectors proper to be carried on in the house, without infringing the rules hereinbefore laid down ; and the inspectors shall provide the tools and implements, and the materials for carrying on such manufactory as they may deem expedient, and shall allow to such of the prisoners as may choose to work thereat three-fourths of the net proceeds of their labour, and shall pay the same as it is earned to the prisoner ; the other fourth shall be deposited in bank in the manner hereinafter directed.

Art. 132. The daily allowance of food to a prisoner in the house of detention shall be the same as is allowed to a soldier in the army of the United States. The bedding shall be the same as is directed for the prisoners in the Penitentiary.

Art. 133. The inspectors shall make prison regulations for the preservation of order in the House of Detention, not inconsistent with this Code, and for the supply of food and other accommodations to such of the persons detained as are allowed to procure the same at their own expense ; but no wine or spirituous liquors shall be introduced but by order of the physician, stating that the health of the party, in whose favour it is given, requires it.

# TITLE II.

### OF THE TREATMENT OF THE PRISONERS IN THE PENITENTIARY.

## CHAPTER I.

### *Of the reception of the convicts.*

Art. 134. Every convict sentenced to imprisonment in the Penitentiary shall, immediately after the sentence shall have been finally pronounced, be conveyed, by the sheriff of the parish in which he was condemned, to the Penitentiary, under secure guard; and when it shall be deemed necessary, the officer commanding the regiment of the place where the court sits, shall furnish a guard for that purpose, on the order of the court entered on its minutes.

Art. 135. On the arrival of a convict, immediate notice shall be given to the physician, who shall examine the state of his health ; he shall then be stripped of his clothes and clothed in the uniform of the prison, that is suited to his offence, in the manner hereinafter provided, being first, if necessary, bathed and cleaned.

Art. 136. The convict shall then be examined by the clerk and the warden, in the presence of as many of the under-keepers as can conveniently attend ; and his height, apparent and alleged age, complexion, colour of hair and eyes, and length of his feet to be accurately measured, shall be entered in a book provided for that purpose, together with such other natural or accidental marks, or peculiarity of feature or appearance, as may serve to identify him ; an instrument shall also be provided by which the profile of his face shall be delineated, and it shall be marked with his name and pasted in the said book, under the description of his person ; and if the convict can write, his signature shall be placed under the said description of his person.

Art. 137. All the effects on the person of the convict, as well as his clothes, shall be taken from him and specially mentioned, and preserved to be restored to him on his discharge, or delivered to his curator, where one shall be appointed, pursuant to the provisions hereinafter contained.

Art. 138. If the convict is not in such ill health as to require being sent to the infirmary, he shall then be conducted to the cell assigned to him, where he shall be kept in solitude for forty-eight hours, interrupted only by the necessary attendance of the keeper ; during this period, designed for reflection, neither books nor employment of any kind shall be allowed him.

Art. 139. On the third day the chaplain shall visit him in his cell, and shall endeavour to impress on his mind as well the wickedness as the danger of vicious and unlawful pursuits, and he shall exhort him to obedience and industry during the term of his service, and urge the utility of acquiring the means of an honest support by labour on his discharge. The warden shall then examine him, and put him to such labour as he shall seem fittest for, consulting his inclinations as well as his physical powers.

## CHAPTER II.

*Of the labour of the male convicts committed for a term of years.*

Art. 140. Although labour forms a part of the sentence, it is annexed as an alleviation, not an aggravation of punishment. The punishment is imprisonment in solitude. All that the law entitles the patient to under this confinement, is food, clothing, and lodging, sufficient for the preservation of health, but all of the coarsest kind ; his health and life are the objects of attention, not his appetite or com-

fort. Other indulgences are the reward of industry, obedience, repentance, and reformation ; these are the effects of labour ; and labour,
therefore, is permitted as the means of attaining them.

Art. 141. The advantages that are to be gained by perseverance in
labour, obedience, moral conduct, and a desire of reform, are :

1. A better diet.

2. A partial relief from solitude, and the means of education by the
visits and lessons of the teacher.

3. Permission to read books of general instruction.

4. The privilege of receiving the visits of friends or relations at
proper periods.

5. Admission into a class for instruction, after a period of good
conduct that shall evince a sincere desire to reform.

6. The privilege, after a long probation, of labouring in society.

7. A proportion of the proceeds of his labour on his discharge.

8. A certificate of good conduct, industry, and skill in the trade he
has learned, which may enable him to regain the confidence of society.

Art. 142. As these advantages are to be gained only by industry
and good conduct, they are suspended and may be forfeited by idleness
or irregularity ; and at the expiration of the two days given for reflection, after the admission of the convict, the articles of this section are
to be read to him, and he shall make his election whether he will avail
himself of the indulgence they offer ; should he consent, he shall be
immediately set to labour ; if he refuse, the offer shall not be repeated
in less than six days ; after the second refusal, it can only be repeated
in fifteen days ; and after a third, he cannot be permitted to accept it
until a month's time shall have elapsed ; after which, he shall be considered as having made his final election.

Art. 143. From among the convicts who have not, before commitment, worked at any trade, the warden shall select a sufficient number
to perform the offices of cooking and other necessary attendance in the
prison. He shall prefer for this purpose those who have the shortest
term to serve; but all these shall be locked up in separate cells at night.

Art. 144. If the convict has been used to any employment or trade
that can be advantageously pursued consistent with the system established by this Code, he shall be furnished with the implements of such
trade, and be allowed to employ himself at it. If his trade is one that
cannot, in the opinion of the inspectors, be conveniently carried on, or
is inconsistent with the system, he shall be taught an employment the
most analogous to the one to which he has been bred.

Art. 145. If the convict has not been bred to any trade, the warden
shall employ him at such business as is best adapted to his habits of life
and his strength, consulting as much as may be possible the inclination
of the convict; and in the selection of employment, regard is to be had
more to giving him an honest mode of subsistence after his discharge,
than to the profit of the prison.

Art. 146. The regular occupation of each convict shall, for the first
six months of his confinement, be carried on in the outer enclosure of
his cell, in solitude, interrupted only by the visits of the inspectors,
the warden, the chaplain, the teacher, the physician, the person (if any)
employed to instruct him in his trade, and the attendants with the
regular meals, and by the exercise mentioned in the next article.

Art. 147. For the preservation of the health of the prisoners, each
of them shall be made to labour one hour in every day at a handcrank

hydraulic machine, or some other, calculated to exert the muscular powers in a manner beneficial to health.  This crank, or other parts of the machine to which bodily power is to be applied, shall be so placed and divided, that each prisoner may labour without having it in his power to have any communication with the others employed in the same labour, and they shall be conducted separately to and from the place, under the care of an under-keeper, who shall prevent any person from having any communication with them by word or otherwise.

Art. 148.  During the first six months of confinement the teacher shall give to the convicts who cannot read or write, a lesson to each, in regular rotation, employing himself at least seven hours in each day, until a class shall be formed, when he shall divide his time equally between the individual prisoners entitled to instruction and the classes.

Art. 149.  At the expiration of six months each convict who has received the lessons of the teacher during that time, and such other convicts as are desirous of receiving further instruction, shall, provided they obtain a certificate of good conduct and industry in labour from the warden, the chaplain, and teacher, have the privilege of being admitted into a class, which shall receive instruction together in the school-room; but no class shall contain more than eight; no more than one class shall be assembled at a time, and the individuals composing it shall be conducted separately to and from the place of instruction.

Art. 150.  The warden may, when necessary for the instruction of a prisoner in any business or trade, with the permission of the inspectors, employ a person of good character for that purpose, who shall, at proper hours, have access to such prisoner.

Art. 151.  The warden may, with the consent of the inspectors, make contracts for the labour of the convicts, or any of them, with mechanics or manufacturers; but a condition of the contract shall be, that the convicts shall be taught, and employed in, some useful trade ; and for that purpose a foreman or instructor, to be employed by the contractor, but approved by the warden and inspectors, shall be admitted to the enclosures adjoining the cells of the convicts, at convenient times during the hours of labour.

Art. 152.  The first contract shall not be for a longer period than eighteen months ; and all subsequent contracts shall be made by auction and for one year; and the applicants for the contract shall be permitted, in the presence of the warden, to examine the convicts as to their skill and ability.

Art. 153.  If any contractor or his agent shall give or promise to any of the convicts any article of food, drink, or other article, not permitted by this Code or by the prison regulation, the contract shall be forfeited, and each offender shall pay a fine of five hundred dollars, and be imprisoned not more than thirty nor less than ten days in close custody.

Art. 154.  After being employed for eighteen months in solitary labour, the convict, if he can procure from the warden, the inspectors, the chaplain, and the teacher (if he have been under his instruction), a certificate of industry, good conduct, and a disposition to reform, may be admitted to a working class, not exceeding ten, to work at some useful trade ; but no one shall enjoy this privilege the value of whose labour during the eighteen months shall not have exceeded the expense of his clothing and food, unless he shall have lost by sickness a number of days' labour, of which the value shall be equal to the deficiency in his account.

Art. 155. Each working class shall be separately employed in a different work-shop, without any communication the one class with another, and shall be under the direction of an under-keeper, who shall permit no communication between the individuals composing it but that necessary for the business, and any breach of this rule shall be punished by close confinement for such time as the warden shall direct, and by a return to solitary labour.

Art. 156. At the dawn of day the convict shall be made to rise and to clear out his sleeping cell, which shall then be locked; he shall then, after washing, commence his labour, which shall continue, including the hour for exercise at the machine and the attendance on the teacher and the time of receiving the visits of the other officers, from the rising to half an hour before the setting of the sun every day except Sundays, excepting one hour for breakfast and one hour and a half for dinner, and the supper shall be given when the work of the day is finished.

Art. 157. After sunset and before it is dark, all the convicts shall be locked up in their separate cells.

## CHAPTER III.

### *Of the treatment of prisoners confined for life.*

Art. 158. The convicts who are confined for life on a third conviction, for an offence which if it had been the first, would have been punishable by imprisonment for a term of years only, shall, in all respects, be treated like the prisoners confined for a term, except that the prison uniform shall be different, and shall designate by three different colours the number of their offences.

Art. 159. Those convicted of murder without any aggravating circumstances, and for rape, shall be strictly confined to their respective cells and adjoining courts; in which last they may be permitted to labour, except for two months consecutively in every year, commencing on the anniversary of their crime, during which period they shall only come into the court during the time necessary to cleanse the cell; and on the anniversary of the commission of their crime the convict shall have no allowance of food for twenty-four hours, during which fast he shall receive the visit of the chaplain, who shall endeavour by exhortation and prayer to bring him to repentance.

Art. 160. Murderers of all description and those convicted of rape, shall receive no visits except from the inspectors, the wardens, officers and attendants of the prison, and from those who are constituted visiters of the prison. They shall have no books, but selections from the Bible and such other books of religion and morality as the chaplain shall deem proper to produce repentance and fix their reliance on a future state. Their uniform and diet shall be such as is hereinafter directed.

Art. 161. Infanticides shall be treated in all respects like those guilty of unaggravated murder, except that the confinement without labour shall continue three months consecutively in each year.

Art. 162. Assassins shall be confined without labour for six months consecutively in every year, and treated in the manner above directed.

Art. 163. Parricides shall not be indulged in the performance of labour at any time, but shall be closely confined in a cell, without a court, but of such dimensions as shall be sufficient for their health, and in other respects shall be treated like other murderers.

Art. 164. When any two of the crimes punishable with imprisonment for life, such as rape and murder, are combined, or where murder under trust is perpetrated by assassination, or parricide by poison, the convict shall receive the same treatment as is directed for parricides, except that on the return in each month of the day on which the crime was committed, they be debarred from all allowance of food for twenty-four hours, and shall, during such fast, receive the visits and exhortation of the chaplain.

Art. 165. The fast shall not be suffered when the physician shall certify that it will be dangerous to the health of the convict.

Art. 166. Those convicts for life who have not learned to read, may be instructed by the teacher.

Art. 167. No murderers, in any degree, shall have any communication with other persons out of the prison than the inspectors and visiters; they are considered dead to the rest of the world.

Art. 168. The cells of murderers (in any degree) shall be painted black within and without, and on the outside thereof shall be inscribed, in large letters, the following sentence :

"In this cell is confined, to pass his life in solitude and sorrow. A. B. convicted of the murder of C. D. [by assassination, parricide, &c. describing the offence, if of an aggravated kind]; his food is bread of the coarsest kind ; his drink is water, mingled with his tears : he is dead to the world; this cell is his grave; his existence is prolonged that he may remember his crime, and repent it, and that the continuance of his punishment may deter others from the indulgence of hatred, avarice, sensuality, and the passions which lead to the crime he has committed. When the Almighty, in his due time, shall exercise towards him that dispensation which he himself arrogantly and wickedly usurped towards another, his body is to be dissected, and his soul will abide that judgment which Divine Justice shall decree."

Art. 169. The same inscription, changing only the words "this cell" for the words "solitary cell in this prison," shall be made on the outside of the prison wall, in large white letters on a black ground. The inscriptions shall be removed on the death of the convicts to which they relate.

Art. 170. Inscriptions shall in like manner be made on the cells of those convicted of rape, and on the outer wall of the prison, to this effect : "In this cell" [or on the outer wall, "In a solitary cell in this prison,] forgotten, or remembered only to be detested and despised, lies A. B. condemned to solitude and abstinence during life, for a cowardly and brutal injury to a woman."

# CHAPTER IV.

## *Of the clothing and diet of the convicts.*

Art. 171. The uniform of the prison shall be a jacket and trousers of cloth or other warm stuff for the winter, and lighter materials for the summer. The form and colour shall be determined by the inspectors; but they shall be the same for all criminals condemned for a term, except those who have been convicted of a repetition of offences; these shall have distinctive marks on their dress, showing the number of their convictions.

Art. 172. Each of the convicts shall have such number of coarse linen shirts and trousers of the same material in summer as will be sufficient to give them a change twice in every week ; and all shall be provided with other articles of clothing sufficient to preserve health and cleanliness.

Art. 173. The convicts for murder shall be clothed in black outer garments, spotted and streaked with red. Those confined for life, for any other crime, shall wear such distinctive marks on their clothing as shall be directed by the inspectors, to designate their respective crimes.

Art. 174. The prison allowance of food is one pound of brown wheaten bread and one pint of mush morning and evening each day; the allowance of bread may be varied by giving three days in the week a pound and a half of Indian corn bread instead of wheaten. Water is the only liquor allowed in the prison ration.

Art. 175. Prisoners who labour and preserve the rules of the prison are allowed, in addition to the prison daily allowance, a gill of molasses, and for four days in the week two pounds of beef or pork without bone, daily, made into six messes, varied from salt to fresh, with vegetables, and for three other days soup.

Art. 176. Those whose labour and industry have entitled them to work in classes, shall also be indulged with a pint of small beer, or cider diluted with water, or a mixture of vinegar and water sweetened with molasses once every day.

Art. 177. No prisoner, while confined to his cell without labour, is to receive any thing but the prison allowance.

Art. 178. No tobacco in any form shall be used by the convicts; and any one who shall supply them with it, or with wine, or spirituous or intoxicating fermented liquor, shall be fined two hundred dollars, and if an officer, be dismissed.

Art. 179. Any convict whose labour shall exceed the expense of his support, according to the account herein directed to be kept, shall have the privilege of directing one-tenth part thereof to be expended in the purchase of books, to be approved by the inspectors, or such articles, excepting food or liquors, as he may desire, and as may not be inconsistent with the prison rules.

Art. 180. Any convict, other than those convicted of murder or rape, who has been steadily employed for eighteen months, and is guilty of no infraction of the prison discipline, may, once in every six months, receive the visit of any friend or relation, of the same sex, for not more than fifteen minutes, in the presence of a keeper, on a written permission signed by two inspectors.

Art. 181. No person, who is not an official visiter of the prisons, or who has not a written permission from one of them ; or from one of the inspectors, is allowed to visit the same. The official visiters are, the governor, president of the senate, members of the general assembly, the secretary of state, the attorney general, the judges of all the courts in the state, the mayor, recorder, and members of the city council of the city of New Orleans, the directors of all the charitable incorporated societies in the city of New Orleans.

Art. 182. None but the official visiters can have any verbal or written communication with the convicts, nor shall any visiter whatever be permitted to deliver or receive from any of the convicts any letter or

4 P

message whatever, or to supply them with any article of any kind, under the penalty of two hundred dollars fine.

Art. 183. It is the duty of any visiter, who shall discover any abuse, infraction of law, or oppression, immediately to make the same known to the board of inspectors, or to the governor if the inspectors or either of them are implicated.

Art. 184. No male visiter shall visit the female convicts but in the presence of the matron.

## CHAPTER V.

### *Of the treatment of the female convicts.*

Art. 185. The female convicts shall, as well as the male, each be lodged in separate cells.

Art. 186. Such of those confined for a term of years as are capable, by their habits or strength, shall be selected by the matron to perform the domestic services of the female division and for the washing of the clothes for the men's department. Those who are so employed shall, during the day, be kept under the inspection of the matron or her assistants, and not suffered to have any conversation but relative to the business in which they are engaged.

Art. 187. The others, not so selected, shall be employed in needle-work, spinning, or other suitable occupations. They shall, on receiving the necessary certificate of order and industry from the matron and chaplain, be entitled to the same advantages of education and social labour that are directed for the male convicts. The classes for education and for labour may consist of such number as the matron, with the approbation of the warden or inspectors, shall desire.

Art. 188. The regulations with respect to diet are applicable to the female department, except that the matron may allow to the industrious and orderly, tea for their breakfast, if they prefer it to mush.

Art. 189. The dress for the female convicts shall be regulated by the matron, with the approbation of the inspectors.

Art. 190. Female convicts for life shall be treated in the same manner as the males, but under the direction of the matron.

## TITLE III.

OF THE SCHOOL OF REFORM.

## CHAPTER I.

### *Of the persons to be admitted into the school of reform.*

Art. 191. All persons under the age of eighteen sentenced to imprisonment and labour (unless for life), and all vagrants under that age and above six years, shall be sent to the School of Reform.

Art. 192. All minors above six and under eighteen years of age, who have no visible means of honest subsistence and are not supported by any friend or relation ; all common beggars within the said age of eighteen ; all females under seventeen years of age, who live by prostitution in a DISORDERLY HOUSE, shall be considered as vagrants under the last article, and may, by order of the mayor of New Orleans, or the parish judge and two other magistrates, be committed to the School of Reform.

Art. 193. All minors above nine and under the age of fifteen, who shall commit an offence of which they shall be acquitted on account of the want of sufficent discretion to know the nature of the offence, may, at the discretion of the court, be committed to the School of Reform.

.Art. 194. In like manner a minor, who being accused of a crime and shall be acquitted by showing that at the time of the commission thereof he was under the age of nine years, may, at the discretion of the court, be sent to the School of Reform.

Art. 195. In cases of misdemeanor, committed by a minor under eighteen years of age, and punishable by simple imprisonment in close custody, the court may also, at their discretion, send the defendant to the School of Reform.

Art. 196. In exercising the discretion given by the three last preceding articles, the court must consider that the object of the School of Reform is not only to punish by restraint, but to separate the juvenile offender from the association of vice, to afford him the means of education, religious and moral instruction, and instruction in some mechanic art, so as to make him a useful member of society ; and that where, from the circumstances of the case, these objects will probably be attained without committing the defendant to the School of Reform, that this public institution ought not to be so burthened.


# CHAPTER II.

## Of the mode of reception.

Art. 197. Every one committed to the School of Reform shall be thoroughly cleansed, and clothed in the uniform of the house, which shall be comfortable and adapted to the season.

Art. 198. The name, age, sex, place of nativity of the person committed, names and place of abode and occupation of his parents, the cause of commitment, and the authority by which it was made, shall be entered in a book specially provided for that purpose by the warden.

Art. 199. The chaplain, or teacher, and the matron (if the person committed be a female), or the warden (if a male), shall interrogate the party as to the course of life he has pursued, and shall make an abstract of his answers in the book above mentioned ; but no other means shall be used, but those of persuasion, to obtain the truth on such interrogatory.

Art. 200. After some time given to solitary reflection, proportioned to the age and degree of depravity of the offender, which shall not exceed, in any case, twelve hours, the advantages of industry, obedience and attention to instruction, and the certainty of punishment for a contrary course, shall be impressed upon him by the warden, or, if a female, by the matron, and he shall then be instructed and employed as is hereinafter directed.

# CHAPTER III.

### *Of the instruction in the school of reform.*

Art. 201. The time of school instruction shall be one hour, to commence at sunrise, and one hour after labour in the afternoon.

Art. 202. The children shall be taught reading and writing in the French and English language, and arithmetic; and such of the boys as show an aptitude for learning, in the opinion of the teacher and warden, shall be taught geography, land surveying, and navigation.

Art. 203. Before the instruction begins, select portions of the scriptures shall be read morning and evening.

Art. 204. Premiums of books and badges of merit shall be given to the scholars by the warden, on the recommendation of the teachers, to the children who shall show the most diligence and be distinguished for orderly conduct.

Art. 205. A small collection of entertaining and instructive books shall also be provided for the use of those who have badges of merit.

Art. 206. The teacher has no greater power of correction than is given by law in ordinary schools, and it extends only to faults committed in relation to the literary instruction.

Art. 207. No punishment shall be inflicted on any of the females for faults committed in school but by the matron, or in her presence.

Art. 208. The boys and girls shall be taught separately, and the matron, or her assistant, shall always be present during the instruction of the girls.

Art. 209. Examinations of the scholars shall be had once every three months, in the presence of the inspectors and such of the visiters as choose to attend.

Art. 210. The teacher shall use the system of mutual instruction, and shall endeavour to qualify such of the children, of both sexes, as show a particular aptitude, to be themselves teachers according to the same method.

# CHAPTER IV.

### *Of employment in the school of reform.*

Art. 211. All the hours between sunrise and sunset that are not hereby appropriated to instruction, to meals, or to relaxation and exercise, must be employed in labour.

Art. 212. The labour to be performed shall be such as, in the opinion of the inspectors, shall be best calculated to procure a subsistence for the prisoners when they shall be restored to liberty.

Art. 213. Each of the boys shall be taught a mechanic art, and for this purpose the warden shall, with the approbation of the inspectors, contract with mechanics to find materials, to send foremen to the prison to superintend their work and teach them the different trades, paying a reasonable sum for the value of their labour. The necessary tools and implements shall be provided by the institution.

Art. 214. The foremen so employed by the mechanics shall be men of good characters, approved by the inspectors; they shall remain in their respective workshops during the hours of labour, preserve order therein, and keep the boys at work, teaching them carefully all the branches of the trade; but they shall inflict no punishment, unless by direction of the warden and in his presence, and such punishment shall be such moderate correction as a master is authorized by law to inflict on an apprentice.

Art. 215. The foremen shall make daily reports to the warden of each boy under his care, for which purpose he shall keep a calendar containing the names of each of them, on which he shall make marks, denoting offences, or extraordinary diligence, or good conduct, which shall be shown daily to the warden.

Art. 216. Great care shall be taken to suit the employment to the physical force and constitution of each boy ; and the warden shall frequently visit the workshops, and see that unreasonable tasks are not imposed by the foremen.

Art. 217. If no such contract should be offered for the labour of the boys as the warden and inspectors shall deem advantageous, proper persons may be employed by the inspectors to instruct them in some mechanic art.

Art. 218. Besides the mechanic arts the boys shall be exercised for two periods in each day (not exceeding half an hour each time) in some laborious employment, that shall require as much as possible the exercise of all the muscular powers, to strengthen and fit them for any hard labour to which they may afterwards be called ; for this purpose a hydraulic or other machine, to be moved by manual labour, shall be constructed in the enclosure of the School of Reform, and a mast, with yards and standing and running rigging, shall be erected, on which they shall be taught to climb, and prepare themselves for a seafaring life.

Art. 219. The tread-mill shall not be introduced into this or any other of the places of confinement established by this Code.

Art. 220. The girls shall be taught needle-work, and be employed in washing, ironing, baking, and other works of housewifery ; and they may also be taught such trades as women are usually employed in, at the time and place in which they are confined. The matron shall superintend this part of their employment, and none but female instructors in any branch, except the school-master, shall be admitted into their department.

Art. 221. The children of both sexes shall, by turns, be employed in the menial service of the establishment to which they belong— waiting at the table, cleaning the workshops and eating-rooms, and other places for the common resort of the persons confined ; but each one is bound to sweep and clean his own cell.

## CHAPTER V.

### *Of the distribution of time in the school of reform.*

Art. 222. At the dawn of day all the prisoners, except those in the infirmary and those confined to solitude for a breach of prison discipline, shall leave their cells ; each one shall put up his bed, remove every thing that ought to be removed, and sweep the cell, which shall be locked.

Art. 223. Each one shall then wash, and twice every week, when the weather will permit, shall bathe. They shall then assemble in the school-room, when a select portion of scripture and prayers shall be read ; the school shall then be opened, and the instruction continue for one hour ; immediately after which breakfast shall be served.

Art. 224. After breakfast half an hour shall be allowed for exercise in the court, but always in the presence of the warden, or some officer of the establishment for the boys, or of the matron or her assistant for the girls ; immediately after the expiration of this half hour, the boys shall be put to labour, for another half hour, on the machine mentioned in the last preceding chapter, and the girls be allowed to continue their exercise.

Art. 225. The boys shall then be conducted to the workshops, where they shall be employed for three hours and a half ; at the expiration of which time they shall wash and go to dinner, and after dinner shall have another half hour for exercise, and labour on the machine, and then be employed in the shops until an hour before sunset, when they shall again assemble for instruction in the school for an hour ; after the evening school, half an hour shall be given for exercise, and then each one shall be locked in his separate cell.

Art. 226. In the summer the inspectors may dispense with the hard labour in the heat of the day, and appropriate it to instruction or relaxation, at their discretion.

Art. 227. On the certificate of the physician, that the labour, or any part of it, cannot be undergone by any one of the persons confined without danger to his health, it shall be remitted or modified by the warden.

## CHAPTER VI.

### *Of diet, lodging, and clothing.*

Art. 228. The diet shall be, for breakfast, coffee made of parched grain, and mush alternately, both sweetened with molasses, and corn bread ; for dinner, beef or mutton soup, with vegetables and corn bread, and a quarter of a pound of the flesh of which the soup is made, for each, for four days in the week—three days, fish or pease soup without meat ; supper, the same as the breakfast. At all the meals, there must be bread of sufficient quantity to satisfy their hunger ;

and when the state of the market will permit, wheat bread may be substituted for corn. Water is the only drink allowed.

Art. 229. The inspectors may, when circumstances require it, change the ration of food, but it must always be coarse, but abundant and nutritive.

Art. 230. Each of the persons confined shall lodge in a separate cell, shut with a door having grates at the top and bottom, which, in cold weather, the occupant may cover with a sliding shutter, on the inside. The cell shall contain a box for a night-pan, and a sheet of canvas, stretched by loops at the four corners and suspended by hooks in the corners of the cell for a hammock, with sheets and one blanket for summer, and two blankets and a corn-husk mat in winter. This bedding shall be aired and washed at such periods as the physician or warden shall direct.

Art. 231. For the boys the clothing shall consist of a cap, a shirt and jacket and trousers of coarse linen or cotton, and shoes, for the summer ; a jacket and trousers of cloth, with socks and shoes, for the winter; the linen to be changed once a week in winter and twice a week in summer. The clothing for the girls shall be directed by the matron with the approbation of the inspectors.


## CHAPTER VII.

### Of the police of the school of reform.

Art. 232. The warden shall see that every one confined in the male department, excepting those in the infirmary, is locked up in his separate cell, at the time for that purpose before designated, and that all the fires in every part of the building are extinguished. No light, under any pretence, is permitted in the cells ; but lights shall be kept during the night in the galleries and passages leading to them.

Art. 233. A reflected light may be thrown into the cells of such as may desire to use the interval between the locking of the cell and nine at night in reading or study, but it shall be continued in favour of those only who can show the teacher on the following morning that they have used it to advantage.

Art. 234. A watch shall be kept at night by one of the under-keepers, and the warden may also employ with the keeper such of the boys, by turns, as may show by their conduct that such confidence may be reposed in them.

Art. 235. The roll shall be called of all the persons confined at the opening of the school in the morning, and at night previous to the retiring ; and the names of all those employed in the different workshops shall also be called at the hours of labour.

Art. 236. The meals shall be taken in the presence of the warden or some other officer of the establishment. The males shall be divided into classes of ten, who shall be seated at separate tables, and one of the boys the most distinguished for his orderly conduct, in each class, to be called the captain of the class, shall preside at each table ; he shall see that silence is observed during the meal, shall designate two of the class, by regular rotation, to wait on the others, and take care that each one receives his full allowance, and he shall report all breaches of order to the warden.

Art. 237. The captain of the class may be degraded for negligence or misbehaviour; and where several boys in a class are equally deserving, they shall have the distinction by turns weekly.

Art. 238. During the hours of recreation, no sports but those which exercise the body shall be allowed, and no wagering permitted; but the warden may award prizes for dexterity or skill.

Art. 239. The utmost attention must be paid to cleanliness in the persons, clothing, and bedding, and every part of the establishment; and it is part of the duty of all the officers employed, of the visiters, and particularly of the physician, to report to the warden every infraction that may be observed of this rule. There shall be a bathing room for each of the sexes, and all the persons confined shall be forced to bathe at least twice in every week during the seasons that will admit of it.


# CHAPTER VIII.

## *Of rewards and punishments.*

Art. 240. The rewards shall consist of badges, prizes of books, the use of the library, and marks of distinction and confidence, such as being made captain of a class, watchmen, or monitors in the school. They shall be conferred by the matron for the female department, by the warden for the male, and by the inspectors for both; but all rewards, for merit in school, shall be on the recommendation of the teacher.

Art. 241. The punishments are, deprivations of distinctions formerly obtained; such moderate personal castigation as does not draw blood, leave a permanent mark, or unfit the child for immediate attention to his instruction or labour; common diet; degradation from the class; confinement in solitude, or in a straight waistcoat or arm straps.

Art. 242. Irons or chains are not permitted under any pretence.

Art. 243. The teacher may preserve order in the school for boys by the moderate chastisement mentioned in the second article of this section; in the female school he may direct it to be done by the female teachers. None of the other punishments can be inflicted but by order of the warden, or, if on a female, but by order of the matron, subject always to the revision of the warden.

Art. 244. All the punishments may be continued, or be directed to cease by the inspectors, or any two of them.

Art. 245. Escape or attempt to escape, violence used towards any officer of the establishment, a refusal to work or receive instruction, or an attempt to persuade others to resist the authority of the officers, shall be punished by all the kinds of punishment above enumerated, for such period as the inspectors and warden, or inspectors and matron may direct.

Art. 246. The warden and the matron, with the approbation of the inspectors, shall frame rules for the preservation of order, not contrary to any thing contained in the Code or this chapter. The said rules shall designate what breaches shall be punishable by any of the penalties above enumerated and in what degree. These rules shall be put up in the different work-rooms, schools, and cells—shall be read to every one on his reception in the house, and shall be rigidly enforced.

# CHAPTER IX.

*Of the discharge from the school of reform.*

Art. 247. Discharges from the School of Reform may be either by the expiration of the term of service or by apprenticeship.

Art. 248. Whatever may be the term of imprisonment designated by law for the offence of which the party sent to the School of Reform is convicted, such party cannot be discharged (unless by apprenticeship), if a female, before she has attained the age of nineteen, or if a male, before twenty-one.

Art. 249. Those who are sentenced for a term that will not expire until after they have respectively attained the ages mentioned in the last preceding article, and whose conduct has not entitled them to the recommendation hereinafter mentioned for apprenticeship, shall, within six months after attaining the ages aforesaid, be transferred to the Penitentiary to serve out the remainder of the term.

Art. 250. Those who are entitled to the recommendation, and who have not been apprenticed for some other cause, shall be discharged after having attained the age of twenty-two if a male, or twenty if a female, although the term of imprisonment in the sentence be for a longer time.

Art. 251. The warden is authorized to bind out, by indentures of apprenticeship, such of the prisoners confined as come within the description contained in the next succeeding article ; and the indentures shall impose the same obligations and give the same rights and remedies as indentures of apprenticeship made by a parent or guardian, with the assent of the minors, under the civil law of the state.

Art. 252. In order to be legally bound, pursuant to the last article, the apprentice must have been two years in the School of Reform ; he must have learned to read, write, and understand the first three rules in arithmetic ; and must have obtained a certificate signed by the warden, (and if a female by the matron), approved by the inspectors, declaring that the moral conduct and diligence of the party has evinced such a reformation as, in their opinion, will render it safe to receive him as an apprentice.

Art. 253. The duration of the apprenticeship shall be until the party bound shall attain the age of twenty-one if a male, or nineteen if a female, unless, at the time of making the indenture, the male apprentice shall have attained nineteen years of age, or the female seventeen ; in which case the indenture may be for three years, if the term of the sentence does not expire before ; but if the term should expire before, the apprentice cannot be bound for a longer term than the attainment of twenty-one years for a male, or nineteen for a female, without his or her consent, and then only for the said term of three years.

Art. 254. The male apprentices shall be put out, if possible, to mechanics of the same trade they have been taught in the School of Reform ; if no mechanic pursuing the same profession offers, some other demanding, as near as may be the same species of labour, shall be preferred ; but whatever trade may have been taught to the apprentice, he may, by his own consent, be apprenticed to a farmer or a mariner.

4 Q

Art. 255. The conditions of the articles of apprenticeship shall be, on the part of the apprentice, obedience to lawful commands, and diligence, sobriety, and honesty ; on the part of the master, that he will perfect the apprentice in the trade he has been taught, or teach him the new business if such be the case, that he will continue his schooling at least one day in the week, that he will provide him necessary food, clothing, lodging, medical assistance, and that, at the end of the period, he will give him new clothing and a sum of money to be specified in the indenture, and such as the warden and the master shall think reasonable.

Art. 256. No one shall be apprenticed to any one residing out of the state, nor shall the indenture be assignable without the assent of the apprentice.

Art. 257. The clause relating to the teaching and perfecting in a trade or business, is not indispensable in the indenture of a female.

Art. 258. No female shall be indented to an unmarried man, or to a married man living apart from his wife.

Art. 259. It shall be a condition in the indenture between the warden and the master, that a report shall be made once in every year of the conduct of the apprentice to the warden ; and if he has reason to believe that his reformation is complete, that he will permit him, if within the city of New Orleans or its suburbs, to visit the school and converse with the others still there.

Art. 260. The convict at the time of his discharge, whether apprenticed or not, shall be comfortably clad, and the inspectors, at their discretion, may make him an allowance in money, or deliver him books or tools, if they are satisfied with his conduct.

## CHAPTER X.

### Of visits.

Art. 261. Besides the persons created visiters of all the places of confinement by this Code, and those who may receive permission from them, the parents or those related in the second degree to the persons confined in the School of Reform, may visit them on stated days, to be appointed by the warden ; but when he is apprehensive that evil counsels may be given, it shall always be in the presence of an officer.

## TITLE IV.

### OF THE PECUNIARY CONCERNS OF THE SEVERAL PLACES OF CONFINEMENT.

Art. 262. The board of inspectors shall appoint an agent, who shall make all purchases and sales on account of all the several places of confinement, including the House of Refuge and Industry, keeping regular sets of mercantile books for each of the said institutions, which may be examined by the inspectors, the wardens, or any of the visiters.

Art. 263. The compensation of the agent shall be fixed by the inspectors, with the approbation of the governor.

Art. 264. The regular supplies of provisions, and of all other articles consumed or used in the said institutions in considerable quantities, shall be furnished by contract, and adjudged after advertisement to the lowest bidder; but the wardens shall examine the articles furnished, and have the right to reject such as are not of the quality contracted for. The physician shall, in like manner, inspect the medicines and hospital furniture.

Art. 265. All the articles manufactured in either of the said places which are not made for manufacturers by contract, in the manner hereinafter provided, shall be sold by the agent to the best advantage, under the direction of the inspectors.

Art. 266. Regular and minute accounts of the receipts and expenditures of each place of confinement, including the House of Refuge, shall be furnished each quarter by the inspectors to the governor, and yearly accounts to the legislature on the first day of their annual meeting.

Art. 267. All moneys appropriated by the legislature for the use of either of the said places, shall be drawn for by the board of inspectors as the same may be wanted, in favour of the cashier of the Louisiana State Bank, and shall by him be carried to the credit of the board of inspectors, in an account to be opened with them in their official capacity, for the use of the particular institution for which the appropriation is made (naming it in the account) between the bank and the inspectors.

Art. 268. Whenever the amount of money in the hands of the agent, received on account of either or all of the institutions, shall exceed three hundred dollars, he shall, within two days, deposit the same in the said bank to the credit of the account opened with the inspectors for the use of the prison to which it belongs.

Art. 269. No money shall be drawn from the bank, on either of the said accounts, but by a draft signed by a majority of the inspectors, specifying on account of which prison it is drawn, for what purpose, and to whom the amount is due.

Art. 270. All accounts or demands against the prisons shall be examined, allowed, and paid by the inspectors; and when they meet to settle such accounts, the agent shall act as their clerk and shall make regular entries in the books of all receipts and expenditures, to the account of the institution to which they belong; but a sum, not exceeding one hundred dollars, may be placed in the hands of each warden, and as much in the hands of the agent, to pay current expenses, to be accounted for monthly to the inspectors.

Art. 271. If either the inspectors or the agent shall fail in making any deposit in the manner and at the time directed by either of the three last preceding articles; or if the inspectors, or either of them, shall draw out of the bank any moneys belonging to or appropriated for either of the said places of confinement, including the House of Refuge, in any other manner than is above directed, the person so offending shall pay a fine of five hundred dollars; and if any of the said moneys which are either not deposited when by the said articles or either of them they ought to be, or are drawn out of the bank contrary to the directions of this chapter, shall be applied to any other use than to that of the said institutions, or one of them, the person guilty of such misapplication shall be dismissed from his office, be imprisoned, in close custody, for sixty days, and pay a fine of one thousand dollars.

Art. 272. The wardens of the several prisons shall deliver to the agent all the articles manufactured in their prisons respectively, which are not necessary for the use of such prison, except those articles manufactured in the House of Detention by the prisoners there who have provided their own materials, or who have made a different arrangement with the inspectors for the disposal of the proceeds of their labour ; and excepting also the articles made for manufacturers by contract, in the Penitentiary, School of Reform, and House of Refuge and Industry.

Art. 273. The wardens of the Penitentiary and of the School of Reform shall each be allowed, in addition to their salaries,
per cent. on the gross amount of sales by the agent of the articles manufactured in their prisons respectively, after deducting only the cost of the materials employed in the articles so sold; and also      per cent. on the amount of sums paid for the labour of the convicts by manufacturers ; but this allowance shall be forfeited for every year in which the wardens shall use any other means than those authorized by this Code to induce the convicts to labour, either by way of punishment or reward.

Art. 274. The average number of deaths in the principal penitentiaries of the United States having been found to be about            in every hundred annually, (taking the average of the number of prisoners confined at all times during the year as the basis of the calculation for the whole number,) as an encouragement to use greater care and attention in lessening this rate of mortality, if the said proportion shall be in any one year reduced in the Penitentiary of this state more than one half of that average, the governor shall present to the physician books, surgical instruments, or plate, of the value of          dollars, which testimonial shall be doubled in value if the proportion be reduced more than three-fourths.

Art. 275. The average number of re-convictions in the principal cities of the Union having been found to be about            in every hundred annually of those committed to the Penitentiary in those cities; to lessen this proportion is the object of the reformatory part of prison discipline. To incite, therefore, the officers to a zealous discharge of this part of their duty, if in any one year, succeeding the third year after this Code shall have gone into operation, the number of re-commitments to the Penitentiary shall be less, in any one year, by one-half than that proportion, an honorary testimonial of that fact, consisting of a piece of plate of the value of          dollars, shall be presented by the governor to the inspectors, the wardens, the chaplains, and teachers, of the said prison ; the value of which plate shall be doubled in any year in which the said proportion is reduced to less than three-fourths of the average above stated.

Art. 276. A similar testimonial shall be given to the matrons, if the like reduction takes place in the re-commitments of the female convicts.

Art. 277. The amount requisite for the purchase of the testimonials aforesaid, shall be taken from the recompense fund, created by the Code of Criminal Procedure.

# TITLE V.

## OF THE DISCHARGE OF THE CONVICTS.

Art. 278. Whenever a convict shall be discharged by the expiration of the term to which he was condemned, or by pardon, he shall take off the prison uniform and have the clothes which he brought to the prison restored to him, together with the other property, if any, that was taken from him on his commitment, that has not been otherwise legally disposed of.

Art. 279. A copy of his account with the prison, made out in the manner hereinbefore directed, shall be given to him ; and if the proceeds of his labour produce any balance in his favour, one half of such balance shall be paid him.

Art. 280. Before the convict is dismissed, the chapter of the Penal Code, "Of the Repetition of Offences," shall be read to him.

Art. 281. If the warden, the chaplain, and the teacher, have been satisfied with the morality, industry, and order of his conduct, they shall give him a certificate to that effect.

Art. 282. One or more of the inspectors shall be present whenever a convict is discharged, who, as well as the officers of the prison, shall inquire into his future prospects and designs ; shall aid him in an endeavour to procure an honest support, or to return to his friends ; shall exhort him to perseverance in habits of industry ; and if he can find no other employment, and is desirous of maintaining himself by labour, the warden shall admit him into the House of Refuge, hereinafter provided for.

Art. 283. If the warden shall discover that any discharged convict, instead of seeking to maintain himself by labour, shall associate with the idle and profligate, he shall immediately proceed against him as a vagrant, under the provisions for that purpose contained in the Code of Criminal Procedure.

# TITLE VI.

HOW THE PROPERTY OF PERSONS CONDEMNED FOR CRIME SHALL BE DISPOSED OF.

## CHAPTER I.

*Of the property of convicts condemned to imprisonment and labour for a term.*

Art. 284. The property of convicts condemned to imprisonment and labour, may be administered by curators during the term for which they are condemned. The letters of curatorship are revoked by their pardon or discharge; but such revocation does not invalidate legal acts done by the curator.

Art. 285. Any person who would be entitled to the curatorship of the convict, had he died on the day judgment was pronounced against him, shall be entitled to the curatorship.

Art. 286. The mode of proceeding to obtain the letters of curatorship shall be the same as that prescribed in case of death, except that, instead of alleging and proving the death of the party, the record of his condemnation shall be produced to the judge.

Art. 287. The curatorship, in case of condemnation, carries with it all the consequences, responsibilities, rights, and duties, that result from a curatorship to a person deceased.

Art. 288. Curators and tutors may also be appointed to the persons and estates of the children of the convict, in the like manner and to the same persons who would have been entitled to the said offices if the convict had been dead.

Art. 289. The curatorships and tutorships, mentioned in the last article, are the same as to all rights, duties, and responsibilities, as they would have been had the appointment been made after the death of the convict; but they are revoked by his pardon or discharge, except in cases where his sentence incapacitates him from exercising those trusts.

Art. 290. Those who would have been the heirs of a convict, sentenced to imprisonment for a term, cannot take the estate out of the hands of the curator; but if he have relations in the ascending or descending line, whom he was bound by law to support, the curator shall, out of the estate, provide for their sustenance.

Art. 291. All property given, or in any manner whatever accruing to a convict in the Penitentiary, shall vest in his curator, if he be sentenced for a term of years, to be disposed of in like manner with his other property; or if he be sentenced for life, shall vest in his heirs.

# CHAPTER II.

*Of the disposition of the property of convicts sentenced to imprisonment for life.*

Art. 292. The same disposition shall be made of the estate of a person sentenced to imprisonment for life, as if he had died on the day sentence was pronounced; and any last will and testament or codicil he may have made prior to that time, shall take effect in the same manner as if he had died on that day.

Art. 293. But no disposition of any estate, either by will or otherwise, after the arrest for crime, of which the prisoner was convicted, in the case of any crime whether the sentence is for life or otherwise, shall be valid against the claim of the person entitled to a suit for the private injury committed by the crime, unless such disposition was made for a valuable and equivalent consideration to a person ignorant of the arrest.

# BOOK III.

## OF THE HOUSE OF REFUGE AND INDUSTRY.

## TITLE I.

### OF THE DESIGN OF THIS ESTABLISHMENT.

Art. 294. The object of this establishment is twofold : the first, to afford the means of voluntary employment to those who are able and willing to labour, and gratuitous support to those who are not; the second object is, to coerce those who, although capable of supporting themselves, prefer a life of idleness, vice, and mendicity, to one of honest labour.

Art. 295. As a House of Refuge, it is intended to afford to the discharged convict the means of support by voluntary labour, until, by degrees, he may regain the confidence of society ; to prevent those offences of which poverty and want of employment are the real or pretended cause ; and to relieve private charity from the unequal burthen of supporting the mendicant poor.

Art. 296. As a House of Industry, the establishment is intended to be a place of coercion and restraint for vagrants and able-bodied beggars ; for the first, because their mode of life raises a just presumption that it is sustained by illegal depredations on a society to which they do not properly belong ; for the second, because, by false pretences of inability, they impose on the charity of the public ; and for both as a measure of preventive justice, because their voluntary idleness, unless corrected, will inevitably conduct them to vice, and crimes, and punishment.

## TITLE II.

### OF THE DIFFERENT DEPARTMENTS OF THE HOUSE OF REFUGE AND INDUSTRY, AND OF THE DESCRIPTION OF PERSONS ADMITTED TO, AND CONFINED IN EACH.

Art. 297. The House of Refuge and Industry shall consist of two departments : the one for voluntary, the other for forced labour ;

both shall be under the direction of the same warden ; and the one shall be called the House of Refuge, and the other the House of Industry.

Art. 298. In the House of Refuge shall be admitted all such discharged convicts as may be desirous of gaining a subsistence by labour; all public mendicants who allege a want of employment as the reason for asking public charity, or who, from age, infirmity, and poverty, are incapable, in part or in the whole, to support themselves, and have no relations who, by law, are bound to support them.

Art. 299. To the House of Industry shall be committed all vagrants above the age of eighteen, and all able-bodied beggars, above that age, who refuse to labour in the House of Refuge, or elsewhere, when employment is offered to them.

Art. 300. In each department the women shall be kept separate from the men, and they shall be under the superintendence of a matron.

Art. 301. The building shall be so constructed as to separate the two departments, and shall contain separate sleeping cells for each of the persons confined in the House of Industry, and for each of the discharged convicts in the House of Refuge. The paupers shall be disposed of in comfortable apartments, in the manner that the warden (subject to the direction of the inspectors) shall direct.

# TITLE III.

### OF THE OFFICERS OF THE HOUSE OF REFUGE AND INDUSTRY, AND OF THEIR DUTIES.

Art. 302. This establishment shall be under the direction of the board of inspectors, in this Code before provided for ; who shall, in relation to this, have the same powers and be subject to the same duties that are before provided in relation to the other places of confinement.

Art. 303. The warden shall be appointed by the governor, and the warden shall appoint so many assistants as the inspectors shall deem necessary.

Art. 304. The matron shall also be appointed by the governor, and shall name such number of female assistants as the inspectors shall direct.

Art. 305. The physician and chaplains shall also attend in their professional capacities on the persons admitted or detained in the House of Refuge and Industry.

Art. 306. The agent of the inspectors shall also be their agent for the sales and purchases of this institution.

Art. 307. The accounts shall be kept by a clerk to be named by the inspectors.

Art. 308. All the above named officers shall perform the same duties and have the same powers, with respect to the House of Refuge and Industry, and to the persons received or committed therein, as are required of and are given to them respectively, with respect to the

Penitentiary and the persons confined therein, except so far as the same are modified by this title.


# TITLE IV.

OF THE ADMISSION INTO THE HOUSE OF REFUGE, AND OF THE EMPLOYMENT OF THE PERSONS ADMITTED.

Art. 309. The House of Refuge and Industry shall be erected as near as conveniently may be to the city of New Orleans, not more than one league distant from the City-Hall of the said city. Annexed to it shall be a garden of at least three superficial acres. The building shall be made on a plan to be approved by the governor, and sufficient in all respects to carry into effect all the provisions of this title.

Art. 310. Discharged convicts shall be admitted on their own application to the warden, and on their agreeing to observe and be bound by the rules of the said house, and the provisions of this title, of which, so far as respects their conduct and obligations, an abstract shall be read to them, and which they shall sign.

Art. 311. Able-bodied paupers, willing to labour but unable to find employment, shall, in like manner, be admitted on their own application, and on their signing an agreement to observe the rules of this house and the provisions of this title which respects them.

Art. 312. All paupers, unable to provide for their own subsistence, shall be admitted to the House of Refuge on the order of the jury of police of the parish to which they belong, or of the city council, if they belong to the city of New Orleans.

Art. 313. The inspectors shall provide the implements, materials, and other means of giving employment to all the persons admitted into the House of Refuge, adapted to their strength, age, sex, and skill respectively, except such as shall, on examination by the physician, be declared incapable of doing any thing towards their support.

Art. 314. No person who shall be admitted into the House of Refuge shall leave the same, without permission of the warden, or without giving at least one month's notice of an intention to leave the same ; and any person absenting himself contrary to this rule, may be arrested on a warrant to be issued by the warden and one of the inspectors, and confined in a solitary cell for a term not exceeding three days.

Art. 315. Any person who shall leave the House of Refuge, either by permission of the warden or otherwise, and shall be found soliciting charity as a PUBLIC BEGGAR, may be arrested, and by the warrant of the parish judge and two magistrates of the parish, where such mendicant may be found, shall be committed to the House of Industry as a vagrant.

Art. 316. Any person admitted into the House of Refuge, who shall refuse or neglect to perform the labour assigned to him, may, if the inspectors shall think that the task assigned is not greater or more difficult than the strength or skill of the person can perform, be committed

4 R

to the House of Industry for such time, not exceeding ten days for each offence, as the inspectors shall direct.

# TITLE V.

## OF THE POLICE OF THE HOUSE OF REFUGE.

Art. 317. The inspectors may make rules for the preservation of order and industry in the House, and may punish breaches thereof in the manner such rules may direct, either by imprisonment in a solitary cell, or by commitment to the House of Industry ; provided that such imprisonment shall not exceed three days, or such commitment be for a longer term than ten days, for any offence against such rules.

Art. 318. The two sexes shall be kept separate in the House of Refuge, in two distinct apartments; but boys, under seven years of age, may be kept with their mothers, or, if they have none, by proper nurses, under the care of the matron.

Art. 319. Children of paupers, between the ages of seven and eighteen, may be sent to the School of Reform by the inspectors, at their discretion, when the friends or relatives of such children do not provide for their education and support.

Art. 320. The matron shall apportion the tasks of the females in both departments of the House of Refuge and Industry, and shall superintend their labour, and report all delinquencies to the warden or inspectors, to be furnished in the same manner as those of the males.

Art. 321. The warden and matron respectively shall appoint, from among the persons admitted into the House of Refuge, a male and female teacher, who shall give lessons in reading, writing, and arithmetic, to such of the persons admitted or confined as may be ignorant of these branches of learning, at such hours as the warden shall direct.

Art. 322. No wine, or spirituous or intoxicating liquors of any kind, shall, under any pretence, be used by those admitted into the House of Refuge or of Industry, unless by prescription of the physician.

Art. 323. Permission may be given to such of the persons as are most orderly and industrious to see their friends out of the House on Sundays, or to attend divine service in the city of New Orleans.

# TITLE VI.

## OF THE HOUSE OF INDUSTRY, ITS POLICE, AND THE EMPLOYMENT OF THE PERSONS CONFINED THEREIN.

Art. 324. The time and place of labour, and the intervals given for other purposes, shall be the same in the House of Industry as that directed by this Code for the convicts in the Penitentiary.

Art. 325. The prison ration for those who labour and for those who are idle shall be the same as in the Penitentiary. The same privations, punishments, and restraints, may be inflicted for idleness, or the breach of any of the rules established by the inspectors or by this chapter.

Art. 326. The same accounts shall be kept with persons confined, and the same allowance for excess of labour above the charges, shall be made.

Art. 327. Whatever is directed for the reception of convicts in the Penitentiary shall be observed when any one, committed to the House of Industry, shall be received, except the prison uniform, which shall not be given unless the clothing of the person convicted is not sufficient for health or cleanliness.

Art. 328. The labour of the persons confined in the House of Industry may be contracted for in the same manner as that of the convicts in the Penitentiary ; or when not contracted for, it is to be carried to the account of the establishment ; and the articles manufactured are to be disposed of in the same way as is directed for the Penitentiary.

## TITLE VII.

OF THE PECUNIARY CONCERNS OF THE HOUSE OF REFUGE AND INDUSTRY.

Art. 329. The accounts of the two departments, the House of Refuge and the House of Industry, shall be kept in separate sets of books by the clerk, under the inspection of the warden and the inspectors.

Art. 330. In the books of the House of Refuge all the expenses of the paupers, sent by any parish or city, shall be charged to such parish or city respectively, and they shall be credited with the amount of the earnings of such paupers.

Art. 331. In the expenses, mentioned in the preceding article, shall be included, not only the food, clothing, medicine, and other articles provided for such paupers, but a just proportion of the salaries of the warden and other officers and attendants of the House of Refuge and Industry, calculated on the average of persons in the said house.

Art. 332. One-fourth part of the salaries of the inspectors, of the chaplains, and physician, shall also, in such account, be considered as chargeable to the House of Refuge and Industry, and a due proportion of that fourth (divided as is above directed by the average number of the persons in the said house) shall be also included in the expenses charged to the parishes as aforesaid.

Art. 333. Whatever sum is found due on such account, if not paid on demand by the city or parish from which it is due, shall be added to the quota of the state taxes, payable by such city or parish, and be collected and paid into the public treasury in like manner with the rest of the state taxes.

Art. 334. All the expenses of the other persons admitted or confined in the said house, shall be paid by the state, without any counter charge.

Art. 335. A detailed account of all the expenditures and receipts of the said house shall be laid before the legislature, by the inspectors, on the first day of every session.

Art. 336. The salary of the warden shall be            dollars per annum, and of the matron           dollars, and each of the assistants shall be paid          a day.

## GENERAL PROVISIONS.

Art. 337. If any one shall, for hire, reward, or emolument of any kind whatever, or the promise of any, solicit the pardon of any one convicted of any offence, or procure any other to sign a petition for such pardon, or to apply for the same, he shall be fined five hundred dollars, and if he be a counsellor or attorney, he shall be suspended from practising as such in any court in the state for one year.

Art. 338. The inspectors, chaplains, teachers, physicians, wardens, matrons, assistants, and under-keepers, appointed by virtue of this Code, shall, before they enter on the performance of their respective duties, take an oath faithfully to perform the same.

# A BOOK OF DEFINITIONS.

# TITLE I.

GENERAL PROVISIONS.

Art. 1. These definitions are intended to show the sense in which the words defined are employed in the system of Penal Law, not to denote or fix their general signification in the language.

Art. 2. The words printed in small capitals in the body of this system, are alphabetically arranged in this Book, with the definition annexed.

Art. 3. Generally the definitions that are incorporated in the other parts of the work are not repeated in this Book; but this rule is departed from when the general use of the term, in other parts of the System than that in which the definition is contained, renders a reference to the explanation necessary.

Art. 4. Corollaries, illustrations, and developments, are used in several instances to fix the attention more strongly to particular parts of the definition: but the omission to employ them, in other cases, is not to be considered as giving any latitude for the construction of any word in a definition beyond the plain import of its meaning in connexion with the context.

# TITLE II.

DEFINITIONS.

ACCIDENT, in this System, means an event happening without the concurrence of the will of the person by whose agency it was caused. It differs from MISTAKE, because the latter always supposes the operation of the human will in producing the event, although that will is caused by erroneous impressions on the mind.—See MISTAKE.

ACT—when applied to a written instrument, is a term used to show the connexion between the instrument and the party who has given it validity by his signature or by his legal assent: when thus perfected, the instrument becomes the ACT of the parties who have signed or assented to it in a form required by law.

ADVANTAGE, applied in different parts of the system to that which is to be gained or lost, means whatever, in the estimation of mankind, causes pleasure by its possession or enjoyment, or uneasiness by its loss or cessation.

AFFIDAVIT—a written declaration, sanctioned by the oath of the declarant administered by a person or court duly authorized for that purpose. The administration of the oath must be duly certified by the official SIGNATURE of the person, or the clerk of the court, before whom it was taken; and the declaration must be SIGNED by the declarant; or it must be certified by the person administering the oath, that the declarant cannot sign.

AFFINITY—a connexion formed by marriage which places the husband in the same degree of nominal propinquity to the relations of the wife as that in which she herself stands towards them, and gives to the wife the same reciprocal connexion with the relations of the husband. It is used in contradistinction to CONSANGUINITY, which is the relationship that exists between several persons who derive their descent in the same or different degrees of propinquity from an ancestor common to all.

AFFIRMATION and OATH. An affirmation is a solemn declaration, made before a person or court authorized to receive it, attesting the truth of a statement already made or about to be made by the affirmant, or the truth or sincerity of a promise made by him. An oath is a similar declaration, accompanied by a religious invocation to the Supreme Being to bear witness to the truth of the declaration or the sincerity of the promise, and by a renunciation of the blessing of God and the respect of man if the engagement should be violated. Vide the Chapter of the Code of Procedure, " Of Oaths and Affirmatiosn." The term " oath," whenever used in this System, as to its effects and consequences and all penalties attending its breach or falsity, includes affirmations, unless the contrary appears from the context.

AMICABLE COMPOUNDER. An arbitrator with extensive equitable powers.

TO APPROPRIATE, in relation to property, is to possess, and to make such use or disposition of it, as none but the owner, or some one legally authorized by him, could do ; and, with respect to rights, to do such acts in relation to them as none but the person entitled to them, or his representatives, could lawfully do.

Appropriations are legal or fraudulent. No appropriations are fraudulent but such as come within the definition of fraud in this book.

*Corollaries.*—I. If the property he destroyed but not possessed, or if the possession be for the purpose of destruction, or be such a possession only, as is necessary for effecting the destruction, it is not an appropriation.

II. If the property be taken possession of and transferred, although it be afterwards destroyed, it is an appropriation.

ARBITRATOR—any one appointed by the parties in any litigated question, either of law or fact, to decide it between them. In this system it is used to include REFEREES, UMPIRES, and AMICABLE COMPOUNDERS, whether they are named by the court, in cases where they are authorized to do so, or by the parties.

ATTEMPT. An attempt to commit an offence, in this system, means an endeavour to accomplish it, which has failed from some other cause than the voluntary relinquishment of the design.

BAILABLE OF RIGHT. Those offences, on a charge for which the magistrate must admit to bail, if good security be offered, are bailable of right. The constitution provides, that bail must be taken for all offences, except those which were punished capitally at the time of its adoption : these were murder, rape, exciting insurrection among the slaves, and stabbing, or shooting, or poisoning with intent to murder. All other offences, therefore, are bailable of right. The offences, above enumerated, are also bailable, when the proof is not evident nor the presumption great.

BREACH OF THE PEACE—any offence against public tranquillity, or against person or property, when accompanied by violence.

BRIBE. The gift or promise which is accepted ; of some ADVANTAGE, as the inducement for an illegal act or omission; or of some illegal EMOLUMENT, as a consideration, for preferring one person to another in the performance of a legal act.

TO BRIBE—to make such gift or promise which is received. If it be not received, it is an OFFER TO BRIBE.

TO RECEIVE A BRIBE, is to accept the gift or promise, and either expressly or impliedly consent to do the act, or be guilty of the omission required. Whatever would be proof of consent in cases of contract, according to the rules of evidence, would show an acceptance in this case.

*Corollaries and Illustrations.*—I. The gift or the promise required by the definition need not be direct : although the gift be clothed in the form of a sale for an inadequate price, or of the payment of a debt ; or the promise be made colourably for some other consideration ; or a wager, or any other device, be used to cover the true intent of the parties, it is a bribe.

II. The gift or the promise must be the inducement for the act or omission ; it must, therefore, precede or accompany such act or omission. If the act be first performed, uninfluenced by any such promise, it is not bribery.

III.  When the act or omission is illegal, the promise or gift of any ADVANTAGE, as the consideration, is bribery.  If a magistrate should discharge, without bail, a person legally accused of a crime, on the promise of that person's influence with the governor for an appointment, this would be bribery ; because, although the inducement, that is to say, the influence with the governor, is only an ADVANTAGE, not an EMOLUMENT, yet the act, that is to say, the discharge without bail, being illegal, it comes within the definition.

IV.  But when the act is legal, but the impropriety consists in the undue preference given to the person offering the inducement, that inducement, to constitute the offence, must not only be an advantage, but an emolument.  If an officer of justice were to promise a magistrate to recommend his friend for an employment, as an inducement for the magistrate to employ him in preference to any other in the business of his office, this would not be bribery ; although it would, if the inducement had been a sum of money or any other emolument.

V.  The emolument, when that is required to constitute the offence, must be illegal, that is to say, either not allowed or more than is allowed by law.  If two persons should apply to a notary, each to have an act of sale drawn, and he should give the preference to the one who paid him double fees, this would come within the definition ; but if he took no more than the tariff allows, the preference would be no offence.

VI.  No acts of bribery, or offer to bribe, are punishable as such, but those which are designated by express law.

VII.  Whenever by the Penal Code bribery, or an offer to bribe, is made punishable, in relation to officers of a particular description, or to persons exercising certain duties, powers, or privileges, it is intended to extend to all official acts and omissions of such officers, and to all acts or omissions of such other persons as relate to their duties, privileges, or powers ; but not to include any other.

BUILDING—any thing erected by art and fixed upon or in the soil, composed of different pieces, connected together, and designed for permanent use in the position in which it is so fixed.

*Corollaries.*—I.  A single piece of timber, although fixed in the ground, is not a building.

II.  A fence or enclosure is a building.

III.  A heap of stones, although some of them may be fixed on the earth, is not a building.

IV.  Every building comes under the description of real estate.

COLOUR.  Doing an act under colour of an office, or other legal power, means the doing it under the false pretence that it is authorized by the duties of such office, or by the due exercise of such legal powers.

CONDITION of a Person—a situation in civil society which creates certain relations between the individual, to whom it is applied, and one or more others, from which mutual rights and obligations arise.  Thus the situation arising from marriage gives rise to the CONDITIONS of husband and wife ; that from paternity to the CONDITIONS of father and child.

COROLLARY, in this system, is used not so much to designate the just consequence that, according to strict reasoning, ought to be drawn from any proposition, as the consequence which is established by law as resulting from the definition or proposition to which it refers.  Those who are to execute or interpret the law, therefore, are forbidden to modify or reject any such consequence under the pretence that it is not a just deduction.

CORPORATION, is an incorporeal being, created, and capable of acting only in the manner prescribed by law.  It is composed of one or more persons having a common name and uninterrupted succession. It may hold property, and for certain purposes specified by law is considered as an individual.

*Corollaries.*—I.  As a corporation, by this definition, is capable of acting only in the manner prescribed by law, no act done in any other manner or form, can be the act of the corporation.  It cannot, therefore, commit an offence.  All such acts, although done under the colour of being corporate acts, are those of the individual members who perform them, and they alone are criminally liable.

II.  Acts which are offences against the property and rights of individuals, are also offences when committed against the property of corporations, and such rights as are vested in them by law.

III.  Corporations are of two kinds : Public, also called Political Corporations, and Private Corporations.  PUBLIC CORPORATIONS are those to which are confided

4 S

certain police powers in a designated portion of the state. PRIVATE CORPORATIONS are all such as are not public.

CORRUPTLY. This adverb is applied to the doing of acts with the intent of gaining some ADVANTAGE inconsistent with official duty or the rights of others.

*Corollaries.*—I. Corruption includes bribery, but is more comprehensive. An act may be corruptly done though the advantage to be derived from it be not offered by another.

II. It is not corruption to do an official act from an expectation of ADVANTAGE, if the act be not contrary to official duty, or does not injure the rights of another.

III. The corruption is not measured by the nature or amount of the ADVANTAGE.

COUNTERFEIT—to make something false in the semblance of that which is true. Whenever this word is used, in this system, it implies fraudulent intent.

COURT—COURT OF JUSTICE. These terms, in this system, are synonymous. A court is an incorporeal political being, which requires for its existence, the presence of the judge and clerk at the time during which, and at the place where, it is by law authorized to be held; and the performance of some public act, indicative of the design to perform the functions of a court.

*Corollaries.*—I. There can be no court without a clerk or some one authorized to perform the duties of a clerk.

II. Executive officers are not essential to the existence of a court.

III. The judge is not the court.

IV. The court cannot exist before the time at which, by law, it is authorized to hold its sessions; nor after the time to which its sitting is limited.

V. All acts done by the persons composing the court, importing to be acts of the court, at any other place than that authorized by law, are not the acts of a court.

VI. A justice of the peace, or any other magistrate authorized to perform judicial duties, without a clerk to record his proceedings, does not constitute a court; but courts may order certain executive acts to be performed at other times and places, such as the issuing of writs and filing of papers.

CRIME, is an offence the punishment of which, in the whole or in part, may be the forfeiture of any civil or political right, or hard labour, or for which hard labour is an alternative, to be inflicted at the discretion of the court.

DAY, given as the period of a notice, prescribed as a necessary interval between two acts or events, excludes the day of the notice and the day the act is to be performed; or of the first and second act or event; so that the full number of days prescribed shall intervene, unless there be a contrary provision in the law.

DAY, used as a period of time, means the period of twenty-four hours, beginning at the expiration of the twelfth hour at night.

DAY, or DAY-TIME, used in contradistinction to night, means the period beginning at half an hour before the rising of the sun, and ending half an hour after its setting.

DEADLY WEAPON—any instrument which, when offensively used against the person, will probably produce death.

DEMUR, is to admit the truth of a fact stated, but to deny the legal consequence for the establishment of which it was alleged. The only case in which a formal demurrer is admitted, in this system, is that of a demurrer to a challenge to the panel of jurors.

DESIGNATED PERSON, is a term used to express one who is either known by name, or by person, or station, or office, or dwelling-place, or in any other way that may designate him to be the person referred to.

DISCRETION—the exercise of sound judgment, directed by what may be supposed would have been the will of the legislature, applied to the case in which the discretion is to be used, had the circumstances of that case been legislated upon: for a development of this definition—See the Code of Procedure, chapter "Of the Judgment."

DISCUSSION of Property, means the using the means prescribed by law for rendering it available to the payment of a debt.

DOMESTIC ANIMALS, means only animals of that kind that are usually employed in hunting, or in husbandry, or which are raised for the purpose of food.

EMOLUMENT—any thing that forms an increase of property.

ESTATE, is used as synonymous with property. See PROPERTY.

EVIDENCE, is that which brings the mind to a just conviction of the truth or falsehood of any substantive proposition which is asserted or denied.

*Illustrations and Developments of the different Parts of this Definition.*—
I. A conviction produced by evidence which ought not, according to the rules of true reason, to have that effect, is not a just conviction : the law, therefore, declares what effect different species of evidence ought to have in producing such conviction ; and that evidence, in its different degrees, is called LEGAL EVIDENCE.

II. Evidence being different according to the different degrees of effect which it ought to produce; those degrees, therefore, receive different denominations, indicative of the operation they each ought to have on the mind. These denominations are—presumptive evidence, direct evidence, and conclusive evidence ; all of which are hereafter defined.

III. The word "substantive," in the definition, is intended to exclude all such abstract propositions as can be demonstrated to be true or false by the reasoning power, without having recourse to the establishment of other facts. The propositions intended by the definition are either of *fact* or of *law*. What is evidence of law, will be shown in the Code of Evidence. The three kinds of evidence enumerated, apply only to propositions of fact.

EVIDENCE (presumptive). Presumptive evidence is that which, by directly establishing the existence of one fact, renders the existence of another probable.

EVIDENCE (direct). Direct evidence is that which, if true, conclusively establishes or destroys the proposition in question.

EVIDENCE (conclusive). Conclusive evidence is that which, by law, is declared to be such proof of that which it asserts, as cannot, while it exists, be contradicted by other testimony.

EXCITE—to offer any persuasion or inducement.

EXTORT, is to obtain some illegal EMOLUMENT or advantage from another, under colour of, or as the consideration for, some official act.

FORCE—VIOLENCE. These terms mean the exertion of physical power, and when unqualified by any thing in the context, the idea of the illegal exercise of such powers is intended to be conveyed.

*Corollaries.*—I. No words, whatever may be their import, can constitute force or violence.

II. Gestures, indicating an intent to apply physical power to the object intended to be affected, when such object is within the reach of the exercise of such power, does amount to force or violence.

III. The exercise of physical power amounts to *force* or *violence*, although it may be insufficient to carry the intent into effect.

IV. Violence and force are, in some instances, considered as offences merely by the intent with which they are used—as in assault, and assault and battery. Sometimes they do not amount to the offence described, unless they are sufficient to carry the intent into effect—as in the offence of violently obstructing the proceedings of a court of justice ; in which case the offence is not complete, unless the violence has produced the obstruction.

FRAUD—TO DEFRAUD—unlawfully, designedly, and knowingly, to appropriate the property of another.

*Illustrations.*—I. Every appropriation of the right of property of another, is not fraud. It must be unlawful; that is to say, such an appropriation as is not permitted by law. Property loaned may, during the time of the loan, be appropriated to the use of the borrower. This is not fraud, because it is permitted by law.

II. The appropriation must be, not only unlawful, but it must be made with a knowledge that the property belongs to another, and with the design to deprive him of the same. It is unlawful to take the property of another ; but if it be done with a design of preserving it for the owners, or if it be taken by mistake, it is not done designedly or knowingly, and, therefore, does not come within the definition of fraud.

III. Every species of unlawful appropriation, enters into this definition when designedly made with a knowledge that the property is another's ; therefore, such an appropriation, intended either for the use of another or for the benefit of the offender himself, is comprehended by the term.

IV. Fraud, however immoral or illegal, is not, in itself, an offence. It only becomes such in the cases specially provided by law.

HABITUALLY—so frequently as to show a design of repeating the same act.

HOUSEHOLDER—one who occupies a house, or part of one, in which he habitually dwells.

*Corollaries.*—I. It is not necessary that the dwelling-place should either be owned or hired; an occupant at sufferance, or in his own wrong, comes within the definition.

II.  By employing the word " dwells," in the definition, it is intended to exclude a sojourner or guest.  The occupant must be provided for at his own table, not board at that of another.

III.  The dwelling must be so habitual as to show an intent of continuance. The quality of householder cannot be assumed, merely for the purpose of using it, in order to do some act for the performance of which that character is required by law, with the intent of relinquishing it when the purpose is attained.

HOUSE—any edifice, which being so built as to come within the definition of REAL PROPERTY, as defined, is closed in on all sides, and has the area, which is enclosed by the sides, covered with a roof.

HOUSE (dwelling).  A dwelling house is one in which some person habitually sleeps or eats his meals; or one that is built and intended for that purpose; although not actually inhabited.

INDUCEMENT—the object, whether of advantage to be obtained or evil to be avoided, which brings the mind to determine on any act or omission.

INFANT—a minor, who has not yet attained the age which usually gives physical and mental power to avoid the ordinary dangers, or without aid to use the ordinary means of sustaining life when they are provided for him.

INJURY, is used in its most enlarged signification, meaning whatever causes evil or detriment, or renders the object of less value.  When it is intended to be used in the restricted sense of an evil or detriment, caused contrary to law, it is called illegal injury, or some other qualifying epithet is annexed to show such intent.

INSANITY—a malady operating on the perceptive or on the reasoning faculties of the mind, which either prevents the person affected from receiving true impressions through his senses, or from drawing just conclusions from what is truly perceived; and existing in such a degree as to render him incapable of performing the usual duties or transacting the ordinary affairs of life. ·

JUDGE—a public officer, appointed to decide litigated questions.  This term, with exceptions that are specially made, is used to designate only such officers as preside in COURTS, and who are designated by that title in their appointments.

*Exceptions and Illustrations.*—I.  Jurors, although they are judges of fact—and ARBITRATORS, although they are private judges, chosen by the parties, and in some cases assigned by the court—are, in this system, not included in the term, unless specially named.

II.  When used in relation to a power to be exercised, or a duty to be performed, in a court having more than one judge, the power or duty is given to or imposed on all the judges, or so many as are necessary for the constitution of the court.  When the term judge is used in relation to a duty or power to be performed or exercised out of court, it is intended to impose the duty or confer the power on any one judge where there are several.

III.  A justice of the peace is included in the term judge in the first two chapters of the title of the Penal Code, " of Offences against the Judiciary Powers."

JUST REASON—to fear—to think—to believe—to doubt—such cause as would produce these effects by their operation on the apprehension or mind of a man of ordinary understanding in the common occurrences of life.  The definition does not call for the exertion of very extraordinary courage, or an unusual degree of intellect.

LAW, as used in this system.  This word signifies all those rules established by the people of the state in their constitution, or necessarily governing them as a member of the Union, or adopted or made by the legislature in conformity with the powers given by the constitution, and according to the forms it prescribes.

*Corollaries, Developments, and Illustrations.*—I.  The laws in force in this state are the following, each having a controlling force over the others in the order in which they are enumerated:

1.  The constitution of the United States, because it was adopted by the people of the state as paramount to their own constitution.

2.  The laws and treaties of the United States, made in conformity with the constitution.

3.  The law of nations, so far as the same has been recognised by the United States.

4.  The constitution of the state.

5. The state laws, passed in conformity with the powers granted by the constitution, and according to the forms prescribed by it.

6. The laws in force in this state, at the time its constitution was adopted, and which have not been since repealed.

II. No other laws or authority for making laws are recognised as having any force to bind the people of this state.

III. No act of the legislature of the United States is law which is not warranted by some power given to them by the constitution of the United States, and which is not made according to the forms it prescribes.

IV. No act of the legislature of this state is law which is not warranted by the powers given to them by the constitution of the state, and is not made according to the forms it prescribes, or which contravenes the constitution of the United States, or laws, or treaties, constitutionally passed or made by the government of the United States.

V. If any provision in the constitution of the State should be found to contravene the constitution of the United States, or any constitutional laws or treaties made under it—the latter must prevail.

VI. Rules, ordinances, and by-laws, made by any court, corporation, body politic, or society, pursuant to powers legally vested in them by the legislature, have the force of law to the extent of those powers, as respects the rights of persons, or property, submitted to their operation.

LAW (penal). A penal law is one having for its immediate object the enforcement of civil or political duties, and the preservation of correspondent rights. It must command certain acts to be done or omitted, and must impose a PENALTY to be enforced in the name of the state for a breach of its provisions.

*Corollaries.*—I. A law which forbids or commands, but without declaring any penalty for disobedience, is not a penal law.

II. Laws authorizing courts to impose fines, or to imprison, for defaults occurring in the administration of justice, or for disobedience to its rules for the maintenance of order, or authorizing corporations or other collective bodies to impose fines on their members, are not penal laws.

III. Ordinances or by-laws of PUBLIC or PRIVATE CORPORATIONS, are not penal laws, although they should impose penalties.

IV. Laws declaring contracts or acts, which want certain formalities, or which are not conformable to the provisions of such laws, to be void, are not penal laws.

V. Laws which impose forfeitures, or pecuniary penalties to be sued for in their own name, and for their own use, or for the joint benefit of the prosecutor and the state, are not penal laws.

LAW (military). Military laws are regulations for the government of the military force ; and although they contain penalties, they are not considered as penal laws, because their immediate object is not the enforcement of civil or political duties.

LAWS (of Nations,) are those rules which, by the general consent of nations, govern them in their intercourse with each other in their national capacity. Offences against those laws, not being cognizable in the courts of this state, they are not detailed in this system.

LAW (civil). Every law which does not come within the description of penal, military, or national law, is, for the purpose of these Codes, called CIVIL LAW.

LAWFUL. Nothing is lawful that contravenes any of the laws in force in this state. All acts or omissions are lawful which are not forbidden by some written law or by the laws of nations.

LYING-IN-WAIT—waiting in or near a place where the property or person of another is expected to come or be brought, for the purpose of committing an offence which shall affect such person or property.

MAGISTRATE. This term means all judges, including justices of the peace.

MAGISTRATE (competent)—one whose legal official powers are sufficient for the execution of the duty required.

MALICE—a malignant design to cause INJURY.

MANIFEST—whatever is apparent of itself, and is not made so by other evidence or by induction.

*Illustration.*—In the chapter of the Penal Code, concerning offences against decency, there is a provision forbidding the exhibition of any work MANIFESTLY designed to corrupt the morals of youth. If this term had not been introduced, the design might be inferred from expressions or figures usually and innocently employed in works of art or science, but at which overstrained delicacy or puritanism might take offence.

MAY—when employed to confer a power, is intended to render the exercise of it discretionary.

MINOR—any person under the age of twenty-one years. All the rules and provisions of penal law, with respect to minors, apply to them, although they may be emancipated.

MISDEMEANOR—any OFFENCE less in degree than a crime.

MISTAKE—a belief in the being of that which does not exist, or in truth of a conclusion that is false.

Mistakes are REAL or INTELLECTUAL. In this system MISTAKE, when not qualified by the context, means exclusively a real mistake, as the same is here defined.

REAL MISTAKES relate to facts, and are caused either by the erroneous operation of the senses, or when the impression on the senses having been true, other circumstances produce a false conclusion in the mind.

INTELLECTUAL MISTAKES are such as are caused wholly by a defective operation of the reasoning faculty, either by drawing false conclusions from true principles, or by adopting false principles, and reasoning either correctly or falsely from them.

*Illustrations and Corollaries.*—I.   If one, intending to shoot an animal in the wood, should fire at a fur cap, and kill the man who wore it, thinking it to be the animal he was hunting, this would be a REAL MISTAKE, produced by a false impression on the organ of sight.   If the same event should be produced by supposing the rush and tread of the man through the bushes to be those of the animal, this would be a mistake of the same description, arising from a false impression on another sense, that of hearing.

II.   One who shoots an innocent but unknown man, believing him to be a robber equally unknown, of whose attempt he has been apprised, gives an example of mistake arising from other circumstances, without any error of the senses.   There was no error in perceiving the man; both men were equally unknown; therefore, the error did not arise from the sight; but the information of the intended robbery, and the entry by night at the time he was expected, were the circumstances from which the erroneous conclusion was drawn, that the innocent man was the robber.

III.   If one should establish in his own mind, the erroneous principle that no human law can rightfully control his revenge for an injury, and from thence deduce a right to challenge and kill the man who has offended him, this is an intellectual mistake, by drawing true conclusions from the establishment of false principles unconnected with the fact.

IV.   If a curator should believe that because he has a right to administer the real property of his ward, he has also that of disposing of it at his pleasure, he commits an intellectual mistake, by drawing a false conclusion from true principles.

V.   In those cases in which the law declares that an act which would otherwise be an offence is not punishable, or is punishable in a less degree when done by mistake, it does not intend intellectual mistakes.

VI.   All mistakes, as to the tenor or the construction of law, are intellectual mistakes.

VII.   No mistake of law can excuse or palliate an offence.

MONTH, in this system—by the term month, a calendar month is always intended.

TO OBSTRUCT, as applied to any proceeding or course of action—means not only to stop altogether, and to interrupt for a time, but to render inconvenient, or to turn out of the usual legal course.

OFFENCE, is the doing what a PENAL LAW forbids to be done, or omitting to do what it commands.   In most cases the contravention must be voluntary to constitute the offence; but there are exceptions to this part of the definition to be found in the description of different offences in the Penal Code.

*Developments.*—I.   Penal law here is not used synonymously with penal statute. If a penal statute should contain any prohibition not SANCTIONED by a penalty, the breach of that part of the statute would not be an offence.

II.   An act, or omission, in contravention of a penal law, is not an offence in any one who does not come within the purview of the law.

OFFICE, is a delegation, either mediately, or immediately, from the state, of powers to perform certain duties; either for carrying the operations of government in some one of its branches, which is called a PUBLIC OFFICE, for performing some duty in relation to some designated individuals, or their property, which is denominated a PRIVATE OFFICE, or for exercising certain functions unconnected with the state government in a public or private corporation, which is designated as a CORPO-RATE OFFICE. In relation to the functions they require, offices are divided into CIVIL and MILITARY ; and civil offices are either LEGISLATIVE, JUDICIAL, or EXE-CUTIVE.

OFFICER (civil). Any one who fills a legislative, executive, or judicial office of the state. No one is an officer until he has received the evidence designated by law of his election or appointment, and (where they are required by law) unless he has taken the oath of office and given security for its faithful performance. But any one performing the functions of an office without being thus qualified, is liable to all the penalties imposed by law for any misconduct of which he may be guilty in the exercise of such office.

OFFICER (military). One who fills an office in the army, or navy, or militia : the last are considered as military officers only when doing military duty.

OFFICERS (legislative). The members of the general assembly are legislative officers. The governor or person acting as such is an executive officer: but performs legislative functions in exercising his right of sending back bills to the general assembly for reconsideration.

OFFICERS (judicial). All those officers whose legal functions are the decision of litigated questions either of law or of fact. Judges, or those who are exclusively employed in the administration of justice, justices of the peace, clerks, and other officers of courts are judicial officers.—ARBITRATORS and jurors are not officers.

OFFICERS (executive). Every PUBLIC OFFICER comes under this description, whose duties are neither military, legislative, nor judicial.

ORDINARY CARE—ORDINARY ATTENTION. These terms signify that degree of attention and care which a man of common prudence and activity employs in his daily occupations : they exclude that deliberation and solicitude which is shown by men of extraordinary circumspection and diligence in common affairs, or which concerns of more than ordinary interest excite in all.

PANEL, is the list formed, according to law, of the names of the grand or petit jurors summoned to attend a court.

PERSONATE—to pretend to be another, either by assuming his name, his addition, designation of office, occupation or place of abode, with an intent to injure or defraud.

POISON—any substance which, by some inherent quality, causes death, when applied to, or received into the human body.

POISONING—the act of administering poison. It is effected by any of the means by which the poisonous substance may operate, whether by swallowing, by respiration, by incision, or by any other mode of application.

*Corollaries from the two last definitions.*—I. Death caused by the deprivation of respirable air, is not poisoning.

II. To suffocate by smoke or steam, or to kill by any of the gaseous fluids, which cause death by stopping respiration, is not poisoning.

III. Death caused by the inhaling of any gaseous fluid, which by some deleterious quality it possesses, causes death when brought into contact with the organs of respiration, is poisoning.

IV. The deadly quality must be inherent in, not adventitious to, the substance. Death occasioned by the administration of a substance, which disorders the functions of the body, but does not usually produce death in the quantity in which it was administered, is not poisoning ; but may be murder, or a less offence, according to the intent.

V. The deleterious effect may be supplied by the quantity. A substance, which given in small quantities may have no deadly effect, may come under the description of poison, if administered in a quantity that usually causes death.

PROPERTY. This term conveys a compound idea composed of that which is its subject, and of the right to be exercised over it. In relation to its object, property is CORPOREAL or INCORPOREAL ; the other part of the definition, the right connected with the object, is that of possessing, and using with respect to corporeal property, or of enforcing or transferring with respect to that which is incorporeal.

PROPERTY (corporeal). Is that property which is material in the physical sense of the word, or which may be perceived by any of the corporeal senses.

PROPERTY (incorporeal). Means the right to enjoy either at the present, or any future time, some species of corporeal property not in the possession of the person having the right ; and for this reason in common parlance, and frequently in this system, it is called a RIGHT.

PROPERTY (real). Is land, and every thing naturally rooted or growing therein, or artificially and permanently erected on, or affixed to the soil.

*Corollaries, Illustrations, and Developments.*—I.  By land or soil is meant not only ground capable of cultivation, but every other matter composing the globe, while it forms a part thereof; therefore rocks and minerals, while they are yet in the quarry or mine, enter into this definition, but cease to form a part of the land when they are dug out or detached.

II.  Trees and all other vegetable matters, while they are rooted in the soil, whether produced by nature alone, or by nature aided by cultivation, and their fruits while they are attached to them are real property: but the plants cease to be real property when they are rooted out or cut down, as do the fruits after they are separated from the plants which produced them.

III.  Land covered with water, and the water standing in or upon or flowing over the soil, is real property.

IV.  Every thing that is constructed upon the land by art, which is not by its construction calculated and intended for locomotion, and all things permanently fixed to such erections as parts thereof, are real property.  Therefore, a BUILDING erected on a foundation of wood or stone, or on posts, is real property ; but one resting on wheels or slides, and intended to be moved from place to place, is not real, but personal property, as are also all furniture, ornaments, or implements of trade which are usually moved, although they may be fastened to the soil or the building.

V.  The rents of real property reserved to the proprietor, while they are unpaid, whether such rent be reserved in money or other things, is real property.

PROPERTY (personal).  Every species of property which is not real property, comes under this description.

*Corollaries.*—I.  Money, bank bills, and public securities, are personal property.

II.  Credits, or the right of demanding or suing for money or other personal property, and the evidence of such debts, are personal property, whether the same be debts of a personal nature or secured on land.

III.  Rents, or annuities charged on hand payable to any one but the proprietor of the land, are personal property.

IV.  The title deeds of real property, are personal property.

V.  Shares in any banking, commercial, or manufacturing corporations or societies, and the certificates and other evidences of ownership thereof, are personal property, although such society or corporation may own real estate.

PUBLIC PRISON—the building designated by law, or used by the sheriff, in each parish, for the confinement of those whose persons are judicially ordered to be kept in custody.

If the prison designated by law should be destroyed, or if none should be provided, the sheriff must find some place for the imprisonment of those who are committed to his custody ; and this place is then a PUBLIC PRISON, although it may be a private house.

PUBLIC PROSECUTOR—the attorney-general, the district attorneys in their respective districts, any person legally performing the duties of either of these officers, and any other officer who may be hereafter appointed by law to prosecute offenders on the part of the state.

PUBLIC RECORD—a written memorial made by a public officer authorized by law to perform that function, and intended to serve as evidence of something written, said, or done.

*Corollaries.*—I.  Every statement in writing, made by a public officer, is not a public record.  It must be one which that officer is specially authorized by law to make and record.

II.  It must be memorial; by which is meant a written statement, intended to preserve the remembrance of what it contains.

III.  It must also be intended to serve as legal evidence, the force of which is provided for in the Code of Evidence.

PUBLISHING, as applied to libels and violations of epistolary correspondence, means the mechanical operation of engraving, copying, painting, printing, or writing, from the dictation or reading of another; and CIRCULATING is the selling, giving, distributing, reading, or exhibiting it to others.

TO RECEIVE—voluntarily to take from another what is voluntarily offered.

RECOGNIZANCE, is an engagement in writing to pay a penalty therein expressed, if the person making the engagement, or some other designated person, shall not do a specified act required by law, or shall not abstain from doing other specified acts.

REPUTATION (general)—estimation for those qualities, the possession of which is essential to happiness in society, not those which render one more agreeable in it.

RIGHT, is in one sense synonymous with INCORPOREAL PROPERTY. In the other and more enlarged sense, it signifies every ADVANTAGE that man ought to enjoy according to the laws of nature, which are called NATURAL RIGHTS; or, according to law, which are called LEGAL RIGHTS.

RIGHTS (political). Political rights form one of the divisions of legal rights. They are those which are given by the constitution or by law of electing, or being elected, or appointed, to fill any PUBLIC OFFICE, or to perform any functions in any branch of the government.

RIGHTS (civil). Civil rights are those which every free person is authorized, by law, to exercise for the preservation either of his own person, property, or reputation; or of the persons, property, or reputation, of certain designated individuals, by virtue of some authority conferred by law, given by consent, or vested in him by the powers annexed to some PRIVATE or CORPORATE OFFICE.

SCHOOL-MASTER, is a person employed for the education of youth, of either sex, in the arts or sciences.

*Corollary and additional Provision.*—I. This definition includes private teachers of any art or science, and professors and tutors in universities, colleges, and academies, as well as in schools.

II. The right of restraint and correction given by the Code to school-masters, may be modified by agreement with their employers.

SECURITIES FOR MONEY, mean the written evidence of the existence of a debt.

SIGNATURE, when used in relation to an instrument in writing, means a name, a firm, or a mark, affixed thereto, in order to give it validity as the act of the party whose name, firm, or mark, is so affixed. The name of a witness, subscribed to an instrument, is also a signature; but it is always, when mentioned in this system, distinguishable by the context from the signature of the party.

TO SIGN, means to affix a signature.

THREAT. When this word occurs without any qualifying expression to show the nature of the evil that is threatened, it means a menace of great and illegal injury to person, property, or reputation.

VERBAL PROCESS, is a written account of any proceeding or operation required by law, signed by the person commissioned to perform the duty, and attested by the signature of witnesses.

TO UTTER, as applied to a false or forged instrument, means not only the declaring it, in words, to be true, but the saying or doing with, or in relation to it, any thing that shows a design, to cause another to believe that the instrument is true.

WARRANT, is the written order of a magistrate, attested by his signature, authorizing the person or officer to whom it is directed to perform certain duties of executive justice therein specified.

WORDS FOLLOWING. This expression, used in relation to the recital of an instrument in writing, includes all numerical figures, or other written signs, or marks, contained in the instrument to which they relate.

WRIT, is a like order, issued by a court, under its seal.

WRITING. Whenever the contrary does not appear from the context, this word means, not only words traced with a pen, or stamped, but printed, or engraved, or made legible by any other device.

YEAR. The year intended in this system is the calendar year.


THE END.

4 T

.

.

www.ingramcontent.com/pod-product-compliance
Lightning Source LLC
Chambersburg PA
CBHW030835300326

41935CB00036B/63